PROFESSIONAL C++

Sixth Edition

Marc Gregoire

WILEY

Published by John Wiley & Sons, Inc., Hoboken, New Jersey.
Published simultaneously in Canada and the United Kingdom.

ISBNs: 9781394193172 (Paperback), 9781394193196 (ePDF), 9781394193189 (ePub)

For general information on our other products and services or for technical support, please contact our Customer Care Department within the United States at (800) 762-2974, outside the United States at (317) 572-3993 or fax (317) 572-4002.

Wiley also publishes its books in a variety of electronic formats. Some content that appears in print may not be available in electronic formats. For more information about Wiley products, visit our web site at www.wiley.com.

Library of Congress Control Number: 2023948608

Cover image: © CSA-Printstock/Getty Images
Cover design: Wiley

SKY10063702_010824

*Dedicated to my amazing parents and brother,
whose continuous support and patience help me in
tackling such a big project as writing this book.*

ABOUT THE AUTHOR

MARC GREGOIRE is a software architect from Belgium. He graduated from the University of Leuven, Belgium, with a degree in "Burgerlijk ingenieur in de computer wetenschappen" (equivalent to a master of science in engineering in computer science). The year after, he received an advanced master's degree in artificial intelligence, *cum laude*, at the same university. After his studies, Marc started working for a software consultancy company called Ordina Belgium. As a consultant, he worked for Siemens and Nokia Siemens Networks on critical 2G and 3G software running on Solaris for telecom operators. This required working in international teams stretching from South America and the United States to Europe, the Middle East, Africa, and Asia. Now, Marc is a software project manager and software architect at Nikon Metrology (`industry.nikon.com`), a division of Nikon and a leading provider of precision optical instruments, X-ray machines, and metrology solutions for X-ray, CT, and 3-D geometric inspection.

His main expertise is C++. He has experience with developing C++ programs running 24/7 on Windows and Linux platforms: for example, KNX/EIB home automation software. In addition to C++, Marc also likes C#.

Since April 2007, he has received the annual Microsoft MVP (Most Valuable Professional) award for his Visual C++ expertise.

Marc is the founder of the Belgian C++ Users Group (`becpp.org`), co-author of *C++ Standard Library Quick Reference* 1st and 2nd editions (Apress 2016 and 2019), a technical editor for numerous books for several publishers, and a regular speaker at the CppCon C++ conference (`cppcon.org`). He maintains a blog at `www.nuonsoft.com/blog` and is passionate about traveling and gastronomic restaurants.

ABOUT THE TECHNICAL EDITORS

BRADLEY JONES has programmed in a variety of languages and tools ranging from C to Unity on platforms ranging from Windows to mobile and including the web as well as a little bit of virtual reality and embedded devices just for fun. In addition to programming, he has authored books on C, C++, C#, Windows, the web, and many more technical topics and a few nontechnical topics. Bradley is the owner of Lots of Software, LLC, and has been recognized in the industry as a community influencer as well as has been recognized as a Microsoft MVP, a CODiE Judge, an international technology speaker, a bestselling technical author, and more.

ARTHUR O'DWYER is a professional C++ trainer, software engineer, author, and WG21 committee member. He authored *Mastering the C++17 STL* (Packt Publishing, 2017), founded CppCon's "Back to Basics" track (2019), implemented libc++'s <memory_resource> header (2022), and is responsible for the simplified "implicit move" semantics in C++20 and C++23. He and his wife live in New York.

ACKNOWLEDGMENTS

I THANK THE JOHN WILEY & SONS editorial and production teams for their support. A special thank-you to Jim Minatel, executive editor at Wiley, for giving me a chance to write this sixth edition; Pete Gaughan, senior managing editor; Ashirvad Moses Thyagarajan, managing editor; Kathryn Hogan, PhD, project manager; Archana Pragash, content refinement specialist; and Kim Wimpsett, copyeditor.

A special thank you to technical editors Bradley Jones and Arthur O'Dwyer for checking the technical accuracy of the book. Their feedback and numerous contributions have strengthened this book and are greatly appreciated.

Of course, the support and patience of my parents and my brother were very important in finishing this book. I would also like to express my sincere gratitude to my employer, Nikon Metrology, for supporting me during this project.

Finally, I thank you, the reader, for supporting me over all these years and across numerous editions with this approach to professional C++ software development.

—Marc Gregoire

CONTENTS

INTRODUCTION

The development of C++ started in 1982 by Bjarne Stroustrup, a Danish computer scientist, as the successor of C with Classes. In 1985, the first edition of *The C++ Programming Language* book was released. The first standardized version of C++ was released in 1998, called C++98. In 2003, C++03 came out and contained a few small updates. After that, it was silent for a while, but traction slowly started building up, resulting in a major update of the language in 2011, called C++11. From then on, the C++ Standard Committee has been on a three-year cycle to release updated versions, giving us C++14, C++17, C++20, and now C++23. All in all, with the release of C++23 in 2023, C++ is almost 40 years old and still going strong. In most rankings of programming languages in 2023, C++ is in the top four. It is being used on an extremely wide range of hardware, going from small devices with embedded microprocessors all the way up to multi-rack supercomputers. Besides wide hardware support, C++ can be used to tackle almost any programming job, be it games on mobile platforms, performance-critical artificial intelligence (AI) and machine learning (ML) software, components for self-driving cars, real-time 3-D graphics engines, low-level hardware drivers, entire operating systems, software stacks for networking equipment, web browsers, and so on. The performance of C++ programs is hard to match with any other programming language, and as such, it is the de facto language for writing fast, powerful, and enterprise-class programs. Big tech companies, such as Microsoft, Facebook, Amazon, Google, and many more, use services written in C++ to run their infrastructure. As popular as C++ has become, the language can be difficult to grasp in full. There are simple, but powerful, techniques that professional C++ programmers use that don't show up in traditional texts, and there are useful parts of C++ that remain a mystery even to experienced C++ programmers.

Too often, programming books focus on the syntax of the language instead of its real-world use. The typical C++ text introduces a major part of the language in each chapter, explaining the syntax and providing an example. *Professional C++* does not follow this pattern. Instead of giving you just the nuts and bolts of the language with little practical context, this book will teach you how to use C++ in the real world. It will show you the little-known features that will make your life easier, as well as the programming techniques that separate novices from professional programmers.

WHO THIS BOOK IS FOR

Even if you have used the language for years, you might still be unfamiliar with the more advanced features of C++, or you might not be using the full capabilities of the language. Maybe you don't yet know all the new features introduced with the latest release, C++23. Perhaps you write competent C++ code but would like to learn more about design and good programming style in C++. Or maybe you're relatively new to C++ but want to learn the "right" way to program from the start. This book will meet those needs and bring your C++ skills to the professional level.

Because this book focuses on advancing from basic or intermediate knowledge of C++ to becoming a professional C++ programmer, it assumes that you have some knowledge about programming.

Chapter 1, "A Crash Course in C++ and the Standard Library," covers the basics of C++ as a refresher, but it is not a substitute for actual training in programming. If you are just starting with C++ but you have experience in another programming language such as C, Java, or C#, you should be able to pick up most of what you need from Chapter 1.

In any case, you should have a solid foundation in programming fundamentals. You should know about loops, functions, and variables. You should know how to structure a program, and you should be familiar with fundamental techniques such as recursion. You should have some knowledge of common data structures such as queues, and useful algorithms such as sorting and searching. You don't need to know about object-oriented programming just yet—that is covered in Chapter 5, "Designing with Classes."

You will also need to be familiar with the compiler you will be using to compile your code. Two compilers, Microsoft Visual C++ and GCC, are introduced later in this introduction. For other compilers, refer to the documentation that came with your compiler.

WHAT THIS BOOK COVERS

Professional C++ uses an approach to C++ programming that will both increase the quality of your code and improve your programming efficiency. You will find discussions on new C++23 features throughout this sixth edition. These features are not just isolated to a few chapters or sections; instead, examples have been updated to use new features when appropriate.

Professional C++ teaches you more than just the syntax and language features of C++. It also emphasizes programming methodologies, reusable design patterns, and good programming style. The *Professional* C++ methodology incorporates the entire software development process, from designing and writing code to debugging and working in groups. This approach will enable you to master the C++ language and its idiosyncrasies, as well as take advantage of its powerful capabilities for large-scale software development.

Imagine users who have learned all of the syntax of C++ without seeing a single example of its use. They know just enough to be dangerous! Without examples, they might assume that all code should go in the `main()` function of the program or that all variables should be global—practices that are generally not considered hallmarks of good programming.

Professional C++ programmers understand the correct way to use the language, in addition to the syntax. They recognize the importance of good design, the theories of object-oriented programming, and the best ways to use existing libraries. They have also developed an arsenal of useful code and reusable ideas.

By reading and understanding this book, you will become a professional C++ programmer. You will expand your knowledge of C++ to cover lesser known and often misunderstood language features. You will gain an appreciation for object-oriented design and acquire top-notch debugging skills. Perhaps most important, you will finish this book armed with a wealth of reusable ideas that you can actually apply to your daily work.

There are many good reasons to make the effort to be a professional C++ programmer as opposed to a programmer who knows C++. Understanding the true workings of the language will improve the quality of your code. Learning about different programming methodologies and processes will help you to work better with your team. Discovering reusable libraries and common design patterns will improve your daily efficiency and help you stop reinventing the wheel. All of these lessons will make you a better programmer and a more valuable employee. While this book can't guarantee you a promotion, it certainly won't hurt.

HOW THIS BOOK IS STRUCTURED

This book is made up of five parts.

Part I, "Introduction to Professional C++," begins with a crash course in C++ basics to ensure a foundation of C++ knowledge. Following the crash course, Part I goes deeper into working with strings, because strings are used extensively in most examples throughout the book. The last chapter of Part I explores how to write *readable* C++ code.

Part II, "Professional C++ Software Design," discusses C++ design methodologies. You will read about the importance of design, the object-oriented methodology, and the importance of code reuse.

Part III, "C++ Coding the Professional Way," provides a technical tour of C++ from the professional point of view. You will read about the best ways to manage memory in C++, how to create reusable classes, and how to leverage important language features such as inheritance. You will also learn techniques for input and output, error handling, string localization, how to work with regular expressions, and how to structure your code in reusable components called modules. You will read about how to implement operator overloading, how to write templates, how to put restrictions on template parameters using concepts, and how to unlock the power of lambda expressions and function objects. This part also explains the C++ Standard Library, including containers, iterators, ranges, and algorithms. You will also read about some additional libraries that are available in the standard, such as the libraries to work with time, dates, time zones, random numbers, and the filesystem.

Part IV, "Mastering Advanced Features of C++," demonstrates how you can get the most out of C++. This part of the book exposes the mysteries of C++ and describes how to use some of its more advanced features. You will read about how to customize and extend the C++ Standard Library to your needs, advanced details on template programming, including template metaprogramming, and how to use multithreading to take advantage of multiprocessor and multicore systems.

Part V, "C++ Software Engineering," focuses on writing enterprise-quality software. You'll read about the engineering practices being used by programming organizations today; how to write efficient C++ code; software testing concepts, such as unit testing and regression testing; techniques used to debug C++ programs; how to incorporate design techniques, frameworks, and conceptual object-oriented design patterns into your own code; and solutions for cross-language and cross-platform code.

The book concludes with a useful chapter-by-chapter guide to succeeding in a C++ technical interview, an annotated bibliography, a summary of the C++ header files available in the standard, and a brief introduction to the Unified Modeling Language (UML).

This book is not a reference of every single class, member function, and function available in C++. The book *C++17 Standard Library Quick Reference* by Peter Van Weert and Marc Gregoire (Apress, 2019. ISBN: 978-1-4842-4923-9) is a condensed reference to all essential data structures, algorithms, and functions provided by the C++ Standard Library up until the C++17 standard.[1] Appendix B, "Annotated Bibliography," lists a couple more references. Two excellent online references are:

- `cppreference.com`: You can use this reference online or download an offline version for use when you are not connected to the Internet.
- `cplusplus.com/reference`

When I refer to a "Standard Library Reference" in this book, I am referring to one of these detailed C++ references.

The following are additional excellent online resources:

- `github.com/isocpp/CppCoreGuidelines`: The C++ *Core Guidelines* are a collaborative effort led by Bjarne Stroustrup, inventor of the C++ language itself. They are the result of many person-years of discussion and design across a number of organizations. The aim of the guidelines is to help people to use modern C++ effectively. The guidelines are focused on relatively higher-level issues, such as interfaces, resource management, memory management, and concurrency.
- `github.com/Microsoft/GSL`: This is an implementation by Microsoft of the *Guidelines Support Library* (GSL) containing functions and types that are suggested for use by the C++ Core Guidelines. It's a header-only library.
- `isocpp.org/faq`: This is a large collection of frequently asked C++ questions.
- `stackoverflow.com`: Search for answers to common programming questions—or ask your own questions.

CONVENTIONS

To help you get the most from the text and keep track of what's happening, a number of conventions are used throughout this book.

> **WARNING** *Boxes like this one hold important, not-to-be-forgotten information that is directly relevant to the surrounding text.*

> **NOTE** *Tips, hints, tricks, and asides to the current discussion are placed in boxes like this one.*

[1] At the time of this writing, an updated edition called *C++23 Standard Library Quick Reference* is being worked on, which is a similar condensed reference but includes all C++20 and C++23 features.

As for styles in the text:

Important words are *italic* when they are introduced.

Keyboard strokes are shown like this: Ctrl+A.

Filenames and code within the text are shown like so: `monkey.cpp`.

URLs are shown like this: `wiley.com`

Code is presented in three different ways:

```
// Comments in code are shown like this.
In code examples, new and important code is highlighted like this.
Code that's less important in the present context or that has been shown before is
formatted like this.
```

Paragraphs or sections that are specific to the C++23 standard have a little C++23 icon on the left, just as this paragraph does. C++11, C++14, C++17, and C++20 features are not marked with any icon.

WHAT YOU NEED TO USE THIS BOOK

All you need to use this book is a computer with a C++ compiler. This book focuses only on parts of C++ that have been standardized, and not on vendor-specific compiler extensions.

Any C++ Compiler

You can use whichever C++ compiler you like. If you don't have a C++ compiler yet, you can download one for free. There are a lot of choices. For example, for Windows, you can download Microsoft Visual Studio Community Edition, which is free and includes Visual C++. For Linux, you can use GCC or Clang, which are also free.

The following two sections briefly explain how to use Visual C++ and GCC. Refer to the documentation that came with your compiler for more details.

COMPILERS AND C++23 FEATURE SUPPORT

This book discusses new features introduced with the C++23 standard. At the time of this writing, no compilers were fully C++23-compliant yet. Some new features were only supported by some compilers and not others, while other features were not yet supported by any compiler. Compiler vendors are hard at work to catch up with all new features, and I'm sure it won't take long before there will be full C++23-compliant compilers available. You can keep track of which compiler supports which features at `en.cppreference.com/w/cpp/compiler_support`.

> **COMPILERS AND C++ MODULE SUPPORT**
>
> At the time of this writing, not all compilers fully support modules yet; though all major compilers do, at least partially. This book uses modules everywhere. If your compiler does not yet support modules, you can convert modularized code to non-modularized code, as explained briefly in Chapter 11, "Modules, Header Files, and Miscellaneous Topics."

Example: Microsoft Visual C++ 2022

First, you need to create a project. Start Visual C++ 2022, and on the welcome screen, click the Create A New Project button. If the welcome screen is not shown, select File ➪ New ➪ Project. In the Create A New Project dialog, search for the Console App project template with tags C++, Windows, and Console, and click Next. Specify a name for the project and a location where to save it and click Create.

Once your new project is loaded, you can see a list of project files in the Solution Explorer. If this docking window is not visible, select View ➪ Solution Explorer. A newly created project will contain a file called `<projectname>.cpp` under the Source Files section in the Solution Explorer. You can start writing your C++ code in that `.cpp` file, or if you want to compile source code files from the downloadable source archive for this book, select the `<projectname>.cpp` file in the Solution Explorer and delete it. You can add new files or existing files to a project by right-clicking the project name in the Solution Explorer and then selecting Add ➪ New Item or Add ➪ Existing Item.

At the time of this writing, Visual C++ 2022 does not yet automatically enable C++23 features. To enable C++23 features, in the Solution Explorer window, right-click your project and click Properties. In the Properties window, go to Configuration Properties ➪ General, set the C++ Language Standard option to ISO C++23 Standard or Preview - Features from the Latest C++ Working Draft, whichever is available in your version of Visual C++, and click OK.

Finally, select Build ➪ Build Solution to compile your code. When it compiles without errors, you can run it with Debug ➪ Start Debugging.

> **NOTE** *Microsoft Visual C++ has full support for modules, including the C++23 standard named module* `std`.

Example: GCC

You can create your source code files with any text editor you prefer and save them to a directory. To compile your code, open a terminal and run the following command, specifying all your `.cpp` files that you want to compile:

```
g++ -std=c++2b -o <executable_name> <source1.cpp> [source2.cpp ...]
```

The `-std=c++2b` option is required to tell GCC to enable C++23 features. This option will change to `-std=C++23` once GCC is fully C++23-compliant.

Module Support

Support for modules in GCC is enabled with the `-fmodules-ts` option.

At the time of this writing, GCC does not yet support the C++23 standard named module `std`, introduced in Chapter 1. To make such code compile, you have to replace `import std;` declarations with `import` declarations of individual Standard Library headers. Once that is done, `import` declarations of Standard Library headers, such as the following, require you to precompile them:

```
import <iostream>;
```

Here is an example of precompiling `<iostream>`:

```
g++ -std=c++2b -fmodules-ts -xc++-system-header iostream
```

As an example, the `AirlineTicket` code from Chapter 1 uses modules. To compile it with GCC, first replace the use of `std::println()` with `std::cout` as GCC does not yet support `<print>` functionality at the time of this writing. After that, replace the `import std;` declarations with the appropriate `import` declarations, `<string>` and `<iostream>` for this example. You can find the adapted code in the `Examples\Ch00\AirlineTicket` directory in the downloadable source code archive.

Then, compile the two standard headers `<iostream>` and `<string>`:

```
g++ -std=c++2b -fmodules-ts -xc++-system-header iostream
g++ -std=c++2b -fmodules-ts -xc++-system-header string
```

Compile the module interface file:

```
g++ -std=c++2b -fmodules-ts -c -x c++ AirlineTicket.cppm
```

Finally, compile the application itself:

```
g++ -std=c++2b -fmodules-ts -o AirlineTicket AirlineTicket.cpp
AirlineTicketTest.cpp AirlineTicket.o
```

When it compiles without errors, you can run it as follows:

```
./AirlineTicket
```

> **NOTE** *The process of compiling C++ code using C++ modules with GCC might change in the future. Also, support for the C++23 standard named module* `std` *will be added. In that case, please consult the GCC documentation for an updated procedure on how to compile such code.*

C++23's Support for Printing Ranges

Chapter 2, "Working with Strings and String Views," explains that you can easily print the entire contents of Standard Library containers, such as `std::vector`, to the screen. This is a new feature since C++23 and not all compilers support this yet at the time of this writing.

As an example, Chapter 2 explains that you can write the contents of an `std::vector` as follows. Don't worry if you don't understand all the syntax yet, you will at the end of Chapter 2.

```
std::vector values { 11, 22, 33 };
std::print("{:n}", values);
```

This outputs:

```
11, 22, 33
```

If your compiler does not yet support this C++23 feature to print the contents of a container using `std::print()`, then you can convert the second line of code to the following:

```
for (const auto& value : values) { std::cout << value << ", "; }
```

This outputs:

```
11, 22, 33,
```

Again, don't worry if you don't understand the syntax yet. All will be clear at the end of Chapter 2.

READER SUPPORT FOR THIS BOOK

The following sections describe different options to get support for this book.

Companion Download Files

As you work through the examples in this book, you may choose either to type in all the code manually or to use the source code files that accompany the book. However, I suggest you type in all the code manually because it greatly benefits the learning process and your memory. All of the source code used in this book is available for download at `www.wiley.com/go/proc++6e` or from GitHub at `github.com/Professional-CPP/edition-6`.

> **NOTE** *Because many books have similar titles, you may find it easiest to search by ISBN; for this book, the ISBN is 978-1-394-19317-2.*

Once you've downloaded the code, just decompress it with your favorite decompression tool.

How to Contact the Publisher

If you believe you've found a mistake in this book, please bring it to our attention. At John Wiley & Sons, we understand how important it is to provide our customers with accurate content, but even with our best efforts an error may occur.

To submit your possible errata, please e-mail it to our Customer Service Team at `wileysupport@wiley.com` with "Possible Book Errata Submission" as a subject line.

How to Contact the Author

If you have any questions while reading this book, the author can easily be reached at `marc.gregoire@nuonsoft.com` and will try to get back to you in a timely manner.

PART I
Introduction to Professional C++

1

A Crash Course in C++ and the Standard Library

WHAT'S IN THIS CHAPTER?

- A brief overview of the most important parts and syntax of the C++ language and the C++ Standard Library
- How to write a basic class
- How scope resolution works
- What uniform initialization is
- The use of `const`
- What pointers, references, exceptions, and type aliases are
- Basics of type inference

WILEY.COM DOWNLOADS FOR THIS CHAPTER

Please note that all the code examples for this chapter are available as a part of the chapter's code download on this book's website at `www.wiley.com/go/proc++6e` on the Download Code tab.

The goal of this chapter is to cover briefly the most important parts of C++ so that you have a foundation of knowledge before embarking on the rest of this book. This chapter is not a comprehensive lesson in the C++ programming language or the Standard Library. Certain basic points, such as what a program is and what recursion is, are not covered. Esoteric points, such as the definition of a `union`, or the `volatile` keyword, are also omitted. Certain parts of the C language that are less relevant in C++ are also left out, as are parts of C++ that get in-depth coverage in later chapters.

This chapter aims to cover the parts of C++ that programmers encounter every day. For example, if you're fairly new to C++ and don't understand what a reference variable is, you'll learn about that kind of variable here. You'll also learn the basics of how to use the functionality available in the Standard Library, such as `vector` containers, `optional` values, `string` objects, and more. These modern constructs from the Standard Library are briefly introduced in this chapter so that they can be used throughout examples in this book from the beginning.

If you already have significant experience with C++, skim this chapter to make sure that there aren't any fundamental parts of the language on which you need to brush up. If you're new to C++, read this chapter carefully and make sure you understand the examples. If you need additional introductory information, consult the titles listed in Appendix B, "Annotated Bibliography."

C++ CRASH COURSE

The C++ language is often viewed as a "better C" or a "superset of C." It was mainly designed to be an object-oriented C, commonly called as "C with classes." Later on, many of the annoyances and rough edges of the C language were addressed as well. Because C++ is based on C, some of the syntax you'll see in this section will look familiar to you if you are an experienced C programmer. The two languages certainly have their differences, though. As evidence, the C23 standard specification document is a little fewer than 800 pages in size, while the C++23 standard specification document is more than 2,000 pages. So, if you're a C programmer but also if you are coming from other languages such as Java, C#, Python, and so on, be on the lookout for new or unfamiliar syntax!

The Obligatory "Hello, World" Program

In all its glory, the following code is the simplest C++ program you're likely to encounter. If you are using an older version of C++, then `import std;` and `std::println()` might not work. In that case, you'll need to use alternatives discussed shortly.

```
// 01_helloworld.cpp
import std;

int main()
{
    std::println("Hello, World!");
    return 0;
}
```

This code, as you might expect, prints the message "Hello, World!" on the screen. It is a simple program and unlikely to win any awards, but it does exhibit the following important concepts about the format of a C++ program:

- Comments
- Importing modules
- The `main()` function
- Printing text
- Returning from a function

These concepts are briefly explained in upcoming sections.

Comments

The first line of the program is a *comment*, a message that exists for the programmer only and is ignored by the compiler. In C++, there are two ways to delineate a comment. You can use two forward slashes to indicate that whatever follows on that line is a comment:

```
// 01_helloworld.cpp
```

The same behavior (this is to say, none) can be achieved by using a *multiline comment*. Multiline comments start with `/*` and end with `*/`. The following code shows a multiline comment in action (or, more appropriately, inaction):

```
/* This is a multiline comment.
   The compiler will ignore it.
 */
```

Comments are covered in detail in Chapter 3, "Coding with Style."

Importing Modules

Support for *modules* was one of the big four new features of C++20, replacing the old mechanism of *header files*. If you want to use functionality from a module, you simply import that module. This is done with an `import` declaration. Starting with C++23, you can get access to the entire C++ Standard Library by importing a single *standard named module* called `std`. The first line of the "Hello, World" application imports this standard module:

```
import std;
```

If the program did not import that module, it would be unable to perform its only task of printing text.

Without C++23's standard named module support, you have to explicitly import all individual header files that your code requires. As there are more than 100 header files in the Standard Library, it's not always obvious to know which specific header you need to import to use a certain feature. As a reference, Appendix C, "Standard Library Header Files," lists all header files of the C++ Standard Library including a short description of their contents. For example, instead of importing the standard named module `std` in the "Hello, World" application, you can import only those header files that the code really needs. In this example, the code only needs to import `<print>` to get access to the text printing functionality. Notice that when importing the named module `std`, you don't use angle brackets, but when importing individual header files, you need to use angle brackets as follows:

```
import <print>;
```

Since this is a book about C++23, this book uses modules everywhere. All functionality provided by the C++ Standard Library is provided in well-defined header files. Most examples in this book simply import the `std` named module, instead of individual header files, but the text always mentions in which header file certain functionality is provided.

Modules are not limited to Standard Library functionality. You can write your own modules to provide custom types and functionality, as you will learn throughout this book.

> **NOTE** *If your compiler does not yet have full support for modules, you can replace explicit header file* `import` *declarations with* `#include` *preprocessor directives, discussed in an upcoming section.*

How the Compiler Processes Your Source Code

In short, building a C++ program is a three-step process. Technically, there are a few more phases in the compilation process, but this simplified view is sufficient for now.

1. First, the code is run through a *preprocessor*, which recognizes meta-information about the code and handles preprocessor directives, such as `#include` directives. A source file in which all preprocessor directives are handled is called a *translation unit*.
2. Next, all translation units are independently *compiled*, or translated, into machine-readable *object files* in which references to functions and so on are not yet defined.
3. Resolving those references is done in the final phase by the *linker*, which links all object files together into the final *executable*.

> **NOTE** *Starting with C++23, the standard mandates that C++ compilers accept source code files saved with UTF-8 encoding. Chapter 21, "String Localization and Regular Expressions," discusses different encodings, including UTF-8. I recommend configuring your toolchain to use UTF-8. This will improve portability of your files between different platforms and will allow you to use non-English characters in your source files.*
>
> *To enable UTF-8 support with Microsoft Visual C++, add the* `/utf-8` *option to the Additional Options setting under Project Properties ⇨ Configuration Properties ⇨ C/C++ ⇨ Command Line. For GCC, use the command-line option* `-finput-charset=UTF-8`*. Clang assumes all files are UTF-8 by default.*

Preprocessor Directives

If your compiler does not yet support modules, then instead of importing modules or header files, you need to `#include` header files. That is, explicit `import` declarations such as `import <print>;`, need to be replaced with `#include` preprocessor directives as follows:

```
#include <print>
```

Directives aimed at the preprocessor start with the # character, as in `#include <print>`. In this case, the `#include` directive tells the preprocessor to take everything from the `<print>` header file and copy it into the current file. The `<print>` header provides the functionality to print text to the screen.

Chapter 11, "Modules, Header Files, and Miscellaneous Topics," discusses preprocessor directives in a bit more detail. But, as mentioned, this book uses modules instead of old-style header files.

The main() Function

`main()` is, of course, where the program starts. The return type of `main()` is an `int`, indicating the result status of the program. The `main()` function either takes no parameters or takes two parameters as follows:

```
int main(int argc, char** argv)
```

`argc` gives the number of arguments passed to the program, and `argv` contains those arguments. Note that `argv[0]` can be the program name, but it might as well be an empty string, so do not rely on it; instead, use platform-specific functionality to retrieve the program name. The important thing to remember is that the actual arguments contained in `argv` start at index 1.

Printing Text

Before C++23, you would use *I/O streams* to output text to the screen. Streams are briefly covered in the next section and in detail in Chapter 13, "Demystifying C++ I/O." However, C++23 introduces a new, easier-to-use mechanism to print text to the screen, which is used in almost every code snippet in this book: `std::print()` and `println()`, both defined in `<print>`.

Chapter 2, "Working with Strings and String Views," discusses the `std::print()` and `println()` string formatting and printing functions in detail. However, their basic use is straightforward and introduced here so that they can already be used in upcoming code snippets. In its most basic form, `println()` can be used to print a line of text that automatically ends with a new line:

```
std::println("Hello, World!");
```

The first argument to `println()` is a format string, which can contain replacement fields to be replaced with values passed in as second and subsequent arguments. You indicate where a replacement field goes by including curly brackets, {}, for each field to be included. For example:

```
std::println("There are {} ways I love you.", 219);
```

In this example, the number 219 is inserted into the string, so the output is:

```
There are 219 ways I love you.
```

You can have as many replacement fields as needed, for example:

```
std::println("{} + {} = {}", 2, 4, 6);
```

In this example, each field is applied in order, so the resulting output is:

```
2 + 4 = 6
```

There is much more to be said about the format of replacement fields, but that's for Chapter 2.

If you use `print()` instead of `println()`, the printed text will not end with a new line character.

I/O Streams

If your compiler does not yet support the C++23 `std::print()` and `println()` functions, you have to rewrite them using I/O streams.

I/O streams are covered in depth in Chapter 13, but the basics of output and input are simple. Think of an output stream as a laundry chute for data. Anything you toss into it will be output appropriately. `std::cout` is the chute corresponding to the user console, or *standard out*. There are other chutes, including `std::cerr`, which outputs to the error console. The `<<` operator tosses data down the chute. Output streams allow multiple types of data to be sent down the stream sequentially on a single line of code. The following code outputs text, followed by a number, followed by more text:

```
std::cout << "There are " << 219 << " ways I love you." << std::endl;
```

Starting with C++20, though, it is recommended to use `std::format()`, defined in `<format>`, to perform string formatting. The `format()` function uses the same concept of replacement fields as `print()` and `println()` and is discussed in detail in Chapter 2. However, using it to rewrite the previous statement is easy enough:

```
std::cout << std::format("There are {} ways I love you.", 219) << std::endl;
```

Thus, if your compiler doesn't support `print()` and `println()` yet, you can easily rewrite such statements to use `cout`, `format()`, and `endl`. For example, suppose you have the following statement:

```
std::println("{} + {} = {}", 2, 4, 6);
```

In this statement, replace `println()` with `format()`, stream the result to `cout`, and add an output of `endl`:

```
std::cout << std::format("{} + {} = {}", 2, 4, 6) << std::endl;
```

`std::endl` represents an end-of-line sequence. When the output stream encounters `std::endl`, it will output everything that has been sent down the chute so far and move to the next line. An alternate way of representing the end of a line is by using the `\n` character. The `\n` character is an *escape sequence*, which refers to a new-line character. Escape sequences can be used within any quoted string of text. The following table shows the most common ones:

ESCAPE SEQUENCE	MEANING
`\n`	New line: moves the cursor to the beginning of the next line
`\r`	Carriage return: moves the cursor to the beginning of the current line, but does not advance to the next line
`\t`	Tab
`\\`	Backslash character
`\"`	Quotation mark

WARNING *Keep in mind that* `endl` *inserts a new line into the stream and flushes everything currently in its buffers down the chute. Overusing* `endl`*, for example in a loop, is not recommended because it will have a performance impact. On the other hand, inserting* `\n` *into the stream also inserts a new line but does not automatically flush the buffers.*

By default, `print()` and `println()` print text to the standard output console, `std::cout`. You can print to the error console, `std::cerr`, as follows:

```
std::println(std::cerr, "Error: {}", 6);
```

Streams can also be used to accept input from the user. The simplest way to do so is to use the >> operator with an input stream. The `std::cin` input stream accepts keyboard input from the user. Here is an example:

```
import std;
int main()
{
    int value;
    std::cin >> value;
    std::println("You entered {}", value);
}
```

The >> operator stops input when it encounters a space character after reading a value. That also means you cannot use the operator to read text containing spaces. Additionally, user input can be tricky because you never know what kind of data the user will enter. Chapter 13 discusses input streams in detail, including how to read text with embedded spaces.

If you're new to C++ and coming from a C background, you're probably wondering what has been done with the trusty old `printf()` and `scanf()` functions. While these functions can still be used in C++, I strongly recommend using the modern `print()`, `println()`, and `format()` functions and the streams library instead, mainly because the `printf()` and `scanf()` family of functions do not provide any type safety.

Returning from a Function

The last line in the "Hello, World" program is as follows:

```
    return 0;
```

Since this is the `main()` function, returning from it returns control to the operating system. When doing so, it passes the value 0, which usually signals to the operating system that there were no errors while executing the program. For error cases, you can return non-zero values.

A `return` statement in `main()` is optional. If you don't write one, the compiler will implicitly add a `return 0;` for you.

Namespaces

Namespaces address the problem of naming conflicts between different pieces of code. For example, you might be writing some code that has a function called `foo()`. One day, you decide to start using a third-party library, which also has a `foo()` function. The compiler has no way of knowing which version of `foo()` you are referring to within your code. You can't change the library's function name, and it would be a big pain to change your own.

Namespaces come to the rescue in such scenarios because you can define the context in which names are defined. To place code in a namespace, enclose it within a namespace block. Here's an example:

```
namespace mycode {
    void foo()
    {
        std::println("foo() called in the mycode namespace");
    }
}
```

By placing your version of `foo()` in the namespace `mycode`, you are isolating it from the `foo()` function provided by the third-party library. To call the namespace-enabled version of `foo()`, prepend the namespace onto the function name by using `::`, also called the *scope resolution operator*, as follows:

```
mycode::foo();    // Calls the "foo" function in the "mycode" namespace
```

Any code that falls within a `mycode` namespace block can call other code within the same namespace without explicitly prepending the namespace. This implicit namespace is useful in making the code more readable. You can also avoid prepending of namespaces with a `using` *directive*. This directive tells the compiler that the subsequent code is making use of names in the specified namespace. The namespace is thus implied for the code that follows:

```
using namespace mycode;

int main()
{
    foo();  // Implies mycode::foo();
}
```

> **NOTE** *The* `main()` *function must never be put in a namespace. It must be in the global namespace.*

A single source file can contain multiple `using` directives, but beware of overusing this shortcut. In the extreme case, if you declare that you're using every namespace known to humanity, you're effectively eliminating namespaces entirely! Name conflicts will again result if you are using two namespaces that contain the same names. It is also important to know in which namespace your code is operating so that you don't end up accidentally calling the wrong version of a function.

You've seen the namespace syntax before—you used it in the "Hello, World" program, where `println` is a name defined in the `std` namespace. You can write "Hello, World" with a `using` directive as shown here:

```
import std;

using namespace std;

int main()
{
    println("Hello, World!");
}
```

> **NOTE** *Most code snippets in this book assume a* `using` *directive for the* `std` *namespace so that everything from the C++ Standard Library can be used without the need to qualify it with* `std::`.

A `using` *declaration* can be used to refer to a particular item within a namespace. For example, if the only part of the `std` namespace that you want to use unqualified is `print`, you can use the following `using` declaration:

```
using std::print;
```

Subsequent code can refer to print without prepending the namespace, but other items in the std namespace, such as println, still need to be explicit:

```
using std::print;
print("Hello, ");
std::println("World!");
```

> **WARNING** *Never put a* using *directive or* using *declaration in a header file at global scope; otherwise, you force it on everyone who includes your header file. Putting it in a smaller scope, for instance at namespace or class scope, is OK, even in a header file. It's also perfectly fine to put a* using *directive or declaration in a module interface file, as long as you don't export it. However, this book always fully qualifies all types in module interface files, as I think it makes it easier to understand an interface. Module interface files and exporting entities from modules are explained later in this chapter.*

Nested Namespace

A *nested namespace* is a namespace inside another one. Each namespace is separated by a double colon. Here's an example:

```
namespace MyLibraries::Networking::FTP {
    /* ... */
}
```

This compact syntax was not available before C++17 in which case you had to resort to the following:

```
namespace MyLibraries {
    namespace Networking {
        namespace FTP {
            /* ... */
        }
    }
}
```

Namespace Alias

A *namespace alias* can be used to give a new and possibly shorter name to another namespace. Here's an example:

```
namespace MyFTP = MyLibraries::Networking::FTP;
```

Literals

Literals are used to write numbers or strings in your code. C++ supports a couple of standard literals. Integral numbers can be written using the following literals (the examples represent the same number, 123):

- Decimal literal, 123
- Octal literal, 0173 (starts with a zero)

- Hexadecimal literal, `0x7B` (starts with 0x)
- Binary literal, `0b1111011` (starts with 0b)

> **WARNING** *Never put a zero, `0`, in front of a numerical literal, unless it's an octal literal!*

Other examples of literals in C++ include the following:

- A floating-point value (such as `3.14f`)
- A double floating-point value (such as `3.14`)
- A hexadecimal floating-point literal (such as `0x3.ABCp-10` and `0Xb.cp121`)
- A single character (such as `'a'`)
- A zero-terminated array of characters (such as `"character array"`)

A literal can have a suffix, such as the `f` in `3.14f`, to force a certain type. In this case, `3.14f` results in a `float`, while `3.14` results in a `double`.

Single quote characters can be used as digit separators in numeric literals. For example:

- `23'456'789`
- `2'34'56'789`
- `0.123'456f`

Multiple string literals separated only by whitespace are automatically concatenated into a single string. For example:

```
std::println("Hello, "
             "World!");
```

is equivalent to:

```
std::println("Hello, World!");
```

It is also possible to define your own type of literals, which is an advanced feature explained in Chapter 15, "Overloading C++ Operators."

Variables

In C++, *variables* can be declared just about anywhere in your code and can be used anywhere in the current block below the line where they are declared. Variables can be declared without being given a value. These uninitialized variables generally end up with a semi-random value based on whatever is in memory at that time, and they are therefore the source of countless bugs. Variables in C++ can alternatively be assigned an initial value when they are declared. The code that follows shows both flavors of variable declaration, both using `int`s, which represent integer values:

```
int uninitializedInt;
int initializedInt { 7 };
```

```
println("{} is a random value", uninitializedInt);
println("{} was assigned as an initial value", initializedInt);
```

> **NOTE** *Most compilers will issue a warning or an error when code is using uninitialized variables. Some compilers will generate code that will report an error at run time.*

The `initializedInt` variable is initialized using the *uniform initialization* syntax. You can also use the following assignment syntax for initializing variables:

```
int initializedInt = 7;
```

Uniform initialization was introduced with the C++11 standard in 2011. It is recommended to use uniform initialization instead of the old assignment syntax, so that's the syntax used in this book. The section "Uniform Initialization" later in this chapter goes deeper in on the benefits and why it is recommended.

Variables in C++ are strongly typed; that is, they always have a specific type. C++ comes with a whole set of built-in types that you can use out of the box. The following table shows the most common types:

TYPE	DESCRIPTION	USAGE

`(signed) int`
`signed`
	Positive and negative integers; the range depends on the compiler (usually 4 bytes)	`int i {-7};`
		`signed int i {-6};`
		`signed i {-5};`

`(signed) short (int)`	Short integer (usually 2 bytes)	`short s {13};`
		`short int s {14};`
		`signed short s {15};`
		`signed short int s {16};`

`(signed) long (int)`	Long integer (usually 4 bytes)	`long l {-7L};`
`(signed) long long (int)`	Long long integer; the range depends on the compiler but is at least the same as for `long` (usually 8 bytes)	`long long ll {14LL};`

`unsigned (int)`
`unsigned short (int)`
`unsigned long (int)`
`unsigned long long (int)`
	Limits the preceding types to values >= 0	`unsigned int i {2U};`
		`unsigned j {5U};`
		`unsigned short s {23U};`
		`unsigned long l {54UL};`
		`unsigned long long ll {140ULL};`

`float`	Single precision floating-point numbers	`float f {7.2f};`

continues

(continued)

TYPE	DESCRIPTION	USAGE
`double`	Double precision floating-point numbers; precision is at least the same as for `float`	`double d {7.2};`
`long double`	Long double precision floating-point numbers; precision is at least the same as for `double`	`long double d {16.98L};`

`char`
`unsigned char`
`signed char`
	A single character	`char ch {'m'};`

`char8_t`
`char16_t`
`char32_t`
	A single *n*-bit UTF-*n*-encoded Unicode character where *n* can be 8, 16, or 32	`char8_t c8 {u8'm'};`
		`char16_t c16 {u'm'};`
		`char32_t c32 {U'm'};`

`wchar_t`	A single wide character; the size depends on the compiler	`wchar_t w {L'm'};`
`bool`	A Boolean type that can have one of two values: `true` or `false`	`bool b {true};`

The range of `signed` and `unsigned` integer and `char` types is as follows:

TYPE	SIGNED	UNSIGNED
`char`	-128 to 127	0 to 255
2-byte integers	-32,768 to 32,767	0 to 65,535
4-byte integers	-2,147,483,648 to 2,147,483,647	0 to 4,294,967,295
8-byte integers	-9,223,372,036,854,775,808 to 9,223,372,036,854,775,807	0 to 18,446,744,073,709,551,615

Type `char` is a different type compared to both the `signed char` and `unsigned char` types. It should be used only to represent characters. Depending on your compiler, it can be either signed or unsigned, so you should not rely on it being signed or unsigned.

The range and precision of floating-point types is discussed in the section "Floating-Point Numbers" later in this chapter.

Related to `char`, `<cstddef>` provides the `std::byte` type representing a single byte. Before C++17, a `char` or `unsigned char` was used to represent a byte, but those types make it look like you are working with characters. `std::byte` on the other hand clearly states your intention, that is, a single byte of memory. A `byte` can be initialized as follows:

```
std::byte b { 42 };
```

> **NOTE** *C++ does not provide a basic string type. However, a standard implementation of a string is provided as part of the Standard Library, as briefly discussed later in this chapter and in detail in Chapter 2.*

Numerical Limits

C++ provides a standard way to obtain information about numeric limits, such as the maximum possible value for an integer on the current platform. In C, you could access constants, such as `INT_MAX`. While those are still available in C++, it's recommended to use the `std::numeric_limits` class template defined in `<limits>`. Class templates are discussed later in this book, but those details are not important to understand how to use `numeric_limits`. For now, you just need to know that, since it is a class template, you have to specify the type you are interested in between a set of angle brackets. For example, to get numeric limits for integers, you write `std::numeric_limits<int>`. Consult a Standard Library reference (see Appendix B) to learn exactly what kind of information you can query using `numeric_limits`.

Here are a few examples:

```
println("int:");
println("Max int value: {}", numeric_limits<int>::max());
println("Min int value: {}", numeric_limits<int>::min());
println("Lowest int value: {}", numeric_limits<int>::lowest());

println("\ndouble:");
println("Max double value: {}", numeric_limits<double>::max());
println("Min double value: {}", numeric_limits<double>::min());
println("Lowest double value: {}", numeric_limits<double>::lowest());
```

The output of this code snippet on my system is as follows:

```
int:
Max int value: 2147483647
Min int value: -2147483648
Lowest int value: -2147483648

double:
Max double value: 1.7976931348623157e+308
Min double value: 2.2250738585072014e-308
Lowest double value: -1.7976931348623157e+308
```

Note the differences between `min()` and `lowest()`. For an integer, the minimum value equals the lowest value. However, for floating-point types, the minimum value is the smallest positive value that can be represented, while the lowest value is the most negative value representable, which equals `-max()`.

Zero Initialization

Variables can be initialized to zero with `{0}`, or with a *zero initializer*, `{}`. Zero initialization initializes primitive integer types (such as `char`, `int`, and so on) to zero, primitive floating-point types to 0.0, pointer types to `nullptr`, and constructs objects with the default constructor (discussed later).

Here is an example of zero initializing a `float` and an `int`:

```
float myFloat {};
int myInt {};
```

Casting

Variables can be converted to other types by *casting* them. For example, a `float` can be cast to an `int`. C++ provides three ways to *explicitly* change the type of a variable. The first method is a holdover from C; it is not recommended but, unfortunately, still commonly used. The second method is rarely used. The third method is the most verbose but is also the cleanest one and is therefore recommended.

```
float myFloat { 3.14f };
int i1 { (int)myFloat };                // method 1
int i2 { int(myFloat) };                // method 2
int i3 { static_cast<int>(myFloat) };   // method 3
```

The resulting integer will be the value of the floating-point number with the fractional part truncated. Chapter 10, "Discovering Inheritance Techniques," describes the different casting methods in more detail. In some contexts, variables can be automatically cast, or *coerced*. For example, a `short` can be automatically converted into a `long` because a `long` represents the same type of data with at least the same precision:

```
long someLong { someShort };            // no explicit cast needed
```

When automatically casting variables, you need to be aware of the potential loss of data. For example, casting a `float` to an `int` throws away the fractional part of the number, and the resulting integer can even be completely wrong if the floating-point value represents a number bigger than the maximum representable integer value. Most compilers will issue a warning or even an error if you assign a `float` to an `int` without an explicit cast. If you are certain that the left-hand side type is fully compatible with the right-hand side type, it's OK to cast implicitly.

Floating-Point Numbers

Working with floating-point numbers can be more complicated than working with integral types. You need to keep a few things in mind. Calculations with floating-point values that are orders of magnitude different can cause errors. Furthermore, calculating the difference between two floating-point numbers that are almost identical will cause the loss of precision. Also keep in mind that a lot of decimal values cannot be represented exactly as floating-point numbers. However, going deeper in on the numerical problems with using floating-point numbers and how to write numerical stable floating-point algorithms is outside the scope of this book, as these topics warrant a whole book on their own.

There are several special floating-point numbers:

- **+/-infinity:** Represents positive and negative infinity, for example the result of dividing a non-zero number by zero
- **NaN:** Abbreviation for not-a-number, for example the result of dividing zero by zero, a mathematically undefined result

To check whether a given floating-point number is not-a-number, use `std::isnan()`. To check for infinity, use `std::isinf()`. Both functions are defined in `<cmath>`.

To obtain one of these special floating-point values, use `numeric_limits`, for example `std::numeric_limits<double>::infinity()`.

Extended Floating-Point Types

As mentioned in the section on variables earlier, C++ provides the following *standard floating-point types*: `float`, `double`, and `long double`.

C++23 introduces the following *extended floating-point types* that have become popular in certain domains. Support for these is optional, and not all compilers provide these types.

TYPE	DESCRIPTION	LITERAL SUFFIX
`std::float16_t`	16-bit format from the IEEE 754 standard.	`F16` or `f16`
`std::float32_t`	32-bit format from the IEEE 754 standard.	`F32` or `f32`
`std::float64_t`	64-bit format from the IEEE 754 standard.	`F64` or `f64`
`std::float128_t`	128-bit format from the IEEE 754 standard.	`F128` or `f128`
`std::bfloat16_t`	Brain floating point.[1] Used in certain AI domains.	`BF16` or `bf16`

Most of the time, the standard types, `float`, `double`, and `long double`, are enough. From these, `double` should be your default type. Using `float` can trigger loss of precision, and, depending on your use case, this might or might not be acceptable.

Range and Accuracy of Floating-Point Types

Floating-point types have a limited range and a limited precision. The following table gives detailed specifications of all standard and extended floating-point types supported by C++. However, the specifications of the standard types, `float`, `double`, and `long double`, are not specified exactly by the C++ standard. The standard says only that `long double` should have at least the same precision as `double`, and `double` should have at least the same precision as `float`. For these three types, the table shows values commonly used by compilers.

TYPE	NAME	MANTISSA BITS	DECIMAL DIGITS	EXPONENT BITS	MIN	MAX
`float`	Single precision	24	7.22	8	1.18×10^{-38}	3.40×10^{38}
`double`	Double precision	53	15.95	11	2.23×10^{-308}	1.80×10^{308}

continues

[1] Developed by Google Brain, an artificial intelligence group at Google. It is used in AI processors and supported in hardware on the latest NVIDIA GPUs.

(continued)

TYPE	NAME	MANTISSA BITS	DECIMAL DIGITS	EXPONENT BITS	MIN	MAX
`long double`	Extended precision	64	19.27	15	3.36×10^{-4932}	1.19×10^{4932}
`std::float16_t`	Half precision	11	3.31	5	6.10×10^{-5}	65504
`std::float32_t`	Single precision	24	7.22	8	1.18×10^{-38}	3.40×10^{38}
`std::float64_t`	Double precision	53	15.95	11	2.23×10^{-308}	1.80×10^{308}
`std::float128_t`	Quadruple precision	113	34.02	15	3.36×10^{-4932}	1.19×10^{4932}
`std::bfloat16_t`	Brain floating point	8	2.41	8	1.18×10^{-38}	3.40×10^{38}

Operators

What good is a variable if you don't have a way to change it? The following table shows common *operators* used in C++ and sample code that makes use of them. Operators in C++ can be *binary* (operate on two expressions), *unary* (operate on a single expression), or even *ternary* (operate on three expressions). There is only one ternary operator in C++, and it is explained in the section "The Conditional Operator" later in this chapter. Furthermore, Chapter 15, "Overloading C++ Operators," is reserved for operators and explains how you can add support for these operators to your own custom types.

OPERATOR	DESCRIPTION	USAGE

`=`	Binary operator to assign the value on the right to the expression on the left.	`int i;`
		`i = 3;`
		`int j;`
		`j = i;`

`!`	Unary operator to complement the true/false (non-0/0) status of an expression.	`bool b {!true};` `bool b2 {!b};`

`+`	Binary operator for addition.	`int i {3 + 2};`
		`int j {i + 5};`
		`int k {i + j};`

`-`
`*`
`/`
	Binary operators for subtraction, multiplication, and division.	`int i {5 - 1};`
		`int j {5 * 2};`
		`int k {j / i};`

<table>
<tr><th>OPERATOR</th><th>DESCRIPTION</th><th>USAGE</th></tr>
<tr><td>%</td><td>Binary operator for the remainder of a division operation. This is also referred to as the mod or modulo operator. For example: 5%2=1.</td><td><code>int rem {5 % 2};</code></td></tr>
<tr><td>++</td><td>Unary operator to increment an expression by 1. If the operator occurs after the expression, or post-increment, the result of the expression is the unincremented value. If the operator occurs before the expression, or pre-increment, the result of the expression is the new value.</td><td><code>i++;</code>
<code>++i;</code></td></tr>
<tr><td>--</td><td>Unary operator to decrement an expression by 1.</td><td><code>i--;</code>
<code>--i;</code></td></tr>
<tr><td>+=
-=
*=
/=
%=</td><td>Shorthand syntax for:
<code>i = i + (j);</code>
<code>i = i - (j);</code>
<code>i = i * (j);</code>
<code>i = i / (j);</code>
<code>i = i % (j);</code></td><td><code>i += j;</code>
<code>i -= j;</code>
<code>i *= j;</code>
<code>i /= j;</code>
<code>i %= j;</code></td></tr>
<tr><td>&
&=</td><td>Takes the raw bits of one expression and performs a bitwise AND with the other expression.</td><td><code>i = j & k;</code>
<code>j &= k;</code></td></tr>
<tr><td>|
|=</td><td>Takes the raw bits of one expression and performs a bitwise OR with the other expression.</td><td><code>i = j | k;</code>
<code>j |= k;</code></td></tr>
<tr><td><<
>>
<<=
>>=</td><td>Takes the raw bits of an expression and "shifts" each bit left (<<) or right (>>) the specified number of places.</td><td><code>i = i << 1;</code>
<code>i = i >> 4;</code>
<code>i <<= 1;</code>
<code>i >>= 4;</code></td></tr>
<tr><td>^
^=</td><td>Performs a bitwise exclusive or, also called XOR operation, on two expressions.</td><td><code>i = i ^ j;</code>
<code>i ^= j;</code></td></tr>
</table>

Operators of the form `op=`, e.g., `+=`, are called *compound assignment operators*.

When a binary operator is applied to two operands of different types, the compiler inserts an *implicit conversion* to convert one of them to the other before applying the operator. You can also use *explicit conversions* to convert one type to another using `static_cast()`.

For implicit conversions, the compiler has certain rules to decide which type it converts to which other type. For example, for a binary operation with a small integer type and a larger integer type, the smaller type will be converted to the larger one. However, the results might not always be as you would expect. Thus, I recommend being careful with implicit conversions and using explicit conversions to make sure the compiler does what you intend.

The following code snippet shows the most common variable types and operators in action. It also shows explicit conversions and explains why they are necessary. If you are unsure about how variables and operators work, try to figure out what the output of this program will be, and then run it to confirm your answer.

```
int someInteger { 256 };
short someShort;
long someLong;
float someFloat;
double someDouble;

someInteger++;
someInteger *= 2;
// Conversion from larger integer type to smaller integer type
// can cause a warning or error, hence static_cast() is required.
someShort = static_cast<short>(someInteger);
someLong = someShort * 10000;
someFloat = someLong + 0.785f;
// To make sure the division is performed with double precision,
// someFloat is explicitly converted to double first.
someDouble = static_cast<double>(someFloat) / 100000;
println("{}", someDouble);
```

The C++ compiler has a recipe for the order in which expressions are evaluated. If you have a complicated expression with many operators, the order of execution may not be obvious. For that reason, it's probably better to break up a complicated expression into several smaller expressions, or explicitly group subexpressions by using parentheses. For example, the following line of code might be confusing unless you happen to know the exact evaluation order of the operators:

```
int i { 34 + 8 * 2 + 21 / 7 % 2 };
```

Adding parentheses makes it clear which operations are happening first:

```
int i { 34 + (8 * 2) + ( (21 / 7) % 2 ) };
```

For those of you playing along at home, both approaches are equivalent and end up with `i` equal to 51. If you assumed that C++ evaluated expressions from left to right, your answer would have been 1. C++ evaluates `/`, `*`, and `%` first (in left-to-right order), followed by addition and subtraction, then bitwise operators. Parentheses let you explicitly tell the compiler that a certain operation should be evaluated first.

Formally, the evaluation order of operators is expressed by their *precedence*. Operators with a higher precedence are executed before operators with a lower precedence. The following list shows the precedence of the operators from the previous table. Operators higher in the list have higher precedence and hence are executed before operators lower in the list.

- `++ --` (postfix)
- `! ++ --` (prefix)
- `* / %`
- `+ -`
- `<< >>`
- `&`

- `^`
- `|`
- `= += -= *= /= %= &= |= ^= <<= >>=`

This is only a selection of the available C++ operators. Chapter 15 gives a complete overview of all available operators, including their precedence.

Enumerations

An integer really represents a single value from a larger set of values—the entire sequence of integral numbers. *Enumerations* are types that let you define your own sequences so that you can declare variables with values in that sequence. For example, in a chess program, you *could* represent each piece as an `int`, with constants for the piece types, as shown in the following code. The integers representing the types are marked `const` to indicate that they can never change.

```
const int PieceTypeKing { 0 };
const int PieceTypeQueen { 1 };
const int PieceTypeRook { 2 };
const int PieceTypePawn { 3 };
//etc.
int myPiece { PieceTypeKing };
```

This representation can become dangerous. Since a piece is just an `int`, what would happen if another programmer added code to increment the value of a piece? By adding 1, a king becomes a queen, which really makes no sense. Worse still, someone could come in and give a piece a value of -1, which has no corresponding constant.

Strongly typed enumerations solve these problems by tightly defining the range of values for a variable. The following code declares a new type, `PieceType`, which has four possible values, called *enumerators*, representing four of the chess pieces:

```
enum class PieceType { King, Queen, Rook, Pawn };
```

This new type can be used as follows:

```
PieceType piece { PieceType::King };
```

Behind the scenes, an enumeration is just an integer value. The underlying values for `King`, `Queen`, `Rook`, and `Pawn` are 0, 1, 2, and 3, respectively. It's possible to specify the integer values for enumerators yourself. The syntax is as follows:

```
enum class PieceType
{
    King = 1,
    Queen,
    Rook = 10,
    Pawn
};
```

If you do not assign a value to an enumerator, the compiler automatically assigns it a value that is the previous enumerator incremented by 1. If you do not assign a value to the first enumerator, the compiler assigns it the value 0. So, in this example, `King` has the integer value 1, `Queen` has the value 2 assigned by the compiler, `Rook` has the value 10, and `Pawn` has the value 11 assigned automatically by the compiler.

Even though enumerators are internally represented by integer values, they are not automatically converted to integers, which means the following is illegal:

```
int underlyingValue { piece };
```

C++23 Starting with C++23, you can use `std::to_underlying()`. For example:

```
int underlyingValue { to_underlying(piece) };
```

By default, the underlying type of an enumerator is an integer, but this can be changed as follows:

```
enum class PieceType : unsigned long
{
    King = 1,
    Queen,
    Rook = 10,
    Pawn
};
```

For an `enum class`, the enumerator names are not automatically exported to the enclosing scope. This means they cannot clash with other names already defined in the parent scope. As a result, different strongly typed enumerations can have enumerators with the same name. For example, the following two enumerations are perfectly legal:

```
enum class State { Unknown, Started, Finished };
enum class Error { None, BadInput, DiskFull, Unknown };
```

A big benefit of this is that you can give short names to the enumerators, for example, `Unknown` instead of `UnknownState` and `UnknownError`. However, it also means that you either have to fully qualify enumerators, or use a `using enum` or `using` declaration. Here's an example of a `using enum` declaration:

```
using enum PieceType;
PieceType piece { King };
```

A `using` declaration can be used if you want to avoid having to fully qualify specific enumerators. For example, in the following code snippet, `King` can be used without full qualification, but other enumerators still need to be fully qualified:

```
using PieceType::King;
PieceType piece { King };
piece = PieceType::Queen;
```

> **WARNING** *Even though C++ allows you to avoid fully qualifying enumerators, I recommend using this feature judiciously. At least try to minimize the scope of the* `using enum` *or* `using` *declaration because if this scope is too big, you risk reintroducing name clashes. The section on the* `switch` *statement later in this chapter shows a properly scoped use of a* `using enum` *declaration.*

Old-Style Enumerations

New code should always use the strongly typed enumerations explained in the previous section. However, in legacy code bases, you might find *old-style enumerations*, also known as *unscoped enumerations*: `enum` instead of `enum class`. Here is the previous `PieceType` defined as an old-style enumeration:

```
enum PieceType { PieceTypeKing, PieceTypeQueen, PieceTypeRook, PieceTypePawn };
```

The enumerators of such old-style enumerations are exported to the enclosing scope. This means that in the parent scope you can use the names of the enumerators without fully qualifying them, for example:

```
PieceType myPiece { PieceTypeQueen };
```

This of course also means that they can clash with other names already defined in the parent scope resulting in a compilation error. Here's an example:

```
bool ok { false };
enum Status { error, ok };
```

This code snippet does not compile because the name `ok` is first defined to be a Boolean variable, and later the same name is used as the name of an enumerator. Visual C++ 2022 emits the following error:

```
error C2365: 'ok': redefinition; previous definition was 'data variable'
```

Hence, you should make sure such old-style enumerations have enumerators with unique names, such as `PieceTypeQueen`, instead of simply `Queen`.

These old-style enumerations are not strongly typed, meaning they are not *type safe*. They are always interpreted as integers, and thus you can inadvertently compare enumerators from completely different enumerations, or pass an enumerator of the wrong enumeration to a function.

> **WARNING** *Always use strongly typed* `enum class` *enumerations instead of old-style, unscoped, type-unsafe* `enum` *enumerations.*

Structs

Structs let you encapsulate one or more existing types into a new type. The classic example of a struct is a database record. If you are building a personnel system to keep track of employee information, you might want to store the first initial, last initial, employee number, and salary for each employee. A struct that contains all of this information is shown in the `employee.cppm` *module interface file* that follows. This is your first self-written module in this book. Module interface files usually have `.cppm` as extension. The first line in the module interface file is a *module declaration* and states that this file is defining a module called `employee`. Furthermore, a module needs to explicitly state what it *exports*, i.e., what will be visible when this module is imported somewhere else. Exporting a type from a module is done with the `export` keyword in front of, for example, a `struct`.

```
export module employee;

export struct Employee {
    char firstInitial;
    char lastInitial;
    int employeeNumber;
    int salary;
};
```

A variable declared with type `Employee` has all of these *fields* built in. The individual fields of a struct can be accessed by using the `.` operator. The example that follows creates and then outputs the record for an employee. Just as with the standard named module `std`, you don't use angle brackets when importing custom modules.

```
import std;
import employee; // Import our employee module

using namespace std;

int main()
{
    // Create and populate an employee.
    Employee anEmployee;
    anEmployee.firstInitial = 'J';
    anEmployee.lastInitial = 'D';
    anEmployee.employeeNumber = 42;
    anEmployee.salary = 80000;
    // Output the values of an employee.
    println("Employee: {}{}", anEmployee.firstInitial,
        anEmployee.lastInitial);
    println("Number: {}", anEmployee.employeeNumber);
    println("Salary: ${}", anEmployee.salary);
}
```

Conditional Statements

Conditional statements let you execute code based on whether something is true. As shown in the following sections, there are two main types of conditional statements in C++: `if/else` statements and `switch` statements.

if/else Statements

The most common conditional statement is the `if` statement, which can be accompanied by an `else`. If the condition given inside the `if` statement is true, the line or block of code is executed. If not, execution continues with the `else` case if present or with the code following the conditional statement. The following code shows a *cascading if statement*, a fancy way of saying that the `if` statement has an `else` statement that in turn has another `if` statement, and so on:

```
if (i > 4) {
    // Do something.
} else if (i > 2) {
    // Do something else.
} else {
    // Do something else.
}
```

The expression between the parentheses of an `if` statement must be a Boolean value or evaluate to a Boolean value. A value of 0 evaluates to `false`, while any non-zero value evaluates to `true`. For example, `if(0)` is equivalent to `if(false)`. Logical evaluation operators, described later, provide ways of evaluating expressions to result in a `true` or `false` Boolean value.

Initializers for if Statements

C++ allows you to include an initializer inside an `if` statement using the following syntax:

```
if (<initializer>; <conditional_expression>) {
    <if_body>
} else if (<else_if_expression>) {
    <else_if_body>
} else {
    <else_body>
}
```

Any variable introduced in the `<initializer>` is available only in the `<conditional_expression>`, in the `<if_body>`, in all `<else_if_expression>`s and `<else_if_body>`s, and in the `<else_body>`. Such variables are not available outside the `if` statement.

It is too early in this book to give a useful example of this feature, but here is an example of how it could be employed:

```
if (Employee employee { getEmployee() }; employee.salary > 1000) { ... }
```

In this example, the initializer gets an employee by calling the `getEmployee()` function. Functions are discussed later in this chapter. The condition checks whether the salary of the retrieved employee exceeds 1000. Only in that case is the body of the `if` statement executed. More concrete examples will be given throughout this book.

switch Statements

The `switch` statement is an alternate syntax for performing actions based on the value of an expression. In C++, the expression of a `switch` statement must be of an integral type, a type convertible to an integral type, an enumeration, or a strongly typed enumeration, and must be compared to constants. Each constant value represents a "case." If the expression matches the case, the subsequent lines of code are executed until a `break` statement is reached. You can also provide a `default` case, which is matched if none of the other cases matches. The following pseudocode shows a common use of the `switch` statement:

```
switch (menuItem) {
    case OpenMenuItem:
        // Code to open a file
        break;
    case SaveMenuItem:
        // Code to save a file
        break;
    default:
        // Code to give an error message
        break;
}
```

A `switch` statement can always be converted into `if/else` statements. The previous `switch` statement can be converted as follows:

```
if (menuItem == OpenMenuItem) {
    // Code to open a file
} else if (menuItem == SaveMenuItem) {
    // Code to save a file
} else {
    // Code to give an error message
}
```

switch statements are generally used when you want to do something based on more than one specific value of an expression, as opposed to some test on the expression. In such a case, the switch statement avoids cascading if/else statements. If you need to inspect only one value, an if or if/else statement is fine.

Once a case expression matching the switch condition is found, all statements that follow it are executed until a break statement is reached. This execution continues even if another case expression is encountered, which is called *fallthrough*. In the following example, a single set of statements is executed for both Mode::Standard and Default. If mode is Custom, then value is first changed from 42 to 84, after which the Standard and Default statements are executed. In other words, the Custom case falls through until it eventually reaches a break statement or the end of the switch statement. This code snippet also shows a nice example of using a properly scoped using enum declaration to avoid having to write Mode::Custom, Mode::Standard, and Mode::Default for the different case labels.

```
enum class Mode { Default, Custom, Standard };

int value { 42 };
Mode mode { /* ... */ };
switch (mode) {
    using enum Mode;

    case Custom:
        value = 84;
    case Standard:
    case Default:
        // Do something with value ...
        break;
}
```

Fallthrough can be a source of bugs, for example if you accidentally forget a break statement. Because of this, some compilers give a warning if a fallthrough is detected in a switch statement, unless the case is empty. In the previous example, no compiler will give a warning that the Standard case falls through to the Default case, but a compiler might give a warning for the Custom case fallthrough. To prevent this warning and to make it clear to a reader and the compiler that the fallthrough is intentional, you can use a [[fallthrough]] attribute as follows:

```
switch (mode) {
    using enum Mode;

    case Custom:
        value = 84;
        [[fallthrough]];
    case Standard:
    case Default:
        // Do something with value ...
        break;
}
```

Surrounding the statements following a case expression with braces is often optional, but sometimes necessary, for example, when defining variables. Here is an example:

```
switch (mode) {
    using enum Mode;
```

```
        case Custom:
            {
                int someVariable { 42 };
                value = someVariable * 2;
                [[fallthrough]];
            }
        case Standard:
        case Default:
            // Do something with value ...
            break;
    }
```

When using a `switch` statement for enumerations, most compilers issue a warning when you don't handle all different enumerators, either by explicitly writing cases for each enumerator or by writing cases for only a selection of the enumerators in combination with a `default` case. However, it's recommended not to include a `default` case in a `switch` statement switching on enumerations. Instead, you should explicitly list all enumerators. The reason is that this makes the code less error prone for when you later add more enumerators to the enumeration. In that case, if you forget to add any new enumerator to specific `switch` statements, the compiler will issue a warning instead of silently handling the new enumerator using the `default` case.

Initializers for switch Statements

Just as for `if` statements, you can use initializers with `switch` statements. The syntax is as follows:

```
switch (<initializer>; <expression>) { <body> }
```

Any variables introduced in the `<initializer>` are available only in the `<expression>` and in the `<body>`. They are not available outside the `switch` statement.

The Conditional Operator

C++ has one operator that takes three arguments, known as a *ternary operator*. It is used as a shorthand conditional expression of the form "if [*something*] then [*perform action*], otherwise [*perform some other action*]." The conditional operator is represented by a `?` and a `:`. The following code outputs "yes" if the variable `i` is greater than 2, and "no" otherwise:

```
println("{}", (i > 2) ? "yes" : "no");
```

The parentheses around `i > 2` are optional, so the following is equivalent:

```
println("{}", i > 2 ? "yes" : "no");
```

The advantage of the conditional operator is that it is an expression, not a statement like the `if` and `switch` statements. Hence, a conditional operator can occur within almost any context. In the preceding example, the conditional operator is used within code that performs output. A convenient way to remember how the syntax is used is to treat the question mark as though the statement that comes before it really is a question. For example, "Is `i` greater than 2? If so, the result is 'yes'; if not, the result is 'no.'"

Logical Evaluation Operators

You have already seen a *logical evaluation operator* without a formal definition. The `>` operator compares two values. The result is `true` if the value on the left is greater than the value on the right. All logical evaluation operators follow this pattern—they all result in a `true` or `false`.

The following table shows common logical evaluation operators:

OP	DESCRIPTION	USAGE

`<`
`<=`
`>`
`>=`
	Determines if the left-hand side is less than, less than or equal to, greater than, or greater than or equal to the right-hand side.	`if (i < 0) {`
		` print("i is negative");`
		`}`

`==`	Determines if the left-hand side equals the right-hand side. Don't confuse this with the = (assignment) operator!	`if (i == 3) {`
		` print("i is 3");`
		`}`

`!=`	Not equals. The result of the statement is `true` if the left-hand side does not equal the right-hand side.	`if (i != 3) {`
		` print("i is not 3");`
		`}`

`<=>`	Three-way comparison operator, also called the spaceship operator. Explained in more detail in the next section.	`result = i <=> 0;`

`!`	Logical NOT. This complements the `true/false` status of a Boolean expression. This is a unary operator.	`if (!bool1) {`
		` print("bool1 is false");`
		`}`

`&&`	Logical AND. The result is `true` if both parts of the expression are `true`.	`if (bool1 && bool2) {`
		` print("both are true");`
		`}`

`||`	Logical OR. The result is `true` if either part of the expression is `true`.	`if (bool1 || bool2) {`
		` print("at least one is true");`
		`}`

C++ uses *short-circuit logic* when evaluating logical expressions. That means that once the final result is certain, the rest of the expression won't be evaluated. For example, if you are performing logical OR operations of several Boolean expressions, as shown in the following code, the result is known to be `true` as soon as one of them is found to be `true`. The rest won't even be checked.

```
bool result { bool1 || bool2 || (i > 7) || (27 / 13 % i + 1) < 2 };
```

In this example, if `bool1` is found to be `true`, the entire expression must be `true`, so the other parts aren't evaluated. In this way, the language saves your code from doing unnecessary work. It can, however, be a source of hard-to-find bugs if the later subexpressions in some way influence the state of the program (for example, by calling a separate function).

The following code shows a statement using `&&` that short-circuits after the second term because 0 always evaluates to `false`:

```
bool result { bool1 && 0 && (i > 7) && !done };
```

Short-circuiting can be beneficial for performance. You can put less resource intensive tests first so that more expensive tests are not even executed when the logic short-circuits. It is also useful in the context of pointers to avoid parts of the expression to be executed when a pointer is not valid. Pointers and short-circuiting with pointers are discussed later in this chapter.

Three-Way Comparisons

The *three-way comparison operator* can be used to determine the order of two values. It is also called the *spaceship operator* because its sign, `<=>`, resembles a spaceship. With a single expression, it tells you whether a value is equal, less than, or greater than another value. Because it has to return more than just `true` or `false`, it cannot return a Boolean type. Instead, it returns an enumeration-like type, defined in `<compare>` in the `std` namespace. If the operands are integral types, the result is a *strong ordering* and can be one of the following:

- `strong_ordering::less`: First operand less than second
- `strong_ordering::greater`: First operand greater than second
- `strong_ordering::equal`: First operand equal to second

Here is an example of its use:

```
int i { 11 };
strong_ordering result { i <=> 0 };
if (result == strong_ordering::less) { println("less"); }
if (result == strong_ordering::greater) { println("greater"); }
if (result == strong_ordering::equal) { println("equal"); }
```

Certain types don't have a total ordering. For example, not-a-number floating-point values are never equal, less than, or greater than any other floating-point value. Thus, such comparisons result in a *partial ordering*:

- `partial_ordering::less`: First operand less than second
- `partial_ordering::greater`: First operand greater than second
- `partial_ordering::equivalent`: First operand equivalent to second, meaning `!(a<b) && !(b<a)`; for example, -0.0 is equivalent to +0.0, but they are not equal
- `partial_ordering::unordered`: If one or both of the operands is not-a-number

If you really need a strong ordering of your floating-point values, e.g., if you know they are never not-a-number, you can use `std::strong_order()`, which always produces an `std::strong_ordering` result.

There is also a *weak ordering*, which is an additional ordering type that you can choose from to implement three-way comparisons for your own types. With a weak ordering, all values are ordered, i.e., there is no `unordered` result, but the ordering is not strong, meaning there can be non-equal values that are equivalent. An example is ordering strings with case-insensitive comparisons. In that case, the strings "Hello World" and "hello world" are certainly not equal, but they are equivalent. Here are the different results of a weak ordering:

- `weak_ordering::less`: First operand less than second
- `weak_ordering::greater`: First operand greater than second
- `weak_ordering::equivalent`: First operand equivalent to second

The three different types of ordering support certain implicit conversions. A `strong_ordering` can be converted implicitly to a `partial_ordering` or a `weak_ordering`. A `weak_ordering` can be converted implicitly to a `partial_ordering`.

For primitive types, using the three-way comparison operator doesn't gain you much compared to just performing individual comparisons using the `==`, `<`, and `>` operators. However, it becomes useful with objects that are more expensive to compare. With the three-way comparison operator, such objects can be ordered with a single operator, instead of potentially having to call two individual comparison operators, triggering two expensive comparisons. Chapter 9, "Mastering Classes and Objects," explains how to add support for three-way comparisons to your own types.

Finally, `<compare>` provides *named comparison functions* to interpret the result of an ordering. These functions are `std::is_eq()`, `is_neq()`, `is_lt()`, `is_lteq()`, `is_gt()`, and `is_gteq()` returning `true` if an ordering represents `==`, `!=`, `<`, `<=`, `>`, or `>=` respectively, `false` otherwise. Here is an example:

```
int i { 11 };
strong_ordering result { i <=> 0 };
if (is_lt(result)) { println("less"); }
if (is_gt(result)) { println("greater"); }
if (is_eq(result)) { println("equal"); }
```

Functions

For programs of any significant size, placing all the code inside of `main()` is unmanageable. To make programs easier to understand, you need to break up, or *decompose*, code into concise functions.

In C++, you first declare a function to make it available for other code to use. If the function is used only inside a particular file, you generally declare and define the function in that source file. If the function is for use by other modules or files, you export a declaration for the function from a module interface file, while the function's definition can be either in the same module interface file or in a module implementation file (discussed later).

> **NOTE** *Function declarations are often called function prototypes or function headers to emphasize that they represent how the function can be accessed, but not the code behind it. The term function signature is used to denote the combination of the function name and its parameter list, but without the return type.*

A function declaration is shown in the following code. This example has a return type of `void`, indicating that the function does not provide a result to the caller. The caller must provide two arguments for the function to work with—an integer and a character.

```
void myFunction(int i, char c);
```

Without an actual definition to match this function declaration, the link stage of the compilation process will fail because code that makes use of the function will be calling nonexistent code. The following definition prints the values of the two parameters:

```
void myFunction(int i, char c)
{
    println("The value of i is {}.", i);
    println("The value of c is {}.", c);
}
```

Elsewhere in the program, you can make calls to `myFunction()` and pass in arguments for the two parameters. Some sample function calls are shown here:

```
int someInt { 6 };
char someChar { 'c' };
myFunction(8, 'a');
myFunction(someInt, 'b');
myFunction(5, someChar);
```

> **NOTE** *In C++, unlike C, a function that takes no parameters just has an empty parameter list. It is not necessary to use* `void` *to indicate that no parameters are taken. However, you must still use* `void` *to indicate when no value is returned.*

C++ functions can also *return* a value to the caller. The following function adds two numbers and returns the result:

```
int addNumbers(int number1, int number2)
{
    return number1 + number2;
}
```

This function can be called as follows:

```
int sum { addNumbers(5, 3) };
```

Function Return Type Deduction

You can ask the compiler to figure out the return type of a function automatically. To make use of this functionality, just specify `auto` as the return type.

```
auto addNumbers(int number1, int number2)
{
    return number1 + number2;
}
```

The compiler deduces the return type based on the expressions used for the `return` statements in the body of the function. There can be multiple `return` statements, but they must all resolve to exactly the same type as the compiler will never insert any implicit conversions to deduce the return type of a function. Such a function can even include recursive calls (calls to itself), but the first `return` statement in the function must be a non-recursive call.

Current Function's Name

Every function has a local predefined variable `__func__` containing the name of the current function. One use of this variable could be for logging purposes.

```
int addNumbers(int number1, int number2)
{
    println("Entering function {}", __func__);
    return number1 + number2;
}
```

Function Overloading

Overloading a function means providing several functions with the same name but with a different set of parameters. Only specifying different return types is not enough, as the returned value can be ignored when calling the function; instead, the number and/or types of the parameters must be different.

Suppose you want to provide versions of `addNumbers()` that work with integers and with `doubles`. Without overloading, you would have to come up with unique names, for example:

```
int addNumbersInts(int a, int b) { return a + b; }
double addNumbersDoubles(double a, double b) { return a + b; }
```

With function overloading, you don't need to come up with different names for the different versions of a function. The following code snippet defines two functions called `addNumbers()`, one defined for integers, the other defined for `doubles`:

```
int addNumbers(int a, int b) { return a + b; }
double addNumbers(double a, double b) { return a + b; }
```

When calling `addNumbers()`, the compiler automatically selects the correct function overload based on the provided arguments. This process is called *overload resolution.*

```
println("{}", addNumbers(1, 2));          // Calls the integer version
println("{}", addNumbers(1.11, 2.22));    // Calls the double version
```

Attributes

Attributes are a mechanism to add optional and/or vendor-specific information into source code. Before attributes were standardized in C++, vendors decided how to specify such information. Examples are `__attribute__`, `__declspec`, and so on. Since C++11, there is standardized support for attributes by using the double square brackets syntax `[[`*attribute*`]]`.

Earlier in this chapter, the `[[fallthrough]]` attribute is introduced to prevent a compiler warning when fallthrough in a `switch case` statement is intentional. The C++ standard defines a couple more standard attributes.

[[nodiscard]]

The [[nodiscard]] attribute can be used on a function that returns a value. The compiler will then issue a warning if the return value from that function is not used by the calling function. Here is an example:

```
[[nodiscard]] int func() { return 42; }

int main()
{
    func();
}
```

The compiler issues a warning similar to the following:

```
warning C4834: discarding return value of function with 'nodiscard' attribute
```

This feature can, for example, be used for functions that return error codes. By adding the [[nodiscard]] attribute to such functions, the error codes returned from them cannot be ignored.

More general, the [[nodiscard]] attribute can be used on classes, structs, functions, and enumerations. An example of applying the attribute to an entire class is when you have a class representing error conditions. By applying [[nodiscard]] to such a class, the compiler will issue a warning for every function call that returns such an error condition and where the caller doesn't do anything with it.

A reason can be provided for the [[nodiscard]] attribute in the form of a string. This reason is then displayed in the warning messages generated by the compiler if the returned value is ignored by the caller of the function. Here is an example:

```
[[nodiscard("Some explanation")]] int func();
```

[[maybe_unused]]

The [[maybe_unused]] attribute can be used to suppress the compiler from issuing a warning when something is unused, as in this example:

```
int func(int param1, int param2)
{
    return 42;
}
```

If the compiler warning level is set high enough, this function definition results in two compiler warnings. For example, Microsoft Visual C++ gives these warnings:

```
warning C4100: 'param2': unreferenced formal parameter
warning C4100: 'param1': unreferenced formal parameter
```

By using the [[maybe_unused]] attribute, you can suppress such warnings:

```
int func(int param1, [[maybe_unused]] int param2)
{
    return 42;
}
```

In this case, the second parameter is marked with the attribute suppressing its warning. The compiler now only issues a warning for param1:

```
warning C4100: 'param1': unreferenced formal parameter
```

The `[[maybe_unused]]` attribute can be used on classes, structs, non-`static` data members, unions, `typedef`s, type aliases, variables, functions, enumerations, and enumerators. Some of these terms you might not know yet but are discussed later in this book.

[[noreturn]]

Adding a `[[noreturn]]` attribute to a function means that it never returns control to the caller. Typically, the function either causes some kind of termination (process termination or thread termination) or throws an exception. Exceptions are discussed later in this chapter. With this attribute, the compiler can avoid giving certain warnings or errors because it now knows more about the intent of the function. Here is an example:

```
import std;
using namespace std;

[[noreturn]] void forceProgramTermination()
{
    exit(1);  // Defined in <cstdlib>
}

bool isDongleAvailable()
{
    bool isAvailable { false };
    // Check whether a licensing dongle is available...
    return isAvailable;
}

bool isFeatureLicensed(int featureId)
{
    if (!isDongleAvailable()) {
        // No licensing dongle found, abort program execution!
        forceProgramTermination();
    } else {
        // Dongle available, perform license check of the given feature...
        bool isLicensed { featureId == 42 };
        return isLicensed;
    }
}

int main()
{
    bool isLicensed { isFeatureLicensed(42) };
    println("{}", isLicensed);
}
```

This code snippet compiles fine without any warnings or errors. However, if you remove the `[[noreturn]]` attribute, the compiler generates the following warning (output from Visual C++):

```
warning C4715: 'isFeatureLicensed': not all control paths return a value
```

[[deprecated]]

`[[deprecated]]` can be used to mark something as deprecated, which means you can still use it, but its use is discouraged. This attribute accepts an optional argument that can be used to explain the reason for the deprecation, as in this example:

```
[[deprecated("Unsafe function, please use xyz")]] void func();
```

If you use this deprecated function, you'll get a compilation error or warning. For example, GCC gives the following warning:

```
warning: 'void func()' is deprecated: Unsafe function, please use xyz
```

[[likely]] and [[unlikely]]

The likelihood attributes `[[likely]]` and `[[unlikely]]` can be used to help the compiler in optimizing code. These attributes can, for example, be used to mark branches of `if` and `switch` statements according to how likely it is that a branch will be taken. However, these attributes are rarely required. Compilers and hardware these days have powerful branch prediction to figure it out themselves, but in certain cases, such as performance critical code, you might have to help the compiler. The syntax is as follows:

```
int value { /* ... */ };
if (value > 11) [[unlikely]] { /* Do something ... */ }
else { /* Do something else ... */ }

switch (value)
{
    [[likely]] case 1:
        // Do something ...
        break;
    case 2:
        // Do something ...
        break;
    [[unlikely]] case 12:
        // Do something ...
        break;
}
```

C++23

[[assume]]

The `[[assume]]` attribute allows the compiler to assume that certain expressions are true without evaluating them at run time. The compiler can use such assumptions to better optimize the code. As an example, let's look at the following function:

```
int divideBy32(int x)
{
    return x / 32;
}
```

The function accepts a signed integer, so the compiler has to produce code to make sure the division works for both positive and negative numbers. If you are sure that `x` will never be negative, and for some reason you cannot make `x` of type `unsigned`, you can add an assumption as follows:

```
int divideBy32(int x)
{
    [[assume(x >= 0)]];
    return x / 32;
}
```

With this assumption in place, the compiler can omit any code to handle negative numbers and optimize the division into a single instruction, a simple right shift of five bits.

C-Style Arrays

> **WARNING** *This section briefly explains C-style arrays, as you will encounter them in legacy code. However, in C++, it is best to avoid C-style arrays and instead use Standard Library functionality, such as* `std::array` *and* `vector`*, discussed in the following two sections.*

Arrays hold a series of values, all of the same type, each of which can be accessed by its position in the array. In C++, you must provide the size of the array when the array is declared. You cannot give a variable as the size—it must be a constant, or a *constant expression (constexpr)*. Constant expressions are discussed in Chapter 9. The code that follows shows the declaration of an array of three integers followed by three lines to initialize the elements to 0:

```
int myArray[3];
myArray[0] = 0;
myArray[1] = 0;
myArray[2] = 0;
```

> **WARNING** *In C++, the first element of an array is always at position 0, not position 1! The last position of the array is always the size of the array minus 1!*

The "Loops" section later in this chapter discusses how you could use loops to initialize each element of an array. However, instead of using loops or the previous initialization mechanism, you can also accomplish *zero initialization* with the following one-liner:

```
int myArray[3] = { 0 };
```

You can even drop the 0.

```
int myArray[3] = {};
```

Finally, the equal sign is optional as well, so you can write this:

```
int myArray[3] {};
```

An array can be initialized with an initializer list, in which case the compiler deduces the size of the array automatically. Here's an example:

```
int myArray[] { 1, 2, 3, 4 }; // The compiler creates an array of 4 elements.
```

If you do specify the size of the array and the initializer list has fewer elements than the given size, the remaining elements are set to 0. For example, the following code sets only the first element in the array to the value 2 and sets all others to 0:

```
int myArray[3] { 2 };
```

To get the size of a stack-based C-style array, you can use the `std::size()` function, defined in `<array>`. It returns an `std::size_t`, which is an unsigned integer type defined in `<cstddef>`. Here is an example:

```
std::size_t arraySize { std::size(myArray) };
```

> **NOTE** *In legacy code, you might see* `size_t` *being used without the* `std` *namespace qualification, without a* `using namespace std` *directive, and without a* `using std::size_t` *declaration. This does not work any longer when you use* `import std`*, as that imports everything into the* `std` *namespace. Hence, you need either to use* `std::size_t` *or to use a proper* `using` *directive or declaration. Alternatively, Chapter 11 explains that you can import the named module* `std.compat` *instead of* `std`*, but this is not recommended for new code.*

> **NOTE** *C++23 introduces a literal suffix* `uz` *for type* `std::size_t`*, for example,* `42uz`*.*

An older trick to get the size of a stack-based C-style array was to use the `sizeof` operator. The `sizeof` operator returns the size of its argument in bytes. To get the number of elements in a stack-based array, you divide the size in bytes of the array by the size in bytes of the first element. Here's an example:

```
std::size_t arraySize { sizeof(myArray) / sizeof(myArray[0]) };
```

The preceding examples show a one-dimensional array of integers, which you can think of as a line of integers, each with its own numbered compartment. C++ allows multidimensional arrays. You might think of a two-dimensional array as a checkerboard, where each location has a position along the x-axis and a position along the y-axis. Three-dimensional arrays can be pictured as a cube, while higher-dimensional arrays are harder to visualize. The following code shows the syntax for creating a two-dimensional array of characters for a tic-tac-toe board and then putting an "o" in the center square:

```
char ticTacToeBoard[3][3];
ticTacToeBoard[1][1] = 'o';
```

Figure 1.1 shows a visual representation of this board with the position of each square.

std::array

The arrays discussed in the previous section come from C and still work in C++. However, C++ has a special type for fixed-size containers called `std::array`, defined in `<array>`. It's basically a thin wrapper around C-style arrays.

ticTacToeBoard[0][0]	ticTacToeBoard[0][1]	ticTacToeBoard[0][2]
ticTacToeBoard[1][0]	ticTacToeBoard[1][1]	ticTacToeBoard[1][2]
ticTacToeBoard[2][0]	ticTacToeBoard[2][1]	ticTacToeBoard[2][2]

FIGURE 1.1

There are a number of advantages to using `std::arrays` instead of C-style arrays. They always know their own size, are not automatically cast to a pointer to avoid certain types of bugs, and have iterators to easily loop over the elements. Iterators are discussed in detail in Chapter 17, "Understanding Iterators and the Ranges Library."

The following example demonstrates how to use the `array` container. The `array` type is a *class template* accepting a number of *class template parameters* that allow you to specify how many elements you want to store in the container and their type. You provide *class template arguments* for class template parameters by specifying them between the angle brackets after `array`, as in `array<int,3>`. Chapter 12, "Writing Generic Code with Templates," discusses templates in detail. However, for now, just remember that you have to specify two arguments between the angle brackets; the first represents the type of the elements in the array, and the second represents the size of the array.

```
array<int, 3> arr { 9, 8, 7 };
println("Array size = {}", arr.size());
println("2nd element = {}", arr[1]);
```

C++ supports *class template argument deduction* (CTAD), as discussed in detail in Chapter 12. For now, it's enough to remember that this allows you to avoid having to specify the template arguments between angle brackets for certain class templates. CTAD works only when using an initializer because the compiler uses this initializer to automatically deduce the template arguments. This works for `std::array`, allowing you to define the previous array as follows:

```
array arr { 9, 8, 7 };
```

> **NOTE** *C-style arrays and* `std::arrays` *have a fixed size, which must be known at compile time. They cannot grow or shrink at run time.*

If you want an array with a dynamic size, it is recommended to use `std::vector`, as explained in the next section. A `vector` automatically increases in size when you add new elements to it.

std::vector

The C++ Standard Library provides a number of different non-fixed-size containers that can be used to store information. `std::vector`, declared in `<vector>`, is an example of such a container. The `vector` class replaces the concept of C-style arrays with a much more flexible and safer mechanism.

As a user, you need not worry about memory management, as a `vector` automatically allocates enough memory to hold its elements. A `vector` is dynamic, meaning that elements can be added and removed at run time. Chapter 18, "Standard Library Containers," goes into more detail regarding containers, but the basic use of a `vector` is straightforward, which is why it's introduced in the beginning of this book so that it can be used in examples. The following code demonstrates the basic functionality of `vector`:

```
// Create a vector of integers.
vector<int> myVector { 11, 22 };

// Add some more integers to the vector using push_back().
myVector.push_back(33);
myVector.push_back(44);

// Access elements.
println("1st element: {}", myVector[0]);
```

`myVector` is declared as `vector<int>`. The angle brackets are required to specify the template arguments, just as with `std::array`. A `vector` is a generic container. It can contain almost any type of object, but all elements in a `vector` must be of the same type. This type is specified between the angle brackets. Templates are discussed in detail in Chapter 12 and Chapter 26, "Advanced Templates."

Just as `std::array`, the `vector` class template supports CTAD, allowing you to define `myVector` as follows:

```
vector myVector { 11, 22 };
```

Again, an initializer is required for CTAD to work. The following is illegal:

```
vector myVector;
```

To add elements to a `vector`, you can use the `push_back()` member function. Individual elements can be accessed using a similar syntax as for arrays, i.e., `operator[]`.

std::pair

The `std::pair` class template is defined in `<utility>`. It groups together two values of possibly different types. The values are accessible through the `first` and `second` public data members. Here is an example:

```
pair<double, int> myPair { 1.23, 5 };
println("{} {}", myPair.first, myPair.second);
```

`pair` also supports CTAD, so you can define `myPair` as follows:

```
pair myPair { 1.23, 5 };
```

> **NOTE** *While you could write a function returning an* `std::pair`*, it is recommended to write a small* `struct` *or* `class` *containing the two values and return that from the function. The downside of returning a* `pair` *is that client code must use* `first` *and* `second` *to access the two values. By returning a proper* `struct` *or* `class`*, you can give more meaningful names to the two values.*

std::optional

`std::optional`, defined in `<optional>`, holds a value of a specific type, or nothing. It is introduced already in this first chapter as it is a useful type to use in some of the examples throughout the book.

Basically, `optional` can be used for parameters of a function if you want to allow for values to be optional. It is also often used as a return type from a function if the function can either return something or not. This removes the need to return "special" values from functions such as `nullptr`, `-1`, `EOF`, and so on. It also removes the need to write the function as returning a Boolean, representing success or failure, while storing the actual result of the function in an argument passed to the function as an output parameter (a parameter of type reference-to-non-`const`, discussed later in this chapter).

The `optional` type is a class template, so you have to specify the actual type that you need between angle brackets, as in `optional<int>`. This syntax is similar to how you specify the type stored in a `vector`, for example `vector<int>`.

Here is an example of a function returning an `optional`:

```
optional<int> getData(bool giveIt)
{
    if (giveIt) {
        return 42;
    }
    return nullopt;  // or simply return {};
}
```

You can call this function as follows:

```
optional<int> data1 { getData(true) };
optional<int> data2 { getData(false) };
```

To determine whether an `optional` has a value, use the `has_value()` member function, or simply use the `optional` in an `if` statement:

```
println("data1.has_value = {}", data1.has_value());
if (!data2) {
    println("data2 has no value.");
}
```

If an `optional` has a value, you can retrieve it with `value()` or with the dereferencing operator `*`. This operator is discussed in detail later in this chapter in the context of pointers.

```
println("data1.value = {}", data1.value());
println("data1.value = {}", *data1);
```

If you call `value()` on an empty `optional`, an `std::bad_optional_access` exception is thrown. Exceptions are introduced later in this chapter.

`value_or()` can be used to return either the value of an `optional` or another value when the `optional` is empty:

```
println("data2.value = {}", data2.value_or(0));
```

You cannot store a reference (discussed later in this chapter) in an `optional`, so `optional<T&>` does not work. Instead, you can store a pointer in an `optional`.

Structured Bindings

A *structured binding* allows you to declare multiple variables that are initialized with elements from a data structure such as an array, struct, or pair.

Assume you have the following std::array:

```
array values { 11, 22, 33 };
```

You can declare three variables, x, y, and z, initialized with the three values from the array as follows. You have to use the auto keyword for structured bindings, i.e., you cannot, for example, specify int instead of auto.

```
auto [x, y, z] { values };
```

The number of variables declared with the structured binding has to match the number of values in the expression on the right.

Structured bindings also work with structs if all non-static members are public. Here's an example:

```
struct Point { double m_x, m_y, m_z; };
Point point;
point.m_x = 1.0; point.m_y = 2.0; point.m_z = 3.0;
auto [x, y, z] { point };
```

As a final example, the following code snippet decomposes the elements of a pair into separate variables:

```
pair myPair { "hello", 5 };
auto [theString, theInt] { myPair };  // Decompose using structured bindings.
println("theString: {}", theString);
println("theInt: {}", theInt);
```

It is also possible to create a set of references-to-non-const or references-to-const using the structured bindings syntax, by using auto& or const auto& instead of auto. Both references-to-non-const and references-to-const are discussed later in this chapter.

Loops

Computers are great for doing the same thing over and over. C++ provides four looping mechanisms: the while loop, do/while loop, for loop, and *range-based* for loop.

The while Loop

The while loop lets you perform a block of code repeatedly as long as an expression evaluates to true. For example, the following completely silly code prints "This is silly." five times:

```
int i { 0 };
while (i < 5) {
    println("This is silly.");
    ++i;
}
```

The keyword `break` can be used within a loop to immediately get out of the loop and resume execution of the program starting at the line of code following the loop. The keyword `continue` can be used to return to the top of the loop and reevaluate the `while` expression. However, using `continue` in loops is often considered poor style because it causes the execution of a program to jump around somewhat haphazardly, so use it sparingly.

The do/while Loop

C++ has a variation on the `while` loop called `do/while`. It works similarly to the `while` loop, except that the code to be executed comes first, and the conditional check for whether to continue happens at the end. In this way, you can use a loop when you want a block of code to always be executed at least once and possibly additional times based on some condition. The example that follows prints the statement, "This is silly." once, even though the condition ends up being false:

```
int i { 100 };
do {
    println("This is silly.");
    ++i;
} while (i < 5);
```

The for Loop

The `for` loop provides another syntax for looping. Any `for` loop can be converted to a `while` loop, and vice versa. However, the `for` loop syntax is often more convenient because it looks at a loop in terms of a starting expression, an ending condition, and a statement to execute at the end of every iteration. In the following code, `i` is initialized to 0; the loop continues as long as `i` is less than 5; and at the end of every iteration, `i` is incremented by 1. This code does the same thing as the `while` loop example earlier but is more readable because the starting value, ending condition, and per-iteration statements are all visible on one line.

```
for (int i { 0 }; i < 5; ++i) {
    println("This is silly.");
}
```

The Range-Based for Loop

The *range-based* `for` loop is the fourth looping mechanism. It allows for easy iteration over elements of a container. This type of loop works for C-style arrays, initializer lists (discussed later in this chapter), and any type that supports `begin()` and `end()` functions returning iterators (see Chapter 17), such as `std::array`, `vector`, and all other Standard Library containers discussed in Chapter 18, "Standard Library Containers."

The following example first defines an `array` of four integers. The range-based `for` loop then iterates over a *copy* of every element in this `array` and prints out each value. To iterate over the elements themselves *without making copies*, use a reference variable, as discussed later in this chapter.

```
array arr { 1, 2, 3, 4 };
for (int i : arr) { println("{}", i); }
```

Initializers for Range-Based for Loops

You can use initializers with range-based for loops, similar to initializers for if and switch statements. The syntax is as follows:

```
for (<initializer>; <range-declaration> : <range-expression>) { <body> }
```

Any variables introduced in the <initializer> are available only in the <range-declaration>, the <range-expression> and in the <body>. They are not available outside the range-based for loop. Here is an example:

```
for (array arr { 1, 2, 3, 4 }; int i : arr) { println("{}", i); }
```

Initializer Lists

Initializer lists are defined in <initializer_list> and make it easy to write functions that can accept a variable number of arguments. The std::initializer_list type is a class template, and so it requires you to specify the type of elements in the list between angle brackets, similar to how you specify the type of elements stored in a vector. The following example shows how to use an initializer list:

```
import std;
using namespace std;

int sum(initializer_list<int> values)
{
    int total { 0 };
    for (int value : values) {
        total += value;
    }
    return total;
}
```

By accepting an initializer list of integers as a parameter, the function sum() can be called with a *braced initializer* of integers as argument. The body of the function uses a range-based for loop to accumulate the total sum. This function can be used as follows:

```
int a { sum({ 1, 2, 3 }) };
int b { sum({ 10, 20, 30, 40, 50, 60 }) };
```

Initializer lists are type safe. All elements in such a list must be of the same type. For the sum() function shown here, all elements of the initializer list must be integers. Trying to call it with a double, as shown next, results in a compilation error or warning stating that converting from double to int requires narrowing.

```
int c { sum({ 1, 2, 3.0 }) };
```

Strings in C++

There are two ways to work with strings in C++:

- **The C style:** Representing strings as arrays of characters
- **The C++ style:** Wrapping a C-style representation in an easier-to-use and safer string type

Chapter 2 provides a detailed discussion. For now, the only thing you need to know is that the C++ `std::string` type is defined in `<string>` and that you can use a C++ `string` almost like a basic type. The following example shows that `strings` can be used just like character arrays:

```
string myString { "Hello, World" };
println("The value of myString is {}", myString);
println("The second letter is {}", myString[1]);
```

C++ as an Object-Oriented Language

If you are a C programmer, you may have viewed the features covered so far in this chapter as convenient additions to the C language. As the name C++ implies, in many ways the language is just a "better C." There is one major point that this view overlooks: unlike C, C++ is an object-oriented language.

Object-oriented programming (OOP) is a different, arguably more natural, way to write code. If you are used to procedural languages such as C or Pascal, don't worry. Chapter 5, "Designing with Classes," covers all the background information you need to know to shift your mindset to the object-oriented paradigm. If you already know the theory of OOP, the rest of this section will get you up to speed (or refresh your memory) on basic C++ object syntax.

Defining Classes

A *class* defines the characteristics of an object. In C++, classes are usually defined and exported from a module interface file (`.cppm`), while their definitions can either be directly in the same module interface file or in a corresponding module implementation file (`.cpp`). Chapter 11 discusses modules in depth.

A basic class definition for an airline ticket class is shown in the following example. The class can calculate the price of the ticket based on the number of miles in the flight and whether the customer is a member of the Elite Super Rewards Program.

The definition begins by declaring the class name. Inside a set of curly braces, the *data members* (properties) of the class and its *member functions* (behaviors) are declared. Each data member and member function is associated with a particular access level: `public`, `protected`, or `private`. These labels can occur in any order and can be repeated. Members that are `public` can be accessed from outside the class, while members that are `private` cannot be accessed from anywhere outside the class. Members that are `protected` can be accessed by derived classes, explained in detail in Chapter 10 in the context of inheritance. It's recommended to make all your data members `private`, and if needed, to give access to them with `public` or `protected` getters to retrieve data from an object and `public` or `protected` setters to set data for an object. This way, you can easily change the representation of your data while keeping the `public`/`protected` interface the same.

Remember, when writing a module interface file, don't forget to use an `export module` declaration to specify which module you are writing, and don't forget to explicitly export the types you want to make available to users of your module.

```
export module airline_ticket;

import std;
```

```
export class AirlineTicket
{
    public:
        AirlineTicket();
        ~AirlineTicket();

        double calculatePriceInDollars();

        std::string getPassengerName();
        void setPassengerName(std::string name);

        int getNumberOfMiles();
        void setNumberOfMiles(int miles);

        bool hasEliteSuperRewardsStatus();
        void setHasEliteSuperRewardsStatus(bool status);
    private:
        std::string m_passengerName;
        int m_numberOfMiles;
        bool m_hasEliteSuperRewardsStatus;
};
```

This book follows the convention to prefix each data member of a class with a lowercase `m` followed by an underscore, such as `m_passengerName`.

The member function that has the same name as the class with no return type is a *constructor*. It is automatically called when an object of the class is created. The member function with a tilde (~) character followed by the class name is a *destructor*. It is automatically called when an object is destroyed.

The .cppm module interface file defines the class, while the implementations of the member functions in this example are in a .cpp module implementation file. This source file starts with the following module declaration to tell the compiler that this is a source file for the `airline_ticket` module:

```
module airline_ticket;
```

There are several ways to initialize data members of a class. One way is to use a *constructor initializer*, which follows a colon after the constructor header. Here is the `AirlineTicket` constructor with a constructor initializer:

```
AirlineTicket::AirlineTicket()
    : m_passengerName { "Unknown Passenger" }
    , m_numberOfMiles { 0 }
    , m_hasEliteSuperRewardsStatus { false }
{
}
```

A second option is to put the initializations in the body of the constructor, as shown here:

```
AirlineTicket::AirlineTicket()
{
    // Initialize data members.
    m_passengerName = "Unknown Passenger";
    m_numberOfMiles = 0;
    m_hasEliteSuperRewardsStatus = false;
}
```

However, if the constructor is only initializing data members without doing anything else, then there is actually no real need for a constructor because data members can be initialized directly inside a class definition, also known as *in-class initializers*. For example, instead of writing an `AirlineTicket` constructor, you can modify the data members in the class definition to initialize them as follows:

```
    private:
        std::string m_passengerName { "Unknown Passenger" };
        int m_numberOfMiles { 0 };
        bool m_hasEliteSuperRewardsStatus { false };
```

If your class additionally needs to perform some other types of initializations, such as opening a file, allocating memory, and so on, then you still need to write a constructor to handle those initializations.

Here is the destructor for the `AirlineTicket` class:

```
AirlineTicket::~AirlineTicket()
{
    // Nothing to do in terms of cleanup
}
```

This destructor doesn't do anything and can simply be removed from this class. It is just shown here so you know the syntax of destructors. Destructors are required if you need to perform some cleanup, such as closing files, freeing memory, and so on. Chapters 8, "Gaining Proficiency with Classes and Objects," and 9 discuss destructors in more detail.

The definitions of the other `AirlineTicket` class member functions are shown here:

```
double AirlineTicket::calculatePriceInDollars()
{
    if (hasEliteSuperRewardsStatus()) {
        // Elite Super Rewards customers fly for free!
        return 0;
    }
    // The cost of the ticket is the number of miles times 0.1.
    // Real airlines probably have a more complicated formula!
    return getNumberOfMiles() * 0.1;
}

string AirlineTicket::getPassengerName() { return m_passengerName; }
void AirlineTicket::setPassengerName(string name) { m_passengerName = name; }

int AirlineTicket::getNumberOfMiles() { return m_numberOfMiles; }
void AirlineTicket::setNumberOfMiles(int miles) { m_numberOfMiles = miles; }

bool AirlineTicket::hasEliteSuperRewardsStatus()
{
    return m_hasEliteSuperRewardsStatus;
}
void AirlineTicket::setHasEliteSuperRewardsStatus(bool status)
{
    m_hasEliteSuperRewardsStatus = status;
}
```

As mentioned in the beginning of this section, it's also possible to put the member function implementations directly in the module interface file. The syntax is as follows:

```
export class AirlineTicket
{
    public:
```

```
        double calculatePriceInDollars()
        {
            if (hasEliteSuperRewardsStatus()) { return 0; }
            return getNumberOfMiles() * 0.1;
        }

        std::string getPassengerName() { return m_passengerName; }
        void setPassengerName(std::string name) { m_passengerName = name; }

        int getNumberOfMiles() { return m_numberOfMiles; }
        void setNumberOfMiles(int miles) { m_numberOfMiles = miles; }

        bool hasEliteSuperRewardsStatus() { return m_hasEliteSuperRewardsStatus; }
        void setHasEliteSuperRewardsStatus(bool status)
        {
            m_hasEliteSuperRewardsStatus = status;
        }
    private:
        std::string m_passengerName { "Unknown Passenger" };
        int m_numberOfMiles { 0 };
        bool m_hasEliteSuperRewardsStatus { false };
};
```

Using Classes

To use the `AirlineTicket` class, you first need to import its module:

```
import airline_ticket;
```

The following sample program makes use of the class. This example shows the creation of a stack-based `AirlineTicket` object:

```
AirlineTicket myTicket;
myTicket.setPassengerName("Sherman T. Socketwrench");
myTicket.setNumberOfMiles(700);
double cost { myTicket.calculatePriceInDollars() };
println("This ticket will cost ${}", cost);
```

The `AirlineTicket` example exposes you to the general syntax for creating and using classes. Of course, there is much more to learn, and that's the topic of Chapters 8, 9, and 10.

Scope Resolution

As a C++ programmer, you need to familiarize yourself with the concept of a *scope*, which defines where an item is visible. Every name in your program, including variable, function, and class names, is in a certain scope. You create scopes with namespaces, function definitions, blocks delimited by curly braces, and class definitions. Variables that are initialized in the initialization statement of `for` loops and range-based `for` loops are scoped to that `for` loop and are not visible outside the `for` loop. Similarly, variables initialized in an initializer for `if` or `switch` statements are scoped to that `if` or `switch` statement and are not visible outside that statement. When you try to access a variable, function, or class, the name is first looked up in the nearest enclosing scope, then the parent scope, and so forth, up to the *global scope*. Any name not in a namespace, function, block delimited by curly braces, or class is assumed to be in the global scope. If it is not found in the global scope, at that point the compiler generates an undefined symbol error.

Sometimes names in scopes hide identical names in other scopes. Other times, the scope you want is not part of the default scope resolution from that particular line in the program. If you don't want the default scope resolution for a name, you can qualify the name with a specific scope using the scope resolution operator `::`. The following example demonstrates this. The example defines a class `Demo` with a `get()` member function, a `get()` function that is globally scoped, and a `get()` function that is in the `NS` namespace.

```
class Demo
{
    public:
        int get() { return 5; }
};

int get() { return 10; }

namespace NS
{
    int get() { return 20; }
}
```

The global scope is unnamed, but you can access it specifically by using the scope resolution operator by itself (with no name prefix). The different `get()` functions can be called as follows. In this example, the code itself is in the `main()` function, which is always in the global scope:

```
int main()
{
    Demo d;
    println("{}", d.get());       // prints 5
    println("{}", NS::get());     // prints 20
    println("{}", ::get());       // prints 10
    println("{}", get());         // prints 10
}
```

If the earlier namespace called `NS` is defined as an *unnamed / anonymous namespace*, that is, a namespace without a name as follows:

```
namespace
{
    int get() { return 20; }
}
```

then the following line will cause a compilation error about ambiguous name resolution because you would have a `get()` defined in the global scope, and another `get()` defined in the unnamed namespace.

```
println("{}", get());
```

The same error occurs if you add the following `using` directive right before the `main()` function:

```
using namespace NS;
```

Uniform Initialization

Before C++11, initialization of types was not always uniform. For example, take the following definitions of a circle, once as a structure, and once as a class:

```
struct CircleStruct
{
    int x, y;
    double radius;
};

class CircleClass
{
    public:
        CircleClass(int x, int y, double radius)
            : m_x { x }, m_y { y }, m_radius { radius } {}
    private:
        int m_x, m_y;
        double m_radius;
};
```

In pre-C++11, initialization of a variable of type `CircleStruct` and a variable of type `CircleClass` looked different:

```
CircleStruct myCircle1 = { 10, 10, 2.5 };
CircleClass myCircle2(10, 10, 2.5);
```

For the structure version, you can use the {...} syntax. However, for the class version, you needed to call the constructor using function notation: `(...)`.

Since C++11, you can more uniformly use the {...} syntax to initialize types, as follows:

```
CircleStruct myCircle3 = { 10, 10, 2.5 };
CircleClass myCircle4 = { 10, 10, 2.5 };
```

The definition of `myCircle4` automatically calls the constructor of `CircleClass`. Even the use of the equal sign is optional, so the following are identical:

```
CircleStruct myCircle5 { 10, 10, 2.5 };
CircleClass myCircle6 { 10, 10, 2.5 };
```

As another example, in the section "Structs" earlier in this chapter, an `Employee` structure is initialized as follows:

```
Employee anEmployee;
anEmployee.firstInitial = 'J';
anEmployee.lastInitial = 'D';
anEmployee.employeeNumber = 42;
anEmployee.salary = 80'000;
```

With uniform initialization, this can be rewritten as follows:

```
Employee anEmployee { 'J', 'D', 42, 80'000 };
```

Uniform initialization is not limited to structures and classes. You can use it to initialize almost anything in C++. For example, the following code initializes all four variables with the value 3:

```
int a = 3;
int b(3);
int c = { 3 };  // Uniform initialization
int d { 3 };    // Uniform initialization
```

Uniform initialization can be used to perform zero-initialization of variables; you just specify an empty set of curly braces, as shown here:

```
int e { };          // Uniform initialization, e will be 0
```

This syntax can also be used with structures. If you create an instance of the `Employee struct` as follows, then its data members are default initialized, which, for primitive types such as `char` and `int`, means they'll contain whatever random data is left in memory:

```
Employee anEmployee;
```

However, if you create the instance as follows, then all data members are zero initialized:

```
Employee anEmployee { };
```

A benefit of using uniform initialization is that it prevents *narrowing*. When using the old-style assignment syntax to initialize variables, C++ implicitly performs narrowing, as shown here:

```
int main()
{
    int x = 3.14;
}
```

For the statement in `main()`, C++ automatically truncates 3.14 to 3 before assigning it to `x`. Some compilers *might* issue a warning about this narrowing, while others won't. In any case, narrowing conversions should not go unnoticed, as they might cause subtle or not so subtle bugs. With uniform initialization, the assignment to `x` *must* generate a compilation error if your compiler fully conforms to the C++11 standard:

```
int x { 3.14 };     // Error because narrowing
```

If a narrowing cast is what you need, I recommend using the `gsl::narrow_cast()` function available in the Guidelines Support Library (GSL).

Uniform initialization can also be used in the constructor initializer to initialize arrays that are members of a class.

```
class MyClass
{
    public:
         MyClass()
            : m_array { 0, 1, 2, 3 }
        {
        }
    private:
        int m_array[4];
};
```

Uniform initialization can be used with the Standard Library containers as well—such as `std::vector`, already demonstrated earlier in this chapter.

> **NOTE** *Considering all these benefits, it is recommended to use uniform initialization over using the assignment syntax to initialize variables. Hence, this book uses uniform initialization wherever possible.*

Designated Initializers

Designated initializers initialize data members of aggregates using their name. An *aggregate type* is an object of an array type, or an object of a structure or class that satisfies the following restrictions: only `public` data members, no user-declared or inherited constructors, no `virtual` functions (see Chapter 10), and no `virtual`, `private`, or `protected` base classes (see Chapter 10). A designated initializer starts with a dot followed by the name of a data member. Designated initializers must be in the same order as the declaration order of the data members. Mixing designated initializers and non-designated initializers is not allowed. Any data members that are not initialized using a designated initializer are initialized with their default values, which means the following:

- Data members that have an in-class initializer will get that value.
- Data members that do not have an in-class initializer are zero initialized.

Let's take a look at a slightly modified `Employee` structure. This time the `salary` data member has a default value of 75,000.

```
struct Employee {
    char firstInitial;
    char lastInitial;
    int  employeeNumber;
    int  salary { 75'000 };
};
```

Earlier in this chapter, such an `Employee` structure is initialized using a uniform initialization syntax as follows:

```
Employee anEmployee { 'J', 'D', 42, 80'000 };
```

Using designated initializers, this can be written as follows:

```
Employee anEmployee {
    .firstInitial = 'J',
    .lastInitial = 'D',
    .employeeNumber = 42,
    .salary = 80'000
};
```

A benefit of using such designated initializers is that it's much easier to understand what a designated initializer is initializing compared to using the uniform initialization syntax.

With designated initializers, you can skip initialization of certain members if you are satisfied with their default values. For example, when creating an employee, you could skip initializing `employeeNumber`, in which case `employeeNumber` is zero initialized as it doesn't have an in-class initializer:

```
Employee anEmployee {
    .firstInitial = 'J',
    .lastInitial = 'D',
    .salary = 80'000
};
```

With the uniform initialization syntax, this is not possible, and you have to specify 0 for the employee number as follows:

```
Employee anEmployee { 'J', 'D', 0, 80'000 };
```

If you skip initializing the `salary` data member as follows, then `salary` gets its default value, which is its in-class initialization value, 75,000:

```
Employee anEmployee {
    .firstInitial = 'J',
    .lastInitial = 'D'
};
```

A final benefit of using designated initializers is that when members are added to the data structure, existing code using designated initializers keeps working. The new data members will just be initialized with their default values.

Pointers and Dynamic Memory

Dynamic memory allows you to build programs with data that is not of fixed size at compile time. Most nontrivial programs make use of dynamic memory in some form.

The Stack and the Free Store

Memory in your C++ application is divided into two parts—the *stack* and the *free store*. One way to visualize the stack is as a deck of cards. The current top card represents the current scope of the program, usually the function that is currently being executed. All variables declared inside the current function will take up memory in the top stack frame, the top card of the deck. If the current function, which I'll call `foo()`, calls another function `bar()`, a new card is put on the deck so that `bar()` has its own *stack frame* to work with. Any parameters passed from `foo()` to `bar()` are copied from the `foo()` stack frame into the `bar()` stack frame. Figure 1.2 shows what the stack might look like during the execution of a hypothetical function `foo()` that has declared two integer values.

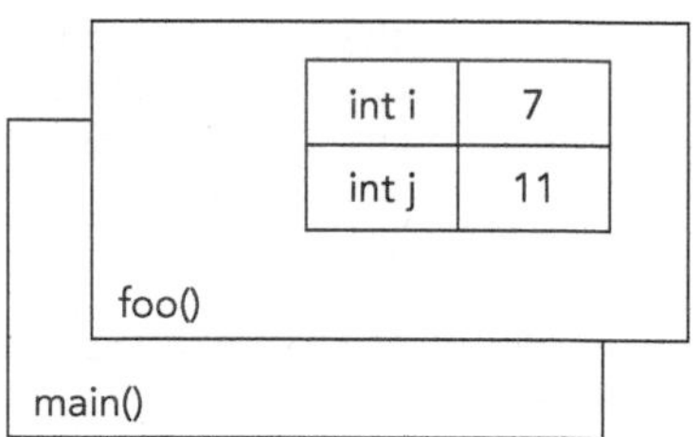

FIGURE 1.2

Stack frames are nice because they provide an isolated memory workspace for each function. If a variable is declared inside the `foo()` stack frame, calling the `bar()` function won't change it unless you specifically tell it to. Also, when the `foo()` function is done running, the stack frame goes away, and all of the variables declared within the function no longer take up memory. Variables that are stack-allocated do not need to be deallocated (deleted) by the programmer; it happens automatically.

The *free store* is an area of memory that is completely independent of the current function or stack frame. You can put variables on the free store if you want them to exist even when the function in which they were created has completed. The free store is less structured than the stack. You can think of it as just a pile of bits. Your program can add new bits to the pile at any time or modify bits that are already on the pile. You have to make sure that you deallocate (delete) any memory that you allocated on the free store. This does not happen automatically, unless you use smart pointers, which are discussed in detail in Chapter 7, "Memory Management."

> **WARNING** *Pointers are introduced here because you will encounter them, especially in legacy code bases. In new code, however, such raw/naked pointers are allowed only if there is no ownership involved. Otherwise, you should use one of the smart pointers explained in Chapter 7.*

Working with Pointers

You can put anything on the free store by explicitly allocating memory for it. For example, to put an integer on the free store, you need to allocate memory for it, but first you need to declare a *pointer*:

```
int* myIntegerPointer;
```

The `*` after the `int` type indicates that the variable you are declaring refers or points to some integer memory. Think of the pointer as an arrow that points at the dynamically allocated free store memory. It does not yet point to anything specific because you haven't assigned it to anything; it is an *uninitialized variable*. Uninitialized variables should be avoided at all times, and especially uninitialized pointers because they point to some random place in memory. Working with such pointers will most likely make your program crash. That's why you should always declare and initialize your pointers at the same time! You can initialize them to a null pointer (`nullptr`—for more information, see the "Null Pointer Constant" section) if you don't want to allocate memory right away:

```
int* myIntegerPointer { nullptr };
```

A null pointer is a special default value that no valid pointer will ever have and converts to `false` when used in a Boolean expression. Here's an example:

```
if (!myIntegerPointer) { /* myIntegerPointer is a null pointer. */ }
```

You use the `new` operator to allocate the memory:

```
myIntegerPointer = new int;
```

In this case, the pointer points to the address of just a single integer value. To access this value, you need to *dereference* the pointer. Think of dereferencing as following the pointer's arrow to the actual value on the free store. To set the value of the newly allocated free store integer, you would use code like the following:

```
*myIntegerPointer = 8;
```

Notice that this is not the same as setting `myIntegerPointer` to the value 8. You are not changing the pointer; you are changing the memory that it points to. If you were to reassign the pointer value, it would point to the memory address 8, which is probably random garbage that will eventually make your program crash.

After you are finished with your dynamically allocated memory, you need to deallocate the memory using the `delete` operator. To prevent the pointer from being used after having deallocated the memory it points to, it's recommended to set it to `nullptr`:

```
delete myIntegerPointer;
myIntegerPointer = nullptr;
```

> **WARNING** *A pointer must be valid before it is dereferenced. Dereferencing a null pointer or an uninitialized pointer causes undefined behavior. Your program might crash, but it might just as well keep running and start giving strange results.*

Pointers don't always point to free store memory. You can declare a pointer that points to a variable on the stack, even another pointer. To get a pointer to a variable, you use the & ("address of") operator:

```
int i { 8 };
int* myIntegerPointer { &i };  // Points to the variable with the value 8
```

C++ has a special syntax for dealing with pointers to structures or classes. Technically, if you have a pointer to a structure or a class, you can access its fields by first dereferencing it with *, and then using the normal . syntax, as in the code that follows. This code snippet also demonstrates how to dynamically allocate and deallocate an Employee instance.

```
Employee* anEmployee { new Employee { 'J', 'D', 42, 80'000 } };
println("{}", (*anEmployee).salary);
delete anEmployee; anEmployee = nullptr;
```

This syntax is a little messy. The -> (arrow) operator lets you perform both the dereference and the field access in one step. The following statement is equivalent to the previous println() call but is easier to read:

```
println("{}", anEmployee->salary);
```

Remember the concept of short-circuiting logic, discussed earlier in this chapter? This can be useful in combination with pointers to avoid using an invalid pointer, as in the following example:

```
bool isValidSalary { anEmployee && anEmployee->salary > 0 };
```

Or, here it is a little bit more verbose:

```
bool isValidSalary { anEmployee != nullptr && anEmployee->salary > 0 };
```

anEmployee is dereferenced to get the salary only if it is a valid pointer. If it is a null pointer, the logical operation short-circuits, and the anEmployee pointer is not dereferenced.

Dynamically Allocated Arrays

The free store can also be used to dynamically allocate arrays. You use the new[] operator to allocate memory for an array.

```
int arraySize { 8 };
int* myVariableSizedArray { new int[arraySize] };
```

This allocates enough memory to hold arraySize integers. Figure 1.3 shows what the stack and the free store both look like after this code is executed. As you can see, the pointer variable still resides on the stack, but the array that was dynamically created lives on the free store.

Now that the memory has been allocated, you can work with myVariableSizedArray as though it were a regular stack-based array:

```
myVariableSizedArray[3] = 2;
```

When your code is done with the array, it should remove the array from the free store so that other variables can use the memory. In C++, you use the delete[] operator to do this:

```
delete[] myVariableSizedArray;
myVariableSizedArray = nullptr;
```

The brackets after delete indicate that you are deleting an array!

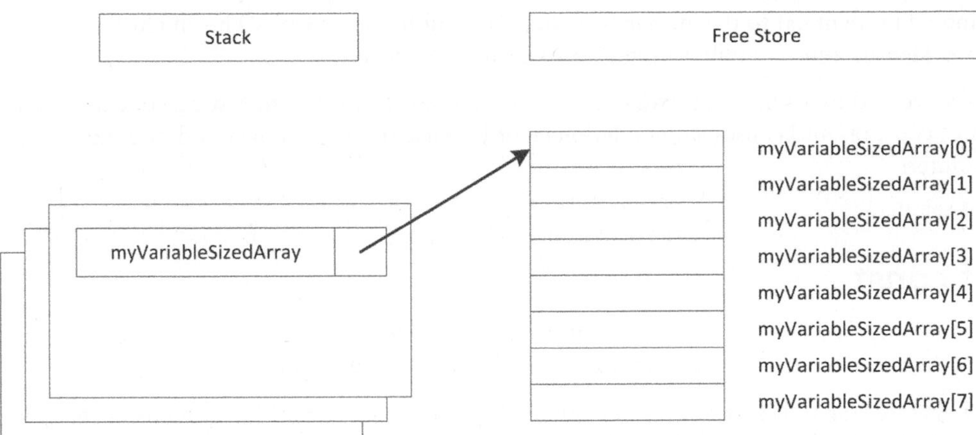

FIGURE 1.3

> **NOTE** *If you do need dynamically allocated memory, avoid using* `malloc()` *and* `free()` *from C. Instead, use* `new` *and* `delete`*, or* `new[]` *and* `delete[]` *from C++. However, in modern C++, the goal is to avoid* `new`*,* `delete`*,* `new[]`*, and* `delete[]` *altogether, and use more modern constructs such as Standard Library containers, e.g.,* `std::vector`*, and smart pointers, discussed in Chapter 7.*

> **WARNING** *To prevent memory leaks, every call to* `new` *should be paired with a call to* `delete`*, and every call to* `new[]` *should be paired with a call to* `delete[]`*. Not calling* `delete` *or* `delete[]`*, or mismatching calls, results in memory leaks or worse. All these intricacies are discussed in Chapter 7.*

Null Pointer Constant

Before C++11, the constant `NULL`, defined in `<cstddef>`, was used for null pointers. You cannot get access to this constant using any `import` declaration; instead, you must use `#include <cstddef>`. `NULL` is simply defined as the constant 0, which can cause problems. Take the following example:

```
#include <cstddef>

void func(int i) { /* ... */ }

int main()
{
    func(NULL);
}
```

The code defines a function `func()` with a single integer parameter. The `main()` function calls `func()` with argument `NULL`, which is supposed to be a null pointer constant. However, since `NULL` is not a real pointer, but identical to the integer 0, it triggers a call to `func(int)`. This might be unexpected behavior. Hence, some compilers even give a warning about this.

This problem is avoided by using a real *null pointer constant*, `nullptr`. The following code uses this real null pointer constant and causes a compilation error because there is no overload of `func()` accepting a pointer:

```
func(nullptr);
```

The Use of const

The keyword `const` can be used in a few different ways in C++. Its uses are related, but there are subtle differences. The subtleties of `const` make for excellent interview questions!

Basically, the keyword `const` is short for "constant" and specifies that something remains unchanged. The compiler enforces this requirement by marking any attempt to change it as an error. Furthermore, when optimizations are enabled, the compiler can take advantage of this knowledge to produce better code.

const as a Qualifier for a Type

If you assumed that the keyword `const` has something to do with constants, you have correctly uncovered one of its uses. In C, programmers often use the preprocessor `#define` mechanism, see Chapter 11, to declare symbolic names for values that won't change during the execution of the program, such as the version number. In C++, programmers are encouraged to avoid `#define` in favor of using `const` to define constants. Defining a constant with `const` is just like defining a variable, except that the compiler guarantees that code cannot change the value. Here are some examples:

```
const int versionNumberMajor { 2 };
const int versionNumberMinor { 1 };
const std::string productName { "Super Hyper Net Modulator" };
const double PI { 3.141592653589793238462 };
```

You can mark any variable `const`, including global variables and class data members.

const with Pointers

When a variable contains one or more levels of indirection via a pointer, applying `const` becomes trickier. Consider the following lines of code:

```
int* ip;
ip = new int[10];
ip[4] = 5;
```

Suppose that you decide to apply `const` to `ip`. Set aside your doubts about the usefulness of doing so for a moment, and consider what it means. Do you want to prevent the `ip` variable itself from being changed, or do you want to prevent the values to which it points from being changed? That is, do you want to prevent the second statement or the third statement?

To prevent the pointed-to values from being modified (as in the third statement), you can add the keyword `const` to the declaration of `ip` like this:

```
const int* ip;
ip = new int[10];
ip[4] = 5; // DOES NOT COMPILE!
```

Now you cannot change the values to which ip points. An alternative but semantically equivalent way to write this is as follows:

```
int const* ip;
ip = new int[10];
ip[4] = 5; // DOES NOT COMPILE!
```

Putting the const before or after the int makes no difference in its functionality.

If you instead want to mark ip itself const (not the values to which it points), you need to write this:

```
int* const ip { nullptr };
ip = new int[10]; // DOES NOT COMPILE!
ip[4] = 5;         // Error: dereferencing a null pointer
```

Now that ip itself cannot be changed, the compiler requires you to initialize it when you declare it, either with nullptr as in the preceding code or with newly allocated memory as follows:

```
int* const ip { new int[10] };
ip[4] = 5;
```

You can also mark both the pointer and the value to which it points const like this:

```
int const* const ip { nullptr };
```

Here is an alternative but equivalent syntax:

```
const int* const ip { nullptr };
```

Although this syntax might seem confusing, there is actually a simple rule: the const keyword applies to whatever is directly to its left. Consider this line again:

```
int const* const ip { nullptr };
```

From left to right, the first const is directly to the right of the word int. Thus, it applies to the int to which ip points. Therefore, it specifies that you cannot change the values to which ip points. The second const is directly to the right of the *. Thus, it applies to the pointer to the int, which is the ip variable. Therefore, it specifies that you cannot change ip (the pointer) itself.

The reason this rule becomes confusing is an exception. That is, the first const can go before the variable like this:

```
const int* const ip { nullptr };
```

This "exceptional" syntax is used much more commonly than the other syntax.

You can extend this rule to any number of levels of indirection, as in this example:

```
const int * const * const * const ip { nullptr };
```

> **NOTE** *Here is another easy-to-remember rule to figure out complicated variable declarations: read from right to left. For example,* `int* const ip` *reads from right to left as "*`ip` *is a* `const` *pointer to an* `int`*." Further,* `int const* ip` *reads as "*`ip` *is a pointer to a* `const int`*," and* `const int* ip` *reads as "*`ip` *is a pointer to an* `int` *constant."*

const to Protect Parameters

In C++, you can cast a non-const variable to a const variable. Why would you want to do this? It offers some degree of protection from other code changing the variable. If you are calling a function that a co-worker of yours is writing and you want to ensure that the function doesn't change the value of an argument you pass in, you can tell your co-worker to have the function take a const parameter. If the function attempts to change the value of the parameter, it will not compile.

In the following code, a string* is automatically cast to a const string* in the call to mysteryFunction(). If the author of mysteryFunction() attempts to change the value of the passed string, the code will not compile. There are ways around this restriction, but using them requires conscious effort. C++ only protects against accidentally changing const variables.

```
void mysteryFunction(const string* someString)
{
    *someString = "Test";  // Will not compile
}

int main()
{
    string myString { "The string" };
    mysteryFunction(&myString);  // &myString is a string*
}
```

You can also use const on primitive-type parameters to prevent accidentally changing them in the body of the function. For example, the following function has a const integer parameter. In the body of the function, you cannot modify the param integer. If you do try to modify it, the compiler will generate an error.

```
void func(const int param) { /* Not allowed to change param... */ }
```

const Member Functions

A second use of the const keyword is to mark class member functions as const, preventing them from modifying data members of the class. The AirlineTicket class introduced earlier can be modified to mark all read-only member functions as const. The const must be added to both the member function declaration and its definition. If any const member function tries to modify one of the AirlineTicket data members, the compiler will emit an error.

```
export class AirlineTicket
{
    public:
        double calculatePriceInDollars() const;

        std::string getPassengerName() const;
        void setPassengerName(std::string name);

        int getNumberOfMiles() const;
        void setNumberOfMiles(int miles);

        bool hasEliteSuperRewardsStatus() const;
        void setHasEliteSuperRewardsStatus(bool status);
    private:
        std::string m_passengerName { "Unknown Passenger" };
        int m_numberOfMiles { 0 };
        bool m_hasEliteSuperRewardsStatus { false };
```

```
};

std::string AirlineTicket::getPassengerName() const
{
    return m_passengerName;
}
// Other member functions omitted...
```

> **NOTE** *To follow the* const*-correctness principle, it's recommended to declare member functions that do not change any data members of the object as being* const*. These member functions are also called* ***inspectors****, compared to* ***mutators*** *for non-*const *member functions.*

References

Professional C++ code, including much of the code in this book, uses references extensively. A *reference* in C++ is an *alias* for another variable. All modifications to the reference change the value of the variable to which it refers. You can think of references as implicit pointers that save you the trouble of taking the address of variables and dereferencing the pointer. Alternatively, you can think of references as just another name for the original variable. You can create stand-alone reference variables, use reference data members in classes, accept references as parameters to functions, and return references from functions.

Reference Variables

Reference variables must be initialized as soon as they are created, like this:

```
int x { 3 };
int& xRef { x };
```

Attaching `&` to a type indicates that the variable is a reference. It is still used as though it was a normal variable, but behind the scenes, it is really a pointer to the original variable. Both the variable `x` and the reference variable `xRef` point to exactly the same value; i.e., `xRef` is just another name for `x`. If you change the value through either one of them, the change is visible through the other one as well. For example, the following code sets `x` to 10 through `xRef`:

```
xRef = 10;
```

You cannot declare a reference variable outside of a class definition without initializing it.

```
int& emptyRef; // DOES NOT COMPILE!
```

> **WARNING** *A reference variable must always be initialized when it's created.*

Modifying References

A reference always refers to the same variable to which it is initialized; references cannot be changed once they are created. The syntax might be confusing for beginning C++ programmers. If you assign a variable to a reference when the reference is declared, the reference refers to that variable. However, if you assign a variable to a reference after that, the variable to which the reference refers is changed to the value of the variable being assigned. The reference is not updated to refer to that variable. Here is a code example:

```
int x { 3 }, y { 4 };
int& xRef { x };
xRef = y; // Changes value of x to 4. Doesn't make xRef refer to y.
```

You might try to circumvent this restriction by taking the address of `y` when you assign it:

```
xRef = &y; // DOES NOT COMPILE!
```

This code does not compile. The address of `y` is a pointer, but `xRef` is declared as a reference to an `int`, not a reference to a pointer.

Some programmers go even further in their attempts to circumvent the intended semantics of references. What if you assign a reference to a reference? Won't that make the first reference refer to the variable to which the second reference refers? You might be tempted to try this code:

```
int x { 3 }, z { 5 };
int& xRef { x };
int& zRef { z };
zRef = xRef; // Assigns values, not references
```

The final statement does not change to what `zRef` refers to. Instead, it sets the value of `z` to 3, because `xRef` refers to `x`, which is 3.

> **WARNING** *Once a reference is initialized to refer to a specific variable, you cannot change the reference to refer to another variable; you can change only the value of the variable the reference refers to.*

References-to-const

`const` applied to references is usually easier than `const` applied to pointers for two reasons. First, references are `const` by default, in that you can't change to what they refer. So, there is no need to mark them `const` explicitly. Second, you can't create a reference to a reference, so there is usually only one level of indirection with references. The only way to get multiple levels of indirection is to create a reference to a pointer.

Thus, when C++ programmers refer to a reference-to-`const`, they mean something like this:

```
int z;
const int& zRef { z };
zRef = 4; // DOES NOT COMPILE
```

By applying `const` to the `int&`, you prevent assignment to `zRef`, as shown. Similar to pointers, `const int& zRef` is equivalent to `int const& zRef`. Note, however, that marking `zRef const` has no effect on `z`. You can still modify the value of `z` by changing it directly instead of through the reference.

You cannot create a reference to an unnamed value, such as an integer literal, unless the reference is to a `const` value. In the following example, `unnamedRef1` does not compile because it is a reference-to-non-`const` referring to a constant. That would mean you could change the value of the constant,

5, which doesn't make sense. `unnamedRef2` works because it's a reference-to-`const`, so you cannot for example write `unnamedRef2 = 7`.

```
int& unnamedRef1 { 5 };          // DOES NOT COMPILE
const int& unnamedRef2 { 5 }; // Works as expected
```

The same holds for temporary objects. You cannot create a reference-to-non-`const` to a temporary object, but a reference-to-`const` is fine. For example, suppose you have the following function returning an `std::string` object:

```
string getString() { return "Hello world!"; }
```

You can create a reference-to-`const` to the result of calling `getString()`, and that reference keeps the temporary `std::string` object alive until the reference goes out of scope:

```
string& string1 { getString() };          // DOES NOT COMPILE
const string& string2 { getString() }; // Works as expected
```

References to Pointers and Pointers to References

You can create references to any type, including pointer types. Here is an example of a reference to a pointer to `int`:

```
int* intP { nullptr };
int*& ptrRef { intP };
ptrRef = new int;
*ptrRef = 5;
delete ptrRef; ptrRef = nullptr;
```

The syntax is a little strange: you might not be accustomed to seeing `*` and `&` right next to each other. However, the semantics are straightforward: `ptrRef` is a reference to `intP`, which is a pointer to `int`. Modifying `ptrRef` changes `intP`. References to pointers are rare but can occasionally be useful, as discussed in the "Reference Parameters" section later in this chapter.

Taking the address of a reference gives the same result as taking the address of the variable to which the reference refers. Here is an example:

```
int x { 3 };
int& xRef { x };
int* xPtr { &xRef }; // Address of a reference is pointer to value.
*xPtr = 100;
```

This code sets `xPtr` to point to `x` by taking the address of a reference to `x`. Assigning 100 to `*xPtr` changes the value of `x` to 100. Writing the comparison `xPtr == xRef` will not compile because of a type mismatch; `xPtr` is a pointer to an `int`, while `xRef` is a reference to an `int`. The comparisons `xPtr == &xRef` and `xPtr == &x` both compile without errors and are both `true`.

Finally, note that you cannot declare a reference to a reference or a pointer to a reference. For example, neither `int& &` nor `int&*` is allowed.

Structured Bindings and References

Structured bindings are introduced earlier in this chapter. One of the examples given was the following:

```
pair myPair { "hello", 5 };
auto [theString, theInt] { myPair };  // Decompose using structured bindings
```

Now that you know about references and `const` variables, it's time to learn that both can be combined with structured bindings as well. Here's an example:

```
auto& [theString, theInt] { myPair };      // Decompose into references-to-non-const
const auto& [theString, theInt] { myPair }; // Decompose into references-to-const
```

Reference Data Members

Data members of classes can be references. As discussed earlier, a reference cannot exist without referring to some other variable, and it is not possible to change where a reference refers to. Thus, reference data members cannot be initialized inside the body of a class constructor, but they must be initialized in the *constructor initializer*. Syntax-wise, a constructor initializer immediately follows the constructor header and starts with a colon. The following is a quick example with the constructor initializer highlighted. Chapter 9 goes in much more detail.

```
class MyClass
{
    public:
        MyClass(int& ref) : m_ref { ref } { /* Body of constructor */ }
    private:
        int& m_ref;
};
```

> **WARNING** *A reference must always be initialized when it's created. Usually, references are created when they are declared, but reference data members need to be initialized in a constructor initializer for the containing class.*

Reference Parameters

C++ programmers do not often use stand-alone reference variables or reference data members. The most common use of references is for parameters to functions. The default parameter-passing semantics is pass-by-value: functions receive copies of their arguments. When those parameters are modified, the original arguments remain unchanged. Pointers to stack variables are often used in C to allow functions to modify variables in other stack frames. By dereferencing the pointer, the function can change the memory that represents the variable even though that variable isn't in the current stack frame. The problem with this approach is that it brings the messiness of pointer syntax into what is really a simple task.

Instead of passing pointers to functions, C++ offers a better mechanism, called *pass-by-reference*, where parameters are references instead of pointers. The following are two implementations of an `addOne()` function. The first one has no effect on the variable that is passed in because it is passed by value, and thus the function receives a copy of the value passed to it. The second one uses a reference and thus changes the original variable.

```
void addOne(int i)
{
    i++;  // Has no real effect because this is a copy of the original
}
```

```
void addOne(int& i)
{
    i++;  // Actually changes the original variable
}
```

The syntax for the call to the addOne() function with an integer reference is no different than if the function just took an integer.

```
int myInt { 7 };
addOne(myInt);
```

> **NOTE** *There is a subtle difference between the two* addOne() *implementations. The version using pass-by-value accepts literals without a problem; for example,* addOne(3); *is legal. However, doing the same with the pass-by-reference version of* addOne() *will result in a compilation error. This can be solved by using reference-to-*const *parameters, discussed in the next section.*

Here is another example where pass-by-reference comes in handy; it's a simple swap function to swap the values of two ints:

```
void swap(int& first, int& second)
{
    int temp { first };
    first = second;
    second = temp;
}
```

You can call it like this:

```
int x { 5 }, y { 6 };
swap(x, y);
```

When swap() is called with the arguments x and y, the first parameter is initialized to refer to x, and the second parameter is initialized to refer to y. When swap() modifies first and second, x and y are actually changed.

A common quandary arises when you have a pointer to something that you need to pass to a function that takes a reference. You can "convert" a pointer to a reference in this case by dereferencing the pointer. This action gives you the value to which the pointer points, which the compiler then uses to initialize the reference parameter. For example, you can call swap() like this:

```
int x { 5 }, y { 6 };
int *xp { &x }, *yp { &y };
swap(*xp, *yp);
```

Finally, if you have a function that needs to return an object of a class that is expensive to copy, you'll often see the function accepting an output parameter of type reference-to-non-const to such a class that the function then modifies, instead of directly returning such an object. Developers thought that this was the recommended way to prevent any performance penalties with creating copies when returning objects from functions. However, even back then, compilers were usually smart enough to avoid any redundant copies. So, we have the following rule:

> **WARNING** *The recommended way to return objects from a function is to return them by value, instead of using output parameters.*

Pass-by-Reference-to-const

The main value in reference-to-`const` parameters is efficiency. When you pass a value into a function, an entire copy is made. When you pass a reference, you are really just passing a pointer to the original so the computer doesn't need to make a copy. By passing a reference-to-`const`, you get the best of both worlds: no copy is made, and the original variable cannot be changed. References-to-`const` become more important when you are dealing with objects because they can be large and making copies of them can have unwanted side effects. The following example shows how to pass an `std::string` to a function as a reference-to-`const`:

```
import std;
using namespace std;
void printString(const string& myString) { println("{}", myString); }

int main()
{
    string someString { "Hello World" };
    printString(someString);
    printString("Hello World");  // Passing literals works.
}
```

Pass-by-Reference vs. Pass-by-Value

Pass-by-reference is required when you want to modify the parameter and see those changes reflected in the variable passed to the function. However, you should not limit your use of pass-by-reference to only those cases. Pass-by-reference avoids copying the arguments to the function, providing two additional benefits:

- **Efficiency:** Large objects could take a long time to copy. Pass-by-reference passes only a reference to the object into the function.
- **Support:** Not all classes allow pass-by-value.

If you want to leverage these benefits but do not want to allow the original objects to be modified, you should mark the parameters `const`, giving you pass-by-reference-to-`const`.

> **NOTE** *These benefits of pass-by-reference imply that you should use pass-by-value only for simple built-in types such as* `int` *and* `double` *for which you don't need to modify the arguments. If you need to pass an object to a function, prefer to pass it by reference-to-*`const` *instead of by value. This prevents unnecessary copying. Pass it by reference-to-non-*`const` *if the function needs to modify the object. Chapter 9 slightly modifies this rule after the introduction of move semantics, allowing pass-by-value of objects in certain cases.*

Reference Return Values

You can return a reference from a function. Of course, you can use this technique only if the variable to which the returned reference refers to continues to exist following the function termination.

> **WARNING** *From a function, never return a reference to a variable that is locally scoped to that function, such as an automatically allocated variable on the stack that will be destroyed when the function ends.*

One of the main reasons to return a reference is if you want to be able to assign to the return value directly as an *lvalue* (the left-hand side of an assignment statement). Several overloaded operators commonly return references, such as operators =, +=, and so on. Chapter 15 goes into more details on how to write such overloaded operators yourself.

Another reason to return a reference from a function is if the return type is expensive to copy. By returning a reference or reference-to-`const`, the copying is avoided, but keep the earlier warning in mind. This is often used to return objects by reference-to-`const` from class member functions, as demonstrated later in this chapter.

Deciding Between References and Pointers

References in C++ could be considered redundant: everything you can do with references, you can accomplish with pointers. For example, you could write the earlier shown `swap()` function like this:

```
void swap(int* first, int* second)
{
    int temp { *first };
    *first = *second;
    *second = temp;
}
```

However, this code is more cluttered than the version with references. References make your programs cleaner and easier to understand. They are also safer than pointers: it's impossible to have a null reference, and you don't explicitly dereference references, so you can't encounter any of the dereferencing errors associated with pointers. Of course, these arguments about references being safer are valid only in the absence of any pointers. For example, take the following function that accepts a reference to an `int`:

```
void refcall(int& t) { ++t; }
```

You could declare a pointer and initialize it to point to some random place in memory. Then you could dereference this pointer and pass it as the reference argument to `refcall()`, as in the following code. This code compiles fine, but it is undefined what will happen when executed. It could for example cause a crash.

```
int* ptr { (int*)8 };
refcall(*ptr);
```

Most of the time, you can use references instead of pointers. References to objects also support *polymorphism*, discussed in detail in Chapter 10, in the same way as pointers to objects. However, there are some use cases in which you need to use a pointer. One example is when you need to change the location to which it points. Recall that you cannot change the variable to which a reference refers. For example, when you dynamically allocate memory, you need to store a pointer to the result in a pointer rather than a reference. A second use case in which you need to use a pointer is when the pointer is optional, that is, when it can be `nullptr`. Yet another use case is if you want to store polymorphic types (discussed in Chapter 10) in a container.

A long time ago, and in legacy code, a way to distinguish between appropriate use of pointers and references in parameters and return types was to consider who *owns* the memory. If the code receiving the variable became the owner and thus became responsible for releasing the memory associated with an object, it had to receive a pointer to the object. If the code receiving the variable didn't have to free the memory, it received a reference. Nowadays, however, raw pointers should be avoided in favor of *smart pointers* (see Chapter 7), which is the recommended way to transfer ownership.

> **NOTE** *Prefer references over pointers; that is, use a pointer only if a reference is not possible.*

Consider a function that splits an array of `int`s into two arrays: one of even numbers and one of odd numbers. The function doesn't know how many numbers in the source array will be even or odd, so it should dynamically allocate the memory for the destination arrays after examining the source array. It should also return the sizes of the two new arrays. Altogether, there are four items to return: pointers to the two new arrays and the sizes of the two new arrays. Obviously, you must use pass-by-reference. The canonical C way to write the function looks like this:

```
void separateOddsAndEvens(const int arr[], size_t size, int** odds,
    size_t* numOdds, int** evens, size_t* numEvens)
{
    // Count the number of odds and evens.
    *numOdds = *numEvens = 0;
    for (size_t i = 0; i < size; ++i) {
        if (arr[i] % 2 == 1) {
            ++(*numOdds);
        } else {
            ++(*numEvens);
        }
    }

    // Allocate two new arrays of the appropriate size.
    *odds = new int[*numOdds];
    *evens = new int[*numEvens];

    // Copy the odds and evens to the new arrays.
    size_t oddsPos = 0, evensPos = 0;
    for (size_t i = 0; i < size; ++i) {
        if (arr[i] % 2 == 1) {
            (*odds)[oddsPos++] = arr[i];
        } else {
            (*evens)[evensPos++] = arr[i];
        }
    }
}
```

The final four parameters to the function are the "reference" parameters. To change the values to which they refer, `separateOddsAndEvens()` must dereference them, leading to some ugly syntax in the function body. Additionally, when you want to call `separateOddsAndEvens()`, you must pass the address of two pointers so that the function can change the actual pointers, and pass the address of two `size_t`s so that the function can change the actual `size_t`s. Note also that the caller is responsible for deleting the two arrays created by `separateOddsAndEvens()`!

```
int unSplit[] { 1, 2, 3, 4, 5, 6, 7, 8, 9, 10 };
int* oddNums { nullptr };
int* evenNums { nullptr };
size_t numOdds { 0 }, numEvens { 0 };

separateOddsAndEvens(unSplit, std::size(unSplit),
    &oddNums, &numOdds, &evenNums, &numEvens);

// Use the arrays...

delete[] oddNums; oddNums = nullptr;
delete[] evenNums; evenNums = nullptr;
```

If this syntax annoys you (which it should), you can write the same function by using references to obtain true pass-by-reference semantics:

```
void separateOddsAndEvens(const int arr[], size_t size, int*& odds,
    size_t& numOdds, int*& evens, size_t& numEvens)
{
    numOdds = numEvens = 0;
    for (size_t i { 0 }; i < size; ++i) {
        if (arr[i] % 2 == 1) {
            ++numOdds;
        } else {
            ++numEvens;
        }
    }

    odds = new int[numOdds];
    evens = new int[numEvens];

    size_t oddsPos { 0 }, evensPos { 0 };
    for (size_t i { 0 }; i < size; ++i) {
        if (arr[i] % 2 == 1) {
            odds[oddsPos++] = arr[i];
        } else {
            evens[evensPos++] = arr[i];
        }
    }
}
```

In this case, the `odds` and `evens` parameters are references to `int*`s. `separateOddsAndEvens()` can modify the `int*`s that are used as arguments to the function (through the reference), without any explicit dereferencing. The same logic applies to `numOdds` and `numEvens`, which are references to `size_t`s. With this version of the function, you no longer need to pass the addresses of the pointers or `size_t`s; the reference parameters handle it for you automatically:

```
separateOddsAndEvens(unSplit, std::size(unSplit),
    oddNums, numOdds, evenNums, numEvens);
```

Even though using reference parameters is already much cleaner than using pointers, it is recommended that you avoid dynamically allocated arrays as much as possible. For example, by using the Standard Library `vector` container, the `separateOddsAndEvens()` function can be rewritten to be much safer, shorter, more elegant, and much more readable, because all memory allocations and deallocations happen automatically.

```
void separateOddsAndEvens(const vector<int>& arr,
    vector<int>& odds, vector<int>& evens)
{
    for (int i : arr) {
        if (i % 2 == 1) {
            odds.push_back(i);
        } else {
            evens.push_back(i);
        }
    }
}
```

This version can be used as follows:

```
vector<int> vecUnSplit { 1, 2, 3, 4, 5, 6, 7, 8, 9, 10 };
vector<int> odds, evens;
separateOddsAndEvens(vecUnSplit, odds, evens);
```

Note that you don't need to deallocate the `odds` and `evens` containers; the `vector` class takes care of this. This version is much easier to use than the versions using pointers or references.

The version using `vectors` is already much better than the versions using pointers or references, but as I recommended earlier, output parameters should be avoided as much as possible. If a function needs to return something, it should just return it instead of using output parameters! Since C++17, a compiler is not allowed to perform any copying or moving of objects for statements of the form `return object;` where `object` is a nameless temporary. This is called *mandatory elision of copy/move operations* and means that there's no performance penalty at all by returning `object` by value. If `object` is a local variable that is not a function parameter, *non-mandatory elision of copy/move operations* is allowed, an optimization also known as *named return value optimization* (NRVO). This optimization is not guaranteed by the standard. Some compilers perform this optimization only for release builds but not for debug builds. With mandatory and non-mandatory elision, compilers can avoid any copying of objects that are returned from functions. This results in *zero-copy pass-by-value* semantics. Note that for NRVO, even though the copy/move constructors won't be called, they still need to be accessible; otherwise, the program is ill-formed according to the standard. Copy/move operations and constructors are discussed in Chapter 9, but those details are not important for the current discussion.

The following version of `separateOddsAndEvens()` returns a simple `struct` of two `vectors`, instead of accepting two output `vectors` as parameters, and uses designated initializers.

```
struct OddsAndEvens { vector<int> odds, evens; };

OddsAndEvens separateOddsAndEvens(const vector<int>& arr)
{
    vector<int> odds, evens;
    for (int i : arr) {
        if (i % 2 == 1) {
            odds.push_back(i);
```

```
            } else {
                evens.push_back(i);
            }
        }
        return OddsAndEvens { .odds = odds, .evens = evens };
    }
```

With these changes, the code to call separateOddsAndEvens() becomes compact yet easy to read and understand:

```
vector<int> vecUnSplit { 1, 2, 3, 4, 5, 6, 7, 8, 9, 10 };
auto oddsAndEvens { separateOddsAndEvens(vecUnSplit) };
// Do something with oddsAndEvens.odds and oddsAndEvens.evens...
```

> **NOTE** *Avoid output parameters. If a function needs to return something, just return it by value.*

const_cast()

In C++ every variable has a specific type. It is possible in certain situations to cast a variable of one type to a variable of another type. To that end, C++ provides five types of casts: const_cast(), static_cast(), reinterpret_cast(), dynamic_cast(), and std::bit_cast(). This section discusses const_cast(). The second type of cast, static_cast(), is briefly introduced earlier in this chapter and discussed in more detail in Chapter 10. The other remaining casts are also discussed in Chapter 10.

const_cast() is the most straightforward of the different casts available. You can use it to add const-ness to a variable or cast away const-ness of a variable. It is the only cast of the five that is allowed to cast away const-ness. Theoretically, of course, there should be no need for a const cast. If a variable is const, it should stay const. In practice, however, you sometimes find yourself in a situation where a function is specified to take a const parameter, which it must then pass to a function that takes a non-const parameter, and you are absolutely sure that the latter function will not modify its non-const argument. The "correct" solution would be to make const consistent in the program, but that is not always an option, especially if you are using third-party libraries. Thus, you sometimes need to cast away the const-ness of a variable, but again you should do this only when you are sure the function you are calling will not modify the object; otherwise, there is no other option than to restructure your program. Here is an example:

```
void thirdPartyLibraryFunction(char* str);

void f(const char* str)
{
    thirdPartyLibraryFunction(const_cast<char*>(str));
}
```

Additionally, the Standard Library provides a helper function called std::as_const(), defined in <utility>, which returns a reference-to-const of its reference parameter. Basically, as_const(obj) is equivalent to const_cast<const T&>(obj), where T is the type of obj. Using as_const() results in shorter and more readable code compared to using `const_cast()`. Concrete use cases for `as_const()` are coming later in this book, but its basic use is as follows:

```
string str { "C++" };
const string& constStr { as_const(str) };
```

Exceptions

C++ is a flexible language, but it does allow you to do unsafe things. For example, the compiler will let you write code that scribbles on random memory addresses or tries to divide by zero (computers don't deal well with infinity). One language feature that attempts to add a degree of safety is *exceptions*.

An exception is an exceptional situation, that is, a situation that you don't expect or want in the normal flow of execution of a program. For example, if you are writing a function that retrieves a web page, several things could go wrong. The Internet host that contains the page might be down, the page might come back blank, or the connection could be lost. One way you could handle this situation is by returning a special value from the function, such as `nullptr` or an error code. Exceptions provide a much better mechanism for dealing with problems.

Exceptions come with some new terminology. When a piece of code detects an exceptional situation, it *throws* an exception. Another piece of code *catches* the exception and takes appropriate action. The following example shows a function, `divideNumbers()`, that throws an exception if the caller passes in a denominator of zero. The `std::invalid_argument` exception is defined in `<stdexcept>`.

```
double divideNumbers(double numerator, double denominator)
{
    if (denominator == 0) {
        throw invalid_argument { "Denominator cannot be 0." };
    }
    return numerator / denominator;
}
```

When the `throw` statement is executed, the function immediately ends without returning a value. If the caller surrounds the function call with a `try/catch` block, as shown in the following code, it receives the exception and is able to handle it. Chapter 14, "Handling Errors," goes into much more detail on exception handling, but for now, just remember that it is recommended to catch exceptions by reference-to-`const`, such as `const invalid_argument&` in the following example. Also note that all Standard Library exception classes have a member function called `what()`, which returns a string containing a brief explanation of the exception.

```
try {
    println("{}", divideNumbers(2.5, 0.5));
    println("{}", divideNumbers(2.3, 0));
    println("{}", divideNumbers(4.5, 2.5));
} catch (const invalid_argument& exception) {
    println("Exception caught: {}", exception.what());
}
```

The first call to `divideNumbers()` executes successfully, and the result is printed on the screen. The second call throws an exception. No value is returned, and the only output is the error message that is printed when the exception is caught. The third call is never executed because the second call throws an exception, causing the program to jump to the catch block. The output for the preceding code snippet is as follows:

```
5
Exception caught: Denominator cannot be 0.
```

Exceptions can get tricky in C++. To use exceptions properly, you need to understand what happens to the stack variables when an exception is thrown, and you have to be careful to properly catch and handle the necessary exceptions. Also, if you need to include more information about an error in an exception, you can write your own exception types. Lastly, the C++ compiler doesn't force you to catch every exception that might occur. If your code never catches any exceptions but an exception is thrown, the program will be terminated. These trickier aspects of exceptions are covered in detail in Chapter 14.

Type Aliases

A *type alias* provides a new name for an existing type declaration. You can think of a type alias as syntax for introducing a synonym for an existing type declaration without creating a new type. The following gives a new name, IntPtr, to the int* type declaration:

```
using IntPtr = int*;
```

You can use the new type name and the definition it aliases interchangeably. For example, the following two lines are valid:

```
int* p1;
IntPtr p2;
```

Variables created with the new type name are completely compatible with those created with the original type declaration. So, it is perfectly valid, given these definitions, to write the following, because they are not just compatible types, they are the same type:

```
p1 = p2;
p2 = p1;
```

The most common use for type aliases is to provide manageable names when the real type declarations become too unwieldy. This situation commonly arises with templates. An example from the Standard Library itself is std::basic_string<T> to represent strings. It's a class template where T is the type of each character in the string, for example char. You have to specify the template type parameter any time you want to refer to such a type. For declaring variables, specifying function parameters, and so on, you would have to write basic_string<char>:

```
void processVector(const vector<basic_string<char>>& vec) { /* omitted */ }

int main()
{
    vector<basic_string<char>> myVector;
    processVector(myVector);
}
```

Since basic_string<char> is used that frequently, the Standard Library provides the following type alias as a shorter, more meaningful name:

```
using string = basic_string<char>;
```

With this type alias, the previous code snippet can be written more elegantly:

```
void processVector(const vector<string>& vec) { /* omitted */ }

int main()
{
    vector<string> myVector;
    processVector(myVector);
}
```

typedefs

Type aliases were introduced in C++11. Before C++11, you had to use `typedefs` to accomplish something similar but in a more convoluted way. This old mechanism is still explained here because you will come across it in legacy code bases.

Just as a type alias, a `typedef` provides a new name for an existing type declaration. For example, take the following type alias:

```
using IntPtr = int*;
```

This can be written as follows with a `typedef`:

```
typedef int* IntPtr;
```

As you can see, it's much less readable. The order is reversed, which causes a lot of confusion, even for professional C++ developers. Other than being more convoluted, a `typedef` behaves the same as a type alias. For example, the `typedef` can be used as follows:

```
IntPtr p;
```

Type aliases and `typedefs` are not entirely equivalent, though. Compared to `typedefs`, type aliases are more powerful when used with templates, but that is a topic covered in Chapter 12 because it requires more details about templates.

> **NOTE** *Always prefer type aliases over* `typedefs`.

Type Inference

Type inference allows the compiler to automatically deduce the type of an expression. There are two keywords for type inference: `auto` and `decltype`.

The auto Keyword

The `auto` keyword has a number of different uses:

- To deduce a function's return type, as explained earlier in this chapter
- To define structured bindings, as explained earlier in this chapter
- To deduce the type of an expression, as discussed in this section

- To deduce the type of non-type template parameters; see Chapter 12
- To define abbreviated function templates; see Chapter 12
- To use with `decltype(auto)`; see Chapter 12
- To write functions using the alternative function syntax; see Chapter 12
- To write generic lambda expressions; see Chapter 19, "Function Pointers, Function Objects, and Lambda Expressions"

`auto` can be used to let the compiler automatically deduce the type of a variable at compile time. The following statement shows the simplest use of the `auto` keyword in that context:

```
auto x { 123 };    // x is of type int.
```

In this example, you don't win much by typing `auto` instead of `int`; however, it becomes useful for more complicated types. Suppose you have a function called `getFoo()` that has a complicated return type. If you want to assign the result of calling `getFoo()` to a variable, you can spell out the complicated type, or you can simply use `auto` and let the compiler figure it out:

```
auto result { getFoo() };
```

This has the added benefit that you can easily change the function's return type without having to update all the places in the code where that function is called.

The auto& Syntax

Using `auto` to deduce the type of an expression strips away reference and `const` qualifiers. Suppose you have the following:

```
const string message { "Test" };
const string& foo() { return message; }
```

You can call `foo()` and store the result in a variable with the type specified as `auto`, as follows:

```
auto f1 { foo() };
```

Because `auto` strips away reference and `const` qualifiers, `f1` is of type `string`, and thus a *copy* is made! If you want a reference-to-`const`, you can explicitly make it a reference and mark it `const`, as follows:

```
const auto& f2 { foo() };
```

Earlier in this chapter, the `as_const()` utility function is introduced. It returns a reference-to-`const` version of its reference parameter. Be careful when using `as_const()` in combination with `auto`. Since `auto` strips away reference and `const` qualifiers, the following `result` variable has type `string`, not `const string&`, and hence a copy is made:

```
string str { "C++" };
auto result { as_const(str) };
```

> **WARNING** *Always keep in mind that* `auto` *strips away reference and* `const` *qualifiers and thus creates a copy! If you do not want a copy, use* `auto&` *or* `const auto&`.

The auto* Syntax

The `auto` keyword can also be used for pointers. Here's an example:

```
int i { 123 };
auto p { &i };
```

The type of `p` is `int*`. There is no danger here to accidentally make a copy, unlike when working with references as discussed in the previous section. However, when working with pointers, I do recommend using the `auto*` syntax as it more clearly states that pointers are involved, for example:

```
auto* p { &i };
```

Additionally, using `auto*` versus just `auto` does resolve a strange behavior when using `auto`, `const`, and pointers together. Suppose you write the following:

```
const auto p1 { &i };
```

Most of the time, this is not doing what you expect it to do!

Often, when you use `const`, you want to protect the thing to which the pointer is pointing to. You would think that `p1` is of type `const int*`, but in fact, the type is `int* const`, so it's a `const` pointer to a non-`const` integer! Putting the `const` after the `auto` as follows doesn't help; the type is still `int* const`:

```
auto const p2 { &i };
```

When you use `auto*` in combination with `const`, then it is behaving as you would expect. Here's an example:

```
const auto* p3 { &i };
```

Now `p3` is of type `const int*`. If you really want a `const` pointer instead of a `const` integer, you put the `const` at the end:

```
auto* const p4 { &i };
```

`p4` has type `int* const`.

Finally, with this syntax you can make both the pointer and the integer constant:

```
const auto* const p5 { &i };
```

`p5` is of type `const int* const`. You cannot achieve this if you omit the `*`.

Copy List vs. Direct List Initialization

There are two types of initializations that use braced initializer lists:

- **Copy list initialization:** `T obj = {arg1, arg2, ...};`
- **Direct list initialization:** `T obj {arg1, arg2, ...};`

In combination with auto type deduction, there is an important difference between copy- and direct list initialization. Here is an example:

```
// Copy list initialization
auto a = { 11 };         // initializer_list<int>
auto b = { 11, 22 };     // initializer_list<int>
```

```
// Direct list initialization
auto c { 11 };              // int
auto d { 11, 22 };          // Error, too many elements.
```

For copy list initialization, all the elements in the braced initializer must be of the same type. For example, the following does not compile:

```
auto b = { 11, 22.33 };  // Compilation error
```

The decltype Keyword

The `decltype` keyword takes an expression as argument and computes the type of that expression, as shown here:

```
int x { 123 };
decltype(x) y { 456 };
```

In this example, the compiler deduces the type of `y` to be `int` because that is the type of `x`.

The difference between `auto` and `decltype` is that `decltype` does not strip reference and `const` qualifiers. Take, again, a function `foo()` returning a reference-to-`const string`. Defining `f2` using `decltype` as follows results in `f2` being of type `const string&`, and thus no copy is made:

```
decltype(foo()) f2 { foo() };
```

On first sight, `decltype` doesn't seem to add much value. However, it is powerful in the context of templates, discussed in Chapters 12 and 26.

The Standard Library

C++ comes with a Standard Library, which contains a lot of useful classes that can readily be used in your code. The benefit of using these classes is that you don't need to reinvent their functionality, and you don't need to waste time on implementing things that have already been implemented for you. Another benefit is that the classes available in the Standard Library are heavily tested and verified for correctness by thousands of users. The Standard Library classes are also optimized for performance, so using them will most likely result in better performance compared to making your own implementation.

A lot of functionality is provided by the Standard Library. Chapters 16 to 24 provide more details; however, when you start working with C++, it is good to have an idea of what the Standard Library can do for you from the beginning. This is especially important if you are a C programmer. As a C programmer, you might try to solve problems in C++ the same way you would solve them in C, but in C++ there is probably an easier and safer solution to the problem that involves using Standard Library classes.

That is the reason why this chapter already introduces some Standard Library classes, such as `std::string`, `array`, `vector`, `pair`, and `optional`. These are used throughout examples in this book from the beginning, to make sure you get into the habit of using Standard Library classes. Many more classes are introduced in Chapters 16 to 24.

YOUR FIRST BIGGER C++ PROGRAM

The following program builds on the employee database example used earlier in the discussion on structs. This time, you will end up with a fully functional C++ program that uses many of the features discussed in this chapter. This real-world example includes the use of classes, exceptions, streams, `vectors`, namespaces, references, and other language features.

An Employee Records System

The next sections implement a program to manage a company's employee records with the following feature set:

- Add and fire employees
- Promote and demote employees
- View all employees, past and present
- View all current employees
- View all former employees

The design for this program divides the code into three parts. The `Employee` class encapsulates the information describing a single employee. The `Database` class manages all the employees of the company. Finally, a separate `UserInterface` file provides the interactivity of the program.

The Employee Class

The `Employee` class maintains all the information about an employee. Its member functions provide a way to query and change that information. An `Employee` also knows how to display herself on the console. Additionally, member functions exist to adjust the employee's salary and employment status.

Employee.cppm

The `Employee.cppm` module interface file defines the `Employee` class. The sections of this file are described individually in the text that follows. The first few lines are as follows:

```
export module employee;
import std;
namespace Records {
```

The first line is a module declaration and states that this file exports a module called `employee`, followed by an import for the Standard Library functionality. This code also declares that the subsequent code, contained within the curly braces, lives in the `Records` namespace. `Records` is the namespace that is used throughout this program for application-specific code.

Next, the following two constants are defined inside the `Records` namespace. This book uses the convention to not prefix constants with any special letter and to start them with a capital letter to better contrast them with variables.

```
    const int DefaultStartingSalary { 30'000 };
    export const int DefaultRaiseAndDemeritAmount { 1'000 };
```

The first constant represents the default starting salary for new employees. This constant is not exported, because code outside this module does not need access to it. Code in the `employee` module can access this constant as `Records::DefaultStartingSalary`.

The second constant is the default amount for promoting or demoting an employee. This constant is exported, so code outside this module could, for example, promote an employee by twice the default amount.

Next, the `Employee` class is defined and exported, along with its public member functions:

```
    export class Employee
    {
        public:
            Employee(const std::string& firstName,
                     const std::string& lastName);

            void promote(int raiseAmount = DefaultRaiseAndDemeritAmount);
            void demote(int demeritAmount = DefaultRaiseAndDemeritAmount);
            void hire(); // Hires or rehires the employee
            void fire(); // Dismisses the employee
            void display() const; // Prints employee info to console

            // Getters and setters
            void setFirstName(const std::string& firstName);
            const std::string& getFirstName() const;

            void setLastName(const std::string& lastName);
            const std::string& getLastName() const;

            void setEmployeeNumber(int employeeNumber);
            int getEmployeeNumber() const;

            void setSalary(int newSalary);
            int getSalary() const;

            bool isHired() const;
```

A constructor is provided that accepts a first and last name. The `promote()` and `demote()` member functions both have integer parameters that have a default value equal to `DefaultRaiseAndDemeritAmount`. In this way, other code can omit the parameter, and the default will automatically be used. Member functions to hire and fire an employee are provided, together with a member function to display information about an employee. A number of setters and getters provide functionality to change the information or to query the current information of an employee.

The data members are declared as `private` so that other parts of the code cannot modify them directly:

```
        private:
            std::string m_firstName;
            std::string m_lastName;
            int m_employeeNumber { -1 };
            int m_salary { DefaultStartingSalary };
            bool m_hired { false };
    };
}
```

The setters and getters provide the only public way of modifying or querying those values. The data members are directly initialized here inside the class definition instead of in a constructor. By default, new employees have no name, an employee number of –1, the default starting salary, and a status of not hired.

Employee.cpp

The first few lines of the module implementation file are as follows:

```
module employee;
import std;
using namespace std;
```

The first line specifies for which module this source file is, followed by an import of `std`, and a `using` directive.

The constructor accepting a first and last name just sets the corresponding data members:

```
namespace Records {
    Employee::Employee(const string& firstName, const string& lastName)
        : m_firstName { firstName }, m_lastName { lastName }
    {
    }
```

The `promote()` and `demote()` member functions simply call `setSalary()` with a new value. The default values for the integer parameters are not repeated here; they are allowed only in a function declaration, not in a definition.

```
    void Employee::promote(int raiseAmount)
    {
        setSalary(getSalary() + raiseAmount);
    }

    void Employee::demote(int demeritAmount)
    {
        setSalary(getSalary() - demeritAmount);
    }
```

The `hire()` and `fire()` member functions just set the `m_hired` data member appropriately:

```
    void Employee::hire() { m_hired = true; }
    void Employee::fire() { m_hired = false; }
```

The `display()` member function uses `println()` to display information about the current employee. Because this code is part of the `Employee` class, it *could* access data members, such as `m_salary`, directly instead of using getters, such as `getSalary()`. However, it is considered good style to make use of getters and setters when they exist, even from within the class.

```
    void Employee::display() const
    {
        println("Employee: {}, {}", getLastName(), getFirstName());
        println("-------------------------");
        println("{}", (isHired() ? "Current Employee" : "Former Employee"));
        println("Employee Number: {}", getEmployeeNumber());
        println("Salary: ${}", getSalary());
        println("");
    }
```

Finally, a number of getters and setters perform the task of getting and setting values:

```
        // Getters and setters
        void Employee::setFirstName(const string& firstName) {m_firstName = firstName;}
        const string& Employee::getFirstName() const { return m_firstName; }

        void Employee::setLastName(const string& lastName) { m_lastName = lastName; }
        const string& Employee::getLastName() const { return m_lastName; }

        void Employee::setEmployeeNumber(int employeeNumber) {
            m_employeeNumber = employeeNumber; }
        int Employee::getEmployeeNumber() const { return m_employeeNumber; }

        void Employee::setSalary(int salary) { m_salary = salary; }
        int Employee::getSalary() const { return m_salary; }

        bool Employee::isHired() const { return m_hired; }
    }
```

Even though these member functions seem trivial, it's better to have trivial getters and setters than to make your data members `public`. For example, in the future, you may want to perform bounds checking in the `setSalary()` member function. Getters and setters also make debugging easier because you can insert a breakpoint in them to inspect values when they are retrieved or set. Another reason is that when you decide to change how you are storing the data in your class, you only need to modify these getters and setters, while other code using your class can remain untouched.

EmployeeTest.cpp

As you write individual classes, it is often useful to test them in isolation. The following code includes a `main()` function that performs some simple operations using the `Employee` class. Once you are confident that the `Employee` class works, you should remove or comment out this file so that you don't attempt to compile your code with multiple `main()` functions.

```
import std;
import employee;

using namespace std;
using namespace Records;

int main()
{
    println("Testing the Employee class.");
    Employee emp { "Jane", "Doe" };
    emp.setFirstName("John");
    emp.setLastName("Doe");
    emp.setEmployeeNumber(71);
    emp.setSalary(50'000);
    emp.promote();
    emp.promote(50);
    emp.hire();
    emp.display();
}
```

Another and much better way to test individual classes is with *unit testing*, discussed in Chapter 30, "Becoming Adept at Testing." Unit tests are small pieces of code to test specific functionality and that remain in the code base. All unit tests are frequently executed; for example, they can automatically be executed by your build system. The benefit of doing this is that if you make some changes to existing functionality, the unit tests will instantly warn you if you break something.

The Database Class

The Database class is implemented next. It uses the std::vector class from the Standard Library to store Employee objects.

Database.cppm

Here are the first few lines of the database.cppm module interface file:

```
export module database;
import std;
import employee;

namespace Records {
    const int FirstEmployeeNumber { 1'000 };
```

Because the database will take care of automatically assigning an employee number to a new employee, a constant defines where the numbering begins.

Next, the Database class is defined and exported:

```
    export class Database
    {
        public:
            Employee& addEmployee(const std::string& firstName,
                                  const std::string& lastName);
            Employee& getEmployee(int employeeNumber);
            Employee& getEmployee(const std::string& firstName,
                                  const std::string& lastName);
```

The database provides an easy way to add a new employee by providing a first and last name. For convenience, this member function returns a reference to the new employee. External code can also get an employee reference by calling the getEmployee() member function. Two overloads of this member function are declared. One allows retrieval by employee number. The other requires a first and last name.

Because the database is the central repository for all employee records, it has the following member functions to display all employees, the employees who are currently hired, and the employees who are no longer hired:

```
            void displayAll() const;
            void displayCurrent() const;
            void displayFormer() const;
```

Finally, the private data members are defined as follows:

```
        private:
            std::vector<Employee> m_employees;
            int m_nextEmployeeNumber { FirstEmployeeNumber };
    };
}
```

The m_employees data member contains the Employee objects, while m_nextEmployeeNumber keeps track of what employee number is assigned to a new employee and is initialized with the FirstEmployeeNumber constant.

Database.cpp

Here is the implementation of the addEmployee() member function:

```
module database;
import std;

using namespace std;

namespace Records {
    Employee& Database::addEmployee(const string& firstName,
                                    const string& lastName)
    {
        Employee theEmployee { firstName, lastName };
        theEmployee.setEmployeeNumber(m_nextEmployeeNumber++);
        theEmployee.hire();
        m_employees.push_back(theEmployee);
        return m_employees.back();
    }
```

The addEmployee() member function creates a new Employee object, fills in its information, and adds it to the vector. The m_nextEmployeeNumber data member is incremented after its use so that the next employee will get a new number. The back() member function of vector returns a reference to the last element in the vector, which is the newly added employee.

One of the getEmployee() member functions is implemented as follows. The second overload is implemented similarly, hence not shown. They both loop over all employees in m_employees using a range-based for loop and check whether an Employee is a match for the information passed to the member function. An exception is thrown if no match is found. Notice the use of auto& in the range-based for loop, because the loop doesn't want to work with copies of Employees but with references to the Employees in the m_employees vector.

```
    Employee& Database::getEmployee(int employeeNumber)
    {
        for (auto& employee : m_employees) {
            if (employee.getEmployeeNumber() == employeeNumber) {
                return employee;
            }
        }
        throw logic_error { "No employee found." };
    }
```

The following display member functions all use a similar algorithm: they loop through all employees and ask each employee to display itself to the console if the criterion for display matches.

```
    void Database::displayAll() const
    {
        for (const auto& employee : m_employees) { employee.display(); }
    }
```

```
    void Database::displayCurrent() const
    {
        for (const auto& employee : m_employees) {
            if (employee.isHired()) { employee.display(); }
        }
    }

    void Database::displayFormer() const
    {
        for (const auto& employee : m_employees) {
            if (!employee.isHired()) { employee.display(); }
        }
    }
}
```

DatabaseTest.cpp

A simple test for the basic functionality of the database is shown here:

```
import std;
import database;

using namespace std;
using namespace Records;

int main()
{
    Database myDB;
    Employee& emp1 { myDB.addEmployee("Greg", "Wallis") };
    emp1.fire();

    Employee& emp2 { myDB.addEmployee("Marc", "White") };
    emp2.setSalary(100'000);

    Employee& emp3 { myDB.addEmployee("John", "Doe") };
    emp3.setSalary(10'000);
    emp3.promote();

    println("All employees:\n==============");
    myDB.displayAll();

    println("\nCurrent employees:\n==================");
    myDB.displayCurrent();

    println("\nFormer employees:\n=================");
    myDB.displayFormer();
}
```

The User Interface

The final part of the program is a menu-based user interface that makes it easy for users to work with the employee database.

The following `main()` function contains a loop that displays the menu, performs the selected action, and then does it all again. For most actions, separate functions are defined. For simpler actions, such as displaying employees, the actual code is put in the appropriate case.

```
import std;
import database;
import employee;

using namespace std;
using namespace Records;

int displayMenu();
void doHire(Database& db);
void doFire(Database& db);
void doPromote(Database& db);

int main()
{
    Database employeeDB;
    bool done { false };
    while (!done) {
        int selection { displayMenu() };
        switch (selection) {
        case 0:
            done = true;
            break;
        case 1:
            doHire(employeeDB);
            break;
        case 2:
            doFire(employeeDB);
            break;
        case 3:
            doPromote(employeeDB);
            break;
        case 4:
            employeeDB.displayAll();
            break;
        case 5:
            employeeDB.displayCurrent();
            break;
        case 6:
            employeeDB.displayFormer();
            break;
        default:
            println(cerr, "Unknown command.");
            break;
        }
    }
}
```

The `displayMenu()` function prints the menu and gets input from the user. One important note is that this code assumes that the user will "play nice" and type a number when a number is requested. When you read about I/O in Chapter 13, you will learn how to protect against bad input.

```
int displayMenu()
{
    int selection;
    println("");
```

```
    println("Employee Database");
    println("-----------------");
    println("1) Hire a new employee");
    println("2) Fire an employee");
    println("3) Promote an employee");
    println("4) List all employees");
    println("5) List all current employees");
    println("6) List all former employees");
    println("0) Quit");
    println("");
    print("---> ");
    cin >> selection;
    return selection;
}
```

The `doHire()` function gets the new employee's name from the user and tells the database to add the employee:

```
void doHire(Database& db)
{
    string firstName;
    string lastName;

    print("First name? ");
    cin >> firstName;

    print("Last name? ");
    cin >> lastName;

    auto& employee { db.addEmployee(firstName, lastName) };
    println("Hired employee {} {} with employee number {}.",
        firstName, lastName, employee.getEmployeeNumber());
}
```

`doFire()` and `doPromote()` both ask the database for an employee by their employee number and then use the `public` member functions of the `Employee` object to make changes:

```
void doFire(Database& db)
{
    int employeeNumber;
    print("Employee number? ");
    cin >> employeeNumber;

    try {
        auto& emp { db.getEmployee(employeeNumber) };
        emp.fire();
        println("Employee {} terminated.", employeeNumber);
    } catch (const std::logic_error& exception) {
        println(cerr, "Unable to terminate employee: {}", exception.what());
    }
}

void doPromote(Database& db)
{
    int employeeNumber;
    print("Employee number? ");
    cin >> employeeNumber;
```

```
        int raiseAmount;
        print("How much of a raise? ");
        cin >> raiseAmount;

        try {
            auto& emp { db.getEmployee(employeeNumber) };
            emp.promote(raiseAmount);
        } catch (const std::logic_error& exception) {
            println(cerr, "Unable to promote employee: {}", exception.what());
        }
    }
```

Evaluating the Program

The preceding program covers a number of topics from the simple to the more complex. There are a number of ways that you could extend this program. For example, the user interface does not expose all the functionality of the `Database` and `Employee` classes. You could modify the UI to include those features. You could also try to implement additional functionality that you can think of for both classes, which would be a great exercise to practice the material you learned in this chapter.

If there are parts of this program that don't make sense, consult the relevant sections in this chapter to review those topics. If something is still unclear, the best way to learn is to play with the code and try things. For example, if you're not sure how to use the conditional operator, write a short `main()` function that uses it.

SUMMARY

After this crash course in C++ and the Standard Library, you are ready to become a professional C++ programmer. When you start getting deeper into the C++ language later in this book, you can refer to this chapter to brush up on parts of the language you may need to review. Going back to some of the sample code in this chapter may be all you need to bring a forgotten concept back to the forefront of your mind.

The next chapter goes deeper in on how strings are handled in C++, because almost every program you'll write will have to work with strings one way or another.

EXERCISES

By solving the following exercises, you can practice the material discussed in this chapter. Solutions to all exercises are available with the code download on the book's website at `www.wiley.com/go/proc++6e`. However, if you are stuck on an exercise, first reread parts of this chapter to try to find an answer yourself before looking at the solution from the website.

Exercise 1-1: Modify the `Employee` structure from the beginning of this chapter by putting it in a namespace called `HR`. What modifications do you have to make to the code in `main()` to work with this new implementation? Additionally, modify the code to use designated initializers.

Exercise 1-2: Build further on the result of Exercise 1-1 and add an enumeration data member `title` to `Employee` to specify whether a certain employee is a Manager, Senior Engineer, or Engineer. Which kind of enumeration will you use and why? Whatever you need to add, add it to the `HR` namespace. Test your new `Employee` data member in the `main()` function. Use a `switch` statement to print out a human-readable string for the title.

Exercise 1-3: Use an `std::array` to store three `Employee` instances from Exercise 1-2 with different data. Subsequently, use a range-based `for` loop to print out the employees in the `array`.

Exercise 1-4: Do the same as Exercise 1-3, but use an `std::vector` instead of an `array`, and use `push_back()` to insert elements into the `vector`.

Exercise 1-5: Take your solution for Exercise 1-4 and replace the data members for the first and last initials with strings to represent the full first and last name.

Exercise 1-6: Now that you know about `const` and references, and what they are used for, modify the `AirlineTicket` class from earlier in this chapter to use references wherever possible and to be `const` correct.

Exercise 1-7: Modify the `AirlineTicket` class from Exercise 1-6 to include an optional frequent-flyer number. What is the best way to represent this optional data member? Add a setter and a getter to set and retrieve the frequent-flyer number. Modify the `main()` function to test your implementation.

2

Working with Strings and String Views

WHAT'S IN THIS CHAPTER?

- The differences between C-style strings and C++ strings
- Details of the C++ `std::string` class
- Why you should use `std::string_view`
- What raw string literals are
- How to produce formatted text
- How to format entire ranges of elements to a string

WILEY.COM DOWNLOADS FOR THIS CHAPTER

Please note all the code examples for this chapter are available as a part of the chapter's code download on this book's website at `www.wiley.com/go/proc++6e` on the Download Code tab.

Every program that you write will use strings of some kind. With the old C language, there is not much choice but to use a dumb null-terminated character array to represent a string. Unfortunately, doing so can cause a lot of problems, such as buffer overflows, which can result in security vulnerabilities. The C++ Standard Library includes a safe and easy-to-use `std::string` class that does not have these disadvantages.

Because strings are so important, this chapter, early in the book, discusses them in more detail.

DYNAMIC STRINGS

Strings in languages that have supported them as first-class objects tend to have a number of attractive features, such as being able to expand to any size or to have substrings extracted or replaced. In other languages, such as C, strings were almost an afterthought; there wasn't a really good string data type, just fixed arrays of bytes. The C string library was nothing more than a collection of rather primitive functions without even bounds checking. C++ provides a string type as a first-class data type. Before discussing what C++ provides for strings, let's take a quick look at C-style strings first.

C-Style Strings

In the C language, strings are represented as an array of characters. The last character of a string is a null character (`\0`) so that code operating on the string can determine where it ends. This null character is officially known as `NUL`, spelled with one L, not two. `NUL` is not the same as the `NULL` pointer. Even though C++ provides a better string abstraction, it is important to understand the C technique for strings because they still arise in C++ programming. One of the most common situations is where a C++ program has to call a C-based interface in some third-party library or as part of interfacing to the operating system.

By far, the most common mistake that programmers make with C strings is that they forget to allocate space for the `\0` character. For example, the string `"hello"` appears to be five characters long, but six characters worth of space are needed in memory to store the value, as shown in Figure 2.1.

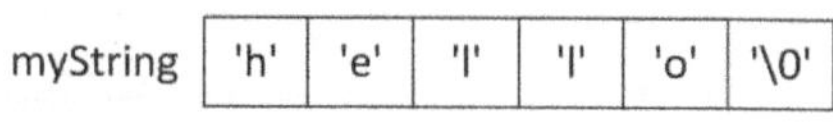

FIGURE 2.1

C++ contains several functions from the C language that operate on strings. These functions are defined in `<cstring>`. As a general rule of thumb, these functions do not handle memory allocation. For example, the `strcpy()` function takes two strings as parameters. It copies the second string onto the first, whether it fits or not. The following code attempts to build a wrapper around `strcpy()` that allocates the correct amount of memory and returns the result, instead of taking in an already allocated string. This initial attempt will turn out to be wrong! It uses the `strlen()` function to obtain the length of the string. The caller is responsible for freeing the memory allocated by `copyString()`.

```
char* copyString(const char* str)
{
    char* result { new char[strlen(str)] };  // BUG! Off by one!
    strcpy(result, str);
    return result;
}
```

The `copyString()` function as written is incorrect. The `strlen()` function returns the length of the string, not the amount of memory needed to hold it. For the string `"hello"`, `strlen()` returns 5, not 6. The proper way to allocate memory for a string is to add 1 to the amount of space needed for the actual characters. It seems a bit unnatural to have +1 all over the place. Unfortunately, that's how it works, so keep this in mind when you work with C-style strings. The correct implementation is as follows:

```
char* copyString(const char* str)
{
    char* result { new char[strlen(str) + 1] };
```

```
        strcpy(result, str);
        return result;
    }
```

One way to remember that `strlen()` returns only the number of actual characters in the string is to consider what would happen if you were allocating space for a string made up of several other strings. For example, if your function took in three strings and returned a string that was the concatenation of all three, how big would it be? To hold exactly enough space, it would be the length of all three strings added together, plus one space for the trailing `\0` character. If `strlen()` included the `\0` in the length of the string, the allocated memory would be too big. The following code uses the `strcpy()` and `strcat()` functions to perform this operation. The `cat` in `strcat()` stands for *concatenate*.

```
char* appendStrings(const char* str1, const char* str2, const char* str3)
{
    char* result { new char[strlen(str1) + strlen(str2) + strlen(str3) + 1] };
    strcpy(result, str1);
    strcat(result, str2);
    strcat(result, str3);
    return result;
}
```

The `sizeof()` operator in C and C++ can be used to get the size of a certain data type or variable. For example, `sizeof(char)` returns 1 because a `char` has a size of 1 byte. However, in the context of C-style strings, `sizeof()` is not the same as `strlen()`. You should never use `sizeof()` to try to get the size of a string. It returns different sizes depending on how the C-style string is stored. If it is stored as a `char[]`, then `sizeof()` returns the actual memory used by the string, including the `\0` character, as in this example:

```
char text1[] { "abcdef" };
size_t s1 { sizeof(text1) };  // is 7
size_t s2 { strlen(text1) };  // is 6
```

However, if the C-style string is stored as a `char*`, then `sizeof()` returns the size of a pointer!

```
const char* text2 { "abcdef" };
size_t s3 { sizeof(text2) };  // is platform-dependent
size_t s4 { strlen(text2) };  // is 6
```

Here, `s3` will be 4 when compiled in 32-bit mode, and 8 when compiled in 64-bit mode because it is returning the size of a `const char*`, which is a pointer.

A complete list of functions to operate on C-style strings can be found in the `<cstring>` header file.

> **WARNING** *When you use the C-style string functions with Microsoft Visual Studio, the compiler is likely to give you security-related warnings or even errors about these functions being deprecated. You can eliminate these warnings by using other C Standard Library functions, such as* `strcpy_s()` *or* `strcat_s()`*, which are part of the "secure C library" standard (ISO/IEC TR 24731). However, the best solution is to switch to the C++* `std::string` *class, discussed in the upcoming "The C++ std::string Class" section, but first a bit more on string literals.*

String Literals

You've probably seen strings written in a C++ program with quotes around them. For example, the following code outputs the string `hello` by including the string itself, not a variable that contains it:

```
println("hello");
```

In the preceding line, `"hello"` is a *string literal* because it is written as a value, not a variable. String literals are actually stored in a read-only part of memory. This allows the compiler to optimize memory usage by reusing references to equivalent string literals. That is, even if your program uses the string literal `"hello"` 500 times, the compiler is allowed to optimize memory by creating just one instance of `hello` in memory. This is called *literal pooling*.

String literals can be *assigned* to variables, but because string literals are in a read-only part of memory and because of the possibility of literal pooling, assigning them to variables can be risky. The C++ standard officially says that string literals are of type "array of *n* `const char`"; however, for backward compatibility with older non-`const`-aware code, some compilers do not force you to assign a string literal to a variable of type `const char*`. They let you assign a string literal to a `char*` without `const`, and the program will work fine unless you attempt to change the string. Generally, the behavior of modifying string literals is undefined. It could, for example, cause a crash, it could keep working with seemingly inexplicable side effects, the modification could silently be ignored, or it could just work; it all depends on your compiler. For example, the following code exhibits undefined behavior:

```
char* ptr { "hello" };        // Assign the string literal to a variable.
ptr[1] = 'a';                 // Undefined behavior!
```

A much safer way to code is to use a pointer to `const` characters when referring to string literals. The following code contains the same bug, but because it assigned the literal to a `const char*`, the compiler catches the attempt to write to read-only memory:

```
const char* ptr { "hello" }; // Assign the string literal to a variable.
ptr[1] = 'a';                 // Error! Attempts to write to read-only memory
```

You can also use a string literal as an initial value for a character array (`char[]`). In this case, the compiler creates an array that is big enough to hold the string and copies the string to this array. The compiler does not put the literal in read-only memory and does not do any literal pooling.

```
char arr[] { "hello" }; // Compiler takes care of creating appropriate sized
                        // character array arr.
arr[1] = 'a';           // The contents can be modified.
```

Raw String Literals

Raw string literals are string literals that can span multiple lines of code, don't require escaping of embedded double quotes, and process escape sequences like `\t` and `\n` as normal text and not as escape sequences. Escape sequences are discussed in Chapter 1, "A Crash Course in C++ and the Standard Library." For example, if you write the following with a normal string literal, you will get a compilation error because the string contains non-escaped double quotes:

```
println("Hello "World"!");    // Error!
```

Normally you have to escape the double quotes as follows:

```
println("Hello \"World\"!");
```

With a raw string literal, you can avoid the need to escape the quotes. A raw string literal starts with `R"(` and ends with `)"`:

```
println(R"(Hello "World"!)");
```

If you need a string consisting of multiple lines, without raw string literals, you need to embed `\n` escape sequences in your string where you want to start a new line. Here's an example:

```
println("Line 1\nLine 2");
```

The output is as follows:

```
Line 1
Line 2
```

With a raw string literal, instead of using `\n` escape sequences to start new lines, you can simply press Enter to start real physical new lines in your source code as follows. The output is the same as the previous code snippet using the embedded `\n`.

```
println(R"(Line 1
Line 2)");
```

Escape sequences are ignored in raw string literals. For example, in the following raw string literal, the `\t` escape sequence is not replaced with a tab character but is kept as the sequence of a backslash followed by the letter `t`:

```
println(R"(Is the following a tab character? \t)");
```

This outputs the following:

```
Is the following a tab character? \t
```

Because a raw string literal ends with `)"`, you cannot embed a `)"` in your string using this syntax. For example, the following string is not valid because it contains the `)"` sequence in the middle of the string:

```
println(R"(Embedded )" characters)");    // Error!
```

If you need embedded `)"` characters, you need to use the extended raw string literal syntax, which is as follows:

```
R"d-char-sequence(r-char-sequence)d-char-sequence"
```

The `r-char-sequence` is the actual raw string. The `d-char-sequence` is an optional delimiter sequence, which should be the same at the beginning and at the end of the raw string literal. This delimiter sequence can have at most 16 characters. You should choose this delimiter sequence as a sequence that will not appear in the middle of your raw string literal.

The previous example can be rewritten using a unique delimiter sequence as follows:

```
println(R"-(Embedded )" characters)-");
```

Raw string literals make it easier to work with database querying strings, regular expressions, file paths, and so on. Regular expressions are discussed in Chapter 21, "String Localization and Regular Expressions."

The C++ std::string Class

C++ provides a much-improved implementation of the concept of a string as part of the Standard Library. In C++, `std::string` is a class (actually an instantiation of the `std::basic_string` class template) that supports many of the same functionalities as the `<cstring>` functions, but that takes care of memory allocations for you. The `string` class is defined in `<string>` and lives in the `std` namespace. It has already been introduced in the previous chapter, but now it's time to take a closer look at it.

What Is Wrong with C-Style Strings?

To understand the necessity of the C++ `string` class, consider the advantages and disadvantages of C-style strings.

Advantages:

- They are simple, making use of the underlying basic character type and array structure.
- They are lightweight, taking up only the memory that they need if used properly.
- They are low level, so you can easily manipulate and copy them as raw memory.
- If you're a C programmer—why learn something new?

Disadvantages:

- They require incredible efforts to simulate a first-class string data type.
- They are unforgiving and susceptible to difficult-to-find memory bugs.
- They don't leverage the object-oriented nature of C++.
- They require knowledge of their underlying representation on the part of the programmer.

The preceding lists were carefully constructed to make you think that perhaps there is a better way. As you'll learn, C++ `string`s solve all the problems of C-style strings and render most of the arguments about the advantages of C strings over a first-class data type irrelevant.

Using the std::string Class

Even though `string` is a class, you can almost always treat it as if it were a built-in type. In fact, the more you think of it that way, the better off you are. Through the magic of operator overloading, C++ `string`s are much easier to use than C-style strings. The next two sections start the discussion by demonstrating how operator overloading makes it easy to concatenate and compare `string`s. Subsequent sections discuss how C++ `string`s handle memory, their compatibility with C-style strings, and some of the built-in operations you can perform on `string`s.

Concatenating Strings

The `+` operator is redefined for `string`s to mean "string concatenation." The following code produces `1234`:

```
string a { "12" };
string b { "34" };
string c { a + b };    // c is "1234"
```

The += operator is also overloaded to allow you to easily append a string:

```
a += b;    // a is "1234"
```

Comparing Strings

Another problem with C strings is that you cannot use == to compare them. Suppose you have the following two strings:

```
char* a { "12" };
char b[] { "12" };
```

Writing a comparison as follows always returns `false`, because it compares the pointer values, not the contents of the strings:

```
if (a == b) { /* ... */ }
```

Note that C arrays and pointers are related. You can think of C arrays, like the `b` array in the example, as pointers to the first element in the array. Chapter 7, "Memory Management," goes deeper in on the array-pointer duality.

To compare C strings, you have to write something like so:

```
if (strcmp(a, b) == 0) { /* ... */ }
```

Furthermore, there is no way to use <, <=, >=, or > to compare C strings, so `strcmp()` performs a three-way comparison, returning a value less than 0, 0, or a value greater than 0, depending on the lexicographic ordering relationship of the strings. This results in clumsy and hard-to-read code, which is also error-prone.

With C++ `strings`, comparison operators (==, !=, <, and so on) are all overloaded to work on the actual characters of the `string`. For example:

```
string a { "Hello" };
string b { "World" };
println("'{}' < '{}' = {}", a, b, a < b);  // 'Hello' < 'World' = true
println("'{}' > '{}' = {}", a, b, a > b);  // 'Hello' > 'World' = false
```

The C++ `string` class additionally provides a `compare()` member function that behaves like `strcmp()` and has a similar return type. Here is an example:

```
string a { "12" };
string b { "34" };

auto result { a.compare(b) };
if (result < 0) { println("less"); }
if (result > 0) { println("greater"); }
if (result == 0) { println("equal"); }
```

Just as with `strcmp()`, this is cumbersome to use. You need to remember the exact meaning of the return value. Furthermore, since the return value is just an integer, it is easy to forget the meaning of this integer and to write the following wrong code to compare for equality:

```
if (a.compare(b)) { println("equal"); }
```

`compare()` returns 0 for equality, anything else for non-equality. So, this line of code does the opposite of what it was intended to do; that is, it outputs "equal" for non-equal strings! If you just want to check whether two `string`s are equal, do not use `compare()`, but simply `==`.

Since C++20, this is improved with the three-way comparison operator, introduced in Chapter 1. The `string` class has full support for this operator. Here's an example:

```
auto result { a <=> b };
if (is_gt(result)) { println("greater"); }
if (is_lt(result)) { println("less"); }
if (is_eq(result)) { println("equal"); }
```

Memory Handling

As the following code shows, when `string` operations require extending the `string`, the memory requirements are automatically handled by the `string` class, so memory overruns are a thing of the past. This code snippet also demonstrates that individual characters can be accessed with the square brackets operator, `[]`, just as with C-style strings.

```
string myString { "hello" };
myString += ", there";
string myOtherString { myString };
if (myString == myOtherString) {
    myOtherString[0] = 'H';
}
println("{}", myString);
println("{}", myOtherString);
```

The output of this code is shown here:

```
hello, there
Hello, there
```

There are several things to note in this example. One point is that there are no memory leaks even though strings are allocated and resized in a few places. All of these `string` objects are created as stack variables. While the `string` class certainly has a bunch of allocating and resizing to do, the `string` destructors clean up this memory when `string` objects go out of scope. How exactly destructors work is explained in detail in Chapter 8, "Gaining Proficiency with Classes and Objects."

Another point to note is that the operators work the way you want them to work. For example, the `=` operator copies the strings, which is most likely what you want. If you are used to working with array-based strings, this will be either refreshingly liberating for you or somewhat confusing. Don't worry—once you learn to trust the `string` class to do the right thing, life gets so much easier.

Compatibility with C-Style Strings

For compatibility, you can use the `c_str()` member function on a `string` to get a `const char` pointer, representing a C-style string. However, the returned `const` pointer becomes invalid whenever the `string` has to perform any memory reallocation or when the `string` object is destroyed. You should call the member function just before using the result so that it accurately reflects the current contents of the `string`, and you must never return the result of `c_str()` called on a stack-based `string` object from a function.

There is also a `data()` member function that, up until C++14, always returned a `const char*` just as `c_str()`. Starting with C++17, however, `data()` returns a `char*` when called on a non-`const` string.

Operations on Strings

The `string` class supports quite a few additional operations. The following list highlights a few. Consult a Standard Library Reference (see Appendix B, "Annotated Bibliography") for a complete list of all supported operations that can be performed on `string` objects.

- `substr(pos,len)`: Returns the substring that starts at a given position and has a given length
- `find(str)`: Returns the position where a given substring is found, or `string::npos` if not found
- `replace(pos,len,str)`: Replaces part of a string (given by a position and a length) with another string
- `starts_with(str)`/`ends_with(str)`: Returns `true` if a string starts/ends with a given substring
-  `contains(str)`/`contains(ch)`: Returns `true` if a `string` contains another `string` or character

Here is a small code snippet that shows some of these operations in action:

```
string strHello { "Hello!!" };
string strWorld { "The World..." };
auto position { strHello.find("!!") };
if (position != string::npos) {
    // Found the "!!" substring, now replace it.
    strHello.replace(position, 2, strWorld.substr(3, 6));
}
println("{}", strHello);
// Test contains().
string toFind { "World" };
println("{}", strWorld.contains(toFind));
println("{}", strWorld.contains('.'));
println("{}", strWorld.contains("Hello"));
```

The output is as follows:

```
Hello World
true
true
false
```

Before C++23, it was possible to construct a `string` object by passing `nullptr` to its constructor. This would then result in undefined behavior at run time. Starting with C++23, trying to construct a `string` from `nullptr` results in a compilation error.

std::string Literals

A string literal in source code is usually interpreted as a `const char*` or a `const char[]`. You can use the standard literal `s` to interpret a string literal as an `std::string` instead.

```
auto string1 { "Hello World" };    // string1 is a const char*.
auto& string2 { "Hello World" };   // string2 is a const char[12].
auto string3 { "Hello World"s };   // string3 is an std::string.
```

The standard literal `s` is defined in the `std::literals::string_literals` namespace. However, both the `string_literals` and `literals` namespaces are *inline namespaces*. As such, you have the following options to make those string literals available to your code:

```
using namespace std;
using namespace std::literals;
using namespace std::string_literals;
using namespace std::literals::string_literals;
```

Basically, everything that is declared in an inline namespace is automatically available in the parent namespace. To define an inline namespace yourself, you use the `inline` keyword. For example, the `string_literals` inline namespace is defined as follows:

```
namespace std {
    inline namespace literals {
        inline namespace string_literals {
            // ...
        }
    }
}
```

CTAD with std::vector and Strings

Chapter 1 explains that `std::vector` supports class template argument deduction (CTAD), allowing the compiler to automatically deduce the type of a `vector` based on an initializer list. You have to be careful when using CTAD for a `vector` of strings. Take the following declaration of a `vector`, for example:

```
vector names { "John", "Sam", "Joe" };
```

The deduced type will be `vector<const char*>`, not `vector<string>`! This is an easy mistake to make and can lead to some strange behavior of your code, or even crashes, depending on what you do with the `vector` afterward.

If you want a `vector<string>`, then use `std::string` literals as explained in the previous section. Note the `s` behind each string literal in the following example:

```
vector names { "John"s, "Sam"s, "Joe"s };
```

Numeric Conversions

The C++ Standard Library provides both high-level and low-level numeric conversion functions, explained in the upcoming sections.

High-Level Numeric Conversions

The `std` namespace includes a number of helper functions, defined in `<string>`, that make it easy to convert numerical values into `string`s or `string`s into numerical values.

Converting to Strings

The following functions are available to convert numerical values into `strings`, where *T* can be `(unsigned) int`, `(unsigned) long`, `(unsigned) long long`, `float`, `double`, or `long double`. All of these functions create and return a new `string` object and manage all necessary memory allocations.

```
string to_string(T val);
```

These functions are straightforward to use. For example, the following code converts a `long double` value into a `string`:

```
long double d { 3.14L };
string s { to_string(d) };  // s contains 3.140000
```

Converting from Strings

Converting in the other direction is done by the following set of functions, also defined in the `std` namespace. In these prototypes, `str` is the `string` that you want to convert, `pos` is a pointer that receives the index of the first unconverted character, and `base` is the mathematical base that should be used during conversion. The `pos` pointer can be `nullptr`, in which case it is ignored. These functions ignore leading whitespace, throw `invalid_argument` if no conversion could be performed, and throw `out_of_range` if the converted value is outside the range of the return type.

```
int stoi(const string& str, size_t *pos = nullptr, int base = 10);
long stol(const string& str, size_t *pos = nullptr, int base = 10);
unsigned long stoul(const string& str, size_t *pos = nullptr, int base = 10);
long long stoll(const string& str, size_t *pos = nullptr, int base = 10);
unsigned long long stoull(const string& str, size_t *pos = nullptr, int base = 10);
float stof(const string& str, size_t *pos = nullptr);
double stod(const string& str, size_t *pos = nullptr);
long double stold(const string& str, size_t *pos = nullptr);
```

Here is an example:

```
const string toParse { "   123USD" };
size_t index { 0 };
int value { stoi(toParse, &index) };
println("Parsed value: {}", value);
println("First non-parsed character: '{}'", toParse[index]);
```

The output is as follows:

```
Parsed value: 123
First non-parsed character: 'U'
```

`stoi()`, `stol()`, `stoul()`, `stoll()`, and `stoull()` accept integral values and have a parameter called `base`, which specifies the base in which the given integral value is expressed. A base of 10, the default, assumes the usual decimal numbers, 0–9, while a base of 16 assumes hexadecimal numbers. If the base is set to 0, the function automatically figures out the base of the given number as follows:

- If the number starts with `0x` or `0X`, it is parsed as a hexadecimal number.
- If the number starts with `0`, it is parsed as an octal number.
- Otherwise, it is parsed as a decimal number.

Low-Level Numeric Conversions

The standard also provides a number of lower-level numerical conversion functions, all defined in `<charconv>`. These functions do not perform any memory allocations and do not work directly with `std::strings`, but instead they use raw buffers provided by the caller. Additionally, they are tuned for high performance and are locale-independent (see Chapter 21 for details on locales). The end result is that these functions can be orders of magnitude faster than other higher-level numerical conversion functions. These functions are also designed for *perfect round-tripping*, which means that serializing a numerical value to a string representation followed by deserializing the resulting string back to a numerical value results in the exact same value as the original one.

You should use these functions if you want highly performant, perfect round-tripping, locale-independent conversions, for example to serialize/deserialize numerical data to/from human-readable formats such as JSON, XML, and so on.

Converting to Strings

For converting integers to characters, the following set of functions is available:

```
to_chars_result to_chars(char* first, char* last, IntegerT value, int base = 10);
```

Here, *`IntegerT`* can be any signed or unsigned integer type or `char`. The result is of type `to_chars_result`, a type defined as follows:

```
struct to_chars_result {
    char* ptr;
    errc ec;
};
```

The `ptr` member is either equal to the one-past-the-end pointer of the written characters if the conversion was successful or equal to `last` if the conversion failed (in which case `ec == errc::value_too_large`). If `ec` is equal to a default constructed `errc`, then the conversion was successful.

Here is an example of its use:

```
const size_t BufferSize { 50 };
string out(BufferSize, ' '); // A string of BufferSize space characters.
auto result { to_chars(out.data(), out.data() + out.size(), 12345) };
if (result.ec == errc{}) { println("{}", out); /* Conversion successful. */ }
```

Using structured bindings introduced in Chapter 1, you can write it as follows:

```
string out(BufferSize, ' '); // A string of BufferSize space characters.
auto [ptr, error] { to_chars(out.data(), out.data() + out.size(), 12345) };
if (error == errc{}) { println("{}", out); /* Conversion successful. */ }
```

Similarly, the following set of conversion functions is available for floating-point types:

```
to_chars_result to_chars(char* first, char* last, FloatT value);
to_chars_result to_chars(char* first, char* last, FloatT value,
                         chars_format format);
to_chars_result to_chars(char* first, char* last, FloatT value,
                         chars_format format, int precision);
```

Here, *FloatT* can be any floating-point type, e.g., `float`, `double`, or `long double`. Formatting can be specified with a combination of `chars_format` flags.

```
enum class chars_format {
    scientific,                  // Style: (-)d.ddde±dd
    fixed,                       // Style: (-)ddd.ddd
    hex,                         // Style: (-)h.hhhp±d (Note: no 0x!)
    general = fixed | scientific // See next paragraph.
};
```

The default format is `chars_format::general`, which causes `to_chars()` to convert the floating-point value to a decimal notation in the style of *(-)ddd.ddd* or to a decimal exponent notation in the style of *(-)d.ddde±dd*, whichever results in the shortest representation with at least one digit before the decimal point (if present). If a format but no precision is specified, the precision is automatically determined to result in the shortest possible representation for the given format, with a maximum precision of six digits. Here is an example:

```
double value { 0.314 };
string out(BufferSize, ' '); // A string of BufferSize space characters.
auto [ptr, error] { to_chars(out.data(), out.data() + out.size(), value) };
if (error == errc{}) { println("{}", out); /* Conversion successful. */ }
```

Converting from Strings

For the opposite conversion—that is, converting character sequences into numerical values—the following set of functions is available[1]:

```
from_chars_result from_chars(const char* first, const char* last, IntegerT& value,
                             int base = 10);
from_chars_result from_chars(const char* first, const char* last, FloatT& value,
                             chars_format format = chars_format::general);
```

Here, `from_chars_result` is a type defined as follows:

```
struct from_chars_result {
    const char* ptr;
    errc ec;
};
```

The `ptr` member of the result type is a pointer to the first character that was not converted, or it equals `last` if all characters were successfully converted. If none of the characters could be converted, `ptr` equals `first`, and the value of the error code will be `errc::invalid_argument`. If the parsed value is too large to be representable by the given type, the value of the error code will be `errc::result_out_of_range`. Note that `from_chars()` does not skip any leading whitespace.

The perfect round-tripping feature of `to_chars()` and `from_chars()` can be demonstrated as follows:

```
double value1 { 0.314 };
string out(BufferSize, ' '); // A string of BufferSize space characters.
auto [ptr1, error1] { to_chars(out.data(), out.data() + out.size(), value1) };
if (error1 == errc{}) { println("{}", out); /* Conversion successful. */ }
```

[1] Starting with C++23, the integer overloads of `to_chars()` and `from_chars()` are marked as `constexpr`. This means that they can be evaluated at compile time in other `constexpr` functions and classes. See Chapter 9, "Mastering Classes and Objects," for a discussion of `constexpr`.

```
    double value2;
    auto [ptr2, error2] { from_chars(out.data(), out.data() + out.size(), value2) };
    if (error2 == errc{}) {
        if (value1 == value2) {
            println("Perfect roundtrip");
        } else {
            println("No perfect roundtrip?!?");
        }
    }
```

The std::string_view Class

Before C++17, there was always a dilemma of choosing the parameter type for a function that accepted a read-only string. Should it be a `const char*`? In that case, if a client had an `std::string` available, they had to call `c_str()` or `data()` on it to get a `const char*`. Even worse, the function would lose the nice object-oriented aspects of `string` and all its nice helper member functions. Maybe the parameter could instead be a `const string&`? In that case, you always needed a `string`. If you passed a string literal, for example, the compiler silently created a temporary `string` object that contained a copy of your string literal and passed a reference to that object to your function, so there was a bit of overhead. Sometimes people would write multiple overloads of the same function—one that accepted a `const char*` and another that accepted a `const string&`—but that was obviously a less-than-elegant solution.

Since C++17, all those problems are solved with the introduction of the `std::string_view` class, which is an instantiation of the `std::basic_string_view` class template, and defined in `<string_view>`. A `string_view` is basically a drop-in replacement for `const string&` but without the overhead. It never copies strings! A `string_view` provides a read-only view of a string and supports an interface similar to `string`, including the `contains()` member function introduced in C++23. One exception is the absence of `c_str()`, but `data()` is available. On the other hand, `string_view` does add the member functions `remove_prefix(size_t)` and `remove_suffix(size_t)`, which shrink a string by advancing the starting pointer by a given offset or by moving the end pointer backward by a given offset. Just like for `string`, starting with C++23, constructing a `string_view` from `nullptr` results in a compilation error.

If you know how to use `std::string`, then using a `string_view` is straightforward, as the following example code demonstrates. The `extractExtension()` function extracts and returns from a given filename the extension including the dot character. Note that `string_views` are usually passed by value because they are extremely cheap to copy. They just contain a pointer to, and the length of, a string. The `rfind()` member function searches a string for another given string or character starting from the back. The `substr()` member function called on a `string_view` returns a `string_view`, which is passed to a `string` constructor to convert it to a `string` and then returned from the function.

```
string extractExtension(string_view filename)
{
    // Return a copy of the extension.
    return string { filename.substr(filename.rfind('.')) };
}
```

This function can be used with all kinds of different strings:

```
string filename { R"(c:\temp\my file.ext)" };
println("C++ string: {}", extractExtension(filename));

const char* cString { R"(c:\temp\my file.ext)" };
println("C string: {}", extractExtension(cString));

println("Literal: {}", extractExtension(R"(c:\temp\my file.ext)"));
```

There is not a single copy of the argument being made in all these calls to `extractExtension()`. The `filename` parameter of the `extractExtension()` function is just a pointer and a length. This is all very efficient.

There is also a `string_view` constructor that accepts any raw buffer and a length. This can be used to construct a `string_view` out of a string buffer that is not `NUL` (`\0`) terminated. It is also useful when you do have a `NUL`-terminated string buffer, but you already know the length of the string, so the `string_view` constructor does not need to count the number of characters again. Here is an example:

```
const char* raw { /* ... */ };
size_t length { /* ... */ };
println("Raw: {}", extractExtension({ raw, length }));
```

The last line can also be written more explicitly as follows:

```
println("Raw: {}", extractExtension(string_view { raw, length }));
```

Finally, you can also construct a `string_view` from a common range, which is a range based on iterators and, since C++23, from a modern range. Iterators, common ranges, and modern ranges are discussed in Chapter 17, "Understanding Iterators and the Ranges Library."

> **NOTE** *Use an* `std::string_view` *instead of* `const string&` *or* `const char*` *whenever a function requires a read-only string as one of its parameters.*

You cannot implicitly construct a `string` from a `string_view`. This is prohibited to prevent accidentally copying the string in a `string_view`, as constructing a `string` from a `string_view` always involves copying the data. To convert a `string_view` to a `string`, use an explicit `string` constructor. That is exactly what the `return` statement in `extractExtension()` does:

```
return string { filename.substr(filename.rfind('.')) };
```

For the same reason, you cannot concatenate a `string` and a `string_view`. The following code does not compile:

```
string str { "Hello" };
string_view sv { " world" };
auto result { str + sv };  // Error, does not compile!
```

Instead, convert the string_view to a string using a string constructor:

```
auto result1 { str + string { sv } };
```

Or, use append():

```
string result2 { str };
result2.append(sv.data(), sv.size());
```

> **WARNING** *Functions returning a string should return a* const string& *or a* string, *but not a* string_view. *Returning a* string_view *would introduce the risk of invalidating the returned* string_view *if, for example, the string to which it refers needs to reallocate.*

> **WARNING** *Storing a* const string& *or a* string_view *as a data member of a class requires you to make sure the string to which they refer stays alive for the duration of the object's lifetime. It's strongly recommended to store an* std::string *instead.*

std::string_view and Temporary Strings

A string_view should not be used to store a view of a temporary string. Take the following example:

```
string s { "Hello" };
string_view sv { s + " World!" };
println("{}", sv);
```

This code snippet has undefined behavior, i.e., what happens when running this code depends on your compiler and compiler settings. It might crash, it might print "ello World!" (without the letter *H*), and so on. Why is this undefined behavior? The initializer expression for the sv string_view results in a temporary string with the "Hello World!" contents. The string_view then stores a pointer to this temporary string. At the end of the second line of code, this temporary string is destroyed, leaving the string_view with a dangling pointer.

> **WARNING** *Never use* std::string_view *to store a view of temporary strings.*

std::string_view Literals

You can use the standard literal sv to interpret a string literal as an std::string_view. Here's an example:

```
auto sv { "My string_view"sv };
```

The standard literal sv requires one of the following using directives:

```
using namespace std::literals::string_view_literals;
using namespace std::string_view_literals;
using namespace std::literals;
using namespace std;
```

Nonstandard Strings

There are several reasons why many C++ programmers don't use C++-style strings. Some programmers simply aren't aware of the string type because it was not always part of the C++ specification. Others have discovered over the years that the C++ string doesn't provide the behavior they need or dislike the fact that std::string is totally agnostic about the character encoding and so have developed their own string type. Chapter 21 returns to the topic of character encodings.

Perhaps the most common reason is that development frameworks and operating systems tend to have their own way of representing strings, such as the CString class in the Microsoft MFC framework. Often, this is for backward compatibility or to address legacy issues. When starting a project in C++, it is important to decide ahead of time how your group will represent strings. Some things are for sure:

- You should never pick the C-style string representation.
- You can standardize on the string functionality available in the framework you are using, such as the built-in string features of MFC, Qt, and so on.
- If you use std::string for your strings, then use std::string_view to pass read-only strings to functions; otherwise, see if your framework has support for something similar like string_views.

FORMATTING AND PRINTING STRINGS

Up until C++20, formatting of strings was usually done with C-style functions like printf() or with C++ I/O streams such as std::cout:

- C-style functions:
  - Not recommended because they are not type safe and are not extensible to support your own custom types
  - Easy to read because of separation of format string and arguments, and hence easy to translate to different languages
  - For example:

```
printf("x has value %d and y has value %d.\n", x, y);
```

- C++ I/O streams:
  - Recommended (before C++20) because they are type safe and extensible

- Harder to read because the strings and arguments are intertwined, and hence harder to translate
- For example:

```
cout << "x has value " << x << " and y has value " << y << '.' << endl;
```

C++20 introduced `std::format()`, defined in `<format>`, to format strings. It basically combines all advantages of the C-style functions and the C++ I/O streams. It's a type-safe and extensible formatting mechanism. For example:

```
cout << format("x has value {} and y has value {}.", x, y) << endl;
```

C++23 makes it even easier with the introduction of `std::print()` and `println()`. For example:

```
println("x has value {} and y has value {}.", x, y);
```

Additionally, `std::print()` and `println()` have better support for writing UTF-8 Unicode text to Unicode-compliant consoles. Unicode is discussed in Chapter 21, but here's a quick example:

```
println("こんにちは世界");
```

This correctly prints the string "こんにちは世界", which is Japanese for "Hello World," to the console.[2] If you try to print this string using C++ I/O streams as follows, depending on your console settings, the output can be something garbled such as "πüôπéôπü½πüíπü»Σ╕ûτòî":

```
cout << "こんにちは世界" << endl;
```

Thanks to the Unicode support, you can even print emojis. The following prints a smiley if your output console properly supports Unicode. Using `cout` for this would likely result in garbled output.

```
println("😀");
```

`std::print()` and `println()` are now the recommended ways to write text to the console; thus, they're used throughout all the examples in this book. They are type safe, are extensible to support user types, are easy to read, support Unicode output, support localization to different languages, and so on. On top of all those benefits, the performance of `print()` and `println()` is also much better compared to doing the same using C++ I/O streams directly, even though, underneath, `print()` and `println()` are still using such streams.

Format Strings

`std::format()`, `print()`, and `println()` use a *format string*, a string specifying how the given arguments must be formatted in the output string. Its basic form is introduced in the previous chapter and already used throughout examples. Now it's time to look at how powerful these format strings really are.

The format string is usually the first argument to `format()`, `print()`, and `println()`. A format string can contain a set of curly brackets, `{}`, which represent a *replacement field*. You can have as many replacement fields as you need. Subsequent arguments to `format()`, `print()`, and `println()`

[2] To compile source code containing Unicode characters, you might need to pass a compiler switch. For Visual C++, you must pass the `/utf-8` compiler switch. For GCC, use the command line option `-finput-charset=UTF-8`. Clang assumes all files are UTF-8 by default. Check your compiler documentation.

are values that are used to fill in those replacement fields. If you need the { and } characters in the output, then you need to escape them as {{ or }}.

Up to now, replacement fields have always been empty sets of curly brackets, {}, but that is just the start. Inside those curly brackets can be a string in the format `[index][:specifier]`:

- The optional `index` is an *argument index*, discussed in the next section.
- The optional `specifier` is a *format specifier* to stipulate how a value must be formatted in the output and explained in detail in the "Format Specifiers" section.

Passing a format string to `format()`, `print()`, and `println()` is mandatory. For example, you cannot directly print a value as follows:

```
int x { 42 };
println(x);
```

Instead, you can write the following:

```
println("{}", x);
```

You also cannot print a single newline by just writing the following:

```
println();
```

Instead, use this:

```
println("");
```

Argument Indices

You can either omit the `index` from all replacement fields or specify, for all replacement fields, the zero-based index of one of the values passed to `format()`, `print()`, or `println()` as second and subsequent arguments that should be used for a replacement field. You are allowed to use a certain `index` multiple times if you want to output that value multiple times. If `index` is omitted, the values passed as second and subsequent arguments are used in their given order for all replacement fields.

The following call to `println()` omits explicit indices in the replacement fields:

```
int n { 42 };
println("Read {} bytes from {}", n, "file1.txt");
```

You can specify manual indices as follows:

```
println("Read {0} bytes from {1}", n, "file1.txt");
```

Mixing manual indices and automatic indices is not allowed. The following uses an invalid format string:

```
println("Read {0} bytes from {}", n, "file1.txt");
```

The order of the formatted values in the output string can be changed without having to change the actual order of the arguments. This is a useful feature if you want to translate strings in your software. Certain languages have different ordering within their sentences. For example, the previous format string can be translated to Chinese as follows. In Chinese, the order of the replacement fields in the sentence is reversed, but thanks to the use of *argument indices* in the format string, the order of the arguments to `println()` remains unchanged.

```
println("从{1}中读取{0}个字节。", n, "file1.txt");
```

Printing to Different Destinations

Up to now, every call to `print()` and `println()` had a format string as the first argument, followed by a number of additional arguments. For example:

```
println("x has value {} and y has value {}.", x, y);
```

This prints the string to the standard output stream, the same stream as `std::cout`.

As Chapter 1 explains, there's also `std::cerr`, which streams to the standard error console. You can use `print()` and `println()` to print to the error console as follows:

```
println(cerr, "x has value {} and y has value {}.", x, y);
```

C++23

Compile-Time Verification of Format Strings

As of C++23, the format string for `format()`,[3] `print()`, and `println()` must be a compile-time constant so that the compiler can check at compile time whether there are any syntax errors in the format string. That means the following does not compile:

```
string s { "Hello World!" };
println(s);    // Error! Does not compile.
```

The error produced is compiler dependent and unfortunately, at the time of this writing, rather cryptic and not always immediately helpful in pinpointing the exact cause of the error. For example, here is the error from the Microsoft Visual C++ 2022 compiler:

```
error C7595: 'std::basic_format_string<char>::basic_format_string': call to
immediate function is not a constant expression
```

The correct use is as follows:

```
string s { "Hello World!" };
println("{}", s);
```

`constexpr` format strings are naturally also allowed as those are compile-time constants. Chapter 9, "Mastering Classes and Objects," discusses the `constexpr` keyword in detail.

```
constexpr auto formatString { "Value: {}" };
println(formatString, 11);  // Value: 11
```

Non-Compile-Time Constant Format Strings

The fact that format strings must be compile-time constants can be a bit cumbersome when you need to localize/translate format strings for different languages. In such a scenario, you can use `std::vprint_unicode()` or `std::vprint_nonunicode()` instead of `std::print()`. It's a little bit harder to use, though. You cannot just pass the arguments as you do with `print()`, but you need to

[3] This is a breaking change for `std::format()`. Prior to C++23, the format string for `format()` was not enforced to be a compile-time constant.

use std::make_format_args() to do so. Here's an example:

```
enum class Language { English, Dutch };

string_view GetLocalizedFormat(Language language)
{
    switch (language) {
        case Language::English: return "Numbers: {0} and {1}.";
        case Language::Dutch:   return "Getallen: {0} en {1}.";
    }
}

int main()
{
    Language language { Language::English };
    vprint_unicode(GetLocalizedFormat(language), make_format_args(1, 2));
    println("");
    language = Language::Dutch;
    vprint_unicode(GetLocalizedFormat(language), make_format_args(1, 2));
}
```

The output is:

```
Numbers: 1 and 2.
Getallen: 1 en 2.
```

The following call using print() does not compile as it requires a compile-time constant format string:

```
print(GetLocalizedFormat(language), 1, 2);
```

Handling Errors in Non-Compile-Time Constant Format Strings

When format strings are verified at run time, instead of at compile time, std::format_error exceptions are thrown for any format string error. As explained earlier, functions such as std::format(), print(), and println() never throw such exceptions as the format strings are all verified at compile time. However, functions such as std::vformat() and vprint_unicode() (see the previous section) don't require the format string to be constant and hence don't verify them at compile time but at run time. These functions might throw format_error exceptions. Here is an example:

```
try {
    vprint_unicode("An integer: {5}", make_format_args(42));
} catch (const format_error& caught_exception) {
    println("{}", caught_exception.what()); // "Argument not found."
}
```

Now, let's investigate how powerful format specifiers really are.

Format Specifiers

As mentioned earlier, a format string can contain replacement fields delimited by curly brackets. Inside those curly brackets can be a string in the format [index][:specifier]. This section discusses the format specifier part of the replacement field. index is discussed earlier.

A *format specifier* is used to manipulate how a value is formatted in the output. A format specifier is prefixed with a colon, `:`. The general form of a format specifier is as follows:

```
[[fill]align][sign][#][0][width][.precision][L][type]
```

All parts between square brackets are optional. The individual specifier parts are discussed in the next subsections.

width

The `width` specifies the minimum width of the field into which the given value should be formatted. This can also be another set of curly brackets, in which case it's called a *dynamic width*. If an index is specified in the curly brackets, for example `{3}`, the value for the dynamic width is taken from the argument with the given index. Otherwise, if no index is specified, for example `{}`, the width is taken from the next argument in the list of arguments.

Here are some examples:

```
int i { 42 };
println("|{:5}|", i);          // |   42|
println("|{:{}}|", i, 7);      // |     42|
println("|{1:{0}}|", 7, i);    // |     42|
```

[fill]align

The `[fill]align` part optionally says what character to use as a fill character, followed by how a value should be aligned in its field:

- `<` means left alignment (default for non-integers and non-floating-point numbers).
- `>` means right alignment (default for integers and floating-point numbers).
- `^` means center alignment.

The fill character is inserted into the output to make sure the field in the output reaches the desired minimum width specified by the `[width]` part of the specifier. If no `[width]` is specified, then `[fill]align` has no effect.

When using center alignment, the same number of fill characters is on the left and on the right of the formatted value. If the total number of fill characters is odd, then the extra fill character is added on the right.

Here are some examples:

```
int i { 42 };
println("|{:7}|", i);     // |     42|
println("|{:<7}|", i);    // |42     |
println("|{:_>7}|", i);   // |_____42|
println("|{:_^7}|", i);   // |__42___|
```

The following is an interesting trick to output a character a specific number of times. Instead of typing a string literal yourself containing the correct number of characters, you specify the number of characters you need explicitly in the format specifier:

```
println("|{:=>16}|", ""); // |================|
```

sign

The `sign` part can be one of the following:

- `-` means to only display the sign for negative numbers (default).
- `+` means to display the sign for negative and positive numbers.
- `space` means that a minus sign should be used for negative numbers, and a space for positive numbers.

Here are some examples:

```
int i { 42 };
println("|{:<5}|", i);   // |42   |
println("|{:<+5}|", i);  // |+42  |
println("|{:< 5}|", i);  // | 42  |
println("|{:< 5}|", -i); // |-42  |
```

#

The `#` part enables the *alternate formatting* rules. If enabled for integral types, and hexadecimal, binary, or octal number formatting is specified as well, then the alternate format inserts a 0x, 0X, 0b, 0B, or 0 in front of the formatted number. If enabled for floating-point types, the alternate format will always output a decimal separator, even if no digits follow it.

The following two sections give examples with alternate formatting.

type

The `type` specifies the type a given value must be formatted in. There are several options:

- **Integer types:** `b` (binary), `B` (binary, but with `0B` instead of `0b` if `#` is specified), `d` (decimal), `o` (octal), `x` (hexadecimal with lowercase `a`, `b`, `c`, `d`, `e`, `f`), `X` (hexadecimal with uppercase `A`, `B`, `C`, `D`, `E`, `F`, and if `#` is specified, with `0X` instead of `0x`). If `type` is unspecified, `d` is used for integer types.
- **Floating-point types:** The following floating-point formats are supported. The result of scientific, fixed, general, and hexadecimal formatting is the same as discussed earlier in this chapter for `std::chars_format::scientific`, `fixed`, `general`, and `hex`.
  - `e`, `E`: Scientific notation with either small `e` or capital `E` as the representation of the exponent, formatted with either a given precision or 6 if no precision is specified.
  - `f`, `F`: Fixed notation formatted with either a given precision or 6 if no precision is specified.
  - `g`, `G`: General notation automatically chooses a representation without an exponent (fixed format) or with an exponent (small `e` or capital `E`), formatted with either a given precision or 6 if no precision is specified.
  - `a`, `A`: Hexadecimal notation with either lowercase letters (`a`) or uppercase letters (`A`)
  - If `type` is unspecified, `g` is used for floating-point types.

- **Booleans:** `s` (outputs `true` or `false` in textual form), `b`, `B`, `c`, `d`, `o`, `x`, `X` (outputs `1` or `0` in integer form). If `type` is unspecified, `s` is used for Boolean types.
- **Characters:** `c` (character is copied to output), `?` (escaped character is copied to output; see section "Formatting Escaped Characters and Strings"), `b`, `B`, `d`, `o`, `x`, `X` (integer representation). If `type` is unspecified, `c` is used for character types.
- **String:** `s` (string is copied to output), `?` (escaped string is copied to output; see section "Formatting Escaped Characters and Strings"). If `type` is unspecified, `s` is used for string types.
- **Pointers:** `p` (hexadecimal notation of the pointer prefixed with `0x`). If `type` is unspecified, `p` is used for pointer types. Only pointers of type `void*` can be formatted. Other pointer types must first be converted to type `void*`, for example using `static_cast<void*>(myPointer)`.

Here are some examples with an integral type:

```
int i { 42 };
println("|{:10d}|", i);    // |        42|
println("|{:10b}|", i);    // |    101010|
println("|{:#10b}|", i);   // |  0b101010|
println("|{:10X}|", i);    // |        2A|
println("|{:#10X}|", i);   // |      0X2A|
```

Here is an example with a string type:

```
string s { "ProCpp" };
println("|{:_^10}|", s); // |__ProCpp__|
```

Examples with floating-point types are given in the next section on precision.

precision

The `precision` can be used only for floating-point and string types. It is specified as a dot followed by the number of decimal digits to output for floating-point types, or the number of characters to output for strings. The number of digits for floating-point types includes all digits, including the ones before the decimal separator, unless fixed floating-point notation (`f` or `F`) is used, in which case `precision` is the number of digits after the decimal point.

Just as with `width`, `precision` can also be another set of curly brackets, in which case it's called a *dynamic precision*. The precision is then taken either from the next argument in the list of arguments or from the argument with given index.

Here are some examples using a floating-point type:

```
double d { 3.1415 / 2.3 };
println("|{:12g}|", d);                              // |     1.36587|
println("|{:12.2}|", d);                             // |         1.4|
println("|{:12e}|", d);                              // |1.365870e+00|

int width { 12 };
int precision { 3 };
println("|{2:{0}.{1}f}|", width, precision, d); // |       1.366|
println("|{2:{0}.{1}}|", width, precision, d);  // |        1.37|
```

0

The 0 part of the specifier means that, for numeric values, zeros are inserted into the formatted value to reach the desired minimum width specified by the [width] part of the specifier (see earlier). These zeros are inserted at the front of the numeric value, but after any sign, and after any 0x, 0X, 0b, or 0B prefix. The 0 specifier is ignored if an alignment is specified.

Here are some examples:

```
int i { 42 };
println("|{:06d}|", i);   // |000042|
println("|{:+06d}|", i);  // |+00042|
println("|{:06X}|", i);   // |00002A|
println("|{:#06X}|", i);  // |0X002A|
```

L

The optional L specifier enables locale-specific formatting. This option is valid only for arithmetic types, such as integers, floating-point types, and Booleans. When used with integers, the L option specifies that the locale-specific digit group separator character must be used. For floating-point types, it means to use the locale-specific digit group and decimal separator characters. For Boolean types output in textual form, it means to use the locale-specific representation of true and false.

When using the L specifier, you have to pass an std::locale instance as the first parameter to std::format(). This works only with format(), not with print() and println(). Here is an example that formats a floating-point number using the nl locale:

```
float f { 1.2f };
cout << format(std::locale{ "nl" }, "|{:Lg}|\n", f);  // |1,2|
```

Locales are discussed in Chapter 21.

Formatting Escaped Characters and Strings

C++23 allows you to format escaped strings and characters by using the ? type specifier. This use case does not occur often, but it can be helpful for logging and debugging purposes. The output resembles how you write string and character literals in your code: they start and end with double or single quotes, and they use escaped character sequences. The following table shows what the output is of certain characters when using escaped formatting:

CHARACTER	ESCAPED OUTPUT
Horizontal tab	\t
New line	\n
Carriage return	\r
Backslash	\\
Double quote	\"
Single quote	\'

The escaping of double quotes happens only when the output is a double-quoted string, while the escaping of single quotes happens only when the output is a single-quoted character. The escaped output of unprintable characters is `\u{hex-code-point}`.

Here are some examples:

```
println("|{:?}|", "Hello\tWorld!\n");  // |Hello\tWorld!\n|
println("|{:?}|", "\"");               // |"\""|
println("|{:?}|", '\'');               // |'\''|
println("|{:?}|", '"');                // |'"'|
```

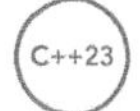

Formatting Ranges

Chapter 1 introduces the `std::vector`, `array`, and `pair` containers to store multiple elements of data. Chapter 18, "Standard Library Containers," introduces quite a few additional containers provided by the Standard Library. Starting with C++23, it's possible to directly format such ranges of elements. For ranges such as `vector`s and `array`s, the output, by default, is surrounded by square brackets and individual elements are separated by commas. If the elements of the range are strings, their output is escaped by default.

The formatting of ranges can be controlled using nested format specifiers. The general form is as follows:

```
[[fill]align][width][n][range-type][:range-underlying-spec]
```

Everything between square brackets is optional. As with other format specifiers, `fill` specifies a fill character, `align` specifies the alignment of the output, and `width` specifies the width of the output field. If `n` is specified, the output will not contain the opening and closing brackets of the range. The `range-type` can be one of the following:

RANGE-TYPE	DESCRIPTION
`m`	Available only for `pair`s and `tuple`s with two elements. By default, these are surrounded by parentheses and separated by commas. If `m` is specified, they are not surrounded by any type of brackets, and the two elements are separated by `": "`.
`s`	Formats the range as a string (cannot be combined with `n` or a `range-underlying-spec`).
`?s`	Formats the range as an escaped string (cannot be combined with `n` or a `range-underlying-spec`).

The `range-underlying-spec` is an optional format specifier for the individual elements of the range. Range specifiers can be nested multiple levels deep. If the elements are again ranges (e.g., a `vector` of `vector`s), then the `range-underlying-spec` is another range format specifier, and so on.

Let's look at some examples. First, let's format a `vector` of numbers:

```
vector values { 11, 22, 33 };
```

```
println("{}", values);          // [11, 22, 33]
println("{:n}", values);        // 11, 22, 33
```

If you want to replace the starting and ending square brackets, you can combine the n specifier with surrounding the format specifier with your own starting and ending characters. For example, the following surrounds the output with curly brackets instead. Curly brackets that you want to appear in the output need to be escaped as {{ and }}.

```
println("{{{:n}}}", values);    // {11, 22, 33}
```

The following provides a format specifier for the entire range. For both, the range is output in the center of a field that is 16 characters wide with * as a fill character. For the second, the n specifies that the opening and closing brackets should be omitted:

```
println("{:*^16}", values);     // **[11, 22, 33]**
println("{:*^16n}", values);    // ***11, 22, 33***
```

The following does not provide an explicit specifier for the entire range, but it does specify how individual elements are to be formatted. In this case, the individual elements are output in the center of a field that's six characters wide with * as a fill character:

```
println("{::*^6}", values);     // [**11**, **22**, **33**]
```

This can again be combined with the n specifier:

```
println("{:n:*^6}", values);    // **11**, **22**, **33**
```

Here are some examples formatting a vector of strings:

```
vector strings { "Hello"s, "World!\t2023"s };
println("{}", strings);         // ["Hello", "World!\t2023"]
println("{:}", strings);        // ["Hello", "World!\t2023"]
println("{::}", strings);       // [Hello, World!    2023]
println("{:n:}", strings);      // Hello, World!    2023
```

If you have a vector of characters, you can format them as individual characters, or you can consider the entire vector as a string using the s or ?s range type:

```
vector chars { 'W', 'o', 'r', 'l', 'd', '\t', '!' };
println("{}", chars);           // ['W', 'o', 'r', 'l', 'd', '\t', '!']
println("{::#x}", chars);       // [0x57, 0x6f, 0x72, 0x6c, 0x64, 0x9, 0x21]
println("{:s}", chars);         // World    !
println("{:?s}", chars);        // "World\t!"
```

Here are some examples of outputting a pair. By default, a pair is surrounded by parentheses instead of square brackets, and the two elements are separated by a comma. Using the n specifier removes the opening and closing parentheses. The m specifier also removes the parentheses and separates the elements with ": ".

```
pair p { 11, 22 };
println("{}", p);               // (11, 22)
println("{:n}", p);             // 11, 22
println("{:m}", p);             // 11: 22
```

Finally, here are some examples of outputting a vector of vectors:

```
vector<vector<int>> vv { {11, 22}, {33, 44, 55} };
```

```
println("{}", vv);          // [[11, 22], [33, 44, 55]]
println("{:n}", vv);        // [11, 22], [33, 44, 55]
println("{:n:n}", vv);      // 11, 22, 33, 44, 55
println("{:n:n:*^4}", vv);  // *11*, *22*, *33*, *44*, *55*
```

Support for Custom Types

The formatting library can be extended to add support for custom types. This involves writing a specialization of the `std::formatter` class template containing two member function templates: `parse()` and `format()`. I know, at this point in the book, you will not understand all the syntax in this example yet, as it uses all of the following techniques:

- `constexpr` functions, discussed in Chapter 9
- Template specialization, member function templates, and abbreviated function template syntax, explained in Chapter 12 "Writing Generic Code with Templates"
- Exceptions, discussed in Chapter 14, "Handling Errors"
- Iterators, discussed in Chapter 17, "Understanding Iterators and the Ranges Library"

Still, for completeness and to give you a taste of what is possible, let's see how you will be able to implement a custom `formatter` once you advance further in the book, at which point you can come back to this example.

Suppose you have the following class to store a key-value pair:

```
class KeyValue
{
    public:
        KeyValue(string_view key, int value) : m_key { key }, m_value { value } {}

        const string& getKey() const { return m_key; }
        int getValue() const { return m_value; }

    private:
        string m_key;
        int m_value { 0 };
};
```

A custom `formatter` for `KeyValue` objects can be implemented by writing the following class template specialization. This `KeyValue` formatter supports:

- Custom format specifiers: `{:k}` outputs only the key, `{:v}` outputs only the value, and `{:b}` and `{}` output both key and value.
- Nested format specifiers: These specify optional formats for the key and or the value. The syntax is as follows: `{:b:`*`KeyFormat`*`:`*`ValueFormat`*`}`.

```
template <>
class std::formatter<KeyValue>
{
    public:
        constexpr auto parse(auto& context)
        {
```

```
        string keyFormat, valueFormat;
        size_t numberOfParsedColons { 0 };
        auto iter { begin(context) };
        for (; iter != end(context); ++iter) {
            if (*iter == '}') { break; }

            if (numberOfParsedColons == 0) { // Parsing output type
                switch (*iter) {
                    case 'k': case 'K':      // {:k format specifier
                        m_outputType = OutputType::KeyOnly;       break;
                    case 'v': case 'V':      // {:v format specifier
                        m_outputType = OutputType::ValueOnly;     break;
                    case 'b': case 'B':      // {:b format specifier
                        m_outputType = OutputType::KeyAndValue;   break;
                    case ':':
                        ++numberOfParsedColons;   break;
                    default:
                        throw format_error { "Invalid KeyValue format." };
                }
            } else if (numberOfParsedColons == 1) { // Parsing key format
                if (*iter == ':') { ++numberOfParsedColons; }
                else { keyFormat += *iter; }
            } else if (numberOfParsedColons == 2) { // Parsing value format
                valueFormat += *iter;
            }
        }
        // Validate key format specifier.
        if (!keyFormat.empty()) {
            format_parse_context keyFormatterContext { keyFormat };
            m_keyFormatter.parse(keyFormatterContext);
        }
        // Validate value format specifier.
        if (!valueFormat.empty()) {
            format_parse_context valueFormatterContext { valueFormat };
            m_valueFormatter.parse(valueFormatterContext);
        }
        if (iter != end(context) && *iter != '}') {
            throw format_error { "Invalid KeyValue format." };
        }
        return iter;
    }

    auto format(const KeyValue& kv, auto& ctx) const
    {
        switch (m_outputType) {
            using enum OutputType;
            case KeyOnly:
                ctx.advance_to(m_keyFormatter.format(kv.getKey(), ctx));
                break;
            case ValueOnly:
                ctx.advance_to(m_valueFormatter.format(kv.getValue(), ctx));
                break;
            default:
                ctx.advance_to(m_keyFormatter.format(kv.getKey(), ctx));
                ctx.advance_to(format_to(ctx.out(), " - "));
```

continues

(continued)

```
                    ctx.advance_to(m_valueFormatter.format(kv.getValue(), ctx));
                    break;
            }
            return ctx.out();
        }
    private:
        enum class OutputType { KeyOnly, ValueOnly, KeyAndValue };
        OutputType m_outputType { OutputType::KeyAndValue };
        formatter<string> m_keyFormatter;
        formatter<int> m_valueFormatter;
};
```

The `parse()` member function is responsible for parsing the format specifier given as a character range [`begin(context)`, `end(context)`). It stores the result of the parsing in data members of the `formatter` class and returns an iterator pointing to the character after the end of the parsed format specifier string. Two of the data members are `m_keyFormatter` of type `formatter<string>` and `m_valueFormatter` of type `formatter<int>` to handle parsing the *`KeyFormat`* and *`ValueFormat`* parts, respectively, of the format specifier.

The `format()` member function formats the value given as first argument according to the format specification parsed by `parse()`, writes the result to `ctx.out()`, and returns an iterator to the end of the output. The function uses `std::format_to()`, which is similar to `std::format()`, except that it accepts an output iterator indicating where the output should be written to.

The `KeyValue` formatter can be tested as follows:

```
const size_t len { 34 }; // Label field length
KeyValue kv { "Key 1", 255 };
println("{:>{}} {}",   "Default:", len, kv);
println("{:>{}} {:k}", "Key only:", len, kv);
println("{:>{}} {:v}", "Value only:", len, kv);
println("{:>{}} {:b}", "Key and value with default format:", len, kv);
println("{:>{}} {:k:*^11}",     "Key only with special format:", len, kv);
println("{:>{}} {:v::#06X}",    "Value only with special format:", len, kv);
println("{:>{}} {::*^11:#06X}", "Key and value with special format:", len, kv);
try {
    auto formatted { vformat("{:cd}", make_format_args(kv)) };
    println("{}", formatted);
} catch (const format_error& caught_exception) {
    println("{}", caught_exception.what());
}
```

The output is as follows:

```
                          Default: Key 1 - 255
                         Key only: Key 1
                       Value only: 255
Key and value with default format: Key 1 - 255
     Key only with special format: ***Key 1***
   Value only with special format: 0X00FF
Key and value with special format: ***Key 1*** - 0X00FF
Invalid KeyValue format.
```

As an exercise, you could add support for a different separator symbol between the key and the value. With custom formatters, the possibilities are endless, and everything is type safe!

SUMMARY

This chapter discussed the C++ `string` and `string_view` classes and what their benefits are compared to plain old C-style character arrays. It also explained how a number of helper functions make it easier to convert numerical values into `string`s and vice versa, and it introduced the concept of raw string literals.

The chapter finished with a discussion of the string formatting library, used throughout examples in this book. It is a powerful mechanism to format strings with fine-grained control over how the formatted output should look.

The next chapter discusses guidelines for good coding style, including code documentation, decomposition, naming, code formatting, and other tips.

EXERCISES

By solving the following exercises, you can practice the material discussed in this chapter. Solutions to all exercises are available with the code download on the book's website at `www.wiley.com/go/proc++6e`. However, if you are stuck on an exercise, first reread parts of this chapter to try to find an answer yourself before looking at the solution from the website.

Exercise 2-1: Write a program that asks the user for two strings and then prints them out in alphabetical order, using the three-way comparison operator. To ask the user for a string, you can use the `std::cin` stream, briefly introduced in Chapter 1. Chapter 13, "Demystifying C++ I/O," explains input and output in detail, but for now, here is how to read in a string from the console. To terminate the line, just press Enter.

```
std::string s;
getline(cin, s1);
```

Exercise 2-2: Write a program that asks the user for a source string (= haystack), a string to find in the source string (= needle), and a replacement string. Write a function with three parameters—the haystack, needle, and replacement string—that returns a copy of the haystack with all needles replaced with the replacement string. Use only `std::string`, no `string_view`. What kind of parameter types will you use and why? Call this function from `main()` and print out all the strings for verification.

Exercise 2-3: Modify the program from Exercise 2-2 and use `std::string_view` on as many places as reasonable.

Exercise 2-4: Write a program that asks the user to enter an unknown number of floating-point numbers and stores all numbers in a `vector`. Each number should be entered followed by a new line. Stop asking for more numbers when the user inputs the number 0. To read a floating-point number from the console, use `cin` in the same way it was used in Chapter 1 to input integer values. Format all numbers in a table with a couple of columns where each column outputs the number in a different format. Each row in the table corresponds to one of the inputted numbers.

Exercise 2-5: Write a program that asks the user to enter an unknown number of words. Stop the input when the user enters `*`. Store all the individual words in a `vector`. You can input individual words using the following:

```
std::string word;
cin >> word;
```

When the input is finished, calculate the length of the longest word. Finally, output all the words in columns, five on a row. The width of the columns is based on the longest word. Output the words centered within their column, and separate the columns with the | character.

3

Coding with Style

WHAT'S IN THIS CHAPTER?

- The importance of documenting your code and what kind of commenting styles you can use
- What decomposition means and how to use it
- What naming conventions are
- What code formatting rules are

If you're going to spend several hours each day in front of a keyboard writing code, you should take some pride in all that work. Writing code that gets the job done is only part of a programmer's work. After all, anybody can learn the fundamentals of coding. It takes a true master to code with style.

This chapter explores the question of what makes stylistically good code. Along the way, you'll see several approaches to C++ style. As you will discover, simply changing the style of code can make it appear very different. For example, C++ code written by Windows programmers often has its own style, using Windows conventions. It almost looks like a completely different language than C++ code written by macOS programmers. Exposure to several different styles will help you avoid that sinking feeling you get when opening a C++ source file that barely resembles the C++ you thought you knew.

THE IMPORTANCE OF LOOKING GOOD

Writing code that is stylistically "good" takes time. You probably don't need much time to whip together a quick-and-dirty program to parse an XML file. Writing the same program with functional decomposition, adequate comments, and a clean structure would take you more time. Is it really worth it?

Thinking Ahead

How confident would you be in your code if a new programmer had to work with it a year from now? A friend of mine, faced with a growing mess of web application code, encouraged his team to think about a hypothetical intern who would be starting in a year. How would this poor intern ever get up to speed on the code base if there were no documentation and scary multiple-page functions? When you're writing code, imagine that somebody new or even you yourself will have to maintain it in the future. Will you even still remember how it works? What if you're not available to help? Well-written code avoids these problems because it is easy to read and understand.

Elements of Good Style

It is difficult to enumerate the characteristics of code that make it "stylistically good." Over time, you'll find styles that you like and notice useful techniques in code that others wrote. Perhaps more important, you'll encounter horrible code that teaches you what to avoid. However, good code shares several universal tenets that are explored in this chapter:

- Documentation
- Decomposition
- Naming
- Use of the language
- Formatting

DOCUMENTING YOUR CODE

In the programming context, documentation usually refers to comments contained in the source files. Comments are your opportunity to tell the world what was going through your head when you wrote the accompanying code. They are a place to say anything that isn't obvious from looking at the code itself.

Reasons to Write Comments

It may seem obvious that writing comments is a good idea, but have you ever stopped to think about why you need to comment your code? Sometimes programmers acknowledge the importance of commenting without fully understanding why comments are important. There are several reasons, all of which are explored in this chapter.

Commenting to Explain Usage

One reason to use comments is to explain how clients should interact with the code. Normally, a developer should be able to understand what a function does simply based on the name of the function, the type of the return value, and the name and type of its parameters. However, not everything can be expressed in code. Function pre- and postconditions[1] and the exceptions a function

[1] *Preconditions* are the conditions that client code must satisfy before calling a function. *Postconditions* are the conditions that must be satisfied by the function when it has finished executing.

can throw are things that you can only explain in a comment. In my opinion, it is OK to only add a comment if it really adds any useful information, such as pre- and postconditions and exceptions; otherwise, it's acceptable to omit the comment. Nevertheless, it's rare for a function to have no pre- or postconditions. Bottom line, it's up to the developer to decide whether a function needs a comment. Experienced programmers will have no problems deciding about this, but less experienced developers might not always make the right decision. That's why some companies have a rule stating that at least each publicly accessible function or member function in a module or header file should have a comment explaining what it does, what its arguments are, what values it returns, which pre- and postconditions need to be satisfied, and which exceptions it can throw.

A comment gives you the opportunity to state, in English, anything that you can't state in code. For example, there's really no way in C++ code to indicate that the `saveRecord()` member function of a database object throws an exception if `openDatabase()` has not been called yet. A comment, however, can be the perfect place to note this restriction, as follows:

```
// Throws:
//    DatabaseNotOpenedException if openDatabase() has not been called yet.
int saveRecord(Record& record);
```

The `saveRecord()` member function accepts a reference-to-non-`const` `Record` object. Users might wonder why it's not a reference-to-`const`, so this is something that needs to be explained in a comment:

```
// Parameters:
//    record: If the given record doesn't yet have a database ID, then saveRecord()
//    modifies the record object to store the ID assigned by the database.
// Throws:
//    DatabaseNotOpenedException if openDatabase() has not been called yet.
int saveRecord(Record& record);
```

The C++ language forces you to specify the return type of a function, but it does not provide a way for you to say what the returned value actually represents. For example, the declaration of `saveRecord()` indicates that it returns an `int` (a bad design decision discussed further in this section), but a client reading that declaration wouldn't know what the `int` means. A comment explains the meaning of it:

```
// Saves the given record to the database.
//
// Parameters:
//    record: If the given record doesn't yet have a database ID, then saveRecord()
//    modifies the record object to store the ID assigned by the database.
// Returns: int
//    An integer representing the ID of the saved record.
// Throws:
//    DatabaseNotOpenedException if openDatabase() has not been called yet.
int saveRecord(Record& record);
```

The previous comment documents everything about `saveRecord()` in a formal way, including a sentence that describes what the member function does. Some companies require such formal and thorough documentation; however, I don't recommend this style of commenting all the time. The first line, for example, is rather useless since the name of the function is self-explanatory. The description of the parameter is important as is the comment about the exception, so these definitely should stay.

Documenting what exactly the return type represents for this version of `saveRecord()` is required since it returns a generic `int`. However, a much better design would be to return a `RecordID` instead of a plain `int`, which removes the need to add any comments for the return type. `RecordID` could be a simple class with a single `int` data member, but it conveys more information, and it allows you to add more data members in the future if need be. So, the following is a much better `saveRecord()`:

```
// Parameters:
//    record: If the given record doesn't yet have a database ID, then saveRecord()
//    modifies the record object to store the ID assigned by the database.
// Throws:
//    DatabaseNotOpenedException if openDatabase() has not been called yet.
RecordID saveRecord(Record& record);
```

> **NOTE** *If your company's coding guidelines don't force you to write formal comments for functions, use common sense when writing them. Only state something in a comment that is not obvious based on the name of the function, the return type, and the name and type of its parameters.*

Sometimes, the parameters to and the return type from a function are generic and can be used to pass all kinds of information. In that case you need to clearly document exactly what type is being passed. For example, message handlers in Windows accept two parameters, `LPARAM` and `WPARAM`, and can return an `LRESULT`. All three can be used to pass almost anything you like, but you cannot change their type. By using type casting, they can, for example, be used to pass simple integers or pointers to some objects. Your documentation could look like this:

```
// Parameters:
//    WPARAM wParam: (WPARAM)(int): An integer representing...
//    LPARAM lParam: (LPARAM)(string*): A string pointer representing...
// Returns: (LRESULT)(Record*)
//    nullptr in case of an error, otherwise a pointer to a Record object
//    representing...
LRESULT handleMessage(WPARAM wParam, LPARAM lParam);
```

Your public documentation should describe the behavior of your code, not the implementation. The behavior includes the inputs, outputs, error conditions and handling, intended uses, and performance guarantees. For example, public documentation describing a call to generate a single random number should specify that it takes no parameters, returns an integer in a previously specified range, and should list all the exceptions that might be thrown when something goes wrong. This public documentation should not explain the details of the linear congruence algorithm for actually generating the number. Providing too much implementation detail in comments targeted for users of your code is probably the single most common mistake in writing public comments.

Commenting to Explain Complicated Code

Good comments are also important inside the actual source code. In a simple program that processes input from the user and writes a result to the console, it is probably easy to read through and understand all of the code. In the professional world, however, you will often need to write code that is algorithmically complex or too esoteric to understand simply by inspection.

Consider the code that follows. It is well-written, but it may not be immediately apparent what it is doing. You might recognize the algorithm if you have seen it before, but a newcomer probably wouldn't understand the way the code works.

```
void sort(int data[], std::size_t size)
{
    for (int i { 1 }; i < size; ++i) {
        int element { data[i] };
        int j { i };
        while (j > 0 && data[j - 1] > element) {
            data[j] = data[j - 1];
            j--;
        }
        data[j] = element;
    }
}
```

A better approach would be to include comments that describe the parameters to the function, the algorithm that is being used, and any (loop) invariants. Invariants are conditions that must be true during the execution of a piece of code, for example, a loop iteration. In the modified function that follows, a comment at the top explains the meaning of the two parameters, a thorough comment at the start of the function explains the algorithm at a high level, and inline comments explain specific lines that may be confusing:

```
// Implements the "insertion sort" algorithm.
// data is an array containing the elements to be sorted.
// size contains the number of elements in the data array.
void sort(int data[], std::size_t size)
{
    // The insertion sort algorithm separates the array into two parts--the
    // sorted part and the unsorted part. Each element, starting at position
    // 1, is examined. Everything earlier in the array is in the sorted part,
    // so the algorithm shifts each element over until the correct position
    // is found to insert the current element. When the algorithm finishes
    // with the last element, the entire array is sorted.

    // Start at position 1 and examine each element.
    for (int i { 1 }; i < size; ++i) {
        // Loop invariant:
        //     All elements in the range 0 to i-1 (inclusive) are sorted.

        int element { data[i] };
        // j marks the position in the sorted part where element will be inserted.
        int j { i };
        // As long as the value in the slot before the current slot in the sorted
        // array is higher than element, shift values to the right to make room
        // for inserting element (hence the name, "insertion sort") in the correct
        // position.
        while (j > 0 && data[j - 1] > element) {
            // invariant: elements in the range j+1 to i are > element.
            data[j] = data[j - 1];
            // invariant: elements in the range j to i are > element.
            j--;
        }
        // At this point the current position in the sorted array
```

continues

(continued)

```
            // is *not* greater than the element, so this is its new position.
            data[j] = element;
        }
    }
```

The new code is certainly more verbose, but a reader unfamiliar with sorting algorithms would be much more likely to understand it with the comments included.

Commenting to Convey Meta-information

> **WARNING** *All meta-information mentioned in this section is from practices from the past. Nowadays, such meta-information is highly discouraged, as the use of a version control system, as discussed in Chapter 28, "Maximizing Software Engineering Methods," is mandatory. Such a solution offers an annotated change history with revision dates, author names, and, if properly used, comments accompanying each modification, including references to change requests and bug reports. You should check in, or commit, each change request or bug fix separately with a descriptive comment. With such a system, you don't need to manually keep track of such meta-information directly in the source code files.*

In old legacy code bases, you might come across comments that were used to provide information at a higher level than the code itself. Such *meta-information* provided details about the creation of the code without addressing the specifics of its behavior, such as the original author of each function, the date a piece of code was written, the specific feature a function addresses, the bug number that corresponds to a line of code, a reminder to revisit a possible problem in the code later, a change-log, and more. Here is an example:

```
// Date       | Change
//------------+--------------------------------------------------
// 2001-04-13 | REQ #005: <marcg> Do not normalize values.
// 2001-04-17 | REQ #006: <marcg> use nullptr instead of NULL.

// Author:  marcg
// Date:    110412
// Feature: PRD version 3, Feature 5.10
RecordID saveRecord(Record& record)
{
    if (!m_databaseOpen) { throw DatabaseNotOpenedException { }; }
    RecordID id { getDB()->saveRecord(record) };
    if (id != -1) {       // Added to address bug #142 - jsmith 110428
        record.setId(id);
    }
    // TODO: What if setId() throws an exception? - akshayr 110501
    return id;
}
```

However, it's worth repeating, such legacy meta-information has no place in new code.

Copyright Comment

Another type of meta-information is a copyright notice. Some companies require such a copyright notice at the beginning of every source file, even though, since the Berne Convention in 1886, it is not required to explicitly write a copyright statement to actually have copyright on your work.

Commenting Styles

Every organization has a different approach to commenting code. In some environments, a particular style is mandated to give the code a common standard for documentation. Other times, the quantity and style of commenting are left up to the programmer. The following examples depict several approaches to commenting code.

Commenting Every Line

One way to avoid lack of documentation is to force yourself to over document by including a comment for every line. Commenting every line of code should ensure that there's a specific reason for everything you write. In reality, such heavy commenting on a large scale is unwieldy, messy, and tedious! For example, consider the following useless comments:

```
int result;                     // Declare an integer to hold the result.
result = doodad.getResult();    // Get the doodad's result.
if (result % 2 ==  0) {         // If the result modulo 2 is 0 ...
   logError();                  // then log an error,
} else {                        // otherwise ...
   logSuccess();                // log success.
}                               // End if/else.
return result;                  // Return the result.
```

The comments in this code express each line as part of an easily readable English story. This is entirely useless if you assume that the reader has at least basic C++ skills. These comments don't add any additional information to code. Specifically, look at this line:

```
if (result % 2 == 0) {          // If the result modulo 2 is 0 ...
```

The comment is just an English translation of the code. It doesn't say *why* the programmer has used the modulo operator on the result with the value 2. The following would be a better comment:

```
if (result % 2 == 0) {          // If the result is even ...
```

The modified comment, while still fairly obvious to most programmers, gives additional information about the code. The modulo operator with 2 is used because the code needs to check whether the result is even.

Even better, if some expression does something that might not be immediately obvious to everyone, I recommend turning it into a function with a well-chosen name. This makes the code self-documenting, removing the need to write comments where the function is used, and results in a piece of reusable code. For example, you can define a function `isEven()` as follows:

```
bool isEven(int value) { return value % 2 == 0; }
```

And then use it like this, without any comments:

```
if (isEven(result)) {
```

Despite its tendency to be verbose and superfluous, heavy commenting can be useful in cases where the code would otherwise be difficult to comprehend. The following code also comments every line, but these comments are actually helpful:

```
// Calculate the doodad. The start, end, and offset values come from the
// table on page 96 of the "Doodad API v1.6."
result = doodad.calculate(Start, End, Offset);
// To determine success or failure, we need to bitwise AND the result with
// the processor-specific mask (see "Doodad API v1.6," page 201).
result &= getProcessorMask();
// Set the user field value based on the "Marigold Formula."
// (see "Doodad API v1.6", page 136)
setUserField((result + MarigoldOffset) / MarigoldConstant + MarigoldConstant);
```

This code is taken out of context, but the comments give you a good idea of what each line does. Without them, the calculations involving `&` and the mysterious "Marigold Formula" would be difficult to decipher.

> **NOTE** *Commenting every line of code is usually not warranted, but if the code is complicated enough to require it, don't just translate the code to English: explain what's really going on.*

Prefix Comments

Your group may decide to begin all source files with a standard comment. This is an opportunity to document important information about the program and a specific file. Examples of information that could be at the top of every file include the following:

- Copyright information
- A brief description of the file/class
- Incomplete features*
- Known bugs*

* These items are usually handled by your bug and feature tracking system (see Chapter 30, "Becoming Adept at Testing").

The following lists some examples of information that should never be included in such comments, as these are automatically handled by your version control system (see Chapter 28).

- The last-modified date
- The original author
- A change-log (as described earlier)
- The feature ID addressed by the file

Here is an example of a prefix comment:

```
// Implements the basic functionality of a watermelon. All units are expressed
// in terms of seeds per cubic centimeter. Watermelon theory is based on the
// white paper "Algorithms for Watermelon Processing."
//
// The following code is (c) copyright 2023, FruitSoft, Inc. ALL RIGHTS RESERVED
```

Fixed-Format Comments

Writing comments in a standard format that can be parsed by external document builders is a popular programming practice. In the Java language, programmers can write comments in a standard format that allows a tool called JavaDoc to automatically create hyperlinked documentation for the project. For C++, a free tool called Doxygen (available at `doxygen.org`) parses comments to automatically build HTML documentation, class diagrams, UNIX man pages, and other useful documents. Doxygen even recognizes and parses JavaDoc-style comments in C++ programs. The code that follows shows JavaDoc-style comments that are recognized by Doxygen:

```
/**
 * Implements the basic functionality of a watermelon
 * TODO: Implement updated algorithms!
 */
export class Watermelon
{
    public:
        /**
         * @param initialSeeds The starting number of seeds, must be > 5.
         * @throws invalid_argument if initialSeeds <= 5.
         */
        Watermelon(std::size_t initialSeeds);

        /**
         * Computes the seed ratio, using the Marigold algorithm.
         * @param slow Whether or not to use long (slow) calculations.
         * @return The marigold ratio.
         */
        double calculateSeedRatio(bool slow);
};
```

Doxygen recognizes the C++ syntax and special comment directives such as `@param`, `@return`, and `@throws` to generate customizable output. Figure 3.1 shows an example of a Doxygen-generated HTML class reference.

Note that you should still avoid writing useless comments, even when you use a tool to automatically generate documentation. Take a look at the `Watermelon` constructor in the previous code. Its comment omits a description and only describes the parameter and the exceptions it throws. Adding a description, as in the following example, is redundant:

```
/**
 * The Watermelon constructor.
 * @param initialSeeds The starting number of seeds, must be > 5.
 * @throws invalid_argument if initialSeeds <= 5.
 */
Watermelon(std::size_t initialSeeds);
```

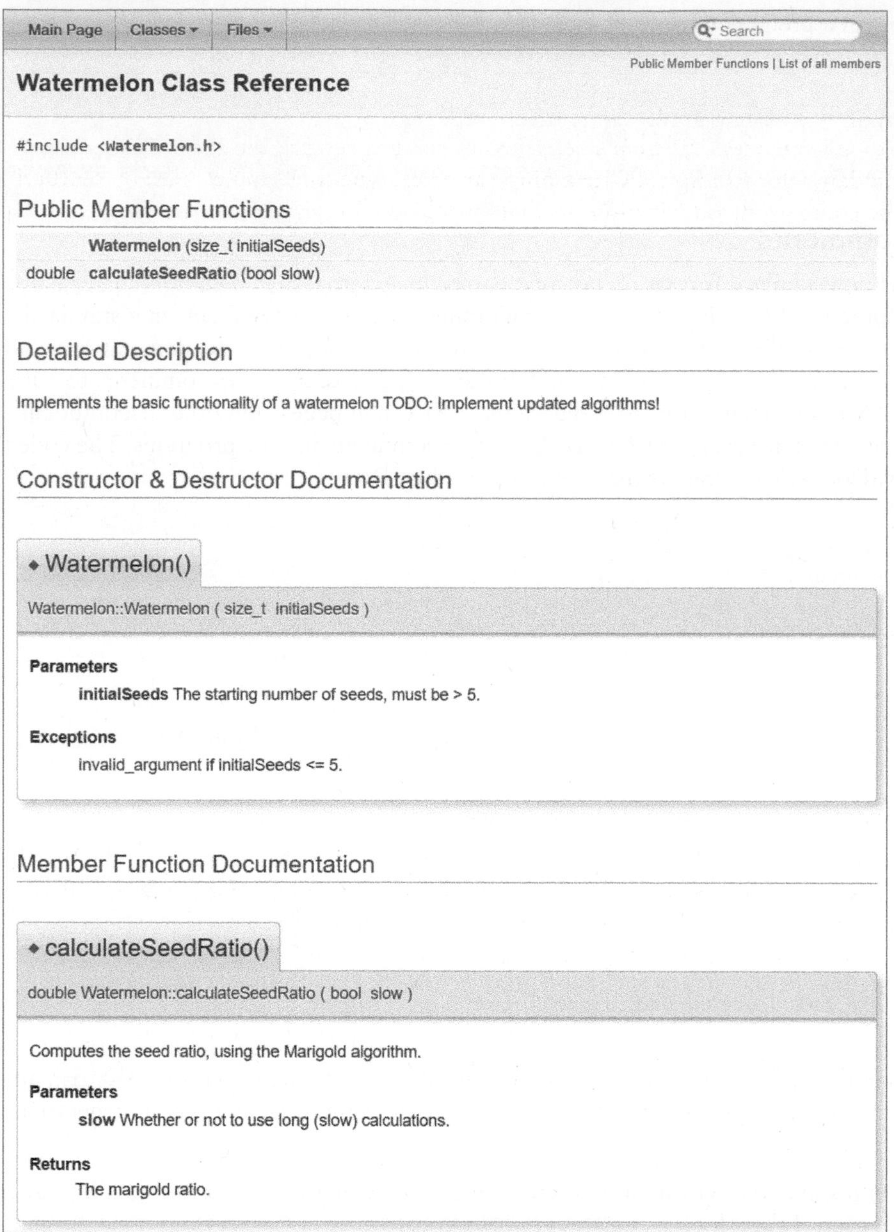

FIGURE 3.1

Automatically generated documentation as shown in Figure 3.1 can be helpful during development because it allows developers to browse through a high-level description of classes and their relationships. Your group can easily customize a tool like Doxygen to work with the style of comments that you have adopted. Ideally, your group would set up a machine that builds documentation on a daily basis.

Ad Hoc Comments

Most of the time, you use comments on an as-needed basis. Here are some guidelines for comments that appear within the body of your code:

- Before adding a comment, first consider whether you can rework the code to make the comment redundant—for example, by renaming variables, functions, and classes; by reordering steps in the code; by introducing intermediate well-named variables; and so on.
- Imagine someone else is reading your code. If there are subtleties that are not immediately obvious, then you should document those.
- Don't put your initials in the code. Version control systems will track that kind of information automatically for you.
- If you are doing something with an API that isn't immediately obvious, include a reference to the documentation of that API where it is explained.
- Remember to update your comments when you update the code. Nothing is more confusing than code that is fully documented with incorrect comments.
- If you use comments to separate a function into sections, consider whether the function can be broken up into multiple, smaller functions.
- Avoid offensive or derogatory language. You never know who might look at your code someday.
- Liberal use of inside jokes is generally considered OK. Check with your manager.

Self-Documenting Code

Well-written code often doesn't need abundant commenting. The best code is written to be readable. If you find yourself adding a comment for every line, consider whether the code could be rewritten to better match what you are saying in the comments. For example, use descriptive names for your functions, parameters, variables, classes, and so on. Properly make use of `const`; that is, if a variable is not supposed to be modified, mark it as `const`. Reorder the steps in a function to make it clearer what it is doing. Introduce intermediate well-named variables to make an algorithm easier to understand. Remember that C++ is a language. Its main purpose is to tell the computer what to do, but the semantics of the language can also be used to explain its meaning to a reader.

Another way to write self-documenting code is to break up, or *decompose*, your code into smaller pieces. That is the topic of the next section.

> **NOTE** *Good code is naturally readable and only requires comments to provide useful additional information.*

DECOMPOSITION

Decomposition is the practice of breaking up code into smaller pieces. There is nothing more daunting in the world of coding than opening up a file of source code to find 300-line functions and massive, nested blocks of code. Ideally, each function should accomplish a single task. Any subtasks of significant complexity should be decomposed into separate functions. For example, if somebody asks you what a function does and you answer, "First it does A, then it does B; then, if C, it does D; otherwise, it does E," you should probably have separate helper functions for A, B, C, D, and E.

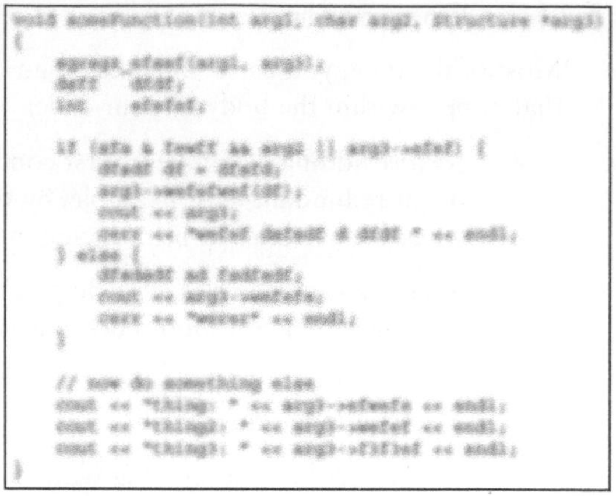

Decomposition is not an exact science. Some programmers will say that no function should be longer than a page of printed code. That may be a good rule of thumb, but you could certainly find a quarter-page of code that is desperately in need of decomposition. Another rule of thumb is that if you squint your eyes and look at the format of the code without reading the actual content, it shouldn't appear too dense in any one area. For example, Figures 3.2 and 3.3 show code that has been purposely blurred so that you don't focus on the content. It should be obvious that the code in Figure 3.3 has better decomposition than the code in Figure 3.2.

FIGURE 3.2

FIGURE 3.3

Decomposition through Refactoring

Sometimes, when you've had a few coffees and you're really in the programming zone, you start coding so fast that you end up with code that does exactly what it's supposed to do but is far from pretty. All programmers do this from time to time. Short periods of vigorous coding are sometimes the most productive times in the course of a project. Dense code also arises over the course of time as code is modified. As new requirements and bug fixes emerge, existing code is amended with small modifications. The computing term *cruft* refers to the gradual accumulation of small amounts of code that eventually turns a once-elegant piece of code into a mess of patches and special cases.

Refactoring is the act of restructuring your code. The book *Refactoring: Improving the Design of Existing Code*, 2nd edition, by Martin Fowler is one of the most influential books about refactoring (see the bibliography in Appendix B, "Annotated Bibliography"). The following list contains some example techniques to refactor code:

- Techniques that allow for more abstraction:
  - **Encapsulate data member:** Make a data member private and give access to it with getter and setter member functions.
  - **Generalize type:** Create more general types to allow for more code sharing.
- Techniques for breaking code apart into more logical pieces:
  - **Extract member function:** Turn part of a larger member function into a new member function to make it easier to understand.
  - **Extract class:** Move part of the code from an existing class into a new class.
- Techniques for improving names and the location of code:
  - **Move member function or move data member:** Move to a more appropriate class or source file.
  - **Rename member function or rename data member:** Change the name to better reveal its purpose.
  - **Pull up:** In object-oriented programming, move to a base class.
  - **Push down:** In object-oriented programming, move to a derived class.

Whether your code starts its life as a dense block of unreadable cruft or it just evolves that way, refactoring is necessary to periodically purge the code of accumulated hacks. Through refactoring, you revisit existing code and rewrite it to make it more readable and maintainable. Refactoring is an opportunity to revisit the decomposition of code. If the purpose of the code has changed or if it was never decomposed in the first place, when you refactor the code, squint at it and determine whether it needs to be broken down into smaller parts.

When refactoring code, it is important to be able to rely on a testing framework that catches any defects that you might introduce. Unit tests, discussed in Chapter 30, are particularly well suited for helping you catch mistakes during refactoring.

Decomposition by Design

If you use modular decomposition and approach every module and function by considering what pieces of it you can put off until later, your programs will generally be less dense and more organized than if you implement every feature in its entirety as you code.

Of course, you should still design your program *before* jumping into the code.

Decomposition in This Book

You will see decomposition in many of the examples in this book. In many cases, functions are referred to for which no implementation is shown because they are not relevant to the example and would take up too much space.

NAMING

The C++ compiler has a few naming rules:

- Names can contain uppercase and lowercase letters, digits, and underscores.
- Letters are not limited to the English alphabet but can be letters from any language, such as Japanese, Arabic, and so on.
- Names cannot start with a number (for example, `9to5`).
- Names that contain a double underscore (such as `my__name`) are reserved for use by the Standard Library and shall not be used.
- Names that begin with an underscore followed by an uppercase letter (such as `_Name`) are always reserved for use by the Standard Library and shall not be used.
- Names in the global namespace that begin with an underscore (such as `_name`) are reserved and shall not be used.

Other than those rules, names exist only to help you and your fellow programmers work with the individual elements of your program. Given this purpose, it is surprising how often programmers use unspecific or inappropriate names.

Choosing a Good Name

The best name for a variable, member function, function, parameter, class, namespace, and so on, accurately describes the purpose of the item. Names can also imply additional information, such as the type or specific usage. Of course, the real test is whether other programmers understand what you are trying to convey with a particular name.

There are no set-in-stone rules for naming other than the rules that work for your organization. However, there are some names that are rarely appropriate. The following table shows some names at both ends of the naming continuum:

GOOD NAMES	BAD NAMES
`sourceName, destinationName` Distinguishes two objects	`thing1, thing2` Too general
`m_nameCounter` Conveys data member status	`m_NC` Too obscure, too brief
`calculateMarigoldOffset()` Simple, accurate	`doAction()` Too general, imprecise
`m_typeString` Easy on the eyes	`typeSTR256` A name only a computer could love
`g_settings` Conveys global status	`m_IHateLarry` Unacceptable inside joke

GOOD NAMES	BAD NAMES
`errorMessage` Descriptive name	`string` Nondescriptive name
`sourceFile, destinationFile` No abbreviations	`srcFile, dstFile` Abbreviations

Naming Conventions

Selecting a name doesn't always require a lot of thought and creativity. In many cases, you'll want to use standard techniques for naming. The following are some of the types of data for which you can make use of standard names.

Counters

Early in your programming career, you probably saw code that used the variable `i` as a counter. It is customary to use `i` and `j` as counters and inner loop counters, respectively. Be careful with nested loops, however. It's a common mistake to refer to the "`i`th" element when you really mean the "`j`th" element. When working with 2-D matrices, it's probably easier to use `row` and `column` as indices instead of `i` and `j`. Some programmers prefer using counters `outerLoopIndex` and `innerLoopIndex`, and some even frown upon using `i` and `j` as loop counters.

Prefixes

Many programmers begin their variable names with a letter that provides some information about the variable's type or usage. On the other hand, there are as many programmers, or even more, who disapprove of using any kind of prefix because this could make evolving code less maintainable in the future. For example, if a member variable is changed from `static` to non-`static`, you have to rename all the uses of that name. If you don't rename them, your names continue to convey semantics, but now they are the wrong semantics.

However, you often don't have a choice, and you need to follow the guidelines of your company. The following table shows some potential prefixes:

PREFIX	EXAMPLE NAME	LITERAL PREFIX MEANING	USAGE
`m` `m_`	`mData` `m_data`	"member"	Data member within a class

`s`
`ms`
`ms_`
	`sLookupTable`
	`msLookupTable`
	`ms_lookupTable`
		"static"	Static variable or data member

`k`	`kMaximumLength`	"konstant" (German for "constant")	A constant value. Some programmers omit any prefix to indicate constants.
`b` `is`	`bCompleted` `isCompleted`	"Boolean"	Designates a Boolean value

Hungarian Notation

Hungarian notation is a variable and data member-naming convention that is popular with Microsoft Windows programmers. The basic idea is that instead of using single-letter prefixes such as `m`, you should use more verbose prefixes to indicate additional information. The following line of code shows the use of Hungarian notation:

```
char* pszName; // psz means "pointer to string, zero-terminated"
```

The term *Hungarian notation* arose from the fact that its inventor, Charles Simonyi, is Hungarian. Some also say that it accurately reflects the fact that programs using Hungarian notation end up looking as if they were written in a foreign language. For this latter reason, some programmers tend to dislike Hungarian notation. In this book, prefixes are used, but not Hungarian notation. Adequately named variables don't need much additional context information besides the prefix. For example, a data member named `m_name` says it all.

> **NOTE** *Good names convey information about their purpose without making the code unreadable.*

Getters and Setters

If your class contains a data member, such as `m_status`, it is customary to provide access to the member via a getter called `getStatus()` and, optionally, a setter called `setStatus()`. To give access to a Boolean data member, you typically use `is` as a prefix instead of `get`, for example `isRunning()`. The C++ language has no prescribed naming for these functions, but your organization will probably want to adopt this or a similar naming scheme.

Capitalization

There are many different ways of capitalizing names in your code. As with most elements of coding style, it is important that your group adopts a standardized approach and that all members adopt that approach. One way to get messy code is to have some programmers naming classes in all lowercase with underscores representing spaces (`priority_queue`) and others using capitals with each subsequent word capitalized (`PriorityQueue`). Variables and data members almost always start with a lowercase letter and use either underscores (`my_queue`) or capitals (`myQueue`) to indicate word breaks. Functions traditionally start with a capital letter in C++, but, as you've seen, in this book I have adopted the style of using a lowercase first letter for functions to distinguish them from class names.

Namespaced Constants

Imagine that you are writing a program with a graphical user interface. The program has several menus, including File, Edit, and Help. To represent the ID of each menu, you may decide to use a constant. A perfectly reasonable name for a constant referring to the Help menu ID is `Help`.

The name `Help` will work fine until you add a Help button to the main window. You also need a constant to refer to the ID of the button, but `Help` is already taken.

A possible solution for this is to put your constants in different namespaces, which are discussed in Chapter 1, "A Crash Course in C++ and the Standard Library." You create two namespaces: `Menu` and `Button`. Each namespace has a `Help` constant, and you use them as `Menu::Help` and `Button::Help`, although in this case, a more recommended solution is to use enumerations, also introduced in Chapter 1.

USING LANGUAGE FEATURES WITH STYLE

The C++ language lets you do all sorts of terribly unreadable things. Take a look at this wacky code:

```
i++ + ++i;
```

This is unreadable, but more importantly, its behavior is undefined by the C++ standard. The problem is that `i++` uses the value of `i` but has a side effect of incrementing it. The standard does not say when this incrementing should be done, only that the side effect (increment) should be visible after the sequence point `;`. However, the compiler can do it at any time during the execution of that statement. It's impossible to know which value of `i` will be used for the `++i` part. Running this code with different compilers and platforms can result in different values.

Expressions such as the following

```
a[i] = ++i;
```

are well-defined since C++17, which guarantees that the evaluation of all operations on the right-hand side of an assignment is finished before evaluating the left-hand side. So, in this case, first `i` is incremented and then used as index in `a[i]`. Even so, for clarity, it remains recommended to avoid such expressions.

With all the power that the C++ language offers, it is important to consider how the language features can be used toward stylistic good instead of evil.

Use Constants

Bad code is often littered with "magic numbers." In some function, the code might be using 2.71828 or 24 or 3600, and so on. Why? What do these values mean? People with a mathematical background might find it obvious that 2.71828 represents an approximation of the transcendental value *e*, but most people don't know this. The C++ language offers constants to give symbolic names to values that don't change, such as 2.71828, 24, 3600, and so on. Here are some examples:

```
const double ApproximationForE { 2.718281828459045235 36 };
const int HoursPerDay { 24 };
const int SecondsPerHour { 3'600 };
```

> **NOTE** *The Standard Library includes a collection of predefined mathematical constants, all defined in* `<numbers>` *in the* `std::numbers` *namespace. For example, it defines* `std::numbers::e`, `pi`, `sqrt2`, `phi`, *and many more.*

Use References Instead of Pointers

In the past, C++ programmers often learned C first. In C, pointers were the only pass-by-reference mechanism, and they certainly worked just fine for many years. Pointers are still required in some cases, but in many situations you can switch to references. If you learned C first, you probably think that references don't really add any new functionality to the language. You might think that they merely introduce a new syntax for functionality that pointers could already provide.

There are several advantages to using references rather than pointers. First, references are safer than pointers because they don't deal directly with memory addresses and cannot be `nullptr`. Second, references are stylistically more pleasing than pointers because they use the same syntax as stack variables; i.e., they do not require you to explicitly take the address of them using `&` or to explicitly dereference them using `*`. They're also easy to use, so you should have no problem adopting references into your style palette. Unfortunately, some programmers think that if they see an `&` in a function call, they know the called function is going to change the object, and if they don't see the `&`, it must be pass-by-value. With references, they say they don't know if the function is going to change the object unless they look at the function prototype. This is a wrong way of thinking. Passing in a pointer does not automatically mean that the object will be modified, because the parameter might be `const T*`. Passing both a pointer and a reference can modify the object, or it may not, depending on whether the function parameter uses `const T*`, `T*`, `const T&`, or `T&`. So, you need to look at the function prototype anyway to know whether the function might change the object.

Another benefit of references is that they clarify ownership of memory. If you are writing a function and another programmer passes you a reference to an object, it is clear that you can read and possibly modify the object, but you have no easy way of freeing its memory. If you are passed a pointer, this might be less clear. Do you need to delete the object to clean up memory? Or will the caller do that? Though in modern C++, the meaning is clear: any raw pointer is non-owning, and handling ownership and ownership transfer is done using smart pointers, discussed in Chapter 7, "Memory Management."

Use Custom Exceptions

C++ makes it easy to ignore exceptions. Nothing about the language syntax forces you to deal with exceptions, and you could in theory write error-tolerant programs with traditional mechanisms such as returning special values (for example, `-1`, `nullptr`, `...`) or setting error flags. When returning special values to signal errors, the `[[nodiscard]]` attribute, introduced in Chapter 1, can be used to force the caller of your function to do something with the returned value.

However, exceptions provide a much richer mechanism for error handling, and custom exceptions allow you to tailor this mechanism to your needs. For example, a custom exception type for a web browser could include fields that specify the web page that contained the error, the network state when the error occurred, and additional context information.

Chapter 14, "Handling Errors," contains a wealth of information about exceptions in C++.

> **NOTE** *Language features exist to help the programmer. Understand and make use of features that contribute to good programming style.*

FORMATTING

Many programming groups have been torn apart and friendships ruined over code-formatting arguments. In college, a friend of mine got into such a heated debate with a peer over the use of spaces in an `if` statement that people were stopping by to make sure that everything was OK.

If your organization has standards in place for code formatting, consider yourself lucky. You may not like the standards they have in place, but at least you won't have to argue about them.

If no standards are in place for code formatting, I recommend introducing them in your organization. Standardized coding guidelines make sure that all programmers on your team follow the same naming conventions, formatting rules, and so on, which makes the code more uniform and easier to understand.

There are automated tools available that can format your code according to certain rules right before committing the code to your version control system. Some IDEs have such tools built-in and can, for example, automatically format the code when saving a file.

If everybody on your team is just writing code their own way, try to be as tolerant as you can. As you'll see, some practices are just a matter of taste, while others actually make it difficult to work in teams.

The Curly Brace Alignment Debate

Perhaps the most frequently debated point is where to put the curly braces that demark a block of code. There are several styles of curly brace use. In this book, the curly brace is put on the same line as the leading statement, except in the case of a class, function, or member function. This style is shown in the code that follows (and throughout this book):

```
void someFunction()
{
    if (condition()) {
        println("condition was true");
    } else {
        println("condition was false");
    }
}
```

This style conserves vertical space while still showing blocks of code by their indentation. Some programmers would argue that preservation of vertical space isn't relevant in real-world coding. A more verbose style is shown here:

```
void someFunction()
{
    if (condition())
    {
        println("condition was true");
    }
    else
    {
        println("condition was false");
    }
}
```

Some programmers are even liberal with the use of horizontal space, yielding code like this:

```
void someFunction()
{
    if (condition())
        {
            println("condition was true");
        }
    else
        {
            println("condition was false");
        }
}
```

Another point of debate is whether to put braces around single statements, for example:

```
void someFunction()
{
    if (condition())
        println("condition was true");
    else
        println("condition was false");
}
```

Obviously, I won't recommend any particular style because I don't want hate mail. Personally, I always use braces, even for single statements, as it protects against certain badly written C-style macros (see Chapter 11, "Modules, Header Files, and Miscellaneous Topics") and is safer against adding statements in the future.

> **NOTE** *When selecting a style for denoting blocks of code, the important consideration is how well you can see which block falls under which condition simply by looking at the code.*

Coming to Blows over Spaces and Parentheses

The formatting of individual lines of code can also be a source of disagreement. Again, I won't advocate a particular approach, but you are likely to encounter a few of the styles shown here.

In this book, I use a space after any keyword, a space before and after any operator, a space after every comma in a parameter list or a call, and parentheses to clarify the order of operations, as follows:

```
if (i == 2) {
    j = i + (k / m);
}
```

An alternative, shown next, treats `if` stylistically like a function, with no space between the keyword and the left parenthesis. Also, the parentheses used to clarify the order of operations inside of the `if` statement are omitted because they have no semantic relevance.

```
if( i == 2 ) {
    j = i + k / m;
}
```

The difference is subtle, and the determination of which is better is left to the reader, yet I can't move on from the issue without pointing out that `if` is not a function.

Spaces, Tabs, and Line Breaks

The use of spaces and tabs is not merely a stylistic preference. If your group does not agree on a convention for spaces and tabs, there are going to be major problems when programmers work jointly. The most obvious problem occurs when Alice uses four-space tabs to indent code and Bob uses five-space tabs; neither will be able to display code properly when working on the same file. An even worse problem arises when Bob reformats the code to use tabs at the same time that Alice edits the same code; many version control systems won't be able to merge in Alice's changes.

Most, but not all, editors have configurable settings for spaces and tabs. Some environments even adapt to the formatting of the code as it is read in or always save using spaces even if the Tab key is used for authoring. If you have a flexible environment, you have a better chance of being able to work with other people's code. Just remember that tabs and spaces are different because a tab can be any length and a space is always a space.

Finally, not all platforms represent a line break in the same way. Windows, for example, uses `\r\n` for line breaks, while Linux-based platforms typically use `\n`. If you use multiple platforms in your company, then you need to agree on which line break style to use. Here also, your IDE can most likely be configured to use the line break style you need, or automated tools can be used to automatically fix line breaks, for example, when committing your code to your version control system.

STYLISTIC CHALLENGES

Many programmers begin a new project by pledging that this time they will do everything right. Any time a variable or parameter shouldn't be changed, it'll be marked `const`. All variables will have clear, concise, readable names. Every developer will put the left curly brace on the subsequent line and will adopt the standard text editor and its conventions for tabs and spaces.

For a number of reasons, it is difficult to sustain this level of stylistic consistency. In the case of `const`, sometimes programmers just aren't educated about how to use it. You will eventually come across old code or a library function that isn't `const`-savvy. For example, suppose you are writing a function accepting a `const` parameter, and you need to call a legacy function accepting a non-`const` parameter. If you cannot modify the legacy code to make it `const` aware, maybe because it's a third-party library, and you are absolutely certain that the legacy function will not modify its non-`const` argument, then a good programmer will use `const_cast()` (see Chapter 1) to temporarily suspend the `const` property of the parameter, but an inexperienced programmer will start to unwind the `const` property back from the calling function, once again ending up with a program that never uses `const`.

Other times, standardization of style comes up against programmers' individual tastes and biases. Perhaps the culture of your team makes it impractical to enforce strict style guidelines. In such situations, you may have to decide which elements you really need to standardize (such as variable names and tabs) and which ones are safe to leave up to individuals (perhaps spacing and commenting style). You can even obtain or write scripts that will automatically correct style "bugs" or flag stylistic problems along with code errors. Some development environments, such as Microsoft Visual C++, support automatic formatting of code according to rules that you specify. This makes it trivial to write code that always follows the guidelines that have been configured.

SUMMARY

The C++ language provides a number of stylistic tools without any formal guidelines on how to use them. Ultimately, any style convention is measured by how widely it is adopted and how much it benefits the readability of the code. When coding as part of a team, you should raise issues of style early in the process as part of the discussion of what language and tools to use.

The most important point about style is to appreciate that it is an important aspect of programming. Teach yourself to check over the style of your code before you make it available to others. Recognize good style in the code you interact with, and adopt the conventions that you and your organization find useful.

To conclude this chapter, keep the following in mind:

> *Always code as if the guy who ends up maintaining your code will be a violent psychopath who knows where you live. Code for readability.*
>
> *John F. Woods, Sep 24, 1991, comp.lang.c++*

This chapter concludes the first part of this book. The next part discusses software design on a high level.

EXERCISES

By solving the following exercises, you can practice the material discussed in this chapter. Solutions to all exercises are available with the code download on the book's website at www.wiley.com/go/proc++6e. However, if you are stuck on an exercise, first reread parts of this chapter to try to find an answer yourself before looking at the solution from the website.

Code comments and coding style are subjective. The following exercises do not have a single perfect answer. The solutions from the website provide one of many possible correct answers to the exercises.

Exercise 3-1: Chapter 1 discusses an example of an employee records system. That system has a database, and one of the member functions of the database is `displayCurrent()`. Here is the implementation of that member function with some comments:

```
void Database::displayCurrent() const     // The displayCurrent() member function
{
    for (const auto& employee : m_employees) {  // For each employee...
        if (employee.isHired()) {               // If the employee is hired
            employee.display();                 // Then display that employee
        }
    }
}
```

Do you see anything wrong with these comments? Why? Can you come up with better comments?

Exercise 3-2: The employee records system from Chapter 1 contains a `Database` class. The following is a snippet of that class with only three member functions. Add proper JavaDoc-style comments to this code snippet. Consult Chapter 1 to brush up on what exactly these member functions do.

```
class Database
{
    public:
        Employee& addEmployee(const std::string& firstName,
            const std::string& lastName);
        Employee& getEmployee(int employeeNumber);
        Employee& getEmployee(const std::string& firstName,
            const std::string& lastName);
    // Remainder omitted...
};
```

Exercise 3-3: The following class has a number of naming issues. Can you spot them all and propose better names?

```
class xrayController
{
    public:
        // Gets the active X-ray current in μA.
        double getCurrent() const;

        // Sets the current of the X-rays to the given current in μA.
        void setIt(double Val);

        // Sets the current to 0 μA.
        void 0Current();

        // Gets the X-ray source type.
        const std::string& getSourceType() const;

        // Sets the X-ray source type.
        void setSourceType(std::string_view _Type);

    private:
        double d; // The X-ray current in μA.
        std::string m_src__type; // The type of the X-ray source.
};
```

Exercise 3-4: Given the following code snippet, reformat the snippet three times: first put curly braces on their own lines, then indent the curly braces themselves, and finally remove the curly braces for single-statement code blocks. This exercise allows you to get a feeling of different formatting styles and what the impact is on code readability.

```
Employee& Database::getEmployee(int employeeNumber)
{
    for (auto& employee : m_employees) {
        if (employee.getEmployeeNumber() == employeeNumber) {
            return employee;
        }
    }
    throw logic_error { "No employee found." };
}
```

PART II
Professional C++ Software Design

Designing Professional C++ Programs

WHAT'S IN THIS CHAPTER?

- The definition of programming design
- The importance of programming design
- The aspects of design that are unique to C++
- The two fundamental themes for effective C++ design: abstraction and reuse
- The different types of code available for reuse
- The advantages and disadvantages of code reuse
- Guidelines for choosing a library to reuse
- Open-source libraries
- The C++ Standard Library

Before writing a single line of code in your application, you should design your program. What data structures will you use? What classes will you write? This plan is especially important when you program in groups. Imagine sitting down to write a program with no idea what your co-worker, who is working on the same program, is planning! In this chapter, you'll learn how to use the *Professional C++* approach to C++ design.

Despite the importance of design, it is probably the most misunderstood and underused aspect of the software-engineering process. Too often, programmers jump into applications without a clear plan: they design as they code. This approach can lead to convoluted and overly complicated designs. It also makes development, debugging, and maintenance tasks more difficult.

Although it seems counterintuitive, investing extra time at the beginning of a project to design it properly actually saves time over the life of the project.

WHAT IS PROGRAMMING DESIGN?

The first step when starting a new program, or a new feature for an existing program, is to analyze the requirements. This involves having discussions with your *stakeholders*. A vital outcome of this analysis phase is a *functional requirements* document describing *what* exactly the new piece of code has to do, but it does not explain *how* it has to do it. Requirement analysis can also result in a *non-functional requirements* document describing how the final system should *be*, compared to what it should *do*. Examples of non-functional requirements are that the system needs to be secure, extensible, satisfy certain performance criteria, and so on.

Once all requirements have been collected, the design phase of the project can start. Your *program design*, or *software design*, is the specification of the architecture that you will implement to fulfill all functional and non-functional requirements of the program. Informally, the design is how you plan to write the program. You should generally write your design in the form of a design document. Although every company or project has its own variation of a desired design document format, most design documents share the same general layout, which includes two main parts:

- The gross subdivision of the program into subsystems, including interfaces and dependencies between the subsystems, data flow between the subsystems, input and output to and from each subsystem, and a general threading model
- The details of each subsystem, including subdivision into classes, class hierarchies, data structures, algorithms, specific threading models, and error-handling specifics

The design documents usually include diagrams and tables showing subsystem interactions and class hierarchies. The Unified Modeling Language (UML) is the industry standard for such diagrams and is used for diagrams in this and subsequent chapters. See Appendix D, "Introduction to UML," for a brief introduction to the UML syntax. With that being said, the exact format of the design document is less important than the process of thinking about your design.

> **NOTE** *The point of designing is to think about your program before you write it.*

You should generally try to make your design as good as possible before you begin coding. The design should provide a map of the program that any reasonable programmer could follow in order to implement the application. Of course, it is inevitable that the design will need to be modified once you begin coding and you encounter issues that you didn't think of earlier. Software-engineering processes have been designed to give you the flexibility to make these changes. Scrum, an agile software development methodology, is one example of such an iterative process whereby the application is developed in cycles, known as *sprints*. With each sprint, designs can be modified, and new requirements can be taken into account. Chapter 28, "Maximizing Software Engineering Methods," describes various software-engineering process models in more detail.

THE IMPORTANCE OF PROGRAMMING DESIGN

It's tempting to skip the analysis and design steps, or to perform them only cursorily, to begin programming as soon as possible. There's nothing like seeing code compiling and running to give you the impression that you have made progress. It seems like a waste of time to formalize a design or to write down functional requirements when you already know, more or less, how you want to structure your program. Besides, writing a design document just isn't as much fun as coding. If you wanted to write papers all day, you wouldn't be a computer programmer! As a programmer myself, I understand this temptation to begin coding immediately and have certainly succumbed to it on occasion. However, it will most likely lead to problems on all but the simplest projects. No matter your experience as a programmer, your proficiency with commonly used design patterns, and how deeply you understand C++, the problem domain, and the requirements, designing ("thinking") is part of your job description. Without this up-front design, it will not work.

If you are working in a team where each team member will work on a different part of the project, it is paramount that there is a design document for all team members to follow. Design documents also help newcomers to get up to speed with the designs of a project. If there are no design documents, anyone new joining the project won't know what the designs are supposed to be and will make changes to the code breaking some undocumented designs, which can then lead to problems later during the project.

Some companies have dedicated functional analysts to write the functional requirements and dedicated software architects to work out the software design. In those companies, developers can usually just focus on the programming aspects of the project. In other companies, the developers have to do the requirements gathering and the designs themselves. Some companies lie in between these two extremes; maybe they only have a software architect making the bigger architectural decisions, while developers do smaller designs themselves.

To help you understand the importance of programming design, imagine that you own a plot of land on which you want to build a house. When the builder shows up, you ask to see the blueprints. "What blueprints?" he responds. "I know what I'm doing. I don't need to plan every little detail ahead of time. Two-story house? No problem. I did a one-story house a few months ago—I'll just start with that model and work from there."

Suppose that you suspend your disbelief and allow the builder to proceed. A few months later, you notice that the plumbing appears to run outside the house instead of inside the walls. When you query the builder about this anomaly, he says, "Oh. Well, I forgot to leave space in the walls for the plumbing. I was so excited about this new drywall technology that it just slipped my mind. But it works just as well outside, and functionality is the most important thing." You're starting to have your doubts about his approach, but, against your better judgment, you allow him to continue.

When you take your first tour of the completed building, you notice that the kitchen lacks a sink. The builder excuses himself by saying, "We were already two-thirds done with the kitchen by the time we realized there wasn't space for the sink. Instead of starting over, we just added a separate sink room next door. It works, right?"

Do the builder's excuses sound familiar if you translate them to the software domain? Have you ever found yourself implementing an "ugly" solution to a problem like putting plumbing outside the house? For example, maybe you forgot to include locking in your queue data structure that is shared between multiple threads. By the time you realize the problem, you decide to just perform the locking manually on all places where the queue is used. Sure, it's ugly, but it works, you say. That is, until someone new joins the project who assumes that the locking is built into the data structure, fails to ensure mutual exclusion in her access to the shared data, and causes a race condition bug that takes three weeks to track down. A professional C++ programmer would never decide to perform the locking manually on each queue access but would instead directly incorporate the locking inside the queue class or make the queue class thread-safe in a lock-free manner.

Formalizing a design before you code helps you determine how everything fits together. Just as blueprints for a house show how the rooms relate to each other and work together to fulfill the requirements of the house, the design for a program shows how the subsystems of the program relate to each other and work together to fulfill the software requirements. Without a design plan, you are likely to miss connections between subsystems, possibilities for reuse or shared information, and the simplest ways to accomplish tasks. Without the "big picture" that the design gives, you might become so bogged down in individual implementation details that you lose track of the overarching architecture and goals. Furthermore, the design provides written documentation to which all members of the project can refer. If you use an iterative process like the agile Scrum methodology mentioned earlier, you need to make sure to keep the design documentation up-to-date during each cycle of the process, for as long as doing so adds value. One of the pillars of the agile methodology states to prefer "Working software over comprehensive documentation." You should at least keep design documentation about how the bigger parts of a project work together up-to-date, while in my opinion, it's up to the team whether maintaining design documentation about smaller aspects of the project adds any value towards the future or not. If not, then make sure to either remove such documents or mark them as out-of-date.

If the preceding analogy still hasn't convinced you to design before you code, here is an example where jumping directly into coding fails to lead to an optimal design. Suppose that you want to write a chess program. Instead of designing the entire program before you begin coding, you decide to jump in with the easiest parts and move slowly to the more difficult parts. Following the object-oriented perspective introduced in Chapter 1, "A Crash Course in C++ and the Standard Library," and covered in more detail in Chapter 5, "Designing with Classes," you decide to model your chess pieces with classes. You figure the pawn is the simplest chess piece, so you opt to start there. After considering the features and behaviors of a pawn, you write a class with the properties and member functions shown in the UML class diagram in Figure 4.1.

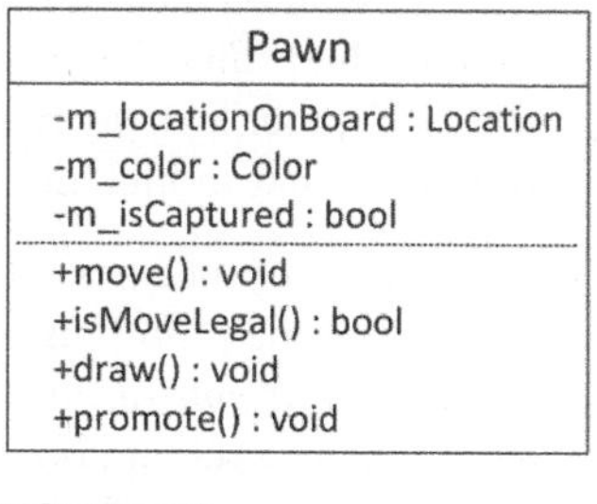

Pawn
-m_locationOnBoard : Location -m_color : Color -m_isCaptured : bool
+move() : void +isMoveLegal() : bool +draw() : void +promote() : void

FIGURE 4.1

In this design, the `m_color` attribute denotes whether the pawn is black or white. The `promote()` member function executes upon reaching the opposing side of the board.

Of course, you haven't actually made this class diagram. You've gone straight to the implementation phase. Happy with that class, you move on to the next easiest piece: the bishop. After considering its attributes and functionality, you write a class with the properties and member functions shown in the class diagram in Figure 4.2.

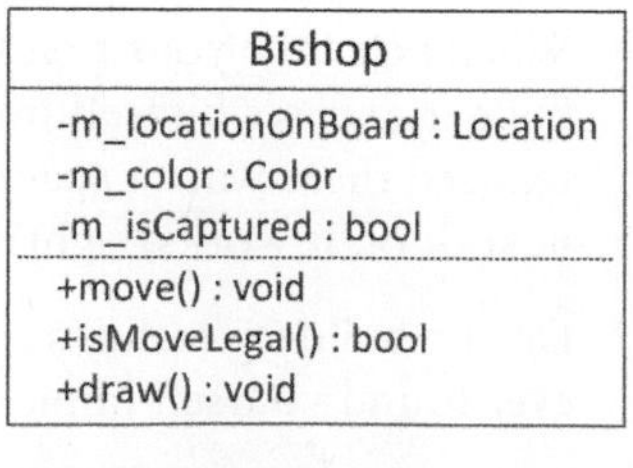

Bishop
-m_locationOnBoard : Location -m_color : Color -m_isCaptured : bool
+move() : void +isMoveLegal() : bool +draw() : void

FIGURE 4.2

Again, you haven't generated a class diagram, because you jumped straight to the coding phase. However, at this point you begin to suspect that you might be doing something wrong. The bishop and the pawn look similar. In fact, their properties are identical, and they share many member functions. Although the implementation of the move member function might differ between the pawn and the bishop, both pieces need the ability to move. If you had designed your program before jumping into coding, you would have realized that the various pieces are actually quite similar and that you should find some way to write the common functionality only once. Chapter 5 explains the object-oriented design techniques for doing that.

Furthermore, several aspects of the chess pieces depend on other subsystems of your program. For example, you cannot accurately represent the location on the board in a chess piece class itself without knowing how you will model the board. On the other hand, perhaps you will design your program so that the board manages pieces in a way that doesn't require them to know their own locations. As another example, how can you write a draw member function for a piece without first deciding your program's user interface? Will it be graphical or text-based? What will the board look like? The problem is that subsystems of a program do not exist in isolation—they interrelate with other subsystems. Most of the design work determines and defines these relationships.

DESIGNING FOR C++

There are several aspects of the C++ language that you need to keep in mind when designing for C++:

- **C++ provides object-oriented capabilities.** This means your designs can include class hierarchies, class interfaces, and object interactions. Object-oriented design is quite different compared to procedural design as used in languages such as C and others. Chapter 5 focuses on object-oriented design in C++.
- **C++ is a multi-paradigm programming language.** Besides object-oriented capabilities as described in the previous point, C++ supports other paradigms, such as procedural. Which paradigm to choose, object-oriented or procedural, is part of the design process.
- **C++ has numerous facilities for designing generic and reusable code.** Next to object-oriented and procedural capabilities, C++ supports other language facilities such as templates for generic programming. Design techniques for reusable code are discussed in more detail later in this chapter and further in Chapter 6, "Designing for Reuse."
- **C++ provides a large Standard Library.** This includes a string class, string formatting, I/O facilities, multithreading building blocks, many common data structures and algorithms, and much more. All of these facilitate coding in C++.
- **C++ readily accommodates many *design patterns*.** In other words, it supports common ways to solve problems.

Tackling a design can be overwhelming. I have spent entire days scribbling design ideas on paper, crossing them out, writing more ideas, crossing those out, and repeating the process. Sometimes this process is helpful, and, at the end of those days (or weeks), it leads to a clean, efficient design. Other times it is frustrating and leads nowhere, but it is not a waste of effort. You will most likely waste more time if you have to re-implement a design that turned out to be broken. It's important to remain aware of whether you are making real progress. If you find that you are stuck, you can take one of the following actions:

- **Ask for help.** Consult a co-worker, mentor, book, newsgroup, or web page.
- **Work on something else for a while.** Come back to this design choice later.
- **Make a decision and move on.** Even if it's not an ideal solution, decide on something and try to work with it. An incorrect choice will soon become apparent. However, it may turn out to be an acceptable solution. Perhaps there is no clean way to accomplish what you want to with this design. Sometimes you have to accept an "ugly" solution if it's the only realistic strategy to fulfill your requirements. Whatever you decide, make sure you document your decision so that you and others in the future know why you made it. This includes documenting designs that you have rejected and the rationale behind the rejection.

> **NOTE** *Keep in mind that good design is hard, and getting it right takes practice. Don't expect to become an expert overnight—and don't be surprised if you find it more difficult to master C++ design than C++ coding.*

TWO RULES FOR YOUR OWN C++ DESIGNS

When you are designing your own C++ programs, there are two fundamental design rules to follow: *abstraction* and *reuse*. These guidelines are so important that they can be considered themes of this book. They come up repeatedly throughout the text and throughout effective C++ program designs in all domains.

Abstraction

The principle of *abstraction* is easiest to understand through a real-world analogy. A television is a piece of technology found in most homes. You are probably familiar with its features: you can turn it on and off, change the channel, adjust the volume, and add external components such as speakers, DVRs, and Blu-ray players. However, can you explain how it works inside the black box? That is, do you know how it receives signals through a cable, translates them, and displays them on the screen? Most people certainly can't explain how a television works, yet are quite capable of using it. That is because the television clearly separates its internal *implementation* from its external *interface*. We interact with the television through its interface: the power button, channel changer, and volume control. We don't know, nor do we care, how the television works; we don't care whether it uses a cathode ray tube or some sort of alien technology to generate the image on our screen. It doesn't matter because it doesn't affect the interface.

Benefiting from Abstraction

The abstraction principle is similar in software. You can use code without knowing the underlying implementation. As a trivial example, your program can make a call to the `sqrt()` function declared in `<cmath>` without knowing what algorithm the function actually uses to calculate the square root.

In fact, the underlying implementation of the square root calculation could change between releases of the library, and as long as the interface stays the same, your function call will still work.

The principle of abstraction extends to classes as well. As introduced in Chapter 1, the `vector` class can be used as a dynamic array; you can add and remove as many elements as you want. For example:

```
vector<int> myVector;
myVector.push_back(33);
myVector.push_back(44);
```

You use the documented interface of the `vector` class to add the elements 33 and 44 to `myVector`. However, you don't need to understand how the `vector` class manages its memory internally. You need to know only the public interface. The underlying implementation of `vector` is free to change, as long as the exposed behavior and interface remain the same.

Incorporating Abstraction in Your Design

You should design functions and classes so that you and other programmers can use them without knowing, or relying on, the underlying implementations. To see the difference between a design that exposes the implementation and one that hides it behind an interface, consider the chess program again. You might want to implement the chessboard with a two-dimensional array of pointers to `ChessPiece` objects. You could declare and use the board like this:

```
ChessPiece* chessBoard[8][8]{};  // Zero-initialized array.
...
chessBoard[0][0] = new Rook{};
```

However, that approach utterly fails to use the concept of abstraction. Every programmer who uses the chessboard knows that it is implemented as a two-dimensional array. Changing that implementation to something else, such as a one dimensional flattened `vector` of size 64, would be difficult, because you would need to change every use of the board in the entire program. Everyone using the chessboard also has to properly take care of memory management. There is no separation of interface from implementation.

A better approach is to model the chessboard as a class. You could then expose an interface that hides the underlying implementation details. Here is an example of the beginnings of a `ChessBoard` class:

```
class ChessBoard
{
    public:
        void setPieceAt(std::size_t x, std::size_t y, ChessPiece* piece);
        ChessPiece* getPieceAt(std::size_t x, std::size_t y) const;
        bool isEmpty(std::size_t x, std::size_t y) const;
        // ...
    private:
        // Private implementation details...
};
```

Note that this interface makes no commitment to any underlying implementation. The `ChessBoard` class could use a two-dimensional array, but the interface does not require it. Changing the implementation does not require changing the interface. Furthermore, the implementation can provide additional functionality, such as bounds checking. This is possible only by strictly adhering to the following rule.

> **WARNING** *All class data members must be* `private`. *Provide* `public` *getters and setters if you want to offer controlled access to data members from outside the class.*

Making all data members `private` is often called *data hiding*. Why is this so important? By following this rule, you provide the highest level of abstraction for your class:

- You can change the underlying implementation without having to change the public interface.
- Allowing external code access to data members only through getters and setters allows you to implement extra steps whenever a value is retrieved or set. For example, you can implement sanity checks to make sure data members are never set to invalid values, you can send out an event whenever a data member changes, and so on.
- With a debugger, you can put breakpoints in getters and setters to make it easier to figure out what other piece of code is retrieving or setting a data member. Debuggers are discussed in Chapter 31, "Conquering Debugging."

Ideally, this example has convinced you that abstraction is an important technique in C++ programming. Chapter 5 covers object-oriented design in more detail, while Chapter 6 goes deeper in on the principles of abstraction. Chapters 8, "Gaining Proficiency with Classes and Objects," 9, "Mastering Classes and Objects," and 10, "Discovering Inheritance Techniques," provide all the details about writing your own classes.

Reuse

The second fundamental rule of design in C++ is *reuse*. Again, it is helpful to examine a real-world analogy to understand this concept. Suppose that you give up your programming career in favor of working as a baker. On your first day of work, the head baker tells you to bake cookies. To fulfill his orders, you find the recipe for chocolate chip cookies, mix the ingredients, form cookies on the cookie sheet, and place the sheet in the oven. The head baker is pleased with the result.

Now, I'm going to point out something so obvious that it will surprise you: you didn't build your own oven in which to bake the cookies. Nor did you churn your own butter, mill your own flour, or form your own chocolate chips. I can hear you think, "That goes without saying." That's true if you're a real cook, but what if you're a programmer writing a baking simulation game? In that case, you would think nothing of writing every component of the program, from the chocolate chips to the oven. Or, you could save yourself time by looking around for code to reuse. Perhaps a co-worker wrote a cooking simulation game and has some nice oven code lying around. Maybe it doesn't do everything you need, but you might be able to modify it and add the necessary functionality.

Something else you took for granted is that you followed a recipe for the cookies instead of making up your own. Again, that goes without saying. However, in C++ programming, it does not go without saying. Although there are standard ways of approaching problems that arise over and over in C++, many programmers persist in reinventing these strategies in each design.

The idea of using existing code is not new. You've been reusing code from the first day you printed something with `std::println()`. You didn't write the code to actually print your data to the screen.

You used the existing `println()` implementation to do the work. Similarly, the employee database from Chapter 1 reused the `std::vector` container from the C++ Standard Library to store a list of `Employees`; you didn't write your own data structure to store the `Employees`.

Unfortunately, not all programmers take advantage of available code, and often reinvent the wheel. Your designs should take into account existing code and reuse it when appropriate.

Writing Reusable Code

The design theme of reuse applies to code you write as well as to code that you use. You should design your programs so that you can reuse your classes, algorithms, and data structures. You and your co-workers should be able to use these components in both the current project and future projects. In general, you should avoid designing overly specific code that is applicable only to the case at hand.

One language technique for writing general-purpose code in C++ is using *templates*. Remember the chess example discussed earlier, but now consider that at some point you might need a `ChessBoard` class storing `ChessPieces`, and a `CheckersBoard` class storing `CheckersPieces`. You could of course write a `ChessBoard` class and a `CheckersBoard` class that are completely independent from each other, but in doing so you'll duplicate quite a bit of code. Such duplicated code can be avoided by writing a generic `GameBoard` class template instead that can then be used for any type of two-dimensional board game such as chess or checkers. You would only need to change the class declaration so that it takes the piece to store as a template parameter, called `PieceType`, instead of hard-coding it in the interface. The class template could look something as follows. If you've never seen this syntax before, don't worry! Chapter 12, "Writing Generic Code with Templates," explains the syntax in depth.

```
template <typename PieceType>
class GameBoard
{
    public:
        void setPieceAt(std::size_t x, std::size_t y, PieceType* piece);
        PieceType* getPieceAt(std::size_t x, std::size_t y) const;
        bool isEmpty(std::size_t x, std::size_t y) const;
        // ...
    private:
        // Private implementation details...
};
```

With this simple change in the interface, you now have a generic game board class that you can use for any two-dimensional board game. Although the code change is simple, it is important to make these decisions in the design phase, so that you are able to implement the code effectively and efficiently.

Chapter 6 goes into more detail on how to design your code with reuse in mind.

Reusing Designs

Learning the C++ language and becoming a good C++ programmer are two very different things. If you sat down and read the C++ standard, memorizing every fact, you would know C++ as well as anybody else. However, until you gained some experience by looking at code and writing your own programs, you wouldn't necessarily be a good programmer. The reason is that the C++ syntax defines what the language can do in its raw form but does not say anything about how each feature should be used.

As the baker example illustrates, it would be ludicrous to reinvent recipes for every baked good that you make. However, programmers often make an equivalent mistake in their designs. Instead of using existing "recipes," or *patterns*, for designing programs, they reinvent these techniques every time they design a program.

As they become more experienced in using the C++ language, C++ programmers develop their own individual ways of using the features of the language. The C++ community at large has also built some standard ways of leveraging the language, some formal and some informal. Throughout this book, I point out these reusable applications of the language, known as *design techniques* and *design patterns*. Additionally, Chapters 32, "Incorporating Design Techniques and Frameworks," and 33, "Applying Design Patterns," focus almost exclusively on design techniques and patterns. Some will seem obvious to you because they are simply a formalization of the obvious solution. Others describe novel solutions to problems you've encountered in the past. Some present entirely new ways of thinking about your program organization.

For example, you might want to design your chess program so that you have a single `ErrorLogger` object that serializes all errors from different components to a log file. When you try to design your `ErrorLogger` class, you realize that you would like to have only a single instance of the `ErrorLogger` class in your program. But you also want several components in your program to be able to use this `ErrorLogger` instance; that is, these components all want to use the same `ErrorLogger` *service*. A standard pattern to implement such a service mechanism is the *strategy pattern* combined with *dependency injection*. With the strategy pattern you create an interface for each service. You can then have multiple implementations of that interface. For example, you could have several logger service implementations, one could log to a file, another could send log messages to a remote server over the Internet, and so on. Once you have defined such interfaces, you then use dependency injection to inject the interfaces a component needs into the component. Thus, a good design at this point would specify that you want to use the strategy pattern with dependency injection.

It is important for you to familiarize yourself with these patterns and techniques so that you can recognize when a particular design problem calls for one of these solutions. There are many more techniques and patterns applicable to C++ than those described in this book. Even though a nice selection is covered here, you may want to consult a book on design patterns for more and different patterns. See Appendix B, "Annotated Bibliography," for suggestions.

REUSING EXISTING CODE

Experienced C++ programmers never start a project from scratch. They incorporate code from a wide variety of sources, such as the Standard Library, open-source libraries, proprietary code bases in their workplace, and their own code from previous projects. You should reuse code liberally in your projects. To make the most of this rule, this section first explains the different types of code that you can reuse, followed by the trade-offs between reusing existing code and writing it yourself. The final part of this section discusses a number of guidelines for choosing a library to reuse, once you have decided not to write the code yourself but to reuse existing code.

> **NOTE** *Reusing code does not mean copying and pasting existing code! In fact, it means quite the opposite: reusing code without duplicating it.*

A Note on Terminology

Before analyzing the advantages and disadvantages of code reuse, it is helpful to specify the terminology involved and to categorize the types of reusable code. There are three categories of code available for reuse:

- Code you wrote yourself in the past
- Code written by a co-worker
- Code written by a third party outside your current organization or company

There are several ways that the code you reuse can be structured:

- **Stand-alone functions or classes.** When you reuse your own code or co-workers' code, you will generally encounter this variety.
- **Libraries.** A *library* is a collection of code used to accomplish a specific task, such as parsing XML, or to handle a specific domain, such as cryptography. Other examples of functionality usually found in libraries include threads and synchronization support, networking, and graphics.
- **Frameworks.** A *framework* is a collection of code around which you design a program. For example, the Microsoft Foundation Classes (MFC) library provides a framework for creating graphical user interface applications for Microsoft Windows. Frameworks usually dictate the structure of your program.
- **Entire applications.** Your project might include multiple applications. Perhaps you need a web server front end to support your new e-commerce infrastructure. It is possible to bundle entire third-party applications, such as a web server, with your software. This approach takes code reuse to the extreme in that you reuse entire applications.

> **NOTE** *A program uses a library but fits into a framework. Libraries provide specific functionality, while frameworks are fundamental to your program design and structure.*

Another term that arises frequently is *application programming interface*, or *API*. An API is an interface to a library or body of code for a specific purpose. For example, programmers often refer to the sockets API, meaning the exposed interface to the sockets networking library, instead of the library itself.

> **NOTE** *Although people use the terms API and library interchangeably, they are not equivalent. The library refers to the implementation, while the API refers to the published interface to the library.*

For the sake of brevity, the rest of this chapter uses the term *library* to refer to any reusable code, whether it is really a library, framework, entire application, or random collection of functions from your co-worker.

Deciding Whether to Reuse Code or Write It Yourself

The rule to reuse code is easy to understand in the abstract. However, it's somewhat vague when it comes to the details. How do you know when it's appropriate to reuse code and which code to reuse? There is always a trade-off, and the decision depends on the specific situation. However, there are some general advantages and disadvantages to reusing code.

Advantages to Reusing Code

Reusing code can provide tremendous advantages to you and to your project:

- You may not know how to or may not be able to justify the time to write the code you need. Would you really want to write code to handle formatted output? Of course not. That's why you use the standard C++ `std::format()` or `print()` functionality.
- Your designs will be simpler because you will not need to design those components of the application that you reuse.
- The code that you reuse usually requires no debugging. You can often assume that library code is bug-free because it has already been tested and used extensively.
- Libraries handle more error conditions than would your first attempt at the code. You might forget obscure errors or edge cases at the beginning of the project and would waste time fixing these problems later. Library code that you reuse has generally been tested extensively and used by many programmers before you, so you can assume that it handles most errors properly.
- Libraries are often tested on a wide range of platforms with different hardware, different operating systems and operating system versions, different graphic cards, and so on; much more than you could possibly have available to test yourself. Sometimes, libraries contain workarounds to make them work on specific platforms.
- Libraries generally are designed to be suspect of bad user inputs. Invalid requests, or requests not appropriate for the current state, usually result in suitable error notifications. For example, a request to seek a nonexistent record in a database, or to read a record from a database that is not open, would have well-specified behavior from a library.
- Reusing code written by domain experts is safer than writing your own code for that area. For example, you should not attempt to write your own security code unless you are a security expert. If you need security or cryptography in your programs, use a library. Many

seemingly minor details in code of that nature could compromise the security of the entire program, and possibly the entire system, if you got them wrong.

- Library code is constantly improving. If you reuse the code, you receive the benefits of these improvements without doing the work yourself. In fact, if the library writers have properly separated the interface from the implementation, you can obtain these benefits by upgrading your library version without changing your interaction with the library. A good upgrade modifies the underlying implementation without changing the interface.

Disadvantages to Reusing Code

Unfortunately, there are also some disadvantages to reusing code:

- When you use libraries that you didn't write yourself, you must spend time understanding the interface and correct usage before you can jump in and use it. This extra time at the beginning of your project will slow down your initial design and coding, but the advantage is that it will save you significant time later because there is less code that needs to be maintained by you, and the final code will be simpler.
- When you write your own code, it does exactly what you want. Library code might not provide the exact functionality that you require.
- Even if the library code provides the exact functionality you need, it might not give you the performance that you desire. The performance might be bad in general, poor for your specific use case, or completely unspecified.
- Using library code introduces a Pandora's box of support issues. If you discover a bug in the library, what do you do? Often you don't have access to the source code, so you couldn't fix it even if you wanted to. If you have already invested significant time in learning the library interface and using the library, you probably don't want to give it up, but you might find it difficult to convince the library developers to fix the bug on your time schedule. Also, if you are using a third-party library, what do you do if the library authors drop support for the library before you stop supporting the product that depends on it? Think carefully about this before you decide to use a library for which you cannot get source code.
- In addition to support problems, libraries present licensing issues, which cover topics such as disclosure of your source code, redistribution fees (often called binary license fees), credit attribution, and development licenses. You should carefully inspect the licensing issues before using any library. For example, some open-source libraries require you to make your own code open-source.
- Reusing code requires a trust factor. You must trust whoever wrote the code by assuming that they did a good job. Some people like to have control over all aspects of their project, including every line of source code.
- Upgrading to a new version of the library can cause problems. The upgrade could introduce bugs, which could have fatal consequences in your product. A performance-related upgrade might optimize performance in certain cases but make it worse in your specific use case.
- Upgrading your compiler to a new version can cause problems when you are using binary-only libraries. You can only upgrade the compiler when the library vendor provides binaries compatible with your new version of the compiler.

Putting It Together to Make a Decision

Now that you are familiar with the terminology, advantages, and disadvantages of reusing code, you are better prepared to make the decision about whether to reuse code. Often, the decision is obvious. For example, if you want to write a graphical user interface (GUI) in C++ for Microsoft Windows, you should use a framework such as MFC or Qt. You probably don't know how to write the underlying code to create a GUI in Windows, and more importantly, you don't want to waste time to learn it. You will save person-years of effort by using a framework in this case.

However, other times the choice is less obvious. For example, if you are unfamiliar with a library and need only a simple data structure, it might not be worth the time to learn the library to reuse only one component that you could write in a few days.

Ultimately, you need to make a decision based on your own particular needs. It often comes down to a trade-off between the time it would take to write it yourself and the time required to find and learn how to use a library to solve the problem. Carefully consider how the advantages and disadvantages listed previously apply to your specific case, and decide which factors are most important to you. Finally, remember that you can always change your mind, which might even be relatively easy if you handled the abstraction correctly.

Guidelines for Choosing a Library to Reuse

When you've decided to reuse libraries, frameworks, co-workers' code, entire applications, or your own code, there are several guidelines you should keep in mind to pick the right code to reuse.

Understand the Capabilities and Limitations

Take the time to familiarize yourself with the code. It is important to understand both its capabilities and its limitations. Start with the documentation and the published interfaces or APIs. Ideally, that will be sufficient to understand how to use the code. However, if the library doesn't provide a clear separation between interface and implementation, you may need to explore the source code itself if it is provided. Also, talk to other programmers who have used the code and who might be able to explain its intricacies. You should begin by learning the basic functionality. If it's a library, what functions does it provide? If it's a framework, how does your code fit in? What classes should you derive from? What code do you need to write yourself? You should also consider specific issues depending on the type of code.

Here are some points to keep in mind when choosing a library:

- Is it safe to use the library in multithreaded programs?
- Does the library impose any specific compiler settings on code using it? If so, is that acceptable in your project?
- On what other libraries does the library depend?

Additionally, you might have to do some more detailed research for specific libraries:

- Which initialization and cleanup calls are needed?
- If you need to derive from a class, which constructor should you call on it? Which virtual member functions should you override?

- If a call returns memory pointers, who is responsible for freeing the memory: the caller or the library? If the library is responsible, when is the memory freed? It's highly recommended to find out whether you can use smart pointers (see Chapter 7, "Memory Management") to manage memory allocated by the library.
- What are all the return values (by value or reference) from a call?
- What are all the possible exceptions thrown?
- What error conditions do library calls check for, and what do they assume? How are errors handled? How is the client program notified about errors? Avoid using libraries that pop up message boxes, print messages on the standard output console, or terminate the program. The client program should decide how to inform users about an error, not the library.

Understand the Learning Cost

The *learning cost* is the amount of time it takes for a developer to learn how to use a library. This is not just an initial cost when starting to use the library, but a recurring cost over time. Whenever a new team member joins the project, she needs to learn how to use that library.

This cost can be substantial for certain libraries. As such, if you find the functionality you need in a well-known library, I recommend using that one over using some exotic, lesser-known library. For example, if the Standard Library provides the data structure or algorithm you need, use that one instead of using another library.

Understand the Performance

It is important to know the performance guarantees that the library or other code provides. Even if your particular program is not performance sensitive, you should make sure that the code you use doesn't have awful performance for your particular use.

Big-O Notation

Programmers generally discuss and document algorithm and library performance using *big-O notation*. This section explains the general concepts of algorithm complexity analysis and big-O notation without a lot of unnecessary mathematics. If you are already familiar with these concepts, you can skip this section.

Big-O notation specifies *relative*, rather than *absolute*, performance. For example, instead of saying that an algorithm runs in a specific amount of time, such as 300 milliseconds, big-O notation specifies how an algorithm performs as its input size increases. Examples of input sizes include the number of items to be sorted by a sorting algorithm, the number of elements in a hash table during a key lookup, and the size of a file to be copied between disks.

> **NOTE** *Big-O notation applies only to algorithms whose speed depends on their inputs. It does not apply to algorithms that take no input or whose running time is random. In practice, you will find that the running times of most algorithms of interest depend on their input, so this limitation is not significant.*

To be more formal, big-O notation specifies an algorithm's run time as a function of its input size, also known as the *complexity* of the algorithm. It's not as complicated as it sounds. For example, an algorithm could take twice as long to process twice as many elements. Thus, if it takes 1 second to process 200 elements, it will take 2 seconds to process 400 elements, and 4 seconds to process 800 elements. Figure 4.3 shows this graphically. It is said that the complexity of such an algorithm is a linear function of its input size, because, graphically, it is represented by a straight line.

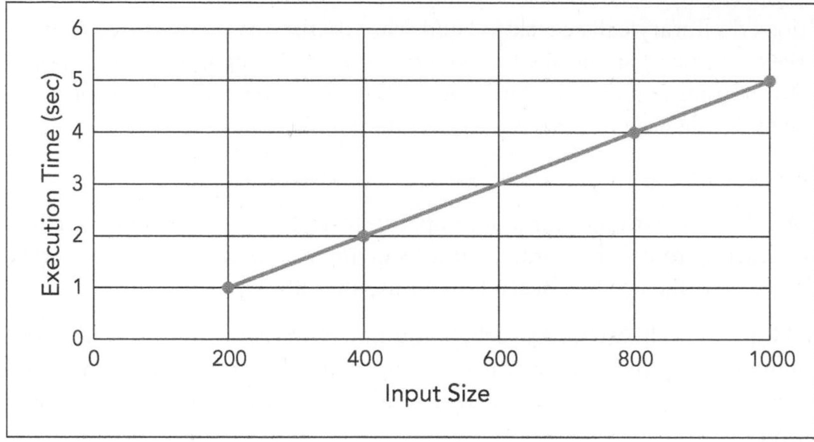

FIGURE 4.3

Big-O notation summarizes the algorithm's linear performance like this: *O(n)*. The O just means that you're using big-O notation, while the *n* represents the input size. *O(n)* specifies that the algorithm speed is a direct linear function of the input size.

Of course, not all algorithms have performance that is linear with respect to their input size. The following table summarizes the common complexities, in order of their performance from best to worst:

ALGORITHM COMPLEXITY	BIG-O NOTATION	EXPLANATION	EXAMPLE ALGORITHMS
Constant	O(1)	The running time is independent of the input size.	Accessing a single element in an array.
Logarithmic	O(log *n*)	The running time is a function of the logarithm base 2 of the input size.	Finding an element in a sorted list using binary search.
Linear	O(*n*)	The running time is directly proportional to the input size.	Finding an element in an unsorted list.
Linear Logarithmic	O(*n* log *n*)	The running time is a function of the linear times the logarithmic function of the input size.	Merge sort.

ALGORITHM COMPLEXITY	BIG-O NOTATION	EXPLANATION	EXAMPLE ALGORITHMS
Quadratic	$O(n^2)$	The running time is a function of the square of the input size.	A slower sorting algorithm like selection sort.
Exponential	$O(2^n)$	The running time is an exponential function of the input size.	Optimized traveling salesman problem.

There are two advantages to specifying performance as a function of the input size instead of in absolute numbers:

- It is platform independent. Specifying that a piece of code runs in 200 milliseconds on one computer says nothing about its speed on a second computer. It is also difficult to compare two different algorithms without running them on the same computer with the exact same load. On the other hand, performance specified as a function of the input size is applicable to any platform.
- Performance as a function of input size covers all possible inputs to the algorithm with one specification. The specific time in seconds that an algorithm takes to run covers only one specific input and says nothing about any other input.

Tips for Understanding Performance

Now that you are familiar with big-O notation, you are prepared to understand most performance documentation. The C++ Standard Library in particular describes its algorithm and data structure performance using big-O notation. However, big-O notation is sometimes insufficient or even misleading. Consider the following issues whenever you think about big-O performance specifications:

- If an algorithm takes twice as long to work on twice as much data, it doesn't say anything about how long it took in the first place! If the algorithm is written badly but scales well, it's still not something you want to use. For example, suppose the algorithm makes unnecessary disk accesses. That probably wouldn't affect the big-O time but would be very bad for overall performance.
- Along those lines, it's difficult to compare two algorithms with the same big-O running time. For example, if two different sorting algorithms both claim to be $O(n \log n)$, it's hard to tell which is really faster without running your own tests.
- The big-O notation describes the time complexity of an algorithm asymptotically, as the input size grows to infinity. For small inputs, big-O time can be very misleading. An $O(n^2)$ algorithm might actually perform better than an $O(\log n)$ algorithm on small input sizes. Consider your likely input sizes before making a decision.

In addition to considering big-O characteristics, you should look at other facets of the algorithm performance. Here are some guidelines to keep in mind:

- You should consider how often you intend to use a particular piece of library code. Some people find the 90/10 rule helpful: 90 percent of the running time of most programs is spent in only 10 percent of the code (Hennessy and Patterson, *Computer Architecture:*

A Quantitative Approach, Fifth Edition, 2011, Morgan Kaufmann). If the library code you intend to use falls in the oft-exercised 10 percent category of your code, you should make sure to analyze its performance characteristics carefully. On the other hand, if it falls into the oft-ignored 90 percent of the code, you should not spend much time analyzing its performance because it will not benefit the overall program performance very much. Chapter 29, "Writing Efficient C++," discusses profilers, tools to help you find performance bottlenecks in your code.

- Don't rely purely on the documentation. Always run performance tests to determine if library code provides acceptable performance characteristics for your specific use case.

Understand Platform Limitations

Before you start using library code, make sure that you understand on which platforms it runs. If you want to write a cross-platform application, make sure the libraries you choose are also cross-platform portable. That might sound obvious, but even libraries that claim to be cross-platform might contain subtle differences on different platforms.

Also, platforms include not only different operating systems but different versions of the same operating system. If you write an application that should run on the operating systems Solaris 8, 9, and 10, ensure that any libraries you use also support all those releases. You cannot assume either forward or backward compatibility across operating system versions. That is, just because a library runs on Solaris 9 doesn't mean that it will run on Solaris 10 and vice versa.

Understand Licensing

Using third-party libraries often introduces complicated licensing issues. You must sometimes pay license fees to third-party vendors for the use of their libraries. There may also be other licensing restrictions, including international export restrictions. Additionally, open-source libraries are sometimes distributed under licenses that require any code that links with them to be open-source as well. A number of licenses commonly used by open-source libraries are discussed later in this chapter.

> **WARNING** *Make sure that you understand the license restrictions of any third-party libraries you use if you plan to distribute or sell the code you develop. When in doubt, consult a legal expert whose specialty is intellectual property.*

Understand Support and Know Where to Find Help

Before you use a library, make sure that you understand the process for submitting bugs and that you realize how long it will take for bugs to get fixed. If possible, determine how long the library will continue to be supported so that you can plan accordingly.

Interestingly, even using libraries from within your own organization can introduce support issues. You may find it just as difficult to convince a co-worker in another part of your company to fix a bug in their library as you would to convince a stranger in another company to do the same thing. In fact, you may even find it harder, because you're not a paying customer. Make sure that you understand the politics and organizational issues within your own organization before using internal libraries.

For reusing entire applications, the support issue might even become more complex. If customers encounter a problem with your bundled web server, should they contact you or the web server vendor? Make sure that you resolve this issue *before* you release the software.

Using libraries and frameworks can sometimes be daunting at first. Fortunately, there are many avenues of support available. First, consult the documentation that accompanies the library. If the library is widely used, such as the Standard Library or the MFC, you should be able to find a good book on the topic. In fact, for help with the Standard Library, you can consult Chapters 16 to 25. If you have specific questions not addressed by books and product documentation, try searching the Web. Type your question in your favorite search engine to find web pages that discuss the library. For example, when you search for the phrase *introduction to C++ Standard Library*, you will find hundreds of websites about C++ and the Standard Library. Also, many websites contain their own private newsgroups or forums on specific topics for which you can register.

> **WARNING** *A note of caution: don't believe everything you read on the Web! Web pages do not necessarily undergo the same review process as printed books and documentation, and may contain inaccuracies.*

Prototype

When you first sit down with a new library or framework, it is often a good idea to write a quick prototype. Trying the code is the best way to familiarize yourself with the library's capabilities. You should consider experimenting with the library even before you tackle your program design so that you are intimately familiar with the library's capabilities and limitations. This empirical testing will allow you to determine the performance characteristics of the library as well.

Even if your prototype application looks nothing like your final application, time spent prototyping is not a waste. Don't feel compelled to write a prototype of your actual application. Write a dummy program that just tests the library capabilities you want to use. The point is only to familiarize yourself with the library.

> **WARNING** *Due to time constraints, programmers sometimes find their prototypes morphing into the final product. If you have hacked together a prototype that is insufficient as the basis for the final product, make sure that it doesn't get used that way.*

Open-Source Libraries

Open-source libraries are an increasingly popular class of reusable code. The general meaning of *open-source* is that the source code is available for anyone to look at. There are formal definitions and legal rules about including source code with all your distributions, but the important thing to remember about open-source software is that anyone (including you) can look at the source code. Note that open-source applies to more than just libraries. In fact, the most famous open-source product is probably the Android operating system. Linux is another open-source operating system. Google Chrome and Mozilla Firefox are two examples of famous open-source web browsers.

The Open-Source Movements

Unfortunately, there is some confusion in terminology in the open-source community. First, there are two competing names for the movement (some would say two separate, but similar, movements). Richard Stallman and the GNU project use the term *free software*. Note that the term *free* does not imply that the finished product must be available without cost. Developers are welcome to charge as much or as little as they want. Instead, the term *free* refers to the freedom for people to examine the source code, modify the source code, and redistribute the software. Think of the free in *free speech* rather than the free in *free beer*. You can read more about Richard Stallman and the GNU project at `www.gnu.org`.

The Open Source Initiative uses the term *open-source software* to describe software in which the source code must be available. As with free software, open-source software does not require the product or library to be available without cost. However, an important difference with free software is that open-source software is not required to give you the freedom to use, modify, and redistribute it. You can read more about the Open Source Initiative at `www.opensource.org`.

There are a lot of licensing options available for open-source projects. For example, a project could use one of the GNU Public License (GPL) versions. However, using a library under the GPL requires you to make your own product open-source under the GPL as well. On the other hand, an open-source project can use a license like Boost Software License, Berkeley Software Distribution (BSD) license, MIT License, Apache License, and so on, which allow using an open-source project in closed-source products. Some of these licenses have different versions. For example, there are actually four versions of the BSD license. Another option for an open-source project is to use one of the six flavors of the Creative Commons (CC) license.

Some licenses require you to include the library's license with your final product. Some licenses require attribution when using the library. Bottom line, all licenses come with subtleties that are important to understand if you want to use libraries in closed-source projects. The `opensource.org/licenses` website gives a thorough overview of approved open-source licenses.

Because the name "open-source" is less ambiguous than "free software," this book uses "open-source" to refer to products and libraries with which the source code is available. The choice of name is not intended to imply endorsement of the open-source philosophy over the free software philosophy: it is only for ease of comprehension.

Finding and Using Open-Source Libraries

Regardless of the terminology, you can gain amazing benefits from using open-source software. The main benefit is functionality. There is a plethora of open-source C++ libraries available for varied tasks, from XML parsing and cross-platform error logging to deep learning and data mining using artificial neural networks.

Although open-source libraries are not required to provide free distribution and licensing, many open-source libraries are available without monetary cost. You will generally be able to save money in licensing fees by using open-source libraries.

Finally, you are often but not always free to modify open-source libraries to suit your exact needs.

Most open-source libraries are available on the Web. For example, searching for *open-source C++ library XML parsing* results in a list of links to XML libraries for C++. There are also a few open-source portals where you can start your search, including the following:

- `www.boost.org`
- `www.gnu.org`
- `github.com/open-source`
- `www.sourceforge.net`

Guidelines for Using Open-Source Code

Open-source libraries present several unique issues and require new strategies. First, open-source libraries are usually written by people in their "free" time. The source base is generally available for any programmer who wants to pitch in and contribute to development or bug fixing. As a good programming citizen, you should try to contribute to open-source projects if you find yourself reaping the benefits of open-source libraries. If you work for a company, you may find resistance to this idea from your management because it does not lead directly to revenue for your company. However, you might be able to convince management that indirect benefits, such as exposure of your company name and perceived support from your company for the open-source movement, should allow you to pursue this activity.

Second, because of the distributed nature of their development and lack of single ownership, open-source libraries often present support issues. If you desperately need a bug fixed in a library, it is often more efficient to make the fix yourself than to wait for someone else to do it. If you do fix bugs, make sure to put those fixes back into the public codebase for the library. Some licenses even require you to do so. Even if you don't fix any bugs, make sure to report problems that you find so that other programmers don't waste time encountering the same issues.

The C++ Standard Library

The most important library that you will use as a C++ programmer is the C++ Standard Library. As its name implies, this library is part of the C++ standard, so any standards-conforming compiler must include it. The Standard Library is not monolithic: it includes several disparate components, some of which you have been using already. You may even have assumed they were part of the core language. Chapters 16 to 25 go into more detail about the Standard Library.

C Standard Library

Because C++ is mostly a superset of C, the C Standard Library is still available. Its functionality includes mathematical functions such as `abs()`, `sqrt()`, and `pow()`, and error-handling helpers such as `assert()` and `errno`. Additionally, the C Standard Library facilities for manipulating character arrays as strings, such as `strlen()` and `strcpy()`, and the C-style I/O functions, such as `printf()` and `scanf()`, are all available in C++. For details on the C libraries, consult a Standard Library Reference; see Appendix B.

> **NOTE** *C++ provides better strings and I/O support than C. Even though the C-style strings and I/O routines are available in C++, you should avoid them in favor of C++ strings and formatting (Chapter 2, "Working with Strings and String Views") and I/O streams (Chapter 13, "Demystifying C++ I/O").*

Deciding Whether or Not to Use the Standard Library

The Standard Library was designed with functionality, performance, and orthogonality as its priorities. The benefits of using it are substantial. Imagine having to track down pointer errors in linked list or balanced binary tree implementations or to debug a sorting algorithm that isn't sorting properly. If you use the Standard Library correctly, you will rarely, if ever, need to perform that kind of coding or debugging yourself. Another benefit is that most C++ developers know how to work with the functionality provided by the Standard Library. Hence, when using the Standard Library in your projects, new team members will get up to speed faster compared to using third-party libraries that might have a substantial learning cost. Chapters 16 to 25 provide in-depth information on the Standard Library functionality.

DESIGNING A CHESS PROGRAM

This section introduces a systematic approach to designing a C++ program in the context of a simple chess game application. To provide a complete example, some of the steps refer to concepts covered in later chapters. You should read this example now to obtain an overview of the design process, but you might also consider rereading it after you have finished later chapters.

Requirements

Before embarking on the design, it is important to possess clear requirements for the program's functionality and efficiency. Ideally, these requirements would be documented in the form of a requirements specification. The requirements for the chess program would contain the following types of specifications, although in more detail and greater number:

- The program shall support the standard rules of chess.
- The program shall support two human players. The program shall not provide an artificially intelligent computer player.
- The program shall provide a text-based interface:
    - The program shall render the game board and pieces in plain text.
    - Players shall express their moves by entering numbers representing locations on the chessboard.

The requirements ensure that you design your program so that it performs as its users expect.

Design Steps

You should take a systematic approach to designing your program, working from the general to the specific. The following steps do not always apply to all programs, but they provide a general guideline. Your design should include diagrams and tables as appropriate. UML is an industry standard for making diagrams. You can refer to Appendix D for a brief introduction, but in short, UML defines a multitude of standard diagrams you can use for documenting software designs, for example, class diagrams, sequence diagrams, and so on. I recommend using UML or at least UML-like diagrams where applicable. However, I don't advocate strictly adhering to the UML syntax because having a clear, understandable diagram is more important than having a syntactically correct one.

Divide the Program into Subsystems

Your first step is to divide your program into its general functional subsystems and to specify the interfaces and interactions between the subsystems. At this point, you should not worry about specifics of data structures and algorithms, or even classes. You are only trying to obtain a general feel for the various parts of the program and their interactions. You can list the subsystems in a table that expresses the high-level behaviors or functionality of the subsystem, the interfaces exported from the subsystem to other subsystems, and the interfaces consumed, or used, by this subsystem from other subsystems.

The recommended design for this chess game is to have a clear separation between storing the data and displaying the data by using the *Model-View-Controller* (MVC) paradigm. This paradigm models the notion that many applications commonly deal with a set of data, one or more views on that data, and manipulation of the data. In MVC, a set of data is called the *model*, a *view* is a particular visualization of the model, and the *controller* is the piece of code that changes the model in response to some event. The three components of MVC interact in a feedback loop: actions are handled by the controller, which adjusts the model, resulting in a change to the view or views. The controller can also directly modify the view, for example UI elements. Figure 4.4 visualizes this interaction. Using this paradigm, the different components are clearly separated, allowing you to modify one component without having to modify others. For example, without having to touch the underlying data model or logic, you can easily switch between having a text-based interface and a graphical user interface, or between an interface for running on a desktop PC and an interface for running on a phone.

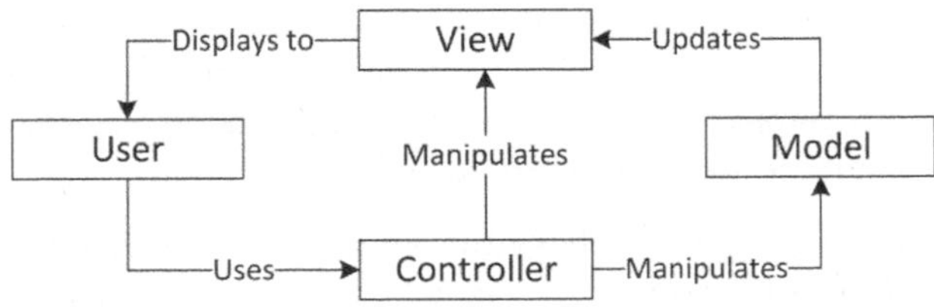

FIGURE 4.4

The following table shows how the possible subsystems for the chess game could look like:

SUBSYSTEM NAME	INSTANCES	FUNCTIONALITY	INTERFACES EXPORTED	INTERFACES CONSUMED
GamePlay	1	Starts game Controls game flow Controls drawing Declares winner Ends game	Game Over	Take Turn (on Player) Draw (on ChessBoardView)
ChessBoard	1	Stores chess pieces Checks for ties and checkmates	Get Piece At Set Piece At	Game Over (on GamePlay)
ChessBoardView	1	Draws the associated ChessBoard	Draw	Draw (on ChessPieceView)
ChessPiece	32	Moves itself Checks for legal moves	Move Check Move	Get Piece At (on ChessBoard) Set Piece At (on ChessBoard)
ChessPieceView	32	Draws the associated ChessPiece	Draw	None
Player	2	Interacts with the user by prompting the user for a move, and obtaining the user's move Moves pieces	Take Turn	Get Piece At (on ChessBoard) Move (on ChessPiece) Check Move (on ChessPiece)
ErrorLogger	1	Writes error messages to a log file	Log Error	None

As this table shows, the functional subsystems of this chess game include a GamePlay subsystem, a ChessBoard and ChessBoardView, 32 ChessPieces and ChessPieceViews, two Players, and one ErrorLogger. However, that is not the only reasonable approach. In software design, as in programming itself, there are often many different ways to accomplish the same goal. Not all solutions are equal; some are certainly better than others. However, there are often several equally valid solutions.

A good division into subsystems separates the program into its basic functional parts. For example, a Player is a subsystem distinct from the ChessBoard, ChessPieces, or GamePlay. It wouldn't make sense to lump the players into the GamePlay subsystem, because they are logically separate subsystems. Other choices might not be as obvious.

In this MVC design, the ChessBoard and ChessPiece subsystems are part of the Model. The Chess-BoardView and ChessPieceView are part of the View, and the Player is part of the Controller.

Because it is often difficult to visualize subsystem relationships from tables, it is usually helpful to show the subsystems of a program in a diagram where lines represent calls from one subsystem to another. Figure 4.5 shows the chess game subsystems visualized as a diagram loosely based on a UML communication diagram.

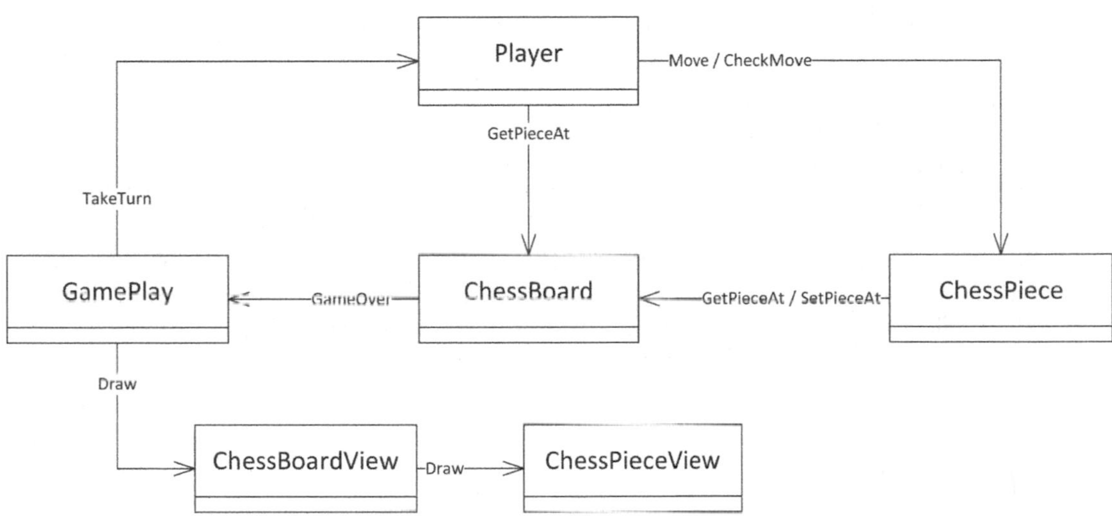

FIGURE 4.5

Choose Threading Models

It's too early in the design phase to think about how to multithread specific loops in algorithms you will write. However, in this step, you choose the number of high-level threads in your program and specify their interactions. Examples of high-level threads are a UI thread, an audio-playing thread, a network communication thread, and so on.

In multithreaded designs, you should try to avoid shared data as much as possible because it will make your designs simpler and safer. If you cannot avoid shared data, you should specify locking requirements.

If you are unfamiliar with multithreaded programs or your platform does not support multithreading, then you should make your programs single-threaded. However, if your program has several distinct tasks, each of which could work in parallel, it might be a good candidate for multiple threads. For example, graphical user interface applications often have one thread performing the main application work and another thread waiting for the user to press buttons or select menu items. Multithreaded programming is covered in Chapter 27, "Multithreaded Programming with C++."

The chess program needs only one thread to control the game flow.

Specify Class Hierarchies for Each Subsystem

In this step, you determine the class hierarchies that you intend to write in your program. The chess program could use a class hierarchy to represent the chess pieces. This hierarchy could work as shown in Figure 4.6. The generic `ChessPiece` class serves as the abstract base class. A similar hierarchy is required for the `ChessPieceView` classes.

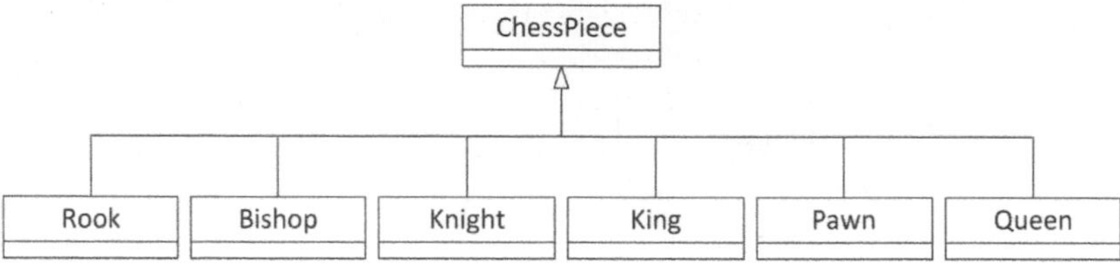

FIGURE 4.6

Another class hierarchy can be used for the `ChessBoardView` class to make it possible to have a text-based interface or a graphical user interface for the game. Figure 4.7 shows an example hierarchy that allows the chessboard to be displayed as text on a console, or with a 2D or 3D graphical user interface. A similar hierarchy is required for the individual classes of the `ChessPieceView` hierarchy.

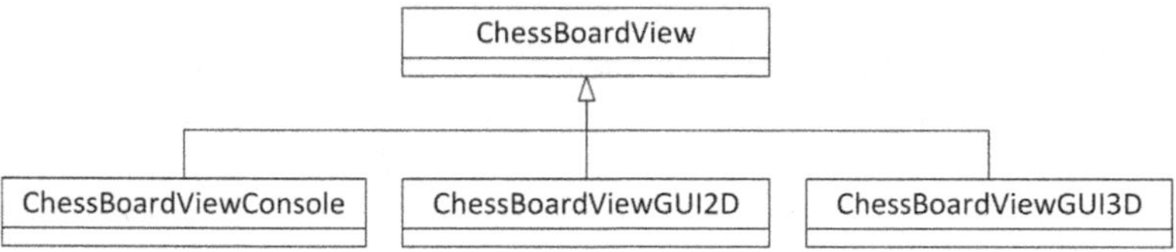

FIGURE 4.7

Chapter 5 explains the details of designing classes and class hierarchies.

Specify Classes, Data Structures, Algorithms, and Patterns for Each Subsystem

In this step, you consider a greater level of detail, and specify the particulars of each subsystem, including the specific classes that you'll write for each subsystem. It may well turn out that you model each subsystem itself as a class. This information can again be summarized in a table.

SUBSYSTEM	CLASSES	DATA STRUCTURES	ALGORITHMS	PATTERNS
GamePlay	`GamePlay` class	`GamePlay` object includes one `ChessBoard` object and two `Player` objects.	Gives each player a turn to play.	None

SUBSYSTEM	CLASSES	DATA STRUCTURES	ALGORITHMS	PATTERNS
ChessBoard	`ChessBoard` class	`ChessBoard` object stores a two-dimensional 8x8 grid containing up to 32 `ChessPieces`.	Checks for a win or tie after each move.	None
ChessBoardView	`ChessBoardView` abstract base class Concrete derived classes `ChessBoardViewConsole`, `ChessBoardViewGUI2D`, and so on	Stores information on how to draw a chessboard.	Draws a chessboard.	Observer
ChessPiece	`ChessPiece` abstract base class `Rook`, `Bishop`, `Knight`, `King`, `Pawn`, and `Queen` derived classes	Each piece stores its location on the chessboard.	Checks for a legal move by querying the chessboard for pieces at various locations.	None
ChessPieceView	`ChessPieceView` abstract base class Derived classes `RookView`, `BishopView`, and so on, and concrete derived classes `RookViewConsole`, `RookViewGUI2D`, and so on	Stores information on how to draw a chess piece.	Draws a chess piece.	Observer
Player	`Player` abstract base class Concrete derived classes `PlayerConsole`, `PlayerGUI2D`, and so on	None.	Prompts the user for a move, checks if the move is legal, and moves the piece.	Mediator

continues

(continued)

SUBSYSTEM	CLASSES	DATA STRUCTURES	ALGORITHMS	PATTERNS
ErrorLogger	`ErrorLogger` class	A queue of messages to log.	Buffers messages and writes them to a log file.	Strategy using dependency injection

Such a table already gives some information about the different classes in a software design, but it doesn't clearly describe the interactions between them. A *UML sequence diagram* can be used to model such interactions. Figure 4.8 shows such a diagram visualizing the interactions of some of the classes from the previous table.

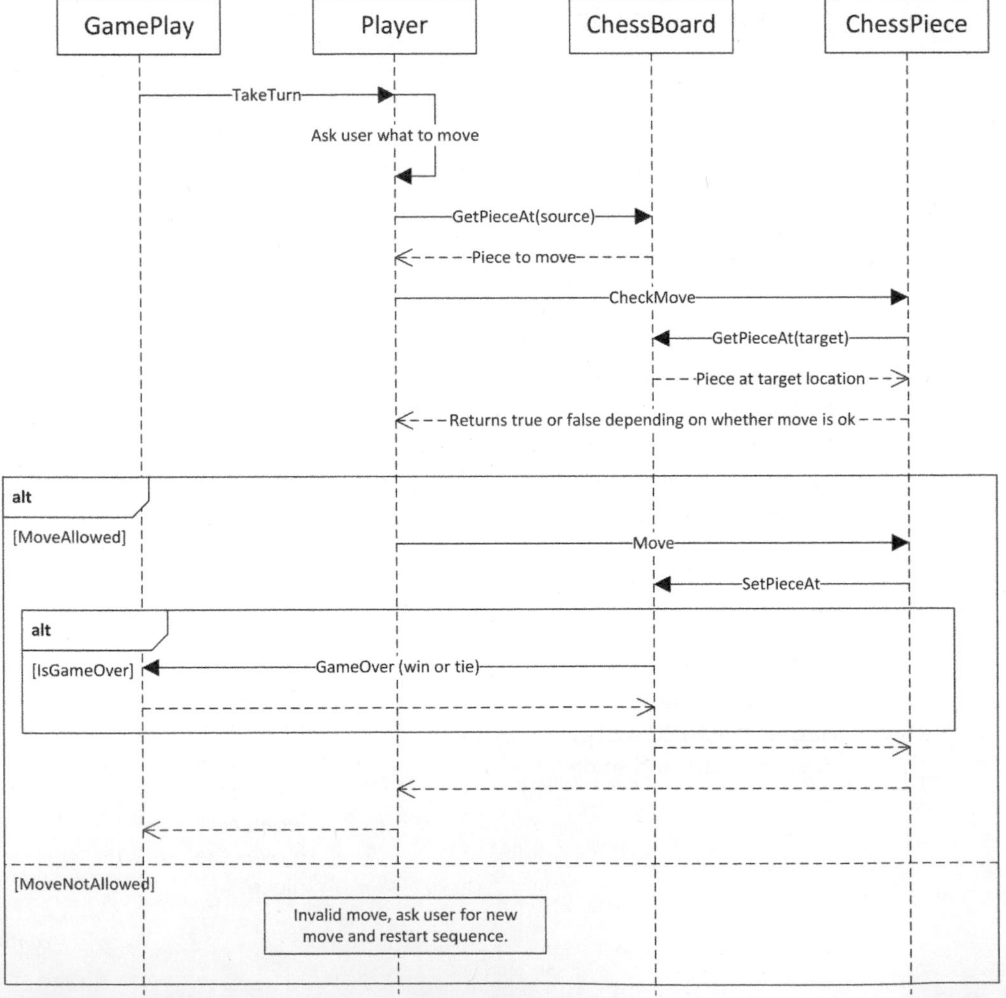

FIGURE 4.8

The diagram in Figure 4.8 shows only a single iteration, a single `TakeTurn` call from `GamePlay` to `Player`; hence, it's only a partial sequence diagram. After a `TakeTurn` call is finished, the `GamePlay` object should ask the `ChessBoardView` to draw itself, which in turn should ask different `ChessPieceViews` to draw themselves. Furthermore, you should extend the sequence diagram to visualize how a chess piece takes an opponent's piece and to include support for a castling move, a move involving a player's king and either of the player's rooks. Castling is the only move for which a player moves two pieces at the same time.

This section of the design document would normally present the actual interfaces for each class, but this example will forgo that level of detail.

Designing classes and choosing data structures, algorithms, and patterns can be tricky. You should always keep in mind the rules of abstraction and reuse discussed earlier in this chapter. For abstraction, the key is to consider the interface and the implementation separately. First, specify the interface from the perspective of the user. Decide *what* you want the component to do. Then decide *how* the component will do it by choosing data structures and algorithms. For reuse, familiarize yourself with standard data structures, algorithms, and patterns, and make sure you are aware of the Standard Library in C++, as well as any proprietary code available at your workplace.

Specify Error Handling for Each Subsystem

In this design step, you delineate the error handling in each subsystem. The error handling should include both system errors, such as network access failures, and user errors, such as invalid entries. You should specify whether each subsystem uses exceptions. You can again summarize this information in a table.

SUBSYSTEM	HANDLING SYSTEM ERRORS	HANDLING USER ERRORS
GamePlay	Logs an error with the `ErrorLogger`, shows a message to the user, and gracefully shuts down the program when an unexpected error occurs.	Not applicable (no direct user interface).
ChessBoard ChessPiece	Logs an error with the `ErrorLogger` and throws an exception when an unexpected error occurs.	Not applicable (no direct user interface).
ChessBoardView ChessPieceView	Logs an error with the `ErrorLogger` and throws an exception if something goes wrong during drawing.	Not applicable (no direct user interface).

continues

(continued)

SUBSYSTEM	HANDLING SYSTEM ERRORS	HANDLING USER ERRORS
Player	Logs an error with the `ErrorLogger` and throws an exception when an unexpected error occurs.	Sanity checks a user's move entry to ensure that it is not off the board; it then prompts the user for another entry. This subsystem checks each move's legality before moving the piece; if illegal, it prompts the user for another move.
ErrorLogger	Attempts to log an error; informs the user when an unexpected error occurs.	Not applicable (no direct user interface).

The general rule for error handling is to handle everything. Think hard about all possible error conditions. If you forget one possibility, it will show up as a bug in your program! Don't treat anything as an "unexpected" error. Expect all possibilities: memory allocation failures, invalid user entries, disk failures, and network failures, to name a few. However, as the table for the chess game shows, you should handle user errors differently from internal errors. For example, a user entering an invalid move should not cause your chess program to terminate. Chapter 14, "Handling Errors," discusses error handling in more depth.

SUMMARY

In this chapter, you learned about the professional C++ approach to design. I hope that it convinced you that software design is an important first step in any programming project. In fact, it is not just the first step, but designs need to be kept up-to-date with each incremental improvement of the code.

You learned about some of the aspects of C++ that make design difficult, including the multi-paradigm capabilities of the language supporting both object-oriented and procedural designs, its large feature set and Standard Library, and its facilities for writing generic code. With this information, you are better prepared to tackle C++ design.

This chapter introduced two design themes. The first theme, the concept of abstraction, or separating interface from implementation, permeates this book and should be a guideline for all your design work.

The second theme, the notion of reuse, both of code and designs, also arises frequently in real-world projects, and in this book. You learned that your C++ designs should include both reuse of code, in the form of libraries and frameworks, and reuse of ideas and designs, in the form of techniques and patterns. You should write your code to be as reusable as possible. Also remember about the trade-offs and about specific guidelines for reusing code, including understanding the capabilities and limitations, the performance, licensing and support models, the platform limitations, prototyping, and where to find help. You also learned about performance analysis and big-O notation. Now that you understand the importance of design and the basic design themes, you are ready for the rest of Part II. Chapter 5 describes strategies for using the object-oriented aspects of C++ in your design.

EXERCISES

By solving the following exercises, you can practice the material discussed in this chapter. Solutions to all exercises are available with the code download on the book's website at `www.wiley.com/go/proc++6e`. However, if you are stuck on an exercise, first reread parts of this chapter to try to find an answer yourself before looking at the solution from the website.

Exercise 4-1: What are the two fundamental design rules to follow when making your own designs in C++?

Exercise 4-2: Suppose you have the following `Card` class. The class supports only the normal cards in a card deck and not joker cards.

```
class Card
{
    public:
        enum class Number { Ace, Two, Three, Four, Five, Six, Seven, Eight,
            Nine, Ten, Jack, Queen, King };
        enum class Figure { Diamond, Heart, Spade, Club };

        Card() {}
        Card(Number number, Figure figure)
            : m_number { number }, m_figure { figure } {}
    private:
        Number m_number { Number::Ace };
        Figure m_figure { Figure::Diamond };
};
```

What do you think of the following use of the `Card` class to represent a deck of cards? Are there any improvements you can think of?

```
int main()
{
    Card deck[52];
    // ...
}
```

Exercise 4-3: Suppose that you, together with a friend, came up with a nice idea for making a 3-D game for mobile devices. You have an Android device, while your friend has an Apple iPhone, and of course you want the game to be playable on both devices. Explain on a high level how you will handle those two different mobile platforms and how you will prepare for starting development of the game.

Exercise 4-4: Given the following big-O complexities: $O(n)$, $O(n^2)$, $O(\log n)$, and $O(1)$, can you order them according to increasing complexity? What are their names? Can you think of any complexities that are even worse than these?

5

Designing with Classes

WHAT'S IN THIS CHAPTER?

- What object-oriented programming design is
- What classes, objects, properties, and behaviors are
- How you can define relationships between different classes

Now that you have developed an appreciation for good software design from Chapter 4, "Designing Professional C++ Programs," it's time to pair the notion of classes with the concept of good design. The difference between programmers who use classes in their code and those who truly grasp object-oriented programming comes down to the way their classes relate to each other and to the overall design of the program.

This chapter begins with a brief description of procedural programming (C-style), followed by a detailed discussion of object-oriented programming (OOP). Even if you've been using classes for years, you will want to read this chapter for some new ideas regarding how to think about classes. I will discuss the different kinds of relationships between classes, including pitfalls programmers often succumb to when building an object-oriented program.

When thinking about procedural programming or object-oriented programming, the most important point to remember is that they just represent different ways of reasoning about what's going on in your program. Too often, programmers get bogged down in the syntax and jargon of OOP before they adequately understand what a class is and what objects are. This chapter is light on code and heavy on concepts and ideas. Chapters 8, "Gaining Proficiency with Classes and Objects," 9, "Mastering Classes and Objects," and 10, "Discovering Inheritance Techniques," go deeper in on C++ class syntax.

AM I THINKING PROCEDURALLY?

A procedural language, such as C, divides code into small pieces, each of which (ideally) accomplishes a single task. Without procedures in C, all your code would be lumped together inside `main()`. Your code would be difficult to read, and your co-workers would be annoyed, to say the least.

The computer doesn't care if all your code is in `main()` or if it's split into bite-sized pieces with descriptive names and comments. Procedures are an abstraction that exists to help you, the programmer, as well as those who read and maintain your code. The concept is built around a fundamental question about your program—*What does this program do?* By answering that question in English, you are thinking procedurally. For example, you might begin designing a stock selection program by answering as follows: First, the program obtains stock quotes from the Internet. Then, it sorts this data by specific metrics. Next, it performs analysis on the sorted data. Finally, it outputs a list of buy and sell recommendations. When you start coding, you might directly turn this mental model into C functions: `retrieveQuotes()`, `sortQuotes()`, `analyzeQuotes()`, and `outputRecommendations()`.

> **NOTE** *Even though C refers to procedures as "functions," C is not a functional language. The term functional is different from procedural and refers to languages like Lisp, which use an entirely different abstraction.*

The procedural approach tends to work well when your program follows a specific list of steps. However, in large, modern applications, there is rarely a linear sequence of events. Often a user is able to perform any command at any time. Procedural thinking also says nothing about data representation. In the previous example, there was no discussion of what a stock quote actually is.

If the procedural mode of thought sounds like the way you approach a program, don't worry. Once you realize that OOP is simply an alternative, more flexible way of thinking about software, it'll come naturally.

THE OBJECT-ORIENTED PHILOSOPHY

Unlike the procedural approach, which is based on the question "What does this program do?" the object-oriented approach asks another question: "What real-world objects am I modeling?" OOP is based on the notion that you should divide your program not into tasks but into models of physical objects. While this seems abstract at first, it becomes clearer when you consider physical objects in terms of their *classes*, *components*, *properties*, and *behaviors*.

Classes

A class helps distinguish an object from its definition. Consider the orange. There's a difference between talking about oranges in general as tasty fruit that grows on trees and talking about a specific orange, such as the one that's currently dripping juice on my keyboard.

When answering the question "What are oranges?" you are talking about the *class* of things known as oranges. All oranges are fruit. All oranges grow on trees. All oranges are some shade of orange. All oranges have some particular flavor. A class is simply the encapsulation of what defines a classification of objects.

When describing a specific orange, you are talking about an *object*. All objects belong to a particular class. Because the object on my desk is an orange, I know that it belongs to the orange class. Thus, I know that it is a fruit that grows on trees. I can further say that it is a medium shade of orange and ranks "mighty tasty" in flavor. An object is an *instance* of a class—a particular item with characteristics that distinguish it from other instances of the same class.

As a more concrete example, reconsider the stock selection application from earlier. In OOP, "stock quote" is a class because it defines the abstract notion of what makes up a quote. A specific quote, such as "current Microsoft stock quote," would be an object because it is a particular instance of the class.

From a C background, think of classes and objects as analogous to types and variables. In fact, Chapter 1, "A Crash Course in C++ and the Standard Library," shows that the syntax for classes is similar to the syntax for C structs.

Components

If you consider a complex real-world object, such as an airplane, it should be fairly easy to see that it is made up of smaller *components*. There's the fuselage, the controls, the landing gear, the engines, and numerous other parts. The ability to think of objects in terms of their smaller components is essential to OOP, just as the breaking up of complicated tasks into smaller procedures is fundamental to procedural programming.

A component is essentially the same thing as a class, just smaller and more specific. A good object-oriented program might have an `Airplane` class, but this class would be huge if it fully described an airplane. Instead, the `Airplane` class deals with many smaller, more manageable, components. Each of these components might have further subcomponents. For example, the landing gear is a component of an airplane, and the wheel is a component of the landing gear.

Properties

Properties are what distinguish one object from another. Going back to the `Orange` class, recall that all oranges are defined as having some shade of orange and a particular flavor. These two characteristics are properties. All oranges have the same properties, just with different values. My orange has a "mighty tasty" flavor, but yours may have a "terribly unpleasant" flavor.

You can also think about properties on the class level. As recognized earlier, all oranges are fruit and grow on trees. These are properties of the fruit class, whereas the specific shade of orange is determined by the particular fruit object. Class properties are shared by all objects of a class, while object properties are present in all objects of the class, but with different values.

In the stock selection example, a stock quote has several object properties, including the name of the company, its ticker symbol, the current price, and other statistics.

Properties are the characteristics that describe an object. They answer the question, "What makes this object different?"

Behaviors

Behaviors answer either of two questions: "What does this object do?" or "What can I do to this object?" In the case of an orange, it doesn't do a whole lot, but we can do things to it. One behavior is that it can be eaten. Like properties, you can think of behaviors on the class level or the object level. All oranges can pretty much be eaten in the same way. However, they might differ in some other behavior, such as being rolled down an incline, where the behavior of a perfectly round orange would differ from that of a more oblate one.

The stock selection example provides some more practical behaviors. If you recall, when thinking procedurally, I determined that my program needed to analyze stock quotes as one of its functions. Thinking in OOP, you might decide that a stock quote object can analyze itself. Analysis becomes a behavior of the stock quote object.

In object-oriented programming, the bulk of functional code is moved out of procedures and into classes. By building classes that have certain behaviors and defining how they interact, OOP offers a much richer mechanism for attaching code to the data on which it operates. Behaviors for classes are implemented in *class member functions*.

As Chapter 4 explains, C++ is a multi-paradigm language supporting both object-oriented programming and procedural programming. Thus, C++ does not force you to put everything into classes, like languages such as Java do. In C++, you are free to use classes when OOP makes sense, but there is nothing wrong with combining it with procedural programming and keeping certain functionality in stand-alone functions. In fact, a lot of the functionality of the C++ Standard Library is provided as stand-alone functions, e.g., all its algorithms.

Bringing It All Together

With these concepts, you could take another look at the stock selection program and redesign it in an object-oriented manner.

As discussed, "stock quote" would be a fine class to start with. To obtain the list of quotes, the program needs the notion of a group of stock quotes, which is often called a *collection*. So, a better design might be to have a class that represents a "collection of stock quotes," which is made up of smaller components that represent a single "stock quote."

Moving on to properties, the collection class would have at least one property—the actual list of quotes received. It might also have additional properties, such as the exact date and time of the most recent retrieval. As for behaviors, the "collection of stock quotes" would be able to talk to a server to get the quotes and provide a sorted list of quotes. These are the "retrieve quotes" and "sort quotes" behaviors.

The stock quote class would have the properties discussed earlier—name, symbol, current price, and so on. Also, it would have an analyze behavior. You might consider other behaviors, such as buying and selling the stock.

It is often useful to create diagrams showing the relationship between components. Figure 5.1 uses the UML class diagram syntax, see Appendix D, "Introduction to UML," to indicate that a `StockQuoteCollection` contains zero or more (0..*) `StockQuote` objects, and that a `StockQuote` object belongs to a single (1) `StockQuoteCollection`.

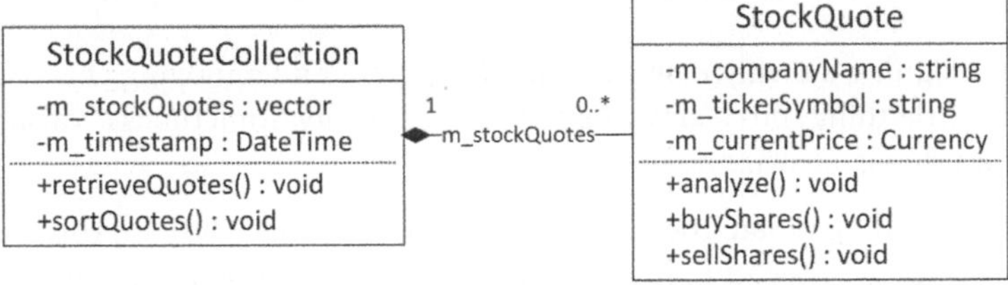

FIGURE 5.1

Let's look at a second example. As described earlier, an orange has properties such as its color and flavor, as well as behaviors such as being eaten and rolled. You can come up with many more behaviors such as being tossed, peeled, or squeezed. Another property of an orange could be a collection of its seeds. Figure 5.2 shows a possible UML class diagram for the `Orange` and `Seed` classes, including the relationship that an `Orange` contains zero or more (0..*) `Seeds` and that a `Seed` belongs to a single (1) `Orange`.

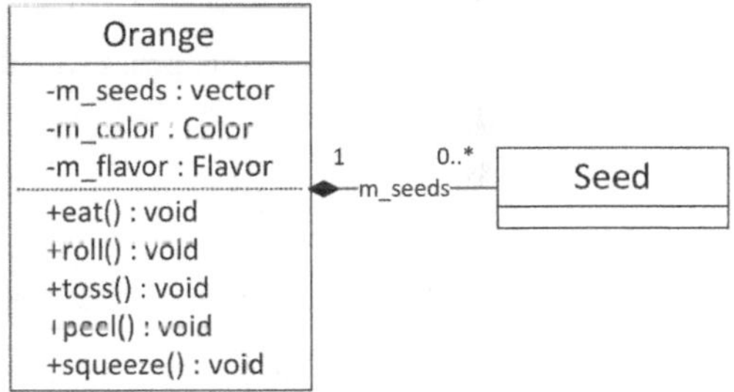

FIGURE 5.2

LIVING IN A WORLD OF CLASSES

Programmers who transition from a procedural thought process to the object-oriented paradigm often experience an epiphany about the combination of properties and behaviors into classes. Some programmers find themselves revisiting the design of programs they're working on and rewriting certain pieces as classes. Others might be tempted to throw all the code away and restart the project as a fully object-oriented application.

There are two major approaches to developing software with classes. To some people, classes simply represent a nice encapsulation of data and functionality. These programmers sprinkle classes throughout their programs to make the code more readable and easier to maintain. Programmers taking this approach slice out isolated pieces of code and replace them with classes like a surgeon implanting a pacemaker. There is nothing inherently wrong with this approach. These people see classes as a tool that is beneficial in many situations. Certain parts of a program just "feel like a class," like the stock quote. These are the parts that can be isolated and described in real-world terms.

Other programmers adopt the OOP paradigm fully and turn everything into a class. In their minds, some classes correspond to real-world things, such as an orange or a stock quote, while others encapsulate more abstract concepts, such as a sorter or an undo class.

The ideal approach is probably somewhere in between these extremes. Your first object-oriented program might really have been a traditional procedural program with a few classes sprinkled in. Or perhaps you went whole hog and made everything a class, from a class representing an `int` to a class representing the main application. Over time, you will find a happy medium.

Over-Classification

There is often a fine line between designing a creative object-oriented system and annoying everybody else on your team by turning every little thing into a class. As Freud used to say, sometimes a variable is just a variable. Okay, that's a paraphrase of what he said.

Perhaps you're designing the next bestselling tic-tac-toe game. You're going all-out OOP on this one, so you sit down with a cup of coffee and a notepad to sketch out your classes and objects. In games like this, there's often a class that oversees game play and is able to detect the winner. To represent the game board, you might envision a `Grid` class that will keep track of the markers and their locations. In fact, a component of the grid could be the `Piece` class that represents an X or an O.

Wait, back up! This design proposes to have a class that represents an X or an O. That is perhaps class overkill. After all, can't a `char` represent an X or an O just as well? Better yet, why can't the `Grid` just use a two-dimensional array of an enumeration type? Does a `Piece` class just complicate the code? Take a look at the following table representing the proposed piece class:

CLASS	ASSOCIATED COMPONENTS	PROPERTIES	BEHAVIORS
Piece	None	X or O	None

The table is a bit sparse, strongly hinting that what we have here may be too granular to be a full-fledged class.

On the other hand, a forward-thinking programmer might argue that while `Piece` is a pretty meager class as it currently stands, making it into a class allows future expansion without any real penalty. Perhaps down the road, additional properties could be added such as the color of the `Piece` or whether the `Piece` was the most recently moved.

Another solution might be to think about the *state* of a grid square instead of using pieces. The state of a square can be Empty, X, or O. To make the design future-proof, you could design an abstract base class `State` with concrete derived classes `StateEmpty`, `StateX`, and `StateO`. With this design, extra properties can be added in the future to the base class or to the individual classes.

Obviously, there is no right answer. The important point is that these are issues that you should consider when designing your application. Remember that classes exist to help programmers manage their code. If classes are being used for no reason other than to make the code "more object-oriented," something is wrong.

Overly General Classes

Perhaps a worse annoyance than classes that shouldn't be classes is classes that are too general. All OOP students start with examples like "orange"—things that are classes, no question about it. In real-life coding, classes can get pretty abstract. Many OOP programs have an "application class," despite that an application isn't really something you can envision in material form. Yet it may be useful to represent the application as a class because the application itself has certain properties and behaviors.

An overly general class is a class that doesn't represent a particular thing at all. The programmer may be attempting to make a class that is flexible or reusable, but ends up with one that is confusing. For example, imagine a program that organizes and displays media. It can catalog your photos, organize your digital music and movie collection, and serve as a personal journal. The overly general approach is to think of all these things as "media" objects and build a single class that can accommodate all of the supported formats. This single class might have a property called "data" that contains the raw bits of the image, song, movie, or journal entry, depending on the type of media. The class might have a behavior called "perform" that appropriately draws the image, plays the song, plays the movie, or brings up the journal entry for editing.

The clues that this single class is too general are in the names of the properties and behaviors. The word *data* has little meaning by itself—you have to use a general term here because this class has been overextended to three very different uses. Similarly, *perform* will do very different things for the different types of media. Clearly, this class is trying to do too much.

Nevertheless, when designing a program to organize media, there for sure will be a `Media` class in your application. This `Media` class will contain the common properties that all types of media have, such as a name, a preview, a link to the corresponding media file, and so on. What this `Media` class should not contain though is the details about handling specific media. It should not contain code to display an image, or to play a song or a movie. Instead, there should be other classes in your design such as a `Picture` class and a `Movie` class. Those specific classes then contain the actual media-specific functionality such as displaying a picture or playing a movie. Obviously, those media-specific classes are somehow related to the `Media` class, and that's exactly the topic of the next section on how to express relationships between classes.

CLASS RELATIONSHIPS

As a programmer, you will certainly encounter cases where different classes have characteristics in common, or seem somehow related to each other. Object-oriented languages provide a number of mechanisms for dealing with such relationships between classes. The tricky part is to understand what the relationship actually is. There are two main types of class relationships—a *has-a* relationship and an *is-a* relationship.

The Has-a Relationship

Classes engaged in a has-a relationship follow the pattern A has a B, or A contains a B. In this type of relationship, you can envision one class as part of another. Components, as defined earlier, generally represent a has-a relationship because they describe classes that are made up of other classes.

A real-world example of this might be the relationship between a zoo and a monkey. You could say that a zoo has a monkey or a zoo contains a monkey. A simulation of a zoo in code would have a zoo class, which has a monkey component.

Often, thinking about user interface scenarios is helpful in understanding class relationships. This is so because even though not all UIs are implemented in OOP (though these days, most are), the visual elements on the screen translate well into classes. One UI analogy for a has-a relationship is a window that contains a button. The button and the window are clearly two separate classes, but they are obviously related in some way. Because the button is inside the window, you say that the window has a button.

Figure 5.3 shows a real-world and a user interface has-a relationship.

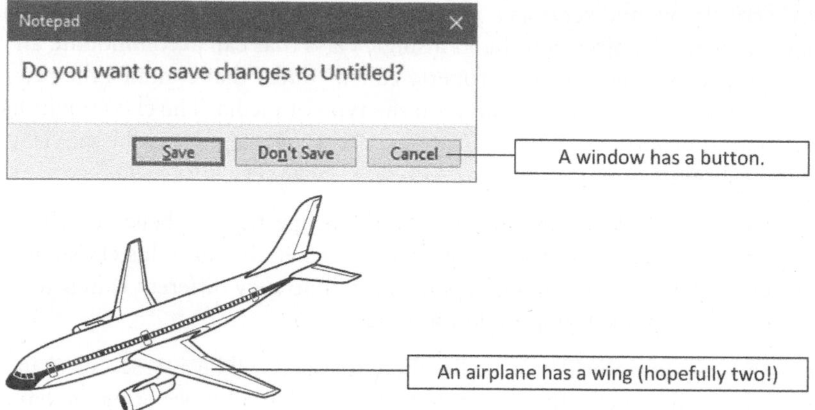

FIGURE 5.3

There are two types of has-a relationships:

- **Aggregation:** With aggregation, the aggregated objects (components) can continue to live when the aggregator is destroyed. For example, suppose a zoo object contains a bunch of animal objects. When the zoo object is destroyed because it went bankrupt, the animal objects are (ideally) not destroyed; they are moved to another zoo.
- **Composition:** With composition, if an object composed of other objects is destroyed, those other objects are destroyed as well. For example, if a window object containing buttons is destroyed, those button objects are destroyed as well.

The Is-a Relationship (Inheritance)

The is-a relationship is such a fundamental concept of object-oriented programming that it has many names, including *deriving*, *subclassing*, *extending*, and *inheriting*. Classes model the fact that the real world contains objects with properties and behaviors. Inheritance models the fact that these objects tend to be organized in hierarchies. These hierarchies indicate is-a relationships.

Fundamentally, inheritance follows the pattern A is a B or A is really quite a bit like B—it can get tricky. To stick with the simple case, revisit the zoo, but assume that there are other animals besides monkeys. That statement alone has already constructed the relationship—a monkey is an animal. Similarly, a giraffe is an animal, a kangaroo is an animal, and a penguin is an animal. So what? Well, the magic of inheritance comes when you realize that monkeys, giraffes, kangaroos, and penguins have certain things in common. These commonalities are characteristics of animals in general.

What this means for the programmer is that you can define an `Animal` class that encapsulates all of the properties (size, location, diet, and so on) and behaviors (move, eat, sleep) that pertain to every animal. The specific animals, such as monkeys, become derived classes of `Animal` because a monkey contains all the characteristics of an animal. Remember, a monkey is an animal plus some additional characteristics that make it distinct. Figure 5.4 shows an inheritance diagram for animals. The arrows indicate the direction of the is-a relationship.

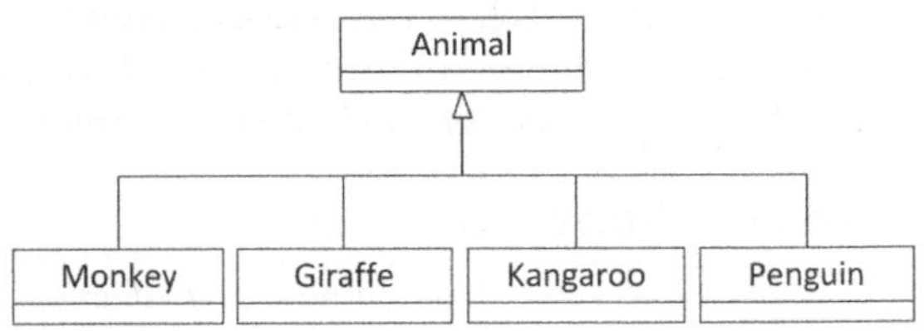

FIGURE 5.4

Just as monkeys and giraffes are different types of animals, a user interface often has different types of buttons. A checkbox, for example, is a button. Assuming that a button is simply a UI element that can be clicked to perform an action, a `Checkbox` extends the `Button` class by adding state—whether the box is checked or unchecked.

When relating classes in an is-a relationship, one goal is to factor common functionality into the *base class*, the class that other classes extend. If you find that all of your derived classes have code that is similar or exactly the same, consider how you could move some or all of that code into the base class. That way, any changes that need to be made only happen in one place and future derived classes get the shared functionality "for free."

> **NOTE** *Sometimes, it is clear whether a relationship represents a has-a or an is-a relationship. Other times, it is not so clear. If you can choose, has-a is preferred over is-a, as explained with an example later in this section.*

Inheritance Techniques

The preceding examples cover a few of the techniques used in inheritance without formalizing them. When deriving classes, there are several ways that the programmer can distinguish a class from its *parent class*, also called *base class* or *superclass*. A derived class may use one or more of these techniques, and they are recognized by completing the sentence, "A is a B that is . . . ."

Adding Functionality

A derived class can augment its parent by adding additional functionality. For example, a monkey is an animal that can swing from trees. In addition to having all of the member functions of `Animal`, the `Monkey` class also has a `swingFromTrees()` member function, which is specific to only the `Monkey` class.

Replacing Functionality

A derived class can replace or *override* a member function of its parent entirely. For example, most animals move by walking, so you might give the `Animal` class a `move()` member function that simulates walking. If that's the case, a kangaroo is an animal that moves by hopping instead of walking. All the other properties and member functions of the `Animal` base class still apply, but the `Kangaroo` derived class simply changes the way that the `move()` member function works. Of course, if you find yourself replacing all of the functionality of your base class, it may be an indication that inheriting was not the correct thing to do after all, unless the base class is an *abstract base class*. An abstract base class forces each of the derived classes to implement all member functions that do not have an implementation in the abstract base class. You cannot create instances of an abstract base class. Abstract base classes are discussed in Chapter 10, "Discovering Inheritance Techniques."

Adding Properties

A derived class can also add new properties to the ones that are inherited from the base class. For example, a penguin has all the properties of an animal but also has a beak size property.

Replacing Properties

C++ provides a way of overriding properties similar to the way you can override member functions. However, doing so is rarely appropriate, because it hides the property from the base class; that is, the base class can have a specific value for a property with a certain name, while the derived class can have another value for another property but with the same name. Hiding is explained in more detail in Chapter 10. It's important not to get the notion of replacing a property confused with the notion of derived classes having different values for properties. For example, all animals have a diet property that indicates what they eat. Monkeys eat bananas and penguins eat fish, but neither of these is replacing the diet property—they simply differ in the value assigned to the property.

Polymorphism

Polymorphism is the notion that objects that adhere to a standard set of properties and member functions can be used interchangeably. A class definition is like a contract between objects and the code that interacts with them. By definition, any `Monkey` object must support the properties and member functions of the `Monkey` class.

This notion extends to base classes as well. Because all monkeys are animals, all `Monkey` objects support the properties and member functions of the `Animal` class as well.

Polymorphism is a beautiful part of object-oriented programming because it truly takes advantage of what inheritance offers. In a zoo simulation, you could programmatically loop through all of the animals in the zoo and have each animal move once. Because all animals are members of the `Animal` class, they all know how to move. Some of the animals have overridden the move member function, but that's the best part—your code simply tells each animal to move without knowing or caring what type of animal it is. Each one moves whichever way it knows how.

The Fine Line Between Has-a and Is-a

In the real world, it's pretty easy to classify has-a and is-a relationships between objects. Nobody would claim that an orange has a fruit—an orange is a fruit. In code, things sometimes aren't so clear.

Consider a hypothetical class that represents an associative array, a data structure that efficiently maps a key to a value. For example, an insurance company could use an `AssociativeArray` class to map member IDs to names so that given an ID, it's easy to find the corresponding member name. The member ID is the *key*, and the member name is the *value*.

In a standard associative array implementation, a key is associated with a single value. If the ID 14534 maps to the member name "Kleper, Scott," it cannot also map to the member name "Kleper, Marni." In most implementations, if you tried to add a second value for a key that already has a value, the first value would go away. In other words, if the ID 14534 mapped to "Kleper, Scott" and you then assigned the ID 14534 to "Kleper, Marni," then Scott would effectively be uninsured. This is demonstrated in the following sequence, which shows two calls to a hypothetical `insert()` member function and the resulting contents of the associative array:

```
myArray.insert(14534, "Kleper, Scott");
```

KEYS	VALUES
14534	"Kleper, Scott" [string]

```
myArray.insert(14534, "Kleper, Marni");
```

KEYS	VALUES
14534	"Kleper, Marni" [string]

It's not difficult to imagine uses for a data structure that's like an associative array but allows multiple values for a given key. In the insurance example, a family might have several names that correspond to the same ID. Because such a data structure is similar to an associative array, it would be nice to leverage that functionality somehow. An associative array can have only a single value as a key, but that value can be anything. Instead of a string, the value could be a collection (such as a `vector`) containing the multiple values for the key. Every time you add a new member for an existing ID, you add the name to the collection. This would work as shown in the following sequence:

```
Collection collection;                // Make a new collection.
collection.insert("Kleper, Scott");   // Add a new element to the collection.
myArray.insert(14534, collection);    // Insert the collection into the array.
```

KEYS	VALUES
14534	{"Kleper, Scott"} [Collection]

```
Collection collection { myArray.get(14534) };  // Retrieve the existing collection.
collection.insert("Kleper, Marni");           // Add a new element to the collection.
myArray.insert(14534, collection); // Replace the collection with the updated one.
```

KEYS	VALUES
14534	{"Kleper, Scott", "Kleper, Marni"} [Collection]

Messing around with a collection instead of a string is tedious and requires a lot of repetitive code. It would be preferable to wrap up this multiple-value functionality in a separate class, perhaps called a `MultiAssociativeArray`. The `MultiAssociativeArray` class would work just like

`AssociativeArray` except that behind the scenes, it would store each value as a collection of strings instead of a single string. Clearly, `MultiAssociativeArray` is somehow related to `AssociativeArray` because it is still using an associative array to store the data. What might be unclear is whether that constitutes an is-a or a has-a relationship.

To start with the is-a relationship, imagine that `MultiAssociativeArray` is a derived class of `AssociativeArray`. This will turn out to be a bad idea, but let's run with it as an example of a bad design. `MultiAssociativeArray` would have to override the member function that adds an entry into the array so that it would either create a collection and add the new element or retrieve the existing collection and add the new element to it. It would also have to override the member function that retrieves a value. There is a complication, though: the overridden `get()` member function should return a single value, not a collection. Which value should a `MultiAssociativeArray` return? One option is to return the first value associated with a given key. An additional `getAll()` member function could be added to retrieve all values associated with a key. This might seem like a reasonable design. Even though it overrides all the member functions of the base class, it still makes use of the base class's member functions from within the derived class. Figure 5.5 shows this approach as a UML class diagram.

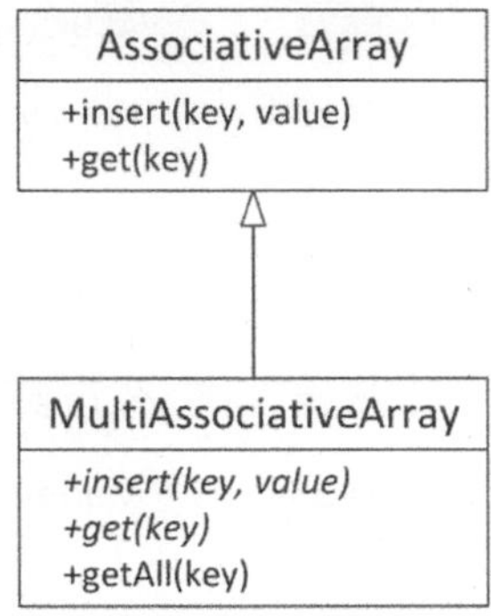

FIGURE 5.5

Now consider it as a has-a relationship. `MultiAssociativeArray` is its own class, but it contains an `AssociativeArray` object. It probably has an interface similar to `AssociativeArray`, but it need not be the same. Behind the scenes, when a user adds something to the `MultiAssociativeArray`, it is really wrapped in a collection and put in an `AssociativeArray` object. This seems perfectly reasonable and is shown in Figure 5.6.

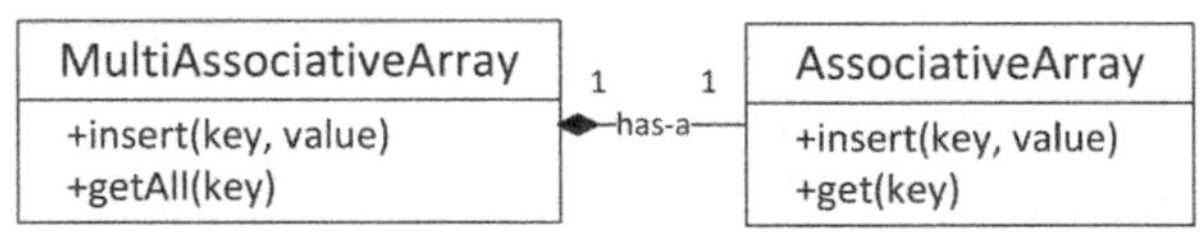

FIGURE 5.6

So, which solution is right? There seems to be no clear answer, but decades of experience have taught us that has-a is usually the better of the two alternatives. The main reason is to allow modifications to the exposed interface without worrying about maintaining associative array functionality. For example, in Figure 5.6, the `get()` member function is changed to `getAll()`, making it clear that this gets all the values for a particular key in a `MultiAssociativeArray`. Additionally, with a has-a relationship, you don't have to worry about any associative array functionality bleeding through. For example, with an is-a relationship, if the associative array class supported a member function that would get the total number of values, it would report the number of collections unless `MultiAssociativeArray` knew to override it.

That said, one could try to make an argument that a `MultiAssociativeArray` actually is an `AssociativeArray` with some new functionality, and it should have been an is-a relationship. The point is that there is sometimes a fine line between the two relationships, and you will need to consider how the class is going to be used and whether what you are building just leverages some functionality from another class or really is that class with modified or new functionality.

The following table represents the arguments for and against taking either approach for the MultiAssociativeArray class:

	IS-A	HAS-A
Reasons For	Fundamentally, it's the same abstraction with different characteristics. It provides (almost) the same member functions as AssociativeArray.	MultiAssociativeArray can have whatever member functions are useful without needing to worry about what member functions AssociativeArray has. The implementation could change to something other than an AssociativeArray without changing the exposed member functions.
Reasons Against	An associative array by definition has one value per key. To say MultiAssociativeArray is an associative array is blasphemy! MultiAssociativeArray overrides both member functions of AssociativeArray, a strong sign that something about the design is wrong. Unknown or inappropriate properties or member functions of AssociativeArray could "bleed through" to MultiAssociativeArray.	In a sense, MultiAssociativeArray reinvents the wheel by coming up with new member functions. Some additional properties and member functions of AssociativeArray might have been useful.

The reasons against using an is-a relationship in this case are very strong. Additionally, the *Liskov substitution principle* (LSP) can help you decide between an is-a and a has-a relationship. This principle states that you should be able to use a derived class instead of a base class without altering the behavior. Applied to this example, it states that this must be a has-a relationship, because you cannot just start using a MultiAssociativeArray where before you were using an AssociativeArray. If you would do so, the behavior would change. For example, the insert() member function of AssociativeArray removes an earlier value with the same key that is already in the array, while MultiAssociativeArray does not remove such values.

The two solutions explained in detail in this section are actually not the only two possible solutions. Other options could be for AssociativeArray to contain a MultiAssociativeArray, or both AssociativeArray and MultiAssociativeArray could inherit from a common base class, and so on. There are often a multitude of solutions that you can come up with for a certain design.

> **WARNING** *If you do have a choice between the two types of relationships, I recommend, after years of experience, opting for a has-a relationship over an is-a relationship.*

Note that the `AssociativeArray` and `MultiAssociativeArray` are used here to demonstrate the difference between the is-a and has-a relationships. In your own code, it is recommended to use one of the standard associative array classes instead of writing your own. The C++ Standard Library provides `std::map`, which you should use instead of `AssociativeArray`, and `std::multimap`, which you should use instead of `MultiAssociativeArray`. Both of these standard classes are discussed in Chapter 18, "Standard Library Containers."

The Not-a Relationship

As you consider what type of relationship classes have, you should consider whether they actually have a relationship at all. Don't let your zeal for object-oriented design turn into a lot of needless class/derived-class relationships.

One pitfall occurs when things are obviously related in the real world but have no actual relationship in code. Object-oriented hierarchies need to model *functional* relationships, not artificial ones. Figure 5.7 shows relationships that are meaningful as ontologies or hierarchies but are unlikely to represent meaningful relationships in code.

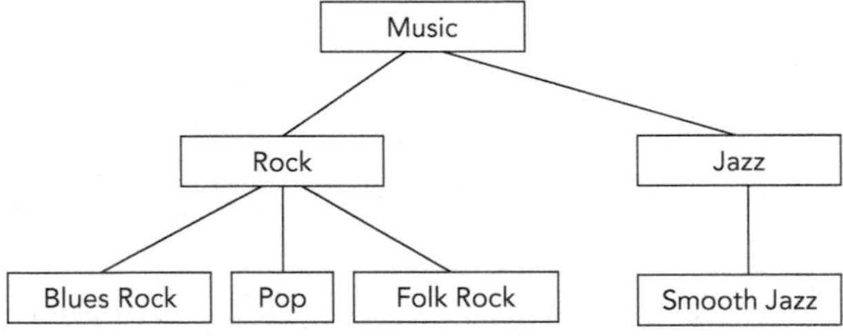

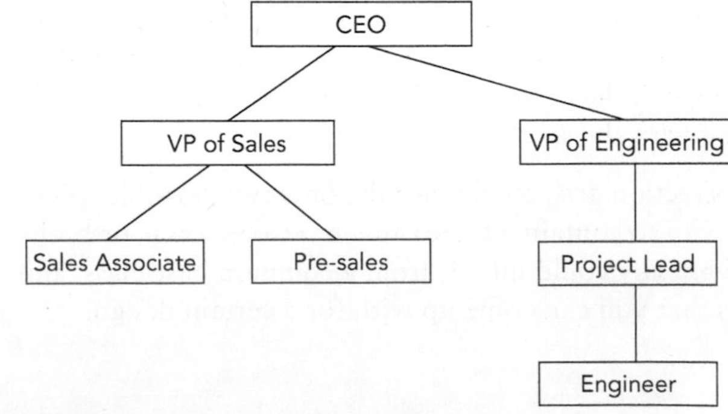

FIGURE 5.7

The best way to avoid needless inheritance is to sketch out your design first. For every class and derived class, write down what properties and member functions you're planning on putting into the class. You should rethink your design if you find that a class has no particular properties or member functions of its own, or if all of those properties and member functions are completely overridden by its derived classes, except when working with abstract base classes as mentioned earlier.

Hierarchies

Just as a class `A` can be a base class of `B`, `B` can also be a base class of `C`. Object-oriented hierarchies can model multilevel relationships like this. A zoo simulation with more animals might be designed with every animal as a derived class of a common `Animal` class, as shown in Figure 5.8.

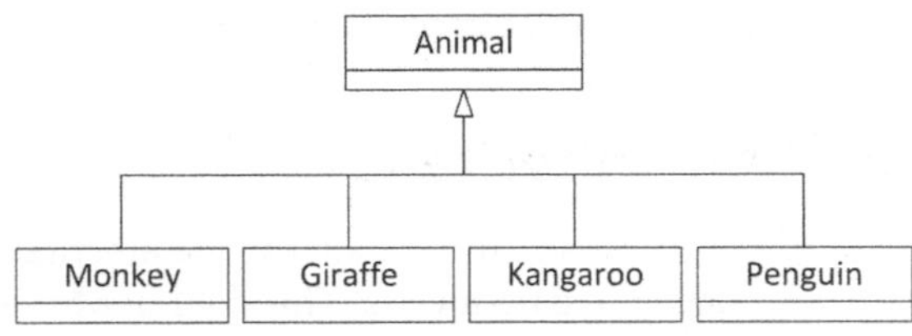

FIGURE 5.8

As you code each of these derived classes, you might find that a lot of them are similar. When this occurs, you should consider putting in a common parent. Realizing that `Lion` and `Panther` both move the same way and have the same diet might indicate a need for a possible `BigCat` class. You could further subdivide the `Animal` class to include `WaterAnimal` and `Marsupial`. Figure 5.9 shows a more hierarchical design that leverages this commonality.

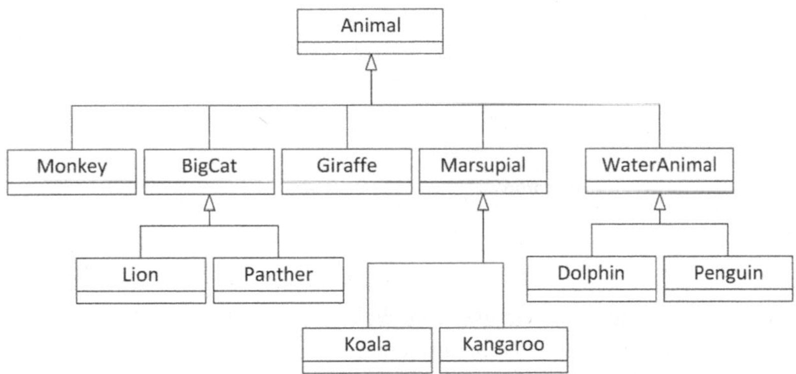

FIGURE 5.9

A biologist looking at this hierarchy may be disappointed—a penguin isn't really in the same family as a dolphin. However, it underlines a good point—in code, you need to balance real-world relationships with shared-functionality relationships. Even though two things might be closely related in the real world, they might have a not-a relationship in code because they really don't share functionality. You could just as easily divide animals into mammals and fish, but that wouldn't factor any commonality to the base class.

Another important point is that there could be other ways of organizing the hierarchy. The preceding design is organized mostly by how the animals move. If it were instead organized by the animals' diet or height, the hierarchy could be very different. In the end, what matters is how the classes will be used. The needs will dictate the design of the class hierarchy.

A good object-oriented hierarchy accomplishes the following:

- Organizes classes into meaningful functional relationships
- Supports code reuse by factoring common functionality to base classes
- Avoids having derived classes that override much of the parent's functionality, unless the parent is an abstract base class

Multiple Inheritance

Every example so far has had a single inheritance chain. In other words, a given class has, at most, one immediate parent class. This does not have to be the case. Through multiple inheritance, a class can have more than one base class.

Figure 5.10 shows a multiple inheritance design. There is still a base class called `Animal`, which is further divided by size. A separate hierarchy categorizes by diet, and a third takes care of movement. Each type of animal is then a derived class of all three of these classes, as shown by different lines.

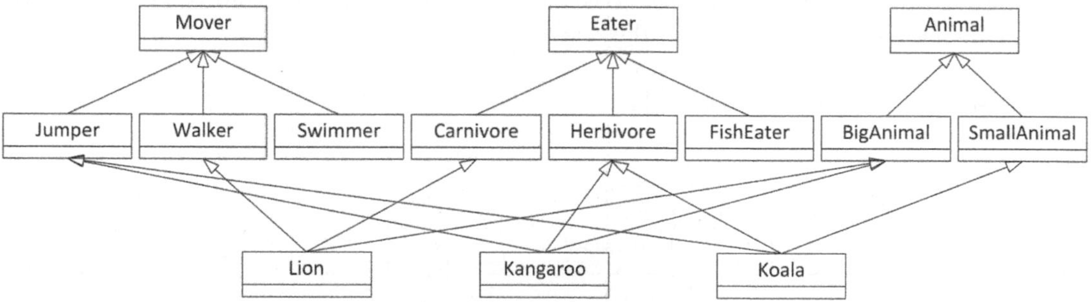

FIGURE 5.10

In a user interface context, imagine an image that the user can click. This class seems to be both a button and an image so the implementation might involve inheriting from both the `Image` class and the `Button` class, as shown in Figure 5.11.

Button
Image
PictureButton

FIGURE 5.11

Multiple inheritance can be useful in certain cases, but it also has a number of disadvantages that you should always keep in mind. Many programmers dislike multiple inheritance. C++ has explicit support for such relationships, though the Java language does away with them altogether, except for inheriting from multiple interfaces (abstract base classes). There are several reasons to which multiple inheritance critics point.

First, visualizing multiple inheritance is complicated. As you can see in Figure 5.10, even a simple class diagram can become complicated when there are multiple hierarchies and crossing lines.

Class hierarchies are supposed to make it easier for the programmer to understand the relationships between code. With multiple inheritance, a class could have several parents that are in no way related to each other. With so many classes contributing code to your object, can you really keep track of what's going on?

Second, multiple inheritance can destroy otherwise clean hierarchies. In the animal example, switching to a multiple inheritance approach means that the `Animal` base class is less meaningful because the code that describes animals is now separated into three separate hierarchies. While the design illustrated in Figure 5.10 shows three clean hierarchies, it's not difficult to imagine how they could get messy. For example, what if you realize that all `Jumpers` not only move in the same way, but they also eat the same things? Because there are separate hierarchies, there is no way to join the concepts of movement and diet without adding yet another derived class.

Third, implementation of multiple inheritance is complicated. What if two of your base classes implement the same member function in different ways? Can you have two base classes that are themselves a derived class of a common base class? These possibilities complicate the implementation because structuring such intricate relationships in code is difficult both for the author and a reader.

The reason that other languages can leave out multiple inheritance is that it is usually avoidable. By rethinking your hierarchies, you can often avoid introducing multiple inheritance when you have control over the design of a project.

Mixin Classes

Mixin classes represent another type of relationship between classes. In C++, one way to implement a mixin class is syntactically just like multiple inheritance, but the semantics are refreshingly different. A mixin class answers the question, "What *else* is this class able to do?" and the answer often ends with "-able." Mixin classes are a way that you can add functionality to a class without committing to a full is-a relationship. You can think of it as a ***shares-with*** relationship.

Going back to the zoo example, you might want to introduce the notion that some animals are "pettable." That is, there are some animals that visitors to the zoo can pet, presumably without being bitten or mauled. You might want all pettable animals to support the behavior "be pet." Because pettable animals don't have anything else in common and you don't want to break the existing hierarchy you've designed, `Pettable` makes a great mixin class.

Mixin classes are used frequently in user interfaces. Instead of saying that a `PictureButton` class is both an `Image` and a `Button`, you might say that it's an `Image` that is `Clickable`. A folder icon on your desktop could be an `Image` that is `Draggable` and `Clickable`. Software developers tend to make up a lot of fun adjectives.

The difference between a mixin class and a base class has more to do with how you think about the class than any code difference. In general, mixin classes are easier to digest than multiple inheritance because they are very limited in scope. The `Pettable` mixin class just adds one behavior to any existing class. The `Clickable` mixin class might just add "mouse down" and "mouse up" behaviors. Additionally, mixin classes rarely have a large hierarchy so there's no cross-contamination of functionality. Chapter 32, "Incorporating Design Techniques and Frameworks," goes into more detail on mixin classes.

SUMMARY

In this chapter, you've gained an appreciation for the design of object-oriented programs without a lot of code getting in the way. The concepts you've learned are applicable to almost any object-oriented language. Some of it may have been a review to you, or it may be a new way of formalizing a familiar concept. Perhaps you picked up some new approaches to old problems or new arguments in favor of the concepts you've been preaching to your team all along. Even if you've never used classes in your code, or have used them only sparingly, you now know more about how to design object-oriented programs than many experienced C++ programmers.

The relationships between classes are important to study, not just because well-linked classes contribute to code reuse and reduce clutter, but also because you will be working in a team. Classes that relate in meaningful ways are easier to read and maintain. You may decide to use the "Class Relationships" section as a reference when you design your programs.

The next chapter continues the design theme by explaining how to design your code with reuse in mind.

EXERCISES

By solving the following exercises, you can practice the material discussed in this chapter. Solutions to all exercises are available with the code download on the book's website at `www.wiley.com/go/proc++6e`. However, if you are stuck on an exercise, first reread parts of this chapter to try to find an answer yourself before looking at the solution from the website.

For the exercises in this chapter, there is no single correct solution. As you have learned in the course of this chapter, a specific problem often has several design solutions with different trade-offs. The solutions accompanying these exercises explain one possible design, but that doesn't mean the solutions you came up with must match those.

Exercise 5-1: Suppose you want to write a car racing game. You will need some kind of model for the car itself. Assume for this exercise there is only one type of car. Each instance of that car needs to keep track of several properties, such as the current power output of its engine, the current fuel usage, the tire pressure, whether or not its driving lights are switched on, whether the windshield wipers are active, and so on. The game should allow players to configure their car with different engines, different tires, custom driving lights and windshield wipers, and so on. How would you model such a car and why?

Exercise 5-2: Continuing the racing game from Exercise 5-1, you of course want to include support for human-driven cars, but also cars driven by an artificial intelligence (AI). How would you model this in your game?

Exercise 5-3: Suppose part of a human resources (HR) application has the following three classes:

- **`Employee`:** Keeping track of employee ID, salary, date when employee started working, and so on
- **`Person`:** Keeping track of a name and address
- **`Manager`:** Keeping track of which employees are in their team

What do you think of the high-level class diagram in Figure 5.12? Are there any changes you would make to it? The diagram doesn't show any properties or behaviors of the different classes, as that's the topic of Exercise 5-4.

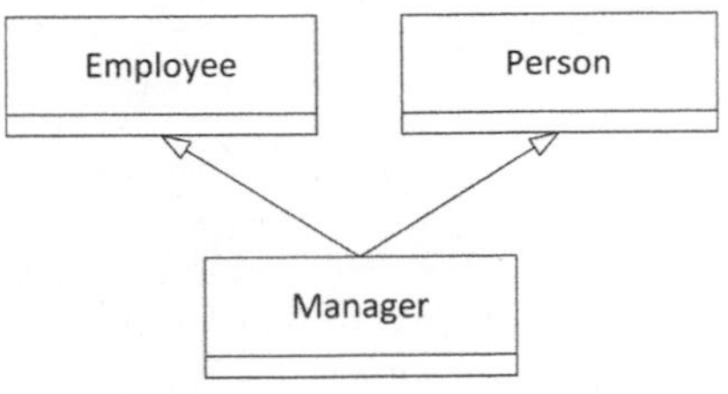

FIGURE 5.12

Exercise 5-4: Start from the final class diagram for Exercise 5-3. Add a couple of behaviors and properties to the class diagram. Finally, model the fact that a manager manages a team of employees.

6 Designing for Reuse

WHAT'S IN THIS CHAPTER?

- The reuse philosophy: Why you should design code for reuse
- How to design reusable code
- How to use abstraction
- Strategies for structuring your code for reuse
- Six strategies for designing usable interfaces
- How to reconcile generality with ease of use
- The SOLID principles

Reusing libraries and other code in your programs as discussed in Chapter 4, "Designing Professional C++ Programs," is an important design strategy. However, it is only half of the *reuse* strategy. The other half is designing and writing your own code that you can reuse in your programs. As you've probably discovered, there is a significant difference between well-designed and poorly designed libraries. Well-designed libraries are a pleasure to use, while poorly designed libraries can prod you to give up in disgust and write the code yourself. Whether you're writing a library explicitly designed for use by other programmers or merely deciding on a class hierarchy, you should design your code with reuse in mind. You never know when you'll need a similar piece of functionality in a subsequent project.

Chapter 4 introduces the design theme of reuse and explains how to apply this theme by incorporating libraries and other code into your designs, but it doesn't explain *how* to design reusable code. That is the topic of this chapter. It builds on the object-oriented design principles described in Chapter 5, "Designing with Classes."

THE REUSE PHILOSOPHY

You should design code that both you and other programmers can reuse. This rule applies not only to libraries and frameworks that you specifically intend for other programmers to use but also to any class, subsystem, or component that you design for a program. You should always keep in mind the following mottos:

- "Write once, use often."
- "Try to avoid code duplication."
- "DRY—Don't Repeat Yourself."

There are several reasons for this:

- **Code is rarely used in only one program.** You can be sure that your code will be used again somehow, so design it correctly to begin with.
- **Designing for reuse saves time and money.** If you design your code in a way that precludes future use, you ensure that you or your partners will spend time reinventing the wheel later when you encounter a need for a similar piece of functionality.
- **Other programmers in your group must be able to use the code that you write.** You are probably not working alone on a project. Your co-workers will appreciate your efforts to offer them well-designed, functionality-packed libraries and pieces of code to use. Designing for reuse can also be called *cooperative coding*.
- **Lack of reuse leads to code duplication; code duplication leads to a maintenance nightmare.** If a bug is found in duplicated code, it has to be fixed in all places where it got duplicated. Whenever you find yourself copy-pasting a piece of code, you have to at least consider moving it out to a helper function or class.
- **You will be the primary beneficiary of your own work.** Experienced programmers never throw away code. Over time, they build a personal library of evolving tools. You never know when you will need a similar piece of functionality in the future.

> **WARNING** *When you design or write code as an employee of a company, the company, not you, generally owns the intellectual property rights. It is often illegal to retain copies of your designs or code when you terminate your employment with the company. The same is also true when you are self-employed and working for clients.*

HOW TO DESIGN REUSABLE CODE

Reusable code fulfills two main goals:

- First, it is general enough to use for slightly different purposes or in different application domains. Program components with details of a specific application are difficult to reuse in other programs.

- Second, reusable code is also easy to use. It doesn't require significant time to understand its interface or functionality. Programmers must be able to incorporate it readily into their applications.

The means of *delivering* your library to clients is also important. You can deliver it in source form, and clients just incorporate your source into their project. Another option is to deliver binaries in the form of static libraries, which they link into their application, or in the form of Dynamic Link Libraries (`.dll`) for Windows clients, or shared objects (`.so`) for Linux clients. Each of these delivery mechanisms can impose additional constraints on how you design your reusable code.

> **NOTE** *This chapter uses the term client to refer to a programmer who uses your interfaces. Don't confuse clients with users who run your programs. This chapter also uses the phrase client code to refer to code that is written to use your interfaces.*

The most important strategy for designing reusable code is *abstraction*.

Use Abstraction

The key to abstraction is effectively separating the *interface* from the *implementation*. The implementation is the code you're writing to accomplish the task you set out to accomplish. The interface is the way that other people use your code. In C, the header file that describes the functions in a library you've written is an interface. In object-oriented programming, the collection of publicly accessible class member functions and class properties is the interface of the class. However, a good interface should contain only public member functions. Properties of a class should never be made public but can be exposed through public member functions, also called *getters* and *setters*.

Chapter 4 introduces the principle of abstraction and presents a real-world analogy of a television, which you can use through its interfaces without understanding how it works inside. Similarly, when you design code, you should clearly separate the interface from the implementation. This separation makes the code easier to use, primarily because clients do not need to understand the internal implementation details to use the functionality.

Using abstraction benefits both you and the clients who use your code. Clients benefit because they don't need to worry about the implementation details; they can take advantage of the functionality you offer without understanding how the code really works. You benefit because you can modify the underlying code without changing the interface to the code. Thus, you can provide upgrades and fixes without requiring clients to change their use. With dynamically linked libraries, clients might not even need to rebuild their executables. Finally, you both benefit because you, as the library writer, can specify in the interface exactly what interactions you expect and what functionality you support. Consult Chapter 3, "Coding with Style," for a discussion on how to write documentation. A clear separation of interfaces and implementations will prevent clients from using the library in ways that you didn't intend, which can otherwise cause unexpected behaviors and bugs.

> **WARNING** *When designing your interface, do not expose implementation details to your clients.*

Sometimes libraries require client code to keep information returned from one interface to pass it to another. This information is sometimes called a *handle* and is often used to keep track of specific instances that require state to be remembered between calls. A real-world example of this is OpenGL, a 2D/3D rendering library. Many functions of OpenGL return and work with handles, which are represented by the type `GLuint`. For example, if you use the OpenGL function `glGenBuffers()` to create a buffer, it returns you the buffer as a `GLuint` handle. Whenever you want to call another function to do something with that buffer, you must pass the `GLuint` handle to that function.

If your library design requires a handle, don't expose its internals. Make that handle into an *opaque* class, in which the programmer can't access the internal data members, neither directly nor through public getters or setters. Don't require the client code to tweak variables inside this handle. An example of a bad design would be a library that requires you to set a specific member of a structure in a supposedly opaque handle in order to turn on error logging.

> **NOTE** *Unfortunately, C++ is fundamentally unfriendly to the principle of good abstraction when writing classes. The syntax requires you to combine your* `public` *interfaces and non-public (*`private` *or* `protected`*) data members and member functions together in one class definition, thereby exposing some of the internal implementation details of the class to its clients. Chapter 9, "Mastering Classes and Objects," describes some techniques for working around this in order to present clean interfaces.*

Abstraction is so important that it should guide your entire design. As part of every decision you make, ask yourself whether your choice fulfills the principle of abstraction. Put yourself in your clients' shoes and determine whether you're requiring knowledge of the internal implementation in the interface. You should rarely, if ever, make exceptions to this rule.

While designing reusable code using abstraction, you should focus on the following:

- First, you must *structure the code* appropriately. What class hierarchies will you use? Should you use templates? How should you divide the code into subsystems?
- Second, you must design the *interfaces*, which are the "entries" into your library to access the functionality you provide.

Both topics are discussed in the upcoming sections.

Structure Your Code for Optimal Reuse

You must consider reuse from the beginning of your design on all levels, that is, from a single function, over a class, to entire libraries and frameworks. In the text that follows, all these different levels are called *components*. The following strategies will help you organize your code properly. Note that all of these strategies focus on making your code general purpose. The second aspect of designing reusable code, providing ease of use, is more relevant to your interface design and is discussed later in this chapter.

Avoid Combining Unrelated or Logically Separate Concepts

When you design a component, you should keep it focused on a single task or group of tasks, that is, you should strive for *high cohesion*. This is also known as the *single responsibility principle* (SRP). Don't combine unrelated concepts such as a random number generator and an XML parser.

Even when you are not designing code specifically for reuse, keep this strategy in mind. Entire programs are rarely reused on their own. Instead, pieces or subsystems of the programs are incorporated directly into other applications or are adapted for slightly different uses. Thus, you should design your programs so that you divide logically separate functionality into distinct components that can be reused in different programs. Each such component should have well-defined responsibilities.

This program strategy models the real-world design principle of discrete, interchangeable parts. For example, you could write a `Car` class and put all properties and behaviors of the engine into it. However, engines are separable components that are not tied to other aspects of the car. The engine could be removed from one car and put into another car. A proper design would include an `Engine` class that contains all engine-specific functionality. A `Car` instance then just contains an instance of `Engine`.

Divide Your Programs into Logical Subsystems

You should design your subsystems as discrete components that can be reused independently, that is, strive for *low coupling*. For example, if you are designing a networked game, keep the networking and graphical user interface aspects in separate subsystems. That way, you can reuse either component without dragging in the other one. For example, you might want to write a non-networked game, in which case you could reuse the graphical interface subsystem but wouldn't need the networking aspect. Similarly, you could design a peer-to-peer file-sharing program, in which case you could reuse the networking subsystem but not the graphical user interface functionality.

Make sure to follow the principle of abstraction for each subsystem. Think of each subsystem as a miniature library for which you must provide a coherent and easy-to-use interface. Even if you're the only programmer who ever uses these miniature libraries, you will benefit from well-designed interfaces and implementations that separate logically distinct functionality.

Use Class Hierarchies to Separate Logical Concepts

In addition to dividing your program into logical subsystems, you should avoid combining unrelated concepts at the class level. For example, suppose you want to write a class for a self-driving car. You decide to start with a basic class for a car and incorporate all the self-driving logic directly into it. However, what if you just want a non-self-driving car in your program? In that case, all the logic related to self-driving is useless and might require your program to link with libraries that it could otherwise avoid, such as vision libraries, LIDAR libraries, and so on. One possible solution is to create a class hierarchy (introduced in Chapter 5) in which a self-driving car is a derived class of a generic car. That way, you can use the car base class in programs that do not need self-driving capabilities without incurring the cost of such algorithms. Figure 6.1 shows this hierarchy.

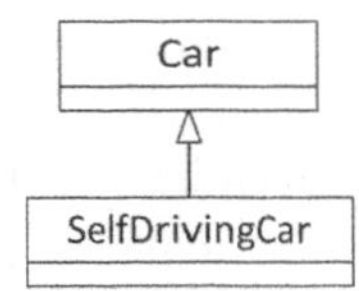

FIGURE 6.1

This strategy works well when there are two logical concepts, such as self-driving and cars. It becomes more complicated when there are three or more concepts. For example, suppose you want to provide both a truck and a car, each of which could be self-driving or not. Logically, both the truck and the car are a special case of a vehicle, and so they could be derived classes of a vehicle class, as shown in Figure 6.2.

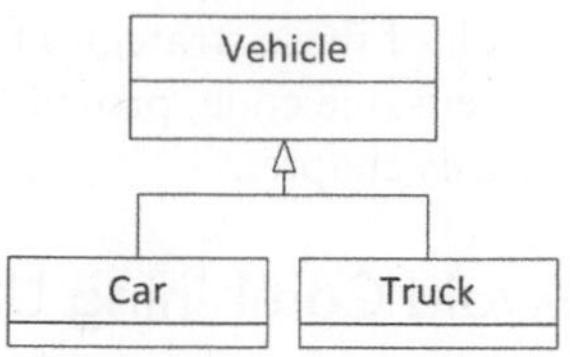

FIGURE 6.2

Similarly, self-driving classes could be derived classes of non-self-driving classes. You can't provide these separations with a linear hierarchy. One possibility is to make the self-driving aspect a mixin class instead. The previous chapter shows one way to implement mixins in C++ by using multiple inheritance. For example, a `PictureButton` could inherit from both an `Image` class and a `Clickable` mixin class. However, for the self-driving design, it's better to use a different kind of mixin implementation, one using class templates.

This example jumps ahead a bit on class template syntax, which is discussed in detail in Chapter 12, "Writing Generic Code with Templates," but those details are not important to follow this discussion. It also jumps ahead a bit on the syntax of inheritance. Chapter 10, "Discovering Inheritance Techniques," discusses inheritance in detail; however, those details are not important to understand this example. For now, you need to know only that the following syntax specifies that the `Derived` class inherits/derives from the `Base` class:

```
class Derived : public Base {};
```

The `SelfDrivable` mixin class template can then be defined as follows:

```
template <typename T>
class SelfDrivable : public T
{
};
```

This `SelfDrivable` mixin class provides all the necessary algorithms for implementing the self-driving functionality. Once you have this `SelfDrivable` mixin class template, you can instantiate one for a car and one for a truck as follows:

```
SelfDrivable<Car> selfDrivingCar;
SelfDrivable<Truck> selfDrivingTruck;
```

The result of these two lines is that the compiler uses the `SelfDrivable` mixin class template to create one instantiation where all `T`'s of the class template are replaced by `Car` and hence is derived from `Car`, and another where the `T`'s are replaced by `Truck` and thus derives from `Truck`. Chapter 32, "Incorporating Design Techniques and Frameworks," goes into more detail on mixin classes.

This solution requires you to write four different classes (`Vehicle`, `Car`, `Truck`, and `SelfDrivable`), but the clear separation of functionality is worth the effort.

Similarly, you should avoid combining unrelated concepts, that is, strive for high cohesion, at any level of your design, not only at the class level. For example, at the level of member functions, a single member function should not perform logically unrelated things, mix mutation (set) and inspection (get), and so on.

Use Aggregation to Separate Logical Concepts

Aggregation, discussed in Chapter 5, models the *has-a* relationship: objects contain other objects to perform some aspects of their functionality. As Chapter 5 explains, if you have a choice, prefer using has-a relationships over is-a relationships.

For example, suppose you want to write a `FamilyTree` class to store the members of a family. Obviously, a tree data structure would be ideal for storing this information. Instead of integrating the tree structure code directly in the `FamilyTree` class, you should write a separate `Tree` class. The `FamilyTree` class can then contain and use a `Tree` instance. To use the object-oriented terminology, `FamilyTree` has-a `Tree`. With this technique, the tree data structure could be reused more easily in another program.

Eliminate User Interface Dependencies

If your library is a data manipulation library, you want to separate data manipulation from the user interface. This means that for those kinds of libraries you should never assume in which type of user interface the library will be used. The library should not use any of the standard console output and input functionality, such as `std::println()` or `cin`, because if the library is used in the context of a graphical user interface, doing so may make no sense. For example, a Windows GUI-based application usually will not have any form of console I/O. If you think your library will only be used in GUI-based applications, you should still never pop up any kind of message box or other kind of notification to the end user, because that is the responsibility of the client code. It's the client code that decides how messages are displayed to the user. These kinds of dependencies not only result in poor reusability, but they also prevent client code from properly responding to an error, for example, to handle it silently.

The Model-View-Controller (MVC) paradigm, introduced in Chapter 4, is a well-known design pattern to separate storing data from visualizing that data. With this paradigm, the model can be in the library, while the client code can provide the view and the controller.

Use Templates for Generic Data Structures and Algorithms

C++ has a concept called *templates* that allows you to create structures that are generic with respect to a type or class. For example, you might have written code for an array of integers. If you subsequently would like an array of `doubles`, you need to rewrite and replicate all the code to work with `doubles`. The notion of a template is that the type becomes a parameter to the specification, and you can create a single body of code that can work on any type. Templates allow you to write both data structures and algorithms that work on any types.

The simplest example of this is the in Chapter 1, "A Crash Course in C++ and the Standard Library," introduced `std::vector` class, which is part of the C++ Standard Library. To create a `vector` of integers, you write `std::vector<int>`; to create a `vector` of `doubles`, you write `std::vector<double>`. Template programming is, in general, extremely powerful but can be very complex. Luckily, it is possible to create rather simple usages of templates that parameterize according to a type. Chapters 12 and 26, "Advanced Templates," explain the techniques to write your own templates, while this section discusses some of their important design aspects.

Whenever possible, you should use a generic design for data structures and algorithms instead of encoding specifics of a particular program. Don't write a balanced binary tree structure that stores only book objects. Make it generic, so that it can store objects of any type. That way, you could use it in a bookstore, a music store, an operating system, or anywhere that you need a balanced binary tree. This strategy underlies the Standard Library, which provides generic data structures and algorithms that work on any types.

However, at the same time, keep in mind that implementing a generic data structure takes more time compared to a non-generic implementation. You will need to think more about requirements, and you will need to test your generic implementation more extensively with many different types. If your data structure is very specific for a specific use case, this extra effort might not pay off, and you might be better off starting with a simple non-generic implementation.

Why Templates Are Better Than Other Generic Programming Techniques

Templates are not the only mechanism for writing generic data structures. Another, albeit older and no longer recommended approach to write generic structures in C and C++ is to store `void*` pointers instead of pointers of a specific type. Clients can use this structure to store anything they want by casting it to a `void*`. However, the main problem with this approach is that it is not *type safe*: the containers are unable to check or enforce the types of the stored elements. You can cast any type to a `void*` to store in the structure, and when you remove the pointers from the data structure, you must cast them back to what you think they are. Because there are no checks involved, the results can be disastrous. Imagine a scenario where one programmer stores pointers to `int` in a data structure by first casting them to `void*`, but another programmer thinks they are pointers to `Process` objects. The second programmer will blithely cast the `void*` pointers to `Process*` pointers and try to use them as `Process*` objects. Needless to say, the program will not work as expected.

Instead of directly using `void*` pointers in your generic non-template-based data structures, you could use the `std::any` class, available since C++17. The `any` class is discussed in Chapter 24, "Additional Vocabulary Types," but for this discussion it's enough to know that you can store any type of object in an instance of the `any` class. The underlying implementation of `std::any` does use a `void*` pointer in certain cases, but it also keeps track of the type stored, so everything remains type safe.

Yet another approach is to write the data structure for a specific class. Through polymorphism, any derived class of that class can be stored in the structure. Java takes this approach to an extreme: it specifies that every class derives directly or indirectly from the `Object` class. The containers in earlier versions of Java store `Objects`, so they can store objects of any type. However, this approach is also not type safe. When you remove an object from the container, you must remember what it really is and down-cast it to the appropriate type. Down casting means casting it to a more specific class in a class hierarchy, that is, casting it downward in the hierarchy.

Templates, on the other hand, are type safe when used correctly. Each instantiation of a template stores only one type. Your program will not compile if you try to store different types in the same template instantiation. Additionally, templates allow the compiler to generate highly optimized code for each template instantiation. Compared to `void*` and `std::any` based data structures, templates can also avoid allocations on the free store, and hence have better performance. Newer versions of Java do support the concept of generics that are type safe just like C++ templates.

> **NOTE** *Templates are ideal for generic programming. They are type safe and result in highly optimized code for each instantiation of the template.*

Problems with Templates

Templates are not perfect. First of all, their syntax might be confusing, especially for someone who has not used them before. Second, templates require homogeneous data structures, in which you can store only objects of the same type in a single structure. That is, if you write a class template for a balanced binary tree, you can create one tree object to store `Process` objects and another tree object to store `int`s. You can't store both `int`s and `Process`es in the same tree. This restriction is a direct result of the type-safe nature of templates.

Another possible disadvantage of templates is called *code bloat*: an increased size of the final binary code. Highly specialized code for each template instantiation takes more code than slightly slower generic code. Usually, however, code bloat is not so much of a problem these days.

Templates vs. Inheritance

Programmers sometimes find it tricky to decide whether to use templates or inheritance. The following are some tips to help you make the decision.

Use templates when you want to provide identical functionality for different types. For example, if you want to write a generic sorting algorithm that works on any type, use a function template. If you want to create a container that can store any type, use a class template. The key concept is that the class- or function template treats all types the same. However, if required, templates can be specialized for specific types to treat those types differently. Template specialization is discussed in Chapter 12.

When you want to provide different behaviors for related types, use inheritance. For example, in a shape-drawing application, use inheritance to support different shapes such as a circle, a square, a line, and so on. The specific shapes then derive from, for example, a `Shape` base class.

Another difference between templates and inheritance is that templates are processed at compile time; thus, all involved types must be known at compile time. This results in compile-time polymorphism. With inheritance, you get run-time polymorphism.

Note that you can combine inheritance and templates. You could write a class template that derives from a base class template. Chapter 12 covers the details of the template syntax.

Provide Appropriate Checks and Safeguards

When you design code with reuse in mind, you need to pay special attention to make sure the code is safe for use in different use cases, not just the use case at hand.

There are two opposite styles for designing safe code. The optimal programming style is probably using a healthy mix of both of them. The first is called *design-by-contract*, which means that the documentation for a function or a class represents a contract with a detailed description of what the responsibility of the client code is and what the responsibility of your function or class is. There are three important aspects of design-by-contract: preconditions, postconditions, and invariants. *Preconditions* list the conditions that client code must satisfy before calling a function. *Postconditions* list the conditions that must be satisfied by the function when it has finished executing. Finally, *invariants* list the conditions that must be satisfied during the whole execution of the function.

Design-by-contract is often used in the Standard Library. For example, `std::vector` defines a contract for using the array notation to get a certain element from a `vector`. The contract states that no bounds checking is performed, but that this is the responsibility of the client code. In other words, a precondition for using array notation to get elements from a `vector` is that the given index is valid. This is done to increase performance for client code that knows their indices are within bounds.

The second style is that you design your functions and classes to be as safe as possible. The most important aspect of this guideline is to perform error checking in your code. For example, if your random number generator requires a seed to be in a specific range, don't just trust the user to pass a valid seed. Check the value that is passed in, and reject the call if it is invalid. As a second example, next to the design-by-contract array notation for retrieving an element from a `vector`, it also defines an `at()` member function to get a specific element while performing bounds checking. If the user provides an invalid index, `at()` throws an exception. So, client code can choose whether it uses the array notation without bounds checking, or `at()` with bounds checking.

As an analogy, consider an accountant who prepares income tax returns. When you hire an accountant, you provide them with all your financial information for the year. The accountant uses this information to fill out forms from the IRS[1]. However, the accountant does not blindly fill out your information on the form, but instead makes sure the information makes sense. For example, if you own a house but forget to specify the property tax you paid, the accountant will remind you to supply that information. Similarly, if you say that you paid $12,000 in mortgage interest but made only $15,000 gross income, the accountant might gently ask you if you provided the correct numbers (or at least recommend more affordable housing).

You can think of the accountant as a "program" where the input is your financial information and the output is an income tax return. However, the value added by an accountant is not just that they fill out the forms. You also choose to employ an accountant because of the checks and safeguards that they provide. Similarly in programming, you could provide as many checks and safeguards as possible in your implementations.

There are several techniques and language features that help you to write safe code and to incorporate checks and safeguards in your programs. To report errors to client code, you can for example return an error code, a distinct value like `false` or `nullptr`, or an `std::optional` as introduced in Chapter 1. Alternatively, you can throw an exception to notify client code of any errors. Chapter 14, "Handling Errors," covers exceptions in detail.

Design for Extensibility

You should strive to design your classes in such a way that they can be extended by deriving another class from them, but they should be closed for modification; that is, the behavior should be extendable without you having to modify its implementation. This is called the *open/closed principle* (OCP).

[1] The Internal Revenue Service (IRS) administers and enforces U.S. federal tax laws.

As an example, suppose you start implementing a drawing application. The first version should only support squares. Your design contains two classes: `Square` and `Renderer`. The former contains the definition of a square, such as the length of its sides. The latter is responsible for drawing the squares. You come up with something as follows:

```
class Square { /* Details not important for this example. */ };

class Renderer
{
    public:
        void render(const vector<Square>& squares)
        {
            for (auto& square : squares) { /* Render this square object... */ }
        }
};
```

Next, you add support for circles, so you create a `Circle` class:

```
class Circle { /* Details not important for this example. */ };
```

To be able to render circles, you have to modify the `render()` member function of the `Renderer` class. You decide to change it as follows:

```
void Renderer::render(const vector<Square>& squares,
                      const vector<Circle>& circles)
{
    for (auto& square : squares) { /* Render this square object... */ }
    for (auto& circle : circles) { /* Render this circle object... */ }
}
```

While doing this, you feel there is something wrong, and you are correct! To extend the functionality to add support for circles, you have to modify the current implementation of `render()`, so it's not closed for modifications.

Your design in this case could use inheritance. Here is a possible design using inheritance:

```
class Shape
{
    public:
        virtual void render() = 0;
};

class Square : public Shape
{
    public:
        void render() override { /* Render square... */ }
    // Other members not important for this example.
};

class Circle : public Shape
{
    public:
        void render() override { /* Render circle... */ }
    // Other members not important for this example.
};
```

```
class Renderer
{
    public:
        void render(const vector<Shape*>& objects)
        {
            for (auto* object : objects) { object->render(); }
        }
};
```

With this design, if you want to add support for a new type of shape, you just need to write a new class that derives from `Shape` and that implements the `render()` member function. You don't need to modify anything in the `Renderer` class. So, this design can be extended without having to modify the existing code; that is, it's open for extension and closed for modification.

Design Usable Interfaces

In addition to abstracting and structuring your code appropriately, designing for reuse requires you to focus on the *interface* with which programmers interact. Even if you have the most beautiful and most efficient implementation, your library will not be any good if it has a wretched interface.

Note that every component in your program should have good interfaces, even if you don't intend them to be used in multiple programs. First, you never know when something will be reused. Second, a good interface is important even for the first use, especially if you are programming in a group and other programmers must use the code you design and write.

In C++, a class's properties and member functions can each be `public`, `protected`, or `private`. Making a property or member function `public` means that any code can access it; `protected` means that only the class itself and its derived classes can access it; `private` is a stricter control, which means that not only is the property or member function locked for other code, but even derived classes don't have access. Note that access specifiers are at the class level, not at the object level. This means that a member function of a class can access, for example, `private` properties or `private` member functions of other objects of the same class.

Designing the exposed interface is all about choosing what to make `public`. You should view the exposed interface design as a process. The main purpose of interfaces is to make the code easy to use, but some interface techniques can help you follow the principle of generality as well.

Consider the Audience

The first step in designing an exposed interface is to consider whom you are designing it for. Is your audience another member of your team? Is this an interface that you will personally be using? Is it something that a programmer external to your company will use? Perhaps a customer or an offshore contractor? In addition to determining who will be coming to you for help with the interface, this should shed some light on some of your design goals.

If the interface is for your own use, you probably have more freedom to iterate on the design. As you're making use of the interface, you can change it to suit your own needs. However, you should keep in mind that roles on an engineering team change, and it is quite likely that, someday, others will be using this interface as well.

Designing an interface for other internal programmers to use is slightly different. In a way, your interface becomes a contract with them. For example, if you are implementing the data store component of a program, others are depending on that interface to support certain operations. You will need to find out all of the things that the rest of the team wants your class to do. Do they need versioning? What types of data can they store?

When designing interfaces for an external customer, ideally the external customer should be involved in specifying what functionality your interfaces expose, just as when designing interfaces for internal customers. You'll need to consider both the specific features they want as well as what customers might want in the future. The terminology used in the interface will have to correspond to the terms that the customer is familiar with, and the documentation will have to be written with that audience in mind. Inside jokes, codenames, and programmer slang should be left out of your design.

Whether your interface is for internal programmers or external customers, the interface is a contract. If the interface is agreed upon before coding begins, you'll receive groans from users of your interface if you decide to change it after code has been written.

The audience for which you are designing an interface also impacts how much time you should invest in the design. For example, if you are designing an interface with just a couple of member functions that will be used only in a few places by a few users, then it could be acceptable to modify the interface later. However, if you are designing a complex interface or an interface that will be used by many users, then you should spend more time on the design and do your best to prevent having to modify the interface once users start using it. This is what is known as Hyrum's law (see `www.hyrumslaw.com`).

Consider the Purpose

There are many reasons for writing an interface. Before putting any code on paper or even deciding on what functionality you're going to expose, you need to understand the purpose of the interface.

Application Programming Interface

An application programming interface (API) is an externally visible mechanism to extend a product or use its functionality within another context. If an internal interface is a contract, an API is closer to a set-in-stone law. Once people who don't even work for your company are using your API, they don't want it to change unless you're adding new features that will help them. So, care should be given to planning the API and discussing it with customers before making it available to them.

The main trade-off in designing an API is usually ease of use versus flexibility. Because the target audience for the interface is not familiar with the internal working of your product, the learning curve to use the API should be gradual. After all, your company is exposing this API to customers because the company wants it to be used. If it's too difficult to use, the API is a failure. Flexibility often works against this. Your product may have a lot of different uses, and you want the customer to be able to leverage all the functionality you have to offer. However, an API that lets the customer do anything that your product can do may be too complicated.

As a common programming adage goes, "A good API makes the *common* case easy and the *advanced/unlikely* case possible." That is, APIs should have a simple learning curve. The things that most programmers will want to do should be accessible. However, the API should allow for more advanced usage, and it's acceptable to trade off complexity of the rare case for simplicity of the common case. The "Design Interfaces That Are Easy to Use" section later in this chapter discusses this strategy in detail with a number of concrete tips to follow for your designs.

Utility Class or Library

Often, your task is to develop some particular functionality for general use elsewhere in the application, for example a logging class. In this case, the interface is somewhat easier to decide on because you tend to expose most or all of the functionality, ideally without giving too much away about its implementation. Generality is an important issue to consider. Because the class or library is general purpose, you'll need to take the possible set of use cases into account in your design.

Subsystem Interface

You may be designing the interface between two major subsystems of the application, such as the mechanism for accessing a database. In these cases, separating the interface from the implementation is paramount for a number of reasons.

One of the most important reasons is *mockability*. In testing scenarios, you will want to replace a certain implementation of an interface with another implementation of the same interface. For example, when writing test code for a database interface, you might not want to access a real database. An interface implementation accessing a real database could be replaced with one simulating all database access.

Another reason is *flexibility*. Even besides testing scenarios, you might want to provide several different implementations of a certain interface that can be used interchangeably. For example, you might want to replace a database interface implementation that uses a MySQL server database, with an implementation that uses a SQL Server database. You might even want to switch between different implementations at run time.

Yet another reason: by finishing the interface first, other programmers can already start programming against your interface before your implementation is complete.

When working on a subsystem, first think about what its main purpose is. Once you have identified the main task your subsystem is charged with, think about specific uses and how it should be presented to other parts of the code. Try to put yourself in their shoes and not get bogged down in implementation details.

Component Interface

Most of the interfaces you define will probably be smaller than a subsystem interface or an API. These will be classes that you use within other code that you've written. In these cases, the main pitfall occurs when your interface evolves gradually and becomes unruly. Even though these interfaces are for your own use, think of them as though they weren't. As with a subsystem interface, consider the main purpose of each class and be cautious of exposing functionality that doesn't contribute to that purpose.

Design Interfaces That Are Easy to Use

Your interfaces should be easy to use. That doesn't mean that they must be trivial, but they should be as simple and intuitive as the functionality allows. This follows the KISS principle: keep it simple, stupid. You shouldn't require consumers of your library to wade through pages of source code or documentation in order to use a simple data structure or to go through contortions in their code to obtain the functionality they need. This section provides four specific strategies for designing interfaces that are easy to use.

Follow Familiar Ways of Doing Things

The best strategy for developing easy-to-use interfaces is to follow standard and familiar ways of doing things. When people encounter an interface similar to something they have used in the past, they will understand it better, adopt it more readily, and be less likely to use it improperly.

For example, suppose that you are designing the steering mechanism of a car. There are a number of possibilities: a joystick, two buttons for moving left or right, a sliding horizontal lever, or a good old steering wheel. Which interface do you think would be easiest to use? Which interface do you think would sell the most cars? Consumers are familiar with steering wheels, so the answer to both questions is, of course, the steering wheel. Even if you developed another mechanism that provided superior performance and safety, you would have a tough time selling your product, let alone teaching people how to use it. When you have a choice between following standard interface models and branching out in a new direction, it's usually better to stick to the interface to which people are accustomed.

Innovation is important, of course, but you should focus on innovation in the underlying implementation, not in the interface. For example, consumers are excited about the innovative fully electric engine in some car models. These cars are selling well in part because the interface to use them is identical to cars with standard gasoline engines.

Applied to C++, this strategy implies that you should develop interfaces that follow standards to which C++ programmers are accustomed. For example, C++ programmers expect a constructor and destructor of a class to initialize and clean up an object, respectively (both discussed in details in Chapter 8, "Gaining Proficiency with Classes and Objects"). If you need to "reinitialize" an existing object, a standard way is to just assign a newly constructed object to it. When you design your classes, you should follow these standards. If you require programmers to call `initialize()` and `cleanup()` member functions for initialization and cleanup instead of placing that functionality in the constructor and destructor, you will confuse everyone who tries to use your class. Because your class behaves differently from other C++ classes, programmers will take longer to learn how to use it and will be more likely to use it incorrectly by forgetting to call `initialize()` or `cleanup()`.

> **NOTE** *Always think about your interfaces from the perspective of someone using them. Do they make sense? Are they what you would expect?*

C++ provides a language feature called *operator overloading* that can help you develop easy-to-use interfaces for your objects. Operator overloading allows you to write classes such that the standard operators work on them just as they work on built-in types like `int` and `double`. For example, you can write a `Fraction` class that allows you to add, subtract, and print fractions like this:

```
Fraction f1 { 3, 4 };
Fraction f2 { 1, 2 };
```

```
Fraction sum { f1 + f2 };
Fraction diff { f1 - f2 };
println("{} {}", f1, f2);
```

Contrast that with the same behavior using member function calls:

```
Fraction f1 { 3, 4 };
Fraction f2 { 1, 2 };
Fraction sum { f1.add(f2) };
Fraction diff { f1.subtract(f2) };
f1.print();
print(" ");
f2.print();
println("");
```

As you can see, operator overloading allows you to provide an easier-to-use interface for your classes. However, be careful not to abuse operator overloading. It's possible to overload the + operator so that it implements subtraction and the - operator so that it implements multiplication. Those implementations would be counterintuitive. This does not mean that each operator should always implement exactly the same behavior. For example, the `string` class implements the + operator to concatenate `strings`, which is an intuitive interface for `string` concatenation. See Chapters 9 and 15, "Overloading C++ Operators," for details on operator overloading.

Don't Omit Required Functionality

As you are designing your interface, keep in mind what the future holds. Is this a design you will be locked into for years? If so, you might need to leave room for expansion by coming up with a plug-in architecture. Do you have evidence that people will try to use your interface for purposes other than what it was designed for? Talk to them and get a better understanding of their use case. The alternative is rewriting it later or, worse, attaching new functionality haphazardly and ending up with a messy interface. Be careful, though! Speculative generality is yet another pitfall. Don't design the be-all, end-all logging class if the future uses are unclear, because it might unnecessarily complicate the design, the implementation, and its public interface.

This strategy is twofold. First, include interfaces for all behaviors that clients could need. That might sound obvious at first. Returning to the car analogy, you would never build a car without a speedometer for the driver to view their speed! Similarly, you would never design a `Fraction` class without a mechanism for client code to access the nominator and denominator values.

However, other possible behaviors might be more obscure. This strategy requires you to anticipate all the uses to which clients might put your code. If you are thinking about the interface in one particular way, you might miss functionality that could be needed when clients use it differently. For example, suppose that you want to design a game board class. You might consider only the typical games, such as chess, and decide to support a maximum of one game piece per spot on the board. However, what if you later decide to write a backgammon game, which allows multiple pieces in one spot on the board? By precluding that possibility, you have ruled out the use of your game board as a backgammon board.

Obviously, anticipating every possible use for your library is difficult, if not impossible. Don't feel compelled to agonize over potential future uses in order to design the perfect interface. Just give it some thought and do the best you can.

The second part of this strategy is to include as much functionality in the implementation as possible. Don't require client code to specify information that you already know in the implementation, or could know if you designed it differently. For example, if your library requires a temporary file, don't make the clients of your library specify that path. They don't care what file you use; find some other way to determine an appropriate temporary file path.

Furthermore, don't require library users to perform unnecessary work to amalgamate results. If your random number library uses a random number algorithm that calculates the low-order and high-order bits of a random number separately, combine all bits into one number before giving it to the user.

Present Uncluttered Interfaces

To avoid omitting functionality in their interfaces, some programmers go to the opposite extreme: they include every possible piece of functionality imaginable. Programmers who use the interfaces are never left without the means to accomplish a task. Unfortunately, the interface might be so cluttered that they never figure out how to do it! Such interfaces are called *fat* interfaces.

Don't provide unnecessary functionality in your interfaces; keep them clean and simple. It might appear at first that this guideline directly contradicts the previous strategy of not omitting necessary functionality. Although one strategy to avoid omitting functionality would be to include every imaginable interface, that is not a sound strategy. You should include *necessary* functionality and omit useless or counterproductive interfaces.

Consider cars again. You drive a car by interacting with only a few components: the steering wheel, the brake and accelerator pedals, the gearshift, the mirrors, the speedometer, and a few other dials on your dashboard. Now, imagine a car dashboard that looked like an airplane cockpit, with hundreds of dials, levers, monitors, and buttons. It would be unusable! Driving a car is so much easier than flying an airplane that the interface can be much simpler: You don't need to view your altitude, communicate with control towers, or control the myriad components in an airplane such as the wings, engines, and landing gear.

A fat interface can be avoided by breaking up the interface into several smaller ones. Alternatively, the *façade design pattern* can be used to provide an easier interface or interfaces on top of a fat interface. For example, a fat car interface would include everything from simple actions such as accelerating, braking, and turning, to more advanced functionality, such as numerous options for tuning the performance of the engine, and many more. A better design is to provide multiple easier to use interfaces: one for basic operations such as accelerating, braking, and turning; another one to provide access to the engine tuning options; and many more.

Additionally, from the library development perspective, smaller libraries are easier to maintain. If you try to make everyone happy, then you have more room to make mistakes, and if your implementation is complicated enough so that everything is intertwined, even one mistake can render the library useless.

Unfortunately, the idea of designing uncluttered interfaces looks good on paper, but is remarkably hard to put into practice. The rule is ultimately subjective: you decide what's necessary and what's not. Of course, your clients will for sure tell you when you get it wrong!

Provide Documentation

Regardless of how easy you make your interfaces to use, you should supply documentation for their use. You can't expect programmers to use your library properly unless you tell them how to do it. Think of your library or code as a product for other programmers to consume. Your product should have documentation explaining its proper use.

There are two ways to provide documentation for your interfaces: comments in the interfaces themselves and external documentation. You should strive to provide both. Most public APIs provide only external documentation: comments are a scarce commodity in many of the standard Unix and Windows header files. In Unix, the documentation usually comes in the form of *man pages*. In Windows, the documentation usually accompanies the integrated development environment or is available on the Internet.

Despite that most APIs and libraries omit comments in the interfaces themselves, I actually consider this form of documentation the most important. You should never give out a "naked" module or header file that contains only code. Even if your comments repeat exactly what's in the external documentation, it is less intimidating to look at a module or header file with friendly comments than one with only code. Even the best programmers still like to see written language every so often! Chapter 3 gives concrete tips for what to comment and how to write comments, and also explains that there are tools available that can write external documentation for you based on the comments you write in your interfaces.

Design General-Purpose Interfaces

The interfaces should be general purpose enough that they can be adapted to a variety of tasks. If you encode specifics of one application in a supposedly general interface, it will be unusable for any other purpose. Here are some guidelines to keep in mind.

Provide Multiple Ways to Perform the Same Functionality

To satisfy all your "customers," it is sometimes helpful to provide multiple ways to perform the same functionality. Use this technique judiciously, however, because over-application can easily lead to cluttered interfaces.

Consider cars again. Most new cars these days provide remote keyless entry systems, with which you can unlock your car by pressing a button on a key fob. However, these cars often provide a standard key that you can use to physically unlock the car, for example, when the battery in the key fob is drained. Although these two methods are redundant, most customers appreciate having both options.

Sometimes there are similar situations in interface design. Remember from earlier in this chapter, `std::vector` provides two member functions to get access to a single element at a specific index. You can use either the `at()` member function, which performs bounds checking, or array notation, which does not. If you know your indices are valid, you can use array notation and forgo the overhead that `at()` incurs due to bounds checking.

Note that this strategy should be considered an exception to the "uncluttered" rule in interface design. There are a few situations where the exception is appropriate, but you should most often follow the uncluttered rule.

Provide Customizability

To increase the flexibility of your interfaces, provide customizability. Customizability can be as simple as allowing a client to turn error logging on or off. The basic premise of customizability is that it allows you to provide the same basic functionality to every client but to give clients the ability to tweak it slightly.

One way to accomplish this is through the use of interfaces to invert dependency relationships, also called *dependency inversion principle* (DIP). *Dependency injection* is one implementation of this principle. Chapter 4, "Designing Professional C++ Programs," briefly mentions an example of an `ErrorLogger` service. You should define an `ErrorLogger` interface and use dependency injection to inject concrete implementations of this interface into each component that wants to use the `ErrorLogger` service.

You can allow greater customizability through callbacks and template parameters. For example, you could allow clients to set their own error-handling callbacks. Chapter 19, "Function Pointers, Function Objects, and Lambda Expressions," discusses callbacks in detail.

The Standard Library takes this customizability strategy to the extreme and allows clients to specify their own memory allocators for containers. If you want to use this feature, you must write a memory allocator class that follows the Standard Library guidelines and adheres to the required interfaces. Most containers in the Standard Library take an allocator as one of their template parameters. Chapter 25, "Customizing and Extending the Standard Library," provides more details.

Reconciling Generality and Ease of Use

The two goals of ease of use and generality sometimes appear to conflict. Often, introducing generality increases the complexity of the interfaces. For example, suppose that you need a graph structure in a map program to store cities. In the interest of generality, you might use templates to write a generic map structure for any type, not just cities. That way, if you need to write a network simulator in your next program, you can employ the same graph structure to store routers in the network. Unfortunately, by using templates, you make the interface a little clumsier and harder to use, especially if the potential client is not familiar with templates.

However, generality and ease of use are not mutually exclusive. Although in some cases increased generality may decrease ease of use, it is possible to design interfaces that are both general purpose and straightforward to use.

To reduce complexity in your interfaces while still providing enough functionality, you can provide multiple separate interfaces. This is called the *interface segregation principle* (ISP). For example, you could write a generic networking library with two separate facets: one presents the networking interfaces useful for games, and the other presents the networking interfaces useful for the Hypertext Transfer Protocol (HTTP) for web browsing. Providing multiple interfaces also helps with making the commonly used functionality easy to use, while still providing the option for the more advanced functionality. Returning to the map program, you might want to provide a separate interface for clients of the map to specify names of cities in different languages, while making English the default as it is so predominant. That way, most clients will not need to worry about setting the language, but those who want to will be able to do so.

Designing a Successful Abstraction

Experience and iteration are essential to good abstractions. Truly well-designed interfaces come from years of writing and using other abstractions. You can also leverage someone else's years of writing and using abstractions by reusing existing, well-designed abstractions in the form of standard design patterns. As you encounter other abstractions, try to remember what worked and what didn't work. What did you find lacking in the Windows file system API you used last week? What would you have done differently if you had written the network wrapper, instead of your co-worker? The best interface is rarely the first one you put on paper, so keep iterating. Bring your design to your peers and ask for feedback. If your company uses code reviews, start by doing a review of the interface specifications before the implementation starts. Don't be afraid to change the abstraction once coding has begun, even if it means forcing other programmers to adapt. Ideally, they'll realize that a good abstraction is beneficial to everyone in the long term.

Sometimes you need to evangelize a bit when communicating your design to other programmers. Perhaps the rest of the team didn't see a problem with the previous design or feels that your approach requires too much work on their part. In those situations, be prepared both to defend your work and to incorporate their ideas when appropriate.

A good abstraction means that the exported interface has only public member functions that are stable and will not change. A specific technique to accomplish this is called the *private implementation idiom*, or *pimpl idiom*, and is discussed in Chapter 9.

Beware of single-class abstractions. If there is significant depth to the code you're writing, consider what other companion classes might accompany the main interface. For example, if you're exposing an interface to do some data processing, consider also writing a result class that provides an easy way to view and interpret the results.

Always turn properties into member functions. In other words, don't allow external code to manipulate the data behind your class directly. You don't want some careless or nefarious programmer to set the height of a bunny object to a negative number. Instead, have a "set height" member function that does the necessary bounds checking.

Iteration is worth mentioning again because it is the most important point. Seek and respond to feedback on your design, change it when necessary, and learn from mistakes.

The SOLID Principles

This chapter and the previous one discuss a number of basic principles of object-oriented design. To summarize these principles, they are often abbreviated with an easy-to-remember acronym: *SOLID*. The following table summarizes the five SOLID principles:

S	**Single Responsibility Principle (SRP)** A single component should have a single, well-defined responsibility and should not combine unrelated functionality.
O	**Open/Closed Principle (OCP)** A class should be open to extension, but closed for modification. Inheritance is one way to accomplish this. Other mechanisms are templates, function overloading, and more. In general, we speak about *customization points* in this context.

L	**Liskov Substitution Principle (LSP)** You should be able to replace an instance of an object with an instance of a subtype of that object. Chapter 5 explains this principle in the section "The Fine Line Between Has-A and Is-A" with an example to decide whether the relationship between `AssociativeArray` and `MultiAssociativeArray` is a has-a or an is-a relationship.
I	**Interface Segregation Principle (ISP)** Keep interfaces clean and simple. It is better to have many smaller, well-defined single-responsibility interfaces than to have broad, general-purpose interfaces.
D	**Dependency Inversion Principle (DIP)** Use interfaces to invert dependency relationships. One way to support the dependency inversion principle is dependency injection, discussed earlier in this chapter and further in Chapter 33, "Applying Design Patterns."

SUMMARY

By reading this chapter, you learned *how* you should design reusable code. You read about the philosophy of reuse, summarized as "write once, use often," and learned that reusable code should be both general purpose and easy to use. You also discovered that designing reusable code requires you to use abstraction, to structure your code appropriately, and to design good interfaces.

This chapter presented specific tips for structuring your code: to avoid combining unrelated or logically separate concepts, to use templates for generic data structures and algorithms, to provide appropriate checks and safeguards, and to design for extensibility.

This chapter also presented six strategies for designing interfaces: to follow familiar ways of doing things, to not omit required functionality, to present uncluttered interfaces, to provide documentation, to provide multiple ways to perform the same functionality, and to provide customizability. It also discussed how to reconcile the often-conflicting demands of generality and ease of use.

The chapter concluded with SOLID, an easy-to-remember acronym that describes the most important design principles discussed in this and other chapters.

This is the last chapter of the second part of the book, which focuses on discussing design themes at a higher level. The next part delves into the implementation phase of the software engineering process, with details of C++ coding.

EXERCISES

By solving the following exercises, you can practice the material discussed in this chapter. Solutions to all exercises are available with the code download on the book's website at `www.wiley.com/go/proc++6e`. However, if you are stuck on an exercise, first reread parts of this chapter to try to find an answer yourself before looking at the solution from the website.

Exercise 6-1: What does it mean to make the common case easy and the unlikely case possible?

Exercise 6-2: What is the number-one strategy for reusable code design?

Exercise 6-3: Suppose you are writing an application that needs to work with information about people. One part of the application needs to keep a list of customers with data such as a list of recent orders, loyalty card number, and so on. Another part of the application needs to keep track of employees of your company that have an employee ID, job title, and so on. To satisfy these requirements, you decide to design a class called `Person` that contains their name, phone number, address, list of recent orders, loyalty card number, salary, employee ID, job title (engineer, senior engineer, . . .), and more. What do you think of such a class? Are there any improvements that you can think of?

Exercise 6-4: Without looking back to the previous pages, explain what SOLID means.

PART III
C++ Coding the Professional Way

7

Memory Management

WHAT'S IN THIS CHAPTER?

- Different ways to use and manage memory
- The often-perplexing relationship between arrays and pointers
- A low-level look at working with memory
- Common memory pitfalls
- Smart pointers and how to use them

WILEY.COM DOWNLOADS FOR THIS CHAPTER

Please note that all the code examples for this chapter are available as part of this chapter's code download on the book's website at `www.wiley.com/go/proc++6e` on the Download Code tab.

When you use modern constructs, such as `std::vector`, `std::string`, and so on, as is done starting from Chapter 1, "A Crash Course in C++ and the Standard Library," and throughout all the other chapters of this book, then C++ is a safe language. The language provides many roads, lines, and traffic lights, such as the C++ Core Guidelines (see Appendix B, "Annotated Bibliography"), static code analyzers to analyze the correctness of code, and many more.

However, C++ does allow you to drive off-road. One example of driving off-road is manual memory management (allocation and deallocation). Such manual memory management is a particularly error-prone area of C++ programming. To write high-quality C++ programs, professional C++ programmers need to understand how memory works behind the scenes. This first chapter of Part III explores the ins and outs of memory management. You will learn about the pitfalls of dynamic memory and some techniques for avoiding and eliminating them.

This chapter discusses low-level memory handling because professional C++ programmers will encounter such code. However, in modern C++ code you should avoid low-level memory operations as much as possible. For example, instead of dynamically allocated C-style arrays, you should use Standard Library containers, such as `vector`, which handle all memory management automatically for you. Instead of raw pointers, you should use smart pointers, such as `unique_ptr` and `shared_ptr` both discussed later in this chapter, which automatically free the underlying resource, such as memory, when it's not needed anymore. Basically, the goal is to avoid having calls to memory allocation routines such as `new`/`new[]` and `delete`/`delete[]` in your code. Of course, it might not always be possible, and in existing code it will most likely not be the case, so as a professional C++ programmer, you still need to know how memory works behind the scenes.

> **WARNING** *In modern C++ code you should avoid low-level memory operations as much as possible, avoid raw pointers when ownership is involved, and avoid using old C-style constructs and functions. Instead, use safe C++ alternatives, such as objects that automatically manage their memory, like the C++* `string` *class, the* `vector` *container, smart pointers, and so on!*

WORKING WITH DYNAMIC MEMORY

Memory is a low-level component of the computer that sometimes unfortunately rears its head even in a high-level programming language like C++. A solid understanding of how dynamic memory really works in C++ is essential to becoming a professional C++ programmer.

How to Picture Memory

Understanding dynamic memory is much easier if you have a mental model for what objects look like in memory. In this book, a unit of memory is shown as a box with a label next to it. The label indicates a variable name that corresponds to the memory. The data inside the box displays the current value of the memory.

For example, Figure 7.1 shows the state of memory after the following line of code is executed. The line should be in a function, so that `i` is a local variable:

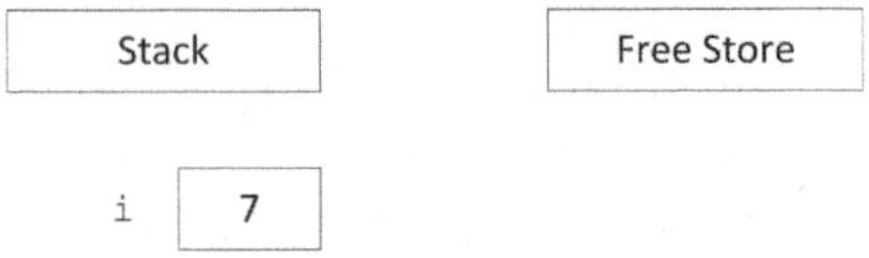

Stack | Free Store

i | 7

FIGURE 7.1

```
int i { 7 };
```

`i` is called an *automatic variable* allocated on the stack. It is automatically deallocated when the program flow leaves the scope in which the variable is declared.

When you use the `new` keyword, memory is allocated on the free store. If not explicitly initialized, memory allocated by a call to `new` is uninitialized; i.e., it contains whatever random data is left at that location in memory. This uninitialized state is represented with a question mark in diagrams in this chapter. The following code creates a variable `ptr` on the stack initialized with `nullptr` and then allocates memory on the free store to which `ptr` points:

```
int* ptr { nullptr };
ptr = new int;
```

This can also be written as a one-liner:

```
int* ptr { new int };
```

Figure 7.2 shows the state of memory after this code is executed. Notice that the variable `ptr` is still on the stack even though it points to memory on the free store. A pointer is just a variable and can live on either the stack or the free store, although this fact is easy to forget. Dynamic memory, however, is always allocated on the free store.

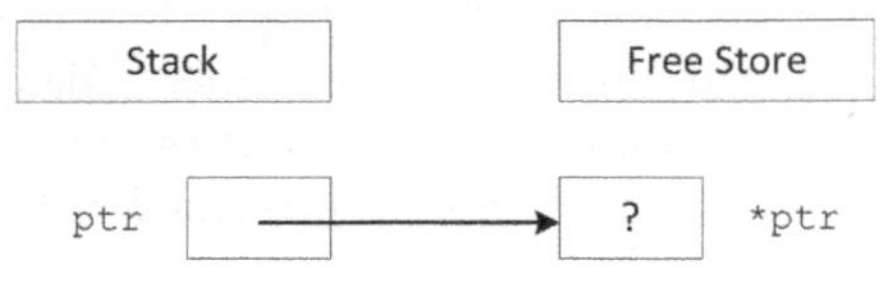

FIGURE 7.2

> **WARNING** *As mandated by the C++ Core Guidelines,[1] every time you declare a pointer variable, you should immediately initialize it with either a proper pointer or* `nullptr`*. Don't leave it uninitialized!*

The next example shows that pointers can exist both on the stack and on the free store:

```
int** handle { nullptr };
handle = new int*;
*handle = new int;
```

This code first declares a pointer to a pointer to an integer as the variable `handle`. It then dynamically allocates enough memory to hold a pointer to an integer, storing the pointer to that new memory in `handle`. Next, that memory (`*handle`) is assigned a pointer to another section of dynamic memory that is big enough to hold the integer. Figure 7.3 shows the two levels of pointers with one pointer residing on the stack (`handle`) and the other residing on the free store (`*handle`).

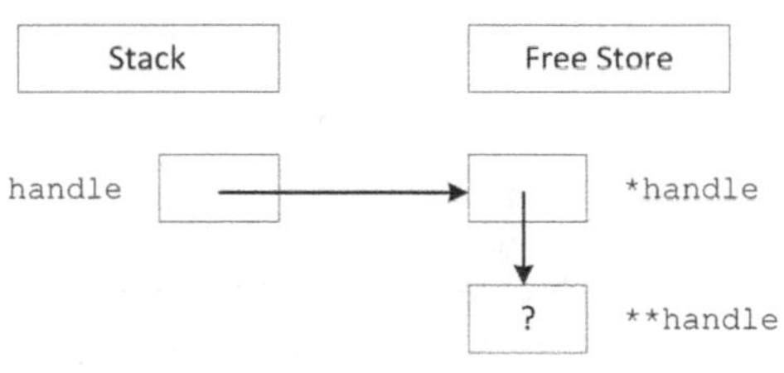

FIGURE 7.3

Allocation and Deallocation

To create space for a variable, you use the `new` keyword. To release that space for use by other parts of the program, you use the `delete` keyword.

Using new and delete

When you want to allocate a block of memory, you call `new` with the type of variable for which you need space. `new` returns a pointer to that memory, although it is up to you to store that pointer in a

[1] Guideline ES.20 of the C++ Core Guidelines, see Appendix B, states "Always initialize an object."

variable. If you ignore the return value of new or if the pointer variable goes out of scope, the memory becomes *orphaned* because you no longer have a way to access it. This is called a *memory leak*.

For example, the following code orphans enough memory to hold an int. Figure 7.4 shows the state of memory after the code is executed. When there are blocks of data on the free store with no access, direct or indirect, from the stack, the memory is orphaned or leaked.

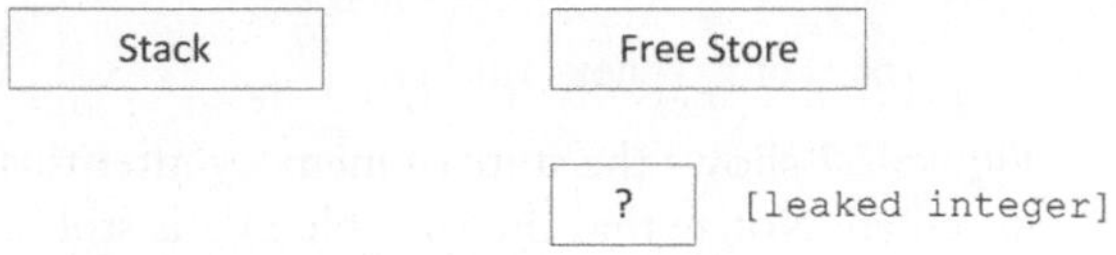

FIGURE 7.4

```
void leaky()
{
    new int;    // BUG! Orphans/leaks memory!
    println("I just leaked an int!");
}
```

Until they find a way to make computers with an infinite supply of fast memory, you will need to tell the compiler when the memory associated with an object can be released and reused for another purpose. To free memory on the free store, you use the delete keyword with a pointer to the memory, as shown here:

```
int* ptr { new int };
delete ptr;
ptr = nullptr;
```

> **WARNING** *As a rule of thumb, every line of code that allocates memory with* new, *and that uses a raw pointer instead of storing the pointer in a smart pointer, should correspond to another line of code that releases the same memory with* delete.

> **NOTE** *It is recommended to set a pointer to* nullptr *after having freed its memory. That way, you do not accidentally use a pointer to memory that has already been deallocated. It's also worth noting that you are allowed to call* delete *on a* nullptr *pointer; it simply will not do anything.*

What About My Good Friend malloc?

If you are a C programmer, you may be wondering what is wrong with the malloc() function. In C, malloc() is used to allocate a given number of bytes of memory. For the most part, using malloc() is simple and straightforward. The malloc() function still exists in C++, but you should avoid it. The main advantage of new over malloc() is that new doesn't just allocate memory, it constructs objects!

For example, consider the following two lines of code, which use a hypothetical class called Foo:

```
Foo* myFoo { (Foo*)malloc(sizeof(Foo)) };
Foo* myOtherFoo { new Foo{} };
```

After executing these lines, both `myFoo` and `myOtherFoo` point to areas of memory on the free store that are big enough for a `Foo` object. Data members and member functions of `Foo` can be accessed using both pointers. The difference is that the `Foo` object pointed to by `myFoo` isn't a proper object because its constructor was never called. The `malloc()` function only sets aside a piece of memory of a certain size. It doesn't know about or care about objects. In contrast, the call to `new` allocates the appropriate size of memory and also calls an appropriate constructor to construct the object.

A similar difference exists between the `free()` function and the `delete` operator. With `free()`, the object's destructor is not called. With `delete`, the destructor is called and the object is properly cleaned up.

> **WARNING** *Avoid the use of* `malloc()` *and* `free()` *in* C++.

When Memory Allocation Fails

Many, if not most, programmers write code with the assumption that `new` will always be successful. The rationale is that if `new` fails, it means that memory is very low and life is very, very bad. It is often an unfathomable state to be in because it's unclear what your program could possibly do in this situation.

By default, an exception is thrown when `new` fails, for example if there is not enough memory available for the request. If this exception is not caught, the program will be terminated. In many programs, this behavior is acceptable. Chapter 1 introduces exceptions, and Chapter 14, "Handling Errors," explains exceptions in more details and provides possible approaches to recover gracefully from an out-of-memory situation.

There is also an alternative version of `new`, which does not throw an exception. Instead, it returns `nullptr` if allocation fails, similar to the behavior of `malloc()` in C. The syntax for using this version is as follows:

```
int* ptr { new(nothrow) int };
```

The syntax is a little strange: you really do write "nothrow" as if it's an argument to `new` (which it is).

Of course, you still have the same problem as the version that throws an exception—what do you do when the result is `nullptr`? The compiler doesn't require you to check the result, so the `nothrow` version of `new` is more likely to lead to other bugs than the version that throws an exception. For this reason, it's suggested that you use the standard version of `new`. If out-of-memory recovery is important to your program, the techniques covered in Chapter 14 give you all the tools you need.

Arrays

Arrays package multiple variables of the same type into a single variable with indices. Working with arrays quickly becomes natural to a novice programmer because it is easy to think about values in numbered slots. The in-memory representation of an array is not far off from this mental model.

Arrays of Primitive Types

When your program allocates memory for an array, it is allocating *contiguous* pieces of memory, where each piece is large enough to hold a single element of the array. For example, a local array of five ints can be declared on the stack as follows:

```
int myArray[5];
```

The individual elements of such a primitive type array are uninitialized; that is, they contain whatever is at that location in memory. Figure 7.5 shows the state of memory after the array is created. When creating arrays on the stack, the size must be a constant value known at compile time.

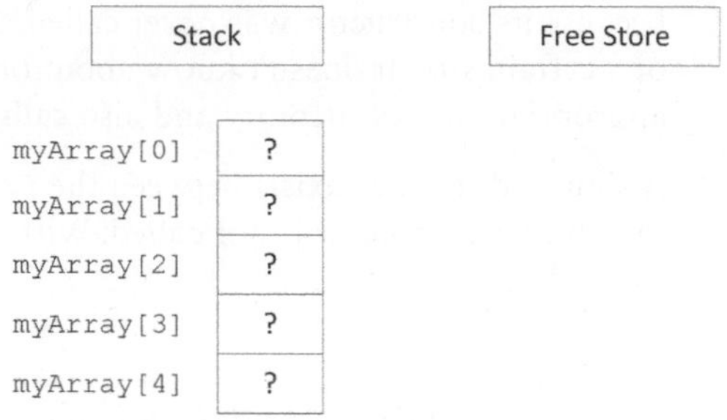

Stack		Free Store
myArray[0]	?	
myArray[1]	?	
myArray[2]	?	
myArray[3]	?	
myArray[4]	?	

FIGURE 7.5

> **NOTE** *Some compilers allow variable-sized arrays on the stack. This is not a standard feature of C++, so I recommend cautiously backing away when you see it.*

When creating an array on the stack, an initializer list can be used to provide initial elements:

```
int myArray[5] { 1, 2, 3, 4, 5 };
```

If the initializer list contains less elements than the size of the array, the remaining elements of the array are zero-initialized (see Chapter 1), for example:

```
int myArray[5] { 1, 2 }; // 1, 2, 0, 0, 0
```

To zero-initialize all elements, you can simply write:

```
int myArray[5] { };       // 0, 0, 0, 0, 0
```

When using an initializer list, the compiler can deduce the number of elements automatically, removing the need to explicitly state the size of the array:

```
int myArray[] { 1, 2, 3, 4, 5 };
```

Declaring arrays on the free store is no different, except that you use a pointer to refer to the location of the array. The following code allocates memory for an array of five uninitialized ints and stores a pointer to the memory in a variable called myArrayPtr:

```
int* myArrayPtr { new int[5] };
```

As Figure 7.6 illustrates, the free store-based array is similar to a stack-based array, but in a different location. The myArrayPtr variable points to the 0th element of the array.

As with the new operator, new[] accepts a nothrow argument to return nullptr instead of throwing an exception if allocation fails:

```
int* myArrayPtr { new(nothrow) int[5] };
```

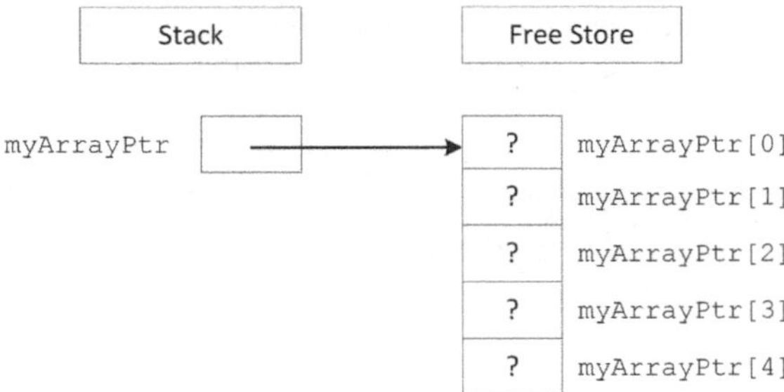

FIGURE 7.6

Dynamically created arrays on the free store can also be initialized with an initializer list:

```
int* myArrayPtr { new int[] { 1, 2, 3, 4, 5 } };
```

Each call to `new[]` should be paired with a call to `delete[]` to clean up the memory. Note the empty square brackets, `[]`, behind `delete[]`!

```
delete [] myArrayPtr;
myArrayPtr = nullptr;
```

The advantage of putting an array on the free store is that you can define its size at run time. For example, the following code snippet receives a desired number of documents from a hypothetical function named `askUserForNumberOfDocuments()` and uses that result to create an array of `Document` objects.

```
Document* createDocumentArray()
{
    size_t numberOfDocuments { askUserForNumberOfDocuments() };
    Document* documents { new Document[numberOfDocuments] };
    return documents;
}
```

Remember that each call to `new[]` should be paired with a call to `delete[]`, so in this example, it's important that the caller of `createDocumentArray()` uses `delete[]` to clean up the returned memory. Another problem is that C-style arrays don't know their size; thus, callers of `createDocumentArray()` have no idea how many elements there are in the returned array!

In the preceding function, `documents` is a dynamically allocated array. Do not get this confused with a *dynamic array*. The array itself is not dynamic because its size does not change once it is allocated. Dynamic memory lets you specify the size of an allocated block at run time, but it does not automatically adjust its size to accommodate the data.

> **NOTE** *There are data structures that do dynamically adjust their size and that do know their actual size, for example Standard Library containers. You should use such containers instead of C-style arrays because they are much safer to use.*

There is a function in C++ called `realloc()`, which is a holdover from the C language. Do not use it! In C, `realloc()` is used to effectively change the size of an array by allocating a new block of memory of the new size, copying all of the old data to the new location, and deleting the original block. This approach is extremely dangerous in C++ because user-defined objects will not respond well to bitwise copying.

> **WARNING** *Never use* `realloc()` *in C++! It is not your friend.*

Arrays of Objects

Arrays of objects are no different than arrays of primitive/fundamental types, except for how their elements are initialized. When you use `new[N]` to allocate an array of *N* objects, enough space is allocated for *N* contiguous blocks where each block is large enough for a single object. For an array of objects, `new[]` automatically calls the zero-argument (= default) constructor for each of the objects, while an array of primitive types by default has uninitialized elements. In this way, allocating an array of objects using `new[]` returns a pointer to an array of fully constructed and initialized objects.

For example, consider the following class:

```
class Simple
{
    public:
        Simple() { println("Simple constructor called!"); }
        ~Simple() { println("Simple destructor called!"); }
};
```

If you allocate an array of four `Simple` objects, the `Simple` constructor is called four times.

```
Simple* mySimpleArray { new Simple[4] };
```

Figure 7.7 shows the memory diagram for this array. As you can see, it is no different than an array of basic types.

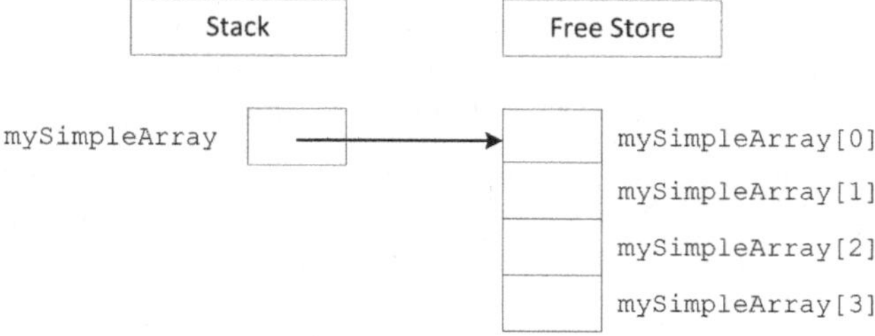

FIGURE 7.7

Deleting Arrays

When you allocate memory with `new[]` (i.e., the array version of `new`), you must release it with `delete[]` (i.e., the array version of `delete`). This version automatically destructs the objects in the array in addition to releasing the memory associated with them.

```
Simple* mySimpleArray { new Simple[4] };
// Use mySimpleArray...
```

```
delete [] mySimpleArray;
mySimpleArray = nullptr;
```

If you do not use the array version of `delete`, your program may behave in odd ways. With some compilers, only the destructor for the first element of the array will be called because the compiler only knows that you are deleting a pointer to an object, and all the other elements of the array will become orphaned objects. With other compilers, memory corruption may occur because `new` and `new[]` can use completely different memory allocation schemes.

WARNING *Always use* `delete` *on anything allocated with* `new`*, and always use* `delete[]` *on anything allocated with* `new[]`.

Of course, the destructors are called only if the elements of the array are objects. If you have an array of pointers, you still need to delete each object pointed to individually just as you allocated each object individually, as shown in the following code:

```
const size_t size { 4 };
Simple** mySimplePtrArray { new Simple*[size] };

// Allocate an object for each pointer.
for (size_t i { 0 }; i < size; ++i) { mySimplePtrArray[i] = new Simple{}; }

// Use mySimplePtrArray...

// Delete each allocated object.
for (size_t i { 0 }; i < size; ++i) {
    delete mySimplePtrArray[i];
    mySimplePtrArray[i] = nullptr;
}

// Delete the array itself.
delete [] mySimplePtrArray;
mySimplePtrArray = nullptr;
```

WARNING *In modern C++ you should avoid using raw C-style pointers when ownership is involved. Instead of storing raw pointers in C-style arrays, you should store smart pointers in modern Standard Library containers, such as* `std::vector`*. Smart pointers, discussed later in this chapter, automatically deallocate the memory associated with them at the right time.*

Multidimensional Arrays

Multidimensional arrays extend the notion of indexed values to multiple indices. For example, a tic-tac-toe game might use a two-dimensional array to represent a three-by-three grid. The following example shows such an array declared on the stack, zero-initialized, and accessed with some test code:

```
char board[3][3] {};
// Test code
board[0][0] = 'X';     // X puts marker in position (0,0).
board[2][1] = 'O';     // O puts marker in position (2,1).
```

You may be wondering whether the first subscript in a two-dimensional array is the x-coordinate or the y-coordinate. The truth is that it doesn't really matter, as long as you are consistent. A four-by-seven grid could be declared as `char board[4][7]` or `char board[7][4]`. For most applications, it is easiest to think of the first subscript as the x-axis and the second as the y-axis.

Multidimensional Stack Arrays

In memory, the three-by-three stack-based two-dimensional `board` array looks like Figure 7.8. Because memory doesn't have two axes (addresses are merely sequential), the computer represents a two-dimensional array just like a one-dimensional array. The difference is in the size of the array and the method used to access it.

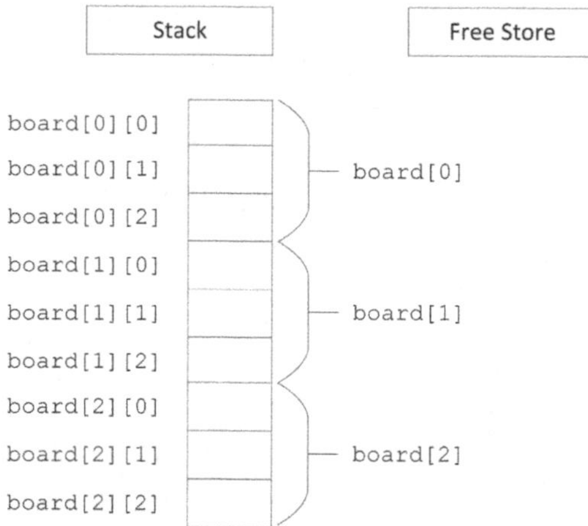

FIGURE 7.8

The size of a multidimensional array is all of its dimensions multiplied together and then multiplied by the size of a single element in the array. In Figure 7.8, the three-by-three board is $3 \times 3 \times 1 = 9$ bytes, assuming that a character is 1 byte. For a four-by-seven board of characters, the array would be $4 \times 7 \times 1 = 28$ bytes.

To access a value in a multidimensional array, the computer treats each subscript as if it were accessing another subarray within the multidimensional array. For example, in the three-by-three grid, the expression `board[0]` actually refers to the subarray highlighted in Figure 7.9. When you add a second subscript, such as `board[0][2]`, the computer is able to access the correct element by looking up the second subscript within the subarray, as shown in Figure 7.10.

These techniques are extended to *N*-dimensional arrays, though dimensions higher than three tend to be difficult to conceptualize and are rarely used.

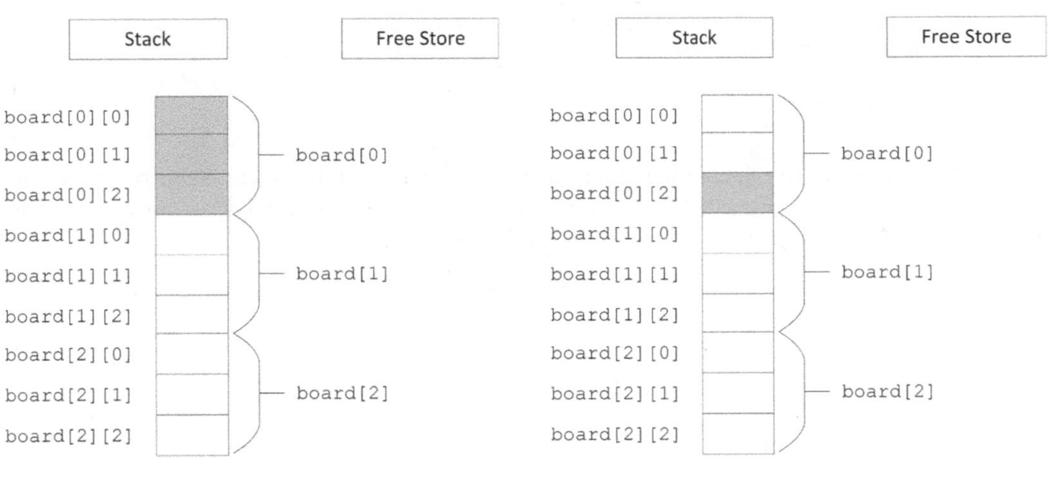

FIGURE 7.9

FIGURE 7.10

Multidimensional Free Store Arrays

If you need to determine the dimensions of a multidimensional array at run time, you can use a free store-based array. Just as a single-dimensional dynamically allocated array is accessed through a pointer, a multidimensional dynamically allocated array is also accessed through a pointer. The only difference is that in a two-dimensional array, you need to start with a pointer-to-a-pointer; and in an *N*-dimensional array, you need *N* levels of pointers. At first, it might seem as if the correct way to declare and allocate a dynamically allocated multidimensional array is as follows:

```
char** board { new char[i][j] }; // BUG! Doesn't compile
```

This code doesn't compile because multidimensional free store-based arrays don't work like stack-based arrays. Their memory layout isn't contiguous. Instead, you start by allocating a single contiguous array for the first subscript dimension of a free store-based array. Each element of that array is actually a pointer to another array that stores the elements for the second subscript dimension. Figure 7.11 shows this layout for a two-by-two dynamically allocated board.

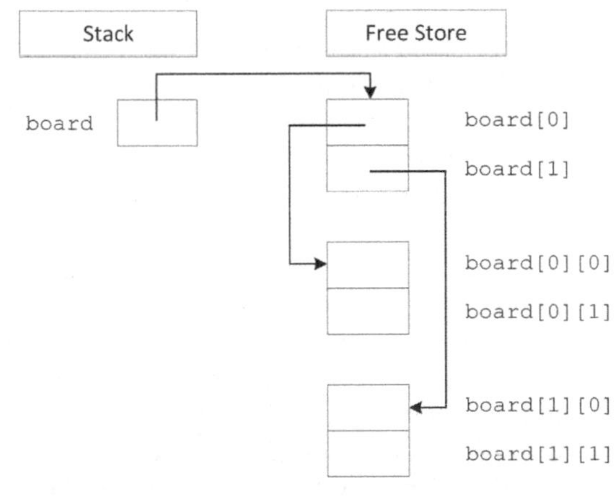

FIGURE 7.11

Unfortunately, the compiler doesn't allocate memory for the subarrays on your behalf. You can allocate the first-dimension array just like a single-dimensional free store-based array, but the individual subarrays must be explicitly allocated. The following function properly allocates memory for a two-dimensional array:

```
char** allocateCharacterBoard(size_t xDimension, size_t yDimension)
{
    char** myArray { new char*[xDimension] }; // Allocate first dimension
```

```
        for (size_t i { 0 }; i < xDimension; ++i) {
            myArray[i] = new char[yDimension];     // Allocate ith subarray
        }
        return myArray;
    }
```

Similarly, when you want to release the memory associated with a multidimensional free store-based array, the array `delete[]` syntax will not clean up the subarrays on your behalf. Your code to release an array should mirror the code to allocate it, as in the following function:

```
void releaseCharacterBoard(char**& myArray, size_t xDimension)
{
    for (size_t i { 0 }; i < xDimension; ++i) {
        delete [] myArray[i];     // Delete ith subarray
        myArray[i] = nullptr;
    }
    delete [] myArray;            // Delete first dimension
    myArray = nullptr;
}
```

> **NOTE** *This example of allocating a multidimensional array is not the most efficient solution. It first allocates memory for the first dimension, followed by allocating memory for each subarray. This results in memory blocks scattered around in memory, which will have a performance impact on algorithms working on such data structures. Algorithms run much faster if they can work with contiguous memory. A better solution is to allocate a single block of memory large enough to store* `xDimension * yDimension` *elements, and to access an element at position (x,y) with a formula such as* `x * yDimension + y`.

Now that you know all the details to work with arrays, it is recommended to avoid these old C-style arrays as much as possible because they do not provide any memory safety. They are explained here because you will encounter them in legacy code. In new code, you should use the C++ Standard Library containers such as `std::array` and `vector`. For example, use `vector<T>` for a one-dimensional dynamic array. For a two-dimensional dynamic array, you could use `vector<vector<T>>`, and similar for higher dimensions. Of course, working directly with data structures such as `vector<vector<T>>` is still tedious, especially for constructing them, and they suffer from the same memory fragmentation problem as discussed in the previous note. So, if you do need N-dimensional dynamic arrays in your application, consider writing helper classes that provide an easier to use interface. For example, to work with two-dimensional data with equally long rows, you should consider writing (or reusing of course) a `Matrix<T>` or `Table<T>` class template that hides the memory allocation/deallocation and element access algorithms from the user. See Chapter 12, "Writing Generic Code with Templates," for details on writing class templates.

> **WARNING** *Use C++ Standard Library containers such as* `std::array, vector,` *and so on, instead of C-style arrays!*

Working with Pointers

Pointers get their bad reputation from the relative ease with which you can abuse them. Because a pointer is just a memory address, you could theoretically change that address manually, even doing something as scary as the following line of code:

```
char* scaryPointer { (char*)7 };
```

This line builds a pointer to the memory address 7, which is likely to be random garbage or memory used elsewhere in the application. If you start to use areas of memory that weren't set aside on your behalf, for example with `new` or on the stack, eventually you will corrupt the memory associated with an object, or the memory involved with the management of the free store, and your program will malfunction. Such a malfunction can manifest itself in several ways. For example, it can reveal itself as invalid results because the data has been corrupted, or as hardware exceptions being triggered due to accessing non-existent memory, or attempting to write to protected memory. If you are lucky, you will get one of the serious errors that usually result in program termination by the operating system or the C++ runtime library; if you are unlucky, you will just get wrong results.

A Mental Model for Pointers

There are two ways to think about pointers. More mathematically minded readers might view pointers as addresses. This view makes pointer arithmetic, covered later in this chapter, a bit easier to understand. Pointers aren't mysterious pathways through memory; they are numbers that happen to correspond to a location in memory. Figure 7.12 illustrates a two-by-two grid in the address-based view of the world.[2]

FIGURE 7.12

Readers who are more comfortable with spatial representations might derive more benefit from the "arrow" view of pointers. A pointer is a level of indirection that says to the program, "Hey! Look over there." With this view, multiple levels of pointers become individual steps on the path to the data. Figure 7.11 shows a graphical view of pointers in memory.

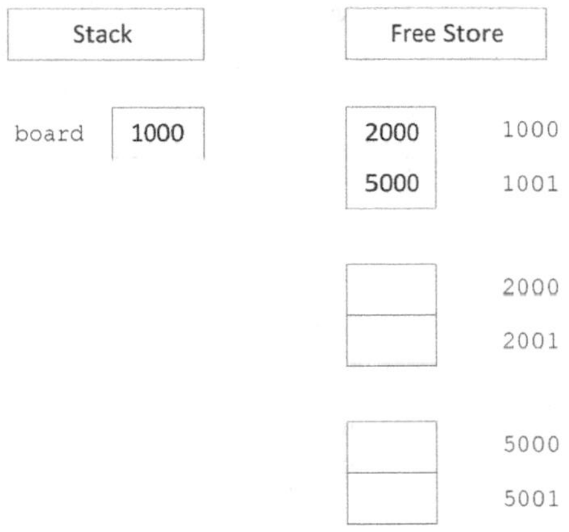

When you *dereference* a pointer, by using the `*` operator, you are telling the program to look one level deeper in memory. In the address-based view, think of a dereference as a jump in memory to the address indicated by the pointer. With the graphical view, every dereference corresponds to following an arrow from its base to its head.

When you take the address of a location, using the `&` operator, you are adding a level of indirection in memory. In the address-based view, the program is noting the numerical address of the location, which can be stored as a pointer. In the graphical view, the `&` operator creates a new arrow whose head ends at the location designated by the expression. The base of the arrow can be stored as a pointer.

[2] The addresses in Figure 7.12 are just for illustrative purpose. Addresses on a real system are highly dependent on the hardware and operating system.

Casting with Pointers

Because pointers are just memory addresses (or arrows to somewhere), they are somewhat weakly typed. A pointer to an XML document is the same size as a pointer to an integer. The compiler lets you easily cast any pointer type to any other pointer type using a *C-style cast*:

```
Document* documentPtr { getDocument() };
char* myCharPtr { (char*)documentPtr };
```

Of course, using the resulting pointer can result in catastrophic run-time errors. A *static cast* offers a bit more safety. The compiler refuses to perform a static cast on pointers to unrelated data types:

```
Document* documentPtr { getDocument() };
char* myCharPtr { static_cast<char*>(documentPtr) };    // BUG! Won't compile
```

Chapter 10, "Discovering Inheritance Techniques," discusses the different styles of casts in detail.

ARRAY-POINTER DUALITY

You have already seen some of the overlap between pointers and arrays. Free store-allocated arrays are referred to by a pointer to their first element. Stack-based arrays are referred to by using the array syntax (`[]`) with an otherwise normal variable declaration. As you are about to learn, however, the overlap doesn't end there. Pointers and arrays have a complicated relationship.

Arrays Decay to Pointers

A free store-based array is not the only place where you can use a pointer to refer to an array. You can also use the pointer syntax to access elements of a stack-based array. The address of an array is really the address of the first element (index 0). The compiler knows that when you refer to an array in its entirety by its variable name, you are really referring to the address of the first element. In this way, the pointer works just like with a free store-based array. The following code creates a zero-initialized array on the stack, and uses a pointer to access it:

```
int myIntArray[10] {};

int* myIntPtr { myIntArray };

// Access the array through the pointer.
myIntPtr[4] = 5;
```

The ability to refer to a stack-based array through a pointer is useful when passing arrays into functions. The following function accepts an array of integers as a pointer. Note that the caller needs to explicitly pass in the size of the array because the pointer implies nothing about size. That is another reason why you should use modern containers such as those provided by the Standard Library.

```
void doubleInts(int* theArray, size_t size)
{
    for (size_t i { 0 }; i < size; ++i) { theArray[i] *= 2; }
}
```

The caller of this function can pass a stack-based or free store-based array. In the case of a free store-based array, the pointer already exists and is passed by value into the function. In the case of a stack-based array, the caller can pass the array variable, and the compiler automatically treats the array variable as a pointer to the array, or you can explicitly pass the address of the first element. All three forms are shown here:

```
size_t arrSize { 4 };
int* freeStoreArray { new int[arrSize]{ 1, 5, 3, 4 } };
doubleInts(freeStoreArray, arrSize);
delete [] freeStoreArray;
freeStoreArray = nullptr;

int stackArray[] { 5, 7, 9, 11 };
arrSize = std::size(stackArray);    // Since C++17, requires <array>
//arrSize = sizeof(stackArray) / sizeof(stackArray[0]); // Pre-C++17, see Ch1
doubleInts(stackArray, arrSize);

doubleInts(&stackArray[0], arrSize);
```

The parameter-passing semantics of arrays is uncannily similar to that of pointers, because the compiler treats an array as a pointer when it is passed to a function. A function that takes an array as an argument and changes values inside the array is actually changing the original array, not a copy. Just like a pointer, passing an array effectively mimics pass-by-reference functionality because what you really pass to the function is the address of the original array, not a copy. The following implementation of `doubleInts()` changes the original array even though the parameter is an array, not a pointer:

```
void doubleInts(int theArray[], size_t size)
{
    for (size_t i { 0 }; i < size; ++i) { theArray[i] *= 2; }
}
```

Any number between the square brackets after `theArray` in the function prototype is simply ignored. The following three versions are identical:

```
void doubleInts(int* theArray, size_t size);
void doubleInts(int theArray[], size_t size);
void doubleInts(int theArray[2], size_t size);
```

You may be wondering why things work this way. Why doesn't the compiler just copy the array when array syntax is used in the function definition? This is done for efficiency—it takes time to copy the elements of an array, and they potentially take up a lot of memory. By always passing a pointer, the compiler doesn't need to include the code to copy the array.

There is a way to pass known-length stack-based arrays "by reference" to a function, although the syntax is non-obvious. This does not work for free store-based arrays. For example, the following `doubleIntsStack()` accepts only stack-based arrays of size 4:

```
void doubleIntsStack(int (&theArray)[4]);
```

A function template, discussed in detail in Chapter 12, can be used to let the compiler deduce the size of the stack-based array automatically:

```
template <size_t N>
void doubleIntsStack(int (&theArray)[N])
{
    for (size_t i { 0 }; i < N; ++i) { theArray[i] *= 2; }
}
```

> **NOTE** *Instead of passing a C-style array directly to a function, it is recommended for the function to have a parameter of type* `std::span`*, discussed in Chapter 18, "Standard Library Containers."* `span` *wraps a pointer to an array and its size!*

Not All Pointers Are Arrays!

Because the compiler lets you pass in an array where a pointer is expected, as in the `doubleInts()` function in the previous section, you may be led to believe that pointers and arrays are the same. In fact, there are subtle, but important, differences. Pointers and arrays share many properties and can sometimes be used interchangeably (as shown earlier), but they are not the same.

A pointer by itself is meaningless. It may point to random memory, a single object, or an array. You can always use array syntax with a pointer, but doing so is not always appropriate because pointers aren't always arrays. For example, consider the following line of code:

```
int* ptr { new int };
```

The pointer `ptr` is a valid pointer, but it is not an array. You can access the pointed-to value using array syntax (`ptr[0]`), but doing so is stylistically questionable and provides no real benefit. In fact, using array syntax with non-array pointers is an invitation for bugs. The memory at `ptr[1]` could be anything!

> **WARNING** *Arrays automatically decay to pointers, but not all pointers are arrays.*

LOW-LEVEL MEMORY OPERATIONS

One of the great advantages of C++ over C is that you don't need to worry quite as much about memory. If you code using objects, you just need to make sure that each individual class properly manages its own memory. Through construction and destruction, the compiler helps you manage memory by telling you when to do it. Hiding the management of memory within classes makes a huge difference in usability, as demonstrated by the Standard Library classes. However, with some applications or with legacy code, you may encounter the need to work with memory at a lower level. Whether for legacy, efficiency, debugging, or curiosity, knowing some techniques for working with raw bytes can be helpful.

Pointer Arithmetic

The C++ compiler uses the declared types of pointers to allow you to perform *pointer arithmetic*. If you declare a pointer to an `int` and increase it by 1, the pointer moves ahead in memory by the size of an `int`, not by a single byte. This type of operation is most useful with arrays, because they contain homogeneous data that is sequential in memory. For example, assume you declare an array of `int`s on the free store:

```
int* myArray { new int[8] };
```

You are already familiar with the following syntax for setting the value at index 2:

```
myArray[2] = 33;
```

With pointer arithmetic, you can equivalently use the following syntax, which obtains a pointer to the memory that is "2 `ints` ahead" of `myArray` and then dereferences it to set the value:

```
*(myArray + 2) = 33;
```

As an alternative syntax for accessing individual elements, pointer arithmetic doesn't seem too appealing. Its real power lies in the fact that an expression like `myArray+2` is still a pointer to an `int` and thus can represent a smaller `int` array.

Let's look at an example using wide strings. Wide strings are discussed in Chapter 21, "String Localization and Regular Expressions," but the details are not important at this point. For now, it is enough to know that wide strings support Unicode characters to represent, for example, Japanese strings. The `wchar_t` type is a character type that can accommodate such Unicode characters, and it is usually bigger than a `char`; i.e., it's more than one byte. To tell the compiler that a string literal is a wide-string literal, prefix it with an `L`. For example, suppose you have the following wide string:

```
const wchar_t* myString { L"Hello, World" };
```

Suppose further that you have a function that takes in a wide string and returns a new string that contains a capitalized version of the input:

```
wchar_t* toCaps(const wchar_t* text);
```

You can capitalize `myString` by passing it into this function. However, if you only want to capitalize *part* of `myString`, you can use pointer arithmetic to refer to only a latter part of the string. The following code calls `toCaps()` on the `World` part of the wide string by just adding 7 to the pointer, even though `wchar_t` is usually more than 1 byte:

```
toCaps(myString + 7);
```

Another useful application of pointer arithmetic involves subtraction. Subtracting one pointer from another of the same type gives you the number of elements of the pointed-to type between the two pointers, not the absolute number of bytes between them.

Custom Memory Management

For 99 percent of the cases you will encounter (some might say 100 percent of the cases), the built-in memory allocation facilities in C++ are adequate. Behind the scenes, `new` and `delete` do all the work of handing out memory in properly sized chunks, maintaining a list of available areas of memory and releasing chunks of memory back to that list upon deletion.

When resource constraints are extremely tight, or under very special conditions, such as managing shared memory, implementing custom memory management may be a viable option. Don't worry—it's not as scary as it sounds. Basically, managing memory yourself means that classes allocate a large chunk of memory and dole out that memory in pieces as it is needed.

How is this approach any better? Managing your own memory can potentially reduce overhead. When you use `new` to allocate memory, the program also needs to set aside a small amount of space to record how much memory was allocated. That way, when you call `delete`, the proper amount of memory can be released. For most objects, the overhead is so much smaller than the memory allocated that it makes little difference. However, for small objects or programs with enormous numbers of objects, the overhead can have an impact.

When you manage memory yourself, you might know the size of each object a priori, so you might be able to avoid the overhead for each object. The difference can be enormous for large numbers of small objects. Performing custom memory management requires overloading the operators `new` and `delete`, a topic for Chapter 15, "Overloading C++ Operators."

Garbage Collection

With environments that support *garbage collection*, the programmer rarely, if ever, explicitly frees memory associated with an object. Instead, objects to which there are no longer any references will be cleaned up automatically at some point by the runtime library.

Garbage collection is not built into the C++ language as it is in C# and Java. In modern C++, you use smart pointers to manage memory, while in legacy code you will see memory management at the object level through `new` and `delete`. Smart pointers such as `shared_ptr` (discussed later in this chapter) provide something very similar to garbage-collected memory; that is, when the last `shared_ptr` instance for a certain resource is destroyed, at that point in time the resource is destroyed as well. It is possible but not easy to implement true garbage collection in C++, but freeing yourself from the task of releasing memory would probably introduce new headaches.

One approach to garbage collection is called *mark and sweep*. With this approach, the garbage collector periodically examines every single pointer in your program and annotates the fact that the referenced memory is still in use. At the end of the cycle, any memory that hasn't been marked is deemed to be not in-use and is freed. Implementing such an algorithm in C++ is not trivial, and if done wrongly, it can be even more error-prone than using `delete`!

Attempts at safe and easy mechanisms for garbage collection have been made in C++, but even if a perfect implementation of garbage collection in C++ came along, it wouldn't necessarily be appropriate to use for all applications. Among the downsides of garbage collection are the following:

- When the garbage collector is actively running, the program might become unresponsive.
- With garbage collectors, you have non-deterministic destructors. Because an object is not destroyed until it is garbage-collected, the destructor is not executed immediately when the object leaves its scope. This means that cleaning up resources (such as closing a file, releasing a lock, and so on), which is done by the destructor, is not performed until some indeterminate time in the future.

Writing a garbage collection mechanism is very hard. You will undoubtedly do it wrong, it will be error prone, and more than likely it will be slow. So, if you do want to use garbage-collected memory in your application, I recommend you to research existing specialized garbage-collection libraries that you can reuse.

Object Pools

Garbage collection is like buying plates for a picnic and leaving any used plates out in the yard where someone at some point will pick them up and throw them away. Surely, there must be a more ecological approach to memory management.

Object pools are the equivalent of recycling. You buy a reasonable number of plates, and after using a plate, you clean it so that it can be reused later. Object pools are ideal for situations where you need to use many objects of the same type over time, and creating each one incurs overhead.

Chapter 29, "Writing Efficient C++," contains further details on using object pools for performance efficiency.

COMMON MEMORY PITFALLS

Handling dynamic memory using `new`/`delete`/`new[]`/`delete[]`, and low-level memory operations are prone to errors. It is difficult to pinpoint the exact situations that can lead to a memory-related bug. Every memory leak or bad pointer has its own nuances. There is no magic bullet for resolving memory issues. This section discusses several common categories of problems and some tools you can use to detect and resolve them.

Underallocating Data Buffers and Out-of-Bounds Memory Access

Underallocation is a common problem with C-style strings, where it arises when the programmer fails to allocate an extra character for the trailing `'\0'` sentinel. Underallocation of strings also occurs when programmers assume a certain fixed maximum size. The basic built-in C-style string functions do not adhere to a fixed size—they will happily write off the end of the string into uncharted memory.

The following code demonstrates underallocation. It reads data off a network connection and puts it in a C-style string. This is done in a loop because the network connection receives only a small amount of data at a time. On each loop, `getMoreData()` is called, which returns a pointer to dynamically allocated memory. When `nullptr` is returned from `getMoreData()`, all of the data has been received. `strcat()` is a C function that concatenates the C-style string given as a second argument to the end of the C-style string given as a first argument. It expects the destination buffer to be big enough.

```
char buffer[1024] { 0 };    // Allocate a whole bunch of memory.
while (true) {
    char* nextChunk { getMoreData() };
    if (nextChunk == nullptr) {
        break;
    } else {
        strcat(buffer, nextChunk); // BUG! No guarantees against buffer overrun!
        delete [] nextChunk;
    }
}
```

There are three ways to resolve the possible underallocation problem in this example. In decreasing order of preference, they are as follows:

1. Use C++-style strings, which handle the memory associated with concatenation on your behalf.
2. Instead of allocating a buffer as a global variable or on the stack, allocate it on the free store. When there is insufficient space left, allocate a new buffer large enough to hold at least the

current contents plus the new chunk, copy the original buffer into the new buffer, append the new contents, and delete the original buffer.

3. Create a version of `getMoreData()` that takes a maximum count (including the `'\0'` character) and returns no more characters than that; then track the amount of space left, and the current position, in the buffer.

Underallocation of data buffers usually leads to out-of-bounds memory access. For example, if you are filling a memory buffer with data, you might start writing outside the allocated data buffer when you assume the buffer is bigger than it actually is. It is only a matter of time before an essential part of memory is overwritten and the program crashes. Consider what might happen if the memory associated with the objects in your program is suddenly overwritten. It's not pretty!

Out-of-bounds memory access also occurs when handling C-style strings that have somehow lost their `'\0'` termination character. For example, if an improperly terminated string is handed to the following function, it will fill the string with `'m'` characters and will happily continue to fill the contents of memory after the string with `'m'`s, overwriting memory outside the bounds of the string.

```
void fillWithM(char* text)
{
    int i { 0 };
    while (text[i] != '\0') {
        text[i] = 'm';
        ++i;
    }
}
```

Bugs that result in writing to memory past the end of an array are often called *buffer overflow errors*. These bugs have been exploited by several high-profile malware programs such as viruses and worms. A devious hacker can take advantage of the ability to overwrite portions of memory to inject code into a running program.

> **WARNING** *Avoid using old C-style strings and arrays that offer no protection whatsoever. Instead, use modern and safe constructs such as C++* `strings` *and* `vectors` *that manage all their memory for you.*

Memory Leaks

In modern C++, there are no memory leaks. All memory management is handled by higher-level classes, such as `std::vector`, `string`, and so on. Only when you drive off-road and perform manual memory allocation and deallocation can memory leaks crop up.

Finding and fixing such memory leaks can be frustrating. Your program finally works and appears to give the correct results. Then, you start to notice that your program gobbles up more and more memory as it runs. Your program has a memory leak.

Memory leaks occur when you allocate memory and neglect to release it. At first, this sounds like the result of careless programming that could easily be avoided. After all, if every `new` has a corresponding delete in every class you write, there should be no memory leaks, right? Actually, that's not always true. For example, in the following code, the Simple class is properly written to release any memory that it allocates. However, when doSomething() is called, the outSimplePtr pointer is changed to another Simple object without deleting the old one to demonstrate a memory leak. Once you lose a pointer to an object, it's nearly impossible to delete it.

```
class Simple
{
    public:
        Simple() { m_intPtr = new int{}; }
        ~Simple() { delete m_intPtr; }
        void setValue(int value) { *m_intPtr = value; }
    private:
        int* m_intPtr;
};

void doSomething(Simple*& outSimplePtr)
{
    outSimplePtr = new Simple{}; // BUG! Doesn't delete the original.
}

int main()
{
    Simple* simplePtr { new Simple{} }; // Allocate a Simple object.
    doSomething(simplePtr);
    delete simplePtr; // Only cleans up the second object.
}
```

> **WARNING** *Keep in mind that this code is only for demonstration purposes! In production-quality code, both* m_intPtr *and* simplePtr *should not be raw pointers, but should be smart pointers discussed later in this chapter.*

In cases like the previous example, the memory leak probably arose from poor communication between programmers or poor documentation of the code. The caller of doSomething() may not have realized that the variable was passed by reference and thus had no reason to expect that the pointer would be reassigned. If they did notice that the parameter was a reference-to-non-const pointer, they may have suspected that something strange was happening, but there is no comment around doSomething() that explains this behavior.

Finding and Fixing Memory Leaks in Windows with Visual C++

Memory leaks are hard to track down because you can't easily look at memory and see what objects are not in use and where they were originally allocated. However, there are programs that can do this for you. Memory leak detection tools range from expensive professional software packages to free downloadable tools. If you work with Microsoft Visual C++, its debug library has built-in support for memory leak detection. This memory leak detection is not enabled by default, unless you create an MFC project. To enable it in other projects, you need to start by including the following three lines at the beginning of your code. These use the #define preprocessor macro, explained in Chapter 11,

"Modules, Header Files, and Miscellaneous Topics." However, for now, just use the three lines verbatim as they are.

```
#define _CRTDBG_MAP_ALLOC
#include <cstdlib>
#include <crtdbg.h>
```

These lines should be in the exact order as shown. Next, you need to redefine the `new` operator as follows. This uses a few other preprocessor macros, all explained in Chapter 11. Again, just use them as is for now.

```
#ifdef _DEBUG
    #ifndef DBG_NEW
        #define DBG_NEW new ( _NORMAL_BLOCK , __FILE__ , __LINE__ )
        #define new DBG_NEW
    #endif
#endif  // _DEBUG
```

The `#ifdef _DEBUG` statement makes sure that the redefinition of `new` is done only when compiling a debug version of your application. This is what you normally want. Release builds usually do not do any memory leak detection, because of the performance penalty.

The last thing you need to do is to add the following line as the first line in your `main()` function:

```
_CrtSetDbgFlag(_CRTDBG_ALLOC_MEM_DF | _CRTDBG_LEAK_CHECK_DF);
```

This tells the Visual C++ CRT (C RunTime) library to write all detected memory leaks to the debug output console when the application exits. For the earlier leaky program, the debug console will contain lines similar to the following:

```
Detected memory leaks!
Dumping objects ->
c:\leaky\leaky.cpp(15) : {147} normal block at 0x014FABF8, 4 bytes long.
 Data: <    > 00 00 00 00
c:\leaky\leaky.cpp(33) : {146} normal block at 0x014F5048, 4 bytes long.
 Data: <Pa > 50 61 20 01
Object dump complete.
```

The output clearly shows in which file and on which line memory was allocated but never deallocated. The line number is between parentheses immediately behind the filename. The number between the curly braces is a counter for the memory allocations. For example, {147} means the 147th allocation in your program since it started. You can use the VC++ `_CrtSetBreakAlloc()` function to tell the VC++ debug runtime to break into the debugger when a certain allocation is performed. For example, you can add the following line to the beginning of your `main()` function to instruct the debugger to break on the 147th allocation:

```
_CrtSetBreakAlloc(147);
```

In this leaky program, there are two leaks: the first `Simple` object that is never deleted (line 33) and the integer on the free store that it creates (line 15). In the Visual C++ debugger output window, you can simply double-click one of the memory leaks, and it will automatically jump to that line in your code.

Of course, programs like Microsoft Visual C++ (discussed in this section) and Valgrind (discussed in the next section) can't actually fix the leak for you—what fun would that be? These tools provide information that you can use to find the actual problem. Normally, that involves stepping through the code to find out where the pointer to an object was overwritten without the original object being released. Most debuggers provide "watch point" functionality that can break execution of the program when this occurs.

Finding and Fixing Memory Leaks in Linux with Valgrind

Valgrind is an example of a free open-source tool for Linux that, among other things, pinpoints the exact line in your code where a leaked object was allocated.

The following output, generated by running Valgrind on the earlier leaky program, pinpoints the exact locations where memory was allocated but never released. Valgrind finds the same two memory leaks—the first `Simple` object never deleted and the integer on the free store that it creates:

```
==15606== ERROR SUMMARY: 0 errors from 0 contexts (suppressed: 0 from 0)
==15606== malloc/free: in use at exit: 8 bytes in 2 blocks.
==15606== malloc/free: 4 allocs, 2 frees, 16 bytes allocated.
==15606== For counts of detected errors, rerun with: -v
==15606== searching for pointers to 2 not-freed blocks.
==15606== checked 4455600 bytes.
==15606==
==15606== 4 bytes in 1 blocks are still reachable in loss record 1 of 2
==15606==    at 0x4002978F: __builtin_new (vg_replace_malloc.c:172)
==15606==    by 0x400297E6: operator new(unsigned) (vg_replace_malloc.c:185)
==15606==    by 0x804875B: Simple::Simple() (leaky.cpp:4)
==15606==    by 0x8048648: main (leaky.cpp:24)
==15606==
==15606==
==15606== 4 bytes in 1 blocks are definitely lost in loss record 2 of 2
==15606==    at 0x4002978F: __builtin_new (vg_replace_malloc.c:172)
==15606==    by 0x400297E6: operator new(unsigned) (vg_replace_malloc.c:185)
==15606==    by 0x8048633: main (leaky.cpp:20)
==15606==    by 0x4031FA46: __libc_start_main (in /lib/libc-2.3.2.so)
==15606==
==15606== LEAK SUMMARY:
==15606==    definitely lost: 4 bytes in 1 blocks.
==15606==    possibly lost:   0 bytes in 0 blocks.
==15606==    still reachable: 4 bytes in 1 blocks.
==15606==         suppressed: 0 bytes in 0 blocks.
```

> **WARNING** *It is strongly recommended to use* `std::vector`, `array`, `string`, *smart pointers (discussed later in this chapter), and other modern C++ constructs to avoid memory leaks.*

Double-Deletion and Invalid Pointers

Once you release memory associated with a pointer using `delete`, the memory is available for use by other parts of your program. Nothing stops you, however, from attempting to continue to use the pointer, which is now a *dangling pointer*. Double deletion is also a problem. If you use `delete` a second time on a pointer, the program could be releasing memory that has since been assigned to another object.

Double deletion and use of already released memory are both difficult problems to track down because the symptoms may not show up immediately. If two deletions occur within a relatively short amount of time, the program potentially could work indefinitely because the associated memory might not have been reused that quickly. Similarly, if a deleted object is used immediately after being deleted, most likely it will still be intact.

Of course, there is no guarantee that such behavior will work or continue to work. The memory allocator is under no obligation to preserve any object once it has been deleted. Even if it does work, it is extremely poor programming style to use objects that have been deleted.

To avoid double deletion and use of already released memory, you should set your pointers to `nullptr` after deallocating their memory.

Many memory leak-detection programs are also capable of detecting double deletion and use of released objects.

SMART POINTERS

As the previous section demonstrated, memory management in C++ is a perennial source of errors and bugs. Many of these bugs arise from the use of dynamic memory allocation and pointers. When you extensively use dynamic memory allocation in your program and pass many pointers between objects, it's difficult to remember to call `delete` on each pointer exactly once and at the right time. The consequences of getting it wrong are severe: when you free dynamically allocated memory more than once or use a pointer to memory that was already free, you can cause memory corruption or a fatal run-time error; when you forget to free dynamically allocated memory, you cause memory leaks.

Smart pointers help you manage your dynamically allocated memory and are the recommended technique for avoiding memory leaks. Conceptually, a smart pointer can hold a dynamically allocated resource, such as memory. When a smart pointer goes out of scope or is reset, it can automatically free the resource it holds. Smart pointers can be used to manage dynamically allocated resources in the scope of a function, or as data members in classes. They can also be used to pass ownership of dynamically allocated resources through function arguments.

C++ provides several language features that make smart pointers attractive. First, you can write a type-safe smart pointer class for any pointer type using templates; see Chapter 12. Second, you can provide an interface to the smart pointer objects using operator overloading (see Chapter 15) that allows code to use the smart pointer objects as if they were dumb raw pointers. Specifically, you can overload the `*`, `->`, and `[]` operators such that client code can dereference a smart pointer object the same way it dereferences a normal pointer.

There are several types of smart pointers. The simplest type takes sole/unique ownership of a resource. Being the single owner of a resource, the smart pointer can automatically free the referenced resource when it goes out of scope or is reset. The Standard Library provides `std::unique_ptr`, which is a smart pointer with *unique ownership* semantics.

A slightly more advanced type of smart pointer allows for *shared ownership*; that is, several of these smart pointers can refer to the same resource. When such a smart pointer goes out of scope or is reset, it frees the referenced resource only if it's the last smart pointer referring to that resource. The Standard Library provides `std::shared_ptr` supporting shared ownership.

Both standard smart pointers, `unique_ptr` and `shared_ptr`, are defined in `<memory>` and are discussed in detail in the next sections.

> **NOTE** *Your default smart pointer should be* `unique_ptr`. *Use* `shared_ptr` *only when you really need to share the resource.*

> **WARNING** *Never assign the result of a resource allocation to a raw pointer! Whatever resource allocation method you use, always immediately store the resource pointer in a smart pointer, either* `unique_ptr` *or* `shared_ptr`, *or use other RAII classes. RAII stands for Resource Acquisition Is Initialization. An RAII class takes ownership of a certain resource and handles its deallocation at the right time. It's a design technique discussed in Chapter 32, "Incorporating Design Techniques and Frameworks."*

unique_ptr

A `unique_ptr` has sole ownership of a resource. When the `unique_ptr` is destroyed or reset, the resource is automatically freed. One advantage is that memory and resources are always freed, even when `return` statements are executed or when exceptions are thrown. This, for example, simplifies coding when a function has multiple `return` statements, because you don't have to remember to free resources before each `return` statement.

As a rule of thumb, always store dynamically allocated resources having a single owner in instances of `unique_ptr`.

Creating unique_ptrs

Consider the following function that blatantly leaks memory by allocating a `Simple` object on the free store and neglecting to release it:

```
void leaky()
{
    Simple* mySimplePtr { new Simple{} };  // BUG! Memory is never released!
    mySimplePtr->go();
}
```

Sometimes you might think that your code is properly deallocating dynamically allocated memory. Unfortunately, it most likely is *not correct* in all situations. Take the following function:

```
void couldBeLeaky()
{
    Simple* mySimplePtr { new Simple{} };
    mySimplePtr->go();
    delete mySimplePtr;
}
```

This function dynamically allocates a `Simple` object, uses the object, and then properly calls `delete`. However, you can still have memory leaks in this example! If the `go()` member function throws an exception, the call to `delete` is never executed, causing a memory leak.

Instead, you should use a `unique_ptr`, created using the `std::make_unique()` helper function. `unique_ptr` is a generic smart pointer that can point to any kind of memory. That's why it is a class template, and `make_unique()` a function template. Both require a template parameter between angle brackets, < >, specifying the type of memory you want the `unique_ptr` to point to. Templates are discussed in detail in Chapter 12, but those details are not important to understand how to use smart pointers.

The following function uses a `unique_ptr` instead of a raw pointer. The `Simple` object is not explicitly deleted; but when the `unique_ptr` instance goes out of scope (at the end of the function, or because an exception is thrown), it automatically deallocates the `Simple` object in its destructor.

```
void notLeaky()
{
    auto mySimpleSmartPtr { make_unique<Simple>() };
    mySimpleSmartPtr->go();
}
```

This code uses `make_unique()`, in combination with the `auto` keyword, so that you only have to specify the type of the pointer, `Simple` in this case, once. This is the recommended way to create a `unique_ptr`. If the `Simple` constructor requires parameters, you pass them as arguments to `make_unique()`.

`make_unique()` uses value initialization. Primitive types, for example, are initialized to zero, and objects are default constructed. If you don't need this value initialization, for instance because you will overwrite the initial value anyway, then you can skip the value initialization and improve performance by using the `make_unique_for_overwrite()` function, which uses default initialization. For primitive types, this means they are not initialized at all and contain whatever is in memory at their location, while objects are still default constructed.

You can also create a `unique_ptr` by directly calling its constructor as follows. Note that `Simple` must now be mentioned twice:

```
unique_ptr<Simple> mySimpleSmartPtr { new Simple{} };
```

As discussed earlier in this book, class template argument deduction (CTAD) can often be used to let the compiler deduce the template type arguments for class templates based on the arguments passed to a constructor of the class template. For example, it allows you to write `vector v{1,2}` instead of `vector<int> v{1,2}`. CTAD does not work with `unique_ptr`, so you cannot omit the template type argument.

Before C++17, you had to use `make_unique()` not only because it meant specifying the type only once, but also because of safety reasons! Consider the following call to a function called `foo()`:

```
foo(unique_ptr<Simple> { new Simple{} }, unique_ptr<Bar> { new Bar { data() } });
```

If the constructor of `Simple` or `Bar`, or the `data()` function, throws an exception, depending on your compiler optimizations, it was possible that either a `Simple` or a `Bar` object would be leaked. With `make_unique()`, nothing would leak:

```
foo(make_unique<Simple>(), make_unique<Bar>(data()))
```

Since C++17, both calls to `foo()` are safe, but I still recommend using `make_unique()` as it results in code that is easier to read.

> **NOTE** *Always use* `make_unique()` *to create a* `unique_ptr`.

Using unique_ptrs

One of the greatest characteristics of the standard smart pointers is that they provide enormous benefit without requiring the user to learn a lot of new syntax. Smart pointers can still be dereferenced (using `*` or `->`) just like standard pointers. For example, in the earlier example, the `->` operator is used to call the `go()` member function:

```
mySimpleSmartPtr->go();
```

Just as with standard pointers, you can also write this as follows:

```
(*mySimpleSmartPtr).go();
```

The `get()` member function can be used to get direct access to the underlying pointer. This can be useful to pass the pointer to a function that requires a raw pointer. For example, suppose you have the following function:

```
void processData(Simple* simple) { /* Use the simple pointer... */ }
```

Then you can call it as follows:

```
processData(mySimpleSmartPtr.get());
```

You can free the underlying pointer of a `unique_ptr` and optionally change it to another pointer using `reset()`. Here's an example:

```
mySimpleSmartPtr.reset();              // Free resource and set to nullptr
mySimpleSmartPtr.reset(new Simple{}); // Free resource and set to a new
                                       // Simple instance
```

You can disconnect the underlying pointer from a `unique_ptr` with `release()` which returns the underlying pointer to the resource and then sets the smart pointer to `nullptr`. Effectively, the smart pointer loses ownership of the resource, and as such, you become responsible for freeing the resource when you are done with it! Here's an example:

```
Simple* simple { mySimpleSmartPtr.release() }; // Release ownership
// Use the simple pointer...
```

```
delete simple;
simple = nullptr;
```

Because a unique_ptr represents unique ownership, it cannot be *copied*! But, spoiler alert, it is possible to *move* one unique_ptr to another one using move semantics, as discussed in detail in Chapter 9, "Mastering Classes and Objects." As a sneak preview, the std::move() utility function can be used to explicitly move ownership of a unique_ptr, as in the following code snippet. Don't worry about the syntax for now; Chapter 9 makes it all clear.

```
class Foo
{
    public:
        Foo(unique_ptr<int> data) : m_data { move(data) } { }
    private:
        unique_ptr<int> m_data;
};

auto myIntSmartPtr { make_unique<int>(42) };
Foo f { move(myIntSmartPtr) };
```

unique_ptr and C-Style Arrays

A unique_ptr can store a dynamically allocated old C-style array. The following example creates a unique_ptr that holds a dynamically allocated C-style array of ten integers:

```
auto myVariableSizedArray { make_unique<int[]>(10) };
```

The type of myVariableSizedArray is unique_ptr<int[]> and supports access to its elements using array notation. Here's an example:

```
myVariableSizedArray[1] = 123;
```

Just as for the non-array case, make_unique() uses value initialization for all elements of an array, similarly as std::vector does. For primitive types, this means initialization to zero. The make_unique_for_overwrite() function can be used instead to create an array with default-initialized values, which means uninitialized for primitive types. Keep in mind, though, that uninitialized data should be avoided as much as possible, so use this judiciously.

Even though it is possible to use a unique_ptr to store a dynamically allocated C-style array, it's recommended to use a Standard Library container instead, such as std::array or vector.

Custom Deleters

By default, unique_ptr uses the standard new and delete operators to allocate and deallocate memory. You can change this behavior to use your own allocation and deallocation functions. This can come in handy when you are working with third-party C libraries. For example, suppose you have a C library that requires you to use my_alloc() for allocation and my_free() for deallocation:

```
int* my_alloc(int value) { return new int { value }; }
void my_free(int* p) { delete p; }
```

To properly call my_free() on an allocated resource at the right time, you can use a unique_ptr with a customer deleter:

```
unique_ptr<int, decltype(&my_free)> myIntSmartPtr { my_alloc(42), my_free };
```

This code allocates memory for an integer with my_alloc(), and the unique_ptr deallocates the memory by calling the my_free() function. This feature of unique_ptr is also useful to manage other resources instead of just memory. For example, it can be used to automatically close a file or network socket or anything when the unique_ptr goes out of scope.

Unfortunately, the syntax for a custom deleter with unique_ptr is a bit clumsy. You need to specify the type of your custom deleter as a template type argument, which should be the type of a pointer to a function accepting a single pointer as argument and returning void. In this example, decltype(&my_free) is used, which returns the type of a pointer to the function my_free(). Using a custom deleter with shared_ptr is easier. The following section on shared_ptr demonstrates how to use a shared_ptr to automatically close a file when it goes out of scope.

shared_ptr

Sometimes, several objects or pieces of code need copies of the same pointer. A unique_ptr cannot be copied and hence cannot be used for such cases. Instead, std::shared_ptr is a smart pointer supporting shared ownership that can be copied. But, if there are multiple instances of shared_ptr referring to the same resource, how can they know when to actually free the resource? This is solved through reference counting, the topic of an upcoming section: "The Need for Reference Counting." But first, let's look at how you can construct and use shared_ptrs.

Creating and Using shared_ptrs

You use shared_ptr in a similar way as unique_ptr. To create one, you use make_shared(), which is more efficient than creating a shared_ptr directly. Here's an example:

```
auto mySimpleSmartPtr { make_shared<Simple>() };
```

> **WARNING** *Always use* make_shared() *to create a* shared_ptr.

Just as with unique_ptr, class template argument deduction does not work for shared_ptr, so you have to specify the template type.

make_shared() uses value initialization, similar to make_unique(). If this is not desired, you can use make_shared_for_overwrite() for default initialization, analogous to make_unique_for_overwrite().

A shared_ptr can be used to store a pointer to a dynamically allocated C-style array, just as you can do with a unique_ptr. You can use make_shared() for this, just as you can use make_unique(). However, even though it is now possible to store C-style arrays in a shared_ptr, I still recommend to use Standard Library containers instead of C-style arrays.

A shared_ptr also supports the get() and reset() member functions, just as a unique_ptr. The only difference is that when calling reset(), the underlying resource is freed only when the last shared_ptr is destroyed or reset. Note that shared_ptr does not support release(). You can use the use_count() member function to retrieve the number of shared_ptr instances that are sharing the same resource.

Just like `unique_ptr`, `shared_ptr` by default uses the standard `new` and `delete` operators to allocate and deallocate memory, or `new[]` and `delete[]` when storing a C-style array. You can change this behavior as follows:

```
// Implementations of my_alloc() and my_free() as before.
shared_ptr<int> myIntSmartPtr { my_alloc(42), my_free };
```

As you can see, you don't have to specify the type of the custom deleter as a template type argument, so this makes it easier than a custom deleter with `unique_ptr`.

The following example uses a `shared_ptr` to store a file pointer. When the `shared_ptr` is destroyed (in this case when it goes out of scope), the file pointer is automatically closed with a call to `close()`. Note that C++ has proper object-oriented classes to work with files (see Chapter 13, "Demystifying C++ I/O"). Those classes already automatically close their files. This example using the old C-style `fopen()` and `fclose()` functions is just to give a demonstration of what `shared_ptr`s can be used for besides pure memory. For example, it comes in handy if you have to use a C-style library, for which there is no C++ alternative, and that has similar functions to open and close resources. You could wrap them in `shared_ptr`s as in this example.

```
void close(FILE* filePtr)
{
    if (filePtr == nullptr) { return; }
    fclose(filePtr);
    println("File closed.");
}
int main()
{
    FILE* f { fopen("data.txt", "w") };
    shared_ptr<FILE> filePtr { f, close };
    if (filePtr == nullptr) {
        println(cerr, "Error opening file.");
    } else {
        println("File opened.");
        // Use filePtr
    }
}
```

The Need for Reference Counting

As briefly mentioned earlier, when a smart pointer with shared ownership, such as `shared_ptr`, goes out of scope or is reset, it should only free the referenced resource if it's the last smart pointer referring to it. How is this accomplished? One solution, used by the `shared_ptr` Standard Library smart pointer, is *reference counting*.

As a general concept, *reference counting* is a technique for keeping track of the number of instances of a class or particular object in use. A reference-counting smart pointer is one that keeps track of how many smart pointers have been constructed to refer to a single real pointer, or single object. Every time such a reference-counted smart pointer is copied, a new instance is created pointing to the same resource, and the reference count is incremented. When such a smart pointer instance goes out of scope or is reset, the reference count is decremented. When the reference count drops to zero, there are no other owners of the resource anymore, so the smart pointer frees the resource.

Reference-counted smart pointers solve a lot of memory management issues, such as double deletion. For example, suppose you have the following two raw pointers pointing to the same memory. The `Simple` class is introduced earlier in this chapter and simply prints out messages when an instance is created and destroyed.

```
Simple* mySimple1 { new Simple{} };
Simple* mySimple2 { mySimple1 };  // Make a copy of the pointer.
```

Deleting both raw pointers will result in a double deletion:

```
delete mySimple2;
delete mySimple1;
```

Of course, you'll (ideally) never find code like this, but it can happen when there are several layers of function calls involved, where one function deletes the memory, while another function has already done so.

By using the `shared_ptr` reference-counted smart pointer, such double deletions are avoided:

```
auto smartPtr1 { make_shared<Simple>() };
auto smartPtr2 { smartPtr1 };  // Make a copy of the pointer.
```

In this case, when both smart pointers go out of scope or are reset, only then is the `Simple` instance freed, exactly once.

All this works correctly only when there are no raw pointers involved! For example, suppose you allocate some memory using `new` and then create two `shared_ptr` instances referring to the same raw pointer:

```
Simple* mySimple { new Simple{} };
shared_ptr<Simple> smartPtr1 { mySimple };
shared_ptr<Simple> smartPtr2 { mySimple };
```

Both these smart pointers will attempt to delete the same object when they are destroyed. Depending on your compiler, this piece of code might crash! If you do get output, it could be as follows:

```
Simple constructor called!
Simple destructor called!
Simple destructor called!
```

Yikes! One call to the constructor and two calls to the destructor? You get the same problem with `unique_ptr`. You might be surprised that even the reference-counted `shared_ptr` class behaves this way. However, this is correct behavior. The only safe way to have multiple `shared_ptr` instances point to the same memory is to simply *copy* such `shared_ptrs`.

Casting a shared_ptr

Just as a raw pointer of a certain type can be cast to a pointer of a different type, a `shared_ptr` storing a certain type can be cast to a `shared_ptr` of another type. Of course, there are restrictions of what type can be cast to what type. Not all casts are valid. The functions that are available to cast `shared_ptrs` are `const_pointer_cast()`, `dynamic_pointer_cast()`, `static_pointer_cast()`, and `reinterpret_pointer_cast()`. These behave and work similar to the non-smart pointer casting functions `const_cast()`, `dynamic_cast()`, `static_cast()`, and `reinterpret_cast()`, which are discussed in detail with examples in Chapter 10.

Note that these casts work only with `shared_ptr` and not with `unique_ptr`.

Aliasing

A shared_ptr supports *aliasing*. This allows a shared_ptr to share ownership over a pointer (*owned pointer*) with another shared_ptr, but pointing to a different object (*stored pointer*). It can, for example, be used to have a shared_ptr pointing to a member of an object while owning the object itself. Here's an example:

```
class Foo
{
    public:
        Foo(int value) : m_data { value } { }
        int m_data;
};

auto foo { make_shared<Foo>(42) };
auto aliasing { shared_ptr<int> { foo, &foo->m_data } };
```

The Foo object is only destroyed when both shared_ptrs (foo and aliasing) are destroyed.

The owned pointer is used for reference counting, while the stored pointer is returned when you dereference the pointer or when you call get() on it.

> **WARNING** *In modern C++ code, raw pointers are allowed only if there is no ownership involved! If there is ownership involved, use* unique_ptr *by default, and* shared_ptr *if ownership needs to be shared. Additionally, use* make_unique() *and* make_shared() *to create these smart pointers. By doing so, there should be almost no need to directly call the* new *operator, and there should never be a need to call* delete.

weak_ptr

There is one more smart pointer class in C++ that is related to shared_ptr, called weak_ptr. A weak_ptr can contain a reference to a resource managed by a shared_ptr. The weak_ptr does not own the resource, so the shared_ptr is not prevented from deallocating the resource. A weak_ptr does not destroy the pointed-to resource when the weak_ptr is destroyed (for example when it goes out of scope); however, it can be used to determine whether the resource has been freed by the associated shared_ptr or not. The constructor of a weak_ptr requires a shared_ptr or another weak_ptr as argument. To get access to the pointer stored in a weak_ptr, you need to convert it to a shared_ptr. There are two ways to do this:

- Use the lock() member function on a weak_ptr instance, which returns a shared_ptr. The returned shared_ptr is nullptr if the shared_ptr associated with the weak_ptr has been deallocated in the meantime.
- Create a new shared_ptr instance and give a weak_ptr as argument to the shared_ptr constructor. This throws an std::bad_weak_ptr exception if the shared_ptr associated with the weak_ptr has been deallocated.

The following example demonstrates the use of weak_ptr:

```
void useResource(weak_ptr<Simple>& weakSimple)
{
    auto resource { weakSimple.lock() };
    if (resource) { println("Resource still alive."); }
    else          { println("Resource has been freed!"); }
}

int main()
{
    auto sharedSimple { make_shared<Simple>() };
    weak_ptr<Simple> weakSimple { sharedSimple };

    // Try to use the weak_ptr.
    useResource(weakSimple);

    // Reset the shared_ptr.
    // Since there is only 1 shared_ptr to the Simple resource, this will
    // free the resource, even though there is still a weak_ptr alive.
    sharedSimple.reset();

    // Try to use the weak_ptr a second time.
    useResource(weakSimple);
}
```

The output of this code is as follows:

```
Simple constructor called!
Resource still alive.
Simple destructor called!
Resource has been freed!
```

weak_ptr also supports C-style arrays, just as shared_ptr.

Passing to Functions

A function accepting a pointer as one of its parameters should accept a smart pointer only if there is ownership transfer or ownership sharing involved. To share ownership of a shared_ptr, simply accept a shared_ptr by value as parameter. Similarly, to transfer ownership of a unique_ptr, simply accept a unique_ptr by value as parameter. The latter requires using move semantics, discussed in detail in Chapter 9.

If neither ownership transfer nor ownership sharing is involved, then the function should simply have a reference-to-non-const or reference-to-const parameter referring to the underlying resource, or a raw pointer to it if nullptr is a valid value for the parameter. Having a parameter type such as const shared_ptr<T>& or const unique_ptr<T>& never makes much sense.

Returning from Functions

The standard smart pointers, shared_ptr, unique_ptr, and weak_ptr, can easily and efficiently be returned from functions by value, thanks to mandatory and non-mandatory copy elision, discussed in Chapter 1, and move semantics, discussed in Chapter 9. Details of move semantics are not important at this time. What is important is that all this means it is efficient to return a smart pointer from a function. For example, you can write the following `create()` function and use it as demonstrated in `main()`:

```
unique_ptr<Simple> create()
{
    auto ptr { make_unique<Simple>() };
    // Do something with ptr...
    return ptr;
}

int main()
{
    unique_ptr<Simple> mySmartPtr1 { create() };
    auto mySmartPtr2 { create() };
}
```

enable_shared_from_this

Deriving a class from `std::enable_shared_from_this` allows a member function called on an object to safely return a `shared_ptr` or `weak_ptr` to itself. Without this base class, one way to return a valid `shared_ptr` or `weak_ptr` to `this` is by adding a `weak_ptr` as a member to the class, and to return copies of it or return `shared_ptr`s constructed from it. The `enable_shared_from_this` class adds the following two member functions to a class deriving from it:

- `shared_from_this()`: Returns a `shared_ptr` that shares ownership of the object
- `weak_from_this()`: Returns a `weak_ptr` that tracks ownership of the object

This is an advanced feature not discussed in detail, but the following code briefly demonstrates its use. Both `shared_from_this()` and `weak_from_this()` are `public` member functions. However, maybe you find the `from_this` part confusing in your `public` interface, so just as a demonstration, the following `Foo` class defines its own member function called `getPointer()`:

```
class Foo : public enable_shared_from_this<Foo>
{
    public:
        shared_ptr<Foo> getPointer() {
            return shared_from_this();
        }
};

int main()
{
    auto ptr1 { make_shared<Foo>() };
    auto ptr2 { ptr1->getPointer() };
}
```

Note that you can use `shared_from_this()` on an object only if its pointer has already been stored in a `shared_ptr`; otherwise, a `bad_weak_ptr` exception is thrown. In the example, `make_shared()` is used in `main()` to create a `shared_ptr` called `ptr1`, which contains an instance of `Foo`. After this `shared_ptr` creation, it is allowed to call `shared_from_this()` on that `Foo` instance. On the other hand, it is always allowed to call weak_from_this(), but it might return an empty weak_ptr if it is called on an object for which its pointer has not been stored in a shared_ptr yet.

The following would be a completely wrong implementation of the getPointer() member function:

```
class Foo
{
    public:
        shared_ptr<Foo> getPointer() {
            return shared_ptr<Foo>(this);
        }
};
```

If you use the same code for main() as shown earlier, this implementation of Foo causes a double deletion. You have two completely independent shared_ptrs (ptr1 and ptr2) pointing to the same object, which will both try to delete the object when they go out of scope.

C++23 Interoperability of Smart Pointers with C-Style Functions

Often, C-style functions use the return type to indicate whether a function executed correctly or whether there was any error. Since the return type is already used for reporting errors, additional output parameters are used to return other data from the function. For example:

```
using errorcode = int;
errorcode my_alloc(int value, int** data) { *data = new int { value }; return 0; }
errorcode my_free(int* data) { delete data; return 0; }
```

With this C-style API, the my_alloc() function returns an errorcode and returns the allocated data in the output parameter called data. Before C++23, you could not directly use a smart pointer, such as unique_ptr, with my_alloc(). Instead, you could do something like this:

```
unique_ptr<int, decltype(&my_free)> myIntSmartPtr(nullptr, my_free);
int* data { nullptr };
my_alloc(42, &data);
myIntSmartPtr.reset(data);
```

That's rather involved for something relatively easy. C++23 introduces the std::out_ptr() and inout_ptr() functions to help with this, both defined in <memory>. Using these, the code snippet can be written more elegantly as follows:

```
unique_ptr<int, decltype(&my_free)> myIntSmartPtr(nullptr, my_free);
my_alloc(42, inout_ptr(myIntSmartPtr));
```

If you're sure that the pointer passed to inout_ptr() is nullptr, then you can use out_ptr instead.

The Old and Removed auto_ptr

The old, pre-C++11 Standard Library included a basic implementation of a smart pointer, called auto_ptr. Unfortunately, auto_ptr has some serious shortcomings. One of these shortcomings is that it does not work correctly when used inside Standard Library containers such as vectors. C++11 officially deprecated auto_ptr, and since C++17, it has been removed entirely from the Standard Library. It is replaced with unique_ptr and shared_ptr. auto_ptr is mentioned here to make sure you know about it and to make sure you never use it.

> **WARNING** *Never use the old* `auto_ptr` *smart pointer! Instead, use* `unique_ptr` *by default or* `shared_ptr` *if you need shared ownership.*

SUMMARY

In this chapter, you learned the ins and outs of dynamic memory. Aside from memory-checking tools and careful coding, there are two key takeaways to avoid dynamic memory-related problems.

First, you need to understand how pointers work under the hood. After reading about two different mental models for pointers, you should now know how the compiler doles out memory.

Second, you should avoid raw pointers when ownership is involved, and avoid using old C-style constructs and functions. Instead, use safe C++ alternatives, such as objects that automatically manage their memory, like the C++ `string` class, the `vector` container, smart pointers, and so on.

EXERCISES

By solving the following exercises, you can practice the material discussed in this chapter. Solutions to all exercises are available with the code download on the book's website at `www.wiley.com/go/proc++6e`. However, if you are stuck on an exercise, first reread parts of this chapter to try to find an answer yourself before looking at the solution from the website.

Exercise 7-1: Analyze the following code snippet. Can you list any problems you find with it? You don't need to fix the problems in this exercise; that will be for Exercise 7-2.

```
const size_t numberOfElements { 10 };
int* values { new int[numberOfElements] };
// Set values to their index value.
for (int index { 0 }; index < numberOfElements; ++index) {
    values[index] = index;
}
// Set last value to 99.
values[10] = 99;
// Print all values.
for (int index { 0 }; index <= numberOfElements; ++index) {
    print("{} ", values[index]);
}
```

Exercise 7-2: Rewrite the code snippet from Exercise 7-1 to use modern and safe C++ constructs.

Exercise 7-3: Write a basic class to store a 3-D point with x, y, and z coordinates. Include a constructor accepting x, y, and z arguments. Write a function that accepts a 3-D point and prints out its coordinates using `std::print()`. In your `main()` function, dynamically allocate an instance of your class and subsequently call your function.

Exercise 7-4: Earlier in this chapter, the following function is shown in the context of out-of-bounds memory access. Can you modernize this function using safe C++ alternatives? Test your solution in your `main()` function.

```
void fillWithM(char* text)
{
    int i { 0 };
    while (text[i] != '\0') {
        text[i] = 'm';
        ++i;
    }
}
```

8

Gaining Proficiency with Classes and Objects

WHAT'S IN THIS CHAPTER?

- How to write your own classes with member functions and data members
- How to control access to your member functions and data members
- How to use objects on the stack and on the free store
- What the life cycle of an object is
- How to write code that is executed when an object is created or destroyed
- How to write code to copy or assign objects

WILEY.COM DOWNLOADS FOR THIS CHAPTER

Please note that all the code examples for this chapter are available as part of this chapter's code download on the book's website at `www.wiley.com/go/proc++6e` on the Download Code tab.

As an object-oriented language, C++ provides facilities for using objects and for writing object blueprints, called *classes*. You can certainly write programs in C++ without classes and objects, but by doing so, you do not take advantage of the most fundamental and useful aspect of the language; writing a C++ program without classes is like traveling to Paris and eating at McDonald's. To use classes and objects effectively, you must understand their syntax and capabilities.

Chapter 1, "A Crash Course in C++ and the Standard Library," reviewed the basic syntax of class definitions. Chapter 5, "Designing with Classes," introduced the object-oriented approach to programming in C++ and presented specific design strategies for classes and objects. This chapter describes the fundamental concepts involved in using classes and objects, including writing class definitions, defining member functions, using objects on the stack and the free store, writing constructors, default constructors, compiler-generated constructors, constructor initializers (also known as *ctor-initializers*), copy constructors, initializer-list constructors, destructors, and assignment operators. Even if you are already comfortable with classes and objects, you should skim this chapter because it contains various tidbits of information with which you might not yet be familiar.

INTRODUCING THE SPREADSHEET EXAMPLE

Both this chapter and the next present a runnable example of a simple spreadsheet application. A spreadsheet is a two-dimensional grid of "cells," and each cell contains a number or a string. Professional spreadsheets such as Microsoft Excel provide the ability to perform mathematical operations, such as calculating the sum of the values of a set of cells. The spreadsheet example in these chapters does not attempt to challenge Microsoft in the marketplace, but it is useful for illustrating the issues of classes and objects.

The spreadsheet application uses two basic classes: `Spreadsheet` and `SpreadsheetCell`. Each `Spreadsheet` object contains `SpreadsheetCell` objects. In addition, a `SpreadsheetApplication` class manages a collection of `Spreadsheets`. This chapter focuses on the `SpreadsheetCell` class. Chapter 9, "Mastering Classes and Objects," develops the `Spreadsheet` and `SpreadsheetApplication` classes.

> **NOTE** *This chapter shows several different versions of the* `SpreadsheetCell` *class in order to introduce concepts gradually. Thus, the various attempts at the class throughout the chapter do not always illustrate the "best" way to do every aspect of class writing. In particular, the early examples omit important features that would normally be included but have not yet been introduced. You can download the final version of the class as described in the beginning of this chapter.*

WRITING CLASSES

When you write a class, you specify the behaviors, or *member functions*, that will apply to objects of that class, and you specify the properties, or *data members*, that each object will contain.

There are two components in the process of writing classes: defining the classes themselves and defining their member functions.

Class Definitions

Here is a first attempt at a simple `SpreadsheetCell` class in a `spreadsheet_cell` module, in which each cell can store only a single number:

```
export module spreadsheet_cell;

export class SpreadsheetCell
{
    public:
        void setValue(double value);
        double getValue() const;
    private:
        double m_value;
};
```

As described in Chapter 1, the first line specifies that this is the definition of a module named `spreadsheet_cell`. Every class definition begins with the keyword `class` followed by the name of the class. If the class is defined in a module and the class must become visible to clients importing the module, then the `class` keyword is prefixed with `export`. A class definition is a *declaration* and ends with a semicolon.

Class definitions usually go in a file named after the class. For example, the `SpreadsheetCell` class definition is put in a file called `SpreadsheetCell.cppm`. Some compilers require the use of a specific extension; others allow you to choose any extension.

Class Members

A class can have several *members*. A member can be a *member function* (which in turn is a *function, constructor*, or *destructor*), a *member variable* (also called a *data member*), member enumerations, type aliases, nested classes, and so on.

The two lines that look like function prototypes declare the member functions that this class supports:

```
void setValue(double value);
double getValue() const;
```

Chapter 1 points out that it is always a good idea to declare member functions that do not change the object as `const`, like the `getValue()` member function.

The line that looks like a variable declaration declares the data member for this class:

```
double m_value;
```

A class defines the member functions and data members that apply. They apply only to a specific *instance* of the class, which is an *object*. The only exceptions to this rule are static members, which are explained in Chapter 9. Classes define concepts; objects contain real bits. So, each object contains its own value for the `m_value` data member. The implementation of the member functions is shared across all objects. Classes can contain any number of member functions and data members. You cannot give a data member the same name as a member function.

Access Control

Every member in a class is subject to one of three *access specifiers*: `public`, `private`, or `protected`. The `protected` access specifier is explained in the context of inheritance in Chapter 10, "Discovering Inheritance Techniques." An access specifier applies to all member declarations that follow it, until the next access specifier. In the `SpreadsheetCell` class, the `setValue()` and `getValue()` member functions have `public` access, while the `m_value` data member has `private` access.

The default access specifier for classes is private: all member declarations before the first access specifier have the private access specification. For example, moving the public access specifier to after the setValue() member function declaration gives the setValue() member function private access instead of public:

```
export class SpreadsheetCell
{
        void setValue(double value); // now has private access
    public:
        double getValue() const;
    private:
        double m_value;
};
```

In C++, a struct can have member functions just like a class. In fact, there is only one difference: for a struct, the default access specifier is public, while it's private for a class.

For example, the SpreadsheetCell class could be rewritten using a struct as follows:

```
export struct SpreadsheetCell
{
        void setValue(double value);
        double getValue() const;
    private:
        double m_value;
};
```

However, it's unconventional to do so. A struct is usually used only if you just need a collection of publicly accessible data members and no member functions. The following is an example of such a simple struct to store 2-D point coordinates:

```
export struct Point
{
    double x;
    double y;
};
```

Order of Declarations

You can declare your members and access control specifiers in any order: C++ does not impose any restrictions, such as member functions before data members or public before private. Additionally, you can repeat access specifiers. For example, the SpreadsheetCell definition could look like this:

```
export class SpreadsheetCell
{
    public:
        void setValue(double value);
    private:
        double m_value;
    public:
        double getValue() const;
};
```

However, for clarity it is a good idea to group declarations based on their access specifier and to group member functions and data members within those declarations.

In-Class Member Initializers

Data members can be initialized directly in the class definition. For example, the `SpreadsheetCell` class can, by default, initialize `m_value` to 0 directly in the class definition as follows:

```
export class SpreadsheetCell
{
    // Remainder of the class definition omitted for brevity
    private:
        double m_value { 0 };
};
```

> **NOTE** *It is recommended to always initialize data members of a class.*

Defining Member Functions

The preceding definition for the `SpreadsheetCell` class is enough for you to create objects of the class. However, if you try to call the `setValue()` or `getValue()` member function, your linker will complain that those member functions are not defined. That's because these member functions only have prototypes so far, but no implementations yet. Usually, a class definition goes in a module interface file. For the member function definitions, you have a choice: they can go in the module interface file or in a *module implementation file*.

Here is the `SpreadsheetCell` class with in-class member function implementations:

```
export module spreadsheet_cell;

export class SpreadsheetCell
{
    public:
        void setValue(double value) { m_value = value; }
        double getValue() const { return m_value; }
    private:
        double m_value { 0 };
};
```

Unlike with header files, with C++ modules there is no harm in putting member function definitions in module interface files. This is discussed in more detail in Chapter 11, "Modules, Header Files, and Miscellaneous Topics." However, this book often puts member function definitions in module implementation files, in the interest of keeping module interface files clean and without any implementation details.

The first line of a module implementation file specifies which module the implementations are for. Here are the definitions for the two member functions of the `SpreadsheetCell` class in the `spreadsheet_cell` module:

```
module spreadsheet_cell;

void SpreadsheetCell::setValue(double value)
{
```

```
    m_value = value;
}

double SpreadsheetCell::getValue() const
{
    return m_value;
}
```

Note that the name of the class followed by two colons precedes each member function name:

```
void SpreadsheetCell::setValue(double value)
```

The `::` is called the *scope resolution operator*. In this context, the syntax tells the compiler that the coming definition of the `setValue()` member function is part of the `SpreadsheetCell` class. Note also that you do not repeat the access specification when you define the member function.

Accessing Data Members

Non-static member functions of a class, such as `setValue()` and `getValue()`, are always executed on behalf of a specific object of that class. Inside a member function's body, you have access to all data members of the class for that object. In the previous definition for `setValue()`, the following line changes the `m_value` variable inside whatever object calls the member function:

```
m_value = value;
```

If `setValue()` is called for two different objects, the same line of code (executed once for each object) changes the variable in two different objects.

Calling Other Member Functions

You can call member functions of a class from inside another member function. For example, consider an extension to the `SpreadsheetCell` class to allow setting and retrieving the value of a cell as a string or as a number. When you try to set the value of a cell with a string, the cell tries to convert the string to a number. If the string does not represent a valid number, the cell value is ignored. In this program, strings that are not numbers will generate a cell value of 0. Here is a first stab at such a class definition for a `SpreadsheetCell`:

```
export module spreadsheet_cell;
import std;
export class SpreadsheetCell
{
    public:
        void setValue(double value);
        double getValue() const;

        void setString(std::string_view value);
        std::string getString() const;
    private:
        std::string doubleToString(double value) const;
        double stringToDouble(std::string_view value) const;
        double m_value { 0 };
};
```

This version of the class stores the data only as a double. If the client sets the data as a string, it is converted to a double. If the text is not a valid number, the double value is set to 0. The class definition shows two new member functions to set and retrieve the text representation of the cell, and two new private *helper member functions* to convert a double to a string and vice versa. Here are the implementations of all the member functions:

```
module spreadsheet_cell;
import std;
using namespace std;

void SpreadsheetCell::setValue(double value)
{
    m_value = value;
}

double SpreadsheetCell::getValue() const
{
    return m_value;
}

void SpreadsheetCell::setString(string_view value)
{
    m_value = stringToDouble(value);
}

string SpreadsheetCell::getString() const
{
    return doubleToString(m_value);
}

string SpreadsheetCell::doubleToString(double value) const
{
    return to_string(value);
}

double SpreadsheetCell::stringToDouble(string_view value) const
{
    double number { 0 };
    from_chars(value.data(), value.data() + value.size(), number);
    return number;
}
```

The std::to_string() and from_chars() functions are explained in Chapter 2, "Working with Strings and String Views."

Note that with this implementation of the doubleToString() member function, a value of, for example, 6.1 is converted to 6.100000. However, because it is a private helper member function, you are free to modify the implementation without having to modify any client code.

Using Objects

The previous class definition says that a SpreadsheetCell consists of one data member, four public member functions, and two private member functions. However, the class definition does not actually create any SpreadsheetCells; it just specifies their shape and behavior. In that sense, a class is like architectural blueprints. The blueprints specify what a house should look like, but drawing the blueprints doesn't build any houses. Houses must be constructed later based on the blueprints.

Similarly, in C++ you can construct a SpreadsheetCell "object" from the SpreadsheetCell class definition by declaring a variable of type SpreadsheetCell. Just as a builder can build more than one house based on a given set of blueprints, a programmer can create more than one SpreadsheetCell object from a SpreadsheetCell class. There are two ways to create and use objects: on the stack and on the free store.

Objects on the Stack

Here is some code that creates and uses SpreadsheetCell objects on the stack:

```
SpreadsheetCell myCell, anotherCell;
myCell.setValue(6);
anotherCell.setString("3.2");
println("cell 1: {}", myCell.getValue());
println("cell 2: {}", anotherCell.getValue());
```

You create objects just as you declare simple variables, except that the variable type is the class name. The . in lines like myCell.setValue(6); is called the *"dot" operator*, also called the *member access operator*; it allows you to call public member functions on the object. If there were any public data members in the object, you could access them with the dot operator as well. Remember that public data members are not recommended.

The output of the program is as follows:

```
cell 1: 6
cell 2: 3.2
```

Objects on the Free Store

You can also dynamically allocate objects by using new:

```
SpreadsheetCell* myCellp { new SpreadsheetCell { } };
myCellp->setValue(3.7);
println("cell 1: {} {}", myCellp->getValue(), myCellp->getString());
delete myCellp;
myCellp = nullptr;
```

When you create an object on the free store, you access its members through the "arrow" operator: ->. The arrow combines dereferencing (*) and member access (.). You could use those two operators instead, but doing so would be stylistically awkward:

```
SpreadsheetCell* myCellp { new SpreadsheetCell { } };
(*myCellp).setValue(3.7);
println("cell 1: {} {}", (*myCellp).getValue(), (*myCellp).getString());
delete myCellp;
myCellp = nullptr;
```

Just as you must free other memory that you allocate on the free store, you must free the memory for objects that you allocate on the free store by calling delete on them, as is done in the previous code snippets! To guarantee safety and to avoid memory problems, you really should use smart pointers, as in the following example:

```
auto myCellp { make_unique<SpreadsheetCell>() };
// Equivalent to:
// unique_ptr<SpreadsheetCell> myCellp { new SpreadsheetCell { } };
myCellp->setValue(3.7);
println("cell 1: {} {}", myCellp->getValue(), myCellp->getString());
```

With smart pointers you don't need to manually free the memory; it happens automatically.

> **WARNING** *When you allocate an object with* `new`*, free it with* `delete` *after you are finished with it, or, better yet, use smart pointers to manage the memory automatically!*

> **NOTE** *If you don't use smart pointers, it is always a good idea to reset a pointer to* `nullptr` *after deleting the object to which it pointed. You are not required to do so, but it will make debugging easier in case the pointer is accidentally used after deleting the object.*

The this Pointer

Every normal member function call implicitly passes a pointer to the object for which it is called as a "hidden" parameter with the name `this`. You can use this pointer to access data members or call member functions, and you can pass it to other member functions or functions. It is sometimes also useful for disambiguating names. For example, you could have defined the `SpreadsheetCell` class with a `value` data member instead of `m_value`. In that case, `setValue()` would look like the following:

```
void SpreadsheetCell::setValue(double value)
{
    value = value; // Confusing!
}
```

That line is confusing. Which `value` do you mean: the `value` that was passed as a parameter or the `value` that is a member of the object?

> **NOTE** *With some compilers or compiler settings, the preceding confusing line compiles without any warnings or errors, but it will not produce the results that you are expecting.*

To disambiguate the names, you can use the `this` pointer:

```
void SpreadsheetCell::setValue(double value)
{
    this->value = value;
}
```

However, if you use the naming conventions described in Chapter 3, "Coding with Style," you will never encounter this type of name collision.

You can also use the `this` pointer to call a function that takes, as a parameter, a pointer to an object from within a member function of that object. For example, suppose you write a `printCell()` stand-alone function (not a member function) like this:

```
void printCell(const SpreadsheetCell& cell)
{
    println("{}", cell.getString());
}
```

If you want to call `printCell()` from the `setValue()` member function, you must pass `*this` as the argument to give `printCell()` a reference to the `SpreadsheetCell` on which `setValue()` operates:

```
void SpreadsheetCell::setValue(double value)
{
    this->value = value;
    printCell(*this);
}
```

> **NOTE** *Instead of writing a* `printCell()` *function, it would be more convenient to write a custom formatter, as explained in Chapter 2. You can then use the following line to print a* `SpreadsheetCell` *called* `myCell`*:*
>
> ```
> std::println("{}", myCell);
> ```
>
> *Alternatively, you can overload the* `<<` *operator, as explained in Chapter 15, "Overloading C++ Operators." You can then write the following:*
>
> ```
> cout << myCell << endl;
> ```

C++23

Explicit Object Parameter

Starting with C++23, instead of relying on the compiler to provide an implicit `this` parameter, you can use an *explicit object parameter*, usually of a reference type. The following code snippet implements the `setValue()` member function of `SpreadsheetCell` from the previous section using an explicit object parameter:

```
void SpreadsheetCell::setValue(this SpreadsheetCell& self, double value)
{
    self.m_value = value;
    printCell(self);
}
```

The first parameter of `setValue()` is now the explicit object parameter, usually called `self`, but you can use any name you want. The type of `self` is prefixed with the `this` keyword. This explicit object parameter must be the first parameter of the member function. Once you use an explicit object parameter, the function no longer has an implicitly defined `this`; hence, in the body of `setValue()`, you now must explicitly use `self` to access anything from the `SpreadsheetCell`.

Calling a member function that uses an explicit object parameter is no different than calling one with an implicit `this` parameter. Even though `setValue()` now specifies two parameters, `self` and `value`, you still call it by passing just a single argument, the `value` that you want to set:

```
SpreadsheetCell myCell;
myCell.setValue(6);
```

Using explicit object parameters as demonstrated in this section has no benefits at all, it even makes the code more verbose. However, they are useful in the following situations:

- To provide a more explicit syntax for writing ref-qualified member functions, discussed in Chapter 9.
- For member function templates where the type of the explicit object parameter is a template type parameter. This can be useful to avoid code duplication when implementing `const` and non-`const` overloads of member functions and is discussed in Chapter 12, "Writing Generic Code with Templates."
- To write recursive lambda expressions, explained in Chapter 19, "Function Pointers, Function Objects, and Lambda Expressions."

UNDERSTANDING OBJECT LIFE CYCLES

The object life cycle involves three activities: *creation*, *destruction*, and *assignment*. It is important to understand how and when objects are created, destroyed, and assigned, and how you can customize these behaviors.

Object Creation

Objects are created at the point you declare them (if they're on the stack) or when you explicitly allocate space for them with a smart pointer, `new`, or `new[]`. When an object is created, all its embedded objects are also created. Here is an example:

```
import std;

class MyClass
{
    private:
        std::string m_name;
};

int main()
{
    MyClass obj;
}
```

The embedded `string` object is created at the point where the `MyClass` object is created in the `main()` function and is destroyed when its containing object is destroyed.

It is often helpful to give variables initial values as you declare them, as so:

```
int x { 0 };
```

Similarly, you could give initial values to objects. You can provide this functionality by declaring and writing a special member function called a *constructor*, in which you can perform initialization work for the object. Whenever an object is created, one of its constructors is executed.

> **NOTE** *C++ programmers sometimes call a constructor a ctor (pronounced "see-tor").*

Writing Constructors

Syntactically, a constructor is specified by a member function name that is the same as the class name. A constructor never has a return type and may or may not have parameters. A constructor that can be called without any arguments is called a *default constructor*. This can be a constructor that does not have any parameters, or a constructor for which all parameters have default values. There are certain contexts in which you may have to provide a default constructor, and you will get compilation errors if you have not provided one. Default constructors are discussed later in this chapter.

Here is a first attempt at adding a constructor to the `SpreadsheetCell` class:

```
export class SpreadsheetCell
{
    public:
        SpreadsheetCell(double initialValue);
        // Remainder of the class definition omitted for brevity
};
```

Just as you must provide implementations for normal member functions, you must provide an implementation for the constructor:

```
SpreadsheetCell::SpreadsheetCell(double initialValue)
{
    setValue(initialValue);
}
```

The `SpreadsheetCell` constructor is a member of the `SpreadsheetCell` class, so C++ requires the normal `SpreadsheetCell::` scope resolution before the constructor name. The constructor name itself is also `SpreadsheetCell`, so the code ends up with the funny-looking `SpreadsheetCell::SpreadsheetCell`. The implementation simply makes a call to `setValue()`.

Using Constructors

Using the constructor creates an object and initializes its values. You can use constructors with both stack-based and free store-based allocation.

Constructors for Objects on the Stack

When you allocate a `SpreadsheetCell` object on the stack, you use the constructor like this:

```
SpreadsheetCell myCell(5), anotherCell(4);
println("cell 1: {}", myCell.getValue());
println("cell 2: {}", anotherCell.getValue());
```

Alternatively, you can use the uniform initialization syntax:

```
SpreadsheetCell myCell { 5 }, anotherCell { 4 };
```

Note that you do *not* call the `SpreadsheetCell` constructor explicitly. For example, do not do something as follows:

```
SpreadsheetCell myCell.SpreadsheetCell(5); // WILL NOT COMPILE!
```

Similarly, you cannot call the constructor later. The following is also incorrect:

```
SpreadsheetCell myCell;
myCell.SpreadsheetCell(5); // WILL NOT COMPILE!
```

Constructors for Objects on the Free Store

When you dynamically allocate a `SpreadsheetCell` object, you use the constructor like this:

```
auto smartCellp { make_unique<SpreadsheetCell>(4) };
// ... do something with the cell, no need to delete the smart pointer

// Or with raw pointers, without smart pointers (not recommended)
SpreadsheetCell* myCellp { new SpreadsheetCell { 5 } };
// Or
// SpreadsheetCell* myCellp{ new SpreadsheetCell(5) };
SpreadsheetCell* anotherCellp { nullptr };
anotherCellp = new SpreadsheetCell { 4 };
// ... do something with the cells
delete myCellp;            myCellp = nullptr;
delete anotherCellp;       anotherCellp = nullptr;
```

Note that you can declare a pointer to a `SpreadsheetCell` object without calling the constructor immediately, which is different from objects on the stack, where the constructor is called at the point of declaration.

Remember to always initialize pointers, either with a proper pointer or with `nullptr`.

Providing Multiple Constructors

You can provide more than one constructor in a class. All constructors have the same name (the name of the class), but different constructors must take a different number of arguments or different argument types. In C++, if you have more than one function with the same name, the compiler selects the one whose parameter types match the types at the call site. This is called *overloading* and is discussed in detail in Chapter 9.

In the `SpreadsheetCell` class, it is helpful to have two constructors: one to take an initial `double` value and one to take an initial string value. Here is the new class definition:

```
export class SpreadsheetCell
{
```

```
    public:
        SpreadsheetCell(double initialValue);
        SpreadsheetCell(std::string_view initialValue);
        // Remainder of the class definition omitted for brevity
};
```

Here is the implementation of the second constructor:

```
SpreadsheetCell::SpreadsheetCell(string_view initialValue)
{
    setString(initialValue);
}
```

Here is some code that uses the two different constructors:

```
SpreadsheetCell aThirdCell { "test" };  // Uses string-arg ctor
SpreadsheetCell aFourthCell { 4.4 };    // Uses double-arg ctor
auto aFifthCellp { make_unique<SpreadsheetCell>("5.5") }; // string-arg ctor
println("aThirdCell: {}", aThirdCell.getValue());
println("aFourthCell: {}", aFourthCell.getValue());
println("aFifthCellp: {}", aFifthCellp->getValue());
```

When you have multiple constructors, it is tempting to try to implement one constructor in terms of another. For example, you might want to call the double constructor from the string constructor as follows:

```
SpreadsheetCell::SpreadsheetCell(string_view initialValue)
{
    SpreadsheetCell(stringToDouble(initialValue));
}
```

That seems to make sense. After all, you can call normal class member functions from within other member functions. The code will compile, link, and run, but will not do what you expect! The explicit call to the `SpreadsheetCell` constructor actually creates a new temporary unnamed object of type `SpreadsheetCell`. It does not call the constructor for the object that you are supposed to be initializing.

However, all is not lost. C++ does support *delegating constructors*. These allow you to call other constructors of the same class from inside the ctor-initializer, but for this, you'll have to wait until later in this chapter after the introduction of ctor-initializers.

Default Constructors

A *default constructor* is a constructor that requires no arguments. It is also called a *zero-argument constructor*.

When You Need a Default Constructor

Consider arrays of objects. The act of creating an array of objects accomplishes two tasks: it allocates contiguous memory space for all the objects, and it calls the default constructor on each object. C++ fails to provide any syntax to tell the array creation code directly to call a different constructor. For example, if you do not define a default constructor for the `SpreadsheetCell` class, the following code does not compile:

```
SpreadsheetCell cells[3]; // FAILS compilation without default constructor
SpreadsheetCell* myCellp { new SpreadsheetCell[10] }; // Also FAILS
```

You can circumvent this restriction by using *initializers* like these:

```
SpreadsheetCell cells[3] { SpreadsheetCell { 0 }, SpreadsheetCell { 23 },
    SpreadsheetCell { 41 } };
```

However, it is usually easier to ensure that your class has a default constructor if you intend to create arrays of objects of that class. If you haven't defined your own constructors, the compiler automatically creates a default constructor for you. This compiler-generated constructor is discussed in a later section.

How to Write a Default Constructor

Here is part of the `SpreadsheetCell` class definition with a default constructor:

```
export class SpreadsheetCell
{
    public:
        SpreadsheetCell();
        // Remainder of the class definition omitted for brevity
};
```

Here is a first crack at an implementation of the default constructor:

```
SpreadsheetCell::SpreadsheetCell()
{
    m_value = 0;
}
```

If you use an in-class member initializer for `m_value`, then the single statement in this default constructor can be left out.

```
SpreadsheetCell::SpreadsheetCell()
{
}
```

You use the default constructor on the stack like this:

```
SpreadsheetCell myCell;
myCell.setValue(6);
println("cell 1: {}", myCell.getValue());
```

The preceding code creates a new `SpreadsheetCell` called `myCell`, sets its value, and prints out its value. Unlike other constructors for stack-based objects, you do not call the default constructor with function-call syntax. Based on the syntax for other constructors, you might be tempted to call the default constructor like this:

```
SpreadsheetCell myCell(); // WRONG, but will compile.
myCell.setValue(6);       // However, this line will not compile.
println("cell 1: {}", myCell.getValue());
```

Unfortunately, the line attempting to call the default constructor compiles. The line following it does not compile. This problem is commonly known as the *most vexing parse*, and it means that your compiler thinks the first line is actually a function declaration for a function with the name `myCell` that takes zero arguments and returns a `SpreadsheetCell` object. When it gets to the second line, it thinks that you're trying to use a function name as an object!

Of course, instead of using function-call-style parentheses, you can use the uniform initialization syntax as follows:

```
SpreadsheetCell myCell { }; // Calls the default constructor.
```

> **WARNING** *When creating an object on the stack with a default constructor, either use curly brackets for the uniform initialization syntax or omit any parentheses.*

For free store-based object allocation, the default constructor can be used as follows:

```
auto smartCellp { make_unique<SpreadsheetCell>() };
// Or with a raw pointer (not recommended)
SpreadsheetCell* myCellp { new SpreadsheetCell { } };
// Or
// SpreadsheetCell* myCellp { new SpreadsheetCell };
// Or
// SpreadsheetCell* myCellp { new SpreadsheetCell() };
// ... use myCellp
delete myCellp;    myCellp = nullptr;
```

Compiler-Generated Default Constructor

The first SpreadsheetCell class definition in this chapter looked like this:

```
export class SpreadsheetCell
{
    public:
        void setValue(double value);
        double getValue() const;
    private:
        double m_value;
};
```

This definition does not declare a default constructor, but still, the code that follows works fine:

```
SpreadsheetCell myCell;
myCell.setValue(6);
```

The following definition is the same as the preceding definition except that it adds an explicit constructor, accepting a double. It still does not explicitly declare a default constructor.

```
export class SpreadsheetCell
{
    public:
        SpreadsheetCell(double initialValue); // No default constructor
        // Remainder of the class definition omitted for brevity
};
```

With this definition, the following code does not compile anymore:

```
SpreadsheetCell myCell;
myCell.setValue(6);
```

What's going on here? The reason it is not compiling is that if you don't specify *any* constructors, the compiler writes one for you that doesn't take any arguments. This *compiler-generated default constructor* calls the default constructor on all object members of the class but does not initialize the language primitives such as `int` and `double`. Nonetheless, it allows you to create objects of that class. However, if you declare any constructor yourself, the compiler no longer generates a default constructor for you.

> **NOTE** *A default constructor is the same as a zero-argument constructor. The term default constructor does not refer only to the constructor that is automatically generated if you fail to declare any constructors yourself. It also refers to the constructor that is defaulted to if no arguments are required.*

Explicitly Defaulted Default Constructors

Before C++11, if your class required a number of explicit constructors accepting arguments but also a default constructor that did nothing, you still had to explicitly write your own empty default constructor as shown earlier.

To avoid having to write empty default constructors manually, C++ supports the concept of *explicitly defaulted default constructors*. This allows you to write the class definition as follows without having to provide an empty implementation for the default constructor:

```
export class SpreadsheetCell
{
    public:
        SpreadsheetCell() = default;
        SpreadsheetCell(double initialValue);
        SpreadsheetCell(std::string_view initialValue);
        // Remainder of the class definition omitted for brevity
};
```

`SpreadsheetCell` defines two custom constructors. However, the compiler still generates a standard compiler-generated default constructor because one is explicitly defaulted using the `default` keyword. You are free to put the `= default` either directly in the class definition or in an implementation file.

Explicitly Deleted Default Constructors

The opposite of explicitly defaulted default constructors is also possible and is called *explicitly deleted default constructors*. For example, you can define a class with only static member functions (see Chapter 9) for which you do not want to write any constructors, and you also do not want the compiler to generate the default constructor. In that case, you need to explicitly delete the default constructor.

```
export class MyClass
{
    public:
        MyClass() = delete;
};
```

> **NOTE** *If a class has data members that have a deleted default constructor, then the default constructor for the class is automatically deleted as well.*

Constructor Initializers aka Ctor-Initializers

Up to now, this chapter initialized data members in the body of a constructor, as in this example:

```
SpreadsheetCell::SpreadsheetCell(double initialValue)
{
    setValue(initialValue);
}
```

C++ provides an alternative method for initializing data members in the constructor, called the *constructor initializer*, also known as the *ctor-initializer* or *member initializer list*. Here is the same `SpreadsheetCell` constructor, rewritten to use the ctor-initializer syntax:

```
SpreadsheetCell::SpreadsheetCell(double initialValue)
    : m_value { initialValue }
{
}
```

As you can see, the ctor-initializer appears syntactically between the constructor parameter list and the opening brace for the body of the constructor. The list starts with a colon and is separated by commas. Each element in the list is an initialization of a data member using function notation or the uniform initialization syntax, a call to a base class constructor (see Chapter 10), or a call to a delegated constructor, discussed later in this chapter.

Initializing data members with a ctor-initializer provides different behavior than does initializing data members inside the constructor body itself. When C++ creates an object, it must create all the data members of the object before calling the constructor. As part of creating these data members, it must call a constructor on any of them that are themselves objects. By the time you assign a value to an object inside your constructor body, you are not actually constructing that object. You are only modifying its value. A ctor-initializer allows you to provide initial values for data members as they are created, which is more efficient than assigning values to them later.

If your class has as data member an object of a class that has a default constructor, then you do not have to explicitly initialize that object in the ctor-initializer. For example, if you have an `std::string` as data member, its default constructor initializes the string to the empty string, so initializing it to `""` in the ctor-initializer is superfluous.

On the other hand, if your class has as a data member an object of a class without a default constructor, you must use the ctor-initializer to properly construct that object. For example, take the following `SpreadsheetCell` class:

```
export class SpreadsheetCell
{
    public:
        SpreadsheetCell(double d);
};
```

This class has only one constructor accepting a `double` and does not include a default constructor. You can use this class as a data member of another class as follows:

```
class SomeClass
{
    public:
        SomeClass();
    private:
        SpreadsheetCell m_cell;
};
```

You can implement the `SomeClass` constructor as follows:

```
SomeClass::SomeClass() { }
```

However, with this implementation, the code does not compile. The compiler does not know how to initialize the `m_cell` data member of `SomeClass` because it does not have a default constructor.

You must initialize the `m_cell` data member in the ctor-initializer as follows:

```
SomeClass::SomeClass() : m_cell { 1.0 } { }
```

> **NOTE** *Ctor-initializers allow initialization of data members at the time of their creation.*

Some programmers prefer to assign initial values in the body of the constructor, even though this might be less efficient. However, several data types must be initialized in a ctor-initializer or with an in-class initializer. The following table summarizes them:

DATA TYPE	EXPLANATION
`const` data members	You cannot legally assign a value to a `const` variable after it is created. Any value must be supplied at the time of creation.
Reference data members	References cannot exist without referring to something, and once created, a reference cannot be changed to refer to something else.
Object data members for which there is no default constructor	C++ attempts to initialize member objects using a default constructor. If no default constructor exists, it cannot initialize the object, and you must tell it explicitly which constructor to call.
Base classes without default constructors	These are covered in Chapter 10.

There is one important caveat with ctor-initializers: they initialize data members in the order that they appear in the class definition, not their order in the ctor-initializer! Take the following definition for a class called `Foo`. Its constructor simply stores a `double` value and prints out the value to the console.

```
class Foo
{
    public:
        Foo(double value);
    private:
        double m_value { 0 };
};

Foo::Foo(double value) : m_value { value }
{
    println("Foo::m_value = {}", m_value);
}
```

Suppose you have another class, `MyClass`, that contains a `Foo` object as one of its data members.

```
class MyClass
{
    public:
        MyClass(double value);
    private:
        double m_value { 0 };
        Foo m_foo;
};
```

Its constructor could be implemented as follows:

```
MyClass::MyClass(double value) : m_value { value }, m_foo { m_value }
{
    println("MyClass::m_value = {}", m_value);
}
```

The ctor-initializer first stores the given `value` in `m_value` and then calls the `Foo` constructor with `m_value` as argument. You can create an instance of `MyClass` as follows:

```
MyClass instance { 1.2 };
```

Here is the output of the program:

```
Foo::m_value = 1.2
MyClass::m_value = 1.2
```

So, everything looks fine. Now make one tiny change to the `MyClass` definition; just reverse the order of the `m_value` and `m_foo` data members. Nothing else is changed.

```
class MyClass
{
    public:
        MyClass(double value);
    private:
        Foo m_foo;
        double m_value { 0 };
};
```

The output of the program now depends on your system. It could, for example, be as follows:

```
Foo::m_value = -9.255963134931783e+61
MyClass::m_value = 1.2
```

This is far from what you expected. You might assume, based on your ctor-initializer, that `m_value` is initialized before using `m_value` in the call to the `Foo` constructor. But C++ doesn't work that way. The data members are initialized in the order they appear in the definition of the class, not the order in the ctor-initializer! So, in this case, the `Foo` constructor is called first with an uninitialized `m_value`.

Note that some compilers issue a warning when the order in the ctor-initializer does not match the order in the class definition.

For this example, there is an easy fix. Don't pass `m_value` to the `Foo` constructor, but simply pass the `value` parameter:

```
MyClass::MyClass(double value) : m_value { value }, m_foo { value }
{
    println("MyClass::m_value = {}", m_value);
}
```

> **WARNING** *Ctor-initializers initialize data members in their declared order in the class definition, not their order in the ctor-initializer list.*

Copy Constructors

There is a special constructor in C++ called a *copy constructor* that allows you to create an object that is an exact copy of another object. Here is the declaration for a copy constructor in the `SpreadsheetCell` class:

```
export class SpreadsheetCell
{
    public:
        SpreadsheetCell(const SpreadsheetCell& src);
        // Remainder of the class definition omitted for brevity
};
```

The copy constructor takes a reference-to-`const` to the source object. Like other constructors, it does not return a value. The copy constructor should copy all the data members from the source object. Technically, of course, you can do whatever you want in a copy constructor, but it's generally a good idea to follow expected behavior and initialize the new object to be a copy of the old one. Here is an example implementation of the `SpreadsheetCell` copy constructor. Note the use of the ctor-initializer.

```
SpreadsheetCell::SpreadsheetCell(const SpreadsheetCell& src)
    : m_value { src.m_value }
{
}
```

If you don't write a copy constructor yourself, C++ generates one for you that initializes each data member in the new object from its equivalent data member in the source object. For object data members, this initialization means that their copy constructors are called. Given a set of data members, called `m1`, `m2`, . . . `mn`, this compiler-generated copy constructor can be expressed as follows:

```
classname::classname(const classname& src)
    : m1 { src.m1 }, m2 { src.m2 }, ... mn { src.mn } { }
```

Therefore, in most circumstances, there is no need for you to specify a copy constructor!

> **NOTE** *The* `SpreadsheetCell` *copy constructor is shown only for demonstration purposes. In fact, in this case, the copy constructor can be omitted because the default compiler-generated one is good enough. However, under certain conditions, this compiler-generated copy constructor is not sufficient. These conditions are covered in Chapter 9.*

When the Copy Constructor Is Called

The default semantics for passing arguments to functions in C++ is pass-by-value. That means that the function receives a copy of the value or object. Thus, whenever you pass an object to a function, the compiler calls the copy constructor of the new object to initialize it. For example, suppose you have the following `printString()` function accepting an `std::string` parameter by value:

```
void printString(string value)
{
    println("{}", value);
}
```

Recall that `std::string` is actually a class, not a built-in type. When your code makes a call to `printString()` passing a `string` argument, the `string` parameter `value` is initialized with a call to its copy constructor. The argument to the copy constructor is the `string` you passed to `printString()`. In the following example, the `string` copy constructor is executed for the `value` object in `printString()` with `name` as its argument:

```
string name { "heading one" };
printString(name); // Copies name
```

When the `printString()` member function finishes, `value` is destroyed. Because it was only a copy of `name`, `name` remains intact. Of course, you can avoid the overhead of copy constructors by passing parameters as references-to-`const`, discussed in an upcoming section.

When returning objects by value from a function, the copy constructor might also get called. This is discussed in the section "Objects as Return Values" later in this chapter.

Calling the Copy Constructor Explicitly

You can use the copy constructor explicitly as well. It is often useful to be able to construct one object as an exact copy of another. For example, you might want to create a copy of a `SpreadsheetCell` object like this:

```
SpreadsheetCell myCell1 { 4 };
SpreadsheetCell myCell2 { myCell1 }; // myCell2 has the same values as myCell1
```

Passing Objects by Reference

To avoid copying objects when you pass them to functions, you should declare that the function takes a *reference* to the object. Passing objects by reference is usually more efficient than passing them by value, because only the address of the object is copied, not the entire contents of the object.

Additionally, pass-by-reference avoids problems with dynamic memory allocation in objects, which is discussed in Chapter 9.

When you pass an object by reference, the function using the object reference could change the original object. When you are only using pass-by-reference for efficiency, you should preclude this possibility by declaring the object `const` as well. This is known as passing objects by reference-to-`const` and has been done in examples throughout this book.

> **NOTE** *For performance reasons, it is best to pass objects by reference-to-*`const` *instead of by value. Chapter 9 slightly modifies this rule after the introduction of move semantics, allowing pass-by-value of objects in certain cases.*

Note that the `SpreadsheetCell` class has a number of member functions accepting an `std::string_view` as parameter. As discussed in Chapter 2, a `string_view` is basically just a pointer and a length. So, it is cheap to copy and is usually passed by value.

Also primitive types, such as `int`, `double`, and so on, should just be passed by value. You don't gain anything by passing such types as reference-to-`const`.

The `doubleToString()` member function of the `SpreadsheetCell` class always returns a `string` by value because the implementation of the member function creates a local `string` object that at the end of the member function is returned to the caller. Returning a reference to this `string` wouldn't work because the `string` to which it refers to will be destroyed when the function exits.

Explicitly Defaulted and Deleted Copy Constructors

Just as you can explicitly default or delete a compiler generated default constructor for a class, you can also explicitly default or delete a compiler-generated copy constructor as follows:

```
SpreadsheetCell(const SpreadsheetCell& src) = default;
```

or

```
SpreadsheetCell(const SpreadsheetCell& src) = delete;
```

By deleting the copy constructor, the object cannot be copied anymore. This can be used to disallow passing the object by value, as discussed in Chapter 9.

> **NOTE** *If a class has data members that have a deleted or* `private` *copy constructor, then the copy constructor for the class is automatically deleted as well, even if you explicitly* `default` *one.*

Initializer-List Constructors

An *initializer-list constructor* is a constructor with an `std::initializer_list<T>` (see Chapter 1) as the first parameter and without any additional parameters or with additional parameters having default values. The `initializer_list<T>` class template is defined in `<initializer_list>`. The following class demonstrates its use. The class accepts only an `initializer_list<double>` with an even number of elements; otherwise, it throws an exception. Chapter 1 introduces exceptions.

```
class EvenSequence
{
    public:
        EvenSequence(initializer_list<double> values)
        {
            if (values.size() % 2 != 0) {
                throw invalid_argument { "initializer_list should "
                    "contain even number of elements." };
            }
            m_sequence.reserve(values.size());
            for (const auto& value : values) {
                m_sequence.push_back(value);
            }
        }

        void print() const
        {
            for (const auto& value : m_sequence) {
                std::print("{}, ", value);
            }
            println("");
        }
    private:
        vector<double> m_sequence;
};
```

Inside the initializer-list constructor you can access the elements of the initializer-list with a range-based `for` loop. You can get the number of elements in an initializer-list with the `size()` member function.

The `EvenSequence` initializer-list constructor uses a range-based `for` loop to copy elements from the given `initializer_list<T>`. You can also use the `assign()` member function of `vector`. The different member functions of `vector`, including `assign()`, are discussed in detail in Chapter 18, "Standard Library Containers." As a sneak preview, to give you an idea of the power of a `vector`, here is the initializer-list constructor using `assign()`:

```
EvenSequence(initializer_list<double> values)
{
    if (values.size() % 2 != 0) {
        throw invalid_argument { "initializer_list should "
            "contain even number of elements." };
    }
    m_sequence.assign(values);
}
```

`EvenSequence` objects can be constructed as follows:

```
try {
    EvenSequence p1 { 1.0, 2.0, 3.0, 4.0, 5.0, 6.0 };
    p1.print();
```

```
    EvenSequence p2 { 1.0, 2.0, 3.0 };
} catch (const invalid_argument& e) {
    println("{}", e.what());
}
```

The construction of `p2` throws an exception because it has an odd number of elements in the initializer-list.

The Standard Library has full support for initializer-list constructors. For example, the `std::vector` container can be initialized with an initializer-list:

```
vector<string> myVec { "String 1", "String 2", "String 3" };
```

Without initializer-list constructors, one way to initialize this `vector` is by using several `push_back()` calls:

```
vector<string> myVec;
myVec.push_back("String 1");
myVec.push_back("String 2");
myVec.push_back("String 3");
```

Initializer lists are not limited to constructors and can also be used with normal functions as explained in Chapter 1.

> **NOTE** *When a class has both an initializer-list constructor and another single-argument constructor, then you should be careful to call the correct one. For example,* `std::vector` *has an initializer-list constructor to initialize a* `vector` *with a given set of elements. It also has a constructor accepting a single argument, the desired size of the new* `vector`*. You call the initializer-list constructor using a braced initializer,* `{}`*, and call the other single-argument constructor using parentheses,* `()`*. For example:*
>
> ```
> vector<int> v1 { 6 }; // Constructs a vector with a single element, 6.
> vector<int> v2 ( 6 ); // Constructs a vector with 6 default-
>                       // initialized elements.
> ```

Delegating Constructors

Delegating constructors allow constructors to call another constructor from the same class. However, this call cannot be placed in the constructor body; it must be in the ctor-initializer, and it must be the only member-initializer in the list. The following is an example:

```
SpreadsheetCell::SpreadsheetCell(string_view initialValue)
    : SpreadsheetCell { stringToDouble(initialValue) }
{
}
```

When this `string_view` constructor (the delegating constructor) is called, it first delegates the call to the target constructor, which is the `double` constructor in this example. When the target constructor returns, the body of the delegating constructor is executed.

Make sure you avoid constructor recursion while using delegating constructors. Here is an example:

```
class MyClass
{
    MyClass(char c) : MyClass { 1.2 } { }
    MyClass(double d) : MyClass { 'm' } { }
};
```

The first constructor delegates to the second constructor, which delegating back to the first one. The behavior of such code is undefined by the standard and depends on your compiler.

Converting Constructors and Explicit Constructors

The current set of constructors for `SpreadsheetCell` is as follows:

```
export class SpreadsheetCell
{
    public:
        SpreadsheetCell() = default;
        SpreadsheetCell(double initialValue);
        SpreadsheetCell(std::string_view initialValue);
        SpreadsheetCell(const SpreadsheetCell& src);
    // Remainder omitted for brevity
};
```

The single-parameter `double` and `string_view` constructors can be used to convert a `double` or a `string_view` into a `SpreadsheetCell`. Such constructors are called *converting constructors*. The compiler can use such constructors to perform implicit conversions for you. Here's an example:

```
SpreadsheetCell myCell { 4 };
myCell = 5;
myCell = "6"sv; // A string_view literal (see Chapter 2).
```

This might not always be the behavior you want. You can prevent the compiler from doing such implicit conversions by marking constructors as `explicit`. The `explicit` keyword goes only in the class definition. Here's an example:

```
export class SpreadsheetCell
{
    public:
        SpreadsheetCell() = default;
        SpreadsheetCell(double initialValue);
        explicit SpreadsheetCell(std::string_view initialValue);
        SpreadsheetCell(const SpreadsheetCell& src);
    // Remainder omitted for brevity
};
```

With this change, a line as follows no longer compiles:

```
myCell = "6"sv; // A string_view literal (see Chapter 2).
```

Prior to C++11, converting constructors could have only a single parameter, as in the `SpreadsheetCell` example. Since C++11, converting constructors can have multiple parameters because of support for list initialization. Let's look at an example. Suppose you have the following class:

```
class MyClass
{
```

```
    public:
        MyClass(int) { }
        MyClass(int, int) { }
};
```

This class has two constructors, and since C++11, both are converting constructors. The following example shows that the compiler automatically converts arguments such as `1`, `{1}`, and `{1,2}`, to instances of `MyClass` using these converting constructors:

```
void process(const MyClass& c) { }

int main()
{
    process(1);
    process({ 1 });
    process({ 1, 2 });
}
```

To prevent these implicit conversions, both converting constructors can be marked as `explicit`:

```
class MyClass
{
    public:
        explicit MyClass(int) { }
        explicit MyClass(int, int) { }
};
```

With this change, you have to perform these conversions explicitly; here's an example:

```
process(MyClass{ 1 });
process(MyClass{ 1, 2 });
```

It is possible to pass a Boolean argument to `explicit` to turn it into a conditional `explicit`. The syntax is as follows:

```
explicit(true) MyClass(int);
```

Of course, just writing `explicit(true)` is equivalent to `explicit`, but it becomes more useful in the context of generic template code using type traits. With type traits you can query certain properties of given types, such as whether a certain type is convertible to another type. The result of such a type trait can be used as argument to `explicit()`. Type traits allow for writing advanced generic code and are discussed in Chapter 26, "Advanced Templates."

> **NOTE** *It is recommended to mark at least any constructor that can be called with a single argument as* `explicit` *to avoid accidental implicit conversions. If there is a real use case for implicit conversions, you can mark the constructor with* `explicit(false)`*. Doing so explains to users of your class that the implicit conversion is consciously allowed.*

Summary of Compiler-Generated Constructors

The compiler can automatically generate a default constructor and a copy constructor for every class. However, the constructors that the compiler automatically generates depend on the constructors that you define yourself according to the rules in the following table:

IF YOU DEFINE. . .	THEN THE COMPILER GENERATES. . .	AND YOU CAN CREATE AN OBJECT. . .
[no constructors]	A default constructor A copy constructor	With no arguments: `SpreadsheetCell a;` As a copy: `SpreadsheetCell b{a};`
A default constructor only	A copy constructor	With no arguments: `SpreadsheetCell a;` As a copy: `SpreadsheetCell b{a};`
A copy constructor only	No constructors	Theoretically, as a copy of another object (practically, you can't create any objects, because there are no non-copy constructors)
A single- or multi-argument non-copy constructor only	A copy constructor	With arguments: `SpreadsheetCell a{6};` As a copy: `SpreadsheetCell b{a};`
A default constructor as well as a single- or multi-argument non-copy constructor	A copy constructor	With no arguments: `SpreadsheetCell a;` With arguments: `SpreadsheetCell b{5};` As a copy: `SpreadsheetCell c{a};`

Note the lack of symmetry between the default constructor and the copy constructor. As long as you don't define a copy constructor explicitly, the compiler creates one for you. On the other hand, as soon as you define *any* constructor, the compiler stops generating a default constructor.

As mentioned before in this chapter, the automatic generation of a default constructor and a default copy constructor can be influenced by defining them as explicitly defaulted or explicitly deleted.

> **NOTE** *A final type of constructor is a move constructor, required to implement move semantics. Move semantics is used to increase performance in certain situations and is discussed in detail in Chapter 9.*

Object Destruction

When an object is destroyed, two events occur: the object's *destructor* member function is called, and the memory it was taking up is freed. The destructor is your chance to perform any cleanup work for the object, such as freeing dynamically allocated memory or closing file handles. If you don't declare a destructor, the compiler writes one for you that does recursive member-wise destruction and allows the object to be deleted. A destructor of a class is a member function with as name the name of the class prefixed with a tilde (~). A destructor does not return anything and does not have any parameters. Here is an example of a destructor that simply writes something to standard output:

```
export class SpreadsheetCell
{
    public:
        ~SpreadsheetCell();  // Destructor.
        // Remainder of the class definition omitted for brevity
};

SpreadsheetCell::~SpreadsheetCell()
{
    println("Destructor called.");
}
```

Objects on the stack are destroyed when they go *out of scope*, which means whenever the current function or other execution *block* ends. In other words, whenever the code encounters an ending curly brace, any objects created on the stack within those curly braces are destroyed. The following program shows this behavior:

```
int main()
{
    SpreadsheetCell myCell { 5 };
    if (myCell.getValue() == 5) {
        SpreadsheetCell anotherCell { 6 };
    } // anotherCell is destroyed as this block ends.

    println("myCell: {}", myCell.getValue());
} // myCell is destroyed as this block ends.
```

Objects on the stack are destroyed in the reverse order of their declaration (and construction). For example, in the following code fragment, `myCell2` is created before `anotherCell2`, so `anotherCell2` is destroyed before `myCell2` (note that you can start a new code block at any point in your program with an opening curly brace):

```
{
    SpreadsheetCell myCell2 { 4 };
    SpreadsheetCell anotherCell2 { 5 }; // myCell2 constructed before anotherCell2
} // anotherCell2 destroyed before myCell2
```

This ordering also applies to objects that are data members of other objects. Recall that data members are initialized in the order of their declaration in the class. Thus, following the rule that objects are destroyed in the reverse order of their construction, data member objects are destroyed in the reverse order of their declaration order in the class.

Objects allocated on the free store without the help of smart pointers are not destroyed automatically. You must call `delete` on the object pointer to call its destructor and free its memory. The following program shows this behavior.

> **WARNING** *Do not write programs like the next example where* `cellPtr2` *is not deleted. Make sure you always free dynamically allocated memory by calling* `delete` *or* `delete[]` *depending on whether the memory was allocated using* `new` *or* `new[]`*. Or better yet, use smart pointers as discussed earlier!*

```
int main()
{
    SpreadsheetCell* cellPtr1 { new SpreadsheetCell { 5 } };
    SpreadsheetCell* cellPtr2 { new SpreadsheetCell { 6 } };
    println("cellPtr1: {}", cellPtr1->getValue());
    delete cellPtr1; // Destroys cellPtr1
    cellPtr1 = nullptr;
} // cellPtr2 is NOT destroyed because delete was not called on it.
```

Assigning to Objects

Just as you can assign the value of one `int` to another in C++, you can assign the value of one object to another. For example, the following code assigns the value of `myCell` to `anotherCell`:

```
SpreadsheetCell myCell { 5 }, anotherCell;
anotherCell = myCell;
```

You might be tempted to say that `myCell` is "copied" to `anotherCell`. However, in the world of C++, "copying" occurs only when an object is being initialized. If an object already has a value that is being overwritten, the more accurate term is "assigned to." Note that the facility that C++ provides for copying is the copy constructor. Because it is a constructor, it can only be used for object creation, not for later assignments to the object.

Therefore, C++ provides another member function in every class to perform assignment. This member function is called the *assignment operator*. Its name is `operator=` because it is actually an overload of the `=` operator for that class. In the preceding example, the assignment operator for `anotherCell` is called, with `myCell` as the argument.

> **NOTE** *The assignment operator as explained in this section is sometimes called the copy assignment operator because data is copied from the right-hand side object to the left-hand side object. Chapter 9 discusses another kind of assignment operator, the move assignment operator, in which data is moved instead of copied, which improves performance for certain use cases.*

As usual, if you don't write your own assignment operator, C++ writes one for you to allow objects to be assigned to one another. The default C++ assignment behavior is almost identical to its default copying behavior: it recursively assigns each data member from the source to the destination object.

Declaring an Assignment Operator

Here is the assignment operator for the `SpreadsheetCell` class:

```
export class SpreadsheetCell
{
    public:
        SpreadsheetCell& operator=(const SpreadsheetCell& rhs);
        // Remainder of the class definition omitted for brevity
};
```

The assignment operator usually takes a reference-to-`const` to the source object, like the copy constructor. In this case, the source object is called `rhs`, which stands for right-hand side of the equal sign, but you are of course free to call it whatever you want. The object on which the assignment operator is called is the left-hand side of the equal sign.

Unlike a copy constructor, the assignment operator returns a reference to a `SpreadsheetCell` object. The reason is that assignments can be *chained*, as in the following example:

```
myCell = anotherCell = aThirdCell;
```

When that line is executed, the first thing that happens is the assignment operator for `anotherCell` is called with `aThirdCell` as its "right-hand side" argument. Next, the assignment operator for `myCell` is called. However, its argument is not `anotherCell`; its right-hand side is the *result* of the assignment of `aThirdCell` to `anotherCell`. The equal sign is simply just shorthand for what is really a member function call. When you look at the line in its full functional syntax shown here, you can see the problem:

```
myCell.operator=(anotherCell.operator=(aThirdCell));
```

Now, you can see that the `operator=` call from `anotherCell` must return a value, which is passed to the `operator=` call for `myCell`. The correct value to return is a reference to `anotherCell` itself, so it can serve as the source for the assignment to `myCell`.

> **WARNING** *You could actually declare the assignment operator to return whatever type you wanted, including* `void`. *However, you should always return a reference to the object on which it is called because that's what clients expect.*

Defining an Assignment Operator

The implementation of the assignment operator is similar to that of a copy constructor but with several important differences. First, a copy constructor is called only for initialization, so the destination object does not yet have valid values. An assignment operator can overwrite the current values in an object. This consideration doesn't really come into play until you have dynamically allocated resources, such as memory, in your objects. See Chapter 9 for details.

Second, it's legal in C++ to assign an object to itself. For example, the following code compiles and runs:

```
SpreadsheetCell cell { 4 };
cell = cell; // Self-assignment
```

Your assignment operator needs to take the possibility of self-assignment into account. In the `SpreadsheetCell` class, this is not important, as its only data member is a primitive type, `double`. However, when your class has dynamically allocated memory or other resources, it's paramount to take self-assignment into account, as is discussed in detail in Chapter 9. To prevent problems in such cases, the first thing assignment operators usually do is check for self-assignment and return immediately if that's the case.

Here is the start of the definition of the assignment operator for the `SpreadsheetCell` class:

```
SpreadsheetCell& SpreadsheetCell::operator=(const SpreadsheetCell& rhs)
{
    if (this == &rhs) {
```

This first line checks for self-assignment, but it might be a bit cryptic. Self-assignment occurs when the left-hand side and the right-hand side of the equal sign are the same. One way to tell whether two objects are the same is if they occupy the same memory location—more explicitly, if pointers to them are equal. Recall that `this` is a pointer to an object accessible from any member function called on the object. Thus, `this` is a pointer to the left-hand side object. Similarly, `&rhs` is a pointer to the right-hand side object. If these pointers are equal, the assignment must be self-assignment, but because the return type is `SpreadsheetCell&`, a correct value must still be returned. All assignment operators return `*this` as follows, and the self-assignment case is no exception:

```
        return *this;
    }
```

`this` is a pointer to the object on which the member function executes, so `*this` is the object itself. The compiler returns a reference to the object to match the declared return type. Now, if it is not self-assignment, you have to do an assignment to every member:

```
    m_value = rhs.m_value;
    return *this;
}
```

Here the member function copies the values, and finally, it returns `*this`, as explained earlier.

Astute readers will notice there's some code duplication between the copy assignment operator and the copy constructor; they both need to copy all data members. Chapter 9 introduces the copy-and-swap idiom to prevent such code duplication.

> **NOTE** *The* `SpreadsheetCell` *assignment operator is shown only for demonstration purposes. In fact, in this case, the assignment operator can be omitted because the default compiler-generated one is good enough; it does simple member-wise assignments of all data members. However, under certain conditions, this compiler-generated assignment operator is not sufficient. These conditions are covered in Chapter 9.*

> **WARNING** *If your class requires special handling for copy operations, always implement both the copy constructor and the copy assignment operator.*

Explicitly Defaulted and Deleted Assignment Operator

You can explicitly default or delete a compiler-generated assignment operator as follows:

```
SpreadsheetCell& operator=(const SpreadsheetCell& rhs) = default;
```

or

```
SpreadsheetCell& operator=(const SpreadsheetCell& rhs) = delete;
```

Compiler-Generated Copy Constructor and Copy Assignment Operator

C++11 deprecated the generation of a copy constructor if the class has a user-declared copy assignment operator or destructor. If you still need a compiler-generated copy constructor in such a case, you can explicitly default one:

```
MyClass(const MyClass& src) = default;
```

C++11 also deprecated the generation of a copy assignment operator if the class has a user-declared copy constructor or destructor. If you still need a compiler-generated copy assignment operator in such a case, you can explicitly default one:

```
MyClass& operator=(const MyClass& rhs) = default;
```

Distinguishing Copying from Assignment

It is sometimes difficult to tell when objects are initialized with a copy constructor rather than assigned to with the assignment operator. Essentially, things that look like a declaration are going to be using copy constructors, and things that look like assignment statements are handled by the assignment operator. Consider the following code:

```
SpreadsheetCell myCell { 5 };
SpreadsheetCell anotherCell { myCell };
```

`AnotherCell` is constructed with the copy constructor. Now consider the following:

```
SpreadsheetCell aThirdCell = myCell;
```

`aThirdCell` is also constructed with the copy constructor, because this is a declaration. The `operator=` is not called for this line! This syntax is just another way to write `SpreadsheetCell aThirdCell{myCell};`. However, consider the following code:

```
anotherCell = myCell; // Calls operator= for anotherCell
```

Here, `anotherCell` has already been constructed, so the compiler calls `operator=`.

Objects as Return Values

When you return objects from functions, it is sometimes difficult to see exactly what copying and assigning is happening. For example, the implementation of `SpreadsheetCell::getString()` looks like this:

```
string SpreadsheetCell::getString() const
{
    return doubleToString(m_value);
}
```

Now consider the following code:

```
SpreadsheetCell myCell2 { 5 };
string s1;
s1 = myCell2.getString();
```

When getString() returns the string, the compiler actually creates an unnamed temporary string object by calling a string copy constructor. When you assign this result to s1, the assignment operator is called for s1 with the temporary string as a parameter. Then, the temporary string object is destroyed. Thus, the single line of code could invoke the copy constructor and the assignment operator (for two different objects).

In case you're not confused enough, consider this code:

```
SpreadsheetCell myCell3 { 5 };
string s2 = myCell3.getString();
```

In this case, getString() still creates a temporary unnamed string object when it returns. But now, s2 gets its copy constructor called, not its assignment operator.

With *move semantics*, the compiler can use a *move constructor* or *move assignment operator* instead of a copy constructor or copy assignment operator to return the string from getString(). This can be more efficient in certain cases and is discussed in Chapter 9. However, even better, compilers are free to (and often even required to) implement *copy elision* to optimize away costly copy operations or move operations when returning values; see Chapter 1.

If you ever forget the order in which these things happen or which constructor or operator is called, you can easily figure it out by temporarily including helpful output in your code or by stepping through your code with a debugger.

Copy Constructors and Object Members

You should also note the difference between assignment operator and copy constructor calls in constructors. If an object contains other objects, the compiler-generated copy constructor calls the copy constructors of each of the contained objects recursively. When you write your own copy constructor, you can provide the same semantics by using a ctor-initializer, as shown previously. If you omit a data member from the ctor-initializer, the compiler performs default initialization on it (a call to the default constructor for objects) before executing your code in the body of the constructor. Thus, by the time the body of the constructor executes, all object data members have already been initialized.

For example, you could write the SpreadsheetCell copy constructor like this:

```
SpreadsheetCell::SpreadsheetCell(const SpreadsheetCell& src)
{
    m_value = src.m_value;
}
```

However, when you assign values to data members in the body of the copy constructor, you are using the assignment operator on them, not the copy constructor, because they have already been initialized.

If you write the copy constructor as follows, then m_value is initialized using the copy constructor:

```
SpreadsheetCell::SpreadsheetCell(const SpreadsheetCell& src)
    : m_value { src.m_value }
{
}
```

SUMMARY

This chapter covered the fundamental aspects of C++'s facilities for object-oriented programming: classes and objects. It first reviewed the basic syntax for writing classes and using objects, including access control. Then, it covered object life cycles: when objects are constructed, destructed, and assigned to, and what member functions those actions invoke. The chapter included details of the constructor syntax, including ctor-initializers and initializer-list constructors, and introduced the notion of copy assignment operators. It also specified exactly which constructors the compiler writes for you and under what circumstances, and it explained that default constructors require no arguments.

You may have found this chapter to be mostly review. Or, it may have opened your eyes to the world of object-oriented programming in C++. In any case, now that you are proficient with objects and classes, read Chapter 9 to learn more about their tricks and subtleties.

EXERCISES

By solving the following exercises, you can practice the material discussed in this chapter. Solutions to all exercises are available with the code download on the book's website at `www.wiley.com/go/proc++6e`. However, if you are stuck on an exercise, first reread parts of this chapter to try to find an answer yourself before looking at the solution from the website.

Exercise 8-1: Implement a `Person` class storing a first and last name as data members. Add a single constructor accepting two parameters, the first and last name. Provide appropriate getters and setters. Write a small `main()` function to test your implementation by creating a `Person` object on the stack and on the free store.

Exercise 8-2: With the set of member functions implemented in Exercise 8-1, the following line of code does not compile:

```
Person persons[3];
```

Can you explain why this does not compile? Modify the implementation of your `Person` class to make this work.

Exercise 8-3: Add the following member functions to your `Person` class implementation: a copy constructor, a copy assignment operator, and a destructor. In all of these member functions, implement what you think is necessary, and additionally, output a line of text to the console so you can trace when they are executed. Modify your `main()` function to test these new member functions. Note: technically, these new member functions are not strictly required for this `Person` class, because the compiler-generated versions are good enough, but this exercise is to practice writing them.

Exercise 8-4: Remove the copy constructor, copy assignment operator, and destructor from your `Person` class, because the default compiler-generated versions are exactly what you need for this simple class. Next, add a new data member to store the initials of a person, and provide a getter and setter. Add a new constructor that accepts three parameters, a first and last name, and a person's initials. Modify the original two-parameter constructor to automatically generate initials for a given first and last name, and delegate the actual construction work to the new three-parameter constructor. Test this new functionality in your `main()` function.

Mastering Classes and Objects

WHAT'S IN THIS CHAPTER?

- How to make classes friends of other classes
- How to use dynamic memory allocation in objects
- What the copy-and-swap idiom is
- What rvalues and rvalue references are
- How move semantics can improve performance
- What the rule of zero means
- How to use the `constexpr` and `consteval` keywords to perform computations at compile time
- The different kinds of data members you can have (`static`, `const`, `constexpr`, reference)
- The different kinds of member functions you can implement (`static`, `const`, `inline`)
- The details of member function overloading
- How to work with default arguments
- How to use nested classes
- What operator overloading is
- How to write separate interface and implementation classes

WILEY.COM DOWNLOADS FOR THIS CHAPTER

Please note that all the code examples for this chapter are available as part of this chapter's code download on the book's website at `www.wiley.com/go/proc++6e` on the Download Code tab.

Chapter 8, "Gaining Proficiency with Classes and Objects," started the discussion on classes and objects. Now it's time to master their subtleties so you can use them to their full potential. By reading this chapter, you will learn how to manipulate and exploit some of the most powerful aspects of the C++ language to write safe, effective, and useful classes.

Many of the concepts in this chapter arise in advanced C++ programming, especially in the C++ Standard Library. Let's start the discussion with the concept of friends in the C++ world.

FRIENDS

C++ allows classes to declare that other classes, member functions of other classes, or non-member functions are *friends*, and can access `protected` and `private` data members and member functions. For example, suppose you have two classes called `Foo` and `Bar`. You can specify that the `Bar` class is a friend of `Foo` as follows:

```
class Foo
{
    friend class Bar;
    // ...
};
```

Now all the member functions of `Bar` can access the `private` and `protected` data members and member functions of `Foo`.

If you only want to make a specific member function of `Bar` a friend, you can do that as well. Suppose the `Bar` class has a member function `processFoo(const Foo&)`. The following syntax is used to make this member function a friend of `Foo`:

```
class Foo
{
    friend void Bar::processFoo(const Foo&);
    // ...
};
```

Stand-alone functions can also be friends of classes. You might, for example, want to write a function that prints all data of a `Foo` object to the console. You might want this function to be outside the `Foo` class because printing is not core functionality of `Foo`, but the function should be able to access the internal data members of the object to print them all. Here is the `Foo` class definition with `printFoo()` as a friend:

```
class Foo
{
    friend void printFoo(const Foo&);
    // ...
};
```

The `friend` declaration in the class serves as the function's prototype. There's no need to write the prototype elsewhere (although it's harmless to do so).

Here is the function definition:

```
void printFoo(const Foo& foo)
{
```

```
        // Print all data of foo to the console, including
        // private and protected data members.
    }
```

You write this function outside the class definition just like any other function, except that you can directly access `private` and `protected` members of `Foo`. You don't repeat the `friend` keyword in the function definition.

Note that a class needs to know which other classes, member functions, or functions want to be its friends; a class, member function, or function cannot declare itself to be a friend of some other class to gain access to non-`public` members of that class.

`friend` classes and functions are easy to abuse; they allow you to violate the principle of encapsulation by exposing internals of your class to other classes or functions. Thus, you should use them only in limited circumstances. Some use cases are shown throughout this chapter.

DYNAMIC MEMORY ALLOCATION IN OBJECTS

Sometimes you don't know how much memory you will need before your program actually runs. As you read in Chapter 7, "Memory Management," the solution is to dynamically allocate as much space as you need during program execution. Classes are no exception. Sometimes you don't know how much memory an object will need when you write the class. In that case, the object should dynamically allocate memory. Dynamically allocated memory in objects provides several challenges, including freeing the memory, handling object copying, and handling object assignment.

The Spreadsheet Class

Chapter 8 introduces the `SpreadsheetCell` class. This chapter moves on to write the `Spreadsheet` class. As with the `SpreadsheetCell` class, the `Spreadsheet` class evolves throughout this chapter. Thus, the various attempts do not always illustrate the best way to do every aspect of class writing.

To start, a `Spreadsheet` is simply a two-dimensional array of `SpreadsheetCells`, with member functions to set and retrieve cells at specific locations in the `Spreadsheet`. Although most spreadsheet applications use letters in one direction and numbers in the other to refer to cells, this `Spreadsheet` uses numbers in both directions.

The first line of the `Spreadsheet.cppm` module interface file defines the name of the module:

```
export module spreadsheet;
```

The `Spreadsheet` class needs access to the `SpreadsheetCell` class, so it needs to import the `spreadsheet_cell` module. Additionally, to make the `SpreadsheetCell` class visible to users of the `spreadsheet` module, the `spreadsheet_cell` module is imported and exported with the following funny-looking syntax:

```
export import spreadsheet_cell;
```

The `Spreadsheet` class uses the `std::size_t` type, which is defined in the C header called `<cstddef>`. You can get access to it with the following import:

```
import std;
```

Finally, here is a first attempt at a definition of the `Spreadsheet` class:

```
export class Spreadsheet
{
    public:
        Spreadsheet(std::size_t width, std::size_t height);
        void setCellAt(std::size_t x, std::size_t y, const SpreadsheetCell& cell);
        SpreadsheetCell& getCellAt(std::size_t x, std::size_t y);
    private:
        bool inRange(std::size_t value, std::size_t upper) const;
        std::size_t m_width { 0 };
        std::size_t m_height { 0 };
        SpreadsheetCell** m_cells { nullptr };
};
```

> **NOTE** *The* `Spreadsheet` *class uses normal pointers for the* `m_cells` *array. This is done throughout this chapter to show the consequences and to explain how to handle resources, such as dynamic memory, in classes. In production code, you should use one of the standard C++ containers, like* `std::vector`*, which greatly simplifies the implementation of* `Spreadsheet`*, but then you wouldn't learn how to correctly handle dynamic memory using raw pointers. In modern C++, you should never use raw pointers with ownership semantics, but you might come across them in existing code, in which case you need to know how to work with them.*

Note that the `Spreadsheet` class does not contain a standard two-dimensional array of `SpreadsheetCells`. Instead, it contains a `SpreadsheetCell**` data member, which is a pointer to a pointer representing an array of arrays. This is because each `Spreadsheet` object might have different dimensions, so the constructor of the class must dynamically allocate the two-dimensional array based on the client-specified height and width.

To dynamically allocate a two-dimensional array, you need to write the following code. Note that in C++, unlike in Java, it's not possible to simply write `new SpreadsheetCell[m_width][m_height]`.

```
Spreadsheet::Spreadsheet(size_t width, size_t height)
    : m_width { width }, m_height { height }
{
    m_cells = new SpreadsheetCell*[m_width];
    for (size_t i { 0 }; i < m_width; ++i) {
        m_cells[i] = new SpreadsheetCell[m_height];
    }
}
```

Figure 9.1 shows the resulting memory layout for a `Spreadsheet` called `s1` on the stack with width 4 and height 3.

The implementations of the `inRange()` and the set and retrieval member functions are straightforward:

```
bool Spreadsheet::inRange(size_t value, size_t upper) const
{
    return value < upper;
}

void Spreadsheet::setCellAt(size_t x, size_t y, const SpreadsheetCell& cell)
{
    if (!inRange(x, m_width)) {
        throw out_of_range {
            format("x ({}) must be less than width ({}).", x, m_width) };
    }
    if (!inRange(y, m_height)) {
        throw out_of_range {
            format("y ({}) must be less than height ({}).", y, m_height) };
    }
    m_cells[x][y] = cell;
}

SpreadsheetCell& Spreadsheet::getCellAt(size_t x, size_t y)
{
    if (!inRange(x, m_width)) {
        throw out_of_range {
            format("x ({}) must be less than width ({}).", x, m_width) };
    }
    if (!inRange(y, m_height)) {
        throw out_of_range {
            format("y ({}) must be less than height ({}).", y, m_height) };
    }
    return m_cells[x][y];
}
```

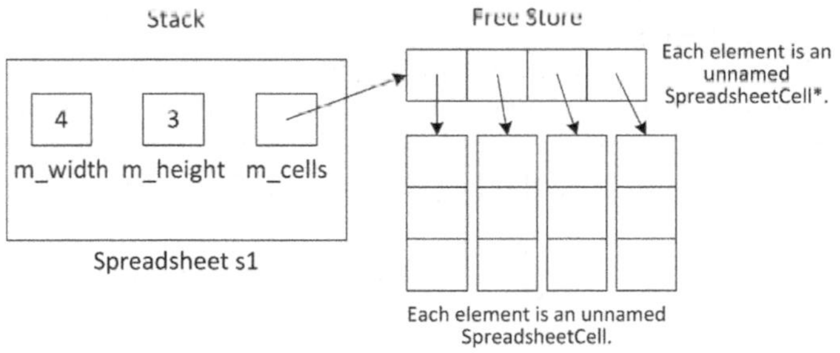

FIGURE 9.1

setCellAt() and getCellAt() both use a helper function called inRange() to check that x and y represent valid coordinates in the spreadsheet. Attempting to access an array element at an out-of-range index will cause the program to malfunction. This example uses exceptions, which are introduced in Chapter 1, "A Crash Course in C++ and the Standard Library," and described in detail in Chapter 14, "Handling Errors."

If you look at the setCellAt() and getCellAt() implementations, you see there is some clear code duplication. Chapter 6, "Designing for Reuse," explains that code duplication should be avoided at all costs. So, let's follow that guideline. Instead of a helper function called `inRange()`, let's define the following `verifyCoordinate()` member function:

```
void verifyCoordinate(std::size_t x, std::size_t y) const;
```

The implementation checks the given coordinate and throws an exception if the coordinate is invalid:

```
void Spreadsheet::verifyCoordinate(size_t x, size_t y) const
{
    if (x >= m_width) {
        throw out_of_range {
            format("x ({}) must be less than width ({}).", x, m_width) };
    }
    if (y >= m_height) {
        throw out_of_range {
            format("y ({}) must be less than height ({}).", y, m_height) };
    }
}
```

The `setCellAt()` and `getCellAt()` implementations can now be simplified:

```
void Spreadsheet::setCellAt(size_t x, size_t y, const SpreadsheetCell& cell)
{
    verifyCoordinate(x, y);
    m_cells[x][y] = cell;
}

SpreadsheetCell& Spreadsheet::getCellAt(size_t x, size_t y)
{
    verifyCoordinate(x, y);
    return m_cells[x][y];
}
```

Freeing Memory with Destructors

Whenever you are finished with dynamically allocated memory, you should free it. If you dynamically allocate memory in an object, the place to free that memory is in the *destructor*. The compiler guarantees that the destructor is called when the object is destroyed. The following is the destructor added to the `Spreadsheet` class definition:

```
export class Spreadsheet
{
    public:
        Spreadsheet(std::size_t width, std::size_t height);
        ~Spreadsheet();
        // Code omitted for brevity
};
```

The destructor has the same name as the name of the class (and of the constructors), preceded by a tilde (~). The destructor takes no arguments, and there can be only one of them. Destructors should never throw any exceptions for reasons explained in detail in Chapter 14.

Here is the implementation of the `Spreadsheet` class destructor:

```
Spreadsheet::~Spreadsheet()
{
    for (size_t i { 0 }; i < m_width; ++i) {
        delete[] m_cells[i];
    }
    delete[] m_cells;
    m_cells = nullptr;
}
```

This destructor frees the memory that was allocated in the constructor. However, no rule requires you to free memory in the destructor. You can write whatever code you want in the destructor, but it is generally a good idea to use it only for freeing memory or disposing of other resources.

Handling Copying and Assignment

Recall from Chapter 8 that if you don't write a copy constructor and a copy assignment operator yourself, C++ writes them for you. These compiler-generated member functions recursively call the copy constructor or copy assignment operator on object data members. However, for primitives, such as `int`, `double`, and pointers, they provide *shallow* or *bitwise* copying or assignment: they just copy or assign the data members from the source object directly to the destination object. That presents problems when you dynamically allocate memory in your object. For example, the following code copies the spreadsheet `s1` to initialize `s` when `s1` is passed to the `printSpreadsheet()` function:

```
import spreadsheet;

void printSpreadsheet(Spreadsheet s) { /* Code omitted for brevity. */ }

int main()
{
    Spreadsheet s1 { 4, 3 };
    printSpreadsheet(s1);
}
```

The `Spreadsheet` contains one pointer variable: `m_cells`. A shallow copy of a `Spreadsheet` gives the destination object a copy of the `m_cells` pointer, but not a copy of the underlying data. Thus, you end up with a situation where both `s` and `s1` have a pointer to the same data, as shown in Figure 9.2.

If `s` changes something to which `m_cells` points, that change shows up in `s1` as well. Even worse, when the `printSpreadsheet()` function exits, `s`'s destructor is called, which frees the memory pointed to by `m_cells`. That leaves the situation where `m_cells` in `s1` no longer points to valid memory, as shown in Figure 9.3. This is called a *dangling pointer*.

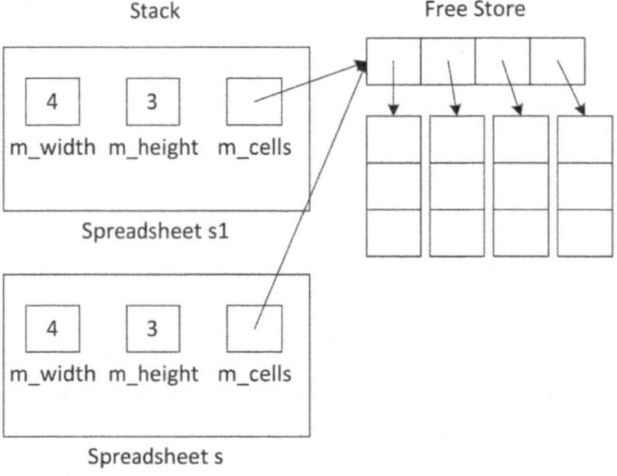

FIGURE 9.2

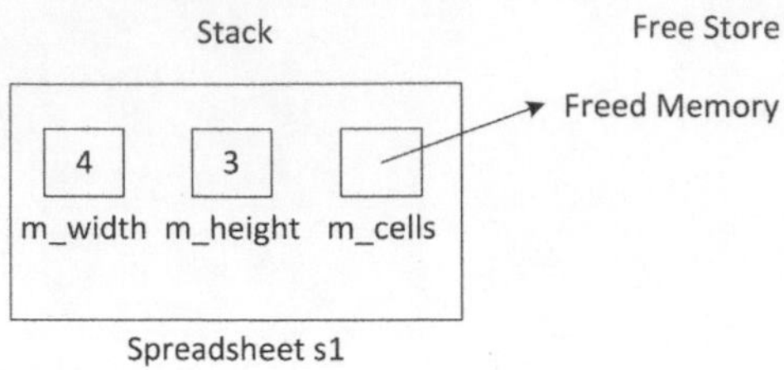

FIGURE 9.3

Unbelievably, the problem is even worse with assignment. Suppose that you have the following code:

```
Spreadsheet s1 { 2, 2 }, s2 { 4, 3 };
s1 = s2;
```

After the first line, when both the `s1` and `s2` `Spreadsheet` objects are constructed, you have the memory layout shown in Figure 9.4.

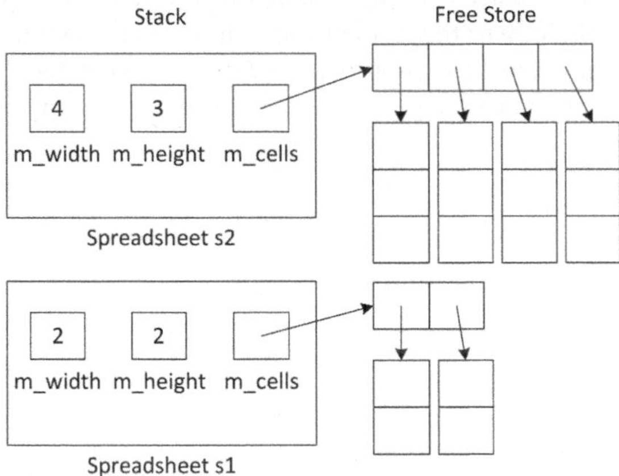

FIGURE 9.4

After the assignment statement, you have the layout shown in Figure 9.5.

Now, not only do the `m_cells` pointers in `s1` and `s2` point to the same memory, but you have also *orphaned* the memory to which `m_cells` in `s1` previously pointed to. This is called a *memory leak*.

It should be clear by now that copy constructors and copy assignment operators must do a *deep copy*; that is, they must not just copy pointer data members, but must copy the actual data to which such pointers point to.

As you can see, relying on C++'s default copy constructor and default copy assignment operator is not always a good idea.

> **WARNING** *Whenever you have dynamically allocated resources in a class, you should write your own copy constructor and copy assignment operator to provide a deep copy of the memory.*

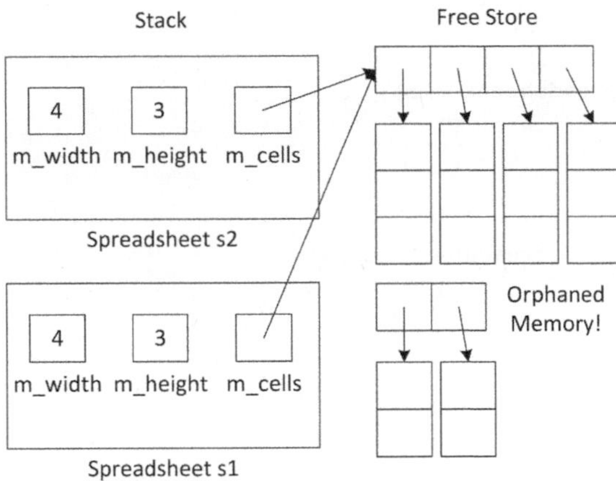

FIGURE 9.5

The Spreadsheet Copy Constructor

Here is a declaration for a copy constructor in the `Spreadsheet` class:

```
export class Spreadsheet
{
    public:
        Spreadsheet(const Spreadsheet& src);
        // Code omitted for brevity
};
```

The definition is as follows:

```
Spreadsheet::Spreadsheet(const Spreadsheet& src)
    : Spreadsheet { src.m_width, src.m_height }
{
    for (size_t i { 0 }; i < m_width; ++i) {
        for (size_t j { 0 }; j < m_height; ++j) {
            m_cells[i][j] = src.m_cells[i][j];
        }
    }
}
```

Note the use of a delegating constructor. The ctor-initializer of this copy constructor delegates first to the non-copy constructor to allocate the proper amount of memory. The body of the copy constructor then copies the actual values. Together, this process implements a deep copy of the `m_cells` dynamically-allocated two-dimensional array.

There is no need to delete any existing `m_cells` because this is a copy constructor, and therefore there is no existing `m_cells` yet in `this` object.

The Spreadsheet Assignment Operator

The following shows the `Spreadsheet` class definition with an assignment operator:

```
export class Spreadsheet
{
    public:
        Spreadsheet& operator=(const Spreadsheet& rhs);
        // Code omitted for brevity
};
```

A naïve implementation could be as follows:

```
Spreadsheet& Spreadsheet::operator=(const Spreadsheet& rhs)
{
    // Check for self-assignment
    if (this == &rhs) {
        return *this;
    }

    // Free the old memory
    for (size_t i { 0 }; i < m_width; ++i) {
        delete[] m_cells[i];
    }
    delete[] m_cells;
    m_cells = nullptr;

    // Allocate new memory
    m_width = rhs.m_width;
    m_height = rhs.m_height;

    m_cells = new SpreadsheetCell*[m_width];
    for (size_t i { 0 }; i < m_width; ++i) {
        m_cells[i] = new SpreadsheetCell[m_height];
    }

    // Copy the data
    for (size_t i { 0 }; i < m_width; ++i) {
        for (size_t j { 0 }; j < m_height; ++j) {
            m_cells[i][j] = rhs.m_cells[i][j];
        }
    }

    return *this;
}
```

The code first checks for self-assignment, then frees the current memory of the `this` object, allocates new memory, and finally copies the individual elements. There is a lot going on in this function, and a lot can go wrong! It is possible that the `this` object gets into an invalid state.

For example, suppose that the memory is successfully freed, that `m_width` and `m_height` are properly set, but that an exception is thrown in the loop that is allocating the memory. When that happens, execution of the remainder of the function is skipped, and the function is exited. Now the `Spreadsheet` instance is corrupt; its `m_width` and `m_height` data members state a certain size, but the `m_cells` data member does not point to the right amount of memory. Basically, this code is not exception-safe!

What we need is an all-or-nothing mechanism; either everything succeeds or the `this` object remains untouched. To implement such an exception-safe assignment operator, the *copy-and-swap* idiom is used. For this, a `swap()` member function is added to the `Spreadsheet` class. Additionally, it's recommended to provide a non-member `swap()` function so that it can also be used by various Standard Library algorithms. Here is the definition of the `Spreadsheet` class with an assignment operator, and the `swap()` member function and non-member function:

```
export class Spreadsheet
{
    public:
        Spreadsheet& operator=(const Spreadsheet& rhs);
        void swap(Spreadsheet& other) noexcept;
        // Code omitted for brevity
};
export void swap(Spreadsheet& first, Spreadsheet& second) noexcept;
```

A requirement for implementing the exception-safe copy-and-swap idiom is that `swap()` never throws any exceptions, so it is marked as `noexcept`.

> **NOTE** *A function can be marked with the* `noexcept` *keyword to specify that it won't throw any exceptions. The* `noexcept` *specifier must appear after any* `const` *keyword. Here's an example:*
>
> ```
> void myNonThrowingConstFunction() const noexcept { /* ... */ }
> ```
>
> *If a* `noexcept` *function does throw an exception, the program is terminated. More details about* `noexcept` *are discussed in Chapter 14, but those details are not important for the remainder of the current chapter.*

The implementation of the `swap()` member function swaps each data member using the `std::swap()` utility function provided by the Standard Library in `<utility>`, which efficiently swaps two values:

```
void Spreadsheet::swap(Spreadsheet& other) noexcept
{
    std::swap(m_width, other.m_width);
    std::swap(m_height, other.m_height);
    std::swap(m_cells, other.m_cells);
}
```

The non-member `swap()` function simply forwards to the `swap()` member function:

```
void swap(Spreadsheet& first, Spreadsheet& second) noexcept
{
    first.swap(second);
}
```

Now that we have an exception-safe `swap()`, it can be used to implement the assignment operator:

```
Spreadsheet& Spreadsheet::operator=(const Spreadsheet& rhs)
{
    Spreadsheet temp { rhs }; // Do all the work in a temporary instance
    swap(temp);               // Commit the work with only non-throwing operations
    return *this;
}
```

The implementation uses the copy-and-swap idiom. First, a *copy* of the right-hand side is made, called `temp`. Then the current object is swapped with this copy. This pattern is the recommended way of implementing assignment operators because it guarantees *strong exception safety*, meaning that if any exception occurs, then the state of the current `Spreadsheet` object remains unchanged. The idiom is implemented in three phases:

- The first phase makes a temporary copy. This does not modify the state of the current `Spreadsheet` object, and so there is no problem if an exception is thrown during this phase.
- The second phase uses the `swap()` function to swap the created temporary copy with the current object. The `swap()` function shall never throw exceptions.
- The third phase is the destruction of the temporary object, which now contains the original object (because of the swap), to clean up any memory.

When you do not use the copy-and-swap idiom for implementing an assignment operator, then for efficiency and sometimes also for correctness, the first line of code in an assignment operator usually checks for self-assignment. Here's an example:

```
Spreadsheet& Spreadsheet::operator=(const Spreadsheet& rhs)
{
    // Check for self-assignment
    if (this == &rhs) { return *this; }
    // ...
    return *this;
}
```

With the copy-and-swap idiom, such a self-assignment test is not needed.

> **WARNING** *When implementing an assignment operator, use the copy-and-swap idiom to avoid code duplication and to guarantee strong exception safety.*

> **NOTE** *The copy-and-swap idiom can be used for more than just assignment operators. It can be used for any operation that takes multiple steps and that you want to turn into an all-or-nothing operation: first, make a copy; then, do all the modifications on the copy; and finally, if there are no errors, perform a non-throwing swap operation.*

Disallowing Assignment and Pass-by-Value

Sometimes when you dynamically allocate memory in your class, it's easiest just to prevent anyone from copying or assigning to your objects. You can do this by explicitly deleting your `operator=` and copy constructor. That way, if anyone tries to pass the object by value, return it from a function, or assign to it, the compiler will complain. Here is a `Spreadsheet` class definition that prevents assignment and pass-by-value:

```
export class Spreadsheet
{
```

```
    public:
        Spreadsheet(std::size_t width, std::size_t height);
        Spreadsheet(const Spreadsheet& src) = delete;
        ~Spreadsheet();
        Spreadsheet& operator=(const Spreadsheet& rhs) = delete;
        // Code omitted for brevity
};
```

You don't provide implementations for deleted member functions. The linker will never look for them because the compiler won't allow code to call them. When you now write code to copy or assign to a `Spreadsheet` object, the compiler will complain with a message like this:

```
'Spreadsheet &Spreadsheet::operator =(const Spreadsheet &)': attempting to
reference a deleted function
```

Handling Moving with Move Semantics

Move semantics for classes requires a *move constructor* and a *move assignment operator*. These can be used by the compiler when the source object is a temporary object that will be destroyed after the operation is finished or, as you will see, explicitly when using `std::move()`. Moving *moves ownership* of memory and other resources from one object to another object. It basically does a *shallow* copy of data members *combined with* switching ownership of allocated memory and other resources to prevent dangling pointers or resources and to prevent memory leaks.

Both the move constructor and the move assignment operator move the data members from a source object to a new object, leaving the source object in some valid but otherwise indeterminate state. Often, data members of the source object are reset to "null" values, but this is not a strict requirement. I do recommend, however, that you make sure your source objects are in a clearly defined empty state after a move operation. To be safe, never use any objects that have been moved from, as this could trigger undefined behavior. Some notable exceptions from the Standard Library are `std::unique_ptr` and `shared_ptr`. The Standard Library explicitly states that these smart pointers must reset their internal pointer to `nullptr` when moving from them, which makes it safe to reuse such smart pointers after a move operation.

Before you can implement move semantics, you need to learn about rvalues and rvalue references.

Rvalue References

In C++, an *lvalue* is something of which you can take an address, for example, a named variable. The name comes from the fact that lvalues can appear on the left-hand side of an assignment. An *rvalue*, on the other hand, is anything that is not an lvalue, such as a literal, or a temporary object or value.[1] Typically, an rvalue is on the right-hand side of an assignment operator. For example, take the following statement:

```
int a { 4 * 2 };
```

In this statement, `a` is an lvalue, it has a name, and you can take the address of it with `&a`. The result of the expression `4*2`, on the other hand, is an rvalue. It is a temporary value that is destroyed when

[1] Technically, the C++ standard defines three more categories (xvalues, prvalues, and glvalues), but those details are not important for the current discussion.

the statement finishes execution. In this example, a copy of this temporary value is stored in the variable with name a.

If a function returns something by value, the result of calling that function is an rvalue, a temporary. If the function returns a reference-to-non-const, then the result of calling the function is an lvalue, as you will be able to use the result on the left-hand side of an assignment.

An *rvalue reference* is a reference to an rvalue. In particular, it is a concept that is applied when the rvalue is a temporary object or an object that is explicitly moved using `std::move()`, explained later in this section. The purpose of an rvalue reference is to make it possible for a particular function overload to be chosen when an rvalue is involved. This allows certain operations that normally involve copying large values to instead copy pointers to those values.

A function can specify an rvalue reference parameter by using `&&` as part of the parameter specification, for example, `type&& name`. Normally, a temporary object will be seen as a `const type&`, but when there is a function overload that uses an rvalue reference, a temporary object can be resolved to that overload. The following example demonstrates this. The code first defines two `handleMessage()` functions, one accepting an lvalue reference and one accepting an rvalue reference:

```
void handleMessage(string& message) // lvalue reference parameter
{
    println("handleMessage with lvalue reference: {}", message);
}

void handleMessage(string&& message) // rvalue reference parameter
{
    println("handleMessage with rvalue reference: {}", message);
}
```

You can call `handleMessage()` with a named variable as an argument:

```
string a { "Hello " };
handleMessage(a);             // Calls handleMessage(string& value)
```

Because a is a named variable, the `handleMessage()` function accepting an lvalue reference is called. Any changes `handleMessage()` does through its reference parameter will change the value of a.

You can also call `handleMessage()` with an expression as an argument:

```
string b { "World" };
handleMessage(a + b);         // Calls handleMessage(string&& value)
```

The `handleMessage()` function accepting an lvalue reference cannot be used, because the expression `a + b` results in a temporary, which is not an lvalue. In this case, the rvalue reference overload is called. Because the argument is a temporary, any changes `handleMessage()` does through its reference parameter will be lost after the call returns.

A literal can also be used as argument to `handleMessage()`. This also triggers a call to the rvalue reference overload because a literal cannot be an lvalue (though a literal can be passed as argument to a reference-to-const parameter):

```
handleMessage("Hello World"); // Calls handleMessage(string&& value)
```

If you remove the `handleMessage()` function accepting an lvalue reference, calling `handleMessage()` with a named variable like `handleMessage(b)` will result in a compilation error because an rvalue reference parameter (`string&&`) will never be bound to an lvalue (`b`). You can force the compiler to call the rvalue reference overload of `handleMessage()` by using `std::move()`. The only thing `move()` does is cast an lvalue to an rvalue reference; that is, it does not do any actual moving. However, by returning an rvalue reference, it allows the compiler to find an overload of `handleMessage()` accepting an rvalue reference, which can then perform the moving. Here is an example of using `move()`:

```
handleMessage(std::move(b));  // Calls handleMessage(string&& value)
```

As I said before, but it's worth repeating, *a named variable is an lvalue*. So, inside the `handleMessage(string&& message)` function, the `message` rvalue reference parameter itself is an lvalue because it has a name! If you want to forward this rvalue reference parameter to another function as an rvalue, then you need to use `std::move()` to cast the lvalue to an rvalue reference. For example, suppose you add the following function with an rvalue reference parameter:

```
void helper(string&& message) { }
```

Calling it as follows does not compile:

```
void handleMessage(string&& message) { helper(message); }
```

The `helper()` function needs an rvalue reference, while `handleMessage()` passes `message`, which has a name, so it's an lvalue, causing a compilation error. Here is the correct way using `std::move()`:

```
void handleMessage(string&& message) { helper(std::move(message)); }
```

WARNING *A named rvalue reference, such as an rvalue reference parameter, itself is an lvalue because it has a name!*

Rvalue references are not limited to parameters of functions. You can declare a variable of an rvalue reference type and assign to it, although this usage is uncommon. Consider the following code, which is illegal in C++:

```
int& i { 2 };          // Invalid: reference to a constant
int a { 2 }, b { 3 };
int& j { a + b };     // Invalid: reference to a temporary
```

Using rvalue references, the following is perfectly legal:

```
int&& i { 2 };
int a { 2 }, b { 3 };
int&& j { a + b };
```

However, such stand-alone rvalue references are rarely used in this way.

NOTE *If a temporary is assigned to an rvalue reference, the lifetime of the temporary is extended for as long as the rvalue reference is in scope.*

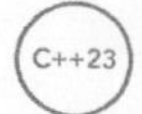

Decay Copy

If you have an object x, writing "auto y{x}" creates a copy of x and gives it a name y; thus, it is an lvalue.

C++23 introduces the auto(x) or auto{x} syntax to create a copy of an object x as an rvalue, not an lvalue.

As an example, assume you have only the rvalue reference handleMessage(string&&) function from the previous section, not the lvalue reference overload. You know that the following won't work in that case:

```
string value { "Hello " };
handleMessage(value);  // Error
```

You could use std::move(), as in:

```
handleMessage(std::move(value));
```

But, after this operation, you should not use the value object any longer, as it might have been moved.

Using C++23 decay-copy syntax, you can write:

```
handleMessage(auto { value });
```

This makes a temporary copy of object value as an rvalue and passes that rvalue to handleMessage(). If handleMessage() moves from the copy, the original object, value, is retained and not impacted

Implementing Move Semantics

Move semantics is implemented using rvalue references. To add move semantics to a class, you need to implement a *move constructor* and a *move assignment operator*. Move constructors and move assignment operators should be marked with the noexcept specifier to tell the compiler that they don't throw any exceptions. This is particularly important for compatibility with the Standard Library, as fully compliant implementations of, for example, the Standard Library containers will only move stored objects if, having move semantics implemented, they also guarantee not to throw. This is done to be able to provide strong exception safety.

The following is the Spreadsheet class definition with a move constructor and move assignment operator. Two helper member functions are introduced as well: cleanup(), which is used from the destructor and the move assignment operator, and moveFrom(), which moves the data members from a source to a destination and then resets the source object.

```
export class Spreadsheet
{
    public:
        Spreadsheet(Spreadsheet&& src) noexcept; // Move constructor
        Spreadsheet& operator=(Spreadsheet&& rhs) noexcept; // Move assignment
        // Remaining code omitted for brevity
    private:
        void cleanup() noexcept;
        void moveFrom(Spreadsheet& src) noexcept;
        // Remaining code omitted for brevity
};
```

The implementations are as follows:

```
void Spreadsheet::cleanup() noexcept
{
    for (size_t i { 0 }; i < m_width; ++i) {
        delete[] m_cells[i];
    }
    delete[] m_cells;
    m_cells = nullptr;
    m_width = m_height = 0;
}

void Spreadsheet::moveFrom(Spreadsheet& src) noexcept
{
    // Shallow copy of data
    m_width = src.m_width;
    m_height = src.m_height;
    m_cells = src.m_cells;

    // Reset the source object, because ownership has been moved!
    src.m_width = 0;
    src.m_height = 0;
    src.m_cells = nullptr;
}

// Move constructor
Spreadsheet::Spreadsheet(Spreadsheet&& src) noexcept
{
    moveFrom(src);
}

// Move assignment operator
Spreadsheet& Spreadsheet::operator=(Spreadsheet&& rhs) noexcept
{
    // Check for self-assignment
    if (this == &rhs) {
        return *this;
    }

    // Free the old memory and move ownership
    cleanup();
    moveFrom(rhs);
    return *this;
}
```

Both the move constructor and the move assignment operator are moving ownership of the memory for `m_cells` from a source object to a new object. They reset the `m_cells` pointer of the source object to a null pointer and set `m_width` and `m_height` of the source object to zero to prevent the source object's destructor from deallocating any memory because the new object is now the owner of it.

Obviously, move semantics is useful only when you know that the source object is not needed anymore.

Note that this implementation includes a self-assignment test in the move assignment operator. Depending on your class and depending on how you are moving one instance of your class to another instance, this self-assignment test might not always be necessary. However, you should always include it, just as the C++ Core Guidelines recommend,[2] to make sure that code as follows never causes a crash at run time:

```
sheet1 = std::move(sheet1);
```

Move constructors and move assignment operators can be explicitly deleted or defaulted, just like copy constructors and copy assignment operators, as explained in Chapter 8.

The compiler automatically generates a default move constructor for a class if and only if the class has no user-declared copy constructor, copy assignment operator, move assignment operator, or destructor. A default move assignment operator is generated for a class if and only if the class has no user-declared copy constructor, move constructor, copy assignment operator, or destructor.

> **WARNING** *When you declare one or more of the special member functions (destructor, copy constructor, move constructor, copy assignment operator, and move assignment operator), then it's recommended to declare all of them. This is called the* ***rule of five****. You either provide explicit implementations for them or explicitly default (*`=default`*) or delete (*`=delete`*) them.*

Using std::exchange

You can use `std::exchange()`, defined in `<utility>`, to replace a value with a new value and return the old value, as in this example:

```
int a { 11 };
int b { 22 };
println("Before exchange(): a = {}, b = {}", a, b);
int returnedValue { exchange(a, b) };
println("After exchange():  a = {}, b = {}", a, b);
println("exchange() returned: {}", returnedValue);
```

The output is as follows:

```
Before exchange(): a = 11, b = 22
After exchange():  a = 22, b = 22
exchange() returned: 11
```

The `exchange()` function is useful in implementing move assignment operators. A move assignment operator needs to move the data from a source object to a destination object, after which the data in the source object is usually nullified. In the previous section, this is done as follows:

```
void Spreadsheet::moveFrom(Spreadsheet& src) noexcept
{
    // Shallow copy of data
    m_width = src.m_width;
```

[2] Guideline C.65 of the C++ Core Guidelines (see Appendix B, "Annotated Bibliography") states, "Make move assignment safe for self-assignment."

```
        m_height = src.m_height;
        m_cells = src.m_cells;

        // Reset the source object, because ownership has been moved!
        src.m_width = 0;
        src.m_height = 0;
        src.m_cells = nullptr;
    }
```

This member function copies the `m_width`, `m_height`, and `m_cells` data members from the source object and then sets them to either `0` or `nullptr`, because ownership has been moved. With `exchange()` this can be written more compactly as follows:

```
void Spreadsheet::moveFrom(Spreadsheet& src) noexcept
{
    m_width = exchange(src.m_width, 0);
    m_height = exchange(src.m_height, 0);
    m_cells = exchange(src.m_cells, nullptr);
}
```

Moving Object Data Members

The `moveFrom()` member function uses direct assignments of the three data members because they are primitive types. If your object contains other objects as data members, then you should move these objects using `std::move()`. Suppose the `Spreadsheet` class has an `std::string` data member called `m_name`. The `moveFrom()` member function should then be implemented as follows:

```
void Spreadsheet::moveFrom(Spreadsheet& src) noexcept
{
    // Move object data members
    m_name = std::move(src.m_name);

    // Move primitives:
    m_width = exchange(src.m_width, 0);
    m_height = exchange(src.m_height, 0);
    m_cells = exchange(src.m_cells, nullptr);
}
```

Move Constructor and Move Assignment Operator in Terms of Swap

The previous implementation of the move constructor and the move assignment operator both use the `moveFrom()` helper function, which moves all data members by performing shallow copies. With this implementation, if you add a new data member to the `Spreadsheet` class, you have to modify both the `swap()` function and the `moveFrom()` function. If you forget to update one of them, you introduce a bug. To avoid such bugs, you can write the move constructor and the move assignment operator in terms of the `swap()` function.

First, the `cleanup()` and `moveFrom()` helper functions can be removed. The code from the `cleanup()` function is moved to the destructor. The move constructor and move assignment operator can then be implemented as follows:

```
Spreadsheet::Spreadsheet(Spreadsheet&& src) noexcept
{
    swap(src);
}
```

```
Spreadsheet& Spreadsheet::operator=(Spreadsheet&& rhs) noexcept
{
    auto moved { std::move(rhs) }; // Move rhs into moved (noexcept)
    swap(moved); // Commit the work with only non-throwing operations
    return *this;
}
```

The move constructor simply swaps the default constructed `*this` with the given source object. The move assignment operator uses the *move-and-swap* idiom, which is similar to the copy-and-swap idiom discussed before.

> **NOTE** *Implementing a move constructor and move assignment operator in terms of* `swap()` *requires less code. It is also less likely bugs are introduced when data members are added, because you only have to update your* `swap()` *implementation to include those new data members.*

The `Spreadsheet` move assignment operator could also be implemented as follows:

```
Spreadsheet& Spreadsheet::operator=(Spreadsheet&& rhs) noexcept
{
    swap(rhs);
    return *this;
}
```

However, doing so does not guarantee that the contents of `this` is immediately cleaned up. Instead, the contents of `this` escapes through `rhs` to the caller of the move assignment operator and thus might stay alive longer than expected.

Testing the Spreadsheet Move Operations

The `Spreadsheet` move constructor and move assignment operator can be tested with the following code:

```
Spreadsheet createObject()
{
    return Spreadsheet { 3, 2 };
}

int main()
{
    vector<Spreadsheet> vec;
    for (size_t i { 0 }; i < 2; ++i) {
        println("Iteration {}", i);
        vec.push_back(Spreadsheet { 100, 100 });
        println("");
    }

    Spreadsheet s { 2, 3 };
```

```
        s = createObject();

        println("");

        Spreadsheet s2 { 5, 6 };
        s2 = s;
    }
```

Chapter 1 introduces the vector. A vector grows dynamically in size to accommodate new objects. This is done by allocating a bigger chunk of memory and then copying or moving the objects from the old vector to the new and bigger vector. If the compiler finds a noexcept move constructor, the objects are moved instead of copied. Because they are moved, there is no need for any deep copying, making it much more efficient.

After adding print statements to all constructors and assignment operators of the Spreadsheet class, the output of the preceding test program can be as follows. The numbers to the right of each line are not part of the actual output but added in this text to make it easier to refer to specific lines in the discussion that follows. This output and the following discussion are based on the version of the Spreadsheet class using the move-and-swap idiom to implement its move operations, and on the Microsoft Visual C++ 2022 compiler for a release build of the code. The C++ standard does not specify the initial capacity of a vector nor its growth strategy, so the output can be different on different compilers.

```
Iteration 0
Normal constructor           (1)
Move constructor             (2)

Iteration 1
Normal constructor           (3)
Move constructor             (4)
Move constructor             (5)

Normal constructor           (6)
Normal constructor           (7)
Move assignment operator     (8)
Move constructor             (9)

Normal constructor          (10)
Copy assignment operator    (11)
Normal constructor          (12)
Copy constructor            (13)
```

On the first iteration of the loop, the vector is still empty. Take the following line of code from the loop:

```
vec.push_back(Spreadsheet { 100, 100 });
```

With this line, a new Spreadsheet object is created, invoking the normal constructor (1). The vector resizes itself to make space for the new object being pushed in. The created Spreadsheet object is then moved into the vector, invoking the move constructor (2).

On the second iteration of the loop, a second Spreadsheet object is created with the normal constructor (3). At this point, the vector can hold one element, so it's again resized to make space for a second object. Because the vector is resized, the previously added elements need to be moved from the old vector to the new and bigger vector. This triggers a call to the move constructor for each previously added element. There is one element in the vector, so the move constructor is called one time (4). Finally, the new Spreadsheet object is moved into the vector with its move constructor (5).

Next, a Spreadsheet object s is created using the normal constructor (6). The createObject() function creates a temporary Spreadsheet object with its normal constructor (7), which is then returned from the function and assigned to the variable s. Because the temporary object returned from createObject() ceases to exist after the assignment, the compiler invokes the move assignment operator (8) instead of the copy assignment operator. The move assignment operator uses the move-and-swap idiom, so it delegates work to the move constructor (9).

Another Spreadsheet object is created, s2, using the normal constructor (10). The assignment s2 = s invokes the copy assignment operator (11) because the right-hand side object is not a temporary object, but a named object. This copy assignment operator uses the copy-and-swap idiom, which creates a temporary copy, triggering a call to the copy constructor, which first delegates to the normal constructor (12 and 13).

If the Spreadsheet class did not implement move semantics, all the calls to the move constructor and move assignment operator would be replaced with calls to the copy constructor and copy assignment operator. In the previous example, the Spreadsheet objects in the loop have 10,000 (100 × 100) elements. The implementations of the Spreadsheet move constructor and move assignment operator don't require any memory allocation, while the copy constructor and copy assignment operator require 101 allocations each. So, using move semantics can increase performance a lot in certain situations.

Implementing a Swap Function with Move Semantics

As another example where move semantics increases performance, take a swap() function that swaps two Objects. The following swapCopy() implementation does not use move semantics:

```
void swapCopy(Object& a, Object& b)
{
    Object temp { a };
    a = b;
    b = temp;
}
```

First, a is copied to temp, then b is copied to a, and finally temp is copied to b. This implementation will hurt performance if Object is expensive to copy. With move semantics, the implementation can avoid all copying:

```
void swapMove(Object& a, Object& b)
{
    Object temp { std::move(a) };
    a = std::move(b);
    b = std::move(temp);
}
```

This is how std::swap() from the Standard Library is implemented.

Using std::move() in Return Statements

As Chapter 1 states, since C++17, a compiler is not allowed to perform any copying or moving of objects for statements of the form `return object;` where `object` is a nameless temporary. This is called *mandatory elision of copy/move operations* and means that there's no performance penalty at all by returning `object` by value. If `object` is a local variable that is not a function parameter, *non-mandatory elision of copy/move operations* is allowed, an optimization also known as *named return value optimization* (NRVO). This optimization is not guaranteed by the standard. Some compilers perform this optimization only for release builds but not for debug builds. With mandatory and non-mandatory elision, compilers can avoid any copying of objects that are returned from functions. This results in *zero-copy pass-by-value* semantics.

> **WARNING** *Note that for NRVO, even though the copy/move constructors won't be called, they still need to be accessible; otherwise, the program is ill-formed according to the standard.*

Now, what happens when using `std::move()` to return an object? Consider you write the following:

```
return std::move(object);
```

With this code, compilers cannot apply mandatory nor non-mandatory (NRVO) elision of copy/move operations anymore, as that works only for statements of the form `return object;`. Since copy/move elision cannot be applied anymore, the next option for the compiler is to use move semantics if the object supports it, and if not, fall back to copy semantics.

Compared to NRVO, falling back to move semantics has a small performance impact, but falling back to copy semantics can have a big performance impact! So, keep the following warning in mind:

> **WARNING** *When returning a local variable or nameless temporary from a function, simply write* `return object;` *and do not use* `std::move()`.

Note that if you want to return a data member of a class from one of its member functions, then you need to use `std::move()` if you want to move it out instead of returning a copy.

Additionally, be careful with expressions such as the following:

```
return condition ? obj1 : obj2;
```

This is not of the form `return object;`, so the compiler cannot apply copy/move elision. Even worse, an expression of the form `condition ? obj1 : obj2` is an lvalue, so the compiler uses a copy constructor instead to return one of the objects. To at least trigger move semantics, you can rewrite the `return` statement as follows:

```
return condition ? std::move(obj1) : std::move(obj2);
```

or

```
return std::move(condition ? obj1 : obj2);
```

However, it's clearer to rewrite the `return` statement as follows for which a compiler can automatically use move semantics without explicitly using `std::move()`:

```
if (condition) {
    return obj1;
} else {
    return obj2;
}
```

Optimal Way to Pass Arguments to Functions

Up to now, the advice has been to use reference-to-`const` parameters for non-primitive function parameters to avoid unnecessary expensive copying of an argument passed to a function. However, with rvalues in the mix, things change slightly. Imagine a function that anyways copies an argument passed as one of its parameters. This situation often pops up with class member functions. Here is a simple example:

```
class DataHolder
{
    public:
        void setData(const vector<int>& data) { m_data = data; }
    private:
        vector<int> m_data;
};
```

`setData()` makes a copy of the data passed in. Now that you are fluent with rvalues and rvalue references, you might want to add an overload to optimize `setData()` to avoid any copying in case of rvalues. Here's an example:

```
class DataHolder
{
    public:
        void setData(const vector<int>& data) { m_data = data; }
        void setData(vector<int>&& data) { m_data = move(data); }
    private:
        vector<int> m_data;
};
```

When `setData()` is called with a temporary, no copies are made; the data is moved instead.

The code in the following code snippet triggers a call to the reference-to-`const` overload of `setData()`, and hence a copy of the data is made:

```
DataHolder wrapper;
vector myData { 11, 22, 33 };
wrapper.setData(myData);
```

On the other hand, the following code snippet calls `setData()` with a temporary, which triggers a call to the rvalue reference overload of `setData()`. The data is subsequently moved instead of copied.

```
wrapper.setData({ 22, 33, 44 });
```

Unfortunately, this way to optimize `setData()` for both lvalues and rvalues requires an implementation of two overloads. Luckily, there is a better way that involves a single member function using pass-by-value. Yes, pass-by-value! Up to now, it has been advised to always pass objects using reference-to-`const` parameters to avoid any unnecessary copying, but now we advise to use pass-by-value. Let's clarify. For parameters that are not copied, passing by reference-to-`const` is still the way to go. The pass-by-value advice *is suitable only* for parameters that the function would copy anyway. In that case, by using pass-by-value semantics, the code is optimal for both lvalues and rvalues. If an lvalue is passed in, it's copied exactly one time, just as with a reference-to-`const` parameter. And, if an rvalue is passed in, no copy is made, just as with an rvalue reference parameter. Let's look at some code:

```
class DataHolder
{
    public:
        void setData(vector<int> data) { m_data = move(data); }
    private:
        vector<int> m_data;
};
```

If an lvalue is passed to `setData()`, it is copied into the `data` parameter and subsequently moved to `m_data`. If an rvalue is passed to `setData()`, it is moved into the `data` parameter, and moved again to `m_data`.

> **NOTE** *Prefer pass-by-value for parameters that a function inherently would copy, but only if the parameter is of a type that supports move semantics and only if you don't need polymorphic behavior on the parameter. Otherwise, use reference-to-*`const` *parameters. Passing polymorphic types by value can result in slicing. This is explained in Chapter 10, "Discovering Inheritance Techniques."*

Rule of Zero

Earlier in this chapter, the rule of five was introduced. It states that once you declare one of the five special member functions (destructor, copy constructor, move constructor, copy assignment operator, and move assignment operator), then you should declare all of them by either implementing, defaulting, or deleting them. The reason is that there are complicated rules that compilers follow to decide whether to automatically provide a compiler-generated version of those special member functions. By declaring all of them yourself, you don't leave anything for the compiler to decide, making your intent much clearer.

All the discussions so far have been to explain how to write those five special member functions. However, in modern C++, you should adopt the *rule of zero*.

The rule of zero states that you should design your classes in such a way that they do not require any of those five special member functions. How do you do that? You can do that for non-polymorphic types in which you avoid using old-style dynamically allocated memory or other resources. Instead, use modern constructs such as Standard Library containers and smart pointers. For example, you can use a `vector<vector<SpreadsheetCell>>` instead of the `SpreadsheetCell**` data member in the `Spreadsheet` class. Or even better, use a `vector<SpreadsheetCell>` storing a linearized representation of a spreadsheet. The `vector` handles memory automatically, so there is no need for any of those five special member functions.

> **WARNING** *In modern C++, adopt the rule of zero!*

The rule of five should be limited to custom resource acquisition is initialization (RAII) classes. An RAII class takes ownership of a resource and handles its deallocation at the right time. It's a design technique used, for example, by `vector` and `unique_ptr` and discussed further in Chapter 32, "Incorporating Design Techniques and Frameworks." Additionally, Chapter 10 explains that polymorphic types require you to follow the rule of five as well.

MORE ABOUT MEMBER FUNCTIONS

C++ provides myriad choices for member functions. This section explains all the tricky details.

static Member Functions

Member functions, like data members, sometimes apply to the class as a whole, not to each object. You can write `static` member functions as well as data members. As an example, consider the `SpreadsheetCell` class from Chapter 8. It has two helper member functions: `stringToDouble()` and `doubleToString()`. These member functions don't access information about specific objects, so they could be `static`. Here is the class definition with these member functions `static`:

```
export class SpreadsheetCell
{
    // Omitted for brevity
    private:
        static std::string doubleToString(double value);
        static double stringToDouble(std::string_view value);
        // Omitted for brevity
};
```

The implementations of these two member functions are identical to the previous implementations. You don't repeat the `static` keyword in front of the member function definitions. Note that `static` member functions are not called on a specific object, so they do not have a `this` pointer and are not executing for a specific object with access to its non-`static` members. In fact, a `static` member function is just like a regular function. The only difference is that it can access `private static` and `protected static` members of the class. Additionally, it can also access `private` and `protected` non-`static` members on objects of the same type, if those objects are made available to the `static` member function, for example, by passing in a reference or pointer to such an object as a parameter.

You call a `static` member function just like a regular member function from within any member function of the class. Thus, the implementation of all the member functions in `SpreadsheetCell` can stay the same.

Outside of the class, you need to qualify the `static` member function name with the class name using the scope resolution operator. Access control applies as usual. For example, if you have a class `Foo` with a `public static` member function called `bar()`, then you can call `bar()` from anywhere in the code as follows:

```
Foo::bar();
```

> **NOTE** *The example defining* `doubleToString()` *and* `stringToDouble()` *as* `private static` *member functions is just to demonstrate how you define and use* `static` *member functions. For this specific case, neither member function accesses any data from specific* `SpreadsheetCell` *instances. Thus, you can also define these helper functions outside of the* `SpreadsheetCell` *class in an unnamed namespace (see Chapter 11, "Modules, Header Files, and Miscellaneous Topics") in the* `spreadsheet_cell` *module implementation file. See the downloadable source code for such an implementation.*

const Member Functions

A `const` object is an object whose value cannot be changed. If you have a `const`, reference to `const`, or pointer to a `const` object, the compiler does not let you call any member functions on that object unless those member functions guarantee that they won't change any data members. The way you guarantee that a member function won't change data members is to mark the member function itself with the `const` keyword. This is already done throughout Chapter 8 during the development of the `SpreadsheetCell` class. As a reminder, here is part of the `SpreadsheetCell` class with the member functions that don't change any data members marked as `const`:

```
export class SpreadsheetCell
{
    public:
        double getValue() const;
        std::string getString() const;
        // Omitted for brevity
};
```

The `const` specification is part of the member function prototype and must accompany its definition as well:

```
double SpreadsheetCell::getValue() const
{
    return m_value;
}

string SpreadsheetCell::getString() const
{
    return doubleToString(m_value);
}
```

Marking a member function as `const` signs a contract with client code guaranteeing that you will not change the internal values of the object from within that member function. If you try to declare a member function const that actually modifies a data member, the compiler will complain. const member functions work by making it appear inside the member function that you have a reference-to-const to each data member. Thus, if you try to change a data member, the compiler will flag an error.

You cannot declare a static member function const, because it is redundant. Static member functions do not work on a specific instance of the class, so it would be impossible for them to change internal values.

You can call const and non-const member functions on a non-const object. However, you can only call const member functions on a const object. Here are some examples:

```
SpreadsheetCell myCell { 5 };
println("{}", myCell.getValue());       // OK
myCell.setString("6");                  // OK

const SpreadsheetCell& myCellConstRef { myCell };
println("{}", myCellConstRef.getValue()); // OK
myCellConstRef.setString("6");              // Compilation Error!
```

You should get into the habit of declaring const all member functions that don't modify the object so that you can use references to const objects in your program.

Note that const objects can still be destroyed, and their destructor can be called. Nevertheless, destructors are not allowed to be declared const.

mutable Data Members

Sometimes you write a member function that is "logically" const but happens to change a data member of the object. This modification has no effect on any user-visible data, but is technically a change, so the compiler won't let you declare the member function const. For example, suppose that you want to profile your spreadsheet application to obtain information about how often data is being read. A crude way to do this would be to add a counter to the SpreadsheetCell class that counts each call to getValue() or getString(). Unfortunately, that makes those member functions non-const in the compiler's eyes, which is not what you intended. The solution is to make your new counter variable mutable, which tells the compiler that it's OK to change it in a const member function. Here is the new SpreadsheetCell class definition:

```
export class SpreadsheetCell
{
    // Omitted for brevity
    private:
        double m_value { 0 };
        mutable unsigned m_numAccesses { 0 };
};
```

Here are the definitions for getValue() and getString():

```
double SpreadsheetCell::getValue() const
{
    ++m_numAccesses;
    return m_value;
}
```

```
string SpreadsheetCell::getString() const
{
    ++m_numAccesses;
    return doubleToString(m_value);
}
```

Member Function Overloading

You've already noticed that you can write multiple constructors in a class, all of which have the same name. These constructors differ only in the number and/or types of their parameters. You can do the same thing for any member function or function in C++. Specifically, you can *overload* a function or member function name by using it for multiple functions, as long as the number and/or types of the parameters differ. For example, in the `SpreadsheetCell` class you can rename both `setString()` and `setValue()` to `set()`. The class definition now looks like this:

```
export class SpreadsheetCell
{
    public:
        void set(double value);
        void set(std::string_view value);
        // Omitted for brevity
};
```

The implementations of the `set()` member functions stay the same. When you write code to call `set()`, the compiler determines which instance to call based on the argument you pass: if you pass a `string_view`, the compiler calls the `string_view` instance; if you pass a `double`, the compiler calls the `double` instance. This is called *overload resolution.*

You might be tempted to do the same thing for `getValue()` and `getString()`: rename each of them to `get()`. However, that does not work. C++ does not allow you to overload a member function name based only on the return type because in many cases it would be impossible for the compiler to determine which instance of the member function to call. For example, if the return value of the member function is not captured anywhere, the compiler has no way to tell which instance of the member function you are trying to call.

Overloading Based on const

You can overload a member function based on `const`. That is, you can write two member functions with the same name and same parameters, one of which is declared `const` and one of which is not. The compiler calls the `const` member function if you have a `const` object and calls the non-`const` overload if you have a non-`const` object. Writing these two overloaded member functions could introduce code duplication, because, often, the implementations of the `const` and non-`const` overloads are identical. As you know, code duplication should be avoided as much as possible, even if it's just a few lines of code. Doing so follows the DRY (Don't Repeat Yourself) principle discussed in Chapter 6 and makes future maintenance of the code easier. For example, imagine that in a few months or years you need to make a small change to duplicated code. When doing so, you need to remember to make the same change to all the places where the code has been duplicated.

The next sections provide two solutions to avoid code duplication when writing such overloaded member functions.

Scott Meyers' const_cast Pattern

To prevent code duplication, you can use the Scott Meyers's `const_cast()` pattern. For example, the `Spreadsheet` class has a member function called `getCellAt()` returning a reference-to-non-`const` to a `SpreadsheetCell`. You can add a `const` overload that returns a reference-to-`const` to a `SpreadsheetCell` as follows:

```
export class Spreadsheet
{
    public:
        SpreadsheetCell& getCellAt(std::size_t x, std::size_t y);
        const SpreadsheetCell& getCellAt(std::size_t x, std::size_t y) const;
        // Code omitted for brevity.
};
```

Scott Meyers' `const_cast()` pattern implements the `const` overload as you normally would and implements the non-`const` overload by forwarding the call to the `const` overload with the appropriate casts, as follows:

```
const SpreadsheetCell& Spreadsheet::getCellAt(size_t x, size_t y) const
{
    verifyCoordinate(x, y);
    return m_cells[x][y];
}

SpreadsheetCell& Spreadsheet::getCellAt(size_t x, size_t y)
{
    return const_cast<SpreadsheetCell&>(as_const(*this).getCellAt(x, y));
}
```

The pattern first casts `*this` (a `Spreadsheet&`) to a `const Spreadsheet&` using `std::as_const()` (defined in `<utility>`). Next, you call the `const` overload of `getCellAt()`, which returns a `const SpreadsheetCell&`. You then cast this to a non-`const SpreadsheetCell&` with a `const_cast()`.

With these two `getCellAt()` overloads, you can now call `getCellAt()` on `const` and non-`const` `Spreadsheet` objects:

```
Spreadsheet sheet1 { 5, 6 };
SpreadsheetCell& cell1 { sheet1.getCellAt(1, 1) };

const Spreadsheet sheet2 { 5, 6 };
const SpreadsheetCell& cell2 { sheet2.getCellAt(1, 1) };
```

Private Helper Member Function

Another option to avoid code duplication when implementing both `const` and non-`const` overloads is to have a `private const` helper member function with a non-`const` return type. The `const` and non-`const` overloaded member functions then both call this helper function. For example, for the `getCellAt()` overloads from the previous section, a `getCellAtHelper()` can be added as follows:

```
export class Spreadsheet
{
    public:
        SpreadsheetCell& getCellAt(std::size_t x, std::size_t y);
        const SpreadsheetCell& getCellAt(std::size_t x, std::size_t y) const;
```

```
        // Code omitted for brevity.
    private:
        SpreadsheetCell& getCellAtHelper(std::size_t x, std::size_t y) const;
};
```

And here are the implementations:

```
SpreadsheetCell& Spreadsheet::getCellAt(size_t x, size_t y)
{
    return getCellAtHelper(x, y);
}

const SpreadsheetCell& Spreadsheet::getCellAt(size_t x, size_t y) const
{
    return getCellAtHelper(x, y);
}

SpreadsheetCell& Spreadsheet::getCellAtHelper(size_t x, size_t y) const
{
    verifyCoordinate(x, y);
    return m_cells[x][y];
}
```

Explicitly Deleting Overloads

Overloaded member functions can be explicitly deleted, which enables you to forbid calling a member function with particular arguments. For example, the `SpreadsheetCell` class has a member function `setValue(double)` that can be called as follows:

```
SpreadsheetCell cell;
cell.setValue(1.23);
cell.setValue(123);
```

For the third line, the compiler converts the integer value (123) to a `double` and then calls `setValue(double)`. If, for some reason, you do not want `setValue()` to be called with integers, you can explicitly delete an integer overload of `setValue()`:

```
export class SpreadsheetCell
{
    public:
        void setValue(double value);
        void setValue(int) = delete;
};
```

With this change, an attempt to call `setValue()` with an integer will be flagged as an error by the compiler.

Ref-Qualified Member Functions

Ordinary class member functions can be called on both non-temporary and temporary instances of a class. Suppose you have the following class that simply remembers the `string` passed as argument to the constructor:

```
class TextHolder
{
    public:
```

```
        explicit TextHolder(string text) : m_text { move(text) } {}
        const string& getText() const { return m_text; }
    private:
        string m_text;
};
```

Of course, there is no doubt that you can call the `getText()` member function on non-temporary instances of `TextHolder`. Here's an example:

```
TextHolder textHolder { "Hello world!" };
println("{}", textHolder.getText());
```

However, `getText()` can also be called on temporary instances:

```
println("{}", TextHolder{ "Hello world!" }.getText());
```

It is possible to explicitly specify on what kind of instances a certain member function can be called, be it temporary or non-temporary instances. This is done by adding a *ref-qualifier* to the member function. If a member function can only be called on non-temporary instances, a `&` qualifier is added after the member function header. Similarly, if a member function can only be called on temporary instances, a `&&` qualifier is added.

The following modified `TextHolder` class implements the `&` qualified `getText()` by returning a reference-to-`const` to `m_text`. The `&&` qualified `getText()`, on the other hand, returns an rvalue reference to `m_text` so that `m_text` can be moved out of a `TextHolder`. This can be more efficient if you, for example, want to retrieve the text from a temporary `TextHolder` instance.

```
class TextHolder
{
    public:
        explicit TextHolder(string text) : m_text { move(text) } {}
        const string& getText() const & { return m_text; }
        string&& getText() && { return move(m_text); }
    private:
        string m_text;
};
```

Suppose you have the following invocations:

```
TextHolder textHolder { "Hello world!" };
println("{}", textHolder.getText());
println("{}", TextHolder{ "Hello world!" }.getText());
```

Then the first call to `getText()` calls the `&` qualified overload, while the second invocation calls the `&&` qualified overload.

A second example of using ref-qualifiers is to prevent a user from assigning a value to a temporary instance of a class. For instance, you can add an assignment operator to `TextHolder`:

```
class TextHolder
{
    public:
        TextHolder& operator=(const string& rhs) { m_text = rhs; return *this; }
    // Remainder of the class definition omitted for brevity
};
```

Once such an assignment operator is added to TextHolder, assigning a new value to a temporary instance of TextHolder, as shown in the next code snippet, does not make much sense, as the object will cease to exist soon:

```
TextHolder makeTextHolder() { return TextHolder { "Hello World!" }; }

int main()
{
    makeTextHolder() = "Pointless!"; // Pointless, object is a temporary.
}
```

Such pointless operations can be prevented by ref-qualifying the assignment operator to only work on lvalues:

```
TextHolder& operator=(const string& rhs) & { m_text = rhs; return *this; }
```

With this assignment operator, the earlier "Pointless!" statement in main() fails to compile. You can now only assign values to lvalues:

```
auto text { makeTextHolder() };
text = "Ok";
```

Ref-Qualification Using Explicit Object Parameters

As Chapter 8 explains, C++23 introduces the concept of explicit object parameters. This allows you to rewrite the ref-qualified member functions from the previous TextHolder class using a slightly different syntax:

```
class TextHolder
{
    public:
        const string& getText(this const TextHolder& self) { return self.m_text; }
        string&& getText(this TextHolder&& self) { return move(self.m_text); }

        TextHolder& operator=(this TextHolder& self, const string& rhs)
        {
            self.m_text = rhs;
            return self;
        }
    // Remainder of the class definition omitted for brevity
};
```

This is certainly more verbose than the syntax used in the previous section, but it makes the ref-qualification more obvious. In the previous section, there's just an & or && at the end of the member function signature, but this is easily overlooked, e.g., when a colleague reviews your code.

Inline Member Functions

C++ gives you the ability to recommend to the compiler that a call to a function should not be implemented in the generated code as a call to a separate block of code. Instead, the compiler should insert the function's body directly into the code where the function is called. This process is called *inlining*, and functions that want this behavior are called *inline functions*.

You can specify an inline member function by placing the `inline` keyword in front of its name in the member function definition. For example, you might want to make the accessor member functions of the `SpreadsheetCell` class `inline`, in which case you would define them like this:

```
inline double SpreadsheetCell::getValue() const
{
    ++m_numAccesses;
    return m_value;
}

inline std::string SpreadsheetCell::getString() const
{
    ++m_numAccesses;
    return doubleToString(m_value);
}
```

This gives a hint to the compiler to replace calls to `getValue()` and `getString()` with the actual member function's body instead of generating code to make a function call. Note that the `inline` keyword is just a hint for the compiler. The compiler can ignore it if it thinks it would hurt performance.

There is one caveat: definitions of `inline` functions should be available in every source file in which they are called. That makes sense if you think about it: how can the compiler substitute the function's body if it can't see the function definition? Thus, if you write `inline` member functions, you should place the definitions of such member functions in the same file as the definition of the class to which the member functions belong.

> **NOTE** *Advanced C++ compilers do not require you to put definitions of* `inline` *member functions in the same file as the class definition. For example, Microsoft Visual C++ supports Link-Time Code Generation (LTCG), which automatically inlines small function bodies, even if they are not declared as* `inline` *and even if they are not defined in the same file as the class definition. GCC and Clang have similar features.*

Outside of C++ modules, if the definition of a member function is placed directly in the class definition, that member function implicitly is marked as inline, even without using the `inline` keyword. With classes exported from modules, this is not the case. If you want such member functions to be inline, you need to mark them with the `inline` keyword. Here's an example:

```
export class SpreadsheetCell
{
    public:
        inline double getValue() const { ++m_numAccesses; return m_value; }

        inline std::string getString() const
        {
            ++m_numAccesses;
```

```
            return doubleToString(m_value);
        }
        // Omitted for brevity
};
```

> **NOTE** *If you single-step with a debugger on a function call that is inlined, some advanced C++ debuggers will jump to the actual source code of the inline function, giving you the illusion of a function call while in reality, the code is inlined.*

Many C++ programmers discover the `inline` function syntax and employ it without understanding the ramifications. Marking a function as `inline` only gives a hint to the compiler. Compilers will only inline the simplest functions. If you define an `inline` function that the compiler doesn't want to inline, it will silently ignore the hint. Modern compilers will take metrics such as code bloat into account before deciding to inline a function, and they will not inline anything that is not cost-effective.

Default Arguments

A feature similar to function overloading in C++ is *default arguments*. You can specify defaults for function parameters in the prototype. If the user provides arguments for those parameters, the default values are ignored. If the user omits those arguments, the default values are used. There is a limitation, though: you can only provide defaults for a continuous list of parameters starting from the *rightmost parameter*. Otherwise, the compiler will not be able to match missing arguments to default arguments. Default arguments can be used in functions, member functions, and constructors. For example, you can assign default values for the width and height in the `Spreadsheet` constructor as follows:

```
export class Spreadsheet
{
    public:
        explicit Spreadsheet(std::size_t width = 100, std::size_t height = 100);
        // Omitted for brevity
};
```

The implementation of the `Spreadsheet` constructor stays the same. Note that you specify the default arguments only in the function declaration, but not in the definition.

Now you can call the `Spreadsheet` constructor with zero, one, or two arguments even though there is only one non-copy constructor:

```
Spreadsheet s1;
Spreadsheet s2 { 5 };
Spreadsheet s3 { 5, 6 };
```

A constructor with defaults for all its parameters can function as a default constructor. That is, you can construct an object of that class without specifying any arguments. If you try to declare both a default constructor and a multi-argument constructor with defaults for all its parameters, the compiler will complain because it won't know which constructor to call if you don't specify any arguments.

> **NOTE** *Anything you can do with default arguments, you can do with function overloading. You could write three different constructors, each of which takes a different number of arguments. However, default arguments allow you to write just one constructor that can take three different number of arguments. You should use the mechanism with which you are most comfortable.*

CONSTEXPR AND CONSTEVAL

In modern C++, it's possible to easily perform computations at compile time instead of at run time. This improves the run-time performance of your code. Two important keywords are used to accomplish this: `constexpr` and `consteval`.

The constexpr Keyword

C++ always had the notion of *constant expressions*, which are expressions evaluated at compile time. In some circumstances, constant expressions are a requirement. For example, when defining an array, the size of the array needs to be a constant expression. Because of this restriction, the following piece of code is not valid in C++:

```
const int getArraySize() { return 32; }

int main()
{
    int myArray[getArraySize()];    // ERROR: Invalid in C++
    println("Size of array = {}", size(myArray));
}
```

Using the `constexpr` keyword, `getArraySize()` can be redefined to allow it to be called from within a constant expression:

```
constexpr int getArraySize() { return 32; }

int main()
{
    int myArray[getArraySize()];    // OK
    println("Size of array = {}", size(myArray));
}
```

You can even do something like this:

```
int myArray[getArraySize() + 1];    // OK
```

Constant expressions can only use `constexpr` entities and integer, Boolean, character, and enumeration constants.

Declaring a function as `constexpr` imposes restrictions on what the function can do because the compiler has to be able to evaluate the function at compile time. For example, a `constexpr` function is not allowed to have any side effects, nor can it let any exceptions escape the function. Throwing exceptions and catching them in `try` blocks inside the function is allowed. A `constexpr` function is allowed to unconditionally call other `constexpr` functions. It is also allowed to call non-`constexpr` functions, but only if those calls are triggered during evaluation at run time, and not during constant evaluation. For example:

```
void log(string_view message) { print("{}", message); }

constexpr int computeSomething(bool someFlag)
{
    if (someFlag) {
        log("someFlag is true");
        return 42;
    }
    else { return 84; }
}
```

The `computeSomething()` function is `constexpr` and includes a call to `log()`, which is non-`constexpr`, but that call is executed only when `someFlag` is `true`. As long as `computeSomething()` is called with `someFlag` set to `false`, it can be called within a constant expression, for example:

```
constexpr auto value1 { computeSomething(false) };
```

Calling the function with `someFlag` set to `true` cannot be done in a constant expression. The following does not compile:

```
constexpr auto value2 { computeSomething(true) };
```

The following works fine, as the evaluation now happens at run time instead of at compile time:

```
const auto value3 { computeSomething(true) };
```

C++23 relaxes the restrictions for `constexpr` functions a bit: `goto` statements, labels (besides `case` labels), and `static` and `static constexpr` variables are now allowed in `constexpr` functions, but were not allowed before.

The consteval Keyword

The `constexpr` keyword specifies that a function *could* be executed at compile time, but it *does not guarantee* compile-time execution. Take the following `constexpr` function:

```
constexpr double inchToMm(double inch) { return inch * 25.4; }
```

If called as follows, the function is evaluated at compile time as desired:

```
constexpr double const_inch { 6.0 };
constexpr double mm1 { inchToMm(const_inch) };    // at compile time
```

However, if called as follows, the function is not evaluated at compile time, but at run time!

```
double dynamic_inch { 8.0 };
double mm2 { inchToMm(dynamic_inch) };  // at run time
```

If you really want the guarantee that a function is always evaluated at compile time, you need to use the `consteval` keyword to turn a function into an *immediate function*. The `inchToMm()` function can be changed as follows:

```
consteval double inchToMm(double inch) { return inch * 25.4; }
```

Now, the call to `inchToMm()` in the definition of `mm1` earlier still compiles fine and results in compile-time evaluation. However, the call in the definition of `mm2` now results in a compilation error because it cannot be evaluated at compile time.

An immediate function can be called only during constant evaluation. For example, suppose you have the following immediate function:

```
consteval int f(int i) { return i; }
```

This immediate function can be called from a `constexpr` function, but only when the `constexpr` function is being executed during constant evaluation. For example, the following function uses an `if consteval` statement to check if constant evaluation is happening in which case it can call `f()`. In the `else` branch, `f()` cannot be called.

```
constexpr int g(int i)
{
    if consteval { return f(i); }
    else         { return 42; }
}
```

constexpr and consteval Classes

By defining a `constexpr` or `consteval` constructor, you can create constant-expression variables of user-defined types. Just as `constexpr` functions, `constexpr` classes may or may not be evaluated at compile time, while `consteval` classes are guaranteed to be evaluated at compile time.

The following `Matrix` class defines a `constexpr` constructor. It also defines a `constexpr getSize()` member function that is performing some calculation.

```
class Matrix
{
    public:
        Matrix() = default; // Implicitly constexpr

        constexpr explicit Matrix(unsigned rows, unsigned columns)
            : m_rows { rows }, m_columns { columns } { }

        constexpr unsigned getSize() const { return m_rows * m_columns; }
    private:
        unsigned m_rows { 0 }, m_columns { 0 };
};
```

Using this class to declare `constexpr` objects is straightforward:

```
constexpr Matrix matrix { 8, 2 };
constexpr Matrix matrixDefault;
```

Such a `constexpr` object can now be used, e.g., to create an array big enough to store the matrix in linear form:

```
int linearizedMatrix[matrix.getSize()];     // OK
```

Compiler-generated (either implicitly or explicitly using `=default`) member functions, such as default constructors, destructors, assignment operators, and so on, are automatically `constexpr` unless the class contains data members where those member functions are not `constexpr`.

The definition of `constexpr` and `consteval` member functions must be available for the compiler so they can be evaluated at compile time. This means that if the class is defined in a module, such member functions must be defined in the module interface file, not in a module implementation file.

> **NOTE** *Several classes from the Standard Library are* `constexpr` *and so can be used within other* `constexpr` *functions and classes. Examples are* `std::vector` *(Chapter 1),* `optional` *(Chapter 1),* `string` *(Chapter 2, "Working with Strings and String Views"),* `unique_ptr` *(Chapter 7, since C++23),* `bitset` *(Chapter 18, "Standard Library Containers"), and* `variant` *(Chapter 24, "Additional Vocabulary Types").*

DIFFERENT KINDS OF DATA MEMBERS

C++ gives you many choices for data members. In addition to declaring simple data members in your classes, you can create `static` data members that all objects of the class share, `const` members, reference members, reference-to-`const` members, and more. This section explains the intricacies of these different kinds of data members.

static Data Members

Sometimes giving each object of a class a copy of a variable is overkill or won't work. The data member might be specific to the class, but not appropriate for each object to have its own copy. For example, you might want to give each spreadsheet a unique numerical identifier. You would need a counter that starts at 0 from which each new object could obtain its ID. This spreadsheet counter really belongs to the `Spreadsheet` class, but it doesn't make sense for each `Spreadsheet` object to have a copy of it, because you would have to keep all the counters synchronized somehow. C++ provides a solution with *static data members*. A `static` data member is a data member associated with a class instead of an object. You can think of `static` data members as global variables specific to a class. Here is the `Spreadsheet` class definition, including the new `static` counter data member:

```
export class Spreadsheet
{
    // Omitted for brevity
    private:
        static std::size_t ms_counter;
};
```

In addition to listing `static` class members in the class definition, you will have to allocate space for them in a source file, usually the source file in which you place your class member function definitions. You can initialize them at the same time, but note that unlike normal variables and data members, they are initialized to 0 by default. Static pointers are initialized to `nullptr`. Here is the code to allocate space for, and zero-initialize, `ms_counter`:

```
size_t Spreadsheet::ms_counter;
```

Static data members are zero-initialized by default, but if you want, you can explicitly initialize them to 0 as follows:

```
size_t Spreadsheet::ms_counter { 0 };
```

This code appears outside of any function or member function bodies. It's almost like declaring a global variable, except that the `Spreadsheet::` scope resolution specifies that it's part of the `Spreadsheet` class.

Just as for normal data members, access control specifiers apply to `static` data members as well. You could make the `ms_counter` data member `public`, but, as you already know, it's not recommended to have `public` data members (`const static` data members discussed in an upcoming section are an exception). You should grant access to data members through `public` getters and setters. If you want to grant access to `static` data members, you can provide `public static` get/set member functions.

Inline Variables

You can declare your static data members as *inline*. The benefit of this is that you do not have to allocate space for them in a source file. Here's an example:

```
export class Spreadsheet
{
    // Omitted for brevity
    private:
        static inline std::size_t ms_counter { 0 };
};
```

Note the `inline` keyword. With this class definition, the following line can be removed from the source file:

```
size_t Spreadsheet::ms_counter;
```

Accessing static Data Members from within Class Member Functions

You can use `static` data members as if they were regular data members from within class member functions. For example, you might want to create an `m_id` data member for the `Spreadsheet` class and initialize it from `ms_counter` in the `Spreadsheet` constructor. Here is the `Spreadsheet` class definition with an `m_id` member:

```
export class Spreadsheet
{
    public:
        // Omitted for brevity
        std::size_t getId() const;
    private:
        // Omitted for brevity
        static inline std::size_t ms_counter { 0 };
        std::size_t m_id { 0 };
};
```

Here is an implementation of the Spreadsheet constructor that assigns the initial ID:

```
Spreadsheet::Spreadsheet(size_t width, size_t height)
    : m_id { ms_counter++ }, m_width { width }, m_height { height }
{
    // Omitted for brevity
}
```

As you can see, the constructor can access ms_counter as if it were a normal member. The copy constructor should also assign a new ID. This is handled automatically because the Spreadsheet copy constructor delegates to the non-copy constructor, which creates the new ID.

For this example, assume that once an ID is assigned to an object, it never changes. So, you should not copy the ID in the copy assignment operator. Thus, it's recommended to make m_id a const data member:

```
export class Spreadsheet
{
    private:
        // Omitted for brevity
        const std::size_t m_id { 0 };
};
```

Since const data members cannot be changed once created, it's, for example, not possible to initialize them inside the body of a constructor. Such data members must be initialized either directly inside the class definition or in the ctor-initializer of a constructor. This also means you cannot assign new values to such data members in an assignment operator. This is not a problem for m_id, because once a Spreadsheet has an ID, it'll never change. However, depending on your use case, if this makes your class unassignable, the assignment operator is typically explicitly deleted.

constexpr static Data Members

Data members in your class can be declared const or constexpr, meaning they can't be changed after they are created and initialized. You should use static constexpr (or constexpr static) data members in place of global constants when the constants apply only to the class, also called *class constants*. static constexpr data members of integral types and enumerations can be defined and initialized inside the class definition even without making them inline variables. For example, you might want to specify a maximum height and width for spreadsheets. If the user tries to construct a spreadsheet with a greater height or width than the maximum, the maximum is used instead. You can make the maximum height and width static constexpr members of the Spreadsheet class:

```
export class Spreadsheet
{
    public:
        // Omitted for brevity
        static constexpr std::size_t MaxHeight { 100 };
        static constexpr std::size_t MaxWidth { 100 };
};
```

You can use these new constants in your constructor as follows:

```
Spreadsheet::Spreadsheet(size_t width, size_t height)
    : m_id { ms_counter++ }
```

```
        , m_width { std::min(width, MaxWidth) } // std::min() defined in <algorithm>
        , m_height { std::min(height, MaxHeight) }
{
    // Omitted for brevity
}
```

> **NOTE** *Instead of automatically clamping the width and height to their maximum, you could also decide to throw an exception when the width or height exceed their maximum. However, the destructor will not be called when you throw an exception from a constructor, so you need to be careful with this. This is further explained in Chapter 14, which discusses error handling in detail.*

Such constants can also be used as default values for parameters. Remember that you can only give default values for a continuous set of parameters starting with the rightmost parameter. Here is an example:

```
export class Spreadsheet
{
    public:
        explicit Spreadsheet(
            std::size_t width = MaxWidth, std::size_t height = MaxHeight);
        // Omitted for brevity
};
```

Accessing static Data Members from Outside Class Member Functions

As mentioned earlier, access control specifiers apply to `static` data members: `MaxWidth` and `MaxHeight` are `public`, so they can be accessed from outside class member functions by specifying that the variable is part of the `Spreadsheet` class using the `::` scope resolution operator. For example:

```
println("Maximum height is: {}", Spreadsheet::MaxHeight);
```

Reference Data Members

`Spreadsheets` and `SpreadsheetCells` are great, but they don't make a useful application by themselves. You need code to control the entire spreadsheet program, which you could package into a `SpreadsheetApplication` class. Suppose further that we want each `Spreadsheet` to store a reference to the application object. The exact definition of the `SpreadsheetApplication` class is not important at this moment, so the following code simply defines it as an empty class. The `Spreadsheet` class is modified to include a new reference data member called `m_theApp`:

```
export class SpreadsheetApplication { };

export class Spreadsheet
{
    public:
        Spreadsheet(std::size_t width, std::size_t height,
            SpreadsheetApplication& theApp);
        // Code omitted for brevity.
```

```
    private:
        // Code omitted for brevity.
        SpreadsheetApplication& m_theApp;
};
```

This definition adds a SpreadsheetApplication reference as a data member. It's recommended to use a reference in this case instead of a pointer because a Spreadsheet should always refer to a SpreadsheetApplication. This would not be guaranteed with a pointer.

Note that storing a reference to the application is done only to demonstrate the use of references as data members. It's not recommended to couple the Spreadsheet and SpreadsheetApplication classes together in this way, but instead to use a paradigm such as Model-View-Controller (MVC), introduced in Chapter 4, "Designing Professional C++ Programs."

The application reference is given to each Spreadsheet in its constructor. A reference cannot exist without referring to something, so m_theApp must be given a value in the ctor-initializer of the constructor.

```
Spreadsheet::Spreadsheet(size_t width, size_t height,
    SpreadsheetApplication& theApp)
    : m_id { ms_counter++ }
    , m_width { std::min(width, MaxWidth) }
    , m_height { std::min(height, MaxHeight) }
    , m_theApp { theApp }
{
    // Code omitted for brevity.
}
```

You must also initialize the reference member in the copy constructor. This is handled automatically because the Spreadsheet copy constructor delegates to the non-copy constructor, which initializes the reference data member.

Remember that after you have initialized a reference, you cannot change the object to which it refers. It's not possible to assign to references in the assignment operator. Depending on your use case, this might mean that an assignment operator cannot be provided for your class with reference data members. If that's the case, the assignment operator is typically marked as deleted.

Finally, a reference data member can also be marked as const. For example, you might decide that Spreadsheets should only have a reference-to-const to the application object. You can simply change the class definition to declare m_theApp as a reference-to-const:

```
export class Spreadsheet
{
    public:
        Spreadsheet(std::size_t width, std::size_t height,
            const SpreadsheetApplication& theApp);
        // Code omitted for brevity.
    private:
        // Code omitted for brevity.
        const SpreadsheetApplication& m_theApp;
};
```

NESTED CLASSES

Class definitions can contain more than just member functions and data members. They can also contain nested classes and `struct`s, type aliases, and enumerations. Anything declared inside a class is in the scope of that class. If it is `public`, you can access it outside the class by scoping it with the *`ClassName::`* scope resolution syntax.

You can provide a class definition inside another class definition. For example, you might decide that the `SpreadsheetCell` class is really part of the `Spreadsheet` class. And since it becomes part of the `Spreadsheet` class, you might as well rename it to `Cell`. You could define both of them like this:

```
export class Spreadsheet
{
    public:
        class Cell
        {
            public:
                Cell() = default;
                Cell(double initialValue);
                // Remainder omitted for brevity
        };

        Spreadsheet(std::size_t width, std::size_t height,
            const SpreadsheetApplication& theApp);
        // Remainder of Spreadsheet declarations omitted for brevity
};
```

Now, the `Cell` class is defined inside the `Spreadsheet` class, so anywhere you refer to a `Cell` outside of the `Spreadsheet` class, you must qualify the name with the `Spreadsheet::` scope. This applies even to the member function definitions. For example, the `double` constructor of `Cell` now looks like this:

```
Spreadsheet::Cell::Cell(double initialValue)
    : m_value { initialValue }
{
}
```

You must even use the syntax for return types (but not parameters) of member functions in the `Spreadsheet` class itself:

```
const Spreadsheet::Cell& Spreadsheet::getCellAt(size_t x, size_t y) const
{
    verifyCoordinate(x, y);
    return m_cells[x][y];
}
```

Fully defining the nested `Cell` class directly inside the `Spreadsheet` class makes the definition of the `Spreadsheet` class a bit bloated. You can alleviate this by only including a forward declaration for `Cell` in the `Spreadsheet` class and then defining the `Cell` class separately, as follows:

```
export class Spreadsheet
{
    public:
        class Cell;
```

```
        Spreadsheet(std::size_t width, std::size_t height,
            const SpreadsheetApplication& theApp);
        // Remainder of Spreadsheet declarations omitted for brevity
};
class Spreadsheet::Cell
{
    public:
        Cell() = default;
        Cell(double initialValue);
        // Omitted for brevity
};
```

Normal access control applies to nested class definitions. If you declare a `private` or `protected` nested class, you can only use it from inside the outer class. A nested class has access to all `protected` and `private` members of the outer class. The outer class on the other hand can only access `public` members of the nested class.

ENUMERATIONS INSIDE CLASSES

Enumerations can also be data members of a class. For example, you can add support for cell coloring to the `SpreadsheetCell` class as follows:

```
export class SpreadsheetCell
{
    public:
        // Omitted for brevity
        enum class Color { Red = 1, Green, Blue, Yellow };
        void setColor(Color color);
        Color getColor() const;
    private:
        // Omitted for brevity
        Color m_color { Color::Red };
};
```

The implementations of the `setColor()` and `getColor()` member functions are straightforward:

```
void SpreadsheetCell::setColor(Color color) { m_color = color; }
SpreadsheetCell::Color SpreadsheetCell::getColor() const { return m_color; }
```

The new member functions can be used as follows:

```
SpreadsheetCell myCell { 5 };
myCell.setColor(SpreadsheetCell::Color::Blue);
auto color { myCell.getColor() };
```

OPERATOR OVERLOADING

You often want to perform operations on objects, such as adding them, comparing them, or streaming them to or from files. For example, spreadsheets are useful only when you can perform arithmetic actions on them, such as summing an entire row of cells. All this can be accomplished by overloading operators.

Many people find the syntax of operator overloading tricky and confusing, at least at first. The irony is that it's supposed to make things simpler. As you will discover in this section, that doesn't mean simpler for the person writing the class, but simpler for the person using the class. The point is to make your new classes as similar as possible to built-in types such as `int` and `double`: it's easier to add objects using + than to remember whether the member function name you should call is `add()` or `sum()`.

> **NOTE** *Provide operator overloading as a service to clients of your class.*

At this point, you might be wondering exactly which operators you can overload. The answer is almost all of them—even some you've never heard of. This chapter just scratches the surface: the assignment operator is explained earlier in this chapter, while this section introduces the basic arithmetic operators, the shorthand arithmetic operators, and the comparison operators. Overloading the stream insertion and extraction operators is also useful. In addition, there are some tricky, but interesting, things you can do with operator overloading that you might not anticipate at first. The Standard Library uses operator overloading extensively. Chapter 15 explains how and when to overload the rest of the operators. Chapters 16 to 24 cover the Standard Library.

Example: Implementing Addition for SpreadsheetCells

In true object-oriented fashion, `SpreadsheetCell` objects should be able to add themselves to other `SpreadsheetCell` objects. Adding one cell to another cell produces a third cell with the result. It doesn't change either of the original cells. The meaning of addition for `SpreadsheetCells` is the addition of the values of the cells.

First Attempt: The add Member Function

You can declare and define an `add()` member function for your `SpreadsheetCell` class like this:

```
export class SpreadsheetCell
{
    public:
        SpreadsheetCell add(const SpreadsheetCell& cell) const;
        // Omitted for brevity
};
```

This member function adds two cells together, returning a new third cell whose value is the sum of the first two. It is declared `const` and takes a reference to a `const SpreadsheetCell` because `add()` does not change either of the source cells. Here is the implementation:

```
SpreadsheetCell SpreadsheetCell::add(const SpreadsheetCell& cell) const
{
    return SpreadsheetCell { getValue() + cell.getValue() };
}
```

You can use the `add()` member function like this:

```
SpreadsheetCell myCell { 4 }, anotherCell { 5 };
```

```
SpreadsheetCell aThirdCell { myCell.add(anotherCell) };
auto aFourthCell { aThirdCell.add(anotherCell) };
```

That works, but it's a bit clumsy. We can do better.

Second Attempt: Overloaded operator+ as a Member Function

It would be convenient to be able to add two cells with the plus sign the way that you add two `int`s or two `double`s—something like this:

```
SpreadsheetCell myCell { 4 }, anotherCell { 5 };
SpreadsheetCell aThirdCell { myCell + anotherCell };
auto aFourthCell { aThirdCell + anotherCell };
```

C++ allows you to write your own version of the plus sign, called the *addition operator*, to work correctly for your classes. To do that, you write a member function with the name `operator+` that looks like this:

```
export class SpreadsheetCell
{
    public:
        SpreadsheetCell operator+(const SpreadsheetCell& cell) const;
        // Omitted for brevity
};
```

> **NOTE** *You are allowed to insert spaces between* `operator` *and the plus sign. For example, instead of writing* `operator+`, *you can write* `operator +`. *This book adopts the style without spaces.*

The definition of the overloaded `operator+` member function is identical to the implementation of the `add()` member function:

```
SpreadsheetCell SpreadsheetCell::operator+(const SpreadsheetCell& cell) const
{
    return SpreadsheetCell { getValue() + cell.getValue() };
}
```

Now you can add two cells together using the plus operator as shown earlier.

This syntax takes a bit of getting used to. Try not to worry too much about the strange member function name `operator+`—it's just a name like `foo` or `add`. To understand the rest of the syntax, it helps to understand what's really going on. When your C++ compiler parses a program and encounters an operator, such as `+`, `-`, `=`, or `<<`, it tries to find a function or member function with the name `operator+`, `operator-`, `operator=`, or `operator<<`, respectively, that takes the appropriate parameters. For example, when the compiler sees the following line, it tries to find a member function in the `SpreadsheetCell` class named `operator+` that accepts another `SpreadsheetCell` as argument (or, as discussed later in this chapter, a global function named `operator+` that accepts two `SpreadsheetCell` arguments):

```
SpreadsheetCell aThirdCell { myCell + anotherCell };
```

If the SpreadsheetCell class contains such an operator+ member function, then the previous line is translated to this:

```
SpreadsheetCell aThirdCell { myCell.operator+(anotherCell) };
```

Note that there's no requirement that operator+ takes as a parameter an object of the same type as the class for which it's written. You could write an operator+ for SpreadsheetCells that takes a Spreadsheet to add to the SpreadsheetCell. That wouldn't make sense to the programmer, but the compiler would allow it. The next section gives an example of an operator+ for SpreadsheetCells accepting a double value.

Note also that you can give operator+ any return type you want. However, you should follow the principle of least astonishment; that is, the return type of your operator+ should generally be what users would expect.

Implicit Conversions

Surprisingly, once you've written the operator+ shown earlier, not only can you add two cells together, but you can also add a cell to a string_view, a double, or an int! Here are some examples:

```
SpreadsheetCell myCell { 4 }, aThirdCell;
string str { "hello" };
aThirdCell = myCell + string_view{ str };
aThirdCell = myCell + 5.6;
aThirdCell = myCell + 4;
```

The reason this code works is that the compiler does more to try to find an appropriate operator+ than just look for one with the exact types specified. The compiler also tries to find an appropriate conversion for the types so that an operator+ can be found. The SpreadsheetCell class has converting constructors (discussed in Chapter 8) to convert a double or a string_view into a SpreadsheetCell. In the preceding example, when the compiler sees a SpreadsheetCell trying to add itself to a double, it finds the SpreadsheetCell constructor that takes a double and constructs a temporary SpreadsheetCell object to pass to operator+. Similarly, when the compiler sees the line trying to add a SpreadsheetCell to a string_view, it calls the string_view SpreadsheetCell constructor to create a temporary SpreadsheetCell to pass to operator+.

Keep in mind, though, that the use of an implicit converting constructor might be inefficient, because temporary objects must be created. In this example, to avoid implicit construction for adding a double, you could write a second operator+ as follows:

```
SpreadsheetCell SpreadsheetCell::operator+(double rhs) const
{
    return SpreadsheetCell { getValue() + rhs };
}
```

Third Attempt: Global operator+

Implicit conversions allow you to use an operator+ member function to add your SpreadsheetCell objects to ints and doubles. However, the operator is not commutative, as shown in the following code:

```
aThirdCell = myCell + 5.6; // Works fine.
aThirdCell = myCell + 4;   // Works fine.
```

```
aThirdCell = 5.6 + myCell; // FAILS TO COMPILE!
aThirdCell = 4 + myCell;   // FAILS TO COMPILE!
```

The implicit conversion works fine when the `SpreadsheetCell` object is on the left of the operator, but it doesn't work when it's on the right. Addition is supposed to be commutative, so something is wrong here. The problem is that the `operator+` member function must be called on a `SpreadsheetCell` object, and that object must be on the left-hand side of the `operator+`. That's just the way the C++ language is defined. So, there's no way you can get this code to work with an `operator+` member function.

However, you can get it to work if you replace the in-class `operator+` member function with a global `operator+` function that is not tied to any particular object. The function looks like this:

```
SpreadsheetCell operator+(const SpreadsheetCell& lhs,
    const SpreadsheetCell& rhs)
{
    return SpreadsheetCell { lhs.getValue() + rhs.getValue() };
}
```

You need to declare this operator in the module interface file and export it:

```
export class SpreadsheetCell { /* Omitted for brevity */ };

export SpreadsheetCell operator+(const SpreadsheetCell& lhs,
    const SpreadsheetCell& rhs);
```

Now all four of the earlier additions work as you expect.

```
aThirdCell = myCell + 5.6; // Works fine.
aThirdCell = myCell + 4;   // Works fine.
aThirdCell = 5.6 + myCell; // Works fine.
aThirdCell = 4 + myCell;   // Works fine.
```

You might be wondering what happens if you write the following code:

```
aThirdCell = 4.5 + 5.5;
```

It compiles and runs, but it's not calling the `operator+` you wrote. It does normal `double` addition of 4.5 and 5.5, which results in the following intermediate statement:

```
aThirdCell = 10;
```

To make this assignment work, there should be a `SpreadsheetCell` object on the right-hand side. The compiler will discover a non-explicit user-defined constructor that takes a `double`, will use this constructor to implicitly convert the `double` value into a temporary `SpreadsheetCell` object, and will then call the assignment operator.

Overloading Arithmetic Operators

Now that you understand how to write `operator+`, the rest of the basic arithmetic operators are straightforward. Here are the declarations of `+`, `-`, `*`, and `/`, where you have to replace *<op>* with `+`, `-`, `*`, and `/`, resulting in four functions. You can also overload `%`, but it doesn't make sense for the `double` values stored in `SpreadsheetCell`s.

```
export class SpreadsheetCell { /* Omitted for brevity */ };

export SpreadsheetCell operator<op>(const SpreadsheetCell& lhs,
    const SpreadsheetCell& rhs);
```

The implementations of `operator-` and `operator*` are similar to the implementation of `operator+`, so these are not shown. For `operator/`, the only tricky aspect is remembering to check for division by zero. This implementation throws an exception if division by zero is detected:

```
SpreadsheetCell operator/(const SpreadsheetCell& lhs,
    const SpreadsheetCell& rhs)
{
    if (rhs.getValue() == 0) {
        throw invalid_argument { "Divide by zero." };
    }
    return SpreadsheetCell { lhs.getValue() / rhs.getValue() };
}
```

C++ does not require you to actually implement multiplication in `operator*`, division in `operator/`, and so on. You could implement multiplication in `operator/`, division in `operator+`, and so forth. However, that would be extremely confusing, and there is no good reason to do so. Whenever possible, stick to the commonly used operator meanings in your implementations.

> **NOTE** *In C++, you cannot change the precedence of operators. For example, `*` and `/` are always evaluated before `+` and `-`. The only thing user-defined operators can do is specify the implementation once the precedence of operations has been determined. C++ also does not allow you to invent new operator symbols or to change the number of arguments for operators. Operator overloading is discussed in more detail in Chapter 15, "Overloading C++ Operators."*

Overloading the Arithmetic Shorthand Operators

In addition to the basic arithmetic operators, C++ provides shorthand operators such as `+=` and `-=`. You might assume that writing `operator+` for your class also provides `operator+=`. No such luck. You have to overload the shorthand arithmetic operators explicitly. These operators differ from the basic arithmetic operators in that they change the object on the left-hand side of the operator instead of creating a new object. A second, subtler difference is that, like the assignment operator, they generate a result that is a reference to the modified object.

The arithmetic shorthand operators always require an object of your class on the left-hand side, so you should write them as member functions, not as global functions. Here are the declarations for the `SpreadsheetCell` class:

```
export class SpreadsheetCell
{
    public:
        SpreadsheetCell& operator+=(const SpreadsheetCell& rhs);
        SpreadsheetCell& operator-=(const SpreadsheetCell& rhs);
        SpreadsheetCell& operator*=(const SpreadsheetCell& rhs);
        SpreadsheetCell& operator/=(const SpreadsheetCell& rhs);
        // Omitted for brevity
};
```

Here is the implementation for operator+=. The others are similar.

```
SpreadsheetCell& SpreadsheetCell::operator+=(const SpreadsheetCell& rhs)
{
    set(getValue() + rhs.getValue());
    return *this;
}
```

The shorthand arithmetic operators are combinations of the basic arithmetic and assignment operators. With the previous definitions, you can now write code like this:

```
SpreadsheetCell myCell { 4 }, aThirdCell { 2 };
aThirdCell -= myCell;
aThirdCell += 5.4;
```

You cannot, however, write code like this (which is a good thing!):

```
5.4 += aThirdCell;
```

> **NOTE** *When you have both a normal and a shorthand version of a certain operator, it's recommended to implement the normal one in terms of the shorthand version to avoid code duplication.*

Here's an example:

```
SpreadsheetCell operator+(const SpreadsheetCell& lhs, const SpreadsheetCell& rhs)
{
    auto result { lhs };   // Local copy
    result += rhs;         // Forward to +=()
    return result;
}
```

Overloading Comparison Operators

The comparison operators, >, <, <=, >=, ==, and !=, are another useful set of operators to define for your classes. The C++20 standard has brought quite a few changes for these operators and has added the three-way comparison operator, also known as the spaceship operator, <=>, introduced in Chapter 1. To make you appreciate more what has changed since C++20, let's first start by looking at what you had to do before C++20 and what you still need to do as long as your compiler does not support the three-way comparison operator yet.

Overloading Comparison Operators Before C++20

Like the basic arithmetic operators, the six pre-C++20 comparison operators should be global functions so that you can use implicit conversion on both the left- and the right-hand side argument of the operator. The comparison operators all return a bool. Of course, you can change the return type, but that's not recommended.

Here are the declarations, where you have to replace *<op>* with `==`, `<`, `>`, `!=`, `<=`, and `>=`, resulting in six functions:

```
class SpreadsheetCell { /* Omitted for brevity */ };

bool operator<op>(const SpreadsheetCell& lhs, const SpreadsheetCell& rhs);
```

Here is the definition of `operator==`. The others are similar.

```
bool operator==(const SpreadsheetCell& lhs, const SpreadsheetCell& rhs)
{
    return (lhs.getValue() == rhs.getValue());
}
```

> **NOTE** *These overloaded comparison operators are comparing* `double` *values. Most of the time, performing equality or inequality tests on floating-point values is not a good idea. You should use an epsilon test, but that falls outside the scope of this book.*

In classes with more data members, it might be painful to compare each data member. However, once you've implemented `==` and `<`, you can write the rest of the comparison operators in terms of those two. For example, here is a definition of `operator>=` that uses `operator<`:

```
bool operator>=(const SpreadsheetCell& lhs, const SpreadsheetCell& rhs)
{
    return !(lhs < rhs);
}
```

You can use these operators to compare `SpreadsheetCell`s to other `SpreadsheetCell`s, and also to `double`s and `int`s:

```
if (myCell > aThirdCell || myCell < 10) {
    cout << myCell.getValue() << endl;
}
```

As you can see, you need to write six separate functions to support the six comparison operators, and that's only to compare two `SpreadsheetCell`s with each other. With the current six implemented comparison functions, it's possible to compare a `SpreadsheetCell` with a `double` because a `double` argument is implicitly converted to a `SpreadsheetCell`. As discussed earlier, such implicit conversions might be inefficient, because temporary objects must be created. Just as with `operator+` earlier, you can avoid this by implementing explicit functions to compare with `double`s. For each operator *<op>*, you would then need the following three overloads:

```
bool operator<op>(const SpreadsheetCell& lhs, const SpreadsheetCell& rhs);
bool operator<op>(double lhs, const SpreadsheetCell& rhs);
bool operator<op>(const SpreadsheetCell& lhs, double rhs);
```

If you want to support all comparison operators, that's a lot of repetitive code to write!

Overloading Comparison Operators Since C++20

Let's now switch gears and see what C++20 and later versions bring to the table. Starting with C++20, adding support for comparison operators to your classes is simplified a lot. First, it is now actually recommended to implement `operator==` as a member function of the class instead of a global function. Note also that it's a good idea to add the `[[nodiscard]]` attribute so the result of the operator cannot be ignored. Here's an example:

```
[[nodiscard]] bool operator==(const SpreadsheetCell& rhs) const;
```

Since C++20, this single `operator==` overload makes the following comparisons work:

```
if (myCell == 10) { println("myCell == 10"); }
if (10 == myCell) { println("10 == myCell"); }
```

An expression such as `10 == myCell` is now rewritten by the compiler as `myCell == 10` for which the `operator==` member function can be called. Additionally, by implementing `operator==`, the compiler automatically adds support for `!=` as well; expressions using `!=` are rewritten to use `==`.

Next, to implement support for the full suite of comparison operators, you just need to implement one additional overloaded operator, `operator<=>`. Once your class has an overload for `operator==` and `<=>`, the compiler automatically provides support for all six comparison operators! For the `SpreadsheetCell` class, `operator<=>` looks as follows:

```
[[nodiscard]] std::partial_ordering operator<=>(const SpreadsheetCell& rhs) const;
```

> **NOTE** *A compiler will not rewrite* `==` *or* `!=` *comparisons in terms of* `<=>`. *This is done to avoid performance issues, as an explicit implementation of* `operator==` *is typically more efficient than using* `<=>`. *For example, take* `std::string`. *Its implementation of* `operator==` *and* `!=` *can first check the lengths of both* `strings` *to compare. If the lengths are different,* `operator==` *and* `!=` *can immediately return* `false`, *respectively* `true`, *without having to check individual characters. However,* `operator<=>` *always has to compare individual characters until it finds two characters that don't match.*

The value stored in a `SpreadsheetCell` is a `double`. Remember from Chapter 1 that floating-point types only have a partial order, so that's why the overload returns `std::partial_ordering`. The implementation is straightforward:

```
partial_ordering SpreadsheetCell::operator<=>(const SpreadsheetCell& rhs) const
{
    return getValue() <=> rhs.getValue();
}
```

By implementing `operator<=>`, the compiler automatically provides support for `>`, `<`, `<=`, and `>=`, by rewriting expressions using those operators to use <=> instead. For example, an expression such as `myCell < aThirdCell` is automatically rewritten to something equivalent to `std::is_lt(myCell <=> aThirdCell)`, where `is_lt()` is a named comparison function; see Chapter 1.

So, by just implementing operator== and operator<=>, the SpreadsheetCell class supports the full set of comparison operators:

```
if (myCell < aThirdCell) { println("myCell < aThirdCell"); }
if (aThirdCell < myCell) { println("aThirdCell < myCell"); }

if (myCell <= aThirdCell) { println("myCell <= aThirdCell"); }
if (aThirdCell <= myCell) { println("aThirdCell <= myCell"); }

if (myCell > aThirdCell) { println("myCell > aThirdCell"); }
if (aThirdCell > myCell) { println("aThirdCell > myCell"); }

if (myCell >= aThirdCell) { println("myCell >= aThirdCell"); }
if (aThirdCell >= myCell) { println("aThirdCell >= myCell"); }

if (myCell == aThirdCell) { println("myCell == aThirdCell"); }
if (aThirdCell == myCell) { println("aThirdCell == myCell"); }

if (myCell != aThirdCell) { println("myCell != aThirdCell"); }
if (aThirdCell != myCell) { println("aThirdCell != myCell"); }
```

Since the SpreadsheetCell class supports implicit conversion from double to a SpreadsheetCell, comparisons such as the following are supported as well:

```
if (myCell < 10) { println("myCell < 10"); }
if (10 < myCell) { println("10 < myCell"); }
if (10 != myCell) { println("10 != myCell"); }
```

As with comparing two SpreadsheetCell objects, the compiler rewrites such expressions in terms of operator== and <=>, and optionally swaps the order of the arguments. For example, 10 < myCell is rewritten first to something equivalent to is_lt(10 <=> myCell), which won't work because we only have an overload for <=> as a member, meaning that the left-hand side argument must be a SpreadsheetCell. Noticing this, the compiler then tries to rewrite the expression to something equivalent to is_gt(myCell <=> 10), which works out fine.

As before, if you want to avoid the slight performance impact of implicit conversions, you can provide specific overloads for doubles. And since C++20, this is not even a lot of work. You only need to provide the following two additional overloaded operators as member functions:

```
[[nodiscard]] bool operator==(double rhs) const;
[[nodiscard]] std::partial_ordering operator<=>(double rhs) const;
```

These are implemented as follows:

```
bool SpreadsheetCell::operator==(double rhs) const
{
    return getValue() == rhs;
}
partial_ordering SpreadsheetCell::operator<=>(double rhs) const
{
    return getValue() <=> rhs;
}
```

Compiler-Generated Comparison Operators

Looking at the implementation of operator== and <=> for SpreadsheetCell, they simply compare all data members. In such a case, you can reduce the number of lines of code needed even further, as

C++20 (and later) can write those for you. Just as, for example, a copy constructor can be explicitly defaulted, `operator==` and `<=>` can also be defaulted in which case the compiler writes them for you and implements them by comparing each data member in turn in the order they are declared in the class definition, also known as a *member-wise lexicographical comparison*.

Additionally, if you just explicitly default `operator<=>`, the compiler automatically includes a defaulted `operator==` as well. So, for the `SpreadsheetCell` version without the explicit `operator==` and `<=>` for `double`s (I'll come back to this later in this section), you can simply write the following *single line* of code to add full support for all six comparison operators to compare two `SpreadsheetCell`s:

```
[[nodiscard]] std::partial_ordering operator<=>(
    const SpreadsheetCell&) const = default;
```

Furthermore, you can use `auto` as the return type for `operator<=>`, in which case the compiler deduces the return type based on the return types of the `<=>` operator for the data members:

```
[[nodiscard]] auto operator<=>(const SpreadsheetCell&) const = default;
```

If not all data members of the class have an accessible `operator==`, then a defaulted `operator==` for the class is implicitly deleted.

If the class has data members that do not support `operator<=>`, a defaulted `operator<=>` falls back to using `operator<` and `==` for those data members. In that case, return type deduction won't work and you need to explicitly specify the return type to be either `strong_ordering`, `partial_ordering`, or `weak_ordering`. If the data members don't even have an accessible `operator<` and `==`, then the defaulted `operator<=>` is implicitly deleted.

To summarize, for the compiler to be able to write a defaulted <=> operator, all data members of the class need to either support `operator<=>`, in which case the return type can be `auto`, or `operator<` and `==`, in which case the return type cannot be `auto`. Since `SpreadsheetCell` has a single `double` as data member, the compiler deduces the return type to be `partial_ordering`.

In the beginning of this section, I mentioned that this single explicitly defaulted `operator<=>` works for the `SpreadsheetCell` version without the explicit `operator==` and `<=>` for `doubles`. If you do add those explicit `double` versions, you are adding a user-declared `operator==(double)`. Because of this, the compiler will no longer automatically generate an `operator==(const SpreadsheetCell&)`, so you have to explicitly default one yourself as follows:

```
export class SpreadsheetCell
{
    public:
        // Omitted for brevity
        [[nodiscard]] auto operator<=>(const SpreadsheetCell&) const = default;
        [[nodiscard]] bool operator==(const SpreadsheetCell&) const = default;

        [[nodiscard]] bool operator==(double rhs) const;
        [[nodiscard]] std::partial_ordering operator<=>(double rhs) const;
        // Omitted for brevity
};
```

If you can explicitly default `operator<=>` for your class, I recommend doing so instead of implementing it yourself. By letting the compiler write it for you, it will stay up-to-date with newly added or modified data members. If you implement the operator yourself, then whenever you add data members or change existing data members, you need to remember to update your implementation of operator<=>. The same holds for operator== in case it's not automatically generated by the compiler.

It is only possible to explicitly default operator== and <=> when they have as parameter a reference-to-const to the class type for which the operators are defined. For example, the following does not work:

```
[[nodiscard]] auto operator<=>(double) const = default;  // Does not work!
```

> **NOTE** *To add support for all six comparison operators to a class in C++20 or later:*
>
> - *If a defaulted* operator<=> *works for your class, then a single line of code to explicitly default* operator<=> *as a member function is all you need to do. In certain cases, you might need to explicitly default* operator== *as well.*
> - *Otherwise, just overload and implement* operator== *and* <=> *as member functions.*
>
> *There is no need to manually implement the other comparison operators.*

BUILDING STABLE INTERFACES

Now that you understand all the syntax of writing classes in C++, it helps to revisit the design principles from Chapter 5, "Designing with Classes," and Chapter 6, "Designing for Reuse." Classes are the main unit of abstraction in C++. You should apply the principles of abstraction to your classes to separate the interface from the implementation as much as possible. Specifically, you should make all data members private and optionally provide getter and setter member functions. This is how the SpreadsheetCell class is implemented: m_value is private, while the public set() member function sets the value, and the public getValue() and getString() retrieve the value.

Using Interface and Implementation Classes

Even with the preceding measures and the best design principles, the C++ language is fundamentally unfriendly to the principle of abstraction. The syntax requires you to combine your public interfaces and private (or protected) data members and member functions together in one class definition, thereby exposing some of the internal implementation details of the class to its clients. The downside of this is that if you have to add new non-public member functions or data members to your class, all the clients of the class have to be recompiled. This can become a burden in bigger projects.

The good news is that you can make your interfaces a lot cleaner and hide all implementation details, resulting in stable interfaces. The bad news is that it takes a bit of coding. The basic principle is to define two classes for every class you want to write: the *interface class* and the *implementation class*. The implementation class is identical to the class you would have written if you were not taking this approach. The interface class presents `public` member functions identical to those of the implementation class, but it has only one data member: a pointer to an implementation class object. This is called the *pimpl idiom*, *private implementation idiom*, or *bridge pattern*. The interface class member function implementations simply call the equivalent member functions on the implementation class object. The result of this is that no matter how the implementation changes, it has no impact on the `public` interface class. This reduces the need for recompilation. None of the clients that use the interface class need to be recompiled if the implementation (and only the implementation) changes. Note that this idiom works only if the single data member is a pointer to the implementation class. If it were a by-value data member, clients would have to recompile when the definition of the implementation class changes.

To use this approach with the `Spreadsheet` class, define the following public interface class, called `Spreadsheet`. The important parts are highlighted.

```
export module spreadsheet;

export import spreadsheet_cell;
import std;

export class Spreadsheet
{
    public:
        explicit Spreadsheet(
            std::size_t width = MaxWidth, std::size_t height = MaxHeight);
        Spreadsheet(const Spreadsheet& src);
        Spreadsheet(Spreadsheet&&) noexcept;
        ~Spreadsheet();

        Spreadsheet& operator=(const Spreadsheet& rhs);
        Spreadsheet& operator=(Spreadsheet&&) noexcept;

        void setCellAt(std::size_t x, std::size_t y, const SpreadsheetCell& cell);
        SpreadsheetCell& getCellAt(std::size_t x, std::size_t y);
        const SpreadsheetCell& getCellAt(std::size_t x, std::size_t y) const;

        std::size_t getId() const;

        static constexpr std::size_t MaxHeight { 100 };
        static constexpr std::size_t MaxWidth { 100 };

        void swap(Spreadsheet& other) noexcept;

    private:
        class Impl;
        std::unique_ptr<Impl> m_impl;
};
export void swap(Spreadsheet& first, Spreadsheet& second) noexcept;
```

The implementation class, `Impl`, is a `private` nested class, because no one else besides the `Spreadsheet` class needs to know about this implementation class. The `Spreadsheet` class now contains only one data member: a pointer to an `Impl` instance. The `public` member functions are identical to the old `Spreadsheet`.

The nested Spreadsheet::Impl class is defined in a spreadsheet module implementation file. It should be hidden from clients, so the Impl class is not exported. The Spreadsheet.cpp module implementation file starts as follows:

```
module spreadsheet;
import std;
using namespace std;

// Spreadsheet::Impl class definition.
class Spreadsheet::Impl
{
    public:
        Impl(size_t width, size_t height);
        // Remainder omitted for brevity.
};
```

This Impl class has almost the same interface as the original Spreadsheet class. You can find the full definition in the downloadable source code archive. For the member function implementations, you need to remember that Impl is a nested class; hence, you need to specify the scope as Spreadsheet::Impl. So, for the constructor, it becomes Spreadsheet::Impl::Impl(...):

```
// Spreadsheet::Impl member function definitions.
Spreadsheet::Impl::Impl(size_t width, size_t height)
    : m_id { ms_counter++ }
    , m_width { min(width, Spreadsheet::MaxWidth) }
    , m_height { min(height, Spreadsheet::MaxHeight) }
{
    m_cells = new SpreadsheetCell*[m_width];
    for (size_t i { 0 }; i < m_width; ++i) {
        m_cells[i] = new SpreadsheetCell[m_height];
    }
}
// Other member function definitions omitted for brevity.
```

Now that the Spreadsheet class has a unique_ptr to an Impl instance, the Spreadsheet class needs to have a user-declared destructor. Since we don't need to do anything in this destructor, it can be defaulted in the implementation file as follows:

```
Spreadsheet::~Spreadsheet() = default;
```

In fact, it must be defaulted in the implementation file and not directly in the class definition. The reason is that the Impl class is only forward declared in the Spreadsheet class definition; that is, the compiler knows there will be a Spreadsheet::Impl class somewhere, but at this time it does not know the definition yet. As such, you cannot default the destructor in the class definition, because then the compiler would try to use the destructor of the as of yet undefined Impl class. The same is true when defaulting other member functions in this case, such as the move constructor and move assignment operator.

The implementations of the Spreadsheet member functions, such as setCellAt() and getCellAt(), just pass the request on to the underlying Impl object:

```
void Spreadsheet::setCellAt(size_t x, size_t y, const SpreadsheetCell& cell)
{
    m_impl->setCellAt(x, y, cell);
}
```

```
const SpreadsheetCell& Spreadsheet::getCellAt(size_t x, size_t y) const
{
    return m_impl->getCellAt(x, y);
}

SpreadsheetCell& Spreadsheet::getCellAt(size_t x, size_t y)
{
    return m_impl->getCellAt(x, y);
}
```

The constructors for the `Spreadsheet` must construct a new `Impl` to do its work:

```
Spreadsheet::Spreadsheet(size_t width, size_t height)
{
    : m_impl { make_unique<Impl>(width, height) }
}
}

Spreadsheet::Spreadsheet(const Spreadsheet& src)
    : m_impl { make_unique<Impl>(*src.m_impl) }
{
}
```

The copy constructor looks a bit strange because it needs to copy the underlying `Impl` from the source `Spreadsheet`. The copy constructor takes a reference to an `Impl`, not a pointer, so you must dereference the `m_impl` pointer to get to the object itself.

The `Spreadsheet` assignment operator must similarly pass on the assignment to the underlying `Impl`:

```
Spreadsheet& Spreadsheet::operator=(const Spreadsheet& rhs)
{
    *m_impl = *rhs.m_impl;
    return *this;
}
```

The first line in the assignment operator looks a little odd. The `Spreadsheet` assignment operator needs to forward the call to the `Impl` assignment operator, which runs only when you copy direct objects. By dereferencing the `m_impl` pointers, you force direct object assignment, which causes the assignment operator of `Impl` to be called.

The `swap()` member function simply swaps the single data member:

```
void Spreadsheet::swap(Spreadsheet& other) noexcept
{
    std::swap(m_impl, other.m_impl);
}
```

This technique to truly separate the interface from the implementation is powerful. Although it is a bit clumsy at first, once you get used to it, you will find it natural to work with. However, it's not common practice in most workplace environments, so you might find some resistance to trying it from your coworkers. The most compelling argument in favor of it is not the aesthetic one of splitting out the interface, but the speedup in build time if the implementation of the class changes. When a class is not using the pimpl idiom, a change to its implementation details might trigger a long rebuild. For example, adding a new data member to a class definition triggers a rebuild of all other source files that use this class definition. With the pimpl idiom, you can modify the implementation class definition as much as you like, and as long as the public interface class remains untouched, it won't trigger a long rebuild.

> **NOTE** *With stable interface classes, build times can be reduced.*

An alternative to separating the implementation from the interface is to use an abstract interface—that is, an interface with only pure virtual member functions—and then have an implementation class that implements that interface. That's a topic for the next chapter.

SUMMARY

This chapter, along with Chapter 8, provided all the tools you need to write solid, well-designed classes, and to use objects effectively.

You discovered that dynamic memory allocation in objects presents new challenges: you need to implement a destructor, copy constructor, copy assignment operator, move constructor, and move assignment operator, which properly copy, move, and free your memory. You learned how to prevent pass-by-value and assignment by explicitly deleting the copy constructor and assignment operator. You discovered the copy-and-swap idiom to implement copy assignment operators and the move-and-swap idiom to implement move assignment operators, as well as learned about the rule of zero.

You read more about different kinds of data members, including `static`, `const`, reference-to-`const`, and `mutable` members. You also learned about `static`, `inline`, and `const` member functions, member function overloading, and default arguments. This chapter also described nested class definitions, and `friend` classes, functions, and member functions.

You encountered operator overloading and learned how to overload the arithmetic and comparison operators, both as global functions and as class member functions. You also discovered how the three-way comparison operator makes adding comparison support to your classes so much easier.

Finally, you learned how to take abstraction to the extreme by providing separate interface and implementation classes.

Now that you're fluent in the language of object-oriented programming, it's time to tackle inheritance, which is covered next in Chapter 10, "Discovering Inheritance Techniques."

EXERCISES

By solving the following exercises, you can practice the material discussed in this chapter. Solutions to all exercises are available with the code download on the book's website at `www.wiley.com/go/proc++6e`. However, if you are stuck on an exercise, first reread parts of this chapter to try to find an answer yourself before looking at the solution from the website.

Exercise 9-1: Take your implementation of the `Person` class from Exercise 8-3 and adapt it to pass strings in the most optimal way you can think of. Additionally, add a move constructor and move assignment operator to it. In both member functions, write a message to the console so you can track when they get called. Implement any additional member functions you need for implementing the move member functions and for improving the implementation of other member functions from Exercise 8-3 to avoid code duplication. Modify `main()` to test your member functions.

Exercise 9-2: Take the `Person` class from Exercise 8-4. Just as for Exercise 9-1, make changes to pass strings in the most optimal way. Then add full support for all six comparison operators to compare two `Person` objects. Try to implement this support in the least amount of code. Test your implementation by performing all kinds of comparisons in `main()`. How are `Persons` ordered? Is the ordering happening based on the first name, based on the last name, or based on a combination?

Exercise 9-3: Before C++20, adding support for all six comparison operators required a bit more lines of code. Start from the `Person` class from Exercise 9-2, remove the `operator<=>`, and add the necessary code to add all comparison operators to compare two `Person` objects without using `<=>`. Perform the same set of tests as you've implemented for Exercise 9-2.

Exercise 9-4: In this exercise, you'll practice writing stable interfaces. Take your `Person` class from Exercise 8-4 and split it into a stable public interface class and a separate implementation class.

Exercise 9-5: Start from your solution for Exercise 9-2, and optimize the `getFirstName()`, `getLastName()`, and `getInitials()` member functions for when these are called on rvalues.

10

Discovering Inheritance Techniques

WHAT'S IN THIS CHAPTER?

- How to extend a class through inheritance
- How to employ inheritance to reuse code
- How to build interactions between base classes and derived classes
- How to use inheritance to achieve polymorphism
- How to work with multiple inheritance
- How to deal with unusual problems in inheritance
- How to cast one type to another type

WILEY.COM DOWNLOADS FOR THIS CHAPTER

Please note that all the code examples for this chapter are available as part of this chapter's code download on the book's website at `www.wiley.com/go/proc++6e` on the Download Code tab.

Without inheritance, classes would simply be data structures with associated behaviors. That alone would be a powerful improvement over procedural languages, but inheritance adds an entirely new dimension. Through inheritance, you can build new classes based on existing ones. In this way, your classes become reusable and extensible components. This chapter teaches you the different ways to leverage the power of inheritance. You will learn about the specific syntax of inheritance as well as sophisticated techniques for making the most of inheritance.

The portion of this chapter relating to polymorphism draws heavily on the spreadsheet example discussed in Chapter 8, "Gaining Proficiency with Classes and Objects," and Chapter 9,

"Mastering Classes and Objects." This chapter also refers to the object-oriented methodologies described in Chapter 5, "Designing with Classes." If you have not read that chapter and are unfamiliar with the theories behind inheritance, you should review Chapter 5 before continuing.

BUILDING CLASSES WITH INHERITANCE

In Chapter 5, you learned that an *is-a* relationship recognizes the pattern that real-world objects tend to exist in hierarchies. In programming, that pattern becomes relevant when you need to write a class that builds on, or slightly changes, another class. One way to accomplish this aim is to copy code from one class and paste it into the other. By changing the relevant parts or amending the code, you can achieve the goal of creating a new class that is slightly different from the original. This approach, however, leaves an OOP programmer feeling sullen and highly annoyed for the following reasons:

- A bug fix to the original class will not be reflected in the new class because the two classes contain completely separate code.
- The compiler does not know about any relationship between the two classes, so they are not polymorphic (see Chapter 5)—they are not just different variations on the same thing.
- This approach does not build a true is-a relationship. The new class is similar to the original because it has similar code, not because it really *is* the same type of object.
- The original code might not be obtainable. It may exist only in a precompiled binary format, so copying and pasting the code might be impossible.

Not surprisingly, C++ provides built-in support for defining a true is-a relationship. The characteristics of C++ is-a relationships are described in the following section.

Extending Classes

When you write a class definition in C++, you can tell the compiler that your class is *inheriting from*, *deriving from*, or *extending* an existing class. By doing so, your class automatically contains the data members and member functions of the original class, which is called the *parent class*, *base class*, or *superclass*. Extending an existing class gives your class (which is now called a *child class*, *derived class*, or *subclass*) the ability to describe only the ways in which it is different from the parent class.

To extend a class in C++, you specify the class you are extending when you write the class definition. To show the syntax for inheritance, two classes are used, `Base` and `Derived`. Don't worry—more interesting examples are coming later. To begin, consider the following definition for the `Base` class:

```
class Base
{
    public:
        void someFunction() {}
    protected:
        int m_protectedInt { 0 };
    private:
        int m_privateInt { 0 };
};
```

If you want to build a new class, called `Derived`, which inherits from `Base`, you use the following syntax:

```
class Derived : public Base
{
    public:
        void someOtherFunction() {}
};
```

`Derived` is a full-fledged class that just happens to share the characteristics of the `Base` class. Don't worry about the word `public` for now—its meaning is explained later in this chapter. Figure 10.1 shows the simple relationship between `Derived` and `Base`. You can declare objects of type `Derived` just like any other object. You could even define a third class that inherits from `Derived`, forming a chain of classes, as shown in Figure 10.2.

FIGURE 10.1

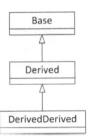

`Derived` doesn't have to be the only derived class of `Base`. Additional classes can also inherit from `Base`, effectively becoming *siblings* to `Derived`, as shown in Figure 10.3.

Internally, a derived class contains an instance of the base class as a *subobject*. Graphically this can be represented as in Figure 10.4.

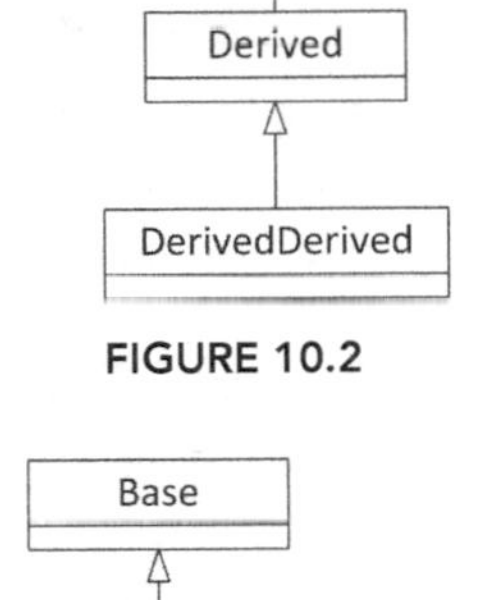

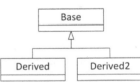

FIGURE 10.2

A Client's View of Inheritance

To a client, or another part of your code, an object of type `Derived` is also an object of type `Base` because `Derived` inherits from `Base`. This means that all the `public` member functions and data members of `Base` *and* all the `public` member functions and data members of `Derived` are available.

FIGURE 10.3

Code that uses the derived class does not need to know which class in your inheritance chain has defined a member function in order to call it. For example, the following code calls two member functions of a `Derived` object, even though one of the member functions is defined by the `Base` class:

```
Derived myDerived;
myDerived.someFunction();
myDerived.someOtherFunction();
```

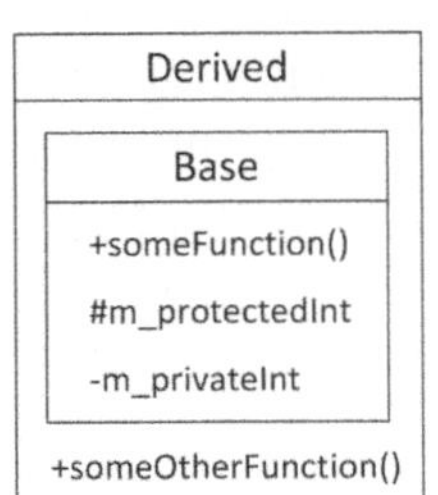

FIGURE 10.4

It is important to understand that inheritance works in only one direction. The `Derived` class has a clearly defined relationship to the `Base` class, but the `Base` class, as written, doesn't know anything about the `Derived` class. That means objects of type `Base` do not have access to member functions and data members of `Derived` because `Base` is *not* a `Derived`.

The following code does not compile because the `Base` class does not contain a `public` member function called `someOtherFunction()`:

```
Base myBase;
myBase.someOtherFunction();  // Error! Base doesn't have a someOtherFunction().
```

> **NOTE** *From the perspective of code using an object, the object belongs to its defined class as well as to any base classes.*

A pointer or reference to a class type can refer to an object of the declared class type or any of its derived classes. This tricky subject is explained in detail later in this chapter. The concept to understand now is that a pointer to `Base` can actually be pointing to a `Derived` object. The same is true for a reference. The client can still access only the member functions and data members that exist in `Base`, but through this mechanism, any code that operates on a `Base` can also operate on a `Derived`.

For example, the following code compiles and works just fine, even though it initially appears that there is a type mismatch:

```
Base* base { new Derived {} }; // Create Derived, store in Base pointer.
```

However, you cannot call member functions from the `Derived` class through the `Base` pointer. The following does not work:

```
base->someOtherFunction();
```

This is flagged as an error by the compiler because, although the object is of type `Derived` and therefore does have `someOtherFunction()` defined, the compiler can only think of it as type `Base`, which does not have `someOtherFunction()` defined.

A Derived Class's View of Inheritance

To the derived class, nothing much has changed in terms of how it is written or how it behaves. You can still define member functions and data members on a derived class just as you would on a regular class. The previous definition of `Derived` declares a member function called `someOtherFunction()`. Thus, the `Derived` class augments the `Base` class by adding an additional member function.

A derived class can access `public` and `protected` member functions and data members declared in its base class as though they were its own, because technically they are. For example, the implementation of `someOtherFunction()` on `Derived` could make use of the data member `m_protectedInt`, which is declared as part of `Base`. The following code shows this. Accessing a base class member is no different than if the member were declared as part of the derived class.

```
void Derived::someOtherFunction()
{
    println("I can access base class data member m_protectedInt.");
    println("Its value is {}", m_protectedInt);
}
```

If a class declares members as `protected`, derived classes have access to them. If they are declared as `private`, derived classes do not have access. The following implementation of `someOtherFunction()` does not compile because the derived class attempts to access a `private` data member from the base class:

```
void Derived::someOtherFunction()
{
```

```
        println("I can access base class data member m_protectedInt.");
        println("Its value is {}", m_protectedInt);
        println("The value of m_privateInt is {}", m_privateInt); // Error!
    }
```

The private access specifier gives you control over how a potential derived class could interact with your class.

Chapter 4, "Designing Professional C++ Programs," gives the following rule: all data members should be private; provide public getters and setters if you want to provide access to data members from outside the class. This rule can now be extended to include the protected access specifier.

> **WARNING** *All data members should be* private. *Provide* public *getters and setters if you want to provide access to data members from outside the class and provide* protected *getters and setters if you want only derived classes to access them.*

The reason to make data members private by default is that this provides the highest level of encapsulation. This means that you can change how you represent your data while keeping the public and protected interfaces unchanged. Additionally, without giving direct access to data members, you can easily add checks on the input data in your public and protected setters. Member functions should also be private by default. Only make those member functions public that are designed to be public and make member functions protected if you want only derived classes to have access to them.

> **NOTE** *From the perspective of a derived class, all* public *and* protected *data members and member functions from the base class are available for use.*

The following table summarizes the meaning of all three access specifiers:

ACCESS SPECIFIER	MEANING	WHEN TO USE
public	Any code can call a public member function or access a public data member of an object.	Behaviors (member functions) that you want clients to use. Access member functions (getters and setters) for private and protected data members.
protected	Any member function of the class can call protected member functions and access protected data members. Member functions of derived classes can access protected members of a base class.	"Helper" member functions that you do not want clients to use.

continues

(continued)

ACCESS SPECIFIER	MEANING	WHEN TO USE
`private`	Only member functions of the class can call `private` member functions and access `private` data members. Member functions in derived classes cannot access `private` members of a base class.	Everything should be `private` by default, especially data members. You can provide `protected` getters and setters if you only want to allow derived classes to access them, and provide `public` getters and setters if you want clients to access them.

Preventing Inheritance

C++ allows you to mark a class as `final`, which means trying to inherit from it will result in a compilation error. A class can be marked as `final` with the `final` keyword right behind the name of the class. For example, if a class tries to inherit from the following `Foo` class, the compiler will produce an error:

```
class Foo final { };
```

Overriding Member Functions

The main reasons to inherit from a class are to add or replace functionality. The definition of `Derived` adds functionality to its parent class by providing an additional member function, `someOtherFunction()`. The other member function, `someFunction()`, is inherited from `Base` and behaves in the derived class exactly as it does in the base class. In many cases, you will want to modify the behavior of a class by replacing, or *overriding*, a member function.

The virtual Keyword

Simply defining a member function from a base class in a derived class does not properly override that member function. To correctly override a member function, we need a new C++ keyword called `virtual`. Only member functions that are declared as `virtual` in the base class can be overridden properly by derived classes. The keyword goes at the beginning of a member function declaration as shown in the modified version of `Base` that follows:

```
class Base
{
    public:
        virtual void someFunction();
        // Remainder omitted for brevity.
};
```

The same holds for the `Derived` class. Its member functions should also be marked `virtual` if you want to override them in further derived classes:

```
class Derived : public Base
{
    public:
        virtual void someOtherFunction();
};
```

The `virtual` keyword is not repeated in front of the member function definition, e.g.:

```
void Base::someFunction()
{
    println("This is Base's version of someFunction().");
}
```

> **WARNING** *Attempting to override a non-`virtual` member function from a base class hides the base class definition, and it will be used only in the context of the derived class.*

Syntax for Overriding a Member Function

To override a member function, you redeclare it in the derived class definition exactly as it was declared in the base class, but you add the `override` keyword and remove the `virtual` keyword. For example, if you want to provide a new definition for `someFunction()` in the `Derived` class, you must first add it to the class definition for `Derived`, as follows:

```
class Derived : public Base
{
    public:
        void someFunction() override; // Overrides Base's someFunction()
        virtual void someOtherFunction();
};
```

The new definition of `someFunction()` is specified along with the rest of `Derived`'s member functions. Just as with the `virtual` keyword, you do not repeat the `override` keyword in the member function definition:

```
void Derived::someFunction()
{
    println("This is Derived's version of someFunction().");
}
```

If you want, you are allowed to add the `virtual` keyword in front of overridden member functions, but it's redundant. Here's an example:

```
class Derived : public Base
{
    public:
        virtual void someFunction() override;   // Overrides Base's someFunction()
};
```

Once a member function or destructor is marked as `virtual`, it is `virtual` for all derived classes even if the `virtual` keyword is removed from derived classes.

A Client's View of Overridden Member Functions

With the preceding changes, other code still calls `someFunction()` the same way it did before. Just as before, the member function could be called on an object of class `Base` or an object of class `Derived`. Now, however, the behavior of `someFunction()` varies based on the class of the object.

For example, the following code works just as it did before, calling Base's version of someFunction():

```
Base myBase;
myBase.someFunction();  // Calls Base's version of someFunction().
```

The output of this code is as follows:

```
This is Base's version of someFunction().
```

If the code declares an object of class Derived, the other version is automatically called:

```
Derived myDerived;
myDerived.someFunction();    // Calls Derived's version of someFunction()
```

The output this time is as follows:

```
This is Derived's version of someFunction().
```

Everything else about objects of class Derived remains the same. Other member functions that might have been inherited from Base still have the definition provided by Base unless they are explicitly overridden in Derived.

As you learned earlier, a pointer or reference can refer to an object of a class or any of its derived classes. The object itself "knows" the class of which it is actually a member, so the appropriate member function is called as long as it was declared virtual. For example, if you have a Base reference that refers to an object that is really a Derived, calling someFunction() actually calls the derived class's version, as shown next. This aspect of overriding does *not* work properly if you omit the virtual keyword in the base class.

```
Derived myDerived;
Base& ref { myDerived };
ref.someFunction();   // Calls Derived's version of someFunction()
```

Remember that even though a Base reference or pointer knows that it is referring to a Derived instance, you cannot access Derived class members that are not defined in Base. The following code does not compile because a Base reference does not have a member function called someOtherFunction():

```
Derived myDerived;
Base& ref { myDerived };
myDerived.someOtherFunction();  // This is fine.
ref.someOtherFunction();        // Error
```

This derived class knowledge characteristic is *not* true for nonpointer or nonreference objects. You can cast or assign a Derived to a Base because a Derived is a Base. However, the object loses any knowledge of the Derived class at that point.

```
Derived myDerived;
Base assignedObject { myDerived };  // Assigns a Derived to a Base.
assignedObject.someFunction();      // Calls Base's version of someFunction()
```

One way to remember this seemingly strange behavior is to imagine what the objects look like in memory. Picture a Base object as a box taking up a certain amount of memory. A Derived object is a box that is slightly bigger because it has everything a Base has plus a bit more. Whether you have a Derived or Base reference or pointer to a Derived, the box doesn't change—you just have a new way of accessing it. However, when you cast a `Derived` into a `Base`, you are throwing out all the "uniqueness" of the `Derived` class to fit it into a smaller box.

> **NOTE** *Derived classes retain all their data members and member functions when referred to by base class pointers or references. They lose their uniqueness when cast to a base class object. The loss of the derived class's data members and member functions is called slicing.*

The override Keyword

The use of the `override` keyword is optional, but highly recommended. Without the keyword, it is possible to accidentally create a new (`virtual`) member function in a derived class instead of overriding a member function from the base class, effectively hiding the member function from the base class. Take the following `Base` and `Derived` classes where `Derived` is properly overriding `someFunction()`, but is not using the `override` keyword:

```
class Base
{
    public:
        virtual void someFunction(double d);
};

class Derived : public Base
{
    public:
        virtual void someFunction(double d);
};
```

You can call `someFunction()` through a reference as follows:

```
Derived myDerived;
Base& ref { myDerived };
ref.someFunction(1.1);  // Calls Derived's version of someFunction()
```

This correctly calls the overridden `someFunction()` from the `Derived` class. Now, suppose you accidentally use an integer parameter instead of a `double` while overriding `someFunction()`, as follows:

```
class Derived : public Base
{
    public:
        virtual void someFunction(int i);
};
```

This code does *not* override `someFunction()` from `Base`, but instead creates a new `virtual` member function. If you try to call `someFunction()` through a `Base` reference as in the following code, `someFunction()` of `Base` is called instead of the one from `Derived`!

```
Derived myDerived;
Base& ref { myDerived };
ref.someFunction(1.1);  // Calls Base's version of someFunction()
```

This type of problem can happen when you start to modify the Base class but forget to update all derived classes. For example, maybe your first version of the Base class has a member function called someFunction() accepting an integer. You then write the Derived class overriding this someFunction() accepting an integer. Later you decide that someFunction() in Base needs a double instead of an integer, so you update someFunction() in the Base class. It could happen that at that time, you forget to update overrides of someFunction() in derived classes to also accept a double instead of an integer. By forgetting this, you are now actually creating a new virtual member function instead of properly overriding the base member function.

You can prevent this situation by using the override keyword as follows:

```
class Derived : public Base
{
    public:
        void someFunction(int i) override;
};
```

This definition of Derived generates a compilation error, because with the override keyword you are saying that someFunction() is supposed to be overriding a member function from a base class, but the Base class has no someFunction() accepting an integer, only one accepting a double.

The problem of accidentally creating a new member function instead of properly overriding one can also happen when you rename a member function in the base class and forget to rename the overriding member functions in derived classes.

> **WARNING** *Always use the* override *keyword on member functions that are meant to be overriding member functions from a base class.*

The Truth about virtual

By now you know that if a member function is not virtual, trying to override it in a derived class will hide the base class's version of that member function. This section explores how virtual member functions are implemented by the compiler and what their performance impact is, as well as discussing the importance of virtual destructors.

How virtual Is Implemented

To understand how member function hiding is avoided, you need to know a bit more about what the virtual keyword actually does. When a class is compiled in C++, a binary object is created that contains all member functions for the class. In the non-virtual case, the code to transfer control to the appropriate member function is hard-coded directly where the member function is called based on the compile-time type. This is called *static binding*, also known as *early binding*.

If the member function is declared virtual, the correct implementation is called through the use of a special area of memory called the *vtable*, or "*virtual table*." Each class that has one or more virtual member functions has a vtable, and every object of such a class contains a pointer to said vtable. This vtable contains pointers to the implementations of the virtual member functions. In this way, when a member function is called on a pointer or reference to an object, its vtable pointer is followed, and the appropriate version of the member function is executed based on the actual type of the object at run time. This is called *dynamic binding*, also known as *late binding*. It's important to remember that this dynamic binding works only when using pointers or references to objects. If you call a `virtual` member function directly on an object, then that call will use static binding resolved at compile time.

To better understand how vtables make overriding of member functions possible, take the following `Base` and `Derived` classes as an example:

```
class Base
{
    public:
        virtual void func1();
        virtual void func2();
        void nonVirtualFunc();
};

class Derived : public Base
{
    public:
        void func2() override;
        void nonVirtualFunc();
};
```

For this example, assume that you have the following two instances:

```
Base myBase;
Derived myDerived;
```

Figure 10.5 shows a high-level view of the vtables of both instances. The `myBase` object contains a pointer to its vtable. This vtable has two entries, one for `func1()` and one for `func2()`. Those entries point to the implementations of `Base::func1()` and `Base::func2()`.

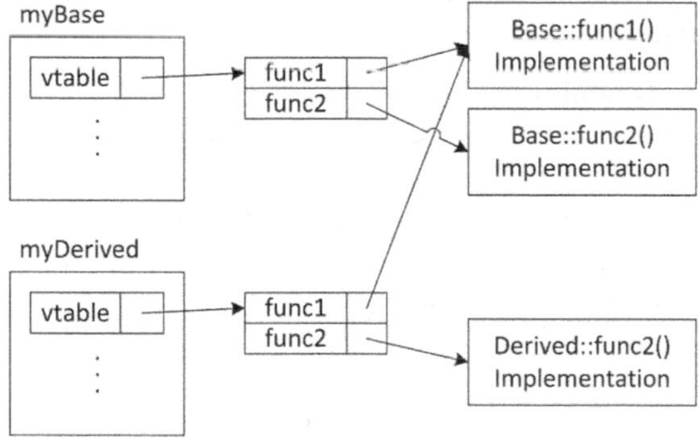

FIGURE 10.5

`myDerived` also contains a pointer to its vtable, which also has two entries, one for `func1()` and one for `func2()`. Its `func1()` entry points to `Base::func1()` because `Derived` does not override `func1()`. On the other hand, its `func2()` entry points to `Derived::func2()`.

Note that both vtables do not contain any entry for the `nonVirtualFunc()` member function because that member function is not `virtual`.

The Justification for virtual

In some languages, such as Java, all member functions are automatically virtual so they can be overridden properly. In C++ that's not the case. The argument against making everything virtual in C++, and the reason that the keyword was created in the first place, has to do with the overhead of the vtable. To call a virtual member function, the program needs to perform an extra operation by dereferencing the pointer to the appropriate code to execute. This is a miniscule performance hit in most cases, but the designers of C++ thought that it was better, at least at the time, to let the programmer decide if the performance hit was necessary. If the member function was never going to be overridden, there was no need to make it virtual and take the performance hit. However, with today's CPUs, the performance hit is measured in fractions of a nanosecond, and this will keep getting smaller with future CPUs. In most applications, you will not have a measurable performance difference between using virtual member functions and avoiding them.

Still, in certain specific use cases, the performance overhead might be too costly, and you may need to have an option to avoid the hit. For example, suppose you have a Point class that has a virtual member function. If you have another data structure that stores millions or even billions of Points, calling a virtual member function on each point creates significant overhead. In that case, it's probably wise to avoid any virtual member functions in your Point class.

There is also a tiny hit to memory usage for each object. In addition to the implementation of the member function, each object also needs a pointer for its vtable, which takes up a tiny amount of space. This is not an issue in the majority of cases. However, sometimes it does matter. Take again the Point class and the container storing billions of Points. In that case, the additional required memory becomes significant.

The Need for virtual Destructors

Destructors should almost always be virtual. Making your destructors non-virtual can easily result in situations in which memory is not freed by object destruction. Only for a class that is marked as final could you make its destructor non-virtual.

For example, if a derived class uses memory that is dynamically allocated in the constructor and deleted in the destructor, it will never be freed if the destructor is never called. Similarly, if your derived class has members that are automatically deleted when an instance of the class is destroyed, such as std::unique_ptrs, then those members will not get deleted either if the destructor is never called.

As the following code shows, it is easy to "trick" the compiler into skipping the call to the destructor if it is non-virtual:

```
class Base
{
    public:
        Base() = default;
        ~Base() {}
};

class Derived : public Base
{
    public:
        Derived()
        {
```

```
            m_string = new char[30];
            println("m_string allocated");
        }

        ~Derived()
        {
            delete[] m_string;
            println("m_string deallocated");
        }
    private:
        char* m_string;
};

int main()
{
    Base* ptr { new Derived {} };   // m_string is allocated here.
    delete ptr; // ~Base is called, but not ~Derived because the destructor
                // is not virtual!
}
```

As you can see from the following output, the destructor of the `Derived` object is never called, that is, the "m_string deallocated" message is never displayed:

```
m_string allocated
```

Technically, the behavior of the `delete` call in the preceding code is undefined by the standard. A C++ compiler could do whatever it wants in such undefined situations. However, most compilers simply call the destructor of the base class, and not the destructor of the derived class.

The fix is to mark the destructor in the base class as `virtual`. If you don't need to do any extra work in that destructor but want to make it `virtual`, you can explicitly default it. Here's an example:

```
class Base
{
    public:
        Base() = default;
        virtual ~Base() = default;
};
```

With this change, the output is as expected:

```
m_string allocated
m_string deallocated
```

Note that since C++11, the generation of a copy constructor and copy assignment operator is deprecated if the class has a user-declared destructor. Basically, once you have a user-declared destructor, the rule of five kicks in. This means you need to declare a copy constructor, copy assignment operator, move constructor, and move assignment operator, possibly by explicitly defaulting them. This is not done in the examples in this chapter in the interest of keeping them concise and to the point.

> **WARNING** *Unless you have a specific reason not to, or the class is marked as* `final`*, destructors should be marked as* `virtual`*. Constructors cannot and need not be* `virtual` *because you always specify the exact class being constructed when creating an object.*

Earlier in this chapter it was advised to use the `override` keyword on member functions that are meant to override base class member functions. It's also possible to use the `override` keyword on a destructor. This makes sure that the compiler will trigger an error if the destructor in the base class is not `virtual`. You can combine `virtual`, `override`, and `default`. Here's an example:

```
class Derived : public Base
{
    public:
        virtual ~Derived() override = default;
};
```

Preventing Overriding

Besides marking an entire class as `final`, C++ also allows you to mark individual member functions as `final`. Such member functions cannot be overridden in a further derived class. For example, overriding `someFunction()` from the following `Derived` class in `DerivedDerived` results in a compilation error:

```
class Base
{
    public:
        virtual ~Base() = default;
        virtual void someFunction();
};
class Derived : public Base
{
    public:
        void someFunction() override final;
};
class DerivedDerived : public Derived
{
    public:
        void someFunction() override;  // Compilation error.
};
```

INHERITANCE FOR REUSE

Now that you are familiar with the basic syntax for inheritance, it's time to explore one of the main reasons that inheritance is an important feature of the C++ language. Inheritance is a vehicle that allows you to leverage existing code. This section presents an example of inheritance for the purpose of code reuse.

The WeatherPrediction Class

Imagine that you are given the task of writing a program to issue simple weather predictions, working with both Fahrenheit and Celsius. Weather predictions may be a little bit out of your area of expertise as a programmer, so you obtain a third-party class library that was written to make weather predictions based on the current temperature and the current distance between Jupiter and Mars (hey, it's plausible). This third-party package is distributed as a compiled library to protect the intellectual property of the prediction algorithms, but you do get to see the class definition. The `weather_prediction` module interface file looks as follows:

```
export module weather_prediction;
import std;
// Predicts the weather using proven new-age techniques given the current
// temperature and the distance from Jupiter to Mars. If these values are
// not provided, a guess is still given but it's only 99% accurate.
export class WeatherPrediction
{
    public:
        // Virtual destructor
        virtual ~WeatherPrediction();
        // Sets the current temperature in Fahrenheit
        virtual void setCurrentTempFahrenheit(int temp);
        // Sets the current distance between Jupiter and Mars
        virtual void setPositionOfJupiter(int distanceFromMars);
        // Gets the prediction for tomorrow's temperature
        virtual int getTomorrowTempFahrenheit() const;
        // Gets the probability of rain tomorrow. 1 means
        // definite rain. 0 means no chance of rain.
        virtual double getChanceOfRain() const;
        // Displays the result to the user in this format:
        // Result: x.xx chance. Temp. xx
        virtual void showResult() const;
        // Returns a string representation of the temperature
        virtual std::string getTemperature() const;
    private:
        int m_currentTempFahrenheit { 0 };
        int m_distanceFromMars { 0 };
};
```

Note that this class marks all member functions as `virtual`, because the class presumes that they might get overridden in derived classes.

This class solves most of the problems for your program. However, as is usually the case, it's not *exactly* right for your needs. First, all the temperatures are given in Fahrenheit. Your program needs to operate in Celsius as well. Also, the `showResult()` member function might not display the result in a way you require.

Adding Functionality in a Derived Class

When you learned about inheritance in Chapter 5, adding functionality was the first technique described. Fundamentally, your program needs something just like the `WeatherPrediction` class but with a few extra bells and whistles. Sounds like a good case for inheritance to reuse code. To begin, define a new class, `MyWeatherPrediction`, that inherits from `WeatherPrediction`:

```
import weather_prediction;

export class MyWeatherPrediction : public WeatherPrediction
{
};
```

The preceding class definition compiles just fine. The `MyWeatherPrediction` class can already be used in place of `WeatherPrediction`. It provides the same functionality, but nothing new yet. For the first modification, you might want to add knowledge of the Celsius scale to the class. There is a bit of a quandary here because you don't know what the class is doing internally. If all of the internal calculations are made using Fahrenheit, how do you add support for Celsius? One way is to use the derived class to act as a go-between, interfacing between the user, who can use either scale, and the base class, which only understands Fahrenheit.

The first step in supporting Celsius is to add new member functions that allow clients to set the current temperature in Celsius instead of Fahrenheit and to get tomorrow's prediction in Celsius instead of Fahrenheit. You also need private helper functions that convert between Celsius and Fahrenheit in both directions. These functions can be `static` because they are the same for all instances of the class.

```
export class MyWeatherPrediction : public WeatherPrediction
{
    public:
        virtual void setCurrentTempCelsius(int temp);
        virtual int getTomorrowTempCelsius() const;
    private:
        static int convertCelsiusToFahrenheit(int celsius);
        static int convertFahrenheitToCelsius(int fahrenheit);
};
```

The new member functions follow the same naming convention as the parent class. Remember that from the point of view of other code, a `MyWeatherPrediction` object has all of the functionality defined in both `MyWeatherPrediction` and `WeatherPrediction`. Adopting the parent class's naming convention presents a consistent interface.

The implementation of the Celsius/Fahrenheit conversion functions is left as an exercise for the reader—and a fun one at that! The other two member functions are more interesting. To set the current temperature in Celsius, you need to convert the temperature first and then present it to the parent class in units that it understands:

```
void MyWeatherPrediction::setCurrentTempCelsius(int temp)
{
    int fahrenheitTemp { convertCelsiusToFahrenheit(temp) };
    setCurrentTempFahrenheit(fahrenheitTemp);
}
```

As you can see, once the temperature is converted, the member function calls the existing functionality from the base class. Similarly, the implementation of `getTomorrowTempCelsius()` uses the parent's existing functionality to get the temperature in Fahrenheit, but converts the result before returning it:

```
int MyWeatherPrediction::getTomorrowTempCelsius() const
{
    int fahrenheitTemp { getTomorrowTempFahrenheit() };
    return convertFahrenheitToCelsius(fahrenheitTemp);
}
```

The two new member functions effectively reuse the parent class because they "wrap" the existing functionality in a way that provides a new interface for using it.

You can also add new functionality completely unrelated to existing functionality of the parent class. For example, you could add a member function that retrieves alternative forecasts from the Internet or a member function that suggests an activity based on the predicted weather.

Replacing Functionality in a Derived Class

The other major technique for inheritance is replacing existing functionality. The `showResult()` member function in the `WeatherPrediction` class is in dire need of a facelift. `MyWeatherPrediction` can override this member function to replace the behavior with its own implementation.

The new class definition for `MyWeatherPrediction` is as follows:

```
export class MyWeatherPrediction : public WeatherPrediction
{
    public:
        virtual void setCurrentTempCelsius(int temp);
        virtual int getTomorrowTempCelsius() const;
        void showResult() const override;
    private:
        static int convertCelsiusToFahrenheit(int celsius);
        static int convertFahrenheitToCelsius(int fahrenheit);
};
```

Here is a new, user-friendlier implementation of the overridden `showResult()` member function:

```
void MyWeatherPrediction::showResult() const
{
    println("Tomorrow will be {} degrees Celsius ({} degrees Fahrenheit)",
        getTomorrowTempCelsius(), getTomorrowTempFahrenheit());
    println("Chance of rain is {}%", getChanceOfRain() * 100);
    if (getChanceOfRain() > 0.5) { println("Bring an umbrella!"); }
}
```

To clients using this class, it's as if the old version of `showResult()` never existed. As long as the object is a `MyWeatherPrediction` object, the new version is called. As a result of these changes, `MyWeatherPrediction` has emerged as a new class with new functionality tailored to a more specific purpose. Yet, it did not require much code because it leveraged its base class's existing functionality.

RESPECT YOUR PARENTS

When you write a derived class, you need to be aware of the interaction between parent classes and child classes. Issues such as order of creation, constructor chaining, and casting are all potential sources of bugs.

Parent Constructors

Objects don't spring to life all at once; they must be constructed along with their parents and any objects that are contained within them. C++ defines the creation order as follows:

1. If the class has a base class, the default constructor of the base class is executed, unless there is a call to a base class constructor in the ctor-initializer, in which case that constructor is called instead of the default constructor.

2. Non-static data members of the class are constructed in the order in which they are declared.
3. The body of the class's constructor is executed.

These rules can apply recursively. If the class has a grandparent, the grandparent is initialized before the parent, and so on. The following code shows this creation order. The proper execution of this code outputs 123.

```
class Something
{
    public:
        Something() { print("2"); }
};

class Base
{
    public:
        Base() { print("1"); }
};

class Derived : public Base
{
    public:
        Derived() { print("3"); }
    private:
        Something m_dataMember;
};

int main()
{
    Derived myDerived;
}
```

When the myDerived object is created, the constructor for Base is called first, outputting the string "1". Next, m_dataMember is initialized, calling the Something constructor, which outputs the string "2". Finally, the Derived constructor is called, which outputs "3".

Note that the Base constructor is called automatically. C++ automatically calls the default constructor for the parent class if one exists. If no default constructor exists in the parent class or if one does exist but you want to use an alternate parent constructor, you can *chain* the constructor just as when initializing data members in the ctor-initializer. For example, the following code shows a version of Base that lacks a default constructor. The associated version of Derived must explicitly tell the compiler how to call the Base constructor or the code will not compile.

```
class Base
{
    public:
        explicit Base(int i) {}
};

class Derived : public Base
{
```

```
    public:
        Derived() : Base { 7 } { /* Other Derived's initialization ... */ }
};
```

The `Derived` constructor passes a fixed value (7) to the `Base` constructor. Of course, `Derived` could also pass a variable:

```
Derived::Derived(int i) : Base { i } { /* Other Derived's initialization ... */ }
```

Passing constructor arguments from the derived class to the base class is perfectly fine and quite normal. Passing data members, however, will not work. The code will compile, but remember that data members are not initialized until *after* the base class is constructed. If you pass a data member as an argument to the parent constructor, it will be uninitialized.

Parent Destructors

Because destructors cannot take arguments, the language can always automatically call the destructor for parent classes. The order of destruction is conveniently the reverse of the order of construction:

1. The body of the class's destructor is called.
2. Any data members of the class are destroyed in the reverse order of their construction.
3. The parent class, if any, is destructed.

Again, these rules apply recursively. The lowest member of the chain is always destructed first. The following code adds destructors to the earlier example. The destructors are all declared `virtual`! If executed, this code outputs `"123321"`.

```
class Something
{
    public:
        Something() { print("2"); }
        virtual ~Something() { print("2"); }
};

class Base
{
    public:
        Base() { print("1"); }
        virtual ~Base() { print("1"); }
};

class Derived : public Base
{
    public:
        Derived() { print("3"); }
        virtual ~Derived() override { print("3"); }
    private:
        Something m_dataMember;
};
```

If the preceding destructors were not declared `virtual`, the code would seem to work fine. However, if code ever called `delete` on a `Base` pointer that was really pointing to a `Derived` instance, the destruction chain would begin in the wrong place. For example, if you remove the `virtual` and `override` keywords from all destructors in the previous code, then a problem arises when a `Derived` object is accessed as a pointer to a `Base` and deleted, as shown here:

```
Base* ptr { new Derived{} };
delete ptr;
```

The output of this code is a shockingly terse `"1231"`. When the `ptr` variable is deleted, only the `Base` destructor is called because the destructor was not declared `virtual`. As a result, the `Derived` destructor is not called, and the destructors for its data members are not called!

Technically, you could fix the preceding problem by marking only the `Base` destructor `virtual`. The "virtualness" automatically applies to any derived classes. However, I advocate explicitly making all destructors `virtual` so that you never have to worry about it.

> **WARNING** *Always make your destructors* `virtual`*! The compiler-generated default destructor is not* `virtual`*, so you should define (or explicitly default) a* `virtual` *destructor, at least for your non-*`final` *base classes.*

virtual Member Function Calls within Constructors and Destructor

`virtual` member functions behave differently in constructors and destructors. If your derived class has overridden a `virtual` member function from a base class, calling that member function from a base class constructor or destructor calls the base class implementation of that `virtual` member function and not your overridden version in the derived class! In other words, calls to `virtual` member functions from within a constructor or destructor are resolved statically at compile time.

The reason for this behavior of constructors has to do with the order of initialization when constructing an instance of a derived class. When creating such an instance, the constructor of any base class is called first, before the derived class instance is fully initialized. Hence, it would be dangerous to already call overridden `virtual` member functions from the not-yet-fully initialized derived class. A similar reasoning holds for destructors due to the order of destruction when destroying an object.

If you really need polymorphic behavior in your constructors, although this is not recommended, you can define an `initialize()` `virtual` member function in your base class, which derived classes can override. Clients creating an instance of your class will have to call this `initialize()` member function after construction has finished.

Similarly, if you need polymorphic behavior in your destructor, again, not recommended, you can define a `shutdown()` `virtual` member function that clients then need to call before the object is destroyed.

Referring to Parent Names

When you override a member function in a derived class, you are effectively replacing the original as far as other code is concerned. However, that parent version of the member function still exists, and you may want to make use of it. For example, an overridden member function would like to keep doing what the base class implementation does, plus something else. Take a look at the `getTemperature()` member function in the `WeatherPrediction` class that returns a `string` representation of the current temperature:

```
export class WeatherPrediction
{
    public:
        virtual std::string getTemperature() const;
        // Remainder omitted for brevity.
};
```

You can override this member function in the `MyWeatherPrediction` class as follows:

```
export class MyWeatherPrediction : public WeatherPrediction
{
    public:
        std::string getTemperature() const override;
        // Remainder omitted for brevity.
};
```

Suppose the derived class wants to add °F to the string by first calling the base class's `getTemperature()` member function and then adding °F to it. You might write this as follows:

```
string MyWeatherPrediction::getTemperature() const
{
    // Note: \u00B0 is the ISO/IEC 10646 representation of the degree symbol.
    return getTemperature() + "\u00B0F";  // BUG
}
```

However, this does not work because, under the rules of name resolution for C++, it first resolves against the local scope, then resolves against the class scope, and as a result ends up calling `MyWeatherPrediction::getTemperature()`. This causes an infinite recursion until you run out of stack space (some compilers detect this error and report it at compile time).

To make this work, you need to use the scope resolution operator as follows:

```
string MyWeatherPrediction::getTemperature() const
{
    // Note: \u00B0 is the ISO/IEC 10646 representation of the degree symbol.
    return WeatherPrediction::getTemperature() + "\u00B0F";
}
```

> **NOTE** *Microsoft Visual C++ supports the non-standard* `__super` *keyword (with two underscores). This allows you to write the following:*
>
> ```
> return __super::getTemperature() + "\u00B0F";
> ```

Calling the parent version of the current member function is a commonly used pattern in C++. If you have a chain of derived classes, each might want to perform the operation already defined by the base class but add their own additional functionality as well.

Let's look at another example. Imagine a class hierarchy of book types, as shown in Figure 10.6.

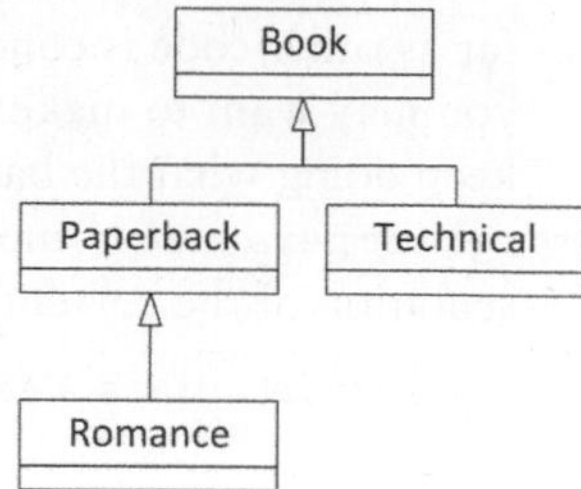

FIGURE 10.6

Because each lower class in the hierarchy further specifies the type of book, a member function that gets the description of a book really needs to take all levels of the hierarchy into consideration. This can be accomplished by chaining to the parent member function. The following code illustrates this pattern:

```
class Book
{
    public:
        virtual ~Book() = default;
        virtual string getDescription() const { return "Book"; }
        virtual int getHeight() const { return 120; }
};

class Paperback : public Book
{
    public:
        string getDescription() const override {
            return "Paperback " + Book::getDescription();
        }
};

class Romance : public Paperback
{
    public:
        string getDescription() const override {
            return "Romance " + Paperback::getDescription();
        }
        int getHeight() const override { return Paperback::getHeight() / 2; }
};

class Technical : public Book
{
    public:
        string getDescription() const override {
            return "Technical " + Book::getDescription();
        }
};

int main()
{
    Romance novel;
    Book book;
    println("{}", novel.getDescription()); // Outputs "Romance Paperback Book"
    println("{}", book.getDescription());  // Outputs "Book"
    println("{}", novel.getHeight());      // Outputs "60"
    println("{}", book.getHeight());       // Outputs "120"
}
```

The `Book` base class has two `virtual` member functions: `getDescription()` and `getHeight()`. All derived classes override `getDescription()`, but only the `Romance` class overrides `getHeight()` by calling `getHeight()` on its parent class (`Paperback`) and dividing the result by two. `Paperback` does not override `getHeight()`, but C++ walks up the class hierarchy to find a class that implements `getHeight()`. In this example, `Paperback::getHeight()` resolves to `Book::getHeight()`.

Casting Up and Down

As you have already seen, an object can be cast or assigned to its parent class. Here's an example:

```
Derived myDerived;
Base myBase { myDerived };  // Slicing!
```

Slicing occurs in situations like this because the end result is a `Base` object, and `Base` objects lack the additional functionality defined in the `Derived` class. However, slicing does *not* occur if a derived class is assigned to a pointer or reference to its base class:

```
Base& myBase { myDerived }; // No slicing!
```

This is generally the correct way to refer to a derived class in terms of its base class, also called *upcasting*. This is why it's always a good idea for functions to take references to classes instead of directly using objects of those classes. By using references, derived classes can be passed in without slicing.

> **WARNING** *When upcasting, use a pointer or reference to the base class to avoid slicing.*

Casting from a base class to one of its derived classes, also called *downcasting*, is often frowned upon by professional C++ programmers because there is no guarantee that the object really belongs to that derived class and because downcasting is a sign of bad design. For example, consider the following code:

```
void presumptuous(Base* base)
{
    Derived* myDerived { static_cast<Derived*>(base) };
    // Proceed to access Derived member functions on myDerived.
}
```

If the author of `presumptuous()` also writes the code that calls `presumptuous()`, everything will probably be OK, albeit still ugly, because the author knows that the function expects the argument to be of type `Derived*`. However, if other programmers call `presumptuous()`, they might pass in a `Base*`. There are no compile-time checks that can be done to enforce the type of the argument, and the function blindly assumes that `base` is actually a pointer to a `Derived` object.

Downcasting is sometimes necessary, and you can use it effectively in controlled circumstances. However, if you are going to downcast, you should use a `dynamic_cast()`, which uses the object's built-in knowledge of its type to refuse a cast that doesn't make sense. This built-in knowledge typically resides in the vtable, which means that `dynamic_cast()` works only for objects with a vtable, that is, objects with at least one `virtual` member. If a `dynamic_cast()` fails on a pointer, the result will be `nullptr` instead of pointing to nonsensical data. If a `dynamic_cast()` fails on an object reference, an `std::bad_cast` exception will be thrown. The last section of this chapter discusses the different options for casting in more detail.

The previous example could have been written as follows:

```
void lessPresumptuous(Base* base)
{
    Derived* myDerived { dynamic_cast<Derived*>(base) };
    if (myDerived != nullptr) {
        // Proceed to access Derived member functions on myDerived.
    }
}
```

However, keep in mind that the use of downcasting is often a sign of a bad design. You should rethink and modify your design so that downcasting can be avoided. For example, the `lessPresumptuous()` function only really works with `Derived` objects, so instead of accepting a `Base` pointer, it should simply accept a `Derived` pointer. This eliminates the need for any downcasting. If the function should work with different derived classes, all inheriting from `Base`, then look for a solution that uses polymorphism, which is discussed next.

> **WARNING** *Use downcasting only when really necessary, and be sure to use* `dynamic_cast()`.

INHERITANCE FOR POLYMORPHISM

Now that you understand the relationship between a derived class and its parent, you can use inheritance in its most powerful scenario—polymorphism. Chapter 5 discusses how polymorphism allows you to use objects with a common parent class interchangeably and to use objects in place of their parents.

Return of the Spreadsheet

Chapters 8 and 9 use a spreadsheet program as an example of an application that lends itself to an object-oriented design. A `SpreadsheetCell` represents a single element of data. Up to now, that element always stored a single `double` value. A simplified class definition for `SpreadsheetCell` follows. Note that a cell can be set either as a `double` or as a `string_view`, but it is always stored as a `double`. The current value of the cell, however, is always returned as a `string` for this example.

```
class SpreadsheetCell
{
    public:
        virtual void set(double value);
        virtual void set(std::string_view value);
        virtual std::string getString() const;
     private:
        static std::string doubleToString(double value);
```

```
        static double stringToDouble(std::string_view value);
        double m_value;
};
```

In a real spreadsheet application, cells can store different things. A cell could store a `double`, but it might just as well store a piece of text. There could also be a need for additional types of cells, such as a formula cell or a date cell. How can you support this?

Designing the Polymorphic Spreadsheet Cell

The `SpreadsheetCell` class is screaming out for a hierarchical makeover. A reasonable approach would be to narrow the scope of the `SpreadsheetCell` to cover only `string`s, perhaps renaming it to `StringSpreadsheetCell` in the process. To handle `double`s, a second class, `DoubleSpreadsheetCell`, would inherit from the `StringSpreadsheetCell` and provide functionality specific to its own format. Figure 10.7 illustrates such a design. This approach models inheritance for reuse because the `DoubleSpreadsheetCell` would be deriving from `StringSpreadsheetCell` only to make use of some of its built-in functionality.

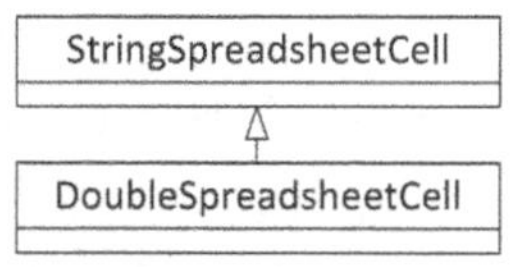

FIGURE 10.7

If you were to implement the design shown in Figure 10.7, you might discover that the derived class would override most, if not all, of the functionality of the base class. Because `double`s are treated differently from `string`s in almost all cases, the relationship may not be quite as it was originally understood. Yet, there clearly is a relationship between a cell containing `string`s and a cell containing `double`s. Rather than using the model in Figure 10.7, which implies that somehow a `DoubleSpreadsheetCell` "is-a" `StringSpreadsheetCell`, a better design would make these classes peers with a common parent, `SpreadsheetCell`. Figure 10.8 shows such a design.

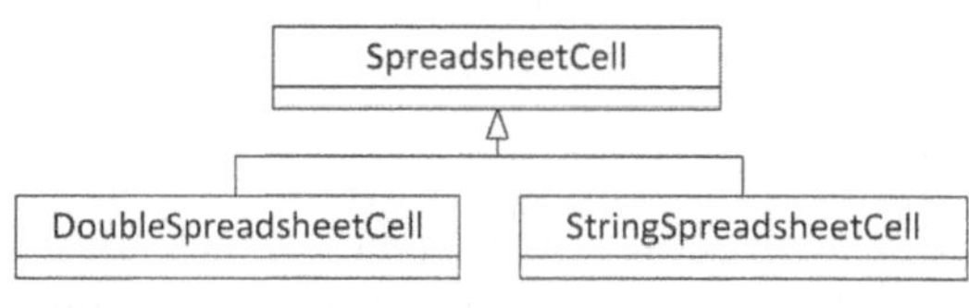

FIGURE 10.8

The design in Figure 10.8 shows a polymorphic approach to the `SpreadsheetCell` hierarchy. Because `DoubleSpreadsheetCell` and `StringSpreadsheetCell` both inherit from a common parent, `SpreadsheetCell`, they are interchangeable in the view of other code. In practical terms, that means the following:

- Both derived classes support the same interface (set of member functions) defined by the base class.
- Code that makes use of `SpreadsheetCell` objects can call any member function in the interface without even knowing whether the cell is a `DoubleSpreadsheetCell` or a `StringSpreadsheetCell`.
- Through the magic of `virtual` member functions, the appropriate instance of every member function in the interface is called depending on the class of the object.
- Other data structures, such as the `Spreadsheet` class described in Chapter 9, can contain a collection of multityped cells by referring to the base type.

The SpreadsheetCell Base Class

Because all spreadsheet cells are deriving from the `SpreadsheetCell` base class, it is probably a good idea to write that class first. When designing a base class, you need to consider how the derived classes relate to each other. From this information, you can derive the commonality that will go inside the parent class. For example, `string` cells and `double` cells are similar in that they both contain a single piece of data. Because the data is coming from the user and will be displayed back to the user, the value is set as a `string` and retrieved as a `string`. These behaviors are the shared functionality that will make up the base class.

A First Attempt

The `SpreadsheetCell` base class is responsible for defining the behaviors that all `SpreadsheetCell`-derived classes will support. In this example, all cells need to be able to set their value as a string. All cells also need to be able to return their current value as a string. The base class definition declares these member functions, as well as an explicitly defaulted `virtual` destructor, but note that it has no data members. The definition is in a `spreadsheet_cell` module.

```
export module spreadsheet_cell;
import std;

export class SpreadsheetCell
{
    public:
        virtual ~SpreadsheetCell() = default;
        virtual void set(std::string_view value);
        virtual std::string getString() const;
};
```

When you start writing the `.cpp` file for this class, you quickly run into a problem. Considering that the base class of the spreadsheet cell contains neither a `double` nor a `string` data member, how can you implement it? More generally, how do you write a base class that declares the behaviors that are supported by derived classes without actually defining the implementation of those behaviors?

One possible approach is to implement "do nothing" functionality for those behaviors. For example, calling the `set()` member function on the `SpreadsheetCell` base class will have no effect because the base class has nothing to set. This approach still doesn't feel right, however. Ideally, there should never be an object that is an instance of the base class. Calling `set()` should always have an effect because it should always be called on either a `DoubleSpreadsheetCell` or a `StringSpreadsheetCell`. A good solution enforces this constraint.

Pure virtual Member Functions and Abstract Base Classes

Pure virtual member functions are member functions that are explicitly undefined in the class definition. By making a member function pure virtual, you are telling the compiler that no definition for the member function exists in the current class. A class with at least one pure virtual member function is said to be an *abstract class* because no other code will be able to instantiate it. The compiler enforces the fact that if a class contains one or more pure virtual member functions, it can never be used to construct an object of that type.

There is a special syntax for designating a pure virtual member function. The member function declaration is followed by =0. No implementation needs to be written.

```
export class SpreadsheetCell
{
    public:
        virtual ~SpreadsheetCell() = default;
        virtual void set(std::string_view value) = 0;
        virtual std::string getString() const = 0;
};
```

Now that the base class is an abstract class, it is impossible to create a SpreadsheetCell object. The following code does not compile and returns an error such as "'SpreadsheetCell': cannot instantiate abstract class":

```
SpreadsheetCell cell; // Error! Attempts creating abstract class instance.
```

However, once the StringSpreadsheetCell class has been implemented, the following code will compile fine because it instantiates a derived class of the abstract base class:

```
unique_ptr<SpreadsheetCell> cell { new StringSpreadsheetCell {} };
```

> **NOTE** *An abstract class provides a way to prevent other code from instantiating an object directly, as opposed to one of its derived classes.*

Note that there is nothing to implement for the SpreadsheetCell class. All member functions are pure virtual, and the destructor is explicitly defaulted.

The Individual Derived Classes

Writing the StringSpreadsheetCell and DoubleSpreadsheetCell classes is just a matter of implementing the functionality that is *defined* in the parent. Because you want clients to be able to instantiate and work with string cells and double cells, the cells can't be abstract—they *must* implement all of the pure virtual member functions inherited from their parent. If a derived class does not implement all pure virtual member functions from the base class, then the derived class is abstract as well, and clients will not be able to instantiate objects of the derived class.

StringSpreadsheetCell Class Definition

The StringSpreadsheetCell class is defined in its own module called string_spreadsheet_cell. The first step in writing the class definition of StringSpreadsheetCell is to inherit from SpreadsheetCell. For this, the spreadsheet_cell module needs to be imported.

Next, the inherited pure virtual member functions are overridden, this time without being set to zero.

Finally, the string cell adds a private data member, m_value, which stores the actual cell data. This data member is an std::optional, introduced in Chapter 1, "A Crash Course in C++ and the Standard Library." By using an optional, it is possible to distinguish whether a value for a cell has never been set or whether it was set to the empty string.

```
export module string_spreadsheet_cell;
export import spreadsheet_cell;
import std;

export class StringSpreadsheetCell : public SpreadsheetCell
{
    public:
        void set(std::string_view value) override;
        std::string getString() const override;
    private:
        std::optional<std::string> m_value;
};
```

StringSpreadsheetCell Implementation

The `set()` member function is straightforward because the internal representation is already a string. The `getString()` member function has to keep into account that `m_value` is of type `optional` and that it might not have a value. When `m_value` doesn't have a value, `getString()` should return a default string, the empty string for this example. This is made easy with the `value_or()` member function of `optional`. By using `m_value.value_or("")`, the real value is returned if `m_value` contains an actual value; otherwise, the empty string is returned.

```
void set(std::string_view value) override { m_value = value; }
std::string getString() const override { return m_value.value_or(""); }
```

DoubleSpreadsheetCell Class Definition and Implementation

The `double` version follows a similar pattern, but with different logic. In addition to the `set()` member function from the base class that takes a `string_view`, it also provides a new `set()` member function that allows a client to set the value with a `double` argument. Additionally, it provides a new `getValue()` member function to retrieve the value as a `double`. Two new `private static` member functions are used to convert between a `string` and a `double`, and vice versa. As in `StringSpreadsheetCell`, it has a data member called `m_value`, this time of type `optional<double>`.

```
export module double_spreadsheet_cell;
export import spreadsheet_cell;
import std;

export class DoubleSpreadsheetCell : public SpreadsheetCell
{
    public:
        virtual void set(double value);
        virtual double getValue() const;

        void set(std::string_view value) override;
        std::string getString() const override;
    private:
        static std::string doubleToString(double value);
        static double stringToDouble(std::string_view value);
        std::optional<double> m_value;
};
```

The set() member function that takes a double is straightforward, as is the implementation of getValue(). The string_view overload uses the private static member function stringToDouble(). The getString() member function returns the stored double value as a string, or returns an empty string if no value has been stored. It uses the has_value() member function of std::optional to query whether the optional has a value. If it has a value, the value() member function is used to retrieve it.

```
virtual void set(double value) { m_value = value; }
virtual double getValue() const { return m_value.value_or(0); }

void set(std::string_view value) override { m_value = stringToDouble(value); }
std::string getString() const override
{
    return (m_value.has_value() ? doubleToString(m_value.value()) : "");
}
```

You may already see one major advantage of implementing spreadsheet cells in a hierarchy—the code is much simpler. Each class can be self-centered and deal only with its own functionality.

Note that the implementations of doubleToString() and stringToDouble() are omitted because they are the same as in Chapter 8.

Leveraging Polymorphism

Now that the SpreadsheetCell hierarchy is polymorphic, client code can take advantage of the many benefits that polymorphism has to offer. The following test program explores many of these features.

To demonstrate polymorphism, the test program declares a vector of three SpreadsheetCell pointers. Remember that because SpreadsheetCell is an abstract class, you can't create objects of that type. However, you can still have a pointer or reference to a SpreadsheetCell because it would actually be pointing to one of the derived classes. This vector, because it is a vector of the parent type SpreadsheetCell, allows you to store a heterogeneous mixture of the two derived classes. This means that elements of the vector could be either a StringSpreadsheetCell or a DoubleSpreadsheetCell.

```
vector<unique_ptr<SpreadsheetCell>> cellArray;
```

The first two elements of the vector are set to point to a new StringSpreadsheetCell, while the third is a new DoubleSpreadsheetCell.

```
cellArray.push_back(make_unique<StringSpreadsheetCell>());
cellArray.push_back(make_unique<StringSpreadsheetCell>());
cellArray.push_back(make_unique<DoubleSpreadsheetCell>());
```

Now that the vector contains multityped data, any of the member functions declared by the base class can be applied to the objects in the vector. The code just uses SpreadsheetCell pointers—the compiler has no idea at compile time what types the objects actually are. However, because the objects are inheriting from SpreadsheetCell, they must support the member functions of SpreadsheetCell.

```
cellArray[0]->set("hello");
cellArray[1]->set("10");
cellArray[2]->set("18");
```

When the getString() member function is called, each object properly returns a string representation of their value. The important, and somewhat amazing, thing to realize is that the different objects do this in different ways. A StringSpreadsheetCell returns its stored value, or an empty string. A DoubleSpreadsheetCell first performs a conversion if it contains a value; otherwise, it returns an empty string. As the programmer, you don't need to know how the object does it—you just need to know that because the object is a SpreadsheetCell, it *can* perform this behavior.

```
println("Vector: [{},{},{}]", cellArray[0]->getString(),
                              cellArray[1]->getString(),
                              cellArray[2]->getString());
```

Future Considerations

The new implementation of the SpreadsheetCell hierarchy is certainly an improvement from an object-oriented design point of view. Yet, it would probably not suffice as an actual class hierarchy for a real-world spreadsheet program for several reasons.

First, despite the improved design, one feature is still missing: the ability to convert from one cell type to another. By dividing them into two classes, the cell objects become more loosely integrated. To provide the ability to convert from a DoubleSpreadsheetCell to a StringSpreadsheetCell, you could add a *converting constructor*, also known as a *typed constructor*. It has a similar appearance as a copy constructor, but instead of a reference to an object of the same class, it takes a reference to an object of a sibling class. Note also that you now have to declare a default constructor, which can be explicitly defaulted, because the compiler stops generating one as soon as you declare any constructor yourself.

```
export class StringSpreadsheetCell : public SpreadsheetCell
{
    public:
        StringSpreadsheetCell() = default;
        StringSpreadsheetCell(const DoubleSpreadsheetCell& cell)
            : m_value { cell.getString() }
        { }
        // Remainder omitted for brevity.
};
```

With a converting constructor, you can easily create a StringSpreadsheetCell given a DoubleSpreadsheetCell. Don't confuse this with casting pointers or references, however. Casting from one sibling pointer or reference to another does not work, unless you overload the cast operator as described in Chapter 15, "Overloading C++ Operators."

> **WARNING** *You can always cast up the hierarchy, and you can sometimes cast down the hierarchy. Casting across the hierarchy is possible by changing the behavior of the cast operator or by using* reinterpret_cast()*, neither of which is recommended.*

Second, the question of how to implement overloaded operators for cells is an interesting one, and there are several possible approaches.

One approach is to implement a version of each operator for every combination of cells. With only two derived classes, this is manageable. There would be an `operator+` function to add two `double` cells, to add two `string` cells, and to add a `double` cell to a `string` cell. For each combination, you decide what the result is. For example, the result of adding two `double` cells could be the result of mathematically adding both values together. The result of adding two `string` cells could be a `string` representing the concatenation of both `string`s, and so on.

Another approach is to decide on a common representation. The earlier implementation already standardizes on a `string` as a common representation of sorts. A single `operator+` could cover all the cases by taking advantage of this common representation.

Yet another approach is a hybrid one. One `operator+` can be provided that adds two `DoubleSpreadsheetCell`s resulting in a `DoubleSpreadsheetCell`. This operator can be implemented in the `double_spreadsheet_cell` module as follows:

```
export DoubleSpreadsheetCell operator+(const DoubleSpreadsheetCell& lhs,
                                       const DoubleSpreadsheetCell& rhs)
{
    DoubleSpreadsheetCell newCell;
    newCell.set(lhs.getValue() + rhs.getValue());
    return newCell;
}
```

This operator can be tested as follows:

```
DoubleSpreadsheetCell doubleCell;     doubleCell.set(8.4);
DoubleSpreadsheetCell result { doubleCell + doubleCell };
println("{}", result.getString());  // Prints 16.800000
```

A second `operator+` can be provided for use when at least one of the two operands is a `StringSpreadsheetCell`. You could decide that the result of this operator should always be a `string` cell. Such an operator can be added to the `string_spreadsheet_cell` module and can be implemented as follows:

```
export StringSpreadsheetCell operator+(const StringSpreadsheetCell& lhs,
                                       const StringSpreadsheetCell& rhs)
{
    StringSpreadsheetCell newCell;
    newCell.set(lhs.getString() + rhs.getString());
    return newCell;
}
```

As long as the compiler has a way to turn a particular cell into a `StringSpreadsheetCell`, the operator will work. Given the previous example of having a `StringSpreadsheetCell` constructor that takes a `DoubleSpreadsheetCell` as an argument, the compiler will automatically perform the conversion if it is the only way to get the `operator+` to work. That means the following code adding a `double` cell to a `string` cell works, even though there are only two `operator+` implementations provided: one adding two `double` cells and one adding two `string` cells.

```
DoubleSpreadsheetCell doubleCell;     doubleCell.set(8.4);
StringSpreadsheetCell stringCell;     stringCell.set("Hello ");
StringSpreadsheetCell result { stringCell + doubleCell };
println("{}", result.getString());  // Prints Hello 8.400000
```

If you are feeling a little unsure about polymorphism, start with the code for this example and try things out. It is a great starting point for experimental code that simply exercises various aspects of polymorphism.

Providing Implementations for Pure virtual Member Functions

Technically, it is possible to provide an implementation for a pure `virtual` member function. This implementation cannot be in the class definition itself but must be provided outside. The class remains abstract though, and any derived classes are still required to provide an implementation of the pure `virtual` member function. Since the class remains abstract, no instances of it can be created. Still, its implementation of the pure `virtual` member function can be called, for example, from a derived class. The following code snippet demonstrates this:

```
class Base
{
public:
    virtual void doSomething() = 0; // Pure virtual member function.
};

// An out-of-class implementation of a pure virtual member function.
void Base::doSomething() { println("Base::doSomething()"); }

class Derived : public Base
{
public:
    void doSomething() override
    {
        // Call pure virtual member function implementation from base class.
        Base::doSomething();
        println("Derived::doSomething()");
    }
};

int main()
{
    Derived derived;
    Base& base { derived };
    base.doSomething();
}
```

The output is as expected:

```
Base::doSomething()
Derived::doSomething()
```

MULTIPLE INHERITANCE

As you read in Chapter 5, multiple inheritance is often perceived as a complicated and unnecessary part of object-oriented programming. I'll leave the decision of whether it is useful up to you and your co-workers. This section explains the mechanics of multiple inheritance in C++.

Inheriting from Multiple Classes

Defining a class to have multiple parent classes is simple from a syntactic point of view. All you need to do is list the base classes individually when declaring the class name.

```
class Baz : public Foo, public Bar { /* Etc. */ };
```

By listing multiple parents, a `Baz` object has the following characteristics:

- A `Baz` object supports the `public` member functions and contains the data members of both `Foo` and `Bar`.
- The member functions of the `Baz` class have access to `protected` data and member functions in both `Foo` and `Bar`.
- A `Baz` object can be upcast to either a `Foo` or a `Bar`.
- Creating a new `Baz` object automatically calls the `Foo` and `Bar` default constructors, in the order in which the classes are listed in the class definition.
- Deleting a `Baz` object automatically calls the destructors for the `Foo` and `Bar` classes, in the reverse order that the classes are listed in the class definition.

The following example shows a class, `DogBird`, that has two parent classes—a `Dog` class and a `Bird` class, as shown in Figure 10.9. The fact that a dog-bird is a ridiculous example should not be viewed as a statement that multiple inheritance itself is ridiculous. Honestly, I leave that judgment up to you.

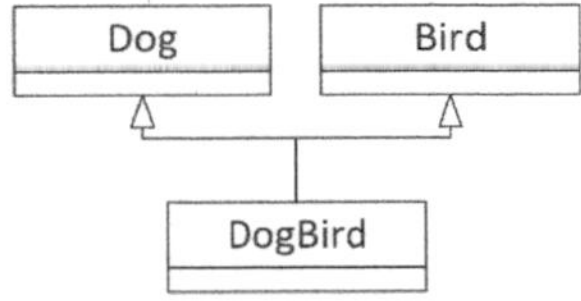

FIGURE 10.9

```
class Dog
{
    public:
        virtual void bark() { println("Woof!"); }
};

class Bird
{
    public:
        virtual void chirp() { println("Chirp!"); }
};

class DogBird : public Dog, public Bird
{
};
```

Using objects of classes with multiple parents is no different from using objects without multiple parents. In fact, the client code doesn't even have to know that the class has two parents. All that really matters are the properties and behaviors supported by the class. In this case, a `DogBird` object supports all of the `public` member functions of `Dog` and `Bird`.

```
DogBird myConfusedAnimal;
myConfusedAnimal.bark();
myConfusedAnimal.chirp();
```

The output of this program is as follows:

```
Woof!
Chirp!
```

Naming Collisions and Ambiguous Base Classes

It's not difficult to construct a scenario where multiple inheritance would seem to break down. The following examples show some of the edge cases that must be considered.

Name Ambiguity

What if the `Dog` class and the `Bird` class both had a member function called `eat()`? Because `Dog` and `Bird` are not related in any way, one version of the member function does not override the other—they both continue to exist in the `DogBird`-derived class.

As long as client code never attempts to call the `eat()` member function, that is not a problem. The `DogBird` class compiles correctly despite having two versions of `eat()`. However, if client code attempts to call the `eat()` member function on a `DogBird`, the compiler gives an error indicating that the call to `eat()` is ambiguous. The compiler does not know which version to call. The following code provokes this ambiguity error:

```
class Dog
{
    public:
        virtual void bark() { println("Woof!"); }
        virtual void eat() { println("The dog ate."); }
};

class Bird
{
    public:
        virtual void chirp() { println("Chirp!"); }
        virtual void eat() { println("The bird ate."); }
};

class DogBird : public Dog, public Bird
{
};

int main()
{
    DogBird myConfusedAnimal;
    myConfusedAnimal.eat();    // Error! Ambiguous call to member function eat()
}
```

If you comment out the last line from `main()` calling `eat()`, the code compiles fine.

The solution to the ambiguity is either to explicitly upcast the object using a `dynamic_cast()`, essentially hiding the undesired version of the member function from the compiler, or to use a *disambiguation syntax*. For example, the following code shows two ways to invoke the `Dog` version of `eat()`:

```
dynamic_cast<Dog&>(myConfusedAnimal).eat(); // Calls Dog::eat()
myConfusedAnimal.Dog::eat();                 // Calls Dog::eat()
```

Member functions of the derived class itself can also explicitly disambiguate between different member functions of the same name by using the same syntax used to access parent member functions, that is, the :: scope resolution operator. For example, the DogBird class could prevent ambiguity errors in other code by defining its own eat() member function. Inside this member function, it would determine which parent version to call.

```
class DogBird : public Dog, public Bird
{
    public:
        void eat() override
        {
            Dog::eat();          // Explicitly call Dog's version of eat()
        }
};
```

Yet another way to prevent the ambiguity error is to use a using declaration to explicitly state which version of eat() should be inherited in DogBird. Here's an example:

```
class DogBird : public Dog, public Bird
{
    public:
        using Dog::eat;  // Explicitly inherit Dog's version of eat()
};
```

Ambiguous Base Classes

Another way to provoke ambiguity is to inherit from the same class twice. This can happen if multiple parents themselves have a common parent. For example, perhaps both Bird and Dog are inheriting from an Animal class, as shown in Figure 10.10.

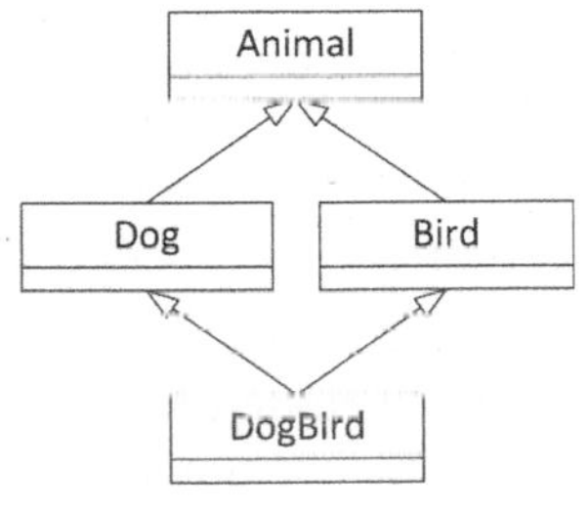

FIGURE 10.10

This type of class hierarchy is permitted in C++, though name ambiguity can still occur. For example, if the Animal class has a public member function called sleep(), that member function cannot be called on a DogBird object because the compiler does not know whether to call the version inherited by Dog or by Bird.

The best way to use these "diamond-shaped" class hierarchies is to make the topmost class an abstract base class with all member functions declared as pure virtual. Because the class only declares member functions without providing definitions, there are no member functions in the base class to call, and thus there are no ambiguities at that level.

The following example implements a diamond-shaped class hierarchy in which the Animal abstract base class has a pure virtual eat() member function that must be defined by each derived class. The DogBird class still needs to be explicit about which parent's eat() member function it uses, but any ambiguity is caused by Dog and Bird having the same member function, not because they inherit from the same class.

```
class Animal
{
    public:
        virtual void eat() = 0;
};
```

```
class Dog : public Animal
{
    public:
        virtual void bark() { println("Woof!"); }
        void eat() override { println("The dog ate."); }
};

class Bird : public Animal
{
    public:
        virtual void chirp() { println("Chirp!"); }
        void eat() override { println("The bird ate."); }
};

class DogBird : public Dog, public Bird
{
    public:
        using Dog::eat;
};
```

A more refined mechanism for dealing with the top class in a diamond-shaped hierarchy, virtual base classes, is explained later in this chapter.

Uses for Multiple Inheritance

At this point, you're probably wondering why programmers would want to tackle multiple inheritance in their code. The most straightforward use case for multiple inheritance is to define a class of objects that is-a something and also is-a something else. As was said in Chapter 5, any real-world objects you find that follow this pattern are unlikely to translate well into code.

One of the most compelling and simple uses of multiple inheritance is for the implementation of mixin classes. Mixin classes are introduced in Chapter 5 and are discussed in more detail in Chapter 32, "Incorporating Design Techniques and Frameworks."

Another reason that people sometimes use multiple inheritance is to model a component-based class. Chapter 5 gives the example of an airplane simulator. The `Airplane` class has an engine, fuselage, controls, and other components. While the typical implementation of an `Airplane` class would make each of these components a separate data member, you could use multiple inheritance. The airplane class would inherit from engine, fuselage, and controls, in effect getting the behaviors and properties of all of its components. I recommend that you stay away from this type of code because it confuses a clear has-a relationship with inheritance, which should be used for is-a relationships. The recommended solution is to have an `Airplane` class that contains data members of type `Engine`, `Fuselage`, and `Controls`.

INTERESTING AND OBSCURE INHERITANCE ISSUES

Extending a class opens up a variety of issues. What characteristics of the class can and cannot be changed? What is non-public inheritance? What are virtual base classes? These questions, and more, are answered in the following sections.

Changing the Overridden Member Function's Return Type

For the most part, the reason you override a member function is to change its implementation. Sometimes, however, you may want to change other characteristics of the member function, such as its return type.

A good rule of thumb is to override a member function with the exact member function declaration, or *member function prototype*, that the base class uses. The implementation can change, but the prototype stays the same.

That does not have to be the case, however. In C++, an overriding member function can change the return type as long as the return type of the member function in the base class is a pointer or reference to a class, and the return type in the derived class is a pointer or reference to a descendant, i.e., more specialized class. Such types are called *covariant return types*. This feature sometimes comes in handy when the base class and derived class work with objects in a *parallel hierarchy*—that is, another group of classes that is tangential, but related, to the first class hierarchy.

For example, consider a basic car simulator. You might have two hierarchies of classes that model different real-world objects but are obviously related. The first is the `Car` hierarchy. The base class, `Car`, has derived classes `GasolineCar` and `ElectricalCar`. Similarly, there is another hierarchy of classes with a base class called `PowerSource` and derived classes `GasolinePowerSource` and `Electrical-PowerSource`. Figure 10.11 shows the two class hierarchies.

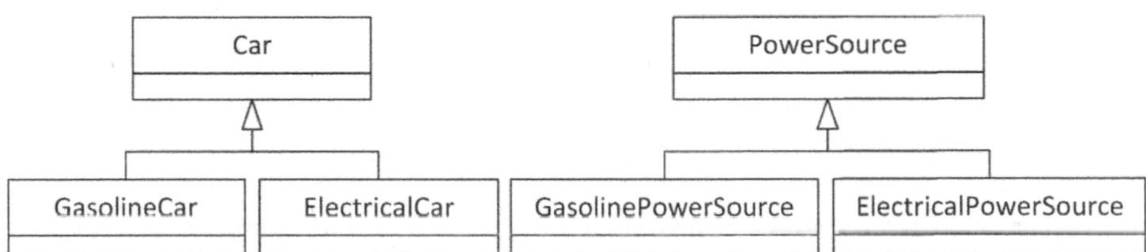

FIGURE 10.11

Let's assume a power source can print its own type and that a gasoline power source has a member function `fillTank()`, while an electrical power source has a member function `chargeBatteries()`:

```
class PowerSource
{
    public:
        virtual void printType() = 0;
};

class GasolinePowerSource : public PowerSource
{
    public:
        void printType() override { println("GasolinePowerSource"); }
        virtual void fillTank() { println("Gasoline tank filled up."); }
};

class ElectricalPowerSource : public PowerSource
{
    public:
```

```
        void printType() override { println("ElectricalPowerSource"); }
        virtual void chargeBatteries() { println("Batteries charged."); }
};
```

Now assume that Car has a virtual member function called getFilledUpPowerSource() that returns a reference to the "filled-up" power source of a specific car:

```
class Car
{
    public:
        virtual PowerSource& getFilledUpPowerSource() = 0;
};
```

This is a pure virtual, abstract member function, as it only makes sense to provide an actual implementation in concrete derived classes. Since a GasolinePowerSource is a PowerSource, the GasolineCar class can implement this member function as follows:

```
class GasolineCar : public Car
{
    public:
        PowerSource& getFilledUpPowerSource() override
        {
            m_engine.fillTank();
            return m_engine;
        }
    private:
        GasolinePowerSource m_engine;
};
```

ElectricalCar can implement it as follows:

```
class ElectricalCar : public Car
{
    public:
        PowerSource& getFilledUpPowerSource() override
        {
            m_engine.chargeBatteries();
            return m_engine;
        }
    private:
        ElectricalPowerSource m_engine;
};
```

These classes can be tested as follows:

```
GasolineCar gc;
gc.getFilledUpPowerSource().printType();
println("");
ElectricalCar ev;
ev.getFilledUpPowerSource().printType();
```

The output is:

```
Gasoline tank filled up.
GasolinePowerSource

Batteries charged.
ElectricalPowerSource
```

This implementation is fine. However, because you know that the `getFilledUpPowerSource()` member function for `GasolineCar` always returns a `GasolinePowerSource`, and for `ElectricalCar` always an `ElectricalPowerSource`, you can indicate this fact to potential users of these classes by changing the return type, as shown here:

```
class GasolineCar : public Car
{
    public:
        GasolinePowerSource& getFilledUpPowerSource() override
        { /* omitted for brevity */ }
};

class ElectricalCar : public Car
{
    public:
        ElectricalPowerSource& getFilledUpPowerSource() override
        { /* omitted for brevity */ }
};
```

A good way to figure out whether you can change the return type of an overridden member function is to consider whether existing code would still work; this is called the *Liskov substitution principle* (LSP). In the preceding example, changing the return type was fine because any code that assumed that the `getFilledUpPowerSource()` member function would always return a `PowerSource` would still compile and work correctly. Because an `ElectricalPowerSource` and a `GasolinePowerSource` are both `PowerSources`, any member functions that were called on the result of `getFilledUpPowerSource()` returning a `PowerSource` could still be called on the result of `getFilledUpPowerSource()` returning an `ElectricalPowerSource` or a `GasolinePowerSource`.

You could not, for example, change the return type to something completely unrelated, such as `int&`. The following code does not compile:

```
class ElectricalCar : public Car
{
    public:
        int& getFilledUpPowerSource() override // Error!
        { /* omitted for brevity */ }
};
```

This generates a compilation error, something like this:

```
'ElectricalCar::getFilledUpPowerSource': overriding virtual function return type
differs and is not covariant from 'Car::getFilledUpPowerSource'
```

This example is using references to `PowerSources` and not smart pointers. Changing the return type does not work when using, for example, `shared_ptr` as return type. Suppose `Car::getFilledUpPowerSource()` returns a `shared_ptr<PowerSource>`. In that case, you cannot change the return type for `ElectricalCar::getFilledUpPowerSource()` to `shared_ptr<ElectricalPowerSource>`. The reason is that `shared_ptr` is a class template. Two instantiations of the `shared_ptr` class template are created, `shared_ptr<PowerSource>` and `shared_ptr<ElectricalPowerSource>`. Both these instantiations are completely different types and are in no way related to each other. You cannot change the return type of an overridden member function to return a completely different type.

Adding Overloads of virtual Base Class Member Functions to Derived Classes

It is possible to add new overloads of `virtual` base class member functions to derived classes. That is, you can add an overload of a `virtual` member function in the derived class with a new prototype but continue to inherit the base class version. This technique uses a `using` declaration to explicitly include the base class definition of the member function within the derived class. Here is an example:

```
class Base
{
    public:
        virtual void someFunction();
};

class Derived : public Base
{
    public:
        using Base::someFunction;          // Explicitly inherits the Base version.
        virtual void someFunction(int i); // Adds a new overload of someFunction().
        virtual void someOtherFunction();
};
```

> **NOTE** *It is rare to find a member function in a derived class with the same name as a member function in the base class but using a different parameter list.*

Inherited Constructors

In the previous section, you saw the use of a `using` declaration to explicitly include the base class definition of a member function within a derived class. This works for normal class member functions, but also for constructors, allowing you to inherit constructors from base classes. Take a look at the following definitions for the `Base` and `Derived` classes:

```
class Base
{
    public:
        virtual ~Base() = default;
        Base() = default;
        explicit Base(int i) {}
};

class Derived : public Base
{
    public:
        explicit Derived(int i) : Base(i) {}
};
```

The only thing the `Derived` constructor is doing is passing its parameter to a `Base` constructor.

You can construct a `Base` object only with the provided `Base` constructors, either the default constructor or the constructor accepting an `int`. On the other hand, constructing a `Derived` object can happen only with the provided `Derived` constructor, which requires a single integer as argument. You cannot construct `Derived` objects using the default constructor from the `Base` class. Here is an example:

```
Base base { 1 };            // OK, calls integer Base ctor.
Derived derived1 { 2 };     // OK, calls integer Derived ctor.
Derived derived2;           // Error, Derived does not have a default ctor.
```

As the `Derived` constructor is just passing its parameter to a `Base` constructor and isn't doing anything else, you can simply inherit the `Base` constructors explicitly with a `using` declaration in the `Derived` class as follows:

```
class Derived : public Base
{
    public:
        using Base::Base;
};
```

The `using` declaration inherits all constructors from `Base`, so now you can construct `Derived` objects in the following ways:

```
Derived derived1 { 2 };     // OK, calls inherited integer Base ctor.
Derived derived2;           // OK, calls inherited default Base ctor.
```

The inherited constructors in a derived class have the same access specifier (`public`, `protected`, or `private`) as the constructors in the base class. Inherited constructors that are explicitly deleted with `=delete` in the base class are deleted in the derived class as well.

Hiding of Inherited Constructors

The `Derived` class can define a constructor with the same parameter list as one of the inherited constructors in the `Base` class. In this case, the constructor of the `Derived` class takes precedence over the inherited constructor. In the following example, the `Derived` class inherits all constructors, from the `Base` class with the `using` declaration. However, because the `Derived` class defines its own constructor with a single parameter of type `float`, the inherited constructor from the `Base` class with a single parameter of type `float` is hidden.

```
class Base
{
    public:
        virtual ~Base() = default;
        Base() = default;
        explicit Base(std::string_view str) {}
        explicit Base(float f) {}
};

class Derived : public Base
{
    public:
        using Base::Base;
        explicit Derived(float f) {}    // Hides inherited float Base ctor.
};
```

With this definition, objects of `Derived` can be created as follows:

```
Derived derived1 { "Hello" };   // OK, calls inherited string_view Base ctor.
Derived derived2 { 1.23f };     // OK, calls float Derived ctor.
Derived derived3;               // OK, calls inherited default Base ctor.
```

A few restrictions apply to inheriting constructors from a base class with a `using` declaration.

- When you inherit a constructor from a base class, you inherit all of them. It is not possible to inherit only a subset of the constructors of a base class.
- When you inherit constructors, they are inherited with the same access specification as they have in the base class, irrespective of which access specification the `using` declaration is under.

Inherited Constructors and Multiple Inheritance

Another restriction with inheriting constructors is related to multiple inheritance. It's not possible to inherit constructors from one of the base classes if another base class has a constructor with the same parameter list, because this leads to ambiguity. To resolve this, the `Derived` class needs to explicitly define the conflicting constructors. For example, the following `Derived` class tries to inherit all constructors from both `Base1` and `Base2`, which results in an ambiguity for the `float`-based constructors.

```
class Base1
{
    public:
        virtual ~Base1() = default;
        Base1() = default;
        explicit Base1(float f) {}
};

class Base2
{
    public:
        virtual ~Base2() = default;
        Base2() = default;
        explicit Base2(std::string_view str) {}
        explicit Base2(float f) {}
};

class Derived : public Base1, public Base2
{
    public:
        using Base1::Base1;
        using Base2::Base2;
        explicit Derived(char c) {}
};

int main()
{
    Derived d { 1.2f };  // Error, ambiguity.
}
```

The first using declaration in Derived inherits all constructors from Base1. This means that Derived gets the following constructor:

```
Derived(float f);    // Inherited from Base1.
```

The second using declaration in Derived tries to inherit all constructors from Base2. However, this means that Derived gets a second Derived(float) constructor. The problem is solved by explicitly declaring conflicting constructors in the Derived class as follows:

```
class Derived : public Base1, public Base2
{
    public:
        using Base1::Base1;
        using Base2::Base2;
        explicit Derived(char c) {}
        explicit Derived(float f) {}
};
```

The Derived class now explicitly declares a constructor with a single parameter of type float, solving the ambiguity. If you want, this explicitly declared constructor in the Derived class accepting a float argument can still forward the call to both the Base1 and Base2 constructors in its ctor-initializer as follows:

```
Derived::Derived(float f) : Base1 { f }, Base2 { f } {}
```

Initialization of Data Members

When using inherited constructors, make sure that all data members are properly initialized. For example, take the following new definitions for Base and Derived. These definitions do not properly initialize the m_int data member in all cases, and, as you know, uninitialized data members are not recommended.

```
class Base
{
    public:
        virtual ~Base() = default;
        explicit Base(std::string_view str) : m_str { str } {}
    private:
        std::string m_str;
};

class Derived : public Base
{
    public:
        using Base::Base;
        explicit Derived(int i) : Base { "" }, m_int { i } {}
    private:
        int m_int;
};
```

You can create a Derived object as follows:

```
Derived s1 { 2 };
```

This calls the `Derived(int)` constructor, which initializes the `m_int` data member of the `Derived` class and calls the `Base` constructor with an empty string to initialize the `m_str` data member.

Because the `Base` constructor is inherited in the `Derived` class, you can also construct a `Derived` object as follows:

```
Derived s2 { "Hello World" };
```

This calls the inherited `Base` constructor in the `Derived` class. However, this inherited `Base` constructor only initializes `m_str` of the `Base` class and does not initialize `m_int` of the `Derived` class, leaving it in an uninitialized state. This is not recommended!

The solution in this case is to use in-class member initializers, which are discussed in Chapter 8. The following code uses an in-class member initializer to initialize `m_int` to 0. Of course, the `Derived(int)` constructor can still change this and initialize `m_int` to the constructor parameter `i`.

```
class Derived : public Base
{
    public:
        using Base::Base;
        explicit Derived(int i) : Base { "" }, m_int { i } {}
    private:
        int m_int { 0 };
};
```

Special Cases in Overriding Member Functions

Several special cases require attention when overriding a member function. This section outlines the cases that you are likely to encounter.

The Base Class Member Function Is static

In C++, you cannot override a `static` member function. For the most part, that's all you need to know. There are, however, a few corollaries that you need to understand.

First of all, a member function cannot be both `static` and `virtual`. This is the first clue that attempting to override a `static` member function will not do what you intend it to do. If you have a `static` member function in your derived class with the same name as a `static` member function in your base class, you actually have two separate member functions.

The following code shows two classes that both happen to have `static` member functions called `beStatic()`. These two member functions are in no way related.

```
class BaseStatic
{
    public:
        static void beStatic() { println("BaseStatic being static."); }
};

class DerivedStatic : public BaseStatic
{
    public:
        static void beStatic() { println("DerivedStatic keepin' it static."); }
};
```

Because a `static` member function belongs to its class, calling the identically named member functions on the two different classes calls their respective member functions.

```
BaseStatic::beStatic();
DerivedStatic::beStatic();
```

This outputs the following:

```
BaseStatic being static.
DerivedStatic keepin' it static.
```

Everything makes perfect sense as long as the member functions are accessed by their class names. The behavior is less clear when objects are involved. In C++, you can call a `static` member function using an object, but because the member function is `static`, it has no `this` pointer and no access to the object itself, so it is equivalent to calling it by its class name. Referring to the previous example classes, you can write code as follows, but the results may be surprising.

```
DerivedStatic myDerivedStatic;
BaseStatic& ref { myDerivedStatic };
myDerivedStatic.beStatic();
ref.beStatic();
```

The first call to `beStatic()` obviously calls the `DerivedStatic` version because it is explicitly called on an object declared as a `DerivedStatic`. The second call might not work as you expect. The object is a `BaseStatic` reference, but it refers to a `DerivedStatic` object. In this case, `BaseStatic`'s version of `beStatic()` is called. The reason is that C++ doesn't care what the object actually is when calling a `static` member function. It only cares about the compile-time type. In this case, the type is a reference to a `BaseStatic`.

The output of the previous example is as follows:

```
DerivedStatic keepin' it static.
BaseStatic being static.
```

> **NOTE** `static` *member functions are scoped by the name of the class in which they are defined, but they are not member functions that apply to a specific object. When you call a* `static` *member function, the version determined by normal name resolution is called. When the member function is called syntactically by using an object, the object is not actually involved in the call, except to determine the type at compile time.*

The Base Class Member Function Is Overloaded

When you override a member function by specifying a name and a set of parameters, the compiler implicitly hides all other instances of the same name in the base class. The idea is that if you have overridden one member function with a given name, you might have intended to override all the member functions with that name, but simply forgot, and therefore this should be treated as an error. It makes sense if you think about it—why would you want to change some overloads of a member function and not others? Consider the following `Derived` class, which overrides a member function without overriding its associated overloaded siblings:

```
class Base
{
    public:
        virtual ~Base() = default;
        virtual void overload() { println("Base's overload()"); }
        virtual void overload(int i) { println("Base's overload(int i)"); }
};

class Derived : public Base
{
    public:
        void overload() override { println("Derived's overload()"); }
};
```

If you attempt to call the version of `overload()` that takes an `int` parameter on a `Derived` object, your code will not compile because it was not explicitly overridden.

```
Derived myDerived;
myDerived.overload(2); // Error! No matching member function for overload(int).
```

It is possible, however, to access this version of the member function from a `Derived` object. All you need is a pointer or a reference to a `Base` object.

```
Derived myDerived;
Base& ref { myDerived };
ref.overload(7);
```

The hiding of unimplemented overloaded member functions is only skin deep in C++. Objects that are explicitly declared as instances of the derived class do not make the member functions available, but a simple cast to the base class brings them right back.

A `using` declaration can be employed to save you the trouble of overriding all the overloads when you really only want to change one. In the following code, the `Derived` class definition uses one version of `overload()` from `Base` and explicitly overrides the other:

```
class Derived : public Base
{
    public:
        using Base::overload;
        void overload() override { println("Derived's overload()"); }
};
```

The `using` declaration has certain risks. Suppose a third `overload()` member function is added to `Base`, which should have been overridden in `Derived`. This will now not be detected as an error, because with the `using` declaration, the designer of the `Derived` class has explicitly said, "I am willing to accept all other overloads of this member function from the parent class."

> **WARNING** *To avoid obscure bugs when overriding a member function from a base class, override all overloads of that member function as well.*

The Base Class Member Function Is private

There's absolutely nothing wrong with overriding a `private` member function. Remember that the access specifier for a member function determines who is able to *call* the member function. Just because a derived class can't call its parent's `private` member functions doesn't mean it can't override them. In fact, the *template member function pattern* is a common pattern in C++ that is implemented by overriding `private` member functions. It allows derived classes to define their own "uniqueness" that is referenced in the base class. Note that, for example, Java and C# only allow overriding `public` and `protected` member functions, not `private` member functions.

For example, the following class is part of a car simulator that estimates the number of miles the car can travel based on its gas mileage and the amount of fuel left. The `getMilesLeft()` member function is the *template member function*. Usually, template member functions are not `virtual`. They typically define some algorithmic skeleton in a base class, calling `virtual` member functions to query for information. A derived class can then override these `virtual` member functions to change aspects of the algorithm without having to modify the algorithm in the base class itself.

```
export class MilesEstimator
{
    public:
        virtual ~MilesEstimator() = default;
        int getMilesLeft() const { return getMilesPerGallon() * getGallonsLeft(); }
        virtual void setGallonsLeft(int gallons) { m_gallonsLeft = gallons; }
        virtual int getGallonsLeft() const { return m_gallonsLeft; }
    private:
        int m_gallonsLeft { 0 };
        virtual int getMilesPerGallon() const { return 20; }
};
```

The `getMilesLeft()` member function performs a calculation based on the results of two of its own member functions: `getGallonsLeft()` which is `public`, and `getMilesPerGallon()` which is `private`. The following code uses the `MilesEstimator` to calculate how many miles can be traveled with two gallons of gas:

```
MilesEstimator myMilesEstimator;
myMilesEstimator.setGallonsLeft(2);
println("Normal estimator can go {} more miles.",
    myMilesEstimator.getMilesLeft());
```

The output of this code is as follows:

```
Normal estimator can go 40 more miles.
```

To make the simulator more interesting, you may want to introduce different types of vehicles, perhaps a more efficient car. The existing `MilesEstimator` assumes that all cars get 20 miles per gallon, but this value is returned from a separate member function specifically so that a derived class can override it. Such a derived class is shown here:

```
export class EfficientCarMilesEstimator : public MilesEstimator
{
    private:
        int getMilesPerGallon() const override { return 35; }
};
```

By overriding this one `private` member function, the new class completely changes the behavior of existing, unmodified, `public` member functions in the base class. The `getMilesLeft()` member function in the base class automatically calls the overridden version of the `private getMilesPerGallon()` member function. An example using the new class is shown here:

```
EfficientCarMilesEstimator myEstimator;
myEstimator.setGallonsLeft(2);
println("Efficient estimator can go {} more miles.",
        myEstimator.getMilesLeft());
```

This time, the output reflects the overridden functionality:

```
Efficient estimator can go 70 more miles.
```

> **NOTE** *Overriding* `private` *and* `protected` *member functions is a good way to change certain features of a class without a major overhaul.*

The Base Class Member Function Has Default Arguments

An overridden member function in a derived class can have different default arguments than in the base class. The arguments that are used depend on the declared type of the variable, not the underlying object. The following is a simple example of a derived class that provides a different default argument in an overridden member function:

```
class Base
{
    public:
        virtual ~Base() = default;
        virtual void go(int i = 2) { println("Base's go with i={}", i); }
};

class Derived : public Base
{
    public:
        void go(int i = 7) override { println("Derived's go with i={}", i); }
};
```

If `go()` is called on a `Derived` object, `Derived`'s version of `go()` is executed with the default argument of 7. If `go()` is called on a `Base` object, `Base`'s version of `go()` is called with the default argument of 2. However (and this is the weird part), if `go()` is called on a `Base` pointer or `Base` reference that really points to a `Derived` object, `Derived`'s version of `go()` is called but with `Base`'s default argument of 2. This behavior is shown in the following example:

```
Base myBase;
Derived myDerived;
Base& myBaseReferenceToDerived { myDerived };
myBase.go();
myDerived.go();
myBaseReferenceToDerived.go();
```

The output of this code is as follows:

```
Base's go with i=2
Derived's go with i=7
Derived's go with i=2
```

The reason for this behavior is that C++ uses the compile-time type of the expression to bind default arguments, not the run-time type. Default arguments are not "inherited" in C++. If the `Derived` class in this example failed to provide a default argument for `go()` as its parent did, it would not be possible to call `go()` on a `Derived` object without passing an argument to it.

> **NOTE** *When overriding a member function that has a default argument, you should provide a default argument as well, and it should probably be the same value. It is recommended to use a named constant for default values so that the same named constant can be used in derived classes.*

The Base Class Member Function Has a Different Access Specification

There are two ways you may want to change the access specification of a member function: you could try to make it more restrictive or less restrictive. Neither case makes much sense in C++, but there are a few legitimate reasons for attempting to do so.

To enforce tighter restrictions on a member function (or on a data member for that matter), there are two approaches you can take. One way is to change the access specifier for the entire base class. This approach is described later in this chapter. The other approach is simply to redefine the access in the derived class, as illustrated in the `Shy` class that follows:

```
class Gregarious
{
    public:
        virtual void talk() { println("Gregarious says hi!"); }
};

class Shy : public Gregarious
{
    protected:
        void talk() override { println("Shy reluctantly says hello."); }
};
```

The `protected` version of `talk()` in `Shy` properly overrides the `Gregarious::talk()` member function. Any client code that attempts to call `talk()` on a `Shy` object gets a compilation error:

```
Shy myShy;
myShy.talk();  // Error! Attempt to access protected member function.
```

However, the member function is not fully protected. One only has to obtain a `Gregarious` reference or pointer to access the member function that you thought was protected:

```
Shy myShy;
Gregarious& ref { myShy };
ref.talk();
```

The output of this code is as follows:

```
Shy reluctantly says hello.
```

This proves that making the member function `protected` in the derived class did override the member function (because the derived class version is correctly called), but it also proves that the `protected` access can't be fully enforced if the base class makes it `public`.

> **NOTE** *There is no reasonable way (or good reason) to restrict access to a* `public` *base class member function.*

> **NOTE** *The previous example redefined the member function in the derived class because it wants to display a different message. If you don't want to change the implementation but instead only want to change the access specification of a member function, the preferred way is to simply add a* `using` *declaration in the derived class definition with the desired access specification.*

It is much easier (and makes more sense) to lessen access restrictions in derived classes. The simplest way is to provide a `public` member function in the derived class that calls a `protected` member function from the base class, as shown here:

```
class Secret
{
    protected:
        virtual void dontTell() { println("I'll never tell."); }
};

class Blabber : public Secret
{
    public:
        virtual void tell() { dontTell(); }
};
```

A client calling the `public tell()` member function of a `Blabber` object effectively accesses the `protected` member function of the `Secret` class. Of course, this doesn't *really* change the access specification of `dontTell()`; it just provides a `public` way of accessing it.

You can also override `dontTell()` explicitly in `Blabber` and give it new behavior with `public` access. This makes a lot more sense than reducing the access specification because it is entirely clear what happens with a reference or pointer to the base class. For example, suppose that `Blabber` actually makes the `dontTell()` member function `public`:

```
class Blabber : public Secret
{
    public:
        void dontTell() override { println("I'll tell all!"); }
};
```

Now you can call `dontTell()` on a `Blabber` object:

```
myBlabber.dontTell(); // Outputs "I'll tell all!"
```

If you don't want to change the implementation of the overridden member function but only change the access specification, then you can use a `using` declaration. Here's an example:

```
class Blabber : public Secret
{
    public:
        using Secret::dontTell;
};
```

This also allows you to call `dontTell()` on a `Blabber` object, but this time the output will be "I'll never tell":

```
myBlabber.dontTell(); // Outputs "I'll never tell."
```

In both previous cases, however, the `protected` member function in the base class stays `protected` because any attempts to call `Secret`'s `dontTell()` member function through a `Secret` pointer or reference will not compile:

```
Blabber myBlabber;
Secret& ref { myBlabber };
Secret* ptr { &myBlabber };
ref.dontTell();  // Error! Attempt to access protected member function.
ptr->dontTell(); // Error! Attempt to access protected member function.
```

> **NOTE** *The only useful way to change a member function's access specification is by providing a less restrictive accessor to a* `protected` *member function.*

Copy Constructors and Assignment Operators in Derived Classes

Chapter 9 explains that providing a copy constructor and assignment operator is a must when you have dynamically allocated memory in a class. When defining a derived class, you need to be careful about copy constructors and `operator=`.

If your derived class does not have any special data (pointers, usually) that require a nondefault copy constructor or `operator=`, you don't need to have one, regardless of whether the base class has one. If your derived class omits the copy constructor or `operator=`, a default copy constructor or `operator=` will be provided for the data members specified in the derived class, and the base class copy constructor or `operator=` will be used for the data members specified in the base class.

On the other hand, if you *do* specify a copy constructor in the derived class, you need to explicitly call the parent copy constructor, as shown in the following code. If you do not do this, the default constructor (not the copy constructor!) will be used for the parent portion of the object.

```
class Base
{
    public:
```

```
        virtual ~Base() = default;
        Base() = default;
        Base(const Base& src) { }
};

class Derived : public Base
{
    public:
        Derived() = default;
        Derived(const Derived& src) : Base { src } { }
};
```

Similarly, if the derived class overrides `operator=`, it is almost always necessary to call the parent's version of `operator=` as well. The only case where you wouldn't do this would be if there was some bizarre reason why you only wanted part of the object assigned when an assignment took place. The following code shows how to call the parent's assignment operator from the derived class:

```
Derived& Derived::operator=(const Derived& rhs)
{
    if (&rhs == this) { return *this; }
    Base::operator=(rhs); // Calls parent's operator=.
    // Do necessary assignments for derived class.
    return *this;
}
```

> **WARNING** *If your derived class does not specify its own copy constructor or* `operator=`, *the base class functionality continues to work. However, if the derived class does provide its own copy constructor or* `operator=`, *it needs to explicitly call the base class versions.*

> **NOTE** *When you need copy functionality in an inheritance hierarchy, a common idiom employed by professional C++ developers is to implement a polymorphic* `clone()` *member function, because relying on the standard copy constructor and copy assignment operators is not sufficient. The polymorphic* `clone()` *idiom is discussed in Chapter 12, "Writing Generic Code with Templates."*

Run-Time Type Facilities

Relative to other object-oriented languages, C++ is very compile-time oriented. As you learned earlier, overriding member functions works because of a level of indirection between a member function and its implementation, not because the object has built-in knowledge of its own class.

There are, however, features in C++ that provide a run-time view of an object. These features are commonly grouped together under a feature set called *run-time type information* (RTTI). RTTI provides a number of useful features for working with information about an object's class membership. One such feature is `dynamic_cast()`, which allows you to safely convert between types within an object-oriented hierarchy; this was discussed earlier in this chapter. Using `dynamic_cast()` on a class without a vtable, that is, without any `virtual` member functions, causes a compilation error.

A second RTTI feature is the `typeid` operator, which lets you query for types at run time. The result of applying the operator is a reference to an `std::type_info` object, defined in `<typeinfo>`. The `type_info` class has a member function called `name()` returning the compiler-dependent name of the type. The `typeid` operator behaves as follows:

- `typeid(type)`: Results in a reference to a `type_info` object representing the given type.
- `typeid(expression)`
    - If evaluating `expression` results in a polymorphic type, then `expression` is evaluated and the result of the `typeid` operator is a reference to a `type_info` object representing the dynamic type of the evaluated `expression`.
    - Otherwise, `expression` is not evaluated, and the result is a reference to a `type_info` object representing the static type.

For the most part, you shouldn't ever need to use `typeid` because any code that is conditionally executed based on the type of the object would be better handled with, for example, `virtual` member functions.

The following code uses `typeid` to print a message based on the type of the object:

```
class Animal { public: virtual ~Animal() = default; };
class Dog : public Animal {};
class Bird : public Animal {};

void speak(const Animal& animal)
{
    if (typeid(animal) == typeid(Dog)) {
        println("Woof!");
    } else if (typeid(animal) == typeid(Bird)) {
        println("Chirp!");
    }
}
```

Whenever you see code like this, you should immediately consider reimplementing the functionality as a `virtual` member function. In this case, a better implementation would be to declare a `virtual` member function called `speak()` in the `Animal` base class. `Dog` would override the member function to print `"Woof!"`, and `Bird` would override it to print `"Chirp!"`. This approach better fits object-oriented programming, where functionality related to objects is given to those objects.

> **WARNING** *The* `typeid` *operator works correctly only if the class has at least one* `virtual` *member function, that is, when the class has a vtable. Additionally, the* `typeid` *operator strips reference and* `const` *qualifiers from its argument.*

One possible use case of the typeid operator is for logging and debugging purposes. The following code makes use of typeid for logging. The logObject() function takes a "loggable" object as a parameter. The design is such that any object that can be logged inherits from the Loggable class and supports a member function called getLogMessage().

```
class Loggable
{
    public:
        virtual ~Loggable() = default;
        virtual string getLogMessage() const = 0;
};

class Foo : public Loggable
{
    public:
        string getLogMessage() const override { return "Hello logger."; }
};

void logObject(const Loggable& loggableObject)
{
    print("{}: ", typeid(loggableObject).name());
    println("{}", loggableObject.getLogMessage());
}
```

logObject() first prints the name of the object's class to the console, followed by its log message. This way, when you read the log later, you can see which object was responsible for every written line. Here is the output generated by Microsoft Visual C++ 2022 when logObject() is called with an instance of Foo:

```
class Foo: Hello logger.
```

As you can see, the name returned by the typeid operator is "class Foo". However, this name depends on your compiler. For example, if you compile and run the same code with GCC, the output is as follows:

```
3Foo: Hello logger.
```

> **NOTE** *If you are using* typeid *for purposes other than logging and debugging, consider changing your design, for example, by using* virtual *member functions.*

Non-public Inheritance

In all previous examples, parent classes were always listed using the public keyword. You may be wondering if a parent can be private or protected. In fact, it can, though neither is as common as public. If you don't specify any access specifier for the parent, then it is private inheritance for a class, and public inheritance for a struct.

Declaring the relationship with the parent to be protected means that all public member functions and data members from the base class become protected in the context of the derived class. Similarly, specifying private inheritance means that all public and protected member functions and data members of the base class become private in the derived class.

There are a handful of reasons why you might want to uniformly degrade the access level of the parent in this way, but most reasons imply flaws in the design of the hierarchy. Some programmers abuse this language feature, often in combination with multiple inheritance, to implement "components" of a class. Instead of making an `Airplane` class that contains an engine data member and a fuselage data member, they make an `Airplane` class that is a `protected` engine and a `protected` fuselage. In this way, the `Airplane` doesn't look like an engine or a fuselage to client code (because everything is `protected`), but it is able to use all of that functionality internally.

> **NOTE** *Non-*`public` *inheritance is rare, and I recommend using it cautiously, if for no other reason than that most programmers are not familiar with it.*

Virtual Base Classes

Earlier in this chapter, you learned about ambiguous base classes, a situation that arises when multiple parents each have a parent in common, as shown again in Figure 10.12. The solution recommended earlier was to make sure that the shared parent doesn't have any functionality of its own. That way, its member functions can never be called, and there is no ambiguity problem.

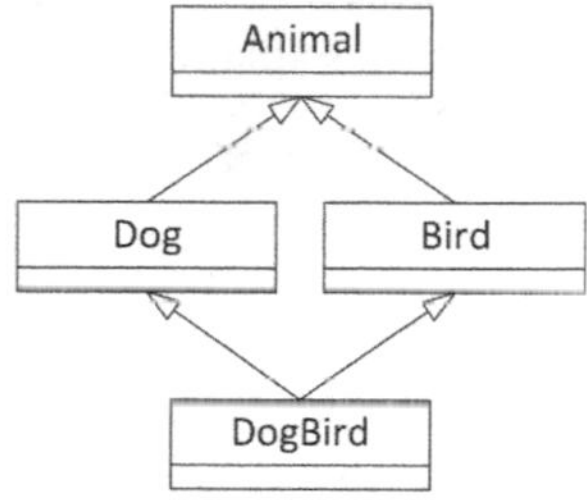

FIGURE 10.12

C++ has another mechanism, called *virtual base classes*, for addressing this problem if you do want the shared parent to have its own functionality. If the shared parent is marked as a virtual base class, there will not be any ambiguity. The following code adds a `sleep()` member function, including an implementation, to the `Animal` base class, and modifies the `Dog` and `Bird` classes to inherit from `Animal` as a virtual base class. Without using a virtual base class, a call to `sleep()` on a `DogBird` object would be ambiguous and would generate a compiler error because `DogBird` would have two subobjects of class `Animal`, one coming from `Dog` and one coming from `Bird`. However, when `Animal` is inherited virtually, `DogBird` has only one subobject of class `Animal`, so there will be no ambiguity with calling `sleep()`.

```
class Animal
{
    public:
        virtual void eat() = 0;
        virtual void sleep() { println("zzzzz...."); }
};

class Dog : public virtual Animal
{
    public:
        virtual void bark() { println("Woof!"); }
        void eat() override { println("The dog ate."); }
};

class Bird : public virtual Animal
{
```

```
    public:
        virtual void chirp() { println("Chirp!"); }
        void eat() override { println("The bird ate."); }
};

class DogBird : public Dog, public Bird
{
    public:
        void eat() override { Dog::eat(); }
};

int main()
{
    DogBird myConfusedAnimal;
    myConfusedAnimal.sleep();  // Not ambiguous because of virtual base class.
}
```

Be careful with constructors in such class hierarchies. For example, the following code adds some data members to the different classes, adds constructors to initialize those data members, and, for reasons explained after the code snippet, adds a `protected` default constructor to `Animal`.

```
class Animal
{
    public:
        explicit Animal(double weight) : m_weight { weight } {}
        virtual double getWeight() const { return m_weight; }
    protected:
        Animal() = default;
    private:
        double m_weight { 0.0 };
};

class Dog : public virtual Animal
{
    public:
        explicit Dog(double weight, string name)
            : Animal { weight }, m_name { move(name) } {}
    private:
        string m_name;
};

class Bird : public virtual Animal
{
    public:
        explicit Bird(double weight, bool canFly)
            : Animal { weight }, m_canFly { canFly } {}
    private:
        bool m_canFly { false };
};

class DogBird : public Dog, public Bird
{
    public:
        explicit DogBird(double weight, string name, bool canFly)
            : Dog { weight, move(name) }, Bird { weight, canFly } {}
};
```

```
int main()
{
    DogBird dogBird { 22.33, "Bella", true };
    println("Weight: {}", dogBird.getWeight());
}
```

When you run this code, the output is unexpected:

```
Weight: 0
```

It seems that the given weight of 22.33 when constructing the `DogBird` in `main()` is lost. Why? This code is using a virtual `Animal` base class; hence, a `DogBird` instance has only one `Animal` subobject. The `DogBird` constructor calls the constructors of both `Dog` and `Bird`, which both forward to their `Animal` base class constructor. This would mean that `Animal` is constructed twice. This is not allowed. In such cases, the compiler disables the call to the `Animal` constructor in the `Dog` and `Bird` constructors when it's being called from a derived class's constructor and, instead, calls a default constructor of the `Animal` base class, thus the need for the `protected` default constructor in `Animal`. All this means that the most derived class itself is responsible for calling a constructor of the shared base class. A correct implementation is as follows:

```
class Animal { /* Same as before. */ };

class Dog : public virtual Animal
{
    public:
        explicit Dog(double weight, string name)
            : Animal { weight }, m_name { move(name) } {}
    protected:
        explicit Dog(string name) : m_name { move(name) } {}
    private:
        string m_name;
};

class Bird : public virtual Animal
{
    public:
        explicit Bird(double weight, bool canFly)
            : Animal { weight }, m_canFly { canFly } {}
    protected:
        explicit Bird(bool canFly) : m_canFly { canFly } {}
    private:
        bool m_canFly { false };
};

class DogBird : public Dog, public Bird
{
    public:
        explicit DogBird(double weight, string name, bool canFly)
            : Animal { weight }, Dog { move(name) }, Bird { canFly } {}
};
```

In this implementation, `protected` single-argument constructors are added to `Dog` and `Bird`. They are `protected` as they should be used only by derived classes. Client code is allowed to construct `Dog`s and `Bird`s only using the two-argument constructors.

After these changes, the output is correct:

```
Weight: 22.33
```

> **NOTE** *Virtual base classes are a great way to avoid ambiguity in class hierarchies. The only drawback is that many C++ programmers are unfamiliar with the concept.*

CASTS

The basic types in C++ are reviewed in Chapter 1, while Chapters 8 through 10 show how to write your own types with classes. This section explores some of the trickier aspects of casting one type to another type.

C++ provides five specific casts: `const_cast()`, `static_cast()`, `reinterpret_cast()`, `dynamic_cast()`, and `std::bit_cast()`. The first one is discussed in Chapter 1. Chapter 1 also introduces `static_cast()` for casting between certain primitive types, but there is more to say about it in the context of inheritance. Now that you are fluent in writing your own classes and understand class inheritance, it's time to take a closer look at these casts.

Note that the old C-style casts such as `(int)myFloat` still work in C++ and are still used extensively in existing code bases. C-style casts cover all C++ casts except `bit_cast()` and thus are more error-prone because it's not always obvious what you are trying to achieve, and you might end up with unexpected results. I strongly recommend you only use the C++ style casts in new code because they are safer and stand out better syntactically and visually in your code.

static_cast()

You can use `static_cast()` to perform explicit conversions that are supported directly by the language. For example, if you write an arithmetic expression in which you need to convert an `int` to a `double` to avoid integer division, use a `static_cast()`. In this example, it's enough to only use `static_cast()` with `i`, because that makes one of the two operands a `double`, making sure C++ performs floating-point division.

```
int i { 3 };
int j { 4 };
double result { static_cast<double>(i) / j };
```

You can also use `static_cast()` to perform explicit conversions that are allowed because of user-defined constructors or conversion routines. For example, if class `A` has a constructor that takes an object of class `B`, you can convert a `B` object to an `A` object using a `static_cast()`. In most situations where you want this behavior, however, the compiler performs the conversion automatically.

Another use for `static_cast()` is to perform downcasts in an inheritance hierarchy, as in this example:

```
class Base
{
```

```
    public:
        virtual ~Base() = default;
};

class Derived : public Base
{
    public:
        virtual ~Derived() = default;
};

int main()
{
    Base* b { nullptr };
    Derived* d { new Derived {} };
    b = d; // Don't need a cast to go up the inheritance hierarchy.
    d = static_cast<Derived*>(b); // Need a cast to go down the hierarchy.

    Base base;
    Derived derived;
    Base& br { derived };
    Derived& dr { static_cast<Derived&>(br) };
}
```

These casts work with both pointers and references. They do not work with objects themselves.

Note that casts using `static_cast()` do not perform run-time type checking. They allow you to convert any `Base` pointer to a `Derived` pointer, or `Base` reference to a `Derived` reference, even if the `Base` really isn't a `Derived` at run time. For example, the following code compiles and executes, but using the pointer `d` can result in potentially catastrophic failure, including memory overwrites outside the bounds of the object.

```
Base* b { new Base {} };
Derived* d { static_cast<Derived*>(b) };
```

To perform such casts safely with run-time type checking, use `dynamic_cast()`, which is explained a bit later in this chapter.

`static_cast()` is not all-powerful. You can't `static_cast()` pointers of one type to pointers of another unrelated type. You can't directly `static_cast()` objects of one type to objects of another type if there is no converting constructor available. You can't `static_cast()` a `const` type to a non-`const` type. You can't `static_cast()` pointers to `int`s. Basically, you can only do things that make sense according to the type rules of C++.

reinterpret_cast()

`reinterpret_cast()` is a bit more powerful, and concomitantly less safe, than `static_cast()`. You can use it to perform some casts that are not technically allowed by the C++ type rules but that might make sense to the programmer in some circumstances. For example, you can use `reinterpret_cast()` to cast a reference to one type to a reference to another type, even if the types are unrelated. Similarly, you can use it to cast a pointer type to any other pointer type, even if they are unrelated by an inheritance hierarchy. However, casting a pointer to a `void*` can be done implicitly, without an explicit cast. To cast a `void*` back to a correctly typed pointer, a `static_cast()` is enough. A `void*` pointer is just a pointer to some location in memory. No type information is associated with a `void*` pointer. Here are some examples:

```
class X {};
class Y {};

int main()
{
    X x;
    Y y;
    X* xp { &x };
    Y* yp { &y };
    // Need reinterpret_cast for pointer conversion from unrelated classes
    // static_cast doesn't work.
    xp = reinterpret_cast<X*>(yp);
    // No cast required for conversion from pointer to void*
    void* p { xp };
    // static_cast is enough for pointer conversion from void*
    xp = static_cast<X*>(p);
    // Need reinterpret_cast for reference conversion from unrelated classes
    // static_cast doesn't work.
    X& xr { x };
    Y& yr { reinterpret_cast<Y&>(x) };
}
```

`reinterpret_cast()` is not all-powerful; it comes with quite a few restrictions on what can be cast to what. These restrictions are not further discussed in this text, as I recommend that you use these kinds of casts judiciously.

In general, you should be careful with `reinterpret_cast()` because it allows you to do conversions without performing any type checking.

> **WARNING** *You can also use* `reinterpret_cast()` *to cast pointers to integral types and back. However, you can only cast a pointer to an integral type that is large enough to hold it. For example, trying to use* `reinterpret_cast()` *to cast a 64-bit pointer to a 32-bit integer results in a compilation error.*

dynamic_cast()

`dynamic_cast()` provides a run-time check on casts within an inheritance hierarchy. You can use it to cast pointers or references. `dynamic_cast()` checks the run-time type information of the underlying object at run time. If the cast doesn't make sense, `dynamic_cast()` returns a null pointer (for the pointer version) or throws an `std::bad_cast` exception (for the reference version).

For example, suppose you have the following class hierarchy:

```
class Base
{
    public:
        virtual ~Base() = default;
```

```
};

class Derived : public Base
{
    public:
        virtual ~Derived() = default;
};
```

The following example shows a correct use of `dynamic_cast()`:

```
Base* b;
Derived* d { new Derived {} };
b = d;
d = dynamic_cast<Derived*>(b);
```

The following `dynamic_cast()` on a reference will cause an exception to be thrown:

```
Base base;
Derived derived;
Base& br { base };
try {
    Derived& dr { dynamic_cast<Derived&>(br) };
} catch (const bad_cast&) {
    println("Bad cast!");
}
```

Note that you can perform the same casts down the inheritance hierarchy with a `static_cast()` or `reinterpret_cast()`. The difference with `dynamic_cast()` is that it performs run-time (dynamic) type checking, while `static_cast()` and `reinterpret_cast()` perform the cast even if they are erroneous.

Remember, the run-time type information is stored in the vtable of an object. Therefore, to use `dynamic_cast()`, your classes must have at least one `virtual` member function. If your classes don't have a vtable, trying to use `dynamic_cast()` will result in a compilation error. Microsoft Visual C++, for example, gives the following error:

```
error C2683: 'dynamic_cast' : 'Base' is not a polymorphic type.
```

std::bit_cast()

`std::bit_cast()` is defined in `<bit>`. It's the only cast that's part of the Standard Library; the other casts are part of the C++ language itself. `bit_cast()` resembles `reinterpret_cast()`, but it creates a new object of a given target type and copies the bits from a source object to this new object. It effectively interprets the bits of the source object as if they are the bits of the target object. `bit_cast()` requires that the size of the source and target objects are the same and that both are *trivially copyable*.

> **NOTE** *A trivially copyable type is a type of which the underlying bytes making up the object can be copied into an array of, for example,* `char`*. If the data of that array is then copied back into the object, the object keeps its original value.*

Here is an example:

```
float asFloat { 1.23f };
auto asUint { bit_cast<unsigned int>(asFloat) };
if (bit_cast<float>(asUint) == asFloat) { println("Roundtrip success."); }
```

A use case for `bit_cast()` is with binary I/O of trivially copyable types. For example, you can write the individual bytes of such types to a file. When you read the file back into memory, you can use `bit_cast()` to correctly interpret the bytes read from the file.

Summary of Casts

The following table summarizes the casts you should use for different situations.

SITUATION	CAST
Remove `const`-ness	`const_cast()`
Explicit cast supported by the language (for example, `int` to `double`, `int` to `bool`)	`static_cast()`
Explicit cast supported by user-defined constructors or conversions	`static_cast()`
Object of one class to object of another (unrelated) class	`bit_cast()`
Pointer-to-object of one class to pointer-to-object of another class in the same inheritance hierarchy	`dynamic_cast()` recommended, or `static_cast()`
Reference-to-object of one class to reference-to-object of another class in the same inheritance hierarchy	`dynamic_cast()` recommended, or `static_cast()`
Pointer-to-type to unrelated pointer-to-type	`reinterpret_cast()`
Reference-to-type to unrelated reference-to-type	`reinterpret_cast()`
Pointer-to-function to pointer-to-function	`reinterpret_cast()`

SUMMARY

This chapter covered numerous details about inheritance. You learned about its many applications, including code reuse and polymorphism. You also learned about its many abuses, including poorly designed multiple-inheritance schemes. Along the way, you uncovered some cases that require special attention.

Inheritance is a powerful language feature that takes some time to get used to. After you have worked with the examples in this chapter and experimented on your own, I hope that inheritance will become your tool of choice for object-oriented design.

EXERCISES

By solving the following exercises, you can practice the material discussed in this chapter. Solutions to all exercises are available with the code download on the book's website at `www.wiley.com/go/proc++6e`. However, if you are stuck on an exercise, first reread parts of this chapter to try to find an answer yourself before looking at the solution from the website.

Exercise 10-1: Take the `Person` class from Exercise 9-2 and add a derived class called `Employee`. You can omit the overload of `operator<=>` from Exercise 9-2. The `Employee` class adds one data member, an employee ID. Provide an appropriate constructor. From `Employee`, derive two more classes called `Manager` and `Director`.

Put all your classes, including the `Person` class, in a namespace called `HR`. Note that you can export everything in a namespace from a module as follows:

```
export namespace HR { /* ... */ }
```

Exercise 10-2: Continuing with your solution from Exercise 10-1, add a `toString()` member function to the `Person` class returning a string representation of a person. Override this member function in the `Employee`, `Manager`, and `Director` classes to build up a complete string representation by delegating part of their work to parent classes.

Exercise 10-3: Practice polymorphic behavior of the classes in your `Person` hierarchy from Exercise 10-2. Define a `vector` to store a mix of persons, employees, managers, and directors, and fill it with some test data. Finally, use a single range-based `for` loop to call `toString()` on all of the elements in the `vector`.

Exercise 10-4: In real companies, employees can get promoted to manager or director positions, and managers can get promoted to director. Do you see a way you can add support for this to your class hierarchy of Exercise 10-3?

11

Modules, Header Files, and Miscellaneous Topics

WHAT'S IN THIS CHAPTER?

- What modules are and how to author and consume them
- Details of preprocessor directives
- What preprocessor macros are and why they are dangerous
- What linkage is and how it affects accessibility of named entities
- The meaning of the one definition rule, ODR
- Details of header files
- What feature-test macros for core language features are
- The different uses of the `static` keyword
- C-style variable-length argument lists

WILEY.COM DOWNLOADS FOR THIS CHAPTER

Please note that all the code examples for this chapter are available as part of this chapter's code download on the book's website at `www.wiley.com/go/proc++6e` on the Download Code tab.

This chapter starts with a detailed discussion on how modules allow you to write reusable components and contrasts this against old-style header files. It also explains what preprocessor directives are and gives some examples of why C-style preprocessor macros are dangerous. The chapter then explains the concept of linkage, which specifies where named entities can be accessed from, and explains the one definition rule. The final part of the chapter discusses the different uses of the `static` and `extern` keywords, as well as C-style variable-length argument lists.

MODULES

Modules are introduced in Chapter 1, "A Crash Course in C++ and the Standard Library," and you have already authored and consumed your own simple modules in previous chapters. However, there are quite a few more things to say about modules. Before the introduction of modules in C++20, header files, discussed later in this chapter, were used to provide the interface to a reusable piece of code. Header files do have a number of problems, though, such as avoiding multiple includes of the same header file and making sure header files are included in the correct order. Additionally, simply #include'ing, for example, <iostream> adds tens of thousands of lines of code that the compiler has to crunch through. If several source files #include <iostream>, all of those translation units grow much bigger. And that is with an include of just a single header file. Imagine if you need <iostream>, <vector>, <format>, and more.

Modules solve all these issues, and more. The order in which modules are imported is not important. Modules are compiled once to a binary format, which the compiler can then use whenever a module is imported in another source file. This is in stark contrast with header files, which the compiler has to compile over and over again, every time it encounters an #include of that header file. Hence, modules can drastically improve compilation times. Incremental compilation times also improve, as certain modifications in modules, for example, modifying an exported function's implementation in a module interface file, do not trigger recompilation of users of that module (discussed in more details later in this chapter). Modules are not influenced by any externally defined macros, and any macros defined inside a module are never visible to any code outside the module, that is, modules are self-isolating. Hence, the following recommendation:

> **NOTE** *With all the discussed benefits, if your compiler supports modules, newly written code should use modules to structure code into building blocks that are logically separated.*

If possible, legacy code can slowly be transitioned to modules as well. However, there is a lot of legacy code in the world, and a lot of third-party libraries don't embrace modules yet, as not all compilers fully support modules at the time of this writing. For these reasons it is still important to know how legacy header files work. That's why this chapter still includes discussions on header files.

> **NOTE** *How to compile modules is compiler dependent. Consult your compiler's documentation to learn how to work with modules with your specific compiler.*

> **NOTE** *As mentioned, at the time of this writing, not all compilers fully support modules yet, though all major compilers do, at least partially. This book uses modules everywhere. If your compiler does not yet fully support modules, you can convert the modularized code to non-modularized code, as explained next.*

Unmodularizing Code

If you want to compile code samples from this book with a compiler that does not yet fully support modules, you can unmodularize the code as follows:

- Rename `.cppm` module interface files to `.h` header files.
- Add a `#pragma once` at the top of each `.h` header file.
- Remove `export module xyz` declarations.
- Replace `module xyz` declarations with an `#include` to include the corresponding header file.
- Replace `import` and `export import` declarations with proper `#include` directives. If the code is using `import std;`, then those need to be replaced with `#include` directives to include all necessary individual header files. See Appendix C, "Standard Library Header Files," for a list of all Standard Library headers and a brief description of their contents.
- Remove any `export` keywords.
- Remove all occurrences of `module;`, which denotes the start of a global module fragment.
- If a function definition or variable definition appears in a `.h` header file, add the `inline` key word in front of it.

Standard Named Modules

As Chapter 1 explains, you get access to everything from the C++ Standard Library by importing the *standard named module* `std`. This named module makes the entire Standard Library available to you, including all C functionality, defined in such headers as `<cstddef>`. However, all C functionality is made available only through the `std` namespace. For legacy code, you can consider importing the `std.compat` named module instead, which imports everything `std` imports but makes all C functionality available both in the `std` namespace and the global namespace. The use of `std.compat` is not recommended in new code.

Module Interface Files

A *module interface file* defines the interface for the functionality provided by a module and usually has `.cppm` as a file extension. A module interface file starts with a declaration stating that the file is defining a module with a certain name. This is called the *module declaration*. A module's name can be any valid C++ identifier. The name can include dots but cannot start or end with a dot and cannot contain multiple dots in a row. Examples of valid names are `datamodel`, `mycompany.datamodel`, `mycompany.datamodel.core`, `datamodel_core`, and so on.

> **NOTE** *Currently, there is no standardized extension for module interface files. However, most compilers support the* `.cppm` *(C++ module) extension, so that's what this book uses. Check the documentation of your compiler to learn which extension to use.*

A module needs to explicitly state what to export, i.e., what should be visible when client code imports the module. A module can export any declaration, such as variable declarations, function declarations, type declarations, `using` directives, and `using` declarations. Additionally, `import` declarations can be exported as well. Exporting entities from a module is done with the `export` keyword. Anything that is not exported from a module is visible only from within the module itself. The collection of all exported entities is called the *module interface*.

Here is an example of a module interface file called `Person.cppm`, defining a `person` module and exporting a `Person` class. Note that it imports the functionality provided by `std`.

```
export module person;  // Named module declaration

import std;            // Import declaration

export class Person    // Export declaration
{
    public:
        Person(std::string firstName, std::string lastName)
            : m_firstName { std::move(firstName) }
            , m_lastName { std::move(lastName) } { }
        const std::string& getFirstName() const { return m_firstName; }
        const std::string& getLastName() const { return m_lastName; }
    private:
        std::string m_firstName;
        std::string m_lastName;
};
```

In standardese terms, everything starting from a named module declaration (the first line in the previous code snippet) until the end of the file is called the *module purview*.

This `Person` class can be made available for use by importing the `person` module as follows (`test.cpp`):

```
import person;     // Import declaration for person module
import std;

using namespace std;

int main()
{
    Person person { "Kole", "Webb" };
    println("{}, {}", person.getLastName(), person.getFirstName());
}
```

Pretty much anything can be exported from a module, as long as it has a name. Examples are class definitions, function prototypes, class enumeration types, `using` declarations and directives, namespaces, and so on. If a namespace is explicitly exported with the `export` keyword, everything inside that namespace is automatically exported as well. For example, the following code snippet exports the entire `DataModel` namespace; hence, there is no need to explicitly export the individual classes and type alias:

```
export module datamodel;
import std;
export namespace DataModel
{
```

```
    class Person { /* ... */ };
    class Address { /* ... */ };
    using Persons = std::vector<Person>;
}
```

You can also export a whole block of declarations using an *export block*. Here's an example:

```
export
{
    namespace DataModel
    {
        class Person { /* ... */ };
        class Address { /* ... */ };
        using Persons = std::vector<Person>;
    }
}
```

Module Implementation Files

A module can be split into a module interface file and one or more *module implementation files*. Module implementation files usually have .cpp as their extension. You are free to decide which implementations you move to module implementation files and which implementations you leave in the module interface file. One option is to move all function and member function implementations to a module implementation file and leave only the function prototypes, class definitions, and so on in the module interface file. Another option is to leave the implementation of small functions and member functions in the interface file, while moving the implementations of other functions and member functions to an implementation file. You have a lot of flexibility here.

A module implementation file again contains a named module declaration to specify for which module the implementations are for, but without the `export` keyword. For example, the previous `person` module can be split into an interface and an implementation file as follows. Here is the module interface file:

```
export module person;  // Module declaration

import std;

export class Person
{
    public:
        Person(std::string firstName, std::string lastName);
        const std::string& getFirstName() const;
        const std::string& getLastName() const;
    private:
        std::string m_firstName;
        std::string m_lastName;
};
```

The implementations now go in a `Person.cpp` module implementation file:

```
module person;  // Module declaration, but without the export keyword

using namespace std;
```

```
Person::Person(string firstName, string lastName)
    : m_firstName { move(firstName) }, m_lastName { move(lastName) }
{
}

const string& Person::getFirstName() const { return m_firstName; }
const string& Person::getLastName() const { return m_lastName; }
```

Note that the implementation file does not have an import declaration for the `person` module. The `module person` declaration implicitly includes an `import person` declaration. Also note that the implementation file does not have any import declaration for `std`, even though it's using `std::string` in the implementation of the member functions. Thanks to the implicit `import person`, and because this implementation file is part of the same `person` module, it implicitly inherits the `std` import declaration from the module interface file. In contrast, adding an `import person` declaration to the `test.cpp` file does not implicitly inherit the `std` import declaration because `test.cpp` is not part of the `person` module. There is more to be said about this, which is the topic of the "Visibility vs. Reachability" section later in this chapter.

> **NOTE** *All* `import` *declarations in module interface and module implementation files must be at the top of the file, after the named module declaration, but before any other declarations.*

> **WARNING** *Module implementation files cannot export anything; only module interface files can.*

Splitting Interface from Implementation

When using header files, discussed later in this chapter, instead of modules, it is strongly recommended to put only declarations in your header file (`.h`) and move all implementations to a source file (`.cpp`). One of the reasons is to improve compilation times. If you were to put your implementations in the header file, any change, even just changing a comment, would require you to recompile all other source files that include that header. For certain header files, this could ripple through the entire code base, causing a full recompile of the program. By putting your implementations in a source file instead, making changes to those implementations without touching the header file means that only that single source file needs to be recompiled.

Modules work differently. A *module interface* consists only of class definitions, function prototypes, and so on, but does not include any function or member function implementations, even if those implementations are directly in the module interface file. This means that changing a function or member function implementation that is inside a module interface file does not require a recompilation of users of that module, as long as you do not touch the interface part, for example, the function header (= function name, parameter list, and return type). Two exceptions are functions marked with the `inline` keyword, and template definitions. For both of these, the compiler needs to know their complete implementations at the time client code using them is compiled. Hence, any change to inline functions or template definitions can trigger recompilation of client code.

> **NOTE** *When class definitions in header files contain member function implementations, those member functions are implicitly inline, even without marking them with the* `inline` *keyword. This is not true for member function implementations in class definitions in module interface files. If these need to be inline, they need to be explicitly marked as such.*

Even though technically, it is not required anymore to split the interface from the implementation, in some cases I still recommend doing so. The main goal should be to have clean and easy-to-read interfaces. Implementations of functions can stay in the interface, as long as they don't obscure the interface and make it harder for users to quickly grasp what the public interface provides. For example, if a module has a rather big public interface, it might be better not to obscure that interface with implementations, so the user can have a better overview of what's being offered. Still, small getter and setter functions can stay in the interface, as they don't really impact the readability of the interface.

Separating the interface from the implementation can be done in several ways. One option is to split a module into interface and implementation files, as discussed in the previous section. Another option is to separate the interface and the implementations within a single module interface file. For example, here is the `Person` class defined in a single module interface file (`person.cppm`), but with the implementations split from the interface:

```
export module person;
import std;
// Class definition
export class Person
{
    public:
        Person(std::string firstName, std::string lastName);
        const std::string& getFirstName() const;
        const std::string& getLastName() const;
    private:
        std::string m_firstName;
        std::string m_lastName;
};
// Implementations
Person::Person(std::string firstName, std::string lastName)
    : m_firstName { std::move(firstName) }, m_lastName { std::move(lastName) } { }
const std::string& Person::getFirstName() const { return m_firstName; }
const std::string& Person::getLastName() const { return m_lastName; }
```

Visibility vs. Reachability

As mentioned earlier, when you import the `person` module in another source file that is not part of the `person` module, for example in a `test.cpp` file, then you are not implicitly inheriting the `std` import declaration from the person module interface file. Without an explicit import for std in test.cpp, the std::string name, for example, is not *visible*, meaning the following highlighted line of code does not compile:

```
import person;
int main()
{
    std::string str;
}
```

Still, even without adding an explicit import for std to test.cpp, the following lines of code work just fine:

```
Person person { "Kole", "Webb" };
const auto& lastName { person.getLastName() };
auto length { lastName.length() };
```

Why is this working? There is a difference between *visibility* and *reachability* of entities in C++. By importing the person module, the functionality from std becomes *reachable* but not *visible*. Member functions of reachable classes automatically become visible. All this means that you can use certain functionality from std, such as storing the result of getLastName() in a variable by using auto type deduction and calling member functions on it such as length().

To make the std::string name properly visible in test.cpp, an explicit import of std or <string> is required.

Submodules

The C++ standard does not speak about *submodules* as such; however, it is allowed to use dots in a module's name, and that makes it possible to structure your modules in any hierarchy you want. For example, earlier, the following example of a DataModel namespace was given:

```
export module datamodel;
import std;
export namespace DataModel
{
    class Person { /* ... */ };
    class Address { /* ... */ };
    using Persons = std::vector<Person>;
}
```

Both the Person and Address classes are inside the DataModel namespace and in the datamodel module. This can be restructured by defining two submodules: datamodel.person and datamodel .address. The module interface file for the datamodel.person submodule is as follows:

```
export module datamodel.person;   // datamodel.person submodule
export namespace DataModel { class Person { /* ... */ }; }
```

Here is the module interface file for datamodel.address:

```
export module datamodel.address;   // datamodel.address submodule
export namespace DataModel { class Address { /* ... */ }; }
```

Finally, a `datamodel` module is defined as follows. It imports and immediately exports both submodules.

```
export module datamodel;            // datamodel module
export import datamodel.person;     // Import and export person submodule
export import datamodel.address;    // Import and export address submodule
import std;
export namespace DataModel { using Persons = std::vector<Person>; }
```

Of course, the member function implementations of classes in submodules can also go into module implementation files. For example, suppose the `Address` class has a default constructor that just prints a statement to standard output. That implementation could be in a file called `datamodel.address.cpp`:

```
module datamodel.address;  // datamodel.address submodule
import std;
using namespace std;
DataModel::Address::Address() { println("Address::Address()"); }
```

A benefit of structuring your code with submodules is that clients can import either everything at once or only specific parts they want to use. For example, if client code needs access to everything in the `datamodel` module, then the following import declaration is the easiest:

```
import datamodel;
```

On the other hand, if client code is only interested in using the `Address` class, then the following import declaration suffices:

```
import datamodel.address;
```

Importing everything at once is more convenient than selectively importing what you need, especially for stable modules that rarely change. However, by using selective imports for less stable modules, it might be possible to improve build times if changes are made to the module. For example, if a change is made to the interface of the `datamodel.address` submodule, then only those files that import that submodule need to be recompiled.

Module Partitions

Another option to structure modules is to split them into separate *partitions*. The difference between submodules and partitions is that the submodule structuring is visible to users of the module, allowing users to selectively import only those submodules they want to use. Partitions, on the other hand, are used to structure a module internally. Partitions are not exposed to users of the module. All partitions declared in *module interface partition files* must ultimately be exported by the *primary module interface file*, either directly or indirectly. A module always has only one such primary module interface file, and that's the interface file containing the `export module` *`name`* declaration.

A module partition is created by separating the name of the module and the name of the partition with a colon. The name of a partition can be any legal identifier. For example, the `DataModel` module from the previous section can be restructured using partitions instead of submodules. Here is the `person` partition in a `datamodel.person.cppm` module interface partition file:

```
export module datamodel:person;  // datamodel:person partition
export namespace DataModel { class Person { /* ... */ }; }
```

Here is the address partition, including a default constructor:

```
export module datamodel:address; // datamodel:address partition
export namespace DataModel
{
    class Address
    {
    public:
        Address();
        /* ... */
    };
}
```

Unfortunately, there is a caveat when using implementation files in combination with partitions: there can be only one file with a certain partition name. So, having an implementation file that starts with the following declaration is ill-formed:

```
module datamodel:address;
```

Instead, you can just put the address partition implementations in an implementation file for the datamodel module as follows:

```
module datamodel;  // Not datamodel:address!
import std;
using namespace std;
DataModel::Address::Address() { println("Address::Address()"); }
```

> **WARNING** *Multiple files cannot have the same partition name. Having multiple module interface partition files with the same partition name is illegal, and implementations for declarations in a module interface partition file cannot go in an implementation file with the same partition name. Instead, just put those implementations in a module implementation file for the module instead.*

An important point to remember when authoring modules structured in partitions is that each module interface partition must ultimately be exported by the primary module interface file, either directly or indirectly. To import a partition, you just specify the name of the partition prefixed with a colon, for example `import :person`. It's illegal to say something like `import datamodel:person`. Remember, partitions are not exposed to users of a module; partitions only structure a module internally. Hence, users cannot import a specific partition; they must import the entire module. Partitions can be imported only within the module itself, so it's redundant (and illegal) to specify the name of the module before the colon. Here is the primary module interface file for the datamodel module:

```
export module datamodel; // datamodel module (primary module interface file)
export import :person;   // Import and export person partition
export import :address;  // Import and export address partition
import std;
export namespace DataModel { using Persons = std::vector<Person>; }
```

This partition-structured datamodel module can be used as follows:

```
import datamodel;
int main() { DataModel::Address a; }
```

> **NOTE** *Partitions are used to structure modules internally and are not visible outside of a module. Thus, users of a module cannot import specific partitions; they must import the entire module. You can use submodules instead of partitions if you want to allow users to selectively import parts of a module.*

Earlier it is explained that a `module name` declaration implicitly includes an `import name` declaration. This is not the case for partitions.

For example, the `datamodel:person` partition does not have an implicit `import datamodel` declaration. In this example, it's even not allowed to add an explicit `import datamodel` to the `datamodel:person` interface partition file. Doing so would result in a circular dependency: the `datamodel` interface file contains an `import :person` declaration, while the `datamodel:person` interface partition file would contain an `import datamodel` declaration.

To break such circular dependencies, you can move the functionality that the `datamodel:person` partition needs from the `datamodel` interface file to another partition, which subsequently can be imported by both the `datamodel:person` interface partition file and the `datamodel` interface file.

Implementation Partitions

A partition does not need to be declared in a module interface partition file, it can also be declared in a *module implementation partition file*, a normal source code file with extension `.cpp`, in which case it's an *implementation partition*, sometimes called an *internal partition*. Such partitions cannot be exported, compared to module interface partitions, which must be exported by the primary module interface file.

For example, suppose you have the following `math` primary module interface file (`math.cppm`):

```
export module math; // math module declaration
export namespace Math
{
    double superLog(double z, double b);
    double lerchZeta(double lambda, double alpha, double s);
}
```

Suppose further that the implementations of the math functions require some helper functions that must not be exported by the module. An implementation partition is the perfect place to put such helper functions. The following defines such an implementation partition in a file called `math_helpers.cpp`:

```
module math:details;  // math:details implementation partition
double someHelperFunction(double a) { return /* ... */ ; }
```

Other `math` module implementation files can get access to these helper functions by importing this implementation partition. For example, a `math` module implementation file (`math.cpp`) could look like this:

```
module math;
import :details;
```

```
double Math::superLog(double z, double b) { return /* ... */; }
double Math::lerchZeta(double lambda, double alpha, double s) { return /* ... */; }
```

With the `import :details;` declaration, the `superLog()` and `lerchZeta()` functions can call `someHelperFunction()`.

Of course, using such implementation partitions with helper functions makes sense only if multiple other source files use those helper functions.

Private Module Fragment

The primary module interface can include a *private module fragment*. This private module fragment starts with the following line:

```
module :private;
```

Everything after this line is part of the private module fragment. Anything that is defined in this private module fragment is not exported and thus not visible to consumers of the module.

Chapter 9, "Mastering Classes and Objects," demonstrates the pimpl idiom, also known as the private implementation idiom. It hides all implementation details from consumers of a class. The solution in Chapter 9 requires two files: a primary module interface file and a module implementation file. Using a private module fragment, you can achieve this separation using a single file. Here is a concise example:

```
export module adder;
import std;
export class Adder
{
    public:
        Adder();
        virtual ~Adder();
        int add(int a, int b) const;
    private:
        class Impl;
        std::unique_ptr<Impl> m_impl;
};

module :private;

class Adder::Impl
{
    public:
        ~Impl() { std::println("Destructor of Adder::Impl"); }
        int add(int a, int b) const { return a + b;}
};

Adder::Adder() : m_impl { std::make_unique<Impl>() } { }
Adder::~Adder() {}
int Adder::add(int a, int b) const { return m_impl->add(a, b); }
```

This class can be tested as follows:

```
Adder adder;
println("Value: {}", adder.add(20, 22));
```

Now, to prove that everything in the private module fragment is truly hidden, let's add a public member function getImplementation() at the end of the Adder class:

```
export class Adder
{
    /* ... as before, omitted for brevity ... */
    private:
        class Impl;
        std::unique_ptr<Impl> m_impl;
    public:
        Impl* getImplementation() { return m_impl.get(); }
};
```

The following compiles and works fine:

```
Adder adder;
auto impl { adder.getImplementation() };
```

From the point of view of consumers of the Adder module, getImplementation() returns a pointer to an incomplete type. The code snippet is storing that pointer in a variable called impl. Simply storing a pointer to an incomplete type is fine, as long as you use auto type deduction. However, you cannot do anything with that pointer. Calling add() on that incomplete pointer results in an error:

```
auto result { impl->add(20, 22) };  // Error!
```

The error is something like: use of undefined type Adder::Impl. The reason is that the Adder::Impl class is part of the private module fragment and hence not accessible from consumers of the Adder module.

If you remove the module :private; line from the module interface file, then the previous code snippet compiles and runs fine. You might be surprised at first sight by this; after all, the Adder::Impl class is not explicitly exported. That's correct—it's not explicitly exported, but it is implicitly exported because the Adder class is exported and the Impl class is declared within the Adder class.

Header Units

When importing a module, you use an import declaration such as the following:

```
import person;
```

If you have legacy code, such as a person.h header file defining a Person class, then you can modularize it by converting it to a proper module, person.cppm, and use import declarations to make it available to client code. However, sometimes you cannot modularize such headers. Maybe your Person class should remain usable by compilers that do not yet have support for modules. Or maybe the person.h header is part of a third-party library that you cannot modify. In such cases, you can import your header file directly, as follows:

```
import "person.h";
```

With such a declaration, everything in the person.h header file becomes implicitly exported. Additionally, macros defined in the header become visible to client code, which is not the case for real modules, neither for your own modules nor for the named std and std.compat modules.

Such an import declaration can include relative or absolute paths to header files, and you can use `< >` instead of `""` to search in the system include directories:

```
import "include/person.h"; // Can include a relative or absolute path.
import <person.h>;         // Search in system include directories.
```

Compared to using `#include` to add a header file, using `import` will improve build throughput, as the `person.h` header will implicitly be converted to a module and hence be compiled only once, instead of every time when the header is included in a source file. As such, it can be used as a standardized way to support *precompiled header files*, instead of using compiler-dependent precompiled header file support.

For each import declaration naming a header file, the compiler creates a module with an exported interface similar to what the header file defines, i.e., it implicitly exports everything from the header file. This is called a *header unit*. The procedure for this is compiler dependent, so check the documentation of your compiler to learn how to work with header units.

> **NOTE** *By importing a header unit, the preprocessor definitions from that header unit become available to you. However, if you* `export import` *a header unit, its preprocessor definitions are not exported further. Any code that needs access to those preprocessor definitions needs to explicitly* `import` *the header unit.*

Importable Standard Library Headers

All C++ headers, such as `<iostream>`, `<vector>`, `<string>`, and so on, are *importable headers* that can be imported with an import declaration. That means you can, for example, write the following:

```
import <vector>;
```

Of course, starting with C++23, it's more convenient to simply import the named module called `std`, instead of manually importing those importable headers that you need. For example, the following makes everything in the Standard Library available for your use:

```
import std;
```

As you know by now, importable C++ Standard Library headers don't have any `.h` extension, e.g., `<vector>`, and they define everything in the `std` namespace or a subnamespace of `std`.

In C, the names of Standard Library header files end with `.h`, such as `<stdio.h>`, and namespaces are not used.

Most of the Standard Library functionality from C is available in C++ but is provided through two different headers:

- The recommended versions without the `.h` extension but with a `c` prefix, for example, `<cstdio>`. These put everything in the `std` namespace.
- The C-style versions with the `.h` extension, for example, `<stdio.h>`. These do not use namespaces. Their use is discouraged, except when you are writing code that needs to be

both valid C++ and valid C at the same time. This use case is not further discussed in this C++ book.

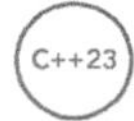

> **NOTE** *Up until C++23, the use of* `<name.h>` *C Standard Library headers was deprecated. Starting with C++23, their use is no longer deprecated, but discouraged.*

Technically, the old versions are allowed to put things in the `std` namespace as well, and the new versions are allowed to additionally put things in the global namespace. This behavior is not standardized, so you should not rely on it.

As mentioned earlier, when using `import std;` you automatically get access to C-style functions, such as the mathematical functions defined in `<cmath>`. They will be in the `std` namespace, e.g., `std::sqrt()`. If you `import std.compat;` these C-style functions will additionally be available in the global namespace, e.g., `::sqrt()`.

However, if you cannot use the `std` or `std.compat` named modules, then keep in mind that the C Standard Library headers are not guaranteed to be importable with an `import` declaration. In that case, to be safe, use `#include <cxyz>` instead of `import <cxyz>;`.

Additionally, as mentioned in the previous section, importing a proper module, e.g., `std` or `std.compat`, won't make any C-style macros defined in the module available to the importing code. This is especially important to remember when you want to use C-style macros from the C Standard Library. Luckily, there aren't many! One of them is `<cassert>`, a C Standard Library header that defines the `assert()` macro, which is explained in more detail in Chapter 31, "Conquering Debugging." Since the named `std` and `std.compat` modules won't make the `assert()` macro available to importing code, and since `<cassert>` is a C Standard Library header and thus not guaranteed to be importable, you must use `#include <cassert>` to get access to `assert()`.

> **NOTE** *If you can* `import` *a header file, it's recommended to do so. Only* `#include` *a header file if it's not importable, for instance, because the content of the header file is dependent on some preprocessor* `#defines` *(see the next section).*

If you do need to `#include` a header in a module interface or module implementation file, the `#include` directives should be placed in the *global module fragment*, which must come before any named module declaration and starts with a nameless module declaration. A global module fragment can only contain preprocessing directives such as `#includes`, `#defines`, and so on. Such a global module fragment and comments are the only things that are allowed to appear before a named module declaration. For example, if you need to use functionality from the `<cassert>` C header file, you can make that available as follows:

```
module;                 // Start of the global module fragment
#include <cassert>      // Include legacy header files

export module person;   // Named module declaration
```

```
import std;
export class Person { /* ... */ };
```

> **WARNING** *Place all* `#include` *directives in a module interface or module implementation file in the global module fragment.*

PREPROCESSOR DIRECTIVES

Chapter 1 introduces the `#include` preprocessor directive to include the contents of a header file. There are a few more preprocessor directives available. The following table shows some of the most commonly used preprocessor directives:

PREPROCESSOR DIRECTIVE	FUNCTIONALITY	COMMON USES
`#include [file]`	The contents of the file with name `[file]` is inserted into the code at the location of the directive.	Almost always used to include header files so that code can make use of functionality defined elsewhere.
`#define [id] [value]`	Every occurrence of the identifier `[id]` is replaced with `[value]`.	Often used in C to define a constant value or a macro. C++ provides better mechanisms for constants and most types of macros. Macros can be dangerous, so use them cautiously. See the next section for some examples.
`#undef [id]`	Undefines the identifier `[id]` previously defined using `#define`.	Used if a defined identifier is only required within a limited scope of the code.

`#if [expression]`
`#elif [expression]`
`#else`
`#endif`
	Conditionally include a block of code based on the result of a given expression.	Often used to provide specific code for specific platforms.

`#ifdef [id]`
`#endif`
 	
`#ifndef [id]`
`#endif`
	Conditionally include code based on whether the specified identifier has been defined with `#define`. `#ifdef [id]` is equivalent to `#if defined(id)` and `#ifndef [id]` is equivalent to `#if !defined(id)`.	Used most frequently to protect against circular includes. Each header file starts with an `#ifndef` checking the absence of an identifier, followed by a `#define` directive to define that identifier. The header file ends with an `#endif`. This prevents the file from being included multiple times; see the Header Files section later in this chapter.

PREPROCESSOR DIRECTIVE	FUNCTIONALITY	COMMON USES
 `#elifdef [id]` `#elifndef [id]`	`#elifdef [id]` is equivalent to `#elif defined(id)` and `#elifndef [id]` is equivalent to `#elif !defined(id)`.	Shorthand notations for other functionality.
`#pragma [xyz]`	Controls compiler-specific behavior. `[xyz]` is compiler dependent. Most compilers support `once` to prevent a header file from being included multiple times.	See the Header Files section later in this chapter for an example.
`#error [message]`	Causes the compilation to stop with the given message.	Can be used to stop the compilation if the user tries to compile code on an unsupported platform.
C++23 `#warning [message]`	Causes the compiler to emit the given message as a warning, but compilation continues.	Used to display a warning to the user without affecting the compilation result.

Preprocessor Macros

You can use the C++ preprocessor to write *macros*, which are like little functions. Here is an example:

```
#define SQUARE(x) ((x) * (x)) // No semicolon after the macro definition!

int main()
{
    println("{}", SQUARE(5));
}
```

Macros are a remnant from C that are quite similar to `inline` functions, except that they are not type-checked, and the preprocessor dumbly replaces any calls to them with their expansions. The preprocessor does not apply true function-call semantics. This behavior can cause unexpected results. For example, consider what would happen if you called the `SQUARE` macro with `2+3` instead of `5`, like this:

```
println("{}", SQUARE(2 + 3));
```

You expect `SQUARE` to calculate `25`, which it does. However, what if you left out some parentheses from the macro definition, so that it looks like this?

```
#define SQUARE(x) (x * x)
```

Now the call to `SQUARE(2+3)` generates `11`, not `25`! Remember that the macro is dumbly expanded without regard to function-call semantics. This means that any `x` in the macro body is replaced by `2 + 3`, leading to this expansion:

```
println("{}", (2 + 3 * 2 + 3));
```

Following proper order of operations, this line performs the multiplication first, followed by the additions, generating `11` instead of `25`!

Macros can also have a performance impact. Suppose you call the `SQUARE` macro as follows:

```
println("{}", SQUARE(veryExpensiveFunctionCallToComputeNumber()));
```

The preprocessor replaces this with the following:

```
println("{}", ((veryExpensiveFunctionCallToComputeNumber()) *
        (veryExpensiveFunctionCallToComputeNumber())));
```

Now you are calling the expensive function twice—another reason to avoid macros.

Macros also cause problems for debugging because the code you write is not the code that the compiler sees or that shows up in your debugger (because of the search-and-replace behavior of the preprocessor). For these reasons, you should avoid macros entirely in favor of inline functions. The details are shown here only because quite a bit of C++ code out there still employs macros. You need to understand them to read and maintain such code.

> **NOTE** *Most compilers can output the preprocessed source to a file or to standard output. You can use that feature to see how the preprocessor is preprocessing your file. For example, with Microsoft Visual C++ you can use the* `/P` *switch. With GCC you can use the* `-E` *switch.*

LINKAGE

This section describes the concept of *linkage* in C++. As Chapter 1 explains, C++ source files are first processed by the preprocessor, which processes all preprocessor directives, resulting in *translation units*. All translation units are then compiled independently into *object files*, which contain the machine executable code but in which references to functions and so on are not yet defined. Resolving those references is done by the final phase, the *linker*, which links all object files together into the final *executable*. Technically, there are a few more phases in the compilation process, but for this discussion, this simplified view is sufficient.

Each name in a C++ translation unit, including functions and global variables, either has linkage or has no linkage, and this specifies where that name can be defined and from where it can be accessed. There are four types of linkage:

- **No linkage:** The name is accessible only from the scope in which it is defined.
- **External linkage:** The name is accessible from any translation unit.

- **Internal linkage (also called static linkage):** The name is accessible only from the current translation unit, but not from other translation units.
- **Module linkage:** The name is accessible from any translation unit from the same module.

Internal Linkage

By default, functions and global variables have external linkage. However, you can specify internal (or static) linkage by employing *anonymous namespaces*. For example, suppose you have two source files: `FirstFile.cpp` and `AnotherFile.cpp`. Here is `FirstFile.cpp`:

```
void f();

int main()
{
    f();
}
```

Note that this file provides a prototype for `f()` but doesn't show the definition. Here is `AnotherFile.cpp`:

```
import std;

void f();

void f()
{
    std::println("f");
}
```

This file provides both a prototype and a definition for `f()`. Note that it is legal to write prototypes for the same function in two different files. That's precisely what the preprocessor does for you if you put the prototypes in a header file that you `#include` in each of the source files. For this example, I don't use a header file. The reason to use header files used to be that it was easier to maintain (and keep synchronized) one copy of the prototype, but now that C++ has support for modules, using modules is recommended over using header files.

Each of these source files compiles without error, and the program links fine: because `f()` has external linkage, `main()` can call it from a different file.

However, suppose you wrap the `f()` function in `AnotherFile.cpp` in an anonymous namespace to give it internal linkage as follows:

```
import std;

namespace
{
    void f();

    void f()
    {
        std::println("f");
    }
}
```

Entities in an anonymous namespace have internal linkage and thus can be accessed anywhere following their declaration in the same translation unit, but cannot be accessed from other translation units. With this change, each of the source files still compiles without error, but the linker step fails because `f()` has internal linkage, making it unavailable from `FirstFile.cpp`.

An alternative to using anonymous namespaces to give a name internal linkage is to prefix the declaration with the keyword `static`. The earlier anonymous namespace example can be written as follows. Note that you don't need to repeat the `static` keyword in front of the definition of `f()`. As long as it precedes the first instance of the function name, there is no need to repeat it.

```
import std;

static void f();

void f()
{
    std::println("f");
}
```

The semantics of this version of the code are exactly the same as the one using an anonymous namespace.

> **WARNING** *If a translation unit needs a helper entity that is only required within that translation unit, wrap it in an anonymous namespace to give it internal linkage. Using the* `static` *keyword for this is discouraged.*

The extern Keyword

A related keyword, `extern`, seems like it should be the opposite of `static`, specifying external linkage for the names it precedes, and it can be used that way in certain cases. For example, `const`s and `typedef`s have internal linkage by default. You can use `extern` to give them external linkage. However, `extern` has some complications. When you specify a name as `extern`, the compiler treats it as a declaration, not a definition. For variables, this means the compiler doesn't allocate space for the variable. You must provide a separate definition for the variable without the `extern` keyword. For example, here is the content of `AnotherFile.cpp`:

```
extern int x;
int x { 3 };
```

Alternatively, you can initialize `x` in the `extern` statement, which then serves as the declaration and the definition:

```
extern int x { 3 };
```

The `extern` in this case is not very useful, because `x` has external linkage by default anyway. The real use of `extern` is when you want to use `x` from another source file, `FirstFile.cpp`:

```
import std;

extern int x;
```

```
int main()
{
    std::println("{}", x);
}
```

Here, `FirstFile.cpp` uses an `extern` declaration so that it can use `x`. The compiler needs a declaration of `x` to use it in `main()`. If you declared `x` without the `extern` keyword, the compiler would think it's a definition and would allocate space for `x`, causing the linkage step to fail (because there are then two `x` variables in the global scope). With `extern`, you can make variables globally accessible from multiple source files.

> **WARNING** *It is not recommended to use global variables at all. They are confusing and error-prone, especially in large programs. Use them judiciously!*
>
> *The only exception are global constants. Don't define the same constants all over the place: define them once and use them from everywhere.*

HEADER FILES

Before the introduction of C++20's modules, *header files*, also called *headers*, were used as a mechanism for providing the interface to a subsystem or piece of code. The most common use of headers is to declare functions that will be defined elsewhere. A *declaration* tells the compiler that an entity (function, variable, etc.) with a certain name exists. For functions, a declaration specifies how a function is called, declaring the number and types of parameters and the function's return type. A *definition* also tells the compiler that an entity with a certain name exists, but also defines the entity itself. For functions, a definition contains the actual code for the function. All definitions are declarations, but not all declarations are definitions. Declarations, and thus also class definitions, which are declarations, see Chapter 8, "Gaining Proficiency with Classes and Objects," usually go into header files, typically with extension `.h`. Definitions, including definitions of non-inline class members, usually go into source files, typically with extension `.cpp`. This book uses modules everywhere, but this section briefly discusses a few trickier aspects of using header files, such as avoiding duplicate definitions and circular dependencies, because you will encounter these in legacy code bases.

One Definition Rule (ODR)

A single translation unit can have exactly one definition of a variable, function, class type, enumeration type, concept, or template. For some types, multiple declarations are allowed, but not multiple definitions. Furthermore, exactly one definition of non-inline functions and non-inline variables is allowed in the entire program.

With header files, it's easy to violate the one definition rule, resulting in duplicate definitions. The next section discusses how such duplicate definitions through header files can be avoided.

Between modules, it's harder to violate the one definition rule, as each module is much better isolated from other modules. A major reason for this is that an entity in a module that is not exported from that module has module linkage and thus is inaccessible from code in other modules. That is, multiple modules can define their own local non-exported entities with the same name without any problem. On the other hand, in non-modular source files, local entities have external linkage by default. Of course, within a module itself, you still need to make sure you don't violate the one definition rule.

Duplicate Definitions

Suppose `A.h` includes `Logger.h`, defining a `Logger` class, and `B.h` also includes `Logger.h`. If you have a source file called `App.cpp`, which includes both `A.h` and `B.h`, you end up with *duplicate definitions* of the `Logger` class because the `Logger.h` header is included through `A.h` and `B.h`.

This problem of duplicate definitions can be avoided with a mechanism known as *include guards*, also known as *header guards*. The following code snippet shows the `Logger.h` header with include guards. At the beginning of each header file, the `#ifndef` directive checks whether a certain key has *not* been defined. If the key has been defined, the compiler skips to the matching `#endif`, which is usually placed at the end of the file. If the key has *not* been defined, the file proceeds to define the key so that a subsequent include of the same file will be skipped.

```
#ifndef LOGGER_H
#define LOGGER_H

class Logger { /* ... */ };

#endif // LOGGER_H
```

Alternatively, nearly all compilers these days support the `#pragma once` directive, which replaces include guards. Placing a `#pragma once` at the beginning of a header file makes sure it'll be included only once and hence avoids duplicate definitions resulting from including the header multiple times. Here's an example:

```
#pragma once

class Logger { /* ... */ };
```

> **NOTE** *Include guards and* `#pragma once` *directives prevent only one definition rule violations when a header file is included multiple times within a single translation unit, not across multiple translation units.*

Circular Dependencies

Another tool for avoiding problems with header files is *forward declarations*. If you need to refer to a class but you cannot include its header file (for example, because it relies heavily on the class you are writing), you can tell the compiler that such a class exists without providing a formal definition through the `#include` mechanism. Of course, you cannot actually use the class in the code because the compiler knows nothing about it, except that the named class will exist after everything is linked together. However, you can still make use of pointers and references to forward-declared classes in your code. You can also declare functions that return such forward-declared classes by value or that have such forward-declared classes as pass-by-value function parameters. Of course, both the code defining the function and any code calling the function will need to include the right header files that properly define the forward-declared classes.

For example, assume that the `Logger` class uses another class called `Preferences` that keeps track of user settings. The `Preferences` class may in turn use the `Logger` class, so you have a *circular dependency* that cannot be resolved with include guards. You need to make use of forward declarations in such cases. In the following code, the `Logger.h` header file uses a forward declaration for the `Preferences` class and subsequently refers to the `Preferences` class without including its header file:

```
#pragma once

#include <string_view>

class Preferences;  // forward declaration

class Logger
{
    public:
        void setPreferences(const Preferences& preferences);
        void logError(std::string_view error);
};
```

It's recommended to use forward declarations as much as possible in your header files instead of including other headers. This can reduce your compilation and recompilation times, because it breaks dependencies of your header file on other headers. Of course, your implementation file needs to include the correct headers for types that you've forward-declared; otherwise, it won't compile.

Querying Existence of Headers

To query whether a certain header file exists, use the `__has_include("filename")` or `__has_include(<filename>)` preprocessor constant expressions. These evaluate to 1 if the header file exists, 0 if it doesn't exist. For example, before the `<optional>` header file was fully approved for C++17, some compilers already had a preliminary version in `<experimental/optional>`. You could use `__has_include()` to check which of the two header files was available on your system:

```
#if __has_include(<optional>)
    #include <optional>
#elif __has_include(<experimental/optional>)
    #include <experimental/optional>
#endif
```

Module Import Declarations

Header files should not contain any module `import` declarations. The standard mandates that module `import` declarations must be at the beginning of a file before any other declarations and must not be coming from header inclusions or preprocessor macro expansions. This makes it easier on build systems to discover module dependencies, which are then used to determine the order modules need to be built.

FEATURE-TEST MACROS FOR CORE LANGUAGE FEATURES

You can use *feature-test macros* to detect which core language features are supported by a compiler. All these macros start with either `__cpp_` or `__has_cpp_`. The following are some examples. Consult your favorite C++ reference for a complete list of all possible core language feature-test macros.

- `__cpp_range_based_for`
- `__cpp_binary_literals`
- `__cpp_char8_t`
- `__cpp_generic_lambdas`
- `__cpp_consteval`
- `__cpp_coroutines`
- `...`
- `__has_cpp_attribute(`*`[attribute_name]`*`)`
- `...`

The value of these macros is a number representing the month and year when a specific feature was added or updated. The date is formatted as `YYYYMM`. For example, the value of `__cpp_binary_literals` is 201304, i.e., April 2013, which is the date when binary literals were introduced. As another example, the value of `__has_cpp_attribute(nodiscard)` can be 201603, i.e., March 2016, which is the date when the `[[nodiscard]]` attribute was first introduced. Or it can be 201907, i.e., July 2019, which is the date when the attribute was updated to allow specifying a reason such as `[[nodiscard("Reason")]]`.

All these core language feature-test macros are available without having to include any specific header. Here is an example use:

```
int main()
{
#ifdef __cpp_range_based_for
    println("Range-based for loops are supported!");
#else
    println("Bummer! Range-based for loops are NOT supported!");
#endif
}
```

Chapter 16, "Overview of the C++ Standard Library," explains that there are similar feature-test macros for Standard Library features.

> **NOTE** *You will rarely need these feature-test macros, unless you are writing cross-platform and cross-compiler code. In that case, you might want to know if certain functionality is supported by a given compiler so that you can provide fallback code in case a feature is missing. Chapter 34, "Developing Cross-Platform and Cross-Language Applications," discusses cross-platform development.*

THE STATIC KEYWORD

There are several uses of the keyword `static` in C++, all seemingly unrelated. Part of the motivation for "overloading" the keyword was attempting to avoid having to introduce new keywords into the language. One use of the keyword is discussed earlier in this chapter in the context of linkage. Other uses are discussed in this section.

static Data Members and Member Functions

You can declare `static` data members and member functions of classes. `static` data members, unlike non-`static` data members, are not part of each object. Instead, there is only one copy of the data member, which exists outside any objects of that class.

`static` member functions are similarly at the class level instead of the object level. A `static` member function does not execute in the context of a specific object; hence, it does not have an implicit `this` pointer. This also means that `static` member functions cannot be marked as `const`.

Chapter 9 provides examples of both `static` data members and member functions.

static Variables in Functions

Another use of the `static` keyword in C++ is to create variables that retain their values between exits and entrances to their scope. For example, a `static` local variable inside a function is like a global variable that is accessible only from within that function. One common use of `static` variables is to "remember" whether a particular initialization has been performed for a certain function. For example, code that employs this technique might look something like this:

```
void performTask()
{
    static bool initialized { false };
    if (!initialized) {
        println("initializing");
        // Perform initialization.
        initialized = true;
    }
    // Perform the desired task.
}
```

However, `static` variables can be confusing, and there are usually better ways to structure your code so that you can avoid them. In this case, you might want to write a class in which the constructor performs the required initialization.

> **NOTE** *Avoid using stand-alone* `static` *variables. Maintain state within an object instead.*

Sometimes, however, they can be useful. One example is for implementing the Meyers' singleton design pattern, as explained in Chapter 33, "Applying Design Patterns."

> **NOTE** *The implementation of* `performTask()` *is not thread-safe; it contains a race condition. In a multithreaded environment, you need to use atomics or other mechanisms for synchronization of multiple threads. Multithreading is discussed in detail in Chapter 27, "Multithreaded Programming with C++."*

Order of Initialization of Nonlocal Variables

Before leaving the topic of `static` variables, consider the order of initialization of such variables. All global and `static` variables in a program are initialized before `main()` begins. The variables in a given source file are initialized in the order they appear in the source file. For example, in the following file, `Demo::x` is guaranteed to be initialized before `y`:

```
class Demo
{
    public:
        static int x;
};
int Demo::x { 3 };
int y { 4 };
```

However, C++ provides no specifications or guarantees about the initialization ordering of nonlocal variables in different source files. If you have a global variable `x` in one source file and a global variable `y` in another, you have no way of knowing which will be initialized first. Normally, this lack of specification isn't cause for concern. However, it can be problematic if one global or `static` variable depends on another. Recall that initialization of objects implies running their constructors. The constructor of one global object might access another global object, assuming that it is already constructed. If these two global objects are declared in two different source files, you cannot count on one being constructed before the other, and you cannot control the order of initialization. This order might not be the same for different compilers or even different versions of the same compiler, and the order might even change when you simply add another file to your project.

> **WARNING** *Initialization order of nonlocal variables in different source files is undefined.*

Order of Destruction of Nonlocal Variables

Nonlocal variables are destroyed in the reverse order they were initialized. Nonlocal variables in different source files are initialized in an undefined order, which means that the order of destruction is also undefined.

C-STYLE VARIABLE-LENGTH ARGUMENT LISTS

In legacy code, you might come across the use of C-style variable-length argument lists. In new code, you should avoid using these and instead use variadic templates for type-safe variable-length argument lists, which are covered in Chapter 26, "Advanced Templates."

So that you are aware of C-style variable-length argument lists, consider the C function `printf()` from `<cstdio>`. You can call it with any number of arguments:

```
printf("int %d\n", 5);
printf("String %s and int %d\n", "hello", 5);
printf("Many ints: %d, %d, %d, %d, %d\n", 1, 2, 3, 4, 5);
```

C/C++ provides the syntax and some utility macros for writing your own functions with a variable number of arguments. These functions usually look a lot like `printf()`. For example, suppose you want to write a quick-and-dirty debug function that prints strings to `stderr` if a debug flag is set but does nothing if the debug flag is not set. Just like `printf()`, this function should be able to print strings with an arbitrary number of arguments and arbitrary types of arguments. A simple implementation looks as follows:

```
import std;
#include <cstdarg>
#include <cstdio>

bool debug { false };

void debugOut(const char* str, ...)
{
    if (debug) {
        va_list ap;
        va_start(ap, str);
        vfprintf(stderr, str, ap);
        va_end(ap);
    }
}
```

The code uses `va_list()`, `va_start()`, and `va_end()`, which are macros defined in `<cstdarg>` and thus require an explicit `#include <cstdarg>`, as `import std;` does not export any macros. Similarly, `stderr` is a macro defined in `<cstdio>` requiring an explicit `#include <cstdio>`.

The prototype for `debugOut()` contains one typed and named parameter `str`, followed by `...` (ellipses). They stand for any number and type of arguments. To access these arguments, you must declare a variable of type `va_list` and initialize it with a call to `va_start`. The second parameter to `va_start()` must be the rightmost *named* variable in the parameter list. All functions with variable-length argument lists require at least one named parameter. The `debugOut()` function simply passes this list to `vfprintf()` (a standard function in `<cstdio>`). After the call to `vfprintf()` returns, `debugOut()` calls `va_end()` to terminate the access of the variable argument list. You must always call `va_end()` after calling `va_start()` to ensure that the function ends with the stack in a consistent state.

You can use the function in the following way:

```
debug = true;
debugOut("int %d\n", 5);
```

```
debugOut("String %s and int %d\n", "hello", 5);
debugOut("Many ints: %d, %d, %d, %d, %d\n", 1, 2, 3, 4, 5);
```

Accessing the Arguments

If you want to access the actual arguments yourself, you can use `va_arg()` to do so. It accepts a `va_list` as first argument, and the type of the argument to interpret. Unfortunately, there is no way to know what the end of the argument list is unless you provide an explicit way of doing so. For example, you can make the first parameter a count of the number of parameters. Or, in the case where you have a set of pointers, you may require the last pointer to be `nullptr`. There are many ways, but they are all burdensome to the programmer.

The following example demonstrates the technique where the caller specifies in the first named parameter how many arguments are provided. The function accepts any number of `int`s and prints them out.

```
void printInts(unsigned num, ...)
{
    va_list ap;
    va_start(ap, num);
    for (unsigned i { 0 }; i < num; ++i) {
        int temp { va_arg(ap, int) };
        print("{} ", temp);
    }
    va_end(ap);
    println("");
}
```

You can call `printInts()` as follows. Note that the first parameter specifies how many integers will follow.

```
printInts(5, 5, 4, 3, 2, 1);
```

Why You Shouldn't Use C-Style Variable-Length Argument Lists

Accessing C-style variable-length argument lists is not very safe. There are several risks, as you can see from the `printInts()` function.

- You don't know the number of parameters. In the case of `printInts()`, you must trust the caller to pass the right number of arguments as the first argument. In the case of `debugOut()`, you must trust the caller to pass the same number of arguments after the `str` string as there are replacement fields in the string.
- You don't know the types of the arguments. `va_arg()` takes a type, which it uses to interpret the value in its current spot. However, you can tell `va_arg()` to interpret the value as any type. There is no way for it to verify the correct type.

> **WARNING** *Avoid using C-style variable-length argument lists. It is preferable to pass in an* `std::array` *or* `vector` *of values, to use initializer lists described in Chapter 1, or to use variadic templates for type-safe variable-length argument lists, as described in Chapter 26.*

SUMMARY

This chapter started with details on authoring and consuming modules and discussed a few trickier aspects of using old-style header files. You also learned about preprocessor directives, preprocessor macros, details of linkage, the one definition rule, and the different uses of the `static` and `extern` keywords. The chapter finished with a discussion on how to write C-style variable-length argument lists.

Preprocessor directives and C-style variable-length argument lists are important to understand, because you might encounter them in legacy code bases. However, they should be avoided in any newly written code.

The next chapter starts a discussion on templates allowing you to write generic code.

EXERCISES

By solving the following exercises, you can practice the material discussed in this chapter. Solutions to all exercises are available with the code download on the book's website at `www.wiley.com/go/proc++6e`. However, if you are stuck on an exercise, first reread parts of this chapter to try to find an answer yourself before looking at the solution from the website.

Exercise 11-1: Write a single-file module called `simulator` containing two classes, `CarSimulator` and `BikeSimulator`, in a `Simulator` namespace. The content of the classes is not important for these exercises. Just provide a default constructor that prints a message to the standard output. Test your code in a `main()` function.

Exercise 11-2: Take your solution from Exercise 11-1 and split the module into several files: a primary module interface file without any implementations and two module implementation files, one for the `CarSimulator` and one for the `BikeSimulator` class.

Exercise 11-3: Take your solution from Exercise 11-2 and convert it to use one primary module interface file and two module interface partition files, one for the `simulator:car` partition containing the `CarSimulator` class, and one for the `simulator:bike` partition containing the `BikeSimulator` class.

Exercise 11-4: Take your solution from Exercise 11-3 and add an implementation partition called `internals`, containing a helper function called `convertMilesToKm(double miles)` in the `Simulator` namespace. One mile is 1.6 kilometers. Add a member function to both the `CarSimulator` and `BikeSimulator` classes called `setOdometer(double miles)`, which uses the helper function to convert the given miles to kilometers and then prints it out to the standard output. Confirm in your `main()` function that the `setOdometer()` works on both classes. Also confirm that `main()` cannot call `convertMilesToKm()`.

Exercise 11-5: Write a source file containing a preprocessor identifier with the value 0 or 1. Use preprocessor directives to check the value of this identifier. If the value is 1, make the compiler output a warning. If it's 0, ignore it. If it's any other value, make the compiler generate an error.

12

Writing Generic Code with Templates

WHAT'S IN THIS CHAPTER?

- How to write class templates
- How the compiler processes templates
- How to organize template source code
- How to use non-type template parameters
- How to write templates of individual class member functions
- How to customize class templates for specific types
- How to combine templates and inheritance
- How to write alias templates
- How to write function templates
- How to make function templates friends of class templates
- How to use the abbreviated function template syntax
- How to use variable templates
- What concepts are
- How to use concepts to type constrain `auto`
- How to use concepts to specify requirements for template type parameters

WILEY.COM DOWNLOADS FOR THIS CHAPTER

Please note that all the code examples for this chapter are available as part of this chapter's code download on the book's website at `www.wiley.com/go/proc++6e` on the Download Code tab.

C++ provides language support not only for object-oriented programming but also for *generic programming*. As discussed in Chapter 6, "Designing for Reuse," the goal of generic programming is to write reusable code. The fundamental tools for generic programming in C++ are *templates*. Although not strictly an object-oriented feature, templates can be combined with object-oriented programming for powerful results. Using existing templates, such as those provided by the Standard Library, e.g., `std::vector`, `unique_ptr`, and so on, is usually straightforward. However, many programmers consider writing their own templates to be the most difficult part of C++ and, for that reason, tend to avoid writing them. However, as a professional C++ programmer, you need to know how to write class and function templates.

This chapter provides the coding details for fulfilling the design principle of generality discussed in Chapter 6, while Chapter 26, "Advanced Templates," delves into some of the more advanced template features.

OVERVIEW OF TEMPLATES

The main programming unit in the procedural paradigm is the *procedure* or *function*. Functions are useful primarily because they allow you to write algorithms that are independent of specific values and can thus be reused for many different values. For example, the `sqrt()` function in C++ calculates the square root of a value supplied by the caller. A square root function that calculates only the square root of one number, such as the number four, would not be particularly useful! The `sqrt()` function is written in terms of a *parameter*, which is a stand-in for whatever value the caller passes. Computer scientists say that functions *parameterize* values.

The object-oriented programming paradigm adds the concept of *objects*, which group related data and behaviors, but it does not change the way functions and member functions parameterize values.

Templates take the concept of parameterization a step further to allow you to parameterize on *types* as well as *values*. Types in C++ include primitives such as `int` and `double`, as well as user-defined classes such as `SpreadsheetCell` and `CherryTree`. With templates, you can write code that is independent not only of the values it will be given, but also of the types of those values. For example, instead of writing separate stack classes to store `int`s, `Car`s, and `SpreadsheetCell`s, you can write one stack class template definition that can be used for any of those types.

Although templates are an amazing language feature, templates in C++ can be syntactically confusing, and thus, many programmers avoid *writing* templates themselves. However, every *professional* C++ programmer needs to know how to write them, and every programmer at least needs to know how to *use* templates, because they are widely used by libraries, such as the C++ Standard Library.

This chapter teaches you about template support in C++ with an emphasis on the aspects that arise in the Standard Library. Along the way, you will learn about some nifty features that you can employ in your programs aside from using the Standard Library.

CLASS TEMPLATES

A *class template* defines a *blueprint* (= template) for a family of class definitions where the types of some of the variables, return types of member functions, and/or parameters to member functions are specified as template type parameters. Class templates are like construction blueprints. They allow the compiler to build (also known as *instantiate*) concrete class definitions by replacing template type parameters with concrete types.

Class templates are useful primarily for containers, or data structures, that store objects. You already used class templates often earlier in this book, e.g., `std::vector`, `unique_ptr`, `string`, and so on. This section discusses how to write your own class templates by using a running example of a `Grid` container. To keep the examples reasonable in length and simple enough to illustrate specific points, different sections of the chapter add features to the `Grid` container that are not used in subsequent sections.

Writing a Class Template

Suppose that you want a generic game board class that you can use as a chessboard, checkers board, tic-tac-toe board, or any other two-dimensional game board. To make it general-purpose, you should be able to store chess pieces, checkers pieces, tic-tac-toe pieces, or any type of game piece.

Coding Without Templates

Without templates, the best approach to build a generic game board is to employ polymorphism to store generic `GamePiece` objects. Then, you could let the pieces for each game inherit from the `GamePiece` class. For example, in a chess game, `ChessPiece` would be a derived class of `GamePiece`. Through polymorphism, the `GameBoard`, written to store `GamePieces`, could also store `ChessPieces`. Because it should be possible to copy a `GameBoard`, the `GameBoard` needs to be able to copy `GamePieces`. This implementation employs polymorphism, so one solution is to add a pure virtual `clone()` member function to the `GamePiece` base class, which derived classes must implement to return a copy of a concrete `GamePiece`. Here is the basic `GamePiece` interface:

```
export class GamePiece
{
    public:
        virtual ~GamePiece() = default;
        virtual std::unique_ptr<GamePiece> clone() const = 0;
};
```

`GamePiece` is an abstract base class. Concrete classes, such as `ChessPiece`, derive from it and implement the `clone()` member function:

```
class ChessPiece : public GamePiece
{
    public:
        std::unique_ptr<GamePiece> clone() const override
        {
            // Call the copy constructor to copy this instance
            return std::make_unique<ChessPiece>(*this);
        }
};
```

A GameBoard represents a two-dimensional grid, so one option to store the GamePieces in GameBoard could be a vector of vectors of unique_ptrs. However, that's not an optimal representation of the data, as the data will be fragmented in memory. It's better to store a linearized representation of the GamePieces as a single vector of unique_ptrs. Converting a two-dimensional coordinate, say (x,y), to a one-dimensional location in the linearized representation is easily done using the formula x+y*width.

```
export class GameBoard
{
    public:
        explicit GameBoard(std::size_t width = DefaultWidth,
            std::size_t height = DefaultHeight);
        GameBoard(const GameBoard& src);    // copy constructor
        virtual ~GameBoard() = default;     // virtual defaulted destructor
        GameBoard& operator=(const GameBoard& rhs); // assignment operator

        // Explicitly default a move constructor and move assignment operator.
        GameBoard(GameBoard&& src) = default;
        GameBoard& operator=(GameBoard&& src) = default;

        std::unique_ptr<GamePiece>& at(std::size_t x, std::size_t y);
        const std::unique_ptr<GamePiece>& at(std::size_t x, std::size_t y) const;

        std::size_t getHeight() const { return m_height; }
        std::size_t getWidth() const { return m_width; }

        static constexpr std::size_t DefaultWidth { 10 };
        static constexpr std::size_t DefaultHeight { 10 };

        void swap(GameBoard& other) noexcept;
    private:
        void verifyCoordinate(std::size_t x, std::size_t y) const;

        std::vector<std::unique_ptr<GamePiece>> m_cells;
        std::size_t m_width { 0 }, m_height { 0 };
};
export void swap(GameBoard& first, GameBoard& second) noexcept;
```

In this implementation, at() returns a reference to the game piece at a given location instead of a copy of the piece. GameBoard serves as an abstraction of a two-dimensional array, so it should provide array access semantics by returning a reference to the actual object at any location, not a copy of the object. Client code should not store this reference for future use because it might become invalid, for example when the m_cells vector needs to be resized. Instead, client code shall call at() right before using the returned reference. This follows the design philosophy of the Standard Library vector class.

> **NOTE** *This implementation provides two versions of* at()*; one returns a reference-to-non-*const *while the other returns a reference-to-*const.

> **NOTE** *Starting with C++23, it is possible to provide a multidimensional subscripting operator for the* `GameBoard` *class. By providing such an operator, clients can write* `myGameBoard[x,y]` *instead of* `myGameBoard.at(x,y)` *to get access to a piece at location* `(x,y)`*. This operator is discussed in Chapter 15, "Overloading C++ Operators."*

Here are the member function definitions. Note that this implementation uses the copy-and-swap idiom for the assignment operator, and Scott Meyers' `const_cast()` pattern to avoid code duplication, both of which are discussed in Chapter 9, "Mastering Classes and Objects."

```
GameBoard::GameBoard(size_t width, size_t height)
    : m_width { width }, m_height { height }
{
    m_cells.resize(m_width * m_height);
}

GameBoard::GameBoard(const GameBoard& src)
    : GameBoard { src.m_width, src.m_height }
{
    // The ctor-initializer of this constructor delegates first to the
    // non-copy constructor to allocate the proper amount of memory.

    // The next step is to copy the data.
    for (size_t i { 0 }; i < m_cells.size(); ++i) {
        if (src.m_cells[i]) {
            m_cells[i] = src.m_cells[i]->clone();
        }
    }
}

void GameBoard::verifyCoordinate(size_t x, size_t y) const
{
    if (x >= m_width) {
        throw out_of_range {
            format("x ({}) must be less than width ({}).", x, m_width) };
    }
    if (y >= m_height) {
        throw out_of_range {
            format("y ({}) must be less than height ({}).", y, m_height) };
    }
}

void GameBoard::swap(GameBoard& other) noexcept
{
    std::swap(m_width, other.m_width);
    std::swap(m_height, other.m_height);
    std::swap(m_cells, other.m_cells);
}
```

```
void swap(GameBoard& first, GameBoard& second) noexcept
{
    first.swap(second);
}

GameBoard& GameBoard::operator=(const GameBoard& rhs)
{
    // Copy-and-swap idiom
    GameBoard temp { rhs }; // Do all the work in a temporary instance.
    swap(temp);             // Commit the work with only non-throwing operations.
    return *this;
}

const unique_ptr<GamePiece>& GameBoard::at(size_t x, size_t y) const
{
    verifyCoordinate(x, y);
    return m_cells[x + y * m_width];
}

unique_ptr<GamePiece>& GameBoard::at(size_t x, size_t y)
{
    return const_cast<unique_ptr<GamePiece>&>(as_const(*this).at(x, y));
}
```

This `GameBoard` class works pretty well:

```
GameBoard chessBoard { 8, 8 };
auto pawn { std::make_unique<ChessPiece>() };
chessBoard.at(0, 0) = std::move(pawn);
chessBoard.at(0, 1) = std::make_unique<ChessPiece>();
chessBoard.at(0, 1) = nullptr;
```

A Template Grid Class

The `GameBoard` class in the previous section is nice but insufficient. One problem is that you cannot use `GameBoard` to store elements by value; it always stores pointers. Another, more serious issue is related to type safety. Each cell in a `GameBoard` stores a `unique_ptr<GamePiece>`. Even if you are storing `ChessPiece`s, when you use `at()` to request a certain piece, you will get back a `unique_ptr<GamePiece>`. This means you have to downcast the retrieved `GamePiece` to a `ChessPiece` to be able to make use of `ChessPiece`'s specific functionality. Additionally, nothing stops you from mixing all kinds of different `GamePiece`-derived objects in a `GameBoard`. For example, suppose there is not only a `ChessPiece` but also a `TicTacToePiece`:

```
class TicTacToePiece : public GamePiece
{
    public:
        std::unique_ptr<GamePiece> clone() const override
        {
            // Call the copy constructor to copy this instance
            return std::make_unique<TicTacToePiece>(*this);
        }
};
```

With the polymorphic solution from the previous section, nothing stops you from storing tic-tac-toe pieces and chess pieces on a single game board:

```
GameBoard gameBoard { 8, 8 };
gameBoard.at(0, 0) = std::make_unique<ChessPiece>();
gameBoard.at(0, 1) = std::make_unique<TicTacToePiece>();
```

The big problem with this is that you somehow need to remember what is stored at a certain location so that you can perform the correct downcast when you call `at()`.

Another shortcoming of `GameBoard` is that it cannot be used to store primitive types, such as `int` or `double`, because the type stored in a cell must derive from `GamePiece`.

It would be nice if you could write a generic `Grid` class that you could use for storing `ChessPieces`, `SpreadsheetCells`, `ints`, `doubles`, and so on. In C++, you can do this by writing a *class template*, which is a blueprint for class definitions. In a class template, not all types are known yet. Clients then *instantiate* the template by specifying the types they want to use. This is called *generic programming*. The biggest advantage of generic programming is type safety. The types used in instantiated class definitions and their member functions are concrete types, and not abstract base class types, as is the case with the polymorphic solution from the previous section.

Let's start by looking at how such a `Grid` class template definition can be written.

The Grid Class Template Definition

To understand class templates, it is helpful to examine the syntax. The following example shows how you can modify the `GameBoard` class to make a parametrized `Grid` class template. The syntax is explained in detail following the code. Note that the name has changed from `GameBoard` to `Grid`. A `Grid` should also be usable with primitive types such as `int` and `double`. That's why I opted to implement this solution using value semantics without polymorphism, compared to the polymorphic pointer semantics used in the `GameBoard` implementation. The `m_cells` container stores actual objects, instead of pointers. A downside of using value semantics compared to pointer semantics is that you cannot have a true empty cell; that is, a cell must always contain some value. With pointer semantics, an empty cell stores `nullptr`. Luckily, `std::optional`, introduced in Chapter 1, "A Crash Course in C++ and the Standard Library," comes to the rescue here. It allows you to use value semantics, while still having a way to represent empty cells.

```
export template <typename T>
class Grid
{
    public:
        explicit Grid(std::size_t width = DefaultWidth,
            std::size_t height = DefaultHeight);
        virtual ~Grid() = default;

        // Explicitly default a copy constructor and copy assignment operator.
        Grid(const Grid& src) = default;
        Grid& operator=(const Grid& rhs) = default;

        // Explicitly default a move constructor and move assignment operator.
        Grid(Grid&& src) = default;
        Grid& operator=(Grid&& rhs) = default;
```

```
        std::optional<T>& at(std::size_t x, std::size_t y);
        const std::optional<T>& at(std::size_t x, std::size_t y) const;

        std::size_t getHeight() const { return m_height; }
        std::size_t getWidth() const { return m_width; }

        static constexpr std::size_t DefaultWidth { 10 };
        static constexpr std::size_t DefaultHeight { 10 };

    private:
        void verifyCoordinate(std::size_t x, std::size_t y) const;

        std::vector<std::optional<T>> m_cells;
        std::size_t m_width { 0 }, m_height { 0 };
};
```

Now that you've seen the full class template definition, take another look at it, starting with the first line.

```
export template <typename T>
```

This first line says that the following class definition is a template on one type, `T`, and that it's being exported from the module. The "`template <typename T>`" part is called the *template header*. Both `template` and `typename` are keywords in C++. As discussed earlier, templates "parameterize" types in the same way that functions "parameterize" values. Just as you use parameter names in functions to represent the arguments that the caller will pass, you use *template type parameter* names (such as `T`) in templates to represent the types that the caller will pass as *template type arguments*. There's nothing special about the name `T`—you can use whatever name you want. Traditionally, when a single type is used, it is called `T`, but that's just a historical convention, like calling the integer that indexes an array `i` or `j`. The template specifier holds for the entire statement, which in this case is the class template definition.

> **NOTE** *For historical reasons, you can use the keyword* `class` *instead of* `typename` *to specify template type parameters. Thus, many books and existing programs use syntax like this:* `template <class T>`*. However, the use of the word class in this context is confusing because it implies that the type must be a class, which is not true. The type can be a class, a struct, a union, a primitive type of the language like* `int` *or* `double`*, and so on. To avoid such confusion, this book uses* `typename`*.*

In the earlier `GameBoard` class, the `m_cells` data member is a `vector` of *pointers*, which requires special code for copying—thus the need for a copy constructor and copy assignment operator. In the `Grid` class, `m_cells` is a `vector` of optional *values*, so the compiler-generated copy constructor and assignment operator are fine. However, as explained in Chapter 8, "Gaining Proficiency with Classes and Objects," once you have a user-declared destructor, it's deprecated for the compiler to implicitly generate a copy constructor or copy assignment operator, so the `Grid` class template explicitly defaults them. It also explicitly defaults the move constructor and move assignment operator. Here is the explicitly defaulted copy assignment operator:

```
Grid& operator=(const Grid& rhs) = default;
```

As you can see, the type of the rhs parameter is no longer a const GameBoard&, but a const Grid&. Within a class definition, the compiler interprets Grid as Grid<T> where needed, but if you want, you can explicitly use Grid<T>:

```
Grid<T>& operator=(const Grid<T>& rhs) = default;
```

However, outside a class definition you must use Grid<T>. When you write a class template, what you used to think of as the class name (Grid) is actually the *template name*. When you want to talk about actual Grid classes or types, you have to use the *template ID*, i.e., Grid<T>, which are *instantiations* of the Grid class template for a certain type, such as int, SpreadsheetCell, or ChessPiece.

Because m_cells is not storing pointers anymore, but optional values, the at() member functions now return optional<T>s instead of unique_ptrs, that is, optionals that can either have a value of type T, or be empty:

```
std::optional<T>& at(std::size_t x, std::size_t y);
const std::optional<T>& at(std::size_t x, std::size_t y) const;
```

The Grid Class Template Member Function Definitions

The template <typename T> template header must precede each member function definition for the Grid class template. The constructor looks like this:

```
template <typename T>
Grid<T>::Grid(std::size_t width, std::size_t height)
    : m_width { width }, m_height { height }
{
    m_cells.resize(m_width * m_height);
}
```

> **NOTE** *Member function definitions of class templates need to be visible to any client code using the class template. This places some restrictions on where such member function definitions can be placed. Usually, they are simply put in the same file as the class template definition itself. Some ways around this restriction are discussed later in this chapter.*

Note that the name before the :: is Grid<T>, not Grid. The body of the constructor is identical to the GameBoard constructor. The rest of the member function definitions are also similar to their equivalents in the GameBoard class with the exception of the appropriate template header and Grid<T> syntax changes:

```
template <typename T>
void Grid<T>::verifyCoordinate(std::size_t x, std::size_t y) const
{
    if (x >= m_width) {
        throw std::out_of_range {
            std::format("x ({}) must be less than width ({}).", x, m_width) };
    }
    if (y >= m_height) {
        throw std::out_of_range {
```

```
            std::format("y ({}) must be less than height ({}).", y, m_height) };
    }
}

template <typename T>
const std::optional<T>& Grid<T>::at(std::size_t x, std::size_t y) const
{
    verifyCoordinate(x, y);
    return m_cells[x + y * m_width];
}

template <typename T>
std::optional<T>& Grid<T>::at(std::size_t x, std::size_t y)
{
    return const_cast<std::optional<T>&>(std::as_const(*this).at(x, y));
}
```

NOTE *If an implementation of a class template member function needs a default value for a certain template type parameter, for example* `T`*, then you can use the* `T{}` *syntax.* `T{}` *calls the default constructor for the object if* `T` *is a class type, or generates zero if* `T` *is a primitive type. This syntax is called the zero-initialization syntax. It's a good way to provide a reasonable default value for a variable whose type you don't know yet.*

Using the Grid Template

When you want to create `Grid` objects, you cannot use `Grid` alone as a type; you must specify the type that is to be stored in that `Grid`. Creating concrete instances of class templates for specific types is called *template instantiation*. Here is an example:

```
Grid<int> myIntGrid; // Declares a grid that stores ints,
                     // using default arguments for the constructor.
Grid<double> myDoubleGrid { 11, 11 }; // Declares an 11x11 Grid of doubles.

myIntGrid.at(0, 0) = 10;
int x { myIntGrid.at(0, 0).value_or(0) };

Grid<int> grid2 { myIntGrid };  // Copy constructor
Grid<int> anotherIntGrid;
anotherIntGrid = grid2;         // Assignment operator
```

Note that the type of `myIntGrid`, `grid2`, and `anotherIntGrid` is `Grid<int>`. You cannot store `SpreadsheetCells` or `ChessPieces` in these grids; the compiler will generate an error if you try to do so.

Note also the use of `value_or()`. The `at()` member functions return an `optional` reference, which can contain a value or not. `value_or()` returns the value inside the `optional` if there is a value; otherwise, it returns the argument given to `value_or()`.

The type specification is important; neither of the following two lines compiles:

```
Grid test;    // WILL NOT COMPILE
Grid<> test; // WILL NOT COMPILE
```

The first line causes the compiler to produce an error like "use of class template requires template argument list." The second line causes an error like "too few template arguments."

If you want to declare a function that takes a `Grid` object, you must specify the type stored in that grid as part of the `Grid` type:

```
void processIntGrid(Grid<int>& grid) { /* Body omitted for brevity */ }
```

Alternatively, you can use function templates, discussed later in this chapter, to write a function parametrized on the type of the elements in the grid.

The `Grid` class template can store more than just `int`s. For example, you can instantiate a `Grid` that stores `SpreadsheetCell`s:

```
Grid<SpreadsheetCell> mySpreadsheet;
SpreadsheetCell myCell { 1.234 };
mySpreadsheet.at(3, 4) = myCell;
```

You can store pointer types as well:

```
Grid<const char*> myStringGrid;
myStringGrid.at(2, 2) = "hello";
```

The type specified can even be another template type:

```
Grid<vector<int>> gridOfVectors;
vector<int> myVector { 1, 2, 3, 4 };
gridOfVectors.at(5, 6) = myVector;
```

You can also dynamically allocate `Grid` objects on the free store:

```
auto myGridOnFreeStore { make_unique<Grid<int>>(2, 2) }; // 2x2 Grid on free store.
myGridOnFreeStore->at(0, 0) = 10;
int x { myGridOnFreeStore->at(0, 0).value_or(0) };
```

How the Compiler Processes Templates

To understand the intricacies of templates, you need to learn how the compiler processes template code. When the compiler encounters class template member function definitions, it performs syntax checking, but doesn't actually compile the templates. It can't compile template definitions because it doesn't know for which types they will be used. It's impossible for a compiler to generate code for something like `x = y` without knowing the types of `x` and `y`. This syntax-checking step is the first step in the *two-phase name lookup* process.

The second step in the two-phase name lookup process happens when the compiler encounters an instantiation of the template, such as `Grid<int>`. At that moment, the compiler writes code for an `int` version of the `Grid` template by replacing each `T` in the class template definition with `int`. When the compiler encounters a different instantiation of the template, such as `Grid<SpreadsheetCell>`, it writes another version of the `Grid` class for `SpreadsheetCell`s. The compiler just writes the code that you would write if you didn't have template support in the language and had to write separate classes for each element type. There's no magic here; templates just automate an annoying process. If you don't instantiate a class template for any types in your program, then the class template member function definitions are never compiled.

This instantiation process explains why you need to use the `Grid<T>` syntax in various places in your definition. When the compiler instantiates the template for a particular type, such as `int`, it replaces `T` with `int`, so that `Grid<int>` is the type.

Selective/Implicit Instantiation

For *implicit class template instantiations* such as the following:

```
Grid<int> myIntGrid;
```

the compiler always generates code for all `virtual` member functions of the class template. However, for non-`virtual` member functions, the compiler generates code only for those non-`virtual` member functions that are actually called. For example, given the earlier `Grid` class template, suppose that you write this code (and only this code) in `main()`:

```
Grid<int> myIntGrid;
myIntGrid.at(0, 0) = 10;
```

The compiler generates only the zero-argument constructor, the destructor, and the non-`const at()` member function for an `int` version of `Grid`. It does not generate other member functions like the copy constructor, the assignment operator, or `getHeight()`. This is called *selective instantiation.*

Explicit Instantiation

The danger exists that there are compilation errors in some class template member functions that go unnoticed with implicit instantiations. Unused member functions of class templates can contain syntax errors, as these will not be compiled. This makes it hard to test all code for syntax errors. You can force the compiler to generate code for all member functions, `virtual` and non-`virtual`, by using *explicit template instantiations.* Here's an example:

```
template class Grid<string>;
```

> **NOTE** *Explicit template instantiations help with finding errors, as they force all your class template member functions to be compiled even when unused.*

When using explicit template instantiations, don't just try to instantiate the class template with basic types like `int`, but try it with more complicated types like `string`, if those are accepted by the class template.

Template Requirements on Types

When you write code that is independent of types, you must assume certain things about those types. For example, in the `Grid` class template, you assume that the element type (represented by `T`) is destructible, copy/move constructible, and copy/move assignable.

When the compiler attempts to instantiate a template with types that do not support all the operations used by class template member functions that are called, the code will not compile, and the error messages will often be quite obscure. However, even if the types you want to use don't support the operations required by all the member functions of the class template, you can exploit selective instantiation to use some member functions but not others.

You can use *concepts* to write requirements for template parameters that the compiler can interpret and validate. The compiler can generate more readable errors if the template arguments passed to instantiate a template do not satisfy these requirements. Concepts are discussed later in this chapter.

Distributing Template Code Between Files

With class templates, both the class template definition and the member function definitions must be available to the compiler from any source file that uses them. There are several mechanisms to accomplish this.

Member Function Definitions in Same File as Class Template Definition

You can place the member function definitions directly in the module interface file where you define the class template itself. When you import this module in another source file where you use the template, the compiler will have access to all the code it needs. This mechanism is used for the previous `Grid` implementation.

Member Function Definitions in Separate File

Alternatively, you can place the class template member function definitions in a separate module interface partition file. You then also need to put the class template definition in its own module interface partition. For example, the primary module interface file for the `Grid` class template could look like this:

```
export module grid;

export import :definition;
export import :implementation;
```

This imports and exports two module interface partitions: `definition` and `implementation`. The class template definition is defined in the `definition` partition:

```
export module grid:definition;

import std;

export template <typename T> class Grid { ... };
```

The implementations of the member functions are in the `implementation` partition, which also needs to import the `definition` partition because it needs the `Grid` class template definition:

```
export module grid:implementation;

import :definition;
import std;
```

```
export template <typename T>
Grid<T>::Grid(std::size_t width, std::size_t height)
    : m_width { width }, m_height { height }
{ /* ... */ }
// Remainder omitted for brevity.
```

Template Parameters

In the `Grid` example, the `Grid` class template has one *template parameter*: the type that is stored in the grid. When you write the class template, you specify the parameter list inside the angle brackets, like this:

```
template <typename T>
```

This parameter list is similar to the parameter list of functions. As with functions, you can write a class template with as many template parameters as you want. Additionally, these parameters don't have to be types, and they can have default values.

Non-type Template Parameters

Non-type template parameters are "normal" parameters such as `int`s and pointers—the kind of parameters which you're familiar with from functions. However, non-type template parameters can only be integral types (`char`, `int`, `long`, and so on), enumerations, pointers, references, `std::nullptr_t`, `auto`, `auto&`, `auto*`, floating-point types, and class types. The latter, however, come with a lot of limitations, not further discussed in this text. Remember that templates are instantiated at compile time; hence, arguments for non-type template parameters are evaluated at compile time. That means such arguments must be literals or compile-time constants.

In the `Grid` class template, you could use non-type template parameters to specify the height and width of the grid instead of specifying them in the constructor. The principal advantage of using non-type template parameters instead of constructor parameters is that the values are known before the code is compiled. Recall that the compiler generates code for template instantiations by substituting the template parameters before compiling. Thus, you can use a normal two-dimensional array in the following implementation instead of a linearized representation using a `vector` that is dynamically resized. Here is the new class template definition with the changes highlighted:

```
export template <typename T, std::size_t WIDTH, std::size_t HEIGHT>
class Grid
{
    public:
        Grid() = default;
        virtual ~Grid() = default;

        // Explicitly default a copy constructor and copy assignment operator.
        Grid(const Grid& src) = default;
        Grid& operator=(const Grid& rhs) = default;

        // Explicitly default a move constructor and move assignment operator.
        Grid(Grid&& src) = default;
        Grid& operator=(Grid&& rhs) = default;

        std::optional<T>& at(std::size_t x, std::size_t y);
```

```
        const std::optional<T>& at(std::size_t x, std::size_t y) const;

        std::size_t getHeight() const { return HEIGHT; }
        std::size_t getWidth() const { return WIDTH; }

    private:
        void verifyCoordinate(std::size_t x, std::size_t y) const;

        std::optional<T> m_cells[WIDTH][HEIGHT];
};
```

The template parameter list now has three parameters: the type of objects stored in the grid, and the width and height of the grid. The width and height are used to create a two-dimensional array to store the objects. Here are the class template member function definitions:

```
template <typename T, std::size_t WIDTH, std::size_t HEIGHT>
void Grid<T, WIDTH, HEIGHT>::verifyCoordinate(std::size_t x, std::size_t y) const
{
    if (x >= WIDTH) {
        throw std::out_of_range {
            std::format("x ({}) must be less than width ({}).", x, WIDTH) };
    }
    if (y >= HEIGHT) {
        throw std::out_of_range {
            std::format("y ({}) must be less than height ({}).", y, HEIGHT) };
    }
}

template <typename T, std::size_t WIDTH, std::size_t HEIGHT>
const std::optional<T>& Grid<T, WIDTH, HEIGHT>::at(
    std::size_t x, std::size_t y) const
{
    verifyCoordinate(x, y);
    return m_cells[x][y];
}

template <typename T, std::size_t WIDTH, std::size_t HEIGHT>
std::optional<T>& Grid<T, WIDTH, HEIGHT>::at(std::size_t x, std::size_t y)
{
    return const_cast<std::optional<T>&>(std::as_const(*this).at(x, y));
}
```

Note that wherever you previously specified `Grid<T>` you must now specify `Grid<T,WIDTH,HEIGHT>` to specify the three template parameters.

You can instantiate this template and use it as follows:

```
Grid<int, 10, 10> myGrid;
Grid<int, 10, 10> anotherGrid;
myGrid.at(2, 3) = 42;
anotherGrid = myGrid;
println("{}", anotherGrid.at(2, 3).value_or(0));
```

This code seems great, but unfortunately, there are more restrictions than you might initially expect. First, you can't use a non-constant integer to specify the height or width. The following code doesn't compile:

```
size_t height { 10 };
Grid<int, 10, height> testGrid; // DOES NOT COMPILE
```

If you define `height` as a constant, it compiles:

```
const size_t height { 10 };
Grid<int, 10, height> testGrid; // Compiles and works
```

`constexpr` functions with the correct return type also work. For example, if you have a `constexpr` function returning a `size_t`, you can use it to initialize the height template parameter:

```
constexpr size_t getHeight() { return 10; }
...
Grid<double, 2, getHeight()> myDoubleGrid;
```

A second restriction might be more significant. Now that the width and height are template parameters, they are part of the type of each grid. That means `Grid<int,10,10>` and `Grid<int,10,11>` are two different types. You can't assign an object of one type to an object of the other, and variables of one type can't be passed to functions that expect variables of another type.

> **NOTE** *Non-type template parameters become part of the type specification of instantiated objects.*

Default Values for Template Parameters

If you continue the approach of making height and width template parameters, you might want to provide defaults for the height and width non-type template parameters just as you did previously in the constructor of the `Grid<T>` class template. C++ allows you to provide defaults for template parameters with a similar syntax. While you are at it, you could also provide a default for the `T` type parameter. Here is the class definition:

```
export template <typename T = int, std::size_t WIDTH = 10, std::size_t HEIGHT = 10>
class Grid
{
    // Remainder is identical to the previous version
};
```

You don't specify the default values for `T`, `WIDTH`, and `HEIGHT` in the template header for the member function definitions. For example, here is the implementation of `at()`:

```
template <typename T, std::size_t WIDTH, std::size_t HEIGHT>
const std::optional<T>& Grid<T, WIDTH, HEIGHT>::at(
    std::size_t x, std::size_t y) const
{
    verifyCoordinate(x, y);
    return m_cells[x][y];
}
```

With these changes, you can instantiate a `Grid` without any template parameters, with only the element type, the element type and the width, or the element type, width, and height:

```
Grid<> myIntGrid;
Grid<int> myGrid;
Grid<int, 5> anotherGrid;
Grid<int, 5, 5> aFourthGrid;
```

Note that if you don't specify any class template parameters, you still need to specify an empty set of angle brackets. For example, the following does not compile!

```
Grid myIntGrid;
```

The rules for default arguments in class template parameter lists are the same as for functions; that is, you can provide defaults for parameters in order starting from the right.

Class Template Argument Deduction

With class template argument deduction, the compiler can automatically deduce the template type parameters from the arguments passed to a class template constructor.

For example, the Standard Library has a class template called `std::pair`, defined in `<utility>` and introduced in Chapter 1. A `pair` stores exactly two values of two possibly different types, which you normally would have to specify as the template type parameters. Here's an example:

```
pair<int, double> pair1 { 1, 2.3 };
```

To avoid having to write the template type parameters explicitly, a helper function template called `std::make_pair()` is available. Details of writing your own function templates are discussed later in this chapter. Function templates have always supported the automatic deduction of template type parameters based on the arguments passed to the function template. Thus, `make_pair()` is capable of automatically deducing the template type parameters based on the values passed to it. For example, the compiler deduces `pair<int, double>` for the following call:

```
auto pair2 { make_pair(1, 2.3) };
```

With class template argument deduction (CTAD), such helper function templates are no longer necessary. The compiler now automatically deduces the template type parameters based on the arguments passed to a constructor. For the `pair` class template, you can simply write the following code:

```
pair pair3 { 1, 2.3 };  // pair3 has type pair<int, double>
```

Of course, this works only when all template type parameters of a class template either have default values or are used as parameters in the constructor so that they can be deduced.

Note that an initializer is required for CTAD to work. The following is illegal:

```
pair pair4;
```

A lot of the Standard Library classes support CTAD, for example, `vector`, `array`, and so on.

> **NOTE** *This type deduction is disabled for* `std::unique_ptr` *and* `shared_ptr`. *You pass a* `T*` *to their constructors, which means that the compiler would have to choose between deducing* `<T>` *or* `<T[]>`*, a dangerous choice to get wrong. So, just remember that for* `unique_ptr` *and* `shared_ptr`*, you need to keep using* `make_unique()` *and* `make_shared()`.

User-Defined Deduction Guides

You can also write your own user-defined *deduction guides* to help the compiler. These allow you to write rules for how the template type parameters have to be deduced. The following is an example demonstrating their use.

Suppose you have this `SpreadsheetCell` class template:

```
template <typename T>
class SpreadsheetCell
{
    public:
        explicit SpreadsheetCell(T t) : m_content { move(t) } { }
        const T& getContent() const { return m_content; }
    private:
        T m_content;
};
```

Thanks to CTAD, you can create a `SpreadsheetCell` with an `std::string` type. The deduced type is `SpreadsheetCell<string>`:

```
string myString { "Hello World!" };
SpreadsheetCell cell { myString };
```

However, if you pass a `const char*` to the `SpreadsheetCell` constructor, then type `T` is deduced as `const char*`, which is not what you want! You can create the following user-defined deduction guide to make sure `T` is deduced as `std::string` when passing a `const char*` as argument to the constructor:

```
SpreadsheetCell(const char*) -> SpreadsheetCell<std::string>;
```

This guide has to be defined outside the class definition but inside the same namespace as the `SpreadsheetCell` class.

The general syntax is as follows. The `explicit` keyword is optional and behaves the same as `explicit` for constructors. Such deduction guides are, more often than not, templates as well.

```
template <...>
explicit TemplateName(Parameters) -> DeducedTemplate<...>;
```

Member Function Templates

C++ allows you to parametrize individual member functions of a class. Such member functions are called *member function templates* and can be inside a normal class or in a class template. When you write a member function template, you are actually writing many different versions of that member function for many different types. Member function templates are useful for assignment operators and copy constructors in class templates.

> **WARNING** *Virtual member functions and destructors cannot be member function templates.*

Consider the original `Grid` template with only one template parameter: the element type. You can instantiate grids of many different types, such as `int`s and `double`s:

```
Grid<int> myIntGrid;
Grid<double> myDoubleGrid;
```

However, `Grid<int>` and `Grid<double>` are two different types. If you write a function that takes an object of type `Grid<double>`, you cannot pass a `Grid<int>`. Even though you know that the elements of an `int` grid could be copied to the elements of a `double` grid, because `int`s can be converted into `double`s, you cannot assign an object of type `Grid<int>` to one of type `Grid<double>` or construct a `Grid<double>` from a `Grid<int>`. Neither of the following two lines compiles:

```
myDoubleGrid = myIntGrid;                     // DOES NOT COMPILE
Grid<double> newDoubleGrid { myIntGrid }; // DOES NOT COMPILE
```

The problem is that the copy constructor and assignment operator for the `Grid` template are as follows:

```
Grid(const Grid& src);
Grid& operator=(const Grid& rhs);
```

which are equivalent to:

```
Grid(const Grid<T>& src);
Grid<T>& operator=(const Grid<T>& rhs);
```

The `Grid` copy constructor and `operator=` both take a reference to a `const Grid<T>`. When you instantiate a `Grid<double>` and try to call the copy constructor and `operator=`, the compiler generates member functions with these prototypes:

```
Grid(const Grid<double>& src);
Grid<double>& operator=(const Grid<double>& rhs);
```

There are no constructors or `operator=` that take a `Grid<int>` within the generated `Grid<double>` class.

Luckily, you can rectify this oversight by adding parametrized versions of the copy constructor and assignment operator to the `Grid` class template to generate member functions that will convert from one grid type to another. Here is the new `Grid` class template definition:

```
export template <typename T>
class Grid
{
    public:
```

```
        template <typename E>
        Grid(const Grid<E>& src);

        template <typename E>
        Grid& operator=(const Grid<E>& rhs);

        void swap(Grid& other) noexcept;

        // Omitted for brevity
};
```

The original copy constructor and copy assignment operator cannot be removed. The compiler will not call these new parametrized copy constructor and parametrized copy assignment operator if `E` equals `T`.

Examine the new parametrized copy constructor first:

```
template <typename E>
Grid(const Grid<E>& src);
```

You can see that there is another template header with a different typename, `E` (short for "element"). The class is parametrized on one type, `T`, and the new copy constructor is additionally parametrized on a different type, `E`. This twofold parametrization allows you to copy grids of one type to another. Here is the definition of the new copy constructor:

```
template <typename T>
template <typename E>
Grid<T>::Grid(const Grid<E>& src)
    : Grid { src.getWidth(), src.getHeight() }
{
    // The ctor-initializer of this constructor delegates first to the
    // non-copy constructor to allocate the proper amount of memory.

    // The next step is to copy the data.
    for (std::size_t i { 0 }; i < m_width; ++i) {
        for (std::size_t j { 0 }; j < m_height; ++j) {
            at(i, j) = src.at(i, j);
        }
    }
}
```

As you can see, you must declare the class template header (with the `T` parameter) before the member template header (with the `E` parameter). You can't combine them like this:

```
template <typename T, typename E> // Wrong for nested template constructor!
Grid<T>::Grid(const Grid<E>& src)
```

In addition to the extra template header before the constructor definition, note that you must use the public accessor member functions `getWidth()`, `getHeight()`, and `at()` to access the elements of `src`. That's because the object you're copying to is of type `Grid<T>`, and the object you're copying from is of type `Grid<E>`. They are not the same type, so you must use public member functions.

The `swap()` member function is straightforward:

```
template <typename T>
void Grid<T>::swap(Grid& other) noexcept
{
```

```
        std::swap(m_width, other.m_width);
        std::swap(m_height, other.m_height);
        std::swap(m_cells, other.m_cells);
    }
```

The parametrized assignment operator takes a `const Grid<E>&` but returns a `Grid<T>&`:

```
template <typename T>
template <typename E>
Grid<T>& Grid<T>::operator=(const Grid<E>& rhs)
{
    // Copy-and-swap idiom
    Grid<T> temp { rhs }; // Do all the work in a temporary instance.
    swap(temp); // Commit the work with only non-throwing operations.
    return *this;
}
```

The implementation of this assignment operator uses the copy-and-swap idiom introduced in Chapter 9. The `swap()` member function can only swap `Grid`s of the same type, but that's OK because this parametrized assignment operator first converts a given `Grid<E>` to a `Grid<T>` called `temp` using the parametrized copy constructor. Afterward, it uses the `swap()` member function to swap this temporary `Grid<T>` with `this`, which is also of type `Grid<T>`.

Member Function Templates with Non-type Template Parameters

A major problem with the earlier `Grid` class template with integer template parameters for `HEIGHT` and `WIDTH` is that the height and width become part of the types. This restriction prevents you from assigning a grid with one height and width to a grid with a different height and width. In some cases, however, it's desirable to assign or copy a grid of one size to a grid of a different size. Instead of making the destination object a perfect clone of the source object, you would copy only those elements from the source array that fit in the destination array, padding the destination array with default values if the source array is smaller in either dimension. With member function templates for the assignment operator and copy constructor, you can do exactly that, thus allowing assignment and copying of different-sized grids. Here is the class definition:

```
export template <typename T, std::size_t WIDTH = 10, std::size_t HEIGHT = 10>
class Grid
{
    public:
        Grid() = default;
        virtual ~Grid() = default;

        // Explicitly default a copy constructor and assignment operator.
        Grid(const Grid& src) = default;
        Grid& operator=(const Grid& rhs) = default;

        // Explicitly default a move constructor and move assignment operator.
        Grid(Grid&& src) = default;
        Grid& operator=(Grid&& rhs) = default;

        template <typename E, std::size_t WIDTH2, std::size_t HEIGHT2>
        Grid(const Grid<E, WIDTH2, HEIGHT2>& src);
```

```
        template <typename E, std::size_t WIDTH2, std::size_t HEIGHT2>
        Grid& operator=(const Grid<E, WIDTH2, HEIGHT2>& rhs);

        void swap(Grid& other) noexcept;

        std::optional<T>& at(std::size_t x, std::size_t y);
        const std::optional<T>& at(std::size_t x, std::size_t y) const;

        std::size_t getHeight() const { return HEIGHT; }
        std::size_t getWidth() const { return WIDTH; }

    private:
        void verifyCoordinate(std::size_t x, std::size_t y) const;

        std::optional<T> m_cells[WIDTH][HEIGHT];
};
```

This new definition includes member function templates for the copy constructor and assignment operator, plus a helper member function `swap()`. Note that the non-parametrized copy constructor and assignment operator are explicitly defaulted (because of the user-declared destructor). They simply copy or assign `m_cells` from the source to the destination, which is exactly the semantics you want for two grids of the same size.

Here is the parametrized copy constructor:

```
template <typename T, std::size_t WIDTH, std::size_t HEIGHT>
template <typename E, std::size_t WIDTH2, std::size_t HEIGHT2>
Grid<T, WIDTH, HEIGHT>::Grid(const Grid<E, WIDTH2, HEIGHT2>& src)
{
    for (std::size_t i { 0 }; i < WIDTH; ++i) {
        for (std::size_t j { 0 }; j < HEIGHT; ++j) {
            if (i < WIDTH2 && j < HEIGHT2) {
                m_cells[i][j] = src.at(i, j);
            } else {
                m_cells[i][j].reset();
            }
        }
    }
}
```

Note that this copy constructor copies only `WIDTH` and `HEIGHT` elements in the x and y dimensions, respectively, from `src`, even if `src` is bigger than that. If `src` is smaller in either dimension, the `std::optional` objects in the extra spots are reset using the `reset()` member function.

Here are the implementations of `swap()` and `operator=`:

```
template <typename T, std::size_t WIDTH, std::size_t HEIGHT>
void Grid<T, WIDTH, HEIGHT>::swap(Grid& other) noexcept
{
    std::swap(m_cells, other.m_cells);
}

template <typename T, std::size_t WIDTH, std::size_t HEIGHT>
template <typename E, std::size_t WIDTH2, std::size_t HEIGHT2>
Grid<T, WIDTH, HEIGHT>& Grid<T, WIDTH, HEIGHT>::operator=(
```

```
        const Grid<E, WIDTH2, HEIGHT2>& rhs)
{
    // Copy-and-swap idiom
    Grid<T, WIDTH, HEIGHT> temp { rhs }; // Do all the work in a temp instance.
    swap(temp); // Commit the work with only non-throwing operations.
    return *this;
}
```

C++23 Using Member Function Templates with Explicit Object Parameters to Avoid Code Duplication

Our running example of the `Grid` class template with a single template type parameter `T` contains two overloads of an `at()` member function, `const` and non-`const`. As a reminder:

```
export template <typename T>
class Grid
{
    public:
        std::optional<T>& at(std::size_t x, std::size_t y);
        const std::optional<T>& at(std::size_t x, std::size_t y) const;
        // Remainder omitted for brevity
};
```

Their implementations use Scott Meyers' `const_cast()` pattern to avoid code duplication:

```
template <typename T>
const std::optional<T>& Grid<T>::at(std::size_t x, std::size_t y) const
{
    verifyCoordinate(x, y);
    return m_cells[x + y * m_width];
}

template <typename T>
std::optional<T>& Grid<T>::at(std::size_t x, std::size_t y)
{
    return const_cast<std::optional<T>&>(std::as_const(*this).at(x, y));
}
```

Although there is no code duplication, you still need to define both the `const` and non-`const` overloads explicitly. Starting with C++23, you can use an *explicit object parameter* (see Chapter 8) to avoid having to provide the two overloads explicitly. The trick is to turn the `at()` member function into a member function template where the type of the explicit object parameter `self` is itself a template type parameter, `Self`, and thus deduced automatically. This feature is called *deducing this*. Here is such a declaration:

```
export template <typename T>
class Grid
{
    public:
        template <typename Self>
        auto&& at(this Self&& self, std::size_t x, std::size_t y);
        // Remainder omitted for brevity
};
```

The implementation uses a *forwarding reference*, Self&&; see the following note. Such a forwarding reference can bind to Grid<T>&, const Grid<T>&, and Grid<T>&&.

> **NOTE** *A reference of type* Self&& *is only a forwarding reference when it is used as a parameter for a function or member function template with* Self *as one of its template type parameters. If a class member function has a* Self&& *parameter, but with* Self *a template type parameter of the class and not of the member function itself, then that* Self&& *is not a forwarding reference, but just an rvalue reference. That's because at the time the compiler starts processing that member function with a* Self&& *parameter, the class template parameter* Self *has already been resolved to a concrete type, for example* int*, and at that time, that member function parameter type has already been replaced with* int&&.

Here is the implementation. Remember from Chapter 8 that in the body of a member function using an explicit object parameter, you need to use the explicit object parameter, self in this case, to get access to the object; there is no this pointer.

```
template <typename T>
template <typename Self>
auto&& Grid<T>::at(this Self&& self, std::size_t x, std::size_t y)
{
    self.verifyCoordinate(x, y);
    return std::forward_like<Self>(self.m_cells[x + y * self.m_width]);
}
```

The implementation uses std::forward_like<Self>(x) introduced in C++23. This returns a reference to x with similar properties as Self&&. Thus, since the type of the elements of m_cells is optional<T>, the following holds:

- If Self&& is bound to a Grid<T>&, the return type will be an optional<T>&.
- If Self&& is bound to a const Grid<T>&, the return type will be a const optional<T>&.
- If Self&& is bound to a Grid<T>&&, the return type will be an optional<T>&&.

To summarize, with a combination of member function templates, explicit object parameters, forwarding references, and forward_like(), it becomes possible to declare and define just a single member function template that provides both const and non-const instantiations.

Class Template Specialization

You can provide alternate implementations of class templates for specific types. For example, you might decide that the Grid behavior for const char*s (C-style strings) doesn't make sense. A Grid<const char*> will store its elements in a vector<optional<const char*>>. The copy constructor and assignment operator will perform shallow copies of this const char* pointer type. For const char*s, it makes more sense to do a deep copy of strings. The easiest solution for this is to write an alternative implementation specifically for const char*s, which converts them to C++ strings and stores them in a vector<optional<string>>.

Alternate implementations of templates are called *template specializations*. You might find the syntax to be a little weird at first. When you write a class template specialization, you must specify that it's based on a template and that you are writing a version of the template for a particular type. Here is the syntax for a `const char*` specialization for `Grid`. For this implementation, the original `Grid` class template is moved to a module interface partition called `main`, while the specialization is in a module interface partition called `string`.

```
export module grid:string;
import std;
// When the template specialization is used, the original template must be
// visible too.
import :main;

export template <>
class Grid<const char*>
{
    public:
        explicit Grid(std::size_t width = DefaultWidth,
            std::size_t height = DefaultHeight);
        virtual ~Grid() = default;

        // Explicitly default a copy constructor and assignment operator.
        Grid(const Grid& src) = default;
        Grid& operator=(const Grid& rhs) = default;

        // Explicitly default a move constructor and assignment operator.
        Grid(Grid&& src) = default;
        Grid& operator=(Grid&& rhs) = default;

        std::optional<std::string>& at(std::size_t x, std::size_t y);
        const std::optional<std::string>& at(std::size_t x, std::size_t y) const;

        std::size_t getHeight() const { return m_height; }
        std::size_t getWidth() const { return m_width; }

        static constexpr std::size_t DefaultWidth { 10 };
        static constexpr std::size_t DefaultHeight { 10 };

    private:
        void verifyCoordinate(std::size_t x, std::size_t y) const;

        std::vector<std::optional<std::string>> m_cells;
        std::size_t m_width { 0 }, m_height { 0 };
};
```

Note that you don't refer to any type variable, such as `T`, in the specialization: you work directly with `const char*`s and `string`s. One obvious question at this point is why this class still has a template header. That is, what good is the following syntax?

```
template <>
class Grid<const char*>
```

This syntax tells the compiler that this class is a `const char*` specialization of the `Grid` class template. Suppose that you didn't use that syntax and just tried to write this:

```
class Grid
```

The compiler wouldn't let you do that because there is already a class template named `Grid` (the original class template). Only by specializing it can you reuse the name. The main benefit of specializations is that they can be invisible to the user. When a user creates a `Grid` of `int`s or `SpreadsheetCell`s, the compiler generates code from the original `Grid` template. When the user creates a `Grid` of `const char*`s, the compiler uses the `const char*` specialization. This can all be "behind the scenes."

The primary module interface file simply imports and exports both module interface partitions:

```
export module grid;

export import :main;
export import :string;
```

The specialization can be tested as follows:

```
Grid<int> myIntGrid;                      // Uses original Grid template.
Grid<const char*> stringGrid1 { 2, 2 }; // Uses const char* specialization.

const char* dummy { "dummy" };
stringGrid1.at(0, 0) = "hello";
stringGrid1.at(0, 1) = dummy;
stringGrid1.at(1, 0) = dummy;
stringGrid1.at(1, 1) = "there";

Grid<const char*> stringGrid2 { stringGrid1 };
```

When you specialize a class template, you don't "inherit" any code; specializations are not like derivations. You must rewrite the entire implementation of the class. There is no requirement that you provide member functions with the same names or behavior. As an example, the `const char*` specialization of `Grid` implements the `at()` member functions by returning an `optional<string>`, not an `optional<const char*>`. As a matter of fact, you could write a completely different class with no relation to the original. Of course, that would abuse the template specialization ability, and you shouldn't do it without good reason. Here are the implementations for the member functions of the `const char*` specialization. Unlike in the class template definition, you do not repeat the template header, `template<>`, before each member function definition.

```
Grid<const char*>::Grid(std::size_t width, std::size_t height)
    : m_width { width }, m_height { height }
{
    m_cells.resize(m_width * m_height);
}

void Grid<const char*>::verifyCoordinate(std::size_t x, std::size_t y) const
{
    if (x >= m_width) {
        throw std::out_of_range {
            std::format("x ({}) must be less than width ({}).", x, m_width) };
    }
    if (y >= m_height) {
        throw std::out_of_range {
            std::format("y ({}) must be less than height ({}).", y, m_height) };
    }
}
```

```
const std::optional<std::string>& Grid<const char*>::at(
    std::size_t x, std::size_t y) const
{
    verifyCoordinate(x, y);
    return m_cells[x + y * m_width];
}

std::optional<std::string>& Grid<const char*>::at(std::size_t x, std::size_t y)
{
    return const_cast<std::optional<std::string>&>(
        std::as_const(*this).at(x, y));
}
```

This section discussed how to use class template specialization to write a special implementation for a class template, with all template type parameters replaced with specific types. This is called *full template specialization*. Such a full class template specialization is no longer a class template itself but a class definition. Chapter 26, "Advanced Templates," continues the discussion of class template specialization with a more advanced feature called *partial specialization*.

Deriving from Class Templates

You can inherit from class templates. If the derived class inherits from the template itself, it must be a template as well. Alternatively, you can derive from a specific instantiation of the class template, in which case your derived class does not need to be a template. As an example of the former, suppose you decide that the generic `Grid` class doesn't provide enough functionality to use as a game board. Specifically, you would like to add a `move()` member function to the game board that moves a piece from one location on the board to another. Here is the class definition for the `GameBoard` template:

```
import grid;

export template <typename T>
class GameBoard : public Grid<T>
{
    public:
        // Inherit constructors from Grid<T>.
        using Grid<T>::Grid;

        void move(std::size_t xSrc, std::size_t ySrc,
            std::size_t xDest, std::size_t yDest);
};
```

This `GameBoard` template derives from the `Grid` template and thereby inherits all its functionality. You don't need to rewrite `at()`, `getHeight()`, or any of the other member functions. You also don't need to add a copy constructor, `operator=`, or destructor, because you don't have any dynamically allocated memory in `GameBoard`. Additionally, `GameBoard` explicitly inherits the constructors from the base class, `Grid<T>`. Inheriting constructors from base classes is explained in Chapter 10, "Discovering Inheritance Techniques."

The inheritance syntax looks normal, except that the base class is `Grid<T>`, not `Grid`. The reason for this syntax is that the `GameBoard` template doesn't really derive from the generic `Grid` template.

Rather, each instantiation of the `GameBoard` template for a specific type derives from the `Grid` instantiation for that same type. For example, if you instantiate a `GameBoard` with a `ChessPiece` type, then the compiler generates code for a `Grid<ChessPiece>` as well. The `: public Grid<T>` syntax says that this class inherits from whatever `Grid` instantiation makes sense for the `T` type parameter.

Here is the implementation of the `move()` member function:

```
template <typename T>
void GameBoard<T>::move(std::size_t xSrc, std::size_t ySrc,
    std::size_t xDest, std::size_t yDest)
{
    Grid<T>::at(xDest, yDest) = std::move(Grid<T>::at(xSrc, ySrc));
    Grid<T>::at(xSrc, ySrc).reset();  // Reset source cell
    // Or:
    // this->at(xDest, yDest) = std::move(this->at(xSrc, ySrc));
    // this->at(xSrc, ySrc).reset();
}
```

> **NOTE** *Although some compilers don't enforce it, the C++ name lookup rules require you to use the* `this` *pointer or* `Grid<T>::` *to refer to data members and member functions in a base class template. Hence, we use* `Grid<T>::at()` *instead of just* `at()`.

You can use the `GameBoard` template as follows:

```
GameBoard<ChessPiece> chessboard { 8, 8 };
ChessPiece pawn;
chessBoard.at(0, 0) = pawn;
chessBoard.move(0, 0, 0, 1);
```

> **NOTE** *Of course, if you want to override member functions from* `Grid`*, you will have to mark them* `virtual` *in the* `Grid` *class template.*

Inheritance vs. Specialization

Some programmers find the distinction between template inheritance and template specialization confusing. The following table summarizes the differences:

	INHERITANCE	SPECIALIZATION
Reuses code?	**Yes:** Derived classes contain all base class data members and member functions.	**No:** You must rewrite all required code in the specialization.

	INHERITANCE	SPECIALIZATION
Reuses name?	**No:** The derived class name must be different from the base class name.	**Yes:** The specialization must have the same name as the original.
Supports polymorphism?	**Yes:** Objects of the derived class can stand in for objects of the base class.	**No:** Each instantiation of a template for a type is a different type.

> **NOTE** *Use inheritance for extending implementations and for polymorphism. Use specialization for customizing implementations for particular types.*

Alias Templates

Chapter 1 introduces the concept of type aliases and `typedef`s. They allow you to give other names to specific types. To refresh your memory, you could, for example, write the following type alias to give a second name to type `int`:

```
using MyInt = int;
```

Similarly, you can use a type alias to give another name to a class template. Suppose you have the following class template:

```
template <typename T1, typename T2>
class MyClassTemplate { /* ... */ };
```

You can define the following type alias in which you specify both class template type parameters:

```
using OtherName = MyClassTemplate<int, double>;
```

A `typedef` can also be used instead of such a type alias.

Additionally, it's also possible to specify only some of the types and keep the other types as template type parameters. This is called an *alias template*. Here's an example:

```
template <typename T1>
using OtherName = MyClassTemplate<T1, double>;
```

This is something you cannot do with a `typedef`.

FUNCTION TEMPLATES

You can also write templates for stand-alone functions. The syntax is similar to the syntax for class templates. For example, you could write the following generic function to find a value in an array and return its index:

```
template <typename T>
optional<size_t> Find(const T& value, const T* arr, size_t size)
{
```

```
        for (size_t i { 0 }; i < size; ++i) {
            if (arr[i] == value) {
                return i; // Found it; return the index.
            }
        }
        return {}; // Failed to find it; return empty optional.
    }
```

The `Find()` function template can work on arrays of any type. For example, you could use it to find the index of an `int` in an array of `int`s or a `SpreadsheetCell` in an array of `SpreadsheetCell`s.

You can call the function in two ways: explicitly specifying the template type parameter with angle brackets or omitting the type and letting the compiler *deduce* the type parameter from the arguments. Here are some examples:

```
int myInt { 3 }, intArray[] {1, 2, 3, 4};
const size_t sizeIntArray { size(intArray) };

optional<size_t> res;
res = Find(myInt, intArray, sizeIntArray);      // calls Find<int> by deduction.
res = Find<int>(myInt, intArray, sizeIntArray); // calls Find<int> explicitly.
if (res) { println("{}", *res); }
else { println("Not found"); }

double myDouble { 5.6 }, doubleArray[] {1.2, 3.4, 5.7, 7.5};
const size_t sizeDoubleArray { size(doubleArray) };

// calls Find<double> by deduction.
res = Find(myDouble, doubleArray, sizeDoubleArray);
// calls Find<double> explicitly.
res = Find<double>(myDouble, doubleArray, sizeDoubleArray);
if (res) { println("{}", *res); }
else { println("Not found"); }

//res = Find(myInt, doubleArray, sizeDoubleArray); // DOES NOT COMPILE!
                                     // Arguments are different types.
// calls Find<double> explicitly, even with myInt.
res = Find<double>(myInt, doubleArray, sizeDoubleArray);

SpreadsheetCell cell1 { 10 }
SpreadsheetCell cellArray[] { SpreadsheetCell { 4 }, SpreadsheetCell { 10 } };
const size_t sizeCellArray { size(cellArray) };

res = Find(cell1, cellArray, sizeCellArray);
res = Find<SpreadsheetCell>(cell1, cellArray, sizeCellArray);
```

The previous implementation of the `Find()` function template requires the size of the array as one of the parameters. Sometimes the compiler knows the exact size of an array, for example, for stack-based arrays. It would be nice to be able to call `Find()` with such arrays without the need to pass it the size of the array. This can be accomplished by adding the following function template. The implementation just forwards the call to the previous `Find()` function template. This also demonstrates that function templates can take non-type parameters, just like class templates.

```
template <typename T, size_t N>
optional<size_t> Find(const T& value, const T(&arr)[N])
{
```

```
        return Find(value, arr, N);
    }
```

The syntax of this overload of `Find()` looks a bit strange, but its use is straightforward, as in this example:

```
int myInt { 3 }, intArray[] {1, 2, 3, 4};
optional<size_t> res { Find(myInt, intArray) };
```

Like class template member function definitions, function template definitions (not just the prototypes) must be available to all source files that use them. Thus, you should put the definitions in module interface files and export them if more than one source file uses them.

Finally, template parameters of function templates can have defaults, just like class templates.

> **NOTE** *The C++ Standard Library provides an* `std::find()` *function template that is more powerful than the* `Find()` *function template shown here. See Chapter 20, "Mastering Standard Library Algorithms," for details.*

Function Overloads vs. Function Template

There are two options when you want to provide a function that can work with different data types: provide function overloads or provide a function template. How do you choose between those two options?

When writing a function that should work with different data types and for which the body of the function is the same for all data types, provide a function template. If the body of the function is different for every data type, provide function overloads.

Function Template Overloading

In theory, the C++ language allows you to write function template specializations, just as you can write class template specializations. However, you rarely want to do this because such function template specializations do not participate in overload resolution and hence might behave unexpectedly.

Instead, you can overload function templates with either non-template functions or other function templates. For example, you might want to write a `Find()` overload for `const char*` C-style strings that compares them with `strcmp()` (see Chapter 2, "Working with Strings and String Views") instead of `operator==`, as `==` would only compare pointers, not the actual strings. Here is such an overload:

```
optional<size_t> Find(const char* value, const char** arr, size_t size)
{
    for (size_t i { 0 }; i < size; ++i) {
        if (strcmp(arr[i], value) == 0) {
            return i; // Found it; return the index.
        }
    }
    return {}; // Failed to find it; return empty optional.
}
```

This function overload can be used as follows:

```
// Using an array for word to make sure no literal pooling happens, see Chapter 2.
const char word[] { "two" };
const char* words[] { "one", "two", "three", "four" };
const size_t sizeWords { size(words) };
optional<size_t> res { Find(word, words, sizeWords) }; // Calls non-template Find.
if (res) { println("{}", *res); }
else { println("Not found"); }
```

The call to `Find()` correctly finds the string "two" at index 1.

If you do explicitly specify the template type parameter as follows, then the function template will be called with `T=const char*`, and not the overload for `const char*`:

```
res = Find<const char*>(word, words, sizeWords);
```

This call of `Find()` does not find any matches, as it doesn't compare the actual strings, but just pointers.

When the overload resolution process of the compiler results in two possible candidates, one being a function template, the other being a non-template function, then the compiler always prefers to use the non-template function.

Function Templates as Friends of Class Templates

Function templates are useful when you want to overload operators in a class template. For example, you might want to overload the addition operator (`operator+`) for the `Grid` class template to be able to add two grids together. The result will be a `Grid` with the same size as the smallest `Grid` of the two operands. Corresponding cells are added together only if both cells contain an actual value. Suppose you want to make your `operator+` a stand-alone function template. The definition, which should go in the `Grid.cppm` module interface file, looks as follows. The implementation uses `std::min()`, defined in `<algorithm>`, to return the minimum value of two given arguments:

```
export template <typename T>
Grid<T> operator+(const Grid<T>& lhs, const Grid<T>& rhs)
{
    std::size_t minWidth { std::min(lhs.m_width, rhs.m_width) };
    std::size_t minHeight { std::min(lhs.m_height, rhs.m_height) };

    Grid<T> result { minWidth, minHeight };
    for (std::size_t y { 0 }; y < minHeight; ++y) {
        for (std::size_t x { 0 }; x < minWidth; ++x) {
            const auto& leftElement { lhs.at(x, y) };
            const auto& rightElement { rhs.at(x, y) };
            if (leftElement.has_value() && rightElement.has_value()) {
                result.at(x, y) = leftElement.value() + rightElement.value();
            }
        }
    }
    return result;
}
```

To query whether an optional contains an actual value, you use the has_value() member function, while value() is used to retrieve this value.

This function template works on any Grid, as long as there is an addition operator for the type of elements stored in the grid. The only problem with this implementation is that it accesses private members m_width and m_height of the Grid class. The obvious solution is to use the public getWidth() and getHeight() member functions, but let's see how you can make a function template a friend of a class template. For this example, you can make the operator a friend of the Grid class template. However, both Grid and the operator+ are templates. What you really want is for each instantiation of operator+ for a particular type T to be a friend of the Grid template instantiation for that same type. The syntax looks like this:

```
export template <typename T>
class Grid
{
    public:
        friend Grid operator+<T>(const Grid& lhs, const Grid& rhs);
        // Omitted for brevity
};
```

This friend declaration is tricky: you're saying that, for an instance of the class template with type T, the T instantiation of operator+ is a friend. In other words, there is a one-to-one mapping of friends between the class instantiations and the function instantiations. Note particularly the explicit template specification <T> on operator+. This syntax tells the compiler that operator+ is itself a template.

This friend operator+ can be tested as follows. The following code first defines two helper function templates: fillGrid(), which fills any Grid with increasing numbers, and printGrid(), which prints any Grid to the console.

```
template <typename T> void fillGrid(Grid<T>& grid)
{
    T index { 0 };
    for (size_t y { 0 }; y < grid.getHeight(); ++y) {
        for (size_t x { 0 }; x < grid.getWidth(); ++x) {
            grid.at(x, y) = ++index;
        }
    }
}

template <typename T> void printGrid(const Grid<T>& grid)
{
    for (size_t y { 0 }; y < grid.getHeight(); ++y) {
        for (size_t x { 0 }; x < grid.getWidth(); ++x) {
            const auto& element { grid.at(x, y) };
            if (element.has_value()) { print("{}\t", element.value()); }
            else { print("n/a\t"); }
        }
        println("");
    }
}
```

```
int main()
{
    Grid<int> grid1 { 2, 2 };
    Grid<int> grid2 { 3, 3 };
    fillGrid(grid1);  println("grid1:");      printGrid(grid1);
    fillGrid(grid2);  println("\ngrid2:");    printGrid(grid2);
    auto result { grid1 + grid2 };
    println("\ngrid1 + grid2:");  printGrid(result);
}
```

More on Template Type Parameter Deduction

The compiler deduces the type of function template parameters based on the arguments passed to the function template. Template parameters that cannot be deduced have to be specified explicitly.

For example, the following `add()` function template requires three template parameters: the type of the return value and the types of the two operands:

```
template <typename RetType, typename T1, typename T2>
RetType add(const T1& t1, const T2& t2) { return t1 + t2; }
```

You can call this function template specifying all three parameters as follows:

```
auto result { add<long long, int, int>(1, 2) };
```

However, because the template parameters `T1` and `T2` are parameters to the function, the compiler can deduce those two parameters, so you can call `add()` by only specifying the type for the return value:

```
auto result { add<long long>(1, 2) };
```

This works only when the parameters to deduce are last in the list of parameters. Suppose the function template is defined as follows:

```
template <typename T1, typename RetType, typename T2>
RetType add(const T1& t1, const T2& t2) { return t1 + t2; }
```

You have to specify `RetType`, because the compiler cannot deduce that type. However, because `RetType` is the second parameter, you have to explicitly specify `T1` as well:

```
auto result { add<int, long long>(1, 2) };
```

You can also provide a default value for the return type template parameter so that you can call `add()` without specifying any types:

```
template <typename RetType = long long, typename T1, typename T2>
RetType add(const T1& t1, const T2& t2) { return t1 + t2; }
...
auto result { add(1, 2) };
```

Return Type of Function Templates

Continuing the example of the `add()` function template, wouldn't it be nice to let the compiler deduce the type of the return value? It would; however, the return type depends on the template type parameters, so how can you do this? For example, take the following function template:

```
template <typename T1, typename T2>
RetType add(const T1& t1, const T2& t2) { return t1 + t2; }
```

In this example, *RetType* should be the type of the expression `t1+t2`, but you don't know this because you don't know what `T1` and `T2` are.

As discussed in Chapter 1, since C++14 you can ask the compiler to automatically deduce the return type for a function. So you can simply write `add()` as follows:

```
template <typename T1, typename T2>
auto add(const T1& t1, const T2& t2) { return t1 + t2; }
```

However, using `auto` to deduce the type of an expression strips away reference and `const` qualifiers, while `decltype` does not strip those. This stripping is fine for the `add()` function template because `operator+` usually returns a new object anyway, but this stripping might not be desirable for certain other function templates, so let's see how you can avoid it.

Before continuing with the function template examples, however, let's first look at the differences between `auto` and `decltype` using a non-template example. Suppose you have the following function:

```
const std::string message { "Test" };

const std::string& getString() { return message; }
```

You can call `getString()` and store the result in a variable with the type specified as `auto` as follows:

```
auto s1 { getString() };
```

Because `auto` strips reference and `const` qualifiers, `s1` is of type `string`, and thus a *copy* is made. If you want a reference-to-`const`, you can explicitly make it a reference and mark it `const` as follows:

```
const auto& s2 { getString() };
```

An alternative solution is to use `decltype`, which does not strip anything:

```
decltype(getString()) s3 { getString() };
```

In this case, `s3` is of type `const string&`; however, there is code duplication because you need to specify `getString()` twice, which can be cumbersome when `getString()` is a more complicated expression. This is solved with `decltype(auto)`:

```
decltype(auto) s4 { getString() };
```

`s4` is also of type `const string&`.

So, with this knowledge, we can write our `add()` function template using `decltype(auto)` to avoid stripping any `const` and reference qualifiers:

```
template <typename T1, typename T2>
decltype(auto) add(const T1& t1, const T2& t2) { return t1 + t2; }
```

Before C++14—that is, before function return type deduction and `decltype(auto)` were supported—the problem was solved using `decltype(`*`expression`*`)`, introduced with C++11. For example, you would think you could write the following:

```
template <typename T1, typename T2>
decltype(t1+t2) add(const T1& t1, const T2& t2) { return t1 + t2; }
```

However, this is wrong. You are using t1 and t2 in the beginning of the prototype line, but these are not yet known. t1 and t2 become known once the semantic analyzer reaches the end of the parameter list.

This problem used to be solved with the *alternative function syntax*. Note that with this syntax, auto is used at the beginning of the prototype line, and the actual return type is specified after the parameter list (*trailing return type*); thus, the names of the parameters (and their types, and consequently, the type t1+t2) are known:

```
template <typename T1, typename T2>
auto add(const T1& t1, const T2& t2) -> decltype(t1+t2)
{
    return t1 + t2;
}
```

Another option is to use std::declval<>(), which returns an rvalue reference to the type you requested. This is not a fully constructed object, as no constructor gets called! You cannot use the object at run time. You should only use it, for example, in combination with decltype(). It comes in handy in generic code and when you need to create an object of some unknown type. In that case, you can't call any sensible constructor as you don't know what constructors the unknown type supports. Let's look at an example. The earlier add() code snippet with an explicit return type of decltype(t1+t2) at the beginning of the prototype line doesn't compile because the names t1 and t2 are not yet known at that time. To remedy this, you can use declval<>() as follows:

```
template <typename T1, typename T2>
decltype(std::declval<T1>() + std::declval<T2>()) add(const T1& t1, const T2& t2)
{
    return t1 + t2;
}
```

> **NOTE** *Now that C++ supports* auto *return type deduction and* decltype(auto)*, it is recommended to use one of these mechanisms, instead of the alternative function syntax or* declval<>().

Abbreviated Function Template Syntax

The *abbreviated function template syntax* makes writing function templates easier. Let's take another look at the add() function template from the previous section:

```
template <typename T1, typename T2>
decltype(auto) add(const T1& t1, const T2& t2) { return t1 + t2; }
```

Looking at this, it's a rather verbose syntax to specify a simple function template. With the abbreviated function template syntax, this can be written more elegantly as follows:

```
decltype(auto) add(const auto& t1, const auto& t2) { return t1 + t2; }
```

With this syntax, there is no template header, template<>, anymore to specify template parameters. Instead, where previously the implementation used T1 and T2 as types for the parameters of the function, they are now specified as auto. This abbreviated syntax is just syntactical sugar; the compiler automatically translates this abbreviated implementation to the longer original code. Basically, every function parameter that is specified as auto becomes a template type parameter.

There are two caveats that you have to keep in mind. First, each parameter specified as auto becomes a different template type parameter. Suppose you have a function template like this:

```
template <typename T>
decltype(auto) add(const T& t1, const T& t2) { return t1 + t2; }
```

This version has only a single template type parameter, and both parameters to the function, t1 and t2, are of type const T&. For such a function template, you cannot use the abbreviated syntax, as that would be translated to a function template having two different template type parameters.

A second issue is that you cannot use the deduced types explicitly in the implementation of the function template, as these automatically deduced types have no name. If you need this, you either need to keep using the longer function template syntax or use decltype() to figure out the type.

VARIABLE TEMPLATES

In addition to class templates, class member function templates, and function templates, C++ supports *variable templates*. The syntax is as follows:

```
template <typename T>
constexpr T pi { T { 3.141592653589793238462643383279502884 } };
```

This is a variable template for the value of π. To get the value of pi in a certain type, you use the following syntax:

```
float piFloat { pi<float> };
auto piLongDouble { pi<long double> };
```

You will always get the closest value of pi representable in the requested type. Just like other types of templates, variable templates can also be specialized.

> **NOTE** *The C++ Standard Library includes* <numbers>*, which defines a selection of commonly used mathematical constants, including π:* std::numbers::pi.

CONCEPTS

Concepts are named requirements used to constrain template arguments of class and function templates. These are written as predicates and evaluated at compile time to verify template arguments passed to a template. The main goal of concepts is to make template-related compiler errors more human readable. Everybody has encountered the situation where the compiler spews out hundreds or even thousands of lines of errors when you provide the wrong argument for a class or function template. It's not always easy to dig through those compiler errors to find the root cause.

The reason why the compiler generates that many errors is that the compiler just blindly instantiates templates with the template arguments you provide. Once a template is instantiated, it is compiled, and only then is the compiler able to find out if the provided template type arguments do not support certain operations required deep down in the template implementation. This can be far away from the place where you instantiated a template, hence the myriad of errors. With concepts, the compiler can verify that provided template arguments satisfy certain constraints before it even starts instantiating a template.

Concepts allow the compiler to output readable error messages if certain type constraints are not satisfied. As such, to get meaningful semantical errors, it's recommended to write concepts to model semantic requirements. Avoid concepts that validate only for syntactic aspects without any semantic meaning, such as a concept that just checks if a type supports `operator+`. Such a concept would check only for syntax, not semantics. An `std::string` supports `operator+`, but obviously, it has a completely different meaning compared to `operator+` for integers. On the other hand, concepts such as sortable and swappable are good examples of concepts modeling some semantic meaning.

> **NOTE** *When writing concepts, make sure they model semantics and not just syntax.*

Let's start by looking at the syntax to write concepts.

Syntax

The syntax of a *concept definition*, a template for a named set of *constraints*, is as follows:

```
template <parameter-list>
concept concept-name = constraints-expression;
```

It starts with a familiar template header, `template<>`, but unlike class and function templates, concepts are never instantiated. Next, a new keyword, `concept`, is used followed by the name of the concept. You can use any name you want. The `constraints-expression` can be any constant expression, that is, any expression that can be evaluated at compile time. The *constraints expression* must result in a Boolean value (exactly `bool` as the compiler will not insert any type conversions). This can also be a conjunction, `&&`, or disjunction, `||`, of constant expressions. The constraints are never evaluated at run time. Constraints expressions are discussed in detail in the next section.

A *concept expression* has the following syntax:

```
concept-name<argument-list>
```

Concept expressions evaluate to either `true` or `false`. If it evaluates to `true`, then it is said that the given template arguments *model the concept*. The next section gives an example.

Constraints Expression

Constant expressions that evaluate to a Boolean can directly be used as constraints for a concept definition. It must evaluate exactly to a Boolean without any type conversions. Here's an example:

```
template <typename T>
concept Big = sizeof(T) > 4;
```

Based on this concept, the concept expressions `Big<char>` and `Big<short>` usually evaluate to `false`, while concept expressions like `Big<long double>` will usually evaluate to `true`. A concept expression evaluates to a Boolean value at compile time that can be verified using a *static assertion*. A static assertion uses `static_assert()` and allows certain conditions to be asserted at compile time. An assertion is something that needs to be `true`. If an assertion is `false`, the compiler issues an error. Chapter 26 discusses static assertions in a bit more detail, but their use with concept expressions is straightforward. The following code asserts that `Big<char>` and `Big<short>` indeed evaluate to `false`, and that `Big<long double>` evaluates to `true`:

```
static_assert(!Big<char>);
static_assert(!Big<short>);
static_assert(Big<long double>);
```

When compiling this, there shouldn't be any compilation errors. However, if you remove the exclamation point in the first line, then the compiler will issue an error similar to the following:

```
error C2607: static assertion failed
01_Big.cpp(4,15): message : the concept 'Big<char>' evaluated to false
01_Big.cpp(2,25): message : the constraint was not satisfied
```

Together with the introduction of concepts, a new type of constant expression is introduced called a *requires expression*, used to define the syntactical requirements of concepts, and explained next.

Requires Expressions

A requires expression has the following syntax:

```
requires (parameter-list) { requirements; }
```

The `(parameter-list)` is optional and is syntactically similar to the parameter list of functions, except that default argument values are not allowed. The parameter list of a requires expression is used to introduce named variables that are local to the body of the requires expression. The body of a requires expression cannot have regular variable declarations.

The `requirements` is a sequence of requirements. Each requirement must end with a semicolon.

There are four types of requirements: simple, type, compound, and nested requirements, all discussed in the upcoming sections.

Simple Requirements

A *simple requirement* is an arbitrary expression statement, not starting with `requires`. Variable declarations, loops, conditional statements, and so on are not allowed. This expression statement is never evaluated; the compiler simply validates that it compiles.

For example, the following concept definition specifies that a type `T` must be incrementable; that is, type `T` must support the post- and prefix `++` operator. Remember, you cannot define local variables in the body of a requires expression; instead, you define those as parameters, `x` in this example.

```
template <typename T>
concept Incrementable = requires(T x) { x++; ++x; };
```

Type Requirements

A *type requirement* verifies that a certain type is valid. It starts with the keyword typename, followed by the type to check. For example, the following concept requires that a certain type T has a value_type member:

```
template <typename T>
concept C = requires { typename T::value_type; };
```

A type requirement can also be used to verify that a certain template can be instantiated with a given type. Here's an example:

```
template <typename T>
concept C = requires { typename SomeTemplate<T>; };
```

Compound Requirements

A compound requirement can be used to verify that something does not throw any exceptions and/or to verify that a certain function returns a certain type. The syntax is as follows:

```
{ expression } noexcept -> type-constraint;
```

Both the noexcept and ->type-constraint are optional. There is no semicolon after expression inside the curly brackets, but there is a semicolon at the end of the compound requirement.

Let's look at an example. The following concept requires that a given type has a non-throwing destructor and non-throwing swap() member function:

```
template <typename T>
concept C = requires (T x, T y) {
    { x.~T() } noexcept;
    { x.swap(y) } noexcept;
};
```

The type-constraint can be any *type constraint.* A type constraint is simply the name of a concept with zero or more template type arguments. The type of the expression on the left of the arrow is automatically passed as the first template type argument to the type constraint. Hence, a type constraint always has one less argument than the number of template type parameters of the corresponding concept definition. For example, a type constraint for a concept definition with a single template type does not require any template arguments; you can either specify empty brackets, <>, or omit them. This might sound tricky, but an example will make this clear. The following concept validates that a given type has a member function called size() returning a type that is convertible to a size_t. It also validates that size() is marked as const because the parameter x is of type const T.

```
template <typename T>
concept C = requires (const T x) {
    { x.size() } -> convertible_to<size_t>;
};
```

std::convertible_to<From, To> is a concept predefined by the Standard Library in <concepts> and has two template type parameters. The type of the expression on the left of the arrow is automatically passed as the first template type argument to the convertible_to type constraint. As such, you only need to specify the To template type argument, size_t in this case.

Here is another example. The following concept requires that instances of a type `T` are comparable:

```
template <typename T>
concept Comparable = requires(const T a, const T b) {
    { a == b } -> convertible_to<bool>;
    { a < b } -> convertible_to<bool>;
    // ... similar for the other comparison operators ...
};
```

> **WARNING** *Remember, the* `type-constraint` *in a compound requirement must be a* ***type constraint****, never a type. The following, for instance, will not compile:*
>
> ```
> { a == b } -> bool;
> ```
>
> *Instead, a correct type constraint could be the following:*
>
> ```
> { a == b } -> convertible_to<bool>;
> ```

Nested Requirements

A requires expression can have *nested requirements*. For example, the following is a concept that requires a type to support the pre- and postfix increment and decrement operations. Additionally, the requires expression has a nested requirement to verify that the size of the type is 4 bytes.

```
template <typename T>
concept C = requires (T t) {
    ++t; --t; t++; t--;
    requires sizeof(t) == 4;
};
```

Combining Concept Expressions

Existing concept expressions can be combined using conjunctions (`&&`) and disjunctions (`||`). For example, suppose you have a `Decrementable` concept, similar to `Incrementable`; the following example shows a concept that requires a type to be both incrementable and decrementable:

```
template <typename T>
concept IncrementableAndDecrementable = Incrementable<T> && Decrementable<T>;
```

Predefined Standard Concepts

The Standard Library defines a whole collection of predefined concepts, more than 100 of them, divided into a number of categories. The following list gives just a few example concepts of each category, all defined in `<concepts>` and in the `std` namespace:

Core language concepts: `same_as`, `derived_from`, `convertible_to`, `integral`, `floating_point`, `copy_constructible`, and so on

Comparison concepts: `equality_comparable`, `totally_ordered`, and so on

Object concepts: `movable`, `copyable`, and so on

Callable concepts: `invocable`, `predicate`, and so on

Additionally, `<iterator>` defines iterator-related concepts such as `random_access_iterator`, `forward_iterator`, `incrementable`, `indirectly_copyable`, `indirectly_swappable`, and so on. A concept such as `indirectly_copyable` is not meant to verify that a given iterator itself is copyable, but rather that the elements pointed to by a given iterator are copyable, hence the "indirectly" part of the name. Finally, `<iterator>` also defines algorithm requirements such as `mergeable`, `sortable`, `permutable`, and so on.

The C++ ranges library also provides a number of standard concepts. Chapter 17, "Understanding Iterators and the Ranges Library," discusses iterators and ranges in detail, while Chapter 20 goes deeper into the algorithms provided by the Standard Library. Consult your favorite Standard Library reference for a full list of available standard concepts.

If any of these standard concepts is what you need, you can use them directly without having to implement your own. For example, the following concept requires that a type `T` is derived from class `Foo`:

```
template <typename T>
concept IsDerivedFromFoo = derived_from<T, Foo>;
```

The following concept requires that type `T` is convertible to `bool`:

```
template <typename T>
concept IsConvertibleToBool = convertible_to<T, bool>;
```

More concrete examples follow in the upcoming sections.

Of course, these standard concepts can also be combined into more specific concepts. The following concept, for example, requires a type `T` to be both default and copy constructible:

```
template <typename T>
concept DefaultAndCopyConstructible =
    default_initializable<T> && copy_constructible<T>;
```

> **NOTE** *Writing semantically complete and correct concepts is not always easy. If possible, use the available standard concepts or combinations of them to constrain your types.*

Type-Constrained auto

Type constraints can be used to constrain variables defined with `auto` type deduction, to constrain return types when using function return type deduction, to constrain parameters in abbreviated function templates and generic lambda expressions, and so on. Using type constraints with `auto` type deduction makes the code more self-documenting. It also results in better error messages if the constraints get violated at some point, as the error then points to the variable definition instead of to some unsupported operation later in the code.

For example, the following compiles without errors because the deduced type is `int`, which models the `Incrementable` concept:

```
Incrementable auto value1 { 1 };
```

However, the following causes a compilation error stating that the constraints are not satisfied. The deduced type is `std::string`, due to the use of the standard literal `s`, and `string` does not model `Incrementable`:

```
Incrementable auto value { "abc"s };
```

Type Constraints and Function Templates

There are several syntactically different ways to use type constraints with function templates. A first syntax is to use a *requires clause* as follows:

```
template <typename T> requires constraints-expression
void process(const T& t);
```

The `constraints-expression` can be any constant expression, or a conjunction and disjunction of constant expressions, resulting in a Boolean type, just as the `constraints-expression` of a concept definition. For example, the constraints expression can be a concept expression:

```
template <typename T> requires Incrementable<T>
void process(const T& t);
```

or a predefined standard concept:

```
template <typename T> requires convertible_to<T, bool>
void process(const T& t);
```

or a requires expression (note the two `requires` keywords):

```
template <typename T> requires requires(T x) { x++; ++x; }
void process(const T& t);
```

or any constant expression resulting in a Boolean:

```
template <typename T> requires (sizeof(T) == 4)
void process(const T& t);
```

or a combination of conjunctions and disjunctions:

```
template <typename T> requires Incrementable<T> && Decrementable<T>
void process(const T& t);
```

or a type trait (see Chapter 26):

```
template <typename T> requires is_arithmetic_v<T>
void process(const T& t);
```

The requires clause can also be specified after the function header, called a *trailing requires clause*:

```
template <typename T>
void process(const T& t) requires Incrementable<T>;
```

Another syntax is to use the familiar `template<>` syntax, but instead of using `typename` (or `class`), you use a type constraint. Here are two examples:

```
template <convertible_to<bool> T>
void process(const T& t);

template <Incrementable T>
void process(const T& t);
```

These are type constraints as discussed in the section on compound requirements, so they require one less template type parameter than usual. Concretely:

```
template <convertible_to<bool> T>
void process(const T& t);
```

is entirely analogous to:

```
template <typename T> requires convertible_to<T, bool>
void process(const T& t);
```

Yet another, more elegant, syntax to use type constraints combines the abbreviated function template syntax, discussed earlier in this chapter, and type constraints, resulting in the following nice and compact syntax. Mind you, even though there is no template header, `template<>`, don't be fooled: `process()` is still a function template.

```
void process(const Incrementable auto& t);
```

Compilation errors when requirements are violated are pretty readable. Calling `process()` with an integer argument works as expected. Calling it with an `std::string`, for instance, results in an error complaining about unsatisfied constraints. As an example, the Clang compiler produces the following errors. On first sight, it might still look a bit verbose, but it's surprisingly readable.

```
<source>:17:2: error: no matching function for call to 'process'
        process(str);
        ^~~~~~~
<source>:9:6: note: candidate template ignored: constraints not satisfied [with T =
std::__cxx11::basic_string<char, std::char_traits<char>, std::allocator<char>>]
void process(const T& t)
     ^
<source>:8:11: note: because 'std::__cxx11::basic_string<char, std::char_
traits<char>, std::allocator<char>>' does not satisfy 'Incrementable'
template <Incrementable T>
          ^
<source>:6:42: note: because 'x++' would be invalid: cannot increment value of type
'std::__cxx11::basic_string<char, std::char_traits<char>, std::allocator<char>>'
concept Incrementable = requires(T x) { x++; ++x; };
```

You are free to use whatever syntax suits you best, but in certain cases, you don't have a choice but to use the trailing requires clause syntax:

- When the constraint uses parameter names of the function, the trailing requires clause syntax must be used; otherwise, the function template's parameter names are not yet in scope.
- To constrain a member function of a class template that is defined directly in the class template's body, the trailing requires clause syntax is required because such a member function doesn't have a template header.

> **NOTE** *With the introduction of type constraints, unconstrained template type parameters for function and class templates should be a thing of the past. Every template type inevitably needs to satisfy certain constraints directly related to what you do with that type in the implementation. Hence, you should put a type constraint on it so the compiler can verify it at compile time.*

Constraint Subsumption

You can overload a function template with different type constraints. The compiler always uses the template with the most specific constraints; the more specific constraints *subsume/imply* the lesser constraints. Here's an example:

```
template <typename T> requires integral<T>
void process(const T& t) { println("integral<T>"); }

template <typename T> requires (integral<T> && sizeof(T) == 4)
void process(const T& t) { println("integral<T> && sizeof(T) == 4"); }
```

Suppose you have the following calls to `process()`:

```
process(int { 1 });
process(short { 2 });
```

Then the output is as follows on a typical system where an `int` has 32 bits and a `short` has 16 bits:

```
integral<T> && sizeof(T) == 4
integral<T>
```

The compiler resolves any subsumption by first normalizing the constraints expressions. During normalization of a constraints expression, all concept expressions are recursively expanded to their definitions until the result is a single constant expression consisting of conjunctions and disjunctions of constant Boolean expressions. A normalized constraints expression then subsumes another one if the compiler can prove that it implies the other one. Only conjunctions and disjunctions are taken into account to prove any subsumption, never negations.

This subsumption reasoning is done only at the syntactical level, not semantically. For example, `sizeof(T)>4` is semantically more specific than `sizeof(T)>=4`, but syntactically the former will not subsume the latter.

One caveat, though, is that type traits, such as the `std::is_arithmetic` trait used earlier, are not expanded during normalization. Hence, if there is a predefined concept and a type trait available, you should use the concept and not the type trait. For example, use the `std::integral` concept instead of the `std::is_integral` type trait.

Type Constraints and Class Templates

All type constraints examples up to now are using function templates. Type constraints can also be used with class templates, using a similar syntax. As an example, let's revisit the `GameBoard` class template from earlier in this chapter. The following is a new definition for it, requiring its template type parameter to be a derived class of `GamePiece`:

```
template <std::derived_from<GamePiece> T>
class GameBoard : public Grid<T>
{
    public:
        // Inherit constructors from Grid<T>.
        using Grid<T>::Grid;

        void move(std::size_t xSrc, std::size_t ySrc,
            std::size_t xDest, std::size_t yDest);
};
```

The member function implementations need to be updated as well. Here's an example:

```
template <std::derived_from<GamePiece> T>
void GameBoard<T>::move(std::size_t xSrc, std::size_t ySrc,
    std::size_t xDest, std::size_t yDest) { /*...*/ }
```

Alternatively, you can also use a requires clause as follows:

```
template <typename T> requires std::derived_from<T, GamePiece>
class GameBoard : public Grid<T> { /*...*/ };
```

Type Constraints and Class Member Functions

It's possible to put additional constraints on specific member functions of a class template. For example, the `move()` member function of the `GameBoard` class template could be further constrained to require that type `T` is moveable:

```
template <std::derived_from<GamePiece> T>
class GameBoard : public Grid<T>
{
    public:
        // Inherit constructors from Grid<T>.
        using Grid<T>::Grid;

        void move(std::size_t xSrc, std::size_t ySrc,
            std::size_t xDest, std::size_t yDest) requires std::movable<T>;
};
```

Such a requires clause also needs to be repeated on the member function definition:

```
template <std::derived_from<GamePiece> T>
void GameBoard<T>::move(std::size_t xSrc, std::size_t ySrc,
    std::size_t xDest, std::size_t yDest) requires std::movable<T>
{ /*...*/ }
```

Remember that, thanks to selective instantiation discussed earlier in this chapter, you can still use this `GameBoard` class template with non-movable types, as long as you never call `move()` on it.

Constraint-Based Class Template Specialization and Function Template Overloading

As described earlier in this chapter, you can write specializations for class templates and overloads for function templates to have a different implementation for certain types. It's also possible to write a specialization or overload for a collection of types satisfying certain constraints.

Let's take one more look at the `Find()` function template from earlier in this chapter. To refresh your memory:

```
template <typename T>
optional<size_t> Find(const T& value, const T* arr, size_t size)
{
    for (size_t i { 0 }; i < size; ++i) {
        if (arr[i] == value) {
```

```
                return i; // Found it; return the index.
            }
        }
        return {}; // Failed to find it; return empty optional.
    }
```

This implementation uses the == operator to compare values. It's usually not advisable to compare floating-point types for equality using ==, but instead to use an *epsilon test*. The following overload of `Find()` for floating-point types uses an epsilon test implemented in an `AreEqual()` helper function instead of `operator==`:

```
template <std::floating_point T>
optional<size_t> Find(const T& value, const T* arr, size_t size)
{
    for (size_t i { 0 }; i < size; ++i) {
        if (AreEqual(arr[i], value)) {
            return i; // Found it; return the index.
        }
    }
    return {}; // Failed to find it; return empty optional.
}
```

`AreEqual()` is defined as follows, also using a type constraint. A detailed discussion of the mathematics behind the epsilon test logic is outside the scope of this book and not important for this discussion.

```
template <std::floating_point T>
bool AreEqual(T x, T y, int precision = 2)
{
    // Scale the machine epsilon to the magnitude of the given values and
    // multiply by the required precision.
    return fabs(x - y) <= numeric_limits<T>::epsilon() * fabs(x + y) * precision
        || fabs(x - y) < numeric_limits<T>::min(); // The result is subnormal.
}
```

Best Practices

As this section shows, concepts are a powerful mechanism to constrain types. They provide for a lot of flexibility. Always keep the following in mind:

- Prefer using predefined Standard Library concepts or combinations of them over writing your own, because writing your own complete and correct concepts is difficult and time-consuming.
- When you do write your own concepts, make sure they model semantic requirements, not just syntactical requirements. For example, if your code technically only requires `operator==` and <, don't write a concept that only requires the availability of those two operators, because that would be a syntactical constraint. Instead, require the type to be orderable—that's a semantic constraint.
- By using proper semantic type requirements up front, you are less likely to have to add more requirements later. For example, if your class template is constrained with a concept that just requires `operator==` and <, then it could be that you might have to add a requirement in

the future for `operator>`. In doing so, you'll break existing code. If you would have used a proper concept from the start modeling orderability, you won't be breaking existing code.

- If a parameter of a requires expression is not meant to be modified, mark the parameter as `const` to capture that requirement.
- When writing new class or function templates, try to put proper type constraints on all template type parameters. Unconstrained template type parameters should be a thing of the past.
- Remember that you can use type constraints with `auto` type deduction.

SUMMARY

This chapter started a discussion on using templates for generic programming. You saw the syntax on how to write templates and examples where templates are really useful. It explained how to write class templates, class member function templates, and how to use template parameters. It further discussed how to use class template specialization to write special implementations of a template where the template parameters are replaced with specific arguments.

You also learned about variable templates, function templates, and the elegant abbreviated function template syntax. The chapter finished with a discussion of concepts, allowing you to put constraints on template parameters.

Chapter 26 continues the discussion on templates with some more advanced features such as class template partial specializations, variadic templates, and metaprogramming.

EXERCISES

By solving the following exercises, you can practice the material discussed in this chapter. Solutions to all exercises are available with the code download on the book's website at `www.wiley.com/go/proc++6e`. However, if you are stuck on an exercise, first reread parts of this chapter to try to find an answer yourself before looking at the solution from the website.

Exercise 12-1: Write a `KeyValuePair` class template with two template type parameters: `Key` and `Value`. The class should have two private data members to store a key and a value. Provide a constructor accepting a key and a value, and add appropriate getters and setters. Test your class by creating a few instantiations in your `main()` function and try class template argument deduction.

Exercise 12-2: The `KeyValuePair` class template from Exercise 12-1 supports all kind of data types for both its key and value template type parameters. For example, the following instantiates the class template with `std::string` as the type for both the key and the value:

```
KeyValuePair<std::string, std::string> kv { "John Doe", "New York" };
```

However, using `const char*` as template type arguments results in data members of type `const char*`, which is not what we want.

Write a class template specialization for `const char*` keys and values that converts the given strings to `std::strings`.

Exercise 12-3: Take your solution from Exercise 12-1 and make the appropriate changes to only allow integer types as the type of the key and only floating-point types as the type of the value.

Exercise 12-4: Write a function template called `concat()` with two template type parameters and two function parameters `t1` and `t2`. The function first converts `t1` and `t2` to a string and then returns the concatenation of those two strings. For this exercise, focus only on types for which `std::to_string()` is supported. Create and use a proper concept to make sure users of the function template don't try to use it with unsupported types. Try to write your function template without using the `template` keyword.

Exercise 12-5: The `concat()` function template from Exercise 12-4 only works with types that are supported by `std::to_string()`. In this exercise, modify your solution to make it also work with strings, and any combinations.

Exercise 12-6: Take the original `Find()` function template from earlier in this chapter and add an appropriate constraint on the type `T`.

13

Demystifying C++ I/O

WHAT'S IN THIS CHAPTER?

- The concept of streams
- How to use streams for input and output of data
- The available standard streams provided by the Standard Library
- How to use the filesystem support library

WILEY.COM DOWNLOADS FOR THIS CHAPTER

Please note that all the code examples for this chapter are available as part of this chapter's code download on the book's website at `www.wiley.com/go/proc++6e` on the Download Code tab.

A program's fundamental job is to accept input and produce output. A program that produces no output of any sort would not be very useful. All languages provide some mechanism for I/O, either as a built-in part of the language or through an OS-specific API. A good I/O system is both flexible and easy to use. Flexible I/O systems support input and output through a variety of devices, such as files and the user console. Files could be standard files but could also be data coming from a variety of sources such as Internet of Things (IoT) devices, web services, and more. It could be weather data from a weather device or stock values from a stockbroker web service. Flexible I/O systems also support reading and writing of different types of data. I/O is error-prone because data coming from a user can be incorrect or the underlying filesystem or other data source can be inaccessible. Thus, a good I/O system is also capable of handling error conditions.

If you are familiar with the C language, you have undoubtedly used `printf()` and `scanf()`. As I/O mechanisms, `printf()` and `scanf()` are certainly flexible. Through escape codes and variable placeholders (similar to format specifiers and replacement fields for `std::format()`, `print()`, and `println()` as discussed in Chapter 2, "Working with Strings and String Views"), they can be customized to read in specially formatted data or output any value that the formatting codes permit. Supported types are limited to integer/character values, floating-point values, and strings. However, `printf()` and `scanf()` falter on other measures of good I/O systems. They do not handle errors particularly well. For example, if you tell them to interpret a floating-point number as an integer, they will happily do so. Additionally, they are not flexible enough to handle custom data types, they are not type safe, and in an object-oriented language like C++, they are not at all object oriented.

C++ provides a more refined, more flexible, and object-oriented approach to I/O. *Streams* are encapsulated in classes that result in a user-friendly and safe solution. In this chapter, you will first learn what streams are and then learn how to use streams for data output and input. You will also learn how to use the stream mechanism to read from various sources and write to various destinations, such as the user console, files, and even strings. This chapter covers the most commonly used I/O features.

Almost all examples in this book use `print()` and `println()` to print text to the user console. An alternative is to use the I/O streaming functionality discussed in this chapter. I recommend using `print()` and `println()` instead of streaming to standard output, as the former is easier to read, more compact, and more performant. However, this chapter discusses I/O streaming in detail, as it's still important to know how it works in C++ because you'll undoubtedly have to work with code that uses I/O streaming.

The last part of this chapter discusses the filesystem support library provided by the C++ Standard Library. This library allows you to work with paths, directories, and files, and it nicely complements the mechanisms provided for I/O by the streams.

USING STREAMS

The stream metaphor takes a bit of getting used to. At first, streams may seem more complex than traditional C-style I/O, such as `printf()`. In reality, they seem complicated initially only because there is a deeper metaphor behind streams than there is behind `printf()`. Don't worry, though: after a few examples, everything will be clear.

What Is a Stream, Anyway?

Chapter 1, "A Crash Course in C++ and the Standard Library," compares the `cout` stream to a laundry chute for data. You throw some variables down the stream, and they are written to the user's screen, or *console*. More generally, all streams can be viewed as data chutes. Streams vary in their direction and their associated source or destination. For example, the `cout` stream that you are already familiar with is an output stream, so its direction is "out." It writes data to the console, so its associated destination is "console." The `c` in `cout` does not stand for "console" as you might expect but stands for "character" as it's a character-based stream. There is another standard stream called `cin` that accepts input from the user. Its direction is "in," and its associated source is "console." As with `cout`, the `c` in `cin` stands for "character." Both `cout` and `cin` are predefined instances of streams available in the `std` namespace. The following table gives a brief description of all predefined streams defined in `<iostream>`.

Streams can be *buffered* or *unbuffered*. The difference between them is that a buffered stream does not immediately send the data to the destination. Instead, it buffers, that is collects, incoming data and then sends it in blocks. An unbuffered stream, on the other hand, immediately sends the data to the destination. Buffering is usually done to improve performance, as certain destinations, such as files, perform better when writing bigger blocks at once. Note that you can always force a buffered stream to send all its currently buffered data to the destination by *flushing* its buffer using the `flush()` member function. Buffering and flushing is discussed in a bit more detail later in this chapter.

STREAM	DESCRIPTION
`cin`	An input stream, reads data from the "input console"
`cout`	A buffered output stream, writes data to the "output console"
`cerr`	An unbuffered output stream, writes data to the "error console," which is often the same as the "output console"
`clog`	A buffered version of `cerr`

Remember from Chapter 1 that `std::print()` and `println()` by default print to `cout` but that you can pass a stream as first argument to these functions if you want to print to a different stream, for example:

```
println(cerr, "This is an error printed to cerr.");
```

There are also wide-character, `wchar_t` versions available of these streams that have names starting with `w`: `wcin`, `wcout`, `wcerr`, and `wclog`. Wide characters can be used to work with languages that have more characters than, for example, English, such as Chinese. Wide characters are discussed in Chapter 21, "String Localization and Regular Expressions."

> **NOTE** *Every input stream has an associated source. Every output stream has an associated destination.*

Another important aspect of streams is that they include data but also have a *current position*. The current position is the position in the stream where the next read or write operation will take place.

> **NOTE** *Graphical user interface applications normally do not have a console; that is, if you write something to* `cout`*, the user will not see it. If you are writing a library, you should never assume the existence of* `cout`*,* `cin`*,* `cerr`*, or* `clog` *because you never know whether your library will be used in a console or a GUI application.*

Stream Sources and Destinations

Streams as a concept can be applied to any object that accepts data or emits data. You could write a stream-based network class or stream-based access to a Musical Instrument Digital Interface (MIDI) instrument. In C++, there are four common sources and destinations for streams: consoles, files, strings, and fixed buffer arrays. Fixed buffer array support is introduced with C++23.

You have already seen many examples of user, or console, streams. Console input streams make programs interactive by allowing input from the user at run time. Console output streams provide feedback to the user and output results.

File streams, as the name implies, read data from and write data to a filesystem. File input streams are useful for reading configuration data and saved files or for batch processing file-based data. File output streams are useful for saving state and providing output. If you are familiar with C-style input and output, then file streams subsume the functionality of the C functions `fprintf()`, `fwrite()`, and `fputs()` for output, and `fscanf()`, `fread()`, and `fgets()` for input. As these C-style functions are not recommended in C++, they are not further discussed.

String streams are an application of the stream metaphor to the string type. With a string stream, you can treat character data just as you would treat any other stream. For the most part, this is merely a handy syntax for functionality that could be handled through member functions on the `string` class. However, using stream syntax provides opportunities for optimization and can be far more convenient and more efficient than direct use of the `string` class. String streams subsume the functionality of `sprintf()`, `sprintf_s()`, `sscanf()`, and other forms of C-style string-formatting functions, not further discussed in this C++ book.

The streams working with fixed buffer arrays allow you to use the stream metaphor on any block of memory, independently of how memory for that buffer was allocated.

The rest of this section deals with console streams (`cin` and `cout`). Examples of file, string, and fixed buffer array streams are provided later in this chapter. Other types of streams, such as printer output or network I/O, are often platform dependent, so they are not covered in this book.

Output with Streams

Output using streams is introduced in Chapter 1. This section briefly revisits some of the basics and introduces material that is more advanced.

Output Basics

Output streams are defined in `<ostream>`. There is also `<iostream>`, which in turn includes the functionality for both input streams and output streams. `<iostream>` also declares all predefined stream instances: `cout`, `cin`, `cerr`, `clog`, and the wide versions.

The `<<` operator is the simplest way to use output streams. C++ basic types, such as `int`s, pointers, `double`s, and characters, can be output using `<<`. In addition, the C++ `string` class is compatible with `<<`, and C-style strings are properly output as well. The following are some examples of using `<<`:

```
int i { 7 };
cout << i << endl;
```

```
char ch { 'a' };
cout << ch << endl;

string myString { "Hello World." };
cout << myString << endl;
```

The output is as follows:

```
7
a
Hello World.
```

The `cout` stream is the built-in stream for writing to the console, or *standard output*. You can "chain" uses of `<<` together to output multiple pieces of data. This is because `operator<<` returns a reference to the stream as its result, so you can immediately use `<<` again on the same stream. Here is an example:

```
int j { 11 };
cout << "The value of j is " << j << "!" << endl;
```

The output is as follows:

```
The value of j is 11!
```

C++ streams correctly parse C-style escape sequences, such as strings that contain `\n`. You can also use `std::endl` to start a new line. The difference between using `\n` and `endl` is that `\n` just starts a new line while `endl` also flushes the buffer. Watch out with `endl` because too many flushes might hurt performance. The following example uses `endl` to output and flush several lines of text with just one line of code:

```
cout << "Line 1" << endl << "Line 2" << endl << "Line 3" << endl;
```

The output is as follows:

```
Line 1
Line 2
Line 3
```

> **WARNING** `endl` *flushes the destination buffer, so use it judiciously in performance critical code, such as tight loops.*

Member Functions of Output Streams

The `<<` operator is, without a doubt, the most useful part of output streams. However, there is additional functionality to be explored. If you look through the contents of `<ostream>`, you'll see many lines of overloaded definitions of the `<<` operator to support outputting all kinds of different data types. You'll also find some useful public member functions.

put() and write()

`put()` and `write()` are *raw output member functions*. Instead of taking an object or variable that has some defined behavior for output, `put()` accepts a single character, while `write()` accepts a character array. The data passed to these member functions is output as is, without any special formatting or processing. For example, the following code snippet shows how to output a C-style string to the console without using the `<<` operator:

```
const char* test { "hello there" };
cout.write(test, strlen(test));
```

The next snippet shows how to write a single character to the console by using the `put()` member function:

```
cout.put('a');
```

flush()

When you write to an output stream, the stream does not necessarily write the data to its destination right away. Most output streams *buffer*, or accumulate, data instead of writing it out as soon as it comes in. This is usually done to improve performance. Certain stream destinations, such as files, are much more performant if data is written in larger blocks, instead of, for example, character by character. The stream *flushes*, or writes out, the accumulated data, when one of the following conditions occurs:

- An `endl` manipulator is encountered.
- The stream goes out of scope and is destructed.
- The stream buffer is full.
- You explicitly tell the stream to flush its buffer.
- Input is requested from a corresponding input stream (that is, when you make use of `cin` for input, `cout` will flush). In the section "File Streams," you will learn how to establish this type of link.

One way to explicitly tell a stream to flush is to call its `flush()` member function, as in the following code:

```
cout << "abc";
cout.flush();    // abc is written to the console.
cout << "def";
cout << endl;    // def is written to the console.
```

> **NOTE** *Not all output streams are buffered. The* `cerr` *stream, for example, does not buffer its output.*

Handling Output Errors

Output errors can arise in a variety of situations. Perhaps you are trying to open a non-existing file. Maybe a disk error has prevented a write operation from succeeding, for example, because the disk is full. None of the streams' code you have seen up until this point has considered these possibilities, mainly for brevity. However, it is vital that you address any error conditions that occur.

When a stream is in its normal usable state, it is said to be "good." The `good()` member function can be called directly on a stream to determine whether the stream is currently good:

```
if (cout.good()) {
    cout << "All good" << endl;
}
```

`good()` provides an easy way to obtain basic information about the validity of the stream, but it does not tell you why the stream is unusable. There is a member function called `bad()` that provides a bit more information. If `bad()` returns `true`, it means that a fatal error has occurred (as opposed to any nonfatal condition like end-of-file, `eof()`). Another member function, `fail()`, returns `true` if the most recent operation has failed; however, it doesn't say anything about the next operation, which can either succeed or fail as well. For example, after calling `flush()` on an output stream, you could call `fail()` to make sure the flush was successful:

```
cout.flush();
if (cout.fail()) {
    cerr << "Unable to flush to standard out" << endl;
}
```

Streams have a conversion operator to convert to type `bool`. This conversion operator returns the same as calling `!fail()`. So, the previous code snippet can be rewritten as follows:

```
cout.flush();
if (!cout) {
    cerr << "Unable to flush to standard out" << endl;
}
```

Important to know is that both `good()` and `fail()` return `false` if the end-of-file is reached. The relation is as follows: `good() == (!fail() && !eof())`.

You can also tell the streams to throw exceptions when a failure occurs. You then write a `catch` handler to catch `ios_base::failure` exceptions, on which you can use the `what()` member function to get a description of the error, and the `code()` member function to get the error code. However, whether or not you get useful information depends on the Standard Library implementation that you use.

```
cout.exceptions(ios::failbit | ios::badbit | ios::eofbit);
try {
    cout << "Hello World." << endl;
} catch (const ios_base::failure& ex) {
    cerr << "Caught exception: " << ex.what()
         << ", error code = " << ex.code() << endl;
}
```

To reset the error state of a stream, use `clear()`:

```
cout.clear();
```

Error checking is performed less frequently for console output streams than for file output or input streams. The member functions discussed here apply for other types of streams as well and are revisited later as each type is discussed.

Output Manipulators

One of the unusual features of streams is that you can throw more than just data down the chute. C++ streams also recognize *manipulators*, objects that make a change to the behavior of the stream instead of, or in addition to, providing data for the stream to work with.

You have already seen one manipulator: `endl`. The `endl` manipulator encapsulates data and behavior. It tells the stream to output an end-of-line sequence and to flush its buffer. The following is a non-exhaustive list of some other useful manipulators, many of which are defined in `<ios>` and `<iomanip>`. An example after this list shows how to use them:

- `boolalpha` and `noboolalpha`: Tells the stream to output `bool` values as *true* and *false* (`boolalpha`) or *1* and *0* (`noboolalpha`). The default is `noboolalpha`.
- `hex`, `oct`, and `dec`: Outputs numbers in hexadecimal, octal, and base 10, respectively.
- `fixed`, `scientific`, and `defaultfloat`: Outputs fractional numbers using fixed, scientific, or default formatting, respectively.
- `setprecision`: Sets the number of decimal places that are output for fractional numbers using fixed or scientific formatting, or else the total number of digits to output. This is a parameterized manipulator (meaning that it takes an argument).
- `setw`: Sets the field width for outputting data. This is a parameterized manipulator.
- `setfill`: Sets a character as the new fill character for the stream. The fill character pads output according to the width set by `setw`. This is a parameterized manipulator.
- `showpoint` and `noshowpoint`: Forces the stream to always or never show the decimal point for floating-point numbers with no fractional part.
- `put_money`: A parameterized manipulator that writes a formatted monetary value to a stream.
- `put_time`: A parameterized manipulator that writes a formatted time to a stream.
- `quoted`: A parameterized manipulator that encloses a given string with quotes and escapes embedded quotes.

All of these manipulators stay in effect for subsequent output to the stream until they are reset, except `setw`, which is active for only the next single output. The following example uses several of these manipulators to customize its output:

```
// Boolean values
bool myBool { true };
cout << "This is the default: " << myBool << endl;
cout << "This should be true: " << boolalpha << myBool << endl;
cout << "This should be 1: " << noboolalpha << myBool << endl;

// Simulate println-style "{:6}" with streams
int i { 123 };
println("This should be '   123': {:6}", i);
cout << "This should be '   123': " << setw(6) << i << endl;
```

```
// Simulate println-style "{:0>6}" with streams
println("This should be '000123': {:0>6}", i);
cout << "This should be '000123': " << setfill('0') << setw(6) << i << endl;

// Fill with *
cout << "This should be '***123': " << setfill('*') << setw(6) << i << endl;
// Reset fill character
cout << setfill(' ');

// Floating-point values
double dbl { 1.452 };
double dbl2 { 5 };
cout << "This should be ' 5': " << setw(2) << noshowpoint << dbl2 << endl;
cout << "This should be @@1.452: " << setw(7) << setfill('@') << dbl << endl;
// Reset fill character
cout << setfill(' ');

// Instructs cout to start formatting numbers according to your location.
// Chapter 21 explains the details of the imbue() call and the locale object.
cout.imbue(locale { "" });

// Format numbers according to your location
cout << "This is 1234567 formatted according to your location: " << 1234567
     << endl;

// Monetary value. What exactly a monetary value means depends on your
// location. For example, in the USA, a monetary value of 120000 means 120000
// dollar cents, which is 1200.00 dollars.
cout << "This should be a monetary value of 120000, "
     << "formatted according to your location: "
     << put_money("120000") << endl;

// Date and time
time_t t_t { time(nullptr) };       // Get current system time.
tm t { *localtime(&t_t) };          // Convert to local time.
cout << "This should be the current date and time "
     << "formatted according to your location: "
     << put_time(&t, "%c") << endl;

// Quoted string
cout << "This should be: \"Quoted string with \\\"embedded quotes\\\".\": "
     << quoted("Quoted string with \"embedded quotes\".") << endl;
```

> **NOTE** *With Microsoft Visual C++, this example might give you a security-related error or warning on the call to* `localtime()`. *You can either switch to using* `localtime_s()` *or temporarily disable this warning using a* `#pragma`. *See the downloadable source code archive.*

If you don't care for the concept of manipulators, you can usually get by without them. Streams provide much of the same functionality through equivalent member functions like `precision()`. For example, take the following line:

```
cout << "This should be '1.2346': " << setprecision(5) << 1.23456789 << endl;
```

This can be converted to use a member function call as follows. The advantage of the member function calls is that they return the previous value, allowing you to restore it, if needed.

```
cout.precision(5);
cout << "This should be '1.2346': " << 1.23456789 << endl;
```

For a detailed description of all stream member functions and manipulators, consult your favorite Standard Library Reference.

Input with Streams

Input streams provide a simple way to read in structured or unstructured data. In this section, the techniques for input are discussed within the context of `cin`, the console input stream.

Input Basics

There are two easy ways to read data by using an input stream. The first is an analog of the `<<` operator that outputs data to an output stream. The corresponding operator for reading data is `>>`. When you use `>>` to read data from an input stream, the variable you provide is the storage for the received value. For example, the following program reads one word from the user and puts it into a string. Then the string is output back to the console:

```
string userInput;
cin >> userInput;
println("User input was {}.", userInput);
```

By default, the `>>` operator tokenizes values according to whitespace. For example, if a user runs the previous program and enters `hello there` as input, only the characters up to the first whitespace character (the space character in this instance) are captured into the `userInput` variable. The output would be as follows:

```
User input was hello.
```

One solution to include whitespace in the input is to use `get()`, which is discussed later in this chapter.

> **NOTE** *Whitespace characters in C++ are space (`' '`), form feed (`'\f'`), line feed (`'\n'`), carriage return (`'\r'`), horizontal tab (`'\t'`), and vertical tab (`'\v'`).*

The `>>` operator works with different variable types, just like the `<<` operator. For example, to read an integer, the code differs only in the type of the variable:

```
int userInput;
cin >> userInput;
println("User input was {}.", userInput);
```

You can use input streams to read in multiple values, mixing and matching types as necessary. For example, the following function, an excerpt from a restaurant reservation system, asks the user for a last name and the number of people in their party:

```
void getReservationData()
{
```

```
        string guestName;
        int partySize;
        print("Name and number of guests: ");
        cin >> guestName >> partySize;
        println("Thank you, {}.", guestName);
        if (partySize > 10) {
            println("An extra gratuity will apply.");
        }
    }
```

Remember that the `>>` operator tokenizes values according to whitespace, so `getReservationData()` does not allow you to enter a name with whitespace. A solution using `unget()` is discussed later in this chapter. Note also that the first use of `cout` does not explicitly flush the buffer using `endl` or `flush()`, but still, the text will be written to the console because the use of `cin` immediately flushes the `cout` buffer; they are linked together in this way.

> **NOTE** *If you get confused between `<<` and `>>`, just think of the angles as pointing toward their destination. In an output stream, `<<` points toward the stream itself because data is being sent to the stream. In an input stream, `>>` points toward the variables because data is being stored.*

Handling Input Errors

Input streams have a number of member functions to detect unusual circumstances. Most of the error conditions related to input streams occur when there is no data available to read. For example, the end of the stream (referred to as *end-of-file*, even for non–file streams) may have been reached. The most common way of querying the state of an input stream is to access it within a conditional statement. For example, the following loop keeps looping as long as `cin` remains in a good state. This pattern takes advantage of the fact that evaluating an input stream within a conditional context results in `true` only if the stream is not in any error state. Encountering an error causes the stream to evaluate to `false`. The underlying details of the conversion operations required to implement such behavior are explained in Chapter 15, "Overloading C++ Operators."

```
while (cin) { ... }
```

You can input data at the same time:

```
while (cin >> ch) { ... }
```

The `good()`, `bad()`, and `fail()` member functions can be called on input streams, just as on output streams. There is also an `eof()` member function that returns `true` if the stream has reached its end. Similar as for output streams, both `good()` and `fail()` return `false` if the end-of-file is reached. The relation is again as follows: `good() == (!fail() && !eof())`.

You should get into the habit of checking the stream state after reading data so that you can recover from bad input.

The following program shows a common pattern for reading data from a stream and handling errors. The program reads numbers from standard input and displays their sum once end-of-file is reached. Note that in command-line environments, the end-of-file is indicated by the user typing a particular character. In Unix and Linux, it is Control+D; in Windows it is Control+Z, both followed by Enter. The exact character is operating-system dependent, so you will need to know what your operating system requires.

```
println("Enter numbers on separate lines to add.");
println("Use Control+D followed by Enter to finish (Control+Z in Windows).");
int sum { 0 };

if (!cin.good()) {
    println(cerr, "Standard input is in a bad state!");
    return 1;
}

while (!cin.bad()) {
    int number;
    cin >> number;
    if (cin.good()) {
        sum += number;
    } else if (cin.eof()) {
        break; // Reached end-of-file.
    } else if (cin.fail()) {
        // Failure!
        cin.clear(); // Clear the failure state.
        string badToken;
        cin >> badToken; // Consume the bad input.
        println(cerr, "WARNING: Bad input encountered: {}", badToken);
    }
}
println("The sum is {}.", sum);
```

Here is some example output of this program. The ^Z characters in the output appear when Control+Z is pressed.

```
Enter numbers on separate lines to add.
Use Control+D followed by Enter to finish (Control+Z in Windows).
1
2
test
WARNING: Bad input encountered: test
3
^Z
The sum is 6.
```

Input Member Functions

Just like output streams, input streams have several member functions that allow a lower level of access than the functionality provided by the more common >> operator.

get()

The get() member function allows raw input of data from a stream. The simplest version of get() returns the next character in the stream, though other versions exist that read multiple characters at once. get() is most commonly used to avoid the automatic tokenization that occurs with the >> operator. For example, the following function reads a name, which can be made up of several words, from an input stream until the end of the stream is reached:

```
string readName(istream& stream)
{
    string name;
    while (stream) { // Or: while (!stream.fail()) {
        int next { stream.get() };
        if (!stream || next == std::char_traits<char>::eof())
            break;
        name += static_cast<char>(next);// Append character.
    }
    return name;
}
```

There are several interesting observations to make about this `readName()` function:

- Its parameter is a reference-to-non-`const` to an `istream`, not a reference-to-`const`. The member functions that read in data from a stream will change the actual stream (most notably, its position), so they are not `const` member functions. Thus, you cannot call them on a reference-to-`const`.
- The return value of `get()` is stored in an `int`, not in a `char`, because `get()` can return special non-character values such as `std::char_traits<char>::eof()` (end-of-file).
- Newline and other escape characters that are read by `get()` will appear in the `string` returned by `readName()`. If the `Ctrl+D` or `Ctrl+Z` isn't done at the beginning of a line, they too will appear in the returned `string`.

`readName()` is a bit strange because there are two ways to get out of the loop: either the stream can get into a failed state or the end of the stream is reached. A more common pattern for reading from a stream uses a different version of `get()` that takes a reference to a character and returns a reference to the stream. Evaluating an input stream within a conditional context results in `true` only if the stream is not in any error state. The following version of the same function is a bit more concise:

```
string readName(istream& stream)
{
    string name;
    char next;
    while (stream.get(next)) {
        name += next;
    }
    return name;
}
```

unget()

For most purposes, the correct way to think of an input stream is as a one-way chute. Data falls down the chute and into variables. The `unget()` member function breaks this model in a way by allowing you to push data back up the chute.

A call to `unget()` causes the stream to back up by one position, essentially putting the previous character read back on the stream. You can use the `fail()` member function to see whether `unget()`

was successful or not. For example, `unget()` can fail if the current position is at the beginning of the stream.

The `getReservationData()` function shown earlier in this chapter did not allow you to enter a name with whitespace. The following code uses `unget()` to allow whitespace in the name. The code reads character by character and checks whether the character is a digit or not. If the character is not a digit, it is added to `guestName`. If it is a digit, the character is put back into the stream using `unget()`, the loop is stopped, and the `>>` operator is used to input an integer, `partySize`. The `noskipws` input manipulator tells the stream not to skip whitespace; that is, whitespace is read like any other characters.

```
void getReservationData()
{
    print("Name and number of guests: ");
    string guestName;
    int partySize { 0 };
    // Read characters until we find a digit
    char ch;
    cin >> noskipws;
    while (cin >> ch) {
        if (isdigit(ch)) {
            cin.unget();
            if (cin.fail()) { println(cerr, "unget() failed."); }
            break;
        }
        guestName += ch;
    }
    // Read partySize, if the stream is not in error state
    if (cin) { cin >> partySize; }
    if (!cin) {
        println(cerr, "Error getting party size.");
        return;
    }

    println("Thank you '{}', party of {}.", guestName, partySize);
    if (partySize > 10) {
        println("An extra gratuity will apply.");
    }
}
```

putback()

The `putback()` member function, like `unget()`, lets you move backward by one character in an input stream. The difference is that `putback()` takes the character being placed back on the stream as a parameter. Here is an example:

```
char c;
cin >> c;
println("Retrieved {}.", c);

cin.putback('e');  // 'e' will be the next character read off the stream.
println("Called putback('e').");

while (cin >> c) { println("Retrieved {}.", c); }
```

The output can be as follows:

```
wow
Retrieved w.
Called putback('e').
Retrieved e.
Retrieved o.
Retrieved w.
```

peek ()

The `peek()` member function allows you to preview the next value that *would* be returned if you were to call `get()`. To take the chute metaphor perhaps a bit too far, you could think of it as looking up the chute without a value actually falling down it.

`peek()` is ideal for any situation where you need to look ahead before reading a value. For example, the following code implements `getReservationData()` that allows whitespace in the name, but uses `peek()` instead of `unget()`:

```
void getReservationData()
{
    print("Name and number of guests: ");
    string guestName;
    int partySize { 0 };
    // Read characters until we find a digit.
    cin >> noskipws;
    while (true) {
        // 'peek' at next character.
        char ch { static_cast<char>(cin.peek()) };
        if (!cin) { break; }
        if (isdigit(ch)) {
            // Next character will be a digit, so stop the loop.
            break;
        }
        // Next character will be a non-digit, so read it.
        cin >> ch;
        if (!cin) { break; }
        guestName += ch;
    }
    // Read partySize, if the stream is not in error state.
    if (cin) { cin >> partySize; }
    if (!cin) {
        println(cerr, "Error getting party size.");
        return;
    }

    println("Thank you '{}', party of {}.", guestName, partySize);
    if (partySize > 10) {
        println("An extra gratuity will apply.");
    }
}
```

getline()

Obtaining a single line of data from an input stream is so common that a member function exists to do it for you. The `getline()` member function fills a character buffer with a line of data up to the specified size. This specified size includes the \0 character. Thus, the following code reads a maximum of BufferSize-1 characters from cin or until an end-of-line sequence is read:

```
char buffer[BufferSize] { 0 };
cin.getline(buffer, BufferSize);
```

When getline() is called, it reads a line from the input stream, up to and including the end-of-line sequence. However, the end-of-line character or characters do not appear in the string. Note that the end-of-line sequence is platform dependent. For example, it can be \r\n, \n, or \n\r.

There is a form of get() that performs the same operation as getline(), except that it leaves the newline sequence in the input stream.

There is also a non-member function called std::getline() that can be used with C++ strings. It is defined in <string> and is in the std namespace. It takes a stream and a string reference. The advantage of using this version of getline() is that it doesn't require you to specify the size of any buffer.

```
string myString;
getline(cin, myString);
```

Both the getline() member function and the std::getline() function accept an optional delimiter as last parameter. The default delimiter is \n. By changing this delimiter, these functions can be used to read in multiple lines of text until a given delimiter is reached. For example, the following code reads in multiple lines of text until it reads an @ character:

```
print("Enter multiple lines of text. "
      "Use an @ character to signal the end of the text.\n> ");
string myString;
getline(cin, myString, '@');
println("Read text: \"{}\"", myString);
```

Here is a possible output:

```
Enter multiple lines of text. Use an @ character to signal the end of the text.
> This is some
text on multiple
lines.@
Read text: "This is some
text on multiple
lines."
```

Input Manipulators

Just as for output streams, input streams support a number of input manipulators. You've already seen one, noskipws, which tells an input stream not to skip any whitespace characters. The following list shows other built-in input manipulators available to you that allow you to customize the way data is read:

- boolalpha and noboolalpha: If boolalpha is used, the string *false* will be interpreted as the Boolean value false; anything else will be treated as the Boolean value true. If noboolalpha is set, zero will be interpreted as false, anything else as true. The default is noboolalpha.

- dec, hex, and oct: Reads numbers in decimal base 10, hexadecimal, or octal notation, respectively. For example, the decimal base 10 number 207 is cf in hexadecimal, and 317 in octal notation.
- skipws and noskipws: Tells the stream to either skip whitespace when tokenizing or to read in whitespace as its own token. The default is skipws.
- ws: A handy manipulator that simply skips over the current series of whitespace at the current position in the stream.
- get_money: A parameterized manipulator that reads a monetary value from a stream.
- get_time: A parameterized manipulator that reads a formatted time from a stream.
- quoted: A parameterized manipulator that reads a string enclosed with quotes and in which embedded quotes are escaped. An example of this manipulator is shown later in this chapter.

Input is locale aware. For example, the following code enables your system locale for cin. Locales are discussed in Chapter 21:

```
cin.imbue(locale { "" });
int i;
cin >> i;
```

If your system locale is U.S. English, you can enter 1,000 and it will be parsed as 1000. If you enter 1.000, it will be parsed as 1. On the other hand, if your system locale is Dutch Belgium, you can enter 1.000 to get the value of 1000, but entering 1,000 will result in 1. In both cases, you can also just enter 1000 without any digit separators to get the value 1000.

Input and Output with Objects

If you are familiar with the old-school printf() function from C for output, you know that it is not flexible and does not support custom types. printf() knows about several types of data, but there really isn't a way to give it additional knowledge. For example, consider the following simple class:

```
class Muffin final
{
    public:
        const string& getDescription() const { return m_description; }
        void setDescription(string description)
        {
            m_description = std::move(description);
        }

        int getSize() const { return m_size; }
        void setSize(int size) { m_size = size; }

        bool hasChocolateChips() const { return m_hasChocolateChips; }
        void setHasChocolateChips(bool hasChips)
        {
            m_hasChocolateChips = hasChips;
        }
    private:
        string m_description;
```

```
        int m_size { 0 };
        bool m_hasChocolateChips { false };
};
```

To output an object of class `Muffin` by using `printf()`, it would be nice if you could specify it as an argument, perhaps using `%m` as a placeholder:

```
printf("Muffin: %m\n", myMuffin); // BUG! printf doesn't understand Muffin.
```

Unfortunately, the `printf()` function knows nothing about the `Muffin` type and is unable to output an object of type `Muffin`. Worse still, because of the way the `printf()` function is declared, this will result in a run-time error, not a compile-time error (though a good compiler will give you a warning).

The best you can do with `printf()` is to add a new `output()` member function to the `Muffin` class:

```
class Muffin final
{
    public:
        void output() const
        {
            printf("%s, size is %d, %s", getDescription().c_str(), getSize(),
                (hasChocolateChips() ? "has chips" : "no chips"));
        }
        // Omitted for brevity
};
```

Using such a mechanism is cumbersome, however. To output a `Muffin` in the middle of another line of text, you'd need to split the line into two calls with a call to `Muffin::output()` in between, as shown here:

```
printf("The muffin is a ");
myMuffin.output();
printf(" -- yummy!\n");
```

A much better and modern option is to write a custom `std::formatter` specialization for `Muffin` objects as explained in Chapter 2. The following is a simple custom `formatter` for `Muffin`s. To keep the example concise, this formatter does not support any format specifiers. Thus, the `parse()` abbreviated member function template does not need to parse anything and can just return `begin(context)`.

```
template <>
class std::formatter<Muffin>
{
    public:
        constexpr auto parse(auto& context) { return begin(context); }

        auto format(const Muffin& muffin, auto& ctx) const
        {
            ctx.advance_to(format_to(ctx.out(), "{}, size is {}, {}",
                muffin.getDescription(), muffin.getSize(),
                (muffin.hasChocolateChips() ? "has chips" : "no chips")));
            return ctx.out();
        }
};
```

With this custom formatter, you can use the modern `std::print()` and `println()` functions to print a muffin. Here is an example:

```
println("The muffin is a {} -- yummy!", myMuffin);
```

Yet another option to print `Muffin`s is to overload the `<<` operator after which you output a `Muffin` just like you output a `string`—by providing it as an argument to `operator<<`. Additionally, you can overload the `>>` operator so that you can input `Muffin`s from an input stream. Chapter 15 covers the details of overloading the `<<` and `>>` operators.

Custom Manipulators

The Standard Library comes with a number of built-in stream manipulators, but, if need be, custom manipulators can be written.

Writing your own non-parameterized manipulator is easy. Here's a simple example defining a `tab` output manipulator which outputs the tab character to a given stream:

```
ostream& tab(ostream& stream) { return stream << '\t'; }

int main()
{
    cout << "Test" << tab << "!" << endl;
}
```

Writing custom parameterized manipulators is more complicated. It involves using functionality exposed by `ios_base`, such as `xalloc()`, `iword()`, `pword()`, and `register_callback()`. Since such manipulators are rarely needed, this text does not further discuss this topic. Consult your favorite Standard Library reference in case you are interested.

STRING STREAMS

String streams provide a way to use stream semantics with `string`s. In this way, you can have an *in-memory stream* that represents textual data. For example, in a GUI application you might want to use streams to build up textual data, but instead of outputting the text to the console or a file, you might want to display the result in a GUI element like a message box or an edit control. Another example could be that you want to pass a string stream around to different functions, while retaining the current read position, so that each function can process the next part of the stream. String streams are also useful for parsing text, because streams have built-in tokenizing functionality.

The `std::ostringstream` class is used to write data to a `string`, while `std::istringstream` is used to read data from a `string`. The o in `ostringstream` stands for output, while the `i` in `istringstream` stands for input. They are both defined in `<sstream>`. Because `ostringstream` and `istringstream` inherit the same behavior as `ostream` and `istream`, working with them is pleasantly similar.

The following program requests words from the user and outputs them to a single `ostringstream`, separated by commas and surrounded by double quotes. At the end of the program, the whole stream is turned into a `string` object using the `str()` member function and is written to the console.

Input of tokens can be stopped by entering the token "done" or by closing the input stream with `Control+D` (Unix) or `Control+Z` (Windows).

```
println("Enter tokens. "
    "Control+D (Unix) or Control+Z (Windows) followed by Enter to end.");
ostringstream outStream;
bool firstLoop { true };
while (cin) {
    string nextToken;
    print("Next token: ");
    cin >> nextToken;

    if (!cin || nextToken == "done") { break; }

    if (!firstLoop) { outStream << ", "; }
    outStream << '"' << nextToken << '"';
    firstLoop = false;
}
println("The end result is: {}", outStream.str());
```

Reading data from a string stream is similarly familiar. The following function creates and populates a `Muffin` object (see the earlier example) from a string input stream. The stream data is in a fixed format so that the function can easily turn its values into calls to `Muffin`'s setters. This fixed format is the description of the muffin between double quotes, followed by the size, followed by true or false depending on whether the muffin has chocolate chips. For example, the following string is a valid muffin:

```
"Raspberry Muffin" 12 true
```

Here is the implementation. Note the use of the `quoted` manipulator to read a quoted string from the input stream.

```
Muffin createMuffin(istringstream& stream)
{
    Muffin muffin;
    // Assume data is properly formatted:
    // "Description" size chips

    string description;
    int size;
    bool hasChips;

    // Read all three values. Note that chips is represented
    // by the strings "true" and "false".
    stream >> quoted(description) >> size >> boolalpha >> hasChips;
    if (stream) { // Reading was successful.
        muffin.setSize(size);
        muffin.setDescription(description);
        muffin.setHasChocolateChips(hasChips);
    }
    return muffin;
}
```

> **NOTE** *Turning an object into a "flattened" type, like a string, is often called marshaling. Marshaling is useful for saving objects to disk or sending them across a network.*

An advantage of string streams over standard C++ `string`s is that, in addition to data, they know where the next read or write operation will take place, also called the *current position*.

Another advantage is that string streams support manipulators and locales to enable more powerful formatting compared to `string`s.

Finally, if you need to build up a string by concatenating several smaller strings, using a string stream will be more performant compared to concatenating `string` objects directly.

SPAN-BASED STREAMS

C++23 introduces *span-based streams*, defined in `<spanstream>`, which allow you to use the stream metaphor on any fixed memory buffer you have available. How memory was allocated for that buffer is not important. The most important classes in this context that you'll use are `ispanstream` for input, `ospanstream` for output, and `spanstream` for input and output. Technically, these are `char` instantiations for the class templates `basic_ispanstream`, `basic_ospanstream`, and `basic_spanstream`. There are also wide-character, `wchar_t` instantiations available called `wispanstream`, `wospanstream`, and `wspanstream`. Wide characters are mentioned earlier in this chapter and covered in more detail in Chapter 21. This section gives examples of the non-wide-character classes, as the others work very similarly.

The constructors of the span-based stream classes require an `std::span`. Chapter 18, "Standard Library Containers," discusses `span` in detail and explains why and when you want to use it, but those details are not important for this section. The use of `span` in the context of span-based streams is straightforward, as you'll see. In a nutshell, a `span` allows you to make a view over a contiguous block of memory. It's a bit similar to how `std::string_view` allows you to create a read-only view over any kind of string, as discussed in Chapter 2. The difference is that a `span` can be a read-only view, but it can also be a writable view allowing modifications to the underlying buffer.

Here is an example of using an `ispanstream` to parse data stored in a fixed memory buffer called `fixedBuffer`. To construct a `span` over that buffer, you simply use the `span` constructor and pass it the location of the buffer.

```
char fixedBuffer[] { "11 2.222 Hello" };
ispanstream stream { span { fixedBuffer } };
int i;   double d;   string str;
stream >> i >> d >> str;
println("Parsed data: int: {}, double: {}, string: {}", i, d, str);
```

The output is as follows:

```
Parsed data: int: 11, double: 2.222, string: Hello
```

Using an ospanstream is similarly straightforward. The following code creates a fixed buffer of 32 chars, constructs a writable ospanstream view over that buffer, uses standard stream insertion operations to output some data to the buffer, and finally prints out the result:

```
char fixedBuffer[32] {};
ospanstream stream { span { fixedBuffer } };
stream << "Hello " << 2.222 << ' ' << 11;
println("Buffer contents: \"{}\"", fixedBuffer);
```

The output is:

```
Buffer contents: "Hello 2.222 11"
```

FILE STREAMS

Files lend themselves well to the stream abstraction because reading and writing files always involves a position in addition to the data. In C++, the std::ofstream and ifstream classes provide output and input functionality for files. They are defined in <fstream>.

When dealing with the filesystem, it is especially important to detect and handle error cases. The file you are working with could be on a network file store that just went offline, or you may be trying to write to a file that is located on a disk that is full. Maybe you are trying to open a file for which the current user does not have permissions. Error conditions can be detected by using the standard error handling mechanisms described earlier.

The only major difference between output file streams and other output streams is that the file stream constructor can take the name of the file and the mode in which you would like to open it. The default mode is write, ios_base::out, which starts writing to a file at the beginning, overwriting any existing data. You can also open an output file stream in append mode by specifying the constant ios_base::app as the second argument to the file stream constructor. The following table lists the different constants that are available:

CONSTANT	DESCRIPTION
ios_base::app	Open, and go to the end before each write operation.
ios_base::ate	Open, and go to the end once immediately after opening.
ios_base::binary	Perform input and output in binary mode as opposed to text mode. See the next section.
ios_base::in	Open for input, start reading at the beginning.
ios_base::out	Open for output, start writing at the beginning, overwriting existing data.
ios_base::trunc	Option for out. Delete all existing data (truncate).
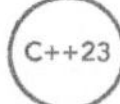 ios_base::noreplace	Option for out. Open in exclusive mode. Open will fail if the file already exists.

Note that modes can be combined. For example, if you want to open a file for output in binary mode, while truncating existing data, you would specify the open mode as follows:

```
ios_base::out | ios_base::binary  | ios_base::trunc
```

An `ifstream` automatically includes the `ios_base::in` mode, while an `ofstream` automatically includes the `ios_base::out` mode, even if you don't explicitly specify `in` or `out` as the mode.

The following program opens the `test.txt` file and writes the program's arguments to it. The `ifstream` and `ofstream` destructors automatically close the underlying file, so there is no need to explicitly call `close()`.

```
int main(int argc, char* argv[])
{
    ofstream outFile { "test.txt", ios_base::trunc };
    if (!outFile.good()) {
        println(cerr, "Error while opening output file!");
        return -1;
    }
    outFile << "There were " << argc << " arguments to this program." << endl;
    outFile << "They are: " << endl;
    for (int i { 0 }; i < argc; i++) {
        outFile << argv[i] << endl;
    }
}
```

Text Mode vs. Binary Mode

By default, a file stream is opened in *text mode*. If you specify the `ios_base::binary` flag, then the file is opened in *binary mode*.

In binary mode, the exact bytes you ask the stream to write are written to the file. When reading, the bytes are returned to you exactly as they are in the file.

In text mode, there is some hidden conversion happening: each line you write to, or read from, a file ends with `\n`. However, how the end of a line is encoded in a file depends on the operating system. For example, on Windows, a line ends with `\r\n` instead of with a single `\n` character. Therefore, when a file is opened in text mode and you write a line ending with `\n` to it, the underlying implementation automatically converts the `\n` to `\r\n` before writing it to the file. Similarly, when reading a line from the file, the `\r\n` that is read from the file is automatically converted back to `\n` before being returned to you.

Jumping Around with seek() and tell()

The `seekx()` and `tellx()` member functions are present on all input and output streams. The `seekx()` member functions let you move to an arbitrary position within an input or output stream. There are several forms of `seekx()`. For an input stream, the member function is called `seekg()` (the *g* is for *get*), and for an output stream, it is called `seekp()` (the *p* is for *put*). You might wonder why there is both a `seekg()` and a `seekp()` member function, instead of one `seek()` member function. The reason is that you can have streams that are both input and output, for example, file streams.

In that case, the stream needs to remember both a read position and a separate write position. This is also called *bidirectional I/O* and is covered later in this chapter.

There are two overloads of `seekg()` and two of `seekp()`. One overload accepts a single argument, an absolute position, and seeks to this absolute position. The second overload accepts an offset and a position and seeks an offset relative to the given position. Positions are of type `std::streampos`, while offsets are of type `std::streamoff`; both are measured in bytes. There are three predefined positions available, as shown in the following table:

POSITION	DESCRIPTION
`ios_base::beg`	The beginning of the stream
`ios_base::end`	The end of the stream
`ios_base::cur`	The current position in the stream

For example, to seek to an absolute position in an output stream, you can use the one-parameter overload of `seekp()`, as in the following case, which uses the constant `ios_base::beg` to move to the beginning of the stream:

```
outStream.seekp(ios_base::beg);
```

Seeking within an input stream is the same, except that the `seekg()` member function is used:

```
inStream.seekg(ios_base::beg);
```

The two-argument overloads move to a relative position in the stream. The first argument prescribes how many positions to move, and the second argument provides the starting point. To move relative to the beginning of the file, the constant `ios_base::beg` is used. To move relative to the end of the file, `ios_base::end` is used. To move relative to the current position, `ios_base::cur` is used. For example, the following line moves to the second byte from the beginning of the output stream. Note that integers are implicitly converted to type `streampos` and `streamoff`.

```
outStream.seekp(2, ios_base::beg);
```

The next example moves to the third-to-last byte of an input stream:

```
inStream.seekg(-3, ios_base::end);
```

You can also query a stream's current location using the `tellx()` member function, which returns a `streampos` that indicates the current position. You can use this result to remember the current marker position before doing a `seekx()` or to query whether you are in a particular location. There are again separate versions of `tellx()` for input streams and output streams. Input streams use `tellg()`, and output streams use `tellp()`.

The following code checks the position of an input stream to determine whether it is at the beginning:

```
streampos curPos { inStream.tellg() };
if (ios_base::beg == curPos) {
    println("We're at the beginning.");
}
```

The following is a sample program that brings it all together. This program writes into a file called `test.out` and performs the following tests:

1. Outputs the string `54321` to the file
2. Verifies that the marker is at position 5 in the stream
3. Moves to position 2 in the output stream
4. Outputs a `0` in position 2 and closes the output stream
5. Opens an input stream on the `test.out` file
6. Reads the first token as an integer
7. Confirms that the value is `54021`

```
ofstream fout { "test.out" };
if (!fout) {
    println(cerr, "Error opening test.out for writing.");
    return 1;
}

// 1. Output the string "54321".
fout << "54321";

// 2. Verify that the marker is at position 5.
streampos curPos { fout.tellp() };
if (curPos == 5) {
    println("Test passed: Currently at position 5.");
} else {
    println("Test failed: Not at position 5!");
}

// 3. Move to position 2 in the output stream.
fout.seekp(2, ios_base::beg);

// 4. Output a 0 in position 2 and close the output stream.
fout << 0;
fout.close();

// 5. Open an input stream on test.out.
ifstream fin { "test.out" };
if (!fin) {
    println(cerr, "Error opening test.out for reading.");
    return 1;
}

// 6. Read the first token as an integer.
int testVal;
fin >> testVal;
if (!fin) {
    println(cerr,  "Error reading from file.");
    return 1;
}
```

```
// 7. Confirm that the value is 54021.
const int expected { 54021 };
if (testVal == expected) {
    println("Test passed: Value is {}.", expected);
} else {
    println("Test failed: Value is not {} (it was {}).", expected, testVal);
}
```

Linking Streams Together

A link can be established between any input and output streams to give them *flush-on-access* behavior. In other words, when data is requested from an input stream, its linked output stream is automatically flushed. This behavior is available to all streams but is particularly useful for file streams that may be dependent upon each other.

Stream linking is accomplished with the `tie()` member function. To tie an output stream to an input stream, call `tie()` on the input stream, and pass the address of the output stream. To break the link, pass `nullptr`.

The following program ties the input stream of one file to the output stream of an entirely different file. You could also tie it to an output stream on the same file, but bidirectional I/O (covered in the next section) is perhaps a more elegant way to read and write the same file simultaneously.

```
ifstream inFile { "input.txt" };  // Note: input.txt must exist.
ofstream outFile { "output.txt" };
// Set up a link between inFile and outFile.
inFile.tie(&outFile);
// Output some text to outFile. Normally, this would
// not flush because std::endl is not send.
outFile << "Hello there!";
// outFile has NOT been flushed.
// Read some text from inFile. This will trigger flush() on outFile.
string nextToken;
inFile >> nextToken;
// outFile HAS been flushed.
```

The `flush()` member function is defined on the `ostream` base class, so you can also link an output stream to another output stream. Here's an example:

```
outFile.tie(&anotherOutputFile);
```

Such a relationship means that every time you write to one file, the buffered data that has been sent to the other file is flushed. You can use this mechanism to keep two related files synchronized.

One example of this stream linking is the link between `cout` and `cin`. Whenever you try to input data from `cin`, `cout` is automatically flushed. There is also a link between `cerr` and `cout`, meaning that any output to `cerr` causes `cout` to flush. The `clog` stream, on the other hand, is not linked to `cout`. The wide versions of these streams have similar links.

Read an Entire File

You can use `getline()` to read the entire contents of a file by specifying `\0` as the delimiter. This works only as long as the file doesn't contain any `\0` characters in its contents. For example:

```
ifstream inputFile { "some_data.txt" };
```

```
if (inputFile.fail()) {
    println(cerr, "Unable to open file for reading.");
    return 1;
}
string fileContents;
getline(inputFile, fileContents, '\0');
println("\"{}\"", fileContents);
```

BIDIRECTIONAL I/O

So far, this chapter has discussed input and output streams as two separate but related classes. However, there is such a thing as a stream that performs both input and output: a *bidirectional stream*.

Bidirectional streams derive from `iostream`, which in turn derives from both `istream` and `ostream`, thus serving as an example of useful multiple inheritance. As you would expect, bidirectional streams support both the `>>` operator and the `<<` operator, as well as the member functions of both input streams and output streams.

The `fstream` class provides a bidirectional file stream. `fstream` is ideal for applications that need to replace data within a file, because you can read until you find the correct position and then immediately switch to writing. For example, imagine a program that stores a list of mappings between ID numbers and phone numbers. It might use a data file with the following format:

```
123 408-555-0394
124 415-555-3422
263 585-555-3490
100 650-555-3434
```

A reasonable approach to such a program would be to read in the entire data file when the program opens and rewrite the file, with any modifications, when the program closes. If the data set is huge, however, you might not be able to keep everything in memory. With `iostreams`, you don't have to. You can easily scan through the file to find a record, and you can add new records by opening the file for output in append mode. To modify an existing record, you could use a bidirectional stream, as in the following function that changes the phone number for a given ID:

```
bool changeNumberForID(const string& filename, int id, string_view newNumber)
{
    fstream ioData { filename };
    if (!ioData) {
        println(cerr, "Error while opening file {}.", filename);
        return false;
    }

    // Loop until the end of file.
    while (ioData) {
        // Read the next ID.
        int idRead;
        ioData >> idRead;
        if (!ioData) { break; }

        // Check to see if the current record is the one being changed.
        if (idRead == id) {
            // Seek the write position to the current read position.
```

```
                ioData.seekp(ioData.tellg());
                // Output a space, then the new number.
                ioData << " " << newNumber;
                break;
            }

            // Read the current number to advance the stream.
            string number;
            ioData >> number;
        }
        return true;
    }
```

Of course, an approach like this only works properly if the data is of a fixed size. When the preceding program switched from reading to writing, the output data overwrote other data in the file. To preserve the format of the file and to avoid writing over the next record, the data had to be the exact same size.

String streams can also be accessed in a bidirectional manner through the `stringstream` class.

> **NOTE** *Bidirectional streams have separate pointers for the read position and the write position. When switching between reading and writing, you need to seek the appropriate position.*

FILESYSTEM SUPPORT LIBRARY

The C++ Standard Library includes a filesystem support library, defined in `<filesystem>` and living in the `std::filesystem` namespace. It allows you to write portable code to work with the filesystem. You can use it for querying whether something is a directory or a file, iterating over the contents of a directory, manipulating paths, and retrieving information about files such as their size, extension, creation time, and so on. The two most important parts of the library—paths and directory entries—are introduced in the next sections.

Path

The basic component of the library is a `path`. A `path` can be absolute or relative and can optionally include a filename. For example, the following code defines a couple of `path`s. Note the use of raw string literals, introduced in Chapter 2, to avoid having to escape backslashes:

```
path p1 { R"(D:\Foo\Bar)" };
path p2 { "D:/Foo/Bar" };
path p3 { "D:/Foo/Bar/MyFile.txt" };
path p4 { R"(..\SomeFolder)" };
path p5 { "/usr/lib/X11" };
```

A `path` can be converted to the native format of the system on which the code is running by calling `string()`. Here's an example:

```
println("{}", p1.string());
println("{}", p2.string());
```

The output on Windows, which supports both forward and backward slashes, is as follows:

```
D:\Foo\Bar
D:/Foo/Bar
```

You can append a component to a `path` with the `append()` member function or with `operator/=`. A platform-dependent path separator is automatically inserted. Here's an example:

```
path p { "D:\\Foo" };
p.append("Bar");
p /= "Bar";
println("{}", p.string());
```

The output on Windows is `D:\Foo\Bar\Bar`.

You can use `concat()` or `operator+=` to concatenate a string to an existing `path`. This does not insert any path separator! Here's an example:

```
path p { "D:\\Foo" };
p.concat("Bar");
p += "Bar";
println("{}", p.string());
```

The output on Windows now is `D:\FooBarBar`.

> **WARNING** `append()` *and* `operator/=` *automatically insert a platform-dependent path separator, while* `concat()` *and* `operator+=` *do not.*

A range-based `for` loop can be used to iterate over the different components of a `path`. Here is an example:

```
path p { R"(C:\Foo\Bar)" };
for (const auto& component : p) {
    println("{}", component.string());
}
```

The output on Windows is as follows:

```
C:
\
Foo
Bar
```

The `path` interface supports operations such as `remove_filename()`, `replace_filename()`, `replace_extension()`, `root_name()`, `parent_path()`, `extension()`, `stem()`, `filename()`, `has_extension()`, `is_absolute()`, `is_relative()`, and more. A few of these are demonstrated in the following code snippet:

```
path p { R"(C:\Foo\Bar\file.txt)" };
println("{}", p.root_name().string());
println("{}", p.filename().string());
println("{}", p.stem().string());
println("{}", p.extension().string());
```

This code produces the following result on Windows:

```
C:
file.txt
file
.txt
```

Consult your favorite Standard Library reference for a full list of all available functionality.

Directory Entry

A `path` just represents a directory or a file on a filesystem. A `path` may refer to a non-existing directory or file. If you want to query an actual directory or file on the filesystem, you need to construct a `directory_entry` from a `path`. The `directory_entry` interface supports operations such as `exists()`, `is_directory()`, `is_regular_file()`, `file_size()`, `last_write_time()`, and others.

The following example constructs a `directory_entry` from a `path` to query the size of a file:

```
path myPath { "c:/windows/win.ini" };
directory_entry dirEntry { myPath };
if (dirEntry.exists() && dirEntry.is_regular_file()) {
    println("File size: {}", dirEntry.file_size());
}
```

Helper Functions

An entire collection of helper functions is available as well. For example, you can use `copy()` to copy files or directories, `create_directory()` to create a new directory on the filesystem, `exists()` to query whether a given directory or file exists, `file_size()` to get the size of a file, `last_write_time()` to get the time the file was last modified, `remove()` to delete a file, `temp_directory_path()` to get a directory suitable for storing temporary files, `space()` to query the available space on a filesystem, and more. Consult a Standard Library reference (see Appendix B, "Annotated Bibliography") for a full list.

The following example prints out the capacity of a filesystem and how much space is still free:

```
space_info s { space("c:\\") };
println("Capacity: {}", s.capacity);
println("Free: {}", s.free);
```

You can find more examples of these helper functions in the following section on directory iteration.

Directory Iteration

If you want to recursively iterate over all files and subdirectories in a given directory, you can use a `recursive_directory_iterator`. To start the iteration process, you need an iterator to the first `directory_entry`. To know when to stop the iteration, you need an end iterator. To create the start iterator, construct a `recursive_directory_iterator` and pass as argument a `path` of the directory over which you want to iterate. To construct the end iterator, default construct a `recursive_directory_iterator`. To get access to the `directory_entry` that an iterator refers to, use the dereferencing operator, `*`. Traversing all elements in the collection is accomplished by simply incrementing the iterator using the `++` operator until it reaches the end iterator. Note that the end iterator is not part of the collection anymore and hence does not refer to a valid `directory_entry` and must not be dereferenced.

```
void printDirectoryStructure(const path& p)
{
    if (!exists(p)) { return; }

    recursive_directory_iterator begin { p };
    recursive_directory_iterator end { };
    for (auto iter { begin }; iter != end; ++iter) {
        const string spacer(iter.depth() * 2, ' ');

        auto& entry { *iter }; // Dereference iter to access directory_entry.

        if (is_regular_file(entry)) {
            println("{}File: {} ({} bytes)",
                spacer, entry.path().string(), file_size(entry));
        } else if (is_directory(entry)) {
            println("{}Dir: {}", spacer, entry.path().string());
        }
    }
}
```

This function can be called as follows:

```
path p { R"(D:\Foo\Bar)" };
printDirectoryStructure(p);
```

You can also use a `directory_iterator` to iterate over the contents of a directory and implement the recursion yourself. Here is an example that does the same thing as the previous example but using a `directory_iterator` instead of a `recursive_directory_iterator`:

```
void printDirectoryStructure(const path& p, unsigned level = 0)
{
    if (!exists(p)) { return; }

    const string spacer(level * 2, ' ');

    if (is_regular_file(p)) {
        println("{}File: {} ({} bytes)", spacer, p.string(), file_size(p));
    } else if (is_directory(p)) {
        println("{}Dir: {}", spacer, p.string());
        for (auto& entry : directory_iterator { p }) {
            printDirectoryStructure(entry, level + 1);
        }
    }
}
```

SUMMARY

Streams provide a flexible and object-oriented way to perform input and output. The most important message in this chapter, even more important than the use of streams, is the concept of a stream. Some operating systems may have their own file access and I/O facilities, but knowledge of how streams and stream-like libraries work is essential to working with any type of modern I/O system.

The chapter finished with an introduction to the filesystem support library, which you can use to work with files and directories in a platform-independent manner.

EXERCISES

By solving the following exercises, you can practice the material discussed in this chapter. Solutions to all exercises are available with the code download on the book's website at `www.wiley.com/go/proc++6e`. However, if you are stuck on an exercise, first reread parts of this chapter to try to find an answer yourself before looking at the solution from the website.

Exercise 13-1: Let's revisit the `Person` class you developed during exercises in previous chapters. Take your implementation from Exercise 9-2 and add an `output()` member function that writes the details of a person to the standard output console.

Exercise 13-2: The `output()` member function from the previous exercise always writes the details of a person to the standard output console. Change the `output()` member function to have an output stream as parameter and write the details of a person to that stream. Test your new implementation in `main()` by writing a person to the standard output console, a string stream, and a file. Notice how it's possible to output a person to all kinds of different targets (output console, string streams, files, and so on) with a single member function using streams.

Exercise 13-3: Develop a class called `Database` that stores `Persons` (from Exercise 13-2) in an `std::vector`. Provide an `add()` member function to add a person to the database. Also provide a `save()` member function, accepting the name of a file to which it saves all persons in the database. Any existing contents in the file is removed. Add a `load()` member function, accepting the name of a file from which the database loads all persons. Provide a `clear()` member function to remove all persons from the database. Finally, add a member function `outputAll()` that calls `output()` on all persons in the database. Make sure your implementation works, even if there are spaces in a person's first or last name.

Exercise 13-4: The `Database` from Exercise 13-3 stores all persons in a single file. To practice the filesystem support library, let's change that to store each person in its own file. Modify the `save()` and `load()` member functions to accept a directory as argument where files should be stored to or loaded from. The `save()` member function saves every person in the database to its own file. The name of each file is the first name of the person followed by an underscore followed by the last name of the person. The extension of the files should be `.person`. If a file already exists, overwrite it. The `load()` member function iterates over all `.person` files in a given directory and loads all of them.

14

Handling Errors

WHAT'S IN THIS CHAPTER?

- How to handle errors in C++, including pros and cons of exceptions
- The syntax of exceptions
- Exception class hierarchies and handling exceptions polymorphically
- How to rethrow caught exceptions
- Stack unwinding and cleanup
- How to embed, inside a custom exception, the exact source code location where an exception occurred
- How to embed the entire stack trace, also known as call stack, in a custom exception
- Common error-handling situations

WILEY.COM DOWNLOADS FOR THIS CHAPTER

Please note that all the code examples for this chapter are available as part of this chapter's code download on the book's website at `www.wiley.com/go/proc++6e` on the Download Code tab.

Inevitably, your C++ programs will encounter errors during execution. The program might be unable to open a file, the network connection might go down, or the user might enter an incorrect value, to name a few possibilities. The C++ language provides a feature called *exceptions* to handle these *exceptional* but not *unexpected* situations.

Most code examples in this book so far have generally ignored error conditions for brevity. This chapter rectifies that simplification by teaching you how to incorporate error handling into your programs from their beginnings. It focuses on C++ exceptions, including the details of their syntax, and describes how to employ them effectively to create well-designed error-handling programs.

The chapter also discusses how you can write your own exception classes. This includes discussing how to automatically embed both, the exact location in your source code where an exception occurred, as well as the full stack trace at the moment the exception was raised. Both of these help tremendously in diagnosing any errors.

ERRORS AND EXCEPTIONS

No program exists in isolation; they all depend on external facilities such as interfaces with the operating system, networks and file systems, external code such as third-party libraries, and user input. Each of these areas can introduce situations that require you to respond to problems your program may encounter. These potential problems can be referred to with the general term *exceptional situations*. Even perfectly written programs encounter errors and exceptional situations. Thus, anyone who writes professional computer programs must include error-handling capabilities. Some languages, such as C, do not include many specific language facilities for error handling. Programmers using these languages generally rely on return values from functions and other ad hoc approaches. Other languages, such as Java, enforce the use of a language feature called *exceptions* as an error-handling mechanism. C++ lies between these extremes. It provides language support for exceptions but does not require their use. However, you can't ignore exceptions entirely in C++ because a few basic facilities, such as memory allocation routines, use them by default, and several classes from the Standard Library use exceptions as well.

What Are Exceptions, Anyway?

Exceptions are a mechanism for a piece of code to notify another piece of code of an "exceptional" situation or error condition without progressing through the normal code paths. The code that encounters the error *throws* the exception, and the code that handles the exception *catches* it. Exceptions do not follow the fundamental rule of step-by-step execution to which you are accustomed. When a piece of code throws an exception, the program control immediately stops executing code step-by-step and transitions to the exception handler, which could be anywhere from the next line in the same function to several function calls up the stack. If you like sports analogies, you can think of the code that throws an exception as an outfielder throwing a baseball back to the infield, where the nearest infielder (closest exception handler) catches it. Figure 14.1 shows a hypothetical stack of three function calls. Function `A()` has the exception handler. It calls function `B()`, which calls function `C()`, which throws the exception.

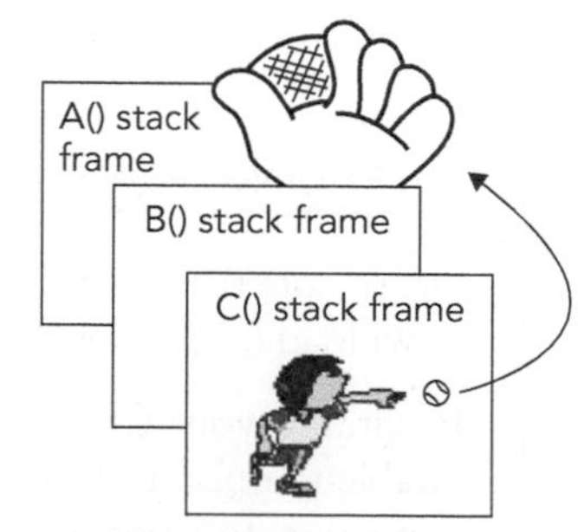

FIGURE 14.1

Figure 14.2 shows the handler catching the exception. The stack frames for `C()` and `B()` have been removed, leaving only `A()`.

Most modern programming languages, such as C# and Java, have support for exceptions, so it's no surprise that C++ has full-fledged support for them as well. However, if you are coming from C, then exceptions are something new; but once you get used to them, you probably don't want to go back.

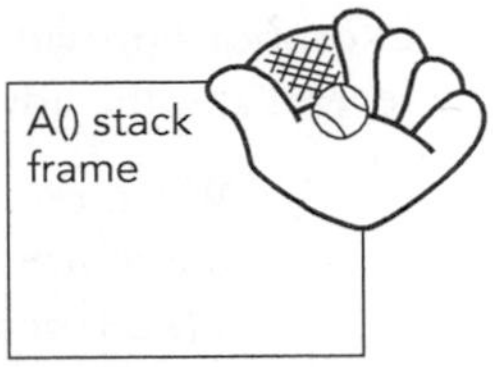

A() stack frame

FIGURE 14.2

Why Exceptions in C++ Are a Good Thing

As mentioned earlier, run-time errors in programs are inevitable. Despite that fact, error handling in most C and C++ programs is messy and ad hoc. The de facto C error-handling standard, which was carried over into many C++ programs, uses integer function return codes, and the `errno` macro to signify errors. Each thread has its own `errno` value. `errno` acts as a thread-local integer variable that functions can use to communicate errors back to calling functions.

Unfortunately, the integer return codes and `errno` are used inconsistently. Some functions might choose to return 0 for success and -1 for an error. If they return -1, they also set `errno` to an error code. Other functions return 0 for success and nonzero for an error, with the actual return value specifying the error code. These functions do not use `errno`. Still others return 0 for failure instead of for success, presumably because 0 always evaluates to `false` in C and C++.

These inconsistencies can cause problems because programmers encountering a new function often assume that its return codes are the same as other similar functions. That is not always true. For example, on the Solaris 11 operating system, there are two different libraries of synchronization objects: the Portable Operating System Interface (POSIX) version and the Solaris version. The function to initialize a semaphore in the POSIX version is called `sem_init()`, and the function to initialize a semaphore in the Solaris version is called `sema_init()`. As if that weren't confusing enough, the two functions handle error codes differently! `sem_init()` returns -1 and sets `errno` on error, while `sema_init()` returns the error code directly as a positive integer and does not set `errno`.

Another problem is that the return type of functions in C++ can be of only one type, so if you need to return both an error and a value, you must find an alternative mechanism. One solution is to return an `std::pair` or `tuple`, an object that you can use to store two or more types. The `pair` class is introduced in Chapter 1, "A Crash Course in C++ and the Standard Library," while `tuple` is discussed in the upcoming chapters that cover the Standard Library. Starting with C++23, you can return an `std::expected` from a function, which can contain either the result of the function or an error if something went wrong. Chapter 24, "Additional Vocabulary Types," discusses `expected` in detail. Another choice is to define your own struct or class that contains several values and return an instance of that struct or class from your function. Yet another option is to return the value or error through a reference parameter or to make the error code one possible value of the return type, such as a `nullptr` pointer. In all these solutions, the caller is responsible for explicitly checking for any errors returned from the function, and if it doesn't handle the error itself, it should propagate the error to its caller. Unfortunately, this often results in the loss of critical details about the error.

C programmers may be familiar with a mechanism known as `setjmp()/longjmp()`. This mechanism cannot be used correctly in C++, because it bypasses scoped destructors on the stack. You should avoid it at all costs, even in C programs; therefore, this book does not explain the details of how to use it.

Exceptions provide an easier, more consistent, and safer mechanism for error handling. There are several specific advantages of exceptions over the ad hoc approaches in C and C++:

- When return codes are used as an error reporting mechanism, you might forget to check the return code and properly handle it either locally or by propagating it upward. The `[[nodiscard]]` attribute, introduced in Chapter 1, offers a possible solution to prevent return codes from being ignored, but it's not foolproof either. Exceptions cannot be forgotten or ignored: if your program fails to catch an exception, it terminates.
- When integer return codes are used, they generally do not contain sufficient information. You can use exceptions to pass as much information as you want from the code that finds the error to the code that handles it. Exceptions can also be used to communicate information other than errors, though many developers, including myself, consider that an abuse of the exception mechanism.
- Exception handling can skip levels of the call stack. That is, a function can handle an error that occurred several function calls down the stack, without error-handling code in the intermediate functions. Return codes require each level of the call stack to clean up explicitly after the previous level and to explicitly propagate the error code.

In some compilers in the past, exception handling added a tiny amount of overhead to any function that had an exception handler. For most modern compilers there is a trade-off in that there is almost no, or even zero, overhead in the non-throwing case, and only some slight overhead when you actually throw something. This trade-off is not a bad thing. Exceptions should not be used for controlling the standard execution flow of a program, such as returning a value from a function. Exceptions should be used only to handle exceptional events that are generally not encountered in normal program use, for example, a failure while reading from a file on disk. All this means that using exceptions actually results in faster code for the non-error case compared to an implementation using error return codes.

Exception handling is not enforced in C++. In Java, for example, it is enforced. A Java function that does not specify a list of exceptions that it can possibly throw is not allowed to throw any exceptions. In C++, it is just the opposite: a function can throw any exception it wants, unless it specifies that it will not throw any exceptions using the `noexcept` keyword, which is discussed later in this chapter!

Recommendation

I recommend exceptions as a useful mechanism for error handling. I feel that the structure and error-handling formalization that exceptions provide outweigh the less desirable aspects. Thus, the remainder of this chapter focuses on exceptions. Also, many popular libraries, such as the Standard Library and Boost, use exceptions, so you need to be prepared to handle them.

EXCEPTION MECHANICS

Exceptional situations arise frequently in file input and output. The following is a function to open a file, read a list of integers from the file, and return the integers in an `std::vector` data structure. The lack of error handling should jump out at you:

```
vector<int> readIntegerFile(const string& filename)
{
```

```
        ifstream inputStream { filename };
        // Read the integers one-by-one and add them to a vector.
        vector<int> integers;
        int temp;
        while (inputStream >> temp) {
            integers.push_back(temp);
        }
        return integers;
    }
```

The following line keeps reading values from the ifstream until the end of the file is reached or until an error occurs:

```
while (inputStream >> temp) {
```

If the >> operator encounters an error, it sets the fail bit of the ifstream object. In that case, the bool() conversion operator returns false, and the while loop terminates. Streams are discussed in more detail in Chapter 13, "Demystifying C++ I/O."

You might use readIntegerFile() like this:

```
const string filename { "IntegerFile.txt" };
vector<int> myInts { readIntegerFile(filename) };
println("{} ", myInts);
```

The rest of this section shows how to add error handling with exceptions, but first, we need to delve a bit deeper into how you throw and catch exceptions.

Throwing and Catching Exceptions

Using exceptions consists of providing two parts in your program: a try/catch construct to handle an exception, and a throw statement that throws an exception. Both must be present in some form to make exceptions work. However, in many cases, the throw happens deep inside some library (including the C++ runtime), and the programmer never sees it, but still has to react to it using a try/catch construct.

The try/catch construct looks like this:

```
try {
    // ... code which may result in an exception being thrown
} catch (exception-type1 exception-name) {
    // ... code which responds to the exception of type 1
} catch (exception-type2 exception-name) {
    // ... code which responds to the exception of type 2
}
// ... remaining code
```

The code that may result in an exception being thrown might contain a throw directly. It might also be calling a function that either directly throws an exception or calls—by some unknown number of layers of calls—a function that throws an exception.

If no exception is thrown, no code from any catch block is executed, and the "remaining code" that follows will follow the last statement executed in the try block.

If an exception is thrown, any code following the `throw` or following the call that resulted in the `throw` is not executed; instead, control immediately goes to the right `catch` block, depending on the type of the exception that is thrown.

If the `catch` block does not do a control transfer—for example, by returning from the function, throwing a new exception, or rethrowing the caught exception—then the "remaining code" is executed after the last statement of that `catch` block.

The simplest example to demonstrate exception handling is avoiding division-by-zero. The following example throws an exception of type `std::invalid_argument`, defined in `<stdexcept>`:

```
double safeDivide(double num, double den)
{
    if (den == 0) { throw invalid_argument { "Divide by zero" }; }
    return num / den;
}

int main()
{
    try {
        println("{}", safeDivide(5, 2));
        println("{}", safeDivide(10, 0));
        println("{}", safeDivide(3, 3));
    } catch (const invalid_argument& e) {
        println("Caught exception: {}", e.what());
    }
}
```

The output is as follows:

```
2.5
Caught exception: Divide by zero
```

`throw` is a keyword in C++ and is the only way to throw an exception. In the code snippet we throw a new instance of `invalid_argument`. It is one of the standard exceptions provided by the C++ Standard Library. All Standard Library exceptions form a hierarchy, which is discussed later in this chapter. Each class in the hierarchy supports a `what()` member function that returns a `const char*` string describing the exception. This is the string you provide in the constructor of the exception.

> **NOTE** *Even though the return type of* `what()` *is* `const char*`, *exceptions can support Unicode strings if you encode them using UTF-8. See Chapter 21, "String Localization and Regular Expressions," for details on Unicode strings.*

Let's go back to the `readIntegerFile()` function. The most likely problem to occur is for the file open to fail. That's a perfect situation for throwing an exception. The following code throws an exception of type `std::exception`, defined in `<exception>`, if the file fails to open:

```
vector<int> readIntegerFile(const string& filename)
{
    ifstream inputStream { filename };
    if (inputStream.fail()) {
```

```
        // We failed to open the file: throw an exception.
        throw exception {};
    }

    // Read the integers one-by-one and add them to a vector.
    vector<int> integers;
    int temp;
    while (inputStream >> temp) {
        integers.push_back(temp);
    }
    return integers;
}
```

> **NOTE** *Always document the possible exceptions a function can throw in its code documentation, because users of the function need to know which exceptions might get thrown so they can properly handle them.*

If the function fails to open the file and executes the `throw exception{};` statement, the rest of the function is skipped, and control transitions to the nearest exception handler.

Throwing exceptions in your code is most useful when you also write code that handles them. Exception handling is a way to "try" a block of code, with another block of code designated to react to any problems that might occur. In the following `main()` function, the `catch` statement reacts to any exception of type `exception` that was thrown within the `try` block by printing an error message. If a `try` block finishes without throwing an exception, the `catch` blocks are skipped. You can think of `try`/`catch` blocks as glorified `if` statements: *if* an exception is thrown in the `try` block, *then* execute a `catch` block, *else* skip all `catch` blocks.

```
int main()
{
    const string filename { "IntegerFile.txt" };
    vector<int> myInts;
    try {
        myInts = readIntegerFile(filename);
    } catch (const exception& e) {
        println(cerr, "Unable to open file {}", filename);
        return 1;
    }
    println("{} ", myInts);
}
```

> **NOTE** *Although by default streams do not throw exceptions, you can tell the streams to throw exceptions for error conditions by calling their* `exceptions()` *member function. However, most compilers give useless information in the stream exceptions they throw. For such compilers, it might be better to deal with the stream state directly instead of using exceptions. This book does not use stream exceptions.*

Exception Types

You can throw an exception of any type. The earlier example throws an object of type `std::exception`, but exceptions do not need to be objects. You could throw a simple `int` like this:

```
vector<int> readIntegerFile(const string& filename)
{
    ifstream inputStream { filename };
    if (inputStream.fail()) {
        // We failed to open the file: throw an exception.
        throw 5;
    }
    // Omitted for brevity
}
```

You would then need to change the `catch` statement as follows:

```
try {
    myInts = readIntegerFile(filename);
} catch (int e) {
    println(cerr, "Unable to open file {} (Error Code {})", filename, e);
    return 1;
}
```

Alternatively, you could throw a `const char*` C-style string. This technique is sometimes useful because the string can contain information about the exception:

```
vector<int> readIntegerFile(const string& filename)
{
    ifstream inputStream { filename };
    if (inputStream.fail()) {
        // We failed to open the file: throw an exception.
        throw "Unable to open file";
    }
    // Omitted for brevity
}
```

When you catch the `const char*` exception, you can print the result as follows:

```
try {
    myInts = readIntegerFile(filename);
} catch (const char* e) {
    println(cerr, "{}", e);
    return 1;
}
```

Despite the previous examples, keep the following in mind:

> **NOTE** *You should generally throw objects rather than other data types as exceptions for two reasons:*
>
> - *Objects convey information by their class name.*
> - *Objects can store all kinds of information, including strings that describe the exception.*

The C++ Standard Library defines a number of predefined exception classes structured in a class hierarchy, discussed later in this chapter. Additionally, you can write your own exception classes and fit them in the standard hierarchy, as you'll also learn later in this chapter.

Catching Exception Objects as Reference-to-const

In the earlier example in which `readIntegerFile()` throws an object of type `exception`, the `catch` handler looks like this:

```
} catch (const exception& e) {
```

However, there is no requirement to catch objects as reference-to-`const`. You could catch the object by value like this:

```
} catch (exception e) {
```

Alternatively, you could catch the object as reference-to-non-`const`:

```
} catch (exception& e) {
```

Also, as you saw in the `const char*` example earlier, you can catch pointers to exceptions, as long as pointers to exceptions are thrown.

Still, I recommend sticking with the following advice:

> **NOTE** *Always throw objects as exceptions, and always catch exception objects as reference-to-*`const`*! This avoids object slicing (see Chapter 10, "Discovering Inheritance Techniques"), which could happen when you catch exception objects by value. Capturing by reference-to-non-*`const` *is not recommended either, as caught exceptions are normally never modified.*

Throwing and Catching Multiple Exceptions

Failure to open the file is not the only problem `readIntegerFile()` could encounter. Reading the data from the file can cause an error if it is formatted incorrectly. Here is an implementation of `readIntegerFile()` that throws an exception if it cannot either open the file or read the data correctly. This time, it uses a `runtime_error`, derived from `exception` and which allows you to specify a descriptive string in its constructor. The `runtime_error` exception class is defined in `<stdexcept>`.

```
vector<int> readIntegerFile(const string& filename)
{
    ifstream inputStream { filename };
    if (inputStream.fail()) {
       // We failed to open the file: throw an exception.
        throw runtime_error { "Unable to open the file." };
    }

    // Read the integers one-by-one and add them to a vector.
    vector<int> integers;
    int temp;
    while (inputStream >> temp) {
        integers.push_back(temp);
    }
```

```
        if (!inputStream.eof()) {
            // We did not reach the end-of-file.
            // This means that some error occurred while reading the file.
            // Throw an exception.
            throw runtime_error { "Error reading the file." };
        }

        return integers;
    }
```

Your code in `main()` does not need to change much because it already catches an exception of type `exception`, from which `runtime_error` derives. However, that exception could now be thrown in two different situations, so we use the `what()` member function to get a proper description of the caught exception:

```
try {
    myInts = readIntegerFile(filename);
} catch (const exception& e) {
    println(cerr, "{}", e.what());
    return 1;
}
```

Alternatively, you could throw two different types of exceptions from `readIntegerFile()`. Here is an implementation of `readIntegerFile()` that throws an exception object of class `invalid_argument` if the file cannot be opened, and an object of class `runtime_error` if the integers cannot be read. Both `invalid_argument` and `runtime_error` are classes defined in `<stdexcept>` as part of the C++ Standard Library.

```
vector<int> readIntegerFile(const string& filename)
{
    ifstream inputStream { filename };
    if (inputStream.fail()) {
        // We failed to open the file: throw an exception.
        throw invalid_argument { "Unable to open the file." };
    }

    // Read the integers one-by-one and add them to a vector.
    vector<int> integers;
    int temp;
    while (inputStream >> temp) {
        integers.push_back(temp);
    }

    if (!inputStream.eof()) {
        // We did not reach the end-of-file.
        // This means that some error occurred while reading the file.
        // Throw an exception.
        throw runtime_error { "Error reading the file." };
    }

    return integers;
}
```

There are no public default constructors for `invalid_argument` and `runtime_error`, only `string` constructors, so you always must pass a string as argument.

Now, `main()` can catch both `invalid_argument` and `runtime_error` exceptions with two `catch` statements:

```
try {
    myInts = readIntegerFile(filename);
} catch (const invalid_argument& e) {
    println(cerr, "{}", e.what());
    return 1;
} catch (const runtime_error& e) {
    println(cerr, "{}", e.what());
    return 2;
}
```

If an exception is thrown inside the `try` block, the compiler matches the type of the exception to the proper `catch` handler. So, if `readIntegerFile()` is unable to open the file and throws an `invalid_argument` object, it is caught by the first `catch` statement. If `readIntegerFile()` is unable to read the file properly and throws a `runtime_error`, then the second `catch` statement catches the exception.

Matching and const

The `const`-ness specified in the type of the exception you want to catch makes no difference for matching purposes. That is, this line matches any exception of type `runtime_error`:

```
} catch (const runtime_error& e) {
```

The following line also matches any exception of type `runtime_error`:

```
} catch (runtime_error& e) {
```

Still, it's advised to always catch exception objects as reference-to-`const`.

Matching Any Exception

You can write a `catch`-all block that matches any possible exception with the special syntax shown in the following example:

```
try {
    myInts = readIntegerFile(filename);
} catch (...) {
    println(cerr, "Error reading or opening file {}", filename);
    return 1;
}
```

The three dots are not a typo. They are a wildcard that matches any exception type. The downside of using a `catch`-all block is that you don't get any details of the caught exception. When you are calling poorly documented code, this technique could be useful to ensure that you catch all possible exceptions. But even then, what would you possibly be able to do to recover from an unknown exception?

One useful use case of a `catch`-all block is to log that an exception was thrown and then rethrow the exception. The following example shows how you can write `catch` handlers that explicitly handle `invalid_argument` and `runtime_error` exceptions, as well as how to include a `catch`-all handler for all other exceptions. In any `catch` block, you can rethrow the currently caught exception using just the `throw` keyword without any arguments. There is more to say about rethrowing exceptions, but that has to wait until later in this chapter.

```
try {
    // Code that can throw exceptions.
} catch (const invalid_argument& e) {
    // Handle invalid_argument exception.
} catch (const runtime_error& e) {
    // Handle runtime_error exception.
} catch (...) {
    // Handle all other exceptions.
    // Log that an exception occurred...
    throw; // Rethrow the caught exception.
}
```

In situations where you have complete information about the set of thrown exceptions, a `catch`-all block is not recommended because it handles every exception type identically. It's better to match exception types explicitly and take appropriate, targeted actions.

Uncaught Exceptions

If your program throws an exception that is not caught anywhere, the program terminates. Basically, there is a `try/catch` construct around the call to your `main()` function, which catches all unhandled exceptions and behaves like the following pseudocode:

```
try {
    main(argc, argv);
} catch (...) {
    // Issue error message and terminate program.
}
// Normal termination code.
```

However, this behavior is usually not what you want. The point of exceptions is to give your program a chance to handle and correct undesirable or unexpected situations.

> **WARNING** *You should catch and handle all exceptions thrown in your programs, as far as possible.*

It is also possible to change the behavior of your program if there is an uncaught exception. When the program encounters an uncaught exception, it calls the built-in `terminate()` function, which calls `abort()` from `<cstdlib>` to kill the program. You can set your own `terminate_handler` by calling `set_terminate()` with a pointer to a function that takes no arguments and returns no value. `terminate()`, `set_terminate()`, and `terminate_handler` are all declared in `<exception>`. The following pseudocode shows a high-level overview of how it works:

```
try {
    main(argc, argv);
```

```
    } catch (...) {
        if (terminate_handler != nullptr) {
            terminate_handler();
        } else {
            terminate();
        }
    }
    // Normal termination code.
```

Before you get too excited about this feature, you should know that your callback function must still terminate the program using either `abort()` or `_Exit()`. It can't just ignore the error. Both `abort()` and `_Exit()` are defined in `<cstdlib>` and terminate the application without cleaning up resources. For example, destructors of objects won't get called. The `_Exit()` function accepts an integer argument that is returned to the operating system and can be used to determine how a process exited. A value of `0` or `EXIT_SUCCESS` means the program exited without any error; otherwise, the program terminated abnormally. The `abort()` function does not accept any arguments. Additionally, there is an `exit()` function that also accepts an integer that is returned to the operating system and that does clean up resources by calling destructors, but it's not recommended to call `exit()` from a `terminate_handler`.

A `terminate_handler` can be used to print a helpful error message before exiting. Here is an example of a `main()` function that doesn't catch the exceptions thrown by `readIntegerFile()`. Instead, it sets the `terminate_handler` to a custom callback. This callback prints an error message and terminates the process by calling `_Exit()`. Note the use of the `[[noreturn]]` attribute, introduced in Chapter 1.

```
[[noreturn]] void myTerminate()
{
    println(cerr, "Uncaught exception!");
    _Exit(1);
}

int main()
{
    set_terminate(myTerminate);

    const string filename { "IntegerFile.txt" };
    vector<int> myInts { readIntegerFile(filename) };
    println("{} ", myInts);
}
```

Although not shown in this example, `set_terminate()` returns the old `terminate_handler` when it sets the new one. The `terminate_handler` applies program-wide, so it's considered good style to restore the old `terminate_handler` when you have completed the code that needed the new `terminate_handler`. In this case, the entire program needs the new `terminate_handler`, so there's no point in restoring it.

While it's important to know about `set_terminate()`, it's not an effective exception-handling approach. It's recommended to catch and handle each exception individually to provide more precise error handling.

> **NOTE** *In professionally written software, a* `terminate_handler` *is usually set up to create a crash dump before terminating the process. A crash dump usually contains information such as the call stack and local variables at the time the uncaught exception was thrown. Such a crash dump can then be loaded into a debugger and allows you to figure out what the uncaught exception was and what caused it. However, writing crash dumps is platform dependent and therefore not further discussed in this book.*

noexcept Specifier

By default, a function is allowed to throw any exception it likes. However, it is possible to mark a function with the `noexcept` specifier, a C++ keyword, to state that it will not throw any exceptions. For example, the following function is marked as `noexcept`, so it is not allowed to throw any exceptions:

```
void printValues(const vector<int>& values) noexcept;
```

> **NOTE** *A function marked with* `noexcept` *must not throw any exceptions.*

When a function marked as `noexcept` throws an exception anyway, C++ calls `terminate()` to terminate the application.

When you override a `virtual` member function in a derived class, you are allowed to mark the overridden member function as `noexcept`, even if the version in the base class is not `noexcept`. The opposite is not allowed.

noexcept(expression) Specifier

The `noexcept(expression)` specifier marks a function as `noexcept` if and only if the given expression returns `true`. In other words, `noexcept` equals `noexcept(true)`, and `noexcept(false)` is the opposite of `noexcept(true)`; that is, a member function marked with `noexcept(false)` can throw any exception it wants, which is the default.

noexcept(expression) Operator

The `noexcept(expression)` operator returns `true` if the given expression is `noexcept`. This evaluation happens at compile time.

Here's an example:

```
void f1() noexcept {}
void f2() noexcept(false) {}
void f3() noexcept(noexcept(f1())) {}
void f4() noexcept(noexcept(f2())) {}
```

```
int main()
{
    println("{} {} {} {}", noexcept(f1()),
                           noexcept(f2()),
                           noexcept(f3()),
                           noexcept(f4()));
}
```

The output of this code snippet is `true false true false`:

- `noexcept(f1())` is `true` because `f1()` is explicitly marked with a `noexcept` specifier.
- `noexcept(f2())` is `false` because `f2()` is explicitly marked as such using a `noexcept(expression)` specifier.
- `noexcept(f3())` is `true` because `f3()` is marked as `noexcept` but only if `f1()` is `noexcept` which it is.
- `noexcept(f4())` is `false` because `f4()` is marked as `noexcept` but only if `f2()` is `noexcept` which it isn't.

Throw Lists

Older versions of C++ allowed you to specify the exceptions a function intended to throw. This specification was called the *throw list* or the *exception specification*.

> **WARNING** *C++11 has deprecated, and C++17 has removed support for exception specifications, apart from* `noexcept` *and* `throw()`*. The latter was equivalent to* `noexcept`*. Since C++20, support for* `throw()` *has been removed as well.*

Because C++17 has officially removed support for exception specifications, this book does not further discuss them.

EXCEPTIONS AND POLYMORPHISM

As described earlier, you can actually throw any type of exception. However, classes are the most useful types of exceptions. In fact, exception classes are usually written in a hierarchy so that you can employ polymorphism when you catch the exceptions.

The Standard Exception Hierarchy

You've already seen several exceptions from the C++ standard exception hierarchy: `exception`, `runtime_error`, and `invalid_argument`. Figure 14.3 shows the full hierarchy. For completeness, all standard exceptions are shown, including those thrown by parts of the Standard Library that are discussed in later chapters.

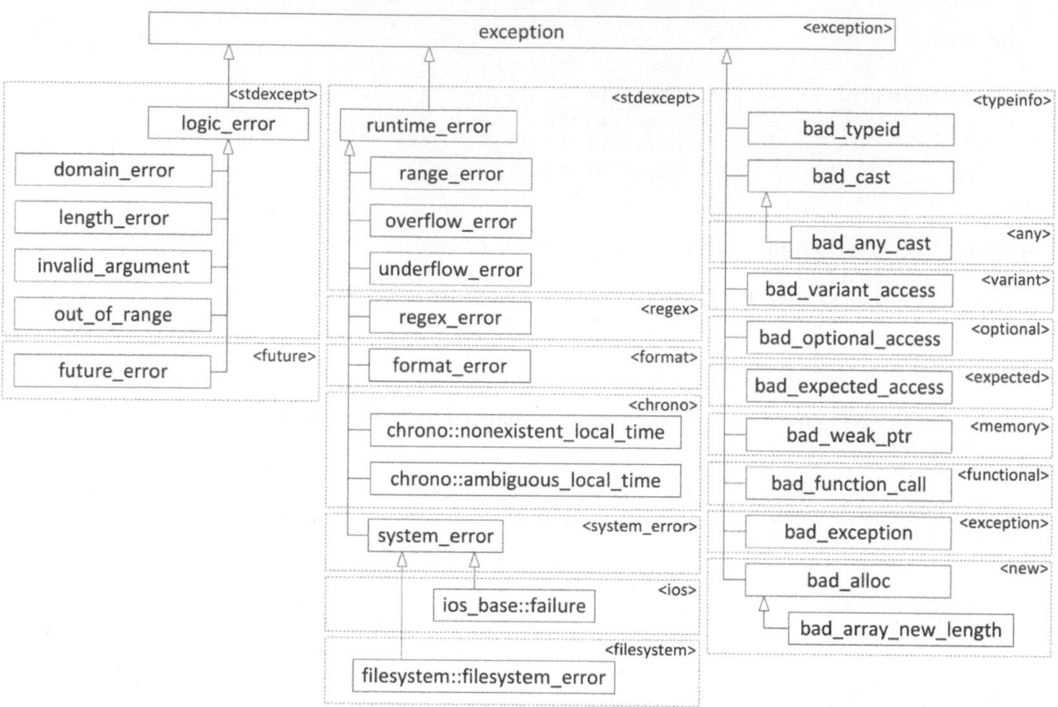

FIGURE 14.3

All of the exceptions thrown by the C++ Standard Library are objects of classes in this hierarchy. Each class in the hierarchy supports a `what()` member function that returns a `const char*` string describing the exception. You can use this string in an error message.

Some of the exception classes require you to set in the constructor the string that is returned by `what()`. That's why you have to specify a string in the constructors for `runtime_error` and `invalid_argument`. This has already been done in examples throughout this chapter. Here is another version of `readIntegerFile()` that includes the filename in the error message:

```
vector<int> readIntegerFile(const string& filename)
{
    ifstream inputStream { filename };
    if (inputStream.fail()) {
        // We failed to open the file: throw an exception.
        const string error { format("Unable to open file {}.", filename) };
        throw invalid_argument { error };
    }

    // Read the integers one-by-one and add them to a vector.
    vector<int> integers;
    int temp;
    while (inputStream >> temp) {
        integers.push_back(temp);
    }

    if (!inputStream.eof()) {
        // We did not reach the end-of-file.
```

```
            // This means that some error occurred while reading the file.
            // Throw an exception.
            const string error { format("Unable to read file {}.", filename) };
            throw runtime_error { error };
        }

        return integers;
    }
```

Catching Exceptions in a Class Hierarchy

A feature of exception hierarchies is that you can catch exceptions polymorphically. For example, if you look at the following two catch statements, you can see that they are identical except for the exception class that they handle:

```
try {
    myInts = readIntegerFile(filename);
} catch (const invalid_argument& e) {
    println(cerr, "{}", e.what());
    return 1;
} catch (const runtime_error& e) {
    println(cerr, "{}", e.what());
    return 1;
}
```

Conveniently, invalid_argument and runtime_error are both derived classes of exception, so you can replace the two catch statements with a single catch statement for exception:

```
try {
    myInts = readIntegerFile(filename);
} catch (const exception& e) {
    println(cerr, "{}", e.what());
    return 1;
}
```

The catch statement for an exception reference matches any derived classes of exception, including both invalid_argument and runtime_error. Note that the higher in the exception hierarchy you catch exceptions, the less specific your error handling can be. You should generally catch exceptions at as specific a level as possible.

> **WARNING** *When you catch exceptions polymorphically, make sure to catch them by reference! If you catch exceptions by value, you can encounter slicing, in which case you lose information from the object. See Chapter 10 for details on slicing.*

When more than one catch clause is used, the catch clauses are matched in syntactic order as they appear in your code; the first one that matches wins. If one catch is more inclusive than a later one, it will match first, and the more restrictive one, which comes later, will never be executed. Therefore, you should place your catch clauses from most restrictive to least restrictive in order. For example, suppose that you want to catch invalid_argument from readIntegerFile() explicitly, but you also want to leave the generic exception handler for any other exceptions. The correct way to do so is like this:

```
try {
    myInts = readIntegerFile(filename);
} catch (const invalid_argument& e) { // List the derived class first.
    // Take some special action for invalid filenames.
} catch (const exception& e) { // Now list exception.
    println(cerr, "{}", e.what());
    return 1;
}
```

The first catch statement catches invalid_argument exceptions, and the second catches any other exceptions of type exception. However, if you reverse the order of the catch statements, you don't get the same result:

```
try {
    myInts = readIntegerFile(filename);
} catch (const exception& e) { // BUG: catching base class first!
    println(cerr, "{}", e.what());
    return 1;
} catch (const invalid_argument& e) {
    // Take some special action for invalid filenames.
}
```

With this order, any exception of a class that derives from exception is caught by the first catch statement; the second catch will never be reached. Some compilers issue a warning in this case, but you shouldn't count on it.

Writing Your Own Exception Classes

There are two advantages to writing your own exception classes:

- The number of exceptions in the C++ Standard Library is limited. Instead of using an exception class with a generic name, such as runtime_error, you can create classes with names that are more meaningful for the particular errors in your program.
- You can add your own information to these exceptions. Most exceptions in the standard hierarchy allow you to set only an error string. You might want to pass different information in the exception.

It's recommended that all the exception classes that you write inherit directly or indirectly from the standard exception class. If everyone on your project follows that rule, you know that every exception in the program will be derived from exception (assuming that you aren't using third-party libraries that break this rule). This guideline makes exception handling via polymorphism significantly easier.

Let's look at an example. invalid_argument and runtime_error don't do a good job at capturing the file opening and reading errors in readIntegerFile(). You can define your own error hierarchy for file errors, starting with a generic FileError class:

```
class FileError : public exception
{
```

```
    public:
        explicit FileError(string filename) : m_filename { move(filename) } {}
        const char* what() const noexcept override { return m_message.c_str(); }
        virtual const string& getFilename() const noexcept { return m_filename; }
    protected:
        virtual void setMessage(string message) { m_message = move(message); }
    private:
        string m_filename;
        string m_message;
};
```

As a good programming citizen, you make `FileError` a part of the standard exception hierarchy. It seems appropriate to integrate it as a child of `exception`. When you derive from `exception`, you can override the `what()` member function, which has the prototype shown and which must return a `const char*` string that is valid until the object is destroyed. In the case of `FileError`, this string comes from the `m_message` data member. Derived classes of `FileError` can set the message using the `protected setMessage()` member function. The generic `FileError` class also contains a filename and a public accessor for that filename.

The first exceptional situation in `readIntegerFile()` occurs when the file cannot be opened. Thus, you might want to write a `FileOpenError` exception derived from `FileError`:

```
class FileOpenError : public FileError
{
    public:
        explicit FileOpenError(string filename) : FileError { move(filename) }
        {
            setMessage(format("Unable to open {}.", getFilename()));
        }
};
```

The `FileOpenError` exception calls `setMessage()` to change the `m_message` string to represent the file-opening error. Note that in the body of the constructor, `getFilename()` is used to get the filename. The `filename` parameter cannot be used for this as the ctor-initializer has moved `filename` in the call to the `FileError` constructor. As you know, after a move operation, you shouldn't use an object any longer.

The second exceptional situation in `readIntegerFile()` occurs if the file cannot be read properly. It might be useful for this exception to include the line number where the error occurred, as well as the filename in the error message string returned from `what()`. Here is a `FileReadError` exception derived from `FileError`:

```
class FileReadError : public FileError
{
    public:
        explicit FileReadError(string filename, size_t lineNumber)
            : FileError { move(filename) }, m_lineNumber { lineNumber }
        {
            setMessage(format("Error reading {}, line {}.",
                getFilename(), lineNumber));
        }

        virtual size_t getLineNumber() const noexcept { return m_lineNumber; }
```

```
    private:
        size_t m_lineNumber { 0 };
};
```

Of course, to set the line number properly, `readIntegerFile()` needs to be modified to track the number of lines read instead of just reading integers directly. Here is a new `readIntegerFile()` function that uses the new exceptions:

```
vector<int> readIntegerFile(const string& filename)
{
    ifstream inputStream { filename };
    if (inputStream.fail()) {
        // We failed to open the file: throw an exception.
        throw FileOpenError { filename };
    }

    vector<int> integers;
    size_t lineNumber { 0 };
    while (!inputStream.eof()) {
        // Read one line from the file.
        string line;
        getline(inputStream, line);
        ++lineNumber;

        // Create a string stream out of the line.
        istringstream lineStream { line };

        // Read the integers one-by-one and add them to the vector.
        int temp;
        while (lineStream >> temp) {
            integers.push_back(temp);
        }

        if (!lineStream.eof()) {
            // We did not reach the end of the string stream.
            // This means that some error occurred while reading this line.
            // Throw an exception.
            throw FileReadError { filename, lineNumber };
        }
    }

    return integers;
}
```

Now, code that calls `readIntegerFile()` can use polymorphism to catch exceptions of type `FileError` like this:

```
try {
    myInts = readIntegerFile(filename);
} catch (const FileError& e) {
    println(cerr, "{}", e.what());
    return 1;
}
```

There is one caveat when writing classes whose objects will be used as exceptions. When a piece of code throws an exception, the object or value thrown is moved or copied, using either the move constructor or the copy constructor. Thus, if you write a class whose objects will be thrown as exceptions, you must make sure those objects are copyable and/or moveable. This means that if you have dynamically allocated memory in your exception class, your class must have a destructor, but also a copy constructor and copy assignment operator and/or a move constructor and move assignment operator, see Chapter 9, "Mastering Classes and Objects."

> **WARNING** *Objects thrown as exceptions are always moved or copied at least once.*

It is possible for exceptions to be copied more than once, but only if you catch the exception by value instead of by reference.

> **NOTE** *Catch exception objects by reference (preferably reference-to-`const`) to avoid unnecessary copying.*

Nested Exceptions

It could happen that during handling of a first exception, a second exceptional situation is triggered that requires a second exception to be thrown. Unfortunately, when you throw the second exception, all information about the first exception that you are currently trying to handle will be lost. The solution provided by C++ for this problem is called *nested exceptions*, which allow you to nest a caught exception in the context of a new exception. This can also be useful if you call a function in a third-party library that throws an exception of a certain type, `A`, but you only want exceptions of another type, `B`, in your code. In such a case, you catch all exceptions from the library and nest them in an exception of type `B`.

You use `std::throw_with_nested()` to throw an exception with another exception nested inside it. A catch handler for this new exception can use a `dynamic_cast()` to get access to the `std::nested_exception` representing the first exception. The upcoming example demonstrates this. It first defines a `MyException` class, which derives from `exception` and accepts a string in its constructor:

```
class MyException : public exception
{
    public:
        explicit MyException(string message) : m_message { move(message) } {}
        const char* what() const noexcept override { return m_message.c_str(); }
    private:
        string m_message;
};
```

The following `doSomething()` function throws a `runtime_error` that is immediately caught in a catch handler. The catch handler writes a message and then uses the `throw_with_nested()` function to throw a second exception that has the first one nested inside it. Note that nesting the exception happens automatically:

```
void doSomething()
{
```

```
        try {
            throw runtime_error { "A runtime_error exception" };
        } catch (const runtime_error& e) {
            println("doSomething() caught a runtime_error");
            println("doSomething() throwing MyException");
            throw_with_nested(
                MyException { "MyException with nested runtime_error" });
        }
    }
```

`throw_with_nested()` works by throwing an unnamed new compiler-generated type that derives from both `nested_exception` and, in this example, from `MyException`. Hence, it's another example of useful multiple inheritance in C++. The default constructor of the `nested_exception` base class automatically captures the exception currently being handled by calling `std::current_exception()` and stores it in an `std::exception_ptr`. An `exception_ptr` is a pointer-like type capable of storing either a null pointer or a pointer to an exception object that was thrown and captured with `current_exception()`. Instances of `exception_ptr` can be passed to functions (usually by value) and across different threads.

Finally, the following code snippet demonstrates how to handle an exception with a nested exception. The code calls `doSomething()` and has one catch handler for exceptions of type `MyException`. When it catches such an exception, it writes a message and then uses a `dynamic_cast()` to get access to the nested exception. If there is no nested exception inside, the result will be a null pointer. If there is a nested exception inside, the `rethrow_nested()` member function on the `nested_exception` is called. This causes the nested exception to be rethrown, which you can then catch in another `try/catch` block.

```
try {
    doSomething();
} catch (const MyException& e) {
    println("main() caught MyException: {}", e.what());

    const auto* nested { dynamic_cast<const nested_exception*>(&e) };
    if (nested) {
        try {
            nested->rethrow_nested();
        } catch (const runtime_error& e) {
            // Handle nested exception.
            println("  Nested exception: {}", e.what());
        }
    }
}
```

The output is as follows:

```
doSomething() caught a runtime_error
doSomething() throwing MyException
main() caught MyException: MyException with nested runtime_error
  Nested exception: A runtime_error exception
```

This code uses a `dynamic_cast()` to check for a nested exception. Because you always have to perform such a `dynamic_cast()` if you want to check for a nested exception, the standard provides a helper function called `std::rethrow_if_nested()` that does it for you. This helper function can be used as follows:

```
try {
    doSomething();
```

```
    } catch (const MyException& e) {
        println("main() caught MyException: {}", e.what());
        try {
            rethrow_if_nested(e);
        } catch (const runtime_error& e) {
            // Handle nested exception.
            println("  Nested exception: {}", e.what());
        }
    }
```

throw_with_nested(), nested_exception, rethrow_if_nested(), current_exception(), and exception_ptr are all defined in <exception>.

RETHROWING EXCEPTIONS

The throw keyword can also be used to rethrow the current exception without copying it, as in the following example:

```
void g() { throw invalid_argument { "Some exception" }; }

void f()
{
    try {
        g();
    } catch (const invalid_argument& e) {
        println("caught in f(): {}", e.what());
        throw;  // rethrow
    }
}

int main()
{
    try {
        f();
    } catch (const invalid_argument& e) {
        println("caught in main(): {}", e.what());
    }
}
```

This example produces the following output:

```
caught in f(): Some exception
caught in main(): Some exception
```

You might think you could rethrow a caught exception e with throw e;. However, that's wrong, because it can cause slicing of your exception object. For example, suppose f() is modified to catch std::exceptions, and main() is modified to catch both exception and invalid_argument exceptions:

```
void g() { throw invalid_argument { "Some exception" }; }

void f()
{
    try {
```

```
        g();
    } catch (const exception& e) {
        println("caught in f(): {}", e.what());
        throw;  // rethrow
    }
}

int main()
{
    try {
        f();
    } catch (const invalid_argument& e) {
        println("invalid_argument caught in main(): {}", e.what());
    } catch (const exception& e) {
        println("exception caught in main(): {}", e.what());
    }
}
```

Remember that `invalid_argument` derives from `exception`, hence it must be caught first. The output of this code is as you would expect, shown here:

```
caught in f(): Some exception
invalid_argument caught in main(): Some exception
```

Now, try replacing the `throw;` statement in `f()` with `throw e;`. The output then becomes as follows:

```
caught in f(): Some exception
exception caught in main(): Some exception
```

`main()` seems to be catching an `exception` object, instead of an `invalid_argument` object. That's because the `throw e;` statement causes slicing, reducing the `invalid_argument` to an `exception`.

> **WARNING** *Always use* `throw;` *to rethrow an exception. Never do something like* `throw e;` *to rethrow a caught exception* `e`*!*

STACK UNWINDING AND CLEANUP

When a piece of code throws an exception, it searches for a catch handler on the stack. This catch handler could be zero or more function calls up the stack of execution. When one is found, the stack is stripped back to the stack level that defines the catch handler by unwinding all intermediate stack frames. *Stack unwinding* means that the destructors for all locally scoped variables are called, and all code remaining in each function past the current point of execution is skipped.

During stack unwinding, pointer variables are obviously not freed, and other cleanup is not performed either. This behavior can present problems. For example, the following code causes a memory leak:

```
void funcOne();
void funcTwo();

int main()
{
    try {
```

```
            funcOne();
        } catch (const exception& e) {
            println(cerr, "Exception caught!");
            return 1;
        }
    }

    void funcOne()
    {
        string str1;
        string* str2 { new string {} };
        funcTwo();
        delete str2;
    }

    void funcTwo()
    {
        ifstream fileStream;
        fileStream.open("filename");
        throw exception {};
        fileStream.close();
    }
```

When `funcTwo()` throws an exception, the closest exception handler is in `main()`. Control then jumps immediately from this line in `funcTwo()`,

```
throw exception {};
```

to this line in `main()`:

```
println(cerr, "Exception caught!");
```

In `funcTwo()`, control remains at the line that threw the exception, so this subsequent line never gets a chance to run:

```
fileStream.close();
```

However, luckily for you, the `ifstream` destructor is called because `fileStream` is a local variable on the stack. The `ifstream` destructor closes the file for you, so there is no resource leak here. If you had dynamically allocated `fileStream`, it would not be destroyed, and the file would not be closed.

In `funcOne()`, control is at the call to `funcTwo()`, so this subsequent line never gets a chance to run:

```
delete str2;
```

In this case, there really is a memory leak. Stack unwinding does not automatically call `delete` on `str2` for you. On the other hand, `str1` is destroyed properly because it is a local variable on the stack. Stack unwinding destroys all local variables correctly.

> **WARNING** *Careless exception handling can lead to memory and resource leaks.*

This is one reason why you should never mix older C models of allocation (even if you are calling `new` so it looks like C++) with modern programming methodologies like exceptions. In C++, this situation should be handled by using stack-based allocations or, if that is not possible, by one of the techniques discussed in the upcoming two sections.

Use Smart Pointers

If stack-based allocation is not possible, then use smart pointers. They allow you to write code that automatically prevents memory or resource leaks during exception handling. Whenever a smart pointer object is destroyed, it frees the underlying resource. Here is a modified `funcOne()` implementation using a `unique_ptr` smart pointer, defined in `<memory>`, and introduced in Chapter 7, "Memory Management":

```
void funcOne()
{
    string str1;
    auto str2 { make_unique<string>("hello") };
    funcTwo();
}
```

The `str2` pointer will automatically be deleted when you return from `funcOne()` or when an exception is thrown.

Of course, you should only allocate something dynamically if you have a good reason to do so. For example, in `funcOne()`, there is no good reason to make `str2` a dynamically allocated string. It should just be a stack-based `string` variable. It's merely shown here as an artificial example of the consequences of throwing exceptions.

> **NOTE** *With smart pointers, or other resource acquisition is initialization (RAII) objects, you never have to remember to free the underlying resource: the destructor of the RAII object does it for you, whether you leave the function normally or via an exception. It's a design technique discussed in Chapter 32, "Incorporating Design Techniques and Frameworks."*

Catch, Cleanup, and Rethrow

Another technique for avoiding memory and resource leaks is for each function to catch any possible exceptions, perform necessary cleanup work, and rethrow the exception for the function higher up the stack to handle. Here is a revised `funcOne()` with this technique:

```
void funcOne()
{
    string str1;
    string* str2 { new string {} };
    try {
        funcTwo();
    } catch (...) {
        delete str2;
        throw; // Rethrow the exception.
    }
    delete str2;
}
```

This function wraps the call to `funcTwo()` with an exception handler that performs the cleanup (calls `delete` on `str2`) and then rethrows the exception. The keyword `throw` by itself rethrows whatever exception was caught most recently. Note that the catch statement uses the `...` syntax to catch all exceptions.

This method works fine but is messy and error prone. In particular, note that there are now two identical lines that call `delete` on `str2`: one while handling the exception and one when the function exits normally.

> **WARNING** *The preferred solution is to use stack-based allocation, or, if not possible, to use smart pointers or other RAII classes instead of the catch, cleanup, and rethrow technique.*

SOURCE LOCATION

Before C++20, you could use the following preprocessor macros to get information about a location in your source code:

MACRO	DESCRIPTION
`__FILE__`	Replaced with the current source code filename
`__LINE__`	Replaced with the current line number in the source code

Additionally, every function has a locally defined `static` character array called `__func__` containing the name of the function.

Since C++20, a proper object-oriented replacement for `__func__` and these C-style preprocessor macros is available in the form of an `std::source_location` class, defined in `<source_location>`. An instance of `source_location` has the following public accessors:

ACCESSOR	DESCRIPTION
`file_name()`	Contains the current source code filename
`function_name()`	Contains the current function name, if the current position is inside a function
`line()`	Contains the current line number in the source code
`column()`	Contains the current column number in the source code

A `static` member function `current()` is provided that creates a `source_location` instance based on the location in the source code where the member function is called.

Source Location for Logging

The source_location class is useful for logging purposes. Previously, logging often involved writing C-style macros to automatically gather the current file name, function name, and line number, so they could be included in the log output. Now, with source_location, you can write a pure C++ function to perform your logging and to automatically collect the location data you require. A nice trick to do this is defining a logMessage() function as follows. This time, the code is prefixed with line numbers to better explain what is happening.

```
5. void logMessage(string_view message,
6.     const source_location& location = source_location::current())
7. {
8.     println("{}({}): {}: {}", location.file_name(),
9.         location.line(), location.function_name(), message);
10. }
11.
12. void foo()
13. {
14.     logMessage("Starting execution of foo().");
15. }
16.
17. int main()
18. {
19.     foo();
20. }
```

The second parameter of logMessage() is a source_location with the result of the static member function current() as default value. The trick here is that the call to current() does not happen on line 6, but actually at the location where logMessage() is called, which is line 14, and that's exactly the location you are interested in.

When executing this program with Microsoft Visual C++, the output is as follows:

```
./01_Logging.cpp(14): void __cdecl foo(void): Starting execution of foo().
```

Line 14 indeed corresponds to the line calling logMessage(). The exact name of the function, void __cdecl foo(void) in this case, is compiler dependent.

Automatically Embed a Source Location in Custom Exceptions

Another interesting use case for source_location is in your own exception classes to automatically store the location where an exception was thrown. Here's an example:

```
class MyException : public exception
{
    public:
        explicit MyException(string message,
            source_location location = source_location::current())
            : m_message { move(message) }
            , m_location { move(location) }
        { }

        const char* what() const noexcept override { return m_message.c_str(); }
        virtual const source_location& where() const noexcept{ return m_location; }
```

```
    private:
        string m_message;
        source_location m_location;
};

void doSomething()
{
    throw MyException { "Throwing MyException." };
}

int main()
{
    try {
        doSomething();
    } catch (const MyException& e) {
        const auto& location { e.where() };
        println(cerr, "Caught: '{}' at line {} in {}.",
            e.what(), location.line(), location.function_name());
    }
}
```

The output with Microsoft Visual C++ is similar to the following:

```
Caught: 'Throwing MyException.' at line 26 in void __cdecl doSomething(void).
```

STACK TRACE

Whenever a function `A()` calls another function `B()`, the arguments to be passed to `B()` are recorded and information about where to return to when the function is finished is recorded as well. The execution of `B()` can again call another function `C()` and so on. All this information is recorded in *frames* on a *stack trace*, also known as a *call stack*. For each function call, a new frame is added to the stack trace. When the execution of the function is finished, its frame is removed from the stack trace. At any given moment in the execution of your program, the stack trace tells you exactly through which function calls you arrived in the currently executing function. Information like this is vital for finding and fixing bugs in your program. Chapter 31, "Conquering Debugging," discusses debugging in detail. This section discusses the functionality provided by the Standard Library to work with stack traces, as well as how this can be very useful in combination with custom exceptions. Everything discussed in this section is new since C++23.

The Stack Trace Library

The stack trace library is defined in `<stacktrace>`. You can retrieve a stack trace at any moment in time using the `static` member function `std::stacktrace::current()`. You can pass an integer to `current()` if you want to skip a certain number of top frames. An example of this is given in the next section. Once you have a stack trace, you can easily print it to the console using `print()` or `println()`. You can also convert a stack trace to a string using `std::to_string()`. Here is an example, with the stack trace–related statements highlighted:

```
void handleStackTrace(const stacktrace& trace)
{
    println("  Stack trace information:");
    println("    There are {} frames in the stack trace.", trace.size());
```

```
        println("    Here are all the frames:");
        println("----------------------------------------------------------");
        println("{}", trace);
        // If the above statement doesn't work yet, you can use the following:
        //println("{}", to_string(trace));
        println("----------------------------------------------------------");
    }

    void C()
    {
        println("Entered C().");
        handleStackTrace(stacktrace::current());
    }

    void B() { println("Entered B()."); C(); }
    void A() { println("Entered A()."); B(); }

    int main()
    {
        A();
    }
```

Compiled with Microsoft Visual C++ and running on Windows, the output resembles the following. Long pathnames have been trimmed to prevent wrapping of lines. The `01_stacktrace.cpp` file is our code. The `exe_common.inl` and `exe_main.cpp` files belong to the Visual C++ runtime. The final two frames, `kernel32` and `ntdll`, are part of the Windows kernel. Function names are highlighted for readability.

```
Entered A().
Entered B().
Entered C().
  Stack trace information:
    There are 10 frames in the stack trace.
    Here are all the frames:
----------------------------------------------------------
0> D:\...\01_stacktrace.cpp(20): TestApp!C+0x77
1> D:\...\01_stacktrace.cpp(27): TestApp!B+0x61
2> D:\...\01_stacktrace.cpp(33): TestApp!A+0x61
3> D:\...\01_stacktrace.cpp(38): TestApp!main+0x20
4> D:\...\exe_common.inl(79): TestApp!invoke_main+0x39
5> D:\...\exe_common.inl(288): TestApp!__scrt_common_main_seh+0x12E
6> D:\...\exe_common.inl(331): TestApp!__scrt_common_main+0xE
7> D:\...\exe_main.cpp(17): TestApp!mainCRTStartup+0xE
8> KERNEL32!BaseThreadInitThunk+0x1D
9> ntdll!RtlUserThreadStart+0x28
----------------------------------------------------------
```

You can iterate over the individual frames of a stack trace and query for information of each frame. A frame is represented by the `std::stacktrace_entry` class, which supports the following member functions:

- `description()`: Returns the description of the frame
- `source_file()` and `source_line()`: The name of the source file and the line number within it that contains the statement represented by the frame

For example, the following implementation of `handleStackTrace()` doesn't just print the entire stack trace all at once but iterates over the individual frames and prints out only the description of each.

```
void handleStackTrace(const stacktrace& trace)
{
    println("  Stack trace information:");
    println("    There are {} frames in the stack trace.", trace.size());
    println("    Here are the descriptions of all the frames:");
    for (unsigned index { 0 }; auto&& frame : trace) {
        println("      {} -> {}", index++, frame.description());
    }
}
```

The output now is as follows:

```
Entered A().
Entered B().
Entered C().
  Stack trace information:
    There are 10 frames in the stack trace.
    Here are the descriptions of all the frames:
      0 -> TestApp!C+0x77
      1 -> TestApp!B+0x61
      2 -> TestApp!A+0x61
      3 -> TestApp!main+0x20
      4 -> TestApp!invoke_main+0x39
      ... <snip> ...
```

Automatically Embed a Stack Trace in Custom Exceptions

We can extend the `MyException` class from an earlier section on `source_location` to include a stack trace in addition to the source location.

```
class MyException : public exception
{
    public:
        explicit MyException(string message,
            source_location location = source_location::current())
            : m_message { move(message) }
            , m_location { move(location) }
            , m_stackTrace { stacktrace::current(1) } // 1 means skip top frame.
        { }

        const char* what() const noexcept override { return m_message.c_str(); }
        virtual const source_location& where() const noexcept{ return m_location; }
        virtual const stacktrace& how() const noexcept { return m_stackTrace; }
    private:
        string m_message;
        source_location m_location;
        stacktrace m_stackTrace;
};
```

Note that the constructor passes `1` to `stacktrace::current()` to skip the top frame of the stack trace. This top frame would be the constructor of `MyException`, which we are not interested in. We're interested only in the stack trace leading up to the construction of this `MyException` instance. This new exception class can be tested as follows:

```
void doSomething()
{
    throw MyException { "Throwing MyException." };
}

int main()
{
    try {
        doSomething();
    } catch (const MyException& e) {
        // Print exception description + location where exception was raised.
        const auto& location { e.where() };
        println(cerr, "Caught: '{}' at line {} in {}.",
            e.what(), location.line(), location.function_name());

        // Print the stack trace at the point where the exception was raised.
        println(cerr, "  Stack trace:");
        for (unsigned index { 0 }; auto&& frame : e.how()) {
            const string& fileName { frame.source_file() };
            println(cerr, "    {}> {}, {}({})", index++, frame.description(),
                (fileName.empty() ? "n/a" : fileName), frame.source_line());
        }
    }
}
```

When compiling with Microsoft Visual C++ and running on Windows, the output resembles the following. Only the top two relevant entries of the stack trace are shown. The stack entries that are inside the Visual C++ runtime or inside Windows itself are omitted for brevity.

```
Caught: 'Throwing MyException.' at line 30 in void __cdecl doSomething(void).
  Stack trace:
    0> TestApp!doSomething+0xD2, D:\...\03_CustomExceptionWithStackTrace.cpp(30)
    1> TestApp!main+0x4D, D:\...\03_CustomExceptionWithStackTrace.cpp(36)
    ... <snip> ...
```

> **NOTE** *If you are using custom exceptions, embed a stack trace in them for easier debugging of errors.*

COMMON ERROR-HANDLING ISSUES

Whether or not you use exceptions in your programs is up to you and your colleagues. However, you are strongly encouraged to formalize an error-handling plan for your programs, regardless of your use of exceptions. If you use exceptions, it is generally easier to come up with a unified error-handling scheme, but it is not impossible without exceptions. The most important aspect of a good plan is uniformity of error handling throughout all the modules of the program. Make sure that every programmer on the project understands and follows the error-handling rules.

This section discusses the most common error-handling issues in the context of exceptions, but the issues are also relevant to programs that do not use exceptions.

Memory Allocation Errors

Despite that all the examples so far in this book have ignored the possibility, memory allocation can fail. On current 64-bit platforms, this will almost never happen, but on mobile or legacy systems, memory allocation can fail. On such systems, you must account for memory allocation failures. C++ provides several different ways to handle memory errors.

The default behaviors of `new` and `new[]` are to throw an exception of type `bad_alloc`, defined in `<new>`, if they cannot allocate memory. Your code could catch these exceptions and handle them appropriately.

It's not realistic to wrap all your calls to `new` and `new[]` with a `try/catch`, but at least you should do so when you are trying to allocate a big block of memory. The following example demonstrates how to catch memory allocation exceptions:

```
int* ptr { nullptr };
size_t integerCount { numeric_limits<size_t>::max() };
println("Trying to allocate memory for {} integers.", integerCount);
try {
    ptr = new int[integerCount];
} catch (const bad_alloc& e) {
    auto location { source_location::current() };
    println(cerr, "{}({}): Unable to allocate memory: {}",
        location.file_name(), location.line(), e.what());
    // Handle memory allocation failure.
    return;
}
// Proceed with function that assumes memory has been allocated.
```

Note that this code uses `source_location` to include the name of the file and the current line number in the error message. This makes debugging easier.

You could, of course, bulk handle many possible new failures with a single `try/catch` block at a higher point in the program, if that works for your program.

Another point to consider is that logging an error might try to allocate memory. If `new` fails, there might not be enough memory left even to log the error message.

Non-throwing new

If you don't like exceptions, you can revert to the old C model in which memory allocation routines return a null pointer if they cannot allocate memory. C++ provides *nothrow* overloads of `new` and `new[]`, which return `nullptr` instead of throwing an exception if they fail to allocate memory. This is done by using the syntax `new(nothrow)` instead of `new`, as shown in the following example:

```
int* ptr { new(nothrow) int[integerCount] };
if (ptr == nullptr) {
    auto location { source_location::current() };
    println(cerr, "{}({}): Unable to allocate memory!",
        location.file_name(), location.line());
    // Handle memory allocation failure.
    return;
}
// Proceed with function that assumes memory has been allocated.
```

> **NOTE** *I do not recommend using non-throwing* `new`*, but the default behavior, which uses exceptions. An exception thrown when allocation fails cannot be ignored, while it's easy to forget checking for* `nullptr` *when using non-throwing* `new`.

Customizing Memory Allocation Failure Behavior

C++ allows you to specify a *new handler* callback function. By default, there is no new handler, so `new` and `new[]` just throw `bad_alloc` exceptions. However, if there is a new handler, the memory allocation routine calls the new handler upon memory allocation failure instead of throwing an exception. If the new handler returns, the memory allocation routine attempts to allocate memory again, calling the new handler again if it fails. This cycle could become an infinite loop unless your new handler changes the situation with one of three alternatives. Practically speaking, some of the options are better than others.

- **Make more memory available.** One trick to expose space is to allocate a large chunk of memory at program start-up and then to free it in the new handler. A practical example is when you hit an allocation error and you need to save the user state so no work gets lost. The key is to allocate a block of memory at program start-up large enough to allow a complete document save operation. When the new handler is triggered, you free this block, save the document, restart the application, and let it reload the saved document.
- **Throw an exception.** The C++ standard mandates that if you throw an exception from your new handler, it must be a `bad_alloc` exception or an exception derived from `bad_alloc`. Here are some examples:
  - **Write and throw a** `document_recovery_alloc` **exception, deriving from** `bad_alloc`. This exception can be caught somewhere in your application to trigger the document save operation and restart of the application.
  - **Write and throw a** `please_terminate_me` **exception, deriving from** `bad_alloc`. In your top-level function—for example, `main()`—you catch this exception and handle it by returning from the top-level function. It's recommended to terminate a program by returning from the top-level function, instead of by calling a function such as `exit()`.
- **Set a different new handler.** Theoretically, you could have a series of new handlers, each of which tries to create memory and sets a different new handler if it fails. However, such a scenario is usually more complicated than useful.

If you don't do one of these things in your new handler, any memory allocation failure will cause an infinite loop.

If there are some memory allocations that can fail but you don't want your new handler to be called, you can simply set the new handler back to its default of `nullptr` temporarily before calling `new` in such cases.

You set the new handler with a call to `set_new_handler()`, declared in `<new>`. Here is an example of a new handler that logs an error message and throws an exception:

```
class please_terminate_me : public bad_alloc { };

void myNewHandler()
{
    println(cerr, "Unable to allocate memory.");
    throw please_terminate_me {};
}
```

The new handler must take no arguments and return no value. This new handler throws a `please_terminate_me` exception, as suggested in the preceding list. You can activate this new handler like this:

```
int main()
{
    try {
        // Set the new new_handler and save the old one.
        new_handler oldHandler { set_new_handler(myNewHandler) };

        // Generate allocation error.
        size_t numInts { numeric_limits<size_t>::max() };
        int* ptr { new int[numInts] };

        // Reset the old new_handler.
        set_new_handler(oldHandler);
    } catch (const please_terminate_me&) {
        auto location { source_location::current() };
        println(cerr, "{}({}): Terminating program.",
            location.file_name(), location.line());
        return 1;
    }
}
```

`new_handler` is a type alias for the type of function pointer that `set_new_handler()` takes.

Errors in Constructors

Before C++ programmers discover exceptions, they are often stymied by error handling and constructors. What if a constructor fails to construct the object properly? Constructors don't have a return value, so the standard pre-exception error-handling mechanism doesn't work. Without exceptions, the best you can do is to set a flag in the object specifying that it is not constructed properly. You can provide a member function, with a name like `checkConstructionStatus()`, which returns the value of that flag, and hope that clients remember to call this member function on the object after constructing it.

Exceptions provide a much better solution. You can throw an exception from a constructor, even though you can't return a value[1]. With exceptions, you can easily tell clients whether construction of an object succeeded. However, there is one major problem: if an exception leaves a constructor, the

[1] There is one caveat, do not throw exceptions from constructors of global objects. Such exceptions cannot be caught because these objects are constructed before `main()` even starts executing.

destructor for that object will never be called! Thus, you must be careful to clean up any resources and free any allocated memory in constructors before allowing exceptions to leave the constructor.

This section describes a `Matrix` class template as an example in which the constructor correctly handles exceptions. Note that this example is using a raw pointer called `m_matrix` to demonstrate the problems. In production-quality code, you should avoid using raw pointers, for example, by using a Standard Library container! The definition of the `Matrix` class template looks like this:

```
export template <typename T>
class Matrix final
{
    public:
        explicit Matrix(std::size_t width, std::size_t height);
        ~Matrix();
        // Copy/move ctors and copy/move assignment operators deleted (omitted).
    private:
        void cleanup();

        std::size_t m_width { 0 };
        std::size_t m_height { 0 };
        T** m_matrix { nullptr };
};
```

The implementation of the `Matrix` class is as follows. The first call to `new` is not protected with a `try/catch` block. It doesn't matter if the first `new` throws an exception because the constructor hasn't allocated anything else yet that needs freeing. If any of the subsequent `new` calls throw an exception, though, the constructor must clean up all of the memory already allocated. The constructor doesn't know what exceptions the `T` constructors themselves might throw, so it catches all exceptions via `...` and then nests the caught exception inside a `bad_alloc` exception. The array allocated with the first call to `new` is zero-initialized using the `{}` syntax; that is, each element will be `nullptr`. This makes the `cleanup()` member function easier, because it is allowed to call `delete` on a `nullptr`.

```
template <typename T>
Matrix<T>::Matrix(std::size_t width, std::size_t height)
{
    m_matrix = new T*[width] {};     // Array is zero-initialized!

    // Don't initialize the m_width and m_height members in the ctor-
    // initializer. These should only be initialized when the above
    // m_matrix allocation succeeds!
    m_width = width;
    m_height = height;

    try {
        for (std::size_t i { 0 }; i < width; ++i) {
            m_matrix[i] = new T[height];
        }
    } catch (...) {
        std::println(std::cerr, "Exception caught in constructor, cleaning up...");
        cleanup();
        // Nest any caught exception inside a bad_alloc exception.
        std::throw_with_nested(std::bad_alloc {});
    }
}
```

```
template <typename T>
Matrix<T>::~Matrix()
{
    cleanup();
}

template <typename T>
void Matrix<T>::cleanup()
{
    for (std::size_t i { 0 }; i < m_width; ++i) {
        delete[] m_matrix[i];
    }
    delete[] m_matrix;
    m_matrix = nullptr;
    m_width = m_height = 0;
}
```

> **WARNING** *Remember, if an exception leaves a constructor, the destructor for that object will never be called!*

The `Matrix` class template can be tested as follows. Catching the `bad_alloc` exception in `main()` is omitted for brevity.

```
class Element
{
    // Kept to a bare minimum, but in practice, this Element class
    // could throw exceptions in its constructor.
    private:
        int m_value;
};

int main()
{
    Matrix<Element> m { 10, 10 };
}
```

You might be wondering what happens when you add inheritance into the mix. Base class constructors run before derived class constructors. If a derived class constructor throws an exception, C++ will execute the destructor of the fully constructed base classes.

> **NOTE** *C++ guarantees that it will run the destructor for all fully constructed "subobjects." Therefore, any constructor that completes without an exception will cause the corresponding destructor to be run.*

Function-Try-Blocks for Constructors

The exception mechanism, as discussed up to now in this chapter, is perfect for handling exceptions within functions. But how should you handle exceptions thrown from inside a ctor-initializer of a constructor? This section explains a feature called *function-try-blocks*, which are capable of catching those exceptions. Function-try-blocks work for normal functions as well as for constructors. This section focuses on the use with constructors. Most C++ programmers, even experienced C++ programmers, don't know of the existence of this feature, even though it was introduced a long time ago.

The following piece of pseudo-code shows the basic syntax for a function-try-block for a constructor:

```
MyClass::MyClass()
try
    : <ctor-initializer>
{
    /* ... constructor body ... */
}
catch (const exception& e)
{
    /* ... */
}
```

As you can see, the `try` keyword should be right before the start of the ctor-initializer. The `catch` statements should be after the closing brace for the constructor, actually putting them outside the constructor body. There are a number of restrictions and guidelines that you should keep in mind when using function-try-blocks with constructors:

- The `catch` statements catch any exception thrown either directly or indirectly by the ctor-initializer or by the constructor body.
- The `catch` statements have to rethrow the current exception or throw a new exception. If a `catch` statement doesn't do this, the runtime automatically rethrows the current exception.
- The `catch` statements can access arguments passed to the constructor.
- When a `catch` statement catches an exception in a function-try-block, all fully constructed base classes and members of the object are destroyed before execution of the `catch` statement starts.
- Inside `catch` statements you should not access data members that are objects because these are destroyed prior to executing the `catch` statements (see the previous bullet). However, if your object contains non-class data members—for example, raw pointers—you can access them if they have been initialized before the exception was thrown. If you have such raw, also called *naked*, resources, you have to take care of them by freeing them in the `catch` statements, as the upcoming example demonstrates.
- The `catch` statements in a function-try-block for a constructor cannot use the `return` keyword.

Based on this list of limitations, function-try-blocks for constructors are useful only in a limited number of situations:

- To convert an exception thrown by the ctor-initializer to another exception
- To log a message to a log file
- To free raw resources that have been allocated in the ctor-initializer prior to the exception being thrown

The following example demonstrates how to use function-try-blocks. The code defines a class called `SubObject`. It has only one constructor, which throws an exception of type `runtime_error`:

```
class SubObject
{
    public:
        explicit SubObject(int i) {
            throw runtime_error { "Exception by SubObject ctor" }; }
};
```

Next, the `MyClass` class has a data member of type `int*` and another one of type `SubObject`:

```
class MyClass
{
    public:
        MyClass();
    private:
        int* m_data { nullptr };
        SubObject m_subObject;
};
```

The `SubObject` class does not have a default constructor. This means you need to initialize `m_subObject` in the `MyClass` ctor-initializer. The constructor of `MyClass` uses a function-try-block to catch exceptions thrown in its ctor-initializer as follows:

```
MyClass::MyClass()
try
    : m_data { new int[42]{ 1, 2, 3 } }, m_subObject { 42 }
{
    /* ... constructor body ... */
}
catch (const exception& e)
{
    // Cleanup memory.
    delete[] m_data;
    m_data = nullptr;
    println(cerr, "function-try-block caught: '{}'", e.what());
}
```

Remember that `catch` statements in a function-try-block for a constructor have to either rethrow the current exception or throw a new exception. The preceding `catch` statement does not throw anything, so the C++ runtime automatically rethrows the current exception. The following is a simple function that uses `MyClass`:

```
int main()
{
    try {
        MyClass m;
    } catch (const exception& e) {
        println(cerr, "main() caught: '{}'", e.what());
    }
}
```

The output is as follows:

```
function-try-block caught: 'Exception by SubObject ctor'
main() caught: 'Exception by SubObject ctor'
```

Note that the code in this example is error prone and not recommended. A proper solution for this example's case is to make the `m_data` member a container, such as `std::vector`, or a smart pointer, such as `unique_ptr`, and to remove the function-try-block.

Function-try-blocks are not limited to constructors. They can be used with ordinary functions as well. However, for normal functions, there is no useful reason to use function-try-blocks because they can just as easily be converted to a simple `try/catch` block inside the function body. One notable difference when using a function-try-block on a normal function compared to a constructor is that rethrowing the current exception or throwing a new exception in the `catch` statements is not required, and the C++ runtime will not automatically rethrow the exception. Using the `return` keyword in such `catch` statements is allowed.

> **WARNING** *Avoid using function-try-blocks!*
>
> *Function-try-blocks are usually necessary only when you have raw resources as data members. Raw resources should be avoided by using RAII classes such as* `std::vector` or `unique_ptr`. *The RAII design pattern is discussed in Chapter 32.*

Errors in Destructors

You should handle all error conditions that arise in destructors in the destructors themselves. You should not let any exceptions be thrown from destructors, for a couple of reasons:

1. What action would clients take? Clients don't call destructors explicitly; destructors are called automatically for them. If you throw an exception from a destructor, what is a client supposed to do? There is no reasonable action the client can take, so there is no reason to burden that code with exception handling.
2. The destructor is your one chance to free memory and resources used in the object. If you waste your chance by exiting the function early due to an exception, you will never be able to go back and free the memory or resources.
3. Destructors are implicitly marked as `noexcept`, unless they are explicitly marked with `noexcept(false)` or the class has any subobjects with a `noexcept(false)` destructor. If you throw an exception from a `noexcept` destructor, the C++ runtime calls `std::terminate()` to terminate the application.
4. Destructors can run during the process of stack unwinding while there is another exception being handled. If you throw an exception from the destructor in the middle of stack unwinding, the C++ runtime calls `std::terminate()` to terminate the application. For the brave and curious, C++ does provide the ability to determine, in a destructor, whether you are executing as a result of a normal function exit or delete call or because of stack unwinding. The function `uncaught_exceptions()`, declared in `<exception>`, returns the number of uncaught exceptions, that is, exceptions that have been thrown but that have not reached a matching `catch` yet. If the result of `uncaught_exceptions()` is greater than zero, then you are in the middle of stack unwinding. However, correct use of this function is complicated, messy, and should be avoided. Note that before C++17, the function was called

`uncaught_exception()` (singular) and returned a `bool` that was `true` if you were in the middle of stack unwinding. This singular version is deprecated since C++17 and removed since C++20.

> **WARNING** *Be careful not to let any exceptions escape from a destructor.*

EXCEPTION SAFETY GUARANTEES

Now that you are fluent in working with exceptions, it's time to discuss *exception safety guarantees*. There are several levels of guarantees you can provide for code you write so that users of your code know what can be expected when an exception is thrown. The following exception safety guarantees can be specified for a function:

- **Nothrow (or nofail) exception guarantee:** The function never throws any exceptions.
- **Strong exception guarantee:** If an exception is thrown, all involved objects are rolled back to the state they were in before the function was called. An example of code providing this guarantee is the copy-and-swap idiom introduced in Chapter 9.
- **Basic exception guarantee:** If an exception is thrown, all involved objects remain in a valid state, and no resources are leaked. However, the objects could be in another state than they were before the function was called.
- **No guarantee:** When an exception is thrown, the application can be in any invalid state, resources might be leaked, memory might be corrupted, and so on.

> **NOTE** *If a function can throw exceptions, then it should provide, at the very least, a basic exception guarantee.*

SUMMARY

This chapter described the issues related to error handling in C++ programs and emphasized that you must design and code your programs with an error-handling plan. By reading this chapter, you learned the details of C++ exceptions syntax and behavior. You learned how to write custom exception classes that automatically embed the location where an exception was raised and the full stack trace at that moment. The chapter also covered some of the areas in which error handling plays a large role, including I/O streaming, memory allocation, constructors, and destructors. The chapter finished with the different kinds of exception safety guarantees a function can provide.

EXERCISES

By solving the following exercises, you can practice the material discussed in this chapter. Solutions to all exercises are available with the code download on the book's website at `www.wiley.com/go/`

proc++6e. However, if you are stuck on an exercise, first reread parts of this chapter to try to find an answer yourself before looking at the solution from the website.

Exercise 14-1: Without compiling and executing, find and correct the errors in the following code:

```
// Throws a logic_error exception if the number of elements
// in the given dataset is not even.
void verifyDataSize(const vector<int>& data)
{
    if (data.size() % 2 != 0)
        throw logic_error { "Number of data points must be even." };
}

// Throws a logic_error exception if the number of elements
// in the given dataset is not even.
// Throws a domain_error exception if one of the datapoints is negative.
void processData(const vector<int>& data)
{
    // Verify the size of the given dataset.
    try {
        verifyDataSize(data);
    } catch (const logic_error& caughtException) {
        // Write message on standard output.
        println(cerr, "Invalid number of data points in dataset. Aborting.");
        // And rethrow the exception.
        throw caughtException;
    }
    // Verify for negative datapoints.
    for (auto& value : data) {
        if (value < 0)
            throw domain_error { "Negative datapoints not allowed." };
    }
    // Process data ...
}

int main()
{
    try {
        vector data { 1, 2, 3, -5, 6, 9 };
        processData(data);
    } catch (const logic_error& caughtException) {
        println(cerr, "logic_error: {}", caughtException.what());
    } catch (const domain_error& caughtException) {
        println(cerr, "domain_error: {}", caughtException.what());
    }
}
```

Exercise 14-2: Take the code from the bidirectional I/O example from Chapter 13. You can find this in the `Ch13\22_Bidirectional` folder in the downloadable source code archive. The example implements a `changeNumberForID()` function. Retrofit the code to use exceptions on all places you deem appropriate. Once your code is using exceptions, do you see a possible change you can make to the `changeNumberForID()` function header?

Exercise 14-3: Add proper error handling using exceptions to your person database solution of Exercise 13-3.

Exercise 14-4: Take a look at the code in Chapter 9 for the `Spreadsheet` example that includes support for move semantics using `swap()`. You can find the entire code in the downloadable source code archive in the folder `Ch09\07_SpreadsheetMoveSemanticsWithSwap`. Add proper error handling to the code, including handling of memory allocation failures. Add a maximum width and height to the class and include the proper verification checks. Write your own exception class, `InvalidCoordinate`, which stores both an invalid coordinate and the range of allowed coordinates. Use it in the `verifyCoordinate()` member function. Write a couple of tests in `main()` to test various error conditions.

15

Overloading C++ Operators

WHAT'S IN THIS CHAPTER?

- What operator overloading is
- Rationale for overloading operators
- Limitations, caveats, and choices in operator overloading
- Summary of operators you can, cannot, and should not overload
- How to overload unary plus, unary minus, increment, and decrement
- How to overload the I/O stream operators (`operator<<` and `operator>>`)
- How to overload the subscripting (array index) operator
- How to write multidimensional subscripting operators
- How to overload the function call operator
- How to overload the dereferencing operators (`*` and `->`)
- How to write conversion operators
- How to overload the memory allocation and deallocation operators
- How to define your own user-defined literal operators
- The available standard literal operators

WILEY.COM DOWNLOADS FOR THIS CHAPTER

Please note that all the code examples for this chapter are available as part of the chapter's code download on this book's website at `www.wiley.com/go/proc++6e` on the Download Code tab.

C++ allows you to redefine the meanings of operators, such as `+`, `-`, and `=`, for your classes. Many object-oriented languages do not provide this capability, so you might be tempted to disregard its usefulness in C++. However, it is instrumental for making your classes behave similarly to built-in types such as `int`s and `double`s. It is even possible to write classes that look like arrays, functions, or pointers.

Chapter 5, "Designing with Classes," and Chapter 6, "Designing for Reuse," introduce object-oriented design and operator overloading, respectively. Chapter 8, "Gaining Proficiency with Classes and Objects," and Chapter 9, "Mastering Classes and Objects," present the syntax details for objects and for basic operator overloading. This chapter picks up operator overloading where Chapter 9 left off.

OVERVIEW OF OPERATOR OVERLOADING

As Chapter 1, "A Crash Course in C++ and the Standard Library," explains, operators in C++ are symbols such as `+`, `<`, `*`, and `<<`. They work on built-in types such as `int` and `double` to allow you to perform arithmetic, logical, and other operations. There are also operators such as `->` and `*` that allow you to dereference pointers. The concept of operators in C++ is broad, and even includes `[]` (array index), `()` (function call), casting, and the memory allocation and deallocation operators. Operator overloading allows you to change the behavior of language operators for your classes. However, this capability comes with rules, limitations, and choices.

Why Overload Operators?

Before learning how to overload operators, you probably want to know why you would ever want to do so. The reasons vary for the different operators, but the general guiding principle is to make your classes behave like built-in types. The closer your classes are to built-in types, the easier they will be for clients to use. For example, if you want to write a class to represent fractions, it's quite helpful to have the ability to define what `+`, `-`, `*`, and `/` mean when applied to objects of that class.

Another reason to overload operators is to gain greater control over the behavior in your program. For example, you can overload memory allocation and deallocation operators for your classes to specify exactly how memory should be distributed and reclaimed for each new object.

It's important to emphasize that operator overloading doesn't necessarily make things easier for you as the class developer; its main purpose is to make things easier for users of the class.

Limitations to Operator Overloading

Here is a list of things you cannot do when you overload operators:

- You cannot add new operator symbols. You can only redefine the meanings of operators already in the language. The table in the section "Summary of Overloadable Operators" later in this chapter lists all of the operators that you can overload.
- There are a few operators that you cannot overload, such as `.` and `.*` (member access in an object), `::` (scope resolution operator), and `?:` (the conditional operator). The table lists all the operators that you *can* overload. The operators that you can't overload are usually not those you would care to overload anyway, so you shouldn't find this restriction limiting.

- The *arity* describes the number of arguments, or *operands*, associated with the operator. You can change the arity only for the function call, new, and delete operators, and, since C++23, also for the subscripting operator (array index), `[]`. For all other operators, you cannot change the arity. Unary operators, such as ++, work on only one operand. Binary operators, such as /, work on two operands.
- You cannot change the *precedence* nor the *associativity* of an operator. The precedence is used to decide which operators need to be executed before other operators, while the associativity can be either left-to-right or right-to-left and specifies in which order operators of the same precedence are executed. Again, this constraint shouldn't be cause for concern in most programs because there are rarely benefits to changing the order of evaluation, but, in certain domains, it's something to keep in mind. For example, if you are writing a class to represent mathematical vectors and would like to overload the ^ operator to be able to raise a vector to a certain power, then keep in mind that ^ has lower precedence compared to many other operators such as +. For instance, suppose `x` and `y` are mathematical vectors, writing `x^3+y` will be evaluated as `x^(3+y)` and not as `(x^3)+y` as you probably intended.
- You cannot redefine operators for built-in types. The operator must be a member function in a class, or at least one of the arguments to a global overloaded operator function must be a user-defined type (for example, a class). This means that you can't do something ridiculous, such as redefine + for `int`s to mean subtraction (though you could do so for your own classes). The one exception to this rule is the memory allocation and deallocation operators; you can replace the global operators for all memory allocations in your program.

Some of the operators already mean two different things. For example, `operator-` can be used as a binary operator (as in `x=y-z;`) or as a unary operator (as in `x=-y;`). The * operator can be used for multiplication or for dereferencing a pointer. The << operator is the stream insertion operator or the left-shift operator, depending on the context. For such dual-meaning operators, you can overload both meanings.

Choices in Operator Overloading

When you overload an operator, you write a global function or member function with the name `operatorX`, where `X` is the symbol for some operator, and with optional whitespace between `operator` and `X`. For example, Chapter 9 declares `operator+` for `SpreadsheetCell` objects like this:

```
SpreadsheetCell operator+(const SpreadsheetCell& lhs, const SpreadsheetCell& rhs);
```

The following sections describe several choices involved in each overloaded operator you write.

Member Function or Global Function

First, you must decide whether your operator should be a member function of your class or a global function. The latter can be a `friend` of the class, although that should be a last resort — adding `friends` to a class should be limited as much as possible, as they can access `private` data members directly and thus circumvent the data-hiding principle.

How do you choose between a member function or a global function? First, you need to understand the difference between these two choices. When the operator is a member function of a class, the left-hand side of the operator expression must always be an object of that class. If you write a global function, the left-hand side can be an object of a different type.

There are three different types of operators:

- **Operators that must be member functions.** The C++ language requires some operators to be member functions of a class because they don't make sense outside of a class. For example, `operator=` is tied so closely to the class that it can't exist anywhere else. The table in the section "Summary of Overloadable Operators" lists those operators that must be member functions. Most operators do not impose this requirement.
- **Operators that must be global functions.** Whenever you need to allow the left-hand side of the operator to be a variable of a different type than your class, you must make the operator a global function. This rule applies specifically to the `<<` and `>>` insertion and extraction streaming operators, where the left-hand side is an `iostream` object, not an object of your class. It also applies to commutative operators like binary `+` and `–`, which should allow variables that are not objects of your class on the left-hand side. A global function is required if implicit conversions are desired for the left operand of a binary operator. Chapter 9 discusses this problem.
- **Operators that can be either member functions or global functions.** There is some disagreement in the C++ community on whether it's better to write member functions or global functions to overload operators. However, I recommend the following rule: make every operator a member function unless you must make it a global function, as described previously. One major advantage to this rule is that member functions can be `virtual`, while global functions obviously cannot. Therefore, when you plan to write overloaded operators in an inheritance tree, you should make them member functions if possible.

When you write an overloaded operator as a member function, you should mark it `const` if it doesn't change the object. That way, it can be called on `const` objects.

When you write an overloaded operator as a global function, put it in the same namespace that contains the class for which the operator is written.

Choosing Argument Types

You are somewhat limited in your choice of argument types because, as stated earlier, for most operators you cannot change the number of arguments. For example, `operator/` must always have two arguments if it is a global function, and one argument if it's a member function. The compiler issues an error if it differs from this standard. In this sense, the operator functions are different from normal functions, which you can overload with any number of parameters. Additionally, although you can write the operator for whichever types you want, the choice is usually constrained by the class for which you are writing the operator. For example, if you want to implement addition for class `T`, you don't write an `operator+` that takes two `string`s! The real choice arises when you try to determine whether to take parameters by value or by reference and whether to make them `const`.

The choice of value versus reference is easy: you should take every non-primitive parameter type by reference, unless the function always makes a copy of the passed object, see Chapter 9.

The `const` decision is also trivial: mark every parameter `const` unless you actually modify it. The table in the section "Summary of Overloadable Operators" shows sample prototypes for each operator, with the arguments marked `const` and reference as appropriate.

Choosing Return Types

C++ doesn't determine overload resolution based on return type. Thus, you can specify any return type you want when you write overloaded operators. However, just because you *can* do something doesn't mean you *should* do it. This flexibility implies that you could write confusing code in which comparison operators return pointers, and arithmetic operators return `bool`s. However, you shouldn't do that. Instead, you should write your overloaded operators such that they return the same types as the operators do for the built-in types. If you write a comparison operator, return a `bool`. If you write an arithmetic operator, return an object representing the result. Sometimes the return type is not obvious at first. For example, as Chapter 8 mentions, `operator=` should return a reference to the object on which it's called in order to support chained assignments. Other operators have similarly tricky return types, all of which are summarized in the table in the section "Summary of Overloadable Operators."

The same choices of reference and `const` apply to return types as well. However, for return values, the choices are more difficult. The general rule for value or reference is to return a reference if you can; otherwise, return a value. How do you know when you can return a reference? This choice applies only to operators that return objects: the choice is moot for the comparison operators that return `bool`, the conversion operators that have no return type, and the function call operator, which may return any type you want. If your operator constructs a new object, then you must return that new object by value. If it does not construct a new object, you can return a reference to the object on which the operator is called, or one of its arguments. The table in the section "Summary of Overloadable Operators" shows examples.

A return value that can be modified as an *lvalue* (e.g., on the left-hand side of an assignment expression) must be non-`const`. Otherwise, it should be `const`. More operators than you might expect require that you return lvalues, including all of the assignment operators (`operator=`, `operator+=`, `operator-=`, and so on).

Choosing Behavior

You can provide whichever implementation you want in an overloaded operator. For example, you could write an `operator+` that launches a game of Scrabble. However, as Chapter 6 describes, you should generally constrain your implementations to provide behaviors that clients expect. Write `operator+` so that it performs addition, or something like addition, such as string concatenation. This chapter explains how you *should* implement your overloaded operators. In exceptional circumstances, you might want to differ from these recommendations; but, in general, you should follow the standard patterns.

Operators You Shouldn't Overload

Some operators should not be overloaded, even though it is permitted. Specifically, the address-of operator (`operator&`) is not particularly useful to overload and leads to confusion if you do because you are changing fundamental language behavior (taking addresses of variables) in potentially unexpected ways. The entire Standard Library, which uses operator overloading extensively, never overloads the address-of operator.

Additionally, you should avoid overloading the binary Boolean operators `operator&&` and `||` because you lose C++'s short-circuit evaluation rules. Short-circuiting is not possible in that case because all operands need to be evaluated before they can be passed to your overloaded operator function. If your class needs logical operators, provide `operator&` and `|` instead.

Finally, you should not overload the comma operator (`operator,`). Yes, you read that correctly: there really is a comma operator in C++. It's also called the *sequencing operator*, and is used to separate two expressions in a single statement, while guaranteeing that they are evaluated left to right. The following snippet demonstrates the comma operator:

```
int x { 1 };
println("{}", (++x, 2 * x)); // Increments x to 2, doubles it, and prints 4.
```

There is rarely a good reason to overload the comma operator.

Summary of Overloadable Operators

The following table lists the operators you can overload, specifies whether they should be member functions of the class or global functions, summarizes when you should (or should not) overload them, and provides sample prototypes showing the proper parameter and return value types. Operators that cannot be overloaded, such as `.`, `.*`, `::`, and `?:` are not in this list.

This table is a useful reference for the future when you want to write an overloaded operator. You're bound to forget which return type you should use and whether or not the function should be a member function.

In this table, `T` is the name of the class for which the overloaded operator is written, and `E` is a different type. The sample prototypes given are not exhaustive; often there are other combinations of `T` and `E` possible for a given operator:

OPERATOR	NAME OR CATEGORY	MEMBER FUNCTION OR GLOBAL FUNCTION	WHEN TO OVERLOAD	SAMPLE PROTOTYPES

`operator+`
`operator-`
`operator*`
`operator/`
`operator%`
	Binary arithmetic	Global function recommended	Whenever you want to provide these operations for your class	`T operator+(const T&, const T&);`
				`T operator+(const T&, const E&);`

`operator-`
`operator+`
`operator~`
	Unary arithmetic and bitwise operators	Member function recommended	Whenever you want to provide these operations for your class	`T operator-() const;`

OPERATOR	NAME OR CATEGORY	MEMBER FUNCTION OR GLOBAL FUNCTION	WHEN TO OVERLOAD	SAMPLE PROTOTYPES
`operator++` `operator--`	Pre-increment and pre-decrement	Member function recommended	Whenever you overload += and -= taking an arithmetic argument (`int`, `long`, . . .)	`T& operator++();`
`operator++` `operator--`	Post-increment and post-decrement	Member function recommended	Whenever you overload += and -= taking an arithmetic argument (`int`, `long`, . . .)	`T operator++(int);`
`operator=`	Assignment operator	Member function required	Whenever your class has dynamically allocated resources, or members that are references	`T& operator=(const T&);`

`operator+=`
`operator-=`
`operator*=`
`operator/=`
`operator%=`
	Shorthand / compound arithmetic assignment operator	Member function recommended	Whenever you overload the binary arithmetic operators and your class is not designed to be immutable	`T& operator+=(const T&);`
				`T& operator+=(const E&);`

`operator<<`
`operator>>`
`operator&`
`operator|`
`operator^`
	Binary bitwise operators	Global function recommended	Whenever you want to provide these operations	`T operator<<(const T&, const T&);`
				`T operator<<(const T&, const E&);`

`operator<<=`
`operator>>=`
`operator&=`
`operator|=`
`operator^=`
	Shorthand / compound bitwise assignment operator	Member function recommended	Whenever you overload the binary bitwise operators and your class is not designed to be immutable	`T& operator<<=(const T&);`
				`T& operator<<=(const E&);`

continues

(continued)

OPERATOR	NAME OR CATEGORY	MEMBER FUNCTION OR GLOBAL FUNCTION	WHEN TO OVERLOAD	SAMPLE PROTOTYPES
`operator<=>`	Three-way comparison operator	Member function recommended	Whenever you want to provide comparison support for your class; if possible, this should be defaulted using `=default`	`auto operator<=>(const T&) const = default;` `partial_ordering operator<=>(const E&) const;`

`operator==`	Binary equality operator	Post-C++20: member function recommended
		Pre-C++20: global function recommended
			Whenever you want to provide comparison support for your class, and you cannot default the three-way comparison operator	`bool operator==(const T&) const;`
				`bool operator==(const E&) const;`
				`bool operator==(const T&, const T&);`
				`bool operator==(const T&, const E&);`

`operator!=`	Binary inequality operator	Post-C++20: member function recommended
		Pre-C++20: global function recommended
			Post-C++20: not needed as the compiler automatically provides `!=` when `==` is supported
			Pre-C++20: Whenever you want to provide comparison support for your class
				`bool operator!=(const T&) const;`
				`bool operator!=(const E&) const;`
				`bool operator!=(const T&, const T&);`
				`bool operator!=(const T&, const E&);`

`operator<`
`operator>`
`operator<=`
`operator>=`
	Binary comparison operators	Global function recommended	Whenever you want to provide these operations; not needed when `<=>` is provided	`bool operator<(const T&, const T&);`
				`bool operator<(const T&, const E&);`

OPERATOR	NAME OR CATEGORY	MEMBER FUNCTION OR GLOBAL FUNCTION	WHEN TO OVERLOAD	SAMPLE PROTOTYPES
`operator<<` `operator>>`	I/O stream operators (insertion and extraction)	Global function required	Whenever you want to provide these operations	`ostream& operator<<(ostream&, const T&);` `istream& operator>>(istream&, T&);`
`operator!`	Boolean negation operator	Member function recommended	Rarely; use `bool` or `void*` conversion instead	`bool operator!() const;`
`operator&&` `operator||`	Binary Boolean operators	Global function recommended	Rarely, if ever, because you lose short-circuiting; it's better to overload `&` and `|` instead, as these never short-circuit	`bool operator&&(const T&, const T&);`
`operator[]`	Subscripting (array index) operator	Member function required	When you want to support subscripting	`E& operator[](size_t); const E& operator[](size_t) const;`
`operator()`	Function call operator	Member function required	When you want objects to behave like function pointers	Return type and parameters can vary; see later examples in this chapter
`operator type()`	Conversion, or cast, operators (separate operator for each type)	Member function required	When you want to provide conversions from your class to other types	`operator double() const;`
`operator ""_x`	User-defined literal operator	Global function required	When you want to support user-defined literals	`T operator""_i(long double d);`

continues

(continued)

OPERATOR	NAME OR CATEGORY	MEMBER FUNCTION OR GLOBAL FUNCTION	WHEN TO OVERLOAD	SAMPLE PROTOTYPES
`operator new` `operator new[]`	Memory allocation routines	Member function recommended	When you want to control memory allocation for your classes (rarely)	`void* operator new(size_t size);` `void* operator new[](size_t size);`
`operator delete` `operator delete[]`	Memory deallocation routines	Member function recommended	Whenever you overload the memory allocation routines (rarely)	`void operator delete(void* ptr) noexcept;` `void operator delete[](void* ptr) noexcept;`
`operator*` `operator->`	Dereferencing operators	Member function recommended for `operator*` Member function required for `operator->`	Useful for smart pointers	`E& operator*() const;` `E* operator->() const;`
`operator&`	Address-of operator	N/A	Never	N/A
`operator->*`	Dereference pointer-to-member	N/A	Never	N/A
`operator,`	Comma operator	N/A	Never	N/A

Rvalue References

Chapter 9 discusses move semantics and rvalue references. It demonstrates these by defining move assignment operators, which are used by the compiler in cases where the source object is a temporary object that will be destroyed after the assignment, or an object that is explicitly moved from using `std::move()`. The normal assignment operator from the preceding table has the following prototype:

```
T& operator=(const T&);
```

The move assignment operator has almost the same prototype, but uses an rvalue reference. It modifies the argument so it cannot be passed as `const`. See Chapter 9 for details.

```
T& operator=(T&&) noexcept;
```

The preceding table does not include sample prototypes with rvalue references. However, for most operators it can make sense to write both a version using normal lvalue references and a version using rvalue references. Whether or not it does make sense depends on implementation details of your class. The `operator=` is one example from Chapter 9. Another example is `operator+` to prevent unnecessary memory allocations. The `std::string` class from the Standard Library, for example, implements an `operator+` using rvalue references as follows (simplified):

```
string operator+(string&& lhs, string&& rhs);
```

The implementation of this operator reuses memory of one of the arguments because they are being passed as rvalue references, meaning both are temporary objects that will be destroyed when this `operator+` is finished. The implementation of this `operator+` has the following effect depending on the size and the capacity of both operands:

```
return move(lhs.append(rhs));
```

or

```
return move(rhs.insert(0, lhs));
```

In fact, `string` defines several `operator+` overloads accepting two `strings` as arguments and different combinations of lvalue and rvalue references. Here is a list (simplified):

```
string operator+(const string& lhs, const string& rhs); // No memory reuse.
string operator+(string&& lhs, const string& rhs); // Can reuse memory of lhs.
string operator+(const string& lhs, string&& rhs); // Can reuse memory of rhs.
string operator+(string&& lhs, string&& rhs); // Can reuse memory of lhs or rhs.
```

Reusing memory of one of the rvalue reference arguments is implemented in the same way as it is explained for move assignment operators in Chapter 9.

Precedence and Associativity

In statements containing multiple operators, the *precedence* of the operators is used to decide which operators need to be executed before other operators. For example, `*` and `/` are always executed before `+` and `-`.

The *associativity* can be either left-to-right or right-to-left and specifies in which order operators of the same precedence are executed.

The following table lists the precedence and associativity of all available C++ operators, including those that you cannot overload and operators you haven't seen mentioned in this book yet. Operators with a lower precedence number are executed before operators with a higher precedence number. In the table, `T` represents a type, while `x`, `y`, and `z` represent objects:

PRECEDENCE	OPERATOR	ASSOCIATIVITY
1	`::`	Left-to-right
2	`x++ x-- x() x[] T() T{} . ->`	Left-to-right
3	`++x --x +x -x ! ~ *x &x (T)` `sizeof co_await new delete new[] delete[]`	Right-to-left

continues

(continued)

PRECEDENCE	OPERATOR	ASSOCIATIVITY
4	.* ->*	Left-to-right
5	x*y x/y x%y	Left-to-right
6	x+y x-y	Left-to-right
7	<< >>	Left-to-right
8	<=>	Left-to-right
9	< <= > >=	Left-to-right
10	== !=	Left-to-right
11	x&y	Left-to-right
12	^	Left-to-right
13	|	Left-to-right
14	&&	Left-to-right
15	||	Left-to-right
16	x?y:z throw co_yield = += -= *= /= %= <<= >>= &= ^= |=	Right-to-left
17	,	Left-to-right

Relational Operators

The following set of function templates for relational operators are defined in <utility> in the std::rel_ops namespace:

```
template<class T> bool operator!=(const T& a, const T& b);// Needs operator==
template<class T> bool operator>(const T& a, const T& b); // Needs operator<
template<class T> bool operator<=(const T& a, const T& b);// Needs operator<
template<class T> bool operator>=(const T& a, const T& b);// Needs operator<
```

These function templates define the operators !=, >, <=, and >= in terms of the == and < operators for any class. So, if you implement operator== and < for your class, you get the other relational operators for free with these templates.

However, there are a lot of problems with this technique. A first problem is that those operators might be created for all classes that you use in relational operations, not only for your own class.

A second problem with this technique is that utility templates such as std::greater<T> (discussed in Chapter 19, "Function Pointers, Function Objects, and Lambda Expressions") do not work with those automatically generated relational operators.

Yet another problem with these is that implicit conversions won't work.

Finally, with C++20's three-way comparison operator and the fact that C++20 has deprecated the `std::rel_ops` namespace, there is no longer any reason to still use `rel_ops`.

> **WARNING** *Never use* `std::rel_ops`*; it has been deprecated since C++20! Instead, to add support for all six comparison operators to a class, just explicitly default or implement* `operator<=>` *and possibly* `operator==` *for the class. See Chapter 9 for details.*

Alternative Notation

C++ supports the following alternative notations for a selection of operators. These were mainly used in the old days when using character sets that didn't include certain characters such as ~, |, and ^.

OPERATOR	ALTERNATIVE NOTATION	OPERATOR	ALTERNATIVE NOTATION
`&&`	`and`	`!=`	`not_eq`
`&=`	`and_eq`	`||`	`or`
`&`	`bitand`	`|=`	`or_eq`
`|`	`bitor`	`^`	`xor`
`~`	`compl`	`^=`	`xor_eq`
`!`	`not`		

OVERLOADING THE ARITHMETIC OPERATORS

Chapter 9 shows how to write the binary arithmetic operators and the shorthand arithmetic assignment operators, but it does not cover how to overload the other arithmetic operators.

Overloading Unary Minus and Unary Plus

C++ has several unary arithmetic operators. Two of these are unary minus and unary plus. Here is an example of these operators using `int`s:

```
int i, j { 4 };
i = -j;    // Unary minus
i = +i;    // Unary plus
j = +(-i); // Apply unary plus to the result of applying unary minus to i.
j = -(-i); // Apply unary minus to the result of applying unary minus to i.
```

Unary minus negates the operand, while unary plus returns the operand directly. Note that you can apply unary plus or unary minus to the result of unary plus or unary minus. These operators don't change the object on which they are called so you should make them `const`.

Here is an example of a unary operator- as a member function for a SpreadsheetCell class. Unary plus is usually an identity operation, so this class doesn't overload it.

```
SpreadsheetCell SpreadsheetCell::operator-() const
{
    return SpreadsheetCell { -getValue() };
}
```

operator- doesn't change the operand, so this member function must construct a new SpreadsheetCell with the negated value and return it. Hence, it can't return a reference. You can use this operator as follows:

```
SpreadsheetCell c1 { 4 };
SpreadsheetCell c3 { -c1 };
```

Overloading Increment and Decrement

There are several ways to add 1 to a variable:

```
i = i + 1;
i = 1 + i;
i += 1;
++i;
i++;
```

The last two forms are called the *increment* operators. The first of these is *prefix increment*, which adds 1 to the variable and then returns the newly incremented value for use in the rest of the expression. The second is *postfix increment*, which also adds 1 to the variable but returns the old (non-incremented) value for use in the rest of the expression. The decrement operators work similarly.

The two possible meanings for operator++ and operator-- (prefix and postfix) present a problem when you want to overload them. When you write an overloaded operator++, for example, how do you specify whether you are overloading the prefix or the postfix version? C++ introduced a hack to allow you to make this distinction: the prefix versions of operator++ and operator-- take no arguments, while the postfix versions take one unused argument of type int.

The prototypes of these overloaded operators for the SpreadsheetCell class look like this:

```
SpreadsheetCell& operator++();    // Prefix
SpreadsheetCell operator++(int); // Postfix
SpreadsheetCell& operator--();    // Prefix
SpreadsheetCell operator--(int); // Postfix
```

The return value in the prefix forms is the same as the end value of the operand, so prefix increment and decrement can return a reference to the object on which they are called. The postfix versions of increment and decrement, however, return values that are different from the end values of the operands, so they cannot return references.

Here are the implementations for operator++:

```
SpreadsheetCell& SpreadsheetCell::operator++()
{
    set(getValue() + 1);
    return *this;
}
```

```
SpreadsheetCell SpreadsheetCell::operator++(int)
{
    auto oldCell { *this }; // Save current value
    ++(*this);              // Increment using prefix ++
    return oldCell;         // Return the old value
}
```

> **NOTE** *It is recommended to implement the postfix operator in terms of the prefix operator.*

The implementations for `operator--` are virtually identical. Now you can increment and decrement `SpreadsheetCell` objects to your heart's content:

```
SpreadsheetCell c1 { 4 };
SpreadsheetCell c2 { 4 };
c1++;
++c2;
```

Increment and decrement operators also work on pointers. When you write classes that are smart pointers, for example, you can overload `operator++` and `operator--` to provide pointer incrementing and decrementing.

OVERLOADING THE BITWISE AND BINARY LOGICAL OPERATORS

The bitwise operators are similar to the arithmetic operators, and the bitwise shorthand assignment operators are similar to the arithmetic shorthand assignment operators. However, they are significantly less common, so no examples are shown here. The table in the section "Summary of Overloadable Operators" shows sample prototypes, so you should be able to implement them easily if the need ever arises.

The logical operators are trickier. It's not recommended to overload `&&` and `||`. These operators don't really apply to individual types: they aggregate results of Boolean expressions. Additionally, when overloading these operators, you lose the short-circuit evaluation, because both the left-hand side and the right-hand side have to be evaluated before they can be bound to the parameters of your overloaded operator `&&` and `||`. Thus, it rarely, if ever, makes sense to overload them for specific types.

OVERLOADING THE INSERTION AND EXTRACTION OPERATORS

In C++, you use operators not only for arithmetic operations but also for reading from, and writing to, streams. For example, when you write `int`s and `string`s to `cout`, you use the insertion operator `<<`:

```
int number { 10 };
cout << "The number is " << number << endl;
```

When you read from streams, you use the extraction operator `>>`:

```
int number;
string str;
cin >> number >> str;
```

You can write insertion and extraction operators that work on your classes as well, so that you can read and write them like this:

```
SpreadsheetCell myCell, anotherCell, aThirdCell;
cin >> myCell >> anotherCell >> aThirdCell;
cout << myCell << " " << anotherCell << " " << aThirdCell << endl;
```

Before you write the insertion and extraction operators, you need to decide how you want to stream your class out and how you want to read it in. In this example, the `SpreadsheetCell`s simply read and write a single `double` value.

The object on the left of an extraction or insertion operator is an `istream` or `ostream` (such as `cin` or `cout`), not a `SpreadsheetCell` object. Because you can't add a member function to the `istream` or `ostream` classes, you must write the extraction and insertion operators as global functions. The declaration of these functions looks like this:

```
export std::ostream& operator<<(std::ostream& ostr, const SpreadsheetCell& cell);
export std::istream& operator>>(std::istream& istr, SpreadsheetCell& cell);
```

By making the insertion operator take a reference to an `ostream` as its first parameter, you allow it to be used for file output streams, string output streams, `cout`, `cerr`, `clog`, and more. See Chapter 13, "Demystifying C++ I/O," for details on streams. Similarly, by making the extraction operator take a reference to an `istream`, you make it work with any input stream, such as a file input stream, string input stream, and `cin`.

The second parameter to `operator<<` and `operator>>` is a reference to the `SpreadsheetCell` object that you want to write or read. The insertion operator doesn't change the `SpreadsheetCell` it writes, so the parameter is of type reference-to-`const`. The extraction operator, however, modifies the `SpreadsheetCell` object, requiring the parameter to be a reference-to-non-`const`.

Both operators return a reference to the stream they were given as their first parameter so that calls to the operator can be nested. Remember that the operator syntax is shorthand for calling the global `operator>>` or `operator<<` functions explicitly. Consider this line:

```
cin >> myCell >> anotherCell >> aThirdCell;
```

This line is shorthand for:

```
operator>>(operator>>(operator>>(cin, myCell), anotherCell), aThirdCell);
```

As you can see, the return value of the first call to `operator>>` is used as input to the next call. Thus, you must return the stream reference so that it can be used in the next nested call. Otherwise, the nesting won't compile.

Here are the implementations for `operator<<` and `>>` for the `SpreadsheetCell` class:

```
ostream& operator<<(ostream& ostr, const SpreadsheetCell& cell)
{
    ostr << cell.getValue();
    return ostr;
}
```

```
istream& operator>>(istream& istr, SpreadsheetCell& cell)
{
    double value;
    istr >> value;
    cell.set(value);
    return istr;
}
```

OVERLOADING THE SUBSCRIPTING OPERATOR

Pretend for a few minutes that you have never heard of the `vector` or `array` class templates in the Standard Library, and so you have decided to write your own dynamically allocated array class. This class would allow you to set and retrieve elements at specified indices and would take care of all memory allocation "behind the scenes." A first stab at the class definition for a dynamically allocated array might look like this:

```
export template <typename T>
class Array
{
    public:
        // Creates an array with a default size that will grow as needed.
        Array();
        virtual ~Array();

        // Disallow copy constructor and copy assignment.
        Array& operator=(const Array& rhs) = delete;
        Array(const Array& src) = delete;

        // Move constructor and move assignment operator.
        Array(Array&& src) noexcept;
        Array& operator=(Array&& rhs) noexcept;

        // Returns the value at index x. Throws an exception of type
        // out_of_range if index x does not exist in the array.
        const T& getElementAt(std::size_t x) const;

        // Sets the value at index x. If index x is out of range,
        // allocates more space to make it in range.
        void setElementAt(std::size_t x, const T& value);

        // Returns the number of elements in the array.
        std::size_t getSize() const noexcept;
    private:
        static constexpr std::size_t AllocSize { 4 };
        void resize(std::size_t newSize);
        T* m_elements { nullptr };
        std::size_t m_size { 0 };
};
```

The interface supports setting and accessing elements. It provides random-access guarantees: a client could create a default array and set elements `1`, `100` and `1000` without worrying about memory management.

Here are the implementations of the member functions:

```
template <typename T> Array<T>::Array()
{
    m_elements = new T[AllocSize] {}; // Elements are zero-initialized!
    m_size = AllocSize;
}

template <typename T> Array<T>::~Array()
{
    delete[] m_elements;
    m_elements = nullptr;
    m_size = 0;
}

template <typename T> Array<T>::Array(Array&& src) noexcept
    : m_elements { std::exchange(src.m_elements, nullptr) }
    , m_size { std::exchange(src.m_size, 0) }
{
}

template <typename T> Array<T>& Array<T>::operator=(Array<T>&& rhs) noexcept
{
    if (this == &rhs) { return *this; }
    delete[] m_elements;
    m_elements = std::exchange(rhs.m_elements, nullptr);
    m_size = std::exchange(rhs.m_size, 0);
    return *this;
}

template <typename T> void Array<T>::resize(std::size_t newSize)
{
    // Create new bigger array with zero-initialized elements.
    auto newArray { std::make_unique<T[]>(newSize) };

    // The new size is always bigger than the old size (m_size).
    for (std::size_t i { 0 }; i < m_size; ++i) {
        // Copy the elements from the old array to the new one.
        newArray[i] = m_elements[i];
    }

    // Delete the old array, and set the new array.
    delete[] m_elements;
    m_size = newSize;
    m_elements = newArray.release();
}

template <typename T> const T& Array<T>::getElementAt(std::size_t x) const
{
    if (x >= m_size) { throw std::out_of_range { "" }; }
    return m_elements[x];
}
```

```
template <typename T> void Array<T>::setElementAt(std::size_t x, const T& val)
{
    if (x >= m_size) {
        // Allocate AllocSize past the element the client wants.
        resize(x + AllocSize);
    }
    m_elements[x] = val;
}

template <typename T> std::size_t Array<T>::getSize() const noexcept
{
    return m_size;
}
```

Pay attention to the exception-safe implementation of the `resize()` member function. First, it creates a new array of appropriate size using `make_unique()` and stores it in a `unique_ptr`. Then, all elements are copied from the old array to the new array. If anything goes wrong while copying the values, the `unique_ptr` cleans up the newly allocated memory automatically. Finally, when both the allocation of the new array and copying all the elements is successful, that is, no exceptions have been thrown, only then do we delete the old `m_elements` array and assign the new array to it. The last line has to use `release()` to release the ownership of the new array from the `unique_ptr`; otherwise, the array would get destroyed when the destructor for the `unique_ptr` is called.

To guarantee strong exception safety (see Chapter 14, "Handling Errors"), `resize()` copies elements from the old array to the newly allocated array. Chapter 26, "Advanced Templates," discusses and implements a `move_assign_if_noexcept()` helper function. This helper function can be used in the implementation of `resize()` so that elements are moved from the old array to the new array, but only if the move assignment operator of the element type is marked as `noexcept`. If that's not the case, the elements are copied. With that change, whether elements are moved or copied, strong exception safety remains guaranteed.

Here is a small example of how you could use this class:

```
Array<int> myArray;
for (size_t i { 0 }; i < 20; i += 2) {
    myArray.setElementAt(i, 100);
}
for (size_t i { 0 }; i < 20; ++i) {
    print("{} ", myArray.getElementAt(i));
}
```

The output is as follows:

```
100 0 100 0 100 0 100 0 100 0 100 0 100 0 100 0 100 0 100 0
```

As you can see, you never have to tell the array how much space you need. It allocates as much space as it requires to store the elements you give it.

> **NOTE** *This is not a memory efficient implementation. If you create an array and only assign a value to the element with index 4000, then it allocates memory for 4004 elements, all zero initialized except for the element with index 4000.*

However, it's inconvenient to always have to use the `setElementAt()` and `getElementAt()` member functions.

This is where the overloaded subscripting operator comes in. You can add an `operator[]` to the class as follows:

```
export template <typename T>
class Array
{
    public:
        T& operator[](std::size_t x);
        // Remainder omitted for brevity.
};
```

Here is the implementation:

```
template <typename T> T& Array<T>::operator[](std::size_t x)
{
    if (x >= m_size) {
        // Allocate AllocSize past the element the client wants.
        resize(x + AllocSize);
    }
    return m_elements[x];
}
```

With this change, you can use conventional array index notation like this:

```
Array<int> myArray;
for (size_t i { 0 }; i < 20; i += 2) {
    myArray[i] = 100;
}
for (size_t i { 0 }; i < 20; ++i) {
    print("{} ", myArray[i]);
}
```

The `operator[]` can be used to both set and get elements because it returns a reference to the element at location `x`. This reference can be used to assign to that element. When `operator[]` is used on the left-hand side of an assignment statement, the assignment actually changes the value at location `x` in the `m_elements` array.

Providing Read-Only Access with operator[]

Although it's sometimes convenient for `operator[]` to return an element that can serve as an lvalue, you don't always want that behavior. It would be nice to be able to provide read-only access to the elements of the array as well, by returning a reference-to-`const`. To provide for this, you need two `operator[]` overloads: one returning a reference-to-non-`const` and one returning a reference-to-`const`:

```
T& operator[](std::size_t x);
const T& operator[](std::size_t x) const;
```

Remember that you can't overload a member function or operator based only on the return type, so the second overload returns a reference-to-`const` *and* is marked as `const`.

Here is the implementation of the const operator[]. It throws an exception if the index is out of range instead of trying to allocate new space. It doesn't make sense to allocate new space when you're only trying to read the element value.

```
template <typename T> const T& Array<T>::operator[](std::size_t x) const
{
    if (x >= m_size) { throw std::out_of_range { "" }; }
    return m_elements[x];
}
```

The following code demonstrates these two forms of operator[]:

```
void printArray(const Array<int>& arr)
{
    for (size_t i { 0 }; i < arr.getSize(); ++i) {
        print("{} ", arr[i]);  // Calls the const operator[] because arr is
                               // a const object.
    }
    println("");
}

int main()
{
    Array<int> myArray;
    for (size_t i { 0 }; i < 20; i += 2) {
        myArray[i] = 100; // Calls the non-const operator[] because
                          // myArray is a non const object.
    }
    printArray(myArray);
}
```

Note that the const operator[] is called in printArray() only because the parameter arr is const. If arr were not const, the non-const operator[] would be called, despite that the result is not modified.

The const operator[] is called for const objects, so it cannot grow the size of the array. The current implementation throws an exception when the given index is out of bounds. An alternative would be to return a zero-initialized element instead of throwing. This can be done as follows:

```
template <typename T> const T& Array<T>::operator[](std::size_t x) const
{
    if (x >= m_size) {
        static T nullValue { T{} };
        return nullValue;
    }
    return m_elements[x];
}
```

The nullValue static variable is initialized using the zero-initialization syntax T{}. It's up to you and your specific use case whether you opt for the throwing version or the version returning a null value.

> **NOTE** *Zero-initialization constructs objects with the default constructor and initializes primitive integer types (such as* `char`, `int`, *and so on) to zero, primitive floating-point types to 0.0, and pointer types to* `nullptr`.

C++23

Multidimensional Subscripting Operator

Starting with C++23, a subscripting operator can support multidimensional indexing. The syntax is straightforward. Instead of writing a subscripting operator accepting a single index parameter, you write a subscripting operator with as many index parameters as dimensions you need.

To demonstrate, let's revisit the `Grid` class template from Chapter 12, "Writing Generic Code with Templates." Its interface contains a `const` and non-`const` overload of an `at(x,y)` member function. These `at()` member functions can be replaced with two-dimensional `const` and non-`const` subscripting operators as follows:

```
template <typename T>
class Grid
{
    public:
        std::optional<T>& operator[](std::size_t x, std::size_t y);
        const std::optional<T>& operator[](std::size_t x, std::size_t y) const;
        // Remainder omitted for brevity.
};
```

The syntax simply specifies two parameters, `x` and `y`, for these two-dimensional subscripting operators. The implementations are almost identical to the implementations of the original `at()` member functions:

```
template <typename T>
const std::optional<T>& Grid<T>::operator[](std::size_t x, std::size_t y) const
{
    verifyCoordinate(x, y);
    return m_cells[x + y * m_width];
}
template <typename T>
std::optional<T>& Grid<T>::operator[](std::size_t x, std::size_t y)
{
    return const_cast<std::optional<T>&>(std::as_const(*this)[x, y]);
}
```

Here is an example of these new operators in action:

```
Grid<int> myIntGrid { 4, 4 };
int counter { 0 };
for (size_t y { 0 }; y < myIntGrid.getHeight(); ++y) {
    for (size_t x { 0 }; x < myIntGrid.getWidth(); ++x) {
        myIntGrid[x, y] = ++counter;
    }
}
for (size_t y { 0 }; y < myIntGrid.getHeight(); ++y) {
    for (size_t x { 0 }; x < myIntGrid.getWidth(); ++x) {
        print("{:3} ", myIntGrid[x, y].value_or(0));
```

```
        }
        println("");
    }
```

The output is:

```
 1   2   3   4
 5   6   7   8
 9  10  11  12
13  14  15  16
```

Non-integral Array Indices

It is a natural extension of the paradigm of "indexing" into a collection to provide a key of some sort; a `vector` (or in general, any linear array) is a special case where the "key" is just a position in the array. Think of the argument of `operator[]` as providing a mapping between two domains: the domain of keys and the domain of values. Thus, you can write an `operator[]` that uses any type as its index. This type does not need to be an integer type. This is done for the Standard Library associative containers, like `std::map`, which are discussed in Chapter 18, "Standard Library Containers."

For example, you could create an *associative array* in which you use `string` keys instead of integral indices. The `operator[]` for such a class would accept a `string`, or better yet `string_view`, as an argument. Implementing such a class is an exercise for you at the end of this chapter.

C++23 static Subscripting Operator

With C++23, the subscripting operator can be marked as `static` as long as the implementation of the operator does not require access to `this`, or, in other words, does not need access to non-`static` data members and non-`static` member functions. This allows the compiler to better optimize the code as it doesn't need to worry about any `this` pointer. Here is an example where `operator[]` is marked as `static`, `constexpr` (see Chapter 9), and `noexcept` (Chapter 14):

```
enum class Figure { Diamond, Heart, Spade, Club };

class FigureEnumToString
{
    public:
        static constexpr string_view operator[](Figure figure) noexcept
        {
            switch (figure) {
                case Figure::Diamond: return "Diamond";
                case Figure::Heart:   return "Heart";
                case Figure::Spade:   return "Spade";
                case Figure::Club:    return "Club";
            }
        }
};

int main()
{
    Figure f { Figure::Spade };
```

```
        FigureEnumToString converter;
        println("{}", converter[f]);
        println("{}", FigureEnumToString{}[f]);
    }
```

OVERLOADING THE FUNCTION CALL OPERATOR

C++ allows you to overload the function call operator, written as `operator()`. If you write an `operator()` for your class, you can use objects of that class as if they were function pointers. An object of a class with a function call operator is called a *function object*, or *functor*, for short. Here is an example of a simple class with an overloaded `operator()` and a class member function with the same behavior:

```
class Squarer
{
    public:
        int operator()(int value) const; // Overloaded function call operator.
        int doSquare(int value) const;   // Normal member function.
};
// Implementation of overloaded function call operator.
int Squarer::operator()(int value) const { return doSquare(value); }
// Implementation of normal member function.
int Squarer::doSquare(int value) const { return value * value; }
```

Here is an example of code that uses the function call operator, contrasted with a call to the normal member function of the class:

```
int x { 3 };
Squarer square;
int xSquared { square(x) };                       // Call the function call operator.
int xSquaredAgain { square.doSquare(xSquared) };// Call the normal member function.
println("{} squared is {}, and squared again is {}.", x, xSquared, xSquaredAgain);
```

The output is as follows:

```
3 squared is 9, and squared again is 81.
```

At first, the function call operator probably seems a little strange. Why would you want to write a special member function for a class to make objects of the class look like function pointers? Why wouldn't you just write a global function or a standard member function of a class?

The advantage of function objects over standard member functions of objects is simple: these objects can sometimes masquerade as function pointers; that is, you can pass function objects as callback functions to other functions. This is discussed in more detail in Chapter 19.

The advantages of function objects over global functions are more intricate. There are two main benefits:

- Objects can retain information in their data members between repeated calls to their function call operators. For example, a function object might be used to keep a running sum of numbers collected from each call to the function call operator.

- You can customize the behavior of a function object by setting data members. For example, you could write a function object to compare an argument to the function call operator against a data member. This data member could be configurable so that the object could be customized for whatever comparison you want.

Of course, you could implement either of the preceding benefits with global or `static` variables. However, function objects provide a cleaner way to do it, and besides, using global or `static` variables should be avoided and can cause problems in a multithreaded application. The true benefits of function objects are demonstrated with the Standard Library in Chapter 20, "Mastering Standard Library Algorithms."

By following the normal member function overloading rules, you can write as many `operator()`s for your classes as you want. For example, you could add an `operator()` to the `Squarer` class that takes a `double`:

```
int operator()(int value) const;
double operator()(double value) const;
```

This `double` overload can be implemented as follows:

```
double Squarer::operator()(double value) const { return value * value; }
```

static Function Call Operator

Starting with C++23, a function call operator can be marked as `static` if its implementation does not require access to `this`, or, in other words, does not need access to non-`static` data members and non-`static` member functions. This is similar to how subscripting operators, discussed earlier in this chapter, can be marked as `static`, and doing so allows the compiler to better optimize the code.

Here is an example, a reduced `Squarer` functor with a `static`, `constexpr`, and `noexcept` function call operator:

```
class Squarer
{
    public:
        static constexpr int operator()(int value) noexcept
        {
            return value * value;
        }
};
```

This functor can be used as follows:

```
int x { 3 };
int xSquared { Squarer::operator()(x) };
int xSquaredAgain { Squarer{}(xSquared) };
println("{} squared is {}, and squared again is {}.", x, xSquared, xSquaredAgain);
```

Another benefit of `static` function call operators is that you can easily take their address, for example, `&Squarer::operator()`, which allows you to use them as if they were function pointers. This can improve the performance when working with the Standard Library algorithms discussed in detail in Chapter 20. Quite a few of those algorithms accept a callable, such as a functor, to customize their behavior. If your functor has a `static` function call operator, then passing the address of that function call operator to such algorithms allows the compiler to generate more performant code than with a non-`static` function call operator. The reason is that with a `static` function call operator, the compiler doesn't need to worry about any `this` pointer.

OVERLOADING THE DEREFERENCING OPERATORS

You can overload three dereferencing operators: `*`, `->`, and `->*`. Ignoring `->*` for the moment (I'll come back to it later), consider the built-in meanings of `*` and `->`. The `*` operator dereferences a pointer to give you direct access to its value, while `->` is shorthand for a `*` dereference followed by a `.` member selection. The following code shows the equivalences:

```
SpreadsheetCell* cell { new SpreadsheetCell };
(*cell).set(5); // Dereference plus member selection.
cell->set(5);   // Shorthand arrow dereference and member selection together.
```

You can overload the dereferencing operators for your classes to make objects of the classes behave like pointers. The main use of this capability is for implementing smart pointers, introduced in Chapter 7, "Memory Management." It is also useful for iterators, which the Standard Library uses extensively. Iterators are discussed in Chapter 17, "Understanding Iterators and the Ranges Library." This chapter teaches you the basic mechanics for overloading the relevant operators in the context of a simple smart pointer class template.

> **WARNING** *C++ has two standard smart pointers called* `std::unique_ptr` *and* `shared_ptr`. *You should use these standard smart pointers instead of writing your own. The example here is given only to demonstrate how to write dereferencing operators.*

Here is an example of a smart pointer class template definition, without the dereferencing operators filled in yet:

```
export template <typename T> class Pointer
{
    public:
        explicit Pointer(T* ptr) : m_ptr { ptr } {}
        virtual ~Pointer() { reset(); }
        // Disallow copy constructor and copy assignment.
        Pointer(const Pointer& src) = delete;
        Pointer& operator=(const Pointer& rhs) = delete;
        // Allow move construction.
        Pointer(Pointer&& src) noexcept : m_ptr{ std::exchange(src.m_ptr, nullptr)}
        { }
        // Allow move assignment.
        Pointer& operator=(Pointer&& rhs) noexcept
        {
            if (this != &rhs) {
```

```
                reset();
                m_ptr = std::exchange(rhs.m_ptr, nullptr);
            }
            return *this;
        }

        // Dereferencing operators will go here...
    private:
        void reset()
        {
            delete m_ptr;
            m_ptr = nullptr;
        }
        T* m_ptr { nullptr };
};
```

This smart pointer is about as simple as you can get. All it does is store a dumb raw pointer, and the storage pointed to by the pointer is deleted when the smart pointer is destroyed. The implementation is equally simple: the constructor takes a raw pointer, which is stored as the only data member in the class. The destructor frees the storage referenced by the pointer.

You want to be able to use the smart pointer class template like this:

```
Pointer<int> smartInt { new int };
*smartInt = 5; // Dereference the smart pointer.
println("{} ", *smartInt);

Pointer<SpreadsheetCell> smartCell { new SpreadsheetCell };
smartCell->set(5); // Dereference and member select the set() member function.
println("{} ", smartCell->getValue());
```

As you can see from this example, you have to provide implementations of `operator*` and `operator->` for this class. These are implemented in the next two sections.

> **WARNING** *You should rarely, if ever, write an implementation of just one of* `operator*` *and* `operator->`*. You should almost always write both operators together. It would confuse the users of your class if you failed to provide both.*

Implementing operator*

When you dereference a pointer, you expect to be able to access the memory to which the pointer points. If that memory contains a simple type such as an `int`, you should be able to change its value directly. If the memory contains a more complicated type, such as an object, you should be able to access its data members or member functions with the `.` operator.

To provide these semantics, you should return a reference from `operator*`. For the `Pointer` class this is done as follows:

```
export template <typename T> class Pointer
{
```

```
    public:
        // Omitted for brevity
        T& operator*() { return *m_ptr; }
        const T& operator*() const { return *m_ptr; }
        // Omitted for brevity
};
```

As you can see, `operator*` returns a reference to the object or variable to which the underlying raw pointer points. As with overloading the subscripting operators earlier in this chapter, it's useful to provide both `const` and non-`const` overloads of the member function, which return a reference-to-`const` and a reference-to-non-`const`, respectively.

Implementing operator–>

The arrow operator is a bit trickier. The result of applying the arrow operator should be a member or member function of an object. However, to implement it like that, you would have to be able to implement the equivalent of `operator*` followed by `operator.`; C++ doesn't allow you to overload `operator.` for good reason: it's impossible to write a single prototype that allows you to capture any possible member or member function selection. Therefore, C++ treats `operator->` as a special case. Consider this line:

```
smartCell->set(5);
```

C++ translates this to the following:

```
(smartCell.operator->())->set(5);
```

As you can see, C++ applies another `operator->` to whatever you return from your overloaded `operator->`. Therefore, you must return a pointer, like this:

```
export template <typename T> class Pointer
{
    public:
        // Omitted for brevity
        T* operator->() { return m_ptr; }
        const T* operator->() const { return m_ptr; }
        // Omitted for brevity
};
```

You may find it confusing that `operator*` and `operator->` are asymmetric, but once you see them a few times, you'll get used to it.

What in the World Are operator.* and operator–>*?

It's perfectly legitimate in C++ to take the address of class data members and member functions to obtain pointers to them. However, you can't access a non-`static` data member or call a non-`static` member function without an object. The whole point of class data members and member functions is that they exist on a per-object basis. Thus, when you want to call the member function or access the data member via the pointer, you must dereference the pointer in the context of an object. The syntax details for using `operator.*` and `->*` is deferred until Chapter 19, as it requires knowledge of how to define function pointers.

C++ does not allow you to overload `operator.*` (just as you can't overload `operator.`), but you could overload `operator->*`. However, it is tricky, and, given that most C++ programmers don't even know that you can access member functions and data members through pointers, it's probably not worth the trouble. The shared_ptr smart pointer in the Standard Library, for example, does not overload operator->*.

WRITING CONVERSION OPERATORS

Going back to the SpreadsheetCell example, consider these two lines of code:

```
SpreadsheetCell cell { 1.23 };
double d1 { cell }; // DOES NOT COMPILE!
```

A SpreadsheetCell contains a double representation, so it seems logical that you could assign it to a double variable. Well, you can't. The compiler tells you that it doesn't know how to convert a SpreadsheetCell to a double. You might be tempted to try forcing the compiler to do what you want, like this:

```
double d1 { (double)cell }; // STILL DOES NOT COMPILE!
```

First, the preceding code still doesn't compile because the compiler still doesn't know *how* to convert the SpreadsheetCell to a double. It already knew from the first line what you wanted it to do, and it would do it if it could. Second, it's a bad idea in general to add gratuitous casts to your program.

If you want to allow this kind of conversion, you must tell the compiler how to perform it. Specifically, you can write a conversion operator to convert SpreadsheetCells to doubles. The prototype looks like this:

```
operator double() const;
```

The name of the function is operator double. It has no return type because the return type is specified by the name of the operator: double. It is const because it doesn't change the object on which it is called. The implementation looks like this:

```
SpreadsheetCell::operator double() const
{
    return getValue();
}
```

That's all you need to do to write a conversion operator from SpreadsheetCell to double. Now the compiler accepts the following lines and does the right thing at run time:

```
SpreadsheetCell cell { 1.23 };
double d1 { cell }; // Works as expected
```

You can write conversion operators for any type with this same syntax. For example, here is an std::string conversion operator for SpreadsheetCell:

```
operator std::string() const;
```

And here is an implementation:

```
SpreadsheetCell::operator std::string() const
{
    return doubleToString(getValue());
}
```

Now you can convert a SpreadsheetCell to a string. However, due to the constructors provided by string, the following does not work:

```
string str { cell };
```

Instead, you can either use normal assignment syntax instead of uniform initialization, or use an explicit static_cast() as follows:

```
string str1 = cell;
string str2 { static_cast<string>(cell) };
```

Operator auto

Instead of explicitly specifying the type that a conversion operator returns, you can specify auto and let the compiler deduce it for you. For example, the double conversion operator of SpreadsheetCell could be written as follows:

```
operator auto() const { return getValue(); }
```

There is one caveat, the implementation of member functions with auto return type deduction must be visible to users of the class. Hence, this example puts the implementation directly in the class definition.

Also, remember from Chapter 1 that auto strips away reference and const qualifiers. So, if your operator auto returns a reference to a type T, then the deduced type will be T returned by value, resulting in a copy being made. If needed, you can explicitly add reference and const qualifiers; here's an example:

```
operator const auto&() const { /* ... */ }
```

Solving Ambiguity Problems with Explicit Conversion Operators

Writing the double conversion operator for the SpreadsheetCell object introduces an *ambiguity* problem. Consider this line:

```
SpreadsheetCell cell { 6.6 };
double d1 { cell + 3.4 }; // DOES NOT COMPILE IF YOU DEFINE operator double()
```

This line now fails to compile. It worked before you wrote operator double(), so what's the problem now? The issue is that the compiler doesn't know if it should convert cell to a double with operator double() and perform double addition, or convert 3.4 to a SpreadsheetCell with the double constructor and perform SpreadsheetCell addition. Before you wrote operator double(), the compiler had only one choice: convert 3.4 to a SpreadsheetCell with the double constructor and perform SpreadsheetCell addition. However, now the compiler could do either. It doesn't want to make a choice you might not like, so it refuses to make any choice at all.

The usual pre-C++11 solution to this conundrum is to make the constructor in question explicit so that the automatic conversion using that constructor is prevented (see Chapter 8). However, you don't want that constructor to be explicit because you generally like the automatic conversion of doubles to SpreadsheetCells. Since C++11, you can solve this problem by making the double conversion operator explicit instead of the constructor:

```
explicit operator double() const;
```

With this change the following line compiles fine:

```
double d1 { cell + 3.4 };  // 10
```

The operator `auto` as discussed in the previous section can also be marked as `explicit`.

Conversions for Boolean Expressions

Sometimes it is useful to be able to use objects in Boolean expressions. For example, programmers often use pointers in conditional statements like this:

```
if (ptr != nullptr) { /* Perform some dereferencing action. */ }
```

Sometimes they write shorthand conditions such as this:

```
if (ptr) { /* Perform some dereferencing action. */ }
```

Other times, you see code as follows:

```
if (!ptr) { /* Do something. */ }
```

Currently, none of the preceding expressions compile with the `Pointer` smart pointer class template defined earlier. To make them work, we can add a conversion operator to the class to convert it to a pointer type. Then, the comparisons to `nullptr`, as well as the object alone in an `if` statement, will trigger the conversion to the pointer type. The usual pointer type for the conversion operator is `void*`, because that's a pointer type with which you cannot do much except test it in Boolean expressions. Here is the implementation:

```
operator void*() const { return m_ptr; }
```

Now the following code compiles and does what you expect:

```
void process(const Pointer<SpreadsheetCell>& p)
{
    if (p != nullptr) { println("not nullptr"); }
    if (p != 0)       { println("not 0"); }
    if (p)            { println("not nullptr"); }
    if (!p)           { println("nullptr"); }
}

int main()
{
    Pointer<SpreadsheetCell> smartCell { nullptr };
    process(smartCell);
    println("");

    Pointer<SpreadsheetCell> anotherSmartCell { new SpreadsheetCell { 5.0 } };
    process(anotherSmartCell);
}
```

The output is as follows:

```
nullptr

not nullptr
not 0
not nullptr
```

Another alternative is to overload `operator bool()` as follows instead of `operator void*()`. After all, you're using the object in a Boolean expression; why not convert it directly to a `bool`?

```
operator bool() const { return m_ptr != nullptr; }
```

The following comparisons still work:

```
if (p != 0)     { println("not 0"); }
if (p)          { println("not nullptr"); }
if (!p)         { println("nullptr"); }
```

However, with `operator bool()`, the following comparison with `nullptr` results in a compilation error:

```
if (p != nullptr) { println("not nullptr"); }  // Error
```

This is because `nullptr` has its own type called `nullptr_t`, which is not automatically converted to the integer 0 (`false`). The compiler cannot find an `operator!=` that takes a `Pointer` object and a `nullptr_t` object. You could implement such an `operator!=` as a `friend` of the `Pointer` class:

```
export template <typename T>
class Pointer
{
    public:
        // Omitted for brevity
        template <typename T>
        friend bool operator!=(const Pointer<T>& lhs, std::nullptr_t rhs);
        // Omitted for brevity
};

export template <typename T>
bool operator!=(const Pointer<T>& lhs, std::nullptr_t rhs)
{
    return lhs.m_ptr != rhs;
}
```

However, after implementing this `operator!=`, the following comparison stops working, because the compiler no longer knows which `operator!=` to use:

```
if (p != 0)     { println("not 0"); }
```

From this example, you might conclude that the `operator bool()` technique only seems appropriate for objects that don't represent pointers and for which conversion to a pointer type really doesn't make sense. Unfortunately, even then, adding a conversion operator to `bool` presents some other unanticipated consequences. C++ applies *promotion* rules to silently convert `bool` to `int` whenever the opportunity arises. Therefore, with the `operator bool()`, the following code compiles and runs:

```
Pointer<SpreadsheetCell> anotherSmartCell { new SpreadsheetCell { 5.0 } };
int i { anotherSmartCell }; // Converts Pointer to bool to int.
```

That's usually not behavior that you expect or desire. To prevent such assignments, you could explicitly delete the conversion operators to `int`, `long`, `long long`, and so on. However, this is getting messy. So, many programmers prefer `operator void*()` instead of `operator bool()`.

As you can see, there is a design element to overloading operators. Your decisions about which operators to overload directly influence the ways in which clients can use your classes.

OVERLOADING THE MEMORY ALLOCATION AND DEALLOCATION OPERATORS

C++ gives you the ability to redefine the way memory allocation and deallocation work in your programs. You can provide this customization both on the global level and the class level. This capability is most useful when you are worried about memory fragmentation, which can occur if you allocate and deallocate a lot of small objects. For example, instead of going to the default C++ memory allocation each time you need memory, you could write a memory pool allocator that reuses fixed-size chunks of memory. This section explains the subtleties of the memory allocation and deallocation routines and shows you how to customize them. With these tools, you should be able to write your own allocator if the need ever arises.

> **WARNING** *Unless you know a lot about memory allocation strategies, attempts to overload the memory allocation routines are rarely worth the trouble. Don't overload them just because it sounds like a neat idea. Only do so if you have a genuine requirement and the necessary knowledge.*

How new and delete Really Work

One of the trickiest aspects of C++ is the details of `new` and `delete`. Consider this line of code:

```
SpreadsheetCell* cell { new SpreadsheetCell {} };
```

The part `new SpreadsheetCell{}` is called the *new-expression*. It does two things. First, it allocates space for the `SpreadsheetCell` object by making a call to `operator new`. Second, it calls the constructor for the object. Only after the constructor has completed does it return the pointer to you.

`delete` works analogously. Consider this line of code:

```
delete cell;
```

This line is called the *delete-expression*. It first calls the destructor for `cell` and then calls `operator delete` to free the memory.

You can overload `operator new` and `operator delete` to control memory allocation and deallocation, but you cannot overload the new-expression or the delete-expression. Thus, you can customize the actual memory allocation and deallocation, but not the calls to the constructor and destructor.

The New-Expression and operator new

There are six different forms of the *new-expression*, each of which has a corresponding `operator new`. Earlier chapters in this book already show four new-expressions: `new`, `new[]`, `new(nothrow)`, and `new(nothrow)[]`. The following list shows the corresponding four `operator new` overloads defined in `<new>`:

```
void* operator new(std::size_t size);
void* operator new[](std::size_t size);
void* operator new(std::size_t size, const std::nothrow_t&) noexcept;
void* operator new[](std::size_t size, const std::nothrow_t&) noexcept;
```

There are two special new-expressions that don't do any allocation but invoke the constructor on an already allocated piece of memory. These are called *placement new operators* (including both single and array forms). They allow you to construct an object in pre-allocated memory like this:

```
void* ptr { allocateMemorySomehow() };
SpreadsheetCell* cell { new (ptr) SpreadsheetCell {} };
```

The two corresponding `operator new` overloads for these look as follows; however, the C++ standard forbids you to overload them:

```
void* operator new(std::size_t size, void* p) noexcept;
void* operator new[](std::size_t size, void* p) noexcept;
```

This feature is a bit obscure, but it's important to know that it exists. It can come in handy if you want to implement memory pools by reusing memory without freeing it in between. This allows you to construct and destruct instances of an object without re-allocating memory for each new instance. Chapter 29, "Writing Efficient C++," gives an example of a memory pool implementation.

The Delete-Expression and operator delete

There are only two different forms of the *delete-expression* that you can call: `delete`, and `delete[]`; there are no `nothrow` or placement forms. However, there are all six overloads of `operator delete`. Why the asymmetry? The two `nothrow` and two placement overloads are used only if an exception is thrown from a constructor. In that case, the `operator delete` is called that matches the `operator new` that was used to allocate the memory prior to the constructor call. However, if you delete a pointer normally, `delete` calls `operator delete` and `delete[]` calls `operator delete[]` (never the `nothrow` or placement forms). Practically, this doesn't really matter because the C++ standard says that throwing an exception from `delete` (for example, from a destructor called by `delete`) results in undefined behavior. This means `delete` should never throw an exception anyway, so the `nothrow` overload of `operator delete` is superfluous. Also, placement `delete` should be a no-op, because placement `new` doesn't allocate any memory, so there's nothing to free.

Here are the prototypes for the six `operator delete` overloads corresponding to the six `operator new` overloads:

```
void operator delete(void* ptr) noexcept;
void operator delete[](void* ptr) noexcept;
void operator delete(void* ptr, const std::nothrow_t&) noexcept;
void operator delete[](void* ptr, const std::nothrow_t&) noexcept;
void operator delete(void* ptr, void*) noexcept;
void operator delete[](void* ptr, void*) noexcept;
```

Overloading operator new and operator delete

You can replace the global `operator new` and `operator delete` routines if you want. These functions are called for every new-expression and delete-expression in the program, unless there are more specific routines in individual classes. However, to quote Bjarne Stroustrup, ". . . replacing the global `operator new` and `operator delete` is not for the fainthearted" (*The C++ Programming Language*, third edition, Addison-Wesley, 1997). I don't recommend it either!

> **WARNING** *If you fail to heed my advice and decide to replace the global* `operator new`, *keep in mind that you cannot put any code in the operator that makes a call to* `new` *because this will cause an infinite recursion. For example, you cannot write a message to the console with* `print()`.

A more useful technique is to overload `operator new` and `operator delete` for specific classes. These overloaded operators will be called only when you allocate and deallocate objects of that particular class. Here is an example of a class that overloads the four non-placement forms of `operator new` and `operator delete`:

```
export class MemoryDemo
{
    public:
        virtual ~MemoryDemo() = default;

        void* operator new(std::size_t size);
        void operator delete(void* ptr) noexcept;

        void* operator new[](std::size_t size);
        void operator delete[](void* ptr) noexcept;

        void* operator new(std::size_t size, const std::nothrow_t&) noexcept;
        void operator delete(void* ptr, const std::nothrow_t&) noexcept;

        void* operator new[](std::size_t size, const std::nothrow_t&) noexcept;
        void operator delete[](void* ptr, const std::nothrow_t&) noexcept;
};
```

Here are implementations of these operators that simply write out a message to the standard output and pass the arguments through to calls to the global versions of the operators. Note that `nothrow` is actually a variable of type `nothrow_t`.

```
void* MemoryDemo::operator new(size_t size)
{
    println("operator new");
    return ::operator new(size);
}
void MemoryDemo::operator delete(void* ptr) noexcept
{
    println("operator delete");
    ::operator delete(ptr);
}
void* MemoryDemo::operator new[](size_t size)
{
    println("operator new[]");
    return ::operator new[](size);
}
void MemoryDemo::operator delete[](void* ptr) noexcept
{
    println("operator delete[]");
    ::operator delete[](ptr);
}
```

```
void* MemoryDemo::operator new(size_t size, const nothrow_t&) noexcept
{
    println("operator new nothrow");
    return ::operator new(size, nothrow);
}
void MemoryDemo::operator delete(void* ptr, const nothrow_t&) noexcept
{
    println("operator delete nothrow");
    ::operator delete(ptr, nothrow);
}
void* MemoryDemo::operator new[](size_t size, const nothrow_t&) noexcept
{
    println("operator new[] nothrow");
    return ::operator new[](size, nothrow);
}
void MemoryDemo::operator delete[](void* ptr, const nothrow_t&) noexcept
{
    println("operator delete[] nothrow");
    ::operator delete[](ptr, nothrow);
}
```

Here is some code that allocates and frees objects of this class in several ways:

```
MemoryDemo* mem { new MemoryDemo{} };
delete mem;
mem = new MemoryDemo[10];
delete [] mem;
mem = new (nothrow) MemoryDemo{};
delete mem;
mem = new (nothrow) MemoryDemo[10];
delete [] mem;
```

Here is the output from running the program:

```
operator new
operator delete
operator new[]
operator delete[]
operator new nothrow
operator delete
operator new[] nothrow
operator delete[]
```

These implementations of `operator new` and `operator delete` are obviously trivial and not particularly useful. They are intended only to give you an idea of the syntax in case you ever want to implement nontrivial versions of them.

> **WARNING** *Whenever you overload* `operator new`, *overload the corresponding form of* `operator delete`. *Otherwise, memory will be allocated as you specify but freed according to the built-in semantics, which may not be compatible.*

It might seem overkill to overload all the various forms of `operator new` and `operator delete`. However, it's generally a good idea to do so to prevent inconsistencies in memory allocations. If you don't want to provide implementations for certain overloads, you can explicitly delete these using `=delete` to prevent anyone from using them. See the next section for more information.

> **WARNING** *Overload all forms of* `operator new` *and* `operator delete`, *or explicitly delete overloads that you don't want to get used, to prevent inconsistencies in the memory allocations.*

Explicitly Deleting or Defaulting operator new and operator delete

Chapter 8 shows how you can explicitly delete or default a constructor or assignment operator. Explicitly deleting or defaulting is not limited to constructors and assignment operators. For example, the following class deletes `operator new` and `new[]`, which means that objects of this class cannot be dynamically allocated using `new` or `new[]`:

```
class MyClass
{
    public:
        void* operator new(std::size_t) = delete;
        void* operator new[](std::size_t) = delete;
        void* operator new(std::size_t, const std::nothrow_t&) noexcept = delete;
        void* operator new[](std::size_t, const std::nothrow_t&) noexcept = delete;
};
```

Using this class as follows results in compilation errors:

```
MyClass* p1 { new MyClass };
MyClass* p2 { new MyClass[2] };
MyClass* p3 { new (std::nothrow) MyClass };
```

Overloading operator new and operator delete with Extra Parameters

In addition to overloading the standard forms of `operator new`, you can write your own versions with extra parameters. These extra parameters can be useful for passing various flags or counters to your memory allocation routines. For instance, some runtime libraries use this in debug mode to provide the filename and line number where an object is allocated, so when there is a memory leak, the offending line that did the allocation can be identified.

As an example, here are the prototypes for an additional `operator new` and `operator delete` with an extra integer parameter for the `MemoryDemo` class:

```
void* operator new(std::size_t size, int extra);
void operator delete(void* ptr, int extra) noexcept;
```

The implementations are as follows:

```
void* MemoryDemo::operator new(std::size_t size, int extra)
{
    println("operator new with extra int: {}", extra);
    return ::operator new(size);
}
void MemoryDemo::operator delete(void* ptr, int extra) noexcept
{
    println("operator delete with extra int: {}", extra);
    return ::operator delete(ptr);
}
```

When you write an overloaded `operator new` with extra parameters, the compiler automatically allows the corresponding new-expression. The extra arguments to `new` are passed with function call syntax (as with `nothrow` overloads). So, you can now write code like this:

```
MemoryDemo* memp { new(5) MemoryDemo{} };
delete memp;
```

The output is as follows:

```
operator new with extra int: 5
operator delete
```

When you define an `operator new` with extra parameters, you should also define the corresponding `operator delete` with the same extra parameters. However, you cannot call this `operator delete` with extra parameters yourself; it will be called only when you use your `operator new` with extra parameters and the constructor of your object throws an exception.

Overloading operator delete with Size of Memory as Parameter

An alternate form of `operator delete` gives you the size of the memory that should be freed as well as the pointer. Simply declare the prototype for `operator delete` with an extra size parameter.

> **WARNING** *If a class declares two overloads of* `operator delete` *with one overload taking the size as a parameter and the other doesn't, the overload without the size parameter will always get called. If you want the overload with the size parameter to be used, write only that overload.*

You can replace `operator delete` with an overload that takes a size for any of the overloads of `operator delete` independently. Here is the `MemoryDemo` class definition with the first `operator delete` modified to take the size of the memory to be deleted:

```
export class MemoryDemo
{
    public:
        // Omitted for brevity
        void* operator new(std::size_t size);
        void operator delete(void* ptr, std::size_t size) noexcept;
        // Omitted for brevity
};
```

The implementation of this `operator delete` again simply calls the global `operator delete`:

```
void MemoryDemo::operator delete(void* ptr, size_t size) noexcept
{
    println("operator delete with size {}", size);
    ::operator delete(ptr, size);
}
```

This capability is useful only if you are writing a complicated memory allocation and deallocation scheme for your classes.

OVERLOADING USER-DEFINED LITERAL OPERATORS

C++ has a number of built-in literal types that you can use in your code. Here are some examples:

- `'a'`: Character
- `"A string"`: Zero-terminated sequence of characters, C-style string
- `3.14f`: `float` single-precision floating-point value
- `0xabc`: Hexadecimal value

C++ also allows you to define your own literals, and the Standard Library does exactly that; it provides a number of additional literal types to construct Standard Library objects. Let's take a look at these first and then see how you can define your own.

Standard Library Literals

The C++ Standard Library defines the following standard literals. Note that these literals do not start with an underscore:

LITERAL	CREATES INSTANCES OF . . .	EXAMPLE	REQUIRES NAMESPACE
`s`	`string`	`auto myString { "Hello"s };`	`string_literals`
`sv`	`string_view`	`auto myStringView { "Hello"sv };`	`string_view_literals`
`h, min, s, ms, us, ns`	`chrono::duration`[1]	`auto myDuration { 42min };`	`chrono_literals`
`y, d`	`chrono::year` and `day`[1]	`auto thisYear { 2024y };`	`chrono_literals`
`i, il, if`	`complex<T>` with `T` equal to `double`, `long double`, `float`, respectively	`auto myComplexNumber { 1.3i };`	`complex_literals`

[1] Discussed in Chapter 22, "Date and Time Utilities."

Technically, all of these are defined in subnamespaces of `std::literals`, for example `std::literals::string_literals`. However, both `string_literals` and `literals` are inline namespaces that automatically make their contents available in their parent namespace. Hence, if you want to use `s` string literals, you can use any of the following `using` directives:

```
using namespace std;
using namespace std::literals;
using namespace std::string_literals;
using namespace std::literals::string_literals;
```

User-Defined Literals

User-defined literals should start with exactly one underscore. Some examples are `_i`, `_s`, `_km`, `_miles`, `_K`, and so on.

User-defined literals are implemented by writing *literal operators*. A literal operator can work in *raw* or *cooked* mode. In raw mode, your literal operator receives a sequence of characters, while in cooked mode your literal operator receives a specific interpreted type. For example, take the C++ literal `123`. A raw literal operator receives this as a sequence of characters `'1'`, `'2'`, `'3'`. A cooked literal operator receives this as the integer 123. The literal `0x23` is received by a raw operator as the characters `'0'`, `'x'`, `'2'`, `'3'`, while a cooked operator receives the integer 35. A literal such as `3.14` is received by a raw operator as `'3'`, `'.'`, `'1'`, `'4'`, while a cooked operator receives the floating-point value 3.14.

Cooked-Mode Literal Operator

A cooked-mode literal operator should have either of the following:

- **To process numeric values:** One parameter of type `unsigned long long`, `long double`, `char`, `wchar_t`, `char8_t`, `char16_t`, or `char32_t`
- **To process strings:** Two parameters where the first is a C-style string and the second is the length of the string, for instance, `(const char* str, std::size_t len)`

For example, the following code defines a `Length` class storing a length in meters. The constructor is `private` because users should only be able to construct a `Length` instance using the provided user-defined literals. The code provides cooked literal operators for user-defined literal operators `_km` and `_m`. Both of these are friends of `Length` so that they can access the `private` constructor. There must not be any space between the `""` and the underscore of these operators.

```
// A class representing a length. The length is always stored in meters.
class Length
{
    public:
        long double getMeters() const { return m_length; }
        // The user-defined literals _km and _m are friends of Length so they
        // can use the private constructor.
        friend Length operator ""_km(long double d);
        friend Length operator ""_m(long double d);
    private:
        // Private constructor because users should only be able to construct a
        // Length using the provided user-defined literals.
        Length(long double length) : m_length { length } {}
        long double m_length;
```

```
};
Length operator ""_km(long double d) // Cooked _km literal operator
{
    return Length { d * 1000 }; // Convert to meters.
}
Length operator ""_m(long double d) // Cooked _m literal operator
{
    return Length { d };
}
```

These literal operators can be used as follows:

```
Length d1 { 1.2_km };
auto d2 { 1.2_m };
println("d1 = {}m; d2 = {}m", d1.getMeters(), d2.getMeters());
```

Here is the output:

```
d1 = 1200m; d2 = 1.2m
```

To demonstrate the variant of a cooked literal operator accepting a `const char*` and a `size_t`, we can re-create the standard string literal, s, provided by the Standard Library, to construct an `std::string`. Let's call the literal _s.

```
string operator ""_s(const char* str, size_t len)
{
    return string { str, len };
}
```

This literal operator can be used as follows:

```
string str1 { "Hello World"_s };
auto str2 { "Hello World"_s };    // str2 has as type string
```

Without the _s literal operator, the `auto` type deduction would result in `const char*`:

```
auto str3 { "Hello World" };      // str3 has as type const char*
```

Raw-Mode Literal Operator

A raw-mode literal operator requires one parameter of type `const char*`, a zero-terminated C-style string. The following example defines the earlier literal operator `_m` as a raw literal operator:

```
Length operator ""_m(const char* str)
{
    // Implementation omitted; it requires parsing the C-style string
    // converting it to a long double, and constructing a Length.
    ...
}
```

Using this raw-mode literal operator is the same as using the cooked version.

> **NOTE** *Raw-mode literal operators work only with non-string literals. For example,* `1.23_m` *could be implemented with a raw-mode literal operator, but* `"1.23"_m` *cannot. The latter one requires a cooked-mode literal with two parameters: the zero-terminated string and its length.*

SUMMARY

This chapter summarized the rationale for operator overloading and provided examples and explanations for overloading the various categories of operators. Ideally, this chapter taught you to appreciate the power that it gives you. Throughout this book, operator overloading is used to provide abstractions and easy-to-use class interfaces.

Now it's time to start delving into the C++ Standard Library. The next chapter starts with an overview of the functionality provided by the C++ Standard Library, followed by chapters that go deeper into specific features of the library.

EXERCISES

By solving the following exercises, you can practice the material discussed in this chapter. Solutions to all exercises are available with the code download on the book's website at `www.wiley.com/go/proc++6e`. However, if you are stuck on an exercise, first reread parts of this chapter to try to find an answer yourself before looking at the solution from the website.

Exercise 15-1: Implement an `AssociativeArray` class template. The class should store a number of elements in a `vector`, where each element consists of a key and a value. The key is always a `string`, while the type of the value can be specified using a template type parameter. Provide overloaded subscripting operators so that elements can be retrieved based on their key. Test your implementation in your `main()` function. Note: this exercise is just to practice implementing subscripting operators using non-integral indices. In practice, you should just use the `std::map` class template provided by the Standard Library and discussed in Chapter 18 for such an associative array.

Exercise 15-2: Take your `Person` class implementation from Exercise 13-2 and add implementations of the insertion and extraction operators to it. Make sure that your extraction operator can read back what your insertion operator writes out.

Exercise 15-3: Add a `string` conversion operator to your solution of Exercise 15-2. The operator simply returns a `string` constructed from the first and last name of the person.

Exercise 15-4: Start from your solution of Exercise 15-3 and add a user-defined literal operator `_p` that constructs a `Person` from a string literal. It should support spaces in last names, but not in first names. For example, `"Peter Van Weert"_p` should result in a `Person` object with first name Peter and last name Van Weert.

16

Overview of the C++ Standard Library

WHAT'S IN THIS CHAPTER?

- The coding principles used throughout the Standard Library
- A high-level overview of the functionality provided by the Standard Library

WILEY.COM DOWNLOADS FOR THIS CHAPTER

Please note that all the code examples for this chapter are available as part of this chapter's code download on the book's website at `www.wiley.com/go/proc++6e` on the Download Code tab.

The most important library that you will use as a C++ programmer is the C++ Standard Library. As its name implies, this library is part of the C++ standard, so any standards-conforming compiler should include it. The Standard Library is not monolithic: it includes several disparate components, some of which you have been using already. You may even have assumed they were part of the core language. All Standard Library classes and functions are declared in the `std` namespace, or a subnamespace of `std`.

The heart of the C++ Standard Library is its generic *containers* and *algorithms*. Some people still call this subset of the library the Standard Template Library, or STL for short, because originally it was based on a third-party library called the Standard Template Library, which used templates abundantly. However, STL is not a term defined by the C++ standard itself, so this book does not use it. The power of the Standard Library is that it provides generic containers and generic algorithms in such a way that most of the algorithms work on most of the containers, no matter what type of data the containers store. Performance is an important aspect of the

Standard Library. The goal is to make the Standard Library containers and algorithms as fast as, or faster than, handwritten code.

The C++ Standard Library also includes most of the C headers that are part of the C11 standard, but with new names. For example, you can access the functionality from the C `<stdio.h>` header by including `<cstdio>`. The former puts everything in the global namespace, while the latter puts everything in the `std` namespace. Though, technically, the former is allowed to put things in the `std` namespace as well, and the latter is allowed to additionally put things in the global namespace. The C11 headers `<stdnoreturn.h>`, `<threads.h>`, and their `<c...>` equivalents are not included in the C++ standard. The `<stdatomic.h>` header from C11 has been available since C++23, but no equivalent `<cstdatomic>` is provided. Furthermore, C++17 has deprecated, and C++20 has removed the following C headers:

- `<ccomplex>` and `<ctgmath>`: Replace the use of these with `<complex>` and/or `<cmath>`.
- `<ciso646>`, `<cstdalign>`, and `<cstdbool>`: These headers were useless in C++ as these were either empty or defined macros that are keywords in C++.

C headers are not guaranteed to be importable. Use `#include` instead of `import` to get access to the functionality defined by them.

> **NOTE** *If there is a C++ equivalent of functionality provided by a C header, it is recommended to use the C++ equivalent.*

A C++ programmer who wants to claim language expertise is expected to be familiar with the Standard Library. You can save yourself immeasurable time and energy by incorporating Standard Library containers and algorithms into your programs instead of writing and debugging your own versions. Now is the time to master this Standard Library.

This first chapter on the Standard Library provides a general overview of the available functionality. The next few chapters go into more detail on several aspects of the Standard Library, including containers, iterators, generic algorithms, predefined function object classes, regular expressions, random number generation, and much more. Additionally, Chapter 25, "Customizing and Extending the Standard Library," is dedicated to customizing and extending the library with your own Standard Library–compliant algorithms and data structures.

Despite the depth of material found in this and the following chapters, the Standard Library is too large for this book to cover exhaustively. You should read these chapters to learn about the Standard Library, but keep in mind that they don't mention every member function and data member that the various classes provide or show you the prototypes of every algorithm. Appendix C, "Standard Library Header Files," summarizes all the header files in the Standard Library. Consult your favorite Standard Library Reference for a complete reference of all provided functionality.

CODING PRINCIPLES

The Standard Library makes heavy use of the C++ features called *templates* and *operator overloading*.

Use of Templates

Templates are used to allow *generic programming*. They make it possible to write code that can work with all kinds of objects, even objects unknown to the programmer when writing the code. The obligation of the programmer writing the template code is to specify the requirements of the classes that define these objects, for example, that they have an operator for comparison or a copy constructor, or whatever is deemed appropriate, and then making sure the code that is written uses only those required capabilities. The obligation of the programmer creating the objects is to supply those operators and member functions that the template requires.

Unfortunately, many programmers consider templates to be the most difficult part of C++ and, for that reason, tend to avoid them. However, even if you never write your own templates, you need to understand their syntax and capabilities to use the Standard Library. Templates are described in detail in Chapter 12, "Writing Generic Code with Templates." If you skipped that chapter and are not familiar with templates, I suggest you first read Chapter 12 and then come back to learn more about the Standard Library.

Use of Operator Overloading

Operator overloading is another feature used extensively by the C++ Standard Library. Chapter 9, "Mastering Classes and Objects," has a whole section devoted to operator overloading. Make sure you read that section and understand it before tackling this and subsequent chapters. In addition, Chapter 15, "Overloading C++ Operators," presents much more detail on the subject of operator overloading, but those details are not required to understand the following chapters.

OVERVIEW OF THE C++ STANDARD LIBRARY

This section introduces the various components of the Standard Library from a design perspective. You will learn what facilities are available for you to use, but you will not learn many coding details. Those details are covered in other chapters.

Strings

C++ provides a built-in `string` class, defined in `<string>`. This C++ `string` class is superior in almost every way compared to C-style strings of character arrays. It handles the memory management; provides some bounds checking, assignment semantics, and comparisons; and supports manipulations such as concatenation, substring extraction, and substring or character replacement.

> **NOTE** *Technically,* `std::string` *is a type alias for a* `char` *instantiation of the* `std::basic_string` *class template. However, you need not worry about these details; you can use* `string` *as if it were a bona fide nontemplate class.*

The Standard Library also provides a `string_view` class, defined in `<string_view>`. It is a read-only view of any kind of string representation and can be used as a drop-in replacement for `const string&`, but without the overhead. It never copies strings!

C++ provides support for *Unicode* and *localization*. Unicode allows you to write programs that work with text in different languages, such as Arabic, Chinese, Japanese, and so on. Locales, defined in `<locale>`, allow you to format data such as numbers and dates according to the rules of a certain country or region.

C++ includes a powerful type-safe string formatting library, accessed through `std::format()` and defined in `<format>`. The library is extensible and allows you to add support for your own custom types. C++23 adds helper functions `std::print()` and `println()` to make it easier to print formatted text to the console.

In case you missed it, Chapter 2, "Working with Strings and String Views," provides all the details of the `string` and `string_view` classes and the string formatting library, while Chapter 21, "String Localization and Regular Expressions," discusses Unicode and localization.

Regular Expressions

Regular expressions are available through functionality provided by `<regex>`. They make it easy to perform *pattern-matching*, often used in text processing. Pattern-matching allows you to search for special patterns in strings and optionally to replace them with a new pattern. Regular expressions are discussed in Chapter 21.

I/O Streams

C++ includes a model for input and output called *streams*. The C++ library provides routines for reading and writing built-in types from and to files, console/keyboard, and strings. C++ also provides the facilities for coding your own routines for reading and writing your own objects. Most of the I/O functionality is defined in `<fstream>`, `<iomanip>`, `<ios>`, `<iosfwd>`, `<iostream>`, `<istream>`, `<ostream>`, `<sstream>`, `<streambuf>`, and `<strstream>`. C++23 introduces span-based streams, defined in `<spanstream>`. Chapter 1, "A Crash Course in C++ and the Standard Library," reviews the basics of I/O streams, and Chapter 13, "Demystifying C++ I/O," discusses streams in detail.

Smart Pointers

One of the problems faced in robust programming is knowing when to delete an object. There are several failures that can happen. A first problem is not deleting the object at all (failing to free the storage). These are known as *memory leaks*, where objects accumulate and take up space but are not used. Another problem is where a piece of code deletes the storage while another piece of code is still pointing to that storage, resulting in pointers to storage that either is no longer in use or has been reallocated for another purpose. These are known as *dangling pointers*. Yet another problem is when one piece of code frees the storage and another piece of code attempts to free the same storage again. This is known as *double deletion*.

All of these problems tend to result in program failures of some sort. Some failures are readily detected and might crash your application; others cause the program to produce erroneous results. Most of these errors are difficult to discover and repair.

C++ addresses all these problems with smart pointers: `unique_ptr`, `shared_ptr`, and `weak_ptr`, all defined in `<memory>`. These smart pointers are discussed in Chapter 7, "Memory Management."

Exceptions

The C++ language supports exceptions, which allow functions to pass errors of various types up to calling functions. The C++ Standard Library provides a class hierarchy of exceptions that you can use in your code as is, or that you can derive from to create your own exception types. Most of the exception support is defined in `<exception>`, `<stdexcept>`, and `<system_error>`. Chapter 14, "Handling Errors," covers the details of exceptions and the standard exception classes.

Standard Integer Types

The `<cstdint>` header file defines a number of standard integer types such as `intx_t` and `uintx_t` with *x* equal to 8, 16, 32, or 64. It also includes macros specifying minimum and maximum values of those types. These integer types are discussed in the context of writing cross-platform code in Chapter 34, "Developing Cross-Platform and Cross-Language Applications."

Numerics Library

The C++ Standard Library provides a collection of mathematical utility classes and functions.

A whole range of common mathematical functions is available, such as `abs()`, `remainder()`, `fma()`, `exp()`, `log()`, `pow()`, `sqrt()`, `sin()`, `atan2()`, `sinh()`, `erf()`, `tgamma()`, `ceil()`, `floor()`, and more. The library also supports a number of mathematical special functions to work with Legendre polynomials, beta functions, elliptic integrals, Bessel functions, cylindrical Neumann functions, and so on. These special functions have established names and notations and are often used in mathematical analysis, functional analysis, geometry, physics, and other applications. The `lerp()` function calculates a linear interpolation or extrapolation: `lerp(a,b,t)` calculates $a+t(b-a)$. Linear interpolation calculates a certain value between given data points, while extrapolation calculates values that are either lower or higher than the minimum or maximum data point. Most of these functions are defined in `<cmath>`, some in `<cstdlib>`.

`<numeric>` defines `gcd()` and `lcm()` that calculate the *greatest common divisor* and *least common multiple* of two integer types, respectively. The `midpoint()` function calculates the midpoint of two values (integers, floating-point numbers, or pointers).

Starting with C++23, quite a few of these functions are marked as `constexpr` (see Chapter 9), so they can be used to perform compile-time computations. Consult your favorite Standard Library reference to learn exactly which functions are `constexpr`.

There is a complex number class called `complex`, defined in `<complex>`, which provides an abstraction for working with numbers that contain both real and imaginary components.

The compile-time rational arithmetic library provides a `ratio` class template, defined in `<ratio>`. This `ratio` class template can exactly represent any finite rational number defined by a numerator and denominator. This library is discussed in Chapter 22, "Date and Time Utilities."

The Standard Library also contains a class called `valarray`, defined in `<valarray>`, which is similar to `vector` but is more optimized for high-performance numerical applications. The library provides several related classes to represent the concept of vector slices. From these building blocks, it is possible to build classes to perform matrix mathematics. There is no built-in matrix class; however, there are third-party libraries like Boost that include matrix support. The `valarray` class is not further discussed in this book.

A selection of often-used mathematical constants is available, all defined in `<numbers>` in the `std::numbers` namespace. Here are just a few of the available constants:

CONSTANT	DESCRIPTION	APPROXIMATION
`pi`	The value of pi (π)	3.141592653589793
`inv_pi`	The inverse of pi	0.3183098861837907
`sqrt2`	The square root of 2	1.4142135623730951
`e`	Euler's number e	2.718281828459045
`phi`	The golden ratio	1.618033988749895

Integer Comparisons

The following comparison functions are available: `std::cmp_equal()`, `cmp_not_equal()`, `cmp_less()`, `cmp_less_equal()`, `cmp_greater()`, and `cmp_greater_equal()`, all defined in `<utility>`. These perform comparisons of two integers and are safe to use on mixed signed and unsigned comparisons.

For example, the following code compares the signed value `-1` and the unsigned value `0u` using `operator>`. The output is `1` (= true), because the -1 is first converted to an unsigned integer and hence becomes a big number such as 4,294,967,295, which is definitely greater than 0:

```
println("{}", (-1 > 0u));              // true
```

Use `cmp_greater()` to get the correct output:

```
println("{}", cmp_greater(-1, 0u));  // false
```

Bit Manipulation

The Standard Library supports the following functions to work with bits, all defined in `<bit>`. All of these functions require an unsigned integral type as first argument:

FUNCTION	DESCRIPTION
`has_single_bit()`	Returns `true` if a given value contains only a single bit, that is, is an integral power of two.
`bit_ceil()`	Returns the smallest integral power of two greater than or equal to a given value.
`bit_floor()`	Returns the largest integral power of two smaller than or equal to a given value.
`bit_width()`	Returns the number of bits needed to store a given value.

FUNCTION	DESCRIPTION
rotl() rotr()	Rotates the bits of a given value to the left or right respectively over a given number of positions.
countl_zero() countl_one()	Returns the number of consecutive zero or one bits respectively in a given value starting from the left, that is, starting with the most-significant bit.
countr_zero() countr_one()	Returns the number of consecutive zero or one bits, respectively, in a given value starting from the right, that is, starting with the least-significant bit.
popcount()	Returns the number of one bits in a given value.
 byteswap()	Reverses the individual bytes of integral types.

Here are a few examples:

```
println("{}", popcount(0b10101010u)); // 4

uint8_t value { 0b11101011u };
println("{}", countl_one(value));      // 3
println("{}", countr_one(value));      // 2

value = 0b10001000u;
println("{:08b}", rotl(value, 2));     // 00100010

value = 0b00001011u;
println("bit_ceil({0:08b} = {0}) = {1:08b} = {1}",
    value, bit_ceil(value));           // bit_ceil(00001011 = 11) = 00010000 = 16
println("bit_floor({0:08b} = {0}) = {1:08b} = {1}",
    value, bit_floor(value));          // bit_floor(00001011 = 11) = 00001000 = 8

uint32_t before { 0x12345678u };
println("{:x}", before);               // 12345678
uint32_t after { byteswap(before) };   // C++23 std::byteswap().
println("{:x}", after);                // 78563412
```

Time and Date Utilities

The Standard Library includes the chrono library, defined in `<chrono>`. This library makes it easy to work with dates and time, to time certain durations, and more. The library supports calendars to work with dates, and time zones, including functionality to convert times between different time zones. The `<ctime>` header provides a number of C-style time and date utilities.

Chapter 22 discusses the time and date utilities in detail.

Random Numbers

C++ already has support for generating pseudo-random numbers for a long time with the `srand()` and `rand()` functions. However, those functions provide only low-quality basic random numbers. For example, you cannot change the distribution of the generated random numbers.

Since C++11, a powerful random number generation library is available. This library is defined in `<random>` and comes with *random number engines*, *random number engine adapters*, and *random number distributions*. These can be used to generate high-quality random numbers and support different distributions, such as normal distributions, negative exponential distributions, and so on.

Consult Chapter 23, "Random Number Facilities," for details on this library.

Initializer Lists

Initializer lists are defined in `<initializer_list>`. They make it easy to write functions that can accept a variable number of arguments and are discussed in Chapter 1.

Pair and Tuple

`<utility>` defines the `pair` class template, which can store two elements of possibly different types. This is known as storing *heterogeneous* elements. All Standard Library containers discussed further in this chapter store *homogeneous* elements, meaning that all the elements in the container must have the same type. A `pair` allows you to store exactly two elements of completely unrelated types in one object. The `pair` class template is introduced in Chapter 1.

`tuple`, defined in `<tuple>`, is a generalization of `pair`. It is a sequence with a fixed size that can have heterogeneous elements. The number and type of elements for a `tuple` instantiation is fixed at compile time. Tuples are discussed in Chapter 24, "Additional Vocabulary Types."

Vocabulary Types

Vocabulary types are types that you will use all the time, just as much as primitive types such as `int` and `double`. Using vocabulary types makes your code safer, more efficient, and easier to write, read, and maintain. Examples of vocabulary types discussed earlier in this book are `vector`, `optional`, `string`, `unique_ptr`, `shared_ptr`, and so on.

Chapter 24 discusses the following additional vocabulary types:

- `variant`, defined in `<variant>`, can hold a single value of one of a given set of types.
- `any`, defined in `<any>`, can hold a single value of any type.
- `tuple`, defined in `<tuple>`, is a generalization of `pair`. It can store any number of values, each with its own specific type.
- `optional`, defined in `<optional>`, holds a value of a specific type or nothing. It can be used for class data members, function parameters, return types of a function, and so on, if you want to allow for values to be optional. It is introduced in Chapter 1. Chapter 24 explains that `optional`s support monadic operations, allowing you to easily chain operations on `optional`s without having to worry whether an `optional` is empty before applying another operation to it.
- C++23 `expected`, defined in `<expected>`, holds a value of a specific type, or an error value of a, possibly different, type. This can be useful as the return type of a function because it allows the function to return either the requested data back to the caller or the reason why something went wrong.

Function Objects

A class that implements a function call operator is called a *function object*. Function objects can, for example, be used as predicates for certain Standard Library algorithms. `<functional>` defines a number of predefined function objects and supports creating new function objects based on existing ones.

Function objects are discussed in detail in Chapter 19, "Function Pointers, Function Objects, and Lambda Expressions."

Filesystem

Everything for the filesystem support library is defined in `<filesystem>` and lives in the `std::filesystem` namespace. It allows you to write portable code to work with a filesystem. You can use it for querying whether something is a directory or a file, iterating over the contents of a directory, manipulating paths, and retrieving information about files such as their size, extension, creation time, and so on. The filesystem support library is discussed in Chapter 13.

Multithreading

All major CPU vendors are selling processors with multiple cores. They are being used for everything from servers to consumer computers and even smartphones. If you want your software to take advantage of all these cores, then you need to write multithreaded code. The Standard Library provides a couple of basic building blocks for writing such code. Individual threads can be created using the `thread` class from `<thread>`. The library also defines `jthread`, a thread that can be cancelled and that automatically performs a join operation when it is destructed.

In multithreaded code you need to take care that several threads are not reading and writing to the same piece of data at the same time, because that will cause data races. To prevent this, you can use atomics, defined in `<atomic>`, which give you thread-safe atomic access to a piece of data. Other thread synchronization mechanisms are provided by `<condition_variable>` and `<mutex>`. There is also support for the following synchronization primitives: semaphores (`<semaphore>`), latches (`<latch>`), and barriers (`<barrier>`).

If you just need to calculate something, possibly on a different thread, and get the result back with proper exception handling, you can use `async` and `future`. These are defined in `<future>` and are easier to use than directly using `thread` or `jthread`.

Writing multithreaded code is discussed in detail in Chapter 27, "Multithreaded Programming with C++."

Type Traits

Type traits are defined in `<type_traits>` and provide information about types at compile time. They are useful when writing advanced templates and are discussed in Chapter 26, "Advanced Templates."

Standard Library Feature-Test Macros

Feature-test macros are available for Standard Library features. These are similar to the feature-test macros for core language features (discussed in Chapter 11, "Modules, Header Files, and

Miscellaneous Topics") and allow you to verify whether a certain feature is supported by your Standard Library implementation. All these macros start with `__cpp_lib_`. The following lists a few examples. Consult your favorite Standard Library Reference for a complete list of all possible Standard Library feature-test macros.

- `__cpp_lib_concepts`
- `__cpp_lib_ranges`
- `__cpp_lib_scoped_lock`
- `__cpp_lib_atomic_float`
- `__cpp_lib_constexpr_vector`
- `__cpp_lib_constexpr_tuple`
- `__cpp_lib_filesystem`
- `__cpp_lib_three_way_comparison`
- `...`

The value of such a macro is a number representing the month and year when a specific feature was added or updated. The date is formatted as `YYYYMM`. For example, the value of `__cpp_lib_filesystem` is 201703, i.e., March 2017.

As Chapter 11 explains, the core language feature-test macros are always available for you to use, without having to include any header. However, the Standard Library feature-test macros are defined in `<version>`. As all feature-test macros are macros, you know from Chapter 11 that importing the named module `std` or `std.compat` will not make those macros available to your code. Chapter 11 also explains that all C++ headers, such as `<version>`, are importable; thus, you have two options to get access to the macros defined in `<version>`:

```
import <version>;
```

or

```
#include <version>
```

Here is a full example:

```
import std;
import <version>; // Important to get access to the feature-test macros!
using namespace std;

int main()
{
#ifdef __cpp_lib_constexpr_vector
    println("std::vector is constexpr!");
#else
    println("Bummer! std::vector is NOT constexpr!");
#endif
}
```

> **NOTE** *You will rarely need these feature-test macros, unless you are writing cross-platform and cross-compiler code. In that case, you might want to know if certain functionality is supported by a given Standard Library implementation so that you can provide fallback code in case a feature is missing. Chapter 34, "Developing Cross-Platform and Cross-Language Applications," discusses cross-platform development.*

<version>

`<version>` can be used to query for implementation-dependent information about the C++ Standard Library that you are using. What exactly your `<version>` provides depends on your library implementation. The following could possibly be exposed: version number, release date, and copyright notice.

Additionally, as explained in the previous section, `<version>` exposes all Standard Library feature-test macros.

Source Location

`std::source_location`, defined in `<source_location>`, can be used to query information about your source code, such as filename, function name, line number, and column number, and replaces the old C-style macros `__FILE__` and `__LINE__`. Example use cases are to provide source code information when logging messages or when throwing exceptions. Chapter 14 gives an example of both these use cases.

Stack Trace

`<stacktrace>` defines the `std::stacktrace` and `std::stacktrace_entry` classes. These can be used to get a stack trace at any given moment in time and to iterate and inspect each individual entry, known as a *frame*. See Chapter 14 for an example.

Containers

The Standard Library provides implementations of commonly used data structures such as linked lists and queues. When you use C++, you should not need to write such data structures again. The data structures are implemented using a concept called *containers*, which store information called *elements*, in a way that implements the data structure (linked list, queue, and so on) appropriately. Different data structures have different insertion, deletion, and access behavior and performance characteristics. It is important to be familiar with the available data structures so that you can choose the most appropriate one for any given task.

All the containers in the Standard Library are class templates, so you can use them to store any type, from built-in types such as `int` and `double` to your own classes. Each container instance stores objects of only one type; that is, they are *homogeneous collections*. If you need non-fixed-sized heterogeneous collections, you can wrap each element in an `std::any` instance and store those `any` instances in a container. Alternatively, you can store `std::variant` instances in a container. A `variant` can be used if the number of different required types is limited and known at compile time. Or you can create a class that has multiple derived classes, and each derived class can wrap an object of your required type. Both `any` and `variant` are discussed in Chapter 24.

> **NOTE** *The C++ Standard Library containers are homogeneous: they allow elements of only one type in each container.*

The C++ standard specifies the *interface*, but not the *implementation*, of each container and algorithm. Thus, different vendors are free to provide different implementations. However, the standard also specifies performance requirements as part of the interface, which the implementations must meet.

This section provides an overview of the various containers available in the Standard Library.

Sequential Containers

The Standard Library provides five sequential containers: `vector`, `list`, `forward_list`, `deque`, and `array`.

vector

`vector` is defined in `<vector>` and stores a sequence of elements while providing random access to these elements. You can think of a `vector` as an array of elements that grows dynamically as you insert elements and additionally provides some bounds checking. Like an array, the elements of a `vector` are stored in contiguous memory.

> **NOTE** *A* `vector` *in C++ is a synonym for a dynamic array: an array that grows and shrinks automatically in response to the number of elements it stores.*

`vector` provides fast element insertion and deletion (amortized constant time) at the end of the `vector`. Amortized constant time insertion means that most of the time insertions are done in constant time O(1) (Chapter 4, "Designing Professional C++ Programs," explains big-O notation). However, sometimes the `vector` needs to grow in size to accommodate new elements, which has a complexity of O(*N*). On average, this results in O(1) complexity or amortized constant time. Details are explained in Chapter 18, "Standard Library Containers." A `vector` has slower (linear time) insertion and deletion anywhere else, because the operation must move all the elements "up" or "down" by one to make room for the new element or to fill the space left by the deleted element. Like arrays, `vector`s provide fast (constant time) access to any of their elements.

Even though inserting and removing elements in the middle of a `vector` requires moving other elements up or down, a `vector` should be your default container! Often, a `vector` will be faster than, for example, a linked list, even for inserting and removing elements in the middle. The reason is that a vector is stored contiguously in memory, while a linked list is scattered around in memory. Computers are extremely efficient to work with contiguous data, which makes vector operations fast. You should only use something like a linked list if a performance profiler (discussed in Chapter 29, "Writing Efficient C++") tells you that it performs better than a vector.

NOTE *The* vector *container should be your default container.*

There is a template specialization available for vector<bool> to store Boolean values in a vector. This specialization optimizes space allocation for the Boolean elements; however, the standard does not specify how an implementation of vector<bool> should optimize space. The difference between the vector<bool> specialization and the bitset discussed later in this chapter is that the bitset container is of fixed size, while vector<bool> automatically grows or shrinks when needed.

list

list is a *doubly linked list* structure and is defined in <list>. Like an array or vector, it stores a sequence of elements. However, unlike an array or vector, the elements of a list are not necessarily contiguous in memory. Instead, each element in the list specifies where to find the next and previous elements in the list (usually via pointers), which is why it's called a *doubly linked list*.

The performance characteristics of a list are the exact opposite of a vector. They provide slow (linear time) element lookup and access, but quick (constant time) insertion and deletion of elements once the relevant position has been found. Still, as discussed in the previous section, a vector is usually faster than a list. Use a profiler (discussed in Chapter 29) to be sure.

forward_list

forward_list, defined in <forward_list>, is a *singly linked list*, compared to the list container, which is doubly linked. forward_list supports forward iteration only and requires a bit less memory than a list. Like list, forward_list allows constant-time insertion and deletion anywhere once the relevant position has been found, and there is no fast random access to elements.

deque

The name deque is an abbreviation for a *double-ended queue*. A deque, defined in <deque>, provides quick (constant time) element access. It also provides fast (constant time) insertion and deletion at both ends of the sequence, but it provides slow (linear time) insertion and deletion in the middle of the sequence. The elements of a deque are not stored contiguously in memory, and thus a deque might be slower than a vector.

You could use a deque instead of a vector when you need to insert or remove elements from either end of the sequence but still need fast access to all elements. However, this requirement does not apply to many programming problems; in most cases, a vector is recommended.

array

array, defined in <array>, is a replacement for standard C-style arrays. Sometimes you know the exact number of elements in your container up front, and you don't need the flexibility of a vector or a `list`, which are able to grow dynamically to accommodate new elements. An `array` is perfect for such fixed-sized collections, and it has a bit less overhead compared to a `vector`; it's basically a thin wrapper around standard C-style arrays. There are a number of advantages in using `arrays` instead of standard C-style arrays: they always know their own size and do not automatically get cast to a pointer to avoid certain types of bugs. Also, `arrays` do not provide insertion or deletion; they have a fixed size. The advantage of having a fixed size is that this allows an `array` to be allocated on the stack, rather than always demanding access to the free store as `vector` does. Access to elements is very fast (constant time), just as with `vectors`.

> **NOTE** *The* `vector`, `list`, `forward_list`, `deque`, *and* `array` *containers are called sequential containers because they store a sequence of elements.*

Sequential Views

The Standard Library provides two sequential views: `span` and `mdspan`.

span

A `span`, defined in `<span>`, represents a view on a contiguous sequence of data. It can be either a read-only view or a view with read/write access to the underlying elements. A `span` allows you to write a single function that can work with data coming from, for example, `vectors`, `arrays`, C-style arrays, and so on. Chapter 18 discusses `span` in more detail.

> **NOTE** *When writing a function accepting, for example, a* `const vector<T>&`, *consider accepting a* `span<const T>` *instead, so the function can work with views and subviews of data sequences coming from* `vectors`, `arrays`, *C-style arrays, and more.*

mdspan

An `mdspan`, defined in `<mdspan>`, is similar to a `span` but represents a multidimensional view on a contiguous sequence of data. Just as a `span`, it can be a read-only view or a view with read/write access to the underlying elements. Chapter 18 discusses `mdspan` in more detail.

Container Adapters

The Standard Library provides three nonassociative container adapters: `queue`, `priority_queue`, and `stack`.

queue

The name `queue` comes directly from the definition of the English word *queue*, which means a line of people or objects. The `queue` container is defined in `<queue>` and provides standard *first in, first out* (or FIFO) semantics. A queue is a container in which you insert elements at one end and take them out at the other end. Both insertion (amortized constant time) and removal (constant time) of elements are quick.

You should use a queue structure when you want to model real-life "first-come, first-served" semantics. For example, consider a bank. As customers arrive at the bank, they get in line. As tellers become available, they serve the next customer in line, thus providing "first-come, first-served" behavior. You could implement a bank simulation by storing customer objects in a queue. As customers arrive at the bank, they are added to the end of the queue. As tellers serve customers, they start with customers at the front of the queue.

priority_queue

A `priority_queue`, also defined in `<queue>`, provides `queue` functionality in which each element has a priority. Elements are removed from the queue in priority order. In the case of priority ties, the order in which elements are removed is undefined. `priority_queue` insertion and deletion are generally slower than simple `queue` insertion and deletion, because the elements must be reordered to support the priority ordering.

You can use `priority_queues` to model "queues with exceptions." For example, in the earlier bank simulation, suppose that customers with business accounts take priority over regular customers. Many real-life banks implement this behavior with two separate lines: one for business customers and one for everyone else. Any customers in the business queue are taken before customers in the other line. However, banks could also provide this behavior with a single line in which business customers move to the front of the line ahead of any non-business customers. In your program, you could use a `priority_queue` in which customers have one of two priorities: business or regular. All business customers would be serviced before all regular customers.

stack

`<stack>` defines the `stack` class, which provides standard *first-in, last-out* (FILO) semantics, also known as *last-in, first-out* (LIFO). Like a `queue`, elements are inserted and removed from the container. However, in a `stack`, the most recent element inserted is the first one removed. The name `stack` derives from a visualization of this structure as a stack of objects in which only the top object is visible. When you add an object to the stack, you hide all the objects underneath it.

The `stack` container provides fast (constant time) insertion and removal of elements. You should use the `stack` structure when you want FILO semantics. For example, an error-processing tool might want to store errors on a `stack` so that the most recent error is the first one available for a human administrator to read. Processing errors in a FILO order is often useful because newer errors sometimes obviate older ones.

> **NOTE** *Technically, the* `queue`, `priority_queue`, *and* `stack` *containers are container adapters. They are simple interfaces built on top of one of the standard sequential containers* `vector`, `list`, *or* `deque`.

Ordered Associative Containers

The Standard Library provides four ordered associative containers: `set`, `multiset`, `map`, and `multimap`. They are called *sorted* or *ordered associative containers* because they sort their elements.

set

The `set` class template is defined in `<set>`, and, as the name suggests, it is a set of elements, loosely analogous to the notion of a mathematical set: each element is unique, and there is at most one instance of the element in the set. One difference between the mathematical concept of set and `set` as implemented in the Standard Library is that in the Standard Library the elements are kept in an order. The reason for the order is that an order makes it much faster to verify whether a certain element is already in a `set`. When a client enumerates the elements, they'll come out in the ordering imposed by the type's `operator<` or a user-defined comparator. The `set` provides logarithmic insertion, deletion, and lookup. This means that, in theory, insertions and deletions are faster than for a `vector` but slower than for a `list`; while lookups are faster than for a `list`, but slower than for a `vector`. As always, use a profiler to make sure which container is faster for your use case.

You could use a `set` when you need the elements to be in an order, to have equal amounts of insertion/deletion and lookups, and you want to optimize performance for both as much as possible. For example, an inventory-tracking program in a busy bookstore might want to use a `set` to store the books. The list of books in stock must be updated whenever books arrive or are sold, so insertion and deletion should be quick. Customers also need the ability to look for a specific book, so the program should provide fast lookup as well.

Elements in a `set` cannot be modified, because this could invalidate the order of the elements. If you need to change an element, remove that element first and insert a new one with the new value.

> **NOTE** *A* `set` *could be an option instead of a* `vector` *or* `list` *if you need order and want equal performance for insertion, deletion, and lookup. It could also be an option if you want to enforce that there are no duplicate elements.*

A `set` does not allow duplicate elements. That is, each element in a `set` must be unique.

multiset

The `multiset` class template, also defined in `<set>`, is almost identical to `set`, except that a `multiset` can store duplicate elements.

map

`<map>` defines the `map` class template, which is an *associative array*. You can use it as an array in which the index can be any type, for example, a `string`. A `map` stores key/value pairs and keeps its elements in sorted order, based on the keys, not the values. It also provides an `operator[]`, which a `set` does not provide. In most other respects, it is identical to a `set`. You could use a `map` when you want to associate keys and values. For example, in the earlier bookstore example, you might want to store the books in a `map` where the key is the ISBN number of the book and the value is a `Book` object containing detailed information for that specific book.

multimap

<map> also defines the `multimap` class template, which is virtually identical to `map`, except that a `multimap` can store elements with duplicate keys.

> **NOTE** *The* `set`, `multiset`, `map`, *and* `multimap` *containers are called associative containers because they associate keys and values. This term might be slightly confusing when applied to* `sets` *and* `multisets`, *because for these the keys are themselves the values.*

Unordered Associative Containers/Hash Tables

The Standard Library supports *hash tables*, also called *unordered associative containers*. There are four unordered associative containers:

- `unordered_map` and `unordered_multimap`
- `unordered_set` and `unordered_multiset`

The first two containers are defined in <unordered_map>, while the latter two are defined in <unordered_set>. Better names would have been `hash_map`, `hash_set`, and so on. Unfortunately, hash tables were not part of the C++ Standard Library before C++11, which means a lot of third-party libraries implemented hash tables themselves by using names with "hash" as a prefix, like `hash_map`. Because of this, the C++ standard committee decided to use the prefix "unordered" instead of "hash" to avoid name clashes.

These unordered associative containers behave similar to their ordered counterparts. An `unordered_map` is similar to a standard `map` except that the standard `map` sorts its elements, while the `unordered_map` doesn't sort its elements.

Insertion, deletion, and lookup with these unordered associative containers can be done on average in constant time. In a worst-case scenario, it will be in linear time. Lookup of elements in an unordered container can be much faster than with a normal `map` or `set`, especially when there are a lot of elements in the container.

Chapter 18 explains how these unordered associative containers work and why they are called hash tables.

Flat Associative Container Adapters

C++23 introduces four flat associative container adapters:

- `flat_map` and `flat_multimap` defined in <flat_map>
- `flat_set` and `flat_multiset` defined in <flat_set>

These are adapters on top of sequential containers and provide an associative container interface. The adapted sequential containers must support random-access iterators, such as `vector` and `deque`. The `flat_map` and `flat_multimap` adapters require two underlying sequential containers, one to store the keys and another one to store the values. `flat_set` and `flat_multiset` require only one underlying sequential container to store their keys.

The interface provided by these adapters is almost identical to their ordered counterpart associative container. The only difference is that the flat adapters don't provide any of the node-related member functions, as the flat adapters are not node-based data structures. Besides that, they are almost an immediate drop-in replacement for their ordered counterparts.

Chapter 18 gives more details about these flat associative container adapters.

bitset

C and C++ programmers commonly store a set of flags in a single `int` or `long`, using one bit for each flag. Bits are set and accessed with the bitwise operators: `&`, `|`, `^`, `~`, `<<`, and `>>`. The C++ Standard Library provides a `bitset` class that abstracts this bit field manipulation, so you shouldn't need to use the bit manipulation operators anymore for such use cases.

`<bitset>` defines the `bitset` container, but this is not a container in the normal sense, in that it does not implement a specific data structure in which you insert and remove elements. A `bitset` has a fixed size. You can think of them as a sequence of Boolean values that you can read and write. However, unlike the C-style way of handling bits, the `bitset` is not limited to the size of an `int` or other elementary data types. Thus, you can have a 40-bit `bitset` or a 213-bit `bitset`. The implementation will use as much storage as it needs to implement *N* bits when you declare your `bitset` with `bitset<N>`.

Summary of Standard Library Containers

The following table summarizes the containers provided by the Standard Library. It uses the big-O notation introduced in Chapter 4 to present the performance characteristics on a container of *N* elements. An N/A entry in the table means that the operation is not part of the container semantics:

NAME	TYPE	INSERT PERFORMANCE	DELETE PERFORMANCE	LOOKUP PERFORMANCE
`vector`	Sequential	Amortized *O*(1) at the end; *O*(*N*) otherwise.	*O*(1) at the end; *O*(*N*) otherwise.	*O*(1)
	When to Use: This should be your default container. Only use another container after using a profiler to confirm it is faster than a `vector`.			
`list`	Sequential	*O*(1) at the beginning and the end, and once you are at the position where you want to insert the element.	*O*(1) at the beginning and the end, and once you are at the position where you want to delete the element.	*O*(1) to access the first or last element; *O*(*N*) otherwise.
	When to Use: Rarely. You should use a `vector`, unless a profiler tells you a `list` is faster for your use case.			

NAME	TYPE	INSERT PERFORMANCE	DELETE PERFORMANCE	LOOKUP PERFORMANCE
`forward_list`	Sequential	*O*(1) at the beginning, and once you are at the position where you want to insert the element.	*O*(1) at the beginning, and once you are at the position where you want to delete the element.	*O*(1) to access the first element; *O*(*N*) otherwise.
	When to Use: Rarely. You should use a `vector`, unless a profiler tells you a `forward_list` is faster for your use case.			
`deque`	Sequential	*O*(1) at the beginning or end; *O*(*N*) otherwise.	*O*(1) at the beginning or end; *O*(*N*) otherwise.	*O*(1)
	When to Use: Not usually needed; use a `vector` instead.			
`array`	Sequential	N/A	N/A	*O*(1)
	When to Use: When you need a fixed-size array to replace a standard C-style array.			
`queue`	Container adapter	Depends on the underlying container; *O*(1) for `list` and `deque`.	Depends on the underlying container; *O*(1) for `list` and `deque`.	N/A
	When to Use: When you want a FIFO structure.			
`priority_queue`	Container adapter	Depends on the underlying container; amortized *O*(log(*N*)) for `vector`, *O*(log(*N*)) for `deque`.	Depends on the underlying container; *O*(log(*N*)) for `vector` and `deque`.	N/A
	When to Use: When you want a queue with priority.			
`stack`	Container adapter	Depends on the underlying container; *O*(1) for `list` and `deque`, amortized *O*(1) for `vector`.	Depends on the underlying container; *O*(1) for `list`, `vector`, and `deque`.	N/A
	When to Use: When you want a FILO/LIFO structure.			

continues

(continued)

NAME	TYPE	INSERT PERFORMANCE	DELETE PERFORMANCE	LOOKUP PERFORMANCE
`set` `multiset`	Sorted associative	$O(\log(N))$	$O(\log(N))$	$O(\log(N))$
	When to Use: When you want a sorted collection of elements with equal lookup, insertion, and deletion times. Use a `set` when you want a collection of elements without duplicates.			
`map` `multimap`	Sorted associative	$O(\log(N))$	$O(\log(N))$	$O(\log(N))$
	When to Use: When you want a sorted collection to associate keys with values, that is, an associative array, with equal lookup, insertion, and deletion times.			
`unordered_map` `unordered_multimap`	Unordered associative / hash table	Average case $O(1)$; worst case $O(N)$.	Average case $O(1)$; worst case $O(N)$.	Average case $O(1)$; worst case $O(N)$.
	When to Use: When you want to associate keys with values with equal lookup, insertion, and deletion times, and you don't require the elements to be sorted. Performance can be better than with a normal `map`, but that depends on the elements.			
`unordered_set` `unordered_multiset`	Unordered associative/ hash table	Average case $O(1)$; worst case $O(N)$.	Average case $O(1)$; worst case $O(N)$.	Average case $O(1)$; worst case $O(N)$.
	When to Use: When you want a collection of elements with equal lookup, insertion, and deletion times, and you don't require the elements to be sorted. Performance can be better than with a normal `set`, but that depends on the elements.			
C++23 `flat_set` `flat_multiset`	Flat set associative container adapter	$O(N)$	$O(N)$	$O(\log(N))$
	When to Use: When you want a sorted collection of elements. Because the adapters use underlying sequential containers that have very cache-friendly memory layout, the performance is often better than the corresponding ordered container.			
C++23 `flat_map` `flat_multimap`	Flat map associative container adapter	$O(N)$	$O(N)$	$O(\log(N))$

NAME	TYPE	INSERT PERFORMANCE	DELETE PERFORMANCE	LOOKUP PERFORMANCE
	When to Use: When you want a sorted collection to associate keys with values. Because the adapters use underlying sequential containers that have very cache-friendly memory layout, the performance is often better than the corresponding ordered container.			
`bitset`	Special	N/A	N/A	O(1)
	When to Use: When you want a collection of flags.			

Note that `strings` are technically containers as well. Thus, some of the algorithms described in the material that follows also work on `strings`.

> **NOTE** `vector` *should be your default container! In practice, insertion and deletion in a* `vector` *are often faster than in a* `list` *or* `forward_list`*. This is because of how memory and caches work on modern CPUs and because of the fact that for a* `list` *or* `forward_list`*, you first need to iterate to the position where you want to insert or delete an element. Memory for a* `list` *or* `forward_list` *might be fragmented, so iteration is much slower than for a* `vector`*.*

Algorithms

In addition to containers, the Standard Library provides implementations of many generic algorithms. An *algorithm* is a strategy for performing a particular task, such as sorting or searching. These algorithms are implemented as function templates, so they work on most of the different container types. Note that the algorithms are not generally part of the containers. The Standard Library takes the approach of separating the *data* (containers) from the *functionality* (algorithms). Although this approach seems counter to the spirit of object-oriented programming, it is necessary in order to support generic programming in the Standard Library. The guiding principle of *orthogonality* maintains that algorithms and containers are independent, with (almost) any algorithm working with (almost) any container.

> **NOTE** *Although the algorithms and containers are theoretically independent, some containers provide certain algorithms in the form of class member functions because the generic algorithms do not perform well on those particular containers. For example,* `set` *provides its own* `find()` *algorithm that is faster than the generic* `find()` *algorithm. You should use the container-specific member function form of an algorithm, if provided, because it is generally more efficient or appropriate for the container at hand.*

Note that the generic algorithms do not work directly on containers; instead, they either use iterators or work on ranges, both discussed in detail in Chapter 17, "Understanding Iterators and the Ranges Library."

This section gives an overview of what kinds of algorithms are available in the Standard Library without going into detail. Chapter 20, "Mastering Standard Library Algorithms," discusses a selection of algorithms with coding examples. For the exact prototypes of all the available algorithms, consult your favorite Standard Library reference.

There are more than 100 algorithms in the Standard Library. The following sections divide these algorithms into different categories. The algorithms are defined in `<algorithm>` unless otherwise noted. Note that whenever the following algorithms are specified as working on a "sequence" of elements, that sequence is presented to the algorithm via iterators.

> **NOTE** *When examining the list of algorithms, remember that the Standard Library is designed with generality in mind, so it adds generality that might never be used but that, if required, would be essential. You may not need every algorithm or need to worry about the more obscure parameters that are there for anticipated generality. It is important only to be aware of what's available in case you ever find it useful.*

Non-modifying Sequence Algorithms

The non-modifying algorithms are those that look at a sequence of elements and return some information about the elements. As "non-modifying" algorithms, they cannot change the values of elements or the order of elements within the sequence. This category contains three types of algorithms: searching, comparing, and counting. The following sections briefly summarize the various non-modifying algorithms. With these algorithms, you should rarely need to write a `for` loop to iterate over a sequence of values.

Searching Algorithms

These algorithms do not require the sequence to be sorted. *N* is the size of the sequence to search in, and *M* is the size of the pattern to find:

NAME	SYNOPSIS	COMPLEXITY
`adjacent_find()`	Finds the first instance of two consecutive elements that are equal to each other or are equivalent to each other as specified by a predicate.	O(*N*)
`find()` `find_if()`	Finds the first element that matches a value or causes a predicate to return `true`.	O(*N*)
`find_first_of()`	Like `find`, but searches for one of several elements at the same time.	O(*N***M*)
`find_if_not()`	Finds the first element that causes a predicate to return `false`.	O(*N*)

NAME	SYNOPSIS	COMPLEXITY
`find_end()`	Finds the last subsequence in a sequence that matches another sequence or whose elements are equivalent, as specified by a predicate.	$O(M*(N-M))$
`search()`	Finds the first subsequence in a sequence that matches another sequence or whose elements are equivalent, as specified by a predicate[1].	$O(N*M)$[1]
`search_n()`	Finds the first instance of *n* consecutive elements that are equal to a given value or relate to that value according to a predicate.	$O(N)$

[1]`search()` accepts an optional extra parameter to specify the searching algorithm to use (`default_searcher`, `boyer_moore_searcher`, or `boyer_moore_horspool_searcher`). With the Boyer–Moore searchers, the worst-case complexity is $O(N+M)$ when the pattern is not found, and $O(N*M)$ when the pattern is found.

Comparison Algorithms

The following comparison algorithms are provided. None of them requires the source sequences to be ordered. All of them have a linear worst-case complexity:

NAME	SYNOPSIS
`equal()`	Determines whether two sequences are equal by checking whether parallel elements are equal or match a predicate.
`mismatch()`	Returns the first element in each sequence that does not match the element in the same location in the other sequence.
`lexicographical_compare()`	Compares two sequences to determine their "lexicographical" ordering. This algorithm compares each element of the first sequence with its equivalent element in the second. If one element is less than the other, that sequence is lexicographically first. If the elements are equal, it compares the next elements in order.
`lexicographical_compare_three_way()`	Compares two sequences to determine their "lexicographical" ordering using three-way comparisons and returns a comparison category type (`strong_ordering`, `weak_ordering`, or `partial_ordering`).
`all_of()`	Returns `true` if a given predicate returns `true` for all the elements in the sequence or if the sequence is empty; `false` otherwise.

continues

(continued)

NAME	SYNOPSIS
`any_of()`	Returns `true` if a given predicate returns `true` for at least one element in the sequence; `false` otherwise.
`none_of()`	Returns `true` if a given predicate returns `false` for all the elements in the sequence or if the sequence is empty; `false` otherwise.

Counting Algorithms

The following counting algorithms are available. None of them requires the source sequences to be ordered. All of them have a linear worst-case complexity:

NAME	SYNOPSIS
`count()` `count_if()`	Counts the number of elements matching a value or that cause a predicate to return `true`.

Modifying Sequence Algorithms

The modifying algorithms modify some or all of the elements in a sequence. Some of them modify elements *in place* so that the original sequence changes. Others copy the results to a different sequence so that the original sequence remains unchanged. All of them have a linear worst-case complexity. The following table summarizes the modifying algorithms:

NAME	SYNOPSIS
`copy()` `copy_backward()`	Copies elements from one sequence to another.
`copy_if()`	Copies elements for which a predicate returns `true` from one sequence to another.
`copy_n()`	Copies *n* elements from one sequence to another.
`fill()`	Sets all elements in the sequence to a new value.
`fill_n()`	Sets the first *n* elements in the sequence to a new value.
`generate()`	Calls a given function to generate a new value for each element in the sequence.
`generate_n()`	Calls a given function to generate a new value for the first *n* elements in the sequence.

NAME	SYNOPSIS
`move()` `move_backward()`	Moves elements from one sequence to another using efficient move semantics (see Chapter 9).

`remove()`
`remove_if()`
`remove_copy()`
`remove_copy_if()`
	Removes all elements that match a given value or that cause a predicate to return `true`, either in place or by copying the results to a different sequence.

`replace()`
`replace_if()`
`replace_copy()`
`replace_copy_if()`
	Replaces all elements matching a value or that cause a predicate to return `true` with a new element, either in place or by copying the results to a different sequence.

`reverse()` `reverse_copy()`	Reverses the order of the elements in the sequence, either in place or by copying the results to a different sequence.
`rotate()` `rotate_copy()`	Swaps the first and second "halves" of the sequence, either in place or by copying the results to a different sequence. The two subsequences to be swapped need not be equal in size.
`sample()`	Selects *n* random elements from the sequence.
`shift_left()` `shift_right()`	Shifts the elements in a sequence left or right by a given number of positions. Elements are moved to their new position. Elements that fall of either end of the sequence are removed. `shift_left()` returns an iterator to the end of the new sequence; `shift_right()` returns an iterator to the beginning of the new sequence.
`shuffle()` `random_shuffle()`	Shuffles the sequence by randomly reordering the elements. It is possible to specify the properties of the random number generator used for shuffling. `random_shuffle()` is deprecated since C++14, and is removed starting with C++17.
`transform()`	Calls a unary function on each element of a sequence or a binary function on parallel elements of two sequences, and stores the results in a destination sequence. If the source and destination sequences are the same, the transformation happens in-place.
`unique()` `unique_copy()`	Removes consecutive duplicates from the sequence, either in place or by copying results to a different sequence.

Operational Algorithms

Operational algorithms execute a function on individual elements of a sequence. There are two operational algorithms provided. Both have a linear complexity and do not require the source sequence to be ordered:

NAME	SYNOPSIS
`for_each()`	Executes a function on each element in the sequence. The sequence is specified with a begin and end iterator.
`for_each_n()`	Similar to `for_each()` but only processes the first *n* elements in the sequence. The sequence is specified by a begin iterator and a number of elements (*n*).

Swap Algorithms

The C++ Standard Library provides the following swap algorithms:

NAME	SYNOPSIS
`iter_swap()` `swap_ranges()`	Swaps two elements or sequences of elements.

Partitioning Algorithms

A sequence is partitioned on a certain predicate, if all elements for which the predicate returns `true` are before all elements for which it returns `false`. The first element in the sequence that does not satisfy the predicate is called the *partition point*. The Standard Library provides the following partition algorithms:

NAME	SYNOPSIS	COMPLEXITY
`is_partitioned()`	Returns `true` if all elements for which a predicate returns `true` are before all elements for which it returns `false`.	Linear
`partition()`	Sorts the sequence such that all elements for which a predicate returns `true` are before all elements for which it returns `false`, without preserving the original order of the elements within each partition.	Linear
`stable_partition()`	Sorts the sequence such that all elements for which a predicate returns `true` are before all elements for which it returns `false`, while preserving the original order of the elements within each partition.	Linear logarithmic
`partition_copy()`	Copies elements from one sequence to two different sequences. The target sequence is selected based on the result of a predicate, either `true` or `false`.	Linear
`partition_point()`	Returns an iterator such that all elements before this iterator return `true` for a predicate and all elements after this iterator return `false` for that predicate.	Logarithmic

Sorting Algorithms

The Standard Library provides several different sorting algorithms with varying performance guarantees:

NAME	SYNOPSIS	COMPLEXITY
`is_sorted()`	Returns `true` if a sequence is sorted, `false` otherwise.	Linear
`is_sorted_until()`	Finds the largest sorted subrange starting at the beginning of the given range of elements.	Linear
`nth_element()`	Relocates the nth element of the sequence such that the element in the position pointed to by n^{th} is the element that would be in that position if the whole range were sorted, and it rearranges all elements such that all elements preceding the nth element are less than the new n^{th} element, and the ones following it are greater than the new n^{th} element.	Linear
`partial_sort()` `partial_sort_copy()`	Partially sorts the sequence: the first *n* elements (specified by iterators) are sorted; the rest are not. They are sorted either in place or by copying them to a new sequence.	Linear logarithmic
`stable_sort()` `sort()`	Sorts elements in place, either preserving the order of duplicate elements (stable) or not.	Linear logarithmic

Binary Search Algorithms

The following binary search algorithms are normally used on sorted sequences. Technically, they only require the sequence to be at least partitioned on the element that is searched for. This could, for example, be achieved by applying `std::partition()`. A sorted sequence also meets this requirement. All these algorithms have logarithmic complexity:

NAME	SYNOPSIS
`lower_bound()`	Finds the first element in a sequence not less than (that is, greater or equal to) a given value.
`upper_bound()`	Finds the first element in a sequence greater than a given value.
`equal_range()`	Returns a `pair` containing the result of both `lower_bound()` and `upper_bound()`.
`binary_search()`	Returns `true` if a given value is found in a sequence; `false` otherwise.

Set Algorithms on Sorted Sequences

Set algorithms are special modifying algorithms that perform set operations on sequences. They are most appropriate on sequences from `set` containers, but work on sorted sequences from most containers:

NAME	SYNOPSIS	COMPLEXITY
`includes()`	Determines whether every element from one sorted sequence is in another sorted sequence.	Linear

`set_union()`
`set_intersection()`
`set_difference()`
`set_symmetric_difference()`
	Performs the specified set operation on two sorted sequences, copying results to a third sorted sequence.	Linear

Other Algorithms on Sorted Sequences

The Standard Library provides the following additional algorithms that work on sorted sequences:

NAME	SYNOPSIS	COMPLEXITY
`inplace_merge()`	Merges two sorted sequences in place.	Linear logarithmic
`merge()`	Merges two sorted sequences by copying them to a new sequence.	Linear

Heap Algorithms

A *heap* is a standard data structure in which the elements of an array or sequence are ordered in a semi-sorted fashion so that finding the "top" element is quick. For example, a heap data structure is typically used to implement a `priority_queue`. Six algorithms allow you to work with heaps:

NAME	SYNOPSIS	COMPLEXITY
`is_heap()`	Returns `true` if a range of elements is a heap, `false` otherwise.	Linear
`is_heap_until()`	Finds the largest subrange that is a heap, starting at the beginning of the given range of elements.	Linear
`make_heap()`	Creates a heap from a range of elements.	Linear
`push_heap()` `pop_heap()`	Adds an element to, or removes an element from, a heap.	Logarithmic
`sort_heap()`	Converts a heap into a range of ascending sorted elements.	Linear logarithmic

Minimum/Maximum Algorithms

The following algorithms are provided to find minimum and maximum elements and to clamp values:

NAME	SYNOPSIS
`clamp()`	Makes sure a value (*v*) is between a given minimum (*lo*) and maximum (*hi*). Returns a reference to *lo* if *v* < *lo*; returns a reference to *hi* if *v* > *hi*; otherwise returns a reference to *v*.
`min()` `max()`	Returns the minimum or maximum of two or more values.
`minmax()`	Returns the minimum and maximum of two or more values as a `pair`.
`min_element()` `max_element()`	Returns the minimum or maximum element in a sequence.
`minmax_element()`	Returns the minimum and maximum element in a sequence as a `pair`.

Numerical Processing Algorithms

The following numerical processing algorithms are defined in `<numeric>`. None of them require the source sequences to be ordered. All of them have a linear complexity:

NAME	SYNOPSIS
`iota()`	Fills a sequence with successively incrementing values starting with a given value.
`adjacent_difference()`	Generates a new sequence in which each element is the difference (or other binary operation) of the second and first of each adjacent pair of elements in the source sequence.
`partial_sum()`	Generates a new sequence in which each element is the sum (or other binary operation) of an element and all its preceding elements in the source sequence.
`exclusive_scan()` `inclusive_scan()`	These are similar to `partial_sum()`. An inclusive scan is identical to a partial sum if the given summation operation is associative. However, `inclusive_scan()` sums in a nondeterministic order, while `partial_sum()` left to right, so for nonassociative summation operations the result of the former is nondeterministic. The `exclusive_scan()` algorithm also sums in a nondeterministic order. For `inclusive_scan()`, the ith element is included in the ith sum, just as for `partial_sum()`. For `exclusive_scan()`, the ith element is not included in the ith sum.
`transform_exclusive_scan()` `transform_inclusive_scan()`	Applies a transformation to each element in a sequence, then performs an exclusive/inclusive scan.

continues

(continued)

NAME	SYNOPSIS
`accumulate()`	"Accumulates" the values of all the elements in a sequence. The default behavior is to sum the elements, but the caller can supply a different binary function instead.
`inner_product()`	Similar to `accumulate()`, but works on two sequences. This algorithm calls a binary function (multiplication by default) on parallel elements in the sequences, accumulating the result using another binary function (addition by default). If the sequences represent mathematical vectors, the algorithm calculates the dot product of the vectors.
`reduce()`	Similar to `accumulate()`, but supports parallel execution. The order of evaluation for `reduce()` is nondeterministic, while it's from left to right for `accumulate()`. This means that the behavior of the former is nondeterministic if the given binary operation is not associative or not commutative.
`transform_reduce()`	Applies a transformation to each element in a sequence, then performs a `reduce()`.

Permutation Algorithms

A *permutation* of a sequence contains the same elements but in a different order. The following algorithms are provided to work with permutations:

NAME	SYNOPSIS	COMPLEXITY
`is_permutation()`	Returns `true` if the elements in one range are a permutation of the elements in another range.	Quadratic
`next_permutation()` `prev_permutation()`	Modifies the sequence by transforming it into its "next" or "previous" lexicographical permutation. Successive calls to one or the other will permute the sequence into all possible permutations of its elements, if you start with a properly sorted sequence. This algorithm returns `false` if no more permutations exist.	Linear

Choosing an Algorithm

The number and capabilities of the algorithms might overwhelm you at first. It can be difficult to see how to apply them in the beginning. However, now that you have an idea of the available options, you are better able to tackle your program designs. The following chapters cover the details of how to use these algorithms in your code.

Ranges Library

The ranges library makes it easier and more elegant to work with sequences of elements. Ranges provide nicer and easier-to-read syntax and eliminate the possibility of mismatching begin/end iterators. Additionally, range adapters allow you to lazily transform and filter underlying sequences, and range factories are provided to build up ranges.

Most algorithms discussed in the previous sections have variants that work with ranges in addition to iterators. Those variants are often called *range-based algorithms* or *constrained algorithms* because they have proper template type parameter constraints in the form of concepts. This allows the compiler to issue better error messages if such a constrained algorithm is used wrongly.

Additionally, C++23 introduces the following algorithms that are available only in a constrained variant. All of them have a linear complexity.

NAME	SYNOPSIS
`contains()` `contains_subrange()`	Returns `true` if a given range contains a given value, respectively, a given subrange, `false` otherwise.
`starts_with()` `ends_with()`	Returns `true` if a given range starts, respectively, ends with another given range, `false` otherwise.

`find_last()`
`find_last_if()`
`find_last_if_not()`
	Finds the last element in a given range that either matches a given value, or for which a given predicate returns `true`, or for which a given predicate returns `false`. The result is a subrange starting at the found element until the end of the range.

`fold_left()`
`fold_left_first()`
`fold_right()`
`fold_right_last()`
`fold_left_with_iter()`
`fold_left_first_with_iter()`
	Folds the elements of a given range left or right. `fold_left()` and `fold_right()` accept an initial value as one of their arguments, and return the result of the fold operation. `fold_left_first()` uses the first element in a given range as the starting value, while `fold_right_last()` uses the last element in a given range as the starting value. Both of these return an `optional` containing the result, or an empty `optional` if applied to an empty range. The last two variants return an instance of `fold_left_with_iter_result`, respectively, `fold_left_first_with_iter_result` that you can use to inspect the result of the fold operation.

The ranges library is defined in `<ranges>` and lives in the `std::ranges` namespace. Chapter 17 discusses the ranges library, while Chapter 20 discusses unconstrained and constrained algorithms with coding examples.

What's Missing from the Standard Library

The Standard Library is powerful, but it's not perfect. Here are two examples of missing functionality:

- The Standard Library does not guarantee any thread safety for accessing containers simultaneously from multiple threads.
- The Standard Library does not provide any generic tree or graph structures. Although `map` and `set` are generally implemented as balanced binary trees, the Standard Library does not expose this implementation in the interface. If you need a tree or graph structure for something like writing a parser, you need to implement your own or find an implementation in another library.

It is important to keep in mind that the Standard Library is *extensible*. You can write your own containers and algorithms that work with existing algorithms and containers. So, if the Standard Library doesn't provide exactly what you need, consider writing your desired code such that it works with the Standard Library. Chapter 25 covers the topic of customizing and extending the Standard Library with custom algorithms and custom containers. Alternatively, you can consider buying or licensing a Standard Library-compliant third-party library that provides the required functionality. See Chapter 4, "Designing Professional C++ Programs," for a discussion on using third-party libraries and licensing options.

SUMMARY

This chapter provided an overview of the C++ Standard Library, which is the most important library that you will use in your code. It subsumes the C library and includes additional facilities for strings, I/O, error handling, and other tasks. It also includes generic containers, algorithms, and the ranges library. The following chapters describe the Standard Library in more detail.

EXERCISES

By solving the following exercises, you can practice the material discussed in this chapter. Solutions to all exercises are available with the code download on the book's website at `www.wiley.com/go/proc++6e`. However, if you are stuck on an exercise, first reread parts of this chapter to try to find an answer yourself before looking at the solution from the website.

Exercise 16-1: The C++ Standard Library provides a whole selection of containers for you to choose from. What should be your preferred container and why?

Exercise 16-2: What are the differences between a `map` and an `unordered_map`?

Exercise 16-3: What are vocabulary types? Besides the vocabulary types already used earlier in this book, this chapter introduced a few additional vocabulary types provided by the C++ Standard Library. What are they?

Exercise 16-4: A self-service restaurant usually has a spring-loaded mechanism containing plates. As a customer, you take a plate from the top. When plates are cleaned and ready to be used again, they are placed on top of any remaining plates in the mechanism. How would you model such a system in C++?

Exercise 16-5: What is a partition?

17

Understanding Iterators and the Ranges Library

WHAT'S IN THIS CHAPTER?

- Details on iterators
- How to use stream iterators
- What iterator adapters are, and how to use the standard iterator adapters
- What the ranges library is, consisting of ranges, range-based and constrained algorithms, projections, views, and factories

WILEY.COM DOWNLOADS FOR THIS CHAPTER

Please note that all the code examples for this chapter are available as part of this chapter's code download on the book's website at `www.wiley.com/go/proc++6e` on the Download Code tab.

Chapter 16, "Overview of the C++ Standard Library," introduces the Standard Library, describes its basic philosophy, and provides an overview of the provided functionality. This chapter begins a more-in-depth tour of the Standard Library by covering the ideas behind iterators used throughout a big part of the library. It also discusses the available stream iterators and iterator adapters. The second part of the chapter discusses the ranges library, a powerful library that allows for more *functional-style programming*: you write code that specifies *what* you want to accomplish instead of *how*.

ITERATORS

The Standard Library uses the iterator pattern to provide a generic abstraction for accessing the elements of a container. Each container provides a container-specific iterator, which is a glorified pointer that knows how to iterate over the elements of that specific container, i.e., an iterator supports traversing the elements of a container. The different iterators for the various containers adhere to standard interfaces defined by the C++ standard. Thus, even though the containers provide different functionality, the iterators present a common interface to code that wants to work with elements of the containers. This results in code that is easier to read and write, less error-prone (e.g., iterators are easier to use correctly compared to pointer arithmetic), more efficient (especially for containers that do not support random access, such as `std::list` and `forward_list`; see Chapter 16), and easier to debug (e.g., iterators could perform bounds checking in debug builds of your code). Additionally, when using iterators to iterate over the contents of a container, the underlying implementation of the container could change completely without any impact on your iterator-based code.

You can think of an iterator as a pointer to a specific element of the container. Like pointers to elements in an array, iterators can move to the next element with `operator++`. Similarly, you can usually use `operator*` and `operator->` on the iterator to access the actual element or field of the element. Some iterators allow comparison with `operator==` and `operator!=`, and support `operator--` for moving to previous elements.

All iterators must be copy constructible, copy assignable, and destructible. Lvalues of iterators must be swappable. Different containers provide iterators with slightly different additional capabilities. The standard defines six categories of iterators, as summarized in the following table:

ITERATOR CATEGORY	OPERATIONS REQUIRED	COMMENTS
Input (also known as Read)	`operator++, *, ->, =, ==, !=` copy constructor	Provides read-only access, forward only (no `operator--` to move backward). Iterators can be assigned, copied, and compared for equality.
Output (also known as Write)	`operator++, *, =` copy constructor	Provides write-only access, forward only. Iterators can be assigned, but cannot be compared for equality. Specific to output iterators is that you can do `*iter = value`. Note the absence of `operator->`. Provides both prefix and postfix `operator++`.
Forward	Capabilities of input iterators, plus default constructor	Provides read access, forward only. Iterators can be assigned, copied, and compared for equality.

ITERATOR CATEGORY	OPERATIONS REQUIRED	COMMENTS
Bidirectional	Capabilities of forward iterators, plus `operator--`	Provides everything a forward iterator provides. Iterators can also move backward to a previous element. Provides both prefix and postfix `operator--`.
Random access	Bidirectional capability, plus the following: `operator+, -, +=, -=, <, >, <=, >=, []`	Equivalent to raw pointers: support pointer arithmetic, array index syntax, and all forms of comparison.
Contiguous	Random-access capability and logically adjacent elements of the container must be physically adjacent in memory	Examples of this are iterators of `std::array`, `vector` (not `vector<bool>`), `string`, and `string_view`.

According to this table, there are six types of iterators: input, output, forward, bidirectional, random access, and contiguous. There is no formal class hierarchy of these iterators. However, one can deduce a hierarchy based on the functionality they are required to provide. Specifically, every contiguous iterator is also random access, every random-access iterator is also bidirectional, every bidirectional iterator is also forward, and every forward iterator is also input. Iterators that additionally satisfy the requirements for output iterators are called *mutable iterators*; otherwise, they are called *constant iterators*. Figure 17.1 shows such hierarchy. Dotted lines are used because the figure is not a real class hierarchy.

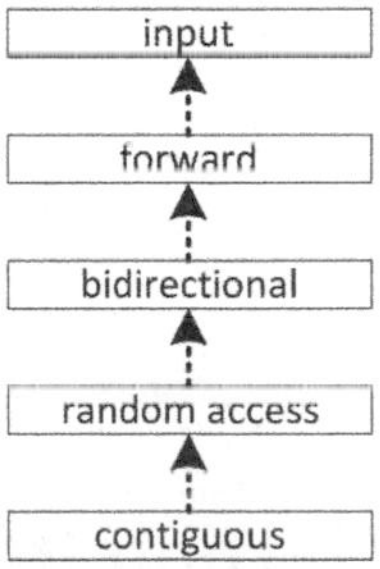

input
forward
bidirectional
random access
contiguous

FIGURE 17.1

The standard technique for an algorithm to specify what kind of iterators it requires is to use names similar to the following for its iterator template type parameters: `InputIterator`, `OutputIterator`, `ForwardIterator`, `BidirectionalIterator`, `RandomAccessIterator`, and `ContiguousIterator`. These names are just names: they don't provide binding type checking. Therefore, you could, for example, try to call an algorithm expecting a `RandomAccessIterator` by passing a bidirectional iterator. The template cannot do type checking, so it would allow this instantiation. However, the code in the function that uses the random-access iterator capabilities would fail to compile on the bidirectional iterator. Thus, the requirement is enforced, just not where you would expect. The error message can therefore be somewhat confusing. For example, attempting to use the generic `sort()` algorithm, which requires a random-access iterator, on a `list`, which provides only a bidirectional iterator, can result in a cryptic error. The following is the error generated by Visual C++ 2022:

```
...\MSVC\14.37.32705\include\algorithm(8061,45): error C2676: binary '-': 'const
std::_List_unchecked_iterator<std::_List_val<std::_List_simple_types<_Ty>>>' does
not define this operator or a conversion to a type acceptable to the
predefined operator
        with
        [
            _Ty=int
        ]
```

Later in this chapter, the ranges library is introduced, which comes with range-based and constrained versions of most Standard Library algorithms. These constrained algorithms have proper type constraints (see Chapter 12, "Writing Generic Code with Templates") for their template type parameters. Hence, the compiler can provide clearer error messages if you try to execute such an algorithm on a container that provides the wrong type of iterators.

> **NOTE** *Iterators mediate between algorithms and containers. They provide a standard interface to traverse the elements of a container in sequence so that any algorithm can work on any container as long as the container provides the algorithm's required iterator category.*

Iterators are implemented similarly to smart pointer classes in that they overload the specific desired operators. Consult Chapter 15, "Overloading C++ Operators," for details on operator overloading.

The basic iterator operations are similar to those supported by raw pointers, so a raw pointer can be a legitimate iterator for certain containers. In fact, the `vector` iterator could technically be implemented as a simple raw pointer. However, as a client of the containers, you need not worry about the implementation details; you can simply use the iterator abstraction.

> **NOTE** *Iterators might, or might not, be implemented internally as pointers, so this text uses the term* **refers to** *instead of* **points to** *when discussing the elements accessible via an iterator.*

Getting Iterators for Containers

Every data structure of the Standard Library that supports iterators provides public type aliases for its iterator types, called `iterator` and `const_iterator`. For example, a `const` iterator for a `vector` of `int`s has as type `std::vector<int>::const_iterator`. Containers that allow you to iterate over their elements in reverse order also provide public type aliases called `reverse_iterator` and `const_reverse_iterator`. This way, clients can use the container iterators without worrying about the actual types.

> **NOTE** `const_iterator`*s and* `const_reverse_iterator`*s provide read-only access to elements of a container.*

The containers also provide a member function `begin()` that returns an iterator referring to the first element in the container. The `end()` member function returns an iterator to the "past-the-end" value of the sequence of elements. That is, `end()` returns an iterator that is equal to the result of applying `operator++` to an iterator referring to the last element in the sequence. Together, `begin()` and `end()` provide a *half-open range* that includes the first element but not the last. The reason for this apparent complication is to support empty ranges (containers without any elements), in which case `begin()` is equal to `end()`. The half-open range bounded by iterators `begin()` and `end()` is often written mathematically like this: [begin, end).

Additionally, the following member functions are available:

- `cbegin()` and `cend()` returning `const` iterators
- `rbegin()` and `rend()` returning reverse iterators
- `crbegin()` and `crend()` returning `const` reverse iterators

> **NOTE** *A sequence specified by two iterators is called a* **common range** *to disambiguate it from ranges defined by the ranges library, discussed later in this chapter.*

`<iterator>` also provides the following global nonmember functions to retrieve specific iterators for a container:

FUNCTION NAME	FUNCTION SYNOPSIS
`begin()` `end()`	Returns a non-`const` iterator to the first, and one past the last, element in a sequence
`cbegin()` `cend()`	Returns a `const` iterator to the first, and one past the last, element in a sequence
`rbegin()` `rend()`	Returns a non-`const` reverse iterator to the last, and one before the first, element in a sequence
`crbegin()` `crend()`	Returns a `const` reverse iterator to the last, and one before the first, element in a sequence

> **NOTE** *It's recommended to use these nonmember functions instead of the member versions.*

These nonmember functions are defined in the `std` namespace; however, especially when writing generic code for class and function templates, it is recommended to use these non-member functions as follows:

```
using std::begin;
begin(...);
```

Note that `begin()` is called without any namespace qualification, as this enables *argument-dependent lookups* (ADL).

> **NOTE** *ADL allows you to call unqualified functions. The compiler tries to find those functions first in the namespace of the arguments passed to them. If not found there, the usual name lookup rules apply.*

When you specialize one of these nonmember functions for your own types, you can either put those specializations in the `std` namespace or put them in the same namespace as the type for which you are specializing them. The latter is recommended as this enables ADL. Thanks to ADL, you can then call your specialization without having to qualify it with any namespace, because the compiler is able to find the correct specialization in your namespace based on the types of arguments passed to the specialized function template.

By combining ADL (calling `begin(...)` without any namespace qualification) with the `using std::begin` declaration, the compiler first looks up the right overload in the namespace of the type of its argument using ADL. If the compiler cannot find an overload using ADL, it tries to find an appropriate overload in the `std` namespace due to the `using` declaration. Just calling `begin()` without the `using` declaration would only call user-defined overloads through ADL, and just calling `std::begin()` would only look in the `std` namespace.

Of course, ADL is not limited to the functions discussed in this section but can be used with any function.

> **NOTE** *Normally it is not allowed to add anything to the* `std` *namespace; however, it is legal to put specializations of Standard Library templates in the* `std` *namespace.*

Iterator Traits

Some algorithm implementations need additional information about their iterators. For example, they might need to know the type of the elements referred to by the iterator to store temporary values, or perhaps they want to know whether the iterator is bidirectional or random access.

C++ provides a class template called `iterator_traits`, defined in `<iterator>`, that allows you to retrieve this information. You instantiate the `iterator_traits` class template with the iterator type of interest, and access one of five type aliases:

- value_type: The type of elements referred to
- difference_type: A type capable of representing the distance, i.e., number of elements, between two iterators
- iterator_category: The type of iterator: `input_iterator_tag`, `output_iterator_tag`, `forward_iterator_tag`, `bidirectional_iterator_tag`, `random_access_iterator_tag`, or `contiguous_iterator_tag`

- pointer: The type of a pointer to an element
- reference: The type of a reference to an element

For example, the following function template declares a temporary variable of the type that an iterator of type `IteratorType` refers to. Note the use of the `typename` keyword in front of `iterator_traits`. You must specify `typename` explicitly whenever you access a type based on one or more template type parameters. In this case, the template type parameter `IteratorType` is used to access the `value_type` type of `iterator_traits`.

```
template <typename IteratorType>
void iteratorTraitsTest(IteratorType it)
{
   typename iterator_traits<IteratorType>::value_type temp;
   temp = *it;
   println("{}", temp);
}
```

This function can be tested with the following code:

```
vector v { 5 };
iteratorTraitsTest(cbegin(v));
```

With this code, the variable `temp` in `iteratorTraitsTest()` is of type `int`. The output is `5`.

Of course, the `auto` keyword could be used in this example to simplify the code, but that wouldn't show you how to use `iterator_traits`.

Examples

The following example simply uses a `for` loop and iterators to iterate over every element in a `vector` and prints them to standard output:

```
vector values { 1, 2, 3, 4, 5, 6, 7, 8, 9, 10 };
for (auto iter { cbegin(values) }; iter != cend(values); ++iter) {
    print("{} ", *iter);
}
```

You might be tempted to test for the end of a common range using `operator<`, as in `iter<cend(values)`. That is not recommended, however. The canonical way to test for the end of a range is to use `!=`, as in `iter!=cend(values)`. The reason is that the `!=` operator works on all types of iterators, while the `<` operator is not supported by bidirectional and forward iterators.

A helper function can be implemented that accepts a common range of elements given as a begin and end iterator and prints all elements in that range to standard output. The `input_iterator` concept is used to constrain the template type parameter to input iterators.

```
template <input_iterator Iter>
void myPrint(Iter begin, Iter end)
{
    for (auto iter { begin }; iter != end; ++iter) { print("{} ", *iter); }
}
```

This helper function can be used as follows:

```
myPrint(cbegin(values), cend(values));
```

A second example is a `myFind()` function template that finds a given value in a given common range. If the value is not found, the end iterator of the range is returned. Note the special type of the `value` parameter. It uses `iterator_traits` to get the type of the values to which the given iterators point to.

```
template <input_iterator Iter>
auto myFind(Iter begin, Iter end,
    const typename iterator_traits<Iter>::value_type& value)
{
    for (auto iter { begin }; iter != end; ++iter) {
        if (*iter == value) { return iter; }
    }
    return end;
}
```

This function template can be used as follows. The `std::distance()` function is used to compute the distance between two iterators of a container.

```
vector values { 11, 22, 33, 44 };
auto result { myFind(cbegin(values), cend(values), 22) };
if (result != cend(values)) {
    println("Found value at position {}", distance(cbegin(values), result));
}
```

More examples of using iterators are given throughout this and subsequent chapters.

Function Dispatching Using Iterator Traits

The Standard Library provides the `std::advance(iter, n)` function to advance a given iterator, `iter`, by `n` positions. This function works on all types of iterators. For random-access iterators, it simply does `iter += n`. For other iterators, it does `++iter` or `--iter` in a loop `n` times, depending on whether `n` is positive or negative. You might wonder how such behavior is implemented. It can be implemented using *function dispatching*. Based on the iterator category, the request is dispatched to a specific helper function. Here's a simplified implementation of our own `myAdvance(iter, n)` function demonstrating such function dispatching:

```
template <typename Iter, typename Distance>
void advanceHelper(Iter& iter, Distance n, input_iterator_tag)
{
    while (n > 0) { ++iter; --n; }
}

template <typename Iter, typename Distance>
void advanceHelper(Iter& iter, Distance n, bidirectional_iterator_tag)
{
    while (n > 0) { ++iter; --n; }
    while (n < 0) { --iter; ++n; }
}

template <typename Iter, typename Distance>
void advanceHelper(Iter& iter, Distance n, random_access_iterator_tag)
{
    iter += n;
}
```

```
template <typename Iter, typename Distance>
void myAdvance(Iter& iter, Distance n)
{
    using category = typename iterator_traits<Iter>::iterator_category;
    advanceHelper(iter, n, category {});
}
```

This implementation of `myAdvance()` can be used on random-access iterators from `vector`s, on bidirectional iterators from `list`s, and so on:

```
template <typename Iter>
void testAdvance(Iter iter)
{
    print("*iter = {} | ", *iter);
    myAdvance(iter, 3); print("3 ahead = {} | ", *iter);
    myAdvance(iter, -2); println("2 back = {}", *iter);
}

int main()
{
    vector vec { 1, 2, 3, 4, 5, 6 };  testAdvance(begin(vec));
    list lst { 1, 2, 3, 4, 5, 6 };    testAdvance(begin(lst));
}
```

The output is as follows:

```
*iter = 1 | 3 ahead = 4 | 2 back = 2
*iter = 1 | 3 ahead = 4 | 2 back = 2
```

With concepts (see Chapter 12), the `myAdvance()` implementation can be simplified. Instead of using helper functions, you can just provide `myAdvance()` overloads with appropriate constraints:

```
template <input_iterator Iter, typename Distance>
void myAdvance(Iter& iter, Distance n)
{
    while (n > 0) { ++iter; --n; }
}

template <bidirectional_iterator Iter, typename Distance>
void myAdvance(Iter& iter, Distance n)
{
    while (n > 0) { ++iter; --n; }
    while (n < 0) { --iter; ++n; }
}

template <random_access_iterator Iter, typename Distance>
void myAdvance(Iter& iter, Distance n)
{
    iter += n;
}
```

STREAM ITERATORS

The Standard Library provides four *stream iterators*. These are iterator-like class templates that allow you to treat input and output streams as input and output iterators. Using these stream iterators, you can adapt input and output streams so that they can serve as sources and destinations, respectively, for various Standard Library algorithms. The following stream iterators are available:

- `ostream_iterator`: Output iterator writing to a `basic_ostream`
- `istream_iterator`: Input iterator reading from a `basic_istream`
- `ostreambuf_iterator`: Output iterator writing to a `basic_streambuf`
- `istreambuf_iterator`: Input iterator reading from a `basic_streambuf`

Output Stream Iterator: ostream_iterator

`ostream_iterator` is an *output stream iterator*. It is a class template that takes the element type as a template type parameter. The constructor takes an output stream and a delimiter string to write to the stream following each element. The `ostream_iterator` class writes elements using `operator<<`.

Let's look at an example. Suppose you have the following `myCopy()` function template that copies a common range given as a begin and end iterator to a target range given as a begin iterator. The second template type parameter is constrained to be an output iterator that accepts values of type `std::iter_reference_t<InputIter>` which is the type of the values referred to by the given `InputIter`.

```
template <input_iterator InputIter,
    output_iterator<iter_reference_t<InputIter>> OutputIter>
void myCopy(InputIter begin, InputIter end, OutputIter target)
{
    for (auto iter { begin }; iter != end; ++iter, ++target) { *target = *iter; }
}
```

The first two parameters of `myCopy()` are the begin and end iterator of the range to copy, and the third parameter is an iterator to the destination range. You have to make sure the destination range is big enough to hold all the elements from the source range. Using the `myCopy()` function template to copy the elements of one `vector` to another one is straightforward.

```
vector myVector { 1, 2, 3, 4, 5, 6, 7, 8, 9, 10 };
// Use myCopy() to copy myVector to vectorCopy.
vector<int> vectorCopy(myVector.size());
myCopy(cbegin(myVector), cend(myVector), begin(vectorCopy));
```

Now, by using an `ostream_iterator`, the `myCopy()` function template can also be used to print elements of a container with just a single line of code. The following code snippet prints the contents of `myVector` and `vectorCopy`:

```
// Use the same myCopy() to print the contents of both vectors.
myCopy(cbegin(myVector), cend(myVector), ostream_iterator<int> { cout, " " });
println("");
myCopy(cbegin(vectorCopy), cend(vectorCopy), ostream_iterator<int> { cout, " " });
println("");
```

The output is as follows:

```
1 2 3 4 5 6 7 8 9 10
1 2 3 4 5 6 7 8 9 10
```

Input Stream Iterator: istream_iterator

You can use the *input stream iterator*, `istream_iterator`, to read values from an input stream using the iterator abstraction. It is a class template that takes the element type as a template type parameter. Its constructor takes an input stream as a parameter. Elements are read using `operator>>`. You can use an `istream_iterator` as a source for algorithms and container member functions.

Suppose you have the following `sum()` function template that calculates the sum of all the elements in a given common range:

```
template <input_iterator InputIter>
auto sum(InputIter begin, InputIter end)
{
    auto sum { *begin };
    for (auto iter { ++begin }; iter != end; ++iter) { sum += *iter; }
    return sum;
}
```

Now, an `istream_iterator` can be used to read integers from the console until the end of the stream is reached. On Windows, this happens when you press Ctrl+Z followed by Enter, while on Linux you press Enter followed by Ctrl+D. The `sum()` function is used to calculate the sum of all the integers. A default constructed `istream_iterator` represents the end iterator.

```
println("Enter numbers separated by whitespace.");
println("Press Ctrl+Z followed by Enter to stop.");
istream_iterator<int> numbersIter { cin };
istream_iterator<int> endIter;
int result { sum(numbersIter, endIter) };
println("Sum: {}", result);
```

Input Stream Iterator: istreambuf_iterator

One use case of the `istreambuf_iterator` input stream iterator is to easily read the contents of an entire file with a single statement. A default constructed `istreambuf_iterator` represents the end iterator. Here is an example:

```
ifstream inputFile { "some_data.txt" };
if (inputFile.fail()) {
    println(cerr, "Unable to open file for reading.");
    return 1;
}
string fileContents {
    istreambuf_iterator<char> { inputFile },
    istreambuf_iterator<char> { }
};
println("{}", fileContents);
```

ITERATOR ADAPTERS

The Standard Library provides a number of *iterator adapters*, which are special iterators, all defined in `<iterator>`. They are split into two groups. The first group of adapters are created from a container and are usually used as output iterators:

- back_insert_iterator: Uses `push_back()` to insert elements into a container
- front_insert_iterator: Uses `push_front()` to insert elements into a container
- insert_iterator: Uses `insert()` to insert elements into a container

Other adapters are created from another iterator, not a container, and are usually used as input iterators. Two common adapters are:

- reverse_iterator: Reverse the iteration order of another iterator.
- move_iterator: The dereferencing operator for a `move_iterator` automatically converts the value to an rvalue reference, so it can be moved to a new destination.

It's also possible to write your own iterator adapters, but this is not covered in this book. Consult one of the Standard Library references listed in Appendix B, "Annotated Bibliography," for details.

Insert Iterators

The `myCopy()` function template as implemented earlier in this chapter does not insert elements into a container; it simply replaces old elements in a range with new ones. To make such algorithms more useful, the Standard Library provides three *insert iterator adapters* that really insert elements into a container: `insert_iterator`, `back_insert_iterator`, and `front_insert_iterator`. They are all parametrized on a container type and take an actual container reference in their constructor. Because they supply the necessary iterator interfaces, these adapters can be used as the destination iterators for algorithms like `myCopy()`. However, instead of replacing elements in the container, they make calls on their container to actually insert new elements.

The basic `insert_iterator` calls `insert(position,element)` on the container, `back_insert_iterator` calls `push_back(element)`, and `front_insert_iterator` calls `push_front(element)`.

The following example uses a `back_insert_iterator` with `myCopy()` to populate `vectorTwo` with copies of all elements from `vectorOne`. Note that `vectorTwo` is not first resized to have enough elements, the insert iterator takes care of properly inserting new elements.

```
vector vectorOne { 1, 2, 3, 4, 5, 6, 7, 8, 9, 10 };
vector<int> vectorTwo;

back_insert_iterator<vector<int>> inserter { vectorTwo };
myCopy(cbegin(vectorOne), cend(vectorOne), inserter);

println("{:n}", vectorTwo);
```

As you can see, when you use insert iterators, you don't need to size the destination containers ahead of time.

You can also use the `std::back_inserter()` utility function to create a `back_insert_iterator`. In the previous example, you can remove the line that defines the `inserter` variable and rewrite the `myCopy()` call as follows. The result remains the same.

```
myCopy(cbegin(vectorOne), cend(vectorOne), back_inserter(vectorTwo));
```

With class template argument deduction (CTAD), this can also be written as follows:

```
myCopy(cbegin(vectorOne), cend(vectorOne), back_insert_iterator { vectorTwo });
```

The front_insert_iterator and insert_iterator work similarly, except that the insert_iterator also takes an initial iterator position in its constructor, which it passes to the first call to insert(position,element). Subsequent iterator position hints are generated based on the return value from each insert() call.

One benefit of using an insert_iterator is that it allows you to use associative containers as destinations of modifying algorithms. Chapter 20, "Mastering Standard Library Algorithms," explains that the problem with associative containers is that you are not allowed to modify the keys over which you iterate. By using an insert_iterator, you insert elements instead of modifying existing ones. Associative containers have an insert() member function that takes an iterator position and can use the position as a "hint," which they can ignore. When you use an insert_iterator on an associative container, you can pass the begin() or end() iterator of the container as the hint. The insert_iterator modifies the iterator hint that it passes to insert() after each call to insert(), such that the position is one past the just-inserted element.

Here is the previous example modified so that the destination container is a set instead of a vector:

```
vector vectorOne { 1, 2, 3, 4, 5, 6, 7, 8, 9, 10 };
set<int> setOne;

insert_iterator<set<int>> inserter { setOne, begin(setOne) };
myCopy(cbegin(vectorOne), cend(vectorOne), inserter);

println("{:n}", setOne);
```

Similar to the back_insert_iterator example, you can use the std::inserter() utility function to create an insert_iterator:

```
myCopy(cbegin(vectorOne), cend(vectorOne), inserter(setOne, begin(setOne)));
```

Or, use class template argument deduction:

```
myCopy(cbegin(vectorOne), cend(vectorOne),
    insert_iterator { setOne, begin(setOne) });
```

Reverse Iterators

The Standard Library provides an std::reverse_iterator class template that iterates through a bidirectional or random-access iterator in a reverse direction. Every reversible container in the Standard Library, which happens to be every container that's part of the standard except forward_list and the unordered associative containers, supplies a reverse_iterator type alias and member functions called rbegin() and rend(). These reverse_iterator type aliases are of type std::reverse_iterator<T> with T equal to the iterator type alias of the container. The member function rbegin() returns a reverse_iterator pointing to the last element of the container, and rend() returns a reverse_iterator pointing to the element before the first element of the container. Applying operator++ to a reverse_iterator calls operator-- on the underlying container iterator, and vice versa. For example, iterating over a collection from the beginning to the end can be done as follows:

```
for (auto iter { begin(collection) }; iter != end(collection); ++iter) {}
```

Iterating over the elements in the collection from the end to the beginning can be done using a reverse_iterator by calling rbegin() and rend(). Note that you still call ++iter.

```
for (auto iter { rbegin(collection) }; iter != rend(collection); ++iter) {}
```

An std::reverse_iterator is useful mostly with algorithms in the Standard Library or your own functions that have no equivalents that work in reverse order. The myFind() function introduced earlier in this chapter searches for the first element in a sequence. If you want to find the last element in the sequence, you can use a reverse_iterator. Note that when you call an algorithm such as myFind() with a reverse_iterator, it returns a reverse_iterator as well. You can always obtain the underlying iterator from a reverse_iterator by calling its base() member function. However, because of how reverse_iterator is implemented, the iterator returned from base() always refers to one element past the element referred to by the reverse_iterator on which it's called. To get to the same element, you must subtract one.

Here is an example of myFind() with a reverse_iterator:

```
vector myVector { 11, 22, 33, 22, 11 };
auto it1 { myFind(begin(myVector), end(myVector), 22) };
auto it2 { myFind(rbegin(myVector), rend(myVector), 22) };
if (it1 != end(myVector) && it2 != rend(myVector)) {
    println("Found at position {} going forward.",
            distance(begin(myVector), it1));
    println("Found at position {} going backward.",
            distance(begin(myVector), --it2.base()));
} else {
    println("Failed to find.");
}
```

The output of this program is as follows:

```
Found at position 1 going forward.
Found at position 3 going backward.
```

Move Iterators

Chapter 9, "Mastering Classes and Objects," discusses *move semantics*, which can be used to prevent unnecessary copying in cases where you know that the source object will be destroyed after an assignment operation or copy construction, or explicitly when using std::move(). The Standard Library provides an iterator adapter called std::move_iterator. The dereferencing operator of a move_iterator automatically converts the value to an *rvalue reference*, which means that the value can be moved to a new destination without the overhead of copying. Before you can use move semantics, you need to make sure your objects are supporting it. The following MoveableClass supports move semantics. For more details, see Chapter 9.

```
class MoveableClass
{
    public:
```

```
        MoveableClass() {
            println("Default constructor");
        }
        MoveableClass(const MoveableClass& src) {
            println("Copy constructor");
        }
        MoveableClass(MoveableClass&& src) noexcept {
            println("Move constructor");
        }
        MoveableClass& operator=(const MoveableClass& rhs) {
            println("Copy assignment operator");
            return *this;
        }
        MoveableClass& operator=(MoveableClass&& rhs) noexcept {
            println("Move assignment operator");
            return *this;
        }
};
```

The constructors and assignment operators are not doing anything useful here, except printing a message to make it easy to see which one is being called. Now that you have this class, you can define a `vector` and store a few `MoveableClass` instances in it as follows:

```
vector<MoveableClass> vecSource;
MoveableClass mc;
vecSource.push_back(mc);
vecSource.push_back(mc);
```

The output could be as follows. The numbers behind each line are not part of the output but are added to make it easier for the upcoming discussion to refer to specific lines.

```
Default constructor  // [1]
Copy constructor     // [2]
Copy constructor     // [3]
Move constructor     // [4]
```

The second line of the code creates a `MoveableClass` instance by using the default constructor, [1]. The first `push_back()` call triggers the copy constructor to copy `mc` into the `vector`, [2]. After this operation, the vector has space for one element, the first copy of `mc`. Note that this discussion is based on the growth strategy and the initial size of a `vector` as implemented by Microsoft Visual C++ 2022. The C++ standard does not specify the initial capacity of a `vector` or its growth strategy, so the output can be different with different compilers.

The second `push_back()` call triggers the `vector` to resize itself, to allocate space for the second element. This resizing causes the move constructor to be called to move every element from the old `vector` to the new resized `vector`, [4]. The copy constructor is triggered to copy `mc` a second time into the `vector`, [3]. The order of moving and copying is undefined, so [3] and [4] could be reversed.

You can create a new `vector` called `vecOne` that contains a copy of the elements from `vecSource` as follows:

```
vector<MoveableClass> vecOne { cbegin(vecSource), cend(vecSource) };
```

Without using move_iterators, this code triggers the copy constructor two times, once for every element in vecSource:

```
Copy constructor
Copy constructor
```

By using std::make_move_iterator() to create move_iterators, the move constructor of MoveableClass is called instead of the copy constructor:

```
vector<MoveableClass> vecTwo { make_move_iterator(begin(vecSource)),
                               make_move_iterator(end(vecSource)) };
```

This generates the following output:

```
Move constructor
Move constructor
```

You can also use class template argument deduction (CTAD) with move_iterator:

```
vector<MoveableClass> vecTwo { move_iterator { begin(vecSource) },
                               move_iterator { end(vecSource) } };
```

> **WARNING** *Remember that you should no longer use an object once it has been moved to another object.*

RANGES

The iterator support of the C++ Standard Library allows algorithms to work independently of the actual containers, as they abstract away the mechanism to navigate through the elements of a container. As you've seen in all iterator examples up to now, most algorithms need an iterator pair consisting of a begin iterator that refers to the first element in the sequence, and an end iterator referring to one past the last element in the sequence. This makes it possible for algorithms to work on all kinds of containers, but it's a bit cumbersome to always have to provide two iterators to specify a sequence of elements and to make sure you don't provide mismatching iterators. *Ranges* provided by the *ranges library* are an abstraction layer on top of iterators, eliminating mismatching iterator errors, and adding extra functionality such as allowing range adapters to lazily filter and transform underlying sequences of elements. The ranges library, defined in <ranges>, consists of the following major components:

- **Ranges:** A range is a concept (see Chapter 12) defining the requirements for a type that allows iteration over its elements. Any data structure that supports begin() and end() is a valid range. For example, std::array, vector, string_view, span, fixed-size C-style arrays, and so on, are all valid ranges.
- **Constrained algorithms:** Chapters 16 and 20 discuss the available Standard Library algorithms accepting iterator pairs to perform their work. For most of these algorithms there are equivalent range-based and constrained variants that accept iterator pairs or ranges.

- **Projection:** A lot of the constrained algorithms accept a projection callback. This callback is called for each element in the range and can transform an element to some other value before it is passed to the algorithm.
- **Views:** A view can be used to transform or filter the elements of an underlying range. Views can be composed together to form pipelines of operations to be applied to a range.
- **Factories:** A range factory is used to construct a view that produces values on demand.

Iteration over the elements in a range can be done with iterators that can be retrieved with accessors such as `ranges::begin()`, `end()`, `rbegin()`, and so on. Ranges also support `ranges::empty()`, `data()`, `cdata()`, and `size()`. The latter returns the number of elements in a range but works only if the size can be retrieved in constant time. Otherwise, use `std::distance()` to calculate the number of elements between a begin and end iterator of a range. All these accessors are not member functions but stand-alone free functions, all requiring a range as argument.

Additionally, `std::format()`, `print()`, and `println()` have full support for formatting and printing ranges, as is demonstrated by numerous examples throughout this section.

Constrained Algorithms

The `std::sort()` algorithm is an example of an algorithm that requires a sequence of elements specified as a begin and end iterator. Algorithms are introduced in Chapter 16 and discussed in detail in Chapter 20. The `sort()` algorithm is straightforward to use. For example, the following code sorts all the elements of a `vector`:

```
vector data { 33, 11, 22 };
sort(begin(data), end(data));
```

This code sorts all the elements in the `data` container, but you have to specify the sequence as a begin/end iterator pair. Wouldn't it be nicer to more accurately describe in your code what you really want to do? That's where the *range-based and constrained algorithms*, simply called *constrained algorithms* in this book, come in. These algorithms live in the `std::ranges` namespace and are defined in the same header file as the corresponding unconstrained variants. With those, you can simply write the following:

```
ranges::sort(data);
```

This code clearly describes your intent, that is, sorting all elements of the `data` container. Since you are not specifying iterators anymore, these constrained algorithms eliminate the possibility of accidentally supplying mismatching begin and end iterators. The constrained algorithms have proper type constraints (see Chapter 12) for their template type parameters. This allows compilers to provide clearer error messages in case you supply a container to a constrained algorithm that does not provide the type of iterator the algorithm requires. For example, calling the `ranges::sort()` algorithm on an `std::list` will result in a compiler error stating more clearly that `sort()` requires a random-access range, which `list` isn't. Similar to iterators, you have input-, output-, forward-, bidirectional-, random-access-, and contiguous ranges, with corresponding concepts such as `ranges::contiguous_range`, `ranges::random_access_range`, and so on.

> **NOTE** *Most Standard Library algorithms, introduced in Chapter 16 and discussed in detail in Chapter 20, have constrained equivalents in the* `std::ranges` *namespace. It's recommended to always use these constrained algorithms, if possible, as the compiler can provide better error messages when such algorithms are used with the wrong types, thanks to their type constraints.*

Projection

A lot of the constrained algorithms have a *projection* parameter, a callback used to transform each element before it is handed over to the algorithm. Let's look at an example. Suppose you have a simple class representing a person:

```
class Person
{
    public:
        explicit Person(string first, string last)
            : m_firstName { move(first) }, m_lastName { move(last) } { }
        const string& getFirstName() const { return m_firstName; }
        const string& getLastName() const { return m_lastName; }
    private:
        string m_firstName;
        string m_lastName;
};
```

The following code stores a couple of `Person` objects in a `vector`:

```
vector persons { Person {"John", "White"}, Person {"Chris", "Blue"} };
```

Since the `Person` class does not implement `operator<`, you cannot sort this `vector` using the normal `std::sort()` algorithm, as it compares elements using `operator<`. So, the following does not compile:

```
sort(begin(persons), end(persons)); // Error: does not compile.
```

Switching to the constrained `ranges::sort()` algorithm doesn't help much at first sight. The following still doesn't compile as the algorithm still doesn't know how to compare elements in the range:

```
ranges::sort(persons); // Error: does not compile.
```

However, you can sort `persons` based on their first name, by specifying a projection function for the sort algorithm to project each person to their first name. The projection parameter is the third one, so we have to specify the second parameter as well, which is the comparator to use, by default `std::ranges::less`. In the following call, the `{}` specifies to use the default comparator, and the projection function is specified as a *lambda expression*, see upcoming note.

```
ranges::sort(persons, {},
    [](const Person& person) { return person.getFirstName(); });
```

Or even shorter:

```
ranges::sort(persons, {}, &Person::getFirstName);
```

> **NOTE** *The discussion on ranges in this chapter uses a few basic lambda expressions. Lambda expressions are discussed in detail in Chapter 19, "Function Pointers, Function Objects, and Lambda Expressions," but all those details are not important for the current discussion. For now, it's enough to know only basic use. A lambda expression, as used in this chapter, has the following syntax:*
>
> ```
> [](const Person& person) { return person.getFirstName(); }
> ```
>
> *The* `[]` *denotes the start of a lambda expression. Next is a comma-separated list of parameters, just as for functions. Finally, the body of the lambda expression is between a set of curly brackets.*
>
> *Basically, lambda expressions allow you to write small, unnamed inline functions at the place where you need them. The previous lambda expression could be replaced with the following standalone function:*
>
> ```
> auto getFirstName(const Person& person) {
>     return person.getFirstName(); }
> ```
>
> *The type of lambda expression parameters can also be* `auto`*. Here is an example:*
>
> ```
> [](const auto& person) { return person.getFirstName(); }
> ```

Views

A *view* allows you to perform operations on an underlying range's elements, such as filtering and transforming. Views can be chained/composed together to form a *pipeline* performing multiple operations on the elements of a range. Composing views is easy, you just combine different operations using the bitwise OR operator, `operator|`. For example, you can easily filter the elements of a range first and then transform the remaining elements. In contrast, if you want to do something similar, filtering followed by transforming, using the unconstrained algorithms, your code will be much less readable and possibly less performant, as you'll have to create temporary containers to store intermediate results.

A view has the following important properties:

- **Lazily evaluated:** Just constructing a view doesn't perform any operations yet. The operations of a view are applied only at the moment you iterate over the elements of the view and dereference such an iterator.
- **Nonowning**[1]**:** A view doesn't own any elements. As the name suggests, it's a view over a range's elements that could be stored in some container, and it's that container that's the owner of the data. A view just allows you to view that data in different ways. As such, the number of elements in a view does not influence the cost of copying, moving, or destroying a view. This is similar to `std::string_view` discussed in Chapter 2, "Working with Strings and String Views," and `std::span` discussed in Chapter 18, "Standard Library Containers."
- **Nonmutating:** A view never modifies the data in the underlying range.

[1] C++23 slightly modifies the definition of a view. It allows for a view to own its elements, but only if it guarantees that it's either non-copyable, or copyable in constant time, O(1). Most views will be nonowning, so owning views are not further discussed in this text.

A view itself is also a range, but not every range is a view. A container is a range but not a view, as it owns its elements.

Views can be created using *range adapters*. A range adapter accepts an underlying sequence of elements, and optionally some arguments, and creates a new view. The following table lists the range adapters provided by the Standard Library. If none of the Standard Library adapters suits your needs, it's possible to write your own range adapters that properly interoperate with existing adapters. However, writing a full-fledged production-quality range adapter is not trivial and would take us a bit too far for the scope of this book. See your favorite Standard Library reference for more details.

RANGE ADAPTER	DESCRIPTION
`views::all`	Creates a view that includes all elements of a range.
`filter_view` `views::filter`	Filters the elements of an underlying sequence based on a given predicate. If the predicate returns `true`, the element is kept, otherwise it is skipped.
`transform_view` `views::transform`	Applies a callback to each element of an underlying sequence to transform the element to some other value, possibly of a different type.
`take_view` `views::take`	Creates a view of the first *n* elements of another view.
`take_while_view` `views::take_while`	Creates a view of the initial elements of an underlying sequence until an element is reached for which a given predicate returns `false`.
`drop_view` `views::drop`	Creates a view by dropping the first *n* elements of another view.
`drop_while_view` `views::drop_while`	Creates a view by dropping all initial elements of an underlying sequence until an element is reached for which a given predicate returns `false`.
`join_view` `views::join`	Flattens a view of ranges into a view. For example, flatten a `vector<vector<int>>` into a `vector<int>`.

`lazy_split_view`
`views::lazy_split`
`split_view`
`views::split`
	Given a delimiter, splits a given view into subranges on the delimiter. The delimiter can be a single element or a view of elements.

`reverse_view` `views::reverse`	Creates a view that iterates over the elements of another view in reverse order. The view must be a bidirectional view.
`elements_view` `views::elements`	Requires a view of tuple-like elements, creates a view of the nth elements of the tuple-like elements.

RANGE ADAPTER	DESCRIPTION
`keys_view` `views::keys`	Requires a view of pair-like elements, creates a view of the first element of each pair.
`values_view` `views::values`	Requires a view of pair-like elements, creates a view of the second element of each pair.
`common_view` `views::common`	Depending on the type of range, `begin()` and `end()` might return different types, such as a begin iterator and an end *sentinel*. This means that you cannot, for example, pass such an iterator pair to functions that expect them to be of the same type. `common_view` can be used to convert such a range to a *common range* which is a range for which `begin()` and `end()` return the same type. You will use this range adapter in one of the exercises.

C++23

C++23 adds the following range adapters:

RANGE ADAPTER	DESCRIPTION
`as_const_view` `views::as_const`	Creates a view through which the elements of an underlying sequence cannot be modified.
`as_rvalue_view` `views::as_rvalue`	Creates a view of rvalues of all elements of an underlying sequence.
`enumerate_view` `views::enumerate`	Creates a view where each element represents the position and value of all elements of an underlying sequence.
`zip_view` `views::zip`	Creates a view consisting of tuples of reference to corresponding elements of all given views.
`zip_transform_view` `views::zip_transform`	Creates a view whose i^{th} element is the result of applying a given callable to the ith elements of all given views.
`adjacent_view` `views::adjacent`	For a given n, creates a view whose i^{th} element is a tuple of references to the ith through $(i + n - 1)^{th}$ elements of a given view.
`adjacent_transform_view` `views::adjacent_transform`	For a given n, creates a view whose i^{th} element is the result of applying a given callable to the ith through $(i + n - 1)^{th}$ elements of a given view.
`views::pairwise` `views::pairwise_transform`	Helper types representing `views::adjacent<2>` and `views::adjacent_transform<2>` respectively.

continues

(continued)

RANGE ADAPTER	DESCRIPTION
`join_with_view` `views::join_with`	Given a delimiter, flattens the elements of a given view, inserting every element of the delimiter in between elements of the view. The delimiter can be a single element or a view of elements.
`stride_view` `views::stride`	For a given *n*, creates a view of an underlying sequence, advancing over *n* elements at a time, instead of one by one.
`slide_view` `views::slide`	For a given *n*, creates a view whose i^{th} element is a view over the ith through $(i + n - 1)^{th}$ elements of the original view. Similar to `views::adjacent`, but the window size, *n*, is a runtime parameter for `slide`, while it's a template argument for `adjacent`.
`chunk_view` `views::chunk`	For a given *n*, creates a range of views that are *n*-sized non-overlapping successive chunks of the elements of the original view, in order.
`chunk_by_view` `views::chunk_by`	Splits a given view into subranges between each pair of adjacent elements for which a given predicate returns `false`.
`cartesian_product_view` `views::cartesian_product`	Given a number of ranges, *n*, creates a view of tuples calculated by the *n*-ary cartesian product of the provided ranges.

The range adapters in the first column of both tables show both the class name in the `std::ranges` namespace and a corresponding *range adapter object* from the `std::ranges::views` namespace. The Standard Library provides a namespace alias called `std::views` equal to `std::ranges::views`.

Each range adapter can be constructed by calling its constructor and passing any required arguments. The first argument is always the range on which to operate, followed by zero or more additional arguments, as follows:

```
std::ranges::operation_view { range, arguments... }
```

Usually, you will not create these range adapters using their constructors, but instead use the range adapter objects from the `std::ranges::views` namespace in combination with the bitwise OR operator, `|`, as follows:

```
range | std::ranges::views::operation(arguments...)
```

Let's see some of these range adapters in action. The following example first defines an abbreviated function template called `printRange()` to print a message followed by all the elements in a given range. Next, the `main()` function starts by creating a `vector` of integers, 1. . .10, and subsequently applies several range adapters on it, each time calling `printRange()` on the result so you can follow what's happening. Afterward, it demonstrates several of the new C++23 range adapters. The example uses the `myCopy()` function introduced earlier in this chapter.

```
void printRange(string_view msg, auto&& range) { println("{}{:n}", msg, range); }

int main()
{
    vector values { 1, 2, 3, 4, 5, 6, 7, 8, 9, 10 };
    printRange("Original sequence: ", values);

    // Filter out all odd values, leaving only the even values.
    auto result1 { values
        | views::filter([](const auto& value) { return value % 2 == 0; }) };
    printRange("Only even values: ", result1);

    // Transform all values to their double value.
    auto result2 { result1
        | views::transform([](const auto& value) { return value * 2.0; }) };
    printRange("Values doubled: ", result2);

    // Drop the first 2 elements.
    auto result3 { result2 | views::drop(2) };
    printRange("First two dropped: ", result3);

    // Reverse the view.
    auto result4 { result3 | views::reverse };
    printRange("Sequence reversed: ", result4);

    // C++23: views::zip
    vector v1 { 1, 2 };
    vector v2 { 'a', 'b', 'c' };
    auto result5 { views::zip(v1, v2) };
    printRange("views::zip: ", result5);

    // C++23: views::adjacent
    vector v3 { 1, 2, 3, 4, 5 };
    auto result6 { v3 | views::adjacent<2> };
    printRange("views::adjacent: ", result6);

    // C++23: views::chunk
    auto result7 { v3 | views::chunk(2) };
    printRange("views::chunk: ", result7);

    // C++23: views::stride
    auto result8 { v3 | views::stride(2) };
    printRange("views::stride: ", result8);

    // C++23: views::enumerate + views::split
    string lorem { "Lorem ipsum dolor sit amet" };
    for (auto [index, word] : lorem | views::split(' ') | views::enumerate) {
        print("{}:'{}' ", index, string_view { word });
    }
    println("");
```

```
    // C++23: views::as_rvalue
    vector<string> words { "Lorem", "ipsum", "dolor", "sit", "amet" };
    vector<string> movedWords;
    auto rvalueView { words | views::as_rvalue };
    myCopy(begin(rvalueView), end(rvalueView), back_inserter(movedWords));
    printRange("movedWords: ", movedWords);

    // C++23: Cartesian product of vector v with itself.
    vector v { 0, 1, 2 };
    for (auto&&[a, b] : views::cartesian_product(v, v)) {print("({},{}) ", a, b);}
}
```

The output of this program is as follows:

```
Original sequence: 1, 2, 3, 4, 5, 6, 7, 8, 9, 10
Only even values: 2, 4, 6, 8, 10
Values doubled: 4, 8, 12, 16, 20
First two dropped: 12, 16, 20
Sequence reversed: 20, 16, 12
views::zip: (1, 'a'), (2, 'b')
views::adjacent: (1, 2), (2, 3), (3, 4), (4, 5)
views::chunk: (1, 2), (3, 4), (5)
views::stride: 1, 3, 5
0:'Lorem' 1:'ipsum' 2:'dolor' 3:'sit' 4:'amet'
movedWords: Lorem, ipsum, dolor, sit, amet
(0,0) (0,1) (0,2) (1,0) (1,1) (1,2) (2,0) (2,1) (2,2)
```

It's worth repeating that views are lazily evaluated. In this example, the construction of the `result1` view does not do any actual filtering yet. The filtering happens at the time when the `printRange()` function iterates over the elements of `result1`.

The code snippet uses the range adapter objects from `std::ranges::views`. You can also construct range adapters using their constructors. For example, the `result1` view can be constructed as follows:

```
auto result1 { ranges::filter_view { values,
    [](const auto& value) { return value % 2 == 0; } } };
```

This example is creating several intermediate views, `result1`, `result2`, `result3`, and `result4`, to be able to output their elements to make it easier to follow what's happening in each step. If you don't need these intermediate views, you can chain them all together in a single pipeline as follows:

```
vector values { 1, 2, 3, 4, 5, 6, 7, 8, 9, 10 };
printRange("Original sequence: ", values);

auto result { values
    | views::filter([](const auto& value) { return value % 2 == 0; })
    | views::transform([](const auto& value) { return value * 2.0; })
    | views::drop(2)
    | views::reverse };
printRange("Final sequence: ", result);
```

The output is as follows. The last line shows that the final sequence is the same as the earlier `result4` view.

```
Original sequence: 1, 2, 3, 4, 5, 6, 7, 8, 9, 10
Final sequence: 20, 16, 12
```

Modifying Elements Through a View

Some ranges are read-only. For example, the result of `views::transform` is a read-only view, because it creates a view with transformed elements but without transforming the actual values in the underlying range. If a range is not read-only, then you can modify the elements of that range through a view. Let's look an example.

The following example constructs a `vector` of ten elements. It then creates a view over the even values, drops the first two even values, and finally reverses the elements. The range-based `for` loop then multiplies the elements in the resulting view with 10. The last line outputs the elements in the original `values vector` to confirm that some elements have been changed through the view.

```
vector values { 1, 2, 3, 4, 5, 6, 7, 8, 9, 10 };
printRange("Original sequence: ", values);

// Filter out all odd values, leaving only the even values.
auto result1 { values
    | views::filter([](const auto& value) { return value % 2 == 0; }) };
printRange("Only even values: ", result1);

// Drop the first 2 elements.
auto result2 { result1 | views::drop(2) };
printRange("First two dropped: ", result2);

// Reverse the view.
auto result3 { result2 | views::reverse };
printRange("Sequence reversed: ", result3);

// Modify the elements using a range-based for loop.
for (auto& value : result3) { value *= 10; }
printRange("After modifying elements through a view, vector contains:\n", values);
```

The output of this program is as follows:

```
Original sequence: 1, 2, 3, 4, 5, 6, 7, 8, 9, 10
Only even values: 2, 4, 6, 8, 10
First two dropped: 6, 8, 10
Sequence reversed: 10, 8, 6
After modifying elements through a view, vector contains:
1, 2, 3, 4, 5, 60, 7, 80, 9, 100
```

Mapping Elements

Transforming elements of a range doesn't need to result in a range with elements of the same type. Instead, you can *map* elements to another type. The following example starts with a range of integers, filters out all odd elements, keeps only the first three even values, and transforms those to strings using `std::format()`:

```
vector values { 1, 2, 3, 4, 5, 6, 7, 8, 9, 10 };
printRange("Original sequence: ", values);

auto result { values
    | views::filter([](const auto& value) { return value % 2 == 0; })
    | views::take(3)
    | views::transform([](const auto& v) { return format("{}", v); }) };
printRange("Result: ", result);
```

The output is as follows:

```
Original sequence: 1, 2, 3, 4, 5, 6, 7, 8, 9, 10
Result: "2", "4", "6"
```

Range Factories

The ranges library provides the following *range factories* to construct views that produce elements lazily on demand:

RANGE FACTORY	DESCRIPTION
`empty_view`	Creates an empty view.
`single_view`	Creates a view with a single given element.
`iota_view`	Creates an infinite or a bounded view containing elements starting with an initial value, and where each subsequent element has a value equal to the value of the previous element incremented by one.
C++23 `repeat_view`	Creates a view that repeats a given value. The resulting view can be unbounded (infinite) or bounded by a given number of values.
`basic_istream_view` `istream_view`	Creates a view containing elements retrieved by calling the extraction operator, `operator>>`, on an underlying input stream.

Just as with the range adapters from the previous section, the names in the range factories table are class names living in the `std::ranges` namespace, which you can directly create using their constructor. Alternatively, you can use the factory functions available in the `std::ranges:views` namespace. For example, the following two statements are equivalent and create an infinite view with elements 10, 11, 12, . . .:

```
std::ranges::iota_view { 10 }
std::ranges::views::iota(10)
```

Let's look at a range factory in practice. The following example is loosely based on an earlier example, but instead of constructing a `vector` with 10 elements in it, this code uses the `iota` range factory to create a lazy infinite sequence of numbers starting at 10. It then removes all odd values, doubles the remaining elements, and finally only keeps the first ten elements that are subsequently output to the console using `printRange()`.

```
// Create an infinite sequence of the numbers 10, 11, 12, ...
auto values { views::iota(10) };
// Filter out all odd values, leaving only the even values.
auto result1 { values
    | views::filter([](const auto& value) { return value % 2 == 0; }) };
// Transform all values to their double value.
auto result2 { result1
    | views::transform([](const auto& value) { return value * 2.0; }) };
// Take only the first ten elements.
auto result3 { result2 | views::take(10) };
printRange("Result: ", result3);
```

The output is as follows:

```
Result: 20, 24, 28, 32, 36, 40, 44, 48, 52, 56
```

The `values` range represents an infinite range, which is subsequently filtered and transformed. Working with infinite ranges is possible because all these operations are lazily evaluated only at the time when `printRange()` iterates over the elements of the view. This also means that in this example you cannot call `printRange()` to output the contents of `values`, `result1`, or `result2` because that would trigger an infinite loop in `printRange()` as those are infinite ranges.

Of course, you can get rid of those intermediate views and simply construct one big pipeline. The following produces the same output as before:

```
auto result { views::iota(10)
    | views::filter([](const auto& value) { return value % 2 == 0; })
    | views::transform([](const auto& value) { return value * 2.0; })
    | views::take(10) };
printRange("Result: ", result);
```

Another range factory example demonstrates how to use a `repeat_view`:

```
printRange("Repeating view: ", views::repeat(42, 5));
```

This outputs the following:

```
Repeating view: 42, 42, 42, 42, 42
```

Input Streams as Views

The `basic_istream_view`/`istream_view` range factory can be used to construct a view over the elements read from an input stream, such as the standard input. Elements are read using `operator>>`.

For example, the following code snippet keeps reading integers from standard input. For each read number that is less than 5, the number is doubled and printed on standard output. Once you enter a number 5 or higher, the loop stops.

```
println("Type integers, an integer >= 5 stops the program.");
for (auto value : ranges::istream_view<int> { cin }
    | views::take_while([](const auto& v) { return v < 5; })
    | views::transform([](const auto& v) { return v * 2; })) {
    println("> {}", value);
}
println("Terminating...");
```

The following is a possible output sequence:

```
Type integers, an integer >= 5 stops the program.
1 2
> 2
> 4
3
> 6
4
> 8
5
Terminating...
```

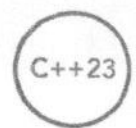

Converting a Range into a Container

Before C++23, it was not easy to convert a range into a container. C++23 introduces `std::ranges::to()` to make such conversions straightforward. This can also be used to convert the elements of a view into a container, as a view is a range. Even more, since a container is a range as well, you can use `ranges::to()` to convert one container into a different container, even with different element types.

The following code snippet demonstrates several uses of `ranges::to()`. The example also demonstrates special constructors for `set` and `string`, which accept the `std::from_range` tag as the first parameter and convert a given range into a `set` or `string`. All Standard Library containers now include such constructors.

```
// Convert a vector to a set with the same element type.
vector vec { 33, 11, 22 };
auto s1 { ranges::to<set>(vec) };
println("{:n}", s1);

// Convert a vector of integers to a set of doubles, using the pipe operator.
auto s2 { vec | ranges::to<set<double>>() };
println("{:n}", s2);

// Convert a vector of integers to a set of doubles, using from_range constructor.
set<double> s3 { from_range, vec };
println("{:n}", s3);

// Lazily generate the integers from 10 to 14, divide these by 2,
// and store the result in a vector of doubles.
auto vec2 { views::iota(10, 15)
    | views::transform([](const auto& v) { return v / 2.0; })
    | ranges::to<vector<double>>() };
println("{:n}", vec2);

// Use views::split() and views::transform() to create a view
// containing individual words of a string, and then convert
// the resulting view to a vector of strings containing all the words.
string lorem { "Lorem ipsum dolor sit amet" };
auto words { lorem | views::split(' ')
    | views::transform([](const auto& v) { return string { from_range, v }; })
    | ranges::to<vector>() };
println("{:n:?}", words);
```

The output is as follows:

```
11, 22, 33
11, 22, 33
11, 22, 33
5, 5.5, 6, 6.5, 7
"Lorem", "ipsum", "dolor", "sit", "amet"
```

C++23 also introduces a number of new member functions for Standard Library containers, providing for interoperability between containers and ranges. These member functions are of the form *xyz*`_range(...)`, where *xyz* can be `insert`, `append`, `prepend`, `assign`, `replace`, `push`, `push_front`, or `push_back`. Chapter 18 discusses all Standard Library containers in detail, but consult a Standard Library reference to learn exactly which member functions are supported by which container. Here is an example demonstrating the `append_range()` and `insert_range()` member functions of `vector`:

```
vector<int> vec3;
vec3.append_range(views::iota(10, 15));
println("{:n}", vec3);
vec3.insert_range(begin(vec3), views::iota(10, 15) | views::reverse);
println("{:n}", vec3);
```

The output is:

```
10, 11, 12, 13, 14
14, 13, 12, 11, 10, 10, 11, 12, 13, 14
```

SUMMARY

This chapter explained the ideas behind iterators, which are an abstraction that allows you to navigate the elements of a container without the need to know the structure of the container. You have seen that output stream iterators can use standard output as a destination for iterator-based algorithms, and similarly that input stream iterators can use standard input as the source of data for algorithms. The chapter also discussed the insert-, reverse-, and move iterator adapters that can be used to adapt other iterators.

The last part of this chapter discussed the ranges library, part of the C++ Standard Library. It allows you to write more functional-style code, by specifying *what* you want to accomplish instead of *how*. You can construct pipelines consisting of a combination of operations applied to the elements of a range. Such pipelines are executed lazily; that is, they don't do anything until you iterate over the resulting view.

EXERCISES

By solving the following exercises, you can practice the material discussed in this chapter. Solutions to all exercises are available with the code download on the book's website at `www.wiley.com/go/proc++6e`. However, if you are stuck on an exercise, first reread parts of this chapter to try to find an answer yourself before looking at the solution from the website.

Exercise 17-1: Write a program that lazily constructs the sequence of elements 10-100, squares each number, removes all numbers dividable by five, and transforms the remaining values to strings using `std::to_string()`.

Exercise 17-2: Write a program that creates a `vector` of `pairs`, where each `pair` contains an instance of the `Person` class introduced earlier in this chapter, and their age. Next, use the ranges library to construct a single pipeline that extracts all ages from all persons from the `vector`, and removes all ages below 12 and above 65. Finally, calculate the average of the remaining ages using the `sum()` algorithm from earlier in this chapter. As you'll pass a range to the `sum()` algorithm, you'll have to work with a common range.

Exercise 17-3: Building further on the solution for Exercise 17-2, add an implementation for `operator<<` for the `Person` class.

Next, create a pipeline to extract the `Person` of each `pair` from the `vector` of `pairs`, and only keep the first four `Persons`. Use the `myCopy()` algorithm introduced earlier in this chapter to print the names of those four persons to the standard output; one name per line.

Finally, create a similar pipeline but one that additionally projects all filtered `Persons` to their last name. This time, use a single `println()` statement to print the last names to the standard output.

Exercise 17-4: Write a program that uses a range-based `for` loop and `ranges::istream_view()` to read integers from the standard input until a -1 is entered. Store the read integers in a `vector`, and afterward, print the content of the `vector` to the console to verify it contains the correct values.

Bonus exercise: Can you find a couple of ways to change the solution for Exercise 17-4 to not use any explicit loops? Hint: one option could be to use the `std::ranges::copy()` algorithm to copy a range from a source to a target. It can be called with a range as first argument and an output iterator as the second argument.

18

Standard Library Containers

WHAT'S IN THIS CHAPTER?

- Containers overview: requirements on elements and general error handling
- Sequential containers: `vector`, `deque`, `list`, `forward_list`, and `array`
- Sequential views: `span` and `mdspan`
- Container adapters: `queue`, `priority_queue`, and `stack`
- The `pair` utility class template
- Associative containers: `map`, `multimap`, `set`, and `multiset`
- Unordered associative containers or hash tables: `unordered_map`, `unordered_multimap`, `unordered_set`, and `unordered_multiset`
- Flat associative container adapters: `flat_map`, `flat_multimap`, `flat_set`, and `flat_multiset`
- Other containers: standard C-style arrays, `string`s, streams, and `bitset`

WILEY.COM DOWNLOADS FOR THIS CHAPTER

Please note that all the code examples for this chapter are available as part of this chapter's code download on the book's website at `www.wiley.com/go/proc++6e` on the Download Code tab.

This chapter of the Standard Library deep-dive chapters covers the available containers. It explains the different containers, their categories, and what the trade-offs are between them.

Some containers are discussed in much more detail compared to others. Once you know how to work with a container of each category, you will have no problems using any of the other containers from the same category. Consult your favorite Standard Library Reference for a complete reference of all member functions of all containers.

CONTAINERS OVERVIEW

Containers in the Standard Library are generic data structures that are useful for storing collections of data. You should rarely need to use a standard C-style array, write a linked list, or design a stack when you use the Standard Library. The containers are implemented as class templates, so you can instantiate them for any type that meets certain basic conditions outlined in the next section. Most of the Standard Library containers, except for `array` and `bitset`, are flexible in size and automatically grow or shrink to accommodate more or fewer elements. This is a huge benefit compared to the old, C-style arrays, which had a fixed size. Because of the fixed-size nature of C-style arrays, they are more vulnerable to overruns, which in the simplest cases merely cause the program to crash because data has been corrupted, but in the worst cases allow certain kinds of security attacks. By using Standard Library containers, you ensure that your programs will be less vulnerable to these kinds of problems.

Chapter 16, "Overview of the C++ Standard Library," gives a high-level overview of the different containers, container adapters, and sequential views provided by the Standard Library. The following table summarizes them.

- **Sequential containers**
  - `vector` (dynamic array)
  - `deque`
  - `list`
  - `forward_list`
  - `array`
- **Sequential views**
  - `span`
  - `mdspan`
- **Container adapters**
  - `queue`
  - `priority_queue`
  - `stack`
- **Ordered associative containers**
  - `map / multimap`
  - `set / multiset`
- **Unordered associative containers or hash tables**
  - `unordered_map / unordered_multimap`
  - `unordered_set / unordered_multiset`
- **Flat set and flat map associative container adapters**
  - `flat_map / flat_multimap`
  - `flat_set / flat_multiset`

Additionally, C++ `strings` and streams can also be used as Standard Library containers to a certain degree, and `bitset` can be used to store a fixed number of bits.

Everything in the Standard Library is in the `std` namespace. As always, the examples in this book usually use the blanket `using namespace std;` directive in source files (never use this in header files!), but you can be more selective in your own programs about which symbols from `std` to use.

Requirements on Elements

Standard Library containers use value semantics on elements. That is, they store a copy of elements that they are given, assign to elements with the assignment operator, and destroy elements with the destructor. Thus, when you write classes that you intend to use with the Standard Library, you need to make sure they are copyable. When requesting an element from the container, a reference to the stored copy is returned.

If you prefer reference semantics, you can store pointers to elements instead of the elements themselves. When the containers copy a pointer, the result still refers to the same element. An alternative is to store `std::reference_wrappers` in the container. A `reference_wrapper` basically exists to make references copyable and can be created using the `std::ref()` and `cref()` helper functions. The `reference_wrapper` class template, and the `ref()` and `cref()` function templates are defined in `<functional>`. An example of this is given in the section "Storing References in a vector" later in this chapter.

It is possible to store move-only types, i.e., non-copyable types, in a container, but when doing so, some operations on the container might not compile. An example of a move-only type is `std::unique_ptr`.

> **WARNING** *If you need to store pointers in containers, if possible, use* `unique_ptrs` *if the container becomes the owner of the pointed-to objects, or use* `shared_ptrs` *if the container shares ownership with other owners. Do not use the old and removed* `auto_ptr` *class in containers because it does not implement copying correctly.*

One of the template type parameters for Standard Library containers is an allocator. The container uses this allocator to allocate and deallocate memory for elements. The allocator type parameter has a default value, so you can almost always just ignore it. For example, the `vector` class template looks as follows:

```
template <typename T, typename Allocator = std::allocator<T>> class vector;
```

Some containers, such as a `map`, additionally accept a comparator as one of the template type parameters. This comparator is used to order elements. It has a default value as well, so you don't always have to specify it. This default is to compare elements using `operator<`. The `map` class template looks like this:

```
template <typename Key, typename T, typename Compare = std::less<Key>,
    typename Allocator = std::allocator<std::pair<const Key, T>>> class map;
```

Both the allocator and the comparator template type parameters are discussed in detail later in this chapter.

The specific requirements on elements in containers using the default allocator and default comparator are shown in the following table:

MEMBER FUNCTION	DESCRIPTION	NOTES
Copy Constructor	Creates a new element that is "equal" to the old one, but that can safely be destructed without affecting the old one.	Used every time you insert an element, except when using an emplace member function (discussed later).
Move Constructor	Creates a new element by moving all content from the source element to the new element.	Used when the source element is an rvalue, and will be destroyed after the construction of the new element; also used when a `vector` grows in size. The move constructor should be `noexcept`; otherwise, it won't be used!
Assignment Operator	Replaces the contents of an element with a copy of the source element.	Used every time you modify an element.
Move Assignment Operator	Replaces the contents of an element by moving all content from the source element.	Used when the source element is an rvalue and will be destroyed after the assignment operation. The move assignment operator should be `noexcept`; otherwise, it won't be used!
Destructor	Cleans up an element.	Used every time you remove an element, or when a `vector` grows in size.
Default Constructor	Constructs an element without any arguments.	Required only for certain operations, such as the `vector::resize()` member function with one argument, and the `map::operator[]` access.
`operator==`	Compares two elements for equality.	Required for keys in unordered associative containers, and for certain operations, such as `operator==` on two containers.
`operator<`	Determines whether one element is less than another.	Required for keys in ordered associative containers and flat associative container adapters, and for certain operations, such as `operator<` on two containers.
`operator>, <=, >=, !=`	Compares two elements.	Required when comparing two containers.

Chapter 9, "Mastering Classes and Objects," explains how to write these member functions.

> **WARNING** *The Standard Library containers often move or copy elements. So, for best performance, make sure the type of objects stored in a container supports move semantics, see Chapter 9. If move semantics is not possible, make sure the copy constructor and copy assignment operator are as efficient as possible.*

Exceptions and Error Checking

The Standard Library containers provide limited error checking. Clients are expected to ensure that their uses are valid. However, some container member functions throw exceptions in certain conditions, such as out-of-bounds indexing. Of course, it is impossible to list exhaustively the exceptions that can be thrown from these member functions because they perform operations on user-specified types with unknown exception characteristics. This chapter mentions exceptions where appropriate. Consult a Standard Library Reference (see Appendix B, "Annotated Bibliography") for a list of possible exceptions thrown from each member function.

SEQUENTIAL CONTAINERS

`vector`, `deque`, `list`, `forward_list`, and `array` are called *sequential containers* because they store a sequence of elements. The best way to learn about sequential containers is to jump in with an example of the `vector` container, which should be your default container anyway. The next section describes the `vector` container in detail, followed by briefer discussions of `deque`, `list`, `forward_list`, and `array`. Once you become familiar with the sequential containers, it's trivial to switch between them.

vector

The Standard Library `vector` container is similar to a standard C-style array: the elements are stored in contiguous memory, each in its own "slot." You can index into a `vector`, as well as add new elements to the back or insert them anywhere else. Inserting and deleting elements into and from a `vector` generally takes linear time, though these operations actually run in *amortized constant* time at the end of a `vector`, as explained in the section "The vector Memory Allocation Scheme," later in this chapter. Random access of individual elements has a constant complexity; see Chapter 4, "Designing Professional C++ Programs," for a discussion on algorithm complexity.

vector Overview

`vector` is defined in `<vector>` as a class template with two type parameters: the element type to store and an *allocator* type:

```
template <typename T, typename Allocator = allocator<T>> class vector;
```

The `Allocator` parameter specifies the type for a memory allocator object that the client can set in order to use custom memory allocation. This template parameter has a default value.

> **NOTE** *The default value for the* `Allocator` *template type parameter is sufficient for most applications. This chapter always uses the default allocator. Chapter 25, "Customizing and Extending the Standard Library," provides more details in case you are interested.*

`std::vector` is `constexpr` (see Chapter 9), just as `std::string`. This means that `vector` can be used to perform operations at compile time and that it can be used in the implementation of `constexpr` functions and other `constexpr` classes.

Fixed-Length vectors

One way to use a `vector` is as a fixed-length array. `vector` provides a constructor that allows you to specify the number of elements and provides an overloaded `operator[]` to access and modify those elements. The result of `operator[]` is undefined when used to access an element outside the `vector` bounds. This means that a compiler can decide how to behave in that case. For example, the default behavior of Microsoft Visual C++ is to give a run-time error message when your program is compiled in debug mode and to disable any bounds checking in release mode for performance reasons. You can change these default behaviors.

> **WARNING** *Like "real" array indexing,* `operator[]` *on a* `vector` *does not provide bounds checking.*

In addition to using `operator[]`, you can access `vector` elements via `at()`, `front()`, and `back()`. The `at()` member function is identical to `operator[]`, except that it performs bounds checking and throws an `out_of_range` exception if the index is out of bounds. `front()` and `back()` return references to the first and last elements of a `vector`, respectively. Calling `front()` or `back()` on an empty container triggers undefined behavior.

> **NOTE** *All* `vector` *element accesses have constant complexity.*

Here is a small example program to "normalize" test scores so that the highest score is set to 100, and all other scores are adjusted accordingly. The program creates a `vector` of ten `doubles`, reads in ten values from the user, divides each value by the max score (times 100), and prints out the new values. To create the `vector`, parentheses, `(10)`, are used and not uniform initialization, `{10}`, as the latter would create a `vector` of just one element with the value 10. For the sake of brevity, the program forsakes error checking.

```
vector<double> doubleVector(10); // Create a vector of 10 doubles.

// Initialize max to smallest number.
double max { -numeric_limits<double>::infinity() };
```

```
for (size_t i { 0 }; i < doubleVector.size(); ++i) {
    print("Enter score {}: ", i + 1);
    cin >> doubleVector[i];
    if (doubleVector[i] > max) {
        max = doubleVector[i];
    }
}

max /= 100.0;
for (auto& element : doubleVector) {
    element /= max;
    print("{} ", element);
}
```

As you can see from this example, you can use a `vector` just as you would use a standard C-style array. Note that the first `for` loop uses the `size()` member function to determine the number of elements in the container. This example also demonstrates the use of a range-based `for` loop with a `vector`. Here, the range-based `for` loop uses `auto&` and not `auto` because a reference is required so that the actual elements can be modified in each iteration.

> **NOTE** `operator[]` *on a* `vector` *normally returns a reference to the element, which can be used on the left-hand side of assignment statements. If* `operator[]` *is called on a* `const vector` *object, it returns a reference to a* `const` *element, which cannot be used as the target of an assignment. See Chapter 15, "Overloading C++ Operators," for details on how this trick is implemented.*

Dynamic-Length vectors

The real power of a `vector` lies in its ability to grow dynamically. For example, consider the test score normalization program from the previous section with the additional requirement that it should handle any number of test scores. Here is the new version:

```
vector<double> doubleVector; // Create a vector with zero elements.

// Initialize max to smallest number.
double max { -numeric_limits<double>::infinity() };

for (size_t i { 1 }; true; ++i) {
    double value;
    print("Enter score {} (-1 to stop): ", i);
    cin >> value;
    if (value == -1) {
        break;
    }
    doubleVector.push_back(value);
    if (value > max) {
        max = value;
    }
}
```

```
max /= 100.0;
for (auto& element : doubleVector) {
    element /= max;
    print("{} ", element);
}
```

This version of the program uses the default constructor to create a vector with zero elements. As each score is read, it's added to the end of the vector with the push_back() member function, which takes care of allocating space for the new element. The range-based for loop doesn't require any changes.

Formatting and Printing Vectors

Starting with C++23, std::format() and the print() functions can be used to format and print entire containers with a single statement. This works for all Standard Library sequential containers, container adapters, and associative containers, and is introduced in Chapter 2, "Working with Strings and String Views." Here is an example:

```
vector values { 1.1, 2.2, 3.3 };
println("{}", values);    // Prints the following: [1.1, 2.2, 3.3]
```

You can specify the n format specifier to omit the surrounding square brackets:

```
println("{:n}", values); // Prints the following: 1.1, 2.2, 3.3
```

If your compiler doesn't support this feature yet, you can use a range-based for loop to iterate over the elements of a vector and to print them, for example:

```
for (const auto& value : values) { std::cout << value << ", "; }
```

vector Details

Now that you've had a taste of vectors, it's time to delve into their details.

Constructors and Destructors

The default constructor creates a vector with zero elements.

```
vector<int> intVector; // Creates a vector of ints with zero elements
```

You can specify a number of elements and, optionally, a value for those elements, like this:

```
vector<int> intVector(10, 100); // Creates vector of 10 ints with value 100
```

If you omit the default value, the new objects are zero-initialized. *Zero-initialization* constructs objects with the default constructor and initializes primitive integer types (such as char, int, and so on) to zero, primitive floating-point types to 0.0, and pointer types to nullptr.

You can create vectors of built-in classes like this:

```
vector<string> stringVector(10, "hello");
```

User-defined classes can also be used as vector elements:

```
class Element { };
...
vector<Element> elementVector;
```

A `vector` can be constructed with an `initializer_list` containing the initial elements:

```
vector<int> intVector({ 1, 2, 3, 4, 5, 6 });
```

Uniform initialization, as discussed in Chapter 1, "A Crash Course in C++ and the Standard Library," works on most Standard Library containers, including `vector`. Here is an example:

```
vector<int> intVector = { 1, 2, 3, 4, 5, 6 };
vector<int> intVector { 1, 2, 3, 4, 5, 6 };
```

Thanks to class template argument deduction (CTAD), you can omit the template type parameter. Here is an example:

```
vector intVector { 1, 2, 3, 4, 5, 6 };
```

Be cautious with uniform initialization, though; usually, when calling a constructor of an object, the uniform initialization syntax can be used. Here's an example:

```
string text { "Hello World." };
```

With `vector` you need be careful. For example, the following line of code calls a `vector` constructor to create a `vector` of 10 integers with value 100:

```
vector<int> intVector(10, 100); // Creates vector of 10 ints with value 100
```

Using uniform initialization here instead as follows does not create a `vector` of 10 integers, but a `vector` with just two elements, initialized to 10 and 100:

```
vector<int> intVector { 10, 100 }; // Creates vector with two elements: 10 and 100
```

You can allocate `vector`s on the free store as well:

```
auto elementVector { make_unique<vector<Element>>(10) };
```

Copying and Assigning vectors

A `vector` stores copies of the objects, and its destructor calls the destructor for each of the objects. The copy constructor and assignment operator of the `vector` class perform deep copies of all the elements in the `vector`. Thus, for efficiency, you should pass `vector`s by reference-to-non-`const` or reference-to-`const` to functions, instead of by value.

In addition to normal copying and assignment, `vector` provides an `assign()` member function that removes all the current elements and adds any number of new elements. This member function is useful if you want to reuse a `vector`. Here is a trivial example. `intVector` is created with 10 elements having the default value 0. Then `assign()` is used to remove all 10 elements and replace them with 5 elements with value 100:

```
vector<int> intVector(10);
println("intVector: {:n}", intVector);  // 0, 0, 0, 0, 0, 0, 0, 0, 0, 0
...
intVector.assign(5, 100);
println("intVector: {:n}", intVector);  // 100, 100, 100, 100, 100
```

`assign()` can also accept an `initializer_list` as follows. After this statement, `intVector` has four elements with the given values:

```
intVector.assign({ 1, 2, 3, 4 });
println("intVector: {:n}", intVector);  // 1, 2, 3, 4
```

vector provides a swap() member function that allows you to swap the contents of two vectors in constant time. Here is a simple example:

```
vector<int> vectorOne(10);
vector<int> vectorTwo(5, 100);
println("vectorOne: {:n}", vectorOne);  // 0, 0, 0, 0, 0, 0, 0, 0, 0, 0
println("vectorTwo: {:n}", vectorTwo);  // 100, 100, 100, 100, 100

vectorOne.swap(vectorTwo);

println("vectorOne: {:n}", vectorOne);  // 100, 100, 100, 100, 100
println("vectorTwo: {:n}", vectorTwo);  // 0, 0, 0, 0, 0, 0, 0, 0, 0, 0
```

Comparing vectors

The Standard Library provides the usual six overloaded comparison operators for vectors: ==, !=, <, >, <=, >=. Two vectors are equal if they have the same number of elements and all the corresponding elements in the two vectors are equal to each other. Two vectors are compared lexicographically; that is, one vector is "less than" another if all elements 0 through i-1 in the first vector are equal to elements 0 through i-1 in the second vector, but element i in the first is less than element i in the second, where i must be in the range 0...n and n must be less than the size() of the smallest of the two vectors.

> **NOTE** *Comparing two* vectors *with* operator== *or* != *requires the individual elements to be comparable with* operator==. *Comparing two* vectors *with* operator<, >, <=, or >= *requires the individual elements to be comparable with* operator<. *If you intend to store objects of a custom class in a* vector, *make sure to write those operators.*

Here is an example of a program that compares vectors of ints:

```
vector<int> vectorOne(10);
vector<int> vectorTwo(10);

if (vectorOne == vectorTwo) { println("equal!"); }
else { println("not equal!"); }

vectorOne[3] = 50;

if (vectorOne < vectorTwo) { println("vectorOne is less than vectorTwo"); }
else { println("vectorOne is not less than vectorTwo"); }
```

The output of the program is as follows:

```
equal!
vectorOne is not less than vectorTwo
```

vector Iterators

Chapter 17, "Understanding Iterators and the Ranges Library," explains the concepts of container iterators. The discussion can get a bit abstract, so it's helpful to jump in and look at a code example. Here is the last for loop of the test score normalization program from earlier in this chapter:

```
for (auto& element : doubleVector) {
    element /= max;
    print("{} ", element);
}
```

This loop can be written using iterators instead of a range-based for loop as follows:

```
for (vector<double>::iterator iter { begin(doubleVector) };
    iter != end(doubleVector); ++iter) {
    *iter /= max;
    print("{} ", *iter);
}
```

First, take a look at the for loop initialization statement:

```
vector<double>::iterator iter { begin(doubleVector) };
```

Recall that every container defines a type named iterator to represent iterators for that type of container. begin() returns an iterator of that type referring to the first element in the container. Thus, the initialization statement obtains in the variable iter an iterator referring to the first element of doubleVector. Next, look at the for loop comparison:

```
iter != end(doubleVector);
```

This statement simply checks whether the iterator is past the end of the sequence of elements in the vector. When it reaches that point, the loop terminates. Always use operator!= in such statements and not operator< as the latter is not supported by all types of iterators; see Chapter 17 for details.

The increment statement, ++iter, increments the iterator to refer to the next element in the vector.

> **NOTE** *Use pre-increment instead of post-increment when possible because pre-increment is at least as efficient and usually more efficient.* iter++ *must return a new iterator object, while* ++iter *can simply return a reference to* iter. *See Chapter 15, "Overloading C++ Operators," for details on implementing both versions of* operator++.

The for loop body contains these two lines:

```
*iter /= max;
print("{} ", *iter);
```

As you can see, your code can both access and modify the elements over which it iterates. The first line uses operator* to dereference iter to obtain the element to which it refers and assigns to that element. The second line dereferences iter again, but this time only to print the element to the standard output console.

The preceding for loop using iterators can be simplified by using the auto keyword:

```
for (auto iter { begin(doubleVector) };
    iter != end(doubleVector); ++iter) {
    *iter /= max;
    print("{} ", *iter);
}
```

With auto, the compiler automatically deduces the type of the variable iter based on the right-hand side of the initializer, which in this case is the result of the call to begin().

vector supports the following member functions to get iterators:

- begin() and end() returning iterators referring to the first and one past the last element
- rbegin() and rend() returning reverse iterators referring to the last and one before the first element
- cbegin(), cend(), crbegin(), and crend() returning const iterators

> **NOTE** *If you need to iterate over all elements in a container, it's recommended to use a range-based* for *loop instead of iterators as the former is easier to read and write, as well as being less error-prone. Use iterators only when you need to iterate over a subrange or when you need an iterator in the body of the loop.*

Accessing Fields of Object Elements

If the elements of your container are objects, you can use the -> operator on iterators to call member functions or access data members of those objects. For example, the following program creates a vector of 10 strings, then iterates over all of them appending a new string to each one:

```
vector<string> stringVector(10, "hello");
for (auto it { begin(stringVector) }; it != end(stringVector); ++it) {
    it->append(" there");
}
```

Often, using a range-based for loop results in more elegant code, as in this example:

```
for (auto& str : stringVector) {
    str.append(" there");
}
```

const_iterator

The normal iterator is read/write. However, if you call begin() or end() on a const object, or you call cbegin() or cend(), you receive a const_iterator. A const_iterator is read-only; you cannot modify the element it refers to. An iterator can always be converted to a const_iterator, so it's always safe to write something like this:

```
vector<type>::const_iterator it { begin(myVector) };
```

However, a const_iterator cannot be converted to an iterator. If myVector is const, the following line doesn't compile:

```
vector<type>::iterator it { begin(myVector) };
```

> **NOTE** *If you do not need to modify the elements of a* vector*, you should use a* const_iterator*. This rule makes it easier to guarantee correctness of your code and helps the compiler to perform better optimizations.*

When using the auto keyword, using const_iterators looks a bit different. Suppose you write the following code:

```
vector<string> stringVector(10, "hello");
for (auto iter { begin(stringVector) }; iter != end(stringVector); ++iter) {
    println("{}", *iter);
}
```

Because of the auto keyword, the compiler deduces the type of the iter variable automatically and makes it a normal iterator because stringVector is not const. If you want a read-only const_iterator in combination with using auto, then you need to use cbegin() and cend() instead of begin() and end() as follows:

```
for (auto iter { cbegin(stringVector) }; iter != cend(stringVector); ++iter) {
    println("{}", *iter);
}
```

Now the compiler uses const_iterator as type for the variable iter because that's what cbegin() returns.

A range-based for loop can also be forced to use const iterators as follows:

```
for (const auto& element : stringVector) {
    println("{}", element);
}
```

Iterator Safety

Generally, iterators are about as safe as pointers—that is, extremely unsafe. For example, you can write code like this:

```
vector<int> intVector;
auto iter { end(intVector) };
*iter = 10; // Bug! Iter doesn't refer to a valid element.
```

Recall that the iterator returned by end() is one element past the end of a vector, not an iterator referring to the last element! Trying to dereference it results in undefined behavior. Iterators are not required to perform any verification.

Another problem can occur if you use mismatched iterators. For example, the following for loop initializes iter with an iterator from vectorTwo and tries to compare it to the end iterator of vectorOne. Needless to say, this loop will not do what you intended and may never terminate. Dereferencing the iterator in the loop will likely produce undefined results.

```
vector<int> vectorOne(10);
vector<int> vectorTwo(10);
// BUG! Possible infinite loop.
for (auto iter { begin(vectorTwo) }; iter != end(vectorOne); ++iter) { /* ... */ }
```

> **NOTE** *Microsoft Visual C++, by default, gives an assertion error at run time for both of the preceding problems when running a debug build of your program. By default, no verification of iterators is performed for release builds. You can enable it for release builds as well, but it has a performance penalty.*

Other Iterator Operations

The `vector` iterator is random access, which means you can move it backward and forward, and jump around. For example, the following code eventually changes the fifth element (index `4`) to the value `4`:

```
vector<int> intVector(10);
auto it { begin(intVector) };
it += 5;
--it;
*it = 4;
```

Iterators vs. Indexing

Given that you can write a `for` loop that uses a simple index variable and the `size()` member function to iterate over the elements of a `vector`, why should you bother using iterators? That's a valid question, for which there are three main answers:

- Iterators allow you to insert and delete elements and sequences of elements at any point in the container. See the section "Adding and Removing Elements" later in this chapter.
- Iterators allow you to use the Standard Library algorithms, which are discussed in Chapter 20, "Mastering Standard Library Algorithms."
- Using an iterator to access each element sequentially is often more efficient than indexing the container to retrieve each element individually. This generalization is not true for `vector`s, but applies to `list`s, `map`s, and `set`s.

Storing References in a vector

As mentioned earlier in this chapter, it is possible to store references in a container, such as a `vector`. To do this, you store `std::reference_wrapper`s in the container. The `std::ref()` and `cref()` function templates are used to create non-const and `const` `reference_wrapper` instances. The `get()` member function is used to get access to the object wrapped by a `reference_wrapper`. All this is defined in `<functional>`. Here is an example:

```
string str1 { "Hello" };
string str2 { "World" };
```

```
// Create a vector of references to strings.
vector<reference_wrapper<string>> vec { ref(str1) };
vec.push_back(ref(str2));  // push_back() works as well.

// Modify the string referred to by the second reference in the vector.
vec[1].get() += "!";

// The end result is that str2 is modified.
println("{} {}", str1, str2);
```

Adding and Removing Elements

As you already know, you can append an element to a `vector` with the `push_back()` member function. The `vector` provides a corresponding remove member function called `pop_back()`.

> **WARNING** `pop_back()` *does not return the element that is removed. If you want that element, you must first retrieve it with* `back()`.

You can also insert elements at any point in the `vector` with the `insert()` member function, which adds one or more elements to a position specified by an iterator, shifting all subsequent elements down to make room for the new ones. There are five different overloads of `insert()` that do the following:

- Insert a single element.
- Insert *n* copies of a single element.
- Insert elements from an iterator range. Recall that the iterator range is half-open, such that it includes the element referred to by the starting iterator but not the one referred to by the ending iterator.
- Insert a single element by moving the given element to a `vector` using move semantics.
- Insert a list of elements into a `vector` where the list of elements is given as an `initializer_list`.

> **NOTE** *There are overloads of* `push_back()` *and* `insert()` *that take an lvalue or an rvalue as a parameter. Both overloads allocate memory as needed to store the new elements. The lvalue overloads store copies of the given elements, while the rvalue overloads use move semantics to move ownership of the given elements to the* `vector` *instead of copying them.*

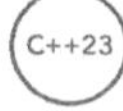

C++23 adds the following member functions: `assign_range()` to replace all elements in a `vector` with the elements of a given range, `insert_range()` to insert all elements of a given range into a `vector` at a given position, and `append_range()` to append all elements of a given range to the end of a `vector`. Chapter 17 discusses ranges in detail.

You can remove elements from any point in a `vector` with `erase()`, and you can remove all elements with `clear()`. There are two overloads of `erase()`: one accepting a single iterator to remove a single element, and one accepting two iterators specifying a range of elements to remove.

Let's look at an example program that demonstrates some of the member functions for adding and removing elements. The following code snippet demonstrates `clear()`, `push_back()`, `pop_back()`, the C++23 `append_range()`, the two-argument version of `erase()`, and the following overloads of `insert()`:

- `insert(const_iterator pos, const T& x)`: The value `x` is inserted at position `pos`.
- `insert(const_iterator pos, size_type n, const T& x)`: The value `x` is inserted `n` times at position `pos`.
- `insert(const_iterator pos, InputIterator first, InputIterator last)`: The elements in the range `[first, last)` are inserted at position `pos`.

Here is the code snippet:

```
vector vectorOne { 1, 2, 3, 5 };
vector<int> vectorTwo;
println("{:n}", vectorOne);

// Oops, we forgot to add 4. Insert it in the correct place.
vectorOne.insert(cbegin(vectorOne) + 3, 4);

// Add elements 6 through 10 to vectorTwo.
for (int i { 6 }; i <= 10; ++i) {
    vectorTwo.push_back(i);
}
println("{:n}", vectorOne);
println("{:n}", vectorTwo);

// Add all elements from vectorTwo to the end of vectorOne.
vectorOne.insert(cend(vectorOne), cbegin(vectorTwo), cend(vectorTwo));
println("{:n}", vectorOne);

// Add all vectorTwo elements to the end of vectorOne using C++23 append_range().
// Note how much clearer this is compared to the previous call to insert().
vectorOne.append_range(vectorTwo);
println("{:n}", vectorOne);

// Now erase the numbers 2 through 5 in vectorOne.
vectorOne.erase(cbegin(vectorOne) + 1, cbegin(vectorOne) + 5);
println("{:n}", vectorOne);

// Clear vectorTwo entirely.
vectorTwo.clear();

// And add 10 copies of the value 100.
vectorTwo.insert(cbegin(vectorTwo), 10, 100);
println("{:n}", vectorTwo);
```

```
// Decide we only want 9 elements.
vectorTwo.pop_back();
println("{:n}", vectorTwo);
```

The output of the program is as follows:

```
1, 2, 3, 5
1, 2, 3, 4, 5
6, 7, 8, 9, 10
1, 2, 3, 4, 5, 6, 7, 8, 9, 10
1, 2, 3, 4, 5, 6, 7, 8, 9, 10, 6, 7, 8, 9, 10
1, 6, 7, 8, 9, 10, 6, 7, 8, 9, 10
100, 100, 100, 100, 100, 100, 100, 100, 100, 100
100, 100, 100, 100, 100, 100, 100, 100, 100
```

Recall that iterator pairs represent half-open ranges, and `insert()` adds elements before the element referred to by a given iterator position. Thus, you can insert the entire contents of `vectorTwo` at the end of `vectorOne`, like this:

```
vectorOne.insert(cend(vectorOne), cbegin(vectorTwo), cend(vectorTwo));
```

> **WARNING** *Member functions such as* `insert()` *and* `erase()` *that take a common iterator range as argument assume that the beginning and ending iterators refer to elements in the same container and that the end iterator refers to an element at or past the begin iterator. The member functions will not work correctly if these preconditions are not met!*

If you want to remove all elements satisfying a condition, one solution would be to write a loop iterating over all the elements and erasing every element that matches the condition. However, this solution has quadratic complexity, which is bad for performance. This quadratic complexity can be avoided by using the *remove-erase-idiom*, which has a linear complexity. The remove-erase-idiom is discussed in Chapter 20.

Starting with C++20, however, there is a more elegant solution in the form of the `std::erase()` and `std::erase_if()` non-member functions, defined for all Standard Library containers. The former is demonstrated in the following code snippet:

```
vector values { 1, 2, 3, 2, 1, 2, 4, 5 };
println("{:n}", values);

erase(values, 2);  // Removes all values equal to 2.
println("{:n}", values);
```

The output is as follows:

```
1, 2, 3, 2, 1, 2, 4, 5
1, 3, 1, 4, 5
```

`erase_if()` works similarly, but instead of passing a value as second argument, a predicate is passed that returns `true` for elements that should be removed, and `false` for elements that should be kept.

The predicate can take the form of a function pointer, a function object, or a lambda expression, all of which are discussed in detail in Chapter 19, "Function Pointers, Function Objects, and Lambda Expressions."

Move Semantics

Adding elements to a `vector` can make use of move semantics to improve performance in certain situations. For example, suppose you have the following `vector` of `string`s:

```
vector<string> vec;
```

You can add an element to this `vector` as follows:

```
string myElement(5, 'a');  // Constructs the string "aaaaa"
vec.push_back(myElement);
```

However, because `myElement` is not a temporary object, `push_back()` makes a copy of `myElement` and puts it into the `vector`.

The `vector` class also defines a `push_back(T&&)`, which is the move equivalent of `push_back(const T&)`. So, copying can be avoided if you call `push_back()` as follows:

```
vec.push_back(move(myElement));
```

This statement explicitly says that `myElement` should be moved into the `vector`. Note that after this call, `myElement` is in a valid but otherwise indeterminate state. You should not use `myElement` anymore, unless you first bring it back to a determinate state, for example by calling `clear()` on it! You can also call `push_back()` as follows:

```
vec.push_back(string(5, 'a'));
```

This call to `push_back()` triggers a call to the move overload because the call to the `string` constructor results in a temporary object. The `push_back()` member function moves this temporary `string` object into the `vector`, avoiding any copying.

Emplace Operations

C++ supports *emplace operations* on most Standard Library containers, including `vector`. Emplace means "to put into place." An example is the `emplace_back()` member function of `vector`, which does not copy or move anything. Instead, it makes space in the container and constructs the object *in place*, as in this example:

```
vec.emplace_back(5, 'a');
```

The emplace member functions take a variable number of arguments as a variadic template. Variadic templates are discussed in Chapter 26, "Advanced Templates," but those details are not required to understand how to use `emplace_back()`. Basically, the arguments passed to `emplace_back()` are forwarded to a constructor of the type stored in the `vector`. The difference in performance between `emplace_back()` and `push_back()` using move semantics depends on how your specific compiler implements these operations. In most situations, you can pick the one based on the syntax that you prefer:

```
vec.push_back(string(5, 'a'));
// Or
vec.emplace_back(5, 'a');
```

The `emplace_back()` member function returns a reference to the inserted element. There is also an `emplace()` member function that constructs an object in place at a specific position in the `vector` and returns an iterator to the inserted element.

Algorithmic Complexity and Iterator Invalidation

Inserting or erasing elements in a `vector` causes all subsequent elements to shift up or down to make room for, or fill in the holes left by, the affected elements. Thus, these operations take linear complexity. Furthermore, all iterators referring to the insertion or removal point or subsequent positions are invalid following the action. The iterators are not "magically" moved to keep up with the elements that are shifted up or down in the `vector`—that's up to you.

Also keep in mind that an internal `vector` reallocation can cause invalidation of all iterators referring to elements in the `vector`, not just those referring to elements past the point of insertion or deletion. See the next section for details.

The vector Memory Allocation Scheme

A `vector` allocates memory automatically to store the elements that you insert. Recall that the `vector` requirements dictate that the elements must be in contiguous memory, like in standard C-style arrays. Because it's impossible to request to add memory to the end of a current chunk of memory, every time a `vector` allocates more memory, it must allocate a new, larger chunk in a separate memory location and copy/move all the elements to the new chunk. This process is time-consuming, so `vector` implementations attempt to avoid it by allocating more space than needed when they have to perform a reallocation. That way, they can avoid reallocating memory every time you insert an element.

One obvious question at this point is why you, as a client of `vector`, care how it manages its memory internally. You might think that the principle of abstraction should allow you to disregard the internals of the `vector` memory allocation scheme. Unfortunately, there are two reasons why you need to understand how it works:

- **Efficiency:** The `vector` allocation scheme can guarantee that an element insertion runs in *amortized constant time*: most of the time the operation is constant, but once in a while (if it requires a reallocation), it's linear. If you are worried about efficiency, you can control when a `vector` performs reallocations.
- **Iterator invalidations:** A reallocation invalidates all iterators referring to elements in a `vector`.

Thus, the `vector` interface allows you to query and control the `vector` reallocations, both explained in the upcoming subsections.

> **WARNING** *If you don't control the reallocations explicitly, you should assume that all insertions cause a reallocation and thus invalidate all iterators.*

Size and Capacity

`vector` provides two member functions for obtaining information about its size: `size()` and `capacity()`. The `size()` member function returns the number of elements in a `vector`, while `capacity()` returns the number of elements that it can hold without a reallocation. Thus, the number of elements that you can insert without causing a reallocation is `capacity() - size()`.

> **NOTE** *You can query whether a* `vector` *is empty with the* `empty()` *member function. A* `vector` *can be empty but have nonzero capacity.*

There are also non-member `std::size()` and `std::empty()` global functions, which can be used with all containers. They can also be used with statically allocated C-style arrays not accessed through pointers, and with `initializer_lists`. Here is an example of using them with a `vector`:

```
vector vec { 1, 2, 3 };
println("{}", size(vec));  // 3
println("{}", empty(vec)); // false
```

Additionally, `std::ssize()`, a global non-member helper function, returns the size as a signed integral type. Here's an example:

```
auto s1 { size(vec) };   // Type is size_t (unsigned)
auto s2 { ssize(vec) };  // Type is long long (signed)
```

Reserving Capacity

If you don't care about efficiency or iterator invalidations, there is never a need to control the `vector` memory allocation explicitly. However, if you want to make your program as efficient as possible or you want to guarantee that iterators will not be invalidated, you can force a `vector` to preallocate enough space to hold all of its elements. Of course, you need to know how many elements it will hold, which is sometimes impossible to predict.

One way to preallocate space is to call `reserve()`, which allocates enough memory to hold the specified number of elements. The upcoming round-robin class example shows the `reserve()` member function in action.

> **WARNING** *Reserving space for elements changes the capacity, but not the size. That is, it doesn't actually create elements. Don't access elements past a* `vector`*'s size.*

Another way to preallocate space is to specify, in the constructor, or with the `resize()` or `assign()` member function, how many elements you want a `vector` to store. This member function actually creates a `vector` of that size (and probably of that capacity).

Reclaiming All Memory

A vector automatically allocates more memory if needed; however, it will never release any memory, unless the vector is destroyed. Removing elements from a vector decreases the size of the vector, but never its capacity. How then can you reclaim its memory?

One option is to use the shrink_to_fit() member function, which requests a vector to reduce its capacity to its size. However, it's just a request, and a Standard Library implementation is allowed to ignore this request.

Reclaiming **all** memory of a vector can be done using the following trick: swap the vector with an empty one. The following code snippet shows how memory of a vector called values can be reclaimed with a single statement. The third line of code constructs a temporary empty default-constructed vector of the same type as values and swaps this with values. All memory that was allocated for values now belongs to this temporary vector, which is automatically destroyed at the end of that statement freeing all its memory. The end result is that all memory that was allocated for values is reclaimed, and values is left with a capacity of zero.

```
vector<int> values;
// Populate values ...
vector<int>().swap(values);
```

Directly Accessing the Data

A vector stores its data contiguously in memory. You can get a pointer to this block of memory with the data() member function.

There is also a non-member std::data() function that can be used to get a pointer to the data. It works for the array and vector containers, strings, statically allocated C-style arrays not accessed through pointers, and initializer_lists. Here is an example for a vector:

```
vector vec { 1, 2, 3 };
int* data1 { vec.data() };
int* data2 { data(vec) };
```

Another way to get access to the memory block of a vector is by taking the address of the first element, as in: &vec[0]. You might find this kind of code in legacy code bases, but it is not safe for empty vectors; as such, I recommend not to use it and instead use data().

Move Semantics

All Standard Library containers support move semantics by including a move constructor and move assignment operator. See Chapter 9 for details on move semantics. Standard Library containers can be returned from functions *by value* without performance penalty. Take a look at the following function:

```
vector<int> createVectorOfSize(size_t size)
{
    vector<int> vec(size);
    for (int contents { 0 }; auto& i : vec) { i = contents++; }
    return vec;
}
...
vector<int> myVector;
myVector = createVectorOfSize(123);
```

Without move semantics, assigning the result of `createVectorOfSize()` to `myVector` might call the copy assignment operator. With the move semantics support in the Standard Library containers, copying of the `vector` is avoided. Instead, the assignment to `myVector` triggers a call to the move assignment operator.

Keep in mind, though, that for move semantics to work properly with Standard Library containers, the move constructor and move assignment operator of the type stored in the container must be marked as `noexcept`! Why are these move member functions not allowed to throw any exceptions? Imagine that they are allowed to throw exceptions. Now, when adding, for example, new elements to a `vector`, it might be that the capacity of the `vector` is not sufficient and that it needs to allocate a bigger block of memory. Subsequently, the `vector` must either copy or move all the data from the original memory block to the new one. If this would be done using a move member function that can potentially throw, then it might happen that an exception gets thrown when part of the data has already been moved to the new memory block. What can we do then? Not much. To avoid these kinds of problems, Standard Library containers will only use move member functions if they guarantee not to throw any exceptions. If they are not marked `noexcept`, the copy member functions will be used instead to guarantee strong exception safety.

When implementing your own Standard Library–like containers, there is a useful helper function available called `std::move_if_noexcept()`, defined in `<utility>`. This can be used to call either the move constructor or the copy constructor depending on whether the move constructor is `noexcept`. In itself, `move_if_noexcept()` doesn't do much. It accepts a reference as a parameter and converts it to either an rvalue reference if the move constructor is `noexcept` or to a reference-to-`const` otherwise, but this simple trick allows you to call the correct constructor with a single call.

The Standard Library does not provide a similar helper function to call the move assignment operator or copy assignment operator depending on whether the former is `noexcept`. Implementing one yourself is not too complicated, but requires some template metaprogramming techniques and type traits to inspect properties of types. Both topics are discussed in Chapter 26, which also gives an example of implementing your own `move_assign_if_noexcept()`.

vector Example: A Round-Robin Class

A common problem in computer science is distributing requests among a finite list of resources. For example, a simple operating system could keep a list of processes and assign a time slice (such as 100ms) to each process to let the process perform some of its work. After the time slice is finished, the OS suspends the process, and the next process in the list is given a time slice to perform some of its work. One of the simplest algorithmic solutions to this problem is *round-robin scheduling*. When the time slice of the last process is finished, the scheduler starts over again with the first process. For example, in the case of three processes, the first-time slice would go to the first process, the second slice to the second process, the third slice to the third process, and the fourth slice back to the first process. The cycle would continue in this way indefinitely.

Suppose that you decide to write a generic round-robin scheduling class that can be used with any type of resource. The class should support adding and removing resources and should support cycling through the resources to obtain the next one. You could use a `vector` directly, but it's often helpful to write a wrapper class that provides more directly the functionality you need for your specific application. The following example shows a `RoundRobin` class template with comments explaining the code.

First, here is the class definition, exported from a module called round_robin:

```
export module round_robin;
import std;

// Class template RoundRobin
// Provides simple round-robin semantics for a list of elements.
export template <typename T>
class RoundRobin final
{
    public:
        // Client can give a hint as to the number of expected elements for
        // increased efficiency.
        explicit RoundRobin(std::size_t numExpected = 0);
        // Prevent copy construction and copy assignment
        RoundRobin(const RoundRobin& src) = delete;
        RoundRobin& operator=(const RoundRobin& rhs) = delete;
        // Explicitly default a move constructor and move assignment operator
        RoundRobin(RoundRobin&& src) noexcept = default;
        RoundRobin& operator=(RoundRobin&& rhs) noexcept = default;
        // Appends element to the end of the list. May be called
        // between calls to getNext().
        void add(const T& element);
        // Removes the first (and only the first) element
        // in the list that is equal (with operator==) to element.
        // May be called between calls to getNext().
        void remove(const T& element);
        // Returns the next element in the list, starting with the first,
        // and cycling back to the first when the end of the list is
        // reached, taking into account elements that are added or removed.
        T& getNext();
    private:
        std::vector<T> m_elements;
        typename std::vector<T>::iterator m_nextElement;
};
```

As you can see, the public interface is straightforward: only three member functions plus the constructor. The resources are stored in a vector called m_elements. The iterator m_nextElement always refers to the element that will be returned with the next call to getNext(). If getNext() hasn't been called yet, m_nextElement is equal to begin(m_elements). Note the use of the typename keyword in front of the line declaring m_nextElement. So far, you've only seen that keyword used to specify template type parameters, but there is another use for it. You must specify typename explicitly whenever you access a type based on one or more template parameters. In this case, the template parameter T is used to access the iterator type. Thus, you must specify typename.

The class also prevents copy construction and copy assignment because of the m_nextElement data member. To make copy construction and copy assignment work, you would have to implement an assignment operator and copy constructor and make sure m_nextElement is valid in the destination object.

The implementation of the RoundRobin class follows with comments explaining the code. Note the use of reserve() in the constructor, and the extensive use of iterators in add(), remove(), and getNext(). The trickiest aspect is handling m_nextElement in the add() and remove() member functions.

```
template <typename T> RoundRobin<T>::RoundRobin(std::size_t numExpected)
{
    // If the client gave a guideline, reserve that much space.
    m_elements.reserve(numExpected);

    // Initialize m_nextElement even though it isn't used until
    // there's at least one element.
    m_nextElement = begin(m_elements);
}

// Always add the new element at the end.
template <typename T> void RoundRobin<T>::add(const T& element)
{
    // Even though we add the element at the end, the vector could
    // reallocate and invalidate the m_nextElement iterator with
    // the push_back() call. Take advantage of the random-access
    // iterator features to save our spot.
    // Note: ptrdiff_t is a type capable of storing the difference
    //       between two random-access iterators.
    std::ptrdiff_t pos { m_nextElement - begin(m_elements) };

    // Add the element.
    m_elements.push_back(element);

    // Reset our iterator to make sure it is valid.
    m_nextElement = begin(m_elements) + pos;
}

template <typename T> void RoundRobin<T>::remove(const T& element)
{
    for (auto it { begin(m_elements) }; it != end(m_elements); ++it) {
        if (*it == element) {
            // Removing an element invalidates the m_nextElement iterator
            // if it refers to an element past the point of the removal.
            // Take advantage of the random-access features of the iterator
            // to track the position of the current element after removal.
            std::ptrdiff_t newPos;

            if (m_nextElement == end(m_elements) - 1 &&
                m_nextElement == it) {
                // m_nextElement refers to the last element in the list,
                // and we are removing that last element, so wrap back to
                // the beginning.
                newPos = 0;
            } else if (m_nextElement <= it) {
                // Otherwise, if m_nextElement is before or at the one
                // we're removing, the new position is the same as before.
                newPos = m_nextElement - begin(m_elements);
            } else {
                // Otherwise, it's one less than before.
                newPos = m_nextElement - begin(m_elements) - 1;
            }
```

```
                // Erase the element (and ignore the return value).
                m_elements.erase(it);

                // Now reset our iterator to make sure it is valid.
                m_nextElement = begin(m_elements) + newPos;

                return;
            }
        }
    }

template <typename T> T& RoundRobin<T>::getNext()
{
    // First, make sure there are elements.
    if (m_elements.empty()) {
        throw std::out_of_range { "No elements in the list" };
    }

    // Store the current element which we need to return.
    auto& toReturn { *m_nextElement };

    // Increment the iterator modulo the number of elements.
    ++m_nextElement;
    if (m_nextElement == end(m_elements)) { m_nextElement = begin(m_elements); }

    // Return a reference to the element.
    return toReturn;
}
```

Here's a simple implementation of a scheduler that uses the `RoundRobin` class template, with comments explaining the code:

```
// Basic Process class.
class Process final
{
    public:
        // Constructor accepting the name of the process.
        explicit Process(string name) : m_name { move(name) } {}

        // Lets a process perform its work for the duration of a time slice.
        void doWorkDuringTimeSlice()
        {
            println("Process {} performing work during time slice.", m_name);
            // Actual implementation omitted.
        }

        // Needed for the RoundRobin::remove() member function to work.
        bool operator==(const Process&) const = default; // = default since C++20.
    private:
        string m_name;
};
```

```
// Basic round-robin based process scheduler.
class Scheduler final
{
    public:
        // Constructor takes a vector of processes.
        explicit Scheduler(const vector<Process>& processes)
        {
            // Add the processes.
            for (auto& process : processes) { m_processes.add(process); }
        }

        // Selects the next process using a round-robin scheduling algorithm
        // and allows it to perform some work during this time slice.
        void scheduleTimeSlice()
        {
            try {
                m_processes.getNext().doWorkDuringTimeSlice();
            } catch (const out_of_range&) {
                println(cerr, "No more processes to schedule.");
            }
        }

        // Removes the given process from the list of processes.
        void removeProcess(const Process& process)
        {
            m_processes.remove(process);
        }
    private:
        RoundRobin<Process> m_processes;
};

int main()
{
    vector processes { Process { "1" }, Process { "2" }, Process { "3" } };

    Scheduler scheduler { processes };
    for (size_t i { 0 }; i < 4; ++i) { scheduler.scheduleTimeSlice(); }

    scheduler.removeProcess(processes[1]);
    println("Removed second process");

    for (size_t i { 0 }; i < 4; ++i) { scheduler.scheduleTimeSlice(); }
}
```

The output should be as follows:

```
Process 1 performing work during time slice.
Process 2 performing work during time slice.
Process 3 performing work during time slice.
Process 1 performing work during time slice.
Removed second process
Process 3 performing work during time slice.
Process 1 performing work during time slice.
Process 3 performing work during time slice.
Process 1 performing work during time slice.
```

The vector<bool> Specialization

The C++ standard requires a partial specialization of `vector` for `bool`s, with the intention that it optimizes space allocation by "packing" the Boolean values. Recall that a `bool` is either `true` or `false` and thus could be represented by a single bit, which can take on exactly two values. C++ does not have a native type that stores exactly one bit. Some compilers represent a Boolean value with a type the same size as a `char`; other compilers use an `int`. The `vector<bool>` specialization is supposed to store the "array of `bool`s" in single bits, thus saving space.

> **NOTE** *You can think of the* `vector<bool>` *as a bit-field instead of a* `vector`. *The* `bitset` *container described later in this chapter provides a more full-featured bit-field implementation than does* `vector<bool>`. *However, the benefit of* `vector<bool>` *is that it can change size dynamically.*

In a half-hearted attempt to provide some bit-field routines for `vector<bool>`, there is one additional member function called `flip()` that complements bits; that is, `true` becomes `false`, and `false` becomes `true`, similar to the logical NOT operator. This member function can be called either on the container—in which case it complements all the elements in the container—or on a single reference returned from `operator[]` or a similar member function, in which case it complements that single element.

At this point, you should be wondering how you can call a member function on a reference to `bool`. The answer is that you can't. The `vector<bool>` specialization actually defines a class called `reference` that serves as a proxy for the underlying `bool` (or bit). When you call `operator[]`, `at()`, or a similar member function, then `vector<bool>` returns a `reference` object, which is a proxy for the real `bool`.

> **WARNING** *The fact that references returned from* `vector<bool>` *are really proxies means that you can't take their addresses to obtain pointers to the actual elements in the container.*

In practice, the little amount of space saved by packing `bool`s hardly seems worth the extra effort. Even worse, accessing and modifying elements in a `vector<bool>` is much slower than, for example, in a `vector<int>`. Many C++ experts recommend avoiding `vector<bool>` in favor of the `bitset`. If you do need a dynamically sized bit field, then just use something like `vector<std::int_fast8_t>` or `vector<unsigned char>`. The `std::int_fast8_t` type is defined in `<cstdint>`. It is a signed integer type for which the compiler has to use the fastest integer type it has that is at least 8 bits.

deque

`deque` (abbreviation for *double-ended queue*) is almost identical to `vector`, but is used far less frequently. It is defined in `<deque>`. The principal differences are as follows:

- Elements are not stored contiguously in memory.
- A `deque` supports true constant-time insertion and removal of elements at both the front and the back (a `vector` supports amortized constant time at just the back).
- A `deque` provides the following member functions that `vector` omits:
  - `push_front()`: Inserts an element at the beginning.
  - `pop_front()`: Removes the first element.
  - `emplace_front()`: Creates a new element in-place at the beginning and returns a reference to the inserted element.
  - `prepend_range()`: Adds all elements of a given range to the beginning of a `deque`. Available since C++23.
- A `deque` never moves its elements to a bigger array (as `vector` does) when inserting elements at the front or at the back. This also means that a `deque` does not invalidate any iterators in such cases.
- A `deque` does not expose its memory management scheme via `reserve()` or `capacity()`.

`deque`s are rarely used, as opposed to `vector`s, so they are not further discussed. Consult a Standard Library Reference for a detailed list of all supported member functions.

list

The Standard Library `list` class template, defined in `<list>`, is a standard doubly linked list. It supports constant-time insertion and deletion of elements at any point in the list but provides slow (linear) time access to individual elements. In fact, the list does not even provide random-access operations like `operator[]`. Only through iterators can you access individual elements.

Most of the `list` operations are identical to those of `vector`, including the constructors, destructor, copying operations, assignment operations, and comparison operations. This section focuses on those member functions that differ from those of `vector`.

Accessing Elements

The only member functions provided by a `list` to access elements are `front()` and `back()`, both of which run in constant time. These member functions return a reference to the first and last elements in a `list`. All other element access must be performed through iterators.

Just as `vector`, `list` supports `begin()`, `end()`, `rbegin()`, `rend()`, `cbegin()`, `cend()`, `crbegin()`, and `crend()`.

> **WARNING** *Lists do not provide random access to elements.*

Iterators

A list iterator is bidirectional, not random access like a vector iterator. That means that you cannot add and subtract list iterators from each other or perform other pointer arithmetic on them. For example, if p is a list iterator, you can traverse through the elements of the list by doing ++p or --p, but you cannot use the addition or subtraction operator; p+n and p-n do not work.

Adding and Removing Elements

A list supports the same add and remove element member functions as a vector, including push_back(), pop_back(), emplace(), emplace_back(), the five forms of insert(), assign_range(), insert_range(), append_range(), the two forms of erase(), and clear(). Like a deque, it also provides push_front(), emplace_front(), pop_front(), and prepend_range(). Member functions adding or removing a single element run in constant time, once you've found the correct position, while member functions adding or removing multiple elements run in linear time. Thus, a list could be appropriate for applications that perform many insertions and deletions from the data structure, but do not need quick index-based element access. But even then, a vector might still be faster. Use a performance profiler to make sure.

list Size

Like deques, and unlike vectors, lists do not expose their underlying memory model. Consequently, they support size(), empty(), and resize(), but not reserve() or capacity(). Note that the size() member function on a list has constant complexity.

Special list Operations

A list provides several special operations that exploit its quick element insertion and deletion. This section provides an overview of some of these operations with examples. Consult a Standard Library Reference for a thorough reference of all the member functions.

Splicing

The linked-list characteristics of a list allow it to *splice*, or insert, an entire list at any position in another list in constant time. The simplest version of this member function works as follows:

```
// Store the a words in the main dictionary.
list<string> dictionary { "aardvark", "ambulance" };
// Store the b words.
list<string> bWords { "bathos", "balderdash" };
// Add the c words to the main dictionary.
dictionary.push_back("canticle");
dictionary.push_back("consumerism");
// Splice the b words into the main dictionary.
if (!bWords.empty()) {
    // Get an iterator to the last b word.
    auto iterLastB { --(cend(bWords)) };
    // Iterate up to the spot where we want to insert b words.
    auto it { cbegin(dictionary) };
    for (; it != cend(dictionary); ++it) {
        if (*it > *iterLastB) { break; }
    }
```

```
        // Add in the b words. This action removes the elements from bWords.
        dictionary.splice(it, bWords);
    }
    // Print out the dictionary.
    println("{:n:}", dictionary);
```

The result from running this program looks like this:

```
aardvark, ambulance, bathos, balderdash, canticle, consumerism
```

There are also two other overloads of `splice()`: one that inserts a single element from another `list` and one that inserts a range from another `list`. Additionally, all overloads of `splice()` are available with either a normal reference or an rvalue reference to the source `list`.

> **WARNING** *Splicing is destructive to the `list` passed as an argument, i.e., it removes the spliced elements from one `list` to insert them into the other.*

More Efficient Versions of Algorithms

In addition to `splice()`, a `list` provides special implementations of several of the generic Standard Library algorithms. The generic forms are covered in Chapter 20. Here, only the specific versions provided by `list` are discussed.

> **NOTE** *When you have a choice, use the `list`-specific member functions rather than the generic Standard Library algorithms because the former are more efficient. Sometimes you don't have a choice, and you must use the `list`-specific member functions; for example, the generic `std::sort()` algorithm requires random-access iterators, which a `list` does not provide.*

The following table summarizes the algorithms for which `list` provides special implementations as member functions. See Chapter 20 for more details on the algorithms.

MEMBER FUNCTION	DESCRIPTION
`remove()` `remove_if()`	Removes all elements matching certain criteria from a `list` and returns the number of removed elements.
`unique()`	Removes duplicate consecutive elements from a `list`, based on `operator==` or a user-supplied binary predicate, and returns the number of removed elements.
`merge()`	Merges two `lists`. Both `lists` must be sorted according to `operator<` or a user-defined comparator. Like `splice()`, `merge()` is destructive to the `list` passed as an argument.

MEMBER FUNCTION	DESCRIPTION
sort()	Performs a stable sort on elements in a list.
reverse()	Reverses the order of the elements in a list.

list Example: Determining Enrollment

Suppose that you are writing a computer registration system for a university. One feature you might provide is the ability to generate a complete list of enrolled students in the university from lists of the students in each class. For the sake of this example, assume that you must write only a single function that takes a `vector` of `list`s of student names (as `string`s), plus a `list` of students that have been dropped from their courses because they failed to pay tuition. This function should generate a complete `list` of all the students in all the courses, without any duplicates, and without those students who have been dropped. Note that students might be in more than one course.

Here is the code for this function, with comments explaining the code. With the power of Standard Library `list`s, the function is practically shorter than its written description! Note that the Standard Library allows you to "nest" containers: in this case, you can use a `vector` of `list`s.

```
// courseStudents is a vector of lists, one for each course. The lists
// contain the students enrolled in those courses. They are not sorted.
//
// droppedStudents is a list of students who failed to pay their
// tuition and so were dropped from their courses.
//
// The function returns a list of every enrolled (non-dropped) student in
// all the courses.
list<string> getTotalEnrollment(const vector<list<string>>& courseStudents,
                                const list<string>& droppedStudents)
{
    list<string> allStudents;

    // Concatenate all the course lists onto the master list
    for (auto& lst : courseStudents) {
        allStudents.append_range(lst);
    }

    // Sort the master list
    allStudents.sort();

    // Remove duplicate student names (those who are in multiple courses).
    allStudents.unique();

    // Remove students who are on the dropped list.
    // Iterate through the dropped list, calling remove on the
    // master list for each student in the dropped list.
    for (auto& str : droppedStudents) {
        allStudents.remove(str);
    }

    // done!
    return allStudents;
}
```

> **NOTE** *This example demonstrates the use of the* list*-specific algorithms. As stated several times before, often a* vector *is faster than a* list*. So, the recommended solution to the student enrollment problem would be to only use* vectors *and to combine these with generic Standard Library algorithms, but those are discussed in Chapter 20.*

forward_list

A forward_list, defined in <forward_list>, is similar to a list except that it is a singly linked list, while list is a doubly linked list. This means that forward_list supports only forward iteration, and because of this, ranges need to be specified differently compared to a list. If you want to modify any list, you need access to the element before the first element of interest. Because a forward_list does not have an iterator that supports going backward, there is no easy way to get to the preceding element. For this reason, ranges that will be modified—for example, ranges supplied to erase() and splice()—must be open at the beginning. The begin() function that was discussed earlier returns an iterator to the first element and thus can only be used to construct a range that is closed at the beginning. The forward_list class therefore provides a before_begin() member function, which returns an iterator that points to an imaginary element before the beginning of the list. You cannot dereference this iterator as it points to invalid data. However, incrementing this iterator by 1 makes it the same as the iterator returned by begin(); as a result, it can be used to make a range that is open at the beginning.

Constructors and assignment operators are similar between a list and a forward_list. The C++ standard requires that forward_list minimizes its memory use. That's the reason why there is no size() member function, because by not providing it, there is no need to store the size of the list. Additionally, a list has to store a pointer to the previous and the next element in the list, while a forward_list only needs to store a pointer to the next element, further reducing memory use. For example, each element in a list<int> on a 64-bit system requires 20 bytes (two 64-bit pointers, 16 bytes, and the int itself, 4 bytes). A forward_list<int> requires only 12 bytes (one 64-bit pointer, 8 bytes, and the int, 4 bytes) per element.

The following table sums up the differences between a list and a forward_list. A filled box (■) means the container supports that operation, while an empty box (□) means the operation is not supported.

OPERATION	list	forward_list
append_range() (C++23)	■	□
assign()	■	■
assign_range() (C++23)	■	■
back()	■	□

OPERATION	list	forward_list
before_begin()	□	■
begin()	■	■
cbefore_begin()	□	■
cbegin()	■	■
cend()	■	■
clear()	■	■
crbegin()	■	□
crend()	■	□
emplace()	■	□
emplace_after()	□	■
emplace_back()	■	□
emplace_front()	■	■
empty()	■	■
end()	■	■
erase()	■	□
erase_after()	□	■
front()	■	■
insert()	■	□
insert_after()	□	■
insert_range() (C++23)	■	□
insert_range_after() (C++23)	□	■
iterator / const_iterator	■	■
max_size()	■	■
merge()	■	■
pop_back()	■	□
pop_front()	■	■
prepend_range() (C++23)	■	■
push_back()	■	□

continues

(continued)

OPERATION	list	forward_list
push_front()	■	■
rbegin()	■	□
remove()	■	■
remove_if()	■	■
rend()	■	□
resize()	■	■
reverse()	■	■
reverse_iterator / const_reverse_iterator	■	□
size()	■	□
sort()	■	■
splice()	■	□
splice_after()	□	■
swap()	■	■
unique()	■	■

The following example demonstrates the use of `forward_lists`:

```
// Create 3 forward lists using an initializer_list
// to initialize their elements (uniform initialization).
forward_list<int> list1 { 5, 6 };
forward_list list2 { 1, 2, 3, 4 };  // CTAD is supported.
forward_list list3 { 7, 8, 9 };

// Insert list2 at the front of list1 using splice.
list1.splice_after(list1.before_begin(), list2);

// Add number 0 at the beginning of the list1.
list1.push_front(0);

// Insert list3 at the end of list1.
// For this, we first need an iterator to the last element.
auto iter { list1.before_begin() };
auto iterTemp { iter };
while (++iterTemp != end(list1)) { ++iter; }
list1.insert_after(iter, cbegin(list3), cend(list3));

// Output the contents of list1.
println("{:n}", list1);
```

To insert `list3` at the end of `list1`, you need an iterator to the last element of `list1`. However, because this is a `forward_list`, you cannot use `--end(list1)`, so you need to iterate over the list from the beginning and stop at the last element. The output is as follows:

```
0, 1, 2, 3, 4, 5, 6, 7, 8, 9
```

array

An `array`, defined in `<array>`, is similar to a `vector` except that it is of a fixed size; it cannot grow or shrink in size. The purpose of a fixed size is to allow an `array` to be allocated on the stack, rather than always demanding access to the free store as `vector` does.

For `array`s containing primitive types (integers, floating-point numbers, characters, Booleans, and so on), initialization of elements is different compared to how they are initialized for containers such as `vector`, `list`, and so on. If no initialization values are given to an `array` when it is created, then the `array` elements will be uninitialized, i.e., contain garbage. For other containers, such as `vector` and `list`, elements are always initialized, either with given values or using zero initialization. As such, `array`s behave virtually identical to C-style arrays.

Just like `vector`s, `array`s support random-access iterators, and elements are stored in contiguous memory. An `array` has support for `front()`, `back()`, `at()`, and `operator[]`. It also supports a `fill()` member function to fill the `array` with a specific element. Because it is fixed in size, it does not support `push_back()`, `pop_back()`, `insert()`, `erase()`, `clear()`, `resize()`, `reserve()`, `capacity()`, or any of the range-based member functions. A disadvantage compared to a `vector` is that the `swap()` member function of an `array` runs in linear time, while it has constant complexity for a `vector`. An `array` can also not be moved in constant time, while a `vector` can. An `array` has a `size()` member function, which is a clear advantage over C-style arrays. The following example demonstrates how to use the `array` class. Note that the `array` declaration requires two template parameters: the first specifies the type of the elements, and the second specifies the fixed number of elements in the `array`.

```
// Create an array of 3 integers and initialize them
// with the given initializer_list using uniform initialization.
array<int, 3> arr { 9, 8, 7 };
// Output the size of the array.
println("Array size = {}", arr.size()); // or std::size(arr)
// Output the contents using C++23's support for formatting ranges.
println("{:n}", arr);
// Output the contents again using a range-based for loop.
for (const auto& i : arr) { print("{} ", i); }
println("");

println("Performing arr.fill(3)...");
// Use the fill member function to change the contents of the array.
arr.fill(3);
// Output the contents of the array using iterators.
for (auto iter { cbegin(arr) }; iter != cend(arr); ++iter) {
    print("{} ", *iter);
}
```

The output is as follows:

```
Array size = 3
9, 8, 7
9 8 7
Performing arr.fill(3)...
3 3 3
```

You can use the `std::get<n>()` function template to retrieve an element from an `std::array` at the given index *n*. The index has to be a constant expression, so it cannot, for example, be a loop variable. The benefit of using `std::get<n>()` is that the compiler checks at compile time that the given index is valid; otherwise, it results in a compilation error, as in this example:

```
array myArray { 11, 22, 33 };  // std::array supports CTAD.
println("{}", std::get<1>(myArray));
println("{}", std::get<10>(myArray));  // BUG! Compilation error!
```

`std::to_array()`, defined in `<array>`, converts a given C-style array to an `std::array`, using copy-initialization of the elements. The function works only for one-dimensional arrays. Here is a quick example:

```
auto arr1 { to_array({ 11, 22, 33 }) }; // Type is array<int, 3>

double carray[] { 9, 8, 7, 6 };
auto arr2 { to_array(carray) };         // Type is array<double, 4>
```

SEQUENTIAL VIEWS

The C++ Standard Library provides two *sequential views*: `std::span` and `std::mdspan`. The latter is new in C++23. A `span` provides a one-dimensional, non-owning view over a contiguous sequence of data. An `mdspan` generalizes this concept and allows the creation of multidimensional, non-owning views over a contiguous sequence of data.

span

Suppose you have this function to print the contents of a `vector`:

```
void print(const vector<int>& values)
{
    for (const auto& value : values) { print("{} ", value); }
    println("");
}
```

Suppose further that you also want to print the contents of C-style arrays. One option is to overload the `print()` function to accept a pointer to the first element of the array, and the number of elements to print:

```
void print(const int values[], size_t count)
{
    for (size_t i { 0 }; i < count; ++i) { print("{} ", values[i]); }
    println("");
}
```

If you also want to print std::arrays, you could provide a third overload, but what would the function parameter type be? For an std::array, you have to specify the type and the number of elements in the array as template parameters. You see, it's getting complicated.

std::span, defined in <span>, comes to the rescue here, as it allows you to write a single function that works with vectors, C-style arrays, and std::arrays of any size. Here is a single implementation of print() using span:

```
void print(span<int> values)
{
    for (const auto& value : values) { print("{} ", value); }
    println("");
}
```

Note that, just as with string_view from Chapter 2, a span is cheap to copy; it basically just contains a pointer to the first element in a sequence and a number of elements. A span never copies data! As such, it is usually passed by value.

There are several constructors for creating a span. For example, one can be created to include all elements of a given vector, std::array, or C-style array. A span can also be created to include only part of a container, by passing the address of the first element and the number of elements you want to include in the span.

A subview can be created from an existing span using the subspan() member function. Its first argument is the offset into the span, and the second argument is the number of elements to include in the subview. There are also two additional member functions called first() and last() returning subviews of a span containing the first n elements or the last n elements respectively.

A span has a couple of member functions that are similar to vector and array: begin(), end(), rbegin(), rend(), front(), back(), operator[], data(), size(), and empty().

The following code snippet demonstrates a few ways to call the print(span) function:

```
vector v { 11, 22, 33, 44, 55, 66 };
// Pass the whole vector, implicitly converted to a span.
print(v);
// Pass an explicitly created span.
span mySpan { v };
print(mySpan);
// Create a subview and pass that.
span subspan { mySpan.subspan(2, 3) };
print(subspan);
// Pass a subview created in-line.
print({ v.data() + 2, 3 });

// Pass an std::array.
array<int, 5> arr { 5, 4, 3, 2, 1 };
print(arr);
print({ arr.data() + 2, 3 });

// Pass a C-style array.
int carr[] { 9, 8, 7, 6, 5 };
print(carr);              // The entire C-style array.
print({ carr + 2, 3 }); // A subview of the C-style array.
```

The output is as follows:

```
11 22 33 44 55 66
11 22 33 44 55 66
33 44 55
33 44 55
5 4 3 2 1
3 2 1
9 8 7 6 5
7 6 5
```

Unlike `string_view` that provides a read-only view of a `string`, a `span` can provide read/write access to the underlying elements. Remember that a `span` just contains a pointer to the first element in a sequence and the number of elements; that is, a `span` never copies data! As such, modifying an element in a `span` actually modifies the element in the underlying sequence. If this is not desired, a `span` of `const` elements can be created. For example, the `print()` function has no reason to modify any of the elements in a given `span`. We can prevent such modifications as follows:

```
void print(span<const int> values)
{
    for (const auto& value : values) { print("{} ", value); }
    println("");
}
```

> **NOTE** *When writing a function accepting a* `const vector<T>&`, *consider accepting a* `span<const T>` *instead, so the function can work with views and subviews of data sequences coming from* `vector`*s,* `array`*s, C-style arrays and more. If the function accepts a* `vector<T>&`, *consider accepting a* `span<T>`, *unless the function needs to add or remove elements from the* `vector`.

mdspan

`std::mdspan`, defined in `<mdspan>`, is similar to `std::span` but allows you to create multidimensional views over a contiguous sequence of data. Just as `span`, an `mdspan` doesn't own the data, so it is cheap to copy. An `mdspan` has four template type parameters:

- `ElementType`: The type of the underlying elements.
- `Extents`: The number of dimensions and their size, a specialization of `std::extents`.
- `LayoutPolicy`: A policy specifying how to convert a multidimensional index to a one-dimensional index into the underlying contiguous sequence of data. You can implement whichever layout policy you need, such as tiled layout, Hilbert curve, and so on. The following standard policies are available:
    - `layout_right`: Row-major multidimensional array layout, where the rightmost extent has stride 1. This is the default policy.

- `layout_left`: Column-major multidimensional array layout, where the leftmost extent has stride 1.
- `layout_stride`: A layout mapping with user-defined strides.

- `AccessorPolicy`: A policy specifying how to convert the one-dimensional index into the underlying contiguous sequence of data into a reference to the actual element at that location. The default is `std::default_accessor`.

There are numerous constructors available. One of them is a constructor accepting a pointer to the contiguous sequence of data as the first parameter, followed by one or more dimension extents. Such extents passed as constructor arguments are called *dynamic extents*. Data can be accessed using a multidimensional `operator[]`. The `size()` member function returns the number of elements in an `mdspan`, and `empty()` returns `true` if an `mdspan` is empty. The `stride(n)` member function can be used to query the stride of dimension `n`. The size of the dimensions can be queried using the `extents()` member function. It returns an `std::extents` instance on which you can call `extent(n)` to query the size of dimension `n`. Here is an example:

```
template <typename T> void print2Dmdspan(const T& mdSpan)
{
    for (size_t i { 0 }; i < mdSpan.extents().extent(0); ++i) {
        for (size_t j { 0 }; j < mdSpan.extents().extent(1); ++j) {
            print("{} ", mdSpan[i, j]);
        }
        println("");
    }
}

int main()
{
    vector data { 1, 2, 3, 4, 5, 6, 7, 8 };
    // View data as a 2D array of 2 rows with 4 integers each,
    // using the default row-major layout policy.
    mdspan data2D { data.data(), 2, 4 };
    print2Dmdspan(data2D);
}
```

The output is as follows:

```
1 2 3 4
5 6 7 8
```

This code uses the default row-major layout policy. The following code snippet uses the column-major layout policy instead. Because the layout policy is the third template type parameter, you have to specify the first and second template type parameters as well. Instead of passing the size of each dimension as an argument to the constructor, the code now passes an `std::extents` as the second template type parameter:

```
mdspan<int, extents<int, 2, 4>, layout_left> data2D { data.data() };
```

The output now is as follows:

```
1 3 5 7
2 4 6 8
```

This mdspan definition specifies the extent of all dimensions as compile-time constants, i.e., *static extents*. It is also possible to combine static and dynamic extents. The following example specifies the first dimension as a compile-time constant, and the second as a dynamic extent. You then must pass the size of all dynamic extents as arguments to the constructor.

```
mdspan<int, extents<int, 2, dynamic_extent>> data2D { data.data(), 4 };
```

The output is again as follows:

```
1 2 3 4
5 6 7 8
```

CONTAINER ADAPTERS

In addition to the standard sequential containers, the Standard Library provides three *container adapters*: queue, priority_queue, and stack. Each of these adapters is a wrapper around one of the sequential containers. They allow you to swap the underlying container without having to change the rest of the code. The intent of the adapters is to simplify the interface and to provide only those features that are appropriate for the stack, queue, or priority_queue abstraction. These adapters do not provide access to the underlying container and hence are a perfect example of the data-hiding principle explained in Chapter 4, "Designing Professional C++ Programs." For instance, the adapters don't provide the capability to erase multiple elements simultaneously, nor do they provide iterators. The latter means you cannot use them with range-based for loops or with any of the standard iterator-based algorithms discussed in Chapter 20. However, starting with C++23, the std::format() and print() functions do support formatting and printing the contents of these container adapters.

queue

The queue container adapter, defined in <queue>, provides standard first-in, first-out semantics. As usual, it's written as a class template, which looks like this:

```
template <typename T, typename Container = deque<T>> class queue;
```

The T template parameter specifies the type that you intend to store in the queue. The second template parameter allows you to stipulate the underlying container that the queue adapts. However, the queue requires the sequential container to support both push_back() and pop_front(), so you have only two built-in choices: deque and list. For most purposes, you can just stick with the default deque.

queue Operations

The queue interface is extremely simple: there are only nine member functions, a set of constructors, and comparison operators. New in C++23 is a constructor accepting an iterator pair, [begin, end), which constructs a queue containing the elements from the given iterator range. The push() and emplace() member functions add a new element to the tail of the queue, while pop() removes the element at the head of the queue. C++23 adds push_range() to add a range of elements to the queue. You can retrieve references to, without removing, the first and last elements with front() and back(), respectively. As usual, when called on const objects, front() and back() return references-to-const; and when called on non-const objects, they return references-to-non-const (read/write).

> **WARNING** pop() *does not return the element popped. If you want to retain a copy, you must first retrieve it with* front().

The queue also supports size(), empty(), and swap().

queue Example: A Network Packet Buffer

When two computers communicate over a network, they send information to each other divided into discrete chunks called *packets*. The networking layer of the computer's operating system must pick up the packets and store them as they arrive. However, the computer might not have enough bandwidth to process all of them at once. Thus, the networking layer usually *buffers*, or stores, the packets until the higher layers have a chance to attend to them. The packets should be processed in the order they arrive, so this problem is perfect for a queue structure. The following is a small PacketBuffer class, with comments explaining the code, which stores incoming packets in a queue until they are processed. It's a class template so that different layers of the networking stack can use it for different kinds of packets, such as IP packets or TCP packets. It allows the client to specify a maximum size because operating systems usually limit the number of packets that can be stored, so as not to use too much memory. When the buffer is full, subsequently arriving packets are ignored.

```
export template <typename T>
class PacketBuffer final
{
    public:
        // If maxSize is 0, the size is unlimited, because creating
        // a buffer of size 0 makes little sense. Otherwise only
        // maxSize packets are allowed in the buffer at any one time.
        explicit PacketBuffer(std::size_t maxSize = 0);

        // Stores a packet in the buffer.
        // Returns false if the packet has been discarded because
        // there is no more space in the buffer, true otherwise.
        bool bufferPacket(const T& packet);

        // Returns the next packet. Throws out_of_range
        // if the buffer is empty.
        [[nodiscard]] T getNextPacket();
    private:
        std::queue<T> m_packets;
        std::size_t m_maxSize;
};

template <typename T> PacketBuffer<T>::PacketBuffer(std::size_t maxSize/*= 0*/)
    : m_maxSize { maxSize }
{
}
```

```
template <typename T> bool PacketBuffer<T>::bufferPacket(const T& packet)
{
    if (m_maxSize > 0 && m_packets.size() == m_maxSize) {
        // No more space. Drop the packet.
        return false;
    }
    m_packets.push(packet);
    return true;
}

template <typename T> T PacketBuffer<T>::getNextPacket()
{
    if (m_packets.empty()) {
        throw std::out_of_range { "Buffer is empty" };
    }
    // Retrieve the head element
    T temp { m_packets.front() };
    // Pop the head element
    m_packets.pop();
    // Return the head element
    return temp;
}
```

A practical application of this class would require multiple threads. However, without explicit synchronization, no Standard Library object can be used safely from multiple threads when at least one of the threads modifies the object. C++ provides synchronization classes to allow thread-safe access to shared objects. This is discussed in Chapter 27, "Multithreaded Programming with C++." The focus in this example is on the queue class, so here is a single-threaded example of using the `PacketBuffer`:

```
class IPPacket final
{
    public:
        explicit IPPacket(int id) : m_id { id } {}
        int getID() const { return m_id; }
    private:
        int m_id;
};

int main()
{
    PacketBuffer<IPPacket> ipPackets { 3 };

    // Add 4 packets
    for (int i { 1 }; i <= 4; ++i) {
        if (!ipPackets.bufferPacket(IPPacket { i })) {
            println("Packet {} dropped (queue is full).", i);
        }
    }

    while (true) {
        try {
            IPPacket packet { ipPackets.getNextPacket() };
            println("Processing packet {}", packet.getID());
        } catch (const out_of_range&) {
```

```
                println("Queue is empty.");
                break;
            }
        }
    }
```

The output of this program is as follows:

```
Packet 4 dropped (queue is full).
Processing packet 1
Processing packet 2
Processing packet 3
Queue is empty.
```

priority_queue

A *priority queue* is a queue that keeps its elements in sorted order. Instead of a strict FIFO ordering, the element at the head of the queue at any given time is the one with the highest priority. This element could be the oldest on the queue or the most recent. If two elements have equal priority, their relative order in the queue is undefined.

The `priority_queue` container adapter is also defined in `<queue>`. Its template definition looks something like this (slightly simplified):

```
template <typename T, typename Container = vector<T>,
          typename Compare = less<T>>;
```

It's not as complicated as it looks. You've seen the first two parameters before: `T` is the element type stored in the `priority_queue`, and `Container` is the underlying container on which the `priority_queue` is adapted. The `priority_queue` uses `vector` as the default, but `deque` works as well. `list` does not work because the `priority_queue` requires random access to its elements. The third parameter, `Compare`, is trickier. As you'll learn more about in Chapter 19, `less` is a class template that supports comparison of two objects of type `T` with `operator<`. This means the priority of elements in a `priority_queue` is determined according to `operator<`. You can customize the comparison used, but that's a topic for Chapter 19. For now, just make sure the types stored in a `priority_queue` support `operator<`. Of course, since C++20 it's enough to provide `operator<=>` which then automatically provides `operator<`.

> **NOTE** *The head element of a* `priority_queue` *is the one with the "highest" priority; by default, this is determined according to* `operator<` *such that elements that are "less" than other elements have lower priority.*

priority_queue Operations

A `priority_queue` provides even fewer operations than does a `queue`. The `push()`, `emplace()`, and `push_range()` (C++23) member functions allow you to insert elements, `pop()` allows you to remove elements, and `top()` returns a reference-to-`const` to the head element.

> **WARNING** `top()` *returns a reference-to-*`const` *even when called on a non-*`const` *object, because modifying the element might change its order, which is not allowed. A* `priority_queue` *provides no mechanism to obtain the tail element.*

> **WARNING** `pop()` *does not return the element popped. If you want to retain a copy, you must first retrieve it with* `top()`.

Like a queue, a `priority_queue` supports `size()`, `empty()`, and `swap()`. However, it does not provide any comparison operators.

priority_queue Example: An Error Correlator

Single failures on a system can often cause multiple errors to be generated from different components. A good error-handling system uses *error correlation* to process the most important errors first. You can use a `priority_queue` to write a simple error correlator. Assume all error events encode their own priority. The error correlator simply sorts error events according to their priority so that the highest-priority errors are always processed first. Here are the class definitions:

```
// Sample Error class with just a priority and a string error description.
export class Error final
{
    public:
        explicit Error(int priority, std::string errorString)
            : m_priority { priority }, m_errorString { std::move(errorString) } { }
        int getPriority() const { return m_priority; }
        const std::string& getErrorString() const { return m_errorString; }
        // Compare Errors according to their priority.
        auto operator<=>(const Error& rhs) const {
            return getPriority() <=> rhs.getPriority(); }
    private:
        int m_priority;
        std::string m_errorString;
};

// Stream insertion overload for Errors.
export std::ostream& operator<<(std::ostream& os, const Error& err)
{
    std::print(os, "{} (priority {})", err.getErrorString(), err.getPriority());
    return os;
}

// Simple ErrorCorrelator class that returns highest priority errors first.
export class ErrorCorrelator final
{
    public:
```

```
        // Add an error to be correlated.
        void addError(const Error& error) { m_errors.push(error); }
        // Retrieve the next error to be processed.
        [[nodiscard]] Error getError()
        {
            // If there are no more errors, throw an exception.
            if (m_errors.empty()) {
                throw std::out_of_range { "No more errors." };
            }
            // Save the top element.
            Error top { m_errors.top() };
            // Remove the top element.
            m_errors.pop();
            // Return the saved element.
            return top;
        }
    private:
        std::priority_queue<Error> m_errors;
};
```

Here is a simple test showing how to use the ErrorCorrelator. Realistic use would require multiple threads so that one thread adds errors, while another processes them. As mentioned earlier with the queue example, this requires explicit synchronization, which is discussed in Chapter 27.

```
ErrorCorrelator ec;
ec.addError(Error { 3, "Unable to read file" });
ec.addError(Error { 1, "Incorrect entry from user" });
ec.addError(Error { 10, "Unable to allocate memory!" });

while (true) {
    try {
        Error e { ec.getError() };
        cout << e << endl;
    } catch (const out_of_range&) {
        println("Finished processing errors");
        break;
    }
}
```

The output of this program is as follows:

```
Unable to allocate memory! (priority 10)
Unable to read file (priority 3)
Incorrect entry from user (priority 1)
Finished processing errors
```

stack

A stack is almost identical to a queue, except that it provides *first-in, last-out* (FILO) semantics, also known as *last-in, first-out* (LIFO), instead of FIFO. It is defined in <stack>. The template definition looks like this:

```
template <typename T, typename Container = deque<T>> class stack;
```

You can use vector, list, or deque as the underlying container for the stack.

stack Operations

Just as for queue, C++23 adds a constructor accepting an iterator pair, [begin, end), which constructs a stack containing the elements from the given iterator range. Also like queue, stack provides push(), emplace(), pop(), and push_range() (C++23). The difference is that push() and push_range() add new elements to the top of the stack, "pushing down" all elements inserted earlier, and pop() removes the element from the top of the stack, which is the most recently inserted element. The top() member function returns a reference-to-const to the top element if called on a const object, and a reference-to-non-const if called on a non-const object.

> **WARNING** pop() *does not return the element popped. If you want to retain a copy, you must first retrieve it with* top().

The stack supports empty(), size(), swap(), and the standard comparison operators.

stack Example: Revised Error Correlator

You can rewrite the previous ErrorCorrelator class so that it gives out the most recent error instead of the one with the highest priority. The only change required is to change m_errors from a priority_queue to a stack. With this change, the errors are distributed in LIFO order instead of priority order. Nothing in the member function definitions needs to change because the push(), pop(), top(), and empty() member functions exist on both a priority_queue and a stack.

ASSOCIATIVE CONTAINERS

The C++ Standard Library provides several different types of associative containers:

- **Ordered associative containers:** map, multimap, set, and multiset.
- **Unordered associative containers:** unordered_map, unordered_multimap, unordered_set, and unordered_multiset. These are also known as hash tables.

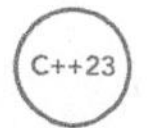

- **Flat associative container adapters:** flat_map, flat_multimap, flat_set, and flat_multiset. These adapt sequential containers to behave as ordered associative containers.

Ordered Associative Containers

Unlike the sequential containers, the *ordered associative containers* do not store elements in a linear configuration. Instead, they provide a mapping of keys to values. They generally offer insertion, deletion, and lookup times that are equivalent to each other.

There are four ordered associative containers provided by the Standard Library: map, multimap, set, and multiset. Each of these containers stores its elements in a *sorted*, tree-like data structure.

The pair Utility Class

Before delving deeper into the ordered associative containers, let's revisit the `pair` class template briefly introduced in Chapter 1. It is defined in `<utility>` and groups together two values of possibly different types. The values are accessible through the `first` and `second` public data members. All comparison operators are supported and compare both the `first` and `second` values. Here are some examples:

```
// Two-argument constructor and default constructor
pair<string, int> myPair { "hello", 5 };
pair<string, int> myOtherPair;

// Can assign directly to first and second
myOtherPair.first = "hello";
myOtherPair.second = 6;

// Copy constructor
pair<string, int> myThirdPair { myOtherPair };

// operator<
if (myPair < myOtherPair) {
    println("myPair is less than myOtherPair");
} else {
    println("myPair is greater than or equal to myOtherPair");
}

// operator==
if (myOtherPair == myThirdPair) {
    println("myOtherPair is equal to myThirdPair");
} else {
    println("myOtherPair is not equal to myThirdPair");
}
```

The output is as follows:

```
myPair is less than myOtherPair
myOtherPair is equal to myThirdPair
```

With class template argument deduction, you can omit the template type arguments. Here is an example. Note the use of the standard string literal `s`.

```
pair myPair { "hello"s, 5 };  // Type is pair<string, int>.
```

Before C++17 introduced support for CTAD, an `std::make_pair()` utility function template could be used to construct a `pair` from two values. The following are three ways to construct a `pair` of an `int` and a `double`:

```
pair<int, double> pair1 { make_pair(5, 10.10) };
auto pair2 { make_pair(5, 10.10) };
pair pair3 { 5, 10.10 };  // CTAD
```

map

A `map`, defined in `<map>`, stores key/value pairs instead of just single values. Insertion, lookup, and deletion are all based on the key; the value is just "along for the ride." The term *map* comes from the conceptual understanding that the container "maps" keys to values.

A map keeps elements in sorted order, based on the keys, so that insertion, deletion, and lookup all take logarithmic time. Because of the order, when you enumerate the elements, they come out in the ordering imposed by the type's operator< or a user-defined comparator. It is usually implemented as some form of balanced tree, such as a red-black tree. However, the tree structure is not exposed to the client.

You should use a map whenever you need to store and retrieve elements based on a "key" and you would like to have them in a certain order.

Constructing maps

The map class template takes four types: the key type, the value type, the comparator type, and the allocator type. As always, the allocator is ignored in this chapter. The comparator is similar to the comparator for a priority_queue described earlier. It allows you to change the default comparator. In this chapter, only the default less comparator is used. When using the default, make sure that your keys all respond to operator< appropriately. If you're interested in further detail, Chapter 19 explains how to write your own comparators.

If you ignore the comparator and allocator parameters, constructing a map is just like constructing a vector or a list, except that you specify the key and value types separately in the template instantiation. For example, the following code constructs a map that uses ints as the key and objects of the Data class as values:

```
class Data final
{
    public:
        explicit Data(int value = 0) : m_value { value } { }
        int getValue() const { return m_value; }
        void setValue(int value) { m_value = value; }
    private:
        int m_value;
};
...
map<int, Data> dataMap;
```

Internally, dataMap stores a pair<int, Data> for each element in the map.

A map also supports uniform initialization. The following map internally stores instances of pair<string, int>:

```
map<string, int> m {
    { "Marc G.", 12 }, { "Warren B.", 34 }, { "Peter V.W.", 56 }
};
```

Class template argument deduction does not work as usual. For example, the following does not compile:

```
map m {
    { "Marc G."s, 12 }, { "Warren B."s, 34 }, { "Peter V.W."s, 56 }
};
```

This does not work because the compiler cannot deduce pair<string, int> from, for example, {"Marc G."s, 12}. If you really want, you can write the following (note the s suffix for the string literals!):

```
map m {
    pair { "Marc G."s, 12 }, pair { "Warren B."s, 34 }, pair { "Peter V.W."s, 56 }
};
```

Formatting and Printing Maps

Just as for vectors, std::format() and the print() functions can be used to format and print entire maps with a single statement. For vectors, the output is surrounded by square brackets, and each element is separated with a comma. For maps, the output is slightly different: the output is surrounded by curly brackets, each key/value pair is separated by a comma, and a colon separates the key and the value. For example, printing the map from the previous section, m, gives the following output:

```
{"Marc G.": 12, "Peter V.W.": 56, "Warren B.": 34}
```

Inserting Elements

Inserting an element into sequential containers such as vector and list always requires you to specify the position at which the element is to be added. A map, along with the other ordered associative containers, is different. The map's internal implementation determines the position in which to store the new element; you need only to supply the key and the value.

> **NOTE** map *and the other ordered associative containers do provide a version of* insert() *that takes an iterator position. However, that position is only a "hint" to the container as to the correct position. The container is not required to insert the element at that position.*

When inserting elements, it is important to keep in mind that maps require unique keys: every element in the map must have a different key. If you want to support multiple elements with the same key, you have two options: either you can use a map and store another container such as a vector as the value for a key or you can use multimaps, described later.

The insert() Member Function

The insert() member function can be used to add elements to a map and has the advantage of allowing you to detect whether a key already exists. You must specify the key/value pair as a pair object or as an initializer_list. The return type of the basic form of insert() is a pair of an iterator and a bool. The reason for the complicated return type is that insert() does not overwrite a value if one already exists with the specified key. The bool element of the returned pair specifies whether the insert() actually inserted the new key/value pair. The iterator refers to the element in the map with the specified key (with a new or old value, depending on whether the insert succeeded or failed). map iterators are discussed in more detail in the next section. Continuing the map example from the previous section, you can use insert() as follows:

```
map<int, Data> dataMap;

auto ret { dataMap.insert({ 1, Data { 4 } }) };   // Using an initializer_list
if (ret.second) { println("Insert succeeded!"); }
else { println("Insert failed!"); }
```

```
ret = dataMap.insert(make_pair(1, Data { 6 })); // Using a pair object
if (ret.second) { println("Insert succeeded!"); }
else { println("Insert failed!"); }
```

The type of the `ret` variable is a `pair` as follows:

```
pair<map<int, Data>::iterator, bool> ret;
```

The first element of the `pair` is a `map` iterator for a `map` with keys of type `int` and values of type `Data`. The second element of the `pair` is a Boolean value.

The output of the program is as follows:

```
Insert succeeded!
Insert failed!
```

With `if` statement initializers, inserting the data into the `map` and checking the result can be done with a single statement as follows:

```
if (auto result { dataMap.insert({ 1, Data { 4 } }) }; result.second) {
    println("Insert succeeded!");
} else {
    println("Insert failed!");
}
```

This can further be combined with structured bindings:

```
if (auto [iter, success] { dataMap.insert({ 1, Data { 4 } }) }; success) {
    println("Insert succeeded!");
} else {
    println("Insert failed!");
}
```

The insert_or_assign() Member Function

`insert_or_assign()` has a similar return type as `insert()`. However, if an element with the given key already exists, `insert_or_assign()` overwrites the old value with the new value, while `insert()` does not overwrite the old value in that case. Another difference with `insert()` is that `insert_or_assign()` has two separate parameters: the key and the value. Here is an example:

```
auto ret { dataMap.insert_or_assign(1, Data { 7 }) };
if (ret.second) { println("Inserted."); }
else { println("Overwritten."); }
```

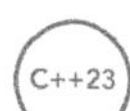

The insert_range() Member Function

C++23 adds `insert_range()` for `map`, which can be used to insert all elements of a given range to the `map`, and returns an iterator to the first element that was added. Here is an example:

```
vector<pair<int, Data>> moreData { {2, Data{22}}, {3, Data{33}}, {4, Data{44}} };
dataMap.insert_range(moreData);
```

operator[]

Another member function to insert elements into a `map` is through the overloaded `operator[]`. The difference is mainly in the syntax: you specify the key and value separately. Additionally, `operator[]`

always succeeds. If no value with the given key exists, it creates a new element with that key and value. If an element with the key already exists, `operator[]` replaces the value with the newly specified value. Here is part of the previous example using `operator[]` instead of `insert()`:

```
map<int, Data> dataMap;
dataMap[1] = Data { 4 };
dataMap[1] = Data { 6 }; // Replaces the element with key 1
```

There is, however, one major caveat to `operator[]`: it always constructs a new value object, even if it doesn't need to use it. Thus, it requires a default constructor for the element values and can be less efficient than `insert()`.

The fact that `operator[]` creates a new element in a `map` if the requested element does not already exist means that this operator is not marked as `const`. This sounds obvious, but might sometimes look counterintuitive. For example, suppose you have the following function:

```
void func(const map<int, int>& m)
{
    println("{}", m[1]);  // Error
}
```

This fails to compile, even though you appear to be just reading the value `m[1]`. It fails because the parameter `m` is a reference-to-`const` to a `map`, and `operator[]` is not marked as `const`. In such cases, you should instead use the `find()` or `at()` member function described in the section "Looking Up Elements."

Emplace Member Functions

A `map` supports `emplace()` and `emplace_hint()` to construct elements in-place, similar to the emplace member functions of a `vector`. There is also a `try_emplace()` member function that inserts an element in-place if the given key does not exist yet, or does nothing if the key already exists in the `map`.

map Iterators

`map` iterators work similarly to the iterators on the sequential containers. The major difference is that the iterators refer to key/value `pair`s instead of just the values. To access the value, you must retrieve the `second` field of the `pair` object. `map` iterators are bidirectional, meaning you can traverse them in both directions. Here is how you can iterate through the `map` from the previous example:

```
for (auto iter { cbegin(dataMap) }; iter != cend(dataMap); ++iter) {
    println("{}", iter->second.getValue());
}
```

Take another look at the expression used to access the value:

```
iter->second.getValue()
```

`iter` refers to a key/value `pair`, so you can use the `->` operator to access the `second` field of that `pair`, which is a `Data` object. You can then call the `getValue()` member function on that `Data` object.

Note that the following code is functionally equivalent:

```
(*iter).second.getValue()
```

Using a range-based `for` loop, the loop can be written more readable and less error prone as follows:

```
for (const auto& p : dataMap) {
    println("{}", p.second.getValue());
}
```

It can be implemented even more elegantly using a combination of a range-based `for` loop and structured bindings:

```
for (const auto& [key, data] : dataMap) {
    println("{}", data.getValue());
}
```

> **WARNING** *You can modify element values through non-`const` iterators, but the compiler will generate an error if you try to modify the key of an element, even through a non-`const` iterator, because it would destroy the sorted order of the elements in the `map`.*

Looking Up Elements

A `map` provides logarithmic lookup of elements based on a supplied key. If you already know that an element with a given key is in a map, the simplest way to look it up is through `operator[]` as long as you call it on a non-`const` `map` or a reference-to-non-`const` `map`. The nice thing about `operator[]` is that it returns a reference to the value that you can use and modify directly, without worrying about pulling the value out of a `pair` object. Here is an extension of the previous example to call the `setValue()` member function on the `Data` object value with key `1`:

```
map<int, Data> dataMap;
dataMap[1] = Data { 4 };
dataMap[1] = Data { 6 };
dataMap[1].setValue(100);
```

As an alternative, `map` provides a `find()` member function that returns an `iterator` referring to the key/value pair with the requested key, if it exists, or the `end()` iterator if the key is not found in the `map`. This can be useful in the following cases:

- If you don't know whether the element exists, you may not want to use `operator[]`, because it will insert a new element with that key if it doesn't find one already.
- If you have a `const` or a reference-to-`const` `map`, in which case you cannot use `operator[]`.

Here is an example using `find()` to perform the same modification to the `Data` object with key `1`:

```
auto it { dataMap.find(1) };
if (it != end(dataMap)) {
    it->second.setValue(100);
}
```

As you can see, using `find()` is a bit clumsier, but it's sometimes necessary.

Alternatively, you can use the `at()` member function, which, just as `operator[]`, returns a reference to the value in the `map` with the requested key, if it exists. It throws an `out_of_range` exception if the requested key isn't found in the `map`. The `at()` member function works fine on a `const` or a reference-to-`const map`. For example:

```
dataMap.at(1).setValue(200);
```

If you only want to know whether an element with a certain key is in a `map`, you can use the `count()` member function. It returns the number of elements in a `map` with a given key. For `map`s, the result will always be `0` or `1` because there can be no elements with duplicate keys.

Additionally, all associative containers (ordered, unordered, and flat) have a member function called `contains()`. It returns `true` if a given key exists in a container, `false` otherwise. With this, it's no longer necessary to use `count()` to figure out whether a certain key is in an associative container. Here is an example:

```
auto isKeyInMap { dataMap.contains(1) };
```

Removing Elements

A `map` allows you to remove an element at a specific iterator position or to remove all elements in a given iterator range, in amortized constant and logarithmic time, respectively. From the client perspective, these two `erase()` member functions are equivalent to those in the sequential containers. A great feature of a `map`, however, is that it also provides a version of `erase()` to remove an element matching a key. Here is an example:

```
map<int, Data> dataMap;
dataMap[1] = Data { 4 };
println("There are {} elements with key 1.", dataMap.count(1));
dataMap.erase(1);
println("There are {} elements with key 1.", dataMap.count(1));
```

The output is as follows:

```
There are 1 elements with key 1.
There are 0 elements with key 1.
```

Nodes

All the ordered and unordered associative containers are *node-based* data structures. The Standard Library provides direct access to *nodes* in the form of *node handles*. The exact type is unspecified, but each container has a type alias called `node_type` that specifies the type of a node handle for that container. A node handle can only be moved and is the owner of the element stored in a node. It provides read/write access to both the key and the value.

Nodes can be extracted from an associative container as a node handle using the `extract()` member function, based either on a given iterator position or on a given key. Extracting a node from a container removes it from the container, because the returned node handle is the sole owner of the extracted element.

New `insert()` overloads are provided that allow you to insert a node handle into a container.

By using `extract()` to extract node handles and using `insert()` to insert node handles, you can effectively transfer data from one associative container to another one without any copying or moving involved. You can even transfer nodes from a `map` to a `multimap` and from a `set` to a `multiset`. Continuing with the example from the previous section, the following code snippet transfers the node with key 1 from `dataMap` to a second `map` called `dataMap2`:

```
map<int, Data> dataMap2;
auto extractedNode { dataMap.extract(1) };
dataMap2.insert(move(extractedNode));
```

The last two lines can be combined into one:

```
dataMap2.insert(dataMap.extract(1));
```

One additional operation is available to move all nodes from one associative container to another one: `merge()`. Nodes that cannot be moved because they would cause, for example, duplicates in a target container that does not allow duplicates, are left in the source container. Here is an example:

```
map<int, int> src { {1, 11}, {2, 22} };
map<int, int> dst { {2, 22}, {3, 33}, {4, 44}, {5, 55} };
dst.merge(src);
println("src = {}", src); // src = {2: 22}
println("dst = {}", dst); // dst = {1: 11, 2: 22, 3: 33, 4: 44, 5: 55}
```

After the merge operation, `src` still contains one element, {2: 22}, because the destination already contains such an element, so it cannot be moved.

map Example: Bank Account

You can implement a simple bank account database using a `map`. A common pattern is for the key to be one field of a `class` or `struct` that is stored in a `map`. In this case, the key is the account number. Here are simple `BankAccount` and `BankDB` classes:

```
export class BankAccount final
{
    public:
        explicit BankAccount(int accountNumber, std::string name)
            : m_accountNumber { accountNumber }, m_clientName { std::move(name) }{}

        void setAccountNumber(int accountNumber) {
            m_accountNumber = accountNumber; }
        int getAccountNumber() const { return m_accountNumber; }

        void setClientName(std::string name) { m_clientName = std::move(name); }
        const std::string& getClientName() const { return m_clientName; }
    private:
        int m_accountNumber;
        std::string m_clientName;
};

export class BankDB final
{
    public:
        // Adds account to the bank database. If an account exists already
        // with that account number, the new account is not added. Returns true
```

```
        // if the account is added, false if it's not.
        bool addAccount(const BankAccount& account);

        // Removes the account with accountNumber from the database.
        void deleteAccount(int accountNumber);

        // Returns a reference to the account represented
        // by its account number or the client name.
        // Throws out_of_range if the account is not found.
        BankAccount& findAccount(int accountNumber);
        BankAccount& findAccount(std::string_view name);

        // Adds all the accounts from db to this database.
        // Deletes all the accounts from db.
        void mergeDatabase(BankDB& db);
    private:
        std::map<int, BankAccount> m_accounts;
};
```

Here are the implementations of the BankDB member functions, with comments explaining the code:

```
bool BankDB::addAccount(const BankAccount& account)
{
    // Do the actual insert, using the account number as the key.
    auto res { m_accounts.emplace(account.getAccountNumber(), account) };
    // or: auto res { m_accounts.insert(
    //         pair { account.getAccountNumber(), account }) };

    // Return the bool field of the pair specifying success or failure.
    return res.second;
}

void BankDB::deleteAccount(int accountNumber)
{
    m_accounts.erase(accountNumber);
}

BankAccount& BankDB::findAccount(int accountNumber)
{
    // Finding an element via its key can be done with find().
    auto it { m_accounts.find(accountNumber) };
    if (it == end(m_accounts)) {
        throw out_of_range { format("No account with number {}.", accountNumber) };
    }
    // Remember that iterators into maps refer to pairs of key/value.
    return it->second;
}

BankAccount& BankDB::findAccount(string_view name)
{
    // Finding an element by a non-key attribute requires a linear
    // search through the elements. The following uses structured bindings.
    for (auto& [accountNumber, account] : m_accounts) {
        if (account.getClientName() == name) {
            return account;  // found it!
```

```
            }
        }
        throw out_of_range { format("No account with name '{}'.", name) };
    }

    void BankDB::mergeDatabase(BankDB& db)
    {
        // Use merge().
        m_accounts.merge(db.m_accounts);
        // Or: m_accounts.insert(begin(db.m_accounts), end(db.m_accounts));

        // Now clear the source database.
        db.m_accounts.clear();
    }
```

You can test the `BankDB` class with the following code:

```
BankDB db;
db.addAccount(BankAccount { 100, "Nicholas Solter" });
db.addAccount(BankAccount { 200, "Scott Kleper" });

try {
    auto& account { db.findAccount(100) };
    println("Found account 100");
    account.setClientName("Nicholas A Solter");

    auto& account2 { db.findAccount("Scott Kleper") };
    println("Found account of Scott Kleper");

    auto& account3 { db.findAccount(1000) };
} catch (const out_of_range& caughtException) {
    println("Unable to find account: {}", caughtException.what());
}
```

The output is as follows:

```
Found account 100
Found account of Scott Kleper
Unable to find account: No account with number 1000.
```

multimap

A `multimap` is a `map` that allows multiple elements with the same key. Like `maps`, `multimaps` support uniform initialization. The interface is almost identical to the `map` interface, with the following differences:

- `multimaps` do not provide `operator[]` and `at()`. The semantics of these do not make sense if there can be multiple elements with a single key.
- Inserts on `multimaps` always succeed. Thus, the `multimap::insert()` member function that adds a single element returns just an `iterator` instead of a `pair`.
- The `insert_or_assign()` and `try_emplace()` member functions supported by `map` are not supported by `multimap`.

> **NOTE** `multimaps` *allow you to insert identical key/value pairs. If you want to avoid this redundancy, you must check explicitly before inserting a new element.*

The trickiest aspect of `multimaps` is looking up elements. You can't use `operator[]`, because it is not provided. `find()` isn't very useful because it returns an `iterator` referring to any one of the elements with a given key (not necessarily the first element with that key).

However, `multimaps` store all elements with the same key together and provide member functions to obtain `iterators` for this subrange of elements with the same key in the container. The `lower_bound()` and `upper_bound()` member functions each return a single `iterator` referring to the first and one-past-the-last elements matching a given key. If there are no elements matching that key, the `iterators` returned by `lower_bound()` and `upper_bound()` will be equal to each other.

If you need to obtain both `iterators` bounding the elements with a given key, it's more efficient to use `equal_range()` instead of calling `lower_bound()` followed by calling `upper_bound()`. The `equal_range()` member function returns a `pair` of the two `iterators` that would be returned by `lower_bound()` and `upper_bound()`.

> **NOTE** *The* `lower_bound()`, `upper_bound()`, *and* `equal_range()` *member functions exist for* `maps` *as well, but their usefulness is limited because a* `map` *cannot have multiple elements with the same key.*

multimap Example: Buddy Lists

Most of the numerous online chat programs allow users to have a "buddy list" or list of friends. The chat program confers special privileges on users in the buddy list, such as allowing them to send unsolicited messages to the user.

One way to implement the buddy lists for an online chat program is to store the information in a `multimap`. One `multimap` could store the buddy lists for every user. Each entry in the container stores one buddy for a user. The key is the user, and the value is the buddy. For example, if Harry Potter and Ron Weasley had each other on their individual buddy lists, there would be two entries of the form "Harry Potter" maps to "Ron Weasley" and "Ron Weasley" maps to "Harry Potter." A `multimap` allows multiple values for the same key, so the same user is allowed multiple buddies. Here is the `BuddyList` class definition:

```
export class BuddyList final
{
    public:
        // Adds buddy as a friend of name.
        void addBuddy(const std::string& name, const std::string& buddy);
        // Removes buddy as a friend of name.
        void removeBuddy(const std::string& name, const std::string& buddy);
        // Returns true if buddy is a friend of name, false otherwise.
        bool isBuddy(const std::string& name, const std::string& buddy) const;
```

```
        // Retrieves a list of all the friends of name.
        std::vector<std::string> getBuddies(const std::string& name) const;
    private:
        std::multimap<std::string, std::string> m_buddies;
};
```

Here are the implementations, with comments explaining the code. It demonstrates the use of `lower_bound()`, `upper_bound()`, and `equal_range()`.

```
void BuddyList::addBuddy(const string& name, const string& buddy)
{
    // Make sure this buddy isn't already there. We don't want
    // to insert an identical copy of the key/value pair.
    if (!isBuddy(name, buddy)) {
        m_buddies.insert({ name, buddy }); // Using initializer_list
    }
}

void BuddyList::removeBuddy(const string& name, const string& buddy)
{
    // Obtain the beginning and end of the range of elements with
    // key 'name'. Use both lower_bound() and upper_bound() to demonstrate
    // their use. Otherwise, it's more efficient to call equal_range().
    auto begin { m_buddies.lower_bound(name) };  // Start of the range
    auto end { m_buddies.upper_bound(name) };    // End of the range

    // Iterate through the elements with key 'name' looking
    // for a value 'buddy'. If there are no elements with key 'name',
    // begin equals end, so the loop body doesn't execute.
    for (auto iter { begin }; iter != end; ++iter) {
        if (iter->second == buddy) {
            // We found a match! Remove it from the map.
            m_buddies.erase(iter);
            break;
        }
    }
}

bool BuddyList::isBuddy(const string& name, const string& buddy) const
{
    // Obtain the beginning and end of the range of elements with
    // key 'name' using equal_range(), and structured bindings.
    auto [begin, end] { m_buddies.equal_range(name) };

    // Iterate through the elements with key 'name' looking
    // for a value 'buddy'.
    for (auto iter { begin }; iter != end; ++iter) {
        if (iter->second == buddy) {
            // We found a match!
            return true;
        }
    }
    // No matches
    return false;
}
```

```
vector<string> BuddyList::getBuddies(const string& name) const
{
    // Obtain the beginning and end of the range of elements with
    // key 'name' using equal_range(), and structured bindings.
    auto [begin, end] { m_buddies.equal_range(name) };

    // Create a vector with all names in the range (all buddies of name).
    vector<string> buddies;
    for (auto iter { begin }; iter != end; ++iter) {
        buddies.push_back(iter->second);
    }
    return buddies;
}
```

Note that `removeBuddy()` can't simply use the version of `erase()` that erases all elements with a given key, because it should erase only one element with the key, not all of them. Note also that `getBuddies()` can't use `insert()` on the `vector` to insert the elements in the range returned by `equal_range()`, because the elements referred to by the `multimap` iterators are key/value pairs, not strings. The `getBuddies()` member function must iterate explicitly through the range extracting the `string` from each key/value `pair` and pushing that onto the new `vector` to be returned.

Alternatively, with the C++23 ranges functionality discussed in Chapter 17, `getBuddies()` can be implemented as follows without any explicit loops:

```
vector<string> BuddyList::getBuddies(const string& name) const
{
    auto [begin, end] { m_buddies.equal_range(name) };
    return ranges::subrange { begin, end } | views::values | ranges::to<vector>();
}
```

Here is a test of the `BuddyList`:

```
BuddyList buddies;
buddies.addBuddy("Harry Potter", "Ron Weasley");
buddies.addBuddy("Harry Potter", "Hermione Granger");
buddies.addBuddy("Harry Potter", "Hagrid");
buddies.addBuddy("Harry Potter", "Draco Malfoy");
// That's not right! Remove Draco.
buddies.removeBuddy("Harry Potter", "Draco Malfoy");
buddies.addBuddy("Hagrid", "Harry Potter");
buddies.addBuddy("Hagrid", "Ron Weasley");
buddies.addBuddy("Hagrid", "Hermione Granger");

auto harrysFriends { buddies.getBuddies("Harry Potter") };

println("Harry's friends: ");
for (const auto& name : harrysFriends) {
    println("\t{}", name);
}
```

The output is as follows:

```
Harry's friends:
        Ron Weasley
        Hermione Granger
        Hagrid
```

set

A set, defined in <set>, is similar to a map. The difference is that instead of storing key/value pairs, in sets the value is the key. sets are useful for storing information in which there is no explicit key, but which you want to have in sorted order without any duplicates, with quick insertion, lookup, and deletion.

The interface supplied by set is almost identical to that of map. The main difference is that set doesn't provide operator[], insert_or_assign(), and try_emplace().

You cannot change the value of elements in a set because modifying elements of a set while they are in the container would destroy the order.

set Example: Access Control List

One way to implement basic security on a computer system is through access control lists. Each entity on the system, such as a file or a device, has a list of users with permissions to access that entity. Users can generally be added to and removed from the permissions list for an entity only by users with special privileges. Internally, a set provides a nice way to represent the access control list. You could use one set for each entity, containing all the usernames that are allowed to access the entity. Here is a class definition for a simple access control list:

```
export class AccessList final
{
    public:
        // Default constructor
        AccessList() = default;
        // Constructor to support uniform initialization.
        AccessList(std::initializer_list<std::string_view> users)
        {
            m_allowed.insert(begin(users), end(users));
        }
        // Adds the user to the permissions list.
        void addUser(std::string user)
        {
            m_allowed.emplace(std::move(user));
        }
        // Removes the user from the permissions list.
        void removeUser(const std::string& user)
        {
            m_allowed.erase(user);
        }
        // Returns true if the user is in the permissions list.
        bool isAllowed(const std::string& user) const
        {
            return m_allowed.contains(user);
        }
```

```
        // Returns all the users who have permissions.
        const std::set<std::string>& getAllUsers() const
        {
            return m_allowed;
        }
        // Returns a vector of all the users who have permissions.
        std::vector<std::string> getAllUsersAsVector() const
        {
            return { begin(m_allowed), end(m_allowed) };
        }
    private:
        std::set<std::string> m_allowed;
};
```

Take a look at the interesting one-line implementation of `getAllUsersAsVector()`. That one line constructs a `vector<string>` to return, by passing a begin and end iterator of `m_allowed` to the `vector` constructor. If you want, you can split this over two lines:

```
std::vector<std::string> users { begin(m_allowed), end(m_allowed) };
return users;
```

Finally, here is a simple test program:

```
AccessList fileX { "mgregoire", "baduser" };
fileX.addUser("pvw");
fileX.removeUser("baduser");

if (fileX.isAllowed("mgregoire")) { println("mgregoire has permissions"); }
if (fileX.isAllowed("baduser")) { println("baduser has permissions"); }

// C++23 supports formatting/printing of ranges, see Chapter 2.
println("Users with access: {:n:}", fileX.getAllUsers());

// Iterating over the elements of a set.
print("Users with access: ");
for (const auto& user : fileX.getAllUsers()) { print("{} ", user); }
println("");

// Iterating over the elements of a vector.
print("Users with access: ");
for (const auto& user : fileX.getAllUsersAsVector()) { print("{} ", user); }
println("");
```

One of the constructors for `AccessList` uses an `initializer_list` as a parameter so that you can use the uniform initialization syntax, as demonstrated in the test program for initializing `fileX`.

The output of this program is as follows:

```
mgregoire has permissions
Users with access: mgregoire, pvw
Users with access: mgregoire pvw
Users with access: mgregoire pvw
```

Note that the m_allowed data member needs to be a set of std::strings, and not of string_views. Changing it to a set of string_views will introduce problems with dangling pointers. For example, suppose you have the following code:

```
AccessList fileX;
{
    string user { "someuser" };
    fileX.addUser(user);
}
```

This code snippet creates a string called user and then adds that to the fileX access control list. However, the string and the call to addUser() are inside a set of curly brackets; that is, the string has a shorter lifetime than fileX. At the closing curly bracket, the string goes out of scope and is destroyed. This would leave the fileX access control list with a string_view pointing to a destroyed string, i.e., a dangling pointer! This problem is avoided by using a set of strings.

multiset

A multiset is to a set what a multimap is to a map. A multiset supports all the operations of a set, but it allows multiple elements that are equal to each other to be stored in the container simultaneously. An example of a multiset is not shown because it's so similar to set and multimap.

Unordered Associative Containers Or Hash Tables

The Standard Library has support for *unordered associative containers* or *hash tables*. There are four of them: unordered_map, unordered_multimap, unordered_set, and unordered_multiset. The map, multimap, set, and multiset containers discussed earlier sort their elements, while these unordered variants do not sort their elements.

Hash Functions

The unordered associative containers are hash tables. That is because the implementation makes use of *hash functions*. The implementation usually consists of some kind of array where each element in the array is called a *bucket*. Each bucket has a specific numerical index like 0, 1, 2, up until the last bucket. A hash function transforms a key into a *hash value*, which is then transformed into a *bucket index*. The value associated with that key is then stored in that bucket.

The result of a hash function is not always unique. The situation in which two or more keys hash to the same bucket index is called a *collision*. A collision can occur when different keys result in the same hash value or when different hash values transform to the same bucket index. There are many approaches to handling collisions, including quadratic re-hashing and linear chaining, among others. If you are interested, consult one of the references in the "Algorithms and Data Structures" section in Appendix B. The Standard Library does not specify which collision-handling algorithm is required, but most current implementations have chosen to resolve collisions by linear chaining. With linear chaining, buckets do not directly contain the data values associated with the keys but contain a pointer to a linked list. This linked list contains all the data values for that specific bucket. Figure 18.1 shows how this works.

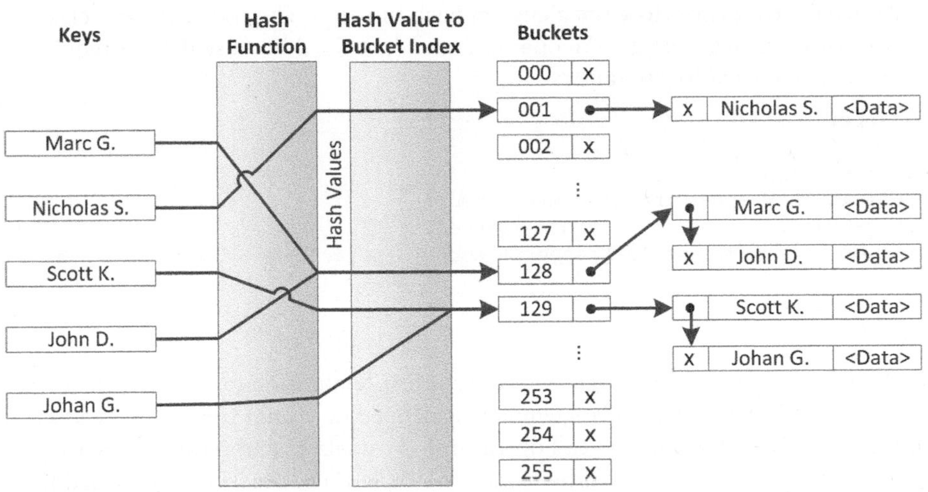

FIGURE 18.1

In Figure 18.1, there are two collisions. The first collision is because applying the hash function to the keys "Marc G." and "John D." results in the same hash value that maps to bucket index 128. This bucket then points to a linked list containing the keys "Marc G." and "John D." together with their associated data values. The second collision is caused by the hash values for "Scott K." and "Johan G." mapping to the same bucket index 129.

From Figure 18.1, it is also clear how lookups based on keys work and what the complexity is. A lookup involves a single hash function call to calculate the hash value. This hash value is then transformed to a bucket index. Once the bucket index is known, one or more equality operations are required to find the right key in the linked list. This shows that lookups can be much faster compared to lookups with normal `map`s, but it all depends on how many collisions there are.

The choice of the hash function is important. A hash function that creates no collisions is known as a *perfect hash*. A perfect hash has a lookup time that is constant; a regular hash has a lookup time that is, on average, close to 1, independent of the number of elements. As the number of collisions increases, the lookup time increases, reducing performance. Collisions can be reduced by increasing the basic hash table size, but you need to take cache sizes into account.

The C++ standard provides hash functions for pointers and all primitive data types such as `bool`, `char`, `int`, `float`, `double`, and so on. Hash functions are also provided for several Standard Library classes, such as `optional`, `bitset`, `unique_ptr`, `shared_ptr`, `string`, `string_view`, `vector<bool>`, and more. If there is no standard hash function available for the type of keys you want to use, then you have to implement your own hash function. Creating a perfect hash is a nontrivial exercise, even when the set of keys is fixed and known. It requires deep mathematical analysis. Even creating a non-perfect one, but one that is good enough and has decent performance, is still challenging. It's outside the scope of this book to explain the mathematics behind hash functions in detail. Instead, only an example of a simple hash function is given.

The following code demonstrates how to write a custom hash function. The code defines a class `IntWrapper` that just wraps a single integer. An `operator==` is provided because that's a requirement for keys used in unordered associative containers.

```
class IntWrapper
{
    public:
        explicit IntWrapper(int i) : m_wrappedInt { i } {}
        int getValue() const { return m_wrappedInt; }
        bool operator==(const IntWrapper&) const = default;// = default since C++20
    private:
        int m_wrappedInt;
};
```

To write the actual hash function for `IntWrapper`, you write a specialization of the `std::hash` class template for `IntWrapper`. The `std::hash` class template is defined in `<functional>`. This specialization needs an implementation of the function call operator that calculates and returns the hash of a given `IntWrapper` instance. For this example, the request is simply forwarded to the standard hash function for integers:

```
namespace std
{
    template<> struct hash<IntWrapper>
    {
        size_t operator()(const IntWrapper& x) const {
            return std::hash<int>{}(x.getValue());
        }
    };
}
```

Note that you normally are not allowed to put anything in the `std` namespace; however, `std` class template specializations are an exception to this rule. The implementation of the function call operator is just one line. It creates an instance of the standard hash function for integers—`std::hash<int>{}`—and then calls the function call operator on it with `x.getValue()` as argument. Note that this forwarding works in this example because `IntWrapper` contains just one data member, an integer. If the class contained multiple data members, then a hash value would need to be calculated taking all those data members into account; however, those details fall outside the scope of this book.

unordered_map

`unordered_map` is defined in `<unordered_map>` as a class template:

```
template <typename Key,
          typename T,
          typename Hash = hash<Key>,
          typename Pred = std::equal_to<Key>,
          typename Alloc = std::allocator<std::pair<const Key, T>>>
    class unordered_map;
```

There are five template type parameters: the key type, the value type, the hash type, the equality comparator type, and the allocator type. The last three parameters have default values. The most important parameters are the first two. As with `map`s, uniform initialization can be used to initialize an unordered_map. Iterating over the elements is also similar to maps, as shown in the following example.

```
unordered_map<int, string> m {
    {1, "Item 1"}, {2, "Item 2"}, {3, "Item 3"}, {4, "Item 4"}
};
// Using C++23 support for formatting/printing ranges.
println("{}", m);
// Using structured bindings.
for (const auto& [key, value] : m) { print("{} = {}, ", key, value); }
println("");
// Without structured bindings.
for (const auto& p : m) { print("{} = {}, ", p.first, p.second); }
```

The output is as follows:

```
{4: "Item 4", 3: "Item 3", 2: "Item 2", 1: "Item 1"}
4 = Item 4, 3 = Item 3, 2 = Item 2, 1 = Item 1,
4 = Item 4, 3 = Item 3, 2 = Item 2, 1 = Item 1,
```

The following table summarizes the differences between map and unordered_map. A filled box (■) means the container supports that operation, while an empty box (□) means the operation is not supported.

OPERATION	map	unordered_map
at()	■	■
begin()	■	■
begin(n)	□	■
bucket()	□	■
bucket_count()	□	■
bucket_size()	□	■
cbegin()	■	■
cbegin(n)	□	■
cend()	■	■
cend(n)	□	■
clear()	■	■
contains()	■	■
count()	■	■
crbegin()	■	□
crend()	■	□

continues

(continued)

OPERATION	map	unordered_map
emplace()	■	■
emplace_hint()	■	■
empty()	■	■
end()	■	■
end(n)	□	■
equal_range()	■	■
erase()	■	■
extract()	■	■
find()	■	■
insert()	■	■
insert_or_assign()	■	■
insert_range() (C++23)	■	■
iterator / const_iterator	■	■
load_factor()	□	■
local_iterator / const_local_iterator	□	■
lower_bound()	■	□
max_bucket_count()	□	■
max_load_factor()	□	■
max_size()	■	■
merge()	■	■
operator[]	■	■
rbegin()	■	□
rehash()	□	■
rend()	■	□
reserve()	□	■
reverse_iterator / const_reverse_iterator	■	□
size()	■	■

OPERATION	map	unordered_map
swap()	■	■
try_emplace()	■	■
upper_bound()	■	□

As with map, all keys in an unordered_map must be unique. The preceding table includes a number of hash-specific member functions. For example, load_factor() returns the average number of elements per bucket to give you an indication of the number of collisions. The bucket_count() member function returns the number of buckets in the container. It also provides a local_iterator and const_local_iterator, allowing you to iterate over the elements in a single bucket; however, these may not be used to iterate across buckets. The bucket(key) member function returns the index of the bucket that contains the given key; begin(n) returns a local_iterator referring to the first element in the bucket with index n, and end(n) returns a local_iterator referring to one-past-the-last element in the bucket with index n. The example in the next section demonstrates how to use some of these member functions.

unordered_map Example: Phone Book

The following example uses an unordered_map to represent a phone book. The name of a person is the key, while the phone number is the value associated with that key.

```
void printMap(const auto& m)  // Abbreviated function template
{
    for (auto& [key, value] : m) {
        println("{} (Phone: {})", key, value);
    }
    println("-------");
}

int main()
{
    // Create a hash table.
    unordered_map<string, string> phoneBook {
        { "Marc G.", "123-456789" },
        { "Scott K.", "654-987321" } };
    printMap(phoneBook);

    // Add/remove some phone numbers.
    phoneBook.insert(make_pair("John D.", "321-987654"));
    phoneBook["Johan G."] = "963-258147";
    phoneBook["Freddy K."] = "999-256256";
    phoneBook.erase("Freddy K.");
    printMap(phoneBook);

    // Find the bucket index for a specific key.
    const size_t bucket { phoneBook.bucket("Marc G.") };
    println("Marc G. is in bucket {} containing the following {} names:",
        bucket, phoneBook.bucket_size(bucket));
    // Get begin and end iterators for the elements in this bucket.
```

```
        // 'auto' is used here. The compiler deduces the type of
        // both as unordered_map<string, string>::const_local_iterator
        auto localBegin { phoneBook.cbegin(bucket) };
        auto localEnd { phoneBook.cend(bucket) };
        for (auto iter { localBegin }; iter != localEnd; ++iter) {
            println("\t{} (Phone: {})", iter->first, iter->second);
        }
        println("-------");

        // Print some statistics about the hash table
        println("There are {} buckets.", phoneBook.bucket_count());
        println("Average number of elements in a bucket is {}.",
            phoneBook.load_factor());
    }
```

A possible output is as follows. Note that the output can be different on different systems, because it depends on the implementation of both the hash function and the `unordered_map` itself being used.

```
Scott K. (Phone: 654-987321)
Marc G. (Phone: 123-456789)
-------
Scott K. (Phone: 654-987321)
Marc G. (Phone: 123-456789)
Johan G. (Phone: 963-258147)
John D. (Phone: 321-987654)
-------
Marc G. is in bucket 1 containing the following 2 names:
        Scott K. (Phone: 654-987321)
        Marc G. (Phone: 123-456789)
-------
There are 8 buckets.
Average number of elements in a bucket is 0.5
```

unordered_multimap

An `unordered_multimap` is an `unordered_map` that allows multiple elements with the same key. Their interfaces are almost identical, with the following differences:

- `unordered_multimaps` do not provide `operator[]` and `at()`. The semantics of these do not make sense if there can be multiple elements with a single key.
- Inserts on `unordered_multimaps` always succeed. Thus, the `unordered_multimap::insert()` member function that adds a single element returns just an `iterator` instead of a `pair`.
- The `insert_or_assign()` and `try_emplace()` member functions supported by `unordered_map` are not supported by an `unordered_multimap`.

> **NOTE** `unordered_multimaps` *allow you to insert identical key/value pairs. If you want to avoid this redundancy, you must check explicitly before inserting a new element.*

As discussed earlier with multimaps, looking up elements in unordered_multimaps cannot be done using operator[] because it is not provided. You can use find(), but it returns an iterator referring to any one of the elements with a given key (not necessarily the first element with that key). Instead, it's best to use the equal_range() member function, which returns a pair of iterators: one referring to the first element matching a given key, and one referring to one-past-the-last element matching that key. The use of equal_range() is the same as discussed for multimaps, so you can look at the example given for multimaps to see how it works.

unordered_set/unordered_multiset

<unordered_set> defines unordered_set and unordered_multiset, which are similar to set and multiset, respectively, except that they do not sort their keys but use a hash function. The differences between unordered_set and unordered_map are similar to the differences between set and map as discussed earlier in this chapter, so they are not discussed in detail here. Consult a Standard Library Reference for a thorough summary of unordered_set and unordered_multiset operations.

Flat Set and Flat Map Associative Container Adapters

C++23 introduces the following new container adapters:

- std::flat_set and flat_multiset defined in <flat_set>
- std::flat_map and flat_multimap defined in <flat_map>

These are adapters providing an associative container interface on top of sequential containers. flat_set and flat_map require unique keys, just as set and map, while flat_multiset and flat_multimap support duplicate keys, just as multiset and multimap. They all store their data sorted on the keys using std::less as the default comparator. flat_set and flat_multiset provide for fast retrieval of a key, while flat_map and flat_multimap provide for fast retrieval of a value based on a key. A flat_set and a flat_multiset require one underlying sequential container to store their keys. A flat_map and a flat_multimap require two underlying containers, one to store the keys and another one to store the values. The underlying container must support random-access iterators, such as vector and deque. By default, vector is used.

All flat associative container adapters have an interface similar to their ordered counterparts, except that the flat container adapters are not *node-based* data structures and thus don't have any concept of node handles as discussed earlier in this chapter in the context of the ordered associative containers. Another difference is that the flat variants provide random-access iterators, while the ordered counterparts provide only bidirectional iterators.

With the addition of these flat container adapters, the Standard Library now provides three variants of each associative container type; e.g., there are now three map containers: map, unordered_map, and flat_map. All three basically work in a similar fashion, but they store their data in drastically different data structures and thus have different time- and space-efficiency. Because the flat associative container adapters store their data sorted in sequential containers, they all have linear time complexity for adding and removing elements, which can potentially be slower than adding and removing elements from ordered and unordered containers. Lookups have logarithmic complexity, just as the ordered associative containers. However, for the flat variants, lookups and especially iteration over the elements are more efficient than for the ordered ones because the former store their data in sequential containers and thus have a much more efficient and cache-friendly memory layout. They also need less memory per element compared to the ordered or unordered variants. Which one of the three flavors per type to choose for a specific use case depends on the exact requirements of your use case. If performance is important, then I recommend profiling all three of them to find out which one is best suited for a specific use. Profiling is explained in Chapter 29, "Writing Efficient C++."

The flat associative container adapters are often just drop-in replacements for their ordered counterparts. For example, the access control list example from earlier has a data member called `m_allowed` of type `set<string>`, an ordered associative container. The code can easily be changed to use a `flat_set` instead. Two changes are necessary. First, the type of `m_allowed` is changed to the following:

```
std::flat_set<std::string> m_allowed;
```

Second, the return type of `getAllUsers()` is changed to a `flat_set`:

```
const std::flat_set<std::string>& getAllUsers() const { return m_allowed; }
```

Everything else remains the same.

Performance of Associative Containers

As is clear from this section, the C++ Standard Library contains several different associative containers. How do you know which one to use for a certain task? If iterating over the contents of an associative container is important for your use case, then the flat associative container adapters have the best performance, because of the way they store their data in continuous memory. If other operations are more important for you, then the unordered associative containers are usually faster compared to the ordered ones. However, if performance is really important, then the only way to decide on the correct container is by benchmarking all of them for your specific use case. Usually, though, you can just pick the one that is easier to work with. To use the ordered versions with your own class types, you must implement comparison operations for your class, while for the unordered versions, you need to write a hash function. The latter is usually harder to implement.

OTHER CONTAINERS

There are several other features of the C++ language and the Standard Library that are somewhat related to containers, including standard C-style arrays, `strings`, streams, and `bitset`.

Standard C-Style Arrays

Recall that raw pointers are bona fide iterators because they support the required operations. This point is more than just a piece of trivia. It means that you can treat standard C-style arrays as Standard Library containers by using pointers to their elements as iterators. Standard C-style arrays, of course, don't provide member functions like `size()`, `empty()`, `insert()`, and `erase()`, so they aren't true Standard Library containers. Nevertheless, because they do support iterators through pointers, you can use them in the algorithms described in Chapter 20 and in some of the member functions described in this chapter.

For example, you could copy all the elements of a standard C-style array into a `vector` using the `insert()` member function of a `vector` that takes an iterator range from any container. This `insert()` member function's prototype looks like this:

```
template <typename InputIterator> iterator insert(const_iterator position,
    InputIterator first, InputIterator last);
```

If you want to use a standard C-style `int` array as the source, then the template type parameter `InputIterator` becomes `int*`. Here is a full example:

```
const size_t count { 10 };
int values[count];      // standard C-style array
// Initialize each element of the array to the value of its index.
for (int i { 0 }; i < count; ++i) { values[i] = i; }

// Insert the contents of the array at the end of a vector.
vector<int> vec;
vec.insert(end(vec), values, values + count);

// Print the contents of the vector.
println("{:n} ", vec);
```

Note that the iterator referring to the first element of the array is the address of the first element, which is `values` in this case. The name of an array alone is interpreted as the address of the first element. The iterator referring to the end must be one-past-the-last element, so it's the address of the first element plus `count`, or `values+count`.

It's easier to use `std::begin()` or `cbegin()` to get an iterator to the first element of a statically allocated C-style array not accessed through pointers, and `std::end()` or `cend()` to get an iterator to one-past-the-last element of such an array. For example, the call to `insert()` in the previous example can be written as follows:

```
vec.insert(end(vec), cbegin(values), cend(values));
```

Starting with C++23, this can be written more elegantly using `append_range()`:

```
vec.append_range(values);
```

> **WARNING** *Functions such as* `std::begin()` *and* `end()` *work only on statically allocated C-style arrays not accessed through pointers. They do not work if pointers are involved or with dynamically allocated C-style arrays.*

Strings

You can think of a `string` as a sequential container of characters. Thus, it shouldn't be surprising to learn that a C++ `string` is a full-fledged sequential container. It has `begin()` and `end()` member functions that return iterators into the `string`; and it has `insert()`, `push_back()`, `erase()`, `size()`, and `empty()` member functions, and all the rest of the sequential container basics. It resembles a `vector` quite closely, even providing the member functions `reserve()` and `capacity()`.

You can use `string` as a Standard Library container just as you would use `vector`. Here is an example:

```
string myString;
myString.insert(cend(myString), 'h');
myString.insert(cend(myString), 'e');
myString.push_back('l');
myString.push_back('l');
myString.push_back('o');

for (const auto& letter : myString) {
    print("{}", letter);
}
println("");

for (auto it { cbegin(myString) }; it != cend(myString); ++it) {
    print("{}", *it);
}
println("");
```

In addition to the Standard Library sequential container member functions, `strings` provide a host of useful member functions and `friend` functions. The `string` interface is actually quite a good example of a cluttered interface, one of the design pitfalls discussed in Chapter 6, "Designing for Reuse." The `string` class is discussed in detail in Chapter 2.

Streams

Input and output streams are not containers in the traditional sense because they do not store elements. However, they can be considered sequences of elements and as such share some characteristics with Standard Library containers. C++ streams do not provide any Standard Library–related member functions directly, but the Standard Library supplies special iterators called `istream_iterator` and `ostream_iterator` that allow you to "iterate" through input and output streams respectively. Chapter 17 explains how to use them.

bitset

A `bitset` is a fixed-length abstraction of a sequence of bits. A bit can represent only two values, 1 and 0, which can be referred to as on/off, true/false, and so on. A `bitset` also uses the terminology *set* and *unset*. You can *toggle* or *flip* a bit from one value to the other.

A `bitset` is not a true Standard Library container: it's of fixed size, it's not parametrized on an element type, and it doesn't support iteration. However, it's a useful utility class, which is often lumped with the containers, so a brief introduction is provided here. Consult a Standard Library Reference for a thorough summary of the `bitset` operations.

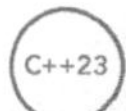

> **NOTE** *Starting with C++23,* `bitset` *is a* `constexpr` *class, and so can be used at compile time.*

bitset Basics

A `bitset`, defined in `<bitset>`, is parametrized on the number of bits it stores. The default constructor initializes all fields of a `bitset` to 0. An alternative constructor creates a `bitset` from a `string` of `0` and `1` characters.

You can adjust the value of individual bits with the `set()`, `reset()`, and `flip()` member functions, and you can access and set individual fields with an overloaded `operator[]`. Note that `operator[]` on a non-`const` object returns a proxy object to which you can assign a Boolean value, call `flip()`, or complement with `operator~`. You can also access individual fields with the `test()` member function. Bits are accessed using a zero-based index. Finally, you can convert a `bitset` to a `string` of `0` and `1` characters using `to_string()`.

Here is a small example:

```
bitset<10> myBitset;

myBitset.set(3);
myBitset.set(6);
myBitset[8] = true;
myBitset[9] = myBitset[3];

if (myBitset.test(3)) { println("Bit 3 is set!"); }
println("{}", myBitset.to_string());
```

The output is as follows:

```
Bit 3 is set!
1101001000
```

Note that the leftmost character in the output `string` is the highest numbered bit. This corresponds to our intuitions about binary number representations, where the low-order bit representing $2^0 = 1$ is the rightmost bit in the printed representation.

Bitwise Operators

In addition to the basic bit manipulation routines, a `bitset` provides implementations of all the bitwise operators: `&`, `|`, `^`, `~`, `<<`, `>>`, `&=`, `|=`, `^=`, `<<=`, and `>>=`. They behave just as they would on a "real" sequence of bits. Here is an example:

```
auto str1 { "0011001100" };
auto str2 { "0000111100" };
bitset<10> bitsOne { str1 };
bitset<10> bitsTwo { str2 };

auto bitsThree { bitsOne & bitsTwo };
println("{}", bitsThree.to_string());
bitsThree <<= 4;
println("{}", bitsThree.to_string());
```

The output of the program is as follows:

```
0000001100
0011000000
```

bitset Example: Representing Cable Channels

One possible use of `bitsets` is tracking channels of cable subscribers. Each subscriber could have a `bitset` of channels associated with their subscription, with set bits representing the channels to which they actually subscribe. This system could also support "packages" of channels, also represented as `bitsets`, which represent commonly subscribed combinations of channels.

The following `CableCompany` class is a simple example of this model. It uses two `maps`, both mapping `strings` to `bitsets`. One stores the cable packages, while the other stores subscriber information.

```
export class CableCompany final
{
    public:
        // Number of supported channels.
        static constexpr std::size_t NumChannels { 10 };
        // Adds package with the channels specified as a bitset to the database.
        void addPackage(const std::string& packageName,
            const std::bitset<NumChannels>& channels);
        // Adds package with the channels specified as a string to the database.
        void addPackage(const std::string& packageName,
            const std::string& channels);
        // Removes the specified package from the database.
        void removePackage(const std::string& packageName);
        // Retrieves the channels of a given package.
        // Throws out_of_range if the package name is invalid.
        const std::bitset<NumChannels>& getPackage(
            const std::string& packageName) const;
        // Adds customer to database with initial channels found in package.
        // Throws out_of_range if the package name is invalid.
        // Throws invalid_argument if the customer is already known.
        void newCustomer(const std::string& name, const std::string& package);
        // Adds customer to database with given initial channels.
        // Throws invalid_argument if the customer is already known.
        void newCustomer(const std::string& name,
            const std::bitset<NumChannels>& channels);
        // Adds the channel to the customer's profile.
        // Throws invalid_argument if the customer is unknown.
        void addChannel(const std::string& name, int channel);
        // Removes the channel from the customer's profile.
        // Throws invalid_argument if the customer is unknown.
        void removeChannel(const std::string& name, int channel);
        // Adds the specified package to the customer's profile.
        // Throws out_of_range if the package name is invalid.
        // Throws invalid_argument if the customer is unknown.
        void addPackageToCustomer(const std::string& name,
            const std::string& package);
        // Removes the specified customer from the database.
        void deleteCustomer(const std::string& name);
        // Retrieves the channels to which a customer subscribes.
        // Throws invalid_argument if the customer is unknown.
        const std::bitset<NumChannels>& getCustomerChannels(
            const std::string& name) const;
```

```
    private:
        // Retrieves the channels for a customer. (non-const)
        // Throws invalid_argument if the customer is unknown.
        std::bitset<NumChannels>& getCustomerChannelsHelper(
            const std::string& name);

        using MapType = std::map<std::string, std::bitset<NumChannels>>;
        MapType m_packages, m_customers;
};
```

Here are the implementations of all member functions, with comments explaining the code:

```
void CableCompany::addPackage(const string& packageName,
    const bitset<NumChannels>& channels)
{
    m_packages.emplace(packageName, channels);
}

void CableCompany::addPackage(const string& packageName, const string& channels)
{
    addPackage(packageName, bitset<NumChannels> { channels });
}

void CableCompany::removePackage(const string& packageName)
{
    m_packages.erase(packageName);
}

const bitset<CableCompany::NumChannels>& CableCompany::getPackage(
    const string& packageName) const
{
    // Get an iterator to the specified package.
    if (auto it { m_packages.find(packageName) }; it != end(m_packages)) {
        // Found package. Note that 'it' is an iterator to a name/bitset pair.
        // The bitset is the second field.
        return it->second;
    }
    throw out_of_range { format("Invalid package '{}'.", packageName) };
}

void CableCompany::newCustomer(const string& name, const string& package)
{
    // Get the channels for the given package.
    auto& packageChannels { getPackage(package) };
    // Create the account with the bitset representing that package.
    newCustomer(name, packageChannels);
}

void CableCompany::newCustomer(const string& name,
    const bitset<NumChannels>& channels)
{
    // Add customer to the customers map.
    if (auto [iter, success] { m_customers.emplace(name, channels) }; !success) {
        // Customer was already in the database. Nothing changed.
        throw invalid_argument { format("Duplicate customer '{}'.", name) };
    }
}
```

```
void CableCompany::addChannel(const string& name, int channel)
{
    // Get the current channels for the customer.
    auto& customerChannels { getCustomerChannelsHelper(name) };
    // We found the customer; set the channel.
    customerChannels.set(channel);
}

void CableCompany::removeChannel(const string& name, int channel)
{
    // Get the current channels for the customer.
    auto& customerChannels { getCustomerChannelsHelper(name) };
    // We found this customer; remove the channel.
    customerChannels.reset(channel);
}

void CableCompany::addPackageToCustomer(const string& name, const string& package)
{
    // Get the channels for the given package.
    auto& packageChannels { getPackage(package) };
    // Get the current channels for the customer.
    auto& customerChannels { getCustomerChannelsHelper(name) };
    // Or-in the package to the customer's existing channels.
    customerChannels |= packageChannels;
}

void CableCompany::deleteCustomer(const string& name)
{
    m_customers.erase(name);
}

const bitset<CableCompany::NumChannels>& CableCompany::getCustomerChannels(
    const string& name) const
{
    // Find an iterator to the customer.
    if (auto it { m_customers.find(name) }; it != end(m_customers)) {
        // Found customer. Note that 'it' is an iterator to a name/bitset pair.
        // The bitset is the second field.
        return it->second;
    }
    throw invalid_argument { format("Unknown customer '{}'.", name) };
}

bitset<CableCompany::NumChannels>& CableCompany::getCustomerChannelsHelper(
    const string& name)
{
    // Forward to const getCustomerChannels() to avoid code duplication.
    return const_cast<bitset<NumChannels>&>(getCustomerChannels(name));
}
```

Finally, here is a simple program demonstrating how to use the `CableCompany` class:

```
CableCompany myCC;
myCC.addPackage("basic",   "1111000000");
```

```
myCC.addPackage("premium",  "1111111111");
myCC.addPackage("sports",   "0000100111");

myCC.newCustomer("Marc G.", "basic");
myCC.addPackageToCustomer("Marc G.", "sports");
println("{}", myCC.getCustomerChannels("Marc G.").to_string());

try { println("{}", myCC.getCustomerChannels("John").to_string()); }
catch (const exception& e) { println("Error: {}", e.what()); }
```

The output is as follows:

```
1111100111
Error: Unknown customer 'John'.
```

SUMMARY

This chapter introduced the Standard Library containers. It also presented sample code illustrating a variety of uses for these containers. Ideally, you appreciate the power of `vector`, `deque`, `list`, `forward_list`, `array`, `span`, `mdspan`, `stack`, `queue`, `priority_queue`, `map`, `multimap`, `set`, `multiset`, `unordered_map`, `unordered_multimap`, `unordered_set`, `unordered_multiset`, `flat_map`, `flat multimap`, `flat_set`, `flat_multiset`, `string`, and `bitset`. I recommend using these containers as much as possible instead of writing your own.

Before we can delve into the true power of the Standard Library with a discussion of its generic algorithms and how they work with the containers discussed in this chapter, we have to explain function pointers, function objects, and lambda expressions. Those are the topics of the next chapter.

EXERCISES

By solving the following exercises, you can practice the material discussed in this chapter. Solutions to all exercises are available with the code download on the book's website at `www.wiley.com/go/proc++6e`. However, if you are stuck on an exercise, first reread parts of this chapter to try to find an answer yourself before looking at the solution from the website.

Exercise 18-1: This exercise is to practice working with `vector`s. Create a program containing a `vector` of `int`s, called `values`, initialized with the numbers 2 and 5. Next, implement the following operations:

1. Use `insert()` to insert the numbers 3 and 4 at the correct place in `values`.
2. Create a second `vector` of `int`s initialized with 0 and 1, and then insert the contents of this new `vector` at the beginning of `values`.
3. Create a third `vector` of `int`s. Loop over the elements of `values` in reverse, and insert them in this third `vector`.
4. Print the contents of the third `vector` using `println()`.
5. Print the contents of the third `vector` using a range-based `for` loop.

Exercise 18-2: Take your implementation of the `Person` class from Exercise 15-4. Add a new module called `phone_book`, defining a `PhoneBook` class that stores one or more phone numbers as `strings` for a person. Provide member functions to add and remove person's phone numbers to/from a phonebook. Also provide a member function that returns a `vector` with all phone numbers for a given person. Test your implementation in your `main()` function. In your tests, use the user-defined person literal developed in Exercise 15-4.

Exercise 18-3: In Exercise 15-1 you developed your own `AssociativeArray`. Modify the test code in `main()` from that exercise to use one of the Standard Library containers instead.

Exercise 18-4: Write an `average()` function (not a function template) to calculate the average of a sequence of `double` values. Make sure it works with a sequence or subsequence from a `vector` or an `array`. Test your code with both a `vector` and an `array` in your `main()` function.

Bonus exercise: Can you convert your `average()` function into a function template? The function template should only be instantiatable with integral or floating-point types. What effect does it have on your test code in `main()`?

19

Function Pointers, Function Objects, and Lambda Expressions

WHAT'S IN THIS CHAPTER?

- How to use function pointers
- How to use pointers to class member functions
- What function objects are
- Which standard function objects are available and how to write your own
- How to use polymorphic function wrappers
- What lambda expressions are

WILEY.COM DOWNLOADS FOR THIS CHAPTER

Please note that all the code examples for this chapter are available as part of this chapter's code download on the book's website at `www.wiley.com/go/proc++6e` on the Download Code tab.

Functions in C++ are *first-class functions*, as functions can be used in the same way as normal variables, such as passing them as arguments to other functions, returning them from other functions, and assigning them to variables. A term that often comes up in this context is a *callback*, representing something that can be called. It can be a function pointer or something that behaves like a function pointer, such as an object with an overloaded `operator()`, or an inline lambda expression. A class that overloads `operator()` is called a *function object*, or *functor* for short. Conveniently, the Standard Library provides a set of classes that can be used to create callback objects and to adapt existing callback objects. Lambda expressions allow you to create small inline callbacks right at the place where you need them, which improves the readability and maintainability of your code. It's time to take a closer look at the concept of callbacks, because many of the algorithms explained in the next chapter accept such callbacks to customize their behavior.

FUNCTION POINTERS

You don't normally think about the location of functions in memory, but each function actually lives at a particular address. In C++, you can use *functions as data*; that is, C++ has first-class functions. In other words, you can take the address of a function and use it like you use a variable.

Function pointers are typed according to the parameter types and return type of compatible functions. Here's an example of a definition for a variable called `fun` capable of pointing to functions returning a Boolean and accepting two `int` arguments:

```
bool (*fun)(int, int);
```

Don't forget the parentheses around `*fun`; otherwise, this statement would not be a variable but a function prototype for a function named `fun`, accepting two `int`s and returning a pointer to a `bool`. The `fun` function pointer is uninitialized. As you know, uninitialized data should be avoided. You could initialize `fun` to `nullptr` as follows:

```
bool (*fun)(int, int) { nullptr };
```

findMatches() Using Function Pointers

Another way to work with function pointers is to use type aliases. A type alias allows you to assign a type name to the family of functions that have the given characteristics. For example, the following defines a type called `Matcher` representing a pointer to any function that has two `int` parameters and returns a `bool`:

```
using Matcher = bool(*)(int, int);
```

The following type alias defines a type called `MatchHandler` for functions accepting a `size_t` and two `int`s and returning nothing:

```
using MatchHandler = void(*)(size_t, int, int);
```

Now that these types are defined, you can write a function that takes two callbacks as parameters: a `Matcher` and a `MatchHandler`. Functions that accept other functions as parameters, or functions that return a function are called *higher-order functions*. For example, the following function accepts two spans of integers, as well as a `Matcher` and `MatchHandler`. It iterates through the `span`s in parallel and calls the `Matcher` on corresponding elements of both `span`s. If the `Matcher` returns `true`, the `MatchHandler` is called with as first argument the position of the match, and as second and third arguments the values that caused the `Matcher` to return `true`. Notice that even though the `Matcher` and `MatchHandler` are passed in as variables, they can be called just like regular functions:

```
void findMatches(span<const int> values1, span<const int> values2,
    Matcher matcher, MatchHandler handler)
{
```

```
        if (values1.size() != values2.size()) { return; } // Must be same size.

        for (size_t i { 0 }; i < values1.size(); ++i) {
            if (matcher(values1[i], values2[i])) {
                handler(i, values1[i], values2[i]);
            }
        }
    }
```

Note that this implementation requires that both spans have the same number of elements. To call the findMatches() function, all you need is any function that adheres to the defined Matcher type—that is, any function that takes in two ints and returns a bool—and a function that adheres to the MatchHandler type. Here is an example of a possible Matcher, returning true if the two parameters are equal:

```
bool intEqual(int value1, int value2) { return value1 == value2; }
```

The following is an example of a MatchHandler that simply prints out the match:

```
void printMatch(size_t position, int value1, int value2)
{
    println("Match found at position {} ({}, {})", position, value1, value2);
}
```

The intEqual() and printMatch() functions can be passed as arguments to findMatches(), as follows:

```
vector values1 { 2, 5, 6, 9, 10, 1, 1 };
vector values2 { 4, 4, 2, 9, 0, 3, 1 };
println("Calling findMatches() using intEqual():");
findMatches(values1, values2, &intEqual, &printMatch);
```

The callback functions are passed to findMatches() by taking their addresses. Technically, the & is optional—if you omit it and only put the function name, the compiler will know that you mean to take its address. The output is as follows:

```
Calling findMatches() using intEqual():
Match found at position 3 (9, 9)
Match found at position 6 (1, 1)
```

The benefit of function pointers lies in the fact that findMatches() is a generic function that compares parallel values in two vectors. As it is used in the previous example, it compares values based on equality. However, because it takes a function pointer, it could compare values based on other criteria. For example, the following function also adheres to the definition of Matcher:

```
bool bothOdd(int value1, int value2) { return value1 % 2 == 1 && value2 % 2 == 1; }
```

The following code snippet shows that bothOdd() can also be used in a call to findMatches():

```
println("Calling findMatches() using bothOdd():");
findMatches(values1, values2, bothOdd, printMatch);
```

The output is as follows:

```
Calling findMatches() using bothOdd():
Match found at position 3 (9, 9)
Match found at position 5 (1, 3)
Match found at position 6 (1, 1)
```

By using function pointers, a single function, `findMatches()`, can be customized to different uses based on functions/callbacks passed in as arguments.

findMatches() As a Function Template

You don't need to use explicit function pointer parameters for `findMatches()` to accept callback parameters. Instead, you can convert `findMatches()` to a function template. The only changes needed are to remove the `Matcher` and `MatchHandler` type aliases and to make `findMatches()` a function template. The changes are highlighted:

```
template <typename Matcher, typename MatchHandler>
void findMatches(span<const int> values1, span<const int> values2,
    Matcher matcher, MatchHandler handler)
{ /* ... */ }
```

Better yet is the following constrained function template. The `Matcher` template type parameter is constrained (see Chapter 12, "Writing Generic Code with Templates") with `predicate<int,int>` to make sure the user supplies a callback that can be called with two `int` arguments and returns a Boolean. Similarly, the `MatchHandler` template type parameter is constrained to callbacks that can be called with one `size_t` argument and two `int` arguments and returns nothing.

```
template <predicate<int, int> Matcher, invocable<size_t, int, int> MatchHandler>
void findMatches(span<const int> values1, span<const int> values2,
    Matcher matcher, MatchHandler handler)
{ /* ... */ }
```

Both these implementations of `findMatches()` require two template type parameters, the type of the `Matcher` and `MatchHandler` callbacks, but thanks to function template argument deduction, calling them is the same as calling the earlier versions.

Using the abbreviated function template syntax, the `findMatches()` function template can be written even more elegantly as follows. Notice there is no longer an explicit template header, `template<...>`.

```
void findMatches(span<const int> values1, span<const int> values2,
    auto matcher, auto handler)
{ /* ... */ }
```

The `matcher` and `handler` parameters can again be constrained:

```
void findMatches(span<const int> values1, span<const int> values2,
    predicate<int, int> auto matcher, invocable<size_t, int, int> auto handler)
{ /* ... */ }
```

> **NOTE** *The* `findMatches()` *function template or abbreviated function template is actually the recommended way to implement the function, instead of using explicit function pointer parameters.*

It should be clear by now that callbacks allow you to write very generic and configurable code. It's exactly such use of callbacks that make many Standard Library algorithms (discussed in Chapter 20, "Mastering Standard Library Algorithms") so powerful.

Windows DLLs and Function Pointers

One common use case for using function pointers is to obtain a pointer to a function in a dynamic link library. The following example obtains a pointer to a function in a Microsoft Windows Dynamic Link Library (DLL). A DLL is basically a library consisting of code and data that can be used by any program. An example of a specific Windows DLL is the User32 DLL, which provides, among a lot of other functionality, a function to show a message box on the screen. Details of Windows DLLs are outside the scope of this book on platform-independent C++, but it is so important to Windows programmers that it is worth discussing briefly, and it is a good example of function pointers in general.

One function in `User32.dll` to show a message box is called `MessageBoxA()`. Suppose you would like to load this library only if you need to show a message box. Loading the library at run time can be done with the Windows `LoadLibraryA()` function (requires `<Windows.h>`):

```
HMODULE lib { ::LoadLibraryA("User32.dll") };
```

The result of this call is a *library handle* and will be `NULL` if there is an error. Before you can load the function from the library, you need to know the prototype for the function. The prototype for `MessageBoxA()` is as follows:

```
int MessageBoxA(HWND, LPCSTR, LPCSTR, UINT);
```

The first parameter is the window that owns the message box (can be NULL), the second is the string to show as the message, the third is the title of the window, and the fourth is the configuration flags for the message box, such as which buttons and which icon to show.

You can now define a type alias `MessageBoxFunction` for a pointer to a function with the required prototype:

```
using MessageBoxFunction = int(*)(HWND, LPCSTR, LPCSTR, UINT);
```

Having successfully loaded the library and defined a type alias for the function pointer, you can get a pointer to the function in the library as follows:

```
MessageBoxFunction messageBox {
    (MessageBoxFunction)::GetProcAddress(lib, "MessageBoxA") };
```

If this fails, `messageBox` will be `nullptr`. If it succeeds, you can call the loaded function as follows. `MB_OK` is a flag to show only a single OK button in the message box.

```
messageBox(NULL, "Hello World!", "ProC++", MB_OK);
```

POINTERS TO MEMBER FUNCTIONS (AND DATA MEMBERS)

As the previous section explains, you can create and use pointers to stand-alone functions. You also know that you can work with pointers to stand-alone variables. Now, consider pointers to class data members and member functions. It's perfectly legitimate in C++ to take the addresses of class data members and member functions in order to obtain pointers to them. However, you can't access a non-`static` data member or call a non-`static` member function without an object. The whole point of class data members and member functions is that they exist on a per-object basis. Thus, when you want to call member functions or access data members via a pointer, you must dereference the pointer in the context of an object. Here is an example using the `Employee` class introduced in Chapter 1, "A Crash Course in C++ and the Standard Library":

```
int (Employee::*functionPtr) () const { &Employee::getSalary };
Employee employee { "John", "Doe" };
println("{}", (employee.*functionPtr)());
```

Don't panic at the syntax. The first line declares a variable called `functionPtr` of type pointer to a non-`static` `const` member function of `Employee` that takes no arguments and returns an `int`. At the same time, it initializes this variable to point to the `getSalary()` member function of the `Employee` class. This syntax is quite similar to declaring a simple function pointer, except for the addition of `Employee::` before the `*functionPtr`. Note also that the `&` is required in this case.

The third line calls the `getSalary()` member function (via the `functionPtr` pointer) on the `employee` object. Note the use of parentheses surrounding `employee.*functionPtr`. They are needed because `operator()` has higher precedence than `.*`.

If you have a pointer to an object, you can use `->*` instead of `.*`, as the following code snippet demonstrates:

```
int (Employee::*functionPtr) () const { &Employee::getSalary };
Employee johnD { "John", "Doe" };
Employee* employee { &johnD };
println("{}", (employee->*functionPtr)());
```

The definition of `functionPtr` can be made easier to read with a type alias:

```
using PtrToGet = int (Employee::*) () const;
PtrToGet functionPtr { &Employee::getSalary };
Employee employee { "John", "Doe" };
println("{}", (employee.*functionPtr)());
```

Finally, it can be simplified even further using `auto`:

```
auto functionPtr { &Employee::getSalary };
Employee employee { "John", "Doe" };
println("{}", (employee.*functionPtr)());
```

> **NOTE** *You can get rid of the* `.*` *or* `->*` *syntax by using* `std::mem_fn()`, *explained later in this chapter in the context of function objects.*

Pointers to member functions and data members won't come up often during your day-to-day programming. However, it's important to keep in mind that you cannot dereference a pointer to a non-`static` member function or data member without an object. Every so often, you may want to try something like passing a pointer to a non-`static` member function to a function such as `qsort()` that requires a function pointer, which simply won't work.

> **NOTE** *C++ does permit you to dereference a pointer to a* `static` *data member or* `static` *member function without an object.*

FUNCTION OBJECTS

You can overload the function call operator in a class such that objects of the class can be used in place of function pointers. These objects are called *function objects*, or *functors* for short. The benefits of using a function object instead of a simple function is that a function object can keep state between calls to it.

Writing Your First Function Object

As Chapter 15, "Overloading C++ Operators," explains, to make any class a function object, you just have to provide an overload for the function call operator. Here is a quick reminder:

```
class IsLargerThan
{
    public:
        explicit IsLargerThan(int value) : m_value { value } {}
        bool operator()(int value1, int value2) const {
            return value1 > m_value && value2 > m_value;
        }
    private:
        int m_value;
};

int main()
{
    vector values1 { 2, 500, 6, 9, 10, 101, 1 };
    vector values2 { 4, 4, 2, 9, 0, 300, 1 };

    findMatches(values1, values2, IsLargerThan { 100 }, printMatch);
}
```

Note that the overloaded function call operator of the `IsLargerThan` class is marked as `const`. This is not strictly necessary in this example, but as the next chapter explains, for most Standard Library algorithms, the function call operator of predicates must be `const`.

Remember also from Chapter 15 that, starting with C++23, an overloaded `operator()` can be marked as `static` if it doesn't require access to any non-`static` data members and member functions of the functor. Doing so allows the compiler to better optimize the code.

Function Objects in the Standard Library

Many of the Standard Library algorithms discussed in the next chapter, such as `find_if()`, `accumulate()`, and so on, accept callbacks, for example function pointers and functors, as parameters to customize the algorithm's behavior. C++ provides several predefined functor classes, defined in `<functional>`, that perform the most commonly used callback operations. This section gives an overview of these predefined functors.

Your `<functional>` might also contain functions like `bind1st()`, `bind2nd()`, `mem_fun()`, `mem_fun_ref()`, and `ptr_fun()`. These functions have officially been removed since the C++17 standard and thus are not further discussed in this book. You should avoid using them.

Arithmetic Function Objects

C++ provides functor class templates for the five binary arithmetic operators: `plus`, `minus`, `multiplies`, `divides`, and `modulus`. Additionally, unary `negate` is supplied. These classes are parametrized on the type of the operands and are wrappers for the actual operators. They take one or two parameters of the template type, perform the operation, and return the result. Here is an example using the `plus` class template:

```
plus<int> myPlus;
int res { myPlus(4, 5) };
println("{}", res);
```

This example is of course silly, because there's no reason to use the `plus` class template when you could just use `operator+` directly. The benefit of the arithmetic function objects is that you can pass them as callbacks to other functions, which you cannot do directly with the arithmetic operators. For example, the following code snippet defines a constrained `accumulateData()` function template accepting an `Operation` as its last parameter. The implementation of `geometricMean()` calls `accumulateData()` with an instance of the predefined `multiplies` function object:

```
template <input_iterator Iter, copy_constructible StartValue,
          invocable<const StartValue&, const StartValue&> Operation>
auto accumulateData(Iter begin, Iter end,
    const StartValue& startValue, Operation op)
{
    auto accumulated { startValue };
    for (Iter iter { begin }; iter != end; ++iter) {
        accumulated = op(accumulated, *iter);
    }
    return accumulated;
}

double geometricMean(span<const int> values)
{
    auto mult {accumulateData(cbegin(values), cend(values), 1, multiplies<int>{})};
    return pow(mult, 1.0 / values.size()); // pow() is defined in <cmath>
}
```

The expression `multiplies<int>{}` creates a new object of the `multiplies` functor class template, instantiating it with type `int`.

The other arithmetic function objects behave similarly.

> **WARNING** *The arithmetic function objects are just wrappers around the arithmetic operators. To use them on objects of a certain type, you have to make sure that those types implement the appropriate operations, such as* `operator*` *or* `operator+`.

Transparent Operator Functors

C++ supports *transparent operator functors*, which allow you to omit the template type argument. For example, you can just specify `multiplies<>{}`, short for `multiplies<void>{}`, instead of `multiplies<int>{}`:

```
double geometricMeanTransparent(span<const int> values)
{
    auto mult { accumulateData(cbegin(values), cend(values), 1, multiplies<>{}) };
    return pow(mult, 1.0 / values.size());
}
```

An important feature of these transparent operators is that they are heterogeneous. That is, they are not only more concise than the non-transparent functors, but they also have real functional advantages. For instance, the following code uses a transparent operator functor, `multiplies<>{}`, and uses 1.1, a `double`, as the start value, while the `vector` contains integers. `accumulateData()` calculates the result as a `double`, and `result` will be 6.6.

```
vector<int> values { 1, 2, 3 };
double result {accumulateData(cbegin(values), cend(values), 1.1, multiplies<>{})};
```

If this code uses a non-transparent operator functor, `multiplies<int>{}`, then `accumulateData()` calculates the result as an integer, and `result` will be 6. When you compile this code, the compiler will give you warnings about possible loss of data.

```
vector<int> values { 1, 2, 3 };
double result {
    accumulateData(cbegin(values), cend(values), 1.1, multiplies<int>{}) };
```

Finally, using transparent operators instead of the non-transparent ones can improve performance, as shown with an example in the next section.

> **NOTE** *It's recommended to always use the transparent operator functors.*

Comparison Function Objects

In addition to the arithmetic function object classes, all standard comparison operations are also available as functors: `equal_to`, `not_equal_to`, `less`, `greater`, `less_equal`, and `greater_equal`. You've already seen `less` in Chapter 18, "Standard Library Containers," as the default comparator for elements in the `priority_queue`, the ordered associative containers, and the flat associative container adapters. Now you can learn how to change that criterion. Here's an example of a `priority_queue` using the default comparator, `std::less`:

```
priority_queue<int> myQueue;
myQueue.push(3);
myQueue.push(4);
myQueue.push(2);
myQueue.push(1);
while (!myQueue.empty()) {
    print("{} ", myQueue.top());
    myQueue.pop();
}
```

Here is the output from the program:

```
4 3 2 1
```

As you can see, the elements of the queue are removed in descending order, according to the `less` comparator. You can change the comparator to `greater` by specifying it as the comparator template type argument. The `priority_queue` template definition looks like this:

```
template <typename T, typename Container = vector<T>, typename Compare = less<T>>;
```

Unfortunately, the `Compare` type parameter is last, which means that to specify it, you must also specify the container type. If you want to use a `priority_queue` that sorts the elements in ascending order using `greater`, then you need to change the definition of the `priority_queue` in the previous example to the following:

```
priority_queue<int, vector<int>, greater<>> myQueue;
```

The output now is as follows:

```
1 2 3 4
```

Note that `myQueue` is defined with a transparent operator, `greater<>`. In fact, it's recommended to always use a transparent operator for Standard Library containers that accept a comparator type. Using a transparent comparator can be more performant compared to using a non-transparent operator. For example, if a `set<string>` uses a non-transparent comparator (which is the default), performing a query for a key given as a string literal causes an unwanted copy to be created, because a `string` instance has to be constructed from the string literal:

```
set<string> mySet;
auto i1 { mySet.find("Key") };        // string constructed, allocates memory!
//auto i2 { mySet.find("Key"sv) };  // Compilation error!
```

When using a transparent comparator, this copying is avoided. This is called *heterogeneous lookups*. Here's an example:

```
set<string, less<>> mySet;
auto i1 { mySet.find("Key") };    // No string constructed, no memory allocated.
auto i2 { mySet.find("Key"sv) }; // No string constructed, no memory allocated.
```

Similarly, C++23 adds support for *heterogeneous erasure and extraction* using `erase()` and `extract()`.

Unordered associative containers, such as `unordered_map` and `unordered_set`, also support transparent operators. Using a transparent operator with unordered associative containers is a bit more involved compared to using them for ordered associative containers. Basically, a custom hash functor needs to be implemented, containing an `is_transparent` type alias defined as `void`:

```
class Hasher
{
    public:
        using is_transparent = void;
        size_t operator()(string_view sv) const { return hash<string_view>{}(sv); }
};
```

When using this custom hasher, you also need to specify the transparent `equal_to<>` functor as the type for the key equality template type parameter. Here is an example:

```
unordered_set<string, Hasher, equal_to<>> mySet;
auto i1 { mySet.find("Key") };    // No string constructed, no memory allocated.
auto i2 { mySet.find("Key"sv) }; // No string constructed, no memory allocated.
```

Logical Function Objects

For the three logical operations, `operator!`, `&&`, and `||`, C++ provides the following function object classes: `logical_not`, `logical_and`, and `logical_or`. These logical operations deal only with the values `true` and `false`. Bitwise function objects are covered in the next section.

Logical functors can, for example, be used to implement an `allTrue()` function that checks whether all the Boolean flags in a container are `true`:

```
bool allTrue(const vector<bool>& flags)
{
    return accumulateData(begin(flags), end(flags), true, logical_and<>{});
}
```

Similarly, the `logical_or` functor can be used to implement an `anyTrue()` function that returns `true` if there is at least one Boolean flag in a container `true`:

```
bool anyTrue(const vector<bool>& flags)
{
    return accumulateData(begin(flags), end(flags), false, logical_or<>{});
}
```

> **NOTE** *The* `allTrue()` *and* `anyTrue()` *functions are just given as examples. In fact, the Standard Library provides the* `std::all_of()` *and* `any_of()` *algorithms (see Chapter 20) that perform the same operations but that have the benefit of short-circuiting (see Chapter 1), so they are more performant.*

Bitwise Function Objects

C++ has function objects `bit_and`, `bit_or`, `bit_xor`, and `bit_not`, corresponding to the bitwise operations `operator&`, `|`, `^`, and `~`. These bitwise functors can, for example, be used together with the `transform()` algorithm (discussed in Chapter 20) to perform bitwise operations on all elements in a container.

Adapter Function Objects

When you try to use the basic function objects provided by the standard, it often feels as if you're trying to put a square peg into a round hole. If you want to use one of the standard function objects, but the signature doesn't quite match your requirements, then you can use *adapter function objects* to attempt to rectify the signature mismatch. They allow you to adapt function objects, function pointers, basically any callable. The adapters provide a modicum of support for *functional composition*, that is, to combine functions together to create the exact behavior you need.

Binders

Binders can be used to *bind* parameters of callables to certain values. A first binder is `std::bind()`, defined in `<functional>`, which allows you to bind parameters of a callable in a flexible way. You can bind parameters to fixed values, and you can even rearrange parameters in a different order.

It is best explained with an example. Suppose you have a function called `func()` accepting two arguments:

```
void func(int num, string_view str)
{
    println("func({}, {})", num, str);
}
```

The following code demonstrates how you can use `bind()` to bind the second argument of `func()` to a fixed value, `myString`. The result is stored in `f1()`. The `auto` keyword is used because the return type of `bind()` is unspecified by the C++ standard and thus is implementation specific. Arguments that are not bound to specific values should be specified as `_1`, `_2`, `_3`, and so on. These are defined in the `std::placeholders` namespace. In the definition of `f1()`, the `_1` specifies where the first argument to `f1()` needs to go when `func()` is called. The result: `f1()` can be called with just a single integer argument:

```
string myString { "abc" };
auto f1 { bind(func, placeholders::_1, myString) };
f1(16);
```

Here is the output:

```
func(16, abc)
```

`bind()` can also be used to rearrange the arguments, as shown in the following code. The `_2` specifies where the second argument to `f2()` needs to go when `func()` is called. In other words, the `f2()` binding means that the first argument to `f2()` will become the second argument to `func()`, and the second argument to `f2()` will become the first argument to `func()`:

```
auto f2 { bind(func, placeholders::_2, placeholders::_1) };
f2("Test", 32);
```

The output is as follows:

```
func(32, Test)
```

As discussed in Chapter 18, `<functional>` defines the `std::ref()` and `cref()` helper function templates. These can be used to bind references-to-non-`const` and references-to-`const`, respectively. For example, suppose you have the following function:

```
void increment(int& value) { ++value; }
```

If you call this function as follows, then the value of `index` becomes 1:

```
int index { 0 };
increment(index);
```

If you use `bind()` to call it as follows, then the value of `index` is not incremented because a copy of `index` is made, and a reference to this copy is bound to the first parameter of the `increment()` function:

```
auto incr { bind(increment, index) };
incr();
```

Using `std::ref()` to pass a proper reference correctly increments `index`:

```
auto incr { bind(increment, ref(index)) };
incr();
```

There is a small issue with binding parameters in combination with overloaded functions. Suppose you have the following two overloaded() functions. One accepts an integer, and the other accepts a floating-point number:

```
void overloaded(int num) {}
void overloaded(float f) {}
```

If you want to use bind() with these overloaded functions, you need to explicitly specify which of the two overloads you want to bind. The following will not compile:

```
auto f3 { bind(overloaded, placeholders::_1) }; // ERROR
```

If you want to bind the parameters of the overloaded function accepting a floating-point argument, you need the following syntax:

```
auto f4 { bind((void(*)(float))overloaded, placeholders::_1) }; // OK
```

Another example of bind() is to use findMatches() (defined earlier in this chapter) with a member function of a class as MatchHandler. For example, suppose you have the following Handler class:

```
class Handler
{
    public:
        void handleMatch(size_t position, int value1, int value2)
        {
            println("Match found at position {} ({}, {})",
                position, value1, value2);
        }
};
```

How to pass the handleMatch() member function as the last argument to findMatches()? The problem here is that a member function must always be called in the context of an object. Technically, every member function of a class has an implicit first parameter, containing a pointer to an object instance and accessible in the member function's body with the name this. So, there is a signature mismatch, as our MatchHandler type accepts only three arguments: a size_t and two ints. The solution is to bind this implicit first parameter as follows:

```
Handler handler;
findMatches(values1, values2, intEqual, bind(&Handler::handleMatch, &handler,
            placeholders::_1, placeholders::_2, placeholders::_3));
```

You can also use bind() to bind parameters of standard function objects. For example, you can bind the second parameter of greater_equal to always compare with a fixed value:

```
auto greaterEqualTo100 { bind(greater_equal<>{}, placeholders::_1, 100) };
```

The Standard Library provides two more binder function objects: std::bind_front() and bind_back(). The latter is introduced with C++23. They both wrap a callable f. When calling a bind_front() wrapper, the first n number of arguments for f are bound to a given set of values. For bind_back(), the last n number of arguments for f are bound. Here are two examples:

```
auto f5 { bind_front(func, 42) };
f5("Hello");

auto f6 { bind_back(func, "Hello")};
f6(42);
```

This generates the following output:

```
func(42, Hello)
func(42, Hello)
```

> **NOTE** *Before C++11 there was* `bind2nd()` *and* `bind1st()`. *Both are removed since the C++17 standard. Use lambda expressions, discussed later in this chapter, or* `bind()`, `bind_front()`, *or* `bind_back()` *instead.*

Negator

`not_fn()` is a *negator*, similar to a binder, but it complements the result of a callable. For example, if you want to use `findMatches()` to find pairs of non-equal values, you can apply the `not_fn()` negator adapter to the result of `intEqual()` like this:

```
findMatches(values1, values2, not_fn(intEqual), printMatch);
```

The `not_fn()` functor complements the result of every call to the callable it takes as a parameter.

> **NOTE** *The* `std::not_fn()` *adapter is available since C++17. Before C++17 you could use the* `std::not1()` *and* `not2()` *adapters. However, both* `not1()` *and* `not2()` *have been deprecated since C++17 and removed from C++20. As such, they are not further discussed, and you should avoid using them.*

Calling Member Functions

You might want to pass a pointer to a class member function as the callback to an algorithm. For example, suppose you have the following algorithm that prints `strings` from a container that match a certain condition. The `Matcher` template type parameter is constrained with `predicate<const string&>` to make sure the user supplies a callback that can be called with a `string` parameter and returns a Boolean.

```
template <predicate<const string&> Matcher>
void printMatchingStrings(const vector<string>& strings, Matcher matcher)
{
    for (const auto& string : strings) {
        if (matcher(string)) { print("'{}' ", string); }
    }
}
```

You could use this algorithm to print all non-empty `strings` by using the `empty()` member function of `string`. However, if you just pass a pointer to `string::empty()` as the second argument to `printMatchingStrings()`, the algorithm has no way of knowing that it received a pointer to a member function instead of a normal function pointer or functor. The code to call a member function pointer is different from that of calling a normal function pointer, because the former must be called in the context of an object.

C++ provides a conversion function called `mem_fn()` that you can call with a member function pointer before passing it to an algorithm. The following example demonstrates this and combines it with `not_fn()` to invert the result of `mem_fn()`. Note that you have to specify the member function pointer as `&string::empty`. The `&string::` part is not optional.

```
vector<string> values { "Hello", "", "", "World", "!" };
printMatchingStrings(values, not_fn(mem_fn(&string::empty)));
```

The output is as follows:

```
'Hello' 'World' '!'
```

`not_fn(mem_fn())` generates a function object that serves as the callback for `printMatchingStrings()`. Each time it is called, it calls the `empty()` member function on its argument and inverts the result.

> **NOTE** `mem_fn()` *is not the most intuitive way to implement the desired behavior. I recommend using lambda expressions, discussed later in this chapter, to implement it in a more elegant and more readable way.*

POLYMORPHIC FUNCTION WRAPPERS

The C++ Standard Library provides `std::function` and `move_only_function`. Both are *polymorphic function wrappers*, which are function objects capable of wrapping anything that is callable such as a function, a function object, or a lambda expression; the latter is discussed later in this chapter.

std::function

The `std::function` functor is defined in `<functional>`. An instance of `std::function` can be used as a function pointer, or as a parameter for a function to implement callbacks, and can be stored, copied, moved, and, of course, executed. The template parameters for the `function` template look a bit different than most template parameters. The syntax is as follows:

```
std::function<R(ArgTypes...)>
```

`R` is the return type of the function, and `ArgTypes` is a comma-separated list of parameter types for the function.

The following example demonstrates how to use `std::function` to implement a function pointer. It creates a function pointer `f1` to point to the function `func()`. Once `f1` is defined, you can use it to call `func()`:

```
void func(int num, string_view str) { println("func({}, {})", num, str); }

int main()
{
    function<void(int, string_view)> f1 { func };
    f1(1, "test");
}
```

A `function<R(ArgTypes...)>` can store a function that has a parameter list exactly matching `ArgTypes` and a return type exactly of type `R`. It can also store any other function that has a parameter list allowing it to be called with a set of `ArgTypes` arguments and returning a type that can be converted to `R`. For example, the `func()` function in the previous example could accept its first parameter by `const int&`, while nothing in `main()` needs to change:

```
void func(const int& num, string_view str) { println("func({}, {})", num, str); }
```

Thanks to class template argument deduction, you can simplify the creation of `f1` as follows:

```
function f1 { func };
```

Of course, in the preceding example, it is possible to just use the `auto` keyword, which removes the need to specify the type of `f1`. The following definition for `f1` works the same and is much shorter, but the compiler-deduced type of `f1` is a function pointer, that is, `void (*f1)(int, string_view)` instead of an `std::function`:

```
auto f1 { func };
```

Because `std::function` types behave as function pointers, they can be passed to functions accepting callbacks. The original `findMatches()` implementation from earlier in this chapter defines two type aliases as function pointers. Those type aliases can be rewritten to use `std::function`, while everything else from that example remains the same:

```
// A type alias for a function accepting two integer values,
// returning true if both values are matching, false otherwise.
using Matcher = function<bool(int, int)>;

// A type alias for a function to handle a match. The first
// parameter is the position of the match,
// the second and third are the values that matched.
using MatchHandler = function<void(size_t, int, int)>;
```

Still, as mentioned earlier in this chapter, the recommended implementation for `findMatches()` uses a function template, instead of function pointers or `std::function`.

So, with all these examples, it looks like `std::function` is not really that useful; however, `std::function` really shines when you need to store a callback as a data member of a class. That's the topic of one of the exercises at the end of this chapter.

std::move_only_function

`std::function` requires that the callable stored in it is copyable. To alleviate this, C++23 introduces the move-only `std::move_only_function` wrapper, also defined in `<functional>`, that can be used to wrap a move-only callable. Additionally, the `move_only_function` functor allows you to explicitly mark its function call operator as `const` and/or `noexcept`. This is not possible with `std::function`, as its function call operator is always `const`.

The following code snippet demonstrates `move_only_function`. Assume the `BigData` class stores a lot of data. The `BigDataProcessor` functor processes the data in an instance of `BigData`. To avoid copying, this functor stores a `unique_ptr` to a `BigData` instance, which it gets through its constructor. The function call operator is marked as `const` for demonstration purposes and simply prints out some text. The `main()` function first creates a `unique_ptr` of a `BigData` instance, creates a const processor, and finally calls the function call operator on processor. Using function instead of move_only_function in this example would not work because BigDataProcessor is a move-only type.

```
class BigData {};

class BigDataProcessor
{
    public:
        explicit BigDataProcessor(unique_ptr<BigData> data)
            : m_data { move(data) } { }
        void operator()() const { println("Processing BigData data..."); }
    private:
        unique_ptr<BigData> m_data;
};

int main()
{
    auto data { make_unique<BigData>() };
    const move_only_function<void() const> processor {
        BigDataProcessor { move(data) } };
    processor();
}
```

LAMBDA EXPRESSIONS

The clumsiness of having to create a function or functor class, give it a name that does not conflict with other names, and then use this name is considerable overhead for what is fundamentally a simple concept. In these cases, using anonymous (unnamed) functions represented by *lambda expressions* is a big convenience. Lambda expressions allow you to write anonymous functions inline. Their syntax is easier and can make your code more compact and easier to read. Lambda expressions are useful to define small callbacks passed to other functions inline, instead of having to define a full function object somewhere else with the callback logic implemented in its overloaded function call operator. This way, all the logic remains in a single place, and it is easier to understand and maintain. Lambda expressions can accept parameters, return values, be templated, access variables from its enclosing scope either by value or by reference, and more. There is a lot of flexibility. Let's start with building up the syntax of lambda expressions step-by-step.

Syntax

Let's start with a simple lambda expression. The following example defines a lambda expression that just writes a string to the console. A lambda expression starts with square brackets, [], called the *lambda introducer*, followed by curly braces, {}, which contain the body of the lambda expression. The lambda expression is assigned to the basicLambda auto-typed variable. The second line executes the lambda expression using normal function-call syntax.

```
auto basicLambda { []{ println("Hello from Lambda"); } };
basicLambda();
```

The output is as follows:

```
Hello from Lambda
```

The compiler automatically transforms any lambda expression to a function object, also called *lambda closure*, with a unique, compiler-generated name. For the previous example, the lambda expression is translated to a function object that behaves like the following function object. Note that the function call operator is a `const` member function and has an `auto` return type to let the compiler automatically deduce the return type based on the body of the member function.

```
class CompilerGeneratedName
{
    public:
        auto operator()() const { println("Hello from Lambda"); }
};
```

The compiler-generated name of a lambda closure can be something exotic like `__Lambda_17Za`. There is no way for you to figure out this name, but luckily, you don't need to know its name.

A lambda expression can accept parameters. Parameters are specified between parentheses and multiple parameters are separated by commas, just as with normal functions. Here is an example using one parameter called `value`:

```
auto parametersLambda { [](int value){ println("The value is {}", value); } };
parametersLambda(42);
```

If a lambda expression does not accept any parameters, you can either specify empty parentheses or simply omit them.

In the compiler-generated function object for this lambda expression, the parameters are simply translated to parameters for the overloaded function call operator:

```
class CompilerGeneratedName
{
    public:
        auto operator()(int value) const { println("The value is {}", value); }
};
```

A lambda expression can return a value. The return type is specified following an arrow, called a *trailing return type*. The following example defines a lambda expression accepting two parameters and returning their sum:

```
auto sumLambda { [](int a, int b) -> int { return a + b; } };
int sum { sumLambda(11, 22) };
```

The return type can be omitted, in which case the compiler deduces the return type of the lambda expression according to the same rules as for function return type deduction (see Chapter 1). In the previous example, the return type can be omitted as follows:

```
auto sumLambda { [](int a, int b){ return a + b; } };
int sum { sumLambda(11, 22) };
```

The closure for this lambda expression behaves as follows:

```
class CompilerGeneratedName
{
    public:
        auto operator()(int a, int b) const { return a + b; }
};
```

The return type deduction strips any reference and `const` qualifiers. For example, suppose you have the following `Person` class:

```
class Person
{
    public:
        explicit Person(std::string name) : m_name { std::move(name) } { }
        const std::string& getName() const { return m_name; }
    private:
        std::string m_name;
};
```

The type of `name1` in the following code snippet is deduced as `string`; hence, a copy of the person's name is made, even though `getName()` returns a `const string&`. See Chapter 12 for a discussion of `decltype(auto)`.

```
Person p { "John Doe" };
decltype(auto) name1 { [] (const Person& person) { return person.getName(); }(p) };
```

You can use a trailing return type in combination with `decltype(auto)` to make it so that the deduced type matches the return type of `getName()`, that is a `const string&`:

```
decltype(auto) name2 { [](const Person& person) -> decltype(auto) {
    return person.getName(); }(p) };
```

The lambda expressions up to now in this section are called *stateless* because they don't capture anything from the enclosing scope. A lambda expression can be *stateful* by capturing variables from its enclosing scope. For example, the following lambda expression captures the variable `data` so that it can be used in its body:

```
double data { 1.23 };
auto capturingLambda { [data]{ println("Data = {}", data); } };
```

The square brackets part serves as a *capture block*. *Capturing* a variable means that the variable becomes available inside the body of the lambda expression. Specifying an empty capture block, `[]`, means that no variables from the enclosing scope are captured. When you just write the name of a variable in the capture block as in the preceding example, then you are capturing that variable by value.

Captured variables become data members of the lambda closure. Variables captured by value are copied into data members of the functor. These data members have the same `const`ness as the captured variables. In the preceding `capturingLambda` example, the functor gets a non-`const` data member called `data`, because the captured variable, `data`, is non-`const`. The compiler-generated functor behaves as follows:

```
class CompilerGeneratedName
{
    public:
        CompilerGeneratedName(const double& d) : data { d } {}
        auto operator()() const { println("Data = {}", data); }
    private:
        double data;
};
```

In the following example, the functor gets a `const` data member called `data`, because the captured variable is `const`:

```
const double data { 1.23 };
auto capturingLambda { [data]{ println("Data = {}", data); } };
```

As mentioned earlier, a lambda closure has an overloaded function call operator that is marked as `const` by default. That means that even if you capture a non-`const` variable by value in a lambda expression, the lambda expression is not able to modify this copy. You can mark the function call operator as non-`const` by specifying the lambda expression as `mutable`, as follows:

```
double data { 1.23 };
auto capturingLambda {
    [data] () mutable { data *= 2; println("Data = {}", data); } };
```

In this example, the non-`const` variable `data` is captured by value; thus, the functor gets a non-`const` data member that is a **copy** of `data`. Because of the `mutable` keyword, the function call operator is marked as non-`const`, and so the body of the lambda expression can modify its **copy** of `data`.

You can prefix the name of a variable with `&` to capture it by reference. The following example captures the variable `data` by reference so that the lambda expression can directly change `data` in the enclosing scope:

```
double data { 1.23 };
auto capturingLambda { [&data]{ data *= 2; } };
```

With this lambda expression, the compiler-generated functor contains a data member called `data` of type reference-to-`double`. When you capture a variable by reference, you have to make sure that the reference is still valid at the time the lambda expression is executed.

There are two ways to capture all variables from the enclosing scope, called *capture defaults*:

- `[=]` captures all variables by value.
- `[&]` captures all variables by reference.

> **NOTE** *When using a capture default, only those variables that are really used in the body of the lambda expression are captured, either by value (*`=`*) or by reference (*`&`*). Unused variables are not captured.*

It is also possible to selectively decide which variables to capture and how, by specifying a *capture list* with an optional *capture default*. Variables prefixed with `&` are captured by reference. Variables without a prefix are captured by value. If present, the capture default must be the first element in the capture list and be either `&` or `=`. Here are some capture block examples:

- `[&x]` captures only `x` by reference and nothing else.
- `[x]` captures only `x` by value and nothing else.
- `[=,&x,&y]` captures by value by default, except variables `x` and `y`, which are captured by reference.

- `[&,x]` captures by reference by default, except variable `x`, which is captured by value.
- `[&x,&x]` is illegal because identifiers cannot be repeated.

When a lambda expression is created in the scope of an object, e.g., inside a member function of a class, then it's possible to capture `this` in several ways:

- `[this]` captures the current object. In the body of the lambda expression you can access this object, even without using `this->`. You need to make sure that the object pointed to stays alive until the last time the lambda expression has been executed.
- `[*this]` captures a copy of the current object. This can be useful in cases where the original object will no longer be alive when the lambda expression is executed.
- `[=,this]` captures everything by value and explicitly captures the `this` pointer. Before C++20, `[=]` would implicitly capture the `this` pointer. In C++20, this has been deprecated, and you need to explicitly capture `this` if you need it.

Here are a few notes on capture blocks:

- If a by-value (`=`) or by-reference (`&`) capture default is specified, then it is not allowed to additionally capture specific variables by value or by reference respectively. For example, `[=,x]` and `[&,&x]` are both invalid.
- Data members of an object cannot be captured, unless by using a lambda capture expression discussed later in this chapter.
- When capturing `this`, either by copying the `this` pointer, `[this]`, or by copying the current object, `[*this]`, the lambda expression has access to all `public`, `protected`, and `private` data members and member functions of the captured object.

> **WARNING** *It is not recommended to use a capture default, even though a capture default only captures those variables that are really used in the body of the lambda expression. By using a `=` capture default, you might accidentally cause an expensive copy. By using an `&` capture default, you might accidentally modify a variable in the enclosing scope. I recommend you explicitly specify which variables you want to capture and how.*

> **WARNING** *Global variables are always captured by reference, even if asked to capture by value! For example, in the following code snippet, a capture default is used to capture everything by value. Yet, the global variable, `global`, is captured by reference, and its value is changed after executing the lambda.*
>
> *continues*

(continued)

```
int global { 42 };
int main()
{
    auto lambda { [=] { global = 2; } };
    lambda();
    // global now has the value 2!
}
```

Additionally, capturing a global variable explicitly as follows is not allowed and results in a compilation error:

```
auto lambda { [global] { global = 2; } };
```

Even besides these problems, global variables are never recommended anyway.

The complete syntax of a lambda expression is as follows:

```
[capture_block] attributes1 (parameters) specifiers noexcept_specifier attributes2
   -> return_type requires1 {body}
```

or

```
[capture_block] <template_params> requires1 attributes1 (parameters) specifiers
   noexcept_specifier attributes2 -> return_type requires2 {body}
```

Everything is optional except the capture block and the body:

- **Capture block:** Called the *lambda introducer* and specifies how variables from the enclosing scope are captured and made available in the body of the lambda.
- **Template parameters:** Allows you to write parametrized lambda expressions, discussed later in this chapter.
- **Parameters:** A list of parameters for the lambda expression. If the lambda expression does not require any parameters, you can omit the set of parentheses or specify an empty set, `()`.[1] The parameter list is similar to the parameter list for normal functions.
- **Specifiers:** The following specifiers are available:
  - `mutable`: Marks the function call operator of the lambda closure as mutable; see earlier examples.
  - `constexpr`: Marks the function call operator of the lambda closure as `constexpr`, so it can be evaluated at compile time. Even if omitted, the function call operator will be `constexpr` implicitly if it satisfies all restrictions for `constexpr` functions.
  - `consteval`: Marks the function call operator of the lambda closure as `consteval`, so it becomes an immediate function that must be evaluated at compile time; see Chapter 9, "Mastering Classes and Objects." `constexpr` and `consteval` cannot be combined.

[1] Prior to C++23, you could only omit the empty set of parentheses if you did not need any parameters and you did not specify `mutable`, `constexpr`, `consteval`, a `noexcept` specifier, attributes, a return type, or a requires clause.

- `static` (C++23): Marks the function call operator of the lambda closure as `static`. This can be specified only for stateless lambda expression, i.e., lambda expressions with an empty capture block! Adding this specifier allows the compiler to better optimize the generated code, especially if such stateless lambda expressions are stored inside an `std::function` or `move_only_function` wrapper.

- `noexcept` **specifier:** Specifies `noexcept` clauses for the function call operator of the lambda closure, similar to `noexcept` clauses for normal functions.

- **Attributes 1 (C++23):** Specifies attributes for the function call operator of the lambda closure, e.g., `[[nodiscard]]`. Attributes are discussed in Chapter 1.
- **Attributes 2:** Specifies attributes for the lambda closure itself.
- **Return type:** The type of the returned value. If omitted, the compiler deduces the return type according to the same rules as for function return type deduction; see Chapter 1.
- **Requires clause 1 and 2:** Specifies template type constraints for the function call operator of the lambda closure. Chapter 12, "Writing Generic Code with Templates," explains how such constraints can be specified.

> **NOTE** *For lambda expressions that do not capture anything, the compiler automatically provides a conversion operator that converts the lambda expression to a function pointer. Such lambda expressions can then, for example, be used to pass to functions that accept a function pointer as one of their arguments.*

Lambda Expressions as Parameters

Lambda expressions can be passed as arguments to functions in two ways. One option is to have a function parameter of type `std::function` that matches the signature of the lambda expression. Another option is to use a template type parameter.

For example, a lambda expression can be passed to the `findMatches()` function from earlier in this chapter:

```
vector values1 { 2, 5, 6, 9, 10, 1, 1 };
vector values2 { 4, 4, 2, 9, 0, 3, 1 };
findMatches(values1, values2,
    [](int value1, int value2) { return value1 == value2; },
    printMatch);
```

Generic Lambda Expressions

It is possible to use auto type deduction for parameters of lambda expressions instead of explicitly specifying concrete types for them. To specify auto-type deduction for a parameter, the type is simply specified as `auto`, `auto&`, or `auto*`. The type deduction rules are the same as for template argument deduction.

The following example defines a generic lambda expression called `areEqual`. This lambda expression is used as callback for the `findMatches()` function from earlier in this chapter:

```
// Define a generic lambda expression to find equal values.
auto areEqual { [](const auto& value1, const auto& value2) {
    return value1 == value2; } };
// Use the generic lambda expression in a call to findMatches().
vector values1 { 2, 5, 6, 9, 10, 1, 1 };
vector values2 { 4, 4, 2, 9, 0, 3, 1 };
findMatches(values1, values2, areEqual, printMatch);
```

The compiler-generated functor for this generic lambda expression behaves like this:

```
class CompilerGeneratedName
{
    public:
        template <typename T1, typename T2>
        auto operator()(const T1& value1, const T2& value2) const {
            return value1 == value2; }
};
```

If the `findMatches()` function is modified to support not only `span`s of `int`s, but also other types, then the `areEqual` generic lambda expression can still be used without requiring any changes to it.

Lambda Capture Expressions

Lambda capture expressions allow you to initialize capture variables with any expression. It can be used to introduce variables in the lambda expression that are not captured from the enclosing scope. For example, the following code creates a lambda expression with two variables in its capture block: one called `myCapture`, initialized with the string "Pi: " using a lambda capture expression, and one called `pi`, which is captured by value from the enclosing scope. Note that non-reference capture variables such as `myCapture` that are initialized with a capture initializer are copy constructed, which means that `const` qualifiers are stripped.

```
double pi { 3.1415 };
auto myLambda { [myCapture = "Pi: ", pi]{ println("{}{}", myCapture, pi); } };
```

A lambda capture variable can be initialized with any expression and thus also with `std::move()`. This is important for objects that cannot be copied, only moved, such as `unique_ptr`. By default, capturing by value uses copy semantics, so it's impossible to capture a `unique_ptr` by value in a lambda expression. Using a lambda capture expression, it is possible to capture it by moving, as in this example:

```
auto myPtr { make_unique<double>(3.1415) };
auto myLambda { [p = move(myPtr)]{ println("{}", *p); } };
```

It is allowed, though not recommended, to have the same name for the capture variable as the name in the enclosing scope. The previous example can be written as follows:

```
auto myPtr { make_unique<double>(3.1415) };
auto myLambda { [myPtr = move(myPtr)]{ println("{}", *myPtr); } };
```

Templated Lambda Expressions

Templated lambda expressions allow you to get easier access to type information of parameters of generic lambda expressions. For example, suppose you have a lambda expression that requires a `vector` to be passed as an argument. However, the type of elements in the `vector` can be anything; hence, it's a generic lambda expression using `auto` for its parameter. The body of the lambda expression wants to figure out what the type of the elements in the `vector` is. Without templated lambda expressions, this could be done using `decltype()` and the `std::decay_t` type trait. Type traits are explained in Chapter 26, "Advanced Templates," but those details are not important to grasp the benefits of templated lambda expressions. It suffices to know that `decay_t` removes, among other things, any `const` and reference qualifications from a type. Here is the generic lambda expression:

```
auto lambda { [](const auto& values) {
    using V = decay_t<decltype(values)>; // The real type of the vector.
    using T = typename V::value_type;    // The type of the elements of the vector.
    T someValue { };
} };
```

You can call this lambda expression as follows:

```
vector values { 1, 2, 100, 5, 6 };
lambda(values);
```

Using `decltype()` and `decay_t` is rather convoluted. A templated lambda expression makes this much easier. The following lambda expression forces its parameter to be a `vector` but still uses a template type parameter for the `vector`'s element type:

```
auto lambda { [] <typename T> (const vector<T> & values) {
    T someValue { };
} };
```

Another use of templated lambda expressions is if you want to put certain restrictions on generic lambda expressions. For example, suppose you have the following generic lambda expression:

```
[](const auto& value1, const auto& value2) { /* ... */ }
```

This lambda expression accepts two parameters, and the compiler deduces the type of each parameter automatically. Since the type of both parameters is deduced separately, the type of `value1` and `value2` could be different. If you want to restrict this and want both parameters to have the same type, you can turn this into a templated lambda expression:

```
[] <typename T> (const T& value1, const T& value2) { /* ... */ }
```

You can also put constraints on the template types by adding a `requires` clause, discussed in Chapter 12. Here's an example:

```
[] <typename T> (const T& value1, const T& value2) requires integral<T> {/* ... */}
```

Lambda Expressions as Return Type

By using `std::function`, discussed earlier in this chapter, lambda expressions can be returned from functions. Take a look at the following definition:

```
function<int(void)> multiplyBy2Lambda(int x)
{
    return [x]{ return 2 * x; };
}
```

The body of this function creates a lambda expression that captures the variable x from the enclosing scope by value and returns an integer that is two times the value passed to `multiplyBy2Lambda()`. The return type of the `multiplyBy2Lambda()` function is `function<int(void)>`, which is a function accepting no arguments and returning an integer. The lambda expression defined in the body of the function exactly matches this prototype. The variable x is captured by value, and thus a copy of the value of x is bound to the x in the lambda expression before the lambda is returned from the function. The function can be called as follows:

```
function<int(void)> fn { multiplyBy2Lambda(5) };
println("{}", fn());
```

You can use the `auto` keyword to make this easier:

```
auto fn { multiplyBy2Lambda(5) };
println("{}", fn());
```

The output is `10`.

Function return type deduction (see Chapter 1) allows you to write the `multiplyBy2Lambda()` function more elegantly, as follows:

```
auto multiplyBy2Lambda(int x)
{
    return [x]{ return 2 * x; };
}
```

The `multiplyBy2Lambda()` function captures the variable x by value, `[x]`. Suppose the function is rewritten to capture the variable by reference, `[&x]`, as follows. This will not work because the lambda expression will be executed later in the program, no longer in the scope of the `multiplyBy2Lambda()` function, at which point the reference to x is not valid anymore.

```
auto multiplyBy2Lambda(int x)
{
    return [&x]{ return 2 * x; }; // BUG!
}
```

Lambda Expressions in Unevaluated Contexts

Lambda expressions can be used in *unevaluated contexts*. For instance, the argument passed to `decltype()` is used only at compile time and never evaluated. Here is an example of using `decltype()` with a lambda expression:

```
using LambdaType = decltype([](int a, int b) { return a + b; });
```

Default Construction, Copying, and Assigning

Stateless lambda expressions can be default constructed, copied, and assigned to. Here is a quick example:

```
auto lambda { [](int a, int b) { return a + b; } }; // A stateless lambda.
```

```
decltype(lambda) lambda2; // Default construction.
auto copy { lambda };      // Copy construction.
copy = lambda2;            // Copy assignment.
```

Combined with using lambda expressions in unevaluated contexts, the following kind of code is valid:

```
using LambdaType = decltype([](int a, int b) { return a + b; }); // Unevaluated.
LambdaType getLambda() { return LambdaType{}; /* Default construction. */ }
```

You can test this function as follows:

```
println("{}", getLambda()(1, 2));
```

Recursive Lambda Expressions

For a normal lambda expression, it is not trivial for it to call itself from within its body, even when you give a name to the lambda expression. For example, the following lambda expression given the name `fibonacci` tries to call itself twice in the second `return` statement. This lambda expression will not compile.

```
auto fibonacci = [](int n) {
    if (n < 2) { return n; }
    return fibonacci(n - 1) + fibonacci(n - 2);  // Error: does not compile!
};
```

With C++23's explicit object parameters feature, introduced in Chapter 8, "Gaining Proficiency with Classes and Objects," it is possible to do exactly that. This allows you to write *recursive lambda expressions*. The following demonstrates such a recursive lambda expression. It uses the explicit object parameter named `self` and calls itself recursively twice in the second `return` statement.

```
auto fibonacci = [](this auto& self, int n) {
    if (n < 2) { return n; }
    return self(n - 1) + self(n - 2);
};
```

This recursive lambda expression can be tested as follows:

```
println("First 20 Fibonacci numbers:");
for (int i { 0 }; i < 20; ++i) { print("{} ", fibonacci(i)); }
```

The output is as expected:

```
First 20 Fibonacci numbers:
0 1 1 2 3 5 8 13 21 34 55 89 144 233 377 610 987 1597 2584 4181
```

INVOKERS

`std::invoke()`, defined in `<functional>`, can be used to call any callable with a set of arguments. The following example uses `invoke()` three times: once to invoke a normal function, once to invoke a lambda expression, and once to invoke a member function on a `string` instance:

```
void printMessage(string_view message) { println("{}", message); }
```

```
int main()
{
    invoke(printMessage, "Hello invoke.");
    invoke([](const auto& msg) { println("{}", msg); }, "Hello invoke.");
    string msg { "Hello invoke." };
    println("{}", invoke(&string::size, msg));
}
```

The output of this code is as follows:

```
Hello invoke.
Hello invoke.
13
```

C++23 adds `std::invoke_r()`, also defined in `<functional>`, allowing you to specify the return type. Here is an example:

```
int sum(int a, int b) { return a + b; }

int main()
{
    auto res1 { invoke(sum, 11, 22) };          // Type of res1 is int.
    auto res2 { invoke_r<double>(sum, 11, 22) }; // Type of res2 is double.
}
```

> **NOTE** *By themselves,* `invoke()` *and* `invoke_r()` *are not that useful because you might as well just call the function or the lambda expression directly. However, they can be very useful when writing generic templated code where you need to invoke some arbitrary callable.*

SUMMARY

This chapter explained the concept of callbacks, which are functions that are passed to other functions to customize their behavior. You've seen that callbacks can be function pointers, function objects, or lambda expressions. You also learned that lambda expressions allow you to write more readable code than composing operations using function objects and adapter function objects. Remember, writing readable code is as important, if not more important, than writing code that works. So, even if a lambda expression is a bit longer than an adapted function object, the lambda expression will be more readable and hence more maintainable.

Now that you are fluent in working with callbacks, it's time to delve into the true power of the Standard Library with a discussion of its generic algorithms.

EXERCISES

By solving the following exercises, you can practice the material discussed in this chapter. Solutions to all exercises are available with the code download on the book's website at `www.wiley.com/go/proc++6e`. However, if you are stuck on an exercise, first reread parts of this chapter to try to find an answer yourself before looking at the solution from the website.

Exercise 19-1: Rewrite the `IsLargerThan` function object example from this chapter using a lambda expression. You can find the code in the downloadable source code archive in `Ch19\03_FunctionObjects\01_IsLargerThan.cpp`.

Exercise 19-2: Rewrite the example given for `bind()` using lambda expressions instead. You can find the code in the downloadable source code archive in `Ch19\03_FunctionObjects\07_bind.cpp`.

Exercise 19-3: Rewrite the example given for binding the class member function `Handler::handleMatch()` using lambda expressions instead. You can find the code in the downloadable source code archive in `Ch19\03_FunctionObjects\10_FindMatchesWithMemberFunctionPointer.cpp`.

Exercise 19-4: Chapter 18 introduces the `std::erase_if()` function to remove elements from a container for which a certain predicate returns `true`. Now that you know everything about callbacks, write a small program that creates a `vector` of integers, and then uses `erase_if()` to remove all odd values from the `vector`. The predicate you need to pass to `erase_if()` should accept a single value and return a Boolean.

Exercise 19-5: Implement a class called `Processor`. The constructor should accept a callback accepting a single integer and returning an integer. Store this callback in a data member of the class. Next, add an overload for the function call operator accepting an integer and returning an integer. The implementation simply forwards the work to the stored callback. Test your class with different callbacks.

Exercise 19-6: Write a recursive lambda expression to calculate the power of a number. For example, 4 to the power 3, written as 4^3, equals 4×4×4. Make sure it works with negative exponents. To help you, 4^-3 equals 1/(4^3). Any number to the power 0 equals 1. Test your lambda expression by generating all powers of two with exponents between -10 and 10.

20

Mastering Standard Library Algorithms

WHAT'S IN THIS CHAPTER?

- What Standard Library algorithms are and what principles they are built on
- Details of the algorithms provided by the Standard Library
- How to execute algorithms in parallel to improve performance
- What constrained algorithms are

WILEY.COM DOWNLOADS FOR THIS CHAPTER

Please note that all the code examples for this chapter are available as part of this chapter's code download on the book's website at `www.wiley.com/go/proc++6e` on the Download Code tab.

As Chapter 18, "Standard Library Containers," shows, the Standard Library provides an impressive collection of generic data structures. Most libraries stop there. The Standard Library, however, contains an additional assortment of generic algorithms that can, with some exceptions, be applied to elements from any container. Using these algorithms, you can find, sort, and process elements in containers and perform a host of other operations. The beauty of the algorithms is that they are independent not only of the types of the underlying elements, but also of the types of the containers on which they operate. Algorithms perform their work using only the iterator or ranges interfaces, discussed in Chapter 17, "Understanding Iterators and the Ranges Library."

The Standard Library comes with a large set of *unconstrained algorithms*, all working solely with iterators. These algorithms don't have any constraints in the form of concepts; see

Chapter 12, "Writing Generic Code with Templates," attached to them. The Standard Library additionally has a large collection of *constrained algorithms*, sometimes called *range-based algorithms*. These are able to work with iterators and ranges and are properly constrained, so the compiler can produce more readable error messages when an algorithm is used wrongly. This chapter focuses first on the unconstrained algorithms, as these are the ones used in most existing and legacy code bases; hence, you need to know how they work. Once you know how they work, it will be refreshing to see how the constrained algorithms make things easier.

Chapter 16, "Overview of the C++ Standard Library," gives a high-level overview of all the Standard Library algorithms, but without any coding details. Combined with the knowledge of Chapter 19, "Function Pointers, Function Objects, and Lambda Expressions," now it's time to look at how those algorithms can be used in practice and discover their true power.

OVERVIEW OF ALGORITHMS

The "magic" behind the unconstrained algorithms is that they work on iterator intermediaries instead of on the containers themselves. In that way, they are not tied to specific container implementations. All the Standard Library algorithms are implemented as function templates, where the template type parameters are usually iterator types. The iterators themselves are specified as arguments to the function. Function templates can usually deduce the template types from the function arguments, so you can generally call the algorithms as if they were normal functions, not templates.

Most algorithms require a source sequence on which to apply the algorithm. For the unconstrained algorithms, a source sequence is specified as an iterator pair, a begin and end iterator, which is called a *common range*. As Chapter 17 explains, common ranges are half-open for most containers such that they include the first element in the range but exclude the last. The end iterator is really a "past-the-end" marker.

Algorithms pose certain requirements on iterators passed to them. For instance, `copy_backward()`, which copies elements from one sequence to another, starting with the last element, is an example of an algorithm that requires a bidirectional iterator. Similarly, `stable_sort()`, which sorts elements in place while preserving the order of duplicate elements, is an example of an algorithm requiring random access iterators. This means that such algorithms cannot work on containers that do not provide the necessary iterators. `forward_list` is an example of a container supporting only forward iterators, no bidirectional or random-access iterators; thus, `copy_backward()` and `stable_sort()` cannot work on `forward_list`.

The majority of the algorithms are defined in `<algorithm>`, with some numerical algorithms defined in `<numeric>`. All of them are in the `std` namespace.

Most algorithms are `constexpr`, which means they can be used in the implementation of `constexpr` functions. Consult a Standard Library Reference (see Appendix B, "Annotated Bibliography") to discover exactly which algorithms are `constexpr`.

The best way to understand the algorithms is to look at some examples in detail first. After you've seen how a few of them work, it's easy to pick up the others. This section describes the `find()`, `find_if()`, and `accumulate()` algorithms in detail. The subsequent sections discuss each of the classes of algorithms with representative samples.

The find and find_if Algorithms

`find()` looks for a specific element in a common range. You can use it on elements in any container type. It returns an iterator referring to the element found or the end iterator of the range in case the element is not found. Note that the range specified in the call to `find()` need not be the entire range of elements in a container; it could be a subset.

> **WARNING** *If* `find()` *fails to find an element, it returns an iterator equal to the end iterator specified in the function call, not the end iterator of the underlying container.*

Before looking at `find()`, let's define a function template to populate a container with integers. This function template is used throughout this chapter. It's a function template parameterized on the type of container. A constraint enforces that the given container type supports `push_back(int)`.

```
template <typename Container>
    requires requires(Container& c, int i) { c.push_back(i); }
void populateContainer(Container& cont)
{
    while (true) {
        print("Enter a number (0 to stop): ");
        int value;
        cin >> value;
        if (value == 0) { break; }
        cont.push_back(value);
    }
}
```

Now we can look at how to use `std::find()`. This example and the `populateContainer()` function template assume that the user plays nice and enters valid numbers; it does not perform any error checking on the user input. Performing error checking on stream input is discussed in Chapter 13, "Demystifying C++ I/O."

```
vector<int> myVector;
populateContainer(myVector);

while (true) {
    print("Enter a number to lookup (0 to stop): ");
    int number;
    cin >> number;
    if (number == 0) { break; }
    auto endIt { cend(myVector) };
    auto it { find(cbegin(myVector), endIt, number) };
    if (it == endIt) {
        println("Could not find {}", number);
    } else {
        println("Found {}", *it);
    }
}
```

To search all the elements of the vector, find() is called with cbegin(myVector) and endIt as iterator arguments, where endIt is defined as cend(myVector). If you want to search in a subrange, you can change these two iterators.

Here is a sample run of the program:

```
Enter a number (0 to stop): 3
Enter a number (0 to stop): 4
Enter a number (0 to stop): 5
Enter a number (0 to stop): 6
Enter a number (0 to stop): 0
Enter a number to lookup (0 to stop): 5
Found 5
Enter a number to lookup (0 to stop): 8
Could not find 8
Enter a number to lookup (0 to stop): 0
```

With initializers for if statements, the call to find() and checking the result can be done with one statement as follows:

```
if (auto it { find(cbegin(myVector), endIt, number) }; it == endIt) {
    println("Could not find {}", number);
} else {
    println("Found {}", *it);
}
```

Some containers, such as map and set, provide their own versions of find() as class member functions, as demonstrated with examples during the discussion of those containers in Chapter 18.

> **WARNING** *If a container provides a member function with the same functionality as a generic algorithm, you should use the member function instead, because it's faster. For example, the generic* find() *algorithm runs in linear time, even on a* map, *while the* find() *member function on a* map *runs in logarithmic time.*

find_if() is similar to find(), except that it accepts a *predicate function callback* returning true or false, instead of a simple element to match. The find_if() algorithm calls the predicate on each element in the range until the predicate returns true, in which case find_if() returns an iterator referring to that element. The following program reads test scores from the user, then checks whether any of the scores are "perfect." A perfect score is a score of 100 or higher. The program is similar to the previous example. Only the major differences are highlighted:

```
bool perfectScore(int num) { return num >= 100; }

int main()
{
    vector<int> myVector;
    populateContainer(myVector);

    auto endIt { cend(myVector) };
    auto it { find_if(cbegin(myVector), endIt, perfectScore) };
```

```
        if (it == endIt) {
            println("No perfect scores");
        } else {
            println("Found a \"perfect\" score of {}", *it);
        }
    }
```

This program passes a pointer to the `perfectScore()` function to `find_if()`, which the algorithm then calls on each element until it returns `true`.

Instead of passing a function pointer to `find_if()`, you can also pass a functor. Chapter 15, "Overloading C++ Operators," explains that, starting with C++23, the function call operator of a functor can be marked as `static` if it doesn't need access to any non-`static` data members and member functions of the functor class. The `perfectScore()` function could be changed to a `PerfectScore` functor with a `static` function call operator as follows:

```
class PerfectScore
{
    public:
        static bool operator()(int num) { return num >= 100; }
};
```

The call to `find_if()` then needs to change as follows:

```
auto it { find_if(cbegin(myVector), endIt, &PerfectScore::operator()) };
```

Finally, instead of a `perfectScore()` function or a `PerfectScore` functor, you can use a lambda expression, discussed in Chapter 19.

```
auto it { find_if(cbegin(myVector), endIt, [](int i){ return i >= 100; }) };
```

The accumulate Algorithm

It's often useful to calculate the sum, or some other arithmetic quantity, of elements in a container. The `accumulate()` function—defined in `<numeric>`, not in `<algorithm>`—does just that. In its most basic form, it calculates the sum of the elements in a specified range. For example, the following function calculates the arithmetic mean of a sequence of integers given as a `span`. The arithmetic mean is simply the sum of all the elements divided by the number of elements:

```
double arithmeticMean(span<const int> values)
{
    double sum { accumulate(cbegin(values), cend(values), 0.0) };
    return sum / values.size();
}
```

The `accumulate()` algorithm takes as its third parameter an initial value for the sum, which in this case should be `0.0` (the identity for addition) to start a fresh sum.

A second overload of `accumulate()` allows the caller to specify an operation to perform instead of the default addition. This operation takes the form of a binary callback. Suppose that you want to calculate the geometric mean, which is the product of all the numbers in the sequence to the power of the inverse of the size. In that case, you would want to use `accumulate()` to calculate the product instead of the sum. You could write it like this:

```
int product(int value1, int value2) { return value1 * value2; }

double geometricMean(span<const int> values)
{
    int mult { accumulate(cbegin(values), cend(values), 1, product) };
    return pow(mult, 1.0 / values.size());  // pow() is defined in <cmath>
}
```

Note that the `product()` function is passed as a callback to `accumulate()` and that the initial value for the accumulation is `1` (the identity for multiplication).

Instead of a separate `product()` function, you could use a lambda expression:

```
double geometricMeanLambda(span<const int> values)
{
    int mult { accumulate(cbegin(values), cend(values), 1,
        [](int value1, int value2) { return value1 * value2; }) };
    return pow(mult, 1.0 / values.size());
}
```

You could also use the transparent `multiplies<>` function object, discussed in Chapter 19, to implement the `geometricMean()` function:

```
double geometricMeanFunctor(span<const int> values)
{
    int mult { accumulate(cbegin(values), cend(values), 1, multiplies<>{}) };
    return pow(mult, 1.0 / values.size());
}
```

Move Semantics with Algorithms

Just like Standard Library containers, Standard Library algorithms are also optimized to use move semantics at appropriate times; that is, they can move objects instead of performing potential expensive copy operations. This can greatly speed up certain algorithms, for example, `remove()`, discussed in detail later in this chapter. For this reason, it is highly recommended that you implement move semantics in your custom element classes that you want to store in containers. Move semantics can be added to any class by implementing a move constructor and a move assignment operator. As discussed in Chapter 18, both should be marked as `noexcept`, otherwise they won't be used by Standard Library containers and algorithms. Consult the "Implementing Move Semantics" section in Chapter 9, "Mastering Classes and Objects," for details on how to add move semantics to your classes.

Algorithm Callbacks

> **WARNING** *The algorithms are allowed to make multiple copies of given callbacks, such as functors and lambda expressions, and call different copies for different elements.*

The fact that multiple copies of a callback can be made places strong restrictions on the side effects of such callbacks. Basically, the callbacks must be stateless. For functors, this means that the function call operator needs to be `const`; thus, you cannot write functors such that they count on any internal state of the object being consistent between calls. Similar for lambda expressions, they cannot be marked as `mutable`.

There are some exceptions. The `generate()` and `generate_n()` algorithms can accept stateful callbacks, but even these make one copy of the callback. On top of that, they don't return that copy, so you don't have access to the changes made to the state once the algorithm is finished. The only exception is `for_each()`. It copies the given predicate once into the `for_each()` algorithm and returns that copy when finished. You can access the changed state through this returned value.

To prevent callbacks from getting copied by algorithms, you can use the `std::ref()` helper function to pass a callback reference to the algorithm instead. This ensures that the algorithm always uses the same callback. For example, the following code snippet is based on an earlier example in this chapter but uses a lambda expression stored in a variable named `isPerfectScore`. The lambda expression counts how often it gets called and writes that to standard output. `isPerfectScore` is passed to the `find_if()` algorithm, not yet using `ref()`. The last statement of the snippet explicitly calls `isPerfectScore` one additional time.

```
auto isPerfectScore { [tally = 0] (int i) mutable {
    println("{}", ++tally);  return i >= 100; } };

auto endIt { cend(myVector) };
auto it { find_if(cbegin(myVector), endIt, isPerfectScore) };
if (it != endIt) { println("Found a \"perfect\" score of {}", *it); }
println("---");
isPerfectScore(1);
```

The output can be as followed:

```
Enter a number (0 to stop): 11
Enter a number (0 to stop): 22
Enter a number (0 to stop): 33
Enter a number (0 to stop): 0
1
2
3
---
1
```

The output shows that the `find_if()` algorithm calls `isPerfectScore` three times producing the output 1, 2, 3. The last line shows that the explicit call to `isPerfectScore` occurs on a different instance of `isPerfectScore` as it starts again at 1.

Now, change the call to `find_if()` as follows:

```
auto it { find_if(cbegin(myVector), endIt, ref(isPerfectScore)) };
```

The output now will be 1, 2, 3, 4, showing that no copies of `isPerfectScore` are made.

ALGORITHM DETAILS

Chapter 16 lists all available Standard Library algorithms, divided into different categories. Most of the algorithms are defined in `<algorithm>`, but a few are located in `<numeric>`. They are all in the `std` namespace.

The goal of this chapter is not to provide a reference-style overview of all available algorithms. Instead, I have picked a number of categories and provided examples for them. Once you know how to use these algorithms, you should have no problems with other algorithms. Consult a Standard Library Reference (see Appendix B) for a full reference of *all* the algorithms.

Non-modifying Sequence Algorithms

Non-modifying sequence algorithms are algorithms that do not modify the sequence of elements they operate on. These include algorithms for searching elements in a range and for comparing two ranges to each other; they also include a number of counting algorithms.

Search Algorithms

You've already seen examples of two search algorithms earlier in this chapter: `find()` and `find_if()`. The Standard Library provides several other variations of the basic `find()` algorithm that work on sequences of elements. The section "Search Algorithms" in Chapter 16 describes the different search algorithms that are available, including their complexity.

All the algorithms use `operator==` or `<` as the default comparison operator, but also provide overloaded versions that allow you to specify a different comparison callback.

Here are examples of some of the search algorithms in action:

```
// The list of elements to be searched.
vector myVector { 5, 6, 9, 8, 8, 3 };
auto beginIter { cbegin(myVector) };
auto endIter { cend(myVector) };

// Find the first element that does not satisfy the given lambda expression.
auto it { find_if_not(beginIter, endIter, [](int i){ return i < 8; }) };
if (it != endIter) {
    println("First element not < 8 is {}", *it);
}

// Find the first pair of matching consecutive elements.
it = adjacent_find(beginIter, endIter);
if (it != endIter) {
    println("Found two consecutive equal elements with value {}", *it);
}

// Find the first of two values.
vector targets { 8, 9 };
it = find_first_of(beginIter, endIter, cbegin(targets), cend(targets));
if (it != endIter) {
    println("Found one of 8 or 9: {}", *it);
}

// Find the first subsequence.
vector sub { 8, 3 };
it = search(beginIter, endIter, cbegin(sub), cend(sub));
if (it != endIter) {
    println("Found subsequence {{8,3}}");
```

```
} else {
    println("Unable to find subsequence {{8,3}}");
}

// Find the last subsequence (which is the same as the first in this example).
auto it2 { find_end(beginIter, endIter, cbegin(sub), cend(sub)) };
if (it != it2) {
    println("Error: search and find_end found different subsequences "
          "even though there is only one match.");
}

// Find the first subsequence of two consecutive 8s.
it = search_n(beginIter, endIter, 2, 8);
if (it != endIter) {
    println("Found two consecutive 8s");
} else {
    println("Unable to find two consecutive 8s");
}
```

Here is the output:

```
First element not < 8 is 9
Found two consecutive equal elements with value 8
Found one of 8 or 9: 9
Found subsequence {8,3}
Found two consecutive 8s
```

> **NOTE** *Remember that some of the containers have member functions equivalent to generic algorithms. If that's the case, it's recommended to use those member functions instead of the generic algorithms, because the member functions are more efficient. An example is the* `find()` *member function of* `std::set` *and* `std::map`.

Specialized Searchers

An optional parameter to the `search()` algorithm allows you to specify which search algorithm to use. You have three options—`default_searcher`, `boyer_moore_searcher`, or `boyer_moore_horspool_searcher`—all defined in `<functional>`. The last two options implement the well-known *Boyer-Moore* and *Boyer-Moore-Horspool* search algorithms. These are more efficient than the default searcher and can be used to find a substring in a larger piece of text. The complexity of the Boyer-Moore searchers is as follows (N is the size of the sequence to search in, the haystack, and M is the size of the pattern to find, the needle):

- If the pattern is not found, the worst-case complexity is $O(N+M)$.
- If the pattern is found, the worst-case complexity is $O(N*M)$.

These are the theoretical worst-case complexities. In practice, these specialized searchers are sublinear, better than $O(N)$, which means they are much faster than the default one! They are sublinear because they are able to skip characters instead of looking at each single character in the haystack. They also have an interesting property that the longer the needle is, the faster they work, as they will be able to skip more characters in the haystack. The difference between the Boyer-Moore and the Boyer-Moore-Horspool algorithm is that the latter has less constant overhead for its initialization and in each loop iteration of its algorithm; however, its worst-case complexity can be significantly higher than for the Boyer-Moore algorithm. So, which one to choose depends on your specific use case.

Here is an example of using a Boyer-Moore searcher:

```
string text { "This is the haystack to search a needle in." };
string toSearchFor { "needle" };
boyer_moore_searcher searcher { cbegin(toSearchFor), cend(toSearchFor) };
auto result { search(cbegin(text), cend(text), searcher) };
if (result != cend(text)) {
    println("Found the needle.");
} else {
    println("Needle not found.");
}
```

Comparison Algorithms

You can compare entire ranges of elements in several different ways: `equal()`, `mismatch()`, `lexicographical_compare()`, and `lexicographical_compare_three_way()`. These algorithms have the advantage that you can compare sequences from different containers. For example, you can compare the contents of a `vector` with the contents of a `list`. In general, these algorithms work best with sequential containers. They work by comparing the values in corresponding positions of the two collections to each other. The following list describes how each algorithm works:

- **`equal()`** returns `true` if all corresponding elements are equal. Originally, `equal()` accepted three iterators: begin and end iterators for the first range, and a begin iterator for the second range. This version required both ranges to have the same number of elements. Since C++14, there is an overload accepting four iterators: begin and end iterators for the first range, and begin and end iterators for the second range. This version can cope with ranges of different sizes. It's recommended to always use the four-iterator version because it's safer!

- **`mismatch()`** returns iterators, one iterator for each range, to indicate where in the range the corresponding elements mismatch. There are three-iterator and four-iterator versions available, just as with `equal()`. It's again recommended to use the four-iterator version, because of safety!

- **`lexicographical_compare()`** compares the elements that have the same position in both supplied ranges against each other (sequentially). It returns `true` if the first unequal element in the first range is less than its corresponding element in the second range, or if the first range has fewer elements than the second and all elements in the first range are equal to their corresponding initial subsequence in the second set. `lexicographical_compare()` gets its name because it resembles the rules for comparing strings in dictionaries, but extends this set of rules to deal with objects of any type.

- **`lexicographical_compare_three_way()`** is similar to `lexicographical_compare()` except that it performs a three-way comparison and returns a comparison category type (`strong_ordering`, `weak_ordering`, or `partial_ordering`, discussed in Chapter 1, "A Crash Course in C++ and the Standard Library") instead of a Boolean.

> **NOTE** *If you want to compare all elements of two containers of the same type, you can just use operators such as* operator== *or* operator< *instead of one of these algorithms. The algorithms are useful for comparing subranges, C-style arrays, sequences of elements from different container types, and so on.*

Here are some examples of these algorithms in action:

```
vector<int> myVector;
list<int> myList;

println("Populate the vector:");
populateContainer(myVector);
println("Populate the list:");
populateContainer(myList);

// Compare the two containers
if (equal(cbegin(myVector), cend(myVector),
          cbegin(myList), cend(myList))) {
    println("The two containers have equal elements");
} else {
    // If the containers were not equal, find out why not
    auto miss { mismatch(cbegin(myVector), cend(myVector),
                         cbegin(myList), cend(myList)) };
    println("The following initial elements are the same in "
        "the vector and the list:");
    for (auto iter { cbegin(myVector) }; iter != miss.first; ++iter) {
        print("{}\t", *iter);
    }
    println("");
}

// Now order them.
if (lexicographical_compare(cbegin(myVector), cend(myVector),
                            cbegin(myList), cend(myList))) {
    println("The vector is lexicographically first.");
} else {
    println("The list is lexicographically first.");
}
```

Here is a sample run of the program:

```
Populate the vector:
Enter a number (0 to stop): 5
Enter a number (0 to stop): 6
Enter a number (0 to stop): 7
Enter a number (0 to stop): 0
Populate the list:
Enter a number (0 to stop): 5
Enter a number (0 to stop): 6
Enter a number (0 to stop): 9
Enter a number (0 to stop): 8
```

```
Enter a number (0 to stop): 0
The following initial elements are the same in the vector and the list:
5       6
The vector is lexicographically first.
```

Additionally, the following comparison algorithms work on a single range: `all_of()`, `any_of()`, and `none_of()`. Here are some examples:

```
// all_of()
vector vec2 { 1, 1, 1, 1 };
if (all_of(cbegin(vec2), cend(vec2), [](int i){ return i == 1; })) {
    println("All elements are == 1");
} else {
    println("Not all elements are == 1");
}

// any_of()
vector vec3 { 0, 0, 1, 0 };
if (any_of(cbegin(vec3), cend(vec3), [](int i){ return i == 1; })) {
    println("At least one element == 1");
} else {
    println("No elements are == 1");
}

// none_of()
vector vec4 { 0, 0, 0, 0 };
if (none_of(cbegin(vec4), cend(vec4), [](int i){ return i == 1; })) {
    println("All elements are != 1");
} else {
    println("Some elements are == 1");
}
```

The output is as follows:

```
All elements are == 1
At least one element == 1
All elements are != 1
```

Counting Algorithms

The non-modifying counting algorithms are `count()` and `count_if()`. The following example uses the `count_if()` algorithm to count the number of elements in a `vector` that satisfy a certain condition. The condition is given in the form of a lambda expression, which captures the `value` variable from its enclosing scope by value:

```
vector values { 1, 2, 3, 4, 5, 6, 7, 8, 9 };
int value { 3 };
auto tally { count_if(cbegin(values), cend(values),
    [value](int i){ return i > value; }) };
println("Found {} values > {}.", tally, value);
```

The output is as follows:

```
Found 6 values > 3
```

The example can be extended to demonstrate capturing variables by reference. The following lambda expression counts the number of times it is called by incrementing a variable in the enclosing scope that is captured by reference:

```
vector values { 1, 2, 3, 4, 5, 6, 7, 8, 9 };
int value { 3 };
int callCounter { 0 };
auto tally { count_if(cbegin(values), cend(values),
    [value, &callCounter](int i){ ++callCounter; return i > value; }) };
println("The lambda expression was called {} times.", callCounter);
println("Found {} values > {}.", tally, value);
```

The output is as follows:

```
The lambda expression was called 9 times.
Found 6 values > 3
```

Modifying Sequence Algorithms

The Standard Library provides a variety of *modifying sequence algorithms* that perform tasks such as copying elements from one range to another, removing elements, or reversing the order of elements in a range.

Some modifying algorithms use the concept of a *source* and a *destination* range. The elements are read from the source range and modified in the destination range. An example of such an algorithm is `copy()`.

Other algorithms perform their work *in-place*; that is, they require only one range, for example the `generate()` algorithm.

> **WARNING** *The modifying algorithms cannot insert elements into a destination. They can only overwrite/modify whatever elements are in the destination already. Chapter 17 describes how iterator adapters can be used to really insert elements into a destination.*

> **NOTE** *Ranges from* `maps` *and* `multimaps` *cannot be used as destinations of modifying algorithms. These algorithms overwrite entire elements, which in a* `map` *consist of key/value pairs. However,* `maps` *and* `multimaps` *mark the key as* `const`*, so it cannot be assigned to. The same holds for* `set` *and* `multiset`*. Your alternative is to use an insert iterator, described in Chapter 17.*

The section "Modifying Sequence Algorithms" in Chapter 16 lists all available modifying algorithms with a description of each one. This section provides code examples for a selection of those algorithms. If you understand how to use the algorithms explained in this section, you should not have any problems using the other algorithms for which no examples are given.

generate

The `generate()` algorithm requires a common range and replaces the values in that range with the values returned from the function callback given as third argument. The following example uses the `generate()` algorithm together with a lambda expression to put the numbers 2, 4, 8, 16, and so on, in a `vector`:

```
vector<int> values(10); // Create a vector of 10 elements.
int value { 1 };
generate(begin(values), end(values), [&value]{ value *= 2; return value; });
println("{:n}", values);
```

The output is as follows:

```
2, 4, 8, 16, 32, 64, 128, 256, 512, 1024
```

transform

There are multiple overloads of the `transform()` algorithm. One overload applies a callback to each element in a range and expects the callback to generate a new element, which it stores in the specified destination range. The source and destination ranges can be the same if you want `transform()` to work in-place. The parameters are a begin and end iterator of the source sequence, a begin iterator of the destination sequence, and the callback. For example, the following code snippet adds 100 to each element in a `vector`. The `populateContainer()` function is the same as defined earlier in this chapter.

```
vector<int> myVector;
populateContainer(myVector);

println("The vector contains: {:n}", myVector);
transform(begin(myVector), end(myVector), begin(myVector),
    [](int i){ return i + 100;});
println("The vector contains: {:n}", myVector);
```

A possible output is as follows:

```
Enter a number (0 to stop): 1
Enter a number (0 to stop): 11
Enter a number (0 to stop): 0
The vector contains: 1, 11
The vector contains: 101, 111
```

Another overload of `transform()` calls a binary function on pairs of elements from two ranges. It requires a begin and end iterator of the first range, a begin iterator of the second range, and a begin iterator of the destination range. The following example creates two `vector`s and uses `transform()` to calculate the sum of pairs of elements and to store the result back in the first `vector`:

```
vector<int> vec1, vec2;
println("Vector1:"); populateContainer(vec1);
println("Vector2:"); populateContainer(vec2);
if (vec2.size() < vec1.size())
{
```

```
        println("Vector2 should be at least the same size as vector1.");
        return 1;
    }

    println("Vector1: {:n}", vec1);
    println("Vector2: {:n}", vec2);
    transform(begin(vec1), end(vec1), begin(vec2), begin(vec1),
        [](int a, int b){ return a + b; });
    println("Vector1: {:n}", vec1);
    println("Vector2: {:n}", vec2);
```

The output could look like this:

```
Vector1:
Enter a number (0 to stop): 1
Enter a number (0 to stop): 2
Enter a number (0 to stop): 0
Vector2:
Enter a number (0 to stop): 11
Enter a number (0 to stop): 22
Enter a number (0 to stop): 33
Enter a number (0 to stop): 0
Vector1: 1, 2
Vector2: 11, 22, 33
Vector1: 12, 24
Vector2: 11, 22, 33
```

> **NOTE** `transform()` *and the other modifying algorithms often return an iterator referring to the past-the-end value of the destination range. The examples in this book usually ignore that return value.*

copy

The `copy()` algorithm allows you to copy elements from one range to another, starting with the first element and proceeding to the last element in the range. The source and destination ranges must be different, but, with restrictions, they can overlap. The restrictions are as follows: for `copy(b,e,d)`, overlapping is fine if `d` is before `b`; however, if `d` is within `[b,e)`, then the behavior is undefined. As with all modifying algorithms, `copy()` cannot insert elements into the destination. It just overwrites whatever elements are there already. Chapter 17 describes how to use iterator adapters to insert elements into a container or stream with `copy()`.

Here is a simple example of `copy()` that uses the `resize()` member function on a `vector` to ensure that there is enough space in the destination container. It copies all elements from `vec1` to `vec2`.

```
vector<int> vec1, vec2;
populateContainer(vec1);
vec2.resize(size(vec1));
copy(cbegin(vec1), cend(vec1), begin(vec2));
println("{:n}", vec2);
```

There is also a `copy_backward()` algorithm, which copies the elements from the source backward to the destination. In other words, it starts with the last element of the source, puts it in the last position in the destination range, and then moves backward after each copy. Also for `copy_backward()`, the source and destination ranges must be different, but, with restrictions, they can again overlap. The restrictions this time are as follows: for `copy_backward(b,e,d)`, overlapping is fine if `d` is after `e`, however, if `d` is within `(b,e]`, then the behavior is undefined. The preceding example can be modified to use `copy_backward()` instead of `copy()`, as follows. Note that you need to specify `end(vec2)` as the third argument instead of `begin(vec2)`. The output is the same as the version using `copy()`.

```
copy_backward(cbegin(vec1), cend(vec1), end(vec2));
```

`copy_if()` works by having an input range specified by two iterators, an output destination specified by one iterator, and a predicate (for example, a function or lambda expression). The algorithm copies all elements that satisfy the given predicate to the destination. Remember, copy does not create or extend containers; it merely replaces existing elements, so the destination should be big enough to hold all elements to be copied. Of course, after copying the elements, it might be desirable to remove the space "beyond" where the last element was copied to. To facilitate this, `copy_if()` returns an iterator to the one-past-the-last-copied element in the destination range. This can be used to determine how many elements should be removed from the destination container. The following example demonstrates this by copying only the even numbers to `vec2`:

```
vector<int> vec1, vec2;
populateContainer(vec1);
vec2.resize(size(vec1));
auto endIterator { copy_if(cbegin(vec1), cend(vec1),
        begin(vec2), [](int i){ return i % 2 == 0; }) };
vec2.erase(endIterator, end(vec2));
println("{:n}", vec2);
```

`copy_n()` copies `n` elements from the source to the destination. The first parameter of `copy_n()` is the start iterator. The second parameter is an integer specifying the number of elements to copy, and the third parameter is the destination iterator. The `copy_n()` algorithm does not perform any bounds checking, so you must make sure that the start iterator, incremented by the number of elements to copy, does not exceed the `end()` of the source collection or your program will have undefined behavior. Here is an example:

```
vector<int> vec1, vec2;
populateContainer(vec1);
size_t tally { 0 };
print("Enter number of elements you want to copy: ");
cin >> tally;
tally = min(tally, size(vec1));
vec2.resize(tally);
copy_n(cbegin(vec1), tally, begin(vec2));
println("{:n}", vec2);
```

move

There are two move-related algorithms: `move()` and `move_backward()`. They both use move semantics, discussed in Chapter 9. You have to provide a move assignment operator in your element classes if you want to use these algorithms on containers with elements of your own types, as demonstrated in the following example. The `main()` function creates a `vector` with three `MyClass` objects and then moves those elements from `vecSrc` to `vecDst`. Note that the code includes two different uses of `move()`. The `move()` function accepting a single argument converts an lvalue into an rvalue and is defined in `<utility>`, while `move()` accepting three arguments is the Standard Library `move()` algorithm to move elements between containers. Consult Chapter 9 for details on implementing move assignment operators and the use of the single parameter version of `std::move()`.

```
class MyClass
{
    public:
        MyClass() = default;
        MyClass(const MyClass& src) = default;
        explicit MyClass(string str) : m_str { move(str) } {}
        virtual ~MyClass() = default;

        // Move assignment operator
        MyClass& operator=(MyClass&& rhs) noexcept {
            if (this == &rhs) { return *this; }
            m_str = move(rhs.m_str);
            println("Move operator= (m_str={})", m_str);
            return *this;
        }

        void setString(string str) { m_str = move(str); }
        const string& getString() const { return m_str; }
    private:
        string m_str;
};

int main()
{
    vector<MyClass> vecSrc { MyClass { "a" }, MyClass { "b" }, MyClass { "c" } };
    vector<MyClass> vecDst(vecSrc.size());
    move(begin(vecSrc), end(vecSrc), begin(vecDst));
    for (const auto& c : vecDst) { print("{} ", c.getString()); }
}
```

The output is as follows:

```
Move operator= (m_str=a)
Move operator= (m_str=b)
Move operator= (m_str=c)
a b c
```

> **NOTE** *Chapter 9 explains that source objects in a move operation are left in some valid but otherwise indeterminate state. For the previous example, this means you should not use the elements from* `vecSrc` *anymore after the move operation, unless you bring them back to a determinate state, for example by calling a member function on them without any preconditions, such as* `setString()`*.*

move_backward() uses the same move mechanism as move(), but it moves the elements starting from the last to the first element. For both move() and move_backward(), the source and destination ranges are allowed to overlap with the same restrictions as for copy() and copy_backward().

replace

The replace() and replace_if() algorithms replace elements in a range matching a value or predicate, respectively, with a new value. Take replace_if() as an example. Its first and second parameters specify the range of elements to process. The third parameter is a callback that returns true or false. If it returns true, the value in the container is replaced with the value given for the fourth parameter; if it returns false, it leaves the original value.

For example, you might want to replace all odd values in a container with the value zero:

```
vector<int> values;
populateContainer(values);
replace_if(begin(values), end(values), [](int i){ return i % 2 != 0; }, 0);
println("{:n}", values);
```

There are also variants of replace() and replace_if() called replace_copy() and replace_copy_if() that copy the results to a different destination range. They are similar to copy(), in that the destination range must already be large enough to hold the copied elements.

erase

As introduced in Chapter 18, std::erase() and std::erase_if() support almost all Standard Library containers. Officially, these operations are called *uniform container erasure*. The erase() function deletes all elements matching a given value from a container, while erase_if() deletes all elements matching a given predicate. These algorithms require a reference to a container, instead of a common range, and are the preferred way to erase elements from containers.

For example, the following code snippet removes all empty strings from a vector of strings and uses erase_if() to do all the work:

```
vector<string> values {"", "one", "", "two", "three", "four"};
println("{:n}", values);
erase_if(values, [](const string& str){ return str.empty(); });
println("{:n}", values);
```

The output is as follows:

```
"", "one", "", "two", "three", "four"
"one", "two", "three", "four"
```

> **NOTE** std::erase() *does not work with ordered and unordered associative containers, because these containers have a member function called* erase(key), *which is much more performant and should be used instead. On the other hand, the* erase_if() *function works with all containers.*

remove

The `erase()` and `erase_if()` algorithms discussed in the previous section have been available since C++20. Still, let's look at your options before C++20, as you will encounter them in legacy code.

A first solution that you might think of is to check the documentation to see whether your container has an `erase()` member function and then iterate over all the elements and call `erase()` for each element that matches the condition. The `vector` is an example of a container that has such an `erase()` member function. However, if applied to the `vector` container, this solution is extremely inefficient as it will cause a lot of memory operations to keep the `vector` contiguous in memory, resulting in a quadratic complexity. This solution is also error-prone, because you need to be careful that you keep your iterators valid after a call to `erase()`. For example, here is a function that removes empty `strings` from a `vector` of `strings` without using algorithms. Note how `iter` is carefully manipulated inside the `for` loop.

```
void removeEmptyStringsWithoutAlgorithms(vector<string>& strings)
{
    for (auto iter { begin(strings) }; iter != end(strings); ) {
        if (iter->empty()) {
            iter = strings.erase(iter);
        } else {
            ++iter;
        }
    }
}
```

> **NOTE** *Quadratic complexity means that the running time is a function of the square of the input size,* $O(n^2)$.

This solution is inefficient and not recommended. A much better solution for this problem is the *remove-erase-idiom*, which runs in linear time and is explained next.

The remove algorithms have access only to the iterator abstraction, not to the container. Thus, they cannot really remove elements from the underlying container. Instead, the algorithms work by replacing the elements that match a given value or predicate with the next element that does not match the given value or predicate. It does so using move assignments. The result is that all elements to be kept are moved toward the beginning of the range. The range becomes partitioned into two sets: the elements to be kept and the elements to be erased. An iterator is returned that points to the first element of the range of elements to be erased. Take care not to use any of the elements in that range, as they might have been moved. The only thing you must do with the returned iterator is to actually erase these elements from the container. So you first use the `remove()` or `remove_if()` algorithm, and then you must call `erase()` on the container to erase all the elements from the returned iterator up to the end of the range. This process is called the *remove-erase-idiom*. Here is an implementation of a `removeEmptyStrings()` function using this idiom:

```
void removeEmptyStrings(vector<string>& strings)
{
    auto it { remove_if(begin(strings), end(strings),
        [](const string& str){ return str.empty(); }) };
```

```
    // Erase the removed elements.
    strings.erase(it, end(strings));
}
```

WARNING *When using the remove-erase-idiom, make sure not to forget the second argument to* `erase()`*! If you forget this second argument,* `erase()` *will erase only a single element from the container, that is, the element referred to by the iterator passed as the first argument.*

The `remove_copy()` and `remove_copy_if()` variations of `remove()` and `remove_if()` do not change the source range. Instead, they copy all kept elements to a different destination range. They are similar to `copy()`, in that the destination range must already be large enough to hold the new elements.

NOTE *The* `remove()` *family of functions are stable; i.e., they maintain the order of elements remaining in the container even while moving the retained elements toward the beginning.*

NOTE *It's recommended to use the* `std::erase_if()` *and* `std::erase()` *algorithms (or the* `erase(key)` *member function for associative containers) over the remove-erase-idiom, and definitely over handwritten loops.*

unique

The `unique()` algorithm is a special case of `remove()` that removes all duplicate contiguous elements. The `list` container provides its own `unique()` member function that implements the same semantics. You should generally use `unique()` on sorted sequences, but nothing prevents you from running it on unsorted sequences.

`unique()` works in a similar way as `remove()`: it moves all elements to be kept to the front of the range and returns an iterator that points to the first element of the range of elements to be erased. As with the remove-erase-idiom, calling `unique()` must be followed by a call to `erase()`.

The basic form of `unique()` runs in place, but there is also a variant of the algorithm called `unique_copy()` that copies its results to a new destination range.

Chapter 18 shows an example of the `list::unique()` algorithm in the section "list Example: Determining Enrollment," so an example of the general form is omitted here.

shuffle

`shuffle()` rearranges the elements of a range in a random order with a linear complexity. It's useful for implementing tasks like shuffling a deck of cards. `shuffle()` requires a start and end iterator for the range that you want to shuffle and a uniform random number generator object that specifies how random numbers should be generated. Here is an example (details on how to use random number generation engines and how to "seed" them are explained in Chapter 23, "Random Number Facilities"):

```
vector values { 1, 2, 3, 4, 5, 6, 7, 8, 9 };

random_device seeder;
default_random_engine generator { seeder() };

for (int i { 0 }; i < 6; ++i) {
    shuffle(begin(values), end(values), generator);
    println("{:n}", values);
}
```

Here is some possible output:

```
8, 6, 7, 5, 4, 1, 2, 9, 3
4, 1, 6, 2, 3, 7, 5, 9, 8
1, 4, 2, 5, 6, 8, 7, 3, 9
8, 4, 2, 7, 5, 9, 1, 6, 3
8, 9, 1, 7, 4, 5, 2, 6, 3
1, 7, 8, 5, 4, 3, 9, 6, 2
```

sample

The `sample()` algorithm returns a selection of *n* randomly chosen elements from a given source range and stores them in a destination range. It requires five parameters:

- A begin and end iterator of the range to sample
- A begin iterator of the destination range where to store the randomly selected elements
- The number of elements to select
- A random number generation engine

Here is an example (details on how to use random number generation engines and how to "seed" them are explained in Chapter 23):

```
vector values { 1, 2, 3, 4, 5, 6, 7, 8, 9 };
const size_t numberOfSamples { 5 };
vector<int> samples(numberOfSamples);

random_device seeder;
default_random_engine generator { seeder() };

for (int i { 0 }; i < 6; ++i) {
    sample(cbegin(values), cend(values), begin(samples),
        numberOfSamples, generator);
    println("{:n}", samples);
}
```

Here is some possible output:

```
1, 4, 7, 8, 9
1, 3, 4, 7, 9
2, 3, 4, 5, 7
3, 5, 6, 7, 9
1, 2, 3, 6, 7
1, 2, 4, 5, 8
```

reverse

The `reverse()` algorithm reverses the order of the elements in a range. The first element in the range is swapped with the last, the second with the second-to-last, and so on.

The basic form of `reverse()` runs in place and requires two arguments: a start and end iterator for the range. There is also a variant of the algorithm called `reverse_copy()` that copies its results to a new destination range and requires three arguments: a start and end iterator for the source range, and a start iterator for the destination range. The destination range must already be large enough to hold the new elements.

Here is an example using `reverse()`:

```
vector<int> values;
populateContainer(values);
reverse(begin(values), end(values));
println("{:n}", values);
```

Shifting Elements

The `shift_left()` and `shift_right()` algorithms shift elements in a given range by moving them to their new position. `shift_left()` returns an iterator to the end of the new range, while `shift_right()` returns an iterator to the beginning of the new range. After calling either algorithm, you must use the returned iterator in a call to `erase()` to delete elements that fell off either end of the range. Here is an example:

```
vector values { 11, 22, 33, 44, 55 };
println("{:n}", values);

// Shift elements to the left by 2 positions.
auto newEnd { shift_left(begin(values), end(values), 2) };
// Resize the vector to its proper size.
values.erase(newEnd, end(values));
println("{:n}", values);

// Shift elements to the right by 2 positions.
auto newBegin { shift_right(begin(values), end(values), 2) };
// Resize the vector to its proper size.
values.erase(begin(values), newBegin);
println("{:n}", values);
```

The output is as follows:

```
11, 22, 33, 44, 55
33, 44, 55
33
```

Operational Algorithms

There are only two algorithms in this category: `for_each()` and `for_each_n()`. They execute a callback on each element of a range, `for_each()`, or on the first *n* elements of a range, `for_each_n()`. The callback can modify elements in the range if the given iterator type is non-`const`. The algorithms are mentioned here so you know they exist; however, it's often easier and more readable to use a simple range-based `for` loop instead.

for_each

The following is an example using a generic lambda expression, printing the elements from a `map`:

```
map<int, int> myMap { { 4, 40 }, { 5, 50 }, { 6, 60 } };
for_each(cbegin(myMap), cend(myMap), [](const auto& p)
    { println("{} -> {}", p.first, p.second); });
```

The type of `p` is `const pair<int, int>&`. The output is as follows:

```
4 -> 40
5 -> 50
6 -> 60
```

The following example shows how to use the `for_each()` algorithm and a lambda expression to calculate the sum and the product of a range of elements at the same time. The lambda expression explicitly captures only those variables it needs. It captures them by reference; otherwise, changes made to `sum` and `product` in the lambda expression would not be visible outside the lambda.

```
vector<int> myVector;
populateContainer(myVector);

int sum { 0 };
int product { 1 };
for_each(cbegin(myVector), cend(myVector),
    [&sum, &product](int i){
        sum += i;
        product *= i;
});
println("The sum is {}", sum);
println("The product is {}", product);
```

This example can also be written with a functor in which you accumulate information that you can retrieve after `for_each()` has finished processing all the elements. For example, you can calculate both the sum and product of the elements in one pass by writing a functor `SumAndProduct` that tracks both at the same time:

```
class SumAndProduct
{
    public:
        void operator()(int value)
        {
            m_sum += value;
            m_product *= value;
        }
```

```
        int getSum() const { return m_sum; }
        int getProduct() const { return m_product; }
    private:
        int m_sum { 0 };
        int m_product { 1 };
};

int main()
{
    vector<int> myVector;
    populateContainer(myVector);

    SumAndProduct calculator;
    calculator = for_each(cbegin(myVector), cend(myVector), calculator);
    println("The sum is {}", calculator.getSum());
    println("The product is {}", calculator.getProduct());
}
```

You might be tempted to ignore the return value of `for_each()` yet still try to read information from `calculator` after the algorithm is finished. However, that doesn't work because `for_each()` copies the functor, and at the end, this copy is returned from the call. You must capture the return value to ensure correct behavior.

Another option is to pass `calculator` by reference using `std::ref()`, see earlier in this chapter:

```
for_each(cbegin(myVector), cend(myVector), ref(calculator));
```

A final point about `for_each()` (that also applies to `for_each_n()` discussed in the next section) is that the callback is allowed to have a reference-to-non-`const` as parameter and modify it. That has the effect of changing values in the actual range. Here is an example:

```
vector values { 11, 22, 33, 44 };
// Double each element in the values vector.
for_each(begin(values), end(values), [](auto& value) { value *= 2; });
println("{:n}", values);
```

for_each_n

The `for_each_n()` algorithm requires a begin iterator of the range, the number of elements to iterate over, n, and a callback. It returns an iterator equal to begin + n. As usual, it does not perform any bounds checking. Here is an example that only iterates over the first two elements of a `map`:

```
map<int, int> myMap { { 4, 40 }, { 5, 50 }, { 6, 60 } };
for_each_n(cbegin(myMap), 2, [](const auto& p)
    { println("{} -> {}", p.first, p.second); });
```

Partition Algorithms

`partition_copy()` copies elements from a source to two different destinations. The destination for each element is selected based on the result of a predicate, either `true` or `false`. The value returned by `partition_copy()` is a pair of iterators: iterators referring to one-past-the-last-copied element in the first and second destination range. These returned iterators can be used in combination with `erase()` to remove excess elements from the two destination ranges, just as in the earlier `copy_if()`

example. The following code snippet asks the user to enter a number of integers, which are then *partitioned* into two destination vectors: one for the even numbers and one for the odd numbers:

```
vector<int> values, vecOdd, vecEven;
populateContainer(values);
vecOdd.resize(size(values));
vecEven.resize(size(values));

auto pairIters { partition_copy(cbegin(values), cend(values),
    begin(vecEven), begin(vecOdd),
    [](int i){ return i % 2 == 0; }) };

vecEven.erase(pairIters.first, end(vecEven));
vecOdd.erase(pairIters.second, end(vecOdd));

println("Even numbers: {:n}", vecEven);
println("Odd numbers: {:n}", vecOdd);
```

The output can be as follows:

```
Enter a number (0 to stop): 11
Enter a number (0 to stop): 22
Enter a number (0 to stop): 33
Enter a number (0 to stop): 44
Enter a number (0 to stop): 0
Even numbers: 22, 44
Odd numbers: 11, 33
```

The `partition()` algorithm sorts a sequence such that all elements for which a predicate returns `true` are before all elements for which it returns `false`, without preserving the original order of the elements within each partition. The following example demonstrates how to partition a `vector` into all even numbers followed by all odd numbers:

```
vector<int> values;
populateContainer(values);
partition(begin(values), end(values), [](int i){ return i % 2 == 0; });
println("Partitioned result: {:n}", values);
```

The output can be as follows:

```
Enter a number (0 to stop): 55
Enter a number (0 to stop): 44
Enter a number (0 to stop): 33
Enter a number (0 to stop): 22
Enter a number (0 to stop): 11
Enter a number (0 to stop): 0
Partitioned result: 22, 44, 33, 55, 11
```

A few more partition algorithms are available as well. See Chapter 16 for a list.

Sorting Algorithms

The Standard Library provides several variations of sorting algorithms. A sorting algorithm reorders the contents of a container such that an ordering is maintained between sequential elements of the collection. Thus, it applies only to sequential collections. Sorting is not relevant for ordered associative containers because they already maintain elements in a sorted order. Sorting is not relevant for the unordered associative containers either, because they have no concept of ordering. Some containers, such as `list` and `forward_list`, provide their own sorting member functions, because these member functions can be implemented more efficiently than a generic sorting mechanism. Consequently, the generic sorting algorithms are most useful for `vector`s, `deque`s, `array`s, and C-style arrays.

The `sort()` algorithm sorts a range of elements in $O(N \log N)$ time in general. Following the application of `sort()` to a range, the elements in the range are in nondecreasing order (lowest to highest), according to `operator<`. If you don't like that order, you can specify a different comparator, such as `greater`.

A variant of `sort()`, called `stable_sort()`, maintains the relative order of equal elements in a range, but it is less efficient than `sort()`.

Here is an example of `sort()` using a transparent `greater<>` comparator:

```
vector<int> values;
populateContainer(values);
sort(begin(values), end(values), greater<>{});
```

There is also `is_sorted()`, returning `true` if a given range is sorted, and `is_sorted_until()`, returning an iterator such that everything before this iterator is sorted.

`nth_element()` is a powerful *selection algorithm*. Given a range of elements and an iterator to the nth element in that range, the algorithm rearranges the elements in the range such that the element in the position pointed to by n^{th} is the element that would be in that position if the whole range were sorted. Additionally, it rearranges all elements such that all elements preceding the nth element are less than the new n^{th} element, and the ones following it are greater than the new n^{th} element. The interesting thing about this algorithm is that it does all this in linear time, $O(n)$. Instead of using `nth_element()`, you could also just sort the whole range and then retrieve the data you are interested in, but that would result in a complexity that is linear logarithmic, $O(n \log n)$.

All this sounds complicated, so let's see this algorithm in action. A first example is to find the third largest element in a given range. It assumes the user enters at least three values.

```
vector<int> values;
populateContainer(values);
// Find the third largest value.
nth_element(begin(values), begin(values) + 2, end(values), greater<>{});
println("3rd largest value: {}", values[2]);
```

Another example is to get the five largest elements from a range in sorted order. It assumes the user enters at least five values.

```
vector<int> values;
populateContainer(values);
// Get the 5 largest elements in sorted order.
nth_element(begin(values), begin(values) + 4, end(values), greater<>{});
// nth_element() has partitioned the elements, now sort the first subrange.
sort(begin(values), begin(values) + 5);
// And finally, output the sorted subrange.
for_each_n(begin(values), 5, [](const auto& element) { print("{}  ", element); });
```

Binary Search Algorithms

There are several search algorithms that work only on sequences that are sorted or that are at least partitioned on the element that is searched for. These algorithms are `binary_search()`, `lower_bound()`, `upper_bound()`, and `equal_range()`. Note that the associative containers, such as `map` and `set`, have equivalent member functions that you should use instead. See Chapter 18 for an example on how to use these member functions on such containers.

The `lower_bound()` algorithm finds the first element in a sorted range not less than (greater or equal to) a given value. It is often used to find at which position in a sorted `vector` a new value should be inserted so that the `vector` remains sorted. Here is an example:

```
vector<int> values;
populateContainer(values);

// Sort the container
sort(begin(values), end(values));
println("Sorted vector: {:n}", values);

while (true) {
    int number;
    print("Enter a number to insert (0 to stop): ");
    cin >> number;
    if (number == 0) { break; }

    auto iter { lower_bound(begin(values), end(values), number) };
    values.insert(iter, number);
    println("New vector: {:n}", values);
}
```

The `binary_search()` algorithm finds a matching element in logarithmic time instead of linear time. It requires a start and end iterator specifying the range to search in, a value to search, and optionally a comparator callback. It returns `true` if the value is found in the specified range, `false` otherwise. Binary search requires the range to be sorted and works by first comparing the middle element of the range. Depending on whether that middle element is greater than or less than the value to search, it continues by comparing the middle element of the left or right half of the range, respectively. This continues until the element is found. Basically, on each iteration, the range is halved, hence the logarithmic complexity. The following example demonstrates this algorithm:

```
vector<int> values;
populateContainer(values);

// Sort the container
sort(begin(values), end(values));

while (true) {
    print("Enter a number to find (0 to stop): ");
    int number;
    cin >> number;
    if (number == 0) { break; }
    if (binary_search(cbegin(values), cend(values), number)) {
        println("That number is in the vector.");
```

```
        } else {
            println("That number is not in the vector.");
        }
    }
```

Set Algorithms

The set algorithms work on any sorted range. The `includes()` algorithm implements standard subset determination, checking whether all the elements of one sorted range are included in another sorted range, in any order.

The `set_union()`, `set_intersection()`, `set_difference()`, and `set_symmetric_difference()` algorithms implement the standard semantics of those operations. In set theory, the result of a union is all the elements in either set. The result of an intersection is all the elements that are in both sets. The result of a difference is all the elements in the first set but not the second. The result of a symmetric difference is the "exclusive or" of sets: all the elements in one, but not both, sets.

> **WARNING** *Make sure that your result range is large enough to hold the result of the operations. For* `set_union()` *and* `set_symmetric_difference()`*, the result is at most the sum of the sizes of the two input ranges. For* `set_intersection()`*, the result is at most the size of the smallest input range, and for* `set_difference()` *it's at most the size of the first range.*

> **WARNING** *You can't use common ranges from associative containers, including* `set`*s, to store the results because they don't allow changes to their keys.*

Let's look at these set algorithms in action. First, a constrained `DumpRange()` function template is defined to write elements of a given range to the standard output stream; it is implemented as follows. `ranges::subrange()` converts a common range, given as a pair of iterators, to a range, which can then be passed to `println()`.

```
template <forward_iterator Iterator>
void DumpRange(string_view message, Iterator begin, Iterator end)
{
    println("{}{:n}", message, ranges::subrange(begin, end));
}
```

With this helper function defined, here are examples on using the set algorithms:

```
vector<int> vec1, vec2, result;
println("Enter elements for set 1:");
populateContainer(vec1);
println("Enter elements for set 2:");
populateContainer(vec2);
```

```
// set algorithms require sorted ranges
sort(begin(vec1), end(vec1));
sort(begin(vec2), end(vec2));

println("Set 1: {:n}", vec1);
println("Set 2: {:n}", vec2);

if (includes(cbegin(vec1), cend(vec1), cbegin(vec2), cend(vec2))) {
    println("The second set is a subset of the first.");
}
if (includes(cbegin(vec2), cend(vec2), cbegin(vec1), cend(vec1))) {
    println("The first set is a subset of the second");
}

result.resize(size(vec1) + size(vec2));
auto newEnd { set_union(cbegin(vec1), cend(vec1), cbegin(vec2),
    cend(vec2), begin(result)) };
DumpRange("The union is: ", begin(result), newEnd);

newEnd = set_intersection(cbegin(vec1), cend(vec1), cbegin(vec2),
    cend(vec2), begin(result));
DumpRange("The intersection is: ", begin(result), newEnd);

newEnd = set_difference(cbegin(vec1), cend(vec1), cbegin(vec2),
    cend(vec2), begin(result));
DumpRange("The difference between set 1 and 2 is: ", begin(result), newEnd);

newEnd = set_symmetric_difference(cbegin(vec1), cend(vec1),
    cbegin(vec2), cend(vec2), begin(result));
DumpRange("The symmetric difference is: ", begin(result), newEnd);
```

Here is a sample run of the program:

```
Enter elements for set 1:
Enter a number (0 to stop): 5
Enter a number (0 to stop): 6
Enter a number (0 to stop): 7
Enter a number (0 to stop): 8
Enter a number (0 to stop): 0
Enter elements for set 2:
Enter a number (0 to stop): 8
Enter a number (0 to stop): 9
Enter a number (0 to stop): 10
Enter a number (0 to stop): 0
Set 1: 5, 6, 7, 8
Set 2: 8, 9, 10
The union is: 5, 6, 7, 8, 9, 10
The intersection is: 8
The difference between set 1 and set 2 is: 5, 6, 7
The symmetric difference is: 5, 6, 7, 9, 10
```

The `merge()` algorithm allows you to merge two sorted ranges together, while maintaining the sorted order. The result is a sorted range containing all the elements of both source ranges. It works in linear time. The following parameters are required:

- Start and end iterator of the first source range
- Start and end iterator of the second source range
- Start iterator of the destination range
- Optionally, a comparator callback

Without `merge()`, you could still achieve the same effect by concatenating the two ranges and applying `sort()` to the result, but that would be less efficient, $O(N \log N)$ instead of the linear complexity of `merge()`.

> **WARNING** *Always ensure that you supply a big enough destination range to store the result of the merge!*

The following example demonstrates `merge()`:

```
vector<int> vectorOne, vectorTwo, vectorMerged;
println("Enter values for first vector:");
populateContainer(vectorOne);
println("Enter values for second vector:");
populateContainer(vectorTwo);

// Sort both containers
sort(begin(vectorOne), end(vectorOne));
sort(begin(vectorTwo), end(vectorTwo));

// Make sure the destination vector is large enough to hold the values
// from both source vectors.
vectorMerged.resize(size(vectorOne) + size(vectorTwo));

merge(cbegin(vectorOne), cend(vectorOne),
      cbegin(vectorTwo), cend(vectorTwo), begin(vectorMerged));

println("Merged vector: {:n}", vectorMerged);
```

Minimum/Maximum Algorithms

The `min()` and `max()` algorithms compare two or more elements of any type using `operator<` or a user-supplied binary predicate, returning a reference-to-`const` to the smallest or largest element, respectively. The `minmax()` algorithm returns a pair containing the minimum and maximum of two or more elements. These algorithms do not work with common ranges or ranges.

The `min_element()` and `max_element()` algorithms work with common ranges and return an iterator to the smallest or largest element in a range, respectively. The `minmax_element()` algorithm also works with a common range and returns a pair containing iterators to the smallest and largest element in a range.

The following program gives some examples:

```
int x { 4 }, y { 5 };
println("x is {} and y is {}", x, y);
```

```
println("Max is {}", max(x, y));
println("Min is {}", min(x, y));

// Using max() and min() on more than two values.
int x1 { 2 }, x2 { 9 }, x3 { 3 }, x4 { 12 };
println("Max of 4 elements is {}", max({ x1, x2, x3, x4 }));
println("Min of 4 elements is {}", min({ x1, x2, x3, x4 }));

// Using minmax().
auto p2 { minmax({ x1, x2, x3, x4 }) }; // p2 is of type pair<int, int>.
println("Minmax of 4 elements is <{},{}>", p2.first, p2.second);

// Using minmax() + structured bindings.
auto [min1, max1] { minmax({ x1, x2, x3, x4 }) };
println("Minmax of 4 elements is <{},{}>", min1, max1);

// Using minmax_element() + structured bindings.
vector values { 11, 33, 22 };
auto [min2, max2] { minmax_element(cbegin(values), cend(values)) };
println("minmax_element() result: <{},{}>", *min2, *max2);
```

Here is the program output:

```
x is 4 and y is 5
Max is 5
Min is 4
Max of 4 elements is 12
Min of 4 elements is 2
Minmax of 4 elements is <2,12>
Minmax of 4 elements is <2,12>
minmax_element() result: <11,33>
```

NOTE *Sometimes you might encounter non-standard macros to find the minimum and maximum. For example, the GNU C Library (glibc) has macros* `MIN()` *and* `MAX()`*, while the* `Windows.h` *header file defines* `min()` *and* `max()` *macros. Because these are macros, they have the potential to evaluate one of their arguments twice, whereas* `std::min()` *and* `std::max()` *evaluate each argument exactly once. Make sure you always use the C++ versions,* `std::min()` *and* `std::max()`.

Even worse, such `min()` *and* `max()` *macros might interfere with using* `std::min()` *and* `std::max()`*. In that case, there are three workarounds:*

- Use `#undef min` and `#undef max` after having included the problematic header, e.g., `Windows.h`.
- Add a `#define NOMINMAX` before you include `Windows.h`.
- Use an extra set of parentheses for `std::min()` and `std::max()`, as follows:

```
auto maxValue { (std::max)(1, 2) };
```

`std::clamp()` is a little helper function, defined in `<algorithm>`, that you can use to make sure that a value (*v*) is between a given minimum (*lo*) and maximum (*hi*). It returns a reference to *lo* if *v* < *lo*, returns a reference to *hi* if *v* > *hi*, and otherwise returns a reference to *v*. Here is an example:

```
println("{}", clamp(-3, 1, 10));
println("{}", clamp(3, 1, 10));
println("{}", clamp(22, 1, 10));
```

The output is as follows:

```
1
3
10
```

Parallel Algorithms

C++ supports executing more than 60 Standard Library iterator-based algorithms in parallel to improve their performance. Examples include `std::for_each()`, `all_of()`, `copy()`, `count_if()`, `find()`, `replace()`, `search()`, `sort()`, `transform()`, and many more.

Algorithms that support parallel execution have an optional *execution policy* as their first parameter. The execution policy allows you to specify whether an algorithm is allowed to be vectorized and/or executed in parallel. When a compiler vectorizes code, it replaces several CPU instructions with a single *vector CPU instruction*. A vector instruction performs some operation on multiple pieces of data with a single hardware instruction. These are also known as *single instruction multiple data* (SIMD) instructions. There are four standard execution policy types, and corresponding global instances of those types, all defined in `<execution>` in the `std::execution` namespace:

EXECUTION POLICY TYPE	GLOBAL INSTANCE	DESCRIPTION
`sequenced_policy`	`seq`	The algorithm is not allowed to parallelize or vectorize its execution.
`parallel_policy`	`par`	The algorithm is allowed to parallelize but not vectorize its execution.
`parallel_unsequenced_policy`	`par_unseq`	The algorithm is allowed to parallelize and vectorize its execution. It's also allowed to migrate its execution across threads.
`unsequenced_policy`	`unseq`	The algorithm is allowed to vectorize but not parallelize its execution.

A Standard Library implementation is free to add additional execution policies.

Let's look at how you can specify an execution policy for an algorithm. Here is an example of sorting the contents of a `vector` using a parallel policy:

```
sort(execution::par, begin(values), end(values));
```

> **WARNING** *Callbacks passed to parallel algorithms are not allowed to throw any uncaught exceptions. Doing so will trigger a call to* `std::terminate()` *which terminates the application.*

For algorithms executing with `parallel_unsequenced_policy` or `unsequenced_policy`, function calls to callbacks are allowed to get interleaved; that is, they are unsequenced. This helps the compiler to vectorize the code. However, this also means there are a lot of restrictions on what a function callback can do. For example, it cannot allocate/deallocate memory, acquire mutexes, use non-lock-free `std::atomics` (see Chapter 27, "Multithreaded Programming with C++"), and more. For the other standard policies, the function calls are sequenced, but in an indeterminate sequence. Such policies do not impose restrictions on what the function callbacks can do.

Parallel algorithms do not take any measures to prevent data races and deadlocks, so it is your responsibility to avoid them when executing an algorithm in parallel. Data race and deadlock prevention are discussed in detail in Chapter 27 in the context of multithreaded programming.

Parallel overloads of algorithms are not `constexpr`, even if the non-parallel overloads are.

The return type of some of the parallel overloads of algorithms can be slightly different compared to the non-parallel overloads. For example, the non-parallel overload of `for_each()` returns the supplied callback, while the parallel overload does not return anything. Consult your favorite Standard Library Reference for a complete overview of all algorithms, including their parameter and return types, for both the parallel and non-parallel overloads.

> **NOTE** *When working with large datasets or when you have to perform a large amount of work on each individual element in a dataset, use the parallel overloads of algorithms to increase performance.*

Keep in mind, though, that using a parallel overload of an algorithm does not guarantee that its execution will be faster compared to a non-parallel overload. For example, when processing a small number of elements, a parallel overload might actually be slower due to the overhead that parallelization brings with it. Another example is when your container does not support random access iterators. To decide whether to use a parallel or a sequential overload for a specific use case, you must profile both and pick the most performant one. Chapter 29, "Writing Efficient C++," discusses profiling.

Numerical Processing Algorithms

You've already seen an example of one numerical processing algorithm: `accumulate()`. The following sections give examples of some more numerical algorithms.

iota

The `iota()` algorithm, defined in `<numeric>`, generates a sequence of values in a specified range starting with a specified value and applying `operator++` to generate each successive value. The following example shows how to use this algorithm on a `vector` of integers, but it works on any element type that implements `operator++`:

```
vector<int> values(10);
iota(begin(values), end(values), 5);
println("{:n}", values);
```

The output is as follows:

```
5, 6, 7, 8, 9, 10, 11, 12, 13, 14
```

Reduce Algorithms

The Standard Library has four *reduce algorithms*: `accumulate()`, `reduce()`, `inner_product()`, and `transform_reduce()`, all defined in `<numeric>`. The `accumulate()` algorithm is discussed earlier in this chapter. All reduce algorithms repeatedly apply an operator to combine two elements of a given range or two given ranges, until only one value remains. These are also called *accumulate*, *aggregate*, *compress*, *inject*, or *fold* algorithms.

reduce

`std::accumulate()` is one of the few algorithms that does not support parallel execution. Instead, you need to use `std::reduce()` to calculate a generalized sum with the option to execute it in parallel.

For example, the following code calculates the same sum twice, once with `accumulate()` and once with `reduce()`. The latter runs a parallel and vectorized version and thus can be much faster on big input ranges. They both require a begin and end iterator of the range, and an initial value, 0 in this example.

```
vector values { 1, 3, 6, 4, 6, 9 };
int result1 { accumulate(cbegin(values), cend(values), 0) };
int result2 { reduce(execution::par_unseq, cbegin(values), cend(values), 0) };
```

In general, both `accumulate()` and `reduce()` calculate the following sum for a range of elements $[x_0, x_n)$, with a given initial value *Init*, and a given binary operator Θ:

$$\text{Init}\ \Theta\ x_0\ \Theta\ x_1\ \Theta \ldots \Theta\ x_{n-1}$$

By default, the binary operator for `accumulate()` is `operator+`, and for `reduce()` it is `std::plus`.

inner_product

`inner_product()` calculates the inner product of two sequences. For example, the inner product in the following example is calculated as `(1*9)+(2*8)+(3*7)+(4*6)`, which is 70:

```
vector v1 { 1, 2, 3, 4 };
vector v2 { 9, 8, 7, 6 };
println("{}", inner_product(cbegin(v1), cend(v1), cbegin(v2), 0));
```

`inner_product()` can accept two additional parameters, which are the two binary operators used in the calculation, by default `operator+` and `operator*`.

`inner_product()` is another algorithm that does not support parallel execution. If parallel execution is required, use `transform_reduce()`, discussed next.

transform_reduce

`transform_reduce()` supports parallel execution and can be executed on a single range of elements or on two ranges. In its first version, it calculates the following sum for a range of elements $[x_0, x_n)$, with a given initial value *Init*, a given unary function *f*, and a given binary operator Θ, `std::plus` by default:

$$\text{Init}\ \Theta\ f(x_0)\ \Theta\ f(x_1)\ \Theta \ldots \Theta\ f(x_{n-1})$$

When executing on two ranges, it behaves the same as `inner_product()`, except by default it uses the binary operators `std::plus` and `std::multiplies`, respectively, instead of `operator+` and `operator*`.

Scan Algorithms

Scan algorithms are also called *prefix sum*, *cumulative sum*, or *partial sum* algorithms. The result of such an algorithm applied to a range is another range containing sums of the elements of the source range.

There are five scan algorithms: `exclusive_scan()`, `inclusive_scan()`/`partial_sum()`, `transform_exclusive_scan()`, and `transform_inclusive_scan()`, all defined in `<numeric>`.

The following table shows which sums $[y_0, y_n)$ are calculated by `exclusive_scan()` and by `inclusive_scan()`/`partial_sum()` for a range of elements $[x_0, x_n)$, with a given initial value *Init* (0 for `partial_sum()`), and a given binary operator Θ:

EXCLUSIVE_SCAN()	INCLUSIVE_SCAN()/PARTIAL_SUM()
$y_0 = \text{Init}$	$y_0 = \text{Init}\ \Theta\ x_0$
$y_1 = \text{Init}\ \Theta\ x_0$	$y_1 = \text{Init}\ \Theta\ x_0\ \Theta\ x_1$
$y_2 = \text{Init}\ \Theta\ x_0\ \Theta\ x_1$	. . .
. . .	$y_{n-1} = \text{Init}\ \Theta\ x_0\ \Theta\ x_1\ \Theta \ldots \Theta\ x_{n-1}$
$y_{n-1} = \text{Init}\ \Theta\ x_0\ \Theta\ x_1\ \Theta \ldots \Theta\ x_{n-2}$	

`transform_exclusive_scan()` and `transform_inclusive_scan()` both first apply a unary function to the elements before calculating the generalized sum, similar to how `transform_reduce()` applies a unary function to the elements before reducing.

Note that these scan algorithms, except `partial_sum()`, can accept an optional execution policy to parallelize their execution. The order of evaluation is non-deterministic, while it is guaranteed left to right for `partial_sum()` and `accumulate()`. That's also the reason why `partial_sum()` and `accumulate()` cannot be parallelized.

Constrained Algorithms

Most of the algorithms have constrained variants in the `std::ranges` namespace. Consult your favorite Standard Library reference to find out exactly which constrained algorithms are available. These algorithms are also defined in `<algorithm>` and `<numeric>`, but unlike the equivalent unconstrained algorithms in the `std` namespace, the constrained variants use concepts (see Chapter 12) to constrain their template type parameters. This means you get better error messages from your compiler if you pass invalid arguments. For example, the `sort()` algorithm requires random-access iterators. Passing a pair of `std::list` iterators as arguments to `std::sort()` can result in a bunch of cryptic errors from your compiler. With the constrained `ranges::sort()` algorithm, the compiler tells you that the passed iterators are not random access.

Another benefit of these constrained algorithms is that they work on a sequence of elements given as either a *begin and end iterator pair*, or as a *range*. Additionally, they can support projections. Ranges and projections are discussed in Chapter 17.

> **NOTE** *Constrained algorithms do not support parallel execution yet, so they do not accept a parallel execution policy as an argument.*

Let's look at a few of these constrained algorithms in action.

Constrained find

As with all constrained algorithms, the `std::ranges::find()` constrained algorithm can be called with a pair of iterators or with a range as argument. Calling it with an iterator pair works the same way as the unconstrained `std::find()`:

```
vector values {1, 2, 3};
auto result { ranges::find(cbegin(values), cend(values), 2) };
if (result != cend(values)) { println("{}", *result); }
```

However, if you want to apply an algorithm on *all* elements of a container, as is often the case, it's rather tedious to always have to specify a begin/end iterator pair to define your sequence. With ranges support, you can just specify a range with a single argument. The previous call to `find()` can be written more readable and less error prone as follows:

```
auto result { ranges::find(values, 2) };
```

Constrained generate

Here is another example, this time using the constrained `std::ranges::generate()` algorithm. The code first creates a lambda expression that simply returns a next number. Then it creates a `vector` of 10 integers and uses the `generate()` algorithm together with the `nextNumber` lambda expression to fill the `vector` with increasing integers. The contents of the `vector` are printed to the console, followed by four more invocations of the `nextNumber` lambda expression.

```
auto nextNumber { [counter = 0] () mutable { return ++counter; } };
vector<int> values(10);
```

```
ranges::generate(values, nextNumber);
println("Vector contains {:n}", values);
print("Four more next numbers: ");
for (unsigned i { 0 }; i < 4; ++i) { print("{}, ", nextNumber()); }
```

The output is as follows:

```
Vector contains 1, 2, 3, 4, 5, 6, 7, 8, 9, 10
Four more next numbers: 1, 2, 3, 4,
```

As the output demonstrates, `generate()` makes a copy of the lambda expression. This can be avoided using `std::ref()`, as explained earlier in this chapter, to pass a reference to the lambda expression instead of making a copy:

```
ranges::generate(values, ref(nextNumber));
```

The output now is:

```
Vector contains 1, 2, 3, 4, 5, 6, 7, 8, 9, 10
Four more next numbers: 11, 12, 13, 14,
```

Constrained for_each

The following example demonstrates using the `std::ranges::for_each()` algorithm on a filtered view created with `std::ranges::views::filter` (defined in `<ranges>`). Only the even values from the `vector` are kept in the view. This filtered view is subsequently passed to `for_each()`, which multiplies the values by 10. Outputting the contents of the `vector` confirms that only the even values in the `vector` have been multiplied.

```
vector values { 1, 2, 3, 4, 5, 6, 7, 8, 9, 10 };
println("Before: {:n}", values);
ranges::for_each(values | views::filter([](int value) { return value % 2 == 0; }),
    [](int& value) { value *= 10; });
println("After:  {:n}", values);
```

The output is as follows:

```
Before: 1, 2, 3, 4, 5, 6, 7, 8, 9, 10
After:  1, 20, 3, 40, 5, 60, 7, 80, 9, 100
```

Constrained-Only Algorithms

C++23 introduces new algorithms that are available only as constrained algorithms. They are all defined in the `std::ranges` namespace. These include the non-modifying sequence algorithms `contains()`, `contains_subrange()`, `starts_with()`, `ends_with()`, `find_last()`, `find_last_if()`, and `find_last_if_not()`, and the fold algorithms `fold_left()`, `fold_left_first()`, `fold_right()`, `fold_right_last()`, `fold_left_with_iter()`, and `fold_left_first_with_iter()`.

Here is an example of some of the non-modifying sequence algorithms:

```
vector values { 11, 22, 33, 44, 55 };
vector v { 11, 22 };
println("{} contains 33 = {}", values, ranges::contains(values, 33));
println("{} contains {} = {}", values, v, ranges::contains_subrange(values, v));
println("{} starts with {} = {}", values, v, ranges::starts_with(values, v));
```

This produces the following output:

```
[11, 22, 33, 44, 55] contains 33 = true
[11, 22, 33, 44, 55] contains [11, 22] = true
[11, 22, 33, 44, 55] starts with [11, 22] = true
```

The following is an example of two of the folding algorithms. `fold_left()` and `fold_right()` accept an initial value as one of their arguments, while `fold_left_first()` uses the first element in a given range as the starting value, and `fold_right_last()` uses the last element in a given range as the starting value. The example demonstrates the difference between a left and a right fold. The `fold_left_first()` and `fold_right_last()` algorithms return an `optional`, so `value_or()` is used to handle an empty result.

```
vector values { 500.0, 10.0, 2.0 };
auto foldedLeft { ranges::fold_left_first(values, divides<>{}) };
auto foldedRight { ranges::fold_right_last(values, divides<>{}) };
println("foldedLeft = {}", foldedLeft.value_or(0.0));
println("foldedRight = {}", foldedRight.value_or(0.0));
```

The output is:

```
foldedLeft = 25
foldedRight = 100
```

The left fold operation calculates ((500.0 / 10.0) / 2.0), while the right fold operation calculates (500.0 / (10.0 / 2.0)).

See your favorite Standard Library reference for more details on all these constrained algorithms.

SUMMARY

This chapter provided coding examples for a selection of Standard Library algorithms. It also showed you that combining these algorithms with lambda expressions allows you to write elegant and easy-to-understand code. Together with the previous chapters, I hope you gained an appreciation for the usefulness and the power of the Standard Library containers and algorithms.

The following chapters continue the discussion of other C++ Standard Library functionality. Chapter 21 discusses regular expressions. Chapter 22 explains the date and time support. Chapter 23 shows how to generate random numbers. Chapter 24 covers a number of additional vocabulary types that are available for you to use. Finally, Chapter 25 gives a taste of some more advanced features, such as allocators and how to write your own Standard Library–compliant algorithms and containers.

EXERCISES

By solving the following exercises, you can practice the material discussed in this chapter. Solutions to all exercises are available with the code download on the book's website at `www.wiley.com/go/proc++6e`. However, if you are stuck on an exercise, first reread parts of this chapter to try to find an answer yourself before looking at the solution from the website.

Exercise 20-1: Use your favorite Standard Library Reference to look up the parameters for the `ranges::fill()` algorithm. Ask the user for a number, and then use `fill()` to fill a `vector` of 10 integers with the given number. Write the contents of the `vector` to the standard output for verification. Provide a second solution using the `std::fill()` algorithm.

Exercise 20-2: Look back at the "Permutation Algorithms" section in Chapter 16, and then use a Standard Library Reference to figure out their parameters. Write a program that asks the user to enter a few numbers, and then use one of the permutation algorithms to print out all possible permutations of those numbers. Provide two solutions, one using only constrained algorithms and a second using legacy, unconstrained algorithms.

Exercise 20-3: Write a function called `trim()` that removes all whitespace at the beginning and end of a given string and returns the result. Use only constrained algorithms. Tip: to check if a character `c` is a whitespace character, you can use `std::isspace(c)`, defined in `<cctype>`. It returns a non-zero value if `c` is a whitespace character, 0 otherwise. Test your implementation with several strings in your `main()` function.

Exercise 20-4: Use a constrained algorithm to create a `vector` containing the numbers 1 to 20. Then, using a single constrained algorithm, copy all even and odd numbers to `evens` and `odds` containers without doing any space reservation on those containers, and, still with this single algorithm call, make sure the even numbers are in ascending sequence, while the odd numbers are in descending sequence. Carefully choose the type for the `evens` and `odds` containers. Hint: maybe there is something in Chapter 17 that you could use.

Exercise 20-5: The solution for Exercise 20-3 uses only constrained algorithms. Can you do the same using only legacy, unconstrained algorithms?

21

String Localization and Regular Expressions

WHAT'S IN THIS CHAPTER?

- How to localize your applications to reach a worldwide audience
- How to use regular expressions to do powerful pattern matching
- How to use regular expressions to validate strings, search substrings, find and replace strings, and more

WILEY.COM DOWNLOADS FOR THIS CHAPTER

Please note that all the code examples for this chapter are available as part of this chapter's code download on the book's website at `www.wiley.com/go/proc++6e` on the Download Code tab.

This chapter starts with a discussion of localization, which allows you to write software that can be localized to different regions around the world. An application that is properly localized displays numbers, dates, currencies, and so on in the appropriate format according to rules for a specific country or region.

The second part of this chapter introduces the *regular expressions library*, which makes it easy to perform pattern matching on strings. It allows you to search for substrings matching a given pattern, but also to validate, parse, and transform strings. Regular expressions are powerful. I recommend that you use them, as they are less error prone than manually writing your own string processing code.

LOCALIZATION

When you're learning how to program in C or C++, it's useful to think of a character as equivalent to a byte and to treat all characters as members of the American Standard Code for Information Interchange (ASCII) character set. ASCII is a 7-bit set usually stored in an 8-bit `char` type. In reality, experienced C++ programmers recognize that successful programs are used throughout the world. Even if you don't initially write your program with international audiences in mind, you shouldn't prevent yourself from *localizing*, or making the software *locale aware*, at a later date.

> **NOTE** *This chapter gives you an introduction to localization, different character encodings, and string code portability. It is outside the scope of this book to discuss all these topics in detail, because they warrant an entire book on their own.*

Wide Characters

The problem with viewing a character as a byte is that not all languages, or *character sets*, can be fully represented in 8 bits, or 1 byte. C++ has a built-in type called `wchar_t` that holds a *wide character*. Languages with non-ASCII (US) characters, such as Japanese and Arabic, can be represented in C++ with `wchar_t`. However, the C++ standard does not define the size for `wchar_t`. Some compilers use 16 bits, while others use 32 bits. Most of the time, it matches the size of the native Unicode character type on the underlying operating system. To write cross-platform code, it is not safe to assume that `wchar_t` is of a particular size.

If there is *any* chance that your program will be used in a non-Western character set context (hint: there is!), you should use wide characters from the beginning. When working with `wchar_t`, string and character literals are prefixed with the letter `L` to indicate that a wide-character encoding should be used. For example, to initialize a `wchar_t` character to the letter `m`, you write it like this:

```
wchar_t myWideCharacter { L'm' };
```

There are wide-character versions of most of your favorite types and classes. The wide `string` class is `wstring`. The "prefix letter w" pattern applies to streams as well. Wide-character file output streams are handled with `wofstream`, and input is handled with `wifstream`. The joy of pronouncing these class names (*woof-stream? whiff-stream?*) is reason enough to make your programs locale aware! Streams are discussed in detail in Chapter 13, "Demystifying C++ I/O."

There are also wide-versions of `cout`, `cin`, `cerr`, and `clog` available, called `wcout`, `wcin`, `wcerr`, and `wclog`. Using them is no different than using the non-wide versions:

```
wcout << L"I am a wide-character string literal." << endl;
```

`print()` and `println()` don't support `wchar_t` string literals, but they do support UTF-8 string literals, discussed later in this chapter. On the other hand, `format()` does support wide-character strings:

```
wcout << format(L"myWideCharacter is {}", myWideCharacter) << endl;
```

Non-Western Character Sets

Wide characters are a great step forward because they increase the amount of space available to define a single character. The next step is to figure out how that space is used. In wide character sets, just like in ASCII, characters are represented by numbers, now called *code points*. The only difference is that each number does not fit in 8 bits. The map of characters to code points is quite a bit larger because it handles many different character sets in addition to the characters that English-speaking programmers are familiar with.

The Universal Character Set (UCS)—defined by the International Standard ISO 10646—and Unicode are both standardized sets of characters. They both identify characters by an unambiguous name and a code point. The same characters with the same numbers exist in both standards. At the time of this writing, the latest version of Unicode was version 15, which defines 149,186 characters. Both UCS and Unicode have specific *encodings* that you can use to represent specific code points. This is important: a code point is just a number; an encoding specifies how to represent that number as one or more bytes. For example, UTF-8 is an example of a Unicode encoding where Unicode characters are encoded using one to four 8-bit bytes. UTF-16 encodes Unicode characters as one or two 16-bit values, and UTF-32 encodes Unicode characters as exactly 32 bits.

Different applications can use different encodings. Unfortunately, as mentioned earlier in this chapter, the C++ standard does not specify a size for wide characters (`wchar_t`). On Windows it is 16 bits, while on other platforms it could be 32 bits. You need to be aware of this when using wide characters for character encoding in cross-platform code. To help solve this issue, there are other character types: `char8_t`, `char16_t`, and `char32_t`. The following list gives an overview of the available character types:

- `char`: Stores 8 bits. This type can be used to store ASCII characters or as a basic building block for storing UTF-8 encoded Unicode characters, where one Unicode character is encoded with up to four `char`s.
- `charx_t`: Stores at least *x* bits where *x* can be 8, 16, or 32. This type can be used as the basic building block for UTF-*x* encoded Unicode characters, encoding one Unicode character with up to four `char8_t`s, up to two `char16_t`s, or one `char32_t`.
- `wchar_t`: Stores a wide character of a compiler-specific size and encoding.

The benefits of using the `charx_t` types instead of `wchar_t` is that the standard guarantees minimum sizes for the `charx_t` types, independent of the compiler. There is no minimum size guaranteed for `wchar_t`.

String literals can have a string prefix to turn them into a specific type. The complete set of supported string prefixes is as follows:

- `u8`: A `char8_t` string literal with UTF-8 encoding
- `u`: A `char16_t` string literal with UTF-16 encoding
- `U`: A `char32_t` string literal with UTF-32 encoding
- `L`: A `wchar_t` string literal with a compiler-dependent encoding

All of these string literals can be combined with the raw string literal prefix, `R`, discussed in Chapter 2, "Working with Strings and String Views." Here are some examples:

```
const char8_t* s1 { u8R"(Raw UTF-8 string literal)" };
const wchar_t* s2 { LR"(Raw wide string literal)" };
const char16_t* s3 { uR"(Raw UTF-16 string literal)" };
const char32_t* s4 { UR"(Raw UTF-32 string literal)" };
```

You can insert specific Unicode code points in non-raw string literals using several different escape sequences. The following table gives an overview of your options. The last column shows the encoding of the superscript two, ^{2}, character.

ESCAPE SEQUENCE	DESCRIPTION	EXAMPLE: ^{2}
\nnn	1 to 3 octal digits	\262
C++23 \o{n...}	Arbitrary number of octal digits	\o{262}
\xn...	Arbitrary number of hexadecimal digits	\xB2 or \x00B2
C++23 \x{n...}	Arbitrary number of hexadecimal digits	\x{B2} or \x{00B2}
\unnnn	4 hexadecimal digits	\u00B2
C++23 \u{n...}	Arbitrary number of hexadecimal digits	\u{B2} or \u{00B2}
\Unnnnnnnn	8 hexadecimal digits	\U000000B2
C++23 \N{name}	Universal character name	\N{SUPERSCRIPT TWO}

The `\o{n...}`, `\x{n...}`, and `\u{n...}` notations introduced with C++23 are useful to avoid problems when the next character in a string literal happens to be a valid octal or hexadecimal digit. For the `\N{name}` notation, the name must be the official Unicode name of the character, which you can look up in any Unicode character reference.

Here are some more examples representing the formula π r^2. The π character has code `3C0`, and the superscript two character has code `B2`.

```
const char8_t* formula1 { u8"\x3C0 r\xB2" };
const char8_t* formula2 { u8"\u03C0 r\u00B2" };
const char8_t* formula3 { u8"\N{GREEK SMALL LETTER PI} r\N{SUPERSCRIPT TWO}" };
```

Besides string literals, character literals can also have a prefix to turn them into specific types. The prefixes `u8`, `u`, `U`, and `L` are supported, for example: `u'a'`, `U'a'`, `L'a'`, and `u8'a'`.

In addition to the `std::string` class, there is also support for `wstring`, `u8string`, `u16string`, and `u32string`. They are defined as follows:

- `using string = basic_string<char>;`
- `using wstring = basic_string<wchar_t>;`
- `using u8string = basic_string<char8_t>;`

- `using u16string = basic_string<char16_t>;`
- `using u32string = basic_string<char32_t>;`

Similarly, the Standard Library provides `std::string_view`, `wstring_view`, `u8string_view`, `u16string_view`, and `u32string_view`, all based on `basic_string_view`.

Multibyte strings are strings with characters composed of one or more bytes using a locale-dependent encoding. Locales are discussed later in this chapter. A multibyte string could use Unicode encoding, or any other kind of encoding such as Shift-JIS, EUC-JP, and so on. Conversion functions are available to convert between `char8_t`/`char16_t`/`char32_t` and multibyte strings, and vice versa: `mbrtoc8()` and `c8rtomb()`, and `mbrtoc16()`, `c16rtomb()`, `mbrtoc32()`, and `c32rtomb()`.

Unfortunately, the support for `char8_t`, `char16_t`, and `char32_t` doesn't go much further. There are some conversion classes available (see later in this chapter), but, for example, there is nothing like a version of `cout`, `cin`, `println()`, `format()`, and so on, that supports these character types; this makes it difficult to print such strings to a console or to read them from user input. If you want to do more with such strings, you need to resort to third-party libraries. International Components for Unicode (ICU) is one well-known library that provides Unicode and globalization support for your applications. (See `icu-project.org`.)

C++23 improves things slightly. It allows a `u8` UTF-8 string literal to initialize an array of type `const char` or `const unsigned char`, and functions like `std::format()` and `print()` do support `const char[]`. For example, the following initializes a `const char[]` array with a UTF-8 string literal and then prints it using `println()`. If your environment is set up to handle Japanese characters, then the output is "Hello world" in Japanese.

```
const char hello[] { u8"こんにちは世界" };
println("{}", hello);
```

If you would use `char8_t[]` instead of `char[]` as follows, you will get a compilation error as `println()` doesn't understand the `char8_t` type.

```
const char8_t hello[] { u8"こんにちは世界" };
println("{}", hello);  // Error: doesn't compile!
```

Localizing String Literals

A critical aspect of localization is that you should never put any native-language string literals in your source code, except maybe for debug strings targeted at the developer. In Microsoft Windows applications, this is accomplished by putting all strings for an application in `STRINGTABLE` resources. Most other platforms offer similar capabilities. If you need to translate your application to another language, translating those resources should be all you need to do, without requiring any source changes. There are tools available that will help you with this translation process.

To make your source code localizable, you should not compose sentences out of string literals, even if the individual literals can be localized. Here is an example:

```
unsigned n { 5 };
wstring filename { L"file1.txt" };
wcout << n << L" bytes read from " << filename << endl;
```

This statement cannot be localized to, for example, German because it requires a reordering of the words. The German translation is as follows:

```
wcout << n << L" Bytes aus " << filename << L" gelezen" << endl;
```

To make sure you can properly localize such strings, you could implement it as follows:

```
vprint_unicode(loadResource(IDS_TRANSFERRED), make_format_args(n, filename));
```

`IDS_TRANSFERRED` is the name of an entry in a string resource table. For the English version, `IDS_TRANSFERRED` could be defined as "{0} bytes read from {1}", while the German version of the resource could be defined as "{0} Bytes aus {1} gelezen". The `loadResource()` function loads the string resource with the given name, and `vprint_unicode()` (see Chapter 2) substitutes `{0}` with the value of `n` and `{1}` with the value of `filename`.

Locales and Facets

Character sets are only one of the differences in data representation between countries. Even countries that use similar character sets, such as Great Britain and the United States, still differ in how they represent certain data, such as dates and monetary values.

The standard C++ mechanism that groups specific data about a particular set of cultural parameters is called a *locale*. An individual component of a locale, such as date format, time format, number format, and so on, is called a *facet*. An example of a locale is US English. An example of a facet is the format used to display a date. Several built-in facets are common to all locales. C++ also provides a way to customize or add facets.

There are third-party libraries available that make it easier to work with locales. One example is `boost.locale` (`boost.org`), which is able to use ICU as its backend, supporting collations and conversions, converting strings to uppercase (instead of converting character by character to uppercase), and so on.

Locales

When using I/O streams, data is formatted according to a particular locale. Locales are objects that can be attached to a stream, and they are defined in `<locale>`. Locale names are implementation specific. The POSIX standard is to separate a language and an area into two-letter sections with an optional encoding. For example, the locale for the English language as spoken in the United States is `en_US`, while the locale for the English language as spoken in Great Britain is `en_GB`. The locale for Japanese spoken in Japan with Japanese Industrial Standard encoding is `ja_JP.jis`.

Locale names on Windows can have two formats. The preferred format is similar to the POSIX format but uses a dash instead of an underscore. The second, old format looks as follows where everything between square brackets is optional:

```
lang[_country_region[.code_page]]
```

The following table shows some examples of the POSIX, preferred Windows, and old Windows locale formats:

LANGUAGE	POSIX	WINDOWS	WINDOWS OLD
US English	en_US	en-US	English_United States

LANGUAGE	POSIX	WINDOWS	WINDOWS OLD
Great Britain English	en_GB	en-GB	English_Great Britain

Most operating systems have a mechanism to determine the locale as defined by the user. In C++, you can pass an empty string to the `std::locale` constructor to create a `locale` from the user's environment. Once this object is created, you can use it to query the `locale`, possibly making programmatic decisions based on it.

Global Locale

The `std::locale::global()` function can be used to replace the global C++ locale in your application with a given locale. The default constructor of `std::locale` returns a copy of this global locale. Keep in mind, though, that the C++ Standard Library objects that use locales, for example streams such as `cout`, store a copy of the global locale at construction time. Changing the global locale afterward does not impact objects that were already created before. If needed, you can use the `imbue()` member function on streams (see the next section) to change their locale after construction.

Here is an example outputting a number with the default locale, changing the global locale to US English and outputting the same number again:

```
void print()
{
    stringstream stream;
    stream << 32767;
    println("{}", stream.str());
}

int main()
{
    print();
    locale::global(locale { "en-US" }); // "en_US" for POSIX
    print();
}
```

The output is as follows:

```
32767
32,767
```

Using Locales

The following code demonstrates how to use the user's locale for a stream by calling the `imbue()` member function on the stream. The result is that everything that is sent to `cout` is formatted according to the formatting rules of the user's environment:

```
cout.imbue(locale { "" });
cout << "User's locale: " << 32767 << endl;
```

This means that if your system locale is English United States and you output the number 32767, the number is displayed as 32,767; however, if your system locale is Dutch Belgium, the same number is displayed as 32.767.

The default locale is the *classic/neutral* locale, and not the user's locale. The classic locale uses ANSI C conventions and has the name C. The classic C locale is similar to US English, but there are slight differences. For example, numbers are handled without any punctuation.

```
cout.imbue(locale { "C" });
cout << "C locale: " << 32767 << endl;
```

The output of this code is as follows:

```
C locale: 32767
```

The following code manually sets the US English locale, so the number 32767 is formatted with US English punctuation, independent of your system locale:

```
cout.imbue(locale { "en-US" }); // "en_US" for POSIX
cout << "en-US locale: " << 32767 << endl;
```

The output of this code is as follows:

```
en-US locale: 32,767
```

By default, `std::print()` and `println()` use the C locale. For example, the following prints 32767:

```
println("println(): {}", 32767);
```

You can specify the `L` format specifier, in which case the global locale is used.

```
println("println() using global locale: {:L}", 32767);
```

`std::format()` also supports locales by using the `L` format specifier and optionally accepts a `locale` as first argument. When the `L` format specifier is used and a `locale` is passed to `format()`, that `locale` is used for formatting. If the `L` format specifier is used without passing a `locale` to `format()`, the global `locale` is used. For example, the following prints 32,767 according to English formatting rules:

```
cout << format(locale { "en-US" }, "format() with en-US locale: {:L}", 32767);
```

A `locale` object allows you to query information about the locale. For example, the following program creates a `locale` matching the user's environment. The `name()` member function is used to get a C++ `string` that describes the locale. Then, the `find()` member function is used on the `string` object to find a given substring, which returns `string::npos` when the given substring is not found. The code checks for the Windows name and the POSIX name. One of two messages is printed, depending on whether the locale appears to be US English.

```
locale loc { "" };
if (loc.name().find("en_US") == string::npos &&
    loc.name().find("en-US") == string::npos) {
    println("Welcome non-US English speaker!");
} else {
    println("Welcome US English speaker!");
}
```

> **NOTE** *When you have to write data to a file that is supposed to be read back by a program, it's recommended to write it using the neutral* `"C"` *locale; otherwise, parsing will be difficult. On the other hand, when displaying data in a user interface, it's recommended to format the data according to the user locale,* `""`.

Character Classification

<locale> contains the following character classification functions: std::isspace(), isblank(), iscntrl(), isupper(), islower(), isalpha(), isdigit(), ispunct(), isxdigit(), isalnum(), isprint(), and isgraph(). They all accept two parameters: the character to classify and the locale to use for the classification. The exact meaning of the different character classes is discussed later in this chapter in the context of regular expressions. Here is an example of using isupper() with a French locale to verify whether a letter is uppercase or not:

```
println("É {}", isupper(L'É', locale{ "fr-FR" }));
println("é {}", isupper(L'é', locale{ "fr-FR" }));
```

The output is as follows:

```
É true
é false
```

Character Conversion

<locale> also defines two character conversion functions: std::toupper() and tolower(). They accept two parameters: the character to convert and the locale to use for the conversion. Here is an example:

```
auto upper { toupper(L'é', locale { "fr-FR" }) };  // É
```

Using Facets

You can use the std::use_facet() function template to obtain a particular facet for a particular locale. The template type argument specifies the facet to retrieve, while the function argument specifies the locale from which to retrieve the facet. For example, the following expression retrieves the standard monetary punctuation facet of the British English locale using the POSIX locale name:

```
use_facet<moneypunct<wchar_t>>(locale { "en_GB" })
```

Note that the innermost template type determines the character type to use. The result is an object that contains all the information you want to know about British monetary punctuation. The data available in the standard facets is defined in <locale>. The following table lists the facet categories defined by the standard. Consult a Standard Library reference (see Appendix B, "Annotated Bibliography") for details about the individual facets.

FACET	DESCRIPTION
ctype	Character classification facets
codecvt	Conversion facets; see next section
collate	Comparing strings lexicographically
time_get	Parsing dates and times
time_put	Formatting dates and times
num_get	Parsing numeric values

continues

(continued)

FACET	DESCRIPTION
`num_put`	Formatting numeric values
`numpunct`	Defines the formatting rules for numeric values
`money_get`	Parsing monetary values
`money_put`	Formatting monetary values
`moneypunct`	Defines the formatting rules for monetary values

The following code snippet brings together locales and facets by printing out the currency symbol in both US English and British English. Note that, depending on your environment, the British currency symbol may appear as a question mark, a box, or not at all. If your environment is set up to handle it, you may actually get the British pound symbol.

```
locale locUSEng { "en-US" };       // "en_US" for POSIX
locale locBritEng { "en-GB" };     // "en_GB" for POSIX

wstring dollars { use_facet<moneypunct<wchar_t>>(locUSEng).curr_symbol() };
wstring pounds { use_facet<moneypunct<wchar_t>>(locBritEng).curr_symbol() };

wcout << L"In the US, the currency symbol is " << dollars << endl;
wcout << L"In Great Britain, the currency symbol is " << pounds << endl;
```

Conversions

The C++ standard provides the `codecvt` class template to help with converting between different character encodings. `<locale>` defines the following four encoding conversion classes:

CLASS	DESCRIPTION
`codecvt<char,char,mbstate_t>`	Identity conversion, that is, no conversion
`codecvt<char16_t,char,mbstate_t>` `codecvt<char16_t,char8_t,mbstate_t>`	Conversion between UTF-16 and UTF-8
`codecvt<char32_t,char,mbstate_t>` `codecvt<char32_t,char8_t,mbstate_t>`	Conversion between UTF-32 and UTF-8
`codecvt<wchar_t,char,mbstate_t>`	Conversion between wide (implementation-specific) and narrow character encodings

Unfortunately, these facets are rather complicated to use. As an example, the following code snippet converts a narrow string to a wide string:

```
auto& facet { use_facet<codecvt<wchar_t, char, mbstate_t>>(locale { }) };
string narrowString { "Hello" };
mbstate_t mb { };
wstring wideString(narrowString.size(), '\0');
const char* fromNext { nullptr };
```

```
wchar_t* toNext { nullptr };
facet.in(mb,
    narrowString.data(), narrowString.data() + narrowString.size(), fromNext,
    wideString.data(), wideString.data() + wideString.size(), toNext);
wideString.resize(toNext - wideString.data());
wcout << wideString << endl;
```

Before C++17, the following three code conversion facets were defined in `<codecvt>`: `codecvt_utf8`, `codecvt_utf16`, and `codecvt_utf8_utf16`. These could be used with two convenience conversion interfaces: `wstring_convert` and `wbuffer_convert`. However, C++17 has deprecated those three conversion facets (the entirety of `<codecvt>`) and the two convenience interfaces, so they are not further discussed in this book. The C++ Standards Committee decided to deprecate this functionality because it does not handle errors very well. Ill-formed Unicode strings are a security risk, and in fact can be and have been used as an attack vector to compromise the security of systems. Also, the API is too obscure and too hard to understand. I recommend using third-party libraries, such as ICU, to work correctly with Unicode strings until the Standards Committee comes up with a suitable, safe, and easier-to-use replacement for the deprecated functionality.

REGULAR EXPRESSIONS

Regular expressions, defined in `<regex>`, are a powerful string related feature of the Standard Library. They support a special mini-language for string processing and might seem complicated at first, but once you get to know them, they make working with strings easier. Regular expressions can be used for several string operations:

- **Validation:** Check if an input string is well formed. For example, is the input string a well-formed phone number?
- **Decision:** Check what kind of string an input represents. For example, is the input string the name of a JPEG or a PNG file?
- **Parsing:** Extract information from an input string. For example, extract the year, month, and day from a date.
- **Transformation:** Search substrings and replace them with a new formatted substring. For example, search all occurrences of "C++23" and replace them with "C++".
- **Iteration:** Search all occurrences of a substring. For example, extract all phone numbers from an input string.
- **Tokenization:** Split a string into substrings based on a set of delimiters. For example, split a string on whitespace, commas, periods, and so on, to extract the individual words.

Of course, you could write your own code to perform any of these operations on strings, but I recommend using the regular expressions functionality, because writing correct and safe code to process strings is tricky.

Before going into more detail on regular expressions, there is some important terminology you need to know. The following terms are used throughout the discussion:

- **Pattern:** The actual regular expression is a pattern represented by a string.

- **Match:** Determines whether there is a match between a given regular expression and all of the characters in a given sequence [first, last).
- **Search:** Determines whether there is some substring within a given sequence [first, last) that matches a given regular expression.
- **Replace:** Identifies substrings in a given sequence and replaces them with a corresponding new substring computed from another pattern, called a *substitution pattern*.

There are several different grammars for regular expressions. C++ includes support for the following grammars:

- **ECMAScript:** The grammar based on the ECMAScript standard. ECMAScript is a scripting language standardized by ECMA-262. The core of JavaScript, ActionScript, Jscript, and so on, all use the ECMAScript language standard.
- **basic:** The basic POSIX grammar.
- **extended:** The extended POSIX grammar.
- **awk:** The grammar used by the POSIX awk utility.
- **grep:** The grammar used by the POSIX grep utility.
- **egrep:** The grammar used by the POSIX grep utility with the `-E` parameter.

If you already know any of these regular expression grammars, you can use it straightaway in C++ by instructing the regular expression library to use that specific syntax (`syntax_option_type`). The default grammar in C++ is ECMAScript, whose syntax is explained in detail in the following section. It is also the most powerful grammar. Explaining the other regular expression grammars falls outside the scope of this book.

> **NOTE** *If this is the first time you're hearing about regular expressions, just use the default ECMAScript syntax.*

ECMAScript Syntax

A regular expression pattern is a sequence of characters representing what you want to match. Any character in the regular expression matches itself except, for the following special characters:

```
^ $ \ . * + ? ( ) [ ] { } |
```

These special characters are explained throughout the following discussion. If you need to match one of these special characters, you need to escape it using the \ character, as in this example:

```
\[ or \. or \* or \\
```

Anchor

The special characters `^` and `$` are called *anchors*. The `^` character matches the position immediately following a line termination character, and `$` matches the position of a line termination character. By default, ^ and $ also match the beginning and ending of a string, respectively, but this behavior can be disabled.

For example, `^test$` matches only the string `test`, and not strings that contain `test` somewhere in the line, such as `1test`, `test2`, `test abc`, and so on.

Wildcard

The *wildcard* character `.` can be used to match any single character except a newline character. For example, the regular expression `a.c` will match `abc`, and `a5c`, but will not match `ab5c`, `ac`, and so on.

Alternation

The `|` character can be used to specify the "or" relationship. For example, `a|b` matches `a` or `b`.

Grouping

Parentheses, `()`, are used to mark *subexpressions*, also called *capture groups*. Capture groups can be used for several purposes:

- Capture groups can be used to identify individual subsequences of the original string; each marked subexpression (capture group) is returned in the result. For example, the regular expression `(.)(ab|cd)(.)` has three marked subexpressions. Performing a search operation with this regular expression on `1cd4` results in a match with four entries. The first entry is the entire match, `1cd4`, followed by three entries for the three marked subexpressions. These three entries are `1`, `cd`, and `4`.
- Capture groups can be used during matching for a purpose called *back references* (explained later).
- Capture groups can be used to identify components during *replace operations* (explained later).

Quantifier

Parts of a regular expression can be repeated by using one of four *quantifiers*:

- `*` matches the preceding part *zero or more* times. For example, `a*b` matches `b`, `ab`, `aab`, `aaaab`, and so on.
- `+` matches the preceding part *one or more* times. For example, `a+b` matches `ab`, `aab`, `aaaab`, and so on, but not `b`.
- `?` matches the preceding part *zero or one* time. For example, `a?b` matches `b` and `ab`, but nothing else.
- `{...}` represents a *bounded quantifier*. `b{n}` matches `b` repeated *exactly n* times; `b{n,}` matches `b` repeated *n times or more*; and `b{n,m}` matches `b` repeated *between n and m* times inclusive. For example, `b{3,4}` matches `bbb` and `bbbb` but not `b`, `bb`, `bbbbb`, and so on.

These quantifiers are called *greedy* because they find the longest match while still matching the remainder of the regular expression. To make them *non-greedy*, a `?` can be added behind the quantifier, as in `*?`, `+?`, `??`, and `{...}?`. A non-greedy quantifier repeats its pattern as few times as possible while still matching the remainder of the regular expression.

For example, the following table shows the difference between a greedy and a non-greedy regular expression, and the resulting submatches when running them on the input sequence `aaabbb`:

REGULAR EXPRESSION	SUBMATCHES
Greedy: `(a+)(ab)*(b+)`	`"aaa" "" "bbb"`
Non-greedy: `(a+?)(ab)*(b+)`	`"aa" "ab" "bb"`

Precedence

Just as with mathematical formulas, it's important to know the precedence of regular expression elements. Precedence is as follows:

- **Elements** like `b` are the basic building blocks of a regular expression.
- **Quantifiers** like `+`, `*`, `?`, and `{...}` bind tightly to the element on the left; for example, `b+`.
- **Concatenation** like `ab+c` binds after quantifiers.
- **Alternation** like `|` binds last.

For example, the regular expression `ab+c|d` matches `abc`, `abbc`, `abbbc`, and so on, and also `d`. Parentheses can be used to change these precedence rules. For example, `ab+(c|d)` matches `abc`, `abbc`, `abbbc`, . . ., `abd`, `abbd`, `abbbd`, and so on. However, by using parentheses, you also mark it as a subexpression or capture group. It is possible to change the precedence rules without creating new capture groups by using `(?:...)`. For example, `ab+(?:c|d)` matches the same as the earlier `ab+(c|d)` but does not create an additional capture group.

Character Set Matches

Instead of writing `(a|b|c|...|z)`, which is clumsy and introduces a capture group, a special syntax for specifying sets of characters or ranges of characters is available. In addition, a "not" form of the match is also available. A *character set* is specified between square brackets and allows you to write $[c_1c_2...c_n]$, which matches any of the characters c_1, c_2, . . ., or c_n. For example, `[abc]` matches any character `a`, `b`, or `c`. If the first character is `^`, it means "any but":

- `ab[cde]` matches `abc`, `abd`, and `abe`.
- `ab[^cde]` matches `abf`, `abp`, and so on, but not `abc`, `abd`, and `abe`.

If you need to match the `^`, `[`, or `]` characters themselves, you need to escape them; for example, `[\[\^\]]` matches the characters `[`, `^`, or `]`.

If you want to specify all letters, you could use a character set like `[abcdefghijklmnopqrstuvwxyz ABCDEFGHIJKLMNOPQRSTUVWXYZ]`; however, this is clumsy, and doing this several times is awkward, especially if you make a typo and omit one of the letters accidentally. There are two solutions to this.

One solution is to use the *range specification* in square brackets; this allows you to write `[a-zA-Z]`, which recognizes all the letters in the range `a` to `z` and `A` to `Z`. If you need to match a hyphen, you need to escape it; for example, `[a-zA-Z\-]+` matches any word including a hyphenated word.

Another solution is to use one of the *character classes*. These are used to denote specific types of characters and are represented as `[:name:]`. Which character classes are available depends on the locale, but the names listed in the following table are always recognized. The exact meaning of these character classes is also dependent on the locale. This table assumes the standard C locale:

CHARACTER CLASS NAME	DESCRIPTION
`digit`	Digits, which are 0, 1, 2, 3, 4, 5, 6, 7, 8, 9.
`d`	Same as `digit`.
`xdigit`	Digits (`digit`) and the following letters used in hexadecimal numbers: a, b, c, d, e, f, A, B, C, D, E, F.
`alpha`	Alphabetic characters. For the C locale, these are all lowercase and uppercase letters.
`alnum`	A combination of the `alpha` class and the `digit` class.
`w`	Same as `alnum`.
`lower`	Lowercase letters, if applicable to the locale.
`upper`	Uppercase letters, if applicable to the locale.
`blank`	Blank characters, which are whitespace characters used to separate words within a line of text. For the C locale, these are space and `\t` (tab).
`space`	Whitespace characters. For the C locale, these are space, `\t`, `\n`, `\r`, `\v`, and `\f`.
`s`	Same as `space`.
`print`	Printable characters. These occupy a printing position—for example, on a display—and are the opposite of control characters (`cntrl`). Examples are lowercase letters, uppercase letters, digits, punctuation characters, and space characters.
`cntrl`	Control characters. These are the opposite of printable characters (`print`), and don't occupy a printing position, for example, on a display. Some examples for the C locale are `\f`, `\n`, and `\r`.
`graph`	Characters with a graphical representation. These are all characters that are printable (`print`), except the space character `' '`.
`punct`	Punctuation characters. For the C locale, these are all graphical characters (`graph`) that are not alphanumeric (`alnum`). Some examples are `!`, `#`, `@`, `}`, and so on.

Character classes are used within character sets; for example, `[[:alpha:]]*` in English means the same as `[a-zA-Z]*`.

Because certain character classes are so common, e.g., digits, there are shorthand patterns for them. For example, `[:digit:]` and `[:d:]` have the same meaning as `[0-9]`. Some classes have an even shorter pattern using the escape notation. For example, `\d` means `[:digit:]`. Therefore, to recognize a sequence of one or more numbers, you can write any of the following patterns:

- `[0-9]+`
- `[[:digit:]]+`
- `[[:d:]]+`
- `\d+`

The following table lists the available escape notations for character classes:

ESCAPE NOTATION	EQUIVALENT TO
`\d`	`[[:d:]]`
`\D`	`[^[:d:]]`
`\s`	`[[:s:]]`
`\S`	`[^[:s:]]`
`\w`	`[_[:w:]]`
`\W`	`[^_[:w:]]`

Here are some examples:

- `Test[5-8]` matches `Test5`, `Test6`, `Test7`, and `Test8`.
- `[[:lower:]]` matches `a`, `b`, and so on, but not `A`, `B`, and so on.
- `[^[:lower:]]` matches any character except lowercase letters like `a`, `b`, and so on.
- `[[:lower:]5-7]` matches any lowercase letter like `a`, `b`, and so on, and the numbers `5`, `6`, and `7`.

Word Boundary

A *word boundary* can mean the following:

- The first character of a word, which is one of the word characters, while the preceding character is not a word character. A word character is a letter, digit, or an underscore. For the standard C locale, this is equal to `[A-Za-z0-9_]`.
- The end of a word, which is a non-word character, while the preceding character is a word character.

- The beginning of the source string if the first character of the source string is one of the word characters. Matching the beginning of the source string is enabled by default, but you can disable it with `regex_constants::match_not_bow`, where `bow` stands for beginning-of-word.
- The end of the source string if the last character of the source string is one of the word characters. Matching the end of the source string is enabled by default, but you can disable it with `regex_constants::match_not_eow`, where `eow` stands for end-of-word.

You can use `\b` to match a word boundary, and you can use `\B` to match anything except a word boundary.

Back Reference

A *back reference* allows you to reference a captured group inside the regular expression itself: `\n` refers to the *n*-th captured group, with `n > 0`. For example, the regular expression `(\d+)-.*-\1` matches a string that has the following format:

- One or more digits captured in a capture group `(\d+)`
- Followed by a dash `-`
- Followed by zero or more characters `.*`
- Followed by another dash `-`
- Followed by the same digits captured by the first capture group `\1`

This regular expression matches `123-abc-123`, `1234-a-1234`, and so on, but does not match `123-abc-1234`, `123-abc-321`, and so on.

Lookahead

Regular expressions support *positive lookahead* (which uses ?=pattern) and *negative lookahead* (which uses ?!pattern). The characters following the lookahead must match (positive) or not match (negative) the lookahead pattern, but those characters are not yet consumed.

For example, the pattern `a(?!b)` contains a negative lookahead to match a letter `a` not followed by a `b`. The pattern `a(?=b)` contains a positive lookahead to match a letter `a` followed by a `b`, but `b` is not consumed so it does not become part of the match.

The following is a more realistic example. The regular expression matches an input sequence that consists of at least one lowercase letter, at least one uppercase letter, at least one punctuation character, and is at least eight characters long. Such a regular expression can, for example, be used to enforce that passwords satisfy certain criteria.

```
(?=.*[[:lower:]])(?=.*[[:upper:]])(?=.*[[:punct:]]).{8,}
```

In one of the exercises at the end of this chapter, you'll experiment with this password-validation regular expression.

Regular Expressions and Raw String Literals

As seen in the preceding sections, regular expressions often use special characters that must be escaped in normal C++ string literals. For example, if you write `\d` in a regular expression, it matches any digit. However, because `\` is a special character in C++, you need to escape it in a regular expression string literal as `\\d`; otherwise, your C++ compiler tries to interpret the `\d`. It gets more complicated if you want a regular expression to match a single backslash character, `\`. Because `\` is a special character in the regular expression syntax itself, you need to escape it as `\\`. The `\` character is also a special character in C++ string literals, so you need to escape it, resulting in `\\\\`.

You can use raw string literals to make complicated regular expressions easier to read in C++ source code. (Raw string literals are discussed in Chapter 2.) For example, take the following regular expression:

```
"( |\\n|\\r|\\\\)"
```

This regular expression matches spaces, newlines, carriage returns, and backslashes. It requires a lot of escape characters. Using raw string literals, this can be replaced with the following more readable regular expression:

```
R"(( |\n|\r|\\))"
```

The raw string literal starts with `R"(` and ends with `)"`. Everything in between is the regular expression. Of course, you still need a double backslash at the end because the backslash needs to be escaped in the regular expression itself.

Common Regular Expressions

Writing correct regular expressions is not always trivial. For common patterns such as validating passwords, phone numbers, Social Security numbers, IP addresses, email addresses, credit card numbers, dates, and so on, you don't have to. When you use your favorite Internet search engine and search for *regular expressions online*, you'll find several websites with collections of predefined patterns, such as `regexr.com`, `regex101.com`, `regextester.com`, and many more. Quite a few of these sites allow you to test patterns online, so you can easily verify whether they are correct before using them in your code.

This concludes a brief description of the ECMAScript grammar. The following sections explain how to actually use regular expressions in C++ code.

The regex Library

Everything for the regular expression library is defined in `<regex>` and in the `std` namespace. The basic template types defined by the regular expression library are:

- `basic_regex`: An object representing a specific regular expression.
- `match_results`: A substring that matched a regular expression, including all the captured groups. It is a collection of `sub_matches`.
- `sub_match`: An object containing a pair of iterators into the input sequence. These iterators represent a matched capture group. The pair is an iterator pointing to the first character of a

matched capture group and an iterator pointing to one-past-the-last character of the matched capture group. It has an `str()` member function that returns the matched capture group as a string.

The library provides three key algorithms: `regex_match()`, `regex_search()`, and `regex_replace()`. All of these algorithms have different overloads that allow you to specify the source string as a `string`, a C-style string, or as a begin/end iterator pair. The iterators can be any of the following:

- `const char*` or `const wchar_t*`
- `string::const_iterator` or `wstring::const_iterator`

In fact, any iterator that behaves as a bidirectional iterator can be used. See Chapters 17, "Understanding Iterators and the Ranges Library," for details on iterators.

The library also defines the following two *regular expression iterators*, which play an important role in finding all occurrences of a pattern in a source string:

- `regex_iterator`: Iterates over all the occurrences of a pattern in a source string.
- `regex_token_iterator`: Iterates over all the capture groups of all occurrences of a pattern in a source string.

To make the library easier to use, the standard defines a number of type aliases for the preceding templates:

```
using regex  = basic_regex<char>;
using wregex = basic_regex<wchar_t>;

using csub_match  = sub_match<const char*>;
using wcsub_match = sub_match<const wchar_t*>;
using ssub_match  = sub_match<string::const_iterator>;
using wssub_match = sub_match<wstring::const_iterator>;

using cmatch  = match_results<const char*>;
using wcmatch = match_results<const wchar_t*>;
using smatch  = match_results<string::const_iterator>;
using wsmatch = match_results<wstring::const_iterator>;

using cregex_iterator  = regex_iterator<const char*>;
using wcregex_iterator = regex_iterator<const wchar_t*>;
using sregex_iterator  = regex_iterator<string::const_iterator>;
using wsregex_iterator = regex_iterator<wstring::const_iterator>;

using cregex_token_iterator  = regex_token_iterator<const char*>;
using wcregex_token_iterator = regex_token_iterator<const wchar_t*>;
using sregex_token_iterator  = regex_token_iterator<string::const_iterator>;
using wsregex_token_iterator = regex_token_iterator<wstring::const_iterator>;
```

The following sections explain the `regex_match()`, `regex_search()`, and `regex_replace()` algorithms, and the `regex_iterator` and `regex_token_iterator` classes.

regex_match()

The `regex_match()` algorithm can be used to compare a given source string with a regular expression pattern. It returns `true` if the pattern matches the entire source string, and `false` otherwise.

There are seven overloads of the `regex_match()` algorithm accepting different kinds of arguments. They all have the following form:

```
template<...>
bool regex_match(InputSequence[, MatchResults], RegEx[, Flags]);
```

The `InputSequence` can be represented as follows:

- A start and end iterator into a source string
- An `std::string`
- A C-style string

The optional `MatchResults` parameter is a reference to a `match_results` and receives the match. If `regex_match()` returns `false`, you are only allowed to call `match_results::empty()` or `match_results::size()`; anything else is undefined. If `regex_match()` returns `true`, a match is found, and you can inspect the `match_results` object for what exactly got matched. This is explained with examples in the following subsections.

The `RegEx` parameter is the regular expression that needs to be matched. The optional `Flags` parameter specifies options for the matching algorithm. In most cases, you can keep the default. For more details, consult a Standard Library Reference.

regex_match() Examples

The following program asks the user to enter a date in the format year/month/day, where year is four digits, month is a number between 1 and 12, and day is a number between 1 and 31. A regular expression together with the `regex_match()` algorithm is used to validate the user input. The details of the regular expression are explained after the code.

```
regex r { "\\d{4}/(?:0?[1-9]|1[0-2])/(?:0?[1-9]|[1-2][0-9]|3[0-1])" };
while (true) {
    print("Enter a date (year/month/day) (q=quit): ");
    string str;
    if (!getline(cin, str) || str == "q") { break; }

    if (regex_match(str, r)) { println("  Valid date."); }
    else { println("  Invalid date!"); }
}
```

The first line creates the regular expression. The expression consists of three parts separated by a forward slash (/) character: one part for year, one for month, and one for day. The following list explains these parts:

- `\d{4}`: Matches any combination of four digits; for example, 1234, 2024, and so on.
- `(?:0?[1-9]|1[0-2])`: This subpart of the regular expression is wrapped inside parentheses to make sure the precedence is correct. We don't need a capture group, so `(?:...)` is used. The inner expression consists of an alternation of two parts separated by the | character.
    - `0?[1-9]`: Matches any number from 1 to 9 with an optional 0 in front of it. For example, it matches 1, 2, 9, 03, 04, and so on. It does not match 0, 10, 11, and so on.
    - `1[0-2]`: Matches 10, 11, or 12, and nothing else.

- `(?:0?[1-9]|[1-2][0-9]|3[0-1])`: This subpart is also wrapped inside a non-capture group and consists of an alternation of three parts.
    - `0?[1-9]`: Again matches any number from 1 to 9 with an optional 0 in front of it.
    - `[1-2][0-9]`: Matches any number between 10 and 29 inclusive and nothing else.
    - `3[0-1]`: Matches 30 or 31 and nothing else.

The example then enters an infinite loop to ask the user to enter a date. Each date entered is given to the `regex_match()` algorithm. When `regex_match()` returns `true`, the user has entered a date that matches the date regular expression pattern.

This example can be extended by asking the `regex_match()` algorithm to return captured subexpressions in a results object. You first have to understand what a capture group does. By specifying a `match_results` object like `smatch` in a call to `regex_match()`, the elements of the `match_results` object are filled in when the regular expression matches the input string. To be able to extract these substrings, you must create capture groups using parentheses.

The first element, `[0]`, in a `match_results` object contains the string that matched the entire pattern. When using `regex_match()` and a match is found, this is the entire source sequence. When using `regex_search()`, discussed in the next section, this can be a substring in the source sequence that matches the regular expression. Element `[1]` is the substring matched by the first capture group, `[2]` by the second capture group, and so on. To get a string representation of the ith capture group from a `match_results` object `m`, you can use `m[i]` as in the following code, or `m[i].str()`.

The following code extracts the year, month, and day digits into three separate integer variables. The regular expression in the revised example has a few small changes. The first part matching the year is wrapped in a capture group, while the month and day parts are now also capture groups instead of non-capture groups. The call to `regex_match()` includes a `smatch` parameter, which receives the matched capture groups. Here is the adapted example:

```
regex r { "(\\d{4})/(0?[1-9]|1[0-2])/(0?[1-9]|[1-2][0-9]|3[0-1])" };
while (true) {
    print("Enter a date (year/month/day) (q=quit): ");
    string str;
    if (!getline(cin, str) || str == "q") { break; }

    if (smatch m; regex_match(str, m, r)) {
        int year { stoi(m[1]) };
        int month { stoi(m[2]) };
        int day { stoi(m[3]) };
        println("  Valid date: Year={}, month={}, day={}", year, month, day);
    } else {
        println("  Invalid date!");
    }
}
```

In this example, there are four elements in the `smatch` results objects:

- `[0]`: The string matching the full regular expression, which in this example is the full date
- `[1]`: The year
- `[2]`: The month
- `[3]`: The day

When you execute this example, you can get the following output:

```
Enter a date (year/month/day) (q=quit): 2024/12/01
  Valid date: Year=2024, month=12, day=1
Enter a date (year/month/day) (q=quit): 24/12/01
  Invalid date!
```

> **NOTE** *These date-matching examples check only if the date consists of a year (four digits), a month (1–12), and a day (1–31). They do not perform any validation for the number of days in a month, leap years, and so on. If you need that, you have to write code to validate the year, month, and day values that are extracted by* `regex_match()`. *If you implement such validation, then the regular expression could be simplified to just match 4 digits for the year, 1 or 2 digits for the month, and 1 or 2 digits for the day.*
>
> ```
> regex r { "(\\d{4})/(\\d{1,2})/(\\d{1,2})" };
> ```

regex_search()

The `regex_match()` algorithm discussed in the previous section returns `true` if the entire source string matches the regular expression and `false` otherwise. If you want to search for a matching substring, you need to use `regex_search()`. There are seven overloads of `regex_search()`, and they all have the following form:

```
template<...>
bool regex_search(InputSequence[, MatchResults], RegEx[, Flags]);
```

All overloads return `true` when a match is found somewhere in the input sequence and `false` otherwise. The parameters are similar to the parameters for `regex_match()`.

Two overloads of `regex_search()` accept a begin and end iterator as the input sequence that you want to process. You might be tempted to use this version of `regex_search()` in a loop to find all occurrences of a pattern in a source string by manipulating these begin and end iterators for each `regex_search()` call. Never do this! It can cause problems when your regular expression uses anchors (`^` or `$`), word boundaries, and so on. It can also cause an infinite loop due to empty matches. Use a `regex_iterator` or `regex_token_iterator` as explained later in this chapter to extract all occurrences of a pattern from a source string.

> **WARNING** *Never use* `regex_search()` *in a loop to find all occurrences of a pattern in a source string. Instead, use a* `regex_iterator` *or* `regex_token_iterator`.

regex_search() Examples

The `regex_search()` algorithm can be used to extract a matching substring from an input sequence. For example, the following program extracts code comments from a string. The regular expression searches for a substring that starts with // followed by optional whitespace, \s*, followed by one or more characters captured in a capture group, (.+). This capture group captures only the comment substring. The smatch object m receives the search results. If successful, m[1] contains the comment that was found. You can check the m[1].first and m[1].second iterators to see where exactly the comment was found in the source string.

```
regex r { "//\\s*(.+)$" };
while (true) {
    print("Enter a string with optional code comments (q=quit):\n> ");
    string str;
    if (!getline(cin, str) || str == "q") { break; }

    if (smatch m; regex_search(str, m, r)) {
        println("  Found comment '{}'", m[1].str());
    } else {
        println("  No comment found!");
    }
}
```

The output of this program can look as follows:

```
Enter a string with optional code comments (q=quit):
> std::string str;   // Our source string
  Found comment 'Our source string'
Enter a string with optional code comments (q=quit):
> int a; // A comment with // in the middle
  Found comment 'A comment with // in the middle'
Enter a string with optional code comments (q=quit):
> std::vector values { 1, 2, 3 };
  No comment found!
```

The match_results object also has a prefix() and suffix() member function, which return the string preceding or following the match, respectively.

regex_iterator

As explained in the previous section, you should never use regex_search() in a loop to extract all occurrences of a pattern from a source sequence. Instead, you should use a regex_iterator or regex_token_iterator. They work similarly to iterators for Standard Library containers.

regex_iterator Examples

The following example asks the user to enter a source string, extracts every word from the string, and prints all words between quotes. The regular expression in this case is [\w]+, which searches for one or more word-letters. This example uses std::string as a source, so it uses sregex_iterator for the iterators. A standard iterator loop is used, but in this case, the end iterator is done slightly differently from the end iterators of Standard Library containers. Normally, you specify an end iterator for a particular container, but for regex_iterator, there is only one "end" iterator. You get this end iterator by default constructing a regex_iterator.

The for loop creates a start iterator called iter, which accepts a begin and end iterator into the source string and a regular expression. The loop body is called for every match found, which is every word in this example. The sregex_iterator iterates over all the matches. By dereferencing a sregex_iterator, you get a smatch object. Accessing the first element of this smatch object, [0], gives you the matched substring:

```
regex reg { "[\\w]+" };
while (true) {
    print("Enter a string to split (q=quit): ");
    string str;
    if (!getline(cin, str) || str == "q") { break; }

    const sregex_iterator end;
    for (sregex_iterator iter { cbegin(str), cend(str), reg };
        iter != end; ++iter) {
        println("\"{}\"", (*iter)[0].str());
    }
}
```

The output of this program can look as follows:

```
Enter a string to split (q=quit): This, is    a test.
"This"
"is"
"a"
"test"
```

As this example demonstrates, even simple regular expressions can perform some powerful string operations!

Note that both regex_iterator, and regex_token_iterator discussed in the next section, internally store a pointer to the given regular expression. Hence, they both explicitly delete any constructors accepting rvalue reference regular expressions to prevent you from constructing them with temporary regex objects. For example, the following does not compile:

```
for (sregex_iterator iter { cbegin(str), cend(str), regex { "[\\w]+" } };
    iter != end; ++iter) { ... }
```

regex_token_iterator

The previous section describes regex_iterator, which iterates through every match. On each iteration, you get a match_results object, which you can use to extract subexpressions for a match that are captured by capture groups.

A regex_token_iterator can be used to automatically iterate over all or selected capture groups across all matches. There are four constructors with the following format:

```
regex_token_iterator(BidirectionalIterator a,
                     BidirectionalIterator b,
                     const regex_type& re
                     [, SubMatches
                     [, Flags]]);
```

All of them require a begin and end iterator as input sequence, and a regular expression. The optional SubMatches parameter is used to specify which capture groups should be iterated over. SubMatches can be specified in four ways:

- As a single integer representing the index of the capture group that you want to iterate over
- As a vector with integers representing the indices of the capture groups that you want to iterate over

- As an `initializer_list` with capture group indices
- As a C-style array with capture group indices

When you omit `SubMatches` or when you specify a 0 for `SubMatches`, you get an iterator that iterates over all capture groups with index 0, which are the substrings matching the full regular expression. The optional `Flags` parameter specifies options for the matching algorithm. In most cases, you can keep the default. Consult a Standard Library Reference for more details.

regex_token_iterator Examples

The earlier `regex_iterator` example can be rewritten using a `regex_token_iterator` as follows. Instead of using `(*iter)[0].str()` in the loop body, you simply use `iter->str()` because a token iterator with 0 (= default) `submatch` index automatically iterates over all capture groups with index 0. The output of this code is the same as the output generated by the earlier `regex_iterator` example.

```
regex reg { "[\\w]+" };
while (true) {
    print("Enter a string to split (q=quit): ");
    string str;
    if (!getline(cin, str) || str == "q") { break; }

    const sregex_token_iterator end;
    for (sregex_token_iterator iter { cbegin(str), cend(str), reg };
        iter != end; ++iter) {
        println("\"{}\"", iter->str());
    }
}
```

The following example asks the user to enter a date and then uses a `regex_token_iterator` to iterate over the second and third capture groups (month and day), which are specified as a `vector` of integers. The regular expression used for dates is explained earlier in this chapter. The only difference is that `^` and `$` anchors are added since we want to match the entire source sequence. Earlier, that was not necessary, because `regex_match()` automatically matches the entire input string.

```
regex reg { "^(\\d{4})/(0?[1-9]|1[0-2])/(0?[1-9]|[1-2][0-9]|3[0-1])$" };
while (true) {
    print("Enter a date (year/month/day) (q=quit): ");
    string str;
    if (!getline(cin, str) || str == "q") { break; }

    vector indices { 2, 3 };
    const sregex_token_iterator end;
    for (sregex_token_iterator iter { cbegin(str), cend(str), reg, indices };
        iter != end; ++iter) {
        println("\"{}\"", iter->str());
    }
}
```

This code prints only the month and day of valid dates. Output generated by this example can look like this:

```
Enter a date (year/month/day) (q=quit): 2024/1/13
"1"
"13"
```

```
Enter a date (year/month/day) (q=quit): 2024/1/32
Enter a date (year/month/day) (q=quit): 2024/12/5
"12"
"5"
```

The `regex_token_iterator` can also be used to perform a *field splitting* or *tokenization*. It is a much safer and more flexible alternative compared to using the old, and not further discussed, `strtok()` function from C. Tokenization is enabled in the `regex_token_iterator` constructor by specifying `-1` as the capture group index to iterate over. In tokenization mode, the iterator iterates over all substrings of the input sequence that *do not match* the regular expression. The following code demonstrates this by tokenizing a string on the delimiters `,` and `;` with zero or more whitespace characters before or after a delimiter. The code demonstrates the tokenization in two ways: first by iterating over the tokens directly and then by creating a new `vector` containing all the tokens followed by printing the contents of the `vector`:

```
regex reg { R"(\s*[,;]\s*)" };
while (true) {
    print("Enter a string to split on ',' and ';' (q=quit): ");
    string str;
    if (!getline(cin, str) || str == "q") { break; }

    // Iterate over the tokens.
    const sregex_token_iterator end;
    for (sregex_token_iterator iter { cbegin(str), cend(str), reg, -1 };
        iter != end; ++iter) {
        print("\"{}\", ", iter->str());
    }
    println("");

    // Store all tokens in a vector.
    vector<string> tokens {
        sregex_token_iterator { cbegin(str), cend(str), reg, -1 },
        sregex_token_iterator {} };
    // Print the contents of the tokens vector.
    println("{:n}", tokens);
}
```

The regular expression in this example is specified as a raw string literal and searches for patterns that match the following:

- Zero or more whitespace characters
- Followed by a `,` or `;` character
- Followed by zero or more whitespace characters

The output can be as follows:

```
Enter a string to split on ',' and ';' (q=quit): This is,   a; test string.
"This is", "a", "test string.",
"This is", "a", "test string."
```

As you can see from this output, the string is split on `,` and `;`. All whitespace characters around the `,` and `;` are removed because the tokenization iterator iterates over all substrings that *do not match* the regular expression and because the regular expression matches `,` and `;` *with* whitespace around them.

regex_replace()

The regex_replace() algorithm requires a regular expression and a formatting string that is used to replace matching substrings. This formatting string can reference parts of the matched substrings by using the escape sequences in the following table.

ESCAPE SEQUENCE	REPLACED WITH
$n	The string matching the nth capture group; for example, $1 for the first capture group, $2 for the second, and so on. *n* must be greater than 0.
$&	The string matching the entire regular expression.
$`	The part of the input sequence that appears to the left of the substring matching the regular expression.
$'	The part of the input sequence that appears to the right of the substring matching the regular expression.
$$	A single dollar sign.

There are six overloads of regex_replace(). The difference between them is in the type of parameters. Four of them have the following format:

```
template<...>
string regex_replace(InputSequence, RegEx, FormatString[, Flags]);
```

These four overloads return the resulting string after performing the replacement. Both the InputSequence and the FormatString can be an std::string or a C-style string. The RegEx parameter is the regular expression that needs to be matched. The optional Flags parameter specifies options for the replace algorithm.

Two overloads of regex_replace() have the following format:

```
OutputIterator regex_replace(OutputIterator,
                             BidirectionalIterator first,
                             BidirectionalIterator last,
                             RegEx, FormatString[, Flags]);
```

These two overloads write the resulting string to the given output iterator and return this output iterator. The input sequence is given as a begin and end iterator. The other parameters are identical to the other four overloads of regex_replace().

regex_replace() Examples

As a first example, take the following HTML source string:

```
<body><h1>Header</h1><p>Some text</p></body>
```

and the following regular expression:

```
<h1>(.*)</h1><p>(.*)</p>
```

The following table shows the different escape sequences and what they will be replaced with:

ESCAPE SEQUENCE	REPLACED WITH
$1	Header
$2	Some text
$&	<h1>Header</h1><p>Some text</p>
$`	<body>
$´	</body>

The following code demonstrates the use of regex_replace():

```
const string str { "<body><h1>Header</h1><p>Some text</p></body>" };
regex r { "<h1>(.*)</h1><p>(.*)</p>" };

const string replacement { "H1=$1 and P=$2" };  // See earlier table.
string result { regex_replace(str, r, replacement) };

println("Original string: '{}'", str);
println("New string      : '{}'", result);
```

The output of this program is as follows:

```
Original string: '<body><h1>Header</h1><p>Some text</p></body>'
New string     : '<body>H1=Header and P=Some text</body>'
```

The regex_replace() algorithm accepts a number of flags to change its behavior. The most important flags are given in the following table:

FLAG	DESCRIPTION
format_default	The default is to replace all occurrences of the pattern and to also copy everything to the output that does not match the pattern.
format_no_copy	Replaces all occurrences of the pattern but does not copy anything to the output that does not match the pattern.
format_first_only	Replaces only the first occurrence of the pattern.

The call to regex_replace() in the previous code snippet can be modified to use the format_no_copy flag:

```
string result { regex_replace(str, r, replacement,
    regex_constants::format_no_copy) };
```

The output now is as follows:

```
Original string: '<body><h1>Header</h1><p>Some text</p></body>'
New string     : 'H1=Header and P=Some text'
```

Another example using regex_replace() is to replace each word boundary in a string with a newline character so that the output contains only one word per line. The following code snippet demonstrates this without using any loops to process a given input string. The code first creates a regular expression that matches individual words. When a match is found with `regex_replace()`, it is substituted with `$1\n` where `$1` is replaced with the matched word. Note also the use of the `format_no_copy` flag to prevent copying whitespace and other non-word characters from the source string to the output.

```
regex reg { "([\\w]+)" };
const string replacement { "$1\n" };
while (true) {
    print("Enter a string to split over multiple lines (q=quit): ");
    string str;
    if (!getline(cin, str) || str == "q") { break; }

    println("{}", regex_replace(str, reg, replacement,
        regex_constants::format_no_copy));
}
```

The output of this program can be as follows:

```
Enter a string to split over multiple lines (q=quit):   This is   a test.
This
is
a
test
```

SUMMARY

This chapter gave you an appreciation for coding with localization in mind. As anyone who has been through a localization effort will tell you, adding support for a new language or locale is infinitely easier if you have planned ahead, for example, by using Unicode characters and being mindful of locales.

The second part of this chapter explained the regular expressions library. Once you know the syntax of regular expressions, it becomes much easier to work with strings. Regular expressions allow you to validate strings, search for substrings inside an input sequence, perform find-and-replace operations, and so on. It is highly recommended that you get to know regular expressions and start using them instead of writing your own string manipulation routines. They will make your life easier.

EXERCISES

By solving the following exercises, you can practice the material discussed in this chapter. Solutions to all exercises are available with the code download on the book's website at `www.wiley.com/go/proc++6e`. However, if you are stuck on an exercise, first reread parts of this chapter to try to find an answer yourself before looking at the solution from the website.

Exercise 21-1: Use an appropriate facet to figure out the decimal separator for formatting numbers according to the user's environment. Consult a Standard Library reference to learn about the exact member functions of your chosen facet.

Exercise 21-2: Write an application that asks the user to enter a phone number as formatted in the United States. Here's an example: 202-555-0108. Use a regular expression to validate the format of the phone number, that is, three digits, followed by a dash, three more digits, another dash, and a final four digits. If it's a valid phone number, print out the three parts on separate lines. For example, for the earlier phone number, the result must be as follows:

```
202
555
0108
```

Exercise 21-3: Write an application that asks the user for a piece of source code that can span multiple lines and that can contain `//` style comments. To signal the end of the input, use a sentinel character, for example `@`. You can use `std::getline()` with `'@'` as delimiter to read in multiple lines of text from the standard input console. Finally, use a regular expression to remove comments from all lines of the code snippet. Make sure your code properly works on a snippet such as the following:

```
string str; // A comment // Some more comments.
str = "Hello"; // Hello.
```

The result for this input must be as follows:

```
string str;
str = "Hello";
```

Exercise 21-4: The section "Lookahead" earlier in this chapter mentioned a password-validation regular expression. Write a program to test this regular expression. Ask the user to enter a password and validate it. Once you've verified that the regular expression works, add one more validation rule to it: a password must also consist of at least two digits.

22

Date and Time Utilities

WHAT'S IN THIS CHAPTER?

- How to work with compile-time rational numbers
- How to work with time
- How to work with dates and calendars
- How to convert time points between different time zones

WILEY.COM DOWNLOADS FOR THIS CHAPTER

Please note that all the code examples for this chapter are available as part of this chapter's code download on the book's website at `www.wiley.com/go/proc++6e` on the Download Code tab.

This chapter discusses the time-related functionality provided by the C++ Standard Library, known collectively as the *chrono library*. It is a collection of classes and functions to work with time and dates. The library consists of the following components:

- Durations
- Clocks
- Time points
- Dates
- Time zones

Everything is defined in `<chrono>` in the `std::chrono` namespace. However, before we can start the discussion of each of these chrono library components, we need a small digression to look at the compile-time rational number support available in C++, as this is heavily used by the chrono library.

COMPILE-TIME RATIONAL NUMBERS

The Ratio library allows you to exactly represent any finite rational number that you can use at compile time. Everything is defined in `<ratio>` and is in the `std` namespace. The numerator and denominator of a rational number are represented as compile-time constants of type `std::intmax_t`, which is a signed integer type with the maximum width supported by a compiler. Because of the compile-time nature of these rational numbers, using them might look a bit different than what you are used to. You cannot define a `ratio` object the same way as you define normal objects, and you cannot call member functions on it. Instead, `ratio` is a class template, and a specific instantiation of the `ratio` class template represents one specific rational number. To name such specific instantiations, you can use type aliases. For example, the following defines a compile-time rational number representing the fraction 1/60:

```
using r1 = ratio<1, 60>;
```

The numerator (`num`) and denominator (`den`) of the `r1` rational number are compile-time constants and can be accessed as follows:

```
intmax_t num { r1::num };
intmax_t den { r1::den };
```

Remember that a `ratio` represents a *compile-time rational number*, which means that the numerator and denominator need to be known at compile time. The following generates a compilation error:

```
intmax_t n { 1 };           // Numerator
intmax_t d { 60 };          // Denominator
using r1 = ratio<n, d>;     // Error
```

Making `n` and `d` constants works fine:

```
const intmax_t n { 1 };     // Numerator
const intmax_t d { 60 };    // Denominator
using r1 = ratio<n, d>;     // Ok
```

Rational numbers are always normalized. For a rational number `ratio<n, d>`, the greatest common divisor, `gcd`, is calculated, and the numerator, `num`, and denominator, `den`, are then defined as follows:

- `num = sign(n)*sign(d)*abs(n)/gcd`
- `den = abs(d)/gcd`

The library supports adding, subtracting, multiplying, and dividing rational numbers. However, you cannot use the standard arithmetic operators because all these operations are again not happening on objects but on types, i.e., instantiations of the `ratio` class template, at compile time. Instead, you need to use specific arithmetic `ratio` class templates. The following arithmetic class templates are available: `ratio_add`, `ratio_subtract`, `ratio_multiply`, and `ratio_divide`, which perform addition, subtraction, multiplication, and division, respectively. These templates calculate the result as a new `ratio` type. This type can be accessed with the embedded type alias called `type`. For example, the following code first defines two `ratio`s, one representing 1/60 and the other representing 1/30. The `ratio_add` template adds those two rational numbers together to produce the `result` rational number, which, after normalization, is 1/20:

```
using r1 = ratio<1, 60>;
```

```
using r2 = ratio<1, 30>;
using result = ratio_add<r1, r2>::type;
```

The standard also defines a number of `ratio` comparison class templates: `ratio_equal`, `ratio_not_equal`, `ratio_less`, `ratio_less_equal`, `ratio_greater`, and `ratio_greater_equal`. Just like the arithmetic `ratio` class templates, the `ratio` comparison class templates are all evaluated at compile time, again not on objects but on `ratio` types. These comparison templates define a new type that is an `std::bool_constant`, representing the result. `bool_constant` is an `std::integral_constant`, a `struct` template that stores a type and a compile-time constant value. For example, `integral_constant<int, 15>` stores an integer with value 15. `bool_constant` is an `integral_constant` with type `bool`. For instance, `bool_constant<true>` is `integral_constant<bool, true>`, which stores a Boolean with value `true`. The result of the `ratio` comparison templates is either `bool_constant<true>` or `bool_constant<false>`. The value associated with a `bool_constant` or an `integral_constant` can be accessed using the `value` data member. The following example demonstrates the use of `ratio_less`:

```
using r1 = ratio<1, 60>;
using r2 = ratio<1, 30>;
using res = ratio_less<r2, r1>;
println("{}", res::value); // false
```

The following code snippet combines everything just covered. Because `ratio`s are not objects but types, you cannot do something like `println("{}", r1);` you need to get the numerator and denominator and print them separately.

```
// Define a compile-time rational number.
using r1 = ratio<1, 60>;

// Get numerator and denominator.
intmax_t num { r1::num };
intmax_t den { r1::den };
println("1) r1 = {}/{}", num, den);

// Add two rational numbers.
using r2 = ratio<1, 30>;
println("2) r2 = {}/{}", r2::num, r2::den);
using result = ratio_add<r1, r2>::type;
println("3) sum = {}/{}", result::num, result::den);

// Compare two rational numbers.
using res = ratio_less<r2, r1>;
println("4) r2 < r1: {}", res::value);
```

The output is as follows:

```
1) r1 = 1/60
2) r2 = 1/30
3) sum = 1/20
4) r2 < r1: false
```

The library provides a number of SI (*Système International*) type aliases for your convenience. They are as follows:

```
using yocto = ratio<1, 1'000'000'000'000'000'000'000'000>; // *
using zepto = ratio<1, 1'000'000'000'000'000'000'000>;     // *
using atto  = ratio<1, 1'000'000'000'000'000'000>;
using femto = ratio<1, 1'000'000'000'000'000>;
```

```
using pico  = ratio<1, 1'000'000'000'000>;
using nano  = ratio<1, 1'000'000'000>;
using micro = ratio<1, 1'000'000>;
using milli = ratio<1, 1'000>;
using centi = ratio<1, 100>;
using deci  = ratio<1, 10>;
using deca  = ratio<10, 1>;
using hecto = ratio<100, 1>;
using kilo  = ratio<1'000, 1>;
using mega  = ratio<1'000'000, 1>;
using giga  = ratio<1'000'000'000, 1>;
using tera  = ratio<1'000'000'000'000, 1>;
using peta  = ratio<1'000'000'000'000'000, 1>;
using exa   = ratio<1'000'000'000'000'000'000, 1>;
using zetta = ratio<1'000'000'000'000'000'000'000, 1>;     // *
using yotta = ratio<1'000'000'000'000'000'000'000'000, 1>; // *
```

The SI units with an asterisk at the end are defined only if your compiler can represent the constant numerator and denominator values for those type aliases as an `intmax_t`. An example of how to use these predefined SI units is given during the discussion of `durations` in the next section.

DURATION

A *duration* is an interval between two points in time. It is represented by the `duration` class template, which stores a number of *ticks* and a *tick period*. The tick period is the time in seconds between two ticks and is represented as a compile-time `ratio` constant, which means it could be a fraction of a second. Ratios are discussed in the previous section. The `duration` template accepts two template type parameters and is defined as follows:

```
template <class Rep, class Period = ratio<1>> class duration {...}
```

The first template parameter, `Rep`, is the type of variable storing the number of ticks and should be an arithmetic type, for example `long`, `double`, and so on. The second template parameter, `Period`, is the rational constant representing the period of a tick. If you don't specify the tick period, the default value `ratio<1>` is used, which represents a tick period of one second.

Three constructors are provided: the default constructor; one that accepts a single value, the number of ticks; and one that accepts another `duration`. The latter constructor can be used to convert from one `duration` to another `duration`, for example, from minutes to seconds. An example is given later in this section.

Durations support arithmetic operations such as `+`, `-`, `*`, `/`, `%`, `++`, `--`, `+=`, `-=`, `*=`, `/=`, and `%=`, and they support the comparison operators `==` and `<=>`. The class also contains the member functions shown in the following table:

MEMBER FUNCTION	DESCRIPTION
`Rep count() const`	Returns the `duration` value as the number of ticks. The return type is the type specified as the first template type parameter for the `duration` template.

MEMBER FUNCTION	DESCRIPTION
`static duration zero()`	Returns a `duration` with a duration value equivalent to zero.
`static duration min()` `static duration max()`	Returns a `duration` with the minimum/maximum possible duration value representable by the type specified as the first template type parameter for the `duration` template.

The library supports `floor()`, `ceil()`, `round()`, and `abs()` operations on `durations` that behave just as they behave with numerical data.

Let's now see how `durations` can be defined. A `duration` where each tick is one second can be defined as follows:

```
duration<long> d1;
```

Because `ratio<1>` is the default tick period, this is the same as writing:

```
duration<long, ratio<1>> d1;
```

The next statement defines a `duration` in minutes (tick period = 60 seconds):

```
duration<long, ratio<60>> d2;
```

Here is a `duration` where each tick period is a sixtieth of a second:

```
duration<double, ratio<1, 60>> d3;
```

As you saw earlier in this chapter, `<ratio>` defines a number of SI rational constants. These predefined constants come in handy for defining tick periods. For example, the next statement defines a `duration` where each tick period is one millisecond:

```
duration<long long, milli> d4;
```

Examples and Converting Durations

Let's see `durations` in action. The following example demonstrates several aspects of `durations`. It shows you how to define them, how to perform arithmetic operations on them, how to print them to the screen, and how to convert one `duration` to another `duration` with a different tick period:

```
// Specify a duration where each tick is 60 seconds.
duration<long, ratio<60>> d1 { 123 };
println("{} ({})", d1, d1.count());

// Specify a duration represented by a double with each tick
// equal to 1 second and assign the largest possible duration to it.
auto d2 { duration<double>::max() };
println("{}", d2);

// Define 2 durations:
// For the first duration, each tick is 1 minute.
// For the second duration, each tick is 1 second.
duration<long, ratio<60>> d3 { 10 };  // = 10 minutes
duration<long, ratio<1>> d4 { 14 };   // = 14 seconds

// Compare both durations.
if (d3 > d4) { println("d3 > d4"); }
else { println("d3 <= d4"); }
```

```
// Increment d4 with 1 resulting in 15 seconds.
++d4;

// Multiply d4 by 2 resulting in 30 seconds.
d4 *= 2;

// Add both durations and store as minutes.
duration<double, ratio<60>> d5 { d3 + d4 };

// Add both durations and store as seconds.
duration<long, ratio<1>> d6 { d3 + d4 };
println("{} + {} = {} or {}", d3, d4, d5, d6);

// Create a duration of 30 seconds.
duration<long> d7 { 30 };

// Convert the seconds of d7 to minutes.
duration<double, ratio<60>> d8 { d7 };
println("{} = {}", d7, d8);
println("{} seconds = {} minutes", d7.count(), d8.count());
```

The output is as follows:

```
123min (123)
1.79769e+308s
d3 > d4
10min + 30s = 10.5min or 630s
30s = 0.5min
30 seconds = 0.5 minutes
```

> **NOTE** *The second line in the output represents the largest possible* `duration` *with type* `double`*. The exact value might be different depending on your compiler.*

Pay special attention to the following two lines of code:

```
duration<double, ratio<60>> d5 { d3 + d4 };
duration<long, ratio<1>> d6 { d3 + d4 };
```

They both calculate `d3+d4`, with `d3` given in minutes and `d4` in seconds, but the first statement stores it as a floating-point value representing minutes, while the second statement stores the result as an integral value representing seconds. Conversion from minutes to seconds, or vice versa, happens automatically.

The following two lines from the example demonstrate how to explicitly convert between different units of time:

```
duration<long> d7 { 30 };                    // seconds
duration<double, ratio<60>> d8 { d7 };  // minutes
```

The first statement defines a `duration` representing 30 seconds. The second statement converts these 30 seconds into minutes, resulting in 0.5 minutes. Converting in this direction can result in a non-integral value and thus requires you to use a `duration` represented by a floating-point type; otherwise, you will get some cryptic compilation errors. The following statements, for example, do not compile because `d8` is using `long` instead of a floating-point type:

```
duration<long> d7 { 30 };                    // seconds
duration<long, ratio<60>> d8 { d7 };    // minutes    // Error!
```

You can, however, force this conversion by using `duration_cast()`:

```
duration<long> d7 { 30 };                               // seconds
auto d8 { duration_cast<duration<long, ratio<60>>>(d7) }; // minutes
```

In this case, `d8` will be 0 minutes, because integer division is used to convert 30 seconds to minutes.

Converting in the other direction does not require floating-point types if the source is an integral type, because the result is always an integral value if you started with an integral value. For example, the following statements convert ten minutes into seconds, both represented by the integral type `long`:

```
duration<long, ratio<60>> d9 { 10 };     // minutes
duration<long> d10 { d9 };               // seconds
```

Predefined Durations

The library provides the following standard `duration` types in the `std::chrono` namespace:

```
using nanoseconds  = duration<X 64 bits, nano>;
using microseconds = duration<X 55 bits, micro>;
using milliseconds = duration<X 45 bits, milli>;
using seconds      = duration<X 35 bits>;
using minutes      = duration<X 29 bits, ratio<60>>;
using hours        = duration<X 23 bits, ratio<3'600>>;
using days   = duration<X 25 bits, ratio_multiply<ratio<24>, hours::period>>;
using weeks  = duration<X 22 bits, ratio_multiply<ratio<7>, days::period>>;
using years  = duration<X 17 bits,
               ratio_multiply<ratio<146'097, 400>, days::period>>;
using months = duration<X 20 bits, ratio_divide<years::period, ratio<12>>>;
```

The exact type of X depends on your compiler, but the C++ standard requires it to be a signed integer type of at least the specified size. The preceding type aliases make use of the predefined SI `ratio` type aliases that are described earlier in this chapter. With these predefined types, instead of writing this:

```
duration<long, ratio<60>> d9 { 10 };     // minutes
```

you can simply write this:

```
minutes d9 { 10 };                       // minutes
```

The following code is another example of how to use these predefined durations. The code first defines a variable `t`, which is the result of 1 hour + 23 minutes + 45 seconds. The `auto` keyword is used to let the compiler automatically figure out the exact type of `t`. The second statement uses the constructor of the predefined `seconds` duration to convert the value of `t` to seconds and writes the result to the console:

```
auto t { hours { 1 } + minutes { 23 } + seconds { 45 } };
println("{}", seconds { t });
```

Because the standard requires that the predefined durations use integer types, there can be compilation errors if a conversion *could* end up with a non-integral value. While integer division normally truncates, in the case of durations, which are implemented with `ratio` types, the compiler declares any computation that *could* result in a non-zero remainder as a compile-time error. For example, the following code does not compile because converting 90 seconds to minutes results in 1.5 minutes:

```
seconds s { 90 };
minutes m { s };
```

However, the following code does not compile either, even though 60 seconds is exactly 1 minute. It is flagged as a compile-time error because converting from seconds to minutes *could* result in non-integral values:

```
seconds s { 60 };
minutes m { s };
```

Converting in the other direction works perfectly fine because the `minutes` duration uses an integral type, and converting it to `seconds` always results in an integral value:

```
minutes m { 2 };
seconds s { m };
```

Standard Literals

You can use the standard literals `h`, `min`, `s`, `ms`, `us`, and `ns` for creating durations. Technically, these are defined in the `std::literals::chrono_literals` namespace, but just as for the standard string literals discussed in Chapter 2, "Working with Strings and String Views," the `chrono_literals` namespace is an inline namespace. So, you can make the chrono literals available with any of the following using directives:

```
using namespace std;
using namespace std::literals;
using namespace std::chrono_literals;
using namespace std::literals::chrono_literals;
```

Additionally, the literals are also made available in the `std::chrono` namespace. Here is an example:

```
using namespace std::chrono;
// ...
auto myDuration { 42min };     // 42 minutes
```

hh_mm_ss

The chrono library provides the `hh_mm_ss` class template, which accepts a `Duration` and splits the given duration into hours, minutes, seconds, and subseconds. It has getters `hours()`, `minutes()`, `seconds()`, and `subseconds()` to retrieve the data, always returning non-negative values. The `is_negative()` member function returns `true` if the duration is a negative duration, `false` otherwise. You'll use the `hh_mm_ss` class template in one of the exercises at the end of this chapter.

CLOCK

A `clock` is a class consisting of a `time_point` and a `duration`. The `time_point` type is discussed in detail in the next section, but those details are not required to understand how `clocks` work. However, `time_points` themselves depend on `clocks`, so it's important to know the details of `clocks` first.

The standard defines several `clocks`, which are described in the following table. The *epoch* of a clock is the time at which the clock starts counting.

CLOCK	DESCRIPTION	EPOCH
`system_clock`	Represents the UTC wall clock time from the system-wide real-time clock.	1970-01-01 00:00:00
`steady_clock`	Guarantees its `time_point` never decreases, which is not guaranteed for `system_clock` because the system clock can be adjusted at any time. In fact, this clock is not required to be related to wall clock time; e.g., it could be the time since the start of the operating system.	Unspecified
`high_resolution_clock`	Has the shortest possible tick period. Depending on your compiler, it is possible for this clock to be a synonym for `steady_clock` or `system_clock`.	Unspecified
`utc_clock`	Represents the Coordinated Universal Time (UTC) wall clock time.	1970-01-01 00:00:00
`tai_clock`	Represents International Atomic Time (TAI), using a weighted average of several atomic clocks.	1958-01-01 00:00:00
`gps_clock`	Represents Global Position System (GPS) time, i.e., the time maintained by the atomic clocks of GPS satellites.	1980-01-06 00:00:00
`file_clock`	Represents file time. It's an alias for `std::filesystem::file_time_type`.	Unspecified, but typically 1970-01-01 on Unix, and 1601-01-01 on Windows.

The `utc_clock` is the only clock that tracks leap seconds, which are seconds that are occasionally added to or subtracted from UTC time to correct for any mismatch between UTC time and true solar time. The other clocks don't track leap seconds, while for `file_clock` it's unspecified.

> **NOTE** *The use of the* `high_resolution_clock` *is discouraged because its implementation is not consistent between different compilers. For some compilers, it might be an alias for* `steady_clock`*, while for others it might be an alias for* `system_clock`*. Hence, for some compilers, the* `high_resolution_clock` *can go backwards, and for others it doesn't.*
>
> *Instead, it's recommended to use* `system_clock` *to work with wall clock time and* `steady_clock` *to measure durations.*

Every clock has a static now() member function to get the current time as a time_point, and an is_steady() member function returning true if the clock is steady, i.e., never goes backwards, false otherwise.

The system_clock also defines two static helper member functions for converting time_points to and from the time_t C-style time representation. The first one is called to_time_t(), and it converts a given time_point to a time_t; the second one, from_time_t(), performs the opposite conversion. The time_t type is defined in <ctime>.

Printing Current Time

The following example demonstrates how to get the current UTC time and print it to the console in a human-readable format:

```
// Set the global locale to the user's local (see Chapter 21).
locale::global(locale { "" });
// Print the current UTC time.
println("UTC: {:L}", system_clock::now());
println("UTC: {:L%c}", system_clock::now());
```

This code snippet first sets the global locale to the user's locale; see Chapter 21, "String Localization and Regular Expressions." This makes sure everything is printed according to the user's preferences. The println() statements use the L format specifier to format the date and time according to the configured global locale. The effect of the %c format specifier is also demonstrated. There are many more format specifiers supported. Consult a Standard Library reference to learn more about them. Here is sample output from the previous code snippet:

```
UTC: 2023-07-19 11:38:44,5521944
UTC: 2023-07-19 11:38:44
```

Execution Timing

To time how long it takes for a piece of code to execute, you want to use a clock that is guaranteed not to go backwards. Hence, you should use a steady_clock. The following code snippet gives an example. The actual type of the variables start and end is steady_clock::time_point, and the actual type of diff is a duration.

```
// Get the start time.
auto start { steady_clock::now() };
// Execute code that you want to time.
const int numberOfIterations { 10'000'000 };
double d { 0 };
for (int i { 0 }; i < numberOfIterations; ++i) { d += sqrt(abs(sin(i) * cos(i))); }
// Get the end time and calculate the difference.
auto end { steady_clock::now() };
auto diff { end - start };
// Use the calculated result, otherwise the compiler might
// optimize away the entire loop!
println("d = {}", d);
```

```
    // Convert the difference into milliseconds and output to the console.
    println("Total: {}", duration<double, milli> { diff });
    // Use duration_cast() if you don't need fractional milliseconds.
    println("Total: {}", duration_cast<milliseconds>(diff));
    // Print the time per iteration in nanoseconds.
    println("{} per iteration", duration<double, nano> { diff / numberOfIterations });
```

Here is the output running on my test system:

```
d = 5393526.082683575
Total: 78.7931ms
Total: 78ms
7ns per iteration
```

The loop in this example is performing some arithmetic operations with `sqrt()`, `abs()`, `sin()`, and `cos()` to make sure the loop doesn't end too fast. If you get really small values for the difference in milliseconds on your system, those values will not be accurate, and you should increase the number of iterations of the loop to make it last longer. Small timings will not be accurate because while timers often have a resolution in milliseconds, on most operating systems, this timer is updated infrequently, for example, every 10 ms or 15 ms. This induces a phenomenon called *gating error*, where any event that occurs in less than one timer tick appears to take place in zero units of time, and any event between one and two timer ticks appears to take place in one timer unit. For example, on a system with a 15 ms timer update, a loop that takes 44 ms will appear to take only 30 ms. When using such timers to time computations, it is important to make sure that the entire computation takes place across a fairly large number of basic timer tick units so that these errors are minimized.

TIME POINT

A point in time is represented by the `time_point` class and stored as a `duration` relative to an *epoch*, representing the beginning of time. A `time_point` is always associated with a certain `clock`, and the epoch is the origin of this associated `clock`. For example, the epoch for the classic Unix/Linux time is January 1, 1970, and durations are measured in seconds. The epoch for Windows is January 1, 1601, and durations are measured in 100-nanosecond units. Other operating systems have different epoch dates and duration units.

The `time_point` class has a function called `time_since_epoch()`, which returns a `duration` representing the time between the epoch of the associated `clock` and the stored point in time.

Arithmetic operations of `time_points` and `durations` that make sense are supported. The following table lists those operations. `tp` is a `time_point`, and `d` is a `duration`:

`tp + d = tp`	`tp - d = tp`
`d + tp = tp`	`tp - tp = d`
`tp += d`	`tp -= d`

An example of an operation that is not supported is `tp+tp`.

Comparison operators `==` and `<=>` to compare two time points are supported. Two static member functions are provided: `min()` and `max()` returning the smallest and largest possible point in time, respectively.

The `time_point` class has three constructors:

- `time_point()`: Constructs a `time_point` initialized with `duration::zero()`. The resulting `time_point` represents the epoch of the associated `clock`.
- `time_point(const duration& d)`: Constructs a `time_point` initialized with the given duration. The resulting `time_point` represents `epoch + d`.
- `template<class Duration2> time_point(const time_point<clock, Duration2>& t)`: Constructs a `time_point` initialized with `t.time_since_epoch()`.

Each `time_point` is associated with a `clock`. To create a `time_point`, you specify the `clock` as the template parameter:

```
time_point<steady_clock> tp1;
```

Each `clock` also knows its `time_point` type, so you can also write it as follows:

```
steady_clock::time_point tp1;
```

The following code snippet demonstrates some operations with `time_points`:

```
// Create a time_point representing the epoch of the associated steady clock.
time_point<steady_clock> tp1;
// Add 10 minutes to the time_point.
tp1 += minutes { 10 };
// Store the duration between epoch and time_point.
auto d1 { tp1.time_since_epoch() };
// Convert the duration to seconds and output to the console.
duration<double> d2 { d1 };
println("{}", d2);
```

The output is as follows:

```
600s
```

Converting `time_points` can be done implicitly or explicitly, similar to `duration` conversions. Here is an example of an implicit conversion. The output is `42000ms`:

```
time_point<steady_clock, seconds> tpSeconds { 42s };
// Convert seconds to milliseconds implicitly.
time_point<steady_clock, milliseconds> tpMilliseconds { tpSeconds };
println("{}", tpMilliseconds.time_since_epoch());
```

If the implicit conversion can result in a loss of data, then you need an explicit conversion using `time_point_cast()`, similar to using `duration_cast()` for explicit `duration` casts as discussed earlier in this chapter. The following example outputs `42000ms`, even though you start from 42,424ms:

```
time_point<steady_clock, milliseconds> tpMilliseconds { 42'424ms };
// Convert milliseconds to seconds explicitly.
time_point<steady_clock, seconds> tpSeconds {
    time_point_cast<seconds>(tpMilliseconds) };
// Or:
// auto tpSeconds { time_point_cast<seconds>(tpMilliseconds) };
```

```
    // Convert seconds back to milliseconds and output the result.
    milliseconds ms { tpSeconds.time_since_epoch() };
    println("{}", ms);
```

The library supports `floor()`, `ceil()`, and `round()` operations for `time_points` that behave just as they behave with numerical data.

DATE

The Standard Library supports working with calendar dates. At this moment, only the Gregorian calendar is supported, but if need be, you can always implement your own calendars that can interoperate with the rest of the `<chrono>` functionality, such as Coptic and Julian calendars.

The Standard Library provides quite a few classes and functions to work with dates (and time zones discussed in a later section). This text discusses the most important classes and functions. Consult a Standard Library reference (see Appendix B, "Annotated Bibliography") to get a complete overview of everything that's available.

Creating Dates

The following calendrical classes are available to create dates, all defined in `std::chrono`:

CLASS	DESCRIPTION
`year`	Represents a year in the range [-32767, 32767]. A `year` has a member function called `is_leap()` returning `true` if a given `year` is a leap year, `false` otherwise. `min()` and `max()` static member functions return the minimum and maximum year, respectively.
`month`	Represents a month in the range [1, 12]. Additionally, there are 12 named constants provided for the 12 months, for example: `std::chrono::January`.
`day`	Represents a day in the range [1, 31].
`weekday`	Represents a day of the week in the range [0, 6], where 0 means Sunday. Additionally, there are seven named constants provided for the seven weekdays, for example: `std::chrono::Sunday`.
`weekday_indexed`	Represents the first, second, third, fourth, or fifth weekday of a month. Can easily be constructed from a `weekday`, for example: `Monday[2]` is the second Monday of a month.
`weekday_last`	Represents the last weekday of some month.
`month_day`	Represents a specific month and day.
`month_day_last`	Represents the last day of a specific month.
`month_weekday`	Represents the nth weekday of a specific month.

continues

(continued)

CLASS	DESCRIPTION
month_weekday_last	Represents the last weekday of a specific month.
year_month	Represents a specific year and month.
year_month_day	Represents a specific year, month, and day.
year_month_day_last	Represents the last day of a specific year and month.
year_month_weekday	Represents the nth weekday of a specific year and month.
year_month_weekday_last	Represents the last weekday of a specific year and month.

All of these classes have a member function called `ok()` that returns `true` if the given object is in a valid range, `false` otherwise. Two additional standard literals are provided in `std::literals::chrono_literals`: `y` to create years, and `d` to create days. Complete dates can be constructed using `operator/` to specify year, month, and day, in three orders: Y/M/D, M/D/Y, D/M/Y. Here are some examples to create dates:

```
year y1 { 2020 };
auto y2 { 2020y };

month m1 { 6 };
auto m2 { June };

day d1 { 22 };
auto d2 { 22d };

// Create a date for 2020-06-22.
year_month_day fulldate1 { 2020y, June, 22d };
auto fulldate2 { 2020y / June / 22d };
auto fulldate3 { 22d / June / 2020y };

// Create a date for the 3rd Monday of June 2020.
year_month_day fulldate4 { Monday[3] / June / 2020 };

// Create a month_day for June 22 of an unspecified year.
auto june22 { June / 22d };
// Create a year_month_day for June 22, 2020.
auto june22_2020 { 2020y / june22 };

// Create a month_day_last for the last day of a June of an unspecified year.
auto lastDayOfAJune { June / last };
// Create a year_month_day_last for the last day of June for the year 2020.
auto lastDayOfJune2020 { 2020y / lastDayOfAJune };

// Create a year_month_weekday_last for the last Monday of June 2020.
auto lastMondayOfJune2020 { 2020y / June / Monday[last] };
```

`sys_time` is a type alias for a `time_point` of a `system_clock` with a certain duration. It's defined as follows:

```
template <typename Duration>
using sys_time = std::chrono::time_point<std::chrono::system_clock, Duration>;
```

Based on the sys_time type alias, two additional type aliases are defined to represent a sys_time with a precision of seconds, and one with a precision of days:

```
using sys_seconds = sys_time<std::chrono::seconds>;
using sys_days = sys_time<std::chrono::days>;
```

sys_days, for example, represents the number of days since the system_clock epoch, and hence, it's a *serial-based type*; that is, it just contains a single number (days since epoch). On the other hand, year_month_day, for example, is a *field-based type*, it stores a year, a month, and a day in separate fields. When doing a lot of arithmetic with dates, a serial-based type will be more performant than a field-based type.

Similar type aliases exist to work with local time: local_time, local_seconds, and local_days. These are demonstrated in a later section on time zones.

You can create a sys_days representing today as follows. floor() is used to truncate a time_point to a precision of days:

```
auto today { floor<days>(system_clock::now()) };
```

sys_days can be used to convert a year_month_day to a time_point, for example:

```
system_clock::time_point t1 { sys_days { 2020y / June / 22d } };
```

The opposite conversion, converting a time_point to a year_month_day, can be done with a year_month_day constructor. The following code snippet gives two examples:

```
year_month_day yearmonthday { floor<days>(t1) };
year_month_day today2 { floor<days>(system_clock::now()) };
```

A complete date including a time can be build up as well. Here's an example:

```
// Full date with time: 2020-06-22 09:35:10 UTC.
auto t2 { sys_days { 2020y / June / 22d } + 9h + 35min + 10s };
```

Printing Dates

Dates can be written to streams using the familiar insertion operator:

```
cout << yearmonthday << endl;
```

Printing and formatting dates are also supported. The L format specifier formats the output according to the current global locale.

```
println("{:L}", yearmonthday);
```

Keep in mind that the output might sometimes be unexpected. For example, lastMondayOfJune2020 is defined earlier as follows:

```
// Create a year_month_weekday_last for the last Monday of June 2020.
auto lastMondayOfJune2020 { 2020y / June / Monday[last] };
```

When you print this, the output is "2020/Jun/Mon[last]":

```
println("{:L}", lastMondayOfJune2020);    // 2020/Jun/Mon[last]
```

If you want to output the exact date, "2020-06-29," then you need to convert the year_month_weekday_last to a year_month_day and then output the result:

```
year_month_day lastMondayOfJune2020YMD { sys_days { lastMondayOfJune2020 } };
println("{:L}", lastMondayOfJune2020YMD);  // 2020-06-29
```

If a date is invalid, printing will insert an error. For example, the string "is not a valid date" is appended to an invalid year_month_day.

Using the L format specifier, names of days and months are correctly localized according to the current global locale. For example, the following code snippet first sets the global locale to Dutch, nl-NL, and then uses the L format specifier to print Monday in Dutch. The %A format specifier causes the full name to be printed instead of the abbreviated name. Consult your favorite Standard Library reference for a full list of all supported date format specifiers.

```
locale::global(locale { "nl-NL" });
println("Monday in Dutch is {:L%A}", Monday);
```

The output is:

```
Monday in Dutch is maandag
```

Arithmetic with Dates

You can perform arithmetic with dates. Here's an example:

```
// Full date with time: 2020-06-22 09:35:10 UTC.
auto t2 { sys_days { 2020y / June / 22d } + 9h + 35min + 10s };
auto t3 { t2 + days { 5 } };     // Add 5 days to t2.
auto t4 { t3 + years { 1 } };    // Add 1 year to t3.
```

Be careful, though, as the result might not always be as expected. For example:

```
auto t5 { sys_days { 2020y / June / 22d } + 9h + 35min + 10s };
auto t6 { t5 + years { 1 } };    // Add 1 year to t5
println("t5 = {:L}", t5);
println("t6 = {:L}", t6);
```

The result is as follows:

```
t5 = 2020-06-22 09:35:10
t6 = 2021-06-22 15:24:22
```

In looking at the results, you can see that the year is updated, but you can also see that the time has changed. The issue here is that we are working with a serial type: sys_days is a time_point, which is a serial type. Adding 1 year to such a serial type does not add 86,400 * 365 = 31,536,000 seconds. Instead, the standard mandates that adding 1 year must add 1 **average year** to keep leap years into account, and hence, it must add 86,400 * ((365 * 400) + 97) / 400 = 31,556,952 seconds.

If you need to add exactly 1 year, then it's best to use a field-based type instead, for example:

```
// Split t5 into days and remaining seconds.
sys_days t5_days { time_point_cast<days>(t5) };
seconds t5_seconds { t5 - t5_days };
// Convert the t5_days serial type to field-based type.
year_month_day t5_ymd { t5_days };
```

```
// Add 1 year.
year_month_day t7_ymd { t5_ymd + years { 1 } };
// Convert back to a serial type.
auto t7 { sys_days { t7_ymd } + t5_seconds };
println("t7 = {:L}", t7);
```

This results in:

```
t7 = 2021-06-22 09:35:10
```

TIME ZONE

To facilitate working with time zones, the C++ Standard Library contains a copy of the Internet Assigned Numbers Authority (IANA) time zone database (`www.iana.org/time-zones`). You can get access to this database by calling `std::chrono::get_tzdb()`, which returns a reference-to-`const` to a single existing instance of type `std::chrono::tzdb`. This database gives access to all known time zones through a public `vector` called `zones`. Each entry in this `vector` is a `time_zone`, which has a name, accessible with `name()`, and member functions `to_sys()` and `to_local()` to convert a `local_time` to a `sys_time`, and vice versa. Due to daylight saving time, it could be that a conversion from `local_time` to `sys_time` is either ambiguous or nonexistent. In such cases, the conversion throws an exception of type `ambiguous_local_time` or `nonexistent_local_time`, respectively.

Here is a code snippet listing all available time zones:

```
const auto& database { get_tzdb() };
for (const auto& timezone : database.zones) {
    println("{}", timezone.name());
}
```

The `std::chrono::locate_zone()` function can be used to retrieve a `time_zone` based on its name and throws a `runtime_error` exception if the requested time zone cannot be found in the database. The `current_zone()` function can be used to get the current time zone. For example:

```
auto* brussels { locate_zone("Europe/Brussels") };
auto* gmt { locate_zone("GMT") };
auto* current { current_zone() };
```

`time_zone` instances can be used to convert times between different zones:

```
// Convert current time (UTC), to time in Brussels, and time in current zone.
auto nowUTC { system_clock::now() };                        // In UTC.
auto nowInBrussels { brussels->to_local(nowUTC) };          // In Brussels' time zone.
auto nowInCurrentZone { current->to_local(nowUTC) }; // In current time zone.
println("Now UTC:          {:L%c}", nowUTC);
println("Now Brussels:     {:L%c}", nowInBrussels);
println("Now in current: {:L%c}", nowInCurrentZone);

// Construct a UTC time. (2020-06-22 09:35:10 UTC)
auto t { sys_days { 2020y / June / 22d } + 9h + 35min + 10s };
// Convert UTC time to Brussels' local time.
auto converted { brussels->to_local(t) };
println("Converted: {:L}", converted);
```

The `zoned_time` class is used to represent a `time_point` in a specific `time_zone`. The following snippet constructs a specific time in the Brussels' time zone and then converts it to New York time:

```
// Construct a local time in the Brussels' time zone.
zoned_time<hours> brusselsTime{ brussels, local_days { 2020y / June / 22d } + 9h };
// Convert to New York time.
zoned_time<hours> newYorkTime { "America/New_York", brusselsTime };
println("Brussels: {:L}", brusselsTime.get_local_time());
println("New York: {:L}", newYorkTime.get_local_time());
```

SUMMARY

This chapter discussed how to use the `ratio` class template to define and work with compile-time rational numbers. You also learned how to work with durations, clocks, time points, dates, and time zones provided by the C++ Standard Library through the chrono library.

The next chapter focusses on the functionality provided by the Standard Library to generate random numbers.

EXERCISES

By solving the following exercises, you can practice the material discussed in this chapter. Solutions to all exercises are available with the code download on the book's website at `www.wiley.com/go/proc++6e`. However, if you are stuck on an exercise, first reread parts of this chapter to try to find an answer yourself before looking at the solution from the website.

Exercise 22-1: Let's play a bit with durations. Create a duration, `d1`, with a precision of seconds, initialized to 42 seconds. Create a second duration, `d2`, with a precision of minutes, initialized to 1.5 minutes. Calculate the sum of `d1` and `d2`. Write out the result to the standard output, once expressed in seconds, once expressed in minutes.

Exercise 22-2: Ask the user to enter a date as yyyy-mm-dd, for example, 2020-06-22. Use a regular expression (see Chapter 21) to extract the year, month, and day components, and finally, use `year_month_day` to validate the date.

Exercise 22-3: Write a `getNumberOfDaysBetweenDates()` function that calculates the number of days between two given dates. Test your implementation in your `main()` function.

Exercise 22-4: Write a program that prints out the day of the week of June 22, 2020.

Exercise 22-5: Construct a UTC time. Convert this time to the local time in Tokyo, Japan. Further convert the resulting time to New York time. And finally convert the resulting time to GMT. Verify that the original UTC time and the final GMT time are equal. Tip: The time zone identifier for Tokyo is Asia/Tokyo, for New York it is America/New_York, and for GMT it is GMT.

Exercise 22-6: Write a `getDurationSinceMidnight()` function that returns the duration between midnight and the current local time in seconds. Use your function to print out the number of seconds since midnight to the standard output console. Finally, use the `hh_mm_ss` class to convert the duration returned by your function to hours, minutes, and seconds, and print the result on standard output.

23

Random Number Facilities

WHAT'S IN THIS CHAPTER?

- The concepts of random number engines and engine adapters
- How to generate random numbers
- How to change the distribution of random numbers

WILEY.COM DOWNLOADS FOR THIS CHAPTER

Please note that all the code examples for this chapter are available as part of this chapter's code download on the book's website at `www.wiley.com/go/proc++6e` on the Download Code tab.

This chapter discusses how to generate random numbers in C++. Generating good random numbers in software is a complex topic. This chapter does not discuss the complex mathematical formulas involved in generating the actual random numbers; however, it does explain how to generate random numbers using the functionality provided by the Standard Library.

The C++ random number generation library can generate random numbers by using different algorithms and distributions. The library is defined by `<random>` in the `std` namespace. It has three big components: *engines*, *engine adapters*, and *distributions*. A random number *engine* is responsible for generating the actual random numbers and storing the state for generating subsequent random numbers. The *distribution* determines the range of the generated random numbers and how they are mathematically distributed within that range. A random number *engine adapter* modifies the results of a random number engine you associate it with.

Before delving into this C++ random number generation library, the old C-style mechanism of generating random numbers and its problems are briefly explained.

C-STYLE RANDOM NUMBER GENERATION

Before C++11, you could generate random numbers using the C-style `srand()` and `rand()` functions. The `srand()` function had to be called once in your application and was used to initialize the random number generator, also called *seeding*. Usually, the current system time would be used as a seed.

> **WARNING** *You need to make sure that you use a good-quality seed for your software-based random number generator. If you initialize the random number generator with the same seed every time, you will create the same sequence of random numbers every time. This is why the seed is usually the current system time.*

Once the generator is initialized, random numbers could be generated with `rand()`. The following example shows how to use `srand()` and `rand()`. The `time()` function, defined in `<ctime>`, returns the system time, usually encoded as the number of seconds since the system's epoch. The epoch represents the beginning of time.

```
srand(static_cast<unsigned int>(time(nullptr)));
println("{}", rand());
```

A random number within a certain range could be generated with the following function:

```
int getRandom(int min, int max)
{
    return static_cast<int>(rand() % (max + 1UL - min)) + min;
}
```

The old C-style `rand()` function generates random numbers in the range 0 to `RAND_MAX`, which is defined by the standard to be at least 32,767. You cannot generate random numbers larger than `RAND_MAX`. On some systems, for example GCC, `RAND_MAX` is 2,147,483,647, which equals the maximum value of a signed integer. To prevent arithmetic overflow on such systems, the formula in `getRandom()` uses `unsigned long` calculations, due to the use of `1UL` instead of just `1`.

Additionally, the low-order bits of `rand()` are often not very random, which means that using the previous `getRandom()` function to generate a random number in a small range, such as 1 to 6, will not result in good randomness.

> **NOTE** *Software-based random number generators can never generate truly random numbers. They are therefore called pseudorandom number generators (PRNGs) because they rely on mathematical formulas to give the impression of randomness.*

Besides generating bad-quality random numbers, the old `srand()` and `rand()` functions don't offer much in terms of flexibility either. You cannot, for example, change the distribution of the generated random numbers. In conclusion, it's highly recommended to stop using `srand()` and `rand()` and start using the classes from `<random>` explained in the upcoming sections.

RANDOM NUMBER ENGINES

The first component of the modern C++ random number generation library is a *random number engine*, responsible for generating the actual random numbers. As mentioned, everything is defined in `<random>`.

The following random number engines are available:

- `random_device`
- `linear_congruential_engine`
- `mersenne_twister_engine`
- `subtract_with_carry_engine`

The `random_device` engine is not a software-based generator; it is a special engine that requires a piece of hardware attached to your computer that generates truly non-deterministic random numbers, for example, by using the laws of physics. A classic mechanism measures the decay of a radioactive isotope by counting alpha-particles-per-time-interval, but there are many other kinds of physics-based random-number generators, including measuring the "noise" of reverse-biased diodes (thus eliminating the concerns about radioactive sources in your computer). The details of these mechanisms fall outside the scope of this book. If no such device is attached to the computer, `random_device` is free to use one of the software algorithms. The choice of algorithm is up to the library designer. Luckily, most modern computers have proper support for a true `random_device`.

The quality of a random number generator is measured by its *entropy*. The `entropy()` member function of the `random_device` engine returns 0.0 if it is using a software-based pseudorandom number generator and returns a non-zero value if it is using a hardware device. The non-zero value is an estimate of the entropy of the hardware device.

Using a `random_device` engine is straightforward:

```
random_device rnd;
println("Entropy: {}", rnd.entropy());
println("Min value: {}, Max value: {}", rnd.min(), rnd.max());
println("Random number: {}", rnd());
```

A possible output of this program could be as follows:

```
Entropy: 32
Min value: 0, Max value: 4294967295
Random number: 3590924439
```

A `random_device` is much slower than a pseudorandom number engine. Therefore, if you need to generate a lot of random numbers, use a pseudorandom number engine and generate a seed for it with a `random_device`. This is demonstrated in the section "Generating Random Numbers" later in this chapter.

Next to the `random_device` engine, there are three pseudorandom number engines:

- **Linear congruential engine:** Requires a minimal amount of memory to store its state. The state is a single integer containing the last generated random number or the initial seed if no random number has been generated yet. The period of this engine depends on an algorithmic parameter and can be up to 2^{64} but is usually less. For this reason, the linear congruential engine should not be used when you need high-quality random numbers.

- **Mersenne twister:** Of the three pseudorandom number engines, this one generates the highest quality of random numbers. The period of a Mersenne twister is a Mersenne prime, which is a prime number one less than a power of two. This period is much bigger than the period of a linear congruential engine. The memory required to store the state of a Mersenne twister also depends on its parameters but is much larger than the single integer state of the linear congruential engine. For example, the predefined Mersenne twister `mt19937` has a period of $2^{19937}-1$, while the state contains 625 integers or 2.5 kilobytes. It is also one of the fastest engines.
- **Subtract with carry engine:** Requires a state of around 100 bytes; however, the quality of the generated random numbers is less than that of the numbers generated by the Mersenne twister, and it is also slower than the Mersenne twister.

The mathematical details of the engines and of the quality of random numbers fall outside the scope of this book. If you want to know more about these topics, you can consult a reference from the "Random Numbers" section in Appendix B, "Annotated Bibliography."

The `random_device` engine is easy to use and doesn't require any parameters. However, creating an instance of one of the three pseudorandom number generators requires you to specify a number of mathematical parameters, which can be daunting. The selection of parameters greatly influences the quality of the generated random numbers. For example, the definition of the `mersenne_twister_engine` class template looks like this:

```
template<class UIntType, size_t w, size_t n, size_t m, size_t r,
        UIntType a, size_t u, UIntType d, size_t s,
        UIntType b, size_t t, UIntType c, size_t l, UIntType f>
    class mersenne_twister_engine {...}
```

It requires 14 parameters. The `linear_congruential_engine` and `subtract_with_carry_engine` class templates also require a number of such mathematical parameters. For this reason, the standard defines a couple of predefined engines. One example is the `mt19937` Mersenne twister, which is defined as follows:

```
using mt19937 = mersenne_twister_engine<uint_fast32_t, 32, 624, 397, 31,
    0x9908b0df, 11, 0xffffffff, 7, 0x9d2c5680, 15, 0xefc60000, 18,
    1812433253>;
```

These parameters are all magic, unless you understand the details of the Mersenne twister algorithm. In general, you do not want to modify any of these parameters unless you are an expert in the mathematics of pseudorandom number generators. Instead, I recommend using the predefined type aliases such as `mt19937`. A complete list of predefined engines is given in a later section.

RANDOM NUMBER ENGINE ADAPTERS

A random number engine adapter modifies the result of a random number engine you associate it with, which is called the *base engine*. This is an example of the *adapter pattern* (see Chapter 33, "Applying design patterns"). The following three adapter templates are defined:

```
template<class Engine, size_t p, size_t r> class discard_block_engine {...}
```

```
template<class Engine, size_t w, class UIntT> class independent_bits_engine {...}
template<class Engine, size_t k> class shuffle_order_engine {...}
```

The `discard_block_engine` adapter generates random numbers by discarding some of the values generated by its base engine. It requires three parameters: the engine to adapt, the block size *p*, and the used block size *r*. The base engine is used to generate *p* random numbers. The adapter then discards *p-r* of those numbers and returns the remaining *r* numbers.

The `independent_bits_engine` adapter generates random numbers with a given number of bits *w* by combining several random numbers generated by the base engine.

The `shuffle_order_engine` adapter generates the same random numbers that are generated by the base engine but delivers them in a different order. The template parameter `k` is the size of an internal table used by the adapter. A random number is randomly selected from this table upon request, and then replaced with a new random number generated by the base engine.

Just as with random number engines, a number of predefined engine adapters are available. The next section gives an overview of the predefined engines and engine adapters.

PREDEFINED ENGINES AND ENGINE ADAPTERS

As mentioned earlier, it is not recommended to specify your own parameters for pseudorandom number engines and engine adapters, but instead to use one of the standard ones. The C++ Standard Library defines the following predefined generators, all in `<random>`. They all have complicated template arguments, but it is not necessary to understand those arguments to be able to use them.

PREDEFINED GENERATOR	CLASS TEMPLATE
`minstd_rand0`	`linear_congruential_engine`
`minstd_rand`	`linear_congruential_engine`
`mt19937`	`mersenne_twister_engine`
`mt19937_64`	`mersenne_twister_engine`
`ranlux24_base`	`subtract_with_carry_engine`
`ranlux48_base`	`subtract_with_carry_engine`
`ranlux24`	`discard_block_engine`
`ranlux48`	`discard_block_engine`
`knuth_b`	`shuffle_order_engine`
`default_random_engine`	*Implementation-defined*

The `default_random_engine` is compiler dependent.

The following section gives an example of how to use these predefined engines.

GENERATING RANDOM NUMBERS

Before you can generate any random number, you first need to create an instance of an engine. If you use a software-based engine, you also need to define a distribution. A distribution is a mathematical formula describing how numbers are distributed within a certain range. The recommended way to create an engine is to use one of the predefined engines discussed in the previous section.

The following example uses the predefined engine called `mt19937`, using a Mersenne twister engine. This is a software-based generator. Just as with the old `rand()` generator, a software-based engine must be initialized with a seed. The seed used with `srand()` was often the current time. In modern C++, it's recommended to use a `random_device` to generate a seed. Here is an example:

```
random_device seeder;
mt19937 engine { seeder() };
```

As mentioned earlier, most modern systems have a `random_device` implementation with proper entropy. If you are not sure that the `random_device` implementation on the system your code will be running on has proper entropy, then you can use a time-based seed as a fallback:

```
random_device seeder;
const auto seed { seeder.entropy() ? seeder() : time(nullptr) };
mt19937 engine { static_cast<mt19937::result_type>(seed) };
```

Next, a distribution is defined. This example uses a uniform integer distribution, for the range 1 to 99. Distributions are explained in detail in the next section, but this uniform distribution is easy enough to use for this example:

```
uniform_int_distribution<int> distribution { 1, 99 };
```

Once the engine and distribution are defined, random numbers can be generated by calling the function call operator of the distribution and passing the engine as an argument. For this example, this is written as `distribution(engine)`:

```
println("{}", distribution(engine));
```

As you can see, to generate a random number using a software-based engine, you always need to specify the engine and distribution. The `std::bind()` utility, introduced in Chapter 19, "Function Pointers, Function Objects, and Lambda Expressions," can be used to remove the need to specify both the distribution and the engine when generating a random number. The following example uses the same `mt19937` engine and uniform distribution as the previous example, but it defines `generator` by using `std::bind()` to bind `engine` as the first argument to `distribution()`. This way, you can call `generator()` without any arguments to generate a random number. The example then demonstrates the use of `generator()` in combination with the constrained `ranges::generate()` algorithm to fill a `vector` of ten elements with random numbers. The `generate()` algorithm is discussed in Chapter 20, "Mastering Standard Library Algorithms."

```
auto generator { bind(distribution, engine) };

vector<int> values(10);
ranges::generate(values, generator);

println("{:n}", values);
```

> **NOTE** *Remember that the* `generate()` *algorithm overwrites existing elements and does not insert new elements. This means you first need to size the* `vector` *to hold the number of elements you need and then call the* `generate()` *algorithm. The previous example sizes the* `vector` *by specifying the size as argument to the constructor.*

Even though you don't know the exact type of `generator`, it's still possible to pass `generator` to another function that wants to use that generator. You have several options: use a parameter of type `std::function<int()>` or use a function template. The previous example can be adapted to generate random numbers in a function called `fillVector()`. Here is an implementation using `std::function`:

```
void fillVector(vector<int>& values, const function<int()>& generator)
{
    ranges::generate(values, generator);
}
```

Here is a constrained function template variant:

```
template <invocable T>
void fillVector(vector<int>& values, const T& generator)
{
    ranges::generate(values, generator);
}
```

This can be simplified using the abbreviated function template syntax:

```
void fillVector(vector<int>& values, const auto& generator)
{
    ranges::generate(values, generator);
}
```

Finally, this function can be used as follows:

```
vector<int> values(10);
fillVector(values, generator);
```

> **WARNING** *The random number generators are not thread safe. If you need to generate random numbers in multiple threads, you should create a generator in each thread and not share one generator among multiple threads. Chapter 27, "Multithreaded Programming with C++," introduces multithreading.*

RANDOM NUMBER DISTRIBUTIONS

A distribution is a mathematical formula describing how numbers are distributed within a certain range. The random number generator library comes with the following distributions that can be used with pseudorandom number engines to define the distribution of the generated random numbers. It's a compacted representation. The first line of each distribution is the name and class template parameters, if any. The next lines are a constructor for the distribution. Only one constructor for each distribution is shown to give you an idea of the class. Consult a Standard Library Reference (see Appendix B) for a detailed list of all constructors and member functions of each distribution.

These are the available uniform distributions:

```
template<class IntType = int> class uniform_int_distribution
    uniform_int_distribution(IntType a = 0,
                             IntType b = numeric_limits<IntType>::max());
template<class RealType = double> class uniform_real_distribution
    uniform_real_distribution(RealType a = 0.0, RealType b = 1.0);
```

These are the available Bernoulli distributions (the first one generates random Boolean values, while the last three generate random non-negative integer values, all of them according to the discrete probability distribution):

```
class bernoulli_distribution
    bernoulli_distribution(double p = 0.5);
template<class IntType = int> class binomial_distribution
    binomial_distribution(IntType t = 1, double p = 0.5);
template<class IntType = int> class geometric_distribution
    geometric_distribution(double p = 0.5);
template<class IntType = int> class negative_binomial_distribution
    negative_binomial_distribution(IntType k = 1, double p = 0.5);
```

These are the available Poisson distributions (generate random non-negative integer values according to the discrete probability distribution):

```
template<class IntType = int> class poisson_distribution
    poisson_distribution(double mean = 1.0);
template<class RealType = double> class exponential_distribution
    exponential_distribution(RealType lambda = 1.0);
template<class RealType = double> class gamma_distribution
    gamma_distribution(RealType alpha = 1.0, RealType beta = 1.0);
template<class RealType = double> class weibull_distribution
    weibull_distribution(RealType a = 1.0, RealType b = 1.0);
template<class RealType = double> class extreme_value_distribution
    extreme_value_distribution(RealType a = 0.0, RealType b = 1.0);
```

These are the available normal distributions:

```
template<class RealType = double> class normal_distribution
    normal_distribution(RealType mean = 0.0, RealType stddev = 1.0);
template<class RealType = double> class lognormal_distribution
    lognormal_distribution(RealType m = 0.0, RealType s = 1.0);
template<class RealType = double> class chi_squared_distribution
    chi_squared_distribution(RealType n = 1);
template<class RealType = double> class cauchy_distribution
    cauchy_distribution(RealType a = 0.0, RealType b = 1.0);
template<class RealType = double> class fisher_f_distribution
    fisher_f_distribution(RealType m = 1, RealType n = 1);
template<class RealType = double> class student_t_distribution
    student_t_distribution(RealType n = 1);
```

These are the available sampling distributions:

```
template<class IntType = int> class discrete_distribution
    discrete_distribution(initializer_list<double> wl);
template<class RealType = double> class piecewise_constant_distribution
    template<class UnaryOperation>
        piecewise_constant_distribution(initializer_list<RealType> bl,
            UnaryOperation fw);
template<class RealType = double> class piecewise_linear_distribution
    template<class UnaryOperation>
        piecewise_linear_distribution(initializer_list<RealType> bl,
            UnaryOperation fw);
```

Each distribution requires a set of parameters. As before, explaining all these mathematical parameters is outside the scope of this book. The rest of this section includes a couple of examples to explain the impact of a distribution on the generated random numbers.

Distributions are easiest to understand when you look at a graphical representation of them. The following code generates one million random numbers between 1 and 99 and keeps track of how many times a certain number is randomly generated in a histogram. The counters are stored in a `map` where the key is a number between 1 and 99, and the value associated with a key is the number of times that that key has been selected randomly. After the loop, the results are written to a semicolon-separated values file (CSV), which can be opened in a spreadsheet application.

```
const unsigned int Start { 1 };
const unsigned int End { 99 };
const unsigned int Iterations { 1'000'000 };

// Uniform distributed Mersenne Twister.
random_device seeder;
mt19937 engine { seeder() };
uniform_int_distribution<int> distribution { Start, End };
auto generator { bind(distribution, engine) };
map<int, int> histogram;
for (unsigned int i { 0 }; i < Iterations; ++i) {
    int randomNumber { generator() };
    // Search map for a key=randomNumber. If found, add 1 to the value associated
    // with that key. If not found, add the key to the map with value 1.
    ++(histogram[randomNumber]);
}

// Write to a CSV file.
ofstream of { "res.csv" };
for (unsigned int i { Start }; i <= End; ++i) {
    of << i << ";" << histogram[i] << endl;
}
```

The resulting data can then be used to generate a graphical representation. Figure 23.1 shows a graph of the generated histogram.

The horizontal axis represents the range in which random numbers are generated. The graph clearly shows that all numbers in the range 1 to 99 are randomly chosen around 10,000 times and that the distribution of the generated random numbers is uniform across the entire range.

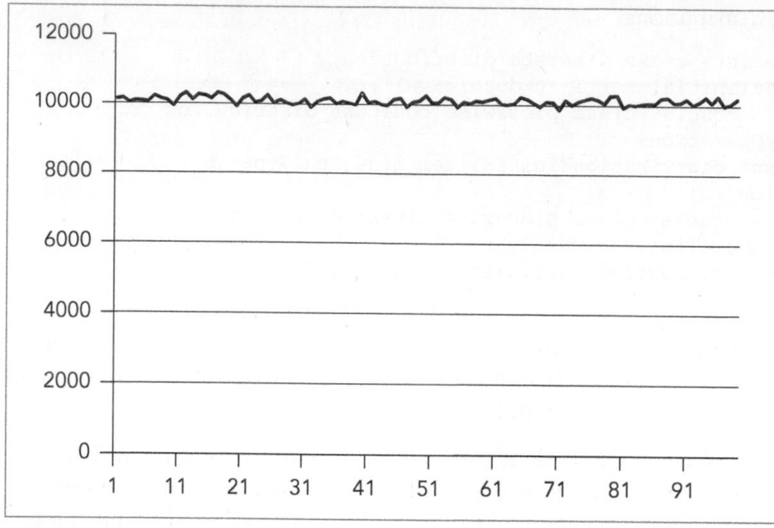

FIGURE 23.1

The example can be modified to generate random numbers according to a normal distribution instead of a uniform distribution. Only two small changes are required. First, you need to modify the creation of the distribution as follows:

```
normal_distribution<double> distribution { 50, 10 };
```

Because normal distributions use `doubles` instead of integers, you also need to modify the call to `generator()`:

```
int randomNumber { static_cast<int>(generator()) };
```

Figure 23.2 shows a graphical representation of the random numbers generated according to this normal distribution.

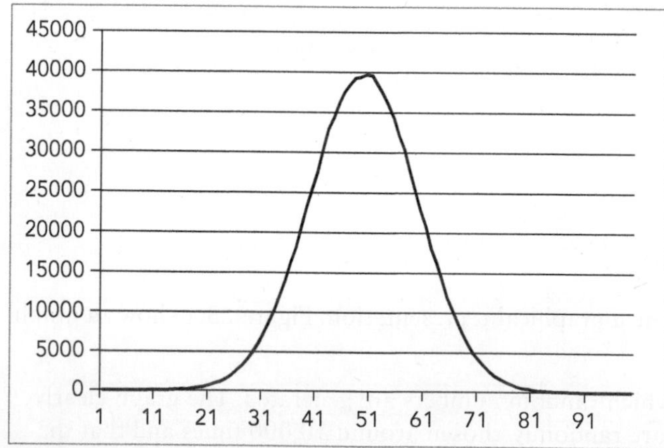

FIGURE 23.2

The graph clearly shows that most of the generated random numbers are around the center of the range. In this example, the value 50 is randomly chosen around 40,000 times, while values like 20 and 80 are chosen only around 500 times.

SUMMARY

In this chapter, you learned how to use the C++ random number generation library provided by the Standard Library to generate good-quality random numbers. You also saw how you can change the distribution of the generated numbers over a given range.

The next chapter is the last chapter of Part 3 of the book and introduces a number of additional vocabulary types that you will use often in your day-to-day coding.

EXERCISES

By solving the following exercises, you can practice the material discussed in this chapter. Solutions to all exercises are available with the code download on the book's website at `www.wiley.com/go/proc++6e`. However, if you are stuck on an exercise, first reread parts of this chapter to try to find an answer yourself before looking at the solution from the website.

Exercise 23-1: Write a loop asking the user if dice should be thrown or not. If yes, throw a die twice using a uniform distribution and print the two numbers on the screen. If no, stop the program. Use the standard `mt19937` Mersenne twister engine. Do not create your random number generator directly in the function where you need it. Instead, write a function `createDiceValueGenerator()` that creates the correct random number generator object and returns it.

Exercise 23-2: Modify your solution to Exercise 23-1 to use a `ranlux48` engine instead of the Mersenne twister.

Exercise 23-3: Modify your solution to Exercise 23-1. Instead of directly using the `mt19937` Mersenne twister engine, adapt the engine with a `shuffle_order_engine` adapter.

Exercise 23-4: Take the source code from earlier in this chapter used to generate histograms to make graphs of a distribution and experiment a bit with different distributions. Try to plot the graphs in a spreadsheet application to see the effects of a distribution. The code can be found in the downloadable source code archive in the folder `Ch23\01_Random`. You can take either the `07_uniform_int_distribution.cpp` or the `08_normal_distribution.cpp` file depending on whether your distribution uses integers or doubles.

Bonus: Besides exporting the data to a CSV file, draw the histogram on the standard output console using characters.

24

Additional Vocabulary Types

WHAT'S IN THIS CHAPTER?

- What vocabulary types are
- How to use the `variant` and `any` data types
- What tuples are and how to use them
- How to use monadic operations with `optional`
- How to represent a value or an error using `expected`

WILEY.COM DOWNLOADS FOR THIS CHAPTER

Please note that all the code examples for this chapter are available as part of this chapter's code download on the book's website at `www.wiley.com/go/proc++6e` on the Download Code tab.

Vocabulary types are types that you are likely to use all the time, just as much as primitive types such as `int` and `double`. They are often used to build more complex types. Using vocabulary types makes your code safer, more efficient, and easier to write, read, and maintain. Examples of vocabulary types discussed earlier in this book are `vector`, `optional`, `string`, `unique_ptr`, `shared_ptr`, and so on.

This chapter starts the discussion with two additional vocabulary types: `variant` and `any`. It then continues with a more in-depth discussion of `tuples`, a generalization of `pairs`, and their operations. Next is monadic operation support for `optionals`, which makes chaining operations on `optionals` so much easier. This is because you won't have to verify whether an `optional` is empty before applying a next operation on it. The chapter finishes with a discussion of `expected`, which is a data type capable of storing either a value of an expected type or an error value. The type used to represent the error can be different than the type of the value.

VARIANT

`std::variant`, defined in `<variant>`, can hold a single value of one of a given set of types. When you define a `variant`, you must specify the types it can potentially contain. For example, the following code defines a `variant` that can contain an integer, a string, or a floating-point value, but only one at a time:

```
variant<int, string, float> v;
```

The template type arguments for a `variant` must be unique; for example, `variant<int,int>` is invalid. A default-constructed `variant` contains a default-constructed value of its first type, `int` in the case of the `variant v`. If you want to be able to default construct a `variant`, you must make sure that the first type of the `variant` is default constructible. For example, the following does not compile because `Foo` is not default constructible:

```
class Foo { public: Foo() = delete; Foo(int) {} };
class Bar { public: Bar() = delete; Bar(int) {} };
...
variant<Foo, Bar> v;
```

In fact, neither `Foo` nor `Bar` is default constructible. If you still want to be able to default construct such a `variant`, then you can use `std::monostate`, a well-behaved empty alternative, as the first type of the `variant`:

```
variant<monostate, Foo, Bar> v;
```

You can use the assignment operator to store something in a `variant`:

```
variant<int, string, float> v;
v = 12;
v = 12.5f;
v = "An std::string"s;
```

A `variant` can contain only one value at any given time. So, with these three assignment statements, first the integer 12 is stored in the `variant`, then the `variant` is modified to contain a single floating-point value, and lastly, the `variant` is modified again to contain a single `string` value.

You can use the `index()` member function to get the zero-based index of the value's type that is currently stored in the `variant`, and you can use the `std::holds_alternative()` function template to figure out whether a `variant` currently contains a value of a certain type:

```
println("Type index: {}", v.index());
println("Contains an int: {}", holds_alternative<int>(v));
```

The output is as follows:

```
Type index: 1
Contains an int: false
```

Use `std::get<index>()` or `get<T>()` to retrieve the value from a `variant`, where *`index`* is the zero-based index of the type you want to retrieve, and *`T`* is the type you want to retrieve. These functions throw a `bad_variant_access` exception if you are using the index of a type, or a type, that does not match the current value in the `variant`:

```
println("{}", get<string>(v));
try {
```

```
        println("{}", get<0>(v));
    } catch (const bad_variant_access& ex) {
        println("Exception: {}", ex.what());
    }
```

This is the output:

```
An std::string
Exception: bad variant access
```

To avoid exceptions, use the `std::get_if<index>()` or `get_if<T>()` helper function. These functions accept a pointer to a `variant` and return a pointer to the requested value, or `nullptr` on error:

```
string* theString { get_if<string>(&v) };
int* theInt { get_if<int>(&v) };
println("Retrieved string: {}", (theString ? *theString : "n/a"));
println("Retrieved int: {}", (theInt ? to_string(*theInt) : "n/a"));
```

Here is the output:

```
Retrieved string: An std::string
Retrieved int: n/a
```

An `std::visit()` helper function is available that you can use to apply the *visitor pattern* to a `variant`. A visitor has to be a callable, e.g., a function, a lambda expression, or a function object, that can accept any type that may be stored in the `variant`. A first example just uses a generic lambda, which can accept any type, as the callable passed as the first argument to `visit()`:

```
visit([](auto&& value) { println("Value = {}", value); }, v);
```

The output is as follows:

```
Value = An std::string
```

If you want to handle each type stored in the `variant` in a different way, then you can write your own visitor class. Suppose you have the following visitor class that defines a number of overloaded function call operators, one for each possible type in the `variant`. This implementation marks all its function call operators as `static` (possible since C++23), as they don't require access to any non-`static` member functions or data members of `MyVisitor`.

```
class MyVisitor
{
    public:
        static void operator()(int i)                  { println("int: {}", i); }
        static void operator()(const string& s) { println("string: {}", s); }
        static void operator()(float f)               { println("float: {}", f); }
};
```

You can use this with `std::visit()` as follows:

```
visit(MyVisitor{}, v);
```

The result is that the appropriate overloaded function call operator is called based on the current value stored in the `variant`. The output for this example is as follows:

```
string: An std::string
```

A `variant` cannot store an array, and as with `optional` introduced in Chapter 1, "A Crash Course in C++ and the Standard Library," it cannot store references. You can store either pointers or instances of `reference_wrapper<T>` or `reference_wrapper<const T>` (see Chapter 18, "Standard Library Containers").

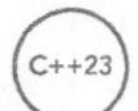

> **NOTE** *Starting with C++23,* `variant` *is a* `constexpr` *class, so it can be used at compile time. See Chapter 9, "Mastering Classes and Objects," for more on* `constexpr` *classes.*

ANY

`std::any`, defined in `<any>`, is a class that can contain a single value of any type. You can create an instance with an `any` constructor or with the `std::make_any()` helper function. Once it is constructed, you can ask an `any` instance whether it contains a value and what the type of the contained value is. To get access to the contained value, you need to use `any_cast()`, which throws an exception of type `bad_any_cast` in the case of failure. Here is an example:

```
any empty;
any anInt { 3 };
any aString { "An std::string."s };

println("empty.has_value = {}", empty.has_value());
println("anInt.has_value = {}\n", anInt.has_value());

println("anInt wrapped type = {}", anInt.type().name());
println("aString wrapped type = {}\n", aString.type().name());

int theInt { any_cast<int>(anInt) };
println("{}", theInt);
try {
    int test { any_cast<int>(aString) };
    println("{}", test);
} catch (const bad_any_cast& ex) {
    println("Exception: {}", ex.what());
}
```

The output is as follows. Note that the wrapped type of `aString` is compiler dependent.

```
empty.has_value = false
anInt.has_value = true

anInt wrapped type = int
aString wrapped type = class std::basic_string<char,struct std::char_
traits<char>,class std::allocator<char>>

3
Exception: Bad any_cast
```

You can assign a new value to an `any` instance and even assign a new value of a different type:

```
any something { 3 };              // Now it contains an integer.
something = "An std::string"s;    // Now the same instance contains a string.
```

Instances of any can be stored in Standard Library containers. This allows you to have heterogeneous data in a single container. The only downside is that you have to perform explicit any_casts to retrieve specific values, as the following example demonstrates:

```
vector<any> v;
v.push_back(42);
v.push_back("An std::string"s);

println("{}", any_cast<string>(v[1]));
```

As with optional and variant, you cannot store references in an any instance. You can again store either pointers or instances of reference_wrapper<T> or reference_wrapper<const T>.

TUPLE

The std::pair class, defined in <utility> and introduced in Chapter 1, can store exactly two values, each with a specific type. The type of each value must be known at compile time. Here is a short reminder:

```
pair<int, string> p1 { 16, "Hello World" };
pair p2 { true, 0.123f };  // Using CTAD.
println("p1 = ({}, {})", p1.first, p1.second);
println("p2 = ({}, {})", p2.first, p2.second);
```

The output is as follows:

```
p1 = (16, Hello World)
p2 = (true, 0.123)
```

Starting with C++23, std::format() and the print() functions have full support for pairs. For example, the two println() statements in the previous code snippet can be written as follows:

```
println("p1 = {}", p1);
println("p2 = {}", p2);
```

The output is as follows, with strings surrounded by double quotes:

```
p1 = (16, "Hello World")
p2 = (true, 0.123)
```

An std::tuple, defined in <tuple>, is a generalization of a pair. It allows you to store any number of values, each with its own specific type. Just like a pair, a tuple has a fixed size and fixed value types, which are determined at compile time.

A tuple can be created with a tuple constructor, specifying both the template types and the actual values. For example, the following code creates a tuple where the first element is an integer, the second element is a string, and the last element is a Boolean:

```
using MyTuple = tuple<int, string, bool>;
MyTuple t1 { 16, "Test", true };
```

Just as for pair, starting with C++23, std::format() and the print() functions fully support tuples:

```
println("t1 = {}", t1);
// Outputs: t1 = (16, "Test", true)
```

`std::get<i>()` is used to get the ith element from a `tuple`, where *i* is a zero-based index; that is, `<0>` is the first element of the tuple, `<1>` is the second element of the tuple, and so on. The value returned has the correct type for that index in the `tuple`:

```
println("t1 = ({}, {}, {})", get<0>(t1), get<1>(t1), get<2>(t1));
// Outputs: t1 = (16, Test, true)
```

You can check that `get<i>()` returns the correct type by using `typeid()`, from `<typeinfo>`. The output of the following code confirms that the value returned by `get<1>(t1)` is indeed an `std::string` (as mentioned before, the exact string returned by `typeid().name()` is compiler dependent):

```
println("Type of get<1>(t1) = {}", typeid(get<1>(t1)).name());
// Outputs: Type of get<1>(t1) = class std::basic_string<char,
//          struct std::char_traits<char>,class std::allocator<char> >
```

You can use the `std::tuple_element` class template to get the type of an element based on the element's index at compile time. `tuple_element` requires you to specify the type of the `tuple` (`MyTuple` in this case) and not an actual `tuple` instance like `t1`. Here is an example:

```
println("Type of element with index 2 = {}",
    typeid(tuple_element<2, MyTuple>::type).name());
// Outputs: Type of element with index 2 = bool
```

You can also retrieve an element from a tuple based on its type with `std::get<T>()`, where *T* is the type of the element you want to retrieve instead of the index. The compiler generates an error if the tuple has several elements with the requested type. For example, you can retrieve the `string` element from `t1` as follows:

```
println("String = {}", get<string>(t1));
// Outputs: String = Test
```

Iterating over the values of a `tuple` is unfortunately not straightforward. You cannot write a simple loop and call something like `get<i>(mytuple)` because the value of `i` must be known at compile time. A possible solution is to use template metaprogramming, which is discussed in detail in Chapter 26, "Advanced Templates," together with an example on how to print `tuple` values.

The size of a tuple can be queried with the `std::tuple_size` class template. As with `tuple_element`, `tuple_size` requires you to specify the type of the `tuple`, not an actual `tuple`:

```
println("Tuple Size = {}", tuple_size<MyTuple>::value);
// Outputs: Tuple Size = 3
```

If you don't know a `tuple`'s exact type, you can always use `decltype()` to query for its type as follows:

```
println("Tuple Size = {}", tuple_size<decltype(t1)>::value);
// Outputs: Tuple Size = 3
```

With class template argument deduction (CTAD) you can omit the template type parameters when constructing a `tuple` and let the compiler deduce them automatically based on the types of the arguments passed to the constructor. For example, the following defines the same `t1` `tuple` consisting of an integer, a `string`, and a Boolean. Note that you now have to specify `"Test"s` using the `s` string literal to make sure it's an `std::string`:

```
tuple t1 { 16, "Test"s, true };
```

With CTAD, you do not explicitly specify the types stored in a `tuple` and so you cannot use `&` to specify references. If you want to use CTAD to generate a `tuple` containing a reference-to-non-`const` or a reference-to-`const`, then you need to use `ref()` or `cref()`, respectively, both defined in `<functional>`. These create instances of `reference_wrapper<T>` or `reference_wrapper<const T>`. For example, the following statements result in a `tuple` of type `tuple<int, double&, const double&, string&>`:

```
double d { 3.14 };
string str1 { "Test" };
tuple t2 { 16, ref(d), cref(d), ref(str1) };
```

To test the `double` reference stored in `t2`, the following code first writes the value of the `double` variable to the console. The call to `get<1>(t2)` returns a reference to `d` because `ref(d)` is used for the second (index 1) `tuple` element. The second statement changes the value of the variable referenced, and the last statement shows that the value of `d` is indeed changed through the reference stored in the `tuple`. Note that the third line fails to compile because `cref(d)` is used for the third `tuple` element; that is, it is a reference-to-`const` to `d`:

```
println("d = {}", d);
get<1>(t2) *= 2;
//get<2>(t2) *= 2;     // ERROR because of cref().
println("d = {}", d);
// Outputs: d = 3.14
//          d = 6.28
```

Without class template argument deduction, you can use the `std::make_tuple()` function template to create a `tuple`. Since it is a function template, it supports function template argument deduction and hence also allows you to create a `tuple` by only specifying the actual values. The types are deduced automatically at compile time. Here's an example:

```
auto t2 { make_tuple(16, ref(d), cref(d), ref(str1)) };
```

Decompose Tuples

There are two ways in which you can *decompose* a `tuple` into its individual elements: structured bindings and `std::tie()`.

Structured Bindings

Structured bindings, available since C++17, make it easy to decompose a `tuple` into separate variables. For example, the following code defines a `tuple` consisting of an integer, a `string`, and a Boolean value, and then uses a structured binding to decompose it into three distinct variables:

```
tuple t1 { 16, "Test"s, true };
auto [i, str, b] { t1 };
println("Decomposed: i = {}, str = \"{}\", b = {}", i, str, b);
```

You can also decompose a `tuple` into references, allowing you to modify the contents of the `tuple` through those references. Here's an example:

```
auto& [i2, str2, b2] { t1 };
i2 *= 2;
str2 = "Hello World";
b2 = !b2;
```

With structured bindings, you cannot ignore specific elements while decomposing a `tuple`. If your `tuple` has three elements, then your structured binding needs three variables.

tie

If you want to decompose a `tuple` without structured bindings, you can use the `std::tie()` utility function, which generates a `tuple` of references. The following example first creates a `tuple` consisting of an integer, a `string`, and a Boolean value. It then creates three variables—an integer, a `string`, and a Boolean—and writes the values of those variables to the console. The `tie(i, str, b)` call creates a `tuple` containing a reference to `i`, a reference to `str`, and a reference to `b`. The assignment operator is used to assign `tuple t1` to the result of `tie()`. Because the result of `tie()` is a `tuple` of references, the assignment actually changes the values in the three separate variables, as is shown by the output of the values after the assignment:

```
tuple t1 { 16, "Test"s, true };
int i { 0 };
string str;
bool b { false };
println("Before: i = {}, str = \"{}\", b = {}", i, str, b);
tie(i, str, b) = t1;
println("After: i = {}, str = \"{}\", b = {}", i, str, b);
```

The result is as follows:

```
Before: i = 0, str = "", b = false
After:  i = 16, str = "Test", b = true
```

With `tie()` you can ignore certain elements that you do not want to be decomposed. Instead of a variable name for the decomposed element, you use the special `std::ignore` value. For example, the `string` element of the `t1 tuple` can be ignored by replacing the `tie()` statement from the previous example with the following:

```
tie(i, ignore, b) = t1;
```

Concatenation

You can use `std::tuple_cat()` to concatenate two `tuple`s into one. In the following example, the type of `t3` is `tuple<int, string, bool, double, string>`:

```
tuple t1 { 16, "Test"s, true };
tuple t2 { 3.14, "string 2"s };
auto t3 { tuple_cat(t1, t2) };
println("t3 = {}", t3);
```

The output is as follows:

```
t3 = (16, "Test", true, 3.14, "string 2")
```

Comparisons

Tuples support all comparison operators. For the comparison operators to work, the element types stored in the `tuple` should support them as well. Here is an example:

```
tuple t1 { 123, "def"s };
tuple t2 { 123, "abc"s };
if (t1 < t2) { println("t1 < t2"); }
else { println("t1 >= t2"); }
```

The output is as follows:

```
t1 >= t2
```

Tuple comparisons can be used to easily implement lexicographical comparison operators for custom types that have several data members. For example, suppose you have the following `class` with three data members:

```
class Foo
{
    public:
        explicit Foo(int i, string s, bool b)
            : m_int { i }, m_str { move(s) }, m_bool { b } { }
    private:
        int m_int;
        string m_str;
        bool m_bool;
};
```

Correctly implementing a full set of comparison operators that compare *all* data members of `Foo` is trivial by explicitly defaulting `operator<=>` as follows:

```
auto operator<=>(const Foo& rhs) const = default;
```

This automatically compares all data members. However, if the semantics of a class are such that a comparison between two instances should take only a subset of the data members into account, then correctly implementing a full set of comparison operators for such a class is not trivial! But, with `std::tie()` and the three-way comparison operator (`operator<=>`), it does become easy, a simple one-liner. The following is an implementation of `operator<=>` for `Foo` comparing only the `m_int` and `m_str` data members and ignoring `m_bool`:

```
auto operator<=>(const Foo& rhs) const
{
    return tie(m_int, m_str) <=> tie(rhs.m_int, rhs.m_str);
}
```

Here is an example of its use:

```
Foo f1 { 42, "Hello", false };
Foo f2 { 42, "World", false };
println("{}", (f1 < f2));  // Outputs true
println("{}", (f2 > f1));  // Outputs true
```

make_from_tuple

`std::make_from_tuple<T>()` constructs an object of a given type `T`, passing the elements of a given `tuple` as arguments to the constructor of `T`. For example, suppose you have the following class:

```
class Foo
{
    public:
        explicit Foo(string str, int i) : m_str { move(str) }, m_int { i } { }
    private:
        string m_str;
        int m_int;
};
```

You can use make_from_tuple() as follows:

```
tuple myTuple { "Hello world.", 42 };
auto foo { make_from_tuple<Foo>(myTuple) };
```

Technically, the argument to make_from_tuple() does not have to be a tuple, but it has to be something that supports std::get<>() and tuple_size. Both std::array and pair satisfy these requirements as well.

This function is not that practical for everyday use, but it comes in handy when writing generic code using templates and template metaprogramming.

apply

std::apply() calls a given callable, passing the elements of a given tuple as arguments. Here is an example:

```
int add(int a, int b) { return a + b; }
...
println("{}", apply(add, tuple { 39, 3 }));
```

As with make_from_tuple(), this function is also more useful when writing generic code using templates and template metaprogramming than for everyday use.

OPTIONAL: MONADIC OPERATIONS

Chapter 1 introduces the basics of std::optional. C++23 adds three new member functions to optional, collectively called *monadic operations*. These allow you to chain operations on an optional without having to check whether the optional has a value before applying each operation.

The following monadic operations are available:

- transform(F): Returns an optional containing the result of invoking F with the value of *this as argument if *this has a value; otherwise, returns an empty optional
- and_then(F): Returns the result (which must be an optional) of invoking F with the value of *this as argument if *this has a value; otherwise, returns an empty optional
- or_else(F): Returns *this if *this has a value; otherwise, returns the result (which must be an optional) of invoking F

Let's look at an example. The following function parses a given string for an integer and returns the result as an optional. If the string cannot be parsed as an integer, an empty optional is returned.

```
optional<int> Parse(const string& str)
{
    try { return stoi(str); }
    catch (...) { return {}; }
}
```

The following loop repeatedly asks the user to give some input. Parse() is called to parse the user's input. If the input is successfully parsed as an integer, the integer is doubled with and_then() and converted back to a string with transform(). If the input cannot be parsed, or_else() is used to return the string "No Integer." Thanks to monadic operations, there is no need to check whether the `optionals` returned from `Parse()` and `and_then()` contain a value before applying the next operation on them. The error handling is taken care of for you. The different operations can simply be chained together.

```
while (true) {
    print("Enter an integer (q to stop): ");
    string str;
    if (!getline(cin, str) || str == "q") { break; }

    auto result { Parse(str)
        .and_then([](int value) -> optional<int> { return value * 2; })
        .transform([](int value) { return to_string(value); })
        .or_else([] { return optional<string> { "No Integer" }; }) };
    println("    > Result: {}", *result);
}
```

Here is some sample output:

```
Enter an integer (q to stop): 21
    > Result: 42
Enter an integer (q to stop): Test
    > Result: No Integer
```

> **NOTE** *Starting with C++23,* `optional` *is a* `constexpr` *class (see Chapter 9) and so can be used at compile time.*

EXPECTED

As Chapter 14, "Handling Errors," explains, a function in C++ can return only a single type. If a function can fail, it should inform the caller about the failure. In the past, you had a couple of options to do so. You could throw an exception with details of the error. Or you could try to come up with a special value of the return type to signal an error.

For example, if a function returns a pointer, the function could return `nullptr` in case of an error. If a function returns only positive integers for its normal operation, you could return negative values to signal different errors, and so on. But coming up with such a special value is not always possible. If the return type of a function is `int` and the valid range of returned values is the entire range of integers, then you don't have any integers left to use as special error values. In such cases, you could use the `std::optional` vocabulary type. It's a type that can either contain a value of a certain type or be empty. A function could then return an empty `optional` to signal an error.

That's all fine, but when a caller of the function receives an empty `optional`, it has no way of knowing what exactly went wrong; i.e., the function cannot return the real reason of the error. These problems are solved with `std::expected`, defined in `<expected>`, and introduced with C++23. It's a class template accepting two template type parameters:

- `T`: The type of the expected value
- `E`: The type of an error value, also known as an unexpected value

An expected is never empty; it always contains either a value of type T or a value of type E. That's the biggest difference compared to optional, which can be empty, leaving you with no clue as to why it's empty. Thus, a function returning an expected should either return a value of the expected type or return a value of the error type to signal the exact reason of the failure. The error type can be whatever you want. It can be a simple integer or a complex class. Often, it's best to encode errors in a class capable of representing as many details about an error as possible, for example, the filename, line number, and column number where parsing of some data file failed.

An instance of expected<T,E> can be created implicitly from a value of type T, just as an optional<T>. To create an instance of expected<T,E> containing a value of the error type E, you must use std::unexpected<E>. A default constructed expected<T,E> contains a default constructed value of the expected type, T. This is different compared to optional. A default constructed optional is empty! In other words, a default constructed expected represents success, while a default constructed optional represents an error.

Let's look at an example. The following is a function receiving a string and trying to parse the string as an integer. The stoi() function throws invalid_argument if the string doesn't represent an integer and throws out_of_range if the parsed integer is larger than what can be represented as an int. Suppose you don't want parseInteger() to throw such exceptions but instead return an expected. The function catches the two exceptions and transforms them to a string, the error type of the returned expected.

```
expected<int, string> parseInteger(const string& str)
{
    try { return stoi(str); }
    catch (const invalid_argument& e) { return unexpected { e.what() }; }
    catch (const out_of_range& e) { return unexpected { e.what() }; }
}
```

expected has the following member functions. All of them, except error(), are analogous to the similarly named member functions for optional.

- has_value() and operator bool: Returns true if the expected has a value of type T, false otherwise.
- value(): Returns the value of type T. Throws std::bad_expected_access if called on an expected containing a value of type E.
- operator* and ->: Accesses the value of type T. The behavior is undefined if the expected doesn't contain a value of type T.
- error(): Returns the error of type E. The behavior is undefined if the expected doesn't contain a value of type E.
- value_or(): Returns the value of type T, or another given value if the expected doesn't contain such a value.

The following example demonstrates most of these member functions:

```
auto result1 { parseInteger("123456789") };
if (result1.has_value()) { println("result1 = {}", result1.value()); }
if (result1) { println("result1 = {}", *result1); }
```

```
println("result1 = {}", result1.value_or(0));

auto result2 { parseInteger("123456789123456") };
if (!result2) { println("result2 contains an error: {}", result2.error()); }

auto result3 { parseInteger("abc") };
if (!result3) { println("result3 contains an error: {}", result3.error()); }
```

Here is the output:

```
result1 = 123456789
result1 = 123456789
result1 = 123456789
result2 contains an error: stoi argument out of range
result3 contains an error: invalid stoi argument
```

Additionally, `expected` supports monadic operations: `and_then()`, `transform()`, `or_else()`, and `transform_error()`. The first three are analogous to the monadic operations supported by `optional`.

- `transform(F)`: Returns an `expected` containing the result of invoking `F` with the expected value as argument if `*this` has an expected value; otherwise, just returns the `expected` as is
- `and_then(F)`: Returns the result (which must be an `expected`) of invoking `F` with the expected value as argument if `*this` has an expected value; otherwise, just returns the `expected` as is
- `or_else(F)`: Returns `*this` if `*this` has an expected value; otherwise, returns the result (which must be an `expected`) of invoking `F` with the unexpected value as argument
- `transform_error(F)`: Returns `*this` if `*this` has an expected value; otherwise, returns an `expected` containing the unexpected value transformed by invoking `F` with the unexpected value as argument

Here is an example of using `and_then()` on an `expected`. Just as for monadic operations on `optionals`, there is no need to explicitly check whether the result of calling `parseInteger()` contains an expected value before applying the operation. The error handling is taken care of for you.

```
auto transformedResult { parseInteger("123456789")
    .and_then([](int value) -> expected<int, string> { return value * 2; }) };
```

The error type of `expected` can be any type you want. Returning multiple error types is also possible by using the `variant` vocabulary type discussed earlier in this chapter. For example, instead of returning a simple `string`, the `parseInteger()` function can return two different error types for the two error cases. The following version returns errors of two custom types `OutOfRange` and `InvalidArgument`:

```
expected<int, variant<OutOfRange, InvalidArgument>>
    parseInteger(const string& str) { ... }
```

To conclude, it's clear that `optional` and `expected` are somewhat related. Use the following rule to decide which one to use in certain use cases.

> **NOTE** *Use* `expected` *when an error is unexpected, in which case the* `expected` *should represent the exact reason for the error, so the caller can handle the error appropriately.*
>
> *Use* `optional` *if it's acceptable that there is no value and without requiring any reason for a missing value. For example, use for functions accepting optional input parameters or return types of functions for which it is not unexpected that there is no value, such as find-related functions.*

Exceptions, Error Return Codes, and expected

There are three major options to handle errors in a function. The function can throw an exception, discussed in detail in Chapter 14; return an error code; or return an `expected`. They all have their own merits. The following table, based on the official proposal paper for `std::expected`, P0323R12, summarizes them:

	EXCEPTION	ERROR RETURN CODE	EXPECTED
VISIBILITY	Not visible, unless you read the function documentation or analyze the code.	Immediately visible from the function prototype. But easy to ignore the return value.	Immediately visible from the function prototype. Cannot be ignored as it contains the result of the function.
DETAILS	Contains as many details about the error as possible.	Often just a simple integer.	Contains as many details about the error as possible.
CODE NOISE	Allows for writing clean code with separate error handling.	Error handling is intertwined with the normal flow, making code harder to read and maintain.	Allows for clean code. Thanks to monadic operations, error handling is not intertwined with normal flow.

SUMMARY

This chapter gave an overview of additional vocabulary types provided by the C++ Standard Library. You learned how to use the `variant` and `any` vocabulary data types. You also learned about `tuples`, which are a generalization of `pairs`, and the operations you can apply to `tuples`. You discovered the power of monadic operations for `optionals` allowing you to easily chain operations on `optionals`. The chapter finished with `expected`, a vocabulary type capable of holding either a value of a certain type or an error.

This chapter concludes Part 3 of the book. The next part discusses some more advanced topics and starts with a chapter showing you how to customize and extend the functionality provided by the C++ Standard Library by implementing your own Standard Library–compliant algorithms and data structures.

EXERCISES

By solving the following exercises, you can practice the material discussed in this chapter. Solutions to all exercises are available with the code download on the book's website at `www.wiley.com/go/proc++6e`. However, if you are stuck on an exercise, first reread parts of this chapter to try to find an answer yourself before looking at the solution from the website.

Exercise 24-1: Chapter 14, "Handling Errors," explains error handling in C++ and explains that there are basically two major options: either you work with error codes or you work with exceptions. I recommend using exceptions for error handling, but for this exercise, you'll use error codes. Write a simple `Error` class that just stores a single message, has a constructor to set the message, and has a getter to retrieve the message. Next, write a `getData()` function with a single Boolean parameter called `fail`. If `fail` is `false`, the function returns a `vector` of some data; otherwise, it returns an instance of `Error`. You are not allowed to use reference-to-non-`const` output parameters. Try to come up with a solution that doesn't use the C++23 `std::expected` class template yet. Test your implementation in your `main()` function.

Exercise 24-2: Modify your solution to Exercise 24-1 to use the C++23 `std::expected` class template and discover how it makes the solution much easier to read and understand.

Exercise 24-3: Most command-line applications accept command-line parameters. In most, if not all, of the sample code in this book the main function is simply `main()`. However, `main()` can also accept parameters: `main(int argc, char** argv)` where `argc` is the number of command-line parameters, and `argv` is an array of strings, one string for each parameter. Assume for this exercise that a command-line parameter is of the form `name=value`. Write a function that can parse a single parameter and that returns a `pair` containing the name of the parameter and a `variant` containing the value as a Boolean if the value can be parsed as a Boolean (`true` or `false`), an integer if the value can be parsed as an integer, or a `string` otherwise. To split the `name=value` string, you can use a regular expression (see Chapter 21, "String Localization and Regular Expressions"). To parse integers, you can use one of the functions explained in Chapter 2, "Working with Strings and String Views." In your `main()` function, loop over all command-line parameters, parse them, and output the parsed results to the standard output using `holds_alternative()`.

Exercise 24-4: Modify your solution to Exercise 24-3. Instead of using `holds_alternative()`, use a visitor to output the parsed results to the standard output.

Exercise 24-5: Modify your solution to Exercise 24-4 to use `tuple`s instead of `pair`s.

PART IV
Mastering Advanced Features of C++

25

Customizing and Extending the Standard Library

WHAT'S IN THIS CHAPTER?

- What allocators are
- How to write Standard Library–compliant custom algorithms, containers, and iterators

WILEY.COM DOWNLOADS FOR THIS CHAPTER

Please note that all the code examples for this chapter are available as part of this chapter's code download on the book's website at `www.wiley.com/go/proc++6e` on the Download Code tab.

Chapters 16, "Overview of the C++ Standard Library," 18, "Standard Library Containers," and 20, "Mastering Standard Library Algorithms," show that the Standard Library contains a powerful general-purpose collection of containers and algorithms. The information covered so far should be sufficient for most applications. However, those chapters show only the functionality of the library that is available out of the box. The Standard Library can be customized and extended however you like. For example, you can write your own Standard Library–compliant containers, algorithms, and iterators, compatible with existing Standard Library functionality. You can even specify your own memory allocation schemes for containers to use. This chapter provides a taste of these advanced features, primarily through the development of a `find_all()` algorithm and a `directed_graph` container.

> **NOTE** *Customizing and extending the Standard Library is rarely necessary. If you're happy with the existing Standard Library containers and algorithms, you can skip this chapter. However, if you really want to understand the Standard Library, not just use it, give this chapter a chance. You should be comfortable with the operator-overloading material from Chapter 15, "Overloading C++ Operators," and because this chapter uses templates extensively, you should also be comfortable with the template material from Chapter 12, "Writing Generic Code with Templates," before continuing.*

ALLOCATORS

Every Standard Library container takes an `Allocator` type as a template type parameter, for which the default usually suffices. For example, the `vector` template definition looks like this:

```
template <class T, class Allocator = allocator<T>> class vector;
```

The container constructors then allow you to pass in an object of type `Allocator`. This permits you to customize the way the containers allocate memory. Every memory allocation performed by a container is made with a call to the `allocate()` member function of the `Allocator` object. Conversely, every deallocation is performed with a call to the `deallocate()` member function of the `Allocator` object. When a Standard Library container takes an `Allocator` parameter, that parameter always defaults to `std::allocator<T>` if not provided. The `allocate()` and `deallocate()` member functions of `std::allocator<T>` are simple wrappers around `new` and `delete`.

Keep in mind that `allocate()` simply allocates a big-enough block of uninitialized memory and does not call any object constructor. Similarly, `deallocate()` simply frees the memory block and does not call any destructor. Once a memory block has been allocated, a placement `new` operator (see Chapter 15) can be used to construct an object in place. The following code snippet shows a contrived example. Chapter 29, "Writing Efficient C++," shows a more realistic use of an allocator for the implementation of an object pool.

```
class MyClass {};
int main()
{
    // Create an allocator to use.
    std::allocator<MyClass> alloc;
    // Allocate an uninitialized memory block for 1 instance of MyClass.
    auto* memory { alloc.allocate(1) };
    // Use placement new operator to construct a MyClass in place.
    ::new (memory) MyClass{};
    // Destroy MyClass instance.
    std::destroy_at(memory);
    // Deallocate memory block.
    alloc.deallocate(memory, 1);
    memory = nullptr;
}
```

If you want containers in your program to use a custom memory allocation and deallocation scheme, you can write your own Allocator class. There are several reasons for using custom allocators. For example, if the underlying allocator has unacceptable performance, there are alternatives. When OS-specific capabilities, such as shared memory segments, must be allocated, using custom allocators allows the use of Standard Library containers in those shared memory segments. The use of custom allocators is complex, and there are many potential problems if you are not careful, so this should not be approached lightly.

Any class that provides allocate(), deallocate(), and several other required member functions and type aliases can be used in place of the default allocator class.

Additionally, the Standard Library has the concept of *polymorphic memory allocators*. Basically, the problem with the allocator for a container being specified as a template type parameter is that two containers that are similar but have different allocator types are completely different types. For example, vector<int, A1> and vector<int, A2> are different and so cannot, e.g., be assigned to one another.

The polymorphic memory allocators, defined in <memory_resource> in the std::pmr namespace, help to solve this problem. The class std::pmr::polymorphic_allocator is a proper Allocator class because it satisfies all the allocator requirements, such as having allocate() and deallocate() member functions. The allocation behavior of a polymorphic_allocator depends on the memory_resource it's given during construction, and not on any template type parameters. As such, different polymorphic_allocators can behave in completely different ways when allocating and deallocating memory, even though they all have the same type, that is, polymorphic_allocator. The standard provides some built-in memory resources that you can use to initialize a polymorphic memory allocator: synchronized_pool_resource, unsynchronized_pool_resource, and monotonic_buffer_resource. The Standard Library also provides template type aliases such as std::pmr::vector<T> for std::vector<T, std::pmr::polymorphic_allocator<T>>. An std::pmr::vector<T> is still a different type from std::vector<T> and cannot be assigned from std::vector<T>. But an std::pmr::vector<T> affiliated with one memory resource is the same type as, and can be assigned from, a second std::pmr::vector<T> object affiliated with a different memory resource.

However, in my experience, both custom allocators and polymorphic memory allocators are rather advanced and rarely used features in day-to-day coding. I've never used them myself, so a detailed discussion falls outside the scope of this book. For more information, consult one of the books listed in Appendix B, "Annotated Bibliography," that specifically covers the C++ Standard Library.

EXTENDING THE STANDARD LIBRARY

The Standard Library includes many useful containers, algorithms, and iterators that you can use in your applications. It is impossible, however, for any library to include all possible utilities that all potential clients might need. Thus, the best libraries are extensible: they allow clients to adapt and add to the basic capabilities to obtain exactly the functionality they require. The Standard Library is inherently extensible because of its fundamental structure of separating data from the algorithms that operate on them. You can write your own containers that can work with the Standard Library algorithms by providing iterators that conform to the Standard Library guidelines. Similarly, you can write your own algorithms that work with iterators from the standard containers. Keep in mind, though, that you are not allowed to put your own containers and algorithms in the `std` namespace.

> **NOTE** *This book usually uses the convention to name functions and member functions without any underscores and where each word of the name is capitalized, except for the first word, for example:* `getIndex()`. *However, this chapter talks about extending the Standard Library, hence it uses the naming conventions used by the Standard Library. This means function and member function names are all lowercase with underscores separating the words, for example* `get_index()`. *Class names are also using the Standard Library naming conventions.*

Why Extend the Standard Library?

If you sit down to write an algorithm or container in C++, you can either make it adhere to the Standard Library conventions or not. For simple containers and algorithms, it might not be worth the extra effort to follow the Standard Library requirements. However, for substantial code that you plan to reuse, the effort pays off. First, the code will be easier for other C++ programmers to understand, because you follow well-established interface guidelines. Second, you will be able to use your container or algorithm with the other parts of the Standard Library (algorithms or containers) without needing to provide special hacks or adapters. Finally, it will force you to employ the necessary rigor required to develop solid code.

Writing a Standard Library Algorithm

Chapters 16 and 20 describe a useful set of algorithms that is part of the Standard Library, but you will inevitably encounter situations in your programs for which you need new algorithms. When that happens, it is usually not difficult to write your own algorithm that works with Standard Library iterators just like the standard algorithms.

find_all

Suppose you want to find all elements, including their position, matching a predicate in a given range. The `find()` and `find_if()` algorithms are the most likely candidates, but each returns an iterator referring to only one element. You can use `copy_if()` to find all elements matching a given predicate, but it fills the output with copies of the found elements, so you lose their position. If you want to avoid copies, you can use `copy_if()` with a `back_insert_iterator` (see Chapter 17, "Understanding Iterators and the Ranges Library") into a `vector<reference_wrapper<T>>`, but this does not give you the position of the found elements either. In fact, there is no standard algorithm to get iterators to all the elements matching a predicate. However, you can write your own version of this functionality called `find_all()`.

In this first section, we'll look at an implementation of find_all() following the model of legacy unconstrained algorithms. Once that implementation is working, we'll see how it can be extended and adapted to follow the model of modern constrained algorithms by adding support for projections and more.

The first task is to define the function prototype. You can follow the model established by copy_if(), that is, a function template with three template type parameters: the input iterator type, the output iterator type, and the predicate type. The parameters of the function are start and end iterators of the input sequence, a start iterator of the output sequence, and a predicate object. As with copy_if(), the algorithm returns an iterator into the output sequence that is one-past-the-last element stored in the output sequence. Of course, in modern C++ code, it's recommended to add proper constraints to template type parameters, so let's follow that advice. Here is the prototype:

```
template <forward_iterator ForwardIterator,
          output_iterator<ForwardIterator> OutputIterator,
          indirect_unary_predicate<ForwardIterator> Predicate>
OutputIterator find_all(ForwardIterator first, ForwardIterator last,
                        OutputIterator dest, Predicate pred);
```

The forward_iterator concept specifies that an iterator must be dereferenceable and incrementable, among others. The output_iterator<ForwardIterator> concept requires that an iterator is an output iterator that accepts values of type ForwardIterator. The indirect_unary_predicate concept is a predefined set of requirements that algorithms can use to specify the requirements for unary predicate arguments. It's "indirect" because the requirements are applied to the type that its template type parameter, ForwardIterator in this case, refers to, and not to ForwardIterator itself.

Another design choice would be to omit the output iterator and return an iterator into the input sequence that iterates over all the matching elements in the input sequence. This would require you to write your own iterator class, which is discussed later in this chapter.

The next task is to write the implementation. The find_all() algorithm iterates over all elements in the input sequence, uses invoke() to call the predicate on each element, and stores iterators of matching elements in the output sequence. Here is the implementation:

```
template <forward_iterator ForwardIterator,
          output_iterator<ForwardIterator> OutputIterator,
          indirect_unary_predicate<ForwardIterator> Predicate>
OutputIterator find_all(ForwardIterator first, ForwardIterator last,
                        OutputIterator dest, Predicate pred)
{
    while (first != last) {
        if (invoke(pred, *first)) {
            *dest = first;
            ++dest;
        }
        ++first;
    }
    return dest;
}
```

Similar to copy_if(), the algorithm only overwrites existing elements in the output sequence, so make sure the output sequence is large enough to hold the result, or use an iterator adapter such as back_insert_iterator, as demonstrated in the following code. After finding all matching elements, the code counts the number of elements found, which is the number of iterators in matches. Then, it iterates through the result, printing each element.

```
vector<int> vec { 5, 4, 5, 4, 10, 6, 5, 8, 10 };
vector<vector<int>::iterator> matches;

find_all(begin(vec), end(vec), back_inserter(matches),
    [](int i){ return i == 10; });

println("Found {} matching elements: ", matches.size());
for (const auto& it : matches) {
    println("{} at position {}", *it, distance(begin(vec), it));
}
```

The output is as follows:

```
Found 2 matching elements:
10 at position 4
10 at position 8
```

Modernized find_all

As Chapter 17 explains, most constrained algorithms accept a projection parameter. The find_all() algorithm can be modernized to support such a projection parameter. Additionally, constrained algorithms usually don't have a begin and end iterator of the same type. Instead, the begin iterator is as usual, but the end marker can be of a different type and is then called a *sentinel*. Here is the updated algorithm:

```
template <forward_iterator ForwardIterator,
    sentinel_for<ForwardIterator> Sentinel,
    output_iterator<ForwardIterator> OutputIterator,
    typename Projection = std::identity,
    indirect_unary_predicate<projected<ForwardIterator, Projection>> Predicate>
OutputIterator find_all(ForwardIterator first, Sentinel last,
                        OutputIterator dest, Predicate pred, Projection proj = {})
{
    while (first != last) {
        if (invoke(pred, invoke(proj, *first))) {
            *dest = first;
            ++dest;
        }
        ++first;
    }
    return dest;
}
```

The sentinel_for constraint ensures that the expression first != last is valid. The Projection template type parameter is new and has a default value, the identity operation. The template type argument for indirect_unary_predicate changed slightly to projected<ForwardIterator, Projection>, which represents the type of applying the Projection function to a dereferenced ForwardIterator.

The modernized `find_all()` can be tested as follows:

```
find_all(begin(vec), end(vec), back_inserter(matches),
    [](int i) { return i == 10; },
    [](int i) { return i * 2; });
```

This invocation of `find_all()` is similar to the one from the previous section, except that it now includes a projection. For each element, the algorithm first transforms it using this projection function, and then passes it to the given predicate. In this case, each element is first doubled, and then checked whether the transformed element is equal to 10. Thus, the output now is as follows. Compare this with the output from the previous section.

```
Found 3 matching elements:
5 at position 0
5 at position 2
5 at position 6
```

Writing a Standard Library Container

The C++ Standard Library contains a list of requirements that any container must fulfill to qualify as a Standard Library container. Additionally, if you want your container to be sequential (like a `vector`), ordered associative (like a `map`), or unordered associative (like an `unordered_map`), it must conform to supplementary requirements.

My suggestion when writing a custom container is to write the basic container first, following the general Standard Library rules such as making it a class template, but without worrying too much yet about the specific details of Standard Library conformity. After developing the basic implementation, add iterator support so that it can work with the Standard Library framework. Next, add member functions and type aliases to fulfill all basic container requirements, and finally, fulfill any additional container requirements. This chapter takes that approach to develop a *directed graph* data structure, also called a *digraph*.

A Basic Directed Graph

Certain C++ Standard Library containers might possibly use a graph in their implementation, but the standard does not make any graph-like data structures available to the user. So, implementing your own graph sounds like a perfect example of writing your own Standard Library–compliant container.

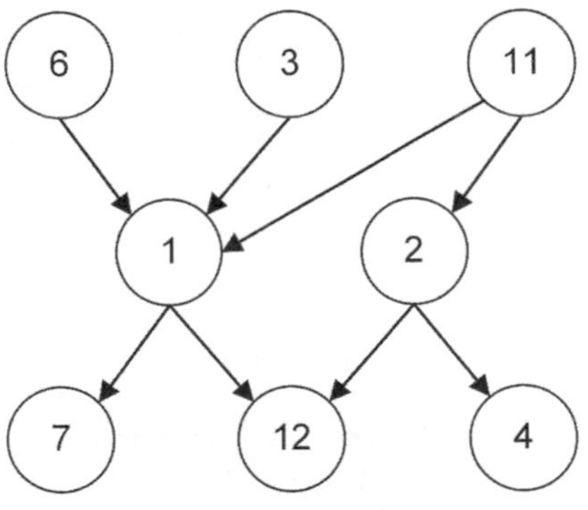

FIGURE 25.1

Before starting with writing any code, let's first take a look at what kind of data structure a directed graph is and how to represent its data in memory. Figure 25.1 shows a visual representation of a directed graph example. Basically, a directed graph consists of a set of *nodes*, also called *vertices*, which are connected by *edges*. Additionally, every edge has a direction, indicated by the arrows, which is why it's called a *directed* graph.

There are multiple ways to store such a data structure in memory, such as edge lists, adjacency matrices, and adjacency lists. This implementation uses *adjacency lists*. Nodes are stored in a vector with each node having an adjacency list listing its neighboring nodes. Let's look at an example. Suppose you have the directed graph from Figure 25.2. Representing this graph with adjacency lists results in the following data structure:

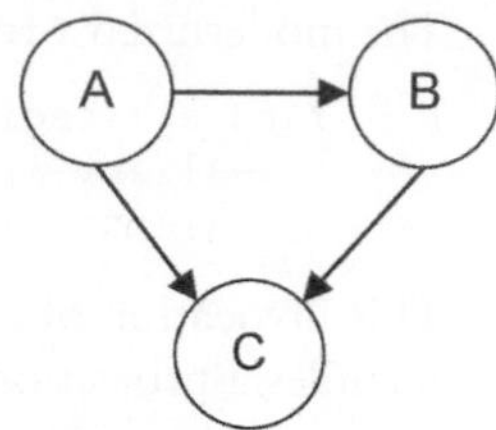

FIGURE 25.2

NODE	ADJACENCY LIST
A	B, C
B	C
C	

This can be stored as a vector where each element in the vector represents one row of the table; that is, each vector element represents a single node and its corresponding adjacency list. Let's start with a basic implementation without worrying too much about Standard Library compliance. This first section implements a simple, but fully functional, directed_graph<T> where T is the type of value to be stored in a single node. All values stored in a directed_graph must be unique. This might not be the best or most performant implementation of a directed graph, but that's not the point of this chapter. The point is to walk through the process of making a data structure following the Standard Library philosophy.

The graph_node Class Template

The directed_graph implementation uses the concept of nodes, so the first piece of code to implement is a data structure representing a single node of a graph. A node has a value and a list of adjacent nodes, stored as a set of indices to those adjacent nodes. Using a set makes sure that no duplicate adjacent indices are stored in the list. The class has a constructor to construct a new graph_node for a given value and has a value() member function to retrieve the value of the node. Only a const overload of value() is provided, as values should never change. The definition is in a directed_graph:node partition file called graph_node.cppm, inside a namespace called details, and is not exported from the module, as users of directed_graphs should not directly use graph_nodes themselves. Here is the interface of graph_node. Note the use of the [[nodiscard]] attribute, introduced in Chapter 1, "A Crash Course in C++ and the Standard Library":

```
export module directed_graph:node;
...
namespace details
{
    template <typename T>
    class graph_node
    {
        public:
            // Constructs a graph_node for the given value.
            explicit graph_node(directed_graph<T>* graph, T t)
                : m_graph { graph }, m_data(std::move(t)) { }
```

```
            // Returns a reference to the stored value.
            [[nodiscard]] const T& value() const noexcept { return m_data; }

            // Type alias for the container type used to store the adjacency list.
            using adjacency_list_type = std::set<std::size_t>;

            // Returns a reference to the adjacency list.
            [[nodiscard]] auto& get_adjacent_nodes_indices() {
                return m_adjacentNodeIndices; }
            [[nodiscard]] const auto& get_adjacent_nodes_indices() const {
                return m_adjacentNodeIndices; }
        private:
            // A pointer to the graph this node is in.
            directed_graph<T>* m_graph;

            T m_data;
            adjacency_list_type m_adjacentNodeIndices;
    };
}
```

In this definition, no constraints are placed on the template type parameter T. The reason is that, just as vector, the element requirements depend on what operations are actually performed on the container.

The initialization of m_data in the constructor initializer uses m_data(std::move(t)). Using the uniform initialization syntax, m_data{std::move(t)}, might not compile because T is a user-defined type.

Now that we have our graph_node implementation, let's look at the directed_graph class itself.

The directed_graph Interface

A directed_graph supports three basic operations: insertion, deletion, and lookup; additionally, it is swappable. It is defined in a directed_graph module. Here is the public portion of the directed_graph class template:

```
export module directed_graph;
...
export template <typename T>
class directed_graph
{
    public:
        // For insert to be successful, the value shall not be in the graph yet.
        // Returns true if a new node with given value has been added to
        // the graph, and false if there was already a node with the given value.
        bool insert(T node_value);

        // Returns true if the given node value was erased, false otherwise.
        bool erase(const T& node_value);

        // Returns true if the edge was successfully created, false otherwise.
        bool insert_edge(const T& from_node_value, const T& to_node_value);

        // Returns true if the given edge was erased, false otherwise.
        bool erase_edge(const T& from_node_value, const T& to_node_value);
```

```
        // Removes all nodes from the graph.
        void clear() noexcept;

        // Returns a reference to the value in the node with given index
        // without bounds checking.
        const T& operator[](std::size_t index) const;

        // Two directed graphs are equal if their sets of nodes are equal (where
        // nodes with the same T value are considered equal) and the same number
        // of edges between each corresponding pair of nodes.
        // The order in which the nodes and edges have been added does not
        // affect equality.
        bool operator==(const directed_graph& rhs) const;

        // Swaps all nodes between this graph and the given graph.
        void swap(directed_graph& other_graph) noexcept;

        // Returns the number of nodes in the graph.
        [[nodiscard]] std::size_t size() const noexcept;

        // Returns a set with the values of the adjacent nodes of a given node.
        // If the given node does not exist, an empty set is returned.
        [[nodiscard]] std::set<T> get_adjacent_nodes_values(
            const T& node_value) const;
    private:
        // Implementation details not shown yet.
};
```

The element type is a template type parameter, similar to the Standard Library `vector` container's. This interface looks straightforward. Note that this interface does not define any user-defined copy and move constructors, copy and move assignment operators, or destructor; i.e., the class follows the Rule of Zero as discussed in Chapter 9, "Mastering Classes and Objects."

Let's now look at concrete implementations of the `public` member functions.

The Implementation

After you finalize the `directed_graph` interface, you need to choose the implementation model. As discussed earlier, this implementation stores a directed graph as a list of nodes where each node contains its value and its set of adjacent node indices. Since the adjacent node lists contain indices to other nodes, nodes should be accessible based on their indices. Thus, a `vector` is the most appropriate container for storing the nodes. Each node is represented as a `graph_node` instance. Thus, the final structure is a `vector` of `graph_nodes`. Here are the first `private` members of the `directed_graph` class:

```
private:
    using node_container_type = std::vector<details::graph_node<T>>;
    node_container_type m_nodes;
```

Searching Nodes

Insert and delete operations on a graph require code to find an element with a given node value. Thus, it is helpful to have a `private` helper member function that performs this task. Both a `const` and a non-`const` overload are provided:

```
// Helper member function to return an iterator to the given node, or the
// end iterator if the given node is not in the graph.
typename node_container_type::iterator find_node(const T& node_value);
typename node_container_type::const_iterator find_node(const T& node_value) const;
```

The implementation of the non-const overload of `find_node()` is as follows. The `const` overload has the same implementation.

```
template <typename T>
typename directed_graph<T>::node_container_type::iterator
    directed_graph<T>::find_node(const T& node_value)
{
    return std::find_if(std::begin(m_nodes), std::end(m_nodes),
        [&](const auto& node) { return node.value() == node_value; });
}
```

The body of the member function is not too complicated. It uses the `find_if()` algorithm from the Standard Library, discussed in Chapter 20, to search all the nodes in the graph for a node with a value equal to the `node_value` parameter. If such a node is found in the graph, an iterator to that node is returned; otherwise, an end iterator is returned.

The syntax in the function header of this member function is somewhat confusing, particularly the use of the `typename` keyword. You must use the `typename` keyword whenever you are using a type that is dependent on a template parameter. Specifically, the type `node_container_type::iterator`, which is `vector<details::graph_node<T>>::iterator`, is dependent on the `T` template type parameter.

Inserting Nodes

`insert()` must first check whether a node with a given value already exists in the graph. If it doesn't exist yet, a new node can be created for the given value. The `public` interface provides an `insert()` member function accepting a `T` by value. This is optimal in this case and follows the recommendation explained in the section "Optimal Way to Pass Arguments to Functions" in Chapter 9. The call to `emplace_back()` constructs a new `graph_node` by passing a pointer to the `directed_graph` and the node's value to the `graph_node` constructor:

```
template <typename T>
bool directed_graph<T>::insert(T node_value)
{
    auto iter { find_node(node_value) };
    if (iter != std::end(m_nodes)) {
        // Value is already in the graph, return false.
        return false;
    }
    m_nodes.emplace_back(this, std::move(node_value));
    // Value successfully added to the graph, return true.
    return true;
}
```

Inserting Edges

Once nodes have been added to the graph, edges between those nodes can be constructed to build up a directed graph. For this, an `insert_edge()` member function is provided that requires two parameters: the value of the node from which the edge should start, and the value of the node to which the edge should point. The first thing the member function does is to search the graph for the from and to nodes. If either one of them is not found in the graph, `false` is returned. If both are found, then the code calculates the index of the node containing `to_node_value` by calling `get_index_of_node()`, a `private` helper function, and finally adds this index to the adjacency list of the node containing `from_node_value`. The `insert_edge()` member function returns `true` if and only if the graph changed as a result of the call. Remember from Chapter 18 that `insert()` on a `set` returns a `pair<iterator,bool>`, where the Boolean represents whether the insert was successful, which is why `.second` is used on the result of `insert()` in the `return` statement.

```
template <typename T>
bool directed_graph<T>::insert_edge(const T& from_node_value,
    const T& to_node_value)
{
    const auto from { find_node(from_node_value) };
    const auto to { find_node(to_node_value) };
    if (from == std::end(m_nodes) || to == std::end(m_nodes)) {
        return false;
    }
    const std::size_t to_index { get_index_of_node(to) };
    return from->get_adjacent_nodes_indices().insert(to_index).second;
}
```

The `get_index_of_node()` helper member function is implemented as follows:

```
template <typename T>
std::size_t directed_graph<T>::get_index_of_node(
    typename node_container_type::const_iterator node) const noexcept
{
    return node - std::cbegin(m_nodes);
}
```

Deleting Nodes

`erase()` follows the same pattern as `insert()`: it first attempts to find the given node by calling `find_node()`. If the node exists, it erases it from the graph. Otherwise, it does nothing. Removing an existing node from the graph is a two-step procedure:

1. Remove the index of the to-be-deleted node from all adjacency lists of all other nodes.
2. Remove the actual node from the list of nodes.

For the first step, a helper member function `remove_node_index()` is added to `graph_node`, which removes a given node index from the adjacency list of a node and updates the remaining indices to account for the shift in indices. The implementation follows. One tricky part is that the adjacency list is a `set`, and a `set` does not allow modifications to its values. Instead, the second step in the implementation converts the `set` into a `vector`, uses the `for_each()` algorithm to update all indices that require updating, and finally clears the `set` and inserts the updated indices. Again, this might not be the most performant implementation, but, as mentioned earlier, that's not the point of this discussion.

```
template <typename T>
void graph_node<T>::remove_node_index(std::size_t node_index)
{
```

```
        // First, remove references to the to-be-deleted node.
        m_adjacentNodeIndices.erase(node_index);

        // Second, modify all adjacency indices to account for the removal of a node.
        // std::set doesn't let us modify its elements in place,
        // so we rebuild the set from scratch.
        std::vector<std::size_t> indices(std::begin(m_adjacentNodeIndices),
            std::end(m_adjacentNodeIndices));
        std::for_each(std::begin(indices), std::end(indices),
            [node_index](std::size_t& index) {
                if (index > node_index) { --index; }
            });
        m_adjacentNodeIndices.clear();
        m_adjacentNodeIndices.insert(std::begin(indices), std::end(indices));
    }
```

Next, a `remove_all_links_to()` helper member function is added to `directed_graph`. This member function updates remaining adjacent node indices in all nodes to account for the removal of a node from the graph. First, it calculates `node_index`, the index of the given node in the `vector` of nodes. Then, it iterates over all nodes and removes `node_index` from the adjacency list of each node.

```
template <typename T>
void directed_graph<T>::remove_all_links_to(
    typename node_container_type::const_iterator node_iter)
{
    const std::size_t node_index { get_index_of_node(node_iter) };
    for (auto&& node : m_nodes) { node.remove_node_index(node_index); }
}
```

With this helper member function, the implementation of the actual `erase()` member function becomes easy:

```
template <typename T>
bool directed_graph<T>::erase(const T& node_value)
{
    auto iter { find_node(node_value) };
    if (iter == std::end(m_nodes)) { return false; }
    remove_all_links_to(iter);
    m_nodes.erase(iter);
    return true;
}
```

Deleting Edges

The procedure to remove edges is quite similar to adding them. If either the from or to node is not found, nothing is done; otherwise, the index of the node with value `to_node_value` is removed from the adjacency list of the node with value `from_node_value`:

```
template <typename T>
bool directed_graph<T>::erase_edge(const T& from_node_value,
    const T& to_node_value)
{
    const auto from { find_node(from_node_value) };
```

```
        const auto to { find_node(to_node_value) };
        if (from == std::end(m_nodes) || to == std::end(m_nodes)) {
            return false; // nothing to erase
        }
        const std::size_t to_index { get_index_of_node(to) };
        from->get_adjacent_nodes_indices().erase(to_index);
        return true;
    }
```

Removing All Elements

`clear()` simply clears the entire graph:

```
template <typename T>
void directed_graph<T>::clear() noexcept
{
    m_nodes.clear();
}
```

Swapping Graphs

Since `directed_graph` has only one data member, a `vector` container, swapping two `directed_graphs` just means swapping their single data member:

```
template <typename T>
void directed_graph<T>::swap(directed_graph& other_graph) noexcept
{
    m_nodes.swap(other_graph.m_nodes);
}
```

The following stand-alone exported `swap()` function is also provided, which simply forwards to the `public swap()` member function:

```
export template <typename T>
void swap(directed_graph<T>& first, directed_graph<T>& second) noexcept
{
    first.swap(second);
}
```

Accessing Nodes

The `public` interface of `directed_graph` supports accessing nodes based on their index with `operator[]`. Its implementation is straightforward. Just as with `vector`, the operator does not perform any bounds checking on the requested index:

```
template <typename T>
const T& directed_graph<T>::operator[](std::size_t index) const
{
    return m_nodes[index].value();
}
```

Comparing Graphs

Two `directed_graphs` are equal if and only if they contain the same set of nodes and the same set of edges between all the nodes. A slight complication arises from the fact that the two `directed_graphs` could have been created by adding nodes to them in different order; as such, the implementation cannot just compare the m_nodes data member but instead needs to do a bit more work.

The code first checks the size of both directed_graphs. If the size is different, both graphs cannot be the same. If they have the same size, the code iterates over all the nodes of one of the graphs. For each node, it tries to find the same node in the other graph. If it doesn't find such a node, the graphs are not equal. If it does find such a node, the adjacent node indices are converted to adjacent node values using a get_adjacent_nodes_values() helper member function, and those values are then compared for equality.

```
template <typename T>
bool directed_graph<T>::operator==(const directed_graph& rhs) const
{
    if (m_nodes.size() != rhs.m_nodes.size()) { return false; }

    for (auto&& node : m_nodes) {
        const auto rhsNodeIter {   rhs.find_node(node.value()) };
        if (rhsNodeIter == std::end(rhs.m_nodes)) { return false; }

        const auto adjacent_values_lhs { get_adjacent_nodes_values(
            node.get_adjacent_nodes_indices()) };
        const auto adjacent_values_rhs { rhs.get_adjacent_nodes_values(
            rhsNodeIter->get_adjacent_nodes_indices()) };
        if (adjacent_values_lhs != adjacent_values_rhs) { return false; }
    }
    return true;
}

template <typename T>
std::set<T> directed_graph<T>::get_adjacent_nodes_values(
    const typename details::graph_node<T>::adjacency_list_type& indices) const
{
    std::set<T> values;
    for (auto&& index : indices) { values.insert(m_nodes[index].value()); }
    return values;
}
```

Getting Adjacent Nodes

The public interface provides a get_adjacent_nodes_values() member function accepting a node_value of type reference-to-const T as parameter. It returns a set containing the values of the nodes adjacent to the given node. If the given node does not exist, an empty set is returned. The implementation uses the get_adjacent_nodes_values() overload accepting a list of indices as implemented in the previous section:

```
template <typename T>
std::set<T> directed_graph<T>::get_adjacent_nodes_values(const T& node_value) const
{
    auto iter { find_node(node_value) };
    if (iter == std::end(m_nodes)) { return {}; }
    return get_adjacent_nodes_values(iter->get_adjacent_nodes_indices());
}
```

Querying the Graph Size

Finally, the `size()` member function returns the number of nodes in the graph:

```
template <typename T>
std::size_t directed_graph<T>::size() const noexcept
{
    return m_nodes.size();
}
```

Printing Graphs

Graphs can be printed in a standard format called *DOT*, a *graph description language*. There are tools available that understand DOT-formatted graphs and that can convert them into graphical representations. To make it easier to test the `directed_graph` code, the following `to_dot()` conversion function can be used. An example of its use is given in the next section.

```
// Returns a given graph in DOT format.
export template <typename T>
std::string to_dot(const directed_graph<T>& graph, std::string_view graph_name)
{
    std::ostringstream output;
    std::println(output, "digraph {} {{", graph_name);
    for (std::size_t index { 0 }; index < graph.size(); ++index) {
        const auto& node_value { graph[index] };
        const auto adjacent_values { graph.get_adjacent_nodes_values(node_value) };
        if (adjacent_values.empty()) {
            std::println(output, "{}", node_value);
        } else {
            for (auto&& neighbor : adjacent_values) {
                std::println(output, "{} -> {}", node_value, neighbor);
            }
        }
    }
    std::println(output, "}}");
    return std::move(output).str();
}
```

Using the Basic Directed Graph

We have now completed the full implementation of a basic directed graph class. It's high time to give this class a test drive. Here is a small program demonstrating the basic `directed_graph` class template:

```
directed_graph<int> graph;
// Insert some nodes and edges.
graph.insert(11);
graph.insert(22);
graph.insert(33);
graph.insert(44);
graph.insert(55);
graph.insert_edge(11, 33);
graph.insert_edge(22, 33);
graph.insert_edge(22, 44);
graph.insert_edge(22, 55);
```

```
graph.insert_edge(33, 44);
graph.insert_edge(44, 55);
println("{}", to_dot(graph, "Graph1"));

// Remove an edge and a node.
graph.erase_edge(22, 44);
graph.erase(44);
println("{}", to_dot(graph, "Graph1"));

// Print the size of the graph.
println("Size: {}", graph.size());
```

The output is as follows:

```
digraph Graph1 {
11 -> 33
22 -> 33
22 -> 44
22 -> 55
33 -> 44
44 -> 55
55
}
digraph Graph1 {
11 -> 33
22 -> 33
22 -> 55
33
55
}
Size: 4
```

Making directed_graph a Standard Library Container

The basic `directed_graph` implemented in the previous sections follows the spirit, but not the letter, of the Standard Library. For most purposes, the preceding implementation is good enough. However, if you want to use the Standard Library algorithms on your `directed_graph`, you must do a bit more work. The C++ standard specifies member functions and type aliases that a class template must provide to qualify as a Standard Library container.

Required Type Aliases

The C++ standard requires that every Standard Library container provide the following `public` type aliases:

TYPE NAME	DESCRIPTION
`value_type`	The element type stored in the container
`reference`	A reference to the element type stored in the container
`const_reference`	A reference-to-`const` to the element type stored in the container
`iterator`	The type for iterating over elements of the container

continues

(continued)

TYPE NAME	DESCRIPTION
`const_iterator`	A version of `iterator` for iterating over `const` elements of the container
`size_type`	A type that can represent the number of elements in the container; this is usually just `size_t` (from `<cstddef>`)
`difference_type`	A type that can represent the difference of two `iterator`s for the container; this is usually just `ptrdiff_t` (from `<cstddef>`)

Here are the definitions for the `directed_graph` class template of all these type aliases except `iterator` and `const_iterator`. Writing iterators is covered in detail later in this chapter.

```
export template <typename T>
class directed_graph
{
    public:
        using value_type = T;
        using reference = value_type&;
        using const_reference = const value_type&;
        using size_type = std::size_t;
        using difference_type = std::ptrdiff_t;
        // Remainder of class definition omitted for brevity.
};
```

With these type aliases, some member functions can be slightly modified. For example, here is the earlier definition for `operator[]`:

```
const T& operator[](std::size_t index) const;
```

With the new type aliases, this can be written as follows:

```
const_reference operator[](size_type index) const;
```

Required Member Functions

In addition to the obligatory type aliases, every container must provide the following member functions:

MEMBER FUNCTION	DESCRIPTION	WORST-CASE COMPLEXITY
Default constructor	Constructs an empty container	Constant
Copy constructor	Performs a deep copy of the container	Linear
Move constructor	Performs a move constructing operation	Constant
Copy assignment operator	Performs a deep copy of the container	Linear
Move assignment operator	Performs a move assignment operation	Constant

MEMBER FUNCTION	DESCRIPTION	WORST-CASE COMPLEXITY
Destructor	Destroys any elements left in the container and frees their heap-allocated memory, if any	Linear
`iterator begin();` `const_iterator begin() const;`	Returns an iterator or `const` iterator referring to the first element in the container	Constant
`iterator end();` `const_iterator end() const;`	Returns an iterator or `const` iterator referring to one-past-the-last element in the container	Constant
`const_iterator cbegin() const;`	Same as `begin() const`	Constant
`const_iterator cend() const;`	Same as `end() const`	Constant
`operator==`	Comparison operator that compares two containers	Linear
`void swap(Container&) noexcept;`	Swaps the contents of the container passed to the member function with the object on which the member function is called	Constant
`size_type size() const;`	Returns the number of elements in the container	Constant
`size_type max_size() const;`	Returns the maximum number of elements the container can hold	Constant
`bool empty() const;`	Returns whether the container has any elements	Constant

As discussed earlier, the `directed_graph` implementation follows the rule of zero (see Chapter 9); that is, it does not need an explicit copy/move constructor, copy/move assignment operator, or destructor.

The following code snippet shows the declarations of the `size()`, `max_size()`, and `empty()` member functions. The iterator-related member functions, `begin()`, `end()`, `cbegin()`, and `cend()`, are covered in the next section on writing iterators.

```
export template <typename T>
class directed_graph
{
    public:
        [[nodiscard]] size_type size() const noexcept;
        [[nodiscard]] size_type max_size() const noexcept;
        [[nodiscard]] bool empty() const noexcept;
        // Other member functions omitted for brevity.
};
```

The implementations of these three member functions are easy because they can simply forward to the similarly named member functions of the m_nodes container. Note that size_type is one of the type aliases defined in the class template. Because it is a member of the class template, such a return type in the implementation must be fully qualified with typename directed_graph<T>.

```
template <typename T>
typename directed_graph<T>::size_type directed_graph<T>::size() const noexcept
{
    return m_nodes.size();
}

template <typename T>
typename directed_graph<T>::size_type directed_graph<T>::max_size() const noexcept
{
    return m_nodes.max_size();
}

template <typename T>
bool directed_graph<T>::empty() const noexcept
{
    return m_nodes.empty();
}
```

The current implementation of directed_graph has operator[] to get access to a node based on its index. This operator, just as with operator[] for vector, does not perform any bounds checking. Passing an out-of-bounds index could make your application crash. As for vector, directed_graph can be augmented with an at() member function that does bounds checking and that throws an std::out_of_range exception if the passed index is out of bounds. Here is the definition:

```
const_reference at(size_type index) const;
```

The implementation just forwards to the m_nodes vector:

```
template <typename T>
typename directed_graph<T>::const_reference
    directed_graph<T>::at(size_type index) const
{
    return m_nodes.at(index).value();
}
```

Writing an Iterator

The most important container requirement is iterator support. To work with the generic algorithms, every container must provide an iterator type for accessing the elements in the container. Your iterator should generally provide overloaded operator++, *, ->, and ==, plus some other operations depending on its specific behavior. As long as your iterator provides the basic iteration operations, everything should be fine.

The first decision to make about your iterator is what kind it will be: forward, bidirectional, random access, or contiguous. Bidirectional iterator support seems like a good choice for a directed_graph iterator. That means you must additionally provide operator--. Another option would be to implement random-access iterators for directed_graph, which involves adding the operators +, -, +=, -=, <, >, <=, >=, and []. This could be a good exercise to practice writing iterators. Consult Chapter 17 for more details on the requirements for random-access iterators.

The second decision is how to order the elements of your container. The `directed_graph` is unsorted, so iterating in a sorted order would not be efficient. The important thing about a Standard Library-compliant container is that iterating over its elements from `begin()` to `end()` will hit every element once; just because it is *a* sequence, doesn't mean that it is a *specific* sequence. Thus, the `directed_graph` iterator can just step through the nodes in the order in which they were added to the graph. This is the same as how iteration for `std::unordered_set` works.

The third decision is how to represent your iterator internally. The representation is usually quite dependent on the internal implementation of the container. The first purpose of an iterator is to refer to a single element in the container. In the case of a `directed_graph`, all nodes are stored in the `m_nodes` vector, so perhaps a `directed_graph` iterator can be a wrapper around a `vector` iterator referring to the element in question.

Once you've chosen your implementation, you must decide on a consistent representation for the end iterator. Recall that the end iterator should really be the "past-the-end" marker: the iterator that's reached by applying ++ to an iterator referring to the final element in the container. A `directed_graph` iterator can use as its end iterator the end iterator of the `m_nodes vector`.

Finally, a container needs to provide both `iterator` and `const_iterator` type aliases. This implementation defines both these type aliases in terms of a `const_directed_graph_iterator_impl` class template. The reason is that values cannot be changed once in the graph. This follows the same principle as `std::set`.

If you do need separate `iterator` and `const_iterator` types for your own data structure, keep in mind that an `iterator` must be convertible to a `const_iterator`.

The const_directed_graph_iterator_impl Class Template

Given the decisions made in the previous section, it's time to define the `const_directed_graph_iterator_impl` class template. The first thing to note is that each `const_directed_graph_iterator_impl` object is an iterator for a specific instantiation of `directed_graph`. To provide this one-to-one mapping, the `const_directed_graph_iterator_impl` must also be a class template with the directed graph type as a template type parameter called `DirectedGraph`.

The main question is how to conform to the bidirectional iterator requirements. Recall that anything that behaves like an iterator is an iterator. Your iterator is not required to derive from another class to qualify as a bidirectional iterator. However, if you want your iterator to be usable by the generic algorithms, you must specify its traits. Chapter 17 explains that `iterator_traits` is a class template that defines, for each iterator type, five type aliases: `value_type`, `difference_type`, `iterator_category`, `pointer`, and `reference`. The default implementation of the `iterator_traits` class template just grabs the five type aliases out of the iterator itself. Thus, you can simply define those type aliases directly for your iterator. The `const_directed_graph_iterator_impl` is a bidirectional iterator, so you specify `bidirectional_iterator_tag` as the iterator category. Other legal iterator categories are `input_iterator_tag`, `output_iterator_tag`, `forward_iterator_tag`, `random_access_iterator_tag`, and `contiguous_iterator_tag`. A contiguous iterator is a random-access iterator for which adjacent elements are also adjacent in memory. For the `const_directed_graph_iterator_impl`, the element type (`value_type`) is `typename DirectedGraph::value_type`.

> **NOTE** *In the past, it was recommended to derive custom iterators from the* `std::iterator` *class template, defined in* `<iterator>`. *This class template has been deprecated and should not be used anymore.*

Here is the `const_directed_graph_iterator_impl` class template definition:

```
template <typename DirectedGraph>
class const_directed_graph_iterator_impl
{
    public:
        using value_type = typename DirectedGraph::value_type;
        using difference_type = std::ptrdiff_t;
        using iterator_category = std::bidirectional_iterator_tag;
        using pointer = const value_type*;
        using reference = const value_type&;
        using node_container_iterator =
            typename DirectedGraph::node_container_type::const_iterator;

        // Bidirectional iterators must supply a default constructor.
        const_directed_graph_iterator_impl() = default;

        explicit const_directed_graph_iterator_impl(node_container_iterator it);

        reference operator*() const;

        // Return type must be something to which -> can be applied.
        // So, return a pointer.
        pointer operator->() const;

        const_directed_graph_iterator_impl& operator++();
        const_directed_graph_iterator_impl operator++(int);

        const_directed_graph_iterator_impl& operator--();
        const_directed_graph_iterator_impl operator--(int);

        // Defaulted operator==.
        bool operator==(const const_directed_graph_iterator_impl&) const = default;

    private:
        friend class directed_graph<value_type>;

        node_container_iterator m_nodeIterator;
};
```

Consult Chapter 15 for details on operator overloading if the definitions and implementations (shown in the next section) of the overloaded operators confuse you. The `const_directed_graph_iterator_impl` implementation does not need copy/move constructors and copy/move assignment operators, as the default behavior is what we want. The class also does not need an explicit destructor, as there's nothing to clean up. Hence, this class also follows the rule of zero.

The const_directed_graph_iterator_impl Member Function Implementations

The const_directed_graph_iterator_impl constructor initializes the data member:

```
template <typename DirectedGraph>
const_directed_graph_iterator_impl<DirectedGraph>::
    const_directed_graph_iterator_impl(node_container_iterator it)
        : m_nodeIterator { it } { }
```

The default constructor is defaulted so that clients can declare const_directed_graph_iterator_impl variables without initializing them. An iterator constructed with the default constructor does not need to refer to any value, and attempting any operations on it is allowed to have undefined results.

The implementations of the dereferencing operators are concise but can look tricky. Chapter 15 explains that operator* and -> are asymmetric:

- operator* returns a reference to the actual underlying value, which in this case is the element to which the iterator refers.
- operator-> must return something to which the arrow operator can be applied again, and thus returns a pointer to the element. The compiler then applies -> to the pointer, which results in accessing a field or member function of the element.

```
// Return a reference to the actual element.
template <typename DirectedGraph>
typename const_directed_graph_iterator_impl<DirectedGraph>::reference
    const_directed_graph_iterator_impl<DirectedGraph>::operator*() const
{
    return m_nodeIterator->value();
}

// Return a pointer to the actual element, so the compiler can
// apply -> to it to access the actual desired field.
template <typename DirectedGraph>
typename const_directed_graph_iterator_impl<DirectedGraph>::pointer
    const_directed_graph_iterator_impl<DirectedGraph>::operator->() const
{
    return &m_nodeIterator->value();
}
```

The increment operators are implemented as follows. The decrement operators are not shown as they are implemented analogously.

```
template <typename DirectedGraph>
const_directed_graph_iterator_impl<DirectedGraph>&
    const_directed_graph_iterator_impl<DirectedGraph>::operator++()
{
    ++m_nodeIterator;
    return *this;
}
```

```
template <typename DirectedGraph>
const_directed_graph_iterator_impl<DirectedGraph>
    const_directed_graph_iterator_impl<DirectedGraph>::operator++(int)
{
    auto oldIt { *this };
    ++*this;
    return oldIt;
}
```

Iterators are not required to be any safer than raw pointers, so error-checking for things like incrementing an iterator already at the end is not required.

The `node_container_iterator` type alias of `const_directed_graph_iterator_impl` uses the private `node_container_type` type alias of `directed_graph`. Thus, the `directed_graph` class template must declare `const_directed_graph_iterator_impl` to be a `friend`:

```
export template <typename T>
class directed_graph
{
    // Other member functions omitted for brevity.
    private:
        friend class const_directed_graph_iterator_impl<directed_graph>;
};
```

Iterator Type Aliases and Access Member Functions

The final piece involved in providing iterator support for `directed_graph` is to supply the necessary type aliases in the `directed_graph` class template, and to write the `begin()`, `end()`, `cbegin()`, and `cend()` member functions. The type aliases and member function prototypes look like this:

```
export template <typename T>
class directed_graph
{
    public:
        // Other type aliases omitted for brevity.
        using iterator = const_directed_graph_iterator_impl<directed_graph>;
        using const_iterator = const_directed_graph_iterator_impl<directed_graph>;

        // Iterator member functions.
        iterator begin() noexcept;
        iterator end() noexcept;
        const_iterator begin() const noexcept;
        const_iterator end() const noexcept;
        const_iterator cbegin() const noexcept;
        const_iterator cend() const noexcept;
        // Remainder of class definition omitted for brevity.
};
```

Both `iterator` and `const_iterator` are type aliases for `const_directed_graph_iterator_impl`, which means users cannot modify the values to which `directed_graph` iterators refer. Node values in a `directed_graph` must be unique. Allowing the user to modify the value of a node through an iterator would allow the possibility of introducing duplicate values. This follows the same principle as `std::set`, in which you also cannot modify elements.

As `iterator` and `const_iterator` are both type aliases for `const_directed_graph_iterator_impl`, the non-`const` `begin()` and `end()` member functions returning `iterator` are not strictly necessary; the `const` overloads are enough. However, the Standard Library requirements state that a container must supply non-`const` `begin()` and `end()` overloads.

The `directed_graph` class template stores all its nodes in a simple `vector`. As such, `begin()` and `end()` can simply forward their work to the identically named member functions on `vector` and wrap those results in a `const_directed_graph_iterator_impl`:

```
template <typename T>
typename directed_graph<T>::iterator
    directed_graph<T>::begin() noexcept { return iterator{ std::begin(m_nodes) }; }

template <typename T>
typename directed_graph<T>::iterator
    directed_graph<T>::end() noexcept { return iterator { std::end(m_nodes) }; }

template <typename T>
typename directed_graph<T>::const_iterator
    directed_graph<T>::begin() const noexcept
{ return const_iterator { std::begin(m_nodes) }; }

template <typename T>
typename directed_graph<T>::const_iterator
    directed_graph<T>::end() const noexcept
{ return const_iterator { std::end(m_nodes) }; }
```

The `cbegin()` and `cend()` member functions forward the request to the `const` overloads of `begin()` and `end()`:

```
template <typename T>
typename directed_graph<T>::const_iterator
    directed_graph<T>::cbegin() const noexcept { return begin(); }

template <typename T>
typename directed_graph<T>::const_iterator
    directed_graph<T>::cend() const noexcept { return end(); }
```

Modifying Other Member Functions to Use Iterators

Now that `directed_graph` supports iterators, other member functions can be slightly modified to work with iterators so that they follow the Standard Library guidelines. Let's look at the `insert()` member function first. In the earlier basic implementation, it is defined as follows:

```
// For an insert to be successful, the value shall not be in the graph yet.
// Returns true if a new node with given value has been added to
// the graph, and false if there was already a node with the given value.
bool insert(T node_value);
```

To follow more closely the spirit of the Standard Library, this can be modified to return an `std::pair<iterator, bool>` where the Boolean is `true` if the element was added to the graph, and `false` if the element was already in the graph. The iterator of the `pair` refers to the newly added element or the element that was already in the graph.

```
std::pair<iterator, bool> insert(T node_value);
```

The implementation is as follows. The changes compared to the version returning a simple `bool` are highlighted.

```
template <typename T>
std::pair<typename directed_graph<T>::iterator, bool>
    directed_graph<T>::insert(T node_value)
{
    auto iter { find_node(node_value) };
    if (iter != std::end(m_nodes)) {
        // Value is already in the graph.
        return { iterator { iter }, false };
    }
    m_nodes.emplace_back(this, std::move(node_value));
    // Value successfully added to the graph.
    return { iterator { std::prev(std::end(m_nodes)) }, true };
}
```

Additionally, an overload of `insert()` is provided that accepts an iterator hint. This hint is useless for a `directed_graph`, but it is provided for symmetry with other Standard Library containers, such as `std::vector`. The hint is ignored, and it merely calls the overload of `insert()` without the hint.

```
template <typename T>
typename directed_graph<T>::iterator
    directed_graph<T>::insert(const_iterator hint, T node_value)
{
    // Ignore the hint, just forward to another insert().
    return insert(std::move(node_value)).first;
}
```

A last overload of `insert()` accepts an iterator range. This overload is a member function template so that it can take an iterator range from any container, not just other `directed_graphs`. The actual implementation uses an `insert_iterator`, described Chapter 17.

```
template <typename T>
template <std::input_iterator Iter>
void directed_graph<T>::insert(Iter first, Iter last)
{
    // Copy each element in the range by using an insert_iterator adapter.
    // Give end() as a dummy position -- insert ignores it anyway.
    std::copy(first, last, std::insert_iterator { *this, end() });
}
```

The `erase()` member functions should be modified to work with iterators. The earlier definition has a node value as parameter and returns a `bool`:

```
// Returns true if the given node value was erased, false otherwise.
bool erase(const T& node_value);
```

To follow Standard Library principles, `directed_graph` is modified to provide two `erase()` member functions: one erasing a node to which an iterator refers and another one erasing a range of nodes given as an iterator range. Both return an iterator to the node after the last deleted node:

```
// Returns an iterator to the element after the last deleted element.
iterator erase(const_iterator pos);
iterator erase(const_iterator first, const_iterator last);
```

Here are the implementations:

```
template <typename T>
typename directed_graph<T>::iterator
    directed_graph<T>::erase(const_iterator pos)
{
    if (pos.m_nodeIterator == std::end(m_nodes)) {
        return end();
    }
    remove_all_links_to(pos.m_nodeIterator);
    return iterator { m_nodes.erase(pos.m_nodeIterator) };
}

template <typename T>
typename directed_graph<T>::iterator
    directed_graph<T>::erase(const_iterator first, const_iterator last)
{
    for (auto iter { first }; iter != last; ++iter) {
        remove_all_links_to(iter.m_nodeIterator);
    }
    return iterator { m_nodes.erase(first.m_nodeIterator, last.m_nodeIterator) };
}
```

Finally, the following public `find()` member function can be implemented returning an iterator. The implementation is left as an exercise at the end of this chapter.

```
const_iterator find(const T& node_value) const;
```

Using the directed_graph Iterators

Now that `directed_graph` supports iterators, you can iterate over its elements just as you would with any other Standard Library container, and you can pass the iterators to member functions and functions. Here are some examples:

```
directed_graph<int> graph;
// Populate the graph, omitted (see downloadable source code archive) ...

// Try to insert a duplicate, and use structured bindings for the result.
auto [iter22, inserted] { graph.insert(22) };
if (!inserted) { println("Duplicate element."); }

// Print nodes using a for loop and iterators.
for (auto iter { graph.cbegin() }; iter != graph.cend(); ++iter) {
    print("{} ", *iter);
}
println("");

// Print nodes using a for loop and iterators retrieved with the non-member
// functions cbegin() and cend().
for (auto iter { cbegin(graph) }; iter != cend(graph); ++iter) {
    print("{} ", *iter);
}
println("");

// Print nodes using a range-based for loop.
for (auto& node : graph) { print("{} ", node); }
println("");
```

```
// Search a node using the find() Standard Library algorithm.
auto result { find(begin(graph), end(graph), 22) };
if (result != end(graph)) { println("Node 22 found.");}
else { println("Node 22 NOT found."); }

// Count all nodes with values > 22.
auto count { count_if(begin(graph), end(graph),
    [](const auto& node) { return node > 22; }) };
println("{} nodes > 22", count);

// Use the iterator-based erase() member function in combination with find().
graph.erase(find(begin(graph), end(graph), 44));
```

This code snippet also shows that, thanks to the support for iterators, Standard Library algorithms can be used with a `directed_graph`. However, since `directed_graph` supports only `const` iterators, only non-modifying Standard Library algorithms are supported, just as with `std::set`. For example, the following code snippet using the remove-erase idiom does not compile:

```
graph.erase(remove_if(begin(graph), end(graph),
    [](const auto& node) { return node > 22; }), end(graph));
```

Adding Support for Reverse Iterators

If your container supplies bidirectional iterators, it is considered *reversible*. Reversible containers should have two additional type aliases:

TYPE NAME	DESCRIPTION
`reverse_iterator`	The type for iterating over elements of the container in reverse order
`const_reverse_iterator`	A version of `reverse_iterator` for iterating over `const` elements of the container in reverse order

Additionally, the container should provide `rbegin()` and `rend()`, which are symmetric with `begin()` and `end()`; and it should provide `crbegin()` and `crend()`, which are symmetric with `cbegin()` and `cend()`.

The `directed_graph` iterators are bidirectional, which means they should support reverse iteration. The following code snippet highlights the necessary changes. The two new type aliases use the `std::reverse_iterator` adapter provided by the Standard Library and described in Chapter 17 to convert the `directed_graph` iterators to behave as reverse iterators.

```
export template <typename T>
class directed_graph
{
    public:
        // Other type aliases omitted for brevity.
        using reverse_iterator = std::reverse_iterator<iterator>;
        using const_reverse_iterator = std::reverse_iterator<const_iterator>;

        // Reverse iterator member functions.
        reverse_iterator rbegin() noexcept;
        reverse_iterator rend() noexcept;
```

```
        const_reverse_iterator rbegin() const noexcept;
        const_reverse_iterator rend() const noexcept;
        const_reverse_iterator crbegin() const noexcept;
        const_reverse_iterator crend() const noexcept;
        // Remainder of class definition omitted for brevity.
};
```

The implementations of the reverse iterator member functions are as follows.

```
template <typename T>
typename directed_graph<T>::reverse_iterator
    directed_graph<T>::rbegin() noexcept { return reverse_iterator { end() }; }

template <typename T>
typename directed_graph<T>::reverse_iterator
    directed_graph<T>::rend() noexcept { return reverse_iterator { begin() }; }

template <typename T>
typename directed_graph<T>::const_reverse_iterator
    directed_graph<T>::rbegin() const noexcept
{ return const_reverse_iterator { end() }; }

template <typename T>
typename directed_graph<T>::const_reverse_iterator
    directed_graph<T>::rend() const noexcept
{ return const_reverse_iterator { begin() }; }

template <typename T>
typename directed_graph<T>::const_reverse_iterator
    directed_graph<T>::crbegin() const noexcept { return rbegin(); }

template <typename T>
typename directed_graph<T>::const_reverse_iterator
    directed_graph<T>::crend() const noexcept { return rend(); }
```

The following code snippet shows how to print all the nodes of a graph in reverse order:

```
for (auto iter { graph.rbegin() }; iter != graph.rend(); ++iter) {
    print("{} ", *iter);
}
```

Iterating over Adjacent Nodes

A `directed_graph` keeps a `vector` of nodes, where each node contains the node's value and a list of adjacent nodes. Let's improve the `directed_graph` interface to support iteration over the adjacent nodes of a given node without copying those nodes into another container as it is done in the earlier implementation of `get_adjacent_nodes_values()`. The first thing to add is a `const_adjacent_nodes_iterator_impl` class template following the same principles as `const_directed_graph_iterator_impl` so the code is not shown. Consult the downloadable source code archive to see the full code.

The next step is to augment the `directed_graph` interface with a new type alias, a helper structure to represent adjacent nodes as a range, and a member function to get access to the adjacent nodes of a given node value. The `nodes_adjacent_to()` member function returns an empty `optional` when the given node value cannot be found.

```
export template <typename T>
class directed_graph
{
    public:
        // Other type aliases omitted for brevity.
        using const_adjacent_nodes_iterator =
            const_adjacent_nodes_iterator_impl<directed_graph>;

        // Helper structure to represent a range of adjacent nodes.
        struct nodes_adjacent_to_result
        {
            const_adjacent_nodes_iterator m_begin;
            const_adjacent_nodes_iterator m_end;
            const_adjacent_nodes_iterator begin() const noexcept{ return m_begin; }
            const_adjacent_nodes_iterator end() const noexcept { return m_end; }
        };

        // Returns a range with the adjacent nodes for the given node value.
        std::optional<nodes_adjacent_to_result> nodes_adjacent_to(
            const T& node_value) const noexcept;
        // Remainder of class definition omitted for brevity.
};
```

Here is the implementation of the `nodes_adjacent_to()` member function:

```
template <typename T>
std::optional<typename directed_graph<T>::nodes_adjacent_to_result>
    directed_graph<T>::nodes_adjacent_to(const T& node_value) const noexcept
{
    auto iter { find_node(node_value) };
    if (iter == std::end(m_nodes)) { return {}; }
    return nodes_adjacent_to_result {
        const_adjacent_nodes_iterator {
            std::cbegin(iter->get_adjacent_nodes_indices()), this },
        const_adjacent_nodes_iterator {
            std::cend(iter->get_adjacent_nodes_indices()), this }
    };
}
```

With `nodes_adjacent_to()`, accessing all adjacent nodes of a given node becomes trivial. Here is an example to print all adjacent nodes of the node with value 22.

```
print("Adjacency list for node 22: ");
auto nodesAdjacentTo22 { graph.nodes_adjacent_to(22) };
if (!nodesAdjacentTo22.has_value()) {
    println("Value 22 not found.");
} else {
    for (const auto& node : *nodesAdjacentTo22) { print("{} ", node); }
}
```

Printing Graphs

Now that directed_graph supports nodes_adjacent_to(), the to_dot() helper function template to print a graph can be simplified:

```
export template <typename T>
std::string to_dot(const directed_graph<T>& graph, std::string_view graph_name)
{
    std::ostringstream output;
    std::println(output, "digraph {} {{", graph_name);
    for (auto&& node : graph) {
        auto adjacent_nodes { graph.nodes_adjacent_to(node) };
        if (adjacent_nodes->begin() == adjacent_nodes->end()) {
            std::println(output, "{}", node);
        } else {
            for (const auto& adjacent_node : *adjacent_nodes) {
                std::println(output, "{} -> {}", node, adjacent_node);
            }
        }
    }
    std::println(output, "}}");
    return std::move(output).str();
}
```

Additional Standard Library–Like Functionality

A few more Standard Library–like features can be added to the directed_graph class template. First, let's add assign() member functions like vector has. The assign() member function accepting an iterator range is again a member function template, just like the iterator-based insert() discussed earlier in this chapter:

```
template <std::input_iterator Iter>
void assign(Iter first, Iter last);

void assign(std::initializer_list<T> il);
```

These allow you to assign all elements of a given iterator range or an initializer_list, discussed in Chapter 1, to a directed graph. Assignment means that the current graph is cleared, and new nodes are inserted. Despite the syntax, the implementations are easy:

```
template <typename T>
template <std::input_iterator Iter>
void directed_graph<T>::assign(Iter first, Iter last)
{
    clear();
    for (auto iter { first }; iter != last; ++iter) { insert(*iter); }
}

template <typename T>
void directed_graph<T>::assign(std::initializer_list<T> il)
{
    assign(std::begin(il), std::end(il));
}
```

An initializer_list overload of insert() is provided as well:

```
template <typename T>
void directed_graph<T>::insert(std::initializer_list<T> il)
{
    insert(std::begin(il), std::end(il));
}
```

With this overload of insert(), nodes can be added as follows:

```
graph.insert({ 66, 77, 88 });
```

Next, an initializer_list constructor and assignment operator can be added. As this is the first explicit directed_graph constructor and assignment operator, the default, copy, and move constructors, and the copy and move assignment operators need to be explicitly defaulted as well.

```
// Default, copy, and move constructors.
directed_graph() = default;
directed_graph(const directed_graph&) = default;
directed_graph(directed_graph&&) noexcept = default;

// initializer_list constructor.
directed_graph(std::initializer_list<T> il);

// Copy and move assignment operators.
directed_graph& operator=(const directed_graph&) = default;
directed_graph& operator=(directed_graph&&) noexcept = default;

// initializer_list assignment operator.
directed_graph& operator=(std::initializer_list<T> il);
```

Here are the implementations of the initializer_list constructor and assignment operator:

```
template <typename T>
directed_graph<T>::directed_graph(std::initializer_list<T> il)
{
    assign(std::begin(il), std::end(il));
}

template <typename T>
directed_graph<T>& directed_graph<T>::operator=(
    std::initializer_list<T> il)
{
    // Use a copy-and-swap-like algorithm to guarantee strong exception safety.
    // Do all the work in a temporary instance.
    directed_graph new_graph { il };
    swap(new_graph); // Commit the work with only non-throwing operations.
    return *this;
}
```

With these in place, a directed_graph can be constructed using uniform initialization, as follows:

```
directed_graph<int> graph { 11, 22, 33 };
```

instead of the following:

```
directed_graph<int> graph;
graph.insert(11);
graph.insert(22);
graph.insert(33);
```

And you can assign to a graph as follows:

```
graph = { 66, 77, 88 };
```

Thanks to the initializer_list constructor and class template argument deduction (CTAD), you can even drop the element type when constructing a directed_graph, just as with vector:

```
directed_graph graph { 11, 22, 33 };
```

A constructor accepting an iterator range of elements can be added as well. This is again a member function template, similar to assign() accepting an iterator range. The implementation simply forwards the work to assign():

```
template <typename T>
template <std::input_iterator Iter>
directed_graph<T>::directed_graph(Iter first, Iter last)
{
    assign(first, last);
}
```

C++23 adds an insert_range() member function to most Standard Library containers, which can be added to directed_graph as well. This implementation uses the std::ranges::input_range concept to constrain the Range template type parameter.

```
template <typename T>
template <std::ranges::input_range Range>
void directed_graph<T>::insert_range(Range&& range)
{
    insert(std::ranges::begin(range), std::ranges::end(range));
}
```

With insert_range() you can easily insert elements from any range, for example, from a vector:

```
vector moreNodes { 66, 77 };
graph.insert_range(moreNodes);
```

Finally, an extra overload of erase() accepting a node value can be added. Similar to std::set, it returns the number of nodes erased, which is always 0 or 1 for directed_graph.

```
template <typename T>
typename directed_graph<T>::size_type directed_graph<T>::erase(
    const T& node_value)
{
    const auto iter { find_node(node_value) };
    if (iter != std::end(m_nodes)) {
        remove_all_links_to(iter);
        m_nodes.erase(iter);
        return 1;
    }
    return 0;
}
```

Further Improvements

There are several improvements that can be made to the `directed_graph` class template. Here are a few:

- The current implementation does not check for cycles in the graph. Such a check could be added to make the graph a *directed acyclic graph*.
- Instead of supporting bidirectional iterators, support for random-access iterators could be implemented.
- The Standard Library associative containers support node-related functionality, see Chapter 18. The `directed_graph` class template could be improved to include a `node_type` type alias and member functions such as `extract()`.
- A more complicated improvement might be to add support for custom allocators, just as all Standard Library containers have. This would require using Standard Library functionality from `std::allocator_traits<A>`, such as `construct()`, `destroy()`, `propagate_on_container_move_assignment`, `propagate_on_container_copy_assignment`, `propagate_on_container_swap`, and more.

Other Container Types

The `directed_graph` class template is basically a sequential container, but due to the nature of graphs, it does implement certain functionality from associative containers, such as the return types of the `insert()` member functions.

You could also write a pure sequential container, unordered associative container, or ordered associative container. In that case, you would need to follow a specific set of requirements mandated by the Standard Library. Instead of listing them here, it's easier to point out that the `deque` container follows the prescribed sequential container requirements almost exactly. The only difference is that it provides an extra `resize()` member function (not required by the standard). An example of an ordered associative container is `map`, on which you can model your own ordered associative containers. And `unordered_map` is an example of an unordered associative container.

SUMMARY

This chapter introduced you to the concept of allocators that allow you to customize how memory is allocated and deallocated for containers. It also showed you how to write your own algorithms that can work with data from Standard Library containers. Finally, the major part of this chapter showed almost the complete development of a Standard Library–compliant `directed_graph` container. Thanks to its iterator support, `directed_graph` is compatible with Standard Library algorithms.

In the process of reading this chapter, you ideally gained an appreciation for the steps involved in developing algorithms and containers. Even if you never write another Standard Library algorithm or container, you understand better the Standard Library's mentality and capabilities, and you can put it to better use.

This chapter concludes the tour of the C++ Standard Library. Even with all the details given in this book, some features are still omitted. If this material excited you, and you would like more information, consult some of the resources in Appendix B. Don't feel compelled to use all the features discussed in these chapters. Forcing them into your programs without a true need will just complicate your code. However, I encourage you to consider incorporating aspects of the Standard Library into your programs where they make sense. Start with the containers, maybe throw in an algorithm or two, and before you know it, you'll be a convert!

EXERCISES

By solving the following exercises, you can practice the material discussed in this chapter. Solutions to all exercises are available with the code download on the book's website at `www.wiley.com/go/proc++6e`. However, if you are stuck on an exercise, first reread parts of this chapter to try to find an answer yourself before looking at the solution from the website.

Exercise 25-1: Write an algorithm called `transform_if()`, similar to the Standard Library's `transform()`, discussed in Chapter 20. The difference is that `transform_if()` should accept an extra predicate and that it only transforms elements for which the predicate returns `true`. Other elements are left untouched. To test your algorithm, create an `array` of integers, and then use `transform_if()` to copy the integers into a `vector` while multiplying all odd values by 2.

Exercise 25-2: Write an algorithm called `generate_fibonacci()`, which fills a given range with a Fibonacci series of numbers.[1] The Fibonacci series starts with 0 and 1, and any subsequent value is the sum of the two previous values, so: 0, 1, 1, 2, 3, 5, 8, 13, 21, 34, 55, 89, and so on. Your implementation is not allowed to contain any manually written loops or be implemented using a recursive algorithm. Instead, you should use the Standard Library's `generate()` algorithm to do most of the work.

Exercise 25-3: Implement a `find(const T&)` member function for the `directed_graph` class template.

Exercise 25-4: All associative containers have a `contains()` member function that returns `true` if a given element is in the container and `false` otherwise. As this could be useful for a `directed_graph` as well, add an implementation of `contains()` to `directed_graph`.

[1] The ratio of two successive Fibonacci numbers converges to the golden ratio, 1.618034 ... The Fibonacci numbers and the golden ratio often occur in nature, such as branching in trees, flowering of artichokes, flower petals, shells, and many more. The golden ratio is artistically attractive for humans, and hence is often used by architects to design rooms, for the arrangements of plants in gardens, and more.

26

Advanced Templates

WHAT'S IN THIS CHAPTER?

- The different kinds of template parameters
- How to use partial specialization
- How to write recursive templates
- How to write variadic templates
- How to write type-safe variable argument functions using variadic templates
- What `constexpr if` statements are
- What fold-expressions are and how to use them
- What metaprogramming is and how to use it
- What type traits are and what they can be used for
- What SFINAE means

WILEY.COM DOWNLOADS FOR THIS CHAPTER

Please note that all the code examples for this chapter are available as part of this chapter's code download on the book's website at `www.wiley.com/go/proc++6e` on the Download Code tab.

Chapter 12, "Writing Generic Code with Templates," covers the most widely used features of class and function templates. If you are interested in only a basic knowledge of templates so that you can better understand how the Standard Library works, or perhaps write your own simple class and function templates, you can skip this chapter on advanced templates. However, if templates interest you and you want to uncover their full power, continue reading this chapter to learn some obscure, but fascinating, details.

MORE ABOUT TEMPLATE PARAMETERS

There are three kinds of template parameters: template type parameters, non-type template parameters, and template template parameters. So far, you've seen examples of type and non-type parameters (in Chapter 12), but not template template parameters. There are also some tricky aspects to both type and non-type parameters that are not covered in Chapter 12. This section goes deeper into all three types of template parameters.

More About Template Type Parameters

Template type parameters are the main purpose of templates. You can declare as many type parameters as you want. For example, you could add to the grid template from Chapter 12 a second type parameter specifying a container on which to build the grid. The Standard Library defines several parametrized container classes, including `vector` and `deque`. The original `Grid` class uses a `vector` to store the elements of a grid. A user of the `Grid` class might want to use a `deque` instead. With another template type parameter, you can allow the user to specify whether they want the underlying container to be a `vector` or a `deque`. The `Grid` implementation requires the underlying container to support random access. It also uses the `resize()` member function of the container and the container's `value_type` type alias. A concept (see Chapter 12) is used to enforce that the provided container type supports these operations. Here is the concept and the class template definition with the additional template type parameter. Changes are highlighted.

```
template <typename Container>
concept GridContainerType =
    std::ranges::random_access_range<Container> &&
    requires(Container c) {
        typename Container::value_type;
        c.resize(1);
    };

export template <typename T, GridContainerType Container>
class Grid
{
    public:
        explicit Grid(std::size_t width = DefaultWidth,
            std::size_t height = DefaultHeight);
        virtual ~Grid() = default;

        // Explicitly default a copy constructor and assignment operator.
        Grid(const Grid& src) = default;
        Grid& operator=(const Grid& rhs) = default;

        // Explicitly default a move constructor and assignment operator.
        Grid(Grid&& src) = default;
        Grid& operator=(Grid&& rhs) = default;

        typename Container::value_type& at(std::size_t x, std::size_t y);
        const typename Container::value_type& at(
           std::size_t x, std::size_t y) const;
```

```
        std::size_t getHeight() const { return m_height; }
        std::size_t getWidth() const { return m_width; }

        static constexpr std::size_t DefaultWidth { 10 };
        static constexpr std::size_t DefaultHeight { 10 };

    private:
        void verifyCoordinate(std::size_t x, std::size_t y) const;

        Container m_cells;
        std::size_t m_width { 0 }, m_height { 0 };
};
```

This template now has two parameters: `T` and `Container`. Thus, wherever you previously referred to `Grid<T>`, you must now refer to `Grid<T, Container>`.

> **NOTE** *Technically, in this implementation of the `Grid` class template, you could remove the `T` template type parameter because the implementation doesn't need it; it only uses the `Container` parameter. However, please bear with me, as the next section builds further on this example to make it more user friendly.*

The `m_cells` data member is now of type `Container` instead of `vector<optional<T>>`. Each `Container` type has a type alias called `value_type`. This is verified with the `GridContainerType` concept. Inside the `Grid` class template definition and its member function definitions, you get access to this `value_type` type name using the scope resolution operator: `Container::value_type`. However, since `Container` is a template type parameter, `Container::value_type` is a *dependent type name*. Usually, a compiler won't treat dependent names as names of types, and this can lead to some rather cryptic compiler error messages. To make sure the compiler does interpret it as the name of a type, you need to prefix it with the `typename` keyword, as in `typename Container::value_type`. This is what is done for the return type of the `at()` member functions; their return type is the type of the elements that is stored inside the given container type, which is `typename Container::value_type`.

Here is the constructor definition:

```
template <typename T, GridContainerType Container>
Grid<T, Container>::Grid(std::size_t width, std::size_t height)
    : m_width { width }, m_height { height }
{
    m_cells.resize(m_width * m_height);
}
```

Here are the implementations of the remaining member functions:

```
template <typename T, GridContainerType Container>
void Grid<T, Container>::verifyCoordinate(std::size_t x, std::size_t y) const
{
    if (x >= m_width) {
        throw std::out_of_range {
            std::format("x ({}) must be less than width ({}).", x, m_width) };
    }
```

```
        if (y >= m_height) {
            throw std::out_of_range {
                std::format("y ({}) must be less than height ({}).", y, m_height) };
        }
    }

    template <typename T, GridContainerType Container>
    const typename Container::value_type&
        Grid<T, Container>::at(std::size_t x, std::size_t y) const
    {
        verifyCoordinate(x, y);
        return m_cells[x + y * m_width];
    }

    template <typename T, GridContainerType Container>
    typename Container::value_type&
        Grid<T, Container>::at(std::size_t x, std::size_t y)
    {
        return const_cast<typename Container::value_type&>(
            std::as_const(*this).at(x, y));
    }
```

Now you can instantiate and use `Grid` objects like this:

```
Grid<int, vector<optional<int>>> myIntVectorGrid;
Grid<int, deque<optional<int>>> myIntDequeGrid;

myIntVectorGrid.at(3, 4) = 5;
println("{}", myIntVectorGrid.at(3, 4).value_or(0));

myIntDequeGrid.at(1, 2) = 3;
println("{}", myIntDequeGrid.at(1, 2).value_or(0));

Grid<int, vector<optional<int>>> grid2 { myIntVectorGrid };
grid2 = myIntVectorGrid;
```

You could try to instantiate the `Grid` class template with `double` for the `Container` template type parameter:

```
Grid<int, double> test; // WILL NOT COMPILE
```

This line does not compile. The compiler complains that the type `double` does not satisfy the constraints of the concept associated with the `Container` template type parameter.

Just as with function parameters, you can give template parameters default values. For example, you might want to say that the default container for a `Grid` is a `vector`. The class template definition then looks like this:

```
export template <typename T,
    GridContainerType Container = std::vector<std::optional<T>>>
class Grid
{
    // Everything else is the same as before.
};
```

You can use the type `T` from the first template type parameter as the argument to the `optional` template in the default value for the second template type parameter. The C++ syntax requires that you do not repeat the default value in the template header line for member function definitions. With this default argument, clients can now instantiate a `Grid` and optionally specify an underlying container. Here are some examples:

```
Grid<int, deque<optional<int>>> myDequeGrid;
Grid<int, vector<optional<int>>> myVectorGrid;
Grid<int> myVectorGrid2 { myVectorGrid };
```

This approach is used by the Standard Library. The `stack`, `queue`, `priority_queue`, `flat_(multi)set`, and `flat_(multi)map` class templates all take a `Container` template type parameter, with a default value, specifying the underlying container.

Introducing Template Template Parameters

There is one problem with the `Container` parameter in the previous section. When you instantiate the class template, you write something like this:

```
Grid<int, vector<optional<int>>> myIntGrid;
```

Note the repetition of the `int` type. You must specify that it's the element type both of the `Grid` and of the `optional` inside the `vector`. What if you wrote this instead:

```
Grid<int, vector<optional<SpreadsheetCell>>> myIntGrid;
```

that wouldn't work very well. It would be nice to be able to write the following, so that you couldn't make that mistake:

```
Grid<int, vector> myIntGrid;
```

The `Grid` class template should be able to figure out that it wants a `vector` of `optional`s of `int`s. The compiler won't allow you to pass that argument to a normal type parameter, though, because `vector` by itself is not a type but a template.

If you want to take a template as a template type parameter, you must use a special kind of parameter called a *template template parameter*. Specifying a template template parameter is sort of like specifying a function pointer parameter in a normal function. Function pointer types include the return type and parameter types of a function. Similarly, when you specify a template template parameter, the full specification of the template template parameter includes the parameters to that template.

For example, containers such as `vector` and `deque` have a template parameter list that looks something like the following. The `E` parameter is the element type. The `Allocator` parameter is covered in Chapter 25, "Customizing and Extending the Standard Library."

```
template <typename E, typename Allocator = std::allocator<E>>
class vector { /* Vector definition */ };
```

To pass such a container as a template template parameter, all you have to do is copy and paste the declaration of the class template (in this example, `template <typename E, typename Allocator = std::allocator<E>> class vector`) and replace the class name (`vector`) with your parameter name (`Container`). Given the preceding template specification, here is the class template definition for `Grid` that takes a container template as its second template parameter:

```
export template <typename T,
  template <typename E, typename Allocator = std::allocator<E>> class Container
    = std::vector>
class Grid
{
    public:
        // Omitted code that is the same as before.
        std::optional<T>& at(std::size_t x, std::size_t y);
        const std::optional<T>& at(std::size_t x, std::size_t y) const;
        // Omitted code that is the same as before.
    private:
        void verifyCoordinate(std::size_t x, std::size_t y) const;

        Container<std::optional<T>> m_cells;
        std::size_t m_width { 0 }, m_height { 0 };
};
```

What is going on here? The first template parameter is the same as before: the element type `T`. The second template parameter is now a template itself for a container such as `vector` or `deque`. As you saw earlier, this "template type" must take two parameters: an element type `E` and an allocator type. The name of this parameter in the `Grid` template is `Container` (as before). The default value is now `vector`, instead of `vector<T>`, because the `Container` parameter is now a template instead of an actual type.

The syntax rule for a template template parameter, more generically, is this:

```
template <..., template <TemplateTypeParams> class ParameterName, ...>
```

> **NOTE** *You can also use the* `typename` *keyword instead of* `class`*, as in the following example:*
>
> ```
> template <..., template <Params> typename ParameterName, ...>
> ```

Instead of using `Container` by itself in the code, you must specify `Container<std::optional<T>>` as the container type. For example, the declaration of `m_cells` is now as follows:

```
Container<std::optional<T>> m_cells;
```

The member function definitions don't need to change, except that you must change the template headers, for example:

```
template <typename T,
  template <typename E, typename Allocator = std::allocator<E>> class Container>
void Grid<T, Container>::verifyCoordinate(std::size_t x, std::size_t y) const
{
    // Same implementation as before...
}
```

This `Grid` class template can be used as follows:

```
Grid<int, vector> myGrid;
myGrid.at(1, 2) = 3;
println("{}", myGrid.at(1, 2).value_or(0));
```

```
Grid<int, vector> myGrid2 { myGrid };
Grid<int, deque> myDequeGrid;
```

This section demonstrated that you can pass templates as type parameters to other templates. However, the syntax looks a bit convoluted, and it is. I recommend avoiding template template parameters. In fact, the Standard Library itself never uses template template parameters.

More About Non-type Template Parameters

You might want to allow the user to specify a default element used to initialize each cell in the grid. Here is a perfectly reasonable approach to implement this goal. It uses the zero-initialization syntax, `T{}`, as the default value for the second template parameter.

```
export template <typename T, T DEFAULT = T{}>
class Grid { /* Identical as before. */ };
```

This definition is legal. You can use the type `T` from the first parameter as the type for the second parameter. You can use this initial value for `T` to initialize each cell in the grid:

```
template <typename T, T DEFAULT>
Grid<T, DEFAULT>::Grid(std::size_t width, std::size_t height)
    : m_width { width }, m_height { height }
{
    m_cells.resize(m_width * m_height, DEFAULT);
}
```

The other member function definitions stay the same, except that you must add the second template parameter to the template headers, and all the instances of `Grid<T>` become `Grid<T, DEFAULT>`. After making those changes, you can instantiate grids with an initial value for all the elements:

```
Grid<int> myIntGrid;          // Initial value is int{}, i.e., 0
Grid<int, 10> myIntGrid2;     // Initial value is 10
```

The initial value can be any integer you want. However, suppose that you try to create a `Grid` for `SpreadsheetCell`s as follows:

```
SpreadsheetCell defaultCell;
Grid<SpreadsheetCell, defaultCell> mySpreadsheet; // WILL NOT COMPILE
```

The second line leads to a compilation error because the value of the template parameter `DEFAULT` must be known at compile time; the value of `defaultCell` can't be known until run time, so it is not an acceptable value for `DEFAULT`.

> **WARNING** *Up until C++20, non-type template parameters cannot be objects, or even* `double`s *or* `float`s. *They are restricted to integral types,* `enum`s, *pointers, and references. Since C++20, these restrictions are relaxed a bit and it is now allowed to have non-type template parameters of floating-point types, and even certain class types. However, such class types have a lot of restrictions, not further discussed in this book. Suffice to say, the* `SpreadsheetCell` *class does not adhere to those restrictions.*

CLASS TEMPLATE PARTIAL SPECIALIZATION

The `const char*` class specialization of the `Grid` class template shown in Chapter 12 is called a *full class template specialization* because it specializes the `Grid` template for every template parameter. There are no template parameters left in the specialization. That's not the only way you can specialize a class; you can also write a *partial class template specialization*, in which you specialize some template parameters but not others. For example, recall the basic version of the `Grid` template with width and height non-type parameters:

```
export template <typename T, std::size_t WIDTH, std::size_t HEIGHT>
class Grid
{
    public:
        Grid() = default;
        virtual ~Grid() = default;

        // Explicitly default a copy constructor and assignment operator.
        Grid(const Grid& src) = default;
        Grid& operator=(const Grid& rhs) = default;

        // Explicitly default a move constructor and assignment operator.
        Grid(Grid&& src) = default;
        Grid& operator=(Grid&& rhs) = default;

        std::optional<T>& at(std::size_t x, std::size_t y);
        const std::optional<T>& at(std::size_t x, std::size_t y) const;

        std::size_t getHeight() const { return HEIGHT; }
        std::size_t getWidth() const { return WIDTH; }
    private:
        void verifyCoordinate(std::size_t x, std::size_t y) const;

        std::optional<T> m_cells[WIDTH][HEIGHT];
};
```

You can specialize this class template for `const char*` C-style strings like this:

```
export template <std::size_t WIDTH, std::size_t HEIGHT>
class Grid<const char*, WIDTH, HEIGHT>
{
    public:
        Grid() = default;
        virtual ~Grid() = default;

        // Explicitly default a copy constructor and assignment operator.
        Grid(const Grid& src) = default;
        Grid& operator=(const Grid& rhs) = default;

        // Explicitly default a move constructor and assignment operator.
        Grid(Grid&& src) = default;
        Grid& operator=(Grid&& rhs) = default;
```

```
        std::optional<std::string>& at(std::size_t x, std::size_t y);
        const std::optional<std::string>& at(std::size_t x, std::size_t y) const;

        std::size_t getHeight() const { return HEIGHT; }
        std::size_t getWidth() const { return WIDTH; }
    private:
        void verifyCoordinate(std::size_t x, std::size_t y) const;

        std::optional<std::string> m_cells[WIDTH][HEIGHT];
};
```

In this case, you are not specializing all the template parameters. Therefore, your template header looks like this:

```
export template <std::size_t WIDTH, std::size_t HEIGHT>
class Grid<const char*, WIDTH, HEIGHT>
```

This class template has only two parameters: `WIDTH` and `HEIGHT`. However, you're writing a `Grid` class for three arguments: `T`, `WIDTH`, and `HEIGHT`. Thus, your template parameter list contains two parameters, and the explicit `Grid<const char*, WIDTH, HEIGHT>` contains three arguments. When you instantiate the template, you must still specify three parameters. You can't instantiate the template with only height and width.

```
Grid<int, 2, 2> myIntGrid;           // Uses the original Grid
Grid<const char*, 2, 2> myStringGrid; // Uses the partial specialization
Grid<2, 3> test;                     // DOES NOT COMPILE! No type specified.
```

Yes, the syntax might be confusing. Additionally, in partial specializations, unlike in full specializations, you must include the template header in front of every member function definition, as in the following example:

```
template <std::size_t WIDTH, std::size_t HEIGHT>
const std::optional<std::string>&
    Grid<const char*, WIDTH, HEIGHT>::at(std::size_t x, std::size_t y) const
{
    verifyCoordinate(x, y);
    return m_cells[x][y];
}
```

You need this template header with two parameters to show that this member function is parameterized on those two parameters. Note that wherever you refer to the full class name, you must use `Grid<const char*, WIDTH, HEIGHT>`.

The previous example does not show the true power of partial specialization. You can write specialized implementations for a subset of possible types without specializing individual types. For example, you can write a specialization of the `Grid` class template for all pointer types. The copy constructor and assignment operator of this specialization perform deep copies of objects to which pointers point, instead of shallow copies.

The following is the class definition, assuming that you're specializing the initial version of `Grid` with only one template parameter. In this implementation, `Grid` becomes the owner of supplied data, so it automatically frees the memory when necessary. Copy/move constructors and copy/move assignment operators are required. As usual, the copy assignment operator uses the copy-and-swap idiom, and the move assignment operator uses the move-and-swap idiom, as discussed in Chapter 9, "Mastering Classes and Objects," which requires a `noexcept swap()` member function.

```
export template <typename U>
class Grid<U*>
{
    public:
        explicit Grid(std::size_t width = DefaultWidth,
            std::size_t height = DefaultHeight);
        virtual ~Grid() = default;

        // Copy constructor and copy assignment operator.
        Grid(const Grid& src);
        Grid& operator=(const Grid& rhs);

        // Move constructor and move assignment operator.
        Grid(Grid&& src) noexcept;
        Grid& operator=(Grid&& rhs) noexcept;

        void swap(Grid& other) noexcept;

        std::unique_ptr<U>& at(std::size_t x, std::size_t y);
        const std::unique_ptr<U>& at(std::size_t x, std::size_t y) const;

        std::size_t getHeight() const { return m_height; }
        std::size_t getWidth() const { return m_width; }

        static constexpr std::size_t DefaultWidth { 10 };
        static constexpr std::size_t DefaultHeight { 10 };

    private:
        void verifyCoordinate(std::size_t x, std::size_t y) const;

        std::vector<std::unique_ptr<U>> m_cells;
        std::size_t m_width { 0 }, m_height { 0 };
};
```

As usual, these two lines are the crux of the matter:

```
export template <typename U>
class Grid<U*>
```

This syntax states that this class template is a specialization of the `Grid` class template for all pointer types. Important to know, when you have an instantiation such as `Grid<int*>`, then `U` is `int`, not `int*`. That might be a bit unintuitive, but that's the way it works.

Here is an example of using this partial specialization:

```
Grid<int> myIntGrid;        // Uses the non-specialized grid.
Grid<int*> psGrid { 2, 2 }; // Uses the partial specialization for pointer types.

psGrid.at(0, 0) = make_unique<int>(1);
psGrid.at(0, 1) = make_unique<int>(2);
psGrid.at(1, 0) = make_unique<int>(3);
```

```
Grid<int*> psGrid2 { psGrid };
Grid<int*> psGrid3;
psGrid3 = psGrid2;

auto& element { psGrid2.at(1, 0) };
if (element != nullptr) {
    println("{}", *element);
    *element = 6;
}
println("{}", *psGrid.at(1, 0));  // psGrid is not modified.
println("{}", *psGrid2.at(1, 0)); // psGrid2 is modified.
```

Here is the output:

```
3
3
6
```

The implementations of the member functions are rather straightforward, except for the copy constructor, which uses the copy constructor of individual elements to make a deep copy of them:

```
template <typename U>
Grid<U*>::Grid(const Grid& src)
    : Grid { src.m_width, src.m_height }
{
    // The ctor-initializer of this constructor delegates first to the
    // non-copy constructor to allocate the proper amount of memory.

    // The next step is to copy the data.
    for (std::size_t i { 0 }; i < m_cells.size(); ++i) {
        // Make a deep copy of the element by using its copy constructor.
        if (src.m_cells[i] != nullptr) {
            m_cells[i] = std::make_unique<U>(*src.m_cells[i]);
        }
    }
}
```

EMULATING FUNCTION PARTIAL SPECIALIZATION WITH OVERLOADING

The C++ standard does not permit partial template specialization of function templates. Instead, you can overload the function template with another function template. As an example, let's look again at the `Find()` algorithm from Chapter 12. It consists of a generic `Find()` function template and a non-template overload for `const char*`s. Here is a reminder:

```
template <typename T>
optional<size_t> Find(const T& value, const T* arr, size_t size)
{
    for (size_t i { 0 }; i < size; ++i) {
        if (arr[i] == value) {
            return i; // found it; return the index.
        }
    }
    return {}; // failed to find it; return empty optional.
}
```

```
optional<size_t> Find(const char* value, const char** arr, size_t size)
{
    for (size_t i { 0 }; i < size; ++i) {
        if (strcmp(arr[i], value) == 0) {
            return i; // found it; return the index.
        }
    }
    return {}; // failed to find it; return empty optional.
}
```

Suppose that you want to customize `Find()` so that it dereferences pointers to use `operator==` directly on the objects pointed to. The correct way to implement this behavior is to overload the `Find()` function template with another, more specialized, function template:

```
template <typename T>
optional<size_t> Find(T* value, T* const* arr, size_t size)
{
    for (size_t i { 0 }; i < size; ++i) {
        if (*arr[i] == *value) {
            return i; // Found it; return the index.
        }
    }
    return {}; // failed to find it; return empty optional.
}
```

> **NOTE** *Between all overloads, the compiler always chooses the "most specific" one to call. If a non-template overload is just as specific as a function template instantiation, then the compiler prefers the non-template overload.*

The following code calls `Find()` several times. The comments say which overload of `Find()` is called.

```
optional<size_t> res;

int myInt { 3 }, intArray[] { 1, 2, 3, 4 };
size_t sizeArray { size(intArray) };
res = Find(myInt, intArray, sizeArray);    // calls Find<int> by deduction
res = Find<int>(myInt, intArray, sizeArray); // calls Find<int> explicitly

double myDouble { 5.6 }, doubleArray[] { 1.2, 3.4, 5.7, 7.5 };
sizeArray = size(doubleArray);
// calls Find<double> by deduction
res = Find(myDouble, doubleArray, sizeArray);
// calls Find<double> explicitly
res = Find<double>(myDouble, doubleArray, sizeArray);

const char* word { "two" };
const char* words[] { "one", "two", "three", "four" };
sizeArray = size(words);
```

```
// calls Find<const char*> explicitly
res = Find<const char*>(word, words, sizeArray);
// calls overloaded Find for const char*s
res = Find(word, words, sizeArray);

int *intPointer { &myInt }, *pointerArray[] { &myInt, &myInt };
sizeArray = size(pointerArray);
// calls the overloaded Find for pointers
res = Find(intPointer, pointerArray, sizeArray);

SpreadsheetCell cell1 { 10 };
SpreadsheetCell cellArray[] { SpreadsheetCell { 4 }, SpreadsheetCell { 10 } };
sizeArray = size(cellArray);
// calls Find<SpreadsheetCell> by deduction
res = Find(cell1, cellArray, sizeArray);
// calls Find<SpreadsheetCell> explicitly
res = Find<SpreadsheetCell>(cell1, cellArray, sizeArray);

SpreadsheetCell *cellPointer { &cell1 };
SpreadsheetCell *cellPointerArray[] { &cell1, &cell1 };
sizeArray = size(cellPointerArray);
// Calls the overloaded Find for pointers
res = Find(cellPointer, cellPointerArray, sizeArray);
```

TEMPLATE RECURSION

Templates in C++ provide capabilities that go far beyond the simple class and function templates you have seen so far in this chapter and Chapter 12. One of these capabilities is *template recursion*. Template recursion is similar to function recursion, in which a function is defined in terms of calling itself with a slightly easier version of the problem. This section first provides a motivation for template recursion and then shows how to implement it.

An N-Dimensional Grid: First Attempt

Up to now, the `Grid` class template supports only two dimensions, which limits its usefulness. What if you want to write a 3-D tic-tac-toe game or write a math program with four-dimensional matrices? You could, of course, write a templated or non-templated class for each of those dimensions. However, that would repeat a lot of code. Another approach would be to write only a single-dimensional grid. Then, you could create a `Grid` of any dimension by instantiating the `Grid` with another `Grid` as its element type. This `Grid` element type could itself be instantiated with a `Grid` as its element type, and so on. Here is the implementation of a `OneDGrid` class template. It's simply a one-dimensional version of the `Grid` class template from earlier examples, with the addition of a `resize()` member function, and the substitution of `operator[]` for `at()`. Just as with Standard Library containers such as `vector`, the `operator[]` implementation does not perform any bounds checking. For this example, `m_elements` stores instances of `T` instead of instances of `std::optional<T>`.

```
export template <typename T>
class OneDGrid final
{
    public:
```

```
        explicit OneDGrid(std::size_t size = DefaultSize) { resize(size); }

        T& operator[](std::size_t x) { return m_elements[x]; }
        const T& operator[](std::size_t x) const { return m_elements[x]; }

        void resize(std::size_t newSize) { m_elements.resize(newSize); }
        std::size_t getSize() const { return m_elements.size(); }

        static constexpr std::size_t DefaultSize { 10 };
    private:
        std::vector<T> m_elements;
};
```

With this implementation of `OneDGrid`, you can create multidimensional grids like this:

```
OneDGrid<int> singleDGrid;
OneDGrid<OneDGrid<int>> twoDGrid;
OneDGrid<OneDGrid<OneDGrid<int>>> threeDGrid;
singleDGrid[3] = 5;
twoDGrid[3][3] = 5;
threeDGrid[3][3][3] = 5;
```

This code works fine, but the declarations are messy. As the next section explains, we can do better.

A Real *N*-Dimensional Grid

You can use template recursion to write a "real" *N*-dimensional grid because dimensionality of grids is essentially recursive. You can see that in this declaration:

```
OneDGrid<OneDGrid<OneDGrid<int>>> threeDGrid;
```

You can think of each nested `OneDGrid` as a recursive step, with the `OneDGrid` of `int` as the base case. In other words, a three-dimensional grid is a single-dimensional grid of single-dimensional grids of single-dimensional grids of `int`s. Instead of requiring the user to do this recursion, you can write a class template that does it for you. You can then create *N*-dimensional grids like this:

```
NDGrid<int, 1> singleDGrid;
NDGrid<int, 2> twoDGrid;
NDGrid<int, 3> threeDGrid;
```

The `NDGrid` class template takes a type for its element and an integer specifying its "dimensionality." The key insight here is that the element type of the `NDGrid` is not the element type specified in the template parameter list, but is in fact another `NDGrid` of dimensionality one less than the current one. In other words, a three-dimensional grid is a `vector` of two-dimensional grids; the two-dimensional grids are each `vector`s of one-dimensional grids.

With recursion, you need a base case. You can write a partial specialization of `NDGrid` for dimensionality of 1, in which the element type is not another `NDGrid`, but is in fact the element type specified by the template parameter.

The following shows the `NDGrid` class template definition and implementation, with highlights showing where it differs from the `OneDGrid` shown in the previous section. The `m_elements` data member is now a `vector` of `NDGrid<T, N-1>`; this is the recursive step. Also, `operator[]` returns a reference to the element type, which is again `NDGrid<T, N-1>`, not `T`.

The trickiest aspect of the implementation, other than the template recursion itself, is appropriately sizing each dimension of the grid. This implementation creates the *N*-dimensional grid with every dimension of equal size. It's significantly more difficult to specify a separate size for each dimension. A user should have the ability to create a grid with a specified size, such as 20 or 50. Thus, the constructor takes an integer size parameter. The `resize()` member function is modified to resize `m_elements` and to initialize each element with `NDGrid<T, N-1> { newSize }`, which recursively resizes all dimensions of the grid to the new size.

```
export template <typename T, std::size_t N>
class NDGrid final
{
    public:
        explicit NDGrid(std::size_t size = DefaultSize) { resize(size); }

        NDGrid<T, N-1>& operator[](std::size_t x) { return m_elements[x]; }
        const NDGrid<T, N-1>& operator[](std::size_t x) const {
            return m_elements[x]; }

        void resize(std::size_t newSize)
        {
            m_elements.resize(newSize, NDGrid<T, N-1> { newSize });
        }

        std::size_t getSize() const { return m_elements.size(); }

        static constexpr std::size_t DefaultSize { 10 };
    private:
        std::vector<NDGrid<T, N-1>> m_elements;
};
```

The template definition for the base case is a partial specialization for dimension 1. The following shows the definition and implementation. You must rewrite a lot of the code because a specialization never inherits any code from the primary template. Highlights show the differences from the non-specialized `NDGrid`.

```
export template <typename T>
class NDGrid<T, 1> final
{
    public:
        explicit NDGrid(std::size_t size = DefaultSize) { resize(size); }

        T& operator[](std::size_t x) { return m_elements[x]; }
        const T& operator[](std::size_t x) const { return m_elements[x]; }

        void resize(std::size_t newSize) { m_elements.resize(newSize); }
        std::size_t getSize() const { return m_elements.size(); }

        static constexpr std::size_t DefaultSize { 10 };
    private:
        std::vector<T> m_elements;
};
```

Here the recursion ends: the element type is `T`, not another template instantiation.

Now, you can write code like this:

```
NDGrid<int, 3> my3DGrid { 4 };
my3DGrid[2][1][2] = 5;
my3DGrid[1][1][1] = 5;
println("{}", my3DGrid[2][1][2]);
```

To avoid the code duplication between the primary template and the specialization, you could pull the duplicate code out into a base class and then derive both the primary template and the specialization from that base class; but in this small example, the overhead added by that technique would outweigh the savings.

VARIADIC TEMPLATES

Normal templates can take only a fixed number of template parameters. *Variadic templates* can take a variable number of template parameters. For example, the following code defines a template that can accept any number of template parameters, using a *parameter pack* called `Types`:

```
template <typename... Types>
class MyVariadicTemplate { };
```

> **NOTE** *The three dots following* `typename` *are not an error. This is the syntax to define a parameter pack for variadic templates. A parameter pack is something that can accept a variable number of arguments.*

You can instantiate `MyVariadicTemplate` with any number of template arguments, as in this example:

```
MyVariadicTemplate<int> instance1;
MyVariadicTemplate<string, double, vector<int>> instance2;
```

It can even be instantiated with zero template arguments:

```
MyVariadicTemplate<> instance3;
```

To disallow instantiating a variadic template with zero template arguments, you can write the template as follows:

```
template <typename T1, typename... Types>
class MyVariadicTemplate { };
```

With this definition, trying to instantiate `MyVariadicTemplate` with zero template arguments results in a compilation error.

It is not possible to directly iterate over the arguments given to a variadic template. The only way you can do this is with the aid of template recursion or fold expressions. The following sections show examples of both.

Type-Safe Variable-Length Argument Lists

Variadic templates allow you to create *type-safe variable-length* argument lists. The following example defines a variadic template called `processValues()`, allowing it to accept a variable number of arguments with different types in a type-safe manner. The `processValues()` function processes each value in the variable-length argument list and executes a function called `handleValue()` for each single argument. This means you have to write an overload of `handleValue()` for each type that you want to handle—`int`, `double`, and `string` in this example:

```
void handleValue(int value) { println("Integer: {}", value); }
void handleValue(double value) { println("Double: {}", value); }
void handleValue(const string& value) { println("String: {}", value); }

void processValues() // Base case to stop recursion
{ /* Nothing to do in this base case. */ }

template <typename T1, typename... Tn>
void processValues(const T1& arg1, const Tn&... args)
{
    handleValue(arg1);
    processValues(args...);
}
```

This example demonstrates a double use of the triple dots (`...`) operator. This operator appears in three places and has two different meanings. First, it is used after `typename` in the template parameter list and after type `Tn` in the function parameter list. In both cases, it denotes a *parameter pack*. A parameter pack can accept a variable number of arguments.

The second use of the `...` operator is following the parameter name `args` in the function body. In this case, it means a *parameter pack expansion*; the operator *unpacks/expands* the parameter pack into separate arguments. It basically takes what is on the left side of the operator and repeats it for every template parameter in the pack, separated by commas. Take the following statement:

```
processValues(args...);
```

This statement expands the `args` parameter pack into its separate arguments, separated by commas, and then calls the `processValues()` function with the list of expanded arguments. The template always requires at least one parameter, `T1`. The act of recursively calling `processValues()` with `args...` is that on each call there is one parameter less.

Because the implementation of the `processValues()` function is recursive, you need to have a way to stop the recursion. This is done by implementing a `processValues()` function that accepts no arguments.

You can test the `processValues()` variadic template as follows:

```
processValues(1, 2, 3.56, "test", 1.1f);
```

The recursive calls generated by this example are as follows:

```
processValues(1, 2, 3.56, "test", 1.1f);
  handleValue(1);
```

```
processValues(2, 3.56, "test", 1.1f);
  handleValue(2);
  processValues(3.56, "test", 1.1f);
    handleValue(3.56);
    processValues("test", 1.1f);
      handleValue("test");
      processValues(1.1f);
        handleValue(1.1f);
        processValues();
```

It is important to remember that this implementation of variable-length argument lists is fully type-safe. The `processValues()` function automatically calls the correct `handleValue()` overload based on the actual type. The compiler will issue an error when you call `processValues()` with an argument of a certain type for which there is no `handleValue()` overload defined.

You can also use *forwarding references*, introduced in Chapter 12, in the implementation of `processValues()`. The following implementation uses forwarding references, `T&&`, and uses `std::forward()` for *perfect forwarding* of all parameters. Perfect forwarding means that if an rvalue is passed to `processValues()`, it is forwarded as an rvalue reference. If an lvalue is passed, it is forwarded as an lvalue reference.

```
void processValues() // Base case to stop recursion
{ /* Nothing to do in this base case.*/ }

template <typename T1, typename... Tn>
void processValues(T1&& arg1, Tn&&... args)
{
    handleValue(forward<T1>(arg1));
    processValues(forward<Tn>(args)...);
}
```

There is one statement that needs further explanation:

```
processValues(forward<Tn>(args)...);
```

The `...` operator is used to unpack the parameter pack. It uses `std::forward()` on each individual argument in the pack and separates them with commas. For example, suppose `args` is a parameter pack with three arguments, `a1`, `a2`, and `a3`, of three types, `A1`, `A2`, and `A3`. The expanded call then looks as follows:

```
processValues(forward<A1>(a1),
              forward<A2>(a2),
              forward<A3>(a3));
```

Inside the body of a function using a parameter pack, you can retrieve the number of arguments in the pack using `sizeof...(pack)`. Notice that this is not doing a pack expansion with `...`, but is using the special keyword-like syntax `sizeof...`

```
int numberOfArguments { sizeof...(args) };
```

A practical example of using variadic templates is to write a secure and type-safe `printf()`-like function template. This would be a good practice exercise for you to try.

constexpr if

`constexpr if` statements are `if` statements executed at compile time, not at run time. If a branch of a `constexpr if` statement is never taken, it is never compiled. Such compile-time decisions can come in handy with variadic templates. For example, the earlier implementation of `processValues()` requires a base case to stop the recursion (`void processValues(){}`). Using `constexpr if`, such a base case can be avoided. Notice that the feature is officially called `constexpr if`, but in actual code you write `if constexpr`.

```
template <typename T1, typename... Tn>
void processValues(T1&& arg1, Tn&&... args)
{
    handleValue(forward<T1>(arg1));
    if constexpr (sizeof...(args) > 0) {
        processValues(forward<Tn>(args)...);
    }
}
```

In this implementation, the recursion stops as soon as the variadic parameter pack, `args`, becomes empty. The only difference with the previous implementations is that you can no longer call `processValues()` without any arguments. Doing so results in a compilation error.

Variable Number of Mixin Classes

Parameter packs can be used almost everywhere. For example, the following code uses a parameter pack to define a variable number of mixin classes for `MyClass`. Chapter 5, "Designing with Classes," discusses the concept of mixin classes.

```
class Mixin1
{
    public:
        explicit Mixin1(int i) : m_value { i } {}
        virtual void mixin1Func() { println("Mixin1: {}", m_value); }
    private:
        int m_value;
};

class Mixin2
{
    public:
        explicit Mixin2(int i) : m_value { i } {}
        virtual void mixin2Func() { println("Mixin2: {}", m_value); }
    private:
        int m_value;
};

template <typename... Mixins>
class MyClass : public Mixins...
{
    public:
        explicit MyClass(const Mixins&... mixins) : Mixins { mixins }... {}
        virtual ~MyClass() = default;
};
```

This code first defines two mixin classes: `Mixin1` and `Mixin2`. They are kept pretty simple for this example. Their constructor accepts an integer, which is stored, and they have a function to print information about a specific instance of the class. The `MyClass` variadic template uses a parameter pack `typename... Mixins` to accept a variable number of mixin classes. The class then inherits from all those mixin classes, and the constructor accepts the same number of arguments to initialize each inherited mixin class. Remember that the `...` expansion operator basically takes what is on the left of the operator and repeats it for every template parameter in the pack, separated by commas. The class can be used as follows:

```
MyClass<Mixin1, Mixin2> a { Mixin1 { 11 }, Mixin2 { 22 } };
a.mixin1Func();
a.mixin2Func();

MyClass<Mixin1> b { Mixin1 { 33 } };
b.mixin1Func();
//b.mixin2Func();    // Error: does not compile.

MyClass<> c;
//c.mixin1Func();    // Error: does not compile.
//c.mixin2Func();    // Error: does not compile.
```

When you try to call `mixin2Func()` on `b`, you will get a compilation error because `b` is not inheriting from the `Mixin2` class. The output of this program is as follows:

```
Mixin1: 11
Mixin2: 22
Mixin1: 33
```

Fold Expressions

C++ supports *fold expressions*. This makes working with parameter packs in variadic templates much easier. Fold expressions can be used to apply a certain operation to every value of a parameter pack, to reduce all values in a parameter pack to a single value, and more.

The following table lists the four types of folds that are supported. In this table, Θ can be any of the following operators: `+ - * / % ^ & | << >> += -= *= /= %= ^= &= |= <<= >>= = == != < > <= >= && || , .* ->*`.

NAME	EXPRESSION	IS EXPANDED TO
Unary right fold	(pack Θ . . .)	pack_0 Θ (. . . Θ (pack_{n-1} Θ pack_n))
Unary left fold	(. . . Θ pack)	((pack_0 Θ pack_1) Θ . . .) Θ pack_n
Binary right fold	(pack Θ . . . Θ Init)	pack_0 Θ (. . . Θ (pack_{n-1} Θ (pack_n Θ Init)))
Binary left fold	(Init Θ . . . Θ pack)	(((Init Θ pack_0) Θ pack_1) Θ . . .) Θ pack_n

Let's look at some examples. Earlier, the `processValue()` function template was defined recursively as follows:

```
void processValues() { /* Nothing to do in this base case.*/ }
```

```
template <typename T1, typename... Tn>
void processValues(T1&& arg1, Tn&&... args)
{
    handleValue(forward<T1>(arg1));
    processValues(forward<Tn>(args)...);
}
```

Because it is defined recursively, it needs a base case to stop the recursion. With fold expressions, this can be implemented with a single function template using a unary right fold over the comma operator:

```
template <typename... Tn>
void processValues(Tn&&... args) { (handleValue(forward<Tn>(args)) , ...); }
```

Basically, the three dots in the function body trigger folding with the comma operator for Θ. That line is expanded to call `handleValue()` for each argument in the parameter pack, and each call to `handleValue()` is separated by a comma. For example, suppose `args` is a parameter pack with three arguments, `a1`, `a2`, and `a3`, of three types, `A1`, `A2`, and `A3`. The expansion of the unary right fold then becomes as follows:

```
(handleValue(forward<A1>(a1)) ,
    (handleValue(forward<A2>(a2)) , handleValue(forward<A3>(a3))));
```

Here is another example. The `printValues()` function template writes all its arguments to the console, separated by newlines.

```
template <typename... Values>
void printValues(const Values&... values) { (println("{}", values) , ...); }
```

Suppose that `values` is a parameter pack with three arguments, `v1`, `v2`, and `v3`. The expansion of the unary right fold then becomes as follows:

```
(println("{}", v1) , (println("{}", v2) , println("{}", v3)));
```

You can call `printValues()` with as many arguments as you want, for example:

```
printValues(1, "test", 2.34);
```

In the examples up to now, the folding is done with the comma operator, but it can be used with almost any kind of operator. For example, the following code defines a variadic function template using a binary left fold to calculate the sum of all the values given to it. A binary left fold always requires an *Init* value (see the overview table earlier). Hence, `sumValues()` has two template type parameters: a normal one to specify the type of *Init*, and a parameter pack that can accept 0 or more arguments.

```
template <typename T, typename... Values>
auto sumValues(const T& init, const Values&... values)
{ return (init + ... + values);}
```

Suppose that `values` is a parameter pack with three arguments, `v1`, `v2`, and `v3`. Here is the expansion of the binary left fold in that case:

```
return (((init + v1) + v2) + v3);
```

The `sumValues()` function template can be tested as follows:

```
println("{}", sumValues(1, 2, 3.3));
println("{}", sumValues(1));
```

The `sumValues()` function template can also be defined in terms of a unary left fold as follows.

```
template <typename... Values>
auto sumValues(const Values&... values) { return (... + values); }
```

Concepts, discussed in Chapter 12, can also be variadic. For example, the `sumValues()` function template can be constrained so that it can be called only with a set of arguments of the same type:

```
template <typename T, typename... Us>
concept SameTypes = (std::same_as<T, Us> && ...);

template <typename T, typename... Values>
    requires SameTypes<T, Values...>
auto sumValues(const T& init, const Values&... values)
{ return (init + ... + values); }
```

Calling this constrained version as follows works fine:

```
println("{}", sumValues(1.1, 2.2, 3.3)); // OK: 3 doubles, output is 6.6
println("{}", sumValues(1));             // OK: 1 integer, output is 1
println("{}", sumValues("a"s, "b"s));    // OK: 2 strings, output is ab
```

However, the following call fails as the argument list contains an integer and two doubles:

```
println("{}", sumValues(1, 2.2, 3.3));    // Error
```

Parameter packs with zero length are allowed for unary folds, but only in combination with the logical AND (`&&`), logical OR (`||`), and comma (`,`) operators. For an empty parameter pack, applying `&&` to it results in `true`, applying `||` results in `false`, and applying `,` results in `void()`, i.e., a no-op. For example:

```
template <typename... Values>
bool allEven(const Values&... values) { return ((values % 2 == 0) && ...); }

template <typename... Values>
bool anyEven(const Values&... values) { return ((values % 2 == 0) || ...); }

int main()
{
    println("{} {} {}", allEven(2,4,6), allEven(2,3), allEven());//true false true
    println("{} {} {}", anyEven(1,2,3), anyEven(1,3), anyEven());//true false false
}
```

METAPROGRAMMING

This section touches on *template metaprogramming*. It is a complicated and broad subject, and there are books written about it explaining all the little details. This book doesn't have the space to go into all of these details. Instead, this section explains the most important concepts, with the aid of a couple of examples.

The goal of template metaprogramming is to perform some computation at compile time instead of at run time. It is basically a programming language on top of another programming language. The following section starts the discussion with a simple example that calculates the factorial of a number at compile time and makes the result available as a simple constant at run time.

Factorial at Compile Time

Template metaprogramming allows you to perform calculations at compile time instead of at run time. The following code is an example that calculates the factorial of a number at compile time. The code uses template recursion, explained earlier in this chapter, which requires a recursive template and a base template to stop the recursion. By mathematical definition, the factorial of 0 is 1, so that is used as the base case.

```
template <int f>
class Factorial
{
    public:
        static constexpr unsigned long long value { f * Factorial<f - 1>::value };
};

template <>
class Factorial<0>
{
    public:
        static constexpr unsigned long long value { 1 };
};

int main()
{
    println("{}", Factorial<6>::value);
}
```

This calculates the factorial of 6, mathematically written as 6!, which is 1×2×3×4×5×6 or 720.

> **NOTE** *It is important to keep in mind that the factorial calculation is happening at compile time. At run time, you simply access the compile-time calculated value through the* `value` *data member, which is just a* `static` *constant value.*

For this specific example of calculating the factorial of a number at compile time, you don't need to use template metaprogramming. You can implement it as a `consteval` immediate function as follows, without any templates, though the template implementation still serves as a good example on how to implement recursive templates.

```
consteval unsigned long long factorial(int f)
{
    if (f == 0) { return 1; }
    else { return f * factorial(f - 1); }
}
```

You can call `factorial()` just as you would call any other function, with the difference that the `consteval` function is guaranteed to be executed at compile time. For example:

```
println("{}", factorial(6));
```

Loop Unrolling

A second example of template metaprogramming is to unroll loops at compile time instead of executing the loop at run time. Note that *loop unrolling* should be done only when you really need it, for example in performance critical code. The compiler is usually smart enough to unroll loops that can be unrolled for you.

This example again uses template recursion because it needs to do something in a loop at compile time. On each recursion, the `Loop` class template instantiates itself with `i-1`. When it hits `0`, the recursion stops.

```
template <int i>
class Loop
{
    public:
        template <typename FuncType>
        static void run(FuncType func) {
            Loop<i - 1>::run(func);
            func(i);
        }
};

template <>
class Loop<0>
{
    public:
        template <typename FuncType>
        static void run(FuncType /* func */) { }
};
```

The `Loop` template can be used as follows:

```
void doWork(int i) { println("doWork({})", i); }

int main()
{
    Loop<3>::run(doWork);
}
```

This code causes the compiler to unroll the loop and to call the function `doWork()` three times in a row. The output of the program is as follows:

```
doWork(1)
doWork(2)
doWork(3)
```

Printing Tuples

This example uses template metaprogramming to print the individual elements of an `std::tuple`. Tuples are explained in Chapter 24, "Additional Vocabulary Types." They allow you to store any number of values, each with its own specific type. A `tuple` has a fixed size and fixed value types, determined at compile time. However, tuples don't have any built-in mechanism to iterate over their elements. The following example shows how you can use template metaprogramming to iterate over the elements of a `tuple` at compile time.

As is often the case with template metaprogramming, this example is again using template recursion. The `TuplePrint` class template has two template parameters: the `tuple` type, and an integer, initialized with the size of the tuple. It then recursively instantiates itself in the constructor and decrements the integer on every call. A partial specialization of `TuplePrint` stops the recursion when this integer hits `0`. The `main()` function shows how this `TuplePrint` class template can be used.

```
template <typename TupleType, int N>
class TuplePrint
{
    public:
        explicit TuplePrint(const TupleType& t) {
            TuplePrint<TupleType, N - 1> tp { t };
            println("{}", get<N - 1>(t));
        }
};

template <typename TupleType>
class TuplePrint<TupleType, 0>
{
    public:
        explicit TuplePrint(const TupleType&) { }
};

int main()
{
    using MyTuple = tuple<int, string, bool>;
    MyTuple t1 { 16, "Test", true };
    TuplePrint<MyTuple, tuple_size<MyTuple>::value> tp { t1 };
}
```

The `TuplePrint` statement in `main()` looks a bit complicated because it requires the exact type and size of the `tuple` as template arguments. This can be simplified by introducing a helper function template that automatically deduces the template parameters. The simplified implementation is as follows:

```
template <typename TupleType, int N>
class TuplePrintHelper
{
    public:
        explicit TuplePrintHelper(const TupleType& t) {
            TuplePrintHelper<TupleType, N - 1> tp { t };
            println("{}", get<N - 1>(t));
        }
};

template <typename TupleType>
class TuplePrintHelper<TupleType, 0>
{
    public:
        explicit TuplePrintHelper(const TupleType&) { }
};
```

```
template <typename T>
void tuplePrint(const T& t)
{
    TuplePrintHelper<T, tuple_size<T>::value> tph { t };
}

int main()
{
    tuple t1 { 16, "Test"s, true };
    tuplePrint(t1);
}
```

The first change made here is renaming the original `TuplePrint` class template to `TuplePrintHelper`. The code then implements a small function template called `tuplePrint()`. It accepts the `tuple`'s type as a template type parameter and accepts a reference to the `tuple` itself as a function parameter. The body of that function instantiates the `TuplePrintHelper` class template. The `main()` function shows how to use this simplified version. You don't need to specify the function template parameter because the compiler can deduce this automatically from the supplied argument.

constexpr if

`constexpr if`, introduced earlier in this chapter, can be used to simplify a lot of template metaprogramming techniques. For example, you can simplify the previous code for printing elements of a `tuple` using `constexpr if`, as follows. The template recursion base case is not needed anymore, because the recursion is stopped with the `constexpr if` statement.

```
template <typename TupleType, int N>
class TuplePrintHelper
{
    public:
        explicit TuplePrintHelper(const TupleType& t) {
            if constexpr (N > 1) {
                TuplePrintHelper<TupleType, N - 1> tp { t };
            }
            println("{}", get<N - 1>(t));
        }
};

template <typename T>
void tuplePrint(const T& t)
{
    TuplePrintHelper<T, tuple_size<T>::value> tph { t };
}
```

Now we can even get rid of the class template itself and replace it with a simple function template called `tuplePrintHelper()`:

```
template <typename TupleType, int N>
void tuplePrintHelper(const TupleType& t)
{
    if constexpr (N > 1) {
        tuplePrintHelper<TupleType, N - 1>(t);
    }
    println("{}", get<N - 1>(t));
}
```

```
template <typename T>
void tuplePrint(const T& t)
{
    tuplePrintHelper<T, tuple_size<T>::value>(t);
}
```

This can be simplified even more. Both function templates can be combined into one, as follows:

```
template <typename TupleType, int N = tuple_size<TupleType>::value>
void tuplePrint(const TupleType& t)
{
    if constexpr (N > 1) {
        tuplePrint<TupleType, N - 1>(t);
    }
    println("{}", get<N - 1>(t));
}
```

It can still be called the same as before:

```
tuple t1 { 16, "Test"s, true };
tuplePrint(t1);
```

Using a Compile-Time Integer Sequence with Folding

C++ supports compile-time integer sequences using `std::integer_sequence`, defined in `<utility>`. A common use case with template metaprogramming is to generate a compile-time sequence of indices, that is, an integer sequence of type `size_t`. For this, a helper `std::index_sequence` is available. You can use `std::make_index_sequence` to generate an index sequence of the same length as the length of a given parameter pack.

The tuple printer can be implemented using variadic templates, compile-time index sequences, and fold expressions as follows:

```
template <typename Tuple, size_t... Indices>
void tuplePrintHelper(const Tuple& t, index_sequence<Indices...>)
{
    (println("{}", get<Indices>(t)) , ...);
}

template <typename... Args>
void tuplePrint(const tuple<Args...>& t)
{
    tuplePrintHelper(t, make_index_sequence<sizeof...(Args)>{});
}
```

It can be called in the same way as before:

```
tuple t1 { 16, "Test"s, true };
tuplePrint(t1);
```

With this call, the unary right fold expression in the `tuplePrintHelper()` function template expands to the following:

```
((println("{}", get<0>(t)) ,
 (println("{}", get<1>(t)) ,
  println("{}", get<2>(t)))));
```

Type Traits

Type traits allow you to make decisions based on types at compile time. For example, you can verify that a type is derived from another type, is convertible to another type, is integral, and so on. The C++ Standard Library comes with a large selection of type traits. All type traits-related functionality is defined in `<type_traits>`. Type traits are divided into separate categories. The following list gives a couple of examples of the available type traits in each category. Consult a Standard Library reference (see Appendix B, "Annotated Bibliography") for a complete list.

- Primary type categories
  - `is_void`
  - `is_integral`
  - `is_floating_point`
  - `is_pointer`
  - `is_function`
  - `...`
- Type properties
  - `is_const`
  - `is_polymorphic`
  - `is_unsigned`
  - `is_constructible`
  - `is_copy_constructible`
  - `is_move_constructible`
  - `is_assignable`
  - `is_trivially_copyable`
  - `is_swappable`
  - `is_nothrow_swappable`
  - `has_virtual_destructor`
  - `has_unique_object_representations`
  - `is_scoped_enum*`
  - `is_implicit_lifetime*`
  - `...`
- Property queries
  - `alignment_of`
  - `rank`
  - `extent`
- Composite type categories
  - `is_arithmetic`
  - `is_reference`
  - `is_object`
  - `is_scalar`
  - `...`
- Type relationships
  - `is_same`
  - `is_base_of`
  - `is_convertible`
  - `is_invocable`
  - `is_nothrow_invocable`
  - `...`
- const-volatile modifications
  - `remove_const`
  - `add_const`
  - `...`
- Sign modifications
  - `make_signed`
  - `make_unsigned`
- Array modifications
  - `remove_extent`
  - `remove_all_extents`
- Logical operator traits
  - `conjunction`
  - `disjunction`
  - `negation`

- Reference modifications
  - remove_reference
  - add_lvalue_reference
  - add_rvalue_reference
- Pointer modifications
  - remove_pointer
  - add_pointer
- Constant evaluation context
  - is_constant_evaluated
- Other transformations
  - enable_if
  - conditional
  - invoke_result
  - type_identity
  - remove_cvref
  - common_reference
  - decay
  - ...

The type traits marked with an asterisk (*) are available only since C++23.

Type traits are a rather advanced C++ feature. By just looking at the preceding list, which is already a shortened version of the list from the C++ standard, it is clear that this book cannot explain all details about all type traits. This section explains just a couple of use cases to show you how type traits can be used.

Using Type Categories

Before an example can be given for a template using type traits, you first need to know a bit more on how classes like `is_integral` work. The C++ standard defines an `integral_constant` class that looks like this:

```
template <class T, T v>
struct integral_constant {
    static constexpr T value = v;
    using value_type = T;
    using type = integral_constant<T, v>;
    constexpr operator value_type() const noexcept { return value; }
    constexpr value_type operator()() const noexcept { return value; }
};
```

It also defines `bool_constant`, `true_type`, and `false_type` type aliases:

```
template <bool B>
using bool_constant = integral_constant<bool, B>;

using true_type = bool_constant<true>;
using false_type = bool_constant<false>;
```

When you access `true_type::value`, you get the value `true`, and when you access `false_type::value`, you get the value `false`. You can also access `true_type::type`, which results in the type of `true_type`. The same holds for `false_type`. Classes like `is_integral`, which checks whether a type is an integral type, and `is_class`, which checks whether a type is a class, inherit from either `true_type` or `false_type`. For example, the Standard Library specializes `is_integral` for type `bool` as follows:

```
template <> struct is_integral<bool> : public true_type { };
```

This allows you to write `is_integral<bool>::value`, which results in the value `true`. Note that you don't need to write these specializations yourself; they are part of the Standard Library.

The following code shows the simplest example of how type categories can be used:

```
if (is_integral<int>::value) { println("int is integral"); }
else { println("int is not integral"); }

if (is_class<string>::value) { println("string is a class"); }
else { println("string is not a class"); }
```

The output is as follows:

```
int is integral
string is a class
```

For each trait that has a `value` member, the Standard Library adds a variable template that has the same name as the trait followed by `_v`. Instead of writing `some_trait<T>::value`, you can write `some_trait_v<T>`—for example, `is_integral_v<T>`, `is_const_v<T>`, and so on. Here is an example of how the `is_integral_v<T>` variable template is defined in the Standard Library:

```
template <class T>
inline constexpr bool is_integral_v = is_integral<T>::value;
```

Using these variable templates, the previous example can be written as follows:

```
if (is_integral_v<int>) { println("int is integral"); }
else { println("int is not integral"); }

if (is_class_v<string>) { println("string is a class"); }
else { println("string is not a class"); }
```

In fact, because the value of `is_integral_v<T>` is a compile-time constant, you could use a `constexpr if` instead of a normal `if`.

Of course, you will likely never use type traits in this way. They become more useful in combination with templates to generate code based on some properties of a type. The following function templates demonstrate this. The code defines two overloaded `processHelper()` function templates that accept a type as template parameter. The first parameter to these functions is a value, and the second is an instance of either `true_type` or `false_type`. The `process()` function template accepts a single parameter and calls `processHelper()`.

```
template <typename T>
void processHelper(const T& t, true_type)
{
    println("{} is an integral type.", t);
}

template <typename T>
void processHelper(const T& t, false_type)
{
    println("{} is a non-integral type.", t);
}
```

```
template <typename T>
void process(const T& t)
{
    processHelper(t, is_integral<T>{});
}
```

The second argument in the call to `processHelper()` is `is_integral<T>{}`. This argument uses `is_integral<T>` to figure out if `T` is an integral type. `is_integral<T>` derives from either `true_type` or `false_type`. The `processHelper()` function needs an instance of a `true_type` or a `false_type` as a second parameter, so that is the reason for the empty set of braces `{}`. The two overloaded `processHelper()` functions don't bother to name the parameters of type `true_type` and `false_type`. They are nameless because they don't use those parameters inside their function body. These parameters are used only for function overload resolution.

The code can be tested as follows:

```
process(123);
process(2.2);
process("Test"s);
```

Here is the output:

```
123 is an integral type.
2.2 is a non-integral type.
Test is a non-integral type.
```

The previous example can be written as a single function template as follows. However, that doesn't demonstrate how to use type traits to select different overloads based on a type.

```
template <typename T>
void process(const T& t)
{
    if constexpr (is_integral_v<T>) {
        println("{} is an integral type.", t);
    } else {
        println("{} is a non-integral type.", t);
    }
}
```

Using Type Relationships

Some examples of type relationships are `is_same`, `is_base_of`, and `is_convertible`. This section gives an example of how to use `is_same`; the other type relationships work similarly.

The following `same()` function template uses the `is_same` type trait to figure out whether two given arguments are of the same type and outputs an appropriate message:

```
template <typename T1, typename T2>
void same(const T1& t1, const T2& t2)
{
    bool areTypesTheSame { is_same_v<T1, T2> };
    println("'{}' and '{}' are {} types.", t1, t2,
        (areTypesTheSame ? "the same" : "different"));
}
```

```
int main()
{
    same(1, 32);
    same(1, 3.01);
    same(3.01, "Test"s);
}
```

The output is as follows:

```
'1' and '32' are the same types.
'1' and '3.01' are different types
'3.01' and 'Test' are different types
```

Alternatively, you can implement this example without using any type traits, but using an overload set of two function templates instead:

```
template <typename T1, typename T2>
void same(const T1& t1, const T2& t2)
{
    println("'{}' and '{}' are different types.", t1, t2);
}
template <typename T>
void same(const T& t1, const T& t2)
{
    println("'{}' and '{}' are the same type.", t1, t2);
}
```

The second function template is more specialized than the first, so it will be preferred by overload resolution whenever it is viable, that is, whenever both arguments are of the same type `T`.

Using the conditional Type Trait

Chapter 18, "Standard Library Containers," explains the Standard Library helper function template `std::move_if_noexcept()`, which can be used to conditionally call either the move constructor or the copy constructor depending on whether the former is marked `noexcept`. The Standard Library does not provide a similar helper function template to easily call the move assignment operator or copy assignment operator depending on whether the former is `noexcept`. Now that you know about template metaprogramming and type traits, let's take a look at how to implement a `move_assign_if_noexcept()` ourselves.

Remember from Chapter 18 that `move_if_noexcept()` just converts a given reference to an rvalue reference if the move constructor is marked `noexcept` and to a reference-to-`const` otherwise.

`move_assign_if_noexcept()` needs to do something similar, convert a given reference to an rvalue reference if the move assignment operator is marked `noexcept`, and to a reference-to-`const` otherwise.

The `std::conditional` type trait can be used to implement the condition. This type trait has three template parameters: a Boolean, a type for when the Boolean is true, and a type for when it is false. The implementation of the `conditional` type trait looks as follows:

```
template <bool B, class T, class F>
struct conditional { using type = T; };

template <class T, class F>
struct conditional<false, T, F> { using type = F; };
```

The is_nothrow_move_assignable type trait can be used to figure out whether a certain type can be move assigned without throwing exceptions. For class types, this means to check if the type has a move assignment operator that is marked with noexcept. Here is the entire implementation of move_assign_if_noexcept():

```
template <typename T>
constexpr conditional<is_nothrow_move_assignable_v<T>, T&&, const T&>::type
    move_assign_if_noexcept(T& t) noexcept
{
    return move(t);
}
```

The Standard Library defines alias templates for traits that have a type member, such as conditional. These have the same name as the trait, but are appended with _t. For example, the conditional_t<B,T,F> alias template for conditional<B,T,F>::type is defined by the Standard Library as follows:

```
template <bool B, class T, class F>
using conditional_t = typename conditional<B,T,F>::type;
```

So, instead of writing this:

```
conditional<is_nothrow_move_assignable_v<T>, T&&, const T&>::type
```

you can write this:

```
conditional_t<is_nothrow_move_assignable_v<T>, T&&, const T&>
```

The move_assign_if_noexcept() function template can be tested as follows:

```
class MoveAssignable
{
    public:
        MoveAssignable& operator=(const MoveAssignable&) {
            println("copy assign"); return *this; }
        MoveAssignable& operator=(MoveAssignable&&) {
            println("move assign"); return *this; }
};

class MoveAssignableNoexcept
{
    public:
        MoveAssignableNoexcept& operator=(const MoveAssignableNoexcept&) {
            println("copy assign"); return *this; }
        MoveAssignableNoexcept& operator=(MoveAssignableNoexcept&&) noexcept {
            println("move assign"); return *this; }
};

int main()
{
    MoveAssignable a, b;
    a = move_assign_if_noexcept(b);
    MoveAssignableNoexcept c, d;
    c = move_assign_if_noexcept(d);
}
```

This outputs the following:

```
copy assign
move assign
```

Using Type Modification Type Traits

A number of type traits modify a given type. For example, the `add_const` type trait adds `const` to a given type, the `remove_pointer` type trait removes the pointer from a type, and so on. Here's an example:

```
println("{}", is_same_v<string, remove_pointer_t<string*>>);
```

The output is `true`.

Implementing such type modification traits yourself is not that hard. Here is an implementation of a `my_remove_pointer` type trait (slightly simplified):

```
// my_remove_pointer class template.
template <typename T> struct my_remove_pointer { using type = T; };
// Partial specialization for pointer types.
template <typename T> struct my_remove_pointer<T*> { using type = T; };
// Partial specialization for const pointer types.
template <typename T> struct my_remove_pointer<T* const> { using type = T; };
// Alias template for ease of use.
template <typename T>
using my_remove_pointer_t = typename my_remove_pointer<T>::type;

int main()
{
    println("{}", is_same_v<string, my_remove_pointer_t<string*>>);
}
```

Using enable_if

The use of `enable_if` is based on a principle called *substitution failure is not an error* (SFINAE), an advanced feature of C++. That principle states that a failure to specialize a function template for a given set of template parameters should not be seen as a compilation error. Instead, such specializations should just be removed from the function overload set. This section explains only the basics of SFINAE.

If you have a set of overloaded functions, you can use `enable_if` to selectively disable certain overloads based on some type traits. The `enable_if` trait is often used on the return types of your set of overloads, or with unnamed non-type template parameters. `enable_if` accepts two template parameters. The first is a Boolean, and the second is a type. If the Boolean is `true`, then the `enable_if` class template has a type alias that you can access using `::type`. The type of this type alias is the type given as the second template parameter. If the Boolean is `false`, then there is no such type alias. Here is the implementation of this type trait:

```
template <bool B, class T = void>
struct enable_if {};

template <class T>
struct enable_if<true, T> { typedef T type; };
```

The same() function template from an earlier section can be rewritten into overloaded checkType() function templates by using enable_if as follows. In this implementation, the checkType() functions return true or false depending on whether the types of the given values are the same. If you don't want to return anything from checkType(), you can remove the return statements and remove the second template argument for enable_if.

```
template <typename T1, typename T2>
enable_if_t<is_same_v<T1, T2>, bool>
    checkType(const T1& t1, const T2& t2)
{
    println("'{}' and '{}' are the same types.", t1, t2);
    return true;
}

template <typename T1, typename T2>
enable_if_t<!is_same_v<T1, T2>, bool>
    checkType(const T1& t1, const T2& t2)
{
    println("'{}' and '{}' are different types.", t1, t2);
    return false;
}

int main()
{
    checkType(1, 32);
    checkType(1, 3.01);
    checkType(3.01, "Test"s);
}
```

The output is the same as before:

```
'1' and '32' are the same types.
'1' and '3.01' are different types.
'3.01' and 'Test' are different types.
```

The code defines two overloads for checkType(). It uses is_same_v to check whether two types are the same. The result is given to enable_if_t. When the first argument to enable_if_t is true, enable_if_t has type bool; otherwise, there is no type. This is where SFINAE comes into play.

When the compiler starts to compile the first statement in main(), it tries to find a function checkType() that accepts two integer values. It finds the first checkType() function template overload and deduces that it can use an instance of this function template by making T1 and T2 both integers. It then tries to figure out the return type. Because both arguments are integers and thus the same types, is_same_v<T1, T2> is true, which causes enable_if_t<true, bool> to be type bool. With this instantiation, everything is fine, and thus the compiler adds this overload to the set of candidates. When it sees the second overload of checkType(), it again deduces that it can use an instance of this function template by making T1 and T2 both integers. However, when trying to figure out the return type, it finds out that !is_same_v<T1, T2> is false. Because of this, enable_if_t<false, bool> does not represent a type, leaving that overload of checkType() without a return type. The compiler notices this error but does not yet generate a real compilation error because of SFINAE. It simply does not add this overload to the set of candidates. Thus, with the first statement in main(), the overload set contains one candidate checkType() function, so it's clear which one the compiler will use.

When the compiler tries to compile the second statement in `main()`, it again tries to find a suitable `checkType()` function. It starts with the first `checkType()` and decides it can use that overload by setting `T1` to type `int` and `T2` to type `double`. It then tries to figure out the return type. This time, `T1` and `T2` are different types, which means that `is_same_v<T1, T2>` is `false`. Because of this, `enable_if_t<false, bool>` does not represent a type, leaving the function `checkType()` without a return type. The compiler notices this error but does not yet generate a real compilation error because of SFINAE. Instead, the compiler simply does not add this overload to the set of candidates. When the compiler sees the second `checkType()` function, it figures out that that one works out fine because `T1` and `T2` are of different types, so `!is_same_v<T1, T2>` is `true`, and thus `enable_if_t<true, bool>` is type `bool`. In the end, the overload set for the second statement in `main()` again contains only one overload, so it's clear which one the compiler will use.

If you don't want to clutter your return types with `enable_if`, then another option is to use `enable_if` with extra non-type template parameters. This actually makes the code easier to read. For example:

```
template <typename T1, typename T2, enable_if_t<is_same_v<T1, T2>>* = nullptr>
bool checkType(const T1& t1, const T2& t2)
{
    println("'{}' and '{}' are the same types.", t1, t2);
    return true;
}

template <typename T1, typename T2, enable_if_t<!is_same_v<T1, T2>>* = nullptr>
bool checkType(const T1& t1, const T2& t2)
{
    println("'{}' and '{}' are different types.", t1, t2);
    return false;
}
```

If you want to use `enable_if` on a set of constructors, you can't use it with the return type because constructors don't have a return type. In that case, you must use it with non-type template parameters, as shown earlier.

The `enable_if` syntax explained in this section was the state of the art prior to C++20. Since C++20, you should prefer to use concepts, discussed in Chapter 12. Notice the syntactic similarity between the earlier `enable_if` code and the following example using concepts. However, it's clear that the version using concepts is more readable.

```
template <typename T1, typename T2> requires is_same_v<T1, T2>
bool checkType(const T1& t1, const T2& t2)
{
    println("'{}' and '{}' are the same types.", t1, t2);
    return true;
}

template <typename T1, typename T2> requires !is_same_v<T1, T2>
bool checkType(const T1& t1, const T2& t2)
{
    println("'{}' and '{}' are different types.", t1, t2);
    return false;
}
```

It is recommended to use SFINAE judiciously. Use it only when you need to resolve overload ambiguities that you cannot possibly resolve using any other technique, such as specializations, concepts, and so on. For example, if you just want compilation to fail when you use a template with the wrong types, use concepts or use `static_assert()`, explained later in this chapter, instead of SFINAE. Of course, there are legitimate use cases for SFINAE, but keep the following in mind.

> **WARNING** *Relying on SFINAE is tricky and complicated. If your use of SFINAE and* `enable_if` *selectively disables the wrong overloads in your overload set, you will get cryptic compiler errors, which will be hard to track down.*

Using constexpr if to Simplify enable_if Constructs

As you can see from earlier examples, using `enable_if` can become quite complicated. The `constexpr if` feature helps to dramatically simplify certain use cases of `enable_if`.

For example, suppose you have the following two classes:

```
class IsDoable
{
    public:
        virtual void doit() const { println("IsDoable::doit()"); }
};

class Derived : public IsDoable { };
```

You can write a function template, `callDoit()`, that calls the `doit()` member function if the member function is available; otherwise, prints an error message. You can do this with `enable_if` by checking whether the given type is derived from `IsDoable`:

```
template <typename T>
enable_if_t<is_base_of_v<IsDoable, T>, void> callDoit(const T& t)
{
    t.doit();
}

template <typename T>
enable_if_t<!is_base_of_v<IsDoable, T>, void> callDoit(const T&)
{
    println("Cannot call doit()!");
}
```

The following code tests this implementation:

```
Derived d;
callDoit(d);
callDoit(123);
```

Here is the output:

```
IsDoable::doit()
Cannot call doit()!
```

You can simplify this enable_if implementation a lot by using constexpr if:

```
template <typename T>
void callDoit(const T& t)
{
    if constexpr (is_base_of_v<IsDoable, T>) {
        t.doit();
    } else {
        println("Cannot call doit()!");
    }
}
```

You cannot accomplish this using a normal if statement. With a normal if statement, both branches need to be compiled, and this will fail if you supply a type T that is not derived from IsDoable. In that case, the statement t.doit() will fail to compile. However, with the constexpr if statement, if a type is supplied that is not derived from IsDoable, then the statement t.doit() won't even be compiled.

Instead of using the is_base_of type trait, you can also use a requires expression; see Chapter 12. Here is an implementation of callDoit() using a requires expression to check whether the doit() member function can be called on object t.

```
template <typename T>
void callDoit(const T& t)
{
    if constexpr (requires { t.doit(); }) {
        t.doit();
    } else {
        println("Cannot call doit()!");
    }
}
```

Logical Operator Traits

There are three logical operator traits: conjunction, disjunction, and negation. Variable templates, ending with _v, are available as well. These traits accept a variable number of template type arguments and can be used to perform logical operations on type traits, as in this example:

```
print("{} ", conjunction_v<is_integral<int>, is_integral<short>>);
print("{} ", conjunction_v<is_integral<int>, is_integral<double>>);

print("{} ", disjunction_v<is_integral<int>, is_integral<double>,
                 is_integral<short>>);

print("{} ", negation_v<is_integral<int>>);
```

The output is as follows:

```
true false true false
```

Static Assertions

static_assert() allows certain conditions to be asserted at compile time. An assertion is something that needs to be true. If an assertion is false, the compiler issues an error. A call to static_assert()

accepts two parameters: an expression to evaluate at compile time and (optionally) a string. When the expression evaluates to `false`, the compiler issues an error that contains the given string. An example is to check that you are compiling with a 64-bit compiler:

```
static_assert(sizeof(void*) == 8, "Requires 64-bit compilation.");
```

If you compile this with a 32-bit compiler where a pointer is four bytes, the compiler issues an error that can look like this:

```
test.cpp(3): error C2338: Requires 64-bit compilation.
```

The string parameter is optional, as in this example:

```
static_assert(sizeof(void*) == 8);
```

In this case, if the expression evaluates to `false`, you get a compiler-dependent error message. For example, Microsoft Visual C++ gives the following error:

```
test.cpp(3): error C2607: static assertion failed
```

`static_assert()` can be combined with type traits. Here is an example:

```
template <typename T>
void foo(const T& t)
{
    static_assert(is_integral_v<T>, "T must be an integral type.");
}
```

Metaprogramming Conclusion

As you have seen in this section, template metaprogramming can be a powerful tool, but it can also get quite complicated. One problem with template metaprogramming, not mentioned before, is that everything happens at compile time so you cannot use a debugger to pinpoint a problem. If you decide to use template metaprogramming in your code, make sure you write good comments to explain exactly what is going on and why you are doing something a certain way. If you don't properly document your template metaprogramming code, it might be difficult for someone else to understand your code, and it might even make it difficult for you to understand your own code in the future.

SUMMARY

This chapter is a continuation of the template discussion from Chapter 12. These chapters show you how to use templates for generic programming and template metaprogramming for compile-time computations. Ideally you have gained an appreciation for the power and capabilities of these features and an idea of how you can apply these techniques to your own code. Don't worry if you didn't understand all the syntax, or didn't follow all the examples, on your first reading. The techniques can be difficult to grasp when you are first exposed to them, and the syntax is tricky whenever you want to write more complicated templates. When you actually sit down to write a class or function template, you can consult this chapter and Chapter 12 for a reference on the proper syntax.

EXERCISES

By solving the following exercises, you can practice the material discussed in this chapter. Solutions to all exercises are available with the code download on the book's website at `www.wiley.com/go/proc++6e`. However, if you are stuck on an exercise, first reread parts of this chapter to try to find an answer yourself before looking at the solution from the website.

Exercise 26-1: In Exercise 12-2, you wrote a full specialization of a `KeyValuePair` class template for `const char*` keys and values. Replace that full specialization with a partial specialization where the values are of type `const char*` but the keys can be of any type.

Exercise 26-2: Calculate the nth number in the Fibonacci series at compile time using template recursion. The Fibonacci series starts with 0 and 1, and any subsequent value is the sum of the two previous values, so: 0, 1, 1, 2, 3, 5, 8, 13, 21, 34, 55, 89, and so on.

Can you also provide a variable template to make your recursive Fibonacci template easier to use?

Exercise 26-3: Take your solution for Exercise 26-2 and modify it so that the calculation still happens at compile time, but without the use of any template or function recursion.

Exercise 26-4: Write a variadic function template called `push_back_values()` accepting a reference to a `vector` and a variable number of values. The function should use a fold expression to push all the values into the given `vector`. Then, write an `insert_values()` function template doing the same thing but in terms of `vector::insert(initializer_list<value_type>)`. What's the difference with the `push_back_values()` implementation?

Exercise 26-5: Write a `multiply()` non-abbreviated function template accepting two template type parameters `T1` and `T2`. Use a type trait to verify that both types are arithmetic. If they are, perform the multiplication and return the result. If they are not, throw an exception containing the names of both types.

Exercise 26-6: Advanced. Transform your solution for Exercise 26-5 to use an abbreviated function template.

27

Multithreaded Programming with C++

WHAT'S IN THIS CHAPTER?

- What multithreaded programming is
- How to launch multiple threads
- How to (sort of) cancel threads
- How to retrieve results from threads
- What deadlocks and race conditions are, and how to use mutual exclusion to prevent them
- How to use atomic types and atomic operations
- What condition variables are
- How to use semaphores, latches, and barriers
- How to use futures and promises for inter-thread communication
- What thread pools are
- What resumable functions, or coroutines, are

WILEY.COM DOWNLOADS FOR THIS CHAPTER

Please note that all the code examples for this chapter are available as part of this chapter's code download on the book's website at `www.wiley.com/go/proc++6e` on the Download Code tab.

Multithreaded programming is important on computer systems with multiple processor units. It allows you to write a program to use all those processor units in parallel. There are multiple ways for a system to have multiple processor units. The system can have multiple discrete processor chips, each one an independent central processing unit (CPU). Or, the system can have a single discrete processor chip that internally consists of multiple independent CPUs, also called *cores*. These kinds of processors are called *multicore processors*. A system can also have a combination of both. Systems with multiple processor units have existed for a long time; however, they were rarely used in consumer systems. Today, all CPU vendors are selling multicore processors, which are being used in everything from servers to consumer computers to smartphones. Because of this proliferation of multicore processors, it is important to know how to write multithreaded applications. A professional C++ programmer needs to know how to write correct multithreaded code to take full advantage of all the available processor units. Writing multithreaded applications used to rely on platform- and operating system–specific APIs. This made it difficult to write platform-independent multithreaded code. C++11 addressed this problem by including a standard threading library.

Multithreaded programming is a complicated subject. This chapter introduces multithreaded programming using the standard threading library, but it cannot go into all of the details due to space constraints. Entire books have been written about developing multithreaded programs. If you are interested in more details, consult one of the references in the multithreading section of Appendix B, "Annotated Bibliography."

There are also third-party C++ libraries that try to make multithreaded programming more platform independent, such as `pthreads` and the `boost::thread` library. However, because these libraries are not part of the C++ standard, they are not discussed in this book.

INTRODUCTION

There are three major styles of executing multiple tasks:

- **Sequential execution:** Each task is executed one after the other.
- **Concurrent execution:** Multiple tasks can be executing seemingly at the same time, but this can be because the operating system is giving a task a tiny amount of time, known as a *time slice*, to do some work, then giving another task a time slice to do its work, and so on. This task switching keeps ongoing until tasks are finished.
- **Parallel execution:** Multiple tasks are truly executing at the same time for example, on multiple processor units.

Multithreaded programming allows you to execute multiple tasks concurrently (perhaps even in parallel). As a result, you can take advantage of the multiple processor units inside virtually all systems today. Two decades ago, the processor market was racing for the highest frequency, which is perfect for single-threaded applications. Around 2005, this race stopped due to a combination of power and heat management problems. Since then, the processor market is racing toward the most cores on a single processor chip. Quad- and octa-core processors are common, but processors with up to 128 and more cores are available.

Similarly, if you look at the processors on graphics cards, called graphical processing units (GPUs), you'll see that they are massively parallel processors. Today, high-end graphics cards have more than 16,000 cores, a number that keeps increasing rapidly! These graphics cards are used not only for gaming, but also to perform computationally intensive tasks, such as artificial intelligence, machine learning, image and video manipulation, protein folding (useful for discovering new drugs), processing signals as part of the Search for Extraterrestrial Intelligence (SETI) project, and so on.

C++98/03 did not have support for multithreaded programming, and you had to resort to third-party libraries or to the multithreading APIs of your target operating system. Since C++11 introduced a standard multithreading library, it became easier to write cross-platform multithreaded applications. However, the current C++ standard targets only CPUs and not GPUs. This might change in the future.

There are two reasons to start writing multithreaded code. First, if you have a computational problem and you manage to separate it into small pieces that can be run in parallel independently from each other, you can expect a huge performance boost when running it on multiple processor units. Second, you can modularize computations along orthogonal axes. For example, you can do long computations in a worker thread instead of blocking the UI thread, so the user interface remains responsive while a long computation occurs in the background.

Figure 27.1 shows a situation that is perfectly suited for running in parallel. An example could be the processing of pixels of an image by an algorithm that does not require information about neighboring pixels. The algorithm could split the image into four parts. On a single-core processor, each part would be processed sequentially; on a dual-core processor, two parts would be processed in parallel; and on a quad-core processor, four parts would be processed in parallel, resulting in an almost linear scaling of the performance with the number of cores.

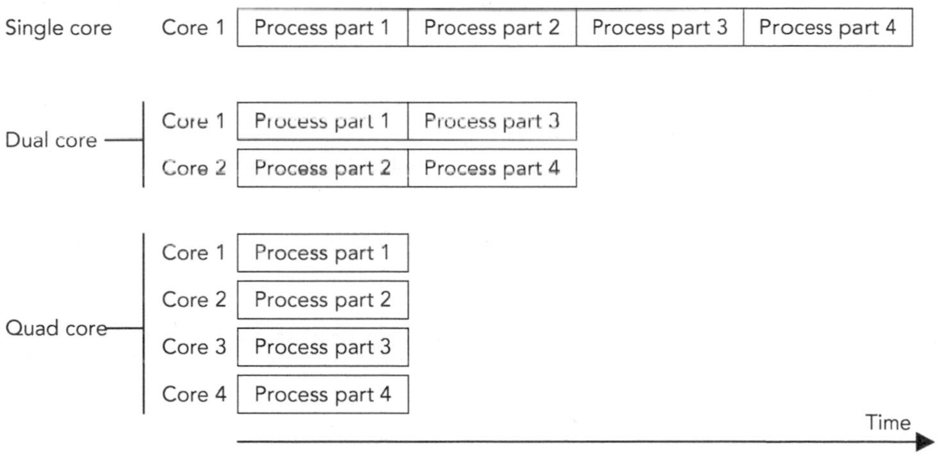

FIGURE 27.1

Of course, it's not always possible to split the problem into parts that can be executed independently of each other in parallel. However, it can often be made parallel, at least partially, resulting in a performance increase. A difficult part of multithreaded programming is making your algorithm parallel, which is highly dependent on the type of the algorithm. Other difficulties are race conditions, deadlocks, tearing, and false sharing. These are discussed in the following sections. Options for making code thread-safe include:

- **Immutable data:** Constant data is inherently safe to be accessed by multiple threads.

- **Atomic operations:** These are low-level types that automatically provide thread-safe operations.
- **Mutual exclusion and other synchronization mechanisms:** These are used to coordinate access to shared data from multiple threads.
- **Thread-local storage:** Variables that are marked as `thread_local` are local to a thread; other threads don't have access to them (at least not by default), so they are generally thread-safe.

All these topics are touched upon in this chapter.

> **NOTE** *To prevent multithreading problems, try to design your programs so that multiple threads need not read and write to shared memory. Or, use a synchronization mechanism (as described in the section "Mutual Exclusion") or atomic operations (as described in the section "Atomic Operations Library").*

Race Conditions

Race conditions can occur when multiple threads want to access any kind of shared resources. Race conditions in the context of memory shared by multiple threads are called *data races*. A data race can occur when multiple threads access the same variable, and at least one of those threads writes to it. For example, suppose you have a shared variable and one thread increments this value while another thread decrements it. Incrementing and decrementing the value means that the current value needs to be retrieved from memory, incremented or decremented, and stored back in memory. Most processors have `INC` and `DEC` instructions to do these operations. On modern x86 processors, these instructions are not atomic, meaning that other instructions can be executed in the middle of the operation, which might cause the code to retrieve a wrong value.

The following table shows the result when the increment is finished before the decrement starts and assumes that the initial value is 1:

THREAD 1 (INCREMENT)	THREAD 2 (DECREMENT)
load value (value = 1)	
increment value (value = 2)	
store value (value = 2)	
	load value (value = 2)
	decrement value (value = 1)
	store value (value = 1)

The final value stored in memory is 1. When the decrement thread is finished before the increment thread starts, the final value is also 1, as shown in the following table:

THREAD 1 (INCREMENT)	THREAD 2 (DECREMENT)
	load value (value = 1)
	decrement value (value = 0)
	store value (value = 0)
load value (value = 0)	
increment value (value = 1)	
store value (value = 1)	

However, when the instructions are interleaved, the result is different, as shown in the following table:

THREAD 1 (INCREMENT)	THREAD 2 (DECREMENT)
load value (value = 1)	
increment value (value = 2)	
	load value (value = 1)
	decrement value (value = 0)
store value (value = 2)	
	store value (value = 0)

The final result in this case is 0. In other words, the effect of the increment operation is lost. This is a data race.

Tearing

Tearing is a specific case or consequence of a data race. There are two kinds of tearing: *torn read* and *torn write*. If a thread has written part of your data to memory, while another part hasn't been written yet, any other thread reading that data at that exact moment sees inconsistent data: a torn read. If two threads are writing to the data at the same time, one thread might have written part of the data, while another thread might have written another part of the data. The final result will be inconsistent: a torn write.

Deadlocks

If you opt to solve a race condition by using a synchronization mechanism, such as mutual exclusion, you might run into another common problem with multithreaded programming: *deadlocks*. Two threads are deadlocked if they are both waiting for the other thread to do something. This can be extended to more than two threads. For example, if two threads want to acquire access to a shared resource, they need to ask for permission to access this resource. If one of the threads currently holds the permission to access the resource, but is blocked indefinitely for some other reason, then the other thread will block indefinitely as well when trying to acquire permission for the same resource.

One mechanism to acquire permission for a shared resource is called a mutual exclusion object, or mutex for short, discussed in detail later in this chapter. For example, suppose you have two threads and two resources protected with two mutexes, A and B. Both threads acquire permission for both resources, but they acquire the permission in different order. The following table shows this situation in pseudo-code:

THREAD 1	THREAD 2
Acquire A Acquire B // . . . compute Release B Release A	Acquire B Acquire A // . . . compute Release A Release B

Now, imagine that the code in the two threads is executed in the following order:

- **Thread 1:** Acquire A (succeeds)
- **Thread 2:** Acquire B (succeeds)
- **Thread 1:** Acquire B (waits/blocks, because B is held by thread 2)
- **Thread 2:** Acquire A (waits/blocks, because A is held by thread 1)

Both threads are now waiting indefinitely in a deadlock situation. Figure 27.2 shows a graphical representation of the deadlock. Thread 1 has acquired permission for resource A and is waiting to acquire permission for resource B. Thread 2 has acquired permission for resource B and is waiting to acquire permission for resource A. In this graphical representation, you see a cycle that depicts the deadlock. Both threads will wait indefinitely.

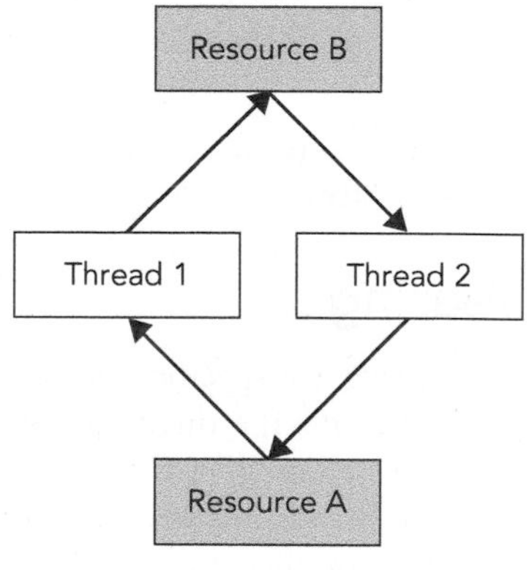

FIGURE 27.2

It's best to always acquire permissions in the same order to avoid these kinds of deadlocks. You could also include mechanisms in your program to break these deadlocks. One possible solution is to try for a certain time to acquire permission for a resource. If the permission cannot be obtained within a certain time interval, the thread can stop waiting and possibly release other permissions it is currently holding. The thread can then sleep for a little bit and try again later to acquire all the resources it needs. This mechanism gives other threads the opportunity to acquire necessary permissions and continue their execution. Whether this mechanism works or not depends heavily on your specific deadlock case.

The previous paragraph describes workarounds to avoid deadlocks. These exact workarounds are implemented in the Standard Library by `std::lock()`, described later in the section "Mutual Exclusion." This function obtains permission for several resources with one call, without the risk of deadlocks. You should use `std::lock()` instead of reinventing the same workarounds. However, it's even better not to get into such a situation in the first place by avoiding having to take multiple locks at once. Ideally, try to avoid patterns that require locking at all.

False Sharing

Most caches work with *cache lines*. For modern CPUs, cache lines are usually 64 bytes. If something needs to be written to a cache line, the entire line needs to be locked. This can bring a serious performance penalty for multithreaded code if your data structure is not properly designed. For example, if two threads are using two different pieces of data, but that data shares a cache line, then when one thread writes something, the other thread is blocked because the entire cache line is locked. Figure 27.3 graphically shows the situation where two threads clearly write to two different blocks of memory while sharing a cache line.

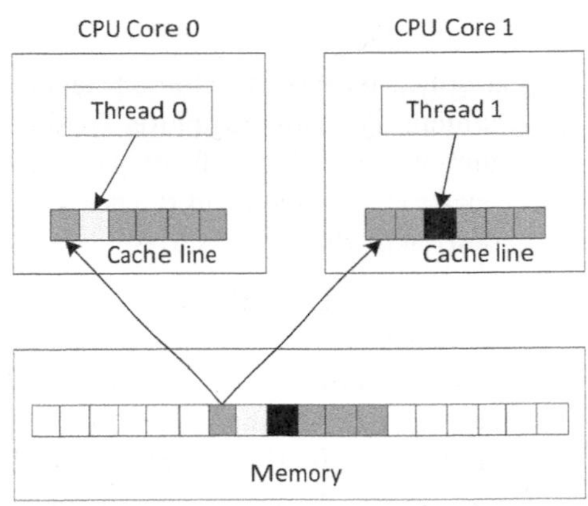

FIGURE 27.3

You can optimize your data structures by using explicit memory alignments to make sure data that is worked on by multiple threads does not share any cache lines. To do this in a portable manner, a constant called `hardware_destructive_interference_size`, defined in `<new>`, can be used, which returns you the minimum recommended offset between two concurrently accessed objects to avoid cache line sharing. You can use that value in combination with the `alignas` keyword to properly align your data.

THREADS

The C++ threading library, defined in `<thread>`, makes it easy to launch new threads. You can specify what needs to be executed in the new thread in several ways. You can let the new thread execute a global function, the `operator()` of a function object, a lambda expression, or even a member function of an instance of some class. The following sections give small examples of all these techniques.

Thread with Function Pointer

Functions such as `CreateThread()`, `_beginthread()`, and so on, on Windows, and `pthread_create()` with the pthreads library, require that the thread function has only one parameter. On the other hand, a function that you want to use with the standard C++ `std::thread` class can have as many parameters as you want.

Suppose you have a `counter()` function accepting two integers: the first representing an ID and the second representing the number of iterations that the function should loop. The body of the function is a single loop that loops the given number of iterations. On each iteration, a message is printed to standard output.

```
void counter(int id, int numIterations)
{
    for (int i { 0 }; i < numIterations; ++i) {
        println("Counter {} has value {}", id, i);
    }
}
```

You can launch multiple threads executing this function using `std::thread`. You can create a thread `t1`, executing `counter()` with arguments 1 and 6 as follows:

```
thread t1 { counter, 1, 6 };
```

The constructor of the `thread` class is a variadic template, which means that it accepts any number of arguments. Variadic templates are discussed in detail in Chapter 26, "Advanced Templates." The first argument is a callable object (such as a function pointer—in this example, a pointer to the function `counter()`) to execute in the new thread. Any subsequent arguments are passed to this callable when execution of the thread starts.

A `thread` object is said to be *joinable* if it represents or represented an active thread in the system. Even when the thread has finished executing, a `thread` object remains in the joinable state. A default-constructed `thread` object is *unjoinable*. Before a joinable `thread` object is destroyed, you need to make sure to call either `join()` or `detach()` on it. A call to `join()` is a blocking call: it waits until the thread has finished its work. A call to `detach()` detaches a `thread` object from its underlying OS thread, in which case the OS thread keeps running independently. Both member functions cause the thread to become unjoinable. If a `thread` object that is still joinable is destroyed, the destructor calls `std::terminate()`, which abruptly terminates all threads and the application itself. The reason for this behavior is that destroying a thread without joining it is almost certainly a bug, and terminating the program is the best available way for the library to indicate the problem.

The following code launches two threads executing the `counter()` function. After launching the threads, `join()` is called on both threads.

```
thread t1 { counter, 1, 6 };
thread t2 { counter, 2, 4 };
t1.join();
t2.join();
```

A possible output of this example looks as follows:

```
Counter 2 has value 0
Counter 1 has value 0
Counter 1 has value 1
Counter 1 has value 2
Counter 1 has value 3
Counter 1 has value 4
Counter 1 has value 5
Counter 2 has value 1
Counter 2 has value 2
Counter 2 has value 3
```

The output on your system will be different, and it will most likely be different every time you run it. This is because two threads are executing the `counter()` function at the same time, so the output depends on the number of processing cores in your machine and on the thread scheduling of the operating system.

Calling `print()` or `println()` from different threads is thread-safe and doesn't cause any data races. However, if you change the single `println()` statement in `counter()` to the following:

```
print("Counter {} has value {}", id, i);
println("");
```

Or:

```
cout << format("Counter {} has value {}", id, i) << endl;
```

Or:

```
cout << format("Counter {} has value {}", id, i);
cout << endl;
```

Then, even though there are still no data races, output from different threads can be interleaved! This means that the output can be mixed together as follows:

```
Counter 1 has value 0Counter 2 has value 0

Counter 2 has value 1
Counter 2 has value 2Counter 1 has value 1
...
```

This can be fixed using synchronization mechanisms, which are discussed later in this chapter.

> **NOTE** *Thread function arguments are always copied into some internal storage for the thread. Use* `std::ref()` *or* `std::cref()` *from* `<functional>` *to pass them by reference.*

Thread with Function Object

Instead of using function pointers, you can also use a function object to execute in a thread. With the function pointer technique of the previous section, the only way to pass information to the thread is by passing arguments to the function. With function objects, you can add data members to your function object class, which you can initialize and use however you want. The following example first defines a class called `Counter`, which has two data members: an ID and the number of iterations for the loop. Both variables are initialized with the constructor. To make the `Counter` class a function object, you need to implement `operator()`, as discussed in Chapter 19, "Function Pointers, Function Objects, and Lambda Expressions." The implementation of `operator()` is the same as the `counter()` function from the previous section. Here is the code:

```
class Counter
{
    public:
        explicit Counter(int id, int numIterations)
            : m_id { id }, m_numIterations { numIterations } { }

        void operator()() const
        {
            for (int i { 0 }; i < m_numIterations; ++i) {
                println("Counter {} has value {}", m_id, i);
            }
        }
    private:
        int m_id { 0 };
        int m_numIterations { 0 };
};
```

Two techniques for initializing threads with a function object are demonstrated in the following code snippet. The first technique uses the uniform initialization syntax. You create an instance of `Counter` with its constructor arguments and give it to the `thread` constructor between curly braces. The second technique defines a named instance of `Counter` and gives this named instance to the constructor of the `thread` class.

```
// Using uniform initialization syntax.
thread t1 { Counter { 1, 20 } };

// Using named variable.
Counter c { 2, 12 };
thread t2 { c };

// Wait for threads to finish.
t1.join();
t2.join();
```

> **NOTE** *Function objects are always copied into some internal storage for the thread. If you want to execute* `operator()` *on a specific instance of your function object instead of on a copy, you should use one of the* `std::ref()` *or* `std::cref()` *helper functions from* `<functional>` *to pass your instance by reference, for example:*
>
> ```
> Counter c { 2, 12 };
> thread t2 { ref(c) };
> ```
>
> *However, since* `t2` *now has a reference to* `c`*, it will be a data race (and thus undefined behavior) to read or write the contents of* `c` *from the main thread before* `t2` *has finished and been joined.*

Thread with Lambda

Lambda expressions fit nicely with the standard C++ threading library. Here is an example that launches a thread to execute a given lambda expression:

```
int id { 1 };
int numIterations { 5 };
thread t1 { [id, numIterations] {
    for (int i { 0 }; i < numIterations; ++i) {
        println("Counter {} has value {}", id, i);
    }
} };
t1.join();
```

Thread with Member Function Pointer

You can specify a member function of a class to be executed in a thread. The following example defines a basic `Request` class with a `process()` member function. The `main()` function creates an instance of the Request class and launches a new thread, which executes the process() member function of the Request instance req.

```
class Request
{
    public:
        explicit Request(int id) : m_id { id } { }
        void process() { println("Processing request {}", m_id); }
    private:
        int m_id { 0 };
};

int main()
{
    Request req { 100 };
    thread t { &Request::process, &req };
    t.join();
}
```

With this technique, you are executing a member function on a specific object in a separate thread. If other threads are accessing the same object, you need to make sure this happens in a thread-safe way to avoid data races. Mutual exclusion, discussed later in this chapter, can be used as a synchronization mechanism to make it thread-safe.

Thread-Local Storage

The C++ standard supports *thread-local storage*. With a keyword called thread_local, you can mark any variable as thread-local, which means that each thread will have its own unique copy of the variable, and it will last for the entire duration of the thread. For each thread, the variable is initialized exactly once. For example, the following code defines two global variables, k and n. Every thread shares one—and only one—copy of k, while each thread has its own unique copy of n.

```
int k;
thread_local int n;
```

The following code snippet verifies this. threadFunction() prints the current values for k and n, and then increments them both. The main() function launches a first thread, waits for it to finish, and then launches a second thread.

```
void threadFunction(int id)
{
    println("Thread {}: k={}, n={}", id, k, n);
    ++n;
    ++k;
}

int main()
{
    thread t1 { threadFunction, 1 }; t1.join();
    thread t2 { threadFunction, 2 }; t2.join();
}
```

From the following output, it's clear that there is only a single instance of k shared across all threads, while each thread has its own copy of n.

```
Thread 1: k=0, n=0
Thread 2: k=1, n=0
```

The previous paragraphs show how thread_local works for global variables. It also works for static data members of classes and static local variables of functions. Inside a function, and only inside a function, declaring a variable as thread_local implies static, but it's recommended to be explicit about this. Here are some examples:

```
static thread_local int x1;     // OK, internal linkage (See Chapter 11)
thread_local int x2;            // OK, external linkage (See Chapter 11)

class Foo
{
    static thread_local int x3; // OK
    thread_local int x4;        // Error!
};

void f()
{
    static thread_local int x5; // OK
    thread_local int x6;        // OK, implicitly static!
}
```

Canceling Threads

The C++ standard does not include any mechanism for canceling a running thread from another thread. One (partial) solution is to use the jthread class, discussed in the next section. If that's not an option, then the best way to achieve this is to provide some communication mechanism that the two threads agree upon. The simplest mechanism is to have a shared variable, which the target thread checks periodically to determine if it should terminate. Other threads can set this shared variable to indirectly instruct the thread to shut down. You have to be careful here, because this shared variable is being accessed by multiple threads, of which at least one is writing to the shared variable. To make this thread safe, it's recommended to use atomic variables or condition variables, both discussed later in this chapter.

Automatically Joining Threads

As discussed earlier, if a thread instance is destroyed that is still joinable, the C++ runtime calls std::terminate() to terminate the application. <thread> also defines std::jthread, which is virtually identical to thread, except:

- It automatically joins in its destructor.
- It supports cooperative cancellation.

Cooperative Cancellation

The cancellation support of jthread is called *cooperative cancellation* because a thread that supports cancellation needs to periodically check if it needs to cancel itself. Before an example can be given, two important classes need to be introduced, both defined in <stop_token>:

- `std::stop_token`: Supports actively checking for a cancellation request. A cancellable thread needs to periodically call `stop_requested()` on a `stop_token` to find out if it needs to stop its work. A `stop_token` can be used with a `condition_variable_any` so a thread can wake up when it needs to stop.
- `std::stop_source`: Used to request a thread to cancel its execution. This is done by calling the `request_stop()` member function on a `stop_source`. If a `stop_source` is used to request a cancellation, that stop request is visible to all associated `stop_sources` and `stop_tokens`. The `stop_requested()` member function can be used to check whether a stop has already been requested.

If you have a `jthread` instance, you can get access to its `stop_token` and `stop_source` by using the `get_stop_token()` and `get_stop_source()` member functions. Additionally, the callable passed to a constructor of `jthread` can have a `stop_token` as its first parameter.

Let's look at an example. The following code defines a `threadFunction()` callable that accepts a `stop_token` as its first parameter. Because this is cooperative cancellation, the body of this thread function uses that `stop_token` to check whether it needs to cancel itself. This code uses `std::this_thread::sleep_for()` to introduce a small delay in each loop. The argument to `sleep_for()` is an `std::chrono::duration`; see Chapter 22, "Date and Time Utilities."

```
void threadFunction(stop_token token, int id)
{
    while (!token.stop_requested()) {
        println("Thread {} doing some work.", id);
        this_thread::sleep_for(500ms);
    }
    println("Stop requested for thread {}.", id);
}
```

The following `main()` function creates two `jthread` instances to execute `threadFunction()`, sleeps for two seconds, writes a message that it's ending, and asks both threads to stop:

```
int main()
{
    jthread job1 { threadFunction, 1 };
    jthread job2 { threadFunction, 2 };

    this_thread::sleep_for(2s);
    println("main() is ending.");

    job1.request_stop();
    job2.request_stop();
}
```

The following is a possible output of this program:

```
Thread 2 doing some work.
Thread 1 doing some work.
Thread 2 doing some work.
Thread 1 doing some work.
Thread 2 doing some work.
Thread 1 doing some work.
Thread 2 doing some work.
```

```
Thread 1 doing some work.
main() is ending.
Stop requested for thread 2.
Stop requested for thread 1.
```

The destructor of `jthread` automatically requests its thread to stop executing before joining it, so the previous `main()` function can be simplified slightly by omitting the two calls to `request_stop()`.

Retrieving Results from Threads

As you saw in the previous examples, launching a new thread is pretty easy. However, in most cases you are probably interested in results produced by the thread. For example, if your thread performs some mathematical calculations, you really would like to get the results out of the thread once the thread is finished. One way is to pass a pointer or reference to a result variable to the thread in which the thread stores the results. Another technique is to store the results inside class data members of a function object, which you can retrieve later once the thread has finished executing. This works only if you use `std::ref()` to pass your function object by reference to the `jthread` constructor. Here is an example:

```
class Calculator
{
    public:
        explicit Calculator(int a, int b) : m_a { a }, m_b { b } {}
        void operator()() { result = m_a * m_b; }
        int getResult() const { return result; }
    private:
        int m_a { 0 };
        int m_b { 0 };
        int result { 0 };
};
int main()
{
    Calculator calculator { 21, 2 };
    jthread job { ref(calculator) };
    job.join();
    println("21*2 = {}", calculator.getResult());
}
```

This correctly outputs:

```
21*2 = 42
```

If you don't use `ref()` and initialize `job` as follows, then the output will be `21*2 = 0`:

```
jthread job { calculator };
```

However, there is another easier mechanism to obtain a result from threads: *futures*. Futures also make it easier to handle errors that occur inside your threads. They are discussed later in this chapter.

Copying and Rethrowing Exceptions

The whole exception mechanism in C++ works perfectly fine, as long as it stays within one single thread. Every thread can throw its own exceptions, but they need to be caught within their own thread. If a thread throws an exception and it is not caught inside the thread, the C++ runtime calls std::terminate(), which terminates the whole application. Exceptions thrown in one thread cannot be caught in another thread. This introduces quite a few problems when you would like to use exception handling in combination with multithreaded programming.

Without the standard threading library, it's difficult if not impossible to gracefully handle exceptions across threads. The standard threading library solves this issue with the following exception-related functions. These functions work not only with std::exceptions, but also with other kinds of exceptions, ints, strings, custom exceptions, and so on:

- `exception_ptr current_exception() noexcept;`

  Intended to be called from inside a catch block. Returns an exception_ptr object that refers to the exception currently being handled, or a copy of the currently handled exception. A null exception_ptr object is returned if no exception is being handled. This referenced exception object is reference counted, similar to std::shared_ptr, and remains valid for as long as there is an object of type exception_ptr that is referencing it.

- `[[noreturn]] void rethrow_exception(exception_ptr p);`

  Rethrows the exception referenced by the exception_ptr parameter (which must not be null). Rethrowing the referenced exception does not have to be done in the same thread that generated the referenced exception in the first place, which makes this feature perfectly suited for handling exceptions across different threads. The [[noreturn]] attribute makes it clear that this function never returns normally.

- `template<class E> exception_ptr make_exception_ptr(E e) noexcept;`

  Creates an exception_ptr object that refers to a copy of the given exception object. This is basically a shorthand notation for the following code:

  ```
  try { throw e; }
  catch(...) { return current_exception(); }
  ```

Let's see how handling exceptions across different threads can be implemented using these functions. The following code defines a function that does some work and throws an exception. This function will ultimately be running in a separate thread.

```
void doSomeWork()
{
    for (int i { 0 }; i < 5; ++i) { println("{}", i); }
    println("Thread throwing a runtime_error exception...");
    throw runtime_error { "Exception from thread" };
}
```

The following threadFunc() function wraps the call to the preceding function in a try/catch block, catching all exceptions that doSomeWork() might throw. A single argument is supplied to threadFunc(), which is of type exception_ptr&. Once an exception is caught, the function current_exception() is used to get a reference to the exception being handled, which is then assigned to the exception_ptr parameter. After that, the thread exits normally.

```
void threadFunc(exception_ptr& err)
{
    try {
```

```
        doSomeWork();
    } catch (...) {
        println("Thread caught exception, returning exception...");
        err = current_exception();
    }
}
```

The following `doWorkInThread()` function is called from within the main thread. Its responsibility is to create a new thread and start executing `threadFunc()` in it. A reference to an object of type `exception_ptr` is given as an argument to `threadFunc()`. Once the thread is created, the `doWorkInThread()` function waits for the thread to finish by using the `join()` member function, after which the error object is examined. Because `exception_ptr` is of type `NullablePointer`, you can easily check it using an `if` statement. If it's a non-null value, the exception is rethrown in the current thread, which is the main thread in this example. Because you are rethrowing the exception in the main thread, the exception has been transferred from one thread to another thread.

```
void doWorkInThread()
{
    exception_ptr error;
    // Launch thread.
    jthread t { threadFunc, ref(error) };
    // Wait for thread to finish.
    t.join();
    // See if thread has thrown any exception.
    if (error) {
        println("Main thread received exception, rethrowing it...");
        rethrow_exception(error);
    } else {
        println("Main thread did not receive any exception.");
    }
}
```

The `main()` function is pretty straightforward. It calls `doWorkInThread()` and wraps the call in a `try/catch` block to catch exceptions thrown by the thread spawned by `doWorkInThread()`.

```
int main()
{
    try {
        doWorkInThread();
    } catch (const exception& e) {
        println("Main function caught: '{}'", e.what());
    }
}
```

The output is as follows:

```
0
1
2
3
4
Thread throwing a runtime_error exception...
Thread caught exception, returning exception...
Main thread received exception, rethrowing it...
Main function caught: 'Exception from thread'
```

To keep the examples in this chapter compact and to the point, their `main()` functions usually use `join()`, either explicitly or implicitly with `jthread`, to block the main thread and to wait until threads have finished. Of course, in real-world applications you do not want to block your main thread. For example, in a GUI application, blocking your main thread means that the UI becomes unresponsive. In that case, you can use a messaging paradigm to communicate between threads. For example, the earlier `threadFunc()` function could send a message to the UI thread with as argument a copy of the result of `current_exception()`.

ATOMIC OPERATIONS LIBRARY

Atomic types allow *atomic access*, which means that concurrent reading and writing without additional synchronization is allowed. Without atomic operations, incrementing a variable is not thread-safe because the compiler first loads the value from memory into a register, increments it, and then stores the result back in memory. Another thread might touch the same memory during this increment operation, which is a data race. For example, the following code is not thread-safe and contains a data race. This type of data race is discussed in the beginning of this chapter.

```
int counter { 0 };    // Global variable
...
++counter;            // Executed in multiple threads
```

You can use the `std::atomic` class template, defined in `<atomic>`, to make this thread-safe without explicitly using any synchronization mechanism. Here is the same code using an atomic integer:

```
atomic<int> counter { 0 } ;  // Global variable
...
++counter;                   // Executed in multiple threads
```

`<atomic>` also defines named integral atomic types for all primitive types. The following table lists just a few:

NAMED ATOMIC TYPE	EQUIVALENT STD::ATOMIC TYPE
`atomic_bool`	`atomic<bool>`
`atomic_char`	`atomic<char>`
`atomic_uchar`	`atomic<unsigned char>`
`atomic_int`	`atomic<int>`
`atomic_uint`	`atomic<unsigned int>`
`atomic_long`	`atomic<long>`
`atomic_ulong`	`atomic<unsigned long>`
`atomic_llong`	`atomic<long long>`
`atomic_ullong`	`atomic<unsigned long long>`
`atomic_wchar_t`	`atomic<wchar_t>`
`atomic_flag`	(none)

You can use atomic types without explicitly using any synchronization mechanism. However, underneath, operations on atomics of a certain type might use a synchronization mechanism such as a mutex. This might happen, for example, when the hardware you are targeting lacks the necessary instructions to perform an operation atomically. You can use the `is_lock_free()` member function on an atomic type to query whether it supports lock-free operations, that is, whether all of its operations run without any explicit synchronization mechanism underneath. There is also a `static` constant called `atomic<T>::is_always_lock_free`, which is `true` if the `atomic<T>` is always lock free, and `false` otherwise.

The `std::atomic` class template can be used with all kinds of types, not only integral types. For example, you can create an `atomic<double>`, or an `atomic<MyType>`, but only if `MyType` is trivially copyable. Depending on the size of the specified type, underneath these might require explicit synchronization mechanisms. In the following example, both `Foo` and `Bar` are trivially copyable, that is, `std::is_trivially_copyable_v` is `true` for both. However, due to the size of `Foo`, `atomic<Foo>` is not lock-free, while `atomic<Bar>` is.

```
struct Foo { int m_array[123]; };
struct Bar { int m_int; };

int main()
{
    atomic<Foo> f;
    println("{} {}", is_trivially_copyable_v<Foo>, f.is_lock_free()); // true false

    atomic<Bar> b;
    println("{} {}", is_trivially_copyable_v<Bar>, b.is_lock_free()); // true true
}
```

When accessing a piece of data from multiple threads, atomics also solve issues with memory ordering, compiler optimizations, and so on. Basically, it's virtually never safe to read and write to the same piece of data from multiple threads without using atomics or explicit synchronization mechanisms!

> **NOTE** *Memory ordering is the order in which memory is accessed. In the absence of any atomics and other synchronization mechanisms, compilers and hardware are allowed to reorder memory accesses as long as this does not affect the outcome. This is known as the* ***as-if rule****, but can cause problems in multithreaded environments.*

`atomic_flag` is an atomic Boolean, always lock-free, guaranteed by the C++ standard. It differs from `atomic<bool>` in that it does not provide an assignment operator; instead, it provides named member functions `clear()`, `test()`, and `test_and_set()`. An example of using `atomic_flag` is given in the mutual exclusion section for the implementation of a spinlock later in this chapter.

Atomic Operations

The C++ standard defines a number of special operations on `atomic<T>`. This section describes a few of those operations. For a full list, consult a Standard Library Reference (see Appendix B).

Our first example of an atomic operation is the following:

```
bool atomic<T>::compare_exchange_strong(T& expected, T desired);
```

The logic implemented atomically by this operation is as follows, in pseudo-code:

```
if (*this == expected) {
    *this = desired;
    return true;
} else {
    expected = *this;
    return false;
}
```

Although this logic might seem fairly strange on first sight, this operation is a key building block for doing any complicated operation on atomics. Here is an example that atomically multiplies an `atomic<int>` with a given number:

```
void atomicallyMultiply(atomic<int>& a, int n)
{
    int expected { a.load() };
    int desired { n * expected };
    while (!a.compare_exchange_strong(expected, desired)) {
        desired = n * expected;
    }
}

int main()
{
    atomic<int> value { 10 };
    println("Value = {}", value.load());
    atomicallyMultiply(value, 3);
    println("Result = {}", value.load());
}
```

A second example is `atomic<T>::fetch_add()`. It fetches the current value of the atomic type, adds the given increment to the atomic value, and returns the original non-incremented value. Here is an example:

```
atomic<int> value { 10 };
println("Value = {}", value.load());
int fetched { value.fetch_add(4) };
println("Fetched = {}", fetched);
println("Value = {}", value.load());
```

If no other threads are touching the contents of the `fetched` and `value` variables, the output is as follows:

```
Value = 10
Fetched = 10
Value = 14
```

Atomic integral types support the following atomic operations: `fetch_add()`, `fetch_sub()`, `fetch_and()`, `fetch_or()`, `fetch_xor()`, `++`, `--`, `+=`, `-=`, `&=`, `^=`, and `|=`. Atomic pointer types support `fetch_add()`, `fetch_sub()`, `++`, `--`, `+=`, and `-=`. Atomic floating-point types support `fetch_add()` and `fetch_sub()`.

Most of the atomic operations can accept an extra parameter specifying the memory ordering that you would like. Here is an example:

```
T atomic<T>::fetch_add(T value, memory_order = memory_order_seq_cst);
```

You can change the default `memory_order`. The C++ standard provides `memory_order_relaxed`, `memory_order_consume`, `memory_order_acquire`, `memory_order_release`, `memory_order_acq_rel`, and `memory_order_seq_cst`, all of which are defined in the `std` namespace. However, you will rarely want to use them instead of the default, unless you're an expert in this domain. While another memory order may perform better than the default according to some metrics, if you use them in a slightly incorrect way, you will again introduce data races or other difficult-to-debug threading-related problems. If you do want to know more about memory orderings, consult one of the multithreading references in Appendix B.

Atomic Smart Pointers

`atomic<std::shared_ptr<T>>` is supported. The control block of a `shared_ptr`, which stores the reference count, among other things, has always been thread-safe, which guarantees that the pointed-to object is deleted exactly once. However, anything else from a `shared_ptr` is not thread-safe. Using the same `shared_ptr` instance concurrently from multiple threads causes data races if non-`const` member functions are called on that `shared_ptr` instance, such as calling `reset()`, assignment, `swap()`, and so on. On the other hand, when using the same `atomic<shared_ptr<T>>` instance from multiple threads, even calling non-`const shared_ptr` member functions is thread-safe. Note that calling non-`const` member functions on the object pointed to by the `shared_ptr` is still not thread-safe and requires manual synchronization.

Atomic References

`std::atomic_ref` is basically the same as `std::atomic`, even with the same interface, but it works with references, while `atomic` always makes a copy of the value it is provided with. An `atomic_ref` instance itself should have a shorter lifetime than the object it references. An `atomic_ref` is copyable, and you can create as many `atomic_ref` instances as you want referring to the same object. Loads and stores done through instances of `atomic_ref` will be atomic and do not race with each other. Loads and stores done concurrently without going through `atomic_ref` can still race with those atomic accesses. The `atomic_ref<T>` class template can be used with any trivially copyable type `T`, just as `std::atomic` can. Additionally, the Standard Library provides the following:

- Partial specializations for pointer types, supporting `fetch_add()` and `fetch_sub()`
- Full specializations for integral types, supporting `fetch_add()`, `fetch_sub()`, `fetch_and()`, `fetch_or()`, and `fetch_xor()`
- Full specializations for floating-point types, supporting `fetch_add()` and `fetch_sub()`

The following section gives an example of how to use an `atomic_ref`.

Using Atomic Types

This section explains in more detail why you should use atomic types. Suppose you have the following function called `increment()` that increments an integer reference parameter in a loop.

```
void increment(int& counter)
{
    for (int i { 0 }; i < 100; ++i) {
        ++counter;
        this_thread::sleep_for(1ms);
    }
}
```

Now, you would like to run several threads in parallel, all executing this `increment()` function on a shared `counter` variable. By implementing this naively without atomic types or without any kind of thread synchronization, you introduce data races. The following code launches 10 `increment()` threads, after which it waits for all threads to finish by calling `join()` on each thread, and then prints the result:

```
int main()
{
    int counter { 0 };
    vector<jthread> threads;
    for (int i { 0 }; i < 10; ++i) {
        threads.emplace_back(increment, ref(counter));
    }

    for (auto& t : threads) { t.join(); }
    println("Result = {}", counter);
}
```

Because `increment()` increments its `counter` parameter 100 times, and 10 threads are launched, each of which executes `increment()` on the same shared `counter`, you might expect the final result to be 1,000. If you execute this program several times, you might get the following output but with different values:

```
Result = 982
Result = 977
Result = 984
```

This code is clearly showing a data race: `counter` is written concurrently from multiple threads without any synchronization. In this example, you can use an atomic type to fix the code. The following code highlights the required changes:

```
void increment(atomic<int>& counter)
{
    for (int i { 0 }; i < 100; ++i) {
        ++counter;
        this_thread::sleep_for(1ms);
    }
}

int main()
{
    atomic<int> counter { 0 };
    vector<jthread> threads;
    for (int i { 0 }; i < 10; ++i) {
        threads.emplace_back(increment, ref(counter));
    }
    for (auto& t : threads) { t.join(); }
    println("Result = {}", counter);
}
```

The only modification is changing the type of the shared `counter` to `std::atomic<int>` instead of `int`. When you run this modified version, you always get 1,000 as the result:

```
Result = 1000
Result = 1000
Result = 1000
```

Without explicitly adding any synchronization mechanism to the code, it is now thread safe and data race free because the `++counter` operation on an atomic type loads, increments, and stores the value in one atomic transaction, which cannot be interrupted.

With `atomic_ref`, you can solve the data race as follows:

```
void increment(int& counter)
{
    atomic_ref<int> atomicCounter { counter };
    for (int i { 0 }; i < 100; ++i) {
        ++atomicCounter;
        this_thread::sleep_for(1ms);
    }
}

int main()
{
    int counter { 0 };
    vector<jthread> threads;
    for (int i { 0 }; i < 10; ++i) {
        threads.emplace_back(increment, ref(counter));
    }
    for (auto& t : threads) { t.join(); }
    println("Result = {}", counter);
}
```

However, there is a new problem with both of these modified implementations: a performance problem. You should try to minimize the amount of synchronization, either atomic or explicit synchronization, because it lowers performance. For this simple example, the best and recommended solution is to let `increment()` calculate its result in a local variable and only after the loop add it to the `counter` reference. Even then, it is still required to use an `atomic` or `atomic_ref` type, because you are still writing to `counter` from multiple threads.

```
void increment(atomic<int>& counter)
{
    int result { 0 };
    for (int i { 0 }; i < 100; ++i) {
        ++result;
        this_thread::sleep_for(1ms);
    }
    counter += result;
}
```

Waiting on Atomic Variables

The following wait-related member functions are available for `std::atomic` and `atomic_ref` to efficiently wait until an atomic variable is modified:

MEMBER FUNCTION	DESCRIPTION
`wait(oldValue)`	Blocks the thread until another thread calls `notify_one()` or `notify_all()`, and the value of the atomic variable has changed, that is, is not equal to `oldValue` anymore. If the current value is already unequal to `oldValue`, then the function doesn't block at all.
`notify_one()`	Wakes up one thread that is blocking on a `wait()` call.
`notify_all()`	Wakes up all threads blocking on a `wait()` call.

Here is an example:

```
atomic<int> value { 0 };

jthread job { [&value] {
    println("Thread starts waiting.");
    value.wait(0);
    println("Thread wakes up, value = {}", value.load());
} };

this_thread::sleep_for(2s);

println("Main thread is going to change value to 1.");
value = 1;
value.notify_all();
```

The output is as follows:

```
Thread starts waiting.
Main thread is going to change value to 1.
Thread wakes up, value = 1
```

MUTUAL EXCLUSION

If you are writing multithreaded applications, you have to be sensitive to the sequencing of operations. If your threads read and write shared data, this can be a problem. There are many ways to avoid this problem, such as never actually sharing data between threads. However, if you can't avoid sharing data, you must provide for synchronization so that only one thread at a time can change the data.

Scalars such as Booleans and integers can often be synchronized properly with atomic operations, as described earlier; however, when your data is more complex and you need to use that data from multiple threads, you can provide explicit synchronization.

The Standard Library has support for mutual exclusion in the form of *mutex* and *lock* classes. These can be used to implement synchronization between threads and are discussed in the following sections.

Mutex Classes

Mutex stands for *mut*ual *ex*clusion. The basic mechanism of using a mutex is as follows:

- A thread that wants to access (read or write) memory shared with other threads tries to lock the mutex object. If another thread is currently holding this lock, the new thread that wants to gain access blocks until the lock is released or until a timeout interval expires.
- Once the thread has obtained the lock, it is free to use the shared memory. Of course, this assumes that all threads that want to use the shared data participate in the mutex-locking scheme.
- After the thread is finished reading/writing to the shared memory, it releases its lock to give some other thread an opportunity to obtain a lock on the mutex. If two or more threads are waiting on the lock, there are no guarantees as to which thread will be granted the lock and thus allowed to proceed.

The C++ Standard Library provides *non-timed* and *timed mutex* classes, both in a *recursive* and *non-recursive* flavor. Before we discuss all these options, let's first have a look at a concept called a *spinlock*.

Spinlock

A spinlock is a synchronization mechanism where a thread uses a busy loop (spinning) to try to acquire a lock, performs its work, and releases the lock. While spinning, the thread remains active but is not doing any useful work. A mutex, on the other hand, might block the thread if the lock cannot be acquired immediately. Blocking a thread is an expensive operation that is avoided with a spinlock. Spinlocks can be useful in situations where you know the lock is going to be held for only a short time. Spinlocks can be implemented entirely in your own code. As the following code snippet demonstrates, a spinlock can be implemented using a single atomic type: `atomic_flag`. The spinlock-related code is highlighted.

```
static constexpr unsigned NumberOfThreads { 50 };
static constexpr unsigned LoopsPerThread { 100 };

void dowork(unsigned threadNumber, vector<unsigned>& data, atomic_flag& spinlock)
{
    for (unsigned i { 0 }; i < LoopsPerThread; ++i) {
        while (spinlock.test_and_set()) { } // Spins until lock is acquired.
        // Safe to handle shared data...
        data.push_back(threadNumber);
        spinlock.clear();                   // Releases the acquired lock.
    }
}

int main()
{
    vector<unsigned> data;
    atomic_flag dataSpinlock;
    vector<jthread> threads;
    for (unsigned i { 0 }; i < NumberOfThreads; ++i) {
        threads.emplace_back(dowork, i, ref(data), ref(dataSpinlock));
    }
```

```
        for (auto& t : threads) { t.join(); }
        println("data contains {} elements, expected {}.", data.size(),
            NumberOfThreads * LoopsPerThread);
    }
```

In this code, each thread tries to acquire a lock by repeatedly calling `test_and_set()` on an `atomic_flag` until it succeeds. This is the busy loop.

> **WARNING** *As spinlocks use a busy waiting loop, they should be an option only when you know for sure that threads will lock the spinlock only for brief moments of time.*

Let's now look at which mutex classes the Standard Library provides.

Non-timed Mutex Classes

The Standard Library has three non-timed mutex classes: `std::mutex`, `recursive_mutex`, and `shared_mutex`. The first two classes are defined in `<mutex>`, and the last one in `<shared_mutex>`. Each mutex supports the following member functions:

- `lock()`: The calling thread tries to obtain the lock and blocks until the lock has been acquired. It blocks indefinitely. If there is a desire to limit the amount of time the thread blocks, you should use a timed mutex, discussed in the next section.
- `try_lock()`: The calling thread tries to obtain the lock. If the lock is currently held by another thread, the call returns immediately. If the lock has been obtained, `try_lock()` returns `true`; otherwise, it returns `false`.
- `unlock()`: The calling thread releases the lock it currently holds, making it available for another thread.

`std::mutex` is a standard mutual exclusion class with exclusive ownership semantics. There can be only one thread owning the mutex. If another thread wants to obtain ownership of this mutex, it either blocks when using `lock()` or fails when using `try_lock()`. A thread already having ownership of a `mutex` is not allowed to call `lock()` or `try_lock()` again on that mutex. This might lead to a deadlock!

`std::recursive_mutex` behaves almost identically to `mutex`, except that a thread already having ownership of a recursive mutex is allowed to call `lock()` or `try_lock()` again on the same recursive mutex. The calling thread should call the `unlock()` member function as many times as it obtained a lock on the recursive mutex.

The `shared_mutex` class supports the concept of *shared lock ownership*, also known as *readers-writer lock*. A thread can get either *exclusive ownership* or *shared ownership* of the lock. Exclusive ownership, also known as a *write lock*, can be acquired only when there are no other threads having exclusive or shared ownership. Shared ownership, also known as a *read lock*, can be acquired if there is no other thread having exclusive ownership, even if other threads have already acquired their own shared ownership. The `shared_mutex` class supports `lock()`, `try_lock()`, and `unlock()`. These member functions acquire and release exclusive locks. Additionally, they have the following shared ownership-related member functions: `lock_shared()`, `try_lock_shared()`, and `unlock_shared()`. These work similarly to the other set of member functions but try to acquire or release shared ownership.

A thread already having a lock on a `shared_mutex` is not allowed to try to acquire a second lock on that mutex. This might lead to a deadlock!

Before examples on how to use these mutex classes can be given, a couple of other topics need to be discussed first. Hence, examples are discussed in the section "Examples Using Mutexes" later in this chapter.

> **WARNING** *Do not manually call the previously discussed lock and unlock member functions on any of the mutex classes discussed in this section and the next one. Mutex locks are resources, and, like all resources, they should almost exclusively be acquired using the Resource Acquisition Is Initialization (RAII) paradigm; see Chapter 32, "Incorporating Design Techniques and Frameworks." The C++ Standard Library provides a number of RAII lock classes, which are discussed in the "Locks" section later in this chapter. Using them is critical to avoid deadlocks. They automatically unlock a mutex when a lock object goes out of scope, so you don't need to remember to manually call* `unlock()` *at the right time.*

Timed Mutex Classes

When calling `lock()` on any of the previously discussed mutex classes, the call blocks until the lock can be obtained. On the other hand, calling `try_lock()` on those mutex classes tries to acquire a lock but returns immediately if not successful. There are also *timed mutex classes* that can try to obtain a lock but give up after a certain amount of time.

The Standard Library provides three timed mutex classes: `std::timed_mutex`, `recursive_timed_mutex`, and `shared_timed_mutex`. The first two classes are defined in `<mutex>`, and the last one in `<shared_mutex>`. They all support the `lock()`, `try_lock()`, and `unlock()` member functions; and `shared_timed_mutex` also supports `lock_shared()`, `try_lock_shared()`, and `unlock_shared()`. All these behave the same as described in the previous section. Additionally, they support the following member functions:

- `try_lock_for(rel_time)`: The calling thread tries to obtain the lock for a certain relative time. If the lock could not be obtained after the given timeout, the call fails and returns `false`. If the lock could be obtained within the timeout, the call succeeds and returns `true`. The timeout is specified as an `std::chrono::duration`; see Chapter 22.
- `try_lock_until(abs_time)`: The calling thread tries to obtain the lock until the system time equals or exceeds the specified absolute time. If the lock could be obtained before this time, the call returns `true`. If the system time passes the given absolute time, the function stops trying to obtain the lock and returns `false`. The absolute time is specified as an `std::chrono::time_point`; see Chapter 22.

A `shared_timed_mutex` also supports `try_lock_shared_for()` and `try_lock_shared_until()`.

A thread already having ownership of a `timed_mutex` or a `shared_timed_mutex` is not allowed to acquire the lock a second time on that mutex. This might lead to a deadlock!

A `recursive_timed_mutex` allows a thread to acquire a lock multiple times, just as with `recursive_mutex`.

Locks

A *lock* class is an RAII class that makes it easier to correctly obtain and release a lock on a mutex; the destructor of the lock class automatically releases the associated mutex. The C++ standard defines four types of locks: `std::lock_guard`, `unique_lock`, `shared_lock`, and `scoped_lock`.

lock_guard

`lock_guard`, defined in `<mutex>`, is a simple lock with two constructors:

- `explicit lock_guard(mutex_type& m);`

  Constructor accepting a reference to a mutex. Tries to obtain a lock on the mutex and blocks until the lock is obtained.

- `lock_guard(mutex_type& m, adopt_lock_t);`

  Constructor accepting a reference to a mutex and a second argument equal to `std::adopt_lock`, which is a global constant of the tag type `std::adopt_lock_t`, which is provided by the Standard Library for exactly this purpose. The lock assumes that the calling thread has already called `lock()` on the referenced mutex. The `lock_guard` "adopts" the mutex and automatically releases the mutex when the `lock_guard` is destroyed.

unique_lock

`std::unique_lock`, defined in `<mutex>`, is a more sophisticated lock that allows you to defer lock acquisition until later in the execution, long after the declaration. You can use the `owns_lock()` member function or the `unique_lock`'s `bool` conversion operator to see if the lock has been acquired. An example of using this conversion operator is given later in this chapter in the section "Using Timed Locks." `unique_lock` has several constructors:

- `explicit unique_lock(mutex_type& m);`

  Accepts a reference to a mutex. Tries to obtain a lock on the mutex and blocks until the lock is obtained.

- `unique_lock(mutex_type& m, defer_lock_t) noexcept;`

  Accepts a reference to a mutex and an instance of `std::defer_lock_t`, for example `std::defer_lock`. The `unique_lock` stores the reference to the mutex, but does not immediately try to obtain a lock. A lock can be obtained later.

- `unique_lock(mutex_type& m, try_to_lock_t);`

  Accepts a reference to a mutex and an instance of `std::try_to_lock_t`, for example `std::try_to_lock`. The lock tries to obtain a lock to the referenced mutex, but if it fails, it does not block, in which case, a lock can be obtained later.

- `unique_lock(mutex_type& m, adopt_lock_t);`

  Accepts a reference to a mutex and an instance of `std::adopt_lock_t`, for example `std::adopt_lock`. The lock assumes that the calling thread has already called `lock()` on the referenced mutex. The lock "adopts" the mutex and automatically releases the mutex when the lock is destroyed.

- `unique_lock(mutex_type& m, const chrono::time_point<Clock, Duration>& abs_time);`

  Accepts a reference to a mutex and an absolute time. Tries to obtain a lock until the system time passes the given absolute time.

- `unique_lock(mutex_type& m, const chrono::duration<Rep, Period>& rel_time);`

  Accepts a reference to a mutex and a relative time. Tries to get a lock on the mutex with the given relative timeout.

The `unique_lock` class also has the member functions `lock()`, `try_lock()`, `try_lock_for()`, `try_lock_until()`, and `unlock()`, which behave as explained in the section "Timed Mutex Classes," earlier in this chapter.

shared_lock

The `shared_lock` class, defined in `<shared_mutex>`, has the same type of constructors and the same member functions as `unique_lock`. The difference is that `shared_lock` calls the shared ownership-related member functions on the underlying shared mutex. Thus, the member functions of `shared_lock` are called `lock()`, `try_lock()`, and so on, but on the underlying shared mutex they call `lock_shared()`, `try_lock_shared()`, and so on. This is done to give `shared_lock` the same interface as `unique_lock`, so it can be used as a drop-in replacement for `unique_lock`, but acquires a shared lock instead of an exclusive lock.

Acquiring Multiple Locks at Once

C++ has two generic lock functions that you can use to obtain locks on multiple mutex objects at once without the risk of creating deadlocks. Both functions are defined in the `std` namespace, and both are variadic function templates, as discussed in Chapter 26.

The first function, `lock()`, locks all the given mutex objects in an unspecified order without the risk of deadlocks. If one of the mutex lock calls throws an exception, `unlock()` is called on all locks that have already been obtained. Its prototype is as follows:

```
template <class L1, class L2, class... Ln> void lock(L1&, L2&, Ln&...);
```

`try_lock()` has a similar prototype, but it tries to obtain a lock on all the given mutex objects by calling `try_lock()` on each of them in sequence. It returns -1 if all calls to `try_lock()` succeed. If any `try_lock()` fails, `unlock()` is called on all locks that have already been obtained, and the return value is the zero-based index of the mutex argument on which `try_lock()` failed.

The following example demonstrates how to use the generic `lock()` function. The `process()` function first creates two locks, one for each mutex, and gives an instance of `std::defer_lock_t` as a second argument to tell `unique_lock` not to acquire the lock during construction. The call to `std::lock()` then acquires both locks without the risk of deadlocks.

```
mutex mut1;
mutex mut2;

void process()
{
    unique_lock lock1 { mut1, defer_lock };
    unique_lock lock2 { mut2, defer_lock };
    lock(lock1, lock2);
    // Locks acquired.
} // Locks automatically released.
```

scoped_lock

`std::scoped_lock`, defined in `<mutex>`, is similar to `lock_guard`, except that it accepts a variable number of mutexes. This greatly simplifies acquiring multiple locks. For instance, the example with the `process()` function from the previous section can be written using a `scoped_lock` as follows:

```
mutex m1;
mutex m2;

void process()
{
    scoped_lock locks { m1, m2 }; // Uses class template argument deduction, CTAD.
    // Locks acquired.
} // Locks automatically released.
```

> **NOTE** `scoped_lock` *simplifies acquiring multiple locks, because you don't need to worry about acquiring them in the right order.*

`scoped_lock` is a variadic class template capable of locking an arbitrary number of mutexes. Suppose that you have an `std::array` with `mutex`es and a need to acquire a lock on all those mutexes at once. To make this easy, you can write a helper variadic function template in combination with using `std::index_sequence` and `make_index_sequence`, both of which are introduced in Chapter 26. Here's an example:

```
// Helper function to create the actual scoped_lock instance.
template <size_t N, size_t... Is>
auto make_scoped_lock(array<mutex, N>& mutexes, index_sequence<Is...>)
{
    return scoped_lock { mutexes[Is]... };
}
```

```
// Helper function to make it easy to use.
template <size_t N>
auto make_scoped_lock(array<mutex, N>& mutexes)
{
    return make_scoped_lock(mutexes, make_index_sequence<N>{});
}

int main()
{
    array<std::mutex, 4> mutexes;
    auto lockAll { make_scoped_lock(mutexes) };
}
```

std::call_once

You can use `std::call_once()` in combination with `std::once_flag` to make sure a certain function or member function is called exactly one time, no matter how many threads try to call `call_once()` with the same `once_flag`. Only one `call_once()` invocation actually calls the given function. If the given function does not throw any exceptions, then this invocation is called the *effective* `call_once()` invocation. If the given function does throw an exception, the exception is propagated back to the caller, and another caller is selected to execute the function. The effective invocation on a specific `once_flag` instance finishes before all other `call_once()` invocations on the same `once_flag`. Other threads calling `call_once()` on the same `once_flag` block until the effective call is finished. Figure 27.4 illustrates this with three threads. Thread 1 performs the effective `call_once()` invocation, thread 2 blocks until the effective invocation is finished, and thread 3 doesn't block because the effective invocation from thread 1 has already finished.

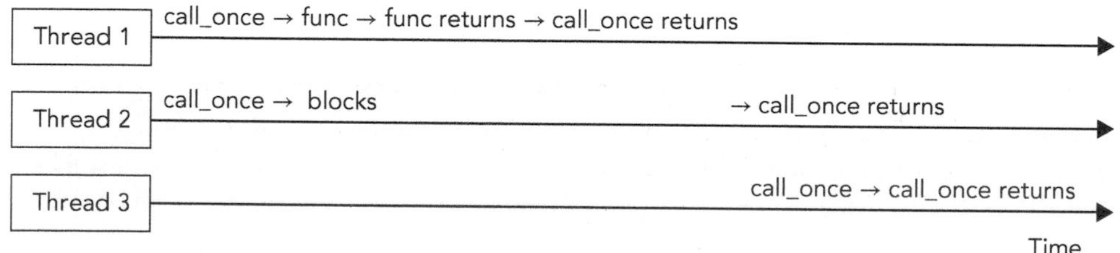

FIGURE 27.4

The following example demonstrates the use of `call_once()`. The example launches three threads running `processingFunction()` that use some shared resources. These shared resources are initialized by calling `initializeSharedResources()` once. To accomplish this, each thread calls `call_once()` with a global `once_flag`. The result is that only one thread effectively executes `initializeSharedResources()`, and exactly one time. While this `call_once()` call is in progress, other threads block until `initializeSharedResources()` returns.

```
once_flag g_onceFlag;

void initializeSharedResources()
{
    // ... Initialize shared resources to be used by multiple threads.
    println("Shared resources initialized.");
}
```

```
void processingFunction()
{
    // Make sure the shared resources are initialized.
    call_once(g_onceFlag, initializeSharedResources);

    // ... Do some work, including using the shared resources
    println("Processing");
}

int main()
{
    // Launch 3 threads.
    vector<jthread> threads { 3 };
    for (auto& t : threads) {
        t = jthread { processingFunction };
    }
    // No need to manually call join(), as we are using jthread.
}
```

The output of this code is as follows:

```
Shared resources initialized.
Processing
Processing
Processing
```

Of course, in this example, you could call `initializeSharedResources()` once in the beginning of the `main()` function before the threads are launched; however, that wouldn't demonstrate the use of `call_once()`.

Examples Using Mutexes

The following sections give a couple of examples on how to use mutexes to synchronize multiple threads.

Thread-Safe Writing to Streams

Earlier in this chapter, in the "Threads" section, there is an example with a class called `Counter`. That example mentions that C++ streams, such as `cout`, are data-race-free by default, but that the output from multiple threads can be interleaved. Here are two solutions to solve this interleaving issue:

- Use a *synchronized stream.*
- Use a mutex to make sure that only one thread at a time is reading/writing to the stream object.

Synchronized Streams

`<syncstream>` defines `std::basic_osyncstream` with predefined type aliases `osyncstream` and `wosyncstream` for `char` and `wchar_t` streams, respectively. The `o` in these class names stands for output. These classes guarantee that all output done through them will appear in the final output stream the moment the synchronized stream is destroyed. It guarantees that the output cannot be interleaved by other output from other threads, as long as those threads are also using their own `osyncstream` objects. As far as thread-safety is concerned, the relationship between `osyncstream` and `ostream` is exactly analogous to the relationship between `atomic_ref<int>` and `int`.

The function call operator of the earlier `Counter` class can be implemented as follows using an `osyncstream` to prevent interleaved output:

```
class Counter
{
    public:
        explicit Counter(int id, int numIterations)
            : m_id { id }, m_numIterations { numIterations } { }

        void operator()() const
        {
            for (int i { 0 }; i < m_numIterations; ++i) {
                osyncstream syncedCout { cout };
                syncedCout << format("Counter {} has value {}", m_id, i);
                syncedCout << endl;
                // Upon destruction, syncedCout atomically flushes
                // its contents into cout.
            }
        }
    private:
        int m_id { 0 };
        int m_numIterations { 0 };
};
```

Using Mutexes

If you cannot use a synchronized stream, you can use a `mutex` as demonstrated in the following code snippet to synchronize all accesses to `cout` in the `Counter` class. For this, a `static mutex` data member is added. It should be `static`, because all instances of the class should use the same `mutex` instance. `lock_guard` is used to obtain a lock on the `mutex` before writing to `cout`.

```
class Counter
{
    public:
        explicit Counter(int id, int numIterations)
            : m_id { id }, m_numIterations { numIterations } { }

        void operator()() const
        {
            for (int i { 0 }; i < m_numIterations; ++i) {
                lock_guard lock { ms_mutex };
                cout << format("Counter {} has value {}", m_id, i) << endl;
            }
        }
    private:
        int m_id { 0 };
        int m_numIterations { 0 };
        inline static mutex ms_mutex;
};
```

This code creates a `lock_guard` instance on each iteration of the `for` loop. It is recommended to limit the time a lock is held as much as possible; otherwise, you are blocking other threads for too long.

For example, if the `lock_guard` instance was created once right before the `for` loop, then you would basically lose all multithreading in this code because one thread would hold a lock for the entire duration of its `for` loop, and all other threads would wait for this lock to be released.

> **WARNING** *Try to hold locks as short as possible. This means you should avoid using slow operations while holding a lock, such as printing messages to the console, reading data from files, accessing databases, performing long calculations, doing explicit sleeps, and so on.*

Using Timed Mutexes

The following example demonstrates how to use a timed mutex. It is the same `Counter` class as before, but this time it uses a `timed_mutex` in combination with a `unique_lock`. A relative time of 200 milliseconds is given to the `unique_lock` constructor, causing it to try to obtain a lock for 200 milliseconds. If the lock cannot be obtained within this timeout interval, the constructor returns. Afterward, you can check whether the lock has been acquired. You can do this with an `if` statement on the `lock` variable, because `unique_lock` defines a `bool` conversion operator. The timeout is specified using the chrono library, discussed in Chapter 22.

```
class Counter
{
    public:
        explicit Counter(int id, int numIterations)
            : m_id { id }, m_numIterations { numIterations } { }

        void operator()() const
        {
            for (int i { 0 }; i < m_numIterations; ++i) {
                unique_lock lock { ms_timedMutex, 200ms };
                if (lock) {
                    cout << format("Counter {} has value {}", m_id, i) << endl;
                } else {
                    // Lock not acquired in 200ms, skip output.
                }
            }
        }
    private:
        int m_id { 0 };
        int m_numIterations { 0 };
        inline static timed_mutex ms_timedMutex;
};
```

Double-Checked Locking

The *double-checked locking pattern* is actually an anti-pattern, which you should avoid! It is shown here because you might come across it in existing code bases. The idea of the double-checked locking pattern is to try to avoid the use of mutexes. It's a half-baked attempt at trying to write more efficient code than using a mutex. It can really go wrong when you try to make it faster than demonstrated in the upcoming example, for instance, by using relaxed atomics (not further discussed), using a regular `bool` instead of an `atomic<bool>`, and so on. The pattern becomes sensitive to data races, and it is hard to get right. The irony is that using `call_once()` will usually be faster, and using a magic static (if applicable) will be even faster.

> **NOTE** *Function-local* `static` *variables are called* ***magic statics*** *or* ***thread-safe statics.*** *C++ guarantees that such local* `static` *variables are initialized in a thread-safe fashion, so you don't need any manual thread synchronization. An example of using a magic static is given in Chapter 33, "Applying Design Patterns," with the discussion of the singleton pattern.*

> **WARNING** *Avoid the double-checked locking pattern! Instead, use other mechanisms such as simple locks, atomic variables,* `call_once()`*, magic statics, and so on.*

Double-checked locking could, for example, be used to make sure that resources are initialized exactly once. The following example shows how you can implement this. It is called the double-checked locking pattern because it is checking the value of the `g_initialized` variable twice, once before acquiring the lock and once right after acquiring the lock. The first `g_initialized` check is used to prevent acquiring a lock when it is not needed. The second check is required to make sure that no other thread performed the initialization between the first `g_initialized` check and acquiring the lock.

```
void initializeSharedResources()
{
    // ... Initialize shared resources to be used by multiple threads.
    println("Shared resources initialized.");
}

atomic<bool> g_initialized { false };
mutex g_mutex;

void processingFunction()
{
    if (!g_initialized) {
        unique_lock lock { g_mutex };
        if (!g_initialized) {
            initializeSharedResources();
            g_initialized = true;
        }
    }
    print("1");
}
```

```
int main()
{
    vector<jthread> threads;
    for (int i { 0 }; i < 5; ++i) {
        threads.emplace_back(processingFunction);
    }
}
```

The output clearly shows that only one thread initializes the shared resources:

```
Shared resources initialized.
11111
```

> **NOTE** *For this example, it's recommended to use* `call_once()` *as demonstrated earlier in this chapter, instead of double-checked locking!*

CONDITION VARIABLES

Condition variables allow a thread to block until a certain condition is set by another thread or until the system time reaches a specified time. These variables allow for explicit inter-thread communication. If you are familiar with multithreaded programming using the Win32 API, you can compare condition variables with *event objects* in Windows.

`<condition_variable>` provides two condition variables:

- `std::condition_variable`: A condition variable that can wait only on a `unique_lock<mutex>`, which, according to the C++ standard, allows for maximum efficiency on certain platforms.
- `std::condition_variable_any`: A condition variable that can wait on any kind of object, including custom lock types.

A `condition_variable` supports the following member functions:

- `notify_one();`

  Wakes up one of the threads waiting on a condition variable. This is similar to an auto-reset event in Windows.

- `notify_all();`

  Wakes up all threads waiting on a condition variable.

- `wait(unique_lock<mutex>& lk);`

  The thread calling `wait()` should already have acquired a lock on `lk`. The effect of calling `wait()` is that it atomically calls `lk.unlock()` and blocks the thread, waiting for a notification. When the thread is unblocked by a `notify_one()` or `notify_all()` call in another thread, the function calls `lk.lock()` again, possibly blocking until the lock has been acquired, and then returns.

- wait_for(unique_lock<mutex>& lk, const chrono::duration<Rep, Period>& rel_time);

  Similar to wait(), except that the thread is unblocked by a notify_one() call, a notify_all() call, or when the given timeout has expired.

- wait_until(unique_lock<mutex>& lk, const chrono::time_point<Clock, Duration>& abs_time);

  Similar to wait(), except that the thread is unblocked by a notify_one() call, a notify_all() call, or when the system time passes the given absolute time.

There are also overloads of wait(), wait_for(), and wait_until() that accept an extra predicate parameter. For instance, the overload of wait() accepting an extra predicate is equivalent to the following:

```
while (!predicate())
    wait(lk);
```

The condition_variable_any class supports the same member functions as condition_variable, except that it accepts any kind of lock class instead of only a unique_lock<mutex>. The used lock class must have a lock() and unlock() member function.

Spurious Wake-Ups

Threads waiting on a condition variable can wake up when another thread calls notify_one() or notify_all(), or after a relative timeout, or when the system time reaches a certain time. However, they can also wake up *spuriously*. This means that a thread can wake up even if no other thread has called any notify member function and no timeouts have been reached yet. Thus, when a thread waits on a condition variable and wakes up, it needs to check why it woke up. One way to check for this is by using one of the versions of wait() accepting a predicate, as demonstrated in the following section.

Using Condition Variables

As an example, condition variables can be used for background threads processing items from a queue. You can define a queue in which you insert items to be processed. A background thread waits until there are items in the queue. When an item is inserted into the queue, the thread wakes up, processes the item, and goes back to sleep, waiting for the next item. Suppose you have the following queue:

```
queue<string> m_queue;
```

To make sure that only one thread is modifying this queue at any given time, we add a mutex:

```
mutex m_mutex;
```

To be able to notify a background thread when an item is added, we also add a condition variable:

```
condition_variable m_condVar;
```

A thread that wants to add an item to the queue first acquires a lock on the mutex, then adds the item to the queue, and notifies the background thread. Calling `notify_one()` or `notify_all()` can be done whether you currently have the lock or not; both work.

```
// Lock mutex and add entry to the queue.
lock_guard lock { m_mutex };
m_queue.push(entry);
// Notify condition variable to wake up thread.
m_condVar.notify_all();
```

The background thread waits for notifications in an infinite loop, as follows. Note the use of `wait()` accepting a predicate to correctly handle spurious wake-ups. The predicate checks if there really is something in the queue. When the call to `wait()` returns, you are sure there is something in the queue.

```
unique_lock lock { m_mutex };
while (true) {
    // Wait for a notification.
    m_condVar.wait(lock, [this]{ return !m_queue.empty(); });
    // Whenever we reach this line, the mutex is locked and the queue is non-empty.
    // Process queue item...
    m_queue.pop();
}
```

The "Example: Multithreaded Logger Class" section toward the end of this chapter, provides a complete example on how to use condition variables to send notifications to other threads.

The C++ standard also defines a helper function called `std::notify_all_at_thread_exit(cond, lk)` where `cond` is a condition variable and `lk` is a `unique_lock<mutex>` instance. A thread calling this function should already have acquired the lock `lk`. When the thread exits, it automatically executes the following:

```
lk.unlock();
cond.notify_all();
```

> **NOTE** *The lock* `lk` *stays locked until the thread exits. So, you need to make sure that this does not cause any deadlocks in your code, for example, due to wrong lock ordering.*

LATCHES

A *latch* is a single-use thread coordination point. A number of threads block at a latch point. Once a given number of threads reach the latch point, all threads are unblocked and allowed to continue execution. Basically, it's a counter that's counting down as each thread arrives at the latch point. Once the counter hits zero, the latch remains "open" indefinitely, all blocking threads are unblocked, and any threads subsequently arriving at the latch point are immediately allowed to continue.

A latch is implemented by `std::latch`, defined in `<latch>`. The constructor accepts the required number of threads that need to reach the latch point. A thread arriving at the latch point can call `arrive_and_wait()`, which decrements the latch counter and blocks until the latch is signaled. Threads can also block on a latch point without decrementing the counter by calling `wait()`. The `try_wait()` member function can be used to check if the counter has reached zero. Finally, if needed, the counter can also be decremented without blocking by calling `count_down()`.

A first example demonstrates a use case for a latch point where data is processed in parallel. The following code snippet launches a number of worker threads, each doing some of the work. Once a worker thread is finished with its work, it calls `count_down()` on the latch to signal that its work is done. The main thread calls `wait()` on the latch to wait until the latch counter reaches zero, signaling that all worker threads have finished.

```
// Launch a number of threads to do some work.
constexpr unsigned numberOfWorkerThreads { 10 };
latch latch { numberOfWorkerThreads };
vector<jthread> threads;
for (unsigned i { 0 }; i < numberOfWorkerThreads; ++i) {
    threads.emplace_back([&latch, i] {
        // Do some work...
        print("{} ", i);
        this_thread::sleep_for(1s);
        print("{} ", i);
        // When work is done, decrease the latch counter.
        latch.count_down();
    });
}
// Wait for all worker threads to finish.
latch.wait();
println("\nAll worker threads are finished.");
```

A second example demonstrates another use case for a latch point in which some data needs to be loaded into memory (I/O bound) that is subsequently processed in parallel in multiple threads. Suppose further that the threads need to perform some CPU-bound initialization when starting up and before they can start processing data. By launching the threads first and letting them do their CPU-bound initialization, and loading the data (I/O bound) in parallel, performance is increased. The code initializes a `latch` object with counter 1 and launches 10 threads that all do some initialization and then block on the `latch` until the latch counter reaches zero. After starting the 10 threads, the code loads some data, for example from disk, that is, an I/O-bound step. Once all data has been loaded, the latch counter is decremented to 0 which unblocks all 10 waiting threads.

```
latch startLatch { 1 };
vector<jthread> threads;
for (int i { 0 }; i < 10; ++i) {
    threads.emplace_back([&startLatch] {
        // Do some initialization... (CPU bound)

        // Wait until the latch counter reaches zero.
        startLatch.wait();

        // Process data...
    });
}
```

```
// Load data... (I/O bound)

// Once all data has been loaded, decrement the latch counter
// which then reaches zero and unblocks all waiting threads.
startLatch.count_down();
```

BARRIERS

A *barrier* is a reusable thread coordination mechanism consisting of a sequence of phases. A number of threads block at the barrier point. Each time a given number of threads reach the barrier, a phase completion callback is executed, all blocking threads are unblocked, the thread counter is reset, and the next phase starts. During each phase, the number of expected threads for the next phase can be adjusted. Barriers are great to perform synchronization between loops. For example, suppose you have a number of threads running concurrently and performing some calculations in a loop. Suppose further that once those calculations are finished, you need to do something with the results before the threads can start a new iteration of their loop. For such a scenario, barriers are perfect. When a thread is done with its work, it blocks at the barrier. When they all arrive at the barrier, the phase completion callback processes the results of the threads and then unblocks all the threads to start their next iteration.

A barrier is implemented by the class template `std::barrier`, defined in `<barrier>`. The most important member function of a `barrier` is `arrive_and_wait()`, which decrements the counter and then blocks the thread until the current phase is finished. Consult a Standard Library reference for a full description of other available member functions.

The following code snippet demonstrates the use of a barrier. It's a simulation of a production environment using robots. For each iteration, all robots need to do some work. When a robot is finished, it waits until all the other robots are finished. Once all robots are done, the next iteration is prepared, and the robots are instructed to start again. The barrier-specific operations are highlighted.

```
constexpr unsigned numberOfRobots { 2 };
constexpr unsigned numberOfIterations { 3 };
unsigned iterationCount { 1 };
vector<jthread> robots;

auto completionCallback { [&] () noexcept {
    if (iterationCount == numberOfIterations) {
        println("Finished {} iterations, stopping robots.", numberOfIterations);
        for (auto& robot : robots) { robot.request_stop(); }
    } else {
        ++iterationCount;
        println("All robots finished. Preparing iteration {}.", iterationCount);
        this_thread::sleep_for(1s);
        println("Iteration {} ready to start. Waking up robots.", iterationCount);
    }
} };
```

```
barrier robotSynchronization { numberOfRobots, completionCallback };

auto robotThreadFunction { [&](stop_token token, string_view name) {
    println("   Thread for robot {} started.", name);
    while (!token.stop_requested()) {
        this_thread::sleep_for(1s);
        println("   {} finished.", name);
        robotSynchronization.arrive_and_wait();
    }
    println("   {} shutting down.", name);
} };

println("Preparing first iteration. Creating {} robot threads.", numberOfRobots);

for (unsigned i { 0 }; i < numberOfRobots; ++i) {
    robots.emplace_back(robotThreadFunction, format("Robot_{}", i));
}

for (auto& robot : robots) { robot.join(); }
println("Done with all work.");
```

The output is as follows:

```
Preparing first iteration. Creating 2 robot threads.
   Thread for robot Robot_0 started.
   Thread for robot Robot_1 started.
   Robot_1 finished.
   Robot_0 finished.
All robots finished. Preparing iteration 2.
Iteration 2 ready to start. Waking up robots.
   Robot_1 finished.
   Robot_0 finished.
All robots finished. Preparing iteration 3.
Iteration 3 ready to start. Waking up robots.
   Robot_1 finished.
   Robot_0 finished.
Finished 3 iterations, stopping robots.
   Robot_0 shutting down.
   Robot_1 shutting down.
Done with all work.
```

In one of the exercises at the end of this chapter, you will improve this robot simulation so that the main thread starts all the robot threads, waits for all the robots to have started, prepares the first iteration, and instructs all waiting robots to start working.

SEMAPHORES

Semaphores are lightweight synchronization primitives that can be used as building blocks for other synchronization mechanisms such as mutexes, latches, and barriers. Basically, a semaphore consists of a counter representing a number of *slots*. The counter is initialized in the constructor. If you acquire a slot, the counter is decremented, while releasing a slot increments the counter. There are two semaphore classes defined in `<semaphore>`: `std::counting_semaphore` and `binary_semaphore`.

The former models a non-negative resource count. The latter has only one slot; hence, the slot is either free or not free, perfectly suitable as building block for a mutex. Both provide the following member functions:

MEMBER FUNCTION	DESCRIPTION
`acquire()`	Decrements the counter. When the counter is zero, blocks until it is able to decrement the counter, and then does so.
`try_acquire()`	Tries to decrement the counter but does not block if the counter is already zero. Returns `true` if the counter could be decremented, `false` otherwise.
`try_acquire_for()`	Same as `try_acquire()` but tries for a given duration.
`try_acquire_until()`	Same as `try_acquire()` but tries until the system time reaches a given time.
`release()`	Increments the counter by a given number and unblocks threads that are blocking in their `acquire()` call.

A counting semaphore allows you to control exactly how many threads you want to allow to run concurrently. For example, the following code snippet allows a maximum of four threads to run in parallel. From the output, you clearly see that only four threads manage to acquire the semaphore concurrently.

```
counting_semaphore semaphore { 4 };
vector<jthread> threads;
for (int i { 0 }; i < 10; ++i) {
    threads.emplace_back([&semaphore] {
        semaphore.acquire();
        // ... Slot acquired ... (at most 4 threads concurrently)
        print("{}", i);
        this_thread::sleep_for(5s);
        semaphore.release();
    });
}
```

Another use case for semaphores is to implement a notification mechanism for threads, instead of condition variables. For example, you could initialize the counter of a semaphore to 0 in its constructor. Any thread that calls `acquire()` will block until some other thread calls `release()` on the semaphore.

FUTURES

As discussed earlier in this chapter, using `std::thread` to launch a thread that calculates a single result does not make it easy to get the computed result back once the thread has finished executing. Another problem with `std::thread` is in how it handles errors like exceptions. If a thread throws an exception and this exception is not caught by the thread itself, the C++ runtime calls `std::terminate()`, which usually terminates the entire application.

A *future* can be used to more easily get the result out of a thread and to transport exceptions from one thread to another thread, which can then handle the exception however it wants.

A *promise* is something in which a thread stores its result. A future is used to get access to the result stored in a promise. That is, a promise is the input side for a result, a future is the output side. Once a function, running in the same thread or in another thread, has calculated the value that it wants to return, it puts this value in a promise. This value can then be retrieved through a future. A promise/future pair is an inter-thread one-shot communication channel for a result.

C++ provides a standard future, called `std::future`. You can retrieve the result from an `std::future` as follows. `T` is the type of the calculated result.

```
future<T> myFuture { ... };   // Is discussed later.
T result { myFuture.get() };
```

The call to `get()` retrieves the result and stores it in the variable `result`. If calculating the result is not finished yet, the call to `get()` blocks until the value becomes available. You can call `get()` only once on a future. The behavior of calling it a second time is undefined by the standard.

If you want to avoid blocking, you can first ask the `future` if there is a result available:

```
if (myFuture.wait_for(0)) {  // Value is available.
    T result { myFuture.get() };
} else {                     // Value is not yet available.
    ...
}
```

std::promise and std::future

C++ provides the `std::promise` class as one way to implement the concept of a promise. You can call `set_value()` on a `promise` to store a result, or you can call `set_exception()` on it to store an exception in the `promise`. You can call `set_value()` or `set_exception()` only once on a specific `promise`. If you call it multiple times, an `std::future_error` exception will be thrown.

Alternatively, you can use `set_value_at_thread_exit()` or `set_exception_at_thread_exit()` to set a value or an exception in a `promise`. Using these, the value or the exception is stored in the `promise` at the time the thread exits and after all thread-local storage variables have been destroyed.

A thread A that launches another thread B to calculate something can create a `promise` and pass it to the launched thread. A `promise` cannot be copied, but it can be moved into a thread! Thread B uses that `promise` to store the result. Before moving the `promise` into thread B, thread A calls `get_future()` on the created `promise` to be able to get access to the result once B has finished. Here is a simple example:

```
void doWork(promise<int> thePromise)
{
    // ... Do some work ...
    // And ultimately store the result in the promise.
    thePromise.set_value(42);
}
```

```
int main()
{
    // Create a promise to pass to the thread.
    promise<int> myPromise;
    // Get the future of the promise.
    auto theFuture { myPromise.get_future() };
    // Create a thread and move the promise into it.
    jthread theThread { doWork, move(myPromise) };

    // Do some more work...

    // Get the result.
    int result { theFuture.get() };
    println("Result: {}", result);
}
```

> **NOTE** *This code is just for demonstration purposes. It starts the calculation in a new thread and then calls* `get()` *on the* `future`*, which blocks until the result is calculated. This sounds like an expensive function call. In real-world applications, you can use* `futures` *by periodically checking if there is a result available or not (using* `wait_for()` *as discussed earlier) or by using a synchronization mechanism such as a condition variable. When the result is not yet available, you can do something else in the meantime, instead of blocking.*

std::packaged_task

A `std::packaged_task` makes it easier to work with promises than explicitly using `std::promise`, as in the previous section. The following code demonstrates this. It creates a `packaged_task` to execute `calculateSum()`. The `future` is retrieved from the `packaged_task` by calling `get_future()`. A thread is launched, and the `packaged_task` is moved into it. A `packaged_task`, like a `std::promise`, is move-only. After the thread is launched, `get()` is called on the retrieved future to get the result. This blocks until the result is available.

`calculateSum()` does not store anything explicitly in any kind of promise. A `packaged_task` automatically creates a promise, and automatically stores the result of the callable—`calculateSum()` in this case—in the promise, no matter whether that result is a value or a thrown exception.

```
int calculateSum(int a, int b) { return a + b; }

int main()
{
    // Create a packaged task to run calculateSum.
    packaged_task task { calculateSum };
    // Get the future for the result of the packaged task.
    auto theFuture { task.get_future() };
    // Create a thread, move the packaged task into it, and
    // execute the packaged task with the given arguments.
    jthread theThread { move(task), 39, 3 };

    // Do some more work...
```

```
    // Get the result.
    int result { theFuture.get() };
    println("Result: {}", result);
}
```

std::async

If you want to give the C++ runtime more control over whether or not a thread is created to calculate something, you can use `std::async()`. It accepts a callable to be executed and returns a `future` that you can use to retrieve the result. There are two ways in which `async()` can run a callable:

- By running it on a separate thread asynchronously
- By running it on the calling thread synchronously at the time you call `get()` on the returned `future`

If you call `async()` without additional arguments, the runtime automatically chooses one of the two mechanisms depending on factors such as the number of CPU cores in your system and the amount of concurrency already taking place. You can influence the runtime's behavior by specifying a policy argument:

- `launch::async`: Forces the runtime to execute the callable asynchronously on a different thread.
- `launch::deferred`: Forces the runtime to execute the callable synchronously on the calling thread when `get()` is called.
- `launch::async | launch::deferred`: Lets the runtime choose (= default behavior).

The following example demonstrates the use of `async()`:

```
int calculateSum(int a, int b) { return a + b; }

int main()
{
    auto myFuture { async(calculateSum, 39, 3) };
    //auto myFuture { async(launch::async, calculateSum, 39, 3) };
    //auto myFuture { async(launch::deferred, calculateSum, 39, 3) };

    // Do some more work...

    // Get the result.
    int result { myFuture.get() };
    println("Result: {}", result);
}
```

As you can see from this code snippet, `std::async()` is one of the easiest techniques to perform some calculations either asynchronously (on a different thread) or synchronously (on the same thread) and retrieve the result afterward.

> **WARNING** *A* `future` *returned by a call to* `async()` *blocks in its destructor until the result is available. (This is not true of ordinary* `futures`*; only the kind returned from* `async()`*.) This means that if you call* `async()` *without capturing the returned* `future`*, the* `async()` *call effectively becomes a blocking call! For example, the following line synchronously calls* `calculateSum()`*:*
>
> ```
> async(calculateSum, 39, 3);
> ```
>
> *What happens with this statement is that* `async()` *creates and returns a* `future`*. This* `future` *is not captured, so it is a temporary. Because it is a temporary* `future`*, its destructor is called at the end of this statement, and this destructor blocks until the result is available.*

Exception Handling

A big advantage of using futures is that they can transport exceptions between threads. Calling `get()` on a `future` either returns the calculated result or rethrows any exception that has been stored in the promise linked to the `future`. When you use `packaged_task` or `async()`, any exception thrown from the launched callable is automatically stored in the promise. If you use `std::promise` directly as your promise, you can call `set_exception()` to store an exception in it. Here is an example using `async()`:

```
int calculate()
{
    throw runtime_error { "Exception thrown from calculate()." };
}

int main()
{
    // Use the launch::async policy to force asynchronous execution.
    auto myFuture { async(launch::async, calculate) };

    // Do some more work...

    // Get the result.
    try {
        int result { myFuture.get() };
        println("Result: {}", result);
    } catch (const exception& ex) {
        println("Caught exception: {}", ex.what());
    }
}
```

std::shared_future

`std::future<T>` only requires `T` to be move-constructible. When you call `get()` on a `future<T>`, the result is moved out of the `future` and returned to you. This means you can call `get()` only once on a `future<T>`.

If you want to be able to call `get()` multiple times, even from multiple threads, then you need to use an `std::shared_future<T>`. A `shared_future` can be created by using `std::future::share()` or by passing a `future` to the `shared_future` constructor. A `future` is not copyable, so you have to move it into the `shared_future` constructor.

`shared_future` can be used to wake up multiple threads at once. For example, the following piece of code defines two lambda expressions to be executed asynchronously on different threads. The first thing each lambda expression does is set a value to their respective `promise` to signal that they have started. Then they both call `get()` on `signalFuture`, which blocks until a parameter is made available through the `future`, after which they continue their execution. Each lambda expression captures their respective `promise` by reference and captures `signalFuture` by value, so both lambda expressions have a copy of `signalFuture`. The main thread uses `async()` to execute both lambda expressions asynchronously on different threads, waits until both threads have started, and then sets the parameter in the `signalPromise`, which wakes up both threads.

```
promise<void> thread1Started, thread2Started;

promise<int> signalPromise;
auto signalFuture { signalPromise.get_future().share() };
//shared_future<int> signalFuture { signalPromise.get_future() };

auto function1 { [&thread1Started, signalFuture] {
    thread1Started.set_value();
    // Wait until parameter is set.
    int parameter { signalFuture.get() };
    // ...
} };

auto function2 { [&thread2Started, signalFuture] {
    thread2Started.set_value();
    // Wait until parameter is set.
    int parameter { signalFuture.get() };
    // ...
} };

// Run both lambda expressions asynchronously.
// Remember to capture the future returned by async()!
auto result1 { async(launch::async, function1) };
auto result2 { async(launch::async, function2) };

// Wait until both threads have started.
thread1Started.get_future().wait();
thread2Started.get_future().wait();

// Both threads are now waiting for the parameter.
// Set the parameter to wake up both of them.
signalPromise.set_value(42);
```

EXAMPLE: MULTITHREADED LOGGER CLASS

This section demonstrates how to use threads, mutexes, locks, and condition variables to write a multithreaded `Logger` class. The class allows log messages to be added to a queue from different threads. The `Logger` class itself processes this queue in a background thread that serially writes the log messages to a file. The class is designed in two iterations to show you some examples of problems you will encounter when writing multithreaded code.

The C++ standard does not have a thread-safe queue, so it is obvious that you must protect access to the queue with some synchronization mechanism to prevent multiple threads from reading/writing to the queue at the same time. This example uses a mutex and a condition variable to provide the synchronization. Based on that, you might define the `Logger` class as follows:

> **WARNING** *This* `Logger` *class uses* `std::thread` *instead of* `jthread` *to demonstrate 1) the catastrophic results when using* `thread` *improperly and 2) how easy it is to use* `thread` *wrongly.*

```
export class Logger
{
    public:
        // Starts a background thread writing log entries to a file.
        Logger();
        // Prevent copy construction and assignment.
        Logger(const Logger&) = delete;
        Logger& operator=(const Logger&) = delete;
        // Add log entry to the queue.
        void log(std::string entry);
    private:
        // The function running in the background thread.
        void processEntries();
        // Helper member function to process a queue of entries.
        void processEntriesHelper(std::queue<std::string>& queue,
            std::ofstream& ofs) const;
        // Mutex and condition variable to protect access to the queue.
        std::mutex m_mutex;
        std::condition_variable m_condVar;
        std::queue<std::string> m_queue;
        // The background thread.
        std::thread m_thread;
};
```

The implementation is as follows. This initial design has a couple of problems. When you try to run it, it might behave incorrect and crash. This is discussed and solved in the next design iteration of the `Logger` class. The `while` loop in the `processEntries()` member function is worth looking at. It processes all messages currently in the queue. While having a lock, it swaps the contents of the current queue of entries with an empty local queue on the stack. After this, it releases the lock so other threads are not blocked anymore to add new entries to the now empty current queue. Once the lock is released, all entries in the local queue are processed. This does not require the lock anymore as other threads will not touch this local queue.

```
Logger::Logger()
{
    // Start background thread.
    m_thread = thread { &Logger::processEntries, this };
}

void Logger::log(string entry)
{
    // Lock mutex and add entry to the queue.
    lock_guard lock { m_mutex };
    m_queue.push(move(entry));
    // Notify condition variable to wake up thread.
    m_condVar.notify_all();
}

void Logger::processEntries()
{
    // Open log file.
    ofstream logFile { "log.txt" };
    if (logFile.fail()) {
        println(cerr, "Failed to open logfile.");
        return;
    }

    unique_lock lock { m_mutex }; // Acquire a lock on m_mutex.
    while (true) { // Start processing loop.
        // Wait for a notification.
        m_condVar.wait(lock);

        // Condition variable is notified, so something might be in the queue.

        // While we still have the lock, swap the contents of the current queue
        // with an empty local queue on the stack.
        queue<string> localQueue;
        localQueue.swap(m_queue);

        // Now that all entries have been moved from the current queue to the
        // local queue, we can release the lock so other threads are not blocked
        // while we process the entries.
        lock.unlock();

        // Process the entries in the local queue on the stack. This happens after
        // having released the lock, so other threads are not blocked anymore.
        processEntriesHelper(localQueue, logFile);

        lock.lock();
    }
}

void Logger::processEntriesHelper(queue<string>& queue, ofstream& ofs) const
{
    while (!queue.empty()) {
        ofs << queue.front() << endl;
        queue.pop();
    }
}
```

> **WARNING** *As you can already see from this rather simple task, writing correct multithreaded code is hard! Unfortunately, at this moment, the C++ Standard Library does not provide any concurrent data structures, at least not yet.*
>
> *The* `Logger` *class is just an example to show these basic building blocks. For production-quality code, I recommend using an appropriate third-party concurrent data structure, instead of writing your own. For example, the open-source boost C++ libraries (*`boost.org`*) have an implementation of a queue that is lock-free and allows concurrent use without the need for any explicit synchronization.*

The `Logger` class can be tested with the following test code. It launches a number of threads, all logging a few messages to the same `Logger` instance.

```
void logSomeMessages(int id, Logger& logger)
{
    for (int i { 0 }; i < 10; ++i) {
        logger.log(format("Log entry {} from thread {}", i, id));
        this_thread::sleep_for(50ms);
    }
}

int main()
{
    Logger logger;
    vector<jthread> threads;
    // Create a few threads all working with the same Logger instance.
    for (int i { 0 }; i < 10; ++i) {
        threads.emplace_back(logSomeMessages, i, ref(logger));
    }
}
```

If you build and run this naive initial version, you will notice that the application is terminated abruptly. That is because the application never calls `join()` or `detach()` on the `Logger` background thread. Remember from earlier in this chapter that the destructor of a joinable `thread` object, that is, neither `join()` nor `detach()` has been called yet, calls `std::terminate()` to terminate all running threads and the application itself. This means that messages still in the queue are not written to the file on disk. Some runtime libraries even issue an error or generate a crash dump when the application is terminated like this. You need to add a mechanism to gracefully shut down the background thread and wait until the background thread is completely shut down before terminating the application. You can do this by adding a destructor and a Boolean data member to the class. The new definition of the class is as follows:

```
export class Logger
{
    public:
        // Gracefully shut down background thread.
        virtual ~Logger();
        // Other public members omitted for brevity.
    private:
```

```
        // Boolean telling the background thread to terminate.
        bool m_exit { false };
        // Other members omitted for brevity.
};
```

The destructor sets `m_exit` to `true`, wakes up the background thread, and then waits until the thread is shut down. The destructor acquires a lock on `m_mutex` before setting `m_exit` to `true`. This is to prevent a race condition and deadlock with `processEntries()`, which could be at the beginning of its `while` loop right after having checked `m_exit` and right before the call to `wait()`. If the main thread calls the `Logger` destructor at that very moment (assuming the destructor hadn't been written to acquire a lock on `m_mutex`), then the destructor sets `m_exit` to `true` and calls `notify_all()` after `processEntries()` has checked `m_exit` and before `processEntries()` is waiting on the condition variable; thus, `processEntries()` will not see the new value of `m_exit`, and it will miss the notification. In that case, the application is deadlocked, because the destructor is waiting on the `join()` call and the background thread is waiting on the condition variable. The destructor can call `notify_all()` while still holding the lock or after having released it, but the lock must certainly be released before calling `join()`, which explains the extra code block using curly brackets.

```
Logger::~Logger()
{
    {
        lock_guard lock { m_mutex };
        // Gracefully shut down the thread by setting m_exit to true.
        m_exit = true;
    }
    // Notify condition variable to wake up thread.
    m_condVar.notify_all();
    // Wait until thread is shut down. This should be outside the above code
    // block because the lock must be released before calling join()!
    m_thread.join();
}
```

The `processEntries()` member function needs to check this Boolean variable and terminate the processing loop when it's `true`. It should also call `wait()` only when the queue is empty.

```
void Logger::processEntries()
{
    // Omitted for brevity.

    unique_lock lock { m_mutex }; // Acquire a lock on m_mutex.
    while (true) { // Start processing loop.
        if (!m_exit) { // Only wait for notifications if we don't have to exit.
            if (m_queue.empty()) { // Only wait if the queue is empty.
                m_condVar.wait(lock);
            }
        } else {
            // We have to exit, process the remaining entries in the queue.
            processEntriesHelper(m_queue, logFile);
            break;
        }

        // Condition variable is notified, so something might be in the queue
```

```
            // and/or we need to shut down this thread.

            queue<string> localQueue;
            localQueue.swap(m_queue);
            lock.unlock();
            processEntriesHelper(localQueue, logFile);

            lock.lock();
        }
    }
```

You cannot just check for `m_exit` in the condition for the outer `while` loop because even when `m_exit` is `true`, there might still be log entries in the queue that need to be written to the log file.

You can add artificial delays in specific places in your multithreaded code to trigger certain behavior. Such delays should only be added for testing and must be removed from your final code! For example, to test that the race condition with the destructor is solved, you can remove any calls to `log()` from the main program, causing it to almost immediately call the destructor of the `Logger` class, and add the following delay:

```
void Logger::processEntries()
{
    // Omitted for brevity.
    while (true) {
        if (!m_exit) { // Only wait for notifications if we don't have to exit.
            this_thread::sleep_for(1000ms);
            if (m_queue.empty()) { // Only wait if the queue is empty.
                m_condVar.wait(lock);
            }
    // Remaining code omitted, same as before.
}
```

> **NOTE** *I recommend using* `jthread` *over* `thread`*, as it automatically joins in its destructor. With* `jthread`*, the explicit call to* `join()` *in the destructor of* `Logger` *is not necessary.*

THREAD POOLS

Instead of creating and deleting threads dynamically throughout your program's lifetime, you can create a pool of threads that can be used as needed. This technique is often used in programs that want to handle some kind of event in a thread. In most environments, the ideal number of threads is equal to the number of processing cores. If there are more threads than cores, threads will have to be suspended to allow other threads to run, and this will ultimately add overhead. Note that while the ideal number of threads is equal to the number of cores, this applies only in the case where the threads are compute bound and cannot block for any other reason, including I/O. When threads can block, it is often appropriate to run more threads than there are cores. Determining the optimal number of threads in such cases is hard and may involve throughput measurements.

Because not all processing is identical, it is not uncommon to have threads from a thread pool receive, as part of their input, a callable that represents the computation to be done.

Because threads from a thread pool are pre-existing, it is much more efficient for the operating system to schedule a thread from the pool to run than it is to create one in response to an input. Furthermore, the use of a thread pool allows you to manage the number of threads that are created, so, depending on the platform, you may have just one thread or thousands of threads.

Several libraries are available that implement thread pools, including Intel Threading Building Blocks (TBB), Microsoft Parallel Patterns Library (PPL), and so on. It's recommended to use such a library for your thread pools instead of writing your own implementation. If you do want to implement a thread pool yourself, it can be done in a similar way as an object pool. Chapter 29, "Writing Efficient C++," gives an example implementation of an object pool.

COROUTINES

A coroutine is a function that can be suspended in the middle of its execution and resumed at a later point in time. Any function with one of the following keywords in its body is a coroutine:

- `co_await`: Suspends the execution of a coroutine while waiting for a computation to finish. Execution is resumed when the computation is finished.
- `co_return`: Returns from a coroutine (just `return` is not allowed in a coroutine). The coroutine cannot be resumed after this.
- `co_yield`: Returns a value from a coroutine back to the caller and suspends the coroutine. Subsequently calling the coroutine again will continue its execution at the point where it was suspended.

In general, there are two types of coroutines: stackful and stackless. A *stackful coroutine* can be suspended from anywhere deep inside a nested call. On the other hand, a *stackless coroutine* can only be suspended from the top stack frame. When a stackless coroutine is suspended, only the variables and temporaries with automatic storage duration in the body of the function are saved; the call stack is not saved. Hence, memory usage for stackless coroutines is minimal, allowing for millions or even billions of coroutines to be running concurrently. C++ only supports the stackless variant.

To be fair, coroutines don't necessarily have anything to do with multithreading; instead, they just provide a way for a function to be suspended and resumed at a later time. Of course, if needed, coroutines can be used in a multithreaded environment just as well.

Coroutines can be used to implement asynchronous operations using a synchronous programming style. Use cases include the following:

- Generators
- Asynchronous I/O
- Lazy computations

- Event-driven applications
- State machines

Unfortunately, while all the low-level language building blocks are available to write your own coroutines, there's not much in terms of high-level coroutine facilities. The C++23 Standard Library introduces one standardized high-level coroutine facility, the *generator* `std::generator`. A generator provides a mechanism to have a single thread switch back and forth between generating results and handling those results, without involving multiple threads.

The following code demonstrates the use of the `std::generator` class template, defined in `<generator>`:

```
generator<int> getSequenceGenerator(int startValue, int numberOfValues)
{
    for (int i { startValue }; i < startValue + numberOfValues; ++i) {
        // Print the local time to standard out, see Chapter 22.
        auto currentTime { system_clock::now() };
        auto localTime { current_zone()->to_local(currentTime) };
        print("{:%H:%M:%OS}: ", localTime);
        // Yield a value to the caller, and suspend the coroutine.
        co_yield i;
    }
}

int main()
{
    auto gen { getSequenceGenerator(10, 5) };
    for (const auto& value : gen) {
        print("{} (Press enter for next value)", value);
        cin.ignore();
    }
}
```

When you run the application, you'll get the following output:

```
16:35:42: 10 (Press enter for next value)
```

Pressing Enter adds another line:

```
16:35:42: 10 (Press enter for next value)
16:36:03: 11 (Press enter for next value)
```

Pressing Enter again adds yet another line:

```
16:35:42: 10 (Press enter for next value)
16:36:03: 11 (Press enter for next value)
16:36:21: 12 (Press enter for next value)
```

Every time after hitting Enter, a new value is requested from the generator. This causes the coroutine to resume, which executes the next iteration of the `for` loop in `getSequenceGenerator()` printing the local time, and returning the next value. Returning a value is done with `co_yield`, which returns the value and then suspends the coroutine. The value itself is printed in the `main()` function, followed by the question to press Enter for the next value. The output clearly shows that the coroutine is suspended and resumed multiple times.

Unfortunately, that's pretty much all there is to say about coroutines in the scope of this book. Writing coroutines yourself, such as `std::generator`, is complicated and way too advanced to discuss in this book. I recommend using existing coroutines, written by experts. If you need other coroutine facilities besides the `generator` provided by the Standard Library, there are third-party libraries available, such as cppcoro[1] and concurrencpp,[2] that provide a collection of high-level coroutines. The goal of this section was to introduce the idea so that you know it exists. Maybe a future C++ standard will introduce more high-level standardized coroutine facilities.

THREADING DESIGN AND BEST PRACTICES

This section lists a few best practices related to multithreaded programming.

- **Use parallel Standard Library algorithms:** The Standard Library contains a large collection of algorithms. More than 60 of them support parallel execution. Whenever possible, use such parallel algorithms instead of writing your own multithreaded code. See Chapter 20, "Mastering Standard Library Algorithms," for details on how to specify parallelization options for algorithms.
- **Prefer using `jthread` over `thread`:** Because `jthread` automatically joins in its destructor, it's harder to use wrong compared to `thread`.
- **Before closing the application, make sure all `thread` objects are unjoinable:** If you do use `thread`, make sure that either `join()` or `detach()` has been called on all `thread` objects. Destructors of `thread`s that are still joinable call `std::terminate()`, which abruptly terminates all threads and the application itself. Also remember that if you detach a thread, it will continue running. If it still accesses any global variables of non-trivial types, then those accesses might race with the destruction of the global variables during process shutdown, causing your program to crash on exit. These kinds of bugs can be hard to debug.
- **The best synchronization is no synchronization:** Multithreaded programming becomes much easier if you manage to design your different threads in such a way that all threads working on shared data read only from that shared data and never write to it, or only write to parts never read by other threads. In that case, there is no need for any synchronization, and you cannot have problems like data races or deadlocks.
- **Try to use the single-thread ownership pattern:** This means that a block of data is owned by no more than one thread at a time. Owning the data means that no other thread is allowed to read from or write to the data. When the thread is finished with the data, the data can be passed off to another thread, which now has sole and complete responsibility/ownership of the data. No synchronization is necessary in this case.
- **Use atomic types and operations when possible:** Atomic types and atomic operations make it easier to write data-race-free and deadlock-free code, because they handle synchronization automatically. If atomic types and operations are not possible in your multithreaded design and you need shared data, you will have to use some synchronization mechanism, such as a mutex.

[1] `https://github.com/lewissbaker/cppcoro`
[2] `https://github.com/David-Haim/concurrencpp`

- **Use locks to protect mutable shared data:** If you need mutable shared data to which multiple threads can write and you cannot use atomic types and operations, you have to use a locking mechanism to make sure that reads and writes between different threads are synchronized.
- **Release locks as soon as possible:** When you need to protect your shared data with a lock, make sure that you release the lock as soon as possible. While a thread is holding a lock, it is blocking other threads waiting for the same lock, possibly hurting performance.
- **Use RAII lock objects:** Use the `lock_guard`, `unique_lock`, `shared_lock`, or `scoped_lock` RAII classes to automatically release locks at the right time.
- **Do not manually acquire multiple locks; instead use `std::lock()`, `try_lock()`, or a `scoped_lock`:** If multiple threads need to acquire multiple locks, they must be acquired in the same order in all threads to prevent deadlock. You should use the generic `std::lock()` or `try_lock()` functions or the `scoped_lock` class to acquire multiple locks.
- **Use a multithreading-aware profiler:** This helps to find performance bottlenecks in your multithreaded applications and to find out if your multiple threads are indeed utilizing all available processing power in your system. An example of a multithreading-aware profiler is the profiler in Microsoft Visual Studio.
- **Understand the multithreading support features of your debugger:** Most debuggers have at least basic support for debugging multithreaded applications. You should be able to get a list of all running threads in your application, and you should be able to switch to any one of those threads to inspect their call stack. You can use this, for example, to inspect deadlocks, because you can see exactly what each thread is doing.
- **Use thread pools instead of creating and destroying a lot of threads dynamically:** Your performance decreases if you dynamically create and destroy a lot of threads. In that case, it's better to use a thread pool to reuse existing threads.
- **Use higher-level multithreading libraries:** The C++ standard, at this moment, only provides basic building blocks for writing multithreaded code. Using those correctly is not trivial. Where possible, use higher-level multithreading libraries such as Intel Threading Building Blocks (TBB), Microsoft Parallel Patterns Library (PPL), and so on, rather than reinventing the wheel. Multithreaded programming is error-prone. More often than not, your wheel may not be as round as you think.

SUMMARY

This chapter gave a brief overview of multithreaded programming using the standard C++ threading support library. You learned how to launch threads using `std::thread`, as well as how `jthread` makes it safer, less error-prone, and so much easier to write cancellable threads. You learned how you can use atomic types and atomic operations to operate on shared data without having to use an explicit synchronization mechanism. In case you cannot use these atomic types and operations, you learned how to use mutexes and condition variables to ensure proper synchronization between different threads that need read/write access to shared data. You learned about the synchronization primitives: semaphores, latches, and barriers. You also saw how promises and futures represent a simple inter-thread communication channel; you can use futures to more easily get a result back from a thread. The chapter finished with a brief introduction to coroutines and a number of best practices for multithreaded application design.

As mentioned in the introduction, this chapter tried to touch on all the basic multithreading building blocks provided by the Standard Library, but due to space constraints, it cannot go into all the details of multithreaded programming. There are books available that discuss nothing but multithreading. See Appendix B for a few references.

EXERCISES

By solving the following exercises, you can practice the material discussed in this chapter. Solutions to all exercises are available with the code download on the book's website at `www.wiley.com/go/proc++6e`. However, if you are stuck on an exercise, first reread parts of this chapter to try to find an answer yourself before looking at the solution from the website.

Exercise 27-1: Write an application that beeps every three seconds indefinitely. The three-second delay must be passed as an argument to your thread function. Tip: You can make your computer beep by printing `\a` to the standard output.

Exercise 27-2: Modify your solution to Exercise 27-1 so that the application can be stopped when the user presses the enter key.

Exercise 27-3: Modify your solution to Exercise 27-1 so that the beeping continues until the user presses the Enter key. Once the Enter key is pressed, beeping should be paused, until the user presses the Enter key again. The user can pause and resume the beeping as many times as she wants.

Exercise 27-4: Write an application that can calculate a number of Fibonacci numbers concurrently. For example, your code should be able to calculate the 4th, 9th, 14th, and 17th number in the Fibonacci series in parallel. The Fibonacci series starts with 0 and 1, and any subsequent value is the sum of the two previous values, so: 0, 1, 1, 2, 3, 5, 8, 13, 21, 34, 55, 89, and so on. Once all results are available, output them to the standard output. Finally, calculate their sum using a constrained Standard Library algorithm.

Exercise 27-5: Improve the robot example from earlier in this chapter. You can find that code in the downloadable source code archive in `Ch27\05_barrier\barrier.cpp`. Improve it so that the main thread starts all the robot threads, waits for all the robots to have started, prepares the first iteration, and then instructs all waiting robots to start working.

Exercise 27-6: Use `compare_exchange_strong()` to implement a function `atomicMin(a, b)` that sets `a` to `min(a, b)` atomically, and where `a` is an `atomic<int>` and `b` an `int`.

PART V
C++ Software Engineering

28

Maximizing Software Engineering Methods

WHAT'S IN THIS CHAPTER?

- What a software life cycle model is, with examples of the waterfall model, the sashimi model, spiral-like models, and agile
- What software engineering methodologies are, with examples of the Unified Process, Rational Unified Process, Scrum, Extreme Programming, and Software Triage
- What version control means

This chapter starts the last part of this book, which is about software engineering. This part describes software engineering methods, code efficiency, testing, debugging, design techniques, design patterns, and how to target multiple platforms.

When you first learned how to program, you were probably on your own schedule. You were free to do everything at the last minute if you wanted to, and you could radically change your design during implementation. When coding in the professional world, however, programmers rarely have such flexibility. Even the most liberal engineering managers admit that some amount of process is necessary. These days, knowing the software engineering process is as important as knowing how to code.

In this chapter, I will survey various approaches to software engineering. I will not go into great depth on any one approach—there are plenty of excellent books on software engineering processes. My intention is to cover some different types of processes in broad strokes so you can compare and contrast them. I will try not to advocate or discourage any particular methodology. Rather, I hope that by learning about the tradeoffs of several different approaches, you'll be able to construct a process that works for you and the rest of your team. Whether you're a contractor working alone on projects or your team consists of hundreds of engineers on several continents, understanding different approaches to software development will help you with your job on a daily basis.

The final part of this chapter discusses version control systems that make it easy to manage source code and keep track of its history. A version control system is mandatory in every company to avoid a source code maintenance nightmare. Even for one-person projects, I highly recommend you use such a system.

THE NEED FOR PROCESS

The history of software development is filled with tales of failed projects. From over-budget and poorly marketed consumer applications to grandiose mega-hyped operating systems, it seems that no area of software development is free from this trend.

Even when software successfully reaches users, bugs have become so commonplace that end users are often forced to endure constant updates and patches. Sometimes the software doesn't accomplish the tasks it is supposed to do or doesn't work the way the user would expect. These issues all point to one fact: writing software is hard.

You may wonder why software engineering seems to differ from other forms of engineering in its frequency of failures. For example, while cars have their share of bugs, you rarely see them stop suddenly and demand a reboot due to a buffer overflow (though as more and more car components become software-driven, you just might). Your TV may not be perfect, but you don't have to upgrade to version 2.3 to get Channel 6 to work.

Is it the case that other engineering disciplines are just more advanced than software development? Is a civil engineer able to construct a working bridge by drawing upon the long history of bridge-building? Are chemical engineers able to build a compound successfully because most of the bugs were worked out in earlier generations? Is software engineering too new, or is it really a different type of discipline with inherent qualities contributing to the frequency of bugs, unusable results, and doomed projects?

It certainly seems as if there's something different about software engineering. For one thing, computer technology changes rapidly, creating uncertainty in the software development process. Even if no earth-shattering breakthrough occurs during your project, the pace at which the IT industry moves can lead to problems. Software also often needs to be developed quickly because competition is fierce.

Software development schedules can also be unpredictable. Accurate scheduling is nearly impossible when a single gnarly bug can take days or even weeks to fix. Even when things seem to be going according to schedule, the widespread tendency of product definition changes (known as *feature creep* or *scope creep*) can throw a wrench in the process. If left unchecked, such scope creep can eventually result in software bloat.

Software is often complex. There is no easy and accurate way to prove that a program is bug-free. Buggy or messy code can have an impact on software for years if it is maintained through several versions. Software systems are often so complex that when staff turnover occurs, nobody wants to get anywhere near some messy legacy code. This leads to a cycle of endless patching, hacks, and workarounds.

Of course, standard business risks apply to software as well. Marketing pressures and miscommunication get in the way. Many programmers try to steer clear of corporate politics, but it's not uncommon to have animosity between the development and product-marketing groups.

All of these factors working against software engineering products indicate the need for some sort of process. Software projects are big, complicated, and fast-paced. To avoid failure, engineering groups need to adopt a system to control this unwieldy process.

Elegantly designed software with clean and maintainable code can be developed. I'm convinced it is possible, but it takes continuous efforts of each individual team member and requires following proper software development processes and practices.

SOFTWARE LIFE CYCLE MODELS

Complexity in software isn't new. The need for a formalized process was recognized decades ago. Several approaches to modeling the *software life cycle* have attempted to bring some order to the chaos of software development by defining the software process in terms of steps from the initial idea to the final product. These models, refined over the years, guide much of software development today.

The Waterfall Model

A classic life cycle model for software is the *waterfall model*. This model is based on the idea that software can be built almost like following a recipe. There is a set of steps that, if followed correctly, will yield a mighty fine chocolate cake — or program, as the case may be. Each stage must be completed before the next stage can begin, as shown in Figure 28.1. You can compare this process to a waterfall, as you can only go downward to the next phase.

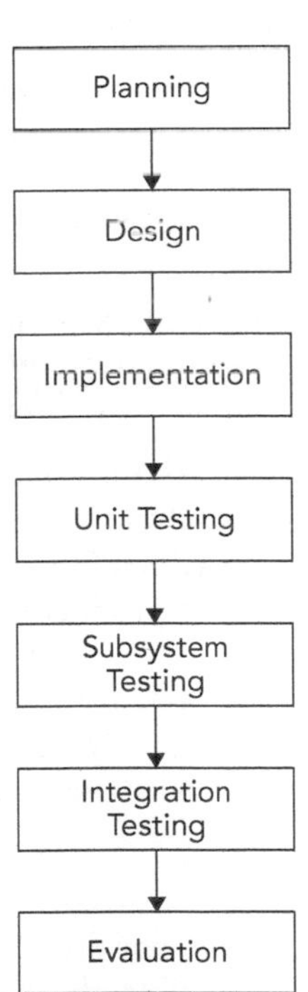

FIGURE 28.1

The process starts with formal planning, which includes gathering an exhaustive list of requirements. This list defines feature completeness for the product. The more specific the requirements are, the more likely it is that the project will succeed. Next, the software is designed and fully specified. The design step, like the requirements step, needs to be as specific as possible to maximize the chance of success. All design decisions are made at this time, often including pseudo-code and the definition of specific subsystems that will need to be written. Subsystem owners work out how their code will interact, and the team agrees on the specifics of the architecture. Implementation of the design occurs next. Because the design has been fully specified, the code needs to adhere closely to the design or else the pieces won't fit together. The final four stages are reserved for unit testing, subsystem testing, integration testing, and evaluation.

The main problem with the waterfall model is that, in practice, it is nearly impossible to complete one stage without at least exploring the next stage. A design cannot be set in stone without writing at least *some* code. Furthermore, if testing reveals bugs, you'll have to go "back up" the waterfall and do some more coding whether your model formally accounted for that or not.

Various incarnations have refined the process in different ways. For example, some plans include a "feasibility" step where experiments are performed before formal requirements are even gathered.

Benefits of the Waterfall Model

The value of the waterfall model lies in its simplicity. You, or your manager, may have followed this approach in past projects without formalizing it or recognizing it by name. The underlying assumption behind the waterfall model is that as long as each step is accomplished as completely and accurately as possible, subsequent steps will go smoothly. As long as all of the requirements are carefully specified in the first step, and all the design decisions and problems are hashed out in the second step, implementation in the third step should be a simple matter of translating the designs into code.

The simplicity of the waterfall model makes project plans based on this system organized and easy to manage. Every project is started the same way: by exhaustively listing all the features that are necessary. For example, managers using this approach can require that by the end of the design phase, all engineers in charge of a subsystem must submit their design as a formal design document or a functional subsystem specification. The benefit for the manager is that by having engineers specify requirements and designs up front, risks are (in theory) minimized.

From the engineer's point of view, the waterfall model forces resolution of major issues up front. All engineers will need to understand their project and design their subsystem before writing a significant amount of code. Ideally, this means that code can be written once instead of being hacked together or rewritten when the pieces don't fit.

For small projects with very specific requirements, the waterfall model can work quite well. Particularly for consulting arrangements, it has the advantage of specifying clearly defined metrics for success at the start of the project. Formalizing requirements helps the consultant to produce exactly what the client wants and forces the client to be specific about the goals for the project.

Drawbacks of the Waterfall Model

In many organizations, and almost all modern software engineering texts, the waterfall model has fallen out of favor. Critics disparage its fundamental premise that software development tasks happen in discrete, linear steps. The waterfall model generally does not allow backward movement. Unfortunately, in many projects today, new requirements are introduced throughout the development of the product. Often, a potential customer will request a feature that is necessary for the sale, or a competitor's product will have a new feature that requires parity.

> **NOTE** *The up-front specification of all requirements makes the waterfall model unusable for many organizations because it is not dynamic enough.*

Another drawback is that in an effort to minimize risk by making decisions as formally and early as possible, the waterfall model may actually be hiding risk. For example, a major design issue might be undiscovered, glossed over, forgotten, or purposely avoided during the design phase. When integration testing finally reveals the mismatch, the team has to go "back up" the waterfall to fix the issues.

A mistake anywhere in the waterfall process will likely lead to delays at the end of the process. Early detection is difficult and occurs rarely.

If you do use the waterfall model, it is often necessary to make it more flexible by taking cues from other approaches.

Sashimi Model

A number of refinements to the waterfall model have been formalized. One such refinement is called the *sashimi model*. The main advancement that the sashimi model brought was the concept of overlap between stages. The name, sashimi model, comes from a Japanese fish dish, called *sashimi*, in which different pieces of fish are overlapping each other. While the model still stresses a rigorous process of planning, designing, coding, and testing, successive stages can partially overlap. Figure 28.2 shows an example of the sashimi model, illustrating the overlapping of stages. Overlap permits activities in two phases to occur simultaneously. This recognizes the fact that one stage can often not be finished completely without at least partially looking at the next stage.

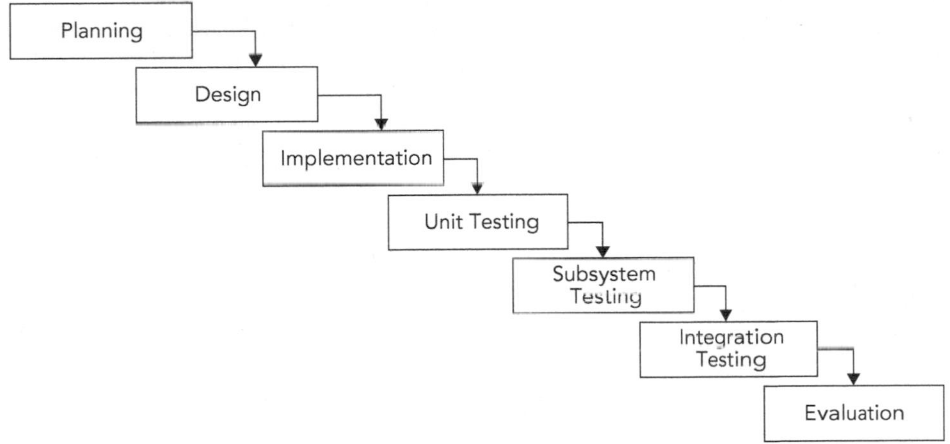

FIGURE 28.2

Spiral-like Models

The *spiral model* was proposed by Barry W. Boehm in 1986 as a risk-driven software development process. Several derivatives have been formulated, which are called *spiral-like models*. The model discussed in this section is part of a family of techniques known as *iterative processes*. The fundamental idea is that it's okay if something goes wrong because you'll fix it in the next iteration. Figure 28.3 shows a single spin through this spiral-like model.

The phases of this model are similar to the steps of the waterfall model. The discovery phase involves discovering requirements, determining objectives, determining alternatives (design alternatives, reuse, buying third-party libraries, and so on), and determining any constraints. During the evaluation phase, implementation alternatives are evaluated, risks are analyzed, and prototype options are considered. In a spiral-like model, particular attention is paid to evaluating and resolving risks in the evaluation phase. The tasks deemed riskiest are the ones that are implemented in the current cycle of the spiral. The tasks in the development phase are determined by the risks identified in the evaluation phase. For example, if evaluation reveals a risky algorithm that may be impossible to implement, the main task for development in the current cycle will be modeling, building, and testing that algorithm. The fourth phase is reserved for analysis and planning. Based on the results of the current cycle, a plan for the subsequent cycle is formed.

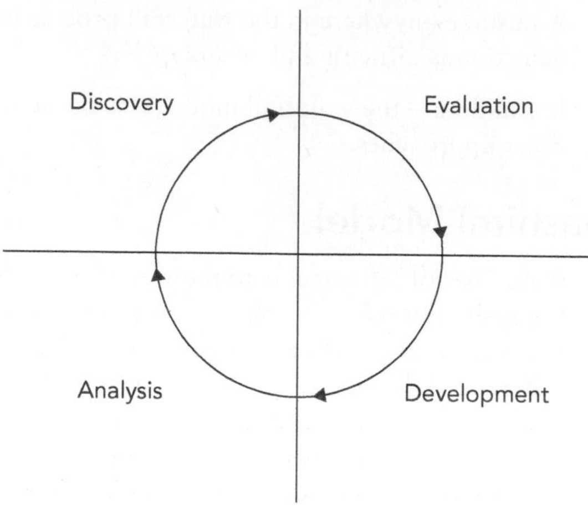

FIGURE 28.3

Figure 28.4 shows an example of three cycles through the spiral in the development of an operating system. The first cycle yields a plan containing the major requirements for the product. The second cycle results in a prototype showing the user experience. The third cycle builds a component that is determined to be a high risk.

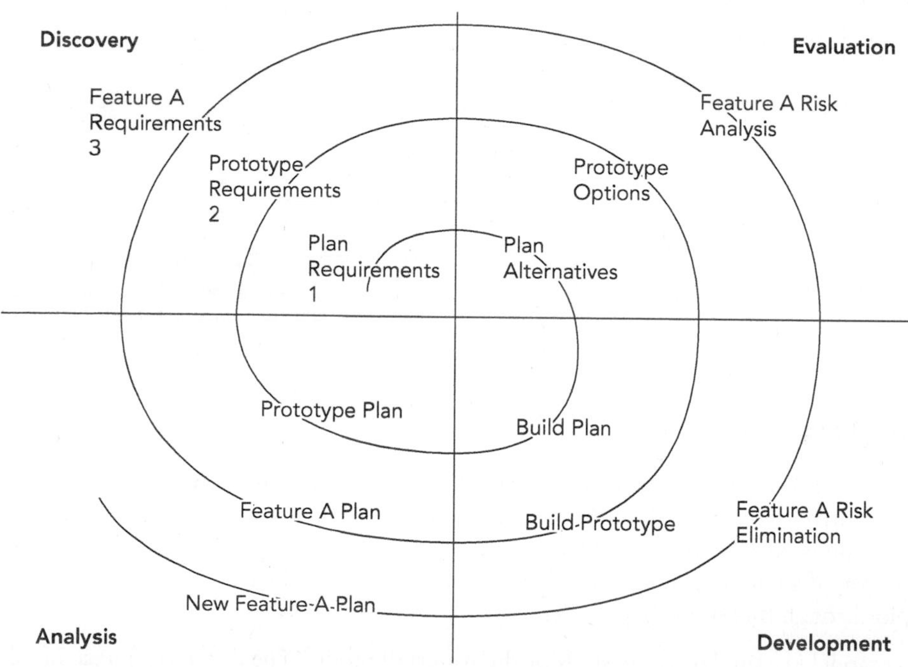

FIGURE 28.4

Benefits of a Spiral-like Model

A spiral-like model can be viewed as the application of an iterative approach to the best that the waterfall model has to offer. Figure 28.5 shows a spiral-like model as a waterfall process that has been modified to allow iteration. Hidden risks and a linear development path, the main drawbacks of the waterfall model, are resolved through iterative cycles.

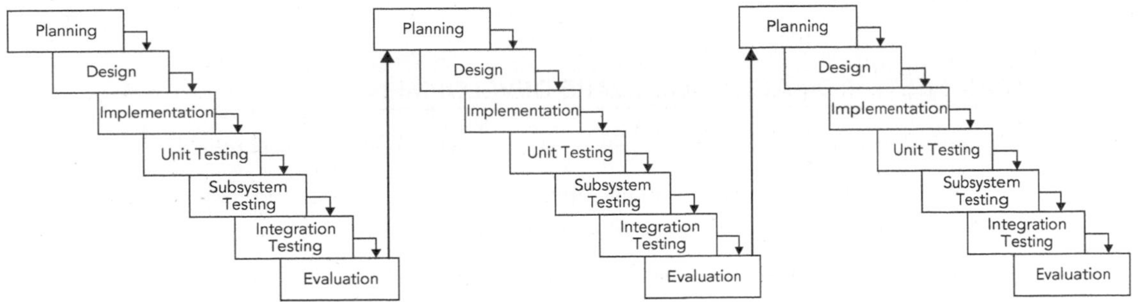

FIGURE 28.5

Performing the riskiest tasks first is another benefit. By bringing risk to the forefront and acknowledging that new conditions can arise at any time, a spiral-like model avoids the hidden time bombs that can occur with the waterfall model. When unexpected problems arise, they can be dealt with by using the same four-stage approach that works for the rest of the process.

This iterative approach also allows to incorporate feedback from testers. For example, an early version of the product can be released for internal or even external evaluation. Testers could, for instance, say that a certain feature is missing or that an existing feature is not working as expected. A spiral-like model has a built-in mechanism to react to such input.

Finally, by repeatedly analyzing after each cycle and building new designs, the practical difficulties with the design-then-implement approach are virtually eliminated. With each cycle, there is more knowledge of the system that can influence the design.

Drawbacks of a Spiral-like Model

The main drawback of a spiral-like model is that it can be difficult to scope each iteration small enough to gain real benefit. In a worst-case scenario, a spiral-like model can degenerate into a waterfall model because the iterations are too long. Unfortunately, a spiral-like model only *models* the software life cycle; it cannot prescribe a specific way to break down a project into single-cycle iterations because that division varies from project to project.

Other possible drawbacks are the overhead of repeating all four phases for each cycle and the difficulty of coordinating cycles. Logistically, it may be difficult to assemble all the group members for design discussions at the right time. If different teams are working on different parts of the product simultaneously, they are probably operating in parallel cycles, which can get out of sync. For example, during the development of an operating system, the user interface group could be ready to start the discovery phase of the Window Manager cycle, but the core OS group could still be in the development phase of the memory subsystem.

Yet another problem is overall time planning for the project. If you continuously keep repeating the four phases, how do you break the cycle to stop the project? Often it will be up to management to decide on an endpoint condition and provide justification for it.

Agile

To address the shortcomings of the waterfall model, the *agile model* was introduced in 2001 in the form of an *Agile Manifesto*.

MANIFESTO FOR AGILE SOFTWARE DEVELOPMENT

The entire manifesto, taken from `http://agilemanifesto.org`, is as follows:

We are uncovering better ways of developing software by doing it and helping others do it. Through this work we have come to value:

- **Individuals and interactions** over processes and tools
- **Working software** over comprehensive documentation
- **Customer collaboration** over contract negotiation
- **Responding to change** over following a plan

That is, while there is value in the items on the right, we value the items on the left more.

As can be understood from this manifesto, the term *agile* is only a high-level description. Basically, it tells you to make the process flexible so that customers' changes can easily be incorporated into the project during development. *Scrum* is one of the most frequently used agile software development methodologies and is discussed in the next section.

SOFTWARE ENGINEERING METHODOLOGIES

Software life cycle models provide a formal way of answering the question, "What do we do next?" but are rarely able to contribute an answer to the logical follow-up question, "How do we do it?" To provide some answers to the how question, a number of *software engineering methodologies* have been developed that provide practical rules of thumb for professional software development. Books and articles on software methodologies abound, but a few of these methodologies deserve particular attention: Scrum, Unified Process, Rational Unified Process, Extreme Programming, and Software Triage.

Scrum

The agile model is just a high-level foundation; it does not specify exactly how the model should be implemented in real life. That's where *Scrum* comes into play; it's an agile methodology with precise descriptions of how to use it on a daily basis. It's one of the most frequently used software engineering methodologies in the industry.

Scrum is an iterative process. It is popular as a means to manage software development projects. In Scrum, each iteration is called a *sprint cycle*. The sprint cycle is the central part of the Scrum process.

The length of sprints, which should be decided at the beginning of the project, is typically between two and four weeks. Before a sprint is started, the team decides on the *sprint goals*. The team makes a commitment to deliver these goals at the end of the sprint. At the end of each sprint, the aim is to have a version of the software available that is fully working and tested and that represents a subset of the customers' requirements. Scrum recognizes that customers will often change their minds during development, so it allows the result of each sprint to be shipped to the customer. This gives customers the opportunity to see iterative versions of the software and allows them to give feedback to the development team about potential issues.

Roles

There are three roles in Scrum. The first role, *product owner*, is the connection to the customer and to other people. The product owner writes high-level *user stories* based on input from the customer, gives each user story a priority, and puts the stories on the Scrum *product backlog*. Actually, everyone on the team is allowed to write high-level user stories for the product backlog, but the product owner decides which user stories are kept and which are removed.

The second role, *Scrum master*, is responsible for keeping the process running and can be part of the team but isn't considered the leader of the team, because with Scrum the team leads itself. The Scrum master is the contact person for the team so that the rest of the team members can concentrate on their tasks. The Scrum master ensures that the Scrum process is followed correctly by the team, for example, by organizing the daily Scrum meetings, discussed in the next section. The Scrum master and product owner should be two different people.

The third and final role in the Scrum process is the *team* itself. Teams develop the software and should be kept small, preferably fewer than 10 members.

The Process

Before the start of each sprint cycle, there is a *sprint planning* meeting in which team members must decide which product features they will implement in the new sprint. This is formalized in a *sprint backlog*. The features are selected from the product backlog containing prioritized user stories, which are high-level requirements of new features. User stories from the product backlog are broken down into smaller tasks with an *effort estimation* and are put on the sprint backlog. The duration of the sprint planning meeting depends on the length of the sprints and the size of the team; typically, there will be two to four hours of sprint planning for each two weeks of a sprint. The sprint planning meeting is usually split into two parts: a meeting with the product owner and the team to discuss the priority of product backlog items and a meeting with only the team to complete the sprint backlog.

In a Scrum team you will sometimes find a physical board, the *Scrum board* or *sprint board*, with three columns: *To Do*, *In Progress*, and *Done*. Every task for the sprint is written on a small piece of paper and stuck on the board in the correct column. Tasks are not assigned to people during a meeting; instead, every team member can go to the board, pick one of the To Do tasks, and move that paper to the In Progress column. When the team member is finished with that task, the paper is moved to the Done column. This method makes it easy for team members to get an overview of the work that still needs to be done and what tasks are in progress or finished. Instead of a physical Scrum board, you can also use software to work with a virtual Scrum board.

The three columns, To Do, In Progress, and Done, are not set in stone. Your team can add any additional columns to include other steps. For example, a Scrum board could contain the following columns:

- **To Do:** The tasks planned for the current sprint that have not been started yet
- **In Progress:** The tasks that are currently being worked on by developers in a development branch (see the "Version Control" section later in this chapter)
- **In Review:** The tasks that have been implemented and that are currently waiting to be reviewed by another team member, also known as *code review*
- **In Testing:** The tasks that have been implemented and code reviewed and that are waiting to be tested by the quality assurance (QA) team for approval
- **In Integration:** The tasks for which the code changes have been validated by a code review and approved by QA and for which the code from the development branch can be integrated into the main code base, but only if all tests are successful on that branch
- **Done:** The tasks that have been fully implemented, reviewed, tested, and integrated

It's recommended to keep individual tasks small. This results in short-lived development branches.

Sometimes, a burn-down chart is also created every day that displays the days of the sprint on the horizontal axis and the remaining development hours on the vertical axis. This gives a quick overview of the progress made and can be used to determine whether all planned tasks are likely to be completed during the sprint.

The Scrum process enforces a daily meeting called the *daily replanning*, *daily Scrum*, or *daily standup*. In this meeting, all team members stand together with the Scrum master. This meeting should start every day at the same time and location but should be no longer than 15 minutes. The sprint board should be visible for all team members during this meeting. In this meeting, the team looks at the current progress toward the sprint goal. Any blocking points or delays are discussed. If need be, the team can remove or add tasks to the current sprint to make sure the sprint goal can be reached at the end of the sprint.

This daily meeting usually includes the following three questions for all team members to answer:

- What did you do yesterday to help the team reach the sprint goal?
- What will you do today to help the team reach the sprint goal?
- Do you see any obstacles that hamper you or the team to reach the sprint goal?

Once a sprint cycle is finished, there are two meetings: the *sprint review* and the *sprint retrospective*. The duration of the sprint review meeting again depends on the length of the sprints and the size of the team, typically two hours per two weeks of a sprint. During the sprint review meeting, a *demo* is given to demonstrate the sprint results and the current state of the software to all interested stakeholders, such as product managers, support engineers, and so on. The sprint review meeting also includes a discussion of the results of the sprint cycle, including what tasks were completed, what tasks were not completed, and why. The sprint retrospective typically takes around one-and-a-half hours for each two weeks of a sprint and allows the team to think about how the last sprint cycle was executed. For example, the team can identify shortcomings in the process and adapt the process for the next sprint. Questions like "What went well?" and "What could be improved?" and "What do we want to start, continue, or stop doing?" are answered. This is called *continuous improvement*; that is, after every sprint, the process itself is examined and improved.

Benefits of Scrum

Scrum is resilient to unforeseen problems that come up during the development stage. When a problem pops up, it can be handled in one of the following sprints. The team is involved in every step of the project. They discuss user stories from the product backlog with the product owner and convert these user stories into smaller tasks for inclusion in a sprint backlog. The team autonomously assigns work to its members with the aid of the Scrum task board. This board makes it easy to see which team member is working on which task, and the daily Scrum meetings ensure that everyone knows what is happening to reach the sprint goals.

A huge benefit to the stakeholders is the demo that follows each sprint, which demonstrates the new iterative version of the project. Stakeholders quickly gets a sense of how the project is progressing and can make changes to the requirements, which usually can be incorporated into a future sprint.

Drawbacks of Scrum

Some companies might find it difficult to accept that the team itself decides who is doing what. Tasks are not assigned to team members by a manager or a team leader. All members pick their own tasks from the Scrum task board.

The Scrum master is a key person to make sure the team stays on track. It is important that the Scrum master trusts the team. Having too much control over the team members will cause the Scrum process to fail.

A possible problem with Scrum is called *feature creep*. Scrum allows new user stories to be added to the product backlog during development. There is a danger that project managers will keep adding new features to the product backlog. This problem is best solved by deciding early on a final release date or the end date of the final sprint.

The Unified Process

The *Unified Process* (UP) is an iterative and incremental software development process. The UP is not set in stone; it's a framework that you should customize to the specific needs of your project. According to the Unified Process, a project can be split into four phases:

- **Inception:** This phase is usually very short. It includes a feasibility study, writing of a business case, deciding whether the project should be developed in-house or bought from a third-party vendor, defining a rough estimate of the cost and timeline, and defining the scope.
- **Elaboration:** Most of the requirements are documented. Risk factors are addressed, and the system architecture is validated. To validate the architecture, the most important parts of the core of the architecture are built as an executable delivery. This should demonstrate that the developed architecture will be able to support the entire system.

- **Construction:** All requirements are implemented on top of the executable architecture delivery from the elaboration phase.
- **Transition:** The product is delivered to the customer. Feedback from the customer is addressed in subsequent transition iterations.

All phases are split into time-boxed *iterations*, each having a tangible result. In each iteration, the teams are working on several *disciplines* of the project at the same time: business modeling, requirements, analysis and design, implementation, testing, and deployment. The amount of work done in each discipline changes with each iteration. Figure 28.6 shows this iterative and overlapping development approach. In this example, the inception phase is done in one iteration, the elaboration phase in two, the construction phase in four, and the transition phase in two iterations.

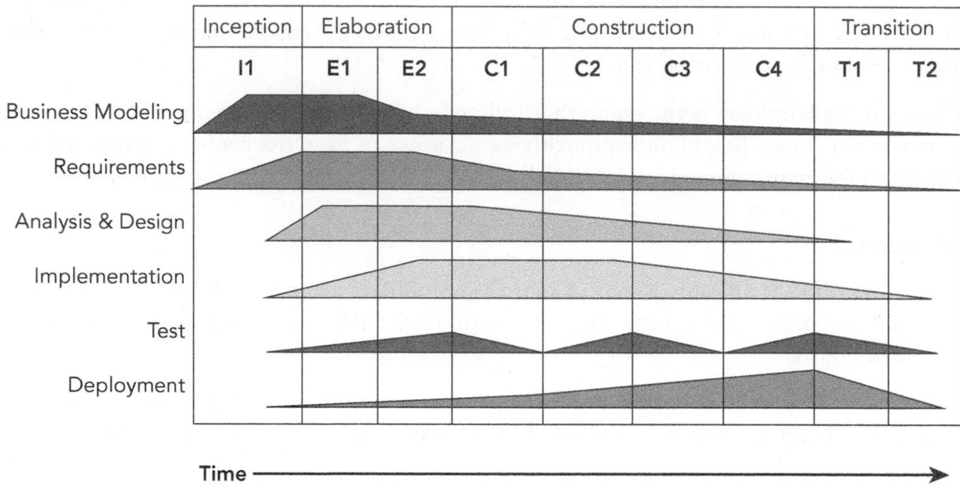

FIGURE 28.6

The Rational Unified Process

The *Rational Unified Process (RUP)* is one of the best-known refinements of the Unified Process. It is a disciplined and formal approach to managing the software development process. The most important characteristic of the RUP is that, unlike the spiral model or the waterfall model, RUP is more than just a theoretical process model. RUP is actually a software product that is sold by Rational Software, a division of IBM. Treating the process itself as software brings about some interesting advantages:

- The process itself can be updated and refined, just as software products periodically have updates.
- Rather than simply suggesting a development framework, RUP includes a set of software tools for working with that framework.
- As a product, RUP can be rolled out to the entire engineering team so that all members are using the exact same processes and tools.
- Like many software products, RUP can be customized to the needs of its users.

RUP as a Product

As a product, RUP takes the form of a suite of software applications that guide developers through the software development process. The product also offers specific guidance for other Rational products, such as the Rational Rose visual modeling tool and the Rational ClearCase configuration management tool. Extensive groupware communication tools are included as part of the "marketplace of ideas" that allows developers to share knowledge.

One of the basic principles behind RUP is that each iteration on a development cycle should have a tangible result. During the Rational Unified Process, users will create numerous designs, requirement documents, reports, and plans. The RUP software provides visualization and development tools for the creation of these artifacts.

RUP as a Process

Defining an accurate model is the central principle of RUP. Models, according to RUP, help explain the complicated structures and relationships in the software development process. In RUP, models are often expressed in Unified Modeling Language (UML) format; see Appendix D, "Introduction to UML."

RUP defines each part of the process as an individual *workflow* (called *discipline* in the earlier discussion of the Unified Process). Workflows represent each step of a process in terms of who is responsible for the step, what tasks are being performed, the artifacts or results of these tasks, and the sequence of events that drives the tasks. Almost everything about RUP is customizable, but several *core process workflows* are defined "out of the box" by RUP.

The core process workflows bear some resemblance to the stages of the waterfall model, but each one is iterative and more specific in definition. The *business modeling workflow* models business processes, usually with the goal of driving software requirements forward. The *requirements workflow* creates the requirements definition by analyzing the problems in the system and iterating on its assumptions. The *analysis and design workflow* deals with system architecture and subsystem design. The *implementation workflow* covers the modeling, coding, and integration of software subsystems. The *testing workflow* models the planning, implementation, and evaluation of software quality tests. The *deployment workflow* is a high-level view of overall planning, releasing, supporting, and testing workflows. The *configuration management workflow* goes from new project conception to iteration and end-of-product scenarios. Finally, the *environment workflow* supports the engineering organization through the creation and maintenance of development tools.

RUP in Practice

RUP is aimed mainly at larger organizations and offers several advantages over the adoption of traditional life cycle models. Once the team has gotten over the learning curve of using the software, all members will be using a common platform for designing, communicating, and implementing their ideas. The process can be customized to the needs of the team, and each stage reveals a wealth of valuable artifacts that document each phase of the development.

A product like RUP can be too heavyweight for some organizations. Teams with diverse development environments or tight engineering budgets might not want to, or be able to, standardize on a software-based development system. The learning curve can also be a factor; new engineers who aren't familiar with the process software will have to learn how to use it, while at the same time getting up to speed on the product and the existing code base.

Extreme Programming

When a friend of mine arrived home from work years ago and told his wife that his company had adopted some of the principles of Extreme Programming, she joked, "I hope you wear a safety harness for that." Despite the somewhat hokey name, Extreme Programming (XP) effectively bundles up the best of other software development guidelines and adds some new material.

XP, popularized by Kent Beck in *Extreme Programming Explained* (Addison-Wesley, 1999), claims to take the best practices of good software development and turn them up a notch. For example, most programmers would agree that testing is a good thing. In XP, testing is deemed so good that you're supposed to write the tests before you write the code.

XP in Theory

The XP methodology is made up of twelve guiding principles, grouped into four categories. These principles are manifested throughout all phases of the software development process and have a direct impact on the daily tasks of engineers.

Category 1: Fine-Scale Feedback

XP provides four fine-grained guidelines related to coding, planning, and testing.

Code in Pairs

XP suggests that all production code should be written by two people working side-by-side, a technique called *pair programming*. Obviously, only one person can actually be in control of the keyboard. The other person reviews the code his peer is writing and takes a high-level approach, thinking about issues such as testing, necessary refactoring, and the overall model of the project.

As an example, if you are in charge of writing the user interface for a particular feature of your application, you might want to ask the original author of the feature to sit down with you. He can advise you about the correct use of the feature, warn you about any "gotchas" you should watch out for, and help oversee your efforts at a high level. Even if you can't acquire the help of the original author, just grabbing another member of the team can help. The theory is that working in pairs builds shared knowledge, ensures proper design, and puts an informal system of checks and balances in place.

Planning Game

In the waterfall model, planning happens once, at the beginning of the process. Under the spiral model, planning is the first phase of each iteration. Under XP, planning is more than just a step—it's a never-ending task. XP teams start with a rough plan that captures the major points of the product being developed. During each iteration of the process, there is a *planning game* meeting. Throughout the development process, the plan is refined and modified as necessary. The theory is that conditions are constantly changing and new information is obtained all the time. There are two major parts in the planning process:

- **Release planning:** This happens with the developers and the customers, and its goal is to determine which requirements need to be included in which upcoming releases.
- **Iteration planning:** This happens only with the developers, and it plans the actual tasks for the developers.

Under XP, estimates for a given feature are always made by the person who will be implementing that particular feature. This helps to avoid situations where the implementer is forced to adhere to an unrealistic and artificial schedule. Initially, estimates are very rough, perhaps on the order of weeks for a feature. As the time horizon shortens, the estimates become more granular. Features are broken down into tasks taking no more than five days.

Test Constantly

According to *Extreme Programming Explained*, "Any program feature without an automated test simply doesn't exist." XP is zealous about testing. Part of your responsibility as an XP engineer is to write the unit tests that accompany your code. A unit test is generally a small piece of code that makes sure that an individual piece of functionality works. For example, individual unit tests for a file-based object store may include `testSaveObject`, `testLoadObject`, and `testDeleteObject`.

XP takes unit testing one step further by suggesting that unit tests should be written before the actual code is written. Of course, the tests won't pass because the code hasn't been written yet. In theory, if your tests are thorough, you should know when your code is complete because all the tests will run successfully. However, it's hard to know if your tests are thorough enough. You have to think about different kinds of bugs that you might introduce when implementing the code and whether your tests would catch those bugs. Writing good tests can be significantly harder than writing good code. The process of writing unit tests before the actual code is called *test-driven development* (TDD). I told you it was "extreme."

Have a Customer On-Site

Because an XP-savvy engineering group constantly refines its product plan and builds only what is currently necessary, having a customer contribute to the process is valuable. Although it is not always possible to convince a customer to be physically present during development, the idea that there should be communication between engineering and the end user is clearly a valuable notion. In addition to assisting with the design of individual features, customers can help prioritize tasks by conveying their individual needs.

Category 2: Continuous Process

XP advocates that you should continuously integrate subsystems so that mismatches between subsystems can be detected early. You should also refactor code whenever necessary and aim to build and deploy small incremental releases.

Integrate Continuously

All programmers are familiar with the dreaded chore of integrating code. This task becomes a nightmare when you discover that your view of a subsystem is a complete mismatch with the way it was actually written. When subsystems come together, problems are exposed. XP recognizes this phenomenon and advocates integrating code into the project frequently as it is being developed.

During development, engineers should run all tests before checking code into the repository. Additionally, a designated machine continually runs automated tests. When the automated tests fail, the team receives an e-mail indicating the problem and listing the most recent check-ins.

With development branches, it is recommended to set up your processes in such a way that a development branch can be merged back into the main code base only if all tests ran successfully on that branch.

Refactor When Necessary

Most programmers *refactor* their code from time to time. Refactoring is the process of redesigning existing working code to take into account new knowledge, new upstream APIs, or alternate uses that have been discovered since the code was written. Refactoring is difficult to build into a traditional software engineering schedule because its results are not as tangible as implementing a new feature. Good managers, however, recognize its importance for long-term code maintainability.

The extreme way of refactoring is to recognize situations during development when refactoring is useful and to do the refactoring at that time. Instead of deciding at the start of a release which existing parts of the product need design work, XP programmers learn to recognize the signs of code that is ready to be refactored. While this practice will almost certainly result in unexpected and unscheduled tasks, restructuring the code when appropriate should make future development easier.

Build Small Releases

One of the theories of XP is that software projects grow risky and unwieldy when they try to accomplish too much at one time. Instead of massive software releases that involve core changes and several pages of release notes, XP advocates smaller releases with a timeframe closer to two months than eighteen months. With such a short release cycle, only the most important features can make it into the product. This forces engineering and marketing to agree on what features are truly important.

Category 3: Shared Understanding

Software is developed by a team. Any code written is not owned by individuals but by the team as a whole. XP gives a couple of guidelines to make sure sharing the code and ideas is possible.

Share Common Coding Standards

Because of the collective ownership guideline and the practice of pair programming, coding in an extreme environment can be difficult if each engineer has their own naming and indenting conventions. XP doesn't advocate any particular style but recommends that if you can look at a piece of code and immediately identify the author, your group probably needs a better definition of its coding standards.

For additional information on various approaches to coding style, see Chapter 3, "Coding with Style."

Share the Code

In many traditional development environments, code ownership is strongly defined and often enforced. A friend of mine once worked in an environment where the manager explicitly forbade checking in changes to code written by any other member of the team. XP takes the extreme opposite approach by declaring that the code is collectively owned by everybody.

Collective ownership is practical for a number of reasons. From a management point of view, it is less detrimental when a single engineer leaves suddenly because there are others who understand that part of the code. This increases the *bus factor* or *bus number*, which represents the minimal number of engineers that need to be hit by a bus to make the project stall. From an engineer's point of view, collective ownership builds a common view of how the system works. This helps with design tasks and frees the individual programmer to make any changes that will add value to the overall project.

One important note about collective ownership is that it is not necessary for every programmer to be familiar with every single line of code. It is more of a mindset that the project is a team effort, and there is no reason for any one person to hoard knowledge.

Simplify Your Designs

A mantra frequently sung by XP-savvy engineers is "avoid speculative generality," also known as KISS, or "Keep It Simple, Stupid." This goes against the natural inclinations of many programmers. If you are given the task of designing a file-based object store, you may start down the path of creating the be-all, end-all solution to all file-based storage problems. Your design might quickly evolve to cover multiple languages and any type of object. XP says you should lean toward the other end of the generality–specificity continuum. Instead of making the ideal object store that will win awards and be celebrated by your peers, design the simplest possible object store that gets the job done. You should understand the current requirements and write your code to those specifications to avoid overly complex code.

It may be hard to get used to simplicity in design. Depending on the type of work you do, your code may need to exist for years and be used by other parts of the code that you haven't even dreamed of. As discussed in Chapter 6, "Designing for Reuse," the problem with building in functionality that *may* be useful in the future is that you don't know what those hypothetical use cases are, and there is no way to craft a good design that is purely speculative. In fact, designing up front for one of these use cases (which might never come to pass) might actually prevent you from being able to accommodate a different use case (which actually could have been useful) unless you refactor the entire design. XP says you should build something that is useful today and leave open the opportunity to modify it later.

Share a Common Metaphor

XP uses the term *metaphor* for the idea that all members of the team (including customers and managers) should share a common high-level view of the system. This does not refer to the specifics of how objects will communicate or the exact APIs that will be written. Rather, the metaphor is the mental model and naming model for the components of the system. Each component should be given a descriptive name so that each member of the team can guess its functionality simply based on its name. Team members should use the metaphor to drive shared terminology when discussing the project.

Category 4: Programmer Welfare

The final guideline of XP is about the welfare of developers.

Work Sane Hours

XP has a thing or two to say about the hours you've been putting in. The claim is that a well-rested programmer is a happy and productive programmer. XP advocates a workweek of approximately 40 hours and warns against putting in overtime for more than two consecutive weeks.

Of course, different people need different amounts of rest. The main idea, though, is that if you sit down to write code without a clear head, you're going to write poor code and abandon many of the XP principles.

XP in Practice

XP purists claim that the twelve tenets of Extreme Programming are so intertwined that adopting some of them without others would largely ruin the methodology. For example, pair programming is vital to testing because if you can't determine how to test a particular piece of code, your partner can help. Also, if you're tired one day and decide to skip the testing, your partner will be there to promote feelings of guilt.

Some of the XP guidelines, however, can prove difficult to implement. To some engineers, the idea of writing tests before code is too abstract. For those engineers, it may be sufficient to *design* the tests without actually writing them until there is code to test. Many of the XP principles are rigidly defined, but if you understand the theory behind them, you may be able to find ways to adapt the guidelines to the needs of your project.

The collaborative aspects of XP can be challenging as well. Pair programming has measurable benefits, but it may be difficult for a manager to rationalize having half as many people actually writing code each day. Some members of the team may even feel uncomfortable with such close collaboration, perhaps finding it difficult to type while others are watching. XP suits some personality types better than others; introverts in particular might dislike pair programming. Pair programming also has obvious challenges if the team is geographically spread out or if members tend to telecommute regularly.

For some organizations, Extreme Programming may be too radical. Large, established companies with formal policies in place for engineering may be slow to adopt approaches like XP. However, even if your company is resistant to the implementation of XP, you can still improve your own productivity by understanding the theory behind it.

Software Triage

In the pessimistically named book *Death March* (Prentice Hall, 1997), Edward Yourdon describes the frequent and scary phenomenon of software that is behind schedule, short on staff, over-budget, or poorly designed. Yourdon's theory is that when software projects get into this state, even the best modern software development methodologies will no longer apply. As you have learned in this chapter, many approaches to software development are built around formalized documents or taking a user-centered approach to design. In a project that's already in "death march" mode, there simply isn't time for these approaches.

The idea behind Software Triage is that when a project is already in a bad state, resources are scarce. Time is scarce, engineers are scarce, and money may be scarce. The main mental obstacle that managers and developers need to overcome when a project is way behind schedule is that it will be impossible to satisfy the original requirements in the allotted time. The task then becomes organizing remaining functionality into must-have, should-have, and nice-to-have lists.

Software Triage is a daunting and delicate process. It often requires the leadership of an outside veteran of "death march" projects to make the tough decisions. For the engineer, the most important point is that in certain conditions, it may be necessary to throw familiar processes (and perhaps some existing code) out the window to finish a project on time.

BUILDING YOUR OWN PROCESS AND METHODOLOGY

It's unlikely that any book or engineering theory will perfectly match the needs of your project or organization. I recommend that you learn from as many approaches as you can and design your own process. Combining concepts from different approaches may be easier than you think. For example, RUP optionally supports an XP-like approach. Here are some tips for building the software engineering process of your dreams.

Be Open to New Ideas

Some engineering techniques seem crazy at first, or unlikely to work. Look at new innovations in software engineering methodologies as a way to refine your existing process. Try things out when you can. If XP sounds intriguing, but you're not sure if it will work in your organization, see if you can work it in slowly, taking a few of the principles at a time or trying it out with a smaller pilot project.

Bring New Ideas to the Table

Most likely, your engineering team is made up of people from varying backgrounds. You may have startup veterans, long-time consultants, recent graduates, and PhDs all on your team. You all have different sets of experiences and different ideas of how a software project should be run. Sometimes the best processes turn out to be a combination of the way things are typically done in these very different environments.

Recognize What Works and What Doesn't Work

At the end of a project (or better yet, during the project, as with the sprint retrospective of the Scrum methodology), get the team together to evaluate the process. Sometimes there's a major problem that nobody notices until the entire team stops to think about it. Perhaps there's a problem that *everybody* knows about but nobody has discussed.

Consider what isn't working and see how those parts can be fixed. Some organizations require formal code reviews prior to any source code check-in. If code reviews are so long and boring that nobody does a good job, discuss code-reviewing techniques as a group.

Also consider what is going well and see how those parts can be extended. For example, if maintaining the feature tasks as a group-editable wiki is working, then maybe devote some time to making the website even better.

Don't Be a Renegade

Whether a process is mandated by your manager or custom-built by the team, it's there for a reason. If your process involves writing formal design documents, make sure you write them. If you think that the process is broken or too complex, talk to your manager about it. Don't just avoid the process—it will come back to haunt you.

VERSION CONTROL

Managing all source code is important for any company, big or small, even for one-person projects. In a company, for example, it would be impractical to store all the source code on the machines of individual developers without it being managed by any *version control* software. This would result in a maintenance nightmare because not everyone would always have the latest code. Instead, all source code **must** be managed by version control software. There are three kinds of such software solutions:

- **Local:** These solutions store all source code files and their history locally on your machine and are not really suitable for use in a team. These are solutions from the '70s and '80s and shouldn't be used anymore. They are not discussed further.
- **Client/server:** These solutions are split into a client component and a server component. For a personal developer, the client and server components can run on the same machine, but the separation makes it easy to move the server component to a dedicated physical server machine if the need arises.
- **Distributed:** These solutions go one step further than the client/server model. There is no central place where everything is stored. Every developer has a copy of all the files, including all the history. A peer-to-peer approach is used instead of a client/server approach. Code is synchronized between peers by exchanging patches.

The client/server solution consists of two parts. The first part is the server software, which is software running on the central server and which is responsible for keeping track of all source code files and their history. The second part is the client software. This client software is installed on every developer's machine and is responsible for communicating with the server software to get the latest version of a source file, get a previous version of a source file, commit local changes back to the server, roll back changes to a previous version, and so on.

A distributed solution doesn't use a central server. The client software uses peer-to-peer protocols to synchronize with other peers by exchanging patches. Common operations such as committing changes, rolling back changes, and so on, are fast because no network access to a central server is involved. The disadvantage is that it requires more space on the client machine because it needs to store all the files, including the entire history.

Most version control systems have a special terminology, but unfortunately, not all systems use the same terms. The following list explains a number of terms that are commonly used:

- **Branch:** The source code can be *branched*, which means that multiple versions can be developed side by side. For example, one branch can be created for every released version. On those branches, bug fixes can be implemented for those released versions, while new features are added to the main branch (often known as the "trunk"). Bug fixes created for released versions can also be merged back to the main branch.
- **Check out:** This is the action of creating a local copy on the developer's machine, coming either from a central server or from peers.
- **Check in, commit, merge, or push:** A developer makes changes to the local copy of the source code. When everything works correctly on the local machine, the developer can check in/commit/merge/push those local changes back to the central server.

- **Conflict and resolve:** When multiple developers make overlapping changes to the same source file, a conflict might occur when committing that source file. The version control software often tries to automatically resolve these conflicts. If that is not possible, the client software asks the user to resolve any conflicts manually.
- **Label or tag:** A human-readable label or tag can be attached to all files or to a specific commit at any given time. This makes it easy to jump back to the version of the source code at that time.
- **Repository:** The collection of all files managed by the version control software, including their history. This also includes metadata about each commit, including when it was committed, by whom, and perhaps even a commit message explaining why.
- **Revision or version:** A revision, or version, is a snapshot of the contents of a file at a specific point in time. Versions represent specific points that the code can be reverted to or compared against.
- **Update or sync:** Updating or synchronizing means that the local copy on the developer's machine is synchronized with a version on the central server or with peers. Note that this requires merging that upstream code into the developer's local copy (with all their local changes), which may result in a conflict that needs to be resolved.
- **Working copy:** The working copy is the local copy on the individual developer's machine.

Several version control software solutions are available. Some of them are free, and some are commercial. The following table lists a few available solutions:

	FREE/OPEN-SOURCE	COMMERCIAL
Local Only	SCCS, RCS	PVCS
Client/Server	CVS, Subversion	IBM Rational ClearCase, Azure DevOps Server, Perforce
Distributed	Git, Mercurial, Bazaar	TeamWare, BitKeeper, Plastic SCM

> **NOTE** *The preceding list is definitely not an exhaustive one. It's just a small selection to give you an idea of what's available.*

This book does not recommend particular software solutions. Most software companies these days have a version control system already in place, which every developer needs to adopt. If this is not the case, the company should definitely invest some time into researching the available solutions and pick one that suits them. The bottom line is that it will be a maintenance nightmare without any version control system in place. Even for your personal projects, I recommend you investigate the available solutions. If you find one that you like, it will make your life easier. It will automatically keep track of different versions and a history of your changes. This makes it easy for you to roll back to an older version if a change didn't work out the way it was supposed to.

SUMMARY

This chapter introduced you to several models and methodologies for the software development process. There are certainly many other ways of building software, both formal and informal. There probably isn't a single correct method for developing software except the method that works for your team. The best way to find this method is to do your own research, learn what you can from various methods, talk to your peers about their experiences, and iterate on your process. Remember, the only metric that matters when examining a process methodology is how much it helps your team to write code.

The final part of this chapter explained the concept of version control. This should be an integral part of any software company, big or small, and is even beneficial for personal projects at home. There are several version control software solutions available, both free and commercial. I recommend that you try a few and see which one of them works for you.

EXERCISES

By solving the following exercises, you can practice the material discussed in this chapter. Solutions to all exercises are available with the code download on the book's website at `www.wiley.com/go/proc++6e`. However, if you are stuck on an exercise, first reread parts of this chapter to try to find an answer yourself before looking at the solution from the website.

Exercise 28-1: Give a few examples of software life cycle models and of software engineering methodologies.

Exercise 28-2: XP advocates to integrate continuously. If this sounds extreme to you, in recent years, some companies go even a step further with *continuous deployment*. Do some research into continuous deployment to find out what it means.

Exercise 28-3: Next to the continuous deployment from Exercise 28-2, there is also *continuous delivery*. Do some research into continuous delivery and contrast it with continuous deployment.

Exercise 28-4: Research the term *rapid application development* (RAD). How does it relate to the contents in this chapter?

29

Writing Efficient C++

WHAT'S IN THIS CHAPTER?

- What *efficiency* and *performance* mean
- What kind of language-level optimizations you can use
- Which design-level guidelines you can follow to design efficient programs
- What profiling tools are

WILEY.COM DOWNLOADS FOR THIS CHAPTER

Please note that all the code examples for this chapter are available as part of this chapter's code download on the book's website at `www.wiley.com/go/proc++6e` on the Download Code tab.

The efficiency of your programs is important regardless of your application domain. If your product competes with others in the marketplace, speed can be a major differentiator: given the choice between a slower and a faster program, which one would you choose? No one would buy an operating system that takes two weeks to boot up. Even if you don't intend to sell your products, they will have users. Those users will not be happy with you if they end up wasting time waiting for your programs to complete tasks.

Now that you understand the concepts of professional C++ design and coding and have tackled some of the more complex facilities that the language provides, you are ready to incorporate performance into your programs. Writing efficient programs involves thought at the design level, as well as details at the implementation level. Although this chapter falls late in this book, remember to consider performance from the beginning of your projects.

OVERVIEW OF PERFORMANCE AND EFFICIENCY

Before delving further into the details, it's helpful to define the terms *performance* and *efficiency*, as used in this book. The *performance* of a program can refer to several areas, such as speed, memory usage, disk access, and network use. This chapter focuses on speed performance. The term *efficiency*, when applied to programs, means running without wasted effort. An efficient program completes its tasks as quickly as possible within the given circumstances. A program can be efficient without being fast, if the application domain is inherently prohibitive to quick execution.

> **NOTE** *An efficient, or high-performance, program runs as fast as possible for its particular task.*

Note that the title of this chapter, "Writing Efficient C++," means writing programs that run efficiently, not efficiently writing programs. That is, the time you learn to save by reading this chapter will be your users', not your own!

Two Approaches to Efficiency

Language-level efficiency involves using the language as efficiently as possible; for example, passing objects by reference instead of by value. However, this will only get you so far. Much more important is *design-level efficiency*, which includes choosing efficient algorithms, avoiding unnecessary steps and computations, and selecting appropriate design optimizations. More often than not, optimizing existing code involves replacing a bad algorithm or data structure with a better, more efficient one.

Two Kinds of Programs

As I've noted, efficiency is important for all application domains. Additionally, there is a small subset of programs, such as system-level software, embedded systems, intensive computational applications, and real-time games, that require extremely high levels of efficiency. Most programs don't. Unless you write those types of high-performance applications, you probably don't need to worry about squeezing every ounce of speed out of your C++ code. Think of it as the difference between building normal family cars and building race cars. Every car must be reasonably efficient, but sports cars require extremely high performance. You wouldn't want to waste your time optimizing family cars for speed when they'll never go faster than 70 miles per hour.

Is C++ an Inefficient Language?

C programmers often resist using C++ for high-performance applications. They claim that the language is inherently less efficient than C or a similar procedural language because C++ includes high-level concepts, such as exceptions and virtual member functions. However, there are problems with this argument.

When discussing the efficiency of a language, you cannot ignore the effect of compilers. Recall that the C or C++ code you write is not the code that the computer executes. A compiler first translates that code into machine language, applying optimizations in the process. This means that you can't simply run benchmarks of C and C++ programs and compare the results. You're really comparing the compiler optimizations of the languages, not the languages themselves. C++ compilers can optimize away many of the high-level constructs in the language to generate machine code similar to, or even better than, the machine code generated from a comparable C program. These days, much more research and development is poured into C++ compilers than into C compilers, so C++ code might actually get better optimized and might run faster than C code.

Critics, however, still maintain that some features of C++ cannot be optimized away. For example, as Chapter 10, "Discovering Inheritance Techniques," explains, virtual member functions require the existence of a vtable, also known as virtual table, and an additional level of indirection at run time, possibly making them slower than regular nonvirtual function calls. However, when you really think about it, this argument is unconvincing. Virtual member function calls provide more than just a function call: they also give you a run-time choice of which function to call. A comparable non-virtual function call would need a conditional statement to decide which function to call. If you don't need those extra semantics, you can use a non-virtual function. A general design rule in the C++ language is that "if you don't use a feature, you don't need to pay for it." If you don't use virtual member functions, you pay no performance penalty for the fact that you *could* use them. Thus, non-virtual function calls in C++ are identical to function calls in C in terms of performance.

Far more important, the high-level constructs of C++ enable you to write cleaner programs that are more efficient at the design level, are more readable, are more easily maintained, and avoid accumulating unnecessary and dead code.

I believe that you will be better served in your development, performance, and code maintenance by choosing C++ instead of a procedural language such as C.

There are also other higher-level object-oriented languages such as C# and Java, both of which run on top of a virtual machine. C++ code is executed directly by a CPU; there is no such thing as a virtual machine to run your code. C++ is closer to the hardware, which means that in most cases it runs faster than languages such as C# and Java.

LANGUAGE-LEVEL EFFICIENCY

Many books, articles, and programmers spend a lot of time trying to convince you to apply language-level optimizations to your code. These tips and tricks are important and can speed up your programs in some cases. However, they are far less important than the overall design and algorithm choices in your program. You can pass-by-reference all you want, but it won't make your program fast if you perform twice as many disk writes as you need to. It's easy to get bogged down in references and pointers and forget about the big picture.

Furthermore, some of these language-level tricks can be performed automatically by good optimizing compilers. A rule of thumb is that you should never spend time optimizing a particular area, unless a profiler, discussed later in this chapter, tells you that that particular area is a bottleneck.

That being said, using certain language-level optimizations, such as pass-by-reference, is just considered good coding style.

In this book, I've tried to present a balance of strategies. So, I've included here what I feel are the most useful language-level optimizations. This list is not comprehensive but is a good start to write optimized code. However, make sure to read, and practice, the design-level efficiency advice that I offer later in this chapter as well.

> **WARNING** *Apply language-level optimizations thoughtfully. I recommend making a clean, well-structured design and implementation first. Then use a profiler, and only invest time optimizing those parts that are flagged by a profiler as being a performance bottleneck.*

Handle Objects Efficiently

C++ does a lot of work for you behind the scenes, particularly with regard to objects. You should always be aware of the performance impact of the code you write. If you follow a few simple guidelines, your code will become more efficient. Note that these guidelines are only relevant for objects, and not for primitive types such as `bool`, `int`, `float`, and so on.

Pass-by-Value or Pass-by-Reference

Chapters 1, "A Crash Course in C++ and the Standard Library," and 9, "Mastering Classes and Objects," present a rule to decide between pass-by-value and pass-by-reference. The rule is worth repeating here.

> **WARNING** *Prefer pass-by-value parameters for parameters that a function inherently would copy, but only if the parameter is of a type that supports move semantics. Otherwise, use reference-to-*`const` *parameters.*

With pass-by-value parameters, you have to keep a few things in mind. When you pass an object of a derived class by value as an argument for a function parameter that has one of the base classes as its type, then the derived object is "sliced" to fit into the base class type. This causes information to be lost; see Chapter 10 for details. Pass-by-value could also incur copying costs that are avoided with pass-by-reference.

However, in certain cases, pass-by-value is actually the optimal way to pass an argument to a function. Consider a class to represent a person that looks as follows:

```
class Person
{
    public:
        Person() = default;
        explicit Person(string firstName, string lastName, int age)
            : m_firstName { move(firstName) }, m_lastName { move(lastName) }
            , m_age { age } { }
        virtual ~Person() = default;
```

```
        const string& getFirstName() const { return m_firstName; }
        const string& getLastName() const { return m_lastName; }
        int getAge() const { return m_age; }

    private:
        string m_firstName, m_lastName;
        int m_age { 0 };
};
```

As the rule recommends, the `Person` constructor accepts `firstName` and `lastName` by value and then moves them to `m_firstName` and `m_lastName`, respectively, because it would make a copy of those anyway. See Chapter 9 for an explanation of this idiom.

Now, take a look at the following function accepting a `Person` object by value:

```
void processPerson(Person p) { /* Process the person. */ }
```

You can call this function like this:

```
Person me { "Marc", "Gregoire", 42 };
processPerson(me);
```

This doesn't look like there's more code than if you write the function like this instead:

```
void processPerson(const Person& p) { /* Process the person. */ }
```

The call to the function remains the same. However, consider what happens when you pass-by-value in the first version of the function. To initialize the `p` parameter of `processPerson()`, `me` must be copied with a call to its copy constructor. Even though you didn't write a copy constructor for the `Person` class, the compiler generates one that copies each of the data members. That still doesn't look so bad: there are only three data members. However, two of them are `string`s, which are themselves objects with copy constructors. So, each of their copy constructors will be called as well. The version of `processPerson()` that takes `p` by reference incurs no such copying costs. Thus, pass-by-reference in this example avoids a lot of overhead when the code enters the function.

And you're still not done. Remember that `p` in the first version of `processPerson()` is a local variable to the `processPerson()` function, and so must be destroyed when the function exits. This destruction requires a call to the `Person` destructor, which will call the destructor of all the data members. `string`s have destructors, so exiting this function (if you passed by value) incurs calls to three destructors. None of those calls are needed if the `Person` object is passed by reference.

> **NOTE** *If a function must modify an object, pass the object by reference-to-non-*`const`*. If the function should not modify the object, pass it by value or by reference-to-*`const`*, as in the preceding example.*

> **NOTE** *Avoid using pass-by-pointer, which is a relatively obsolete technique for pass-by-reference. It is a throwback to the C language and thus rarely suitable in C++ (unless passing* `nullptr` *has meaning in your design).*

Return-by-Value or Return-by-Reference

You could return objects by reference from functions to avoid copying the objects unnecessarily. Unfortunately, it is sometimes impossible to return objects by reference, such as when you write overloaded `operator+` and other similar operators. And, you should never return a reference or a pointer to a local object that will be destroyed when the function exits!

However, returning objects by value from functions is usually fine. This is due to mandatory and non-mandatory elision of copy/move operations and move semantics, both of which optimize returning objects by value, and both are discussed Chapter 9.

Catch Exceptions by Reference

As noted in Chapter 14, "Handling Errors," you should catch exceptions by reference to avoid slicing and unnecessary copying. Throwing exceptions is heavy in terms of performance, so any little thing you can do to improve their efficiency will help.

Use Move Semantics

You should make sure your classes support move semantics (see Chapter 9), either through the compiler-generated move constructor and move assignment operator or by implementing them yourself. According to the rule of zero (see Chapter 9), you should try to design your classes such that the compiler-generated copy and move constructors and copy and move assignment operators are sufficient. If the compiler cannot implicitly define these for a class, try to explicitly default them if that works for your class. If that is also not an option, you should implement them yourself. With move semantics for your objects, lots of operations will be more efficient, especially in combination with Standard Library containers and algorithms.

Avoid Creating Temporary Objects

The compiler creates temporary, unnamed objects in several circumstances. Chapter 9 explains that after writing a global `operator+` for a class, you can add objects of that class to other types, as long as those types can be converted to objects of that class. For example, the `SpreadsheetCell` class definition from Chapter 9, which includes support for the arithmetic operators, looks in part like this:

```
export class SpreadsheetCell
{
    public:
        // Other constructors omitted for brevity.
        SpreadsheetCell(double initialValue);
        // Remainder omitted for brevity.
};

export SpreadsheetCell operator+(const SpreadsheetCell& lhs,
    const SpreadsheetCell& rhs);
```

The non-`explicit` constructor that takes a `double` allows you to write code like this:

```
SpreadsheetCell myCell { 4 }, aThirdCell;
aThirdCell = myCell + 5.6;
aThirdCell = myCell + 4;
```

The second statement constructs a temporary `SpreadsheetCell` object from the `5.6` argument; it then calls the `operator+` with `myCell` and this temporary object as arguments. The result is stored in `aThirdCell`. The third statement does the same thing, except that `4` must be coerced to a `double` to call the `double` constructor of the `SpreadsheetCell`.

The important point in this example is that the compiler generates code to create an extra, unnamed `SpreadsheetCell` object for both addition operations in this example. That object must be constructed and destructed with calls to its constructor and destructor. If you're still skeptical, try inserting `print()` statements in your constructor and destructor, and watch the printout.

In general, the compiler constructs a temporary object whenever your code converts a variable of one type to another type for use in a larger expression. This rule applies mostly to function calls. For example, suppose that you write a function with the following prototype:

```
void doSomething(const SpreadsheetCell& s);
```

You can call this function like this:

```
doSomething(5.56);
```

The compiler constructs a temporary `SpreadsheetCell` object from `5.56` using the `double` constructor. This temporary object is then passed to `doSomething()`. Note that if you remove the `const` from the `s` parameter, you can no longer call `doSomething()` with a constant; you must pass an lvalue.

You should generally attempt to avoid cases in which the compiler is forced to construct temporary objects. Although it is impossible to avoid in some situations, you should at least be aware of the existence of this "feature" so you aren't surprised by performance and profiling results.

Move semantics is used by the compiler to make working with temporary objects more efficient. That's another reason to make sure your classes support move semantics. See Chapter 9 for details.

Pre-allocate Memory

One of the main advantages of using containers such as those from the C++ Standard Library discussed in Chapter 18, "Standard Library Containers," is that they handle all memory management for you. The containers grow automatically when you add more elements to them. However, sometimes this causes a performance penalty. For example, an `std::vector` container stores its elements contiguously in memory. If it needs to grow in size, it needs to allocate a new block of memory and then move (or copy) all elements to this new memory. This has serious performance implications, for example, if you use `push_back()` in a loop to add millions of elements to a `vector`.

If you know in advance how many elements you are going to add to a `vector` or if you have a rough estimate, you should pre-allocate enough memory before starting to add your elements. A `vector` has a capacity, that is, the number of elements that can be added without reallocation, and a size, that is, the actual number of elements in the container. You can pre-allocate memory by changing the capacity using the `reserve()` member function or by resizing the `vector` using `resize()`. See Chapter 18 for details.

Use Inline Functions

Some compilers use the `inline` keyword as a hint to the optimizer to more aggressively optimize a marked function (especially at low optimization levels). If you notice that a particular small function is a performance bottleneck, try marking it `inline`. Do not overuse this feature, because it throws away a fundamental design principle stating that the interface and the implementation should be separated such that the implementation can evolve without changes to the interface.

Mark Unreachable Code

The C++ Standard Library includes `std::unreachable`, defined in `<utility>`, to mark source code locations as being *unreachable*. Doing so helps the compiler to better optimize the final executable code. For example,[1] the following function accepts an integer parameter, and the programmer of this function knows for a fact that this parameter can only ever have the values 0, 1, 2, or 3, nothing else.

```
void doSomething(int number_that_is_only_0_1_2_or_3)
{
    switch (number_that_is_only_0_1_2_or_3) {
        case 0:
        case 2:
            handle0Or2(); break;
        case 1:
            handle1();    break;
        case 3:
            handle3();    break;
    }
}
```

However, all the compiler sees is an `int` parameter, so it doesn't know that the value can be only 0, 1, 2, or 3. The `switch` statement in the function handles all possible values of the parameter. However, the compiler does not know this and thus must generate executable code to check that the value is 0, 1, 2, or 3, before it executes the jump to the correct `case` block; for any other value, it has to jump to the first statement after the `switch` statement.

By adding a `default` case to the `switch` statement and specifying to the compiler that this `default` case will never be reached, the compiler can omit the executable code to check that the parameter value is 0, 1, 2, or 3, and just immediately jump to the correct `case` block. In certain cases, for example in tight loops, this can improve the performance of the final executable code.

```
void doSomething(int number_that_is_only_0_1_2_or_3)
{
    switch (number_that_is_only_0_1_2_or_3) {
        // Same cases for 0, 1, 2, and 3 as before, omitted for brevity...
        default:
            unreachable();
    }
}
```

If a call to `unreachable()` is ever reached at run time, the result is undefined behavior. For example, calling `doSomething()` with argument 8 triggers undefined behavior, and a compiler is free to choose what to do in such a case.

[1] This example comes from the official proposal paper of `std::unreachable()`, P0627R6.

DESIGN-LEVEL EFFICIENCY

The design choices in your program affect its performance far more than do language details such as pass-by-reference. For example, if you choose an algorithm for a fundamental task in your application that runs in $O(n^2)$ time instead of a simpler one that runs in $O(n)$ time, you could potentially perform the square of the number of operations that you really need. To put numbers on that, a task that uses an $O(n^2)$ algorithm and performs 1 million operations would perform only 1,000 with an $O(n)$ algorithm. Even if that operation is optimized beyond recognition at the language level, the simple fact that you perform 1 million operations when a better algorithm would use only 1,000 will make your program very inefficient. Always choose your algorithms carefully. Refer to Part II, specifically Chapter 4, "Designing Professional C++ Programs," of this book for a detailed discussion of algorithm design choices and big-O notation.

In addition to your choice of algorithms, design-level efficiency includes specific tips and tricks. Instead of writing your own data structures and algorithms, you should use existing ones, such as those from the C++ Standard Library, the Boost libraries (`boost.org`), or other libraries, as much as possible because they are written by experts. These libraries have been, and are being, used a lot, so you can expect most bugs to have been discovered and fixed. You should also think about incorporating multithreading in your design to take full advantage of all the processing power available on a machine. See Chapter 27, "Multithreaded Programming with C++," for more details. The remainder of this section presents two more design techniques for optimizing your program: caching and using object pools.

Cache Where Necessary

Caching means storing items for future use to avoid retrieving or recalculating them. You might be familiar with the principle from its use in computer hardware. Modern computer processors are built with memory caches that store recently and frequently accessed memory values in a location that is quicker to access than main memory. Most memory locations that are accessed at all are accessed more than once in a short time period, so caching at the hardware level can significantly speed up computations.

Caching in software follows the same approach. If a task or computation is particularly slow, you should make sure that you are not performing it more than necessary. Store the results in memory the first time you perform the task so that they are available for future needs. Here is a list of tasks that are usually slow:

- **Disk access:** You should avoid opening and reading the same file more than once in your program. If memory is available, save the file contents in RAM if you need to access it frequently.
- **Network communication:** Whenever you need to communicate over a network, your program is subject to the vagaries of the network. Treat network accesses like file accesses, and cache as much static information as possible.
- **Mathematical computations:** If you need the result of a complex computation in more than one place, perform the calculation once and share the result. However, if it's not very complex, then it's probably faster to just calculate it instead of retrieving it from a cache. Use a profiler to be sure.

- **Object allocation:** If you need to create and use a large number of short-lived objects in your program, consider using an object pool, described later in this chapter.
- **Thread creation:** Creating threads is slow. You can "cache" threads in a thread pool, similar to caching objects in an object pool.

One common problem with caching is that the data you store often comprises only copies of the underlying information. The original data might change during the lifetime of the cache. For example, you might want to cache the values in a configuration file so that you don't need to read it repeatedly. However, the user might be allowed to change the configuration file while your program is running, which would make your cached version of the information obsolete. In cases like this, you need a mechanism for *cache invalidation*: when the underlying data changes, you must either stop using your cached information or repopulate your cache.

One technique for cache invalidation is to request that the entity managing the underlying data notifies your program of every change. It could do this through a *callback* that your program registers with the manager. Alternatively, your program could poll for certain events that would trigger it to repopulate the cache automatically. Regardless of your specific cache invalidation technique, make sure that you think about these issues before relying on a cache in your program.

When adding caching to a data structure, make sure your design hides any details of this caching from the `public` interface. Client code should not be aware that the underlying implementation uses any kind of caching. This also allows you to change the caching mechanism without affecting the `public` interface.

> **NOTE** *Always keep in mind that maintaining caches takes code, memory, and processing time. On top of that, caches can be a source of subtle bugs. You should only add caching to a particular area when a profiler clearly shows that that area is a performance bottleneck. First write clean and correct code, then profile it, and only then optimize parts of it.*

Use Object Pools

There are different kinds of object pools. This section discusses one kind of object pool where it allocates a large chunk of memory at once, in which the pool creates smaller objects in-place. These objects can be handed out to clients and reused when clients are done with them, without incurring any additional calls to the memory manager to allocate or deallocate memory for individual objects.

Where the following object pool implementation shines, as will be demonstrated with benchmarks, is for objects with big data members. Whether or not an object pool is the right solution for a specific use case can only be decided by profiling your code.

An Object Pool Implementation

This section provides an implementation of an object pool class template that you can use in your programs. The implementation keeps a `vector` of chunks of objects of type `T`. Additionally, it also keeps track of free objects in a `vector` that contains pointers to all free objects. The pool hands out objects via the `acquireObject()` member function. If `acquireObject()` is called but there are no free objects anymore, then the pool allocates another chunk of objects. `acquireObject()` returns a `shared_ptr`.

This implementation is using the `vector` Standard Library container without any synchronization. As such, this version is not thread-safe. See Chapter 27 for a discussion on how you can make the implementation thread-safe.

Here is the class definition with comments explaining the details. The class template is parameterized on the type that is to be stored in the pool and on the type of allocator to use for allocating and deallocating chunks of memory.

```
// Provides an object pool that can be used with any class.
//
// acquireObject() returns an object from the list of free objects. If
// there are no more free objects, acquireObject() creates a new chunk
// of objects.
// The pool only grows: objects are never removed from the pool, until
// the pool is destroyed.
// acquireObject() returns an std::shared_ptr with a custom deleter that
// automatically puts the object back into the object pool when the
// shared_ptr is destroyed and its reference count reaches 0.
export
template <typename T, typename Allocator = std::allocator<T>>
class ObjectPool final
{
    public:
        ObjectPool() = default;
        explicit ObjectPool(const Allocator& allocator);
        ~ObjectPool();

        // Prevent move construction and move assignment.
        ObjectPool(ObjectPool&&) = delete;
        ObjectPool& operator=(ObjectPool&&) = delete;

        // Prevent copy construction and copy assignment.
        ObjectPool(const ObjectPool&) = delete;
        ObjectPool& operator=(const ObjectPool&) = delete;

        // Reserves and returns an object from the pool. Arguments can be
        // provided which are perfectly forwarded to a constructor of T.
        template <typename... Args>
        std::shared_ptr<T> acquireObject(Args&&... args);

    private:
        // Creates a new block of uninitialized memory, big enough to hold
        // m_newChunkSize instances of T.
        void addChunk();
        // Contains chunks of memory in which instances of T will be created.
        // For each chunk, the pointer to its first object is stored.
        std::vector<T*> m_pool;
        // Contains pointers to all free instances of T that
        // are available in the pool.
        std::vector<T*> m_freeObjects;
```

```
        // The number of T instances that should fit in the first allocated chunk.
        static constexpr std::size_t ms_initialChunkSize { 5 };
        // The number of T instances that should fit in a newly allocated chunk.
        // This value is doubled after each newly created chunk.
        std::size_t m_newChunkSize { ms_initialChunkSize };
        // The allocator to use for allocating and deallocating chunks.
        Allocator m_allocator;
};
```

When using this object pool, you have to make sure that the object pool itself outlives all the objects handed out by the pool.

The constructor is trivial and just stores the given allocator in a data member:

```
template <typename T, typename Allocator>
ObjectPool<T, Allocator>::ObjectPool(const Allocator& allocator)
    : m_allocator { allocator }
{
}
```

The `addChunk()` member function to allocate a new chunk is implemented as follows. The first part of `addChunk()` does the actual allocation of a new chunk. A "chunk" is just a block of *uninitialized* memory, allocated using an allocator and big enough to hold `m_newChunkSize` instances of `T`. By adding a chunk of objects, no objects are actually constructed yet; i.e., no object constructors are called. That is done later in `acquireObject()` when instances are handed out. The second part of `addChunk()` creates pointers to the new instances of `T`. It uses the `iota()` algorithm, defined in `<numeric>`. To refresh your memory, `iota()` fills a range given by its first two arguments with values. The values start with the value of the third argument and are incremented by one for each subsequent value. Since we are working with `T*` pointers, incrementing a `T*` pointer by one jumps ahead to the next `T` in the memory block. Finally, the `m_newChunkSize` value is doubled so that the next block that will be added is double the size of the currently added block. This is done for performance reasons and follows the principle of `std::vector`. Here is the implementation:

```
template <typename T, typename Allocator>
void ObjectPool<T, Allocator>::addChunk()
{
    std::println("Allocating new chunk...");

    // Allocate a new chunk of uninitialized memory big enough to hold
    // m_newChunkSize instances of T, and add the chunk to the pool.
    // Care is taken that everything is cleaned up in the event of an exception.
    m_pool.push_back(nullptr);
    try {
        m_pool.back() = m_allocator.allocate(m_newChunkSize);
    } catch (...) {
        m_pool.pop_back();
        throw;
    }

    // Create pointers to each individual object in the new chunk
    // and store them in the list of free objects.
    auto oldFreeObjectsSize { m_freeObjects.size() };
    m_freeObjects.resize(oldFreeObjectsSize + m_newChunkSize);
    std::iota(begin(m_freeObjects) + oldFreeObjectsSize, end(m_freeObjects),
        m_pool.back());
```

```
        // Double the chunk size for next time.
        m_newChunkSize *= 2;
    }
```

acquireObject(), a variadic member function template, returns a free object from the pool, allocating a new chunk if there are no more free objects available. As explained earlier, adding a new chunk just allocates a block of uninitialized memory. It is the responsibility of acquireObject() to properly construct a new instance of T at the right place in memory. This is done using a placement new operator. Any arguments passed to acquireObject() are perfectly forwarded to a constructor of type T.

acquireObject() uses a placement new operator to construct a new instance of an object of type T at an explicitly specified memory location. If type T contains any const or reference members, accessing the newly constructed object through the original pointer triggers undefined behavior. To turn this into defined behavior, you need to launder the memory using std::launder(), defined in <new>.[2]

Finally, the laundered T* pointer is wrapped in a shared_ptr with a custom deleter. This deleter does not deallocate any memory; instead, it manually calls the destructor by using std::destroy_at() and then puts the pointer back on the list of available objects.

```
template <typename T, typename Allocator>
template <typename... Args>
std::shared_ptr<T> ObjectPool<T, Allocator>::acquireObject(Args&&... args)
{
    // If there are no free objects, allocate a new chunk.
    if (m_freeObjects.empty()) { addChunk(); }

    // Get a free object.
    T* object { m_freeObjects.back() };

    // Initialize, i.e. construct, an instance of T in an
    // uninitialized block of memory using placement new, and
    // perfectly forward any provided arguments to the constructor.
    ::new(object) T { std::forward<Args>(args)... };

    // Launder the object pointer.
    T* constructedObject { std::launder(object) };

    // Remove the object from the list of free objects.
    m_freeObjects.pop_back();

    // Wrap the constructed object and return it.
    return std::shared_ptr<T> { constructedObject, [this](T* object) {
        // Destroy object.
        std::destroy_at(object);
        // Put the object back in the list of free objects.
        m_freeObjects.push_back(object);
    } };
}
```

[2] C++23 introduces a slightly related function called std::start_lifetime_as(). The difference with launder() is that launder() doesn't create a new object, it just launders a pointer to an already constructed object. On the other hand, start_lifetime_as() actually creates a new object but without running any constructor code. This can be useful if you have a block of memory that you know represents an object, maybe received over the network, and that you want to turn into an object, e.g., start_lifetime_as<MyObjectType>(networkBuffer).

Finally, the destructor of the pool must deallocate any allocated memory using the given allocator:

```
template <typename T, typename Allocator>
ObjectPool<T, Allocator>::~ObjectPool()
{
    // Note: this implementation assumes that all objects handed out by this
    //       pool have been returned to the pool before the pool is destroyed.
    //       The following statement asserts if that is not the case.
    assert(m_freeObjects.size() ==
        ms_initialChunkSize * (std::pow(2, m_pool.size()) - 1));

    // Deallocate all allocated memory.
    std::size_t chunkSize { ms_initialChunkSize };
    for (auto* chunk : m_pool) {
        m_allocator.deallocate(chunk, chunkSize);
        chunkSize *= 2;
    }
    m_pool.clear();
}
```

`assert()` is a macro defined in `<cassert>`. It takes a Boolean expression and, if the expression evaluates to `false`, prints an error message and terminates the program. Chapter 31, "Conquering Debugging," gives more details. The formula used in the `assert()` statement is based on the fact that each allocated chunk is double in size compared to the previous chunk.

Using the Object Pool

Consider an application that uses a lot of short-lived objects with big data members and hence are expensive to allocate. Let's assume we have an `ExpensiveObject` class definition that looks as follows:

```
class ExpensiveObject
{
    public:
        ExpensiveObject() { /* ... */ }
        virtual ~ExpensiveObject() = default;
        // Member functions to populate the object with specific information.
        // Member functions to retrieve the object data.
        // (not shown)
    private:
        // An expensive data member.
        array<double, 4 * 1024 * 1024> m_data;
        // Other data members (not shown)
};
```

Instead of allocating and deallocating large numbers of such objects throughout the lifetime of your program, you can use the object pool developed in the previous section. We can benchmark the pool using the chrono library (see Chapter 22, "Date and Time Utilities") as follows:

```
using MyPool = ObjectPool<ExpensiveObject>;

shared_ptr<ExpensiveObject> getExpensiveObject(MyPool& pool)
{
    // Obtain an ExpensiveObject object from the pool.
    auto object { pool.acquireObject() };
```

```
        // Populate the object. (not shown)
        return object;
    }

    void processExpensiveObject(ExpensiveObject& object) { /* ... */ }

    int main()
    {
        const size_t NumberOfIterations { 500'000 };

        println("Starting loop using pool...");
        MyPool requestPool;
        auto start1 { chrono::steady_clock::now() };
        for (size_t i { 0 }; i < NumberOfIterations; ++i) {
            auto object { getExpensiveObject(requestPool) };
            processExpensiveObject(*object.get());
        }
        auto end1 { chrono::steady_clock::now() };
        auto diff1 { end1 - start1 };
        println("{}", chrono::duration<double, milli>(diff1));


        println("Starting loop using new/delete...");
        auto start2 { chrono::steady_clock::now() };
        for (size_t i { 0 }; i < NumberOfIterations; ++i) {
            auto object { std::make_unique<ExpensiveObject>() };
            processExpensiveObject(*object);
        }
        auto end2 { chrono::steady_clock::now() };
        auto diff2 { end2 - start2 };
        println("{}", chrono::duration<double, milli>(diff2));
    }
```

The `main()` function contains a small benchmark of the pool's performance. It asks for 500,000 objects in a loop and times how long it takes. The loop is done twice, once using our pool and once using the standard `new`/`delete` operators. The results on a test machine with a release build of the code are as follows:

```
Starting loop using pool...
Allocating new chunk...
54.526ms
Starting loop using new/delete...
9463.2393ms
```

In this example, using the object pool is around 170 times faster. Keep in mind, though, that this object pool is tailored to work with objects with big data members. This is the case for the `ExpensiveObject` class used in the example, which contains a 32MB `array` as one of its data members.

PROFILING

It is good to think about efficiency as you design and code. There is no point in writing obviously inefficient programs if this can be avoided with some common sense or experience-based intuition.

However, I urge you not to get too obsessed with performance during the design and coding phases. It's best to first make a clean, well-structured design and implementation, then use a profiler, and only optimize parts that are flagged by the profiler as being performance bottlenecks. Remember the "90/10" rule, introduced in Chapter 4, which states that 90 percent of the running time of most programs is spent in only 10 percent of the code (Hennessy and Patterson, *Computer Architecture, A Quantitative Approach, Fourth Edition*, [Morgan Kaufmann, 2006]). This means you could optimize 90 percent of your code, but still only improve the running time of the program by 10 percent. Obviously, you want to optimize the parts of the code that are exercised the most for the specific workload that you expect the program to run.

Consequently, it is often helpful to *profile* your program to determine which parts of the code require optimization. There are many *profiling tools* available that analyze programs as they run to generate data about their performance. Most profiling tools provide analysis at the function level by specifying the amount of time (or percent of total execution time) spent in each function in the program. After running a profiler on your program, you can usually tell immediately which parts of the program need optimization. Profiling before and after optimizing is essential to prove that your optimizations had an effect.

If you are using Microsoft Visual C++, you already have a great built-in profiler, which is discussed later in this chapter. If you are not yet using Visual C++, Microsoft has a community edition available (`visualstudio.microsoft.com`) that is free of charge for students, open-source developers, and individual developers to create both free and paid applications. It's also free of charge for up to five users in small organizations. Another great profiling tool is Rational PurifyPlus from IBM (`www.almtoolbox.com/purify.php`). There are also a number of smaller free profiling tools available: Very Sleepy (`www.codersnotes.com/sleepy`) and Luke Stackwalker (`lukestackwalker.sourceforge.net`) are popular profilers for Windows, Valgrind (`valgrind.org`) and gprof (GNU profiler, `sourceware.org/binutils/docs/gprof`) are well-known profilers for Unix/Linux systems, and there are plenty of other choices. This section demonstrates two profilers: gprof for Linux, and the profiler that comes with Visual C++ 2022.

Profiling Example with gprof

The power of profiling can best be seen with a real coding example. As a disclaimer, the performance bugs in the first implementation shown are not subtle! Real efficiency issues would probably be more complex, but a program long enough to demonstrate them would be too lengthy for this book.

Suppose that you work for the US Social Security Administration. Every year the administration puts up a website that allows users to look up the popularity of new baby names from the previous year. Your job is to write the backend program that looks up names for users. Your input is a file containing the name of every new baby. This file will obviously contain duplicate names. For example, in the file for boys for 2003, the name Jacob was the most popular, showing up 29,195 times. Your program must read the file to construct an in-memory database. A user may then request the absolute number of babies with a given name or the rank of that name among all the babies.

First Design Attempt

A logical design for this program consists of a `NameDB` class with the following public member functions:

```
export class NameDB
{
```

```
        public:
            // Reads list of baby names in nameFile to populate the database.
            // Throws invalid_argument if nameFile cannot be opened or read.
            explicit NameDB(const std::string& nameFile);

            // Returns the rank of the name (1st, 2nd, etc).
            // Returns -1 if the name is not found.
            int getNameRank(const std::string& name) const;

            // Returns the number of babies with a given name.
            // Returns -1 if the name is not found.
            int getAbsoluteNumber(const std::string& name) const;

            // Private members not shown yet ...
    };
```

The hard part is choosing a good data structure for the in-memory database. A first attempt is a `vector` of name/count `pair`s. Remember, `pair` is a utility class that combines two values of possibly different types. Each entry in the `vector` stores one of the names, along with a count of the number of times that name shows up in the raw data file. Here is the complete class definition with this design:

```
export class NameDB
{
    public:
        explicit NameDB(const std::string& nameFile);
        int getNameRank(const std::string& name) const;
        int getAbsoluteNumber(const std::string& name) const;
    private:
        std::vector<std::pair<std::string, int>> m_names;

        // Helper member functions
        bool nameExists(const std::string& name) const;
        void incrementNameCount(const std::string& name);
        void addNewName(const std::string& name);
};
```

Here are the implementations of the constructor and the helper member functions `nameExists()`, `incrementNameCount()`, and `addNewName()`. The loops in `nameExists()` and `incrementNameCount()` iterate over all the elements of the `vector`.

```
// Reads the names from the file and populates the database.
// The database is a vector of name/count pairs, storing the
// number of times each name shows up in the raw data.
NameDB::NameDB(const string& nameFile)
{
    // Open the file and check for errors.
    ifstream inputFile { nameFile };
    if (!inputFile) {
        throw invalid_argument { "Unable to open file" };
    }

    // Read the names one at a time.
    string name;
    while (inputFile >> name) {
        // Look up the name in the database so far.
        if (nameExists(name)) {
```

```
                // If the name exists in the database, just increment the count.
                incrementNameCount(name);
            } else {
                // If the name doesn't yet exist, add it with a count of 1.
                addNewName(name);
            }
        }
}

// Returns true if the name exists in the database, false otherwise.
bool NameDB::nameExists(const string& name) const
{
    // Iterate through the vector of names looking for the name.
    for (auto& entry : m_names) {
        if (entry.first == name) {
            return true;
        }
    }
    return false;
}

// Precondition: name exists in the vector of names.
// Postcondition: the count associated with name is incremented.
void NameDB::incrementNameCount(const string& name)
{
    for (auto& entry : m_names) {
        if (entry.first == name) {
            entry.second += 1;
            return;
        }
    }
}

// Adds a new name to the database.
void NameDB::addNewName(const string& name)
{
    m_names.emplace_back(name, 1);
}
```

Note that you could use an algorithm like `std::find_if()`, discussed in Chapter 20, "Mastering Standard Library Algorithms," to accomplish the same thing as the loops in `nameExists()` and `incrementNameCount()`. The loops are shown explicitly to emphasize the performance problems.

You might have noticed some performance problems already. What if there are hundreds of thousands of names? The many linear searches involved in populating the database will become slow.

To complete the example, here are the implementations of the two public member functions:

```
// Returns the rank of the name.
// First looks up the name to obtain the number of babies with that name.
// Then iterates through all the names, counting all the names with a higher
// count than the specified name. Returns that count as the rank.
int NameDB::getNameRank(const string& name) const
{
    // Make use of the getAbsoluteNumber() member function.
    int num { getAbsoluteNumber(name) };
```

```
    // Check if we found the name.
    if (num == -1) {
        return -1;
    }

    // Now count all the names in the vector that have a
    // count higher than this one. If no name has a higher count,
    // this name is rank number 1. Every name with a higher count
    // decreases the rank of this name by 1.
    int rank { 1 };
    for (auto& entry : m_names) {
        if (entry.second > num) {
            ++rank;
        }
    }
    return rank;
}

// Returns the count associated with the given name.
int NameDB::getAbsoluteNumber(const string& name) const
{
    for (auto& entry : m_names) {
        if (entry.first == name) {
            return entry.second;
        }
    }
    return -1;
}
```

Profiling the First Design Attempt

To test the program, you need a `main()` function:

```
import name_db;
import std;
using namespace std;

int main()
{
    NameDB boys { "boys_long.txt" };
    println("{}", boys.getNameRank("Daniel"));
    println("{}", boys.getNameRank("Jacob"));
    println("{}", boys.getNameRank("William"));
}
```

This `main()` function creates one `NameDB` database called `boys`, telling it to populate itself with the file `boys_long.txt`, which contains 500,500 names.

There are three steps to using gprof:

1. After having compiled the `name_db` module, you should compile the main program with a special flag that causes it to log raw execution information when it is run. When using GCC as your compiler, the flag is `-pg`, as in this example:

```
> gcc -lstdc++ -std=c++2b -pg -fmodules-ts -o namedb NameDB.cpp NameDBTest.cpp
```

> **NOTE** *At the time of this writing, GCC does not yet have full support for C++ modules. Once GCC fully supports modules, check its documentation to learn how to compile and work with modules.*
>
> *Additionally, at this moment, you have to specify* `-std=c++2b` *to enable C++23 features. This will change in the future to* `-std=c++23`*. Check the documentation.*

2. Run your program. This should generate a file called `gmon.out` in the working directory. Be patient when you run the program because this first version is slow.
3. Run the `gprof` command. This final step enables you to analyze the `gmon.out` profiling information and produce a (somewhat) readable report. gprof outputs to standard out, so you should redirect the output to a file:

```
> gprof namedb gmon.out > gprof_analysis.out
```

Now you can analyze the data. Unfortunately, the output file is somewhat cryptic and intimidating, so it takes a little while to learn how to interpret it. gprof provides two separate sets of information. The first set summarizes the amount of time spent executing each function in the program. The second and more useful set summarizes the amount of time spent executing each function *and its descendants*; this set is also called a *call graph*. Here is some of the output from the `gprof_analysis.out` file, edited to make it more readable. Note that the numbers will be different on your machine.

```
index  %time    self  children     called     name
[1]    100.0    0.00   14.06                  main [1]
                0.00   14.00        1/1           NameDB::NameDB [2]
                0.00    0.04        3/3           NameDB::getNameRank [25]
                0.00    0.01        1/1           NameDB::~NameDB [28]
```

The following list explains the different columns:

- `index`: An index to be able to refer to this entry in the call graph.
- `%time`: The percentage of the total execution time of the program required by this function and its descendants.
- `self`: How many seconds the function itself was executing.
- `children`: How many seconds the descendants of this function were executing.
- `called`: How often this function was called.
- `name`: The name of the function. If the name of the function is followed by a number between square brackets, that number refers to another index in the call graph.

The preceding extract tells you that `main()` and its descendants took 100 percent of the total execution time of the program, for a total of 14.06 seconds. The second line shows that the `NameDB` constructor took 14.00 seconds of the total 14.06 seconds. So, it's immediately clear where the performance issue is situated. To track down which part of the constructor is taking that long, you need to jump to the call graph entry with index 2, because that's the index in square brackets behind the name in the last column. The call graph entry with index 2 is as follows on my test system:

```
[2] 99.6    0.00    14.00         1           NameDB::NameDB [2]
            1.20     6.14   500500/500500        NameDB::nameExists [3]
            1.24     5.24   499500/499500        NameDB::incrementNameCount [4]
            0.00     0.18     1000/1000          NameDB::addNewName [19]
            0.00     0.00        1/1             vector::vector [69]
```

The nested entries below `NameDB::NameDB` show which of its descendants took the most time. Here you can see that `nameExists()` took 6.14 seconds, and `incrementNameCount()` took 5.24 seconds. These times are the sums of all the calls to the functions. The fourth column in those lines shows the number of calls to the function (500,500 to `nameExists()` and 499,500 to `incrementNameCount()`). No other function took a significant amount of time.

Without going any further in this analysis, two things should jump out at you:

- Taking 14 seconds to populate the database of approximately 500,000 names is slow. Perhaps you need a better data structure.
- `nameExists()` and `incrementNameCount()` take an almost identical amount of time and are called almost the same number of times. If you think about the application domain, that makes sense: most names in the input text file are duplicates, so the vast majority of the calls to `nameExists()` are followed by a call to `incrementNameCount()`. If you look back at the code, you can see that these functions are almost identical; they could probably be combined. In addition, most of what they are doing is searching the `vector`. It would probably be better to use a sorted data structure to reduce the searching time.

Second Design Attempt

With these two observations from the gprof output, it's time to redesign the program. The new design uses a `map` instead of a `vector`. Chapter 18 explains that the Standard Library `map` keeps the entries sorted and provides O(log n) lookup instead of the O(n) searches in a `vector`. A good exercise for you to try would be to use an `std::unordered_map`, which has an expected O(1) for lookups, and to use a profiler to see if that is faster than `std::map` for this application.

The new version of the program also combines `nameExists()` and `incrementNameCount()` into one `incrementIfExists()`.

Here is the new class definition:

```
export class NameDB
{
    public:
        explicit NameDB(const std::string& nameFile);
        int getNameRank(const std::string& name) const;
        int getAbsoluteNumber(const std::string& name) const;
    private:
        std::map<std::string, int> m_names;
        bool incrementIfExists(const std::string& name);
        void addNewName(const std::string& name);
};
```

Here are the new member function implementations:

```
// Reads the names from the file and populates the database.
// The database is a map associating names with their frequency.
NameDB::NameDB(const string& nameFile)
{
    // Open the file and check for errors.
    ifstream inputFile { nameFile };
    if (!inputFile) {
        throw invalid_argument { "Unable to open file" };
    }

    // Read the names one at a time.
    string name;
    while (inputFile >> name) {
        // Look up the name in the database so far.
        if (!incrementIfExists(name)) {
            // If the name exists in the database, the
            // member function incremented it, so we just continue.
            // We get here if it didn't exist, in which case
            // we add it with a count of 1.
            addNewName(name);
        }
    }
}

// Returns true if the name exists in the database, false
// otherwise. If it finds it, it increments it.
bool NameDB::incrementIfExists(const string& name)
{
    // Find the name in the map.
    auto res { m_names.find(name) };
    if (res != end(m_names)) {
        res->second += 1;
        return true;
    }
    return false;
}

// Adds a new name to the database.
void NameDB::addNewName(const string& name)
{
    m_names[name] = 1;
}

int NameDB::getNameRank(const string& name) const { /* Omitted, same as before */ }

// Returns the count associated with the given name.
int NameDB::getAbsoluteNumber(const string& name) const
{
    auto res { m_names.find(name) };
    if (res != end(m_names)) {
        return res->second;
    }
    return -1;
}
```

Profiling the Second Design Attempt

By following the same steps shown earlier, you can obtain the gprof performance data on the new version of the program. The data is quite encouraging:

```
index %time  self  children    called          name
[1]   100.0  0.00    0.21                      main [1]
             0.02    0.18       1/1            NameDB::NameDB [2]
             0.00    0.01       1/1            NameDB::~NameDB [13]
             0.00    0.00       3/3            NameDB::getNameRank [28]
[2]    95.2  0.02    0.18       1              NameDB::NameDB [2]
             0.02    0.16 500500/500500        NameDB::incrementIfExists
[3]          0.00    0.00    1000/1000         NameDB::addNewName [24]
             0.00    0.00       1/1            map::map [87]
```

If you run this on your machine, the output will be different. It's even possible that you will not see any data for `NameDB` member functions in your output. Because of the efficiency of this second attempt, the timings are getting so small that you might see more `map` member functions in the output than `NameDB` member functions.

On my test system, `main()` now takes only 0.21 seconds—a 67-fold improvement! There are certainly further improvements that you could make to this program. For example, the current constructor performs a lookup to see if the name is already in the `map`, and if not, adds it to the `map`. You could combine these two operations simply with the following single line:

```
m_names[name] += 1;
```

If the name is already in the `map`, this statement just increments its counter. If the name is not yet in the `map`, this statement first adds an entry to the `map` with the given name as key and a zero-initialized value, and then increments the value, resulting in a counter of 1.

With this improvement, you can remove the `incrementIfExists()` and `addNewName()` member functions and change the constructor as follows:

```
NameDB::NameDB(const string& nameFile)
{
    // Open the file and check for errors.
    ifstream inputFile { nameFile };
    if (!inputFile) {
        throw invalid_argument { "Unable to open file" };
    }

    // Read the names one at a time.
    string name;
    while (inputFile >> name) {
        m_names[name] += 1;
    }
}
```

`getNameRank()` still uses a loop that iterates over all elements in the `map`. A good exercise for you to try is to come up with another data structure so that the linear iteration in `getNameRank()` can be avoided.

Profiling Example with Visual C++ 2022

Most editions of Microsoft Visual C++ 2022 come with a great built-in profiler, which is briefly discussed in this section. The VC++ profiler has a complete graphical user interface. This book does not recommend one profiler over another, but it is always good to have an idea of what a command line–based profiler like gprof can provide in comparison with a GUI-based profiler like the one included with VC++.

To start profiling an application in Visual C++ 2022, you first need to open the project in Visual Studio. This example uses the same `NameDB` code as in the first inefficient design attempt from the previous sections. That code is not repeated here. Once your project is opened in Visual Studio, make sure the configuration is set to Release instead of Debug, then click the Debug menu, and choose Performance Profiler. A new window appears, similar to the one shown in Figure 29.1.

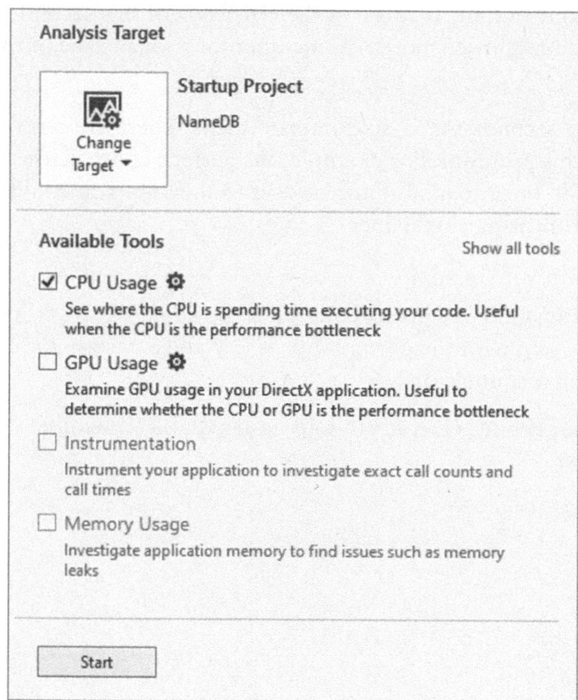

FIGURE 29.1

Depending on your version of VC++, there will be a number of different analysis tools available from this window. The following non-exhaustive list explains two of them:

- **CPU Usage:** Used to monitor applications with low overhead. This means that the act of profiling the application will not have a big performance impact on the target application.
- **Instrumentation:** Adds extra code to the application to be able to accurately count the number of function calls and to time individual function calls. However, this tool has a much bigger performance impact on the application. It is recommended to use the CPU Usage tool first to get an idea about the bottlenecks in your application. If that tool does not give you enough information, you can try the Instrumentation tool.

For this profiling example, enable only the CPU Usage tool and click the Start button. This executes your program and analyzes its CPU usage. When the program execution is finished, Visual Studio automatically opens the profiling report. Figure 29.2 shows how this report might look like when profiling the first attempt of the `NameDB` application.

From this report, you can immediately see the hot path. Just like with gprof, it shows that the `NameDB` constructor takes up most of the running time of the program. The Visual Studio profiling report is interactive. For example, you can drill down the `NameDB::NameDB` constructor by clicking on it in the hot path tree in Figure 29.2. This results in a drill-down report for that function, as show in Figure 29.3.

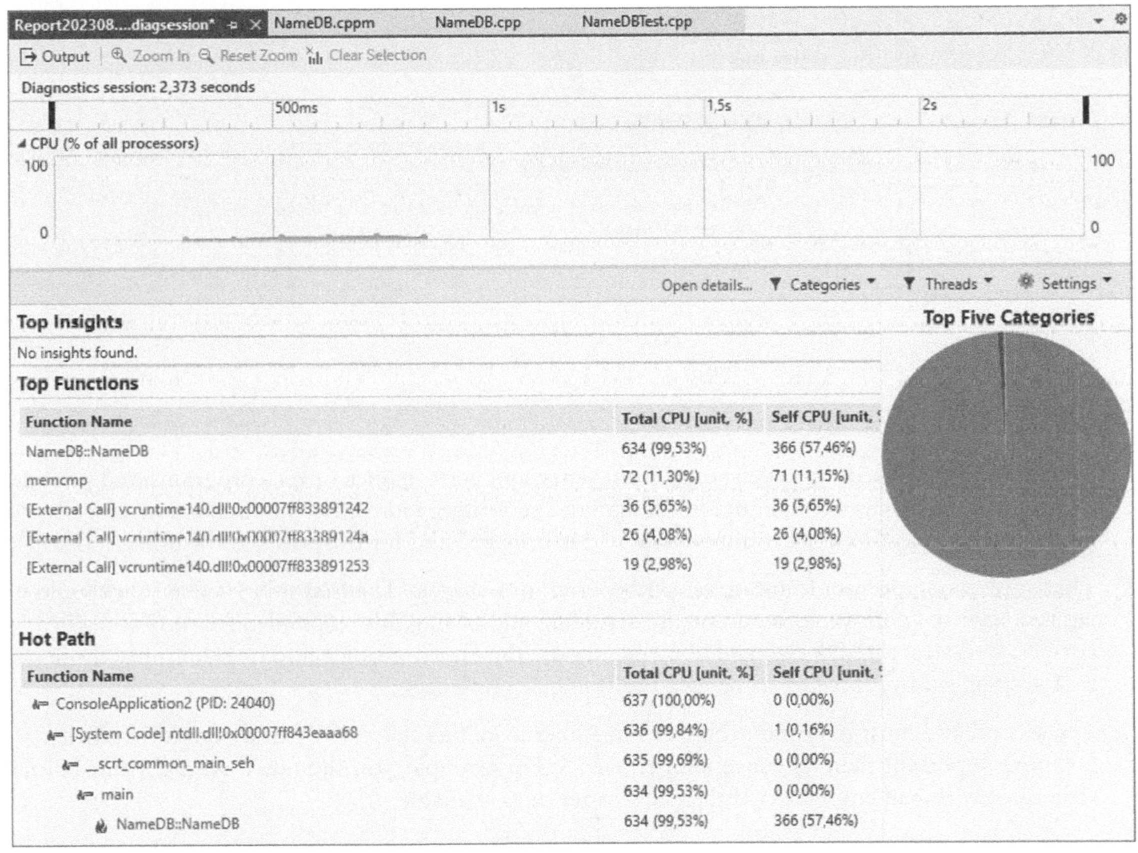

FIGURE 29.2

This drill-down view shows the hot path at the top and the actual code of the member function at the bottom. The code view shows the percentage of the running time that a line of code needed. The lines using up most of the time are shown in shades of red. This view instantly makes it clear that `incrementNameCount()` and `nameExists()` both roughly take the same time.

At the top of this report, there is a drop-down called Current View, which you can use to get different views of the profiling data.

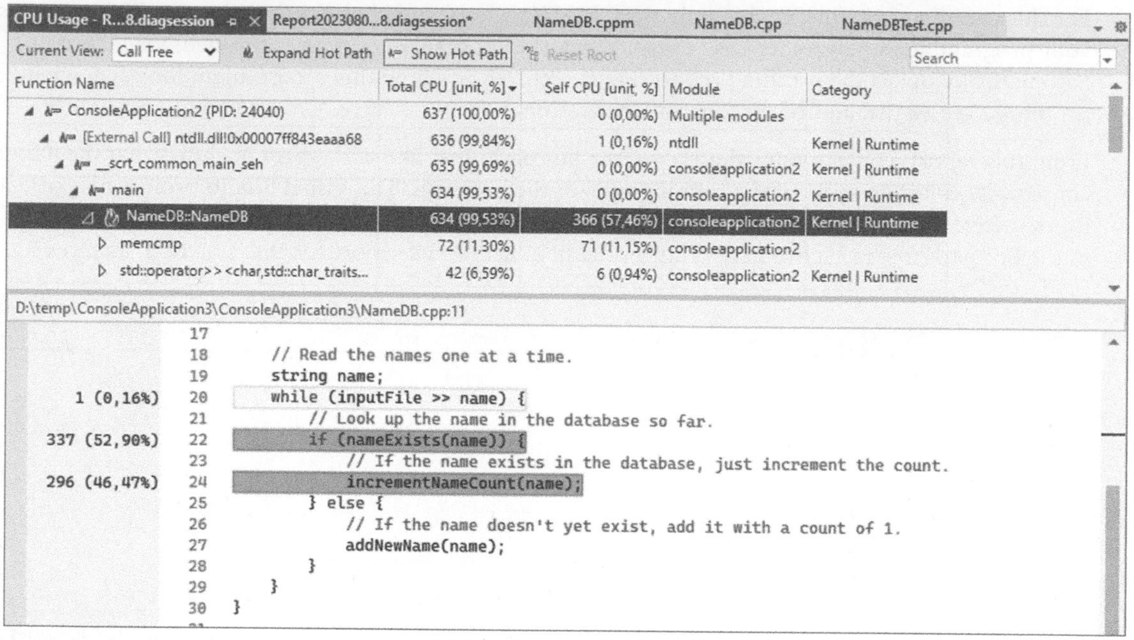

FIGURE 29.3

SUMMARY

This chapter discussed the key aspects of efficiency and performance in C++ programs and provided several specific tips and techniques for designing and writing more efficient applications. Ideally, you gained an appreciation for the importance of performance and for the power of profiling tools.

There are two important things to remember from this chapter. The first thing is that you should not get too obsessed with performance while designing and coding. It's recommended to first make a correct, well-structured design and implementation, then use a profiler, and only optimize those parts that are flagged by a profiler as being a performance bottleneck.

The second and most important thing to remember from this chapter is that design-level efficiency is far more important than language-level efficiency. For example, you shouldn't use algorithms or data structures with bad complexity if there are better ones available.

EXERCISES

By solving the following exercises, you can practice the material discussed in this chapter. Solutions to all exercises are available with the code download on the book's website at `www.wiley.com/go/proc++6e`. However, if you are stuck on an exercise, first reread parts of this chapter to try to find an answer yourself before looking at the solution from the website.

Exercise 29-1: What are the two most important things to remember from this chapter?

Exercise 29-2: Modify the final `NameDB` solution from the "Profiling" section to use an `std::unordered_map` instead of a `map`. Profile your code before and after your changes and compare the results.

Exercise 29-3: From the profiling results of Exercise 29-2, it now looks like `operator>>` in the `NameDB` constructor is the bottleneck. Can you change the implementation to avoid using `operator>>`? Since each line in the input file contains one name, maybe it's faster to simply use `std::getline()`? Try to modify your implementation as such and compare the profiling results before and after your changes.

30

Becoming Adept at Testing

WHAT'S IN THIS CHAPTER?

- What software quality control is and how to track bugs
- What unit testing means
- Unit testing in practice using the Visual C++ Testing Framework
- What fuzz testing or fuzzing means
- What integration, system, and regression testing means

WILEY.COM DOWNLOADS FOR THIS CHAPTER

Please note that all the code examples for this chapter are available as part of this chapter's code download on the book's website at `www.wiley.com/go/proc++6e` on the Download Code tab.

A programmer has overcome a major hurdle in her career when she realizes that testing is part of the software development process. Bugs are not an occasional occurrence. They are found in *every* project of significant size. A good *quality assurance* (QA) team is invaluable, but the full burden of testing cannot be placed on QA alone. Your responsibility as a programmer is to write code that works and to write tests to prove its correctness.

A distinction is often made between *white-box testing*, in which the tester is aware of the inner workings of the program, and *black-box testing*, which tests the program's functionality without any knowledge of its implementation. Both forms of testing are important to professional-quality projects. Black-box testing is the most fundamental approach because it typically models the behavior of a user. For example, a black-box test can examine interface components such as buttons. If the tester clicks the button and nothing happens, there is obviously a bug in the program.

Black-box testing cannot cover everything. Modern programs are too large to employ a simulation of clicking every button, providing every kind of input, and performing all combinations of commands. White-box testing is necessary, because when you know the code—when tests are written to exercise a specific object or subsystem—then it is easier to make sure all code paths in the code are exercised by tests. This helps to ensure test coverage. White-box tests are often easier to write and automate than black-box tests. This chapter focuses on topics that would generally be considered white-box testing techniques because the programmer can use these techniques during the development.

This chapter begins with a high-level discussion of quality control, including some approaches to viewing and tracking bugs. A section on unit testing, one of the simplest and most useful types of testing, follows this introduction. You then read about the theory and practice of unit testing, as well as several examples of unit tests in action, and what fuzz testing is. Next, higher-level tests are covered, including integration tests, system tests, and regression tests. Finally, this chapter ends with a list of tips for successful testing.

QUALITY CONTROL

Large programming projects are rarely finished when a feature-complete goal is reached. There are always bugs to find and fix, both during and after the main development phase. It is essential to understand the shared responsibility of quality control and the life cycle of a bug to perform well in a group.

Whose Responsibility Is Testing?

Software development organizations have different approaches to testing. In a small startup, there may not be a group of people whose full-time job is testing the product. Testing may be the responsibility of the individual developers, or all the employees of the company may be asked to lend a hand and try to break the product before its release. In larger organizations, a full-time quality assurance staff probably qualifies a release by testing it according to a set of criteria. Nonetheless, some aspects of testing may still be the responsibility of the developers. Even in organizations where the developers have no role in formal testing, you still need to be aware of what your responsibilities are in the larger process of quality assurance.

The Life Cycle of a Bug

All good engineering groups recognize that bugs will occur in software both before and after its release. There are many different ways to deal with these problems. Figure 30.1 shows a formal bug process, expressed as a flow chart. In this particular process, a bug is always filed by a member of the QA team. The bug reporting software sends a notification to the development manager, who sets the priority of the bug and assigns the bug to the appropriate module owner. The module owner can accept the bug or explain why the bug actually belongs to a different module or is invalid, giving the development manager the opportunity to assign it to someone else.

Once the bug has found its rightful owner, a fix is made, and the developer marks the bug as "fixed." At this point, the QA engineer verifies that the bug no longer exists and marks the bug as "closed" or reopens the bug if it is still present.

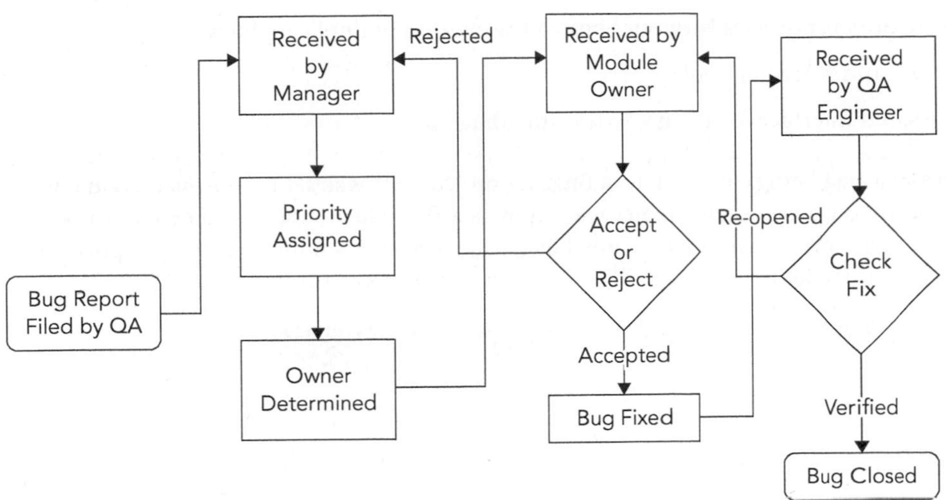

FIGURE 30.1

Figure 30.2 shows a less formal approach. In this workflow, anybody can file a bug and assign an initial priority and a module. The module owner receives the bug report and can either accept it or reassign it to another engineer or module. When a correction is made, the bug is marked as "fixed." Toward the end of the testing phase, all the developers and QA engineers divide up the fixed bugs and verify that each bug is no longer present in the current build. The release is ready when all bugs are marked as "closed."

FIGURE 30.2

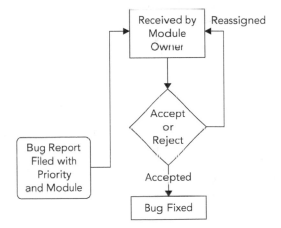

Bug-Tracking Tools

There are many ways to keep track of software bugs, from informal spreadsheet- or e-mail-based schemes to expensive third-party bug-tracking software. The appropriate solution for your organization depends on the group's size, the nature of the software, and the level of formality you want to build around bug fixing.

There are also a number of free open-source bug-tracking solutions available. One of the more popular free tools for bug tracking is *Bugzilla* (`bugzilla.org`), written by the authors of the Mozilla and Firefox web browser. As an open-source project, Bugzilla has gradually accumulated a number of useful features to the point where it now rivals expensive bug-tracking software packages. Here are just a few of its many features:

- Customizable settings for a bug, including its priority, associated component, status, and so on
- E-mail notification of new bug reports or changes to an existing report

- Tracking of dependencies between bugs and resolution of duplicate bugs
- Reporting and searching tools
- A web-based interface for filing and updating bugs

Figure 30.3 shows a bug being entered into a Bugzilla project that was set up for the second edition of this book. For my purposes, each chapter was input as a Bugzilla component. The filer of the bug can specify the severity of the bug (that is, how big of a deal it is). A summary and description are included to make it possible to search for the bug or list it in a report format.

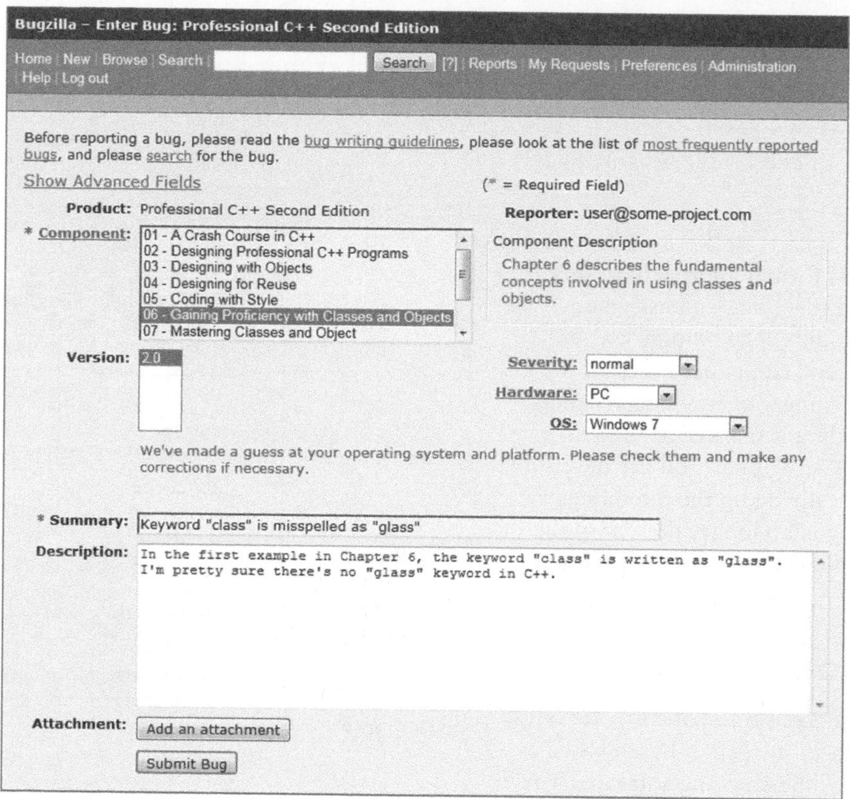

FIGURE 30.3

When writing a bug report, make sure to include as much information as possible in the report. For example, if your bug report is about an error you get, put the full error message in the bug report as text, not only as a screenshot. This allows other people to find your bug report if they come across the same error.

Bug-tracking tools like Bugzilla are essential components of a professional software development environment. In addition to supplying a central list of currently open bugs, bug-tracking tools provide an important archive of previous bugs and their fixes. A support engineer, for instance, might use the tool to search for a problem similar to one reported by a customer. If a fix was made, the support person will be able to tell the customer which version they need to update to or how to work around the problem.

UNIT TESTING

The only way to find bugs is through testing. One of the most important types of tests from a developer's point of view is the *unit test*. Unit tests are pieces of code that exercise specific functionality of a class or subsystem. These are the finest-grained tests that you could possibly write. Ideally, one or more unit tests should exist for every low-level task that your code can perform. For example, imagine that you are writing a math library that can perform addition and multiplication. Your suite of unit tests might contain the following tests:

- Test a simple addition like 1+2
- Test addition of large numbers
- Test addition of negative numbers
- Test addition of zero to a number
- Test the commutative property of addition
- Test a simple multiplication
- Test multiplication of large numbers
- Test multiplication of negative numbers
- Test multiplication with zero
- Test the commutative property of multiplication

Well-written unit tests protect you in many ways:

- They prove that a piece of functionality actually works. Until you have some code that actually makes use of your class, its behavior is a major unknown.
- They provide a first alert when a recently introduced change breaks something. This specific usage, called a *regression test*, is covered later in this chapter.
- When used as part of the development process, they force the developer to fix problems from the start. If you are prevented from checking in your code with failed unit tests, then you're forced to address problems right away.
- Unit tests let you try code before other code is in place. When you first started programming, you could write an entire program and then run it for the first time. Professional programs are too big for that approach, so you need to be able to test components in isolation.
- Last, but certainly not least, they provide an example of usage. Almost as a side effect, unit tests make great reference code for other programmers. If a co-worker wants to know how to perform matrix multiplication by using your math library, you can point her to the appropriate test.

Approaches to Unit Testing

It's hard to go wrong with unit tests, unless you don't write them or you write them poorly. In general, the more tests you have, the more coverage you have. The more coverage you have, the less likely it is for bugs to fall through the cracks and for you to have to tell your boss, or worse, your customer, "Oh, we never tested that."

There are several methodologies for writing unit tests most effectively. The Extreme Programming methodology, explained in Chapter 28, "Maximizing Software Engineering Methods," instructs its followers to write unit tests *before* writing code.

Writing tests first helps you to solidify the requirements for the component and to provide a metric that can be used to determine when coding is done. However, writing tests first can be tricky and requires diligence on the part of the programmer. For some programmers, it simply doesn't mesh well with their coding style. A less rigid approach is to *design* the tests before coding but *implement* them later in the process. This way, the programmer is still forced to understand the requirements of the module but doesn't have to write code that makes use of nonexistent classes.

In some groups, the author of a particular subsystem doesn't write the unit tests for that subsystem. The idea is that if you write the tests for your own code, you might subconsciously work around problems that you know about or only cover certain cases that you know your code handles well. In addition, it's sometimes difficult to get excited about finding bugs in code you just wrote, so you might only put in a half-hearted effort. Having one developer write unit tests for another developer's code requires a lot of extra overhead and coordination. When such coordination is accomplished, however, this approach helps guarantee more effective tests.

Code coverage is a metric to measure how much of the code is covered by unit tests. Such a metric allows you to maximize code coverage when writing unit tests. You can use a code coverage tool, such as `gcov` (`gcc.gnu.org/onlinedocs/gcc/Gcov.html`), that tells you what percentage of the code is called by unit tests. The idea is that a properly tested piece of code has unit tests to test all possible code paths that can be taken through that piece of code and thus reaches 100 percent unit-test code coverage. Different code coverage tools have different definitions of code coverage. Does the tool consider a line to be covered if it's an `if` statement written on a single line and the body was never executed? How does the tool define coverage for templates? Does the tool support branch coverage to make sure each possible direction of a branch is covered? Always do some research on any tool you intend to use.

The Unit Testing Process

The process of providing unit tests for your code starts from the beginning, long before any code is written. Keeping unit testability in mind during the design phase can influence the design decisions you make for your software. Even if you do not subscribe to the methodology of writing unit tests before you write code, you should at least take the time to consider what sorts of tests you will provide, even while still in the design phase. This way, you can break the task up into well-defined chunks, each of which has its own test-validated criteria. For example, if your task is to write a database access class, you might first write the functionality that inserts data into the database. Once that is fully tested with a suite of unit tests, you can continue to write the code to support updates, deletes, and selects, testing each piece as you go.

The following list of steps is a suggested approach for designing and implementing unit tests. As with any programming methodology, the best process is the one that yields the best results. I suggest that you experiment with different ways of using unit tests to discover what works best for you.

Define the Granularity of Your Tests

Writing unit tests takes time; there is no way around this. Software developers are often crunched for time. To reach deadlines, developers tend to skip writing unit tests, because they think they will finish faster that way. Unfortunately, this thinking does not take the whole picture into account. Omitting unit tests will backfire in the long run. The earlier a bug is detected in the software development process, the less it costs. If a developer finds a bug during unit testing, it can be fixed immediately, before anyone else encounters it. However, if the bug is discovered by QA, then it becomes a much costlier bug. The bug can cause an extra development cycle, requiring bug management; it has to go back to the development team for a fix and then back to QA to verify the fix. If a bug slips through the QA process and finds its way to the customer, then it becomes even more expensive.

The *granularity* of tests refers to their scope. As the following table illustrates, you can initially unit test a database class with just a few test functions and then gradually add more tests to ensure that everything works as it should:

LARGE-GRAINED TESTS	MEDIUM-GRAINED TESTS	FINE-GRAINED TESTS
`testConnection()`	`testConnectionDropped()`	`testConnectionThroughHTTP()`
`testInsert()`	`testInsertBadData()`	`testConnectionLocal()`
`testUpdate()`	`testInsertStrings()`	`testConnectionErrorBadHost()`
`testDelete()`	`testInsertIntegers()`	`testConnectionErrorServerBusy()`
`testSelect()`	`testUpdateStrings()`	`testInsertWideCharacters()`
	`testUpdateIntegers()`	`testInsertLargeData()`
	`testDeleteNonexistentRow()`	`testInsertMalformed()`
	`testSelectComplicated()`	`testUpdateWideCharacters()`
	`testSelectMalformed()`	`testUpdateLargeData()`
		`testUpdateMalformed()`
		`testDeleteWithoutPermissions()`
		`testDeleteThenUpdate()`
		`testSelectNested()`
		`testSelectWideCharacters()`
		`testSelectLargeData()`

As you can see, each successive column brings in more-specific tests. As you move from large-grained tests to more finely grained tests, you start to consider error conditions, different input data sets, and different modes of operation.

Of course, the decisions you make initially when choosing the granularity of your tests are not set in stone. Perhaps the database class is just being written as a proof of concept and might not even be used. A few simple tests may be adequate now, and you can always add more later. Or perhaps the use cases will change at a later date. For example, the database class might not initially have been written with international characters in mind. Once such features are added, they should be tested with specific targeted unit tests.

Consider the unit tests to be part of the actual implementation of a feature. When you make a modification, don't just modify the tests so that they continue to work (although of course you should do this too). Write new tests and re-evaluate the existing ones. When bugs are uncovered and fixed, add new unit tests that specifically test those fixes, called regression tests.

> **WARNING** *Unit tests are part of the subsystem that they are testing. As you enhance and refine the subsystem, enhance and refine the tests.*

Brainstorm the Individual Tests

Over time, you will gain an intuition for which aspects of a piece of code should turn into a unit test. Certain functions or inputs will just feel like they should be tested. This intuition is gained through trial and error and by looking at unit tests that other people in your group have written. It should be pretty easy to pick out which programmers are the best unit testers. Their tests tend to be organized and frequently modified.

Until unit test creation becomes second nature, approach the task of figuring out which tests to write by brainstorming. To get some ideas flowing, consider the following questions:

- What are the things that this piece of code was written to do?
- What are the typical ways each function would be called?
- What preconditions of the functions could be violated by the caller?
- How could each function be misused?
- What kinds of data are you expecting as input?
- What kinds of data are you not expecting as input?
- What are the edge cases or exceptional conditions?

You don't need to write formal answers to those questions (unless your manager is a particularly fervent devotee of this book or of certain testing methodologies), but they should help you generate some ideas for unit tests. The table of tests for the database class contained test functions, each of which arose from one of these questions.

Once you have generated ideas for some of the tests you would like to use, consider how you might organize them into categories; the breakdown of tests will fall into place. In the database class example, the tests could be split into the following categories:

- Basic tests
- Error tests
- Localization tests
- Bad input tests
- Complicated tests

Splitting your tests into categories makes them easier to identify and augment. It might also make it easier to realize which aspects of the code are well tested and which could use a few more unit tests.

> **WARNING** *It's easy to write a massive number of simple tests, but don't forget about the more complicated cases!*

Create Sample Data and Results

The most common trap to fall into when writing unit tests is to match the test to the behavior of the code, instead of using the test to validate the code. If you write a unit test that performs a database select for a piece of data that is definitely in the database, and the test fails, is it a problem with the code or a problem with the test? It's often easier to assume that the code is right and to modify the test to match. This approach is usually wrong.

To avoid this pitfall, you should understand the inputs to the test and the expected output before you try it. This is sometimes easier said than done. For example, say you wrote some code to encrypt an arbitrary block of text using a particular key. A reasonable unit test would take a fixed string of text and pass it in to the encryption module. Then, it would examine the result to see if it was correctly encrypted.

When you go to write such a test, it is tempting to try the behavior with the encryption module first and see the result. If it looks reasonable, you might write a test to look for that value. Doing so really doesn't prove anything, however! You haven't actually tested the code; you've just written a test that guarantees it will continue to return that same value. Oftentimes, writing the test requires some real work; you would need to encrypt the text independently of your encryption module to get an accurate result. If you don't know the encryption algorithm being used, e.g., because it's coming from a third-party library, then you can at least write tests such as `decrypt(encrypt(x))==x` and `encrypt(a)!=encrypt(b)`.

> **WARNING** *Decide on the correct output for your test before you ever run the test.*

Write the Tests

The exact code behind a test varies depending on what type of test framework you have in place. One framework, the Microsoft Visual C++ Testing Framework, is discussed later in this chapter. Independent of the actual implementation, however, the following guidelines will help ensure effective tests:

- Make sure that you're testing only one thing in each test. That way, if a test fails, it will point to a specific piece of functionality.
- Be specific inside the test. Did the test fail because an exception was thrown or because the wrong value was returned?
- Use logging extensively inside of test code. If the test fails someday, you will have some insight into what happened.

- Avoid tests that depend on earlier tests or are otherwise interrelated. Tests should be as atomic and isolated as possible.
- If the test requires the use of other subsystems, consider writing *stubs* or *mocks* to simulate those subsystems. A stub or mock implements the same interface as the subsystem it simulates. They can then be used in place of any concrete subsystem implementation. For example, if a unit test requires a database but that database is not the subsystem being tested by that unit test, then a stub or mock can implement the database interface and simulate a real database. This way, running the unit test does not require a connection to a real database, and errors in the real database implementation won't have any impact on this specific unit test. In fact, you can use a mock to simulate error conditions that might be difficult or impossible to reliably achieve using the real database!
- Code reviewers must not only review the code but review the unit tests as well. When you do a code review, tell the other engineer where you think additional tests could be added.

As you will see later in this chapter, unit tests are usually small and simple pieces of code. In most cases, writing a single unit test will take only a few minutes, making unit tests one of the most productive uses of your time.

Run the Tests

When you're done writing a test, you should run it right away before the anticipation of the results becomes too much to bear. The joy of a screen full of passing unit tests shouldn't be minimized. For most programmers, this is the easiest way to see quantitative data that declares your code useful and (as far as you know) correct.

Even if you adopt the methodology of writing tests before writing code, you should still run the tests immediately after they are written. This way, you can prove to yourself that the tests fail initially. Once the code is in place, you have tangible data that shows that it accomplished what it was supposed to accomplish.

It's unlikely that every test you write will have the expected result the first time. In theory, if you are writing tests before writing code, all of your tests should fail. If one passes, either the code magically appeared or there is a problem with the test. If the coding is done and tests still fail (some would say that if tests fail, the coding is actually *not* done), there are two possibilities: the code could be wrong, or the tests could be wrong.

Running unit tests must be automated. This can be done in several ways. One option is to have a dedicated system that automatically runs all unit tests after every continuous integration build, or at least once a night. Such a system must send out e-mails to notify developers when unit tests are failing. Another option is to set up your local development environment so that unit tests are executed every time you compile your code. For this, unit tests should be kept small and very efficient. If you do have longer-running unit tests, put these separate, and let these be tested by a dedicated test system.

Unit Testing in Action

Now that you've read about unit testing in theory, it's time to actually write some tests. The following example draws on the object pool implementation from Chapter 29, "Writing Efficient C++." As a brief recap, the object pool is a class that can be used to avoid allocating an excessive number of objects. By keeping track of already-allocated objects, the pool acts as a broker between code that needs a certain type of object and such objects that already have been allocated.

The public interface for the `ObjectPool` class template is as follows; consult Chapter 29 for all the details:

```
export
template <typename T, typename Allocator = std::allocator<T>>
class ObjectPool final
{
    public:
        ObjectPool() = default;
        explicit ObjectPool(const Allocator& allocator);
        ~ObjectPool();

        // Prevent move construction and move assignment.
        ObjectPool(ObjectPool&&) = delete;
        ObjectPool& operator=(ObjectPool&&) = delete;

        // Prevent copy construction and copy assignment.
        ObjectPool(const ObjectPool&) = delete;
        ObjectPool& operator=(const ObjectPool&) = delete;

        // Reserves and returns an object from the pool. Arguments can be
        // provided which are perfectly forwarded to a constructor of T.
        template <typename... Args>
        std::shared_ptr<T> acquireObject(Args&&... args);
};
```

Introducing the Microsoft Visual C++ Testing Framework

Microsoft Visual C++ comes with a built-in testing framework. The advantage of using a unit testing framework is that it allows the developer to focus on writing tests instead of dealing with setting up tests, building logic around tests, and gathering results. The following discussion is written for Visual C++ 2022.

> **NOTE** *If you are not using Visual C++, there are a number of open-source unit testing frameworks available.* Google Test *(`github.com/google/googletest`) is one such framework for C++, and the* Boost Test Library *(`www.boost.org/doc/libs/1_82_0/libs/test/`) is another one. They both include a number of helpful utilities for test developers and options to control the automatic output of results.*

To get started with the *Visual C++ Testing Framework*, you have to create a test project. The following steps explain how to test the `ObjectPool` class template:

1. Start Visual C++, create a new project, select Native Unit Test Project, and click Next.
2. Give the project a name and click Create.

3. The wizard creates a new test project, which includes a file called `<ProjectName>.cpp`. Select this file in the Solution Explorer and delete it, because you will add your own files. If the Solution Explorer docking window is not visible, go to View ➪ Solution Explorer.
4. Right-click your project in the Solution Explorer and click Properties. Go to Configuration Properties ➪ C/C++ ➪ Precompiled Headers, set the Precompiled Header option to Not Using Precompiled Headers, and click OK. Additionally, select the `pch.cpp` and `pch.h` files in the Solution Explorer and delete them. Using precompiled headers is a feature of Visual C++ to improve build times but is not used for this test project.
5. Add empty files called `ObjectPoolTest.h` and `ObjectPoolTest.cpp` to the test project.

Now you are ready to start adding unit tests to the code.

The most common technique is to divide your unit tests into logical groups of tests, called *test classes*. You will now create a test class called `ObjectPoolTest`. The basic code in `ObjectPoolTest.h` for getting started is as follows:

```
#pragma once
#include <CppUnitTest.h>

TEST_CLASS(ObjectPoolTest)
{
    public:
};
```

This code defines a test class called `ObjectPoolTest`, but the syntax is a bit different compared to standard C++. This is so that the framework can automatically discover all the tests.

If you need to perform any tasks that need to happen prior to running the tests defined in a test class or to perform any cleanup after the tests have been executed, then you can implement an initialize and a cleanup member function. Here is an example:

```
TEST_CLASS(ObjectPoolTest)
{
    public:
        TEST_CLASS_INITIALIZE(setUp);
        TEST_CLASS_CLEANUP(tearDown);
};
```

Because the tests for the `ObjectPool` class template are relatively simple and isolated, empty definitions will suffice for `setUp()` and `tearDown()`, or you can simply remove them altogether. If you do need them, the beginning stage of the `ObjectPoolTest.cpp` source file is as follows:

```
#include "ObjectPoolTest.h"

void ObjectPoolTest::setUp() { }
void ObjectPoolTest::tearDown() { }
```

That's all the initial code you need to start developing unit tests.

> **NOTE** *In real-world scenarios, you usually divide the testing code and the code you want to test into separate projects. In the interest of keeping this example succinct, I have not done this here.*

Writing the First Test

Because this may be your first exposure to the Visual C++ Testing Framework, or to unit tests at large, the first test will be a simple one. It tests whether 0 < 1.

An individual unit test is just a member function of a test class. To create a simple test, add its declaration to the `ObjectPoolTest.h` file:

```
TEST_CLASS(ObjectPoolTest)
{
    public:
        TEST_CLASS_INITIALIZE(setUp);
        TEST_CLASS_CLEANUP(tearDown);

        TEST_METHOD(testSimple);  // Your first test!
};
```

The implementation of the `testSimple` test uses `Assert::IsTrue()`, defined in the `Microsoft::VisualStudio::CppUnitTestFramework` namespace, to perform the actual test. `Assert::IsTrue()` validates that a given expression returns `true`. If the expression returns `false`, the test fails. `Assert` provides many more helper functions, such as `AreEqual()`, `IsNull()`, `Fail()`, `ExpectException()`, and so on. In the `testSimple` case, the test claims that 0 is less than 1. Here is the updated `ObjectPoolTest.cpp` file:

```
#include "ObjectPoolTest.h"

using namespace Microsoft::VisualStudio::CppUnitTestFramework;

void ObjectPoolTest::setUp() { }
void ObjectPoolTest::tearDown() { }

void ObjectPoolTest::testSimple()
{
    Assert::IsTrue(0 < 1);
}
```

That's it. Of course, most of your unit tests will do something a bit more interesting than a simple assert. As you will see, the common pattern is to perform some sort of calculation and then assert that the result is the value you expect. With the Visual C++ Testing Framework, you don't even need to worry about exceptions; the framework catches and reports them as necessary.

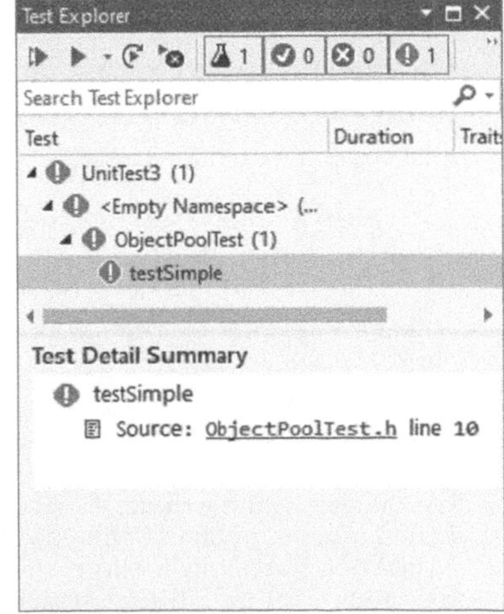

FIGURE 30.4

Building and Running Tests

Build your solution by clicking Build ➪ Build Solution, and open the Test Explorer (Test ➪ Test Explorer), shown in Figure 30.4.

After having built the solution, the Test Explorer automatically displays all discovered unit tests. In this case, it displays the `testSimple` unit test. You can run all tests by clicking the Run All Tests button in the upper-left corner of the window. When you do that, the Test Explorer shows whether the unit tests succeed or fail. In this case, the single unit test succeeds, as shown in Figure 30.5.

If you modify the code to assert that 1 < 0, the test fails, and the Test Explorer reports the failure, as shown in Figure 30.6.

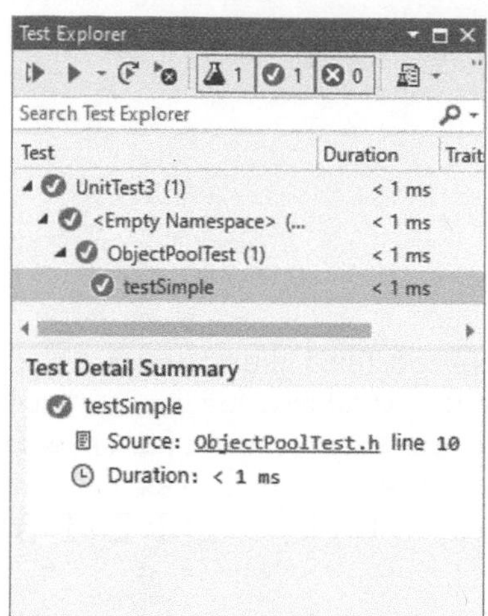

FIGURE 30.5

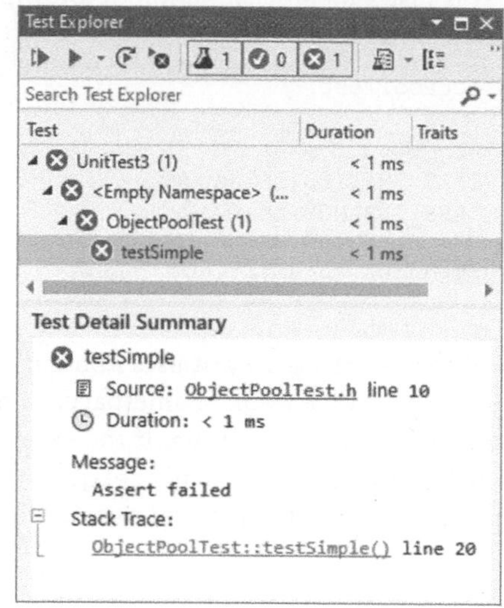

FIGURE 30.6

The lower part of the Test Explorer window displays useful information related to the selected unit test. In case of a failed unit test, it tells you exactly what failed. In this case, it says that an assertion failed. There is also a stack trace that was captured at the time the failure occurred. You can click the hyperlinks in that stack trace to jump directly to the offending line—very useful for debugging.

Negative Tests

You can write *negative tests*, tests that do something that *should* fail. For example, you can write a negative test to test that a certain function throws an expected exception. The Visual C++ Testing Framework provides the `Assert::ExpectException()` function to handle expected exceptions. For example, the following unit test uses `ExpectException()` to execute a lambda expression that throws an `std::invalid_argument` exception, defined in `<stdexcept>`[1]. The template type parameter for `ExpectException()` specifies the type of exception to expect.

```
void ObjectPoolTest::testException()
{
    Assert::ExpectException<std::invalid_argument>(
        []{ throw std::invalid_argument { "Error" }; });
}
```

[1] At the time of this writing, Visual C++ 2022 contained a bug which prevents combining `#include <CppUnitTest.h>` and `import std;`. As a workaround, replace `import std;` statements with `#include` statements for the required header files, e.g., `#include <stdexcept>`. See the downloadable source code archive for the full set of required header files in the different source code files.

Adding the Real Tests

Now that the framework is all set up and a simple test is working, it's time to turn your attention to the ObjectPool class template and write some code that actually tests it. All of the following tests will be added to ObjectPoolTest.h and ObjectPoolTest.cpp, just like the earlier initial tests.

First, copy the ObjectPool.cppm module interface file next to the ObjectPoolTest.h file you created, and then add it to the project. ObjectPool.cppm uses C++23 functionality, which is not yet enabled by default in Visual C++ 2022 at the time of this writing. To enable it, open the project properties, go to Configuration Properties ➪ General, and set the C++ Language Standard to "Preview - Features from the Latest C++ Working Draft." In a future version of Visual C++, you will be able to set this option to "ISO C++23 Standard."

Before you can write the tests, you'll need a helper class to use with the ObjectPool. The ObjectPool creates objects of a certain type and hands them out to the caller as requested. Some of the tests will need to check if a retrieved object is the same as a previously retrieved object. One way to do this is to create a pool of serial objects—objects that have a monotonically increasing serial number. The following code shows the Serial.cppm module interface file defining such a class:

```
export module serial;

export class Serial
{
    public:
        // A new object gets a next serial number.
        Serial() : m_serialNumber { ms_nextSerial++ } { }
        unsigned getSerialNumber() const { return m_serialNumber; }
    private:
        static inline unsigned ms_nextSerial { 0 }; // The first serial number is 0
        unsigned m_serialNumber { 0 };
};
```

Now, on to the tests! As an initial sanity check, you might want a test that creates an object pool. If any exceptions are thrown during creation, the Visual C++ Testing Framework will report an error. The code is written according to the *AAA principle*: Arrange, Act, Assert; the test first sets up everything for the test to run, then does some work, and finally asserts the expected result. This is also often called the *if-when-then principle*. I recommend adding comments to your unit test that actually start with IF, WHEN, and THEN so the three phases of a test clearly stand out.

```
void ObjectPoolTest::testCreation()
{
    // IF nothing

    // WHEN creating an ObjectPool
    ObjectPool<Serial> myPool;

    // THEN no exception is thrown
}
```

Don't forget to add a TEST_METHOD(testCreation); statement to the header file. This holds for all subsequent tests as well. You also need to add an import declaration for the object_pool and serial modules to the ObjectPoolTest.cpp source file.

```
import object_pool;
import serial;
```

A second test, `testAcquire()`, tests a specific piece of public functionality: the ability of the `ObjectPool` to give out an object. In this case, there is not much to assert. To prove the validity of the resulting `Serial` object, the test asserts that its serial number is greater than or equal to zero.

```
void ObjectPoolTest::testAcquire()
{
    // IF an ObjectPool has been created for Serial objects
    ObjectPool<Serial> myPool;
    // WHEN acquiring an object
    auto serial { myPool.acquireObject() };
    // THEN we get a valid Serial object
    Assert::IsTrue(serial->getSerialNumber() >= 0);
}
```

The next test is a bit more interesting. The `ObjectPool` should not give out the same `Serial` object twice. This test checks the exclusivity property of the `ObjectPool` by retrieving a number of objects from the pool. The serial numbers of all retrieved objects are stored in a `set`. If the pool is properly dishing out unique objects, none of their serial numbers should match.

```
void ObjectPoolTest::testExclusivity()
{
    // IF an ObjectPool has been created for Serial objects
    ObjectPool<Serial> myPool;
    // WHEN acquiring several objects from the pool
    const size_t numberOfObjectsToRetrieve { 20 };
    set<unsigned> seenSerialNumbers;

    for (size_t i { 0 }; i < numberOfObjectsToRetrieve; ++i) {
        auto nextSerial { myPool.acquireObject() };
        seenSerialNumbers.insert(nextSerial->getSerialNumber());
    }

    // THEN all retrieved serial numbers are different.
    Assert::AreEqual(numberOfObjectsToRetrieve, seenSerialNumbers.size());
}
```

The final test (for now) checks the release functionality. Once an object is released, the `ObjectPool` can give it out again. The pool shouldn't allocate additional objects until it has *recycled* all released objects.

The test first acquires 10 `Serial` objects from the pool, stores them in a `vector` to keep them alive, and records the raw pointer of each acquired `Serial`. Once all 10 objects have been retrieved, they are released back to the pool.

The second phase of the test again retrieves 10 objects from the pool and stores them in a `vector` to keep them alive. All these retrieved objects must have a raw pointer that has already been seen during the first phase of the test. This validates that objects are properly reused by the pool.

```
void ObjectPoolTest::testRelease()
{
    // IF an ObjectPool has been created for Serial objects
    ObjectPool<Serial> myPool;
    // AND we acquired and released 10 objects from the pool, while
```

```
    //     remembering their raw pointers
    const size_t numberOfObjectsToRetrieve { 10 };
    // A set to remember all raw pointers that have been handed out by the pool.
    set<Serial*> retrievedSerialPointers;
    vector<shared_ptr<Serial>> retrievedSerials;
    for (size_t i { 0 }; i < numberOfObjectsToRetrieve; ++i) {
        auto object { myPool.acquireObject() };
        retrievedSerialPointers.push_back(object.get());
        // Add the retrieved Serial to the vector to keep it 'alive'.
        retrievedSerials.push_back(object);
    }
    // Release all objects back to the pool.
    retrievedSerials.clear();

    // The above loop has created 10 Serial objects, with 10 different
    // addresses, and released all 10 Serial objects back to the pool.

    // WHEN again retrieving 10 objects from the pool, and
    //     remembering their raw pointers.
    set<Serial*> newlyRetrievedSerialPointers;
    for (size_t i { 0 }; i < numberOfObjectsToRetrieve; ++i) {
        auto object { myPool.acquireObject() };
        newlyRetrievedSerialPointers.push_back(object.get());
        // Add the retrieved Serial to the vector to keep it 'alive'.
        retrievedSerials.push_back(object);
    }
    // Release all objects back to the pool.
    retrievedSerials.clear();

    // THEN all addresses of the 10 newly acquired objects must have been
    //     seen already during the first loop of acquiring 10 objects.
    //     This makes sure objects are properly re-used by the pool.
    Assert::IsTrue(retrievedSerialPointers == newlyRetrievedSerialPointers);
}
```

If you add all these tests and run them, the Test Explorer should look like Figure 30.7. Of course, if one or more tests fail, you are presented with the quintessential issue in unit testing: is it the test or the code that is broken?

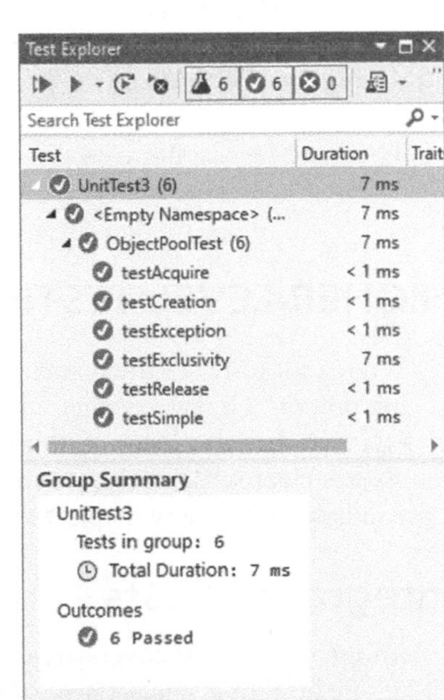

FIGURE 30.7

Debugging Tests

The Visual C++ Testing Framework makes it easy to debug unit tests that are failing. The Test Explorer shows a stack trace captured at the time a unit test failed, containing hyperlinks pointing directly to offending lines.

However, sometimes it is useful to run a unit test directly in the debugger so that you can inspect variables at run time, step through the code line by line, and so on. To do this, put a breakpoint on some line of code in a unit test. Then, right-click the unit test in the Test Explorer and click Debug. The testing framework starts running the selected tests in the debugger and breaks at your breakpoint. From then on, you can step through the code however you want.

Basking in the Glorious Light of Unit Test Results

The tests in the previous section should have given you a good idea of how to start writing professional-quality tests for real code. It's just the tip of the iceberg, though. The previous examples should help you think of additional tests that you could write for the `ObjectPool` class template.

For example, you could add a `capacity()` member function to `ObjectPool` that returns the sum of the number of objects that have been handed out and the number of objects that are still available without allocating a new chunk of memory. This is similar to the `capacity()` member function of `vector` that returns the total number of elements that can be stored in a `vector` without reallocation. Once you have such a member function, you can include a test that verifies that the pool always grows by double the number of elements compared to the previous time the pool grew.

There is no end to the number of unit tests you could write for a given piece of code, and that's the best thing about unit tests. If you find yourself wondering how your code might react to a certain situation, that's a unit test. If a particular aspect of your subsystem seems to be presenting problems, increase unit test coverage of that particular area. Even if you simply want to put yourself in the client's shoes to see what it's like to work with your class, writing unit tests is a great way to get a different perspective. You might even decide to write your unit tests before you implement your code. That way, you start using your planned interface before it is implemented, which could uncover use cases and error conditions that you didn't think about before.

FUZZ TESTING

Fuzz testing, also known as *fuzzing*, involves a *fuzzer* that automatically generates random input data for a program or component to try to find unhandled edge cases. Typically, a recipe is provided that specifies how input data needs to be structured so it can be used as input for the program. If clearly wrongly structured input is provided to a program, its input data parser will likely immediately reject it. A fuzzer's job then is to try to generate input data that is not obviously wrongly structured, so it won't be rejected immediately by the program, but that could trigger some faulty logic further along during the execution of the program. Since a fuzzer generates random input data, it requires a lot of resources to cover the entire input space. An option is to run such fuzz testing scenarios in a cloud. There are several libraries available for implementing fuzz testing, for example libFuzzer (`llvm.org/docs/LibFuzzer.html`) and honggfuzz (`github.com/google/honggfuzz`).

HIGHER-LEVEL TESTING

While unit tests are the best first line of defense against bugs, they are only part of the larger testing process. Higher-level tests focus on how pieces of the product work together, as opposed to the relatively narrow focus of unit tests. In a way, higher-level tests are more challenging to write because it's less clear what tests need to be written. Still, you cannot really claim that the program works until you have tested how its pieces work together.

Integration Tests

An *integration test* covers areas where components meet. Unlike a unit test, which generally acts on the level of a single class, an integration test usually involves two or more classes. Integration tests excel at testing interactions between two components, often written by two different programmers. In fact, the process of writing an integration test often reveals important incompatibilities between designs.

Sample Integration Tests

Because there are no hard-and-fast rules to determine what integration tests you should write, some examples might help you get a sense of when integration tests are useful. The following scenarios depict cases where an integration test is appropriate, but they do not cover every possible case. Just as with unit tests, over time you will refine your intuition for useful integration tests.

A JSON-Based File Serializer

Suppose that your project includes a persistence layer that is used to save certain types of objects to disk and to read them back in. The hip way to serialize data is to use the JSON format, so a logical breakdown of components might include a JSON conversion layer sitting on top of a custom file API. Both of these components can be thoroughly unit tested. The JSON layer can have unit tests that ensure that different types of objects are correctly converted to JSON and populated from JSON. The file API can have tests that read, write, update, and delete files on disk.

When these modules start to work together, integration tests are appropriate. At the least, you should have an integration test that saves an object to disk through the JSON layer and then reads it back in and does a comparison to the original. Because the test covers both modules, it is a basic integration test.

Readers and Writers to a Shared Resource

Imagine a program that contains a data structure shared by different components. For example, a stock-trading program can have a queue of buy-and-sell requests. Components related to receiving stock transaction requests can add orders to the queue, and components related to performing stock trades can take data off the queue. You can unit test the heck out of the queue class, but until it is tested with the actual components that will be using it, you really don't know if any of your assumptions are wrong.

A good integration test uses the stock request components and the stock trade components as clients of the queue class. You can write some sample orders and make sure that they successfully enter and exit the queue through the client components.

Wrapper Around a Third-Party Library

Integration tests do not always need to occur at integration points in your own code. Many times, integration tests are written to test the interaction between your code and a third-party library.

For example, you may be using a database connection library to talk to a relational database system. Perhaps you built an object-oriented wrapper around the library that adds support for connection caching or provides a friendlier interface. This is an important integration point to test because, even though the wrapper probably provides a more useful interface to the database, it introduces possible misuse of the original library.

In other words, writing a wrapper is a good thing, but writing a wrapper that introduces bugs will be a disaster.

Integration Testing Techniques

When it comes to actually writing integration tests, there is often a fine line between integration and unit tests. If a unit test is modified so that it touches another component, is it suddenly an integration test? In a way, the answer is moot because a good test is a good test, regardless of the type of test. I recommend you use the concepts of integration and unit testing as two *approaches* to testing, but avoid getting caught up in labeling the category of every single test.

In terms of implementation, integration tests are often written by using a unit testing framework, further blurring their distinction. As it turns out, unit testing frameworks provide an easy way to write a yes/no test and produce useful results. Whether the test is looking at a single unit of functionality or the intersection of two components hardly makes a difference from the framework's point of view.

However, for performance reasons or organizational reasons, you may want to attempt to separate unit tests from integration tests. For example, your group may decide that everybody must run integration tests before checking in new code, but be a bit laxer on running unrelated unit tests. Separating the two types of tests also increases the value of results. If a test failure occurs within the JSON class tests, it will be clear that it's a bug in that class, not in the interaction between that class and the file API.

System Tests

System tests operate at an even higher level than integration tests. These tests examine the program as a whole. System tests often make use of a *virtual user* that simulates a human being working with the program. Of course, the virtual user must be programmed with a script of actions to perform. Other system tests rely on scripts or a fixed set of inputs and expected outputs.

Much like unit and integration tests, an individual system test performs a specific test and expects a specific result. It is not uncommon to use system tests to make sure that different features work in combination with one another.

In theory, a fully system-tested program would contain a test for every permutation of every feature. This approach quickly grows unwieldy, but you should still make an effort to test many features in combination. For example, a graphics program could have a system test that imports an image, rotates it, performs a blur filter, converts it to black and white, and then saves it. The test would compare the saved image to a file that contains the expected result.

Unfortunately, few specific rules can be stated about system tests because they are highly dependent on the actual application. For applications that process files with no user interaction, system tests can be written much like unit and integration tests. For graphical programs, a virtual user approach may be best. For server applications, you might need to build stub clients that simulate network traffic. The important part is that you are actually testing real use of the program, not just a piece of it.

Regression Tests

Regression testing is more of a testing concept than a specific type of test. The idea is that once a feature works, developers tend to put it aside and assume that it will continue to work. Unfortunately, new features and other code changes often conspire to break previously working functionality.

Regression tests are often put in place as a sanity check for features that are, more or less, complete and working. If the regression test is well written, it will cease to pass when a change is introduced that breaks the feature.

If your company has an army of quality-assurance testers, regression testing may take the form of manual testing. The tester acts as a user would and goes through a series of steps, gradually testing every feature that worked in the previous release. This approach is thorough and accurate if carefully performed, but is not particularly scalable.

At the other extreme, you could build a completely automated system that performs each function as a virtual user. This would be a scripting challenge, though several commercial and noncommercial packages exist to ease the scripting of various types of applications.

A middle ground is known as *smoke testing*. Some tests will only test a subset of the most important features that should work. The idea is that if something is broken, it should show up right away. If smoke tests pass, they could be followed by more rigorous manual or automated testing. The term *smoke testing* was introduced a long time ago, in electronics. After a circuit was built, with different components like vacuum tubes, resistors, and so on, the question was, "Is it assembled correctly?" A solution was to "plug it in, turn it on, and see if smoke comes out." If smoke came out, the design might be wrong, or the assembly might be wrong. By seeing what part went up in smoke, the error could be determined.

Some bugs are like nightmares: they are both terrifying and recurring. Recurring bugs are frustrating and a poor use of engineering resources. To prevent bugs from recurring, you should write regression tests for bugs that you fix. By writing a test for a bug fix, you both prove that the bug is fixed and set up an alert that is triggered if the bug ever comes back—for example, if your change is rolled back or otherwise undone, or if two branches are not merged correctly into the main development branch. When a regression test of a previously fixed bug fails, it should be easy to fix because the regression test can refer to the original bug number and describe how it was fixed the first time.

TIPS FOR SUCCESSFUL TESTING

As a software engineer, your role in testing may range anywhere from basic unit testing responsibility to complete management of an automated test system. Because testing roles and styles vary so much, here are several tips from my experience that may help you in different testing situations:

- Spend some time designing your automated test system. A system that runs constantly throughout the day will detect failures quickly. A system that sends e-mails to engineers automatically or sits in the middle of the room loudly playing show tunes when a failure occurs, will result in increased visibility of problems.
- Don't forget about stress testing. Even if a full suite of unit tests passes for your database access class, it could still fall down when used by several dozen threads simultaneously. You should test your product under the most extreme conditions it could face in the real world.
- Test on a variety of platforms or a platform that closely mirrors the customer's system. One technique of testing on multiple platforms is to use a virtual machine environment that allows you to run several different platforms on the same physical machine.

- Some tests can be written to intentionally inject faults in a system. For example, you could write a test that deletes a file while it is being read, or that simulates a network outage during a network operation.
- Bugs and tests are closely related. Bug fixes should be proven by writing regression tests. A comment with a test could refer to the original bug number.
- Don't remove tests that are failing. When a co-worker is slaving over a bug and finds out you removed tests, he will come looking for you.

> **WARNING** *The most important tip I can give you is to remember that testing is part of software development. If you agree with that and accept it before you start coding, it won't be quite as unexpected when the feature is finished, but there is still more work to do to prove that it works.*

SUMMARY

This chapter covered the basic information that all professional programmers should know about testing. Unit testing in particular is the easiest and most effective way to increase the quality of your own code. Higher-level tests provide coverage of use cases, synchronicity between modules, and protection against regressions. No matter what your role is with regard to testing, you should now be able to confidently design, create, and review tests at various levels.

Now that you know how to find bugs, it's time to learn how to fix them. To that end, Chapter 31, "Conquering Debugging," covers techniques and strategies for effective debugging.

EXERCISES

By solving the following exercises, you can practice the material discussed in this chapter. Solutions to all exercises are available with the code download on the book's website at `www.wiley.com/go/proc++6e`. However, if you are stuck on an exercise, first reread parts of this chapter to try to find an answer yourself before looking at the solution from the website.

Exercise 30-1: What are the three types of testing?

Exercise 30-2: Make a list of unit tests that you can think of for the following piece of code:

```
export class Foo
{
    public:
        // Constructs a Foo. Throws invalid_argument if a >= b.
        explicit Foo(int a, int b) : m_a { a }, m_b { b }
        {
            if (a >= b) {
                throw std::invalid_argument { "a should be less than b." };
            }
        }
```

```
        int getA() const { return m_a; }
        int getB() const { return m_b; }

    private:
        int m_a { 0 };
        int m_b { 0 };
};
```

Exercise 30-3: If you are using Visual C++, implement the unit tests that you've listed in Exercise 30-2 using the Visual C++ Testing Framework.

Exercise 30-4: Suppose you have written a function to calculate the factorial of a number. The factorial of a number *n*, written as *n*!, is the product of all numbers 1 to *n*. For example, 3! equals 1×2×3. You decide to follow the advice given in this chapter and to write unit tests for your code. You run the code to calculate 10!; it produces 36288000. You write a unit test that verifies that the code produces 36288000 when asked to calculate the factorial of 10. What do you think of such a unit test?

31 Conquering Debugging

WHAT'S IN THIS CHAPTER?

- The fundamental law of debugging, and bug taxonomies
- Tips for avoiding bugs
- How to plan for bugs
- The different kinds of memory errors
- How to use a debugger to pinpoint code causing a bug

WILEY.COM DOWNLOADS FOR THIS CHAPTER

Please note that all the code examples for this chapter are available as part of this chapter's code download on the book's website at `www.wiley.com/go/proc++6e` on the Download Code tab.

Your code will contain bugs. Every professional programmer would like to write bug-free code, but the reality is that few software engineers succeed in this endeavor. As computer users know, bugs are endemic in computer software. The software that you write is probably no exception. Therefore, unless you plan to bribe your co-workers into fixing all your bugs, you cannot be a professional C++ programmer without knowing how to debug C++ code. One factor that often distinguishes experienced programmers from novices is their debugging skills.

Despite the obvious importance of debugging, it is rarely given enough attention in courses and books. Debugging seems to be the type of skill that everyone wants you to know, but no one knows how to teach. This chapter attempts to provide concrete debugging guidelines and techniques.

This chapter starts with the fundamental law of debugging and bug taxonomies, followed by tips for avoiding bugs. Techniques for planning for bugs include error logging, debug traces, assertions, and crash dumps. Specific tips are given for debugging the problems that arise, including techniques for reproducing bugs and debugging reproducible bugs, nonreproducible bugs, memory errors, and multithreaded programs. The chapter concludes with a step-by-step debugging example.

THE FUNDAMENTAL LAW OF DEBUGGING

The first rule of debugging is to be honest with yourself and admit that your code will contain bugs! This realistic assessment enables you to put your best effort into preventing bugs from crawling into your code in the first place, while you simultaneously include the necessary features to make debugging as easy as possible.

> **WARNING** *The fundamental law of debugging states that you should avoid bugs when you're coding, but plan for bugs in your code.*

BUG TAXONOMIES

A *bug* in a computer program is incorrect run-time behavior. This undesirable behavior includes both *catastrophic* and *noncatastrophic bugs*. Examples of catastrophic bugs are program crashes, data corruption, operating system failures, or some other horrific outcome. A catastrophic bug can also manifest itself external to the software or computer system running the software; for example, medical software might contain a catastrophic bug causing a massive radiation overdose to a patient. Noncatastrophic bugs are bugs that cause the program to behave incorrectly in more subtle ways; for example, a web browser might return the wrong web page, or a spreadsheet application might calculate the standard deviation of a column incorrectly. These are also called *logical bugs*.

There are also *cosmetic bugs*, where something is visually not correct, but otherwise works correctly. For example, a button in a user interface is kept enabled when it shouldn't be—but clicking it does nothing. All computations are perfectly correct, the program does not crash, but it doesn't look as "nice" as it should.

The underlying cause, or *root cause*, of a bug is the mistake in the program that causes this incorrect behavior. The process of debugging a program includes both determining the root cause of the bug and fixing the code so that the bug will not occur again.

AVOID BUGS

It's impossible to write completely bug-free code, so debugging skills are important. However, a few tips can help you to minimize the number of bugs:

- **Read this book from cover to cover:** Learn the C++ language intimately, especially pointers and memory management. Then, recommend this book to your friends and co-workers so they avoid bugs too.
- **Design before you code:** Starting to write code for a feature without thinking about the design at all tends to lead to convoluted designs that are harder to understand and are more

error prone. It also makes you more likely to omit possible edge cases and error conditions. Thus, before you start writing code, think about the design. And, once you start the implementation, don't be afraid to change the design if you come across an issue that you didn't think of before. There is nothing wrong with making changes to the design once you start the implementation.

- **Do code reviews:** In a professional environment, every single line of code should be peer reviewed. Sometimes it takes a fresh perspective to notice problems.
- **Test, test, and test again:** Thoroughly test your code, and have *others* test your code! They are more likely to find problems you haven't thought of.
- **Write automated unit tests:** Unit tests are designed to test isolated functionality. You should write unit tests for all implemented features. Run these unit tests automatically as part of your continuous integration setup, or automatically after each local compilation. Chapter 30, "Becoming Adept at Testing," discusses unit testing in detail.
- **Expect error conditions, and handle them appropriately:** In particular, plan for and handle errors when working with files and network connections. They will occur. See chapters 13, "Demystifying C++ I/O," and 14, "Handling Errors."
- **Use smart pointers to avoid resource leaks:** Smart pointers automatically free resources when they are not needed anymore.
- **Don't ignore compiler warnings:** Configure your compiler to compile with a high warning level. Do not blindly ignore warnings. Ideally, you should enable an option in your compiler to treat warnings as errors. This forces you to address each warning immediately. With GCC or Clang you can pass `-Werror` to the compiler to treat all warnings as errors. In Visual C++, open the properties of your project, go to Configuration Properties ➪ C/C++ ➪ General, and enable the option Treat Warnings As Errors.
- **Use static code analysis:** A static code analyzer helps to pinpoint problems in your code by analyzing your source code. Ideally, static code analysis is done in real time while typing code in your integrated development environment (IDE) to detect problems early. It can also be set up to run automatically by your build process. There are quite a few different analyzers available on the Internet, both free and commercial.
- **Use good coding style:** Strive for readability and clarity, use meaningful names, don't use abbreviations, add code comments (not only interface comments), use the `override` and `explicit` keywords, and so on. This makes it easier for other people to understand your code.

PLAN FOR BUGS

Your programs should contain functionality that enables easier debugging when the inevitable bugs arise. This section describes some examples of such functionality and presents sample implementations, where appropriate, that you can incorporate into your own programs.

Error Logging

Imagine this scenario: You have just released a new version of your flagship product, and one of the first users reports that the program "stopped working." You attempt to pry more information from the user and eventually discover that the program died in the middle of an operation. The user can't quite remember what he was doing or if there were any error messages. How will you debug this problem?

Now imagine the same scenario, but in addition to the limited information from the user, you are also able to examine the error log on the user's computer. In the log you see a message from your program that says, "Error: unable to open config.xml file." Looking at the code near the spot where that error message was generated, you find a line in which you read from the file without checking whether the file was opened successfully. You've found the root cause of your bug!

Error logging is the process of writing error messages to persistent storage so that they will be available following an application, or even machine, crash. Despite the example scenario, you might still have doubts about this strategy. Won't it be obvious by your program's behavior if it encounters errors? Won't the user notice if something goes wrong? As the preceding example shows, user reports are not always accurate or complete. In addition, many programs, such as the operating system kernel and long-running daemons like `inetd` (internet service daemon) or `syslogd` on Unix, are not interactive and run unattended on a machine. The only way these programs can communicate with users is through error logging. In many cases, a program might also want to automatically recover from certain errors and hide those errors from the user. Still, having logs of those errors available can be invaluable to improve the overall stability of the program.

Thus, your program should log errors as it encounters them. That way, if a user reports a bug, you will be able to examine the log files on the machine to see if your program reported any errors prior to encountering the bug. Unfortunately, error logging is platform-dependent: C++ does not contain a standard logging mechanism. Examples of platform-specific logging mechanisms include the `syslog` facility in Unix and the event reporting API in Windows. You should consult the documentation for your development platform. There are also some open-source implementations of cross-platform logging frameworks. Here are two examples:

- log4cpp at `log4cpp.sourceforge.net`
- Boost.Log at `boost.org`

Now that you're convinced that logging is a great feature to add to your programs, you might be tempted to log messages every few lines in your code so that, in the event of any bug, you'll be able to trace the code path that was executing. These types of log messages are appropriately called *traces*.

However, you should not write these traces to log files for two reasons. First, writing to persistent storage is slow. Even on systems that write the logs asynchronously, logging that much information will slow down your program. Second, and most important, most of the information that you would put in your traces is not appropriate for the end user to see. It will just confuse the user, leading to unwarranted service calls. That said, tracing is an important debugging technique under the correct circumstances, as described in the next section.

Here are some specific guidelines for the types of errors you should log:

- Unrecoverable errors, such as a system call failing unexpectedly.
- Errors for which an administrator can take action, such as low memory, an incorrectly formatted data file, an inability to write to disk, or a network connection being down.

- Unexpected errors such as a code path that you never expected to take or variables with unexpected values. On the other hand, your code should "expect" users to enter invalid data and should handle it appropriately. An unexpected error represents a bug in your program.
- Potential security breaches, such as a network connection attempted from an unauthorized address, or too many network connections attempted (denial of service).

A natural question you might be asking yourself is: What should be included in a logged error? At the very least, each logged error should contain the date and time the error occurred and the error message itself. In multithreaded applications, it's useful to log the ID of the thread that caused the error as well. Starting with C++23, the Standard Library includes `std::stacktrace`, discussed in Chapter 14, which allows you to get a stack trace at any moment during the execution of your program. You could include such a stack trace, or at least part of it, with each logged error.

It is also useful to log warnings, or recoverable errors, giving you the option to investigate if they can possibly be avoided.

Most logging APIs allow you to specify a *log level* or *error level*, typically at least "error," "warning," or "info". You can log non-error conditions under a log level that is less severe than "error." For example, you might want to log significant state changes in your application, or startup and shutdown of the program. You also might consider giving your users a way to adjust the log level of your program at run time so that they can customize the amount of logging that occurs.

Debug Traces

When debugging complicated problems, public error messages generally do not contain enough information. You often need a complete trace of the code path taken, or values of variables before the bug showed up. In addition to basic messages, it's sometimes helpful to include the following information in debug traces:

- The thread ID, if it's a multithreaded program
- The name of the function that generates the trace
- The name of the source file in which that function lives

You can add this tracing to your program through a special *debug mode*, or via a *ring buffer*. Both of these techniques are explained in detail in the following sections. Note that in multithreaded programs you have to make your trace logging thread-safe. See Chapter 27, "Multithreaded Programming with C++," for details on multithreaded programming.

> **WARNING** *Trace files can be written in text format, but if you do, be careful with logging too much detail. You don't want to leak intellectual property through your log files! Logging too much implementation details can also be dangerous if hackers can get a hold of the trace output!*

Debug Mode

A first technique to add debug traces is to provide a debug mode for your program. In debug mode, the program writes trace output to standard error or to a file, and perhaps does extra checking during execution. There are several ways to add a debug mode to your program. All following examples are writing traces in text format.

Start-Time Debug Mode

Start-time debug mode allows your application to run with or without debug mode depending on a command-line argument. This strategy includes the debug code in the "release" binary and allows debug mode to be enabled at a customer site. However, it does require users to restart the program to run it in debug mode, which may prevent you from obtaining useful information about certain bugs.

The following example is a simple program implementing a start-time debug mode. This program doesn't do anything useful; it is only for demonstrating the technique.

All logging functionality is wrapped in a `Logger` class. This class has two `static` data members: the name of the log file and a Boolean saying whether logging is enabled or disabled. The class has a public `static log()` member function template. Variadic templates like this one are discussed in Chapter 26, "Advanced Templates." The log file is opened, flushed, and closed on each call to `log()`. This might lower performance a bit; however, it does guarantee correct logging, which is more important.

```
class Logger
{
    public:
        static void enableLogging(bool enable) { ms_loggingEnabled = enable; }
        static bool isLoggingEnabled() { return ms_loggingEnabled; }

        template <typename... Args>
        static void log(const Args&... args)
        {
            if (!ms_loggingEnabled) { return; }

            ofstream logfile { ms_debugFilename, ios_base::app };
            if (logfile.fail()) {
                println(cerr, "Unable to open debug file!");
                return;
            }
            print(logfile, "{:L} UTC: ", chrono::system_clock::now());
            // Use a fold-expression; see Chapter 26.
            (logfile << ... << args);
            logfile << endl;
        }
    private:
        static inline const string ms_debugFilename { "debugfile.out" };
        static inline bool ms_loggingEnabled { false };
};
```

The following helper macro is defined to make it easy to log something. It's a macro accepting a variable number of arguments. You get access to those arguments using `__VA_ARGS__`. The macro uses `__func__`, a predefined variable defined by the C++ standard that contains the name of the current function.

```
#define LOG(...) Logger::log(__func__, "(): ", __VA_ARGS__)
```

This macro replaces every call to `LOG()` in your code with a call to `Logger::log()`. The macro automatically includes the function name as first argument to `Logger::log()`. For example, suppose you call the macro as follows:

```
LOG("The value is: ", value);
```

The `LOG()` macro replaces this with the following:

```
Logger::log(__func__, "(): ", "The value is: ", value);
```

Start-time debug mode needs to parse the command-line arguments to find out whether it should enable debug mode. Unfortunately, there is no standard functionality in C++ for parsing command-line arguments. This program uses a simple `isDebugSet()` function to check for the debug flag among all the command-line arguments, but a function to parse all command-line arguments would need to be more sophisticated.

```
bool isDebugSet(int argc, char** argv)
{
    auto parameters { views::counted(argv, argc) };
    return ranges::contains(parameters, string_view { "-d" });
}
```

Some arbitrary test code is used to exercise the debug mode in this example. Two classes are defined, `ComplicatedClass` and `UserCommand`. Both classes define an `operator<<` to write instances of them to a stream. The `Logger` class uses this operator to dump objects to the log file.

```
class ComplicatedClass { /* ... */ };
ostream& operator<<(ostream& outStream, const ComplicatedClass& src)
{
    outStream << "ComplicatedClass";
    return outStream;
}

class UserCommand { /* ... */ };
ostream& operator<<(ostream& outStream, const UserCommand& src)
{
    outStream << "UserCommand";
    return outStream;
}
```

Here is some test code with a number of log calls:

```
UserCommand getNextCommand(ComplicatedClass* obj)
{
    UserCommand cmd;
    return cmd;
}
```

```
void processUserCommand(const UserCommand& cmd)
{
    // Details omitted for brevity.
}

void trickyFunction(ComplicatedClass* obj)
{
    LOG("given argument: ", *obj);

    for (size_t i { 0 }; i < 100; ++i) {
        UserCommand cmd { getNextCommand(obj) };
        LOG("retrieved cmd ", i, ": ", cmd);

        try {
            processUserCommand(cmd);
        } catch (const exception& e) {
            LOG("exception from processUserCommand(): ", e.what());
        }
    }
}

int main(int argc, char** argv)
{
    Logger::enableLogging(isDebugSet(argc, argv));

    if (Logger::isLoggingEnabled()) {
        // Print the command-line arguments to the trace.
        for (size_t i { 0 }; i < argc; ++i) {
            LOG("Argument: ", argv[i]);
        }
    }

    ComplicatedClass obj;
    trickyFunction(&obj);

    // Rest of the function not shown.
}
```

There are two ways to run this application:

```
> STDebug
> STDebug -d
```

Debug mode is activated only when the `-d` argument is specified on the command line.

> **WARNING** *Macros in C++ should be avoided as much as possible because they can be hard to debug. However, for logging purposes, using a simple macro can be acceptable, and it makes using the logging code much easier. Even so, with* `std::source_location`, *discussed in Chapter 14, the example can be modified to avoid the use of a macro. This is the topic of one of the exercises at the end of this chapter.*

Compile-Time Debug Mode

Instead of enabling or disabling debug mode through a command-line argument, you could also use a preprocessor symbol such as `DEBUG_MODE` and `#ifdefs` to selectively compile the debug code into your program. To generate a debug version of this program, you would have to compile it with the symbol `DEBUG_MODE` defined. Your compiler allows you to define symbols during compilation; consult your compiler's documentation for details. For example, GCC allows you to specify `-Dsymbol` through the command line. Microsoft Visual C++ allows you to specify the symbols through the Visual Studio IDE or by specifying `/D symbol` if you use the Visual C++ command-line tools. Instead of using a custom `DEBUG_MODE` symbol, you could also use the `NDEBUG` symbol, which is defined by a compiler for release builds and not for debug builds.

The advantage of this technique is that your debug code is not compiled into the "release" binary and so does not increase its size. The disadvantage is that there is no way to enable debugging at a customer site for testing or following the discovery of a bug.

An example implementation is given in `CTDebug.cpp` in the downloadable source code archive. One important remark on this implementation is that it contains the following definition for the `LOG()` macro:

```
#ifdef DEBUG_MODE
    #define LOG(...) Logger::log(__func__, "(): ", __VA_ARGS__)
#else
    #define LOG(...) (void)0
#endif
```

That is, if `DEBUG_MODE` is not defined, then all calls to `LOG()` are replaced with nothing, called *no-ops*.

> **WARNING** *Be careful not to put any code that must be executed for correct program functioning inside your* `LOG()` *calls. For example, the following line of code could be asking for trouble:*
>
> ```
> LOG("Result: ", calculateResult());
> ```
>
> *If* `DEBUG_MODE` *is not defined, the preprocessor replaces all* `LOG()` *calls with no-ops, which means that the call to* `calculateResult()` *is removed as well!*

As logging code is removed if `DEBUG_MODE` is not defined, it could mean that certain variables might be unused, which can trigger compiler warnings. Using the `[[maybe_unused]]` attribute (see Chapter 1, "A Crash Course in C++ and the Standard Library") avoids such warnings. For example:

```
int main([[maybe_unused]] int argc, [[maybe_unused]] char** argv)
{
#ifdef DEBUG_MODE
    // Print the command-line arguments to the trace.
    for (size_t i { 0 }; i < argc; ++i) { LOG("Argument: ", argv[i]); }
#endif
    ComplicatedClass obj;
```

```
        trickyFunction(&obj);
        // Rest of the function not shown.
    }
```

Run-Time Debug Mode

The most flexible way to provide a debug mode is to allow it to be enabled or disabled at run time. One way to provide this feature is to supply an asynchronous interface that controls debug mode on the fly. This interface could be an asynchronous command that makes an interprocess call into the application (for example, using sockets, signals, or remote procedure calls). This interface could also take the form of a menu command in the user interface. C++ provides no standard way to perform interprocess communication or to implement user interfaces, so an example of this technique is not shown.

Ring Buffers

Debug mode is useful for debugging reproducible problems and for running tests. However, bugs often appear when the program is running in non-debug mode, and by the time you or the customer enables debug mode, it is too late to gain any information about the bug. One solution to this problem is to enable tracing in your program at all times. You usually need only the most recent traces to debug a program, so you should store only the most recent traces at any point in a program's execution. One way to provide for this is through careful use of log file rotations.

However, for performance reasons, it's better that you don't log these traces continuously to disk. Instead, store them in memory and provide a mechanism to dump all the trace messages to standard error or to a log file if the need arises.

A common technique is to use a *ring buffer*, or *circular buffer*, to store a fixed number of messages, or messages in a fixed amount of memory. When the buffer fills up, it starts writing messages at the beginning of the buffer again, overwriting the older messages. This cycle can repeat indefinitely. The following sections provide an implementation of a ring buffer and show you how you can use it in your programs.

Ring Buffer Interface

The following `RingBuffer` class provides a simple ring buffer storing messages. The client specifies the number of entries in the constructor and adds messages with the `addEntry()` member function. Once the number of entries exceeds the number allowed, new entries overwrite the oldest entries in the buffer. The buffer also provides the option to output entries to a stream as they are added to the buffer. The client can specify an output stream in the constructor and can reset it with the `setOutput()` member function. Finally, the `operator<<` streams the entire buffer to an output stream. This implementation uses a variadic template member function, discussed in Chapter 26.

```
export class RingBuffer final
{
    public:
        // Constructs a ring buffer with space for numEntries.
        // Entries are written to *outStream as they are queued (optional).
        explicit RingBuffer(std::size_t numEntries = DefaultNumEntries,
            std::ostream* outStream = nullptr);
```

```
        // Adds an entry to the ring buffer, possibly overwriting the
        // oldest entry in the buffer (if the buffer is full).
        template <typename... Args>
        void addEntry(const Args&... args)
        {
            std::ostringstream oss;
            std::print(oss, "{:L} UTC: ", std::chrono::system_clock::now());
            // Use a fold-expression; see Chapter 26.
            (oss << ... << args);
            addStringEntry(std::move(oss).str());
        }

        // Streams the buffer entries, separated by newlines, to outStream.
        friend std::ostream& operator<<(std::ostream& outStream, RingBuffer& rb);

        // Streams entries as they are added to the given stream.
        // Specify nullptr to disable this feature.
        // Returns the old output stream.
        std::ostream* setOutput(std::ostream* newOutStream);

    private:
        std::vector<std::string> m_entries;
        std::vector<std::string>::iterator m_next;

        std::ostream* m_outStream { nullptr };
        bool m_wrapped { false };

        static constexpr std::size_t DefaultNumEntries { 500 };

        void addStringEntry(std::string entry);
};
```

Ring Buffer Implementation

This implementation of the ring buffer stores a fixed number of `string` objects. This approach certainly is not the most efficient solution. Other possibilities would be to provide a fixed number of bytes of memory for the buffer. However, this implementation should be sufficient unless you're writing a high-performance application.

For multithreaded programs, it's useful to add the ID of the thread to each trace entry. Of course, the ring buffer has to be made thread-safe before using it in a multithreaded application. See Chapter 27 for multithreaded programming.

Here are the implementations:

```
// Initialize the vector to hold exactly numEntries. The vector size
// does not need to change during the lifetime of the object.
// Initialize the other members.
RingBuffer::RingBuffer(size_t numEntries, ostream* outStream)
    : m_entries { numEntries }, m_outStream { outStream }, m_wrapped { false }
{
    if (numEntries == 0) {
        throw invalid_argument { "Number of entries must be > 0." };
    }
```

```
    m_next = begin(m_entries);
}

// The addStringEntry algorithm is pretty simple: add the entry to the next
// free spot, then reset m_next to indicate the free spot after
// that. If m_next reaches the end of the vector, it starts over at 0.
//
// The buffer needs to know if the buffer has wrapped or not so
// that it knows whether to print the entries past m_next in operator<<.
void RingBuffer::addStringEntry(string entry)
{
    // If there is a valid m_outStream, write this entry to it.
    if (m_outStream) { *m_outStream << entry << endl; }

    // Move the entry to the next free spot and increment
    // m_next to point to the free spot after that.
    *m_next = move(entry);
    ++m_next;

    // Check if we've reached the end of the buffer. If so, we need to wrap.
    if (m_next == end(m_entries)) {
        m_next = begin(m_entries);
        m_wrapped = true;
    }
}

// Set the output stream.
ostream* RingBuffer::setOutput(ostream* newOutStream)
{
    return exchange(m_outStream, newOutStream);
}

// operator<< uses an ostream_iterator to "copy" entries directly
// from the vector to the output stream.
//
// operator<< must print the entries in order. If the buffer has wrapped,
// the earliest entry is one past the most recent entry, which is the entry
// indicated by m_next. So, first print from entry m_next to the end.
//
// Then (even if the buffer hasn't wrapped) print from beginning to m_next-1.
ostream& operator<<(ostream& outStream, RingBuffer& rb)
{
    if (rb.m_wrapped) {
        // If the buffer has wrapped, print the elements from
        // the earliest entry to the end.
        copy(rb.m_next, end(rb.m_entries),
            ostream_iterator<string>{ outStream, "\n" });
    }

    // Now, print up to the most recent entry.
    // Go up to m_next because the range is not inclusive on the right side.
    copy(begin(rb.m_entries), rb.m_next,
        ostream_iterator<string>{ outStream, "\n" });

    return outStream;
}
```

Using the Ring Buffer

To use the ring buffer, you can create an instance of it and start adding messages to it. When you want to print the buffer, just use `operator<<` to print it to the appropriate `ostream`. Here is the earlier start-time debug mode program modified to use a ring buffer instead. Changes are highlighted. The definitions of the `ComplicatedClass` and `UserCommand` classes, and the functions `getNextCommand()`, `processUserCommand()`, and `trickyFunction()` are not shown. They are the same as before.

```
RingBuffer debugBuffer;

#define LOG(...) debugBuffer.addEntry(__func__, "(): ", __VA_ARGS__)

int main(int argc, char** argv)
{
    // Log the command-line arguments.
    for (size_t i { 0 }; i < argc; ++i) {
        LOG("Argument: ", argv[i]);
    }

    ComplicatedClass obj;
    trickyFunction(&obj);

    // Print the current contents of the debug buffer to cout.
    cout << debugBuffer;
}
```

Displaying the Ring Buffer Contents

Storing trace debug messages in memory is a great start, but for them to be useful, you need a way to access these traces for debugging.

Your program should provide a "hook" to tell it to export the messages. This hook could be similar to the interface you would use to enable debugging at run time. Additionally, if your program encounters a fatal error that causes it to exit, it could export the ring buffer automatically to a log file before exiting.

Another way to retrieve these messages is to obtain a memory dump of the program. Each platform handles memory dumps differently, so you should consult a reference or expert for your platform.

Assertions

`<cassert>` defines an `assert()` macro. It takes a Boolean expression and, if the expression evaluates to `false`, prints an error message and terminates the program. If the expression evaluates to `true`, it does nothing.

> **WARNING** *Normally, you should avoid any library functions or macros that can terminate your program. The* `assert()` *macro is an exception. If an assertion triggers, it means that some assumption is wrong or that something is catastrophically, unrecoverably wrong, and the only sane thing to do is to terminate the application at that very moment, instead of continuing.*

Assertions allow you to "force" your program to exhibit a bug at the exact point where that bug originates. If you didn't assert at that point, your program might proceed with those incorrect values, and the bug might not show up until much later. Thus, assertions allow you to detect bugs earlier than you otherwise would.

> **NOTE** *The behavior of the standard* `assert()` *macro depends on the* `NDEBUG` *preprocessor symbol: if the symbol is not defined, the assertion takes place; otherwise, it is ignored. Compilers often define this symbol when compiling "release" builds. If you want to leave assertions in release builds, you may have to change your compiler settings or write your own version of* `assert()` *that isn't affected by the value of* `NDEBUG`.

`assert()` is a C-style macro whose implementation depends on whether client code defines the `NDEBUG` preprocessor symbol or not. That makes `<cassert>` an example of a *non-modular, non-importable header*, as explained in Chapter 11, "Modules, Header Files, and Miscellaneous Topics." Use `#include <cassert>` instead of `import <cassert>` to get access to the `assert()` macro.

You could use assertions in your code whenever you are "assuming" something about the state of your variables. For example, if you call a library function that is supposed to return a pointer and claims never to return `nullptr`, throw in an `assert()` after the function call to make sure that the pointer isn't `nullptr`.

However, you should assume as little as possible. For example, if you are writing a library function, don't assert that the parameters are valid. Instead, check the parameters, and return an error code or throw an exception if they are invalid.

As a rule, assertions should be used only for cases that are truly problematic and should therefore never be ignored when they occur during development. If you hit an assertion during development, fix it, don't just disable the assertion.

Let's look at a couple of examples on how to use `assert()`. Here is a `process()` function that requires three elements in a `vector` passed to the function:

```
void process(const vector<int>& coordinate)
{
    assert(coordinate.size() == 3);
    // ...
}
```

If the `process()` function is called with a `vector` that has less or more elements than three, the assertion fails and generates a message similar to the following (the exact message depends on the compiler that is used):

```
Assertion failed: coordinate.size() == 3, file D:\test\test.cpp, line 12
```

If you want a custom error message, you can use the following trick using the comma operator and a set of extra parentheses:

```
assert(("A custom message...", coordinate.size() == 3));
```

The output then will be something as follows:

```
Assertion failed: ("A custom message...", coordinate.size() == 3), file D:\test\
test.cpp, line 106
```

If at some point in your code you want that an assert always fails with a certain error message, you can use the following trick:

```
assert(!"This should never happen.");
```

> **WARNING** *Be careful not to put any code that must be executed for correct program functioning inside assertions. For example, the following line of code could be asking for trouble:*
>
> ```
> assert(calculateResult() != 0);
> ```
>
> *If a release build of your code strips assertions, then the call to* `calculateResult()` *is stripped as well!*

Crash Dumps

Make sure your programs create *crash dumps*, also called *memory dumps* or *core dumps*. A crash dump is a dump file that is created when your application crashes. It contains information about which threads were running at the time of the crash, a call stack of all the threads, and so on. How you create such dumps is platform dependent, so you should consult the documentation of your platform or use a third-party library that takes care of it for you. Breakpad (`github.com/google/breakpad/`) is an example of such an open-source cross-platform library that can write and process crash dumps.

Also make sure you set up a *symbol server* and a *version control server*. The symbol server is used to store debugging symbols of released binaries of your software. These symbols are used later to interpret crash dumps received from customers. The version control server, discussed in Chapter 28, "Maximizing Software Engineering Methods," stores all revisions of your source code. When debugging crash dumps, this version control server is used to download the correct source code for the revision of your software that created the crash dump.

The exact procedure of analyzing crash dumps depends on your platform and compiler, so consult their documentation.

From my personal experience, I have found that a crash dump is often worth more than a thousand bug reports.

DEBUGGING TECHNIQUES

Debugging a program can be incredibly frustrating. However, with a systematic approach it becomes significantly easier. Your first step in trying to debug a program should always be to reproduce the bug. Depending on whether you can reproduce the bug, your subsequent approach will differ. The next four sections explain how to reproduce bugs, how to debug reproducible bugs, how to debug nonreproducible bugs, and how to debug regressions. Additional sections explain details about debugging memory errors and debugging multithreaded programs. The final sections show a step-by-step debugging example.

Reproducing Bugs

If you can reproduce a bug consistently, it will be much easier to determine the root cause. Sometimes a bug might be reproducible by Alice but not by Bob. That in itself can be a clue for Alice to find the root cause. Finding the root cause of bugs that are not reproducible is difficult, if not impossible.

As a first step to reproduce the bug, run the program on a similar environment (hardware, operating system, and so on) and with the same inputs as the run when the bug first appeared. Be sure to include all inputs, from the program's startup to the time of the bug's appearance. A common mistake is to attempt to reproduce the bug by performing only the triggering action. This technique may not reproduce the bug because the bug might be caused by an entire sequence of actions.

For example, if your web browser dies when you request a certain web page, it may be due to memory corruption triggered by that particular request's network address. On the other hand, it may be because your program records all requests in a queue, with space for one million entries, and this entry was number 1,000,001. Starting the program over and sending one request certainly wouldn't trigger the bug in that case.

Sometimes it is impossible to emulate the entire sequence of events that leads to the bug. Perhaps the bug was reported by someone who can't remember everything that she did. Alternatively, maybe the program was running for too long to emulate every input. In that case, do your best to reproduce the bug. It takes some guesswork and can be time-consuming, but effort at this point will save time later in the debugging process. Here are some techniques you can try:

- Repeat the triggering action in the correct environment and with as many inputs as possible similar to the initial report.
- Do a quick review of the code related to the bug. More often than not, you'll find a likely cause that will guide you in reproducing the problem.
- Run automated tests that exercise similar functionality. Reproducing bugs is one benefit of automated tests. If it takes 24 hours of testing before the bug shows up, it's preferable to let those tests run on their own rather than spend 24 hours of your time trying to reproduce the bug.
- If you have the necessary hardware available, running slight variations of tests concurrently on different machines can sometimes save time.
- Run stress tests that exercise similar functionality. If your program is a web server that died on a particular request, try running as many browsers as possible simultaneously that make that request.

After you are able to reproduce the bug consistently, you should attempt to find the smallest sequence that triggers the bug. You can start with the minimum sequence, containing only the triggering action, and slowly expand the sequence to cover the entire sequence from startup until the bug is triggered. This will result in the simplest and most efficient test case to reproduce it, which makes it simpler to find the root cause of the problem and easier to verify the fix.

Debugging Reproducible Bugs

When you can reproduce a bug consistently and efficiently, it's time to figure out the problem in the code that causes the bug. Your goal at this point is to find the exact lines of code that trigger the problem. You can use two different strategies:

- **Use a debugger:** Debuggers allow you to step through the execution of your program and to view the state of memory and the values of variables at various points. They are often indispensable tools for finding the root cause of bugs. When you have access to the source code, you should use a *symbolic debugger*: a debugger that utilizes the variable names, class names, and other symbols in your code. To use a symbolic debugger, you must instruct your compiler to generate debug symbols. Check the documentation of your compiler for details on how to enable symbol generation.
- **Log debug messages:** By adding enough debug messages to your program and watching its output when you reproduce the bug, you should be able to pinpoint the exact lines of code where the bug occurs. If you have a debugger at your disposal, adding debug messages is usually not recommended because it requires modifications to the program and can be time-consuming. However, if you have already instrumented your program with debug messages as described earlier, you might be able to find the root cause of your bug by running your program in debug mode while reproducing the bug. Note that bugs sometimes disappear simply when you enable logging because the act of enabling logging can slightly change the timings of your application.

The debugging example at the end of this chapter demonstrates both these approaches.

Debugging Nonreproducible Bugs

Fixing bugs that are not reproducible is significantly more difficult than fixing reproducible bugs. You often have little information and must employ a lot of guesswork. Nevertheless, a few strategies can aid you:

- Try to turn a nonreproducible bug into a reproducible bug. By using educated guesses, you can often determine approximately where the bug lies. It's worthwhile to spend some time trying to reproduce the bug. Once you have a reproducible bug, you can figure out its root cause by using the techniques described earlier.
- Analyze error logs. This is easy to do if you have instrumented your program with error log generation, as described earlier. You should sift through this information because any errors that were logged directly before the bug occurred are likely to have contributed to the bug itself. If you're lucky (or if you coded your program well), your program will have logged the exact reason for the bug at hand.
- Obtain and analyze traces. Again, this is easy to do if you have instrumented your program with tracing output, for example, via a ring buffer as described earlier. At the time of the bug's occurrence, you ideally obtained a copy of the traces. These traces should lead you right to the location of the bug in your code.
- Examine a *crash/memory dump* file, if it exists. Some platforms automatically generate memory dump files of applications that terminate abnormally. On Unix and Linux, these

memory dumps are called *core files*. Each platform provides tools for analyzing these memory dumps. They can, for example, be used to view the stack trace of the application and the contents of its memory before the application died.

- Inspect the code. Unfortunately, this is often the only strategy to determine the cause of a nonreproducible bug. Surprisingly, it often works. When you examine code, even code that you wrote yourself, with the perspective of the bug that just occurred, you can often find mistakes that you overlooked previously. I don't recommend spending hours staring at your code, but tracing through the code path manually can often lead you directly to the problem.
- Use a memory-watching tool, such as one of the tools described in the section "Debugging Memory Problems," later in this chapter. Such tools often alert you to memory errors that don't always cause your program to misbehave but could potentially be the cause of the bug in question.
- File or update a bug report. Even if you can't find the root cause of the bug right away, the report will be a useful record of your attempts if the problem is encountered again.
- If you are unable to find the root cause of the bug, be sure to add extra logging or tracing so that you will have a better chance next time the bug occurs.

Once you have found the root cause of a nonreproducible bug, you should create a reproducible test case and move it to the "reproducible bugs" category. It is important to be able to reproduce a bug before you actually fix it. Otherwise, how will you test the fix? A common mistake when debugging nonreproducible bugs is to fix the wrong problem in the code. Because you can't reproduce the bug, you don't know if you've really fixed it, so you shouldn't be surprised when it shows up again a month later.

Debugging Regressions

If a feature contains a *regression* bug, it means that the feature used to work correctly, but at some point unexpectedly stopped working.

A useful debugging technique for investigating regressions is to look at the change log of relevant files. If you know at what time the feature was still working, look at all the change logs since that time. You might notice something suspicious that could lead you to the root cause.

Another approach that can save you a lot of time when debugging regressions is to use a binary search approach with older versions of the software (often called *bisecting*) to try to figure out when it started to go wrong. You can use binaries of older versions if you keep them, or you can revert the source code to an older revision. Once you know when it started to go wrong, inspect the change logs to see what changed at that time. This mechanism is possible only when you can reproduce the bug.

Debugging Memory Problems

Most catastrophic bugs, such as application crashes, are caused by memory errors. Many noncatastrophic bugs are triggered by memory errors as well. Some memory bugs are obvious. For example, if your program attempts to dereference a null pointer, the default action is to terminate the program. However, nearly every platform enables you to respond to catastrophic errors and take remedial action. The amount of effort you devote to the response depends on the importance of this kind of recovery to your end users. For example, a text editor really needs to make a best attempt to save the modified buffers (possibly under a "recovered" name), while for other programs, users may find the default behavior acceptable, even if it is unpleasant.

Some memory bugs are more insidious. If you write past the end of an array in C++, your program will probably not crash at that point. However, if that array was on the stack, you may have written into a different variable or array, changing values that won't show up until later in the program. Alternatively, if the array was on the free store, you could cause memory corruption in the free store, which will cause errors later when you attempt to allocate or free more memory dynamically.

Chapter 7, "Memory Management," introduces some of the common memory errors from the perspective of what to avoid when you're coding. This section discusses memory errors from the perspective of identifying problems in code that exhibits bugs. You should be familiar with the discussion in Chapter 7 before continuing with this section.

> **WARNING** *Most, if not all, of the following memory problems can be avoided by using smart pointers instead of raw pointers.*

Categories of Memory Errors

To debug memory problems, you should be familiar with the types of errors that can occur. This section describes the major categories of memory errors. Each category lists different types of memory errors, including a small code example demonstrating each error, and a list of possible *symptoms* that you might observe. Note that a symptom is not the same thing as a bug: a symptom is an observable behavior caused by a bug.

Memory-Freeing Errors

The following table summarizes five major errors that involve freeing memory:

ERROR TYPE	SYMPTOMS	EXAMPLE

Memory leak	Process memory usage grows over time. Process runs more slowly over time. Eventually, depending on the OS, operations and system calls fail because of lack of memory.	`void memoryLeak()`
		`{`
		`  int* p { new int[1000] };`
		`  return; // Not freeing p!`
		`}`

Using mismatched allocation and free operations	Does not usually cause a crash immediately. This type of error can cause memory corruption on some platforms, which might show up as a crash later in the program. Certain mismatches can also cause memory leaks.	`void mismatchedFree()`
		`{`
		`  int* p1{(int*)malloc(sizeof(int))};`
		`  int* p2{new int};`
		`  int* p3{new int[1000]};`
		`  delete p1;  // Should use free()!`
		`  delete[] p2;// Should use delete!`
		`  free(p3);   // Should use delete[]!`
		`}`

continues

(continued)

ERROR TYPE	SYMPTOMS	EXAMPLE

Freeing memory more than once	Can cause a crash if the memory at that location has been handed out in another allocation between the two calls to delete.	`void doubleFree()`
		`{`
		`  int* p1 { new int[1000] };`
		`  delete[] p1;`
		`  int* p2 { new int[1000] };`
		`  delete[] p1; // Freeing p1 twice!`
		`} // Leaking memory of p2!`

Freeing unallocated memory	Usually causes a crash.	`void freeUnallocated()`
		`{`
		`  int* p{reinterpret_cast<int*>(10)};`
		`  delete p; // p not a valid pointer!`
		`}`

Freeing stack memory	Technically a special case of freeing unallocated memory. This usually causes a crash.	`void freeStack()`
		`{`
		`  int x;`
		`  int* p { &x };`
		`  delete p; // Freeing stack memory!`
		`}`

The crashes mentioned in this table can have different manifestations depending on your platform, such as segmentation faults, bus errors, access violations, and so on.

As you can see, some of the errors do not cause immediate program termination. These bugs are more subtle, leading to problems later in the program's execution.

Memory-Access Errors

Another category of memory errors involves the actual reading and writing of memory:

ERROR TYPE	SYMPTOMS	EXAMPLE

Accessing invalid memory	Almost always causes the program to crash immediately.	`void accessInvalid()`
		`{`
		`  int* p {reinterpret_cast<int*>(10)};`
		`  *p = 5; // p is not a valid pointer!`
		`}`

Accessing freed memory	Does not usually cause a crash. If the memory has been handed out in another allocation, this error type can cause "strange" and potentially dangerous values to appear unexpectedly.	`void accessFreed()`
		`{`
		`  int* p1 { new int };`
		`  delete p1;`
		`  *p1 = 5; // The memory pointed to`
		`          // by p1 has been freed!`
		`}`

ERROR TYPE	SYMPTOMS	EXAMPLE

Accessing memory in a different allocation	Does not usually cause a crash. This error type can cause "strange" and potentially dangerous values to appear unexpectedly in other variables or temporary objects, or even change the control flow of the program.	`void accessElsewhere()`
		`{`
		`  int x, y[10], z;`
		`  x = 0;`
		`  z = 0;`
		`  for (int i { 0 }; i <= 10; ++i) {`
		`    y[i] = 5; // BUG for i==10! element`
		`              // 10 is past end of array`
		`  }`
		`}`

Reading uninitialized memory	Does not cause a crash, unless you use the uninitialized value as a pointer or array index and dereference it (as in the example). Even then, it will not always cause a crash.	`void readUninitialized()`
		`{`
		`  int* p;`
		`  print("{}",*p);// p is uninitialized!`
		`}`

Memory-access errors don't always cause a crash. They can instead lead to subtle errors, in which the program does not terminate but instead produces erroneous results. Erroneous results can lead to serious consequences, for example, when external devices—such as robotic arms, X-ray machines, radiation treatments, life support systems, and so on—are being controlled by the computer.

Note that the symptoms discussed here for both memory-freeing and memory-access errors are the default symptoms for release builds of your program. Debug builds will most likely behave differently, and when you run the program inside a debugger, the debugger might break into the code when an error occurs.

Tips for Debugging Memory Errors

Memory-related bugs often show up in slightly different places in the code each time you run the program. This is usually the case with free store memory corruption. Free store memory corruption is like a time bomb, ready to explode at some attempt to allocate, free, or use memory on the free store. So, when you see a bug that is reproducible but that shows up in slightly different places, you should suspect memory corruption.

If you suspect a memory bug, your best option is to use a memory-checking tool for C++. Debuggers often provide options to run the program while checking for memory errors. For example, if you run a debug build of your application in the Microsoft Visual C++ debugger, it will catch almost all types of errors discussed in the previous sections. Additionally, there are some excellent third-party tools such as Purify from Rational Software (now owned by IBM) and Valgrind for Linux (discussed in Chapter 7). Microsoft also provides a free download called *Application Verifier* (Part of the Windows SDK, `https://developer.microsoft.com/windows/downloads/windows-sdk`), which can be used with release builds of your applications in a Windows environment. It is a run-time verification tool to help you find subtle programming errors like the previously discussed memory errors. These debuggers and tools work by interposing their own memory-allocation and -freeing routines to check for any misuse of dynamic memory, such as freeing unallocated memory, dereferencing unallocated memory, or writing off the end of an array.

If you don't have a memory-checking tool at your disposal and the normal strategies for debugging are not helping, you may need to resort to code inspection. First, narrow down the part of the code containing the bug. Then, as a general rule, look at all raw pointers. Provided that you work on moderate- to good-quality code, most pointers should already be wrapped in smart pointers. If you do encounter raw pointers, take a closer look at how they are used, because they might be the cause of the error. Here are some more items to look for in your code.

Object and Class-Related Errors

- Verify that your classes with dynamically allocated memory have destructors that free exactly the memory that's allocated in the object: no more, and no less.
- Ensure that your classes handle copying and assignment correctly with copy constructors and assignment operators, as described in Chapter 9, "Mastering Classes and Objects." Make sure move constructors and move assignment operators properly set pointers in the source object to `nullptr` so that their destructors don't try to free that memory.
- Check for suspicious casts. If you are casting a pointer to an object from one type to another, make sure that it's valid. When possible, use `dynamic_casts`.

> **WARNING** *Whenever you see raw pointers being used to handle ownership of resources, I highly recommend you replace those raw pointers with smart pointers and try to refactor your classes to follow the rule of zero, as discussed in Chapter 9. This removes the types of errors explained in the first and second bullet points in the preceding list.*

General Memory Errors

- Make sure that every call to `new` is matched with exactly one call to `delete` and every call to `new[]` is matched with one call to `delete[]`. Similarly, every call to `malloc`, `alloc`, or `calloc` should be matched with one call to `free`. To avoid freeing memory multiple times or using freed memory, it's recommended to set your pointer to `nullptr` after freeing its memory. Of course, the best solution is to simply avoid using raw pointers to handle ownership of resources and instead use smart pointers.
- Check for buffer overruns. Whenever you iterate over an array or write into or read from a C-style string, verify that you are not accessing memory past the end of the array or string. These problems can often be avoided by using Standard Library containers and strings.
- Check for dereferencing of invalid pointers.

- When declaring a pointer (or really any scalar type) on the stack, make sure you always initialize it as part of its declaration. For example, use `T* p{nullptr};` or `T* p{new T};` but never `T* p;`. Better yet, use smart pointers!
- Similarly, make sure your classes always initialize pointer data members with in-class initializers or in their constructors, by either allocating memory in the constructor or setting the pointers to `nullptr`. Also here, the best solution is to use smart pointers.

Debugging Multithreaded Programs

C++ includes a threading support library that provides mechanisms for threading and synchronization between threads. This threading support library is discussed in Chapter 27. Multithreaded C++ programs are common, so it is important to think about the special issues involved in debugging a multithreaded program. Bugs in multithreaded programs are often caused by variations in timings in the operating system scheduling and can be difficult to reproduce. Thus, debugging multithreaded programs requires a special set of techniques:

- **Use a debugger:** A debugger makes it relatively easy to diagnose certain multithreaded problems, for example, deadlocks. When a deadlock appears, break into the debugger and inspect the different threads. You will be able to see which threads are blocked and on which line in the code they are blocked. Combining this with trace logs that show you how you came into the deadlock situation should be enough to fix deadlocks.
- **Use log-based debugging:** When debugging multithreaded programs, log-based debugging can sometimes be more effective than using a debugger to debug certain problems. You can add log statements to your program before and after critical sections, and before acquiring and after releasing locks. Log-based debugging is extremely useful in investigating race conditions. However, the act of adding log statements slightly changes run-time timings, which might hide the bug.
- **Insert forced sleeps and context switches:** If you are having trouble consistently reproducing a problem or you have a hunch about the root cause but want to verify it, you can force certain thread-scheduling behavior by making your threads sleep for specific amounts of time. `<thread>` defines `sleep_until()` and `sleep_for()` in the `std::this_thread` namespace, which you can use to sleep. The time to sleep is specified as an `std::time_point` or an `std::duration` respectively, both part of the chrono library discussed in Chapter 22, "Date and Time Utilities." Sleeping for several seconds right before releasing a lock, immediately before signaling a condition variable, or directly before accessing shared data can reveal race conditions that would otherwise go undetected. If this debugging technique reveals the root cause, it must be fixed so that it works correctly after removing these forced sleeps and context switches. Never leave these forced sleeps and context switches in your code! That would be the wrong "fix" for the problem.
- **Perform code review:** Reviewing your thread synchronization code often helps in finding and fixing race conditions. Try to prove over and over that what happened is not possible, until you see how it is. It doesn't hurt to write down these "proofs" in code comments. Also, ask a co-worker to do pair debugging; she might see something you are overlooking.

Debugging Example: Article Citations

This section presents a buggy program and shows you the steps to take in order to debug it and fix the problem.

Suppose that you're part of a team writing a web page that allows users to search for research articles that cite a particular paper. This type of service is useful for authors who are trying to find work similar to their own. Once they find one paper representing a related work, they can look for every paper that cites that one to find other related work.

In this project, you are responsible for the code that reads the raw citation data from text files. For simplicity, assume that the citation information for each paper is found in its own file. Furthermore, assume that the first line of each file contains the author, title, and publication information for the paper; that the second line is always empty; and that all subsequent lines contain the citations from the article (one on each line). Here is an example file for one of the most important papers in computer science:

```
Alan Turing, "On Computable Numbers, with an Application to the
Entscheidungsproblem", Proceedings of the London Mathematical Society, Series 2,
Vol.42 (1936-37), 230-265.

Gödel, "Über formal unentscheidbare Sätze der Principia Mathematica und verwandter
Systeme, I", Monatshefte Math. Phys., 38 (1931), 173-198.
Alonzo Church. "An unsolvable problem of elementary number theory", American J. of
Math., 58 (1936), 345-363.
Alonzo Church. "A note on the Entscheidungsproblem", J. of Symbolic Logic, 1
(1936), 40-41.
E.W. Hobson, "Theory of functions of a real variable (2nd ed., 1921)", 87-88.
```

Buggy Implementation of an ArticleCitations Class

You may decide to structure your program by writing an `ArticleCitations` class that reads the file and stores the information. This class stores the article information from the first line in one string, and the citations in a C-style array of strings.

> **WARNING** *The design decision to use a C-style array is obviously a* bad one! *You should opt for one of the Standard Library containers to store the citations. This is just used here as a demonstration of memory problems. There are other obvious issues with this implementation, such as not using the copy-and-swap idiom (see Chapter 9) to implement the assignment operator. But, for the purpose of illustrating a buggy application, it's perfect.*

The `ArticleCitations` class definition, defined in an `article_citations` module, looks like this:

```
export class ArticleCitations
{
    public:
        explicit ArticleCitations(const std::string& filename);
        virtual ~ArticleCitations();
```

```
        ArticleCitations(const ArticleCitations& src);
        ArticleCitations& operator=(const ArticleCitations& rhs);

        const std::string& getArticle() const;
        int getNumCitations() const;
        const std::string& getCitation(int i) const;
    private:
        void readFile(const std::string& filename);
        void copy(const ArticleCitations& src);

        std::string m_article;
        std::string* m_citations { nullptr };
        int m_numCitations { 0 };
};
```

The implementation is as follows. Keep in mind that this program is buggy! Don't use it verbatim or as a model.

```
ArticleCitations::ArticleCitations(const string& filename)
{
    // All we have to do is read the file.
    readFile(filename);
}

ArticleCitations::ArticleCitations(const ArticleCitations& src)
{
    copy(src);
}

ArticleCitations& ArticleCitations::operator=(const ArticleCitations& rhs)
{
    // Check for self-assignment.
    if (this == &rhs) {
        return *this;
    }
    // Free the old memory.
    delete [] m_citations;
    // Copy the data.
    copy(rhs);
    return *this;
}

void ArticleCitations::copy(const ArticleCitations& src)
{
    // Copy the article name, author, etc.
    m_article = src.m_article;
    // Copy the number of citations.
    m_numCitations = src.m_numCitations;
    // Allocate an array of the correct size.
    m_citations = new string[m_numCitations];
    // Copy each element of the array.
    for (int i { 0 }; i < m_numCitations; ++i) {
        m_citations[i] = src.m_citations[i];
    }
}
```

```
ArticleCitations::~ArticleCitations()
{
    delete [] m_citations;
}

void ArticleCitations::readFile(const string& filename)
{
    // Open the file and check for failure.
    ifstream inputFile { filename };
    if (inputFile.fail()) {
        throw invalid_argument { "Unable to open file" };
    }
    // Read the article author, title, etc. line.
    getline(inputFile, m_article);

    // Skip the whitespace before the citations start.
    inputFile >> ws;

    int count { 0 };
    // Save the current position so we can return to it.
    streampos citationsStart { inputFile.tellg() };
    // First count the number of citations.
    while (!inputFile.eof()) {
        // Skip whitespace before the next entry.
        inputFile >> ws;
        string temp;
        getline(inputFile, temp);
        if (!temp.empty()) {
            ++count;
        }
    }

    if (count != 0) {
        // Allocate an array of strings to store the citations.
        m_citations = new string[count];
        m_numCitations = count;
        // Seek back to the start of the citations.
        inputFile.seekg(citationsStart);
        // Read each citation and store it in the new array.
        for (count = 0; count < m_numCitations; ++count) {
            string temp;
            getline(inputFile, temp);
            if (!temp.empty()) {
                m_citations[count] = temp;
            }
        }
    } else {
        m_numCitations = -1;
    }
}

const string& ArticleCitations::getArticle() const { return m_article; }

int ArticleCitations::getNumCitations() const { return m_numCitations; }

const string& ArticleCitations::getCitation(int i) const { return m_citations[i]; }
```

Testing the ArticleCitations Class

The following program asks the user for a filename, constructs an `ArticleCitations` instance for that file, and passes this instance by value to the `processCitations()` function, which prints out all the information. Passing the instance by value to the function is done for this buggy example. In production code, you should pass by reference-to-`const`.

```
void processCitations(ArticleCitations cit)
{
    println("{}", cit.getArticle());
    for (int i { 0 }; i < cit.getNumCitations(); ++i) {
        println("{}", cit.getCitation(i));
    }
}

int main()
{
    while (true) {
        print("Enter a file name (\"STOP\" to stop): ");
        string filename;
        cin >> filename;
        if (filename == "STOP") { break; }

        ArticleCitations cit { filename };
        processCitations(cit);
    }
}
```

You decide to test the program on the Alan Turing example (stored in a file called `paper1.txt`). Here is the output:

```
Enter a file name ("STOP" to stop): paper1.txt
Alan Turing, "On Computable Numbers, with an Application to the
Entscheidungsproblem", Proceedings of the London Mathematical Society, Series 2,
Vol.42 (1936-37), 230-265.
[ 4 empty lines omitted for brevity ]
Enter a file name ("STOP" to stop): STOP
```

That doesn't look right. There are supposed to be four citations printed instead of four blank lines.

Message-Based Debugging

For this bug, you decide to try log-based debugging, and because this is a console application, you decide to just print messages using `println()`. In this case, it makes sense to start by looking at the function that reads the citations from the file. If that doesn't work right, then obviously the object won't have the citations. You can modify `readFile()` as follows:

```
void ArticleCitations::readFile(const string& filename)
{
    // Code omitted for brevity.

    // First count the number of citations.
    println("readFile(): counting number of citations");
    while (!inputFile.eof()) {
        // Skip whitespace before the next entry.
```

```
            inputFile >> ws;
            string temp;
            getline(inputFile, temp);
            if (!temp.empty()) {
                println("Citation {}: {}", count, temp);
                ++count;
            }
        }

        println("Found {} citations", count);
        println("readFile(): reading citations");
        if (count != 0) {
            // Allocate an array of strings to store the citations.
            m_citations = new string[count];
            m_numCitations = count;
            // Seek back to the start of the citations.
            inputFile.seekg(citationsStart);
            // Read each citation and store it in the new array.
            for (count = 0; count < m_numCitations; ++count) {
                string temp;
                getline(inputFile, temp);
                if (!temp.empty()) {
                    println("{}", temp);
                    m_citations[count] = temp;
                }
            }
        } else {
            m_numCitations = -1;
        }
        println("readFile(): finished");
    }
```

Running the same test with this program gives the following output:

```
Enter a file name ("STOP" to stop): paper1.txt
readFile(): counting number of citations
Citation 0: Gödel, "Über formal unentscheidbare Sätze der Principia Mathematica und
verwandter Systeme, I", Monatshefte Math. Phys., 38 (1931), 173-198.
Citation 1: Alonzo Church. "An unsolvable problem of elementary number theory",
American J. of Math., 58 (1936), 345-363.
Citation 2: Alonzo Church. "A note on the Entscheidungsproblem", J. of Symbolic
Logic, 1 (1936), 40-41.
Citation 3: E.W. Hobson, "Theory of functions of a real variable (2nd ed.,
1921)", 87-88.
Found 4 citations
readFile(): reading citations
readFile(): finished
Alan Turing, "On Computable Numbers, with an Application to the
Entscheidungsproblem", Proceedings of the London Mathematical Society, Series 2,
Vol.42 (1936-37), 230-265.
[ 4 empty lines omitted for brevity ]
Enter a file name ("STOP" to stop): STOP
```

As you can see from the output, the first time the program reads the citations from the file, to count them, it reads them correctly. However, the second time, they are not read correctly; nothing is printed between "readFile(): reading citations" and "readFile(): finished" — why not? One way to delve deeper into this issue is to add some debugging code to check the state of the file stream after each attempt to read a citation:

```
void printStreamState(const istream& inputStream)
{
    if (inputStream.good()) { println("stream state is good"); }
    if (inputStream.bad()) { println("stream state is bad"); }
    if (inputStream.fail()) { println("stream state is fail"); }
    if (inputStream.eof()) { println("stream state is eof"); }
}

void ArticleCitations::readFile(const string& filename)
{
    // Code omitted for brevity.

    // First count the number of citations.
    println("readFile(): counting number of citations");
    while (!inputFile.eof()) {
        // Skip whitespace before the next entry.
        inputFile >> ws;
        printStreamState(inputFile);
        string temp;
        getline(inputFile, temp);
        printStreamState(inputFile);
        if (!temp.empty()) {
            println("Citation {}: {}", count, temp);
            ++count;
        }
    }

    println("Found {} citations", count);
    println("readFile(): reading citations");
    if (count != 0) {
        // Allocate an array of strings to store the citations.
        m_citations = new string[count];
        m_numCitations = count;
        // Seek back to the start of the citations.
        inputFile.seekg(citationsStart);
        // Read each citation and store it in the new array.
        for (count = 0; count < m_numCitations; ++count) {
            string temp;
            getline(inputFile, temp);
            printStreamState(inputFile);
            if (!temp.empty()) {
                println("{}", temp);
                m_citations[count] = temp;
            }
        }
```

```
        } else {
            m_numCitations = -1;
        }
        println("readFile(): finished");
    }
```

When you run your program this time, you find some interesting information:

```
Enter a file name ("STOP" to stop): paper1.txt
readFile(): counting number of citations
stream state is good
stream state is good
Citation 0: Gödel, "Über formal unentscheidbare Sätze der Principia Mathematica und
verwandter Systeme, I", Monatshefte Math. Phys., 38 (1931), 173-198.
stream state is good
stream state is good
Citation 1: Alonzo Church. "An unsolvable problem of elementary number theory",
American J. of Math., 58 (1936), 345-363.
stream state is good
stream state is good
Citation 2: Alonzo Church. "A note on the Entscheidungsproblem", J. of Symbolic
Logic, 1 (1936), 40-41.
stream state is good
stream state is good
Citation 3: E.W. Hobson, "Theory of functions of a real variable (2nd ed.,
1921)", 87-88.
stream state is eof
stream state is fail
stream state is eof
Found 4 citations
readFile(): reading citations
stream state is fail
stream state is fail
stream state is fail
stream state is fail
readFile(): finished
Alan Turing, "On Computable Numbers, with an Application to the
Entscheidungsproblem", Proceedings of the London Mathematical Society, Series 2,
Vol.42 (1936-37), 230-265.
[ 4 empty lines omitted for brevity ]
Enter a file name ("STOP" to stop): STOP
```

It looks like the stream state is good until after the final citation is read for the first time. Because the `paper1.txt` file contains an empty last line, the `while` loop is executed one more time after having read the last citation. In this last loop, `inputFile >> ws` reads the whitespace of the last line, which causes the stream state to become `eof`. Then, the code still tries to read a line using `getline()`, which causes the stream state to become `fail` and `eof`. That is expected. What is not expected is that the stream state remains `fail` after all attempts to read the citations a second time. That doesn't appear to make sense at first: the code uses `seekg()` to seek back to the beginning of the citations before reading them a second time.

However, Chapter 13 explains that streams maintain their error states until you clear them explicitly; `seekg()` doesn't clear the `fail` state automatically. When in an error state, streams fail to read data correctly, which explains why the stream state is also `fail` after trying to read the citations a second time.

A closer look at the code reveals that it fails to call `clear()` on the `istream` after reaching the end of the file. If you modify the code by adding a call to `clear()`, it will read the citations properly.

Here is the corrected `readFile()` implementation without the debugging print statements:

```
void ArticleCitations::readFile(const string& filename)
{
    // Code omitted for brevity.

    if (count != 0) {
        // Allocate an array of strings to store the citations.
        m_citations = new string[count];
        m_numCitations = count;
        // Clear the stream state.
        inputFile.clear();
        // Seek back to the start of the citations.
        inputFile.seekg(citationsStart);
        // Read each citation and store it in the new array.
        for (count = 0; count < m_numCitations; ++count) {
            string temp;
            getline(inputFile, temp);
            if (!temp.empty()) {
                m_citations[count] = temp;
            }
        }
    } else {
        m_numCitations = -1;
    }
}
```

Running the same test again on `paper1.txt` now shows the correct four citations.

Using the GDB Debugger on Linux

Now that your `ArticleCitations` class seems to work well on one citations file, you decide to blaze ahead and test some special cases, starting with a file with no citations. The file looks like this and is stored in a file named `paper2.txt`:

```
Author with no citations
```

When you try to run your program on this file, depending on your version of Linux and your compiler, you might get a crash that looks something like the following:

```
Enter a file name ("STOP" to stop): paper2.txt
terminate called after throwing an instance of 'std::bad_alloc'
  what():  std::bad_alloc
Aborted (core dumped)
```

The message "core dumped" means that the program crashed. This time you decide to give the debugger a shot. The Gnu Debugger (GDB) is widely available on Unix and Linux platforms. First, you must compile your program with debugging information (`-g` with g++). Then you can launch the program under GDB. Here's an example session using the debugger to find the root cause of this problem. This example assumes your compiled executable is called `buggyprogram`. Text that you have to type is shown in bold.

```
> gdb buggyprogram
[ Start-up messages omitted for brevity ]
```

```
Reading symbols from /home/marc/c++/gdb/buggyprogram...done.
(gdb) run
Starting program: buggyprogram
Enter a file name ("STOP" to stop): paper2.txt
terminate called after throwing an instance of 'std::bad_alloc'
  what():  std::bad_alloc
Program received signal SIGABRT, Aborted.
0x00007ffff7535c39 in raise () from /lib64/libc.so.6
(gdb)
```

When the program crashes, the debugger breaks the execution and allows you to poke around in the state of the program at that time. The `backtrace` or `bt` command shows the current stack trace. The last operation is at the top, with frame number zero (#0).

```
(gdb) bt
#0  0x00007ffff7535c39 in raise () from /lib64/libc.so.6
#1  0x00007ffff7537348 in abort () from /lib64/libc.so.6
#2  0x00007ffff7b35f85 in __gnu_cxx::__verbose_terminate_handler() () from /lib64/
libstdc++.so.6
#3  0x00007ffff7b33ee6 in ?? () from /lib64/libstdc++.so.6
#4  0x00007ffff7b33f13 in std::terminate() () from /lib64/libstdc++.so.6
#5  0x00007ffff7b3413f in __cxa_throw () from /lib64/libstdc++.so.6
#6  0x00007ffff7b346cd in operator new(unsigned long) () from /lib64/libstdc++.so.6
#7  0x00007ffff7b34769 in operator new[](unsigned long) () from /lib64/
libstdc++.so.6
#8  0x00000000004016ea in ArticleCitations::copy (this=0x7fffffffe090, src=...) at
ArticleCitations.cpp:39
#9  0x00000000004015b5 in ArticleCitations::ArticleCitations
(this=0x7fffffffe090, src=...)
    at ArticleCitations.cpp:15
#10 0x0000000000401d0c in main () at ArticleCitationsTest.cpp:23
```

When you get a stack trace like this, you should try to find the first stack frame from the top that is in your own code. In this example, this is stack frame #8. From this frame, you can see that there seems to be a problem in the `copy()` member function of `ArticleCitations`. This member function is invoked because `main()` calls `processCitations()` and passes the argument by value, which triggers a call to the copy constructor, which calls `copy()`. Of course, in production code you should pass a reference-to-`const`, but pass-by-value is used in this example of a buggy program. You can tell the debugger to switch to stack frame #8 with the `frame` command, which requires the index of the frame that you want to jump to:

```
(gdb) frame 8
#8  0x00000000004016ea in ArticleCitations::copy (this=0x7fffffffe090, src=...) at
ArticleCitations.cpp:39
39      m_citations = new string[m_numCitations];
```

This output shows that the following line caused a problem:

```
m_citations = new string[m_numCitations];
```

Now, you can use the `list` command to show the code in the current stack frame around the offending line:

```
(gdb) list
34      // Copy the article name, author, etc.
35      m_article = src.m_article;
36      // Copy the number of citations.
```

```
m_numCitations = src.m_numCitations;
// Allocate an array of the correct size.
m_citations = new string[m_numCitations];
// Copy each element of the array.
for (int i { 0 }; i < m_numCitations; ++i) {
    m_citations[i] = src.m_citations[i];
}
```

In GDB, you can print values available in the current scope with the `print` command. To find the root cause of the problem, you can try printing some of the variables. The error happens inside the `copy()` member function, so checking the value of the `src` parameter is a good start:

```
(gdb) print src
$1 = (const ArticleCitations &) @0x7fffffffe060: {
  _vptr.ArticleCitations = 0x401fb0 <vtable for ArticleCitations+16>,
  m_article = "Author with no citations", m_citations = 0x000000000000,
  m_numCitations = -1}
```

A-ha! Here's the problem. This article isn't supposed to have any citations. Why is `m_numCitations` set to the strange value `-1`? Take another look at the code in `readFile()` for the case where there are no citations. In that case, it looks like `m_numCitations` is erroneously set to `-1`. The fix is easy: you always need to initialize `m_numCitations` to `0`, instead of setting it to `-1` when there are no citations. Another problem is that `readFile()` can be called multiple times on the same `ArticleCitations` object, so you also need to free a previously allocated `m_citations` array. Here is the fixed code:

```
void ArticleCitations::readFile(const string& filename)
{
    // Code omitted for brevity.

    delete [] m_citations;  // Free previously allocated citations.
    m_citations = nullptr;
    m_numCitations = 0;
    if (count != 0) {
        // Allocate an array of strings to store the citations.
        m_citations = new string[count];
        m_numCitations = count;

        // Code omitted for brevity.
    }
}
```

As this example shows, bugs don't always show up right away. It often takes a debugger and some persistence to find them.

Using the Visual C++ 2022 Debugger

This section explains the same debugging procedure as described in the previous section but uses the Microsoft Visual C++ 2022 debugger instead of GDB.

First, you need to create a project. Either click the New Project button in the Visual Studio 2022's welcome screen or select File ⇨ New ⇨ Project. In the Create A New Project dialog, search for the Console App project template with tags C++, Windows, and Console, and click Next. Enter **ArticleCitations** as the name for the project, choose a folder where to save the project, and click Create. Once your project is created, you can see a list of project files in the Solution Explorer. If this docking window is not visible, select View ⇨ Solution Explorer. The project will already contain a file called

`ArticleCitations.cpp` listed under Source Files in the Solution Explorer tree. Select this file in the Solution Explorer and delete it, as you will add your own files.

Now let's add our files. Right-click the ArticleCitations project in the Solution Explorer and select Add ⇨ Existing Item. Add all the files from the `06_ArticleCitations\04_AfterLogDebugging` folder in the downloadable source code archive to the project. Your Solution Explorer should look similar to Figure 31.1.

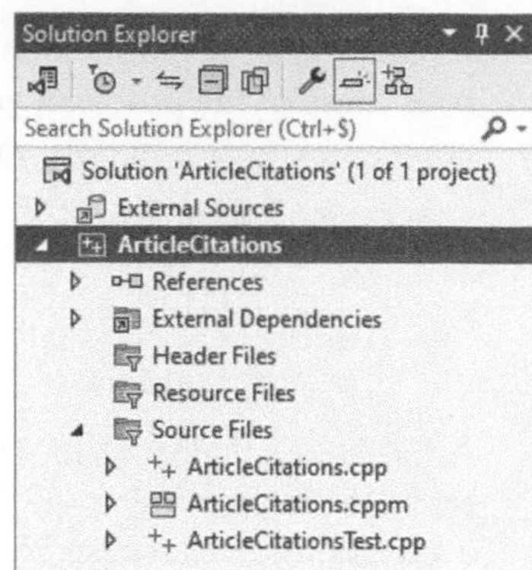

FIGURE 31.1

This example uses C++23 features which are not yet enabled by default in Visual C++ 2022 at the time of this writing. To enable them, right-click the ArticleCitations project in the Solution Explorer window and click Properties. In the Properties window, select Configuration Properties ⇨ General and set the C++ Language Standard option to "ISO C++23 Standard" or "Preview - Features From The Latest C++ Working Draft", whichever is available in your version of Visual C++. The ISO C++23 Standard option is not currently there yet, but it will appear in a future update of Visual C++. While still in the Properties window, go to Configuration Properties ⇨ C/C++ ⇨ Command Line and add /utf-8 as Additional Options. This makes sure that characters such as the ö in Gödel are properly printed.

Make sure the configuration is set to Debug and not Release and then compile the whole program by selecting Build ⇨ Build Solution. Then copy the `paper1.txt` and `paper2.txt` test files to your `ArticleCitations` project folder, which is the folder containing the `ArticleCitations.vcxproj` file.

Run the application with Debug ⇨ Start Debugging and test the program by first specifying the `paper1.txt` file. It should properly read the file and output the result to the console. Then, test `paper2.txt`. The debugger breaks the execution with a message similar to Figure 31.2.

```
void ArticleCitations::copy(const ArticleCitations& src)
{
    // Copy the article name, author, etc.
    m_article = src.m_article;
    // Copy the number of citations.
    m_numCitations = src.m_numCitations;
    // Allocate an array of the correct size.
    m_citations = new string[m_numCitations];
    // Copy each element of the array.
    for (int i{ 0 }; i < m_numCitations; ++i)
        m_citations[i] = src.m_citations[i];
    }
}

ArticleCitations::~ArticleCitations()
{
    delete [] m_citations;
```


FIGURE 31.2

This shows that an `std::bad_array_new_length` exception is thrown. If the code you see is not code you have written, then you need to find the line in your code that caused the exception. To do so, use the call stack window (Debug ➪ Windows ➪ Call Stack). In the call stack, you need to find the first line that contains code you wrote. This is shown in Figure 31.3. You can double-click a line in the call stack window to jump to that line in the code.

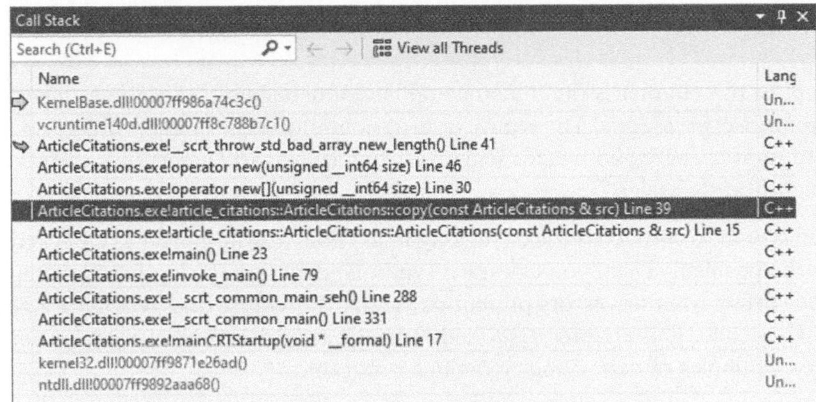

FIGURE 31.3

Just as with GDB, you see that the problem is in `ArticleCitations::copy()`.

You can now inspect variables by simply hovering your mouse over the name of a variable. If you hover over `src`, you'll notice that `m_numCitations` is `-1`. The reason and the fix are the same as in the GDB example.

Instead of hovering over variables to inspect their values, you can also use the Debug ➪ Windows ➪ Autos window, which shows a list of variables. Figure 31.4 shows this list with the `src` variable expanded to show its data members. From this window, you can also see that `m_numCitations` is `-1`.

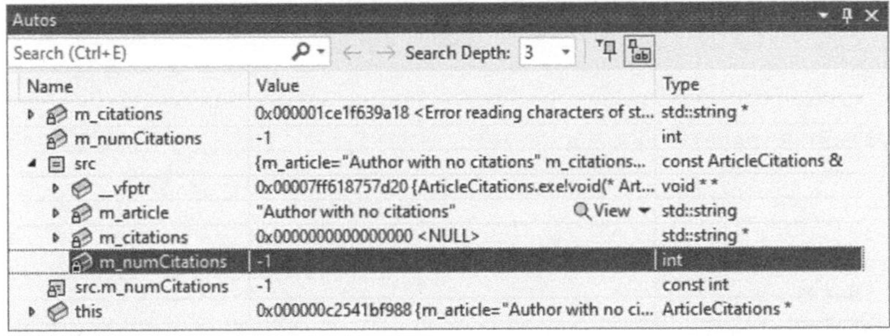

FIGURE 31.4

Lessons from the ArticleCitations Example

You might be inclined to disregard this example as too small to be representative of real debugging. Although the buggy code is not lengthy, many classes that you write will not be much bigger, even in large projects. Imagine if you had failed to test this example thoroughly before integrating it with the rest of the project. If these bugs showed up later, you and other engineers would spend more time narrowing down the problem before you could debug it as shown here. Additionally, the techniques shown in this example apply to all debugging, whether on a large or small scale.

SUMMARY

The most important concept in this chapter is the fundamental law of debugging: *avoid bugs when you're coding, but plan for bugs in your code.* The reality of programming is that bugs will appear. If you've prepared your program properly, with error logging, debug traces, and assertions, then the actual debugging will be significantly easier.

This chapter also presented specific approaches for debugging bugs. The most important rule when debugging is to reproduce the problem. Then, you can use a symbolic debugger, or log-based debugging, to track down the root cause. Memory errors present particular difficulties and account for the majority of bugs in legacy C++ code. This chapter described various categories of memory bugs and their symptoms and showed examples of debugging errors in a program.

Debugging is a hard skill to learn. To take your C++ skills to a professional level, you will have to practice debugging a lot.

EXERCISES

By solving the following exercises, you can practice the material discussed in this chapter. Solutions to all exercises are available with the code download on the book's website at `www.wiley.com/go/proc++6e`. However, if you are stuck on an exercise, first reread parts of this chapter to try to find an answer yourself before looking at the solution from the website.

Exercise 31-1: What is the fundamental law of debugging?

Exercise 31-2: Can you spot any problems with the following piece of code?

```
import std;
using namespace std;

int* getData(int value) { return new int { value * 2 }; }

int main()
{
    int* data { getData(21) };
    println("{}", *data);

    data = getData(42);
    println("{}", *data);
}
```

Exercise 31-3: Given the following code snippet:

```
import std;
using namespace std;
```

```
int sum(int* values, int count)
{
    int total { 0 };
    for (int i { 0 }; i <= count; ++i) { total += values[i]; }
    return total;
}

int main()
{
    int values[] { 1, 2, 3 };
    int total { sum(values, sizeof(values)) };
    println("{}", total);
}
```

It calculates the sum of a set of values. For the values 1, 2, and 3, you expect the sum to be 6; however, when running the code on my machine, the result is -2 for a debug build and some different random number each time I execute a release build, e.g., 920865056, -321371431, and so on. What's going on? Use a symbolic debugger and its step-by-step execution mode to pinpoint the root cause of the wrong result. Consult the documentation of your debugger to learn how to step through individual lines of your code.

Exercise 31-4: (*advanced*) Modify the start-time debug mode example from earlier in this chapter to use `std::source_location`, discussed in Chapter 14, to get rid of the old-style `LOG()` macro. This is trickier than it sounds. The problem is that `Logger::log()` is a variadic function template, so you cannot just add a named `source_location` parameter after the variadic parameter pack. One trick is to use a helper class, for example `Log`. The constructor accepts a variadic parameter pack and a `source_location` and forwards the work to `Logger::log()`. The final part of the trick is the following deduction guide; see Chapter 12, "Writing Generic Code with Templates":

```
template <typename... Ts>
Log(Ts&&...) -> Log<Ts...>;
```

32

Incorporating Design Techniques and Frameworks

WHAT'S IN THIS CHAPTER?

- An overview of C++ language features that are common, but for which you might have forgotten the syntax
- What RAII is and why it is a powerful concept
- What the double dispatch technique is and how to use it
- Various techniques to implement and use mixin classes
- What frameworks are
- The model-view-controller paradigm

WILEY.COM DOWNLOADS FOR THIS CHAPTER

Please note that all the code examples for this chapter are available as part of this chapter's code download on the book's website at `www.wiley.com/go/proc++6e` on the Download Code tab.

One of the major themes of this book has been the adoption of reusable techniques and patterns. As a programmer, you tend to face similar problems repeatedly. With an arsenal of diverse approaches, you can save yourself time by applying the proper technique or pattern to a given problem.

This chapter is about *design techniques*, while the next chapter is about *design patterns*. Both represent standard approaches for solving particular problems; however, design techniques are specific to C++, whereas design patterns are less language-specific. Often, a design technique aims to overcome an annoying feature or language deficiency. Other times, a design technique is a piece of code that you use in many different programs to solve a common C++ problem.

Design techniques are C++ idioms that aren't necessarily built-in parts of the language but are nonetheless frequently used. The first part of this chapter covers the language features in C++ that are common, but for which you might have forgotten the syntax. This material is a review, but it is a useful reference tool when the syntax escapes you. The topics covered include the following:

- Starting a class from scratch
- Extending a class by deriving from it
- Writing a lambda expression
- Implementing the copy-and-swap idiom
- Throwing and catching exceptions
- Defining a class template
- Constraining class and function template parameters
- Writing to a file
- Reading from a file

The second part of this chapter focuses on higher-level techniques that build upon C++ language features. These techniques offer a better way to accomplish everyday programming tasks. Topics include the following:

- Resource Acquisition Is Initialization (RAII)
- The double dispatch technique
- Mixin classes

The chapter concludes with an introduction to frameworks, a coding technique that greatly eases the development of large applications.

"I CAN NEVER REMEMBER HOW TO. . ."

Chapter 1, "A Crash Course in C++ and the Standard Library," explains that the C++ standard specification is more than 2,000 pages long. The standard defines a lot of keywords and a very large number of language features. It is impossible to memorize it all. Even C++ experts need to look things up sometimes. With that in mind, this section presents examples of coding techniques that are used in almost all C++ programs. When you remember the concept but forgot the syntax, turn to the following sections for a refresher.

. . .Write a Class

Don't remember how to get started? No problem—here is the definition of a `Simple` class defined in a module interface file:

```
export module simple;

// A simple class that illustrates class definition syntax.
export class Simple
{
    public:
        Simple();                              // Constructor
        virtual ~Simple() = default;           // Defaulted virtual destructor

        // Disallow copy construction and copy assignment.
        Simple(const Simple& src) = delete;
        Simple& operator=(const Simple& rhs) = delete;

        // Explicitly default move constructor and move assignment operator.
        Simple(Simple&& src) = default;
        Simple& operator=(Simple&& rhs) = default;

        virtual void publicMemberFunction();   // Public member function
        int m_publicInteger;                   // Public data member

    protected:
        virtual void protectedMemberFunction();// Protected member function
        int m_protectedInteger { 41 };         // Protected data member

    private:
        virtual void privateMemberFunction();  // Private member function
        int m_privateInteger { 42 };           // Private data member
        static constexpr int Constant { 2 };   // Private constant
        static inline int ms_staticInt { 3 };  // Private static data member
};
```

> **NOTE** *This class definition shows some things that are possible but not recommended. In your own class definitions, you should avoid having* `public` *or* `protected` *data members. A class should encapsulate its data; hence, you should make data members* `private` *and provide* `public` *or* `protected` *getter and setter member functions.*

As explained in Chapter 10, "Discovering Inheritance Techniques," if your class is meant to be a base class for other classes, you must make at least your destructor `virtual`. It's allowed to leave the destructor non-`virtual`, but then I recommend to mark the class as `final` so that no other classes can derive from it. If you only want to make your destructor `virtual` but you don't need any code inside the destructor, then you can explicitly default it, as in the `Simple` class example.

This example also demonstrates that you can explicitly delete or default special member functions. The copy constructor and copy assignment operator are deleted to prevent unintentional copying, while the move constructor and move assignment operator are explicitly defaulted.

Next, here is the module implementation file:

```
module simple;

Simple::Simple() : m_publicInteger { 40 }
```

```
{
    // Implementation of constructor
}

void Simple::publicMemberFunction() { /* Implementation */ }
void Simple::protectedMemberFunction() { /* Implementation */ }
void Simple::privateMemberFunction() { /* Implementation */ }
```

> **NOTE** *Class member function definitions can also appear directly in the module interface file as demonstrated in the next section. You are not required to split a class up into a module interface file and a module implementation file.*

Chapters 8, "Gaining Proficiency with Classes and Objects," and 9, "Mastering Classes and Objects," provide all the details for writing your own classes.

. . .Derive from an Existing Class

To derive from an existing class, you declare a new class that is an extension of another class. Here is the definition for a class called `DerivedSimple`, deriving from `Simple`, and defined in a `derived_simple` module:

```
export module derived_simple;

export import simple;

// A class derived from the Simple class.
export class DerivedSimple : public Simple
{
    public:
        DerivedSimple() : Simple{} // Constructor
        { /* Implementation of constructor */ }

        void publicMemberFunction() override // Overridden member function
        {
            // Implementation of overridden member function
            Simple::publicMemberFunction(); // Access the base class implementation
        }

        virtual void anotherMemberFunction() // New member function
        { /* Implementation of new member function */ }
};
```

Consult Chapter 10 for details on inheritance techniques.

. . .Write a Lambda Expression

Lambda expressions allow you to write small anonymous inline functions. They are especially powerful in combination with the C++ Standard Library algorithms. The following code snippet shows an example. It uses the `count_if()` algorithm and a lambda expression to count the number of even values in a vector. Additionally, the lambda expression captures the callCount variable by reference from its enclosing scope to keep track of the number of times it gets called.

```
vector values { 1, 2, 3, 4, 5, 6, 7, 8, 9 };
int callCount { 0 };
auto evenCount { ranges::count_if(values,
    [&callCount](int value) {
        ++callCount;
        return value % 2 == 0;
    })
};
println("There are {} even elements in the vector.", evenCount);
println("Lambda was called {} times.", callCount);
```

Chapter 19, "Function Pointers, Function Objects, and Lambda Expressions," discusses lambda expressions in detail.

. . .Use the Copy-and-Swap Idiom

The copy-and-swap idiom is discussed in detail in Chapter 9. It's an idiom to implement a possibly throwing operation on an object with a strong exception-safety guarantee, that is, all-or-nothing. You simply create a copy of the object, modify that copy (can be a complex algorithm, possibly throwing exceptions), and finally, when no exceptions have been thrown, swap the copy with the original object using a non-throwing swap(). An assignment operator is an example of an operation for which you can use the copy-and-swap idiom. Your assignment operator first makes a local copy of the source object and then swaps this copy with the current object using only a non-throwing swap() implementation.

Here is a concise example of the copy-and-swap idiom used for a copy assignment operator. The class defines a copy constructor, a copy assignment operator, and a swap() member function marked as noexcept.

```
export module copy_and_swap;

export class CopyAndSwap final
{
    public:
        CopyAndSwap() = default;
        ~CopyAndSwap();                               // Destructor

        CopyAndSwap(const CopyAndSwap& src);          // Copy constructor
        CopyAndSwap& operator=(const CopyAndSwap& rhs); // Copy assignment operator

        void swap(CopyAndSwap& other) noexcept; // noexcept swap() member function

    private:
        // Private data members...
};
// Standalone noexcept swap() function
export void swap(CopyAndSwap& first, CopyAndSwap& second) noexcept;
```

Here are the implementations:

```
CopyAndSwap::~CopyAndSwap() { /* Implementation of destructor. */ }

CopyAndSwap::CopyAndSwap(const CopyAndSwap& src)
{
    // This copy constructor can first delegate to a non-copy constructor
    // if any resource allocations have to be done. See the Spreadsheet
    // implementation in Chapter 9 for an example.

    // Make a copy of all data members...
}

void swap(CopyAndSwap& first, CopyAndSwap& second) noexcept
{
    first.swap(second);
}

void CopyAndSwap::swap(CopyAndSwap& other) noexcept
{
    using std::swap;

    // Swap each data member, for example:
    // swap(m_data, other.m_data);
}

CopyAndSwap& CopyAndSwap::operator=(const CopyAndSwap& rhs)
{
    // Copy-and-swap idiom.
    auto copy { rhs };  // Do all the work in a temporary instance.
    swap(copy);         // Commit the work with only non-throwing operations.
    return *this;
}
```

Consult Chapter 9 for a more detailed discussion.

. . .Throw and Catch Exceptions

If you've been working on a team that doesn't use exceptions (for shame!) or if you've gotten used to Java-style exceptions, the C++ syntax may escape you. Here's a refresher that uses the built-in exception class `std::runtime_error`. In most larger programs, you will write your own exception classes.

```
import std;
using namespace std;
void throwIf(bool should)
{
    if (should) {
        throw runtime_error { "Here's my exception" };
    }
}

int main()
{
    try {
```

```
        throwIf(false); // Doesn't throw.
        throwIf(true);  // Throws.
    } catch (const runtime_error& e) {
        println(cerr, "Caught exception: {}", e.what());
        return 1;
    }
}
```

Chapter 14, "Handling Errors," discusses exceptions in more detail.

. . .Write a Class Template

Template syntax can be confusing. The most forgotten piece of the template puzzle is that code that uses a class template needs to be able to see the class template definition as well as the member function implementations. The same holds for function templates. One technique to accomplish this is to simply put the class member function implementations directly in the interface file containing the class template definition. The following example demonstrates this and implements a class template that wraps a reference to an object and includes a getter. Here is the module interface file:

```
export module simple wrapper;

export template <typename T>
class SimpleWrapper
{
    public:
        explicit SimpleWrapper(T& object) : m_object { object } { }
        T& get() const { return m_object; }
    private:
        T& m_object;
};
```

The code can be tested as follows:

```
import simple_wrapper;
import std;
using namespace std;

int main()
{
    // Try wrapping an integer.
    int i { 7 };
    SimpleWrapper intWrapper { i };  // Using CTAD.
    // Or without class template argument deduction (CTAD).
    SimpleWrapper<int> intWrapper2 { i };
    i = 2;
    println("wrapped value is {}", intWrapper.get());
    println("wrapped value is {}", intWrapper2.get());

    // Try wrapping a string.
    string str { "test" };
    SimpleWrapper stringWrapper { str };
    str += "!";
    println("wrapped value is {}", stringWrapper.get());
}
```

Details about templates can be found in Chapter 12, "Writing Generic Code with Templates," and Chapter 26, "Advanced Templates."

. . .Constrain Template Parameters

With concepts, you can put constraints on template parameters of class and function templates. For example, the following code snippet constrains the template type parameter `T` of the `SimpleWrapper` class template from the previous section to be either a floating-point or an integral type. Specifying a type for `T` that does not satisfy these constraints will cause a compilation error.

```
import std;

export template <typename T> requires (std::floating_point<T> || std::integral<T>)
class SimpleWrapper
{
    public:
        explicit SimpleWrapper(T& object) : m_object { object } { }
        T& get() const { return m_object; }
    private:
        T& m_object;
};
```

Chapter 12 explains concepts in detail.

. . .Write to a File

The following program outputs a message to a file and then reopens the file and appends another message. Additional details can be found in Chapter 13, "Demystifying C++ I/O."

```
import std;
using namespace std;

int main()
{
    ofstream outputFile { "FileWrite.out" };
    if (outputFile.fail()) {
        println(cerr, "Unable to open file for writing.");
        return 1;
    }
    outputFile << "Hello!" << endl;
    outputFile.close();

    ofstream appendFile { "FileWrite.out", ios_base::app };
    if (appendFile.fail()) {
        println(cerr, "Unable to open file for appending.");
        return 2;
    }
    appendFile << "World!" << endl;
}
```

. . .Read from a File

Details for file input are discussed in Chapter 13. Here is a quick sample program for file reading basics. It reads the file written by the program in the previous section and outputs it one whitespace-separated token at a time.

```
import std;
using namespace std;

int main()
{
    ifstream inputFile { "FileWrite.out" };
    if (inputFile.fail()) {
        println(cerr, "Unable to open file for reading.");
        return 1;
    }

    string nextToken;
    while (inputFile >> nextToken) {
        println("Token: {}", nextToken);
    }
}
```

The following reads an entire text file with a single call to `getline()`. This doesn't work with binary files, as they might contain `\0` characters in their contents.

```
string fileContents;
getline(inputFile, fileContents, '\0');
println("{}", fileContents);
```

An alternative is to use an `istreambuf_iterator` (see Chapter 17, "Understanding Iterators and the Ranges Library"):

```
string fileContents {
    istreambuf_iterator<char> { inputFile },
    istreambuf_iterator<char> { }
};
println("{}", fileContents);
```

THERE MUST BE A BETTER WAY

As you read this paragraph, thousands of C++ programmers throughout the world are solving problems that have already been solved. Someone in a cubicle in San Jose is writing a smart pointer implementation from scratch that uses reference counting. A young programmer on a Mediterranean island is designing a class hierarchy that could benefit immensely from the use of mixin classes.

As a professional C++ programmer, you ought to spend less of your time reinventing the wheel and more of your time adapting reusable concepts in new ways. This section gives some examples of general-purpose approaches that you can apply directly to your own programs or customize for your needs.

Resource Acquisition Is Initialization

Resource acquisition is initialization (RAII) is a simple yet powerful concept. It is used to acquire ownership of some resources and to automatically free these acquired resources when an RAII instance goes out of scope. Both initialization and destruction happen at a deterministic point in time. Basically, the constructor of a new RAII instance *acquires ownership* of a certain resource and *initializes* the instance with that resource, which is why it's called *resource acquisition is initialization*. The destructor automatically frees the acquired resource when the RAII instance is destroyed.

Here is an example of a `File` RAII class that safely wraps a C-style file handle (`std::FILE`) and automatically closes the file when the RAII instance goes out of scope. The RAII class also provides `get()`, `release()`, and `reset()` member functions that behave similarly to the same member functions on certain Standard Library classes, such as `std::unique_ptr`. RAII classes usually disallow copy construction and copy assignment; hence, this implementation deletes those members.

```
import std;

class File final
{
    public:
        explicit File(std::FILE* file) : m_file { file } { }
        ~File() { reset(); }

        // Prevent copy construction and copy assignment.
        File(const File& src) = delete;
        File& operator=(const File& rhs) = delete;

        // Allow move construction.
        File(File&& src) noexcept : m_file { std::exchange(src.m_file, nullptr) }
        {
        }

        // Allow move assignment.
        File& operator=(File&& rhs) noexcept
        {
            if (this != &rhs) {
                reset();
                m_file = std::exchange(rhs.m_file, nullptr);
            }
            return *this;
        }

        // get(), release(), and reset()
        std::FILE* get() const noexcept { return m_file; }

        [[nodiscard]] std::FILE* release() noexcept
        {
            return std::exchange(m_file, nullptr);
        }

        void reset(std::FILE* file = nullptr) noexcept
        {
            if (m_file) { std::fclose(m_file); }
            m_file = file;
        }

    private:
        std::FILE* m_file { nullptr };
};
```

It can be used as follows:

```
File myFile { std::fopen("input.txt", "r") };
```

As soon as the myFile instance goes out of scope, its destructor is called, and the file is automatically closed.

There is one important pitfall with using RAII classes that you need to be aware of. You can accidentally write a statement that you think is properly creating an RAII instance within a certain scope, but that is instead creating a temporary object, which is immediately destroyed when that statement has finished executing. For example, the following statement correctly uses the File RAII class:

```
File myFile { std::fopen("input.txt", "r") };
```

However, you could accidentally forget to give the RAII instance a name as follows:

```
File { std::fopen("input.txt", "r") };
```

This statement creates a temporary File instance, which is immediately destroyed at the end of the statement. This does not trigger any warning or error from the compiler. To avoid this, you should mark the constructor of RAII classes with the [[nodiscard]] attribute. For example:

```
[[nodiscard]] explicit File(std::FILE* file) : m_file{ file } { }
```

With this change, creating a File instance without giving it a name triggers a compiler warning such as the following:

```
warning C4834: discarding return value of function with 'nodiscard' attribute
```

Of course, with the File RAII class, you probably will never forget to give it a name as you most likely will want to do something with the opened file. However, sometimes you need to create an instance of an RAII class in a certain scope, without having to directly interact any further with that created instance, e.g., mutex locks. Let's look at such an example using an RAII class from the Standard Library, std::unique_lock (see Chapter 27, "Multithreaded Programming with C++"). The following code snippet shows proper use of a unique_lock. I'm initially not using the uniform initialization syntax to initialize the unique_lock but will get back to this in the subsequent discussion.

```
class Foo
{
    public:
        void setData()
        {
            unique_lock<mutex> lock(m_mutex);
            // ...
        }
    private:
        mutex m_mutex;
};
```

The setData() member function uses the unique_lock RAII class to construct a local lock object that locks the m_mutex data member and automatically unlocks that mutex at the end of the function.

However, because you do not directly use the lock variable after it has been defined, it is easy to make the following mistake:

```
unique_lock<mutex>(m_mutex);
```

In this code, you accidentally forgot to give the unique_lock a name. This compiles, but it does not do what you intended it to do! It actually declares a local variable called m_mutex (hiding the `m_mutex` data member) and initializes it with a call to the `unique_lock`'s default constructor. The result is that the `m_mutex` data member is *not* locked! The compiler will give a warning, though, if the warning level is set high enough. Something along the lines of:

```
warning C4458: declaration of 'm_mutex' hides class member
```

If you use uniform initialization syntax as follows, the compiler doesn't generate the "hiding class member" warning, but it also does not do what you want. The following creates a temporary lock on `m_mutex`, but since it's temporary, the lock is immediately released at the end of this statement.

```
unique_lock<mutex> { m_mutex };
```

Recently, some compilers actually do mark the `unique_lock` constructors with `[[nodiscard]]`, just as I recommended with the `File` RAII example. One such compiler is Visual C++ 2022. If you use such a compiler, the previous statement generates a warning about the fact that the return value of the constructor is discarded.

Additionally, you could make a typo in the name passed as argument, for example as follows:

```
unique_lock<mutex>(m);
```

Here you forgot to give a name for the lock, and you made a typo in the name of the argument. This code simply declares a local variable called `m` and initializes it with the default constructor of `unique_lock`. The compiler does not even generate a warning, unless maybe a warning that `m` is an unreferenced local variable. In this case, though, if you would use uniform initialization syntax as follows, then the compiler issues an error complaining about an undeclared identifier `m`:

```
unique_lock<mutex> { m };
```

> **WARNING** *Make sure you always name your RAII instances! Additionally, I recommend not to include a default constructor in an RAII class. That avoids some of the issues discussed here.*

Double Dispatch

Double dispatch is a technique that adds an extra dimension to the concept of polymorphism. As described in Chapter 5, "Designing with Classes," polymorphism lets the program determine behavior based on types at run time. For example, you could have an `Animal` class with a `move()` member function. All `Animals` move, but they differ in terms of *how* they move. The `move()` member function is defined for every derived class of `Animal` so that the appropriate member function can be called, or can be dispatched to, for the appropriate animal at run time without knowing the type of the animal at compile time. Chapter 10 explains how to use virtual member functions to implement this run-time polymorphism.

Sometimes, however, you need a member function to behave according to the run-time type of two objects, instead of just one. For example, suppose you want to add a member function to the `Animal` class that returns `true` if the animal eats another animal, and `false` otherwise. The decision is based on two factors: the type of animal doing the eating and the type of animal being eaten. Unfortunately, C++ provides no language mechanism to choose a behavior based on the run-time type of more than one object. Virtual member functions alone are insufficient for modeling this scenario because they determine a member function, or behavior, depending on the run-time type of only the receiving object.

Some object-oriented languages provide the ability to choose a member function at run time based on the run-time types of two or more objects. They call this feature *multimethods*. In C++ there is no core language feature to support multimethods, but you can use the *double dispatch* technique, which provides a way to make functions virtual for more than one object.

> **NOTE** *Double dispatch is really a special case of multiple dispatch, in which a behavior is chosen depending on the run-time types of two or more objects. In practice, double dispatch, which chooses a behavior based on the run-time types of exactly two objects, is usually sufficient.*

Attempt #1: Brute Force

The most straightforward way to implement a member function whose behavior depends on the run-time types of two different objects is to take the perspective of one of the objects and use a series of `if/else` constructs to check the type of the other. For example, you could implement a member function called `eats()` in each class derived from `Animal` that takes the other animal as a parameter. The member function is declared pure virtual in the base class as follows:

```
class Animal
{
    public:
        virtual bool eats(const Animal& prey) const = 0;
};
```

Each derived class implements the `eats()` member function and returns the appropriate value based on the type of the parameter. The implementation of `eats()` for several derived classes follows. Note that the `TRex` avoids any `if` statements because—according to the author—a T-rex, like any carnivorous dinosaur, eats anything.

```
bool Bear::eats(const Animal& prey) const
{
    if (typeid(prey) == typeid(Fish)) { return true; }
    return false;
}

bool Fish::eats(const Animal& prey) const
{
    if (typeid(prey) == typeid(Fish)) { return true; }
    return false;
}

bool TRex::eats(const Animal& prey) const
{
    return true;
}
```

This brute-force approach works, and it's probably the most straightforward technique for a small number of classes. However, there are several reasons why you might want to avoid this approach.

- Object-oriented programming (OOP) purists often frown upon explicitly querying the type of an object because it implies a design that is lacking a proper object-oriented structure.
- As the number of types grows, such code can become messy and repetitive.
- This approach does not force derived classes to consider new types. For example, if you added a `Donkey`, the `Bear` class would continue to compile but would return `false` when told to eat a `Donkey`, even though everybody knows that bears eat donkeys. A bear would refuse to eat a donkey because there is no `else if` statement checking explicitly for `Donkeys`.

Attempt #2: Single Polymorphism with Overloading

You could attempt to use polymorphism with overloading to circumvent all of the cascading `if/else` constructs. Instead of giving each class a single `eats()` member function that takes an `Animal` reference, why not overload the member function for each derived class of `Animal`? The base class definition would look like this:

```
class Animal
{
    public:
        virtual bool eats(const Bear&) const = 0;
        virtual bool eats(const Fish&) const = 0;
        virtual bool eats(const TRex&) const = 0;
};
```

Because the member functions are pure virtual in the base class, each derived class is forced to implement the behavior for every other type of `Animal`. For example, the `Bear` class contains the following member functions:

```
class Bear : public Animal
{
    public:
        bool eats(const Bear&) const override { return false; }
        bool eats(const Fish&) const override { return true; }
        bool eats(const TRex&) const override { return false; }
};
```

This approach initially appears to work, but it really solves only half of the problem. To call the proper `eats()` member function on an `Animal`, the compiler needs to know the compile-time type of the animal being eaten. A call such as the following will be successful because the compile-time types of both the animal that eats and the animal that is eaten are known:

```
Bear myBear;
Fish myFish;
println("Bear eats fish? {}", myBear.eats(myFish));
```

The missing piece is that the solution is polymorphic in only one direction. You can access `myBear` through an `Animal` reference, and the correct member function will be called:

```
Animal& animalRef { myBear };
println("Bear eats fish? {}", animalRef.eats(myFish));
```

However, the reverse is not true. If you pass an `Animal` reference to the `eats()` member function, you will get a compilation error because there is no `eats()` member function that takes an `Animal`. The compiler cannot determine, at compile time, which version to call. The following example does not compile:

```
Animal& animalRef { myFish };
println("Bear eats fish? {}",
    myBear.eats(animalRef)); // BUG! No member function Bear::eats(Animal&)
```

Because the compiler needs to know which overloaded version of the `eats()` member function is going to be called at compile time, this solution is not truly polymorphic. It would not work, for example, if you were iterating over an array of `Animal` references and passing each one to a call to `eats()`.

Attempt #3: Double Dispatch

The *double dispatch* technique is a truly polymorphic solution to the multiple-type problem. In C++, polymorphism is achieved by overriding member functions in derived classes. At run time, member functions are called based on the actual type of the object. The preceding single polymorphic attempt didn't work because it attempted to use polymorphism to determine which overloaded version of a member function to call instead of using it to determine on which class to call the member function.

To begin, focus on a single derived class, perhaps the `Bear` class. The class needs a member function with the following declaration:

```
bool eats(const Animal& prey) const override;
```

The key to double dispatch is to determine the result based on a member function call on the argument. Suppose that the `Animal` class has a member function called `eatenBy()`, which takes an `Animal` reference as a parameter. This member function returns `true` if the current `Animal` gets eaten by the one passed in. With such a member function, the definition of `eats()` becomes simple:

```
bool Bear::eats(const Animal& prey) const
{
    return prey.eatenBy(*this);
}
```

At first, it looks like this solution adds another layer of member function calls to the single polymorphic member function. After all, each derived class still has to implement a version of `eatenBy()` for every derived class of `Animal`. However, there is a key difference. Polymorphism is occurring twice! When you call the `eats()` member function on an `Animal`, polymorphism determines whether you are calling `Bear::eats()`, `Fish::eats()`, or one of the others. When you call `eatenBy()`, polymorphism again determines which class's version of the member function to call. It calls `eatenBy()` on the run-time type of the `prey` object. Note that the run-time type of `*this` is always the same as the compile-time type so that the compiler can call the correct overloaded version of `eatenBy()` for the argument (in this case `Bear`).

The following are the class definitions for the `Animal` hierarchy using double dispatch. The forward class declarations are necessary because the base class uses references to the derived classes. Note that each `Animal`-derived class implements the `eats()` member function in the same way, but it cannot be factored up into the base class. The reason is that if you attempt to do so, the compiler won't know which overloaded version of the `eatenBy()` member function to call because `*this` would be an `Animal`, not a particular derived class. Member function overload resolution is determined according to the compile-time type of the object, not its run-time type.

```
// Forward declarations.
class Fish;
class Bear;
class TRex;

class Animal
{
    public:
        virtual bool eats(const Animal& prey) const = 0;

        virtual bool eatenBy(const Bear&) const = 0;
        virtual bool eatenBy(const Fish&) const = 0;
        virtual bool eatenBy(const TRex&) const = 0;
};

class Bear : public Animal
{
    public:
        bool eats(const Animal& prey) const override{ return prey.eatenBy(*this); }

        bool eatenBy(const Bear&) const override { return false; }
        bool eatenBy(const Fish&) const override { return false; }
        bool eatenBy(const TRex&) const override { return true; }
};

class Fish : public Animal
{
    public:
        bool eats(const Animal& prey) const override{ return prey.eatenBy(*this); }

        bool eatenBy(const Bear&) const override { return true; }
        bool eatenBy(const Fish&) const override { return true; }
        bool eatenBy(const TRex&) const override { return true; }
};

class TRex : public Animal
{
    public:
        bool eats(const Animal& prey) const override{ return prey.eatenBy(*this); }

        bool eatenBy(const Bear&) const override { return false; }
        bool eatenBy(const Fish&) const override { return false; }
        bool eatenBy(const TRex&) const override { return true; }
};
```

Double dispatch is a concept that takes a bit of getting used to. I suggest playing with this code to familiarize yourself with the concept and its implementation.

Mixin Classes

Chapters 5 and 6, "Designing for Reuse," introduce mixin classes. They answer the question, "What else is this class able to do?" and the answer often ends with "-able." Examples are `Clickable`, `Drawable`, `Printable`, `Lovable`, and so on. Mixin classes are a way that you can add functionality to a class without committing to a full *is-a* relationship. There are several techniques to implement mixin classes in C++. This section looks at the following:

- Using multiple inheritance
- Using class templates
- Using CRTP
- Using CRTP and "deducing `this`"

Using Multiple Inheritance

This section examines how to design, implement, and use a mixin class using the multiple inheritance technique.

Designing a Mixin Class

Mixin classes contain actual code that can be reused by other classes. A single mixin class implements a well-defined piece of functionality. For example, you might have a mixin class called `Playable` that is mixed into certain types of media objects. The mixin class could, for example, contain most of the code to communicate with the computer's sound drivers. By mixing in the class, the media object would get that functionality for free.

When designing a mixin class, you need to consider what behavior you are adding and whether it belongs in the object hierarchy or in a separate class. Using the previous example, if all media classes are playable, the base class should derive from `Playable` instead of mixing the `Playable` class into all of the derived classes. If only certain media classes are playable and they are scattered throughout the hierarchy, a mixin class makes sense.

One of the cases where mixin classes are particularly useful is when you have classes organized into a hierarchy on one axis, but they also contain similarities on another axis. For example, consider a war simulation game played on a grid. Each grid location can contain an `Item` with attack and defense capabilities and other characteristics. Some items, such as a `Castle`, are stationary. Others, such as a `Knight` or `FloatingCastle`, can move throughout the grid. When initially designing the object hierarchy, you might end up with something like Figure 32.1, which organizes the classes according to their attack and defense capabilities.

The hierarchy in Figure 32.1 ignores the movement functionality that certain classes contain. Building your hierarchy around movement would result in a structure similar to Figure 32.2.

Of course, the design of Figure 32.2 throws away all the organization of Figure 32.1. What's a good object-oriented programmer to do?

Assuming that you go with the first hierarchy, organized around attackers and defenders, you need some way to work movement into the equation. One possibility is that, even though only a portion of the derived classes support movement, you *could* add a `move()` member function to the `Item` base class. The default implementation would do nothing, but certain derived classes would override `move()` to actually change their location on the grid.

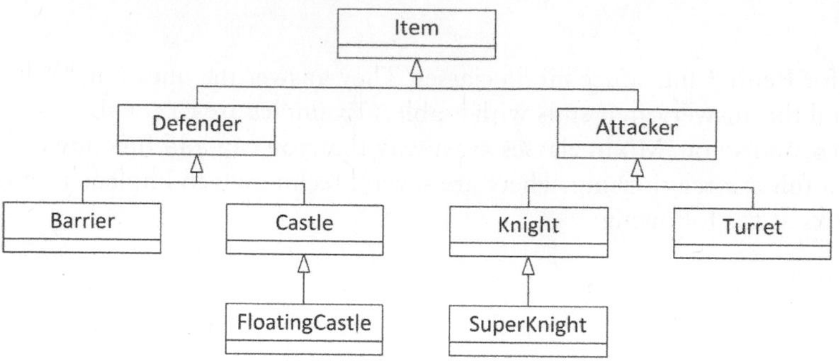

FIGURE 32.1

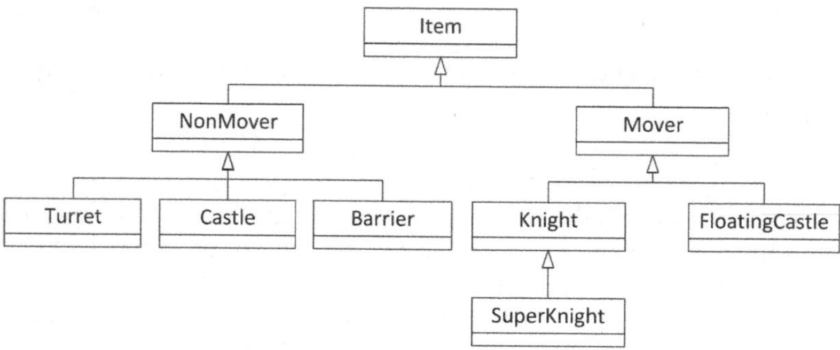

FIGURE 32.2

Another approach is to write a `Movable` mixin class. The elegant hierarchy from Figure 32.1 could be preserved, but certain classes in the hierarchy would derive from `Movable` in addition to their parent. Figure 32.3 shows this design.

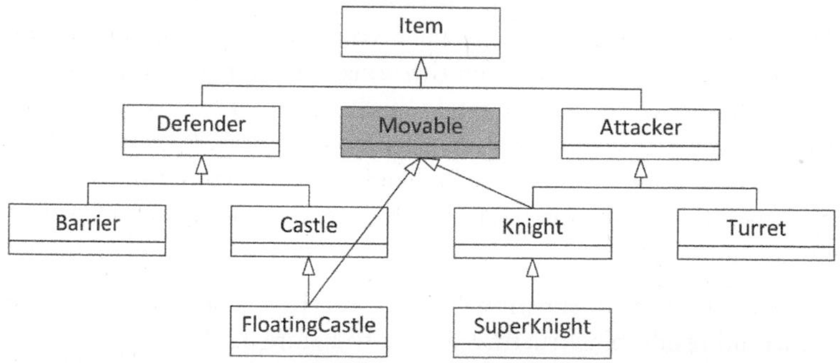

FIGURE 32.3

Yet another approach is to flatten the hierarchy and don't use run time polymorphism at all. Instead, you can use static polymorphism and/or type-erasure whenever you need to deal polymorphically with a subset of your types. These approaches are not further discussed in this text.

Implementing a Mixin Class

Writing a mixin class is no different from writing a normal class. In fact, it's usually much simpler. Using the earlier war simulation, the `Movable` mixin class might look as follows:

```
class Movable
{
    public:
        virtual void move() { /* Implementation to move an item... */ }
};
```

This `Movable` mixin class implements the actual code to move an item on the grid. It also provides a type for `Items` that can be moved. This allows you to create, for example, an array of all movable items without knowing or caring what actual derived class of `Item` they belong to.

Using a Mixin Class

The code for using a mixin class is syntactically equivalent to multiple inheritance. In addition to deriving from your parent class in the main hierarchy, you also derive from the mixin class. Here's an example:

```
class FloatingCastle : public Castle, public Movable { /* ... */ };
```

This *mixes in* the functionality provided by the `Movable` mixin class into the `FloatingCastle` class. Now you have a class that exists in the most logical place in the hierarchy, but still shares commonality with objects elsewhere in the hierarchy.

Using Class Templates

A second option to implement a mixin class in C++ is to make the mixin class itself a class template accepting a template type parameter and then deriving itself from that type.

Chapter 6 explains the mechanism for implementing a `SelfDrivable` mixin class template that can then be used to create self-drivable cars and trucks. Now that you are fluent in class templates (Chapters 12 and 26), the `SelfDrivable` mixin example from Chapter 6 should hold no surprises anymore. The mixin class is defined as follows:

```
template <typename T>
class SelfDrivable : public T { /* ... */ };
```

If you then have a `Car` and a `Truck` class, you can easily define a self-drivable car and truck as follows:

```
SelfDrivable<Car> selfDrivingCar;
SelfDrivable<Truck> selfDrivingTruck;
```

This way, functionality can be added to existing classes, `Car` and `Truck`, without having to modify those classes at all.

Here is a complete example:

```
template <typename T>
class SelfDrivable : public T
{
    public:
```

```
        void drive() { this->setSpeed(1.2); }
};

class Car
{
    public:
        void setSpeed(double speed) { println("Car speed set to {}.", speed); }
};

class Truck
{
    public:
        void setSpeed(double speed) { println("Truck speed set to {}.", speed); }
};

int main()
{
    SelfDrivable<Car> car;
    SelfDrivable<Truck> truck;
    car.drive();
    truck.drive();
}
```

Using CRTP

Another technique to implement a mixin class in C++ is to use the *curiously recurring template pattern* (CRTP).

The mixin class itself is again a class template, but this time it accepts a template type parameter representing the type of a derived class and doesn't inherit itself from any other class. In the implementation a `static_cast()` is required to cast `this` to the type of the derived class.

```
template <typename Derived>
class SelfDrivable
{
    public:
        void drive()
        {
            auto& self { static_cast<Derived&>(*this) };
            self.setSpeed(1.2);
        }
};
```

Concrete classes, such as `Car` and `Truck`, then inherit from `SelfDrivable` and pass their own type as the template type argument for `SelfDrivable`.

```
class Car : public SelfDrivable<Car>
{
    public:
        void setSpeed(double speed) { println("Car speed set to {}.", speed); }
};

class Truck : public SelfDrivable<Truck>
{
```

```
    public:
        void setSpeed(double speed) { println("Truck speed set to {}.", speed); }
};
```

These can be used as follows:

```
Car car;
Truck truck;
car.drive();
truck.drive();
```

Using CRTP and Deducing this

The implementation of `SelfDrivable::drive()` in the previous CRTP example requires a `static_cast()` to get access to the correct derived type. Thanks to the C++23 "deducing `this`" feature, the `SelfDrivable` class can be implemented more elegantly as follows using an explicit object parameter. In this implementation, the `SelfDrivable` mixin class is no longer a class template, but `SelfDrivable::drive()` is now a member function template. The parameter annotated with `this` is known as an explicit object parameter (see Chapter 8, "Gaining Proficiency with Classes and Objects").

```
class SelfDrivable
{
    public:
        void drive(this auto& self) { self.setSpeed(1.2); }
};
```

`Car` and `Truck` then simply derive from `SelfDrivable`:

```
class Car : public SelfDrivable { /* Same as before */ };
class Truck : public SelfDrivable { /* Same as before */ };
```

OBJECT-ORIENTED FRAMEWORKS

When graphical operating systems first came on the scene in the 1980s, procedural programming was the norm. At the time, writing a GUI application usually involved manipulating complex data structures and passing them to OS-provided functions. For example, to draw a rectangle in a window, you might have had to populate a `Window` struct with the appropriate information and pass it to a `drawRect()` function.

As object-oriented programming (OOP) grew in popularity, programmers looked for a way to apply the OOP paradigm to GUI development. The result is known as an *object-oriented framework*. In general, a framework is a set of classes that are used collectively to provide an object-oriented interface to some underlying functionality. By frameworks, programmers usually mean large class libraries that are used for general application development. However, a framework can really represent functionality of any size. If you write a suite of classes that provides database functionality for your application, those classes could be considered a framework.

Working with Frameworks

The defining characteristic of a framework is that it provides its own set of techniques and patterns. Frameworks usually require a bit of learning to get started with because they have their own mental model. Before you can work with a large application framework, such as the Microsoft Foundation Classes (MFC), you need to understand its view of the world.

Frameworks vary greatly in their abstract ideas and in their actual implementation. Many frameworks are built on top of legacy procedural APIs, which may affect various aspects of their design. Other frameworks are written from the ground up with object-oriented design in mind. Some frameworks might ideologically oppose certain aspects of the C++ language. For example, a framework could consciously shun the notion of multiple inheritance.

When you start working with a new framework, your first task is to find out what makes it tick. To what design principles does it subscribe? What mental model are its developers trying to convey? What aspects of the language does it use extensively? These are all vital questions, even though they may sound like things that you'll pick up along the way. If you fail to understand the design, model, or language features of the framework, you will quickly get into situations where you overstep the bounds of the framework.

An understanding of the framework's design will also make it possible for you to extend it. For example, if the framework omits a feature, such as support for printing, you could write your own printing classes using the same model as the framework. By doing so, you retain a consistent model for your application, and you have code that can be reused by other applications.

Additionally, a framework might use certain specific data types. For example, the MFC framework uses the `CString` data type to represent strings, instead of using the Standard Library `std::string` class. This does not mean you have to switch to the data types provided by the framework for your entire code base. Instead, you could convert the data types on the boundaries between the framework code and the rest of your code.

The Model-View-Controller Paradigm

As I mentioned earlier, frameworks vary in their approaches to object-oriented design. One common paradigm is known as *model-view-controller* (MVC). This paradigm models the notion that many applications commonly deal with a set of data, one or more views on that data, and manipulation of the data.

In MVC, a set of data is called the *model*. In a race car simulator, the model would keep track of various statistics, such as the current speed of the car and the amount of damage it has sustained. In practice, the model often takes the form of a class with many getters and setters. The class definition for the model of the race car might look as follows:

```
class RaceCar
{
    public:
        RaceCar();
        virtual ~RaceCar() = default;

        virtual double getSpeed() const;
```

```
        virtual void setSpeed(double speed);

        virtual double getDamageLevel() const;
        virtual void setDamageLevel(double damage);
    private:
        double m_speed { 0.0 };
        double m_damageLevel { 0.0 };
};
```

A *view* is a particular visualization of the model. For example, there could be two views on a RaceCar. The first view could be a graphical view of the car, and the second could be a graph that shows the level of damage over time. The important point is that both views are operating on the same data—they are different ways of looking at the same information. This is one of the main advantages of the MVC paradigm: by keeping data separated from its display, you can keep your code more organized and easily create additional views.

The final piece to the MVC paradigm is the *controller*. The controller is the piece of code that changes the model in response to some event. For example, when the driver of the race car simulator runs into a concrete barrier, the controller instructs the model to bump up the car's damage level and reduce its speed. The controller can also manipulate the view. For example, when the user scrolls a scrollbar in the user interface, the controller instructs the view to scroll its content.

The three components of MVC interact in a feedback loop. Actions are handled by the controller, which adjusts the model and/or views. If the model changes, it notifies the views to update themselves. Figure 32.4 shows this interaction.

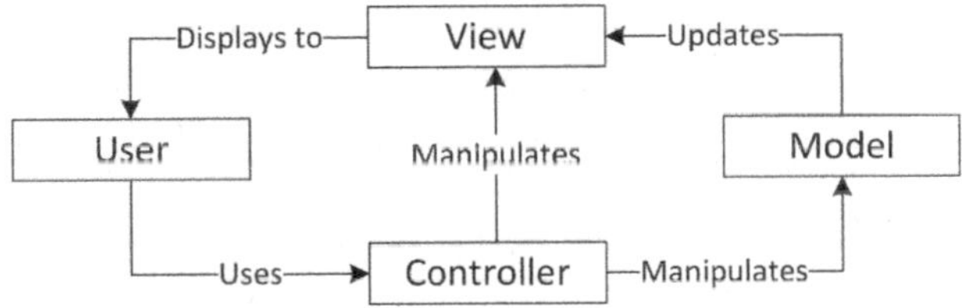

FIGURE 32.4

The model-view-controller paradigm has gained widespread support within many popular frameworks. Even nontraditional applications, such as web applications, are moving in the direction of MVC because it enforces a clear separation between data, the manipulation of data, and the displaying of data.

The MVC pattern has evolved into several different variants, such as model-view-presenter (MVP), model-view-adapter (MVA), model-view-viewmodel (MVVM), and so on.

SUMMARY

In this chapter, you've read about some of the common techniques that professional C++ programmers use consistently in their projects. As you advance as a software developer, you will undoubtedly form your own collection of reusable classes and libraries. Discovering design techniques opens the door to developing and using *patterns*, which are higher-level reusable constructs. You will experience the many applications of patterns next in Chapter 33, "Applying Design Patterns."

EXERCISES

By solving the following exercises, you can practice the material discussed in this chapter. Solutions to all exercises are available with the code download on the book's website at `www.wiley.com/go/proc++6e`. However, if you are stuck on an exercise, first reread parts of this chapter to try to find an answer yourself before looking at the solution from the website.

Exercise 32-1: Write an RAII class template, `Pointer<T>`, that can store a pointer to a `T` and automatically deletes the memory when such an RAII instance goes out of scope. Provide a `reset()` and `release()` member function, and an overloaded `operator*`.

Exercise 32-2: Modify your class template from Exercise 32-1 so that it throws an exception if the argument given to the constructor is `nullptr`.

Exercise 32-3: Take your solution from Exercise 32-2 and add a member function template called `assign()` with a template type parameter `E`. The function should accept an argument of type `E` and assign this argument to the data to which the wrapped pointer is pointing. Add a constraint to the member function template to make sure type `E` is in fact assignable to an lvalue of type `T`.

Exercise 32-4: Write a lambda expression returning the sum of two arguments. Both arguments must be of the same type. The lambda expression should work with all kind of data types, such as integral types, floating-point types, and even `std::strings`. Try out your lambda expression by calculating the sum of 11 and 22, 1.1 and 2.2, and "Hello " and "world!"

33

Applying Design Patterns

WHAT'S IN THIS CHAPTER?

- What a pattern is and what the difference is with a design technique
- How to use the following patterns:
    - Strategy
    - Abstract factory
    - Factory method
    - Adapter
    - Proxy
    - Iterator
    - Observer
    - Decorator
    - Chain of responsibility
    - Singleton

WILEY.COM DOWNLOADS FOR THIS CHAPTER

Please note that all the code examples for this chapter are available as part of this chapter's code download on the book's website at `www.wiley.com/go/proc++6e` on the Download Code tab.

A *design pattern* is a standard approach to program organization that solves a general problem. Design patterns are less language-specific than are techniques. The difference between a pattern and a technique is admittedly fuzzy, and different books employ different definitions. This book defines a technique as a strategy particular to the C++ language, while a pattern is a more general strategy for object-oriented design applicable to any object-oriented language, such as C++, C#, Java, or Smalltalk. In fact, if you are familiar with C# or Java programming, you will recognize many of these patterns.

Design patterns have names, and that's a big advantage. The name carries meaning and therefore helps to more easily communicate about solutions. The names of patterns also help developers to more quickly understand a solution. However, certain patterns have several different names, and the distinctions between certain patterns is sometimes a bit vague with different sources describing and categorizing them slightly differently. In fact, depending on the books or other sources you use, you may find the same name applied to different patterns. There is even disagreement as to which design approaches qualify as patterns. With a few exceptions, this book follows the terminology used in the seminal book *Design Patterns: Elements of Reusable Object-Oriented Software*, by Erich Gamma et al. (Addison-Wesley Professional, 1994). Other pattern names and variations are noted when appropriate.

The design pattern concept is a simple but powerful idea. Once you are able to recognize the recurring object-oriented interactions that occur in a program, finding an elegant solution often becomes a matter of selecting the appropriate pattern to apply.

As there are books available discussing nothing but design patterns, this chapter briefly describes just a small selection of the more important design patterns in detail and presents sample implementations. This gives you a pretty good idea about what design patterns are all about.

Any aspect of design is likely to provoke debate among programmers, and I believe that is a good thing. Don't simply accept these patterns as the only way to accomplish a task—draw on their approaches and ideas to refine them and form new patterns.

THE STRATEGY PATTERN

The *strategy design pattern* is one way to support the *dependency inversion principle* (DIP); see Chapter 6, "Designing for Reuse." With this pattern, interfaces are used to invert dependency relationships. Interfaces are created for every provided service. If a component needs a set of services, interfaces to those services are injected into the component, a mechanism called *dependency injection*. Using the strategy pattern makes unit testing easier, as you can easily mock services away. As an example, this section discusses a logging mechanism implemented with the strategy pattern.

Example: A Logging Mechanism

The strategy-based logger example uses an interface, or abstract base class, called `ILogger`. Any code that wants to log something uses this `ILogger` interface. Subsequently, a concrete implementation of this interface is then injected into any code that needs to be able to use the logging functionality. With this pattern, a unit test can, for example, inject a special mock implementation for the `ILogger` interface to verify that the right information gets logged. A huge advantage of this pattern is that concrete loggers can easily be swapped without having to modify any library code; client code simply passes in the logger it wants to use.

Implementation of a Strategy-Based Logger

This implementation provides a `Logger` class with the following features:

- It can log single strings.
- Each log message is prefixed with the current system time and an associated log level.
- The logger can be set up to only log messages above a certain log level.
- Every logged message is flushed to disk so that it will appear in the file immediately.

Let's first define the `ILogger` interface:

```
export class ILogger
{
    public:
        virtual ~ILogger() = default; // Virtual destructor.

        // Enumeration for the different log levels.
        enum class LogLevel { Debug, Info, Error };

        // Sets the log level.
        virtual void setLogLevel(LogLevel level) = 0;

        // Logs a single message at the given log level.
        virtual void log(std::string_view message, LogLevel logLevel) = 0;
};
```

Next, a concrete `Logger` class is implemented as follows:

```
export class Logger : public ILogger
{
    public:
        explicit Logger(const std::string& logFilename);
        void setLogLevel(LogLevel level) override;
        void log(std::string_view message, LogLevel logLevel) override;
    private:
        // Converts a log level to a human readable string.
        std::string_view getLogLevelString(LogLevel level) const;

        std::ofstream m_outputStream;
        LogLevel m_logLevel { LogLevel::Error };
};
```

The implementation of the `Logger` class is straightforward. Once the log file has been opened, each log message is written to it with the log level prepended and then flushed to disk.

```
Logger::Logger(const string& logFilename)
{
    m_outputStream.open(logFilename, ios_base::app);
    if (!m_outputStream.good()) {
        throw runtime_error { "Unable to initialize the Logger!" };
    }
    println(m_outputStream, "{}: Logger started.", chrono::system_clock::now());
}
```

```
void Logger::setLogLevel(LogLevel level)
{
    m_logLevel = level;
}

string_view Logger::getLogLevelString(LogLevel level) const
{
    switch (level) {
        case LogLevel::Debug: return "DEBUG";
        case LogLevel::Info: return "INFO";
        case LogLevel::Error: return "ERROR";
    }
    throw runtime_error { "Invalid log level." };
}

void Logger::log(string_view message, LogLevel logLevel)
{
    if (m_logLevel > logLevel) { return; }
    println(m_outputStream, "{}: [{}] {}", chrono::system_clock::now(),
        getLogLevelString(logLevel), message);
}
```

Using the Strategy-Based Logger

Suppose you have a class called `Foo` that wants to use the logging functionality. With the strategy pattern, a concrete `ILogger` instance is injected into the class, for example through the constructor:

```
class Foo
{
    public:
        explicit Foo(ILogger* logger) : m_logger { logger }
        {
            if (m_logger == nullptr) {
                throw invalid_argument { "ILogger cannot be null." };
            }
        }
        void doSomething()
        {
            m_logger->log("Hello strategy!", ILogger::LogLevel::Info);
        }
    private:
        ILogger* m_logger;
};
```

When a `Foo` instance is created, a concrete `ILogger` is injected into it:

```
Logger concreteLogger { "log.out" };
concreteLogger.setLogLevel(ILogger::LogLevel::Debug);

Foo f { &concreteLogger };
f.doSomething();
```

THE ABSTRACT FACTORY PATTERN

A factory in real life constructs tangible objects, such as tables or cars. Similarly, a *factory* in object-oriented programming constructs objects. When you use factories in your program, portions of code that want to create a particular object ask a factory for an instance of the object instead of calling the object constructor themselves. For example, an interior decorating program might have a `FurnitureFactory` object. When part of the code needs a piece of furniture such as a table, it calls the `createTable()` member function of the `FurnitureFactory` object, returning a new table. This is the main benefit of factories; they abstract the object creation process.

At first glance, factories seem to lead to complicated designs. It appears that you're only adding another layer of indirection to the program. Instead of calling `createTable()` on a `FurnitureFactory`, you could simply create a new `Table` object directly. However, a benefit of using factories is that they can be used alongside class hierarchies to construct objects without knowing their exact type. As you'll see in the following example, factories can run parallel to class hierarchies. This is not to say they must run parallel to class hierarchies. Factories may as well just create any number of concrete types.

Another benefit of factories is that instead of directly creating various objects all over your code, you pass around factories that allow different parts of the program to create objects of the same kind for a particular domain.

Another reason to use a factory is when the creation of your objects requires certain information, states, resources, and so on, owned by the factory, and which clients of the factory should not know about. A factory can also be used if creating your objects requires a complex series of steps to be executed in the right order, or if all created objects need to be linked to other objects in a correct manner, and so on.

Factories can be swapped; using dependency injection, you can easily substitute a different factory in your program. And, just as you can use polymorphism with the created objects, you can use polymorphism with factories. The following example demonstrates this.

There are two major types of factory-related patterns in object-oriented programming: the *abstract factory pattern* and the *factory method pattern*. This section discusses the abstract factory pattern, while the next section discusses the factory method pattern.

Example: A Car Factory Simulation

Imagine a factory capable of producing cars. The factory creates the type of car that is requested from it. First, a hierarchy is needed to represent several types of cars. Figure 33.1 introduces an `ICar` interface with a `virtual` member function to retrieve information about a specific car. The `Toyota` and `Ford` cars derive from `ICar`, and finally, both Ford and Toyota have a sedan and an SUV model.

Next to the car hierarchy, we need a factory hierarchy. An abstract factory just exposes an interface to create a sedan or an SUV independent of the brand, with concrete factories constructing concrete models from concrete brands. Figure 33.2 shows this hierarchy.

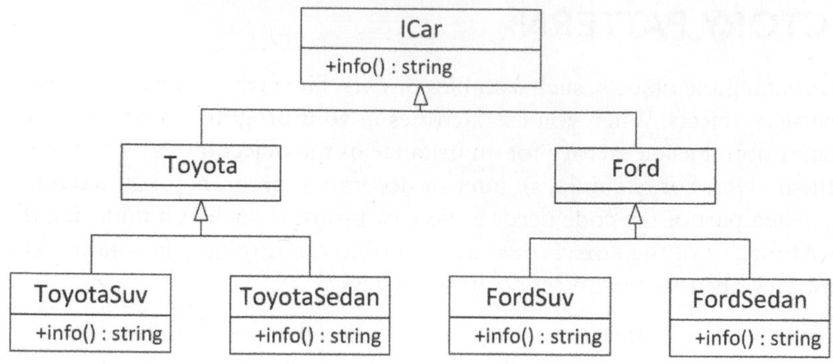

FIGURE 33.1

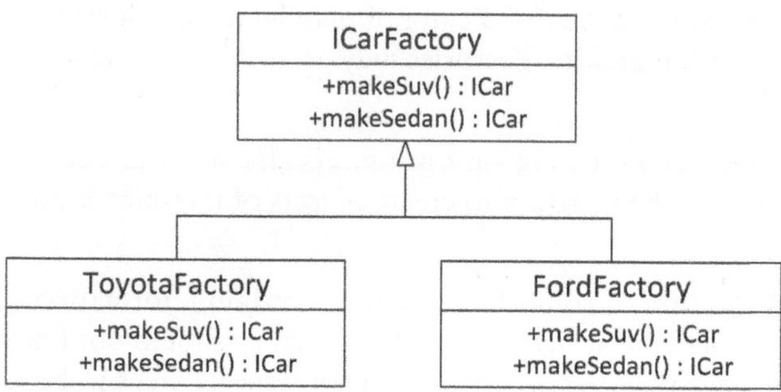

FIGURE 33.2

Implementation of an Abstract Factory

The implementation of the car hierarchy is straightforward:

```
export class ICar
{
    public:
        virtual ~ICar() = default;  // Always a virtual destructor!
        virtual std::string info() const = 0;
};

export class Ford : public ICar { };

export class FordSedan : public Ford
{
    public:
        std::string info() const override { return "Ford Sedan"; }
};

export class FordSuv : public Ford
{
    public:
        std::string info() const override { return "Ford SUV"; }
};
```

```
export class Toyota : public ICar { };

export class ToyotaSedan : public Toyota
{
    public:
        std::string info() const override { return "Toyota Sedan"; }
};

export class ToyotaSuv : public Toyota
{
    public:
        std::string info() const override { return "Toyota SUV"; }
};
```

Next up is the `ICarFactory` interface. It simply exposes member functions to create a sedan or an SUV without knowing any concrete factory or car.

```
export class ICarFactory
{
    public:
        virtual ~ICarFactory() = default;  // Always a virtual destructor!
        virtual std::unique_ptr<ICar> makeSuv() = 0;
        virtual std::unique_ptr<ICar> makeSedan() = 0;
};
```

Then finally we have the concrete factories, creating concrete car models. Only the `FordFactory` is shown; the `ToyotaFactory` is similar.

```
export class FordFactory : public ICarFactory
{
    public:
        std::unique_ptr<ICar> makeSuv() override {
            return std::make_unique<FordSuv>(); }
        std::unique_ptr<ICar> makeSedan() override {
            return std::make_unique<FordSedan>(); }
};
```

The approach used in this example is called an *abstract factory* because the type of object created depends on which *concrete* factory is being used.

Using an Abstract Factory

The following example shows how to use the implemented factories. It has a function that accepts an abstract car factory and uses that to build both a sedan and an SUV and prints out information about each produced car. This function has no idea about any concrete factory or any concrete cars; i.e., it only uses interfaces. The `main()` function creates two factories, one for Fords and one for Toyotas, and then asks the `createSomeCars()` function to use each of these factories to create some cars.

```
void createSomeCars(ICarFactory& carFactory)
{
    auto sedan { carFactory.makeSedan() };
    auto suv { carFactory.makeSuv() };
    println("Sedan: {}", sedan->info());
    println("SUV: {}", suv->info());
}
```

```
int main()
{
    FordFactory fordFactory;
    ToyotaFactory toyotaFactory;
    createSomeCars(fordFactory);
    createSomeCars(toyotaFactory);
}
```

The output of this code snippet is as follows:

```
Sedan: Ford Sedan
SUV: Ford SUV
Sedan: Toyota Sedan
SUV: Toyota SUV
```

THE FACTORY METHOD PATTERN

The second type of factory-related pattern is called the *factory method pattern*. With this pattern, it is entirely up to the concrete factory to decide what kind of object to create. In the earlier abstract factory example, the `ICarFactory` had a member function to either create an SUV or create a sedan. With the factory method pattern, you just ask for a car from the factory, and the concrete factories decide what exactly to build. Let's look at another car factory simulation.

Example: A Second Car Factory Simulation

In the real world, when you talk about driving a car, you can do so without referring to the specific type of car. You could be discussing a Toyota or a Ford. It doesn't matter, because both Toyotas and Fords are drivable. Now, suppose that you want a new car. You would then need to specify whether you wanted a Toyota or a Ford, right? Not always. You could just say, "I want a car," and depending on where you were, you would get a specific car. If you said "I want a car" in a Toyota factory, chances are you'd get a Toyota. (Or you'd get arrested, depending on how you asked.) If you said "I want a car" in a Ford factory, you'd get a Ford.

The same concepts apply to C++ programming. The first concept, a generic car that's drivable, is nothing new; it's standard polymorphism, described in Chapter 5, "Designing with Classes." You could write an abstract `ICar` interface that defines a virtual `drive()` member function. Both `Toyota` and `Ford` could be implementing such an interface.

Your program could drive cars without knowing whether they were really `Toyota`s or `Ford`s. However, with standard object-oriented programming, the one place that you'd need to specify `Toyota` or `Ford` would be when you created the car. Here, you would need to call the constructor for one or the other. You couldn't just say, "I want a car." However, suppose that you also had a parallel class hierarchy of car factories. The `CarFactory` base class could define a `public` non-virtual `requestCar()` member function that forwards the work to a `private` virtual `createCar()` member function. The `ToyotaFactory` and `FordFactory` derived classes override the `createCar()` member function to build a `Toyota` or a `Ford`. Figure 33.3 shows the `ICar` and `CarFactory` hierarchies.

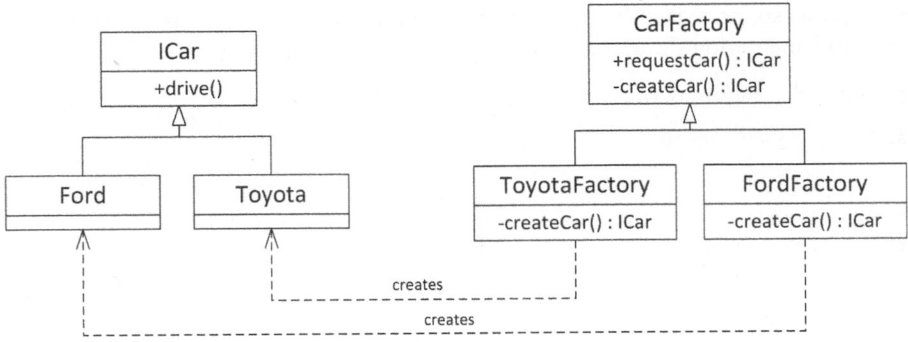

FIGURE 33.3

Now, suppose that there is one `CarFactory` object in a program. When code in the program, such as a car dealer, wants a new car, it calls `requestCar()` on the `CarFactory` object. Depending on whether that car factory is really a `ToyotaFactory` or a `FordFactory`, the code gets either a `Toyota` or a `Ford`. Figure 33.4 shows the objects in a car dealer program using a `ToyotaFactory`.

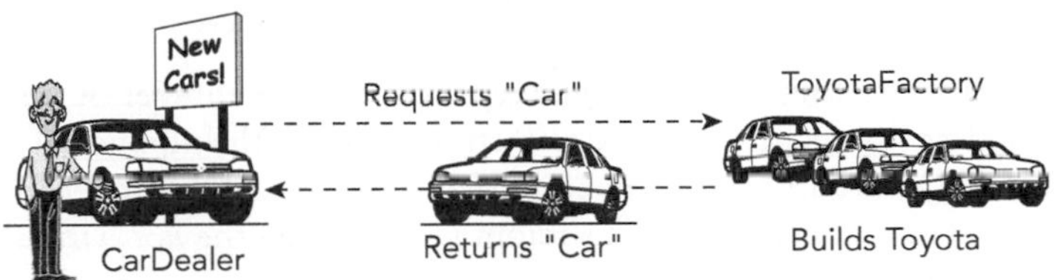

FIGURE 33.4

Figure 33.5 shows the same program, but with a `FordFactory` instead of a `ToyotaFactory`. Note that the `CarDealer` object and its relationship with the factory stay the same.

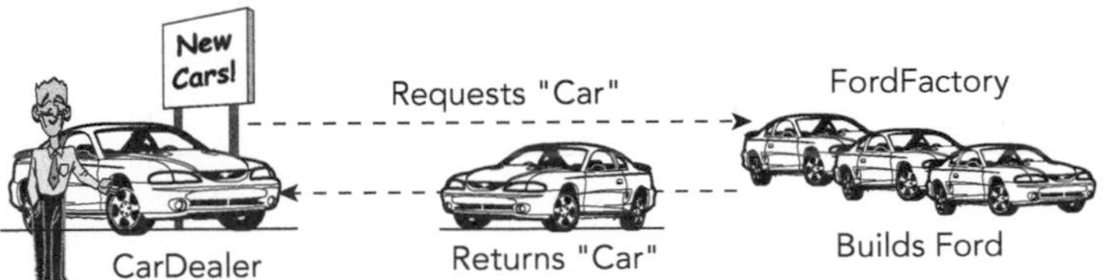

FIGURE 33.5

This example demonstrates using polymorphism with factories. When you ask the car factory for a car, you might not know whether it's a Toyota factory or a Ford factory, but either way it will give you a car that you can drive. This approach leads to easily extensible programs; simply changing the factory instance can allow the program to work on a completely different set of objects and classes.

Implementation of a Factory Method

One reason for using factories is that the type of the object you want to create may depend on some condition. For example, if you want a car, you might want to put your order into the factory that has received the fewest requests so far, regardless of whether the car you eventually get is a Toyota or a Ford. The following implementation shows how to write such factories in C++.

The first thing we need is the hierarchy of cars:

```
export class ICar
{
    public:
        virtual ~ICar() = default;  // Always a virtual destructor!
        virtual std::string info() const = 0;
};

export class Ford : public ICar
{
    public:
        std::string info() const override { return "Ford"; }
};

export class Toyota : public ICar
{
    public:
        std::string info() const override { return "Toyota"; }
};
```

The CarFactory base class is a bit more interesting. Each factory keeps track of the number of cars produced. When the public non-virtual requestCar() member function is called, the number of cars produced at the factory is increased by one, and the private virtual createCar() member function is called, which creates and returns a new concrete car. This idiom is also called the *non-virtual interface idiom (NVI)*. The idea is that individual factories override createCar() to return the appropriate type of car. The CarFactory itself implements requestCar(), which takes care of updating the number of cars produced. The requestCar() member function is an example of the *template method design pattern*.

The CarFactory also provides a public member function to query the number of cars produced at each factory. The class definitions for the CarFactory class and derived classes are as follows:

```
export class CarFactory
{
    public:
        virtual ~CarFactory() = default;  // Always a virtual destructor!
        // Omitted defaulted default ctor, copy/move ctor, copy/move assignment op.

        std::unique_ptr<ICar> requestCar()
        {
            // Increment the number of cars produced and return the new car.
            ++m_numberOfCarsProduced;
            return createCar();
        }

        unsigned getNumberOfCarsProduced() const { return m_numberOfCarsProduced; }
    private:
        virtual std::unique_ptr<ICar> createCar() = 0;
        unsigned m_numberOfCarsProduced { 0 };
};
```

```
export class FordFactory final : public CarFactory
{
    private:
        std::unique_ptr<ICar> createCar() override {
            return std::make_unique<Ford>(); }
};

export class ToyotaFactory final : public CarFactory
{
    private:
        std::unique_ptr<ICar> createCar() override {
            return std::make_unique<Toyota>(); }
};
```

As you can see, the derived classes simply override `createCar()` to return the specific type of car that they produce.

> **NOTE** *Factory methods are one way to implement virtual constructors, which are member functions that create objects of different types. For example, the* `requestCar()` *member function creates both* `Toyota`*s and* `Ford`*s, depending on the concrete factory object on which it is called.*

Using a Factory Method

The simplest way to use a factory is to instantiate it and to call the appropriate member function, as in the following piece of code:

```
ToyotaFactory myFactory;
auto myCar { myFactory.requestCar() };
println("{}", myCar->info());    // Outputs Toyota
```

A more interesting example makes use of the virtual constructor idea to build a car in the factory that has the fewest cars produced. To do this, you can create a new factory, called `LeastBusyFactory`, that derives from `CarFactory` and that accepts a number of other `CarFactory` objects in its constructor. As all `CarFactory` classes have to do, `LeastBusyFactory` overrides the `createCar()` member function. Its implementation finds the least busy factory in the list of factories passed to the constructor and asks that factory to create a car. Here is the implementation of such a factory:

```
class LeastBusyFactory final : public CarFactory
{
    public:
        // Constructs an instance, taking ownership of the given factories.
        explicit LeastBusyFactory(vector<unique_ptr<CarFactory>> factories);
    private:
        unique_ptr<ICar> createCar() override;
        vector<unique_ptr<CarFactory>> m_factories;
};

LeastBusyFactory::LeastBusyFactory(vector<unique_ptr<CarFactory>> factories)
    : m_factories { move(factories) }
{
```

```
        if (m_factories.empty()) {
            throw runtime_error { "No factories provided." };
        }
    }

    unique_ptr<ICar> LeastBusyFactory::createCar()
    {
        auto leastBusyFactory { ranges::min_element(m_factories,
            [](const auto& factory1, const auto& factory2) {
                return factory1->getNumberOfCarsProduced() <
                       factory2->getNumberOfCarsProduced(); }) };
        return (*leastBusyFactory)->requestCar();
    }
```

The following code makes use of this factory to build 10 cars, whatever brand they might be, from the factory that has produced the least number of cars:

```
vector<unique_ptr<CarFactory>> factories;

// Create 3 Ford factories and 1 Toyota factory.
factories.push_back(make_unique<FordFactory>());
factories.push_back(make_unique<FordFactory>());
factories.push_back(make_unique<FordFactory>());
factories.push_back(make_unique<ToyotaFactory>());

// To get more interesting results, preorder some cars from specific factories.
for (size_t i : {0, 0, 0, 1, 1, 2}) { factories[i]->requestCar(); }

// Create a factory that automatically selects the least busy
// factory from a list of given factories.
LeastBusyFactory leastBusyFactory { move(factories) };

// Build 10 cars from the least busy factory.
for (unsigned i { 0 }; i < 10; ++i) {
    auto theCar { leastBusyFactory.requestCar() };
    println("{}", theCar->info());
}
```

When executed, the program prints out the make of each car produced.

```
Toyota
Ford
Toyota
Ford
Ford
Toyota
Ford
Ford
Ford
Toyota
```

Other Uses

You can use a factory method pattern for more than just modeling real-world factories. For example, consider a word processor in which you want to support documents in different languages, where each document uses a single language. There are many aspects of the word processor in which the choice of document language requires different support: the character set used in the document (whether accented characters are needed), the spell checker, the thesaurus, and the way the document is displayed, to name just a few. You could use factories to design a clean word processor by writing a `LanguageFactory` base class and derived factories for each language of interest, such as `EnglishLanguageFactory` and `FrenchLanguageFactory`. When the user specifies a language for a document, the program uses the appropriate `LanguageFactory` to create language-specific instances of certain functionality. For example, it calls the `createSpellchecker()` member function on the factory to create a language-specific spell checker. It then replaces the current spell checker for the previous language attached to the document with the newly constructed spell checker for the new language.

OTHER FACTORY PATTERNS

The previous sections describe two concrete patterns related to factories: the abstract factory pattern and the factory method pattern.

There are other types of factories. For example, a factory can also be implemented in a single class instead of a class hierarchy. In that case, a single `create()` member function on the factory takes a type or string parameter from which it decides which object to create, instead of delegating that work to concrete subclasses. Such a function is commonly called a *factory function*. This factory pattern does not provide dependency inversion and does not allow customization of the construction process.

An example of using a factory function is an alternative implementation of the pimpl idiom, discussed in Chapter 9, "Mastering Classes and Objects." It provides a wall between the public interface and the concrete implementation of the provided functionality. This use of a factory function looks as follows. First, the following is publicly exposed, with a `create()` factory function:

```
// Public interface (to be included in the rest of the program,
// shared from a library, ...)
class Foo
{
    public:
        virtual ~Foo() = default;  // Always a virtual destructor!
        // Omitted defaulted copy/move ctor, copy/move assignment op.
        static unique_ptr<Foo> create();  // Factory function.
        // Public functionality...
        virtual void bar() = 0;
    protected:
        Foo() = default; // Protected default constructor.
};
```

Next, the implementation is hidden from the outside world:

```
// Implementation
class FooImpl : public Foo
{
    public:
        void bar() override { /* ... */ }
};
```

```
unique_ptr<Foo> Foo::create()
{
    return make_unique<FooImpl>();
}
```

Any client code that needs a `Foo` instance can create one as follows:

```
auto fooInstance { Foo::create() };
fooInstance->bar();
```

THE ADAPTER PATTERN

Sometimes, the abstraction given by a class doesn't suit the current design and can't be changed. In this case, you can build an *adapter* class. The adapter provides the abstraction that the rest of the code uses and serves as the link between the desired abstraction and the actual underlying code. There are two main use cases:

- Implementing a certain interface by reusing some existing implementation. In this use case, the adapter typically creates an instance of the implementation behind the scenes.
- Allowing existing functionality to be used through a new interface. In this use case, the constructor of the adapter typically receives an instance of the underlying object in its constructor.

Chapter 18, "Standard Library Containers," discusses how the Standard Library uses the adapter pattern to implement containers like `stack` and `queue` in terms of other containers, such as `deque` and `list`.

Example: Adapting a Logger Class

For this adapter pattern example, let's assume a very basic `Logger` class. Here is the interface and class definition:

```
// Definition of a logger interface.
export class ILogger
{
    public:
        virtual ~ILogger() = default;  // Always a virtual destructor!
        enum class LogLevel { Debug, Info, Error };
        // Logs a single message at the given log level.
        virtual void log(LogLevel level, const std::string& message) = 0;
};

// Concrete implementation of ILogger.
export class Logger : public ILogger
{
    public:
        Logger();
        void log(LogLevel level, const std::string& message) override;
    private:
        // Converts a log level to a human readable string.
        std::string_view getLogLevelString(LogLevel level) const;
};
```

The `Logger` class has a constructor, which outputs a line of text to the standard console, and a member function called `log()` that writes the given message to the console prefixed with the current system time and a log level. Here are the implementations:

```
Logger::Logger() { println("Logger constructor"); }

void Logger::log(LogLevel level, const string& message)
{
    println("{}: [{}] {}", chrono::system_clock::now(),
        getLogLevelString(level), message);
}

string_view Logger::getLogLevelString(LogLevel level) const
{ /* See the strategy-based logger earlier in this chapter. */ }
```

One reason why you might want to write an adapter class around this basic `Logger` class is to change its interface. Maybe you are not interested in the log level and you would like to call the `log()` member function with just one argument, the actual message. You might also want to change the interface to accept an `std::string_view` instead of a `string` as the argument for the `log()` member function.

Implementation of an Adapter

The first step in implementing the adapter pattern is to define the new interface for the underlying functionality. This new interface is called `IAdaptedLogger` and looks like this:

```
export class IAdaptedLogger
{
    public:
        virtual ~IAdaptedLogger() = default; // Always virtual destructor!
        // Logs a single message with Info as log level.
        virtual void log(std::string_view message) = 0;
};
```

This class is an abstract class, which declares the desired interface that you want for your new logger. The interface defines only one pure virtual member function, that is, a `log()` member function accepting just a single argument of type `string_view`.

The next step is to write the concrete new logger class, `AdaptedLogger`, which implements `IAdaptedLogger` so that it has the interface that you designed. The implementation wraps a `Logger` instance, i.e., it uses composition.

```
export class AdaptedLogger : public IAdaptedLogger
{
    public:
        AdaptedLogger();
        void log(std::string_view message) override;
    private:
        Logger m_logger;
};
```

The constructor of the new class writes a line to the standard output to keep track of which constructors are being called. The code then implements the `log()` member function from `IAdaptedLogger` by forwarding the call to the `log()` member function of the `Logger` instance that is wrapped. In that call, the given `string_view` is converted to a `string`, and the log level is hard-coded as `Info`.

```
AdaptedLogger::AdaptedLogger() { println("AdaptedLogger constructor"); }

void AdaptedLogger::log(string_view message)
{
    m_logger.log(Logger::LogLevel::Info, string { message });
}
```

Using an Adapter

Because adapters exist to provide a more appropriate interface for the underlying functionality, their use should be straightforward and specific to the particular case. Given the previous implementation, the following code snippet uses the new simplified interface for the logging functionality:

```
AdaptedLogger logger;
logger.log("Testing the logger.");
```

It produces the following output:

```
Logger constructor
AdaptedLogger constructor
2023-08-12 14:06:53.3694244: [INFO] Testing the logger.
```

THE PROXY PATTERN

The *proxy* pattern is one of several patterns that divorce the abstraction of a class from its underlying representation. A proxy object serves as a stand-in for a real object. Such objects are generally used when using the real object would be time-consuming or impossible. For example, take a document editor. A document could contain several big objects, such as images. Instead of loading all those images when opening the document, the document editor could substitute *proxy objects* for all the images. These proxies don't immediately load the images. Only when the user scrolls down in the document and reaches an image does the document editor ask the image proxy to draw itself. At that time, the proxy delegates the work to the real image object, which loads the image.

Proxies can also be used to properly shield certain functionality from clients, while at the same time making sure that clients can't even use casts to get around the shielding.

Example: Hiding Network Connectivity Issues

Consider a networked game with a `Player` class that represents a person on the Internet who has joined the game. The `Player` class includes functionality that requires network connectivity, such as an instant messaging feature. If a player's connection becomes unresponsive, the `Player` object representing that person can no longer receive instant messages.

Because you don't want to expose network problems to the user, it may be desirable to have a separate class that hides the networked parts of a `Player`. This `PlayerProxy` object would substitute for the actual `Player` object. Either clients of the class would use the `PlayerProxy` class at all times as a gatekeeper to the real `Player` class, or the system would substitute a `PlayerProxy` when a `Player` became unavailable. During a network failure, the PlayerProxy object could still display the player's name and last known state and could continue to function when the original Player object could not. Thus, the proxy class hides some undesirable semantics of the underlying Player class.

Implementation of a Proxy

The first step is defining an IPlayer interface containing the public interface for a Player:

```
class IPlayer
{
    public:
        virtual ~IPlayer() = default; // Always virtual destructor.
        virtual string getName() const = 0;
        // Sends an instant message to the player over the network and
        // returns the reply as a string.
        virtual string sendInstantMessage(string_view message) const = 0;
};
```

The Player class implements the IPlayer interface as follows. Imagine for this example that sendInstantMessage() requires network connectivity to properly function and raises an exception if the network connection is down.

```
class Player : public IPlayer
{
    public:
        string getName() const override;
        // Network connectivity is required.
        // Throws an exception if network connection is down.
        string sendInstantMessage(string_view message) const override;
};
```

The PlayerProxy class also implements the IPlayer interface and contains another IPlayer instance (the "real" Player):

```
class PlayerProxy : public IPlayer
{
    public:
        // Create a PlayerProxy, taking ownership of the given player.
        explicit PlayerProxy(unique_ptr<IPlayer> player);
        string getName() const override;
        // Network connectivity is optional.
        string sendInstantMessage(string_view message) const override;
    private:
        bool hasNetworkConnectivity() const;
        unique_ptr<IPlayer> m_player;
};
```

The constructor takes ownership of the given IPlayer:

```
PlayerProxy::PlayerProxy(unique_ptr<IPlayer> player)
    : m_player { move(player) } { }
```

The getName() member function just forwards to the underlying player:

```
string PlayerProxy::getName() const { return m_player->getName(); }
```

The implementation of the PlayerProxy's sendInstantMessage() member function checks the network connectivity and either returns a default string or forwards the request. This hides the fact that the sendInstantMessage() member function on the underlying Player object raises an exception when the network connection is down.

```
string PlayerProxy::sendInstantMessage(string_view message) const
{
    if (hasNetworkConnectivity()) { return m_player->sendInstantMessage(message); }
    else { return "The player has gone offline."; }
}
```

Using a Proxy

If a proxy is well written, using it should be no different from using any other object. For the PlayerProxy example, the code that uses the proxy could be completely unaware of its existence. The following function, designed to be called when the Player has won, could be dealing with an actual Player or a PlayerProxy. The code is able to handle both cases in the same way because the proxy ensures a valid result.

```
bool informWinner(const IPlayer& player)
{
    auto result { player.sendInstantMessage("You have won! Play again?") };
    if (result == "yes") {
        println("{} wants to play again.", player.getName());
        return true;
    } else {
        // The player said no, or is offline.
        println("{} does not want to play again.", player.getName());
        return false;
    }
}
```

THE ITERATOR PATTERN

The *iterator* pattern provides a mechanism for separating algorithms or operations from the structure of the data on which they operate. Basically, an iterator allows algorithms to navigate a data structure without having to know the actual structure of the data. At first glance, this pattern seems to contradict the fundamental principle in object-oriented programming of grouping together in classes data and the behaviors that operate on that data. While that argument is true on a certain level, the iterator pattern does not advocate removing fundamental behaviors from classes. Instead, it solves two problems that commonly arise with tight coupling of data and behaviors.

The first problem with tightly coupling data and behaviors is that it precludes generic algorithms that work on a variety of data structures. To write generic algorithms, you need some standard mechanism to navigate/access the contents of a data structure without knowledge of the concrete structure.

The second problem with tightly coupled data and behaviors is that it's sometimes difficult to add new behaviors. At the least, you need access to the source code for the data objects. However, what if the class hierarchy of interest is part of a third-party framework or library that you cannot change? It would be nice to be able to add an algorithm or operation that works on the data without modifying the original hierarchy of classes that hold the data.

You've already seen an example of the iterator pattern in the Standard Library. Conceptually, Standard Library *iterators* provide a mechanism for an operation or algorithm to access a container of elements in a sequence. The name comes from the English word *iterate*, which means "repeat." It applies to iterators because they repeat the action of moving forward in a sequence to reach each new element. In the Standard Library, the generic algorithms use iterators to access the elements of the containers on which they operate. By defining a standard iterator interface, the Standard Library allows you to write algorithms that can work on any container that supplies an iterator with the appropriate interface. You can even provide several different iterators for a single data structure. This allows an algorithm to navigate that data in different ways, for example, top-down and bottom-up traversal for a tree data structure. Thus, iterators allow you to write generic algorithms that can traverse the contents of a data structure without having to know anything about the structure. Figure 33.6 shows an iterator as the central coordinator; operations depend on iterators, and data objects provide iterators.

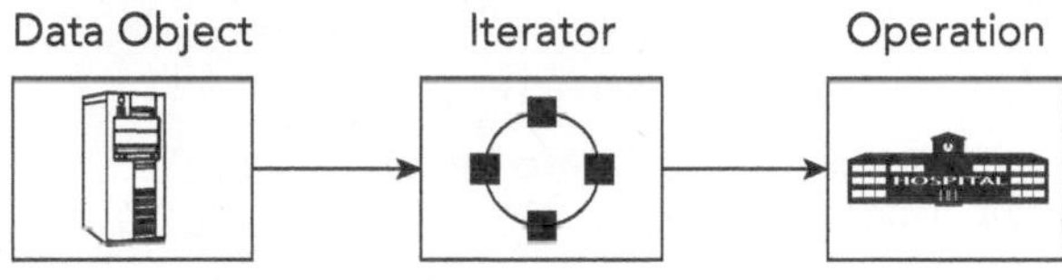

FIGURE 33.6

Chapter 25, "Customizing and Extending the Standard Library," illustrates a detailed example of how to implement a Standard Library-compliant iterator for a data structure, which means that the iterator can be used by the generic Standard Library algorithms.

THE OBSERVER PATTERN

The *observer* pattern is used to have observers be notified by observable objects (= subjects). Concrete observers are *registered* with the observable object they are interested in. When the observable object's state changes, it notifies all registered observers of this change. The main benefit of using the observer pattern is that it decreases coupling. The observable class does not need to know the concrete observer types that are observing it.

Example: Exposing Events from Subjects

This example consists of generic-purpose events with a variadic number of arguments. Subjects can expose specific events, for example an event raised when the subject's data is modified, an event raised when the subject's data is deleted, and so on.

Implementation of an Observable

First, a variadic class template `Event` is defined. Variadic class templates are discussed in Chapter 26, "Advanced Templates." The class stores a `map` of `functions` with a variadic number of arguments. An `addObserver()` member function is provided to register a new observer in the form of a `function` that should be notified when this event is raised. `addObserver()` returns an `EventHandle` that subsequently can be passed to `removeObserver()` to unregister the observer. This `EventHandle` is just a number that is increased with every registered observer. Finally, the `raise()` member function notifies all registered observers that the event has been raised.

```
using EventHandle = unsigned int;

template <typename... Args>
class Event final
{
    public:
        // Adds an observer. Returns an EventHandle to unregister the observer.
        [[nodiscard]] EventHandle addObserver(
            function<void(const Args&...)> observer)
        {
            auto number { ++m_counter };
            m_observers[number] = move(observer);
            return number;
        }

        // Unregisters the observer pointed to by the given handle.
        void removeObserver(EventHandle handle)
        {
            m_observers.erase(handle);
        }

        // Raise event: notifies all registered observers.
        void raise(const Args&... args)
        {
            for (const auto& [_, callback] : m_observers) { callback(args...); }
        }
    private:
        unsigned int m_counter { 0 };
        map<EventHandle, function<void(const Args&...)>> m_observers;
};
```

Any class that wants to expose events on which observers can register themselves just needs to provide register and unregister member functions. Thanks to the use of a variadic class template, `Event` instances can be created with any number of parameters. This allows an observable object to pass any relevant information to observers. Here is an example:

```
class ObservableSubject
{
    public:
        EventHandle registerDataModifiedObserver(const auto& observer) {
            return m_eventDataModified.addObserver(observer); }
        void unregisterDataModifiedObserver(EventHandle handle) {
            m_eventDataModified.removeObserver(handle); }

        EventHandle registerDataDeletedObserver(const auto& observer) {
            return m_eventDataDeleted.addObserver(observer); }
        void unregisterDataDeletedObserver(EventHandle handle) {
            m_eventDataDeleted.removeObserver(handle); }
```

```
        void modifyData()
        {
            // ...
            m_eventDataModified.raise(1, 2.3);
        }

        void deleteData()
        {
            // ...
            m_eventDataDeleted.raise();
        }
    private:
        Event<int, double> m_eventDataModified;
        Event<> m_eventDataDeleted;
};
```

Using an Observer

The following is some test code that demonstrates how to use the implemented observer pattern. Suppose we have the following stand-alone global function `modified()` that can handle modification events:

```
void modified(int a, double b) { println("modified({}, {})", a, b); }
```

Suppose that we also have a class `Observer` capable of handling modification events:

```
class Observer final
{
    public:
        explicit Observer(ObservableSubject& subject) : m_subject { subject }
        {
            m_subjectModifiedHandle = m_subject.registerDataModifiedObserver(
                [this](int i, double d) { onSubjectModified(i, d); });
        }

        ~Observer()
        {
            m_subject.unregisterDataModifiedObserver(m_subjectModifiedHandle);
        }
    private:
        void onSubjectModified(int a, double b)
        {
            println("Observer::onSubjectModified({}, {})", a, b);
        }
        ObservableSubject& m_subject;
        EventHandle m_subjectModifiedHandle;
};
```

Finally, we can construct an `ObservableSubject` instance and register some observers:

```
ObservableSubject subject;

auto handleModified { subject.registerDataModifiedObserver(modified) };
auto handleDeleted { subject.registerDataDeletedObserver(
    []{ println("deleted"); }) };
Observer observer { subject };
```

```
    subject.modifyData();
    subject.deleteData();

    println("");

    subject.unregisterDataModifiedObserver(handleModified);
    subject.modifyData();
    subject.deleteData();
```

The output is as follows:

```
modified(1, 2.3)
Observer::onSubjectModified(1, 2.3)
deleted

Observer::onSubjectModified(1, 2.3)
deleted
```

> **NOTE** *One issue with the observer pattern that you need to keep in mind is the lifetime coupling between observers and subjects. In the previous example, for instance, the destructor of* `Observer` *works only if the subject is still alive.*

THE DECORATOR PATTERN

The *decorator* pattern is exactly what it sounds like: a "decoration" on a class. The pattern is used to augment or change the behavior of a class at run time. Decorators are a lot like derived classes but are able to dynamically change the decorated class's behavior. The trade-off is that decorators have fewer ways to change behavior compared to derived classes, because, for example, a decorator cannot override certain helper member functions. On the other hand, the major benefit of decorators is that they are non-intrusive; that is, they allow you to adapt behavior without having to change code in the underlying class. Decorators can also easily be composed to accomplish exactly what you need without having to write derived classes for each combination.

For example, if you have a stream of data that you are parsing and you reach data that represents an image, you could temporarily decorate the stream object with an `ImageStream` object. The `ImageStream` constructor would take the stream object as a parameter and would have built-in knowledge of image parsing. Once the image is parsed, you could continue using the original object to parse the remainder of the stream. The `ImageStream` acts as a decorator because it adds new functionality (image parsing) to an existing object (a stream).

Example: Defining Styles in Web Pages

As you may already know, web pages are written in a simple text-based structure called HyperText Markup Language (HTML). In HTML, you can apply styles to a text by using style tags, such as `<b>` and `</b>` for bold and `<i>` and `</i>` for italic. The following line of HTML displays the message in bold:

```
<b>A party? For me? Thanks!</b>
```

The following line displays the message in bold and italic:

```
<i><b>A party? For me? Thanks!</b></i>
```

Paragraphs in HTML are wrapped in `<p>` and `</p>` tags. Here's an example:

```
<p>This is a paragraph.</p>
```

Suppose you are writing an HTML editing application. Your users should be able to type in paragraphs of text and apply one or more styles to them. You *could* make each type of paragraph a new derived class, as shown in Figure 33.7, but that design is cumbersome and would grow exponentially as new styles are added.

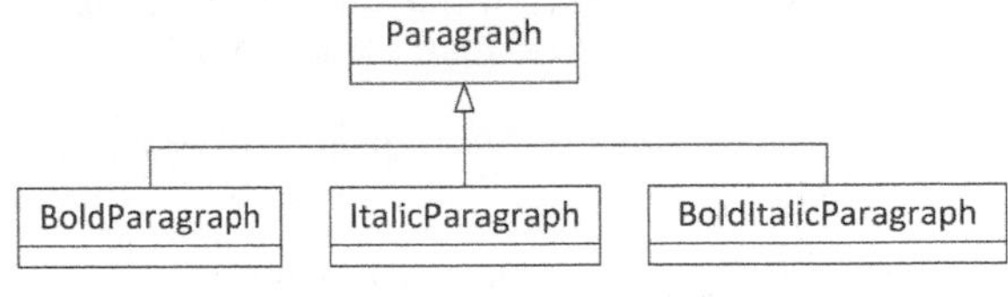

FIGURE 33.7

The alternative is to consider styled paragraphs not as *types* of paragraphs, but as *decorated* paragraphs. This leads to situations like the one shown in Figure 33.8, where an `ItalicParagraph` operates on a `BoldParagraph`, which in turn operates on a `Paragraph`. The recursive decoration of objects nests the styles in code just as they are nested in HTML.

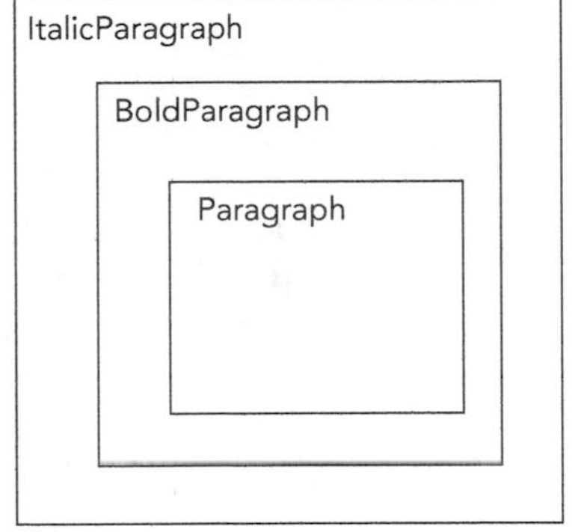

FIGURE 33.8

Implementation of a Decorator

To start, you need an `IParagraph` interface:

```
class IParagraph
{
    public:
        virtual ~IParagraph() = default;  // Always a virtual destructor!
        virtual std::string getHTML() const = 0;
};
```

The `Paragraph` class implements this `IParagraph` interface:

```
class Paragraph : public IParagraph
{
    public:
        explicit Paragraph(std::string text) : m_text { std::move(text) } {}
        std::string getHTML() const override {return format("<p>{}</p>", m_text); }
    private:
        std::string m_text;
};
```

To decorate a `Paragraph` with zero or more styles, you need styled `IParagraph` classes, each one constructible from an existing `IParagraph`. This way, they can all decorate a `Paragraph` or a styled `IParagraph`. The `BoldParagraph` class derives from `IParagraph` and implements `getHTML()`. The key here is that since you only intend to use it as a decorator, its single `public` non-copy constructor takes a reference-to-const to an `IParagraph`.

```
class BoldParagraph : public IParagraph
{
    public:
        explicit BoldParagraph(const IParagraph& paragraph)
            : m_wrapped { paragraph } { }

        std::string getHTML() const override {
            return format("<b>{}</b>", m_wrapped.getHTML()); }
    private:
        const IParagraph& m_wrapped;
};
```

The `ItalicParagraph` class is similar:

```
class ItalicParagraph : public IParagraph
{
    public:
        explicit ItalicParagraph(const IParagraph& paragraph)
            : m_wrapped { paragraph } { }

        std::string getHTML() const override {
            return format("<i>{}</i>", m_wrapped.getHTML()); }
    private:
        const IParagraph& m_wrapped;
};
```

Using a Decorator

From the user's point of view, the decorator pattern is appealing because it is easy to apply and is transparent once applied. A `BoldParagraph` behaves just like a `Paragraph`. Keep in mind, though, that since a `BoldParagraph` contains just a reference to an `IParagraph`, if you somehow change the text of that `IParagraph`, that change will be visible through the `BoldParagraph` as well.

Here is an example that creates and outputs a paragraph, first in bold and then in bold and italic:

```
Paragraph text { "A party? For me? Thanks!" };
// Bold
println("{}", BoldParagraph{text}.getHTML());
// Bold and Italic
println("{}", ItalicParagraph{BoldParagraph{text}}.getHTML());
```

The output is as follows:

```
<b><p>A party? For me? Thanks!</p></b>
<i><b><p>A party? For me? Thanks!</p></b></i>
```

THE CHAIN OF RESPONSIBILITY PATTERN

A *chain of responsibility* is used when you want a number of objects to get a crack at performing a particular action. Chains of responsibility are perhaps most commonly used for event handling. Many modern applications, particularly those with graphical user interfaces, are designed as a series of events and responses. For example, when a user clicks the *File* menu and selects *Open*, an "open" event is triggered. When the user moves the mouse over the drawable area of a paint program, mouse move events are generated continuously. If the user presses down a button on the mouse, a "mouse down" event for that button-press is generated. The program can then start paying attention to the mouse move events, allowing the user to "draw" some object and continue doing this until the "mouse up" event occurs. Each operating system has its own way of naming and using these events, but the overall idea is the same: when an event occurs, it is somehow propagated to different objects to take appropriate action.

You might find the chain of responsibility pattern to be similar to the decorator pattern. However, there is a difference. You should see the chain of responsibility pattern as the architectural equivalent of an if-else cascade; that is, find a first match. The decorator pattern on the other hand extends functionality.

As you know, C++ does not have any built-in facilities for graphical programming. It also has no notion of events, event transmission, or event handling. A chain of responsibility is a reasonable approach to give different objects a chance to handle certain events.

Example: Event Handling

Consider a drawing program: an application with a window in which shapes can be drawn. The user can press a mouse button somewhere in the application's window. If that happens, the application should figure out whether the user clicked a shape. If so, the shape is asked to handle the "mouse button down" event. If it decides it doesn't need to handle the event, it passes the event to the window, which gets the next crack at the event. If the window is also not interested in the event, it forwards it to the application itself, which is the final object in the chain to handle the event. It's a chain of responsibility because each handler may either handle the event or pass the event to the next handler in the chain.

Implementation of a Chain of Responsibility

Suppose all possible events are defined in an enumeration as follows:

```
enum class Event { LeftMouseButtonDown, LeftMouseButtonUp,
    RightMouseButtonDown, RightMouseButtonUp };
```

Next, the following `Handler` base class is defined:

```
class Handler
{
    public:
        virtual ~Handler() = default;
        // Omitted defaulted default ctor, copy/move ctor, copy/move assignment op.
        explicit Handler(Handler* nextHandler) : m_nextHandler { nextHandler } { }
        virtual void handleMessage(Event message) = 0;
    protected:
        void nextHandler(Event message)
        {
            if (m_nextHandler) { m_nextHandler->handleMessage(message); }
        }
    private:
        Handler* m_nextHandler { nullptr };
};
```

Next, the `Application`, `Window`, and `Shape` classes are concrete handlers, all deriving from the `Handler` class. In this example, `Application` handles only `RightMouseButtonDown` messages, `Window` handles only `LeftMouseButtonUp` messages, and `Shape` handles only `LeftMouseButtonDown` messages. If any of the handlers receives a message it doesn't know about, it calls the next handler in the chain.

```
class Application : public Handler
{
    public:
        explicit Application(Handler* nextHandler) : Handler { nextHandler } { }

        void handleMessage(Event message) override
        {
            println("Application::handleMessage()");
            if (message == Event::RightMouseButtonDown) {
                println("   Handling message RightMouseButtonDown");
            } else { nextHandler(message); }
        }
};

class Window : public Handler
{
    public:
        explicit Window(Handler* nextHandler) : Handler { nextHandler } { }

        void handleMessage(Event message) override
        {
            println("Window::handleMessage()");
            if (message == Event::LeftMouseButtonUp) {
                println("   Handling message LeftMouseButtonUp");
            } else { nextHandler(message); }
        }
};

class Shape : public Handler
{
    public:
        explicit Shape(Handler* nextHandler) : Handler { nextHandler } { }

        void handleMessage(Event message) override
        {
            println("Shape::handleMessage()");
            if (message == Event::LeftMouseButtonDown) {
                println("   Handling message LeftMouseButtonDown");
            } else { nextHandler(message); }
        }
};
```

Using a Chain of Responsibility

The chain of responsibility implemented in the previous section can be tested as follows:

```
Application application { nullptr };
Window window { &application };
Shape shape { &window };
```

```
shape.handleMessage(Event::LeftMouseButtonDown);
println("");

shape.handleMessage(Event::LeftMouseButtonUp);
println("");

shape.handleMessage(Event::RightMouseButtonDown);
println("");

shape.handleMessage(Event::RightMouseButtonUp);
```

The output is as follows:

```
Shape::handleMessage()
   Handling message LeftMouseButtonDown

Shape::handleMessage()
Window::handleMessage()
   Handling message LeftMouseButtonUp

Shape::handleMessage()
Window::handleMessage()
Application::handleMessage()
   Handling message RightMouseButtonDown

Shape::handleMessage()
Window::handleMessage()
Application::handleMessage()
```

Of course, in a real application there must be some other class that *dispatches* the events to the correct object, i.e., calls `handleMessage()` on the correct object. Because this task varies greatly by framework or platform, the following example shows pseudo-code for handling a left mouse button down event, in lieu of platform-specific C++ code:

```
MouseLocation location { getMouseLocation() };
Shape* clickedShape { findShapeAtLocation(location) };
if (clickedShape) {
    clickedShape->handleMessage(Event::LeftMouseButtonDown);
} else {
    window.handleMessage(Event::LeftMouseButtonDown);
}
```

The chained approach is flexible and has an appealing structure for object-oriented hierarchies. The downside is that it requires diligence on the part of the programmer. If a class forgets to chain to the next handler in the chain, events will effectively get lost. Worse, if you chain to the wrong class, you could end up in an infinite loop!

THE SINGLETON PATTERN

The *singleton* is one of the simplest design patterns. In English, the word *singleton* means "one of a kind" or "individual." It has a similar meaning in programming. The singleton pattern is a strategy for enforcing the existence of exactly one instance of a class in a program. Applying the singleton pattern to a class guarantees that only one object of that class type will ever be created. The singleton pattern also specifies that the one object is globally accessible from anywhere in the program. Programmers usually refer to a class following the singleton pattern as a *singleton class*.

If your program relies on the assumption that there will be exactly one instance of a class, you could enforce that assumption with the singleton pattern. Technically, in C++, you could achieve the same thing using global variables and free functions in some namespace instead of a class, but other languages, such as Java, don't have the concept of global variables.

However, the singleton pattern has a number of disadvantages that you need to be aware of. If you have multiple singletons, it's not always easy to guarantee that they are initialized in the right order at program startup. It's also not easy to ensure a singleton is still there when callers need it during program shutdown. On top of that, singleton classes introduce hidden dependencies, cause tight coupling, and complicate unit testing. In a unit test, for example, you might want to write a mock version (see Chapter 30, "Becoming Adept at Testing") of a singleton that accesses the network or a database, but given the nature of a typical singleton implementation, that's hard to do.

A more appropriate design pattern is the strategy design pattern, discussed earlier in this chapter. With the strategy design pattern, you create an interface for each service you provide and inject the interfaces a component needs into the component. Strategy makes it easy to introduce different implementations which helps with mocking (stub versions) for unit testing. Still, the singleton pattern is discussed here because you will encounter it, especially in legacy code bases.

> **WARNING** *Avoid using the singleton pattern in new code because of its numerous problems. Prefer other patterns, such as the strategy design pattern.*

Example: A Logging Mechanism

Many applications have a notion of a logger—a class that is responsible for writing status information, debugging data, and errors to a central location. A logging class could have the following characteristics:

- It is available at all times.
- It is easy to use.
- There is only one instance.

The singleton pattern could be used to accomplish these requirements. But again, in new code I recommend avoiding introducing new singletons.

Implementation of a Singleton

There are two approaches to implement singleton behavior in C++. The first approach uses a class with only static member functions. Such a class needs no instantiation and is accessible from anywhere. The problem with this technique is that it lacks a built-in mechanism for construction and destruction. And, technically, a class that uses all static member functions doesn't really follow the singleton design pattern but the *monostate* design pattern; that is, such a class can have multiple instances but only one state. The term *singleton* implies that there is exactly one instance of the class. The monostate design pattern is not further discussed in this section.

The second approach uses access control levels to regulate the creation and access of one single instance of a class. This is a true singleton and illustrated with the example of a `Logger` class, providing similar features as the strategy-based `Logger` discussed earlier in this chapter.

To build a true singleton in C++, you can use the access control mechanisms as well as the `static` keyword. An actual `Logger` instance exists at run time, and the class enforces that only one instance is ever instantiated. Clients can always get a hold of that single instance through a `static` member function called `instance()`. The class definition looks like this:

```
export class Logger final
{
    public:
        enum class LogLevel { Debug, Info, Error };

        // Sets the name of the log file.
        // Note: needs to be called before the first call to instance()!
        static void setLogFilename(std::string logFilename);

        // Returns a reference to the singleton Logger object.
        static Logger& instance();

        // Prevent copy/move construction.
        Logger(const Logger&) = delete;
        Logger(Logger&&) = delete;

        // Prevent copy/move assignment operations.
        Logger& operator=(const Logger&) = delete;
        Logger& operator=(Logger&&) = delete;

        // Sets the log level.
        void setLogLevel(LogLevel level);

        // Logs a single message at the given log level.
        void log(std::string_view message, LogLevel logLevel);
    private:
        // Private constructor and destructor.
        Logger();
        ~Logger();

        // Converts a log level to a human-readable string.
        std::string_view getLogLevelString(LogLevel level) const;

        static inline std::string ms_logFilename;
        std::ofstream m_outputStream;
        LogLevel m_logLevel { LogLevel::Error };
};
```

This implementation is based on Scott Meyers' singleton pattern. This means that the `instance()` member function contains a local `static` instance of the `Logger` class. C++ guarantees that this local `static` instance is initialized in a thread-safe fashion, so you don't need any manual thread synchronization in this version of the singleton pattern. These are called *magic statics* or *thread-safe static local variables*. Note that only the initialization is thread-safe! If multiple threads are going to call member functions on the Logger class, then you should make the Logger member functions themselves thread safe as well. See Chapter 27, "Multithreaded Programming with C++," for a detailed discussion on synchronization mechanisms to make a class thread-safe.

The implementation of the Logger class is straightforward. Once the log file has been opened, each log message is written to it with a timestamp and the log level prepended, and then flushed to disk. The constructor and destructor are called automatically when the static instance of the Logger class in the instance() member function is created and destroyed. Because the constructor and destructor are private, no external code can create or delete a Logger.

Here are the implementations of the setLogFilename() and instance() member functions and the constructor and destructor. The other member functions have the same implementations as in the strategy-based logger example earlier in this chapter.

```
void Logger::setLogFilename(string logFilename)
{ ms_logFilename = move(logFilename); }

Logger& Logger::instance()
{
    static Logger instance; // Thread-safe static local variable.
    return instance;
}

Logger::Logger()
{
    m_outputStream.open(ms_logFileName, ios_base::app);
    if (!m_outputStream.good()) {
        throw runtime_error { "Unable to initialize the Logger!" };
    }
    println(m_outputStream, "{}: Logger started.", chrono::system_clock::now());
}


Logger::~Logger()
{ println(m_outputStream, "{}: Logger stopped.", chrono::system_clock::now()); }
```

Using a Singleton

The singleton Logger class can be tested as follows:

```
// Set the log filename before the first call to instance().
Logger::setLogFilename("log.out");
// Set log level to Debug.
Logger::instance().setLogLevel(Logger::LogLevel::Debug);
// Log some messages.
Logger::instance().log("test message", Logger::LogLevel::Debug);
// Set log level to Error.
Logger::instance().setLogLevel(Logger::LogLevel::Error);
// Now that the log level is set to Error, logging a Debug
// message will be ignored.
Logger::instance().log("A debug message", Logger::LogLevel::Debug);
```

After executing, the file `log.out` contains the following lines:

```
2023-08-12 17:36:15.1370238: Logger started.
2023-08-12 17:36:15.1372522: [DEBUG] test message
2023-08-12 17:36:15.1373057: Logger stopped.
```

SUMMARY

This chapter has given you just a taste of how patterns can help you organize object-oriented concepts into high-level designs. A lot of design patterns are cataloged and discussed on Wikipedia (`en.wikipedia.org/wiki/Software_design_pattern`). It's easy to get lost with the sheer number of available patterns. I recommend that you concentrate on a few patterns that interest you and slowly build up your arsenal of patterns.

I would like to conclude this chapter with the following quote, which expresses the reason why we use patterns:

> *The use of [design patterns] provides us in our daily lives with decisive speed advantages for understanding complex structures. This is also why patterns found their way into software development years ago. . . . Consistently applied patterns help us deal with the complexity of source code.*
>
> Carola Lilienthal, Software Architecture Metrics, O'Reilly Media

EXERCISES

By solving the following exercises, you can practice the material discussed in this chapter. Solutions to all exercises are available with the code download on the book's website at `www.wiley.com/go/proc++6e`. However, if you are stuck on an exercise, first reread parts of this chapter to try to find an answer yourself before looking at the solution from the website.

The concept of the exercises for this chapter is different compared to other chapters. The following exercises briefly introduce new patterns and ask you to do research into those patterns to learn more about them.

Exercise 33-1: Although this chapter discussed a nice selection of patterns, there are of course many more patterns available. One such pattern is the *command pattern*. It encapsulates an operation or operations in an object. One major use case of this pattern is to implement undoable operations. Use one of the patterns-related references in Appendix B, "Annotated Bibliography," to research and learn about the command pattern, or, alternatively, start from the Wikipedia article, `en.wikipedia.org/wiki/Software_design_pattern`, to start your research.

Exercise 33-2: Another pattern is the *facade pattern*. With this pattern, you provide an easy-to-use higher-level interface to hide the complexity of a subsystem. This makes the subsystem easier to use. Research the facade pattern to learn more about it.

Exercise 33-3: With the *prototype pattern*, you specify different kinds of objects that can be created by constructing prototypical instances of those objects. These prototypical instances are usually registered in some kind of registry. A client can then ask the registry for the prototype of a specific kind of object and subsequently clone the prototype for further use. Research the prototype pattern to learn more about it.

Exercise 33-4: The *mediator pattern* is used to control the interactions between a set of objects. It advocates loose coupling between the different subsystems in play. Research the mediator pattern to learn more about it.

34

Developing Cross-Platform and Cross-Language Applications

WHAT'S IN THIS CHAPTER?

- How to write code that runs on multiple platforms
- How to mix different programming languages together

WILEY.COM DOWNLOADS FOR THIS CHAPTER

Please note that all the code examples for this chapter are available as part of the chapter's code download on this book's website at `www.wiley.com/go/proc++6e` on the Download Code tab.

C++ programs can be compiled to run on a variety of computing platforms, and the language has been rigorously defined to ensure that programming in C++ for one platform is similar to programming in C++ for another. Yet, despite the standardization of the language, platform differences eventually come into play when writing professional-quality programs in C++. Even when development is limited to a particular platform, small differences in compilers can elicit major headaches. This chapter examines the necessary complication of programming in a world with multiple platforms and multiple programming languages.

The first part of this chapter surveys the platform-related issues that C++ programmers encounter. A *platform* is the collection of all the details that make up your development and/or run-time system. For example, your platform may be the Microsoft Visual C++ 2022 compiler running on Windows 11 on an Intel Core i7 processor. Alternatively, your platform might be the GCC 13.2 compiler running on Linux on a PowerPC processor. Both of these platforms are able to compile and run C++ programs, but there are significant differences between them.

The second part of this chapter looks at how C++ can interact with other programming languages. While C++ is a general-purpose language, it may not always be the right tool for the job. Through a variety of mechanisms, you can integrate C++ code with other languages that may better serve your needs.

CROSS-PLATFORM DEVELOPMENT

There are several reasons why the C++ language encounters platform issues. C++ is a high-level language, and the standard does not specify certain low-level details. For example, the layout of an object in memory is unspecified by the standard and left to the compiler[1]. Different compilers can use different memory layouts for objects.

C++ also faces the challenge of providing a standard language and a Standard Library without a standard implementation. Varying interpretations of the specification among C++ compiler and library vendors can lead to trouble when moving from one system to another.

Finally, C++ is selective in what the language provides as standard. Despite the existence of the Standard Library, programs often need functionality that is not provided by the language or the Standard Library. This functionality generally comes from third-party libraries or the platform itself, and can vary greatly.

Architecture Issues

The term *architecture* generally refers to the processor, or family of processors, on which a program runs. A standard PC running Windows or Linux generally runs on the x86 or x64 architecture, and older versions of macOS were usually found on the PowerPC architecture. As a high-level language, C++ shields you from the differences between these architectures. For example, a Core i7 processor may have a single instruction that performs the same functionality as six PowerPC instructions. As a C++ programmer, you don't need to know what this difference is or even that it exists. One advantage to using a high-level language is that the compiler takes care of converting your code into the processor's native assembly code format.

However, processor differences do sometimes rise up to the level of C++ code. The first one discussed, the size of integers, is important if you are writing cross-platform code. The others you won't face often, unless you are doing particularly low-level work, but still, you should be aware that they exist.

Size of Integers

The C++ standard does not define the exact size of integer types. The standard just says the following in section [basic.fundamental]:

> *There are five standard signed integer types:* `signed char`, `short int`, `int`, `long int`, *and* `long long int`. *In this list, each type provides at least as much storage as those preceding it in the list.*

[1] Starting with C++23, the order of members is defined by the standard and must be in the same order as they are declared in the class definition—older standards allowed compilers to reorder members. However, other aspects of object layout, such as padding and alignment, are platform-specific.

The standard does give a few additional hints for the size of these types, but never an exact size. The actual size is compiler-dependent. Thus, if you want to write truly cross-platform code, you cannot rely on these types. One of the exercises at the end of this chapter asks you to investigate this further.

Besides these core language integer types, the C++ Standard Library does define a number of types that have clearly specified sizes, all defined in the `std` namespace in `<cstdint>`, although some of the types are optional. Here is an overview:

TYPE	DESCRIPTION

`int8_t`
`int16_t`
`int32_t`
`int64_t`
	Signed integers of which the size is exactly 8, 16, 32, or 64 bits. On exotic platforms, some of these types might be absent. For example, if your exotic platform doesn't support an 8-bit type, `int8_t` will simply be absent.

`int_fast8_t`
`int_fast16_t`
`int_fast32_t`
`int_fast64_t`
	Signed integers with sizes of at least 8, 16, 32, or 64 bits. For these, the compiler should use the fastest integer type it has that satisfies the requirements.

`int_least8_t`
`int_least16_t`
`int_least32_t`
`int_least64_t`
	Signed integers with sizes of at least 8, 16, 32, or 64 bits — the smallest such types that exist. These types are guaranteed always to exist, even on exotic platforms. For example, a hypothetical platform with 24-bit bytes would alias both `int_least8_t` and `int_least16_t` to its 24-bit `char` type.

`intmax_t`	An integer type with the maximum size supported by the compiler.
`intptr_t`	An integer type big enough to store a pointer. This type is also optional, but most compilers support it.

There are also unsigned variants available, such as `uint8_t`, `uint_fast8_t`, and so on.

> **NOTE** *When writing cross-platform code, I recommend using the* `<cstdint>` *types instead of the basic integer types.*

Binary Compatibility

As you probably already know, you cannot take a program compiled for a Core i7 computer and run it on a PowerPC-based Mac. These two platforms are not *binary compatible* because their processors do not support the same set of instructions. When you compile a C++ program, your source code is turned into binary instructions that the computer executes. That binary format is defined by the platform, not by the C++ language.

One solution to support platforms that are not binary compatible is to build each version separately with a compiler on each target platform.

Another solution is *cross-compilation*. When you are using platform X for your development, but you want your program to run on platforms Y and Z, you can use a cross-compiler on your platform X that generates binary code for platforms Y and Z.

You can also make your program *open source*. When you make your source code available to end users, they can compile it natively on their systems and build a version of the program that is in the correct binary format for their machines. As discussed in Chapter 4, "Designing Professional C++ Programs," open-source software has become increasingly popular. One of the major reasons is that it allows programmers to collaboratively develop software and increase the number of platforms on which it can run.

Address Sizes

When someone describes an architecture as *64-bit*, they most likely mean that the *address* size is 64 bits, or 8 bytes. In general, a system with a larger address size can handle more memory and might operate more quickly on complex programs.

Because pointers are memory addresses, they are inherently tied to address sizes. Sometimes, programmers are taught that pointers are always 8 bytes, but this is wrong. For example, consider the following code snippet, which outputs the size of a pointer:

```
int *ptr { nullptr };
println("ptr size is {} bytes", sizeof(ptr));
```

If this program is compiled and executed on a 32-bit x86 system, the output will be as follows:

```
ptr size is 4 bytes
```

If you compile and run it on an x86-64 system, the output will be as follows:

```
ptr size is 8 bytes
```

From a programmer's point of view, the upshot of varying pointer sizes is that you cannot equate a pointer with either 4 or 8 bytes. More generally, you need to be aware that most sizes are not prescribed by the C++ standard. The standard only says that a `long` is at least as long as an `int`, which is at least as long as a `short`, and so on.

The size of a pointer is also not necessarily the same as the size of an integer. For example, on a 64-bit platform, pointers are 64-bit, but integers could be 32-bit. Casting a 64-bit pointer to a 32-bit integer results in losing 32 critical bits! The standard does define an `std::uintptr_t` type alias in `<cstdint>` which is an integer type at least big enough to hold a pointer. The definition of this type is optional according to the standard, but virtually all compilers support it.

> **WARNING** *Never assume that a pointer is 32 bits or 64 bits. Never cast a pointer to an integer, unless you use* `std::uintptr_t`.

Byte Order

All modern computers store numbers in a binary representation, but the representation of the same number on two platforms may not be identical. This sounds contradictory, but as you'll see, there are two approaches to representing numbers that both make sense.

Most computers these days are *byte-addressable*, meaning that every byte in memory has a unique memory address. Numeric types in C++ usually occupy multiple bytes. For example, a `short` may occupy 2 bytes. Imagine that your program contains the following line:

```
short myShort { 513 };
```

In binary, the number 513 is 0000 0010 0000 0001. This number contains 16 ones and zeros, or 16 bits. Because there are 8 bits in a byte, the computer needs 2 bytes to store the number. Because each individual memory address contains 1 byte, the computer needs to split the number up into multiple bytes. Assuming that a `short` is 2 bytes, the number is split into two parts. The higher part of the number is put into the *high-order byte*, and the lower part of the number is put into the *low-order byte*. In this case, the high-order byte is 0000 0010 and the low-order byte is 0000 0001.

Now that the number has been split up into memory-sized parts, the only question that remains is how to store them in memory. Two bytes are needed, but the order of the bytes is underdetermined and, in fact, depends on the architecture of the system in question.

One way to represent the number is to put the high-order byte first in memory and the low-order byte next. This strategy is called *big-endian ordering* because the bigger part of the number comes first. PowerPC and SPARC processors use a big-endian approach. Some other processors, such as x86, arrange the bytes in the opposite order, putting the low-order byte first in memory. This approach is called *little-endian ordering* because the smaller part of the number comes first. An architecture may choose one approach or the other, usually based on backward compatibility. For the curious, the terms *big-endian* and *little-endian* predate modern computers by several hundred years. Jonathan Swift coined the terms in his eighteenth-century novel *Gulliver's Travels* to describe the opposing camps of a debate about the proper end on which to break an egg.

Regardless of the *endianness* a particular architecture uses, your programs can continue to use numerical values without paying any attention to whether the machine uses big-endian ordering or little-endian ordering. That ordering only comes into play when data moves between architectures. For example, if you are sending binary data across a network, you may need to consider the endianness of the other system. One solution is to use the standard network byte ordering, which is always big-endian. So, before sending data across a network, you convert it to big-endian, and whenever you receive data from a network, you convert it from big-endian to the native endianness of your system.

Similarly, if you are writing binary data to a file, you may need to consider what happens when that file is opened on a system with opposite byte ordering.

The Standard Library includes the `std::endian` enumeration, defined in `<bit>`, which can be used to determine whether the current system is a big- or little-endian system. The following code snippet outputs the native byte ordering of your system:

```
switch (endian::native)
{
    case endian::little:
        println("Native ordering is little-endian.");
        break;
    case endian::big:
        println("Native ordering is big-endian.");
        break;
}
```

Implementation Issues

When a C++ compiler is written, it is designed by a human being who attempts to adhere to the C++ standard. Unfortunately, the C++ standard is more than 2,000 pages long and written in a combination of prose, pseudocode, and examples. Two human beings implementing a compiler according to such a standard are unlikely to interpret every piece of prescribed information in the same way or to catch every single edge case. As a result, compilers will have bugs.

Compiler Quirks and Extensions

There is no simple rule for finding or avoiding compiler bugs. The best you can do is to stay up to speed on compiler updates and perhaps subscribe to a mailing list or newsgroup for your compiler. If you suspect that you have encountered a compiler bug, a simple web search for the error message or condition you have witnessed could uncover a workaround or patch.

One area that compilers are notorious for having trouble with is language features that are added by recent updates to the standard. Although in recent years, vendors of major compilers are pretty quick in adding support for the latest features.

Another issue to be aware of is that compilers often include their own language extensions without making it obvious to the programmer. For example, variable-length stack-based arrays (VLAs) are not part of the C++ language; however, they are part of the C language. Some compilers support both the C and C++ standards and can allow the use of VLAs in C++ code. One such compiler is g++. The following compiles and runs as expected with the g++ compiler:

```
int i { 4 };
char myStackArray[i];  // Not a standard language feature!
```

Some compiler extensions may be useful, but if there is a chance that you will switch compilers at some point, you should see if your compiler has a strict mode where it avoids using such extensions. For example, compiling the previous code with the `-pedantic` flag passed to g++ yields the following warning:

```
warning: ISO C++ forbids variable length array 'myStackArray' [-Wvla]
```

The C++ specification allows for a certain type of compiler-defined language extension through the `#pragma` mechanism. `#pragma` is a preprocessor directive whose behavior is defined by the implementation. If the implementation does not understand the directive, it ignores it. For example, some compilers allow the programmer to turn compiler warnings off temporarily with `#pragma`.

Library Implementations

Most likely, your compiler includes an implementation of the C++ Standard Library. Because the Standard Library is written in C++, however, you aren't required to use the implementation that came bundled with your compiler. You could use a third-party Standard Library that, for example, has been optimized for speed, or you could even write your own.

Of course, Standard Library implementers face the same problems that compiler writers face: the standard is subject to interpretation. In addition, certain implementations may make tradeoffs that are incompatible with your needs. For example, one implementation may optimize for speed, while another implementation may focus on optimizing for being able to catch misuses at run time.

When working with a Standard Library implementation, or indeed any third-party library, it is important to consider the tradeoffs that the designers made during the development. Chapter 4 contains a more detailed discussion of the issues involved in using libraries.

Handling Different Implementations

As discussed in the previous sections, not all compilers and Standard Library implementations behave exactly the same. This is something you need to keep in mind when doing cross-platform development. Concretely, as a developer, you are most likely using a single toolchain, that is, a single compiler with a single Standard Library implementation. It's unlikely that you will personally verify all your code changes with all toolchains that your product must build with. The solution: *continuous integration* and *automated testing*.

You should set up a continuous integration environment that automatically builds all code changes on all toolchains that you need to support. The moment a build breaks on one of the toolchains, the developer who broke the build should automatically be informed.

Not all development environments use the same project files to describe all the source files, compiler switches, and so on. If you need to support multiple environments, manually maintaining separate project files for each is a maintenance nightmare. Instead, it's better to a use a single type of project file or single set of build scripts that can then automatically be transformed to concrete project files or concrete build scripts for specific toolchains. One such tool is called *CMake*. The collection of source files, compiler switches, libraries to link with, and so on, are described in CMake configuration files, which also have support for scripting. The CMake tool then automatically generates project files, for example for Visual C++ for development on Windows, or Xcode for development on macOS.

Once the continuous integration environment produces a build, automated testing should be triggered for that build. This should run a suite of test scripts on the produced executable to verify its correct behavior. Also in this step, if something goes wrong, the developer should automatically be informed.

Platform-Specific Features

C++ is a great general-purpose language. Thanks to the Standard Library, the language is packed with so many features that a casual programmer could happily code in C++ for years without going beyond what is built in. However, professional programs require facilities that C++ does not provide. This section lists several important features that are provided by the platform or third-party libraries, not by the C++ language or the C++ Standard Library:

- **Graphical user interfaces:** Most commercial programs today run on an operating system that has a graphical user interface, containing such elements as clickable buttons, movable windows, and hierarchical menus. C++, like the C language, has no notion of these elements. To write a graphical application in C++, you can use platform-specific libraries that allow you to draw windows, accept input through the mouse, and perform other graphical tasks. A better option is to use a third-party library, such as wxWidgets (`wxwidgets.org`), Qt (`qt.io`), Uno (`platform.uno`), and many more that provide an abstraction layer for building graphical applications. These libraries often provide support for many different target platforms.
- **Networking:** The Internet has changed the way we write applications. These days, most applications check for updates through the web, and games provide a networked multiplayer mode.

C++ does not provide a mechanism for networking yet, though several standard libraries exist. The most common means of writing networking software is through an abstraction called *sockets*. A socket library implementation can be found on most platforms, and it provides a simple procedure-oriented way to transfer data over a network. Some platforms support a stream-based networking system that operates like I/O streams in C++. There are also third-party networking libraries available that provide a networking abstraction layer. These libraries often support many different target platforms. Choosing a networking library that is IPv-independent would be a better choice than choosing one that only supports IPv4, as IPv6 is already being used.

- **OS events and application interaction:** In pure C++ code, there is little interaction with the surrounding operating system and other applications. The command-line arguments are about all you get in a standard C++ program without platform extensions. For example, operations such as copy and paste (which interact with the operating system's "clipboard") are not directly supported in C++. You can either use platform-provided libraries or use third-party libraries that support multiple platforms. For example, both wxWidgets and Qt are examples of libraries that abstract the clipboard operations and support multiple platforms.
- **Low-level files:** Chapter 13, "Demystifying C++ I/O," explains standard I/O in C++, including reading and writing files. Many operating systems provide their own file APIs, which are usually incompatible with the standard file classes in C++. These libraries often provide OS-specific file tools, such as a mechanism to get the home directory of the current user.
- **Threads:** Concurrent threads of execution within a single program were not directly supported in C++03 or earlier. Since C++11, a threading support library has been included with the Standard Library, as explained in Chapter 27, "Multithreaded Programming with C++," and C++17 has added parallel algorithms, as discussed in Chapter 20, "Mastering Standard Library Algorithms." If you need more powerful threading functionality besides what the Standard Library provides, then you need to use third-party libraries. Two examples are Intel's Threading Building Blocks (TBB) and the STE||AR Group's High Performance ParalleX (HPX) library.

NOTE *If you are doing cross-platform development and you need functionality not provided by the C++ language or the C++ Standard Library, you should try to find a third-party cross-platform library that provides the functionality you require. If, instead, you start using platform-specific APIs directly, then you are complicating your cross-platform code a lot, as you will have to implement the functionality for each platform you need to support.*

NOTE *When using third-party libraries, if possible, get these libraries as source code and build them yourself with the exact toolchains you need.*

CROSS-LANGUAGE DEVELOPMENT

For certain types of programs, C++ may not be the best tool for the job. For example, if your Unix program needs to interact closely with the shell environment, you may be better off writing a shell script than a C++ program. If your program performs heavy text processing, you may decide that the Perl language is the way to go. If you need a lot of database interaction, then C# or Java might be a better choice. C# in combination with the WPF framework or the Uno platform might be better suited to write modern graphical user interface applications, and so on. Still, if you do decide to use another language, you sometimes might want to be able to call into C++ code, for example, to perform some computational-expensive operations; or the other way around, you might want to call non-C++ code from C++. Fortunately, there are some techniques you can use to get the best of both worlds—the specific specialty of another language combined with the power and flexibility of C++.

Mixing C and C++

As you already know, the C++ language is almost a superset of the C language. Most C code can easily be converted to C++, but there are a few things to keep in mind. A handful of C features are not supported by C++; for example, C supports variable-length arrays (VLAs), while C++ does not. Other things to keep in mind are the use of reserved words. In C, for example, the term *class* has no particular meaning. Thus, it could be used as a variable name, as in the following C code:

```
int class = 1; // Compiles in C, not C++
printf("class is %d\n", class);
```

This program compiles and runs in C but yields an error when compiled as C++ code. When you translate, or *port*, a program from C to C++, these are the types of errors you will face. Fortunately, the fixes are usually quite simple. In this case, rename the `class` variable to, e.g., `classID` and the code will compile.

On the other hand, every C++ compiler is also a C compiler. There is no reason to compile "C as C++"; you can just compile "C as C". If your project consists of a mixture of C and C++, you can simply link the C and C++ object files together into the final executable. This ease of incorporating C code in a C++ program comes in handy when you encounter a useful library or legacy code that was written in C. Functions and classes, as you've seen many times in this book, work just fine together. A class member function can call a function, and a function can make use of objects.

Shifting Paradigms

One of the dangers of mixing C and C++ is that your program may start to lose its object-oriented properties. For example, if your object-oriented web browser is implemented with a procedural networking library, the program will be mixing these two paradigms. Given the importance and quantity of networking tasks in such an application, you might consider writing an *object-oriented wrapper* around the procedural library. A typical design pattern that can be used for this is called the *façade*.

For example, imagine that you are writing a web browser in C++, but you are using a networking library that has a C-style API and contains the functions declared in the following code. Note that the `HostHandle` and `ConnectionHandle` data structures have been omitted for brevity.

```
// networklib.h
#include "HostHandle.h"
#include "ConnectionHandle.h"

// Gets the host record for a particular Internet host given
// its hostname (i.e. www.host.com).
HostHandle* lookupHostByName(const char* hostName);
// Frees the given HostHandle.
void freeHostHandle(HostHandle* host);

// Connects to the given host.
ConnectionHandle* connectToHost(HostHandle* host);
// Closes the given connection.
void closeConnection(ConnectionHandle* connection);

// Retrieves a web page from an already-opened connection.
char* retrieveWebPage(ConnectionHandle* connection, const char* page);
// Frees the memory pointed to by page.
void freeWebPage(char* page);
```

The `networklib.h` interface is fairly simple and straightforward. However, it is not object-oriented, and a C++ programmer who uses such a library is bound to feel *icky*, to use a technical term. This library isn't organized into a cohesive class. Of course, the authors of the library could have written a better interface, but as the user of a library, you have to accept what you are given. Writing a wrapper is your opportunity to customize the interface.

Before you build an object-oriented wrapper for this library, take a look at how it might be used as-is to gain an understanding of its actual usage. In the following program, the `networklib` library is used to retrieve the web page at `www.example.com/index.html`:

```
HostHandle* myHost { lookupHostByName("www.example.com") };
ConnectionHandle* myConnection { connectToHost(myHost) };
char* result { retrieveWebPage(myConnection, "/index.html") };

println("The result is:\n{}", result);

freeWebPage(result); result = nullptr;
closeConnection(myConnection); myConnection = nullptr;
freeHostHandle(myHost); myHost = nullptr;
```

A possible way to make the library more object-oriented is to provide a single abstraction that recognizes the commonality between looking up a host, connecting to the host, and retrieving a web page. A good object-oriented wrapper hides the needless complexity of the `HostHandle` and `ConnectionHandle` types.

This example follows the design principles described in Chapters 5, "Designing with Classes," and 6, "Designing for Reuse": the new class should capture the common use case for the library. The previous example shows the most frequently used pattern: first a host is looked up, then a connection is established, and finally a page is retrieved. It is also likely that subsequent pages will be retrieved from the same host, so a good design will accommodate that mode of use as well.

To start, the `HostRecord` class wraps the functionality of looking up a host. It's an RAII class. Its constructor uses `lookupHostByName()` to perform the lookup. The `unique_ptr` data member uses a custom deleter to automatically free the retrieved `HostHandle` by calling `freeHostHandle()`. See Chapter 7, "Memory Management," for a discussion of using custom deleters with `unique_ptr`. Here is the code:

```
export class HostRecord final
{
    public:
        // Looks up the host record for the given host.
        explicit HostRecord(const std::string& host)
            : m_hostHandle { lookupHostByName(host.c_str()), freeHostHandle }
        { }
        // Returns the underlying handle.
        HostHandle* get() const noexcept { return m_hostHandle.get(); }
    private:
        std::unique_ptr<HostHandle, decltype(&freeHostHandle)> m_hostHandle;
};
```

Next, a `WebHost` class is implemented that uses the `HostRecord` class. The `WebHost` class creates a connection to a given host and supports retrieving webpages. It's also an RAII class. When the `WebHost` object is destroyed, it automatically closes the connection to the host. The `getPage()` member function calls `retrieveWebPage()` and immediately stores the result in a `unique_ptr` with a custom deleter, `freeWebPage()`. Here is the code:

```
export class WebHost final
{
    public:
        // Connects to the given host.
        explicit WebHost(const std::string& host);
        // Obtains the given page from this host.
        std::string getPage(const std::string& page);
    private:
        std::unique_ptr<ConnectionHandle, decltype(&closeConnection)> m_connection
            { nullptr, closeConnection };
};

WebHost::WebHost(const std::string& host)
{
    HostRecord hostRecord { host };
    if (hostRecord.get()) {
        m_connection = { connectToHost(hostRecord.get()), closeConnection };
    }
}

std::string WebHost::getPage(const std::string& page)
{
    std::string resultAsString;
    if (m_connection) {
        std::unique_ptr<char[], decltype(&freeWebPage)> result {
            retrieveWebPage(m_connection.get(), page.c_str()),
            freeWebPage };
        resultAsString = result.get();
    }
    return resultAsString;
}
```

The `WebHost` class effectively encapsulates the behavior of a host and provides useful functionality without unnecessary calls and data structures. The implementation of the `WebHost` class makes extensive use of the `networklib` library without exposing any of its workings to the user. The constructor of `WebHost` uses a `HostRecord` RAII object for the specified host. The resulting `HostRecord` is used to set up a connection to the host, which is stored in the `m_connection` data member for later use. The `HostRecord` RAII object is automatically destroyed at the end of the constructor. The `WebHost` destructor destroys `m_connection` which closes the connection. The `getPage()` member function uses `retrieveWebPage()` to retrieve a web page, converts it to an `std::string`, uses `freeWebPage()` to free memory, and returns the retrieved page as an `std::string`.

The `WebHost` class makes the common case easy for the client programmer. Here is an example:

```
WebHost myHost { "www.example.com" };
string result { myHost.getPage("/index.html") };
println("The result is:\n{}", result);
```

> **NOTE** *Networking-savvy readers may note that keeping a connection open to a host indefinitely is considered bad practice and doesn't adhere to the HTTP specification. You should not do this in production-quality code. However, for this example, I've chosen elegance over etiquette.*

As you can see, the `WebHost` class provides an object-oriented wrapper around the C-style library. By providing an abstraction, you can change the underlying implementation without affecting client code, and you can provide additional features. These features can include connection reference counting, automatically closing connections after a specific time to adhere to the HTTP specification, automatically reopening the connection on the next `getPage()` call, and so on.

You'll explore writing wrappers a bit more in one of the exercises at the end of this chapter.

Linking with C Code

The previous example assumed that you had the raw C code to work with. The example took advantage of the fact that most C code will successfully compile with a C++ compiler. If you only have compiled C code, perhaps in the form of a library, you can still use it in your C++ program, but you need to take a few extra steps.

Before you can start using compiled C code in your C++ programs, you first need to know about a concept called *name mangling*. To implement function overloading, the complex C++ namespace is "flattened." For example, if you have a C++ program, it is legitimate to write the following:

```
void myFunc(double);
void myFunc(int);
void myFunc(int, int);
```

However, this would mean that the linker would see several different functions, all called `myFunc`, and would not know which one you want to call. Therefore, all C++ compilers perform an operation that is referred to as *name mangling* and is the logical equivalent of generating names, as follows:

```
myFunc_double
myFunc_int
myFunc_int_int
```

To avoid conflicts with other names you might have defined, the compiler might generate names that are reserved as identifiers, for example, names beginning with double underscores or names beginning with an underscore followed by an uppercase letter. Alternatively, some compilers generate names that have characters that are legal to the linker but not legal in C++ source code. For example, Microsoft VC++ generates names as follows:

```
?myFunc@@YAXN@Z
?myFunc@@YAXH@Z
?myFunc@@YAXHH@Z
```

This encoding is complex and often vendor specific. The C++ standard does not specify how function overloading should be implemented on a given platform, so there is no standard for name mangling algorithms.

In C, function overloading is not supported (the compiler will complain about duplicate definitions). So, names generated by the C compiler are quite simple, for example, `_myFunc`.

Now, if you compile a simple program with the C++ compiler, even if it has only one instance of the `myFunc` name, it still generates a request to link to a mangled name. However, when you link with the C library, it cannot find the desired mangled name, and the linker complains. Therefore, it is necessary to tell the C++ compiler to not mangle that name. This is done by using the `extern "C"` qualification both in the header file (to instruct the client code to create a name compatible with C) and, if your library source is in C++, at the definition site (to instruct the library code to generate a name compatible with C).

Here is the syntax of `extern "C"`:

```
extern "C" declaration1();
extern "C" declaration2();
```

or:

```
extern "C" {
    declaration1();
    declaration2();
}
```

The C++ standard says that any language specification can be used, so in principle, the following could be supported by a compiler:

```
extern "C" void myFunc(int i);
extern "Fortran" Matrix* matrixInvert(Matrix* M);
extern "Pascal" void someLegacySubroutine(int n);
extern "Ada" bool aimMissileDefense(double angle);
```

In practice, many compilers only support `"C"`. Each compiler vendor will inform you which language designators they support.

As an example, the following code specifies the function prototype for `cFunction()` as an external C function:

```
extern "C" {
    void cFunction(int i);
}

int main()
{
    cFunction(8); // Calls the C function.
}
```

The actual definition for `cFunction()` is provided in a compiled binary file attached in the link phase. The `extern` keyword informs the compiler that the linked-in code was compiled in C.

A more common pattern for using `extern` is at the header level. For example, if you are using a graphics library written in C, it probably came with an `.h` file for you to include. The author of this header file should condition it on whether it is being compiled for C or C++. A C++ compiler predefines the symbol `__cplusplus` if you are compiling for C++. The symbol is not defined for C compilations. This symbol can be used to condition a header file as follows:

```
#ifdef __cplusplus
    extern "C" {
#endif
        drawCircle();
        drawSquare();
#ifdef __cplusplus
    } // matches extern "C"
#endif
```

This means that `drawCircle()` and `drawSquare()` are functions that are in a library compiled by the C compiler. Using this technique, the same header file can be used in both C and C++ clients.

Whether you are including C code in your C++ program or linking against a compiled C library, remember that even though C++ is almost a superset of C, they are different languages with different design goals. Adapting C code to work in C++ is quite common, but providing an object-oriented C++ wrapper around procedural C code is often much better.

Calling C++ Code from C#

Even though this is a C++ book, I won't pretend that there aren't other languages out there. One example is C#. By using the *Interop services* from C#, it's pretty easy to call C++ code from within your C# applications. An example scenario could be that you develop parts of your application, like the graphical user interface, in C#, but use C++ to implement certain performance-critical or computational-expensive components. To make Interop work, you need to write a library in C++, which can be called from C#. On Windows, the library will be in a `.dll` file. The following C++ example defines a `functionInDLL()` function that is compiled into a library. The function accepts a Unicode string and returns an integer. The implementation writes the received string to the console and returns the value 42 to the caller:

```
import std;
using namespace std;
```

```
extern "C"
{
    __declspec(dllexport) int functionInDLL(const wchar_t* p)
    {
        wcout << format(L"The following string was received by C++: '{}'", p)
              << endl;
        return 42;    // Return some value...
    }
}
```

Keep in mind that you are implementing a function in a library, not writing a program, so you do not need a `main()` function. How you compile this code depends on your development environment. If you are using Microsoft Visual C++, you need to go to the properties of your project and select Dynamic Library (.dll) as the configuration type. The example uses `__declspec(dllexport)` to tell the linker that this function should be made available to clients of the library. This is the way you do it with Microsoft Visual C++. Other linkers might use a different mechanism to export functions.

Once you have the library, you can call it from C# by using the Interop services. First, you need to include the Interop namespace:

```
using System.Runtime.InteropServices;
```

Next, you define the function prototype and tell C# where it can find the implementation of the function. This is done with the following statement, assuming you have compiled the library as `HelloCpp.dll`:

```
[DllImport("HelloCpp.dll", CharSet = CharSet.Unicode)]
public static extern int functionInDLL(String s);
```

The first line is saying that C# should import this function from a library called `HelloCpp.dll` and that it should use Unicode strings. The second line specifies the actual prototype of the function, which is a function accepting a string as parameter and returning an integer. The following code shows a complete example of how to use the C++ library from C#:

```
using System;
using System.Runtime.InteropServices;

namespace HelloCSharp
{
    class Program
    {
        [DllImport("HelloCpp.dll", CharSet = CharSet.Unicode)]
        public static extern int functionInDLL(String s);

        static void Main(string[] args)
        {
            Console.WriteLine("Written by C#.");
            int result = functionInDLL("Some string from C#.");
            Console.WriteLine("C++ returned the value " + result);
        }
    }
}
```

The output is as follows:

```
Written by C#.
The following string was received by C++: 'Some string from C#.'
C++ returned the value 42
```

The details of the C# code are outside the scope of this C++ book, but the general idea should be clear with this example.

This section only talked about calling C++ functions from C# and didn't say anything about using C++ classes from C#. That will be remedied in the next section with the introduction of C++/CLI.

Use C# Code from C++ and C++ from C# with C++/CLI

To use C# code from C++, you can use C++/CLI. CLI stands for *Common Language Infrastructure* and is the backbone of all .NET languages such as C#, Visual Basic .NET, and so on. C++/CLI was created by Microsoft in 2005 to be a version of C++ that supports the CLI. In December 2005, C++/CLI has been standardized as the ECMA-372 standard. You can write your C++ programs in C++/CLI and gain access to any other piece of functionality written in any other language that supports the CLI, such as C#. Keep in mind, though, that C++/CLI might lag behind the latest C++ standard, meaning that it does not necessarily support all latest C++ features. Discussing the C++/CLI language in detail is outside the scope of this pure C++ book. Only a few small examples are given.

Suppose you have the following C# class in a C# library:

```
namespace MyLibrary
{
    public class MyClass
    {
        public double DoubleIt(double value) { return value * 2.0; }
    }
}
```

You can consume this C# library from your C++/CLI code as follows. The important bits are highlighted. CLI objects are managed by a memory garbage collector that automatically cleans up memory when memory is not needed anymore. As such, you cannot just use the standard C++ `new` operator to create managed objects; you have to use `gcnew`, an abbreviation for "garbage collect new." Instead of storing the resulting pointer in a normal C++ pointer variable such as `MyClass*` or in a smart pointer such as `std::unique_ptr<MyClass>`, you have to store it using a *handle*, `MyClass^`, usually pronounced as "MyClass hat."

```
#include <iostream>

using namespace System;
using namespace MyLibrary;

int main(array<System::String^>^ args)
{
    MyClass^ instance { gcnew MyClass() };
    auto result { instance->DoubleIt(1.2) };
    std::cout << result << std::endl;
}
```

C++/CLI can also be used in the other direction; you can write managed C++ *ref classes*, which are then accessible by any other CLI language. Here is a simple example of a managed C++ ref class:

```
#pragma once
```

```
using namespace System;

namespace MyCppLibrary
{
    public ref class MyCppRefClass
    {
        public:
            double TripleIt(double value) { return value * 3.0; }
    };
}
```

This C++/CLI ref class can then be used from C# as follows:

```
using MyCppLibrary;

namespace MyLibrary
{
    public class MyClass
    {
        public double TripleIt(double value)
        {
            // Ask C++ to triple it.
            MyCppRefClass cppRefClass = new MyCppRefClass();
            return cppRefClass.TripleIt(value);
        }
    }
}
```

As you can see, the basics are not that complicated, but these examples all use primitive datatypes, such as `double`. It starts to become more complicated if you need to work with non-primitive datatypes such as strings, vectors, and so on, because then you need to start marshaling objects between C# and C++/CLI, and vice versa. However, this would take us too far for this brief introduction to C++/CLI.

Calling C++ Code from Java with JNI

The *Java Native Interface* (JNI) is part of the Java language that allows programmers to access functionality that was not written in Java. Because Java is a cross-platform language, the original intent was to make it possible for Java programs to interact with the operating system. JNI also allows programmers to make use of libraries written in other languages, such as C++. Access to C++ libraries may be useful to a Java programmer who has a performance-critical or computational-expensive piece of code or who needs to use legacy code.

JNI can also be used to execute Java code within a C++ program, but such a use is far less common. Because this is a C++ book, I do not include an introduction to the Java language. This section is recommended if you already know Java and want to incorporate C++ code into your Java code.

To begin your Java cross-language adventure, start with the Java program. For this example, the simplest of Java programs will suffice:

```
public class HelloCpp
{
    public static void main(String[] args)
    {
```

```
        System.out.println("Hello from Java!");
    }
}
```

Next, you need to declare a Java method that will be written in another language. To do this, you use the `native` keyword and leave out the implementation:

```
// This will be implemented in C++.
public static native void callCpp();
```

The C++ code will eventually be compiled into a shared library that gets dynamically loaded into the Java program. You can load this library inside a Java static block so that it is loaded when the Java program begins executing. The name of the library can be whatever you want, for example, `hellocpp.so` on Linux systems, or `hellocpp.dll` on Windows systems.

```
static { System.loadLibrary("hellocpp"); }
```

Finally, you need to actually call the C++ code from within the Java program. The `callCpp()` Java method serves as a placeholder for the not-yet-written C++ code. Here is the complete Java program:

```
public class HelloCpp
{
    static { System.loadLibrary("hellocpp"); }

    // This will be implemented in C++.
    public static native void callCpp();

    public static void main(String[] args)
    {
        System.out.println("Hello from Java!");
        callCpp();
    }
}
```

That's all for the Java side. Now, just compile the Java program as you normally would:

```
javac HelloCpp.java
```

Then use the `javah` program (I like to pronounce it as *jav-AHH!*) to create a header file for the native function:

```
javah HelloCpp
```

After running `javah`, you will find a file named `HelloCpp.h`, which is a fully working (if somewhat ugly) C/C++ header file. Inside of that header file is a C function definition for a function called `Java_HelloCpp_callCpp()`. Your C++ program will need to implement this function. The full prototype is as follows:

```
JNIEXPORT void JNICALL Java_HelloCpp_callCpp(JNIEnv*, jclass);
```

Your C++ implementation of this function can make full use of the C++ language. This example just outputs some text from C++. First, you need to include the `jni.h` header file and the `HelloCpp.h` file that was created by `javah`. You also need to include any C++ headers that you intend to use.

```
#include <jni.h>
#include "HelloCpp.h"
#include <iostream>
```

The C++ function is written as normal. The parameters to the function allow interaction with the Java environment and the object that called the native code. They are beyond the scope of this example.

```
JNIEXPORT void JNICALL Java_HelloCpp_callCpp(JNIEnv*, jclass)
{
    std::cout << "Hello from C++!" << std::endl;
}
```

How to compile this code into a library depends on your environment, but you will most likely need to tweak your compiler's settings to include the JNI headers. Using the GCC compiler on Linux, your compile command might look like this:

```
g++ -shared -I/usr/java/jdk/include/ -I/usr/java/jdk/include/linux \
HelloCpp.cpp -o hellocpp.so
```

The output from the compiler is the library used by the Java program. As long as the shared library is somewhere in the Java class path, you can execute the Java program as you normally would:

```
java HelloCpp
```

You should see the following result:

```
Hello from Java!
Hello from C++!
```

Of course, this example just scratches the surface of what is possible through JNI. You could use JNI to interface with OS-specific features or hardware drivers. For complete coverage of JNI, you should consult a Java text.

Calling Scripts from C++ Code

The original Unix OS included a rather limited C library, which did not support certain common operations. Unix programmers therefore developed the habit of launching *scripts* from applications to accomplish tasks that should have had API or library support. Scripts can be written in languages such as Perl and Python, but they can also be shell scripts for executing in a shell such as Bash.

Today, many of these Unix programmers still insist on using scripts as a form of subroutine call. To enable these kinds of interoperabilities, C++ provides the `std::system()` function defined in `<cstdlib>`. It requires only a single argument, a string representing the command you want to execute. Here are some examples:

```
system("python my_python_script.py"); // Launch a Python script.
system("perl my_perl_script.pl");     // Launch a Perl script.
system("my_shell_script.sh");         // Launch a Shell script.
```

However, there are significant risks to this approach. For example, if there is an error in the script, the caller may or may not get a detailed error indication. The `system()` call is also exceptionally heavy-duty, because it has to create an entire new process to execute the script. This may ultimately be a serious performance bottleneck in your application.

Using `system()` to launch scripts is not further discussed in this text. In general, you should explore the features of C++ libraries to see if there are better ways to do something. There are some platform-independent wrappers around a lot of platform-specific libraries, for example, the Boost Asio library, which provides portable networking and other low-level I/O, including sockets, timers, serial ports, and so on. If you need to work with a filesystem, you can use the platform-independent `<filesystem>` API available as part of the C++ Standard Library since C++17, and discussed in Chapter 13. Concepts like launching a Perl script with `system()` to process some textual data may not be the best choice. Using techniques like the regular expressions library of C++, see Chapter 21, "String Localization and Regular Expressions," might be a better choice for your string processing needs.

Calling C++ Code from Scripts

C++ contains a built-in general-purpose mechanism to interface with other languages and environments. You've already used it many times, probably without paying much attention to it—it's the arguments to and return value from the `main()` function.

C and C++ were designed with command-line interfaces in mind. The `main()` function receives the arguments from the command line and returns a status code that can be interpreted by the caller. In a scripting environment, arguments to and status codes from your program can be a powerful mechanism that allows you to interface with the environment.

A Practical Example: Encrypting Passwords

Assume that you have a system that writes everything a user sees and types to a file for auditing purposes. The file can be read only by the system administrator so that she can figure out who to blame if something goes wrong. An excerpt of such a file might look like this:

```
Login: bucky-bo
Password: feldspar

bucky-bo> mail
bucky-bo has no mail
bucky-bo> exit
```

While the system administrator may want to keep a log of all user activity, she may also want to obscure everybody's passwords in case the file is somehow obtained by a hacker. She decides to write a script to parse the log files and to use C++ to perform the actual encryption. The script then calls out to a C++ program to perform the encryption.

The following script uses the Perl language, though almost any scripting language could accomplish this task. Note also that these days, there are libraries available for Perl that perform encryption, but, for the sake of this example, let's assume the encryption is done in C++. If you don't know Perl, you will still be able to follow along. The most important element of the Perl syntax for this example is the ` character. The ` character instructs the Perl script to *shell out* to an external command. In this case, the script will shell out to a C++ program called `encryptString`.

> **NOTE** *Launching an external process causes a big performance overhead because a completely new process has to be created. You shouldn't use it when you need to call the external process often. In this password encryption example, it is okay, because you can assume that a log file will contain only a few password lines.*

The strategy for the script is to loop over every line of a file, `userlog.txt`, looking for lines that contain a password prompt. The script writes a new file, `userlog.out`, which contains the same text as the source file, except that all passwords are encrypted. The first step is to open the input file for reading and the output file for writing. Then, the script needs to loop over all the lines in the file. Each line in turn is placed in a variable called `$line`.

```
open (INPUT, "userlog.txt") or die "Couldn't open input file!";
open (OUTPUT, ">userlog.out") or die "Couldn't open output file!";
while ($line = <INPUT>) {
```

Next, the current line is checked against a *regular expression* to see if this particular line contains the `Password:` prompt. If it does, Perl stores the password in the variable `$1`.

```
    if ($line =~ m/^Password: (.*)/) {
```

If a match is found, the script calls the `encryptString` program with the detected password to obtain an encrypted version of it. The output of the program is stored in the `$result` variable, and the result status code from the program is stored in the variable `$?`. The script checks `$?` and quits immediately if there is a problem. If everything is okay, the password line is written to the output file with the encrypted password instead of the original one.

```
        $result = `./encryptString $1`;
        if ($? != 0) { exit(-1); }
        print OUTPUT "Password: $result\n";
    } else {
```

If the current line is not a password prompt, the script writes the line as is to the output file. At the end of the loop, it closes both files and exits.

```
        print OUTPUT "$line";
    }
}
close (INPUT);
close (OUTPUT);
```

That's it. The only other required piece is the actual C++ program. Implementation of a cryptographic algorithm is beyond the scope of this book. The important piece is the `main()` function because it accepts the string that should be encrypted as an argument.

Arguments are contained in the `argv` array of C-style strings. You should always check the `argc` parameter before accessing an element of `argv`. If `argc` is 1, there is one element in the argument list, and it is accessible as `argv[0]`. Actual command-line parameters begin at `argv[1]`. The zeroth element of the `argv` array is generally the name of the program, but because it is controlled by whoever spawned the current process, e.g., by the Linux `execve()` system call, it can technically hold any data at all. All you're guaranteed is that each argument in `argv[0]` through `argv[argc-1]` is a null-terminated string, and `argv[argc]` itself is a null pointer.

The following is the `main()` function for a C++ program that encrypts the input string. Notice that the program returns 0 for success and non-0 for failure, as is standard in Linux.

```
int main(int argc, char** argv)
{
    if (argc < 2) {
```

```
        println(cerr, "Usage: {} string-to-be-encrypted", argv[0]);
        return 1;
    }
    print("{}", encrypt(argv[1]));
}
```

> **NOTE** *There is actually a subtle security hole in this code. When the to-be-encrypted string is passed to the C++ program as a command-line argument, it may be visible to other users through the process table. One example of a more secure way to get the information into the C++ program would be to send it through standard input.*

Now that you've seen how easily C++ programs can be incorporated into scripting languages, you can combine the strengths of the two languages for your own projects. You can use a scripting language to interact with the operating system and control the flow of the script, and a traditional programming language like C++ for the heavy lifting.

> **NOTE** *This example is just to demonstrate how to use Perl and C++ together. The C++ Standard Library includes regular expressions support, which makes it easy to convert this Perl/C++ solution into a pure C++ solution. This pure C++ solution will run much faster because it avoids calling an external program. See Chapter 21 for details on the regular expressions library.*

Calling Assembly Code from C++

C++ is considered a fast language, especially relative to other languages. Yet, in some rare cases, you might want to use raw assembly code when speed is absolutely critical. The compiler generates assembly code from your source files, and this generated assembly code is fast enough for virtually all purposes. Both the compiler and the linker (when it supports link time code generation) use optimization algorithms to make the generated assembly code as fast as possible. These optimizers are getting more and more powerful by using special processor instruction sets such as MMX, SSE, and AVX. These days, it's hard to write your own assembly code that outperforms the code generated by the compiler, unless you know all the little details of these enhanced instruction sets.

However, in case you do need it, the keyword `asm` can be used by a C++ compiler to allow the programmer to insert raw assembly code. The keyword is part of the C++ standard, but its implementation is compiler-defined. In some compilers, you can use `asm` to drop from C++ down to the level of assembly right in the middle of your program. Sometimes, the support for the `asm` keyword depends on your target architecture, and sometimes a compiler uses a non-standard keyword instead of the `asm` keyword. For example, Microsoft Visual C++ 2022 does not support the `asm` keyword. Instead, it supports the `__asm` keyword when compiling in 32-bit mode, and does not support inline assembly at all when compiling in 64-bit mode.

Assembly code can be useful in some applications, but I don't recommend it for most programs. There are several reasons to avoid assembly code:

- Your code is no longer portable to another processor once you start including raw assembly code for your platform.
- Most programmers don't know assembly languages and won't be able to modify or maintain your code.
- Assembly code is not known for its readability. It can hurt your program's use of style.
- Most of the time, it is not necessary. If your program is slow, look for algorithmic problems, or consult some of the other performance suggestions from Chapter 29, "Writing Efficient C++."

> **WARNING** *When you encounter performance issues in your application, use a profiler to determine the real hotspot, and look into algorithmic speed-ups! Only start thinking about using assembly code if you have exhausted all other options, and even then, think about the disadvantages of assembly code.*

Practically, if you have a computationally expensive block of code, you should move it to its own C++ function. If you determine, using performance profiling (see Chapter 29), that this function is a performance bottleneck, and there is no way to write the code smaller and faster, you might use raw assembly code to try to increase its performance.

In such a case, one of the first things you want to do is declare the function `extern "C"` so the C++ name mangling is suppressed. Then, you can write a separate module in assembly code that performs the function more efficiently. The advantage of a separate module is that there is both a "reference implementation" in C++ that is platform-independent, and also a platform-specific high-performance implementation in raw assembly code. The use of `extern "C"` means that the assembly code can use a simple naming convention (otherwise, you have to reverse-engineer your compiler's name mangling algorithm). Then, you can link with either the C++ version or the assembly code version.

You would write this module in assembly code and run it through an assembler, rather than using the inline `asm` keyword in C++. This is particularly true in many of the popular x86-compatible 64-bit compilers, where the inline `asm` keyword is not supported.

Even though it is possible, you should use raw assembly code only if there are significant performance improvements. Additionally, don't forget *Amdahl's law*. For example, a 10x speedup in your encryption routine sounds great, but if your program spends 90 percent of its time not doing encryption, that means that 10x speedup is for 10 percent of the program only—just a 9 percent overall improvement!

SUMMARY

If you take away one point from this chapter, it should be that C++ is a flexible language. It exists in the sweet spot between languages that are too tied to a particular platform, and languages that are too high-level and generic. Rest assured that when you develop code in C++, you aren't locking yourself into the language forever. C++ can be mixed with other technologies and has a solid history and code base that will help guarantee its relevance in the future.

In Part V of this book, I discussed software engineering methods, writing efficient C++, testing and debugging techniques, design techniques and patterns, and cross-platform and cross-language application development. This is a terrific way to end your journey through professional C++ programming because these topics help good C++ programmers become great C++ programmers. By thinking through your designs, experimenting with different approaches in object-oriented programming, selectively adding new techniques to your coding repertoire, and practicing testing and debugging techniques, you'll be able to take your C++ skills to the professional level.

EXERCISES

By solving the following exercises, you can practice the material discussed in this chapter. Solutions to all exercises are available with the code download on the book's website at `www.wiley.com/go/proc++6e`. However, if you are stuck on an exercise, first reread parts of this chapter to try to find an answer yourself before looking at the solution from the website.

Exercise 34-1: Write a program that outputs the sizes of all standard C++ integer types. If possible, try to compile and execute it with different compilers on different platforms.

Exercise 34-2: This chapter introduces the concept of big- and little-endian encoding of integer values. It also explained that over a network, it's recommended to always use big-endian encoding and to convert as necessary. Write a program that can convert 16-bit unsigned integers between little- and big-endian encoding in both directions. Pay special attention to the data types you use. Write a `main()` function to test your function.

Bonus exercise: Can you do the same for 32-bit integers?

Exercise 34-3: The networking example in the Shifting Paradigms section showing how to use a C-style API with C++ might be a bit abstract. It doesn't present an entire implementation as that would require networking code which is neither provided by the C nor the C++ Standard Library. In this exercise, let's look at a much smaller C-style library that you might want to use in your C++ code. The C-style library basically consists of two functions. The first function, `reverseString()`, allocates a new string and initializes it with the reverse of a given source string. The second function, `freeString()`, frees the memory allocated by `reverseString()`. Here are their declarations with descriptive comments:

```
/// <summary>
/// Allocates a new string and initializes it with the reverse of a given string.
/// </summary>
/// <param name="string">The source string to reverse.</param>
/// <returns>A newly allocated buffer filled with the reverse of the
/// given string.
/// The returned memory needs to be freed with freeString().</returns>
char* reverseString(const char* string);

/// <summary>Frees the memory allocated for the given string.</summary>
/// <param name="string">The string to deallocate.</param>
void freeString(char* string);
```

How would you use this "library" from your C++ code?

Exercise 34-4: All examples about mixing C and C++ code in this chapter have been about calling C code from C++. Of course, the opposite is also possible when limiting yourself to data types known by C. In this exercise, you'll combine both directions. Write a C function called `writeTextFromC(const char*)` that calls a C++ function called `writeTextFromCpp(const char*)` that uses `std::println()` to print out the given string to the standard output. To test your code, write a `main()` function in C++ that calls the C function `writeTextFromC()`.

PART VI
Appendices

C++ Interviews

Reading this book will surely give your C++ career a kick-start, but employers will want you to prove yourself before they offer the big bucks. Interview methodologies vary from company to company, yet many aspects of technical interviews are predictable. A thorough interviewer will want to test your basic coding skills, your debugging skills, your design and style skills, and your problem-solving skills. The set of questions you might be asked is quite large. In this appendix, you'll read about some of the different types of questions you may encounter and the best tactics for landing that high-paying C++ programming job you're after.

This appendix iterates through all chapters of the book, discussing the aspects of each chapter that are likely to come up in an interview situation. Each section also includes a discussion of the types of questions that could be designed to test those skills, and the best ways to deal with those questions.

CHAPTER 1: A CRASH COURSE IN C++ AND THE STANDARD LIBRARY

A technical interview will often include some basic C++ questions to weed out the candidates who put C++ on their résumé simply because they've heard of the language. These questions might be asked during a *phone screen*, when a developer or recruiter calls you before bringing you in for an in-person interview. They could also be asked via e-mail or in person. When answering these questions, remember that the interviewer is just trying to establish that you've actually learned and used C++. You generally don't need to get every detail right to earn high marks.

Things to Remember

- Use of functions
- Uniform initialization
- Basic use of modules
- Use of the standard named module `std` (C++23)

- How to print text to the screen using the modern `std::print()` and `println()` functions (C++23)
- How to print text to the screen using `std::cout`
- Use of namespaces and nested namespaces
- Language basics, such as loop syntax, including the range-based `for` loop, conditional statements, the conditional operator, and variables
- Use of the three-way comparison operator
- Enumerations
- The difference between the stack and the free store
- The many uses of `const`
- What pointers and references are and their differences
- The need for references to be bound to a variable when they are declared and that the binding cannot be changed
- The advantages of pass-by-reference over pass-by-value
- Structured bindings
- The `auto` keyword, and its use with structured bindings and to deduce the type of an expression or a function's return type
- Basic use of Standard Library containers such as `std::array` and `vector`
- Using `std::pair` and `optional`
- How type aliases and `typedef`s work
- The general idea behind attributes

Types of Questions

Basic C++ questions will often come in the form of a vocabulary test. The interviewer may ask you to define C++ terms, such as `auto` or `enum class`. She may be looking for the textbook answer, but you can often score extra points by giving sample usage or extra detail. For example, when asked to define the `auto` keyword, you can score extra points by not only explaining the use of `auto` to define variables, but also its use with function return type deduction and structured bindings.

The other form that basic C++ competence questions can take is a short program that you write in front of the interviewer. An interviewer may give you a warm-up question, such as, "Write *Hello, World* in C++." When you get a seemingly simple question like this, make sure that you score all the extra points you can by showing that you are namespace-savvy and up-to-date with the latest standards; i.e., you use the modern `std::print()` and `println()` functions instead of the C-style `printf()` function, and you know that a single import of `std` gives access to the entire Standard Library. However, upgrading a code base with every new C++ standard takes time, so a lot of companies don't always use the latest C++ standard. That means you still need to know how to do things using older standards. For the "Hello, World" program, you should also demonstrate that you can write it using `std::cout` and `#include` instead of `std::println()` and `import`.

Asking a candidate to define const is a classic C++ interview question. The keyword provides a sliding scale with which an interviewer can assess an answer. For example, a fair candidate will talk about const variables. A good candidate will explain const member functions and pass-by-reference-to-const and explain why this can be more efficient than pass-by-value. A great candidate might talk about the relationship of const to thread-safety (discussed in Chapter 27, "Multithreaded Programming with C++"), show how to define static const data members (discussed in Chapter 9, "Mastering Classes and Objects"), or differentiate const from constexpr (see Chapter 9).

Certain topics described in this chapter also come in find-the-bug type problems. Be on the lookout for misuse of references. For example, imagine a class that contains a reference as a data member:

```
class Gwenyth
{
    private:
        int& m_caversham;
};
int main()
{
    Gwenyth g;
}
```

The statement in main() won't compile, and the compiler will spit out an error saying that it attempts to reference a deleted function. Because m_caversham is a reference, it needs to be bound to a variable when the class is constructed. The compiler-generated default constructor cannot do that, so the compiler implicitly deletes the default constructor of Gwenyth. You need to provide a constructor and initialize the reference in the constructor initializer. The class could take the variable to be referenced as a parameter to the constructor:

```
class Gwenyth
{
    public:
        explicit Gwenyth(int& i) : m_caversham { i } { }
    private:
        int& m_caversham;
};
```

CHAPTERS 2 AND 21: WORKING WITH STRINGS AND STRING VIEWS, AND STRING LOCALIZATION AND REGULAR EXPRESSIONS

Strings are important and are used in almost every kind of application. An interviewer will most likely ask at least one question related to string handling in C++.

Things to Remember

- The std::string and string_view classes
- To prefer const string& or string as function return type instead of string_view
- Differences between the C++ std::string class and C-style (char*) strings, including why C-style strings should be avoided

- Conversion of strings to numeric types such as integers and floating-point numbers, and vice versa
- String formatting using `std::format()`
- String printing using `std::print()` and `println()` (C++23)
- How to format and print entire ranges at once (C++23)
- Raw string literals
- The importance of localization
- Ideas behind Unicode
- The high-level concepts of locales and facets
- What regular expressions are

Types of Questions

An interviewer could ask you to explain how you can append two strings together. With this question, the interviewer wants to find out whether you are thinking as a C++ programmer or as a C programmer. If you get such a question, you should explain the `std::string` class and show how to use it to append two strings. It's also worth mentioning that the `string` class handles all memory management for you automatically, and contrasting this to C-style strings.

Most interviewers won't ask specific details about localization. If you do receive a question about your experience with localization, be sure to mention the importance of considering worldwide use from the beginning of the project.

You might also be asked about the general idea behind locales and facets. Most likely, you will not have to explain the exact syntax, but you should explain that they allow you to format text and numbers according to the rules of a certain language or country.

You might get a question about Unicode, but almost certainly it will be a question to explain the ideas and the basic concepts behind Unicode instead of implementation details. So, make sure you understand the high-level concepts of Unicode and that you can explain their use in the context of localization. You should also know about the different options for encoding Unicode characters, such as UTF-8 and UTF-16, without specific details.

As discussed in Chapter 21, regular expressions can have a daunting syntax. It is unlikely that an interviewer will ask you about little details of regular expressions. However, you should be able to explain the concept of regular expressions and what kind of string manipulations you can do with them.

CHAPTER 3: CODING WITH STYLE

Anybody who's coded in the professional world has had a co-worker who writes messy code. That is something companies don't want, so interviewers sometimes attempt to determine a candidate's style skills.

Things to Remember

- Style matters, even during interview questions that aren't explicitly style related.
- Well-written code doesn't need extensive comments.
- Comments can be used to convey meta information.
- Decomposition is the practice of breaking up code into smaller pieces.
- Refactoring is the act of restructuring your code, for example to clean up previously written code.
- Naming techniques are important, so pay attention to how you name your variables, classes, and so on.

Types of Questions

Style questions can come in a few different forms. A friend of mine was once asked to write the code for a relatively complex algorithm on a whiteboard. As soon as he wrote the first variable name, the interviewer stopped him and told him he passed. The question wasn't about the algorithm; it was just a red herring to see how well he named his variables. More commonly, you may be asked to submit code that you've written or to give your opinions on style.

You need to be careful when a potential employer asks you to submit a code sample. You probably cannot legally submit code that you wrote for a previous employer. You also have to find a piece of code that shows off your skills without requiring too much background knowledge. For example, you wouldn't want to submit your master's thesis on high-speed image rendering to a company that is interviewing you for a database administration position. If the company gives you a specific program to write, that's a perfect opportunity to show off what you've learned in this book. If the potential employer doesn't specify the program, you could consider writing a small program specifically to submit to the company. Instead of selecting some code you've already written, start from scratch to produce code that is relevant to the job and highlights good style.

If you have documentation that you have written and that can be released, meaning it is not confidential, use it to show your skills to *communicate*; it will give you extra points. Websites you have built or maintained, and articles you have submitted to places like Stack Overflow (`stackoverflow.com`), CodeGuru (`codeguru.com`), CodeProject (`codeproject.com`), and so on, are useful. This tells the interviewer that you can not only *write code*, but also *communicate* to others how to *use* that code effectively.

If you are contributing to active open-source projects, for example on GitHub (`github.com`), you can score extra points. Even better would be if you have your own open-source project that you actively maintain. That's the perfect opportunity to show off your coding style and your communication skills. Profile pages on websites such as GitHub are taken as part of your résumé by certain employers.

CHAPTER 4: DESIGNING PROFESSIONAL C++ PROGRAMS

Your interviewer will want to make sure that in addition to knowing the C++ language, you are skilled at applying it. You might not be asked a design question explicitly, but good interviewers have a variety of techniques to sneak design into other questions, as you'll see.

A potential employer will also want to know that you're able to work with code that you didn't write yourself. If you've listed third-party libraries on your résumé, then you should be prepared to answer questions about them. If you didn't list specific libraries, a general understanding of the importance of libraries will probably suffice.

Things to Remember

- Design is subjective. Be prepared to defend design decisions you make during the interview.
- Before the interview, recall the details of a design you've done in the past in case you are asked for an example.
- Be prepared to sketch out a design visually, including class hierarchies.
- Be prepared to tout the benefits and disadvantages of code reuse.
- Understand the concept of libraries.
- Know the tradeoffs between building from scratch and reusing existing code.
- Know the basics of big-O notation, or at least remember that $O(n \log n)$ is better than $O(n^2)$.
- Understand the functionality that is included in the C++ Standard Library.
- Know the high-level definition of design patterns.

Types of Questions

Design questions are hard for an interviewer to come up with; any program that you could design in an interview setting is probably too simple to demonstrate real-world design skills. Design questions may come in a fuzzier form, such as "Tell me the steps in designing a good program" or "Explain the fundamental rule of code reuse." They can also be less explicit. When discussing your previous job, the interviewer may ask, "Can you explain the design of that project to me?" Be careful not to expose intellectual property from your previous jobs, though.

If the interviewer is asking you about a specific library, he will probably focus on the high-level aspects of the library as opposed to technical specifics. For example, you may be asked to explain what the strengths and weaknesses of the Standard Library are from a library design point of view. The best candidates talk about the Standard Library's breadth and standardization as strengths and its sometimes-complex usage as a drawback.

You may also be asked a design question that initially doesn't sound as if it's related to libraries. For example, the interviewer could ask how you would go about creating an application that downloads MP3 music from the web and plays it on a local computer. This question isn't explicitly related to libraries, but that's what it's getting at; the question is really asking about process.

You should begin by talking about how you would gather requirements and do initial prototypes. Because the question mentions two specific technologies, the interviewer would like to know how you would deal with them. This is where libraries come into play. If you tell the interviewer that you would write your own web classes and MP3-playing code, you won't fail the test, but you will be challenged to justify the time and expense of reinventing these tools.

A better answer is to say that you would survey existing libraries that perform web and MP3 functionality to see if one exists that suits the project. You might want to name some technologies that you would start with, such as libcurl (`curl.haxx.se`) for web retrieval in Linux or the Windows Media library for music playback in Windows.

Mentioning some websites with free libraries, and some ideas of what those websites provide, might also get you extra points. Some examples are `codeguru.com` and `codeproject.com` for Windows libraries, `boost.org` and `github.com` for platform-independent C++ libraries, and so on. Giving examples of some of the licenses that are available for open-source software, such as the GNU General Public License, Boost Software License, Creative Commons license, MIT license, OpenBSD license, and so on, might score you extra credit.

CHAPTER 5: DESIGNING WITH CLASSES

Object-oriented design questions are used to weed out C programmers who merely know what a class is, from C++ programmers who actually use the object-oriented features of the language. Interviewers don't take anything for granted; even if you've been using object-oriented languages for years, they may still want to see evidence that you understand the methodology.

Things to Remember

- The differences between the procedural and object oriented paradigms
- The difference between a class and an object
- Expressing classes in terms of components, properties, and behaviors
- Is-a and has-a relationships
- The tradeoffs involved in multiple inheritance

Types of Questions

There are typically two ways to ask object-oriented design questions: you can be asked to define an object-oriented concept, or you can be asked to sketch out an object-oriented hierarchy. The former is pretty straightforward. Remember that examples might earn you extra credit.

If you're asked to sketch out an object-oriented hierarchy, the interviewer will usually provide a simple application, such as a card game, for which you should design a class hierarchy. Interviewers often ask design questions about games because those are applications with which most people are already familiar. They also help lighten the mood a bit when compared to questions about things like database implementations. The hierarchy you generate will, of course, vary based on the game or application they are asking you to design. Here are some points to consider:

- The interviewer wants to see your thought process. It is very important to think aloud, brainstorm, and engage the interviewer in a discussion. Don't be afraid to erase and go in a different direction!
- The interviewer may assume that you are familiar with the application. If you've never heard of blackjack and you get a question about it, ask the interviewer to clarify or change the question.

- Unless the interviewer gives you a specific format to use when describing the hierarchy, it's recommended that your class diagrams take the form of inheritance trees with rough lists of member functions and data members for each class.
- You may have to defend your design or revise it to take added requirements into consideration. Try to gauge whether the interviewer sees actual flaws in your design, or whether she just wants to put you on the defensive to see your skills of persuasion.

CHAPTER 6: DESIGNING FOR REUSE

Interviewers rarely ask questions about designing reusable code. This omission is unfortunate because having programmers on staff who can write only single-purpose code can be detrimental to a programming organization. Occasionally, you'll find a company that is savvy on code reuse and asks about it in their interviews. Such a question is an indication that it might be a good company to work for.

Things to Remember

- The principle of abstraction
- The creation of subsystems and class hierarchies
- The general rules for good interface design, which are interfaces with no implementation details and no `public` data members
- When to use templates for polymorphism and when to use inheritance

Types of Questions

The interviewer might ask you to explain the principle of abstraction and its benefits and to give some concrete examples.

Questions about reuse will almost certainly be about previous projects on which you have worked. For example, if you worked at a company that produced both consumer and professional video-editing applications, the interviewer may ask how code was shared between the two applications. Even if you aren't explicitly asked about code reuse, you might be able to sneak it in. When you're describing some of your past work, tell the interviewer if the modules you wrote were used in other projects. Even when answering apparently straight coding questions, make sure to consider and mention the interfaces involved. As always, be careful not to expose intellectual property from your previous jobs, though.

CHAPTER 7: MEMORY MANAGEMENT

You can be sure that an interviewer will ask you some questions related to memory management, including your knowledge of smart pointers. Besides smart pointers, you will also get more low-level questions. The goal is to determine whether the object-oriented aspects of C++ have distanced you too much from the underlying implementation details. Memory management questions will give you a chance to prove that you know what's really going on.

Things to Remember

- Know how to draw the stack and the free store; this can help you understand what's going on.
- Avoid using low-level memory allocation and deallocation functions. In modern C++, there should be no calls to `new`, `delete`, `new[]`, `delete[]`, `malloc()`, `free()`, and so on. Instead, use smart pointers.
- Understand smart pointers; use `std::unique_ptr` by default, `shared_ptr` for shared ownership.
- Use `std::make_unique()` to create a `unique_ptr`.
- Use `std::make_shared()` to create a `shared_ptr`.
- Never use `auto_ptr`; it has been removed since C++17.
- If you do need to use low-level memory allocation functions, use `new`, `delete`, `new[]`, and `delete[]`, never `malloc()` and `free()`.
- If you have an array of pointers to objects, you still need to allocate memory for each individual pointer and delete the memory—the array allocation syntax doesn't take care of pointers.
- Be aware of the existence of memory allocation problem detectors, such as Valgrind, to expose memory problems.

Types of Questions

Find-the-bug questions often contain memory issues, such as double deletion, `new`/`delete`/`new[]`/`delete[]` mix-up, and memory leaks. When you are tracing through code that makes heavy use of pointers and arrays, you should draw and update the state of the memory as you process each line of code.

Another good way to find out if a candidate understands memory is to ask how pointers and arrays differ. At this point, the question might catch you off guard for a moment. If that's the case, skim Chapter 7 again for the discussion on pointers and arrays.

When answering questions about memory allocation, it's always a good idea to mention the concept of smart pointers and their benefits for automatically cleaning up memory and other resources. You should also mention that it's much better to use Standard Library containers, such as `std::vector`, instead of C-style arrays, because the Standard Library containers handle memory management for you automatically.

CHAPTERS 8 AND 9: GAINING PROFICIENCY WITH CLASSES AND OBJECTS, AND MASTERING CLASSES AND OBJECTS

There is no limit to the types of questions you can be asked about classes and objects. Some interviewers are syntax-fixated and might throw some complicated code at you. Others are less concerned with the implementation and more interested in your design skills.

Things to Remember

- Basic class definition syntax.
- Access specifiers for member functions and data members.
- The use of the `this` pointer.
- How name resolution works.
- Object creation and destruction, both on the stack and the free store.
- Cases when the compiler generates a constructor for you.
- Constructor initializers.
- Copy constructors and assignment operators.
- Delegating constructors.
- The `mutable` keyword.
- Member function overloading and default arguments.
- `const` members.
- Friend classes and member functions.
- Managing dynamically allocated memory in classes.
- `static` member functions and data members.
- Inline member functions and the fact that the `inline` keyword is just a hint for the compiler, which can ignore the hint.
- The key idea of separating interface and implementation classes, which says that interfaces should only contain `public` member functions, should be as stable as possible, and should not contain any data members or `private`/`protected` member functions. Thus, interfaces can remain stable while implementations are free to change under them.
- In-class member initializers.
- Explicitly defaulted and deleted special member functions.
- The difference between rvalues and lvalues.
- Rvalue references.
- Move semantics with move constructors and move assignment operators.
- The copy-and-swap idiom and what it is used for.
- The rule of zero versus the rule of five.
- Basic operator overloading syntax.
- The three-way comparison operator for classes.
- What explicit object parameters are (C++23).
- What `constexpr` and `consteval` functions and classes are.

Types of Questions

Questions such as "What does the keyword `mutable` mean?" are great for phone screening. A recruiter may have a list of C++ terms and will move candidates to the next stage of the process based on the number of terms that they get right. You might not know all of the terms thrown at you, but keep in mind that other candidates are facing the same questions, and it's one of the few metrics available to a recruiter.

The find-the-bug style of questions is popular among interviewers and course instructors alike. You will be presented with some nonsense code and asked to point out its flaws. Interviewers struggle to find quantitative ways to analyze candidates, and this is one of the few ways to do it. In general, your approach should be to read each line of code and voice your concerns, brainstorming aloud. The types of bugs can fall into several categories:

- **Syntax errors:** These are rare; interviewers know you can find compile-time bugs with a compiler.
- **Memory problems:** These include problems such as leaks and double deletion.
- **"You wouldn't do that" problems:** This category includes things that are technically correct but are not recommended. For example, you wouldn't use C-style character arrays; you would use `std::string` instead.
- **Style errors:** Even if the interviewer doesn't count it as a bug, point out poor comments or variable names.

Here's a find-the-bug problem that demonstrates each of these areas:

```
class Buggy
{
        Buggy(int param);
        ~Buggy();
        void turtle(int i = 7, int j);
    protected:
        double fjord(double val);
        int fjord(double val);
        int param;
        double* m_graphicDimension;
};

Buggy::Buggy(int param)
{
    param = param;
    m_graphicDimension = new double;
}

Buggy::~Buggy()
{
}

double Buggy::fjord(double val)
{
    return val * param;
}
```

```
int Buggy::fjord(double val)
{
    return (int)fjord(val);
}

void Buggy::turtle(int i, int j)
{
    cout << "i is " << i << ", j is " << j << endl;
}
```

Take a careful look at the code, and then consult the following improved version:

```
import std; // Import the Standard Library functionality.

class Buggy final // Mark as final, or provide a virtual destructor.
{
    public: // These should most likely be public.
        explicit Buggy(int param);  // Constructor should be explicit.

        // Destructor not necessary as there's nothing to clean up.

        void turtle(int i, int j); // Only last parameters can have defaults.
    private: // Use private by default.
        // int version won't compile. Overloaded member functions
        // cannot differ only in return type.
        double fjord(double val);
        int m_param; // Data member naming.
        double m_graphicDimension; // Use value semantics!
};

Buggy::Buggy(int param)
    : m_param{ param } // Prefer using constructor initializer.
{
}

void Buggy::turtle(int i, int j)
{
    // Namespaces + use std::println().
    std::println("i is {}, j is {}", i, j);
}

double Buggy::fjord(double val)
{
    return val * m_param; // Changed data member name.
}
```

You should explain why you changed `m_graphicDimension` from a `double*` pointer to a `double` value. If you do need to use pointers, you should explain why you should never use raw pointers that represent ownership but smart pointers instead.

CHAPTER 10: DISCOVERING INHERITANCE TECHNIQUES

Questions about inheritance usually come in the same forms as questions about classes. The interviewer might also ask you to implement a class hierarchy to show that you have worked with C++ enough to write derived classes without looking it up in a book.

Things to Remember

- The syntax for inheritance
- The difference between `private` and `protected` from the derived class's point of view
- Member function overriding and `virtual`
- The difference between overloading, overriding, and hiding
- The reason why base-class destructors should be `virtual`
- Chained constructors
- The ins and outs of upcasting and downcasting
- The different types of casts in C++
- The principle of polymorphism
- Pure `virtual` member functions and abstract base classes
- Multiple inheritance
- Run-time type information (RTTI)
- Inherited constructors
- The `final` keyword on classes
- The `override` and `final` keywords on member functions

Types of Questions

Many of the pitfalls in inheritance questions are related to getting the details right. When you are writing a base class, don't forget to make the member functions `virtual`. If you mark all member functions `virtual`, be prepared to justify that decision. You should be able to explain what `virtual` means and how it works. Also, don't forget the `public` keyword before the name of the parent class in the derived class definition (for example, `class Derived : public Base`). It's unlikely that you'll be asked to perform nonpublic inheritance during an interview.

More challenging inheritance questions have to do with the relationship between a base class and a derived class. Be sure you know how the different access levels work, especially the difference between `private` and `protected`. Remind yourself of the phenomenon known as *slicing*, when certain types of casts cause a class to lose its derived class information.

CHAPTER 11: MODULES, HEADER FILES, AND MISCELLANEOUS TOPICS

This chapter is mostly focused on modules, but it also discusses header files, linkage, feature test macros for core language features, the `static` keyword, C-style variable-length argument lists, and preprocessor macros.

Things to Remember

- The many uses of `static`
- What modules are and why their use is preferred over using header files
- Header file syntax and `#include`
- The concept of preprocessor macros and their disadvantages
- The use of `#define` and `#pragma once`
- The different types of linkage: no linkage, external linkage, internal linkage, and module linkage
- Why you shouldn't use C-style variable-length argument lists

Types of Questions

Asking a candidate to define `static` is a classic C++ interview question. Because the keyword has several uses, it can be used to assess the breadth of your knowledge. You should definitely talk about `static` member functions and `static` data members and give good examples of them. You'll get extra points if you also explain `static` linkage and `static` function-local variables.

Modules are the perfect way to make code reusable and bolster clear separation of responsibilities. Be sure to know how to consume modules and how to author a basic module.

CHAPTERS 12 AND 26: WRITING GENERIC CODE WITH TEMPLATES, AND ADVANCED TEMPLATES

As one of the most arcane parts of C++, templates are a good way for interviewers to separate the C++ novices from the pros. While most interviewers will forgive you for not remembering some of the advanced template syntax, you should go into an interview knowing the basics.

Things to Remember

- How to use a class or function template
- How to write a simple class or function template
- The abbreviated function template syntax
- Function template argument deduction
- Class template argument deduction (CTAD)
- Alias templates and why `using` is better than `typedef`
- The ideas behind concepts, and their basic use
- What variadic templates and fold-expressions are
- The ideas behind template metaprogramming
- Type traits and what they can be used for

Types of Questions

Many interview questions start out with a simple problem and gradually add complexity. Often, interviewers have an endless amount of complexity that they are prepared to add, and they simply want to see how far you get. For example, an interviewer might begin a problem by asking you to create a class that provides sequential access to a fixed number of `ints`. Next, the class will need to grow to accommodate an arbitrary number of elements. Then, it will need to work with arbitrary data types, which is where templates come in. From there, the interviewer could take the problem in a number of directions, asking you to use operator overloading to provide array-like syntax or continuing down the template path by asking you to provide a default type for the template type parameters or to put type constraints on them. However, most interviewers understand that the template syntax can be difficult and will forgive you for syntactical errors.

The interviewer might ask you high-level questions related to template metaprogramming to find out whether you have heard about it. While explaining, you could give a small example such as calculating the factorial of a number at compile time. Don't worry if the syntax is not entirely correct. As long as you explain what it is supposed to do, you should be fine.

CHAPTER 13: DEMYSTIFYING C++ I/O

If you're interviewing for a job writing GUI applications, you probably won't get too many questions about I/O streams, because GUI applications tend to use other mechanisms for I/O. However, streams can come up in other problems, and as a standard part of C++, they are fair game as far as the interviewer is concerned.

Things to Remember

- The definition of a stream
- Basic input and output using streams
- The concept of manipulators
- Types of streams (console, file, string, and so on)
- Error-handling techniques
- The existence of a standard filesystem API

Types of Questions

I/O may come up in the context of any question. For example, the interviewer could ask you to read in a file containing test scores and put them in a `vector`. This question tests basic C++, Standard Library, and I/O skills.

CHAPTER 14: HANDLING ERRORS

Managers sometimes shy away from hiring recent graduates or novice programmers for vital (and high-paying) jobs because it is assumed that they don't write production-quality code. You can prove to an interviewer that your code won't keel over randomly by demonstrating your error-handling skills during an interview.

Things to Remember

- Syntax of exceptions
- Catching exceptions as references-to-`const`
- Why hierarchies of exceptions are preferable to a few generic ones
- The basics of how stack unwinding works when an exception gets thrown
- How to handle errors in constructors and destructors
- How smart pointers help to avoid memory leaks when exceptions are thrown
- The `std::source_location` class as a replacement for certain C-style preprocessor macros
- The `std::stacktrace` class to get a stack trace at any moment during the execution of a program and to inspect individual stack frames (C++23)

Types of Questions

Be prepared to discuss error handling if the interviewer brings it up. But don't try to shoehorn error handling into the discussion yourself and force the interviewer to talk about it if they're really trying to focus the interview on something else, like data structures or algorithms.

Interviewers might ask you about different error handling strategies. Additionally, you might be asked to give a high-level overview of how stack unwinding works when an exception is thrown, without implementation details.

Of course, not all programmers appreciate exceptions. Some may even have a bias against them for performance reasons. If the interviewer asks you to do something without exceptions, you'll have to revert to traditional `nullptr` checks and error codes.

Knowledge of the `source_location` and `stacktrace` classes and their most important use cases will score you extra points.

An interviewer can also ask you whether you would avoid using exceptions because of their performance impact. You should explain that with modern compilers, throwing an exception might possibly have a performance penalty, but just having code that can handle potential exceptions has close to zero performance penalty.

CHAPTER 15: OVERLOADING C++ OPERATORS

It's possible, though somewhat unlikely, that you will have to perform something more difficult than a simple operator overload during an interview. Some interviewers like to have an advanced question on hand that they don't really expect anybody to answer correctly. The intricacies of operator overloading make great, nearly impossible questions because few programmers get the syntax right without looking it up. That means it's a great area to review before an interview.

Things to Remember

- Overloading stream operators, because they are commonly overloaded operators, and are conceptually unique
- What a functor is (a callable object) and how to create one
- What the benefit is of making a class's function call operator `static` (C++23)
- Choosing between a member function operator and a global function
- How some operators can be expressed in terms of others (for example, `operator<=` can be written by negating the result of `operator>`)
- The multidimensional subscript operator and what it can be used for (C++23)
- The fact that you can define your own user-defined literals, but without the syntactical details

Types of Questions

It's impossible to predict the exact questions that you'll get, but the number of operators is finite. As long as you've seen an example of overloading each operator that makes sense to overload, you'll do fine!

One possible question is to write a simple class, for instance, a `Fraction` class to store mathematical fractions. The interviewer might then ask you to add support for some operators such as addition and subtraction. If you're unsure how to add or subtract fractions, ask the interviewer as that's not the point of the question; the point is writing overloaded operators.

Besides asking you to implement an overloaded operator, you could be asked high-level questions about operator overloading. A find-the-bug question could contain an operator that is overloaded to do something that is conceptually wrong for that particular operator. In addition to syntax, keep the use cases and theory of operator overloading in mind.

CHAPTERS 16–20 AND 25: THE STANDARD LIBRARY

As you've seen, certain aspects of the Standard Library can be difficult to work with. Few interviewers would expect you to recite the details of Standard Library classes unless you claim to be a Standard Library expert. If you know that the job you're interviewing for makes heavy use of the Standard Library, you might want to write some Standard Library code the day before to refresh your memory. Otherwise, recalling the high-level design of the Standard Library and its basic usage should suffice.

Things to Remember

- The different types of containers and their relationships with iterators
- Use of `vector`, which is the most frequently used Standard Library class
- The `span` class and why you should use it
- What an `mdspan` is (C++23)

- Use of associative containers, such as `map`
- The differences between associative containers, e.g., `map`, unordered associative containers, e.g., `unordered_map`, and flat associative container adapters (C++23), e.g., `flat_map`
- How to work with function pointers, function objects (callable objects), and lambda expressions
- What transparent operator functors are
- The purpose of Standard Library algorithms and some of the built-in algorithms
- The use of lambda expressions in combination with Standard Library algorithms
- The remove-erase idiom
- The fact that a lot of Standard Library algorithms have an option to execute them in parallel to improve performance
- The ways in which you can extend the Standard Library (details are most likely unnecessary)
- What ranges, projections, views, and range factories are
- The expressiveness of the Ranges library
- Your own opinions about the Standard Library

Types of Questions

If interviewers are dead set on asking detailed Standard Library questions, there really are no bounds to the types of questions they could ask. If you're feeling uncertain about syntax, though, you should state the obvious during the interview: "In real life, of course, I'd look that up in *Professional C++*, but I'm pretty sure it works like this . . ." At least that way, the interviewer is reminded that he should forgive the details, as long as you get the basic idea right.

High-level questions about the Standard Library are often used to gauge how much you've used the Standard Library without making you recall all the details. For example, casual users of the Standard Library may be familiar with associative and non-associative containers. A slightly more advanced user would be able to define an iterator, describe how iterators work with containers, and describe the remove-erase idiom. Other high-level questions could ask you about your experience with Standard Library algorithms, or whether you've customized the Standard Library. An interviewer might also gauge your knowledge about function objects and lambda expressions, and their use with Standard Library algorithms. When talking about lambda expressions, you can score extra points if you explain the use of the `auto` keyword to define generic lambda expressions.

You might also be asked to explain the benefits of using the ranges library. Remember, it basically allows you to write code that describes *what* you want to do instead of *how* you want to do it.

CHAPTER 22: DATE AND TIME UTILITIES

The C++ Standard Library provides the chrono library, which allows you to work with dates and times. It is unlikely that an interviewer will ask detailed questions about this functionality, but she might gauge whether you've heard about this part of the Standard Library.

Things to Remember

- Compile-time rational numbers
- What durations, clocks, and time points are
- What dates and calendars are
- The possibility of converting dates and times between different time zones

Types of Questions

Instead of asking you any detailed questions about the chrono library, an interviewer might explain a problem involving dates and times and ask you how you would tackle it. If you explain that you would implement your own classes to work with dates and times, be prepared to explain why. A better approach is to explain that you would use the functionality provided by the chrono library. Remember, reuse of code is an important programming paradigm.

CHAPTER 23: RANDOM NUMBER FACILITIES

Generating good random numbers in software is a complex topic, and interviewers know this. They will not ask any syntactical details about it, but you need to know the basics and concepts behind the `<random>` library, which is part of the C++ Standard Library.

Things to Remember

- Using the `<random>` library as the preferred technique of generating random numbers
- How random number engines and distributions work together to generate random numbers
- What seeding means and why it is important

Types of Questions

An interviewer might show you a piece of code that is using the C functions `rand()` and `srand()` to generate random numbers and ask you to comment on the code snippet. You should explain that those C functions are not recommended anymore and why it's better to use the functionality provided by `<random>`.

In the context of questions related to random numbers, it is important to explain the differences between true random numbers and pseudorandom numbers. You will score extra points if you explain that you can use a `random_device` to generate a truly random seed for a pseudorandom number generator, as well as why you would use a pseudorandom number generator instead of just using a `random_device` all the time.

CHAPTER 24: ADDITIONAL VOCABULARY TYPES

This chapter discusses a few additional vocabulary types provided by the C++ Standard Library. An interviewer might touch on a few of these topics to get an idea of the breadth of your Standard Library knowledge.

Things to Remember

- The `std::variant` and `any` vocabulary data types, and how they complement `optional`
- `std::tuple` as a generalization of `pair`
- What the `std::expected` vocabulary type is and how to use it (C++23)
- What monadic operations for `optional` and `expected` are (C++23)

Types of Questions

You might be asked what the use cases are for the `variant`, `any`, and `tuple` data structures. While explaining `variant` and `any`, you can also contrast these with the `optional` vocabulary type from Chapter 1.

You will impress the interviewer if you can explain the C++23 `expected` data type and show its use with a small example.

CHAPTER 27: MULTITHREADED PROGRAMMING WITH C++

Almost any system, from servers to laptops and even cellphones, has processors with multiple cores these days. Multithreaded programming is crucial to harness the power of all those cores. An interviewer might ask you a couple of multithreading questions. C++ includes a standard threading support library, so it's a good idea to know how it works.

Things to Remember

- What race conditions and deadlocks are and how to prevent them
- `std::jthread` to spawn threads, and why it can be better than using `std::thread`
- The atomic types and atomic operations
- The concept of mutual exclusion, including the use of the different mutex and lock classes, to provide synchronization between threads
- Condition variables and how to use them to signal other threads
- The concepts of semaphores, latches, and barriers
- Futures and promises
- Copying and rethrowing of exceptions across thread boundaries

- What coroutines are, including a high-level overview of how they work
- The standard `std::generator` awaitable (C++23)

Types of Questions

Multithreaded programming is a complicated subject, so you don't need to expect detailed questions, unless you are interviewing for a specific multithreaded programming position.

Instead, an interviewer might ask you to explain the different kinds of problems you can encounter with multithreaded code: problems such as race conditions, deadlocks, and tearing. She might ask you to explain the need for atomic types and atomic operations. You may also be asked to explain the general concepts behind multithreaded programming. This is a broad question, but it allows the interviewer to get an idea of your multithreading knowledge. Explaining the concepts of mutexes, semaphores, latches, and barriers will earn you extra points. You can also mention that a lot of the Standard Library algorithms have an option to run in parallel to improve their performance.

Writing your own coroutines is complicated, but since C++23, the Standard Library comes with a standard `std::generator` type. If you can explain how `generator` works with a small example, you will earn extra points.

CHAPTER 28: MAXIMIZING SOFTWARE ENGINEERING METHODS

You should be suspicious if you go through the complete interview process with a company and the interviewers do *not* ask any process questions—it may mean that they don't have any process in place or that they don't care about it. Alternatively, they might not want to scare you away with their process behemoth.

Having a well defined process in place is important. Similarly, version control should be mandatory for any project of any size.

Most of the time, you'll get a chance to ask questions regarding the company. I suggest you consider asking about the company's engineering processes and version control solution as one of your standard questions.

Things to Remember

- Traditional life-cycle models
- The trade-offs of different models
- The main principles behind Extreme Programming
- Scrum as an example of an agile process
- Other processes you have used in the past
- What version control is

Types of Questions

The most common question you'll be asked is to describe the process that your previous employer used. Be careful, though, not to disclose any confidential information. When answering, you should mention what worked well and what failed, but try not to denounce any particular methodology. The methodology you criticize could be the one that your interviewer uses.

Almost every candidate is listing Scrum/Agile as a skill these days. If the interviewer asks you about Scrum, she probably doesn't want you to simply recite the textbook definition—the interviewer knows that you can read the table of contents of a Scrum book. Instead, pick a few ideas from Scrum that you find appealing. Explain each one to the interviewer along with your thoughts on it. Try to engage the interviewer in a conversation, proceeding in a direction in which she is interested based on the cues that she gives.

If you get a question regarding version control, it will most likely be a high-level question. You should explain why it should be used and what its benefits are. You could also explain the difference between local, client/server, and distributed solutions, and possibly explain how version control was implemented by your previous employer.

CHAPTER 29: WRITING EFFICIENT C++

Efficiency questions are quite common in interviews because many organizations are facing scalability issues with their code and need programmers who are savvy about performance.

Things to Remember

- Language-level efficiency is important, but it can only go so far; design-level choices are ultimately much more significant.
- Algorithms with bad complexity, such as quadratic algorithms, should be avoided.
- Reference parameters are more efficient because they avoid copying.
- Object pools can help avoid the overhead of creating and destroying objects.
- Profiling is vital to determine which operations are really consuming the most time, so you don't waste effort trying to optimize code that is not a performance bottleneck.

Types of Questions

Often, the interviewer will use her own product as an example to drive efficiency questions. Sometimes the interviewer will describe an older design and some performance-related symptoms she experienced. The candidate is supposed to come up with a new design that alleviates the problem. Unfortunately, there is a major problem with a question like this: what are the odds that you're going to come up with the same solution that the company did when the problem was actually solved? Because the odds are slim, you need to be extra careful to justify your designs. You might not come up with the actual solution, but you could still have an answer that is correct or even better than the company's newer design.

Other types of efficiency questions may ask you to tweak some C++ code for performance or iterate on an algorithm. For example, the interviewer could show you code that contains extraneous copies or inefficient loops.

The interviewer might also ask you for a high-level description of profiling tools (such as gprof or Visual C++), what their benefits are, and why you should use them.

CHAPTER 30: BECOMING ADEPT AT TESTING

Potential employers value strong testing abilities. Because your résumé probably doesn't indicate your testing skills, unless you have explicit quality assurance (QA) experience, you might face interview questions about testing.

Things to Remember

- The difference between black-box and white-box testing
- The concept of unit testing, integration testing, system testing, and regression testing
- Techniques for higher-level tests
- Testing and QA environments in which you've worked before: what worked and what didn't?

Types of Questions

An interviewer could ask you to write some tests during the interview, but it's unlikely that a program presented during an interview would contain the depth necessary for interesting tests. It's more likely that you will be asked high-level testing questions. Be prepared to describe how testing was done at your last job and what you liked and didn't like about it. Again, be careful not to disclose any confidential information. After you've answered the interviewer's questions about testing, a good question for you to ask the interviewer is to ask how testing is done at their company. It might start a conversation about testing and give you a better idea of the environment at your potential job.

CHAPTER 31: CONQUERING DEBUGGING

Engineering organizations look for candidates who are able to debug their own code as well as code that they've never seen before. Technical interviews often attempt to size up your debugging muscles.

Things to Remember

- Debugging doesn't start when bugs appear; you should instrument your code ahead of time, so you're prepared for bugs when they arrive.
- Logs and debuggers are your best tools.
- You should know how to use assertions.
- The symptoms that a bug exhibits may appear to be unrelated to the actual cause.
- Object diagrams can be helpful in debugging, especially during an interview.

Types of Questions

During an interview, you might be challenged with an obscure debugging problem. Remember that the process is the most important thing, and the interviewer probably knows that. Even if you don't find the bug during the interview, make sure that the interviewer knows what steps you would go through to track it down. If the interviewer hands you a function and tells you that it crashes during execution, she should award you just as many points or even more if you properly discuss the sequence of steps to find the bug, as if you find the bug right away.

CHAPTER 32: INCORPORATING DESIGN TECHNIQUES AND FRAMEWORKS

Each of the techniques presented in Chapter 32 makes a fine interview question. Rather than repeat what you already read in the chapter, I suggest that you skim over Chapter 32 prior to an interview to make sure that you are able to understand each of the techniques.

If you are being interviewed for a GUI-based job, you should know about the existence of frameworks such as MFC, Qt, and possibly others.

CHAPTER 33: APPLYING DESIGN PATTERNS

Because design patterns are popular in the professional world (many candidates even list them as skills), it's likely that you'll encounter an interviewer who wants you to explain a pattern, give a use case for a pattern, or implement a pattern.

Things to Remember

- The basic idea of a pattern as a reusable object-oriented design concept
- The patterns you have read about in this book, as well as others that you've used in your work
- The fact that you and your interviewer may use different words for the same pattern, given that there are hundreds of patterns with often-conflicting names

Types of Questions

Answering questions about design patterns is usually a walk in the park, unless the interviewer expects you to know the details of every single pattern known to humankind. Luckily, most interviewers who appreciate design patterns will just want to chat with you about them and get your opinions. After all, looking up concepts in a book or online instead of memorizing them is a good pattern in itself.

CHAPTER 34: DEVELOPING CROSS-PLATFORM AND CROSS-LANGUAGE APPLICATIONS

Few programmers submit résumés that list only a single language or technology, and few large applications rely on only a single language or technology. Even if you're only interviewing for a C++ position, the interviewer may still ask questions about other languages, especially as they relate to C++.

Things to Remember

- The ways in which platforms can differ (architecture, integer sizes, and so on)
- The fact that you should try to find a cross-platform library to accomplish a certain task, instead of starting to implement the functionality yourself for different kinds of platforms
- The fact that C++ can interoperate with other languages, such as C#, Java, scripting languages, and so on

Types of Questions

The most popular cross-language question is to compare and contrast two different languages. You should avoid saying only positive or negative things about a particular language, even if you really love or hate that language. The interviewer wants to know that you are able to see trade-offs and make decisions based on them.

Cross-platform questions are more likely to be asked while discussing previous work. If your résumé indicates that you once wrote C++ applications that ran on a custom hardware platform, you should be prepared to talk about the compiler you used and the challenges of that platform.

B

Annotated Bibliography

This appendix contains a list of books and online resources on various C++-related topics that either were consulted while writing this book or are recommended for further or background reading.

C++

Beginning C++ Without Previous Programming Experience

- Ivor Horton and Peter Van Weert. *Beginning C++23: From Beginner to Pro*, 7th ed. Apress, 2023. ISBN: 978-1484293423.

  This book starts with the basics and progresses through step-by-step examples to become a proficient C++ programmer. This edition includes new features from C++23. There is no assumption of prior programming knowledge.

- Bjarne Stroustrup. *Programming: Principles and Practice Using* C++, 2nd ed. Addison-Wesley Professional, 2014. ISBN: 0-321-99278-4.

  An introduction to programming in C++ by the inventor of the language. This book assumes no previous programming experience, but even so, it is also a good read for experienced programmers.

- Steve Oualline. *Practical C++ Programming,* 2nd ed. O'Reilly Media, 2003. ISBN: 0-596-00419-2.

  An introductory C++ text that assumes no prior programming experience.

- Walter Savitch. *Problem Solving with C++*, 10th ed. Pearson, 2017. ISBN: 978-0134448282.

  Assumes no prior programming experience. This book is often used as a textbook in introductory programming courses.

Beginning C++ with Previous Programming Experience

- Bjarne Stroustrup. *A Tour of C++*, 3rd ed. Addison-Wesley Professional, 2022. ISBN: 978-0136816485.

  A quick (about 320 pages) tutorial-based overview of the entire C++ language and Standard Library at a moderately high level for people who already know C++ or are at least experienced programmers. This book includes C++20 features.

- Stanley B. Lippman, Josée Lajoie, and Barbara E. Moo. *C++ Primer*, 5th ed. Addison-Wesley Professional, 2012. ISBN: 0-321-71411-3.

  A thorough introduction to C++ that covers just about everything in the language in an accessible format and in great detail.

- Andrew Koenig and Barbara E. Moo. *Accelerated C++: Practical Programming by Example*. Addison-Wesley Professional, 2000. ISBN: 0-201-70353-X.

  Covers the same material as *C++ Primer*, but in much less space, because it assumes that the reader has programmed in another language before.

- Bruce Eckel. *Thinking in C++, Volume 1: Introduction to Standard C++*, 2nd ed. Prentice Hall, 2000. ISBN: 0-139-79809-9.

  An excellent introduction to C++ programming that expects the reader to know C already.

General C++

- The C++ Programming Language. `isocpp.org` (accessed August 15, 2023).

  The home of Standard C++ on the web, containing news, status, and discussions about the C++ standard on all compilers and platforms.

- The C++ Super-FAQ. isocpp.org/fag (accessed August 15, 2023).

  A huge collection of frequently asked questions about C++.

- Klaus Iglberger. *C++ Software Design*, O'Reilly Media, Inc, 2022. ISBN: 9781098113162.

  Excellent book on good software design. With this book, experienced C++ developers will get a thorough, practical, and unparalleled overview of software design.

- Marius Bancila. *Modern C++ Programming Cookbook*, 2nd ed. Packt, 2020. ISBN: 9781800208988.

  This book is organized in the form of practical recipes covering a wide range of problems faced by C++ developers. This 2nd edition comes with 30 new or updated recipes for C++20.

- Paul Deitel, Harvey Deitel. *C++20 for Programmers*, 3rd ed. O'Reilly, 2020. ISBN: 9780136905776.

  This book is an introductory-through-intermediate-level tutorial-based presentation of programming in the C++ programming language, covers C++20.

- Scott Meyers. *Effective Modern C++: 42 Specific Ways to Improve Your Use of C++11 and C++14*. O'Reilly, 2014. ISBN: 1-491-90399-6.
- Scott Meyers. *Effective C++: 55 Specific Ways to Improve Your Programs and Designs*, 3rd ed. Addison-Wesley Professional, 2005. ISBN: 0-321-33487-6.
- Scott Meyers. *More Effective C++: 35 New Ways to Improve Your Programs and Designs*. Addison-Wesley Professional, 1996. ISBN: 0-201-63371-X.

  Three books that provide excellent tips and tricks on commonly misused and misunderstood features of C++.
- Bjarne Stroustrup. *The C++ Programming Language*, 4th ed. Addison-Wesley Professional, 2013. ISBN: 0-321-56384-0.

  The "bible" of C++ books, written by the designer of C++. Every C++ programmer should own a copy of this book, although it can be a bit obscure in places for the C++ novice.
- Herb Sutter. *Exceptional C++: 47 Engineering Puzzles, Programming Problems, and Solutions*. Addison-Wesley Professional, 1999. ISBN: 0-201-61562-2.

  Presented as a set of puzzles, with one of the best, most thorough discussions of proper resource management and exception safety in C++ through resource acquisition is initialization (RAII). This book also includes in-depth coverage of a variety of topics, such as the pimpl idiom, name lookup, good class design, and the C++ memory model.
- Herb Sutter. *More Exceptional C++: 40 New Engineering Puzzles, Programming Problems, and Solutions*. Addison-Wesley Professional, 2001. ISBN: 0-201-70434-X.

  Covers additional exception safety topics not covered in *Exceptional C++: 47 Engineering Puzzles, Programming Problems, and Solutions*. This book also discusses effective object-oriented programming and correct use of certain aspects of the Standard Library.
- Herb Sutter. *Exceptional C++ Style: 40 New Engineering Puzzles, Programming Problems, and Solutions*. Addison-Wesley Professional, 2004. ISBN: 0-201-76042-8.

  Discusses generic programming, optimization, and resource management. This book also has an excellent exposition of how to write modular code in C++ by using nonmember functions and the single responsibility principle.
- Stephen C. Dewhurst. *C++ Gotchas: Avoiding Common Problems in Coding and Design*. Addison-Wesley Professional, 2002. ISBN: 0-321-12518-5.

  Provides 99 specific tips for C++ programming.
- Bruce Eckel and Chuck Allison. *Thinking in C++, Volume 2: Practical Programming*. Prentice Hall, 2003. ISBN: 0-130-35313-2.

  The second volume of Eckel's book, which covers more advanced C++ topics.
- Ray Lischner. *C++ in a Nutshell*. O'Reilly, 2003. ISBN: 0-596-00298-X.

  A C++ reference covering everything from the basics to more-advanced material.

- Stephen Prata, *C++ Primer Plus*, 6th ed. Addison-Wesley Professional, 2011. ISBN: 0-321-77640-2.

  One of the most comprehensive C++ books available.

- The C++ Reference. `cppreference.com` (accessed August 15, 2023).

  An excellent reference of C++98, C++03, C++11, C++14, C++17, C++20, and C++23.

- The C++ Resources Network. `cplusplus.com` (accessed August 15, 2023).

  A website containing a lot of information related to C++, with a complete reference of the language, including C++23.

I/O Streams and Strings

- Cameron Hughes and Tracey Hughes. *Stream Manipulators and Iterators in C++*. `www.informit.com/articles/article.aspx?p=171014` (accessed August 15, 2023).

  A well-written article that takes the mystery out of defining custom stream manipulators in C++.

- Philip Romanik and Amy Muntz. *Applied C++: Practical Techniques for Building Better Software*. Addison-Wesley Professional, 2003. ISBN: 0-321-10894-9.

  A unique blend of software development advice and C++ specifics, as well as a very good explanation of locale and Unicode support in C++.

- Joel Spolsky. *The Absolute Minimum Every Software Developer Absolutely, Positively Must Know About Unicode and Character Sets (No Excuses!)*. `www.joelonsoftware.com/articles/Unicode.html` (accessed August 15, 2023).

  A treatise by Joel Spolsky on the importance of localization. After reading this, you'll want to check out the other entries on his *Joel on Software* website.

- The Unicode Consortium. *The Unicode Standard 5.0*, 5th ed. Addison-Wesley Professional, 2006. ISBN: 0-321-48091-0.

  The definitive book on Unicode, which all developers using Unicode must have.

- Unicode, Inc. *Where is my Character?* `www.unicode.org/standard/where` (accessed August 15, 2023).

  The best resource for finding Unicode characters, charts, and tables.

- Wikipedia contributors. *Universal Coded Character Set*. Wikipedia, The Free Encyclopedia, `en.wikipedia.org/wiki/Universal_Character_Set` (accessed August 15, 2023).

  An explanation of what the Universal Character Set (UCS) is, including the Unicode standard.

The C++ Standard Library

- Peter Van Weert and Marc Gregoire. *C++17 Standard Library Quick Reference*. Apress, 2019. ISBN: 978-1-4842-4922-2.

  This quick reference is a condensed guide to all essential data structures, algorithms, and functions provided by the C++17 Standard Library.

- Rainer Grimm. *The C++ Standard Library: What Every Professional C++ Programmer Should Know about the C++ Standard Library*. Independently published, 2023. ISBN: 979-8386658595.

  The goal of this book is to provide a concise reference of the C++23 Standard Library in about 350 pages. This book assumes that you are familiar with C++.

- Nicolai M. Josuttis. *The C++ Standard Library: A Tutorial and Reference*, 2nd ed. Addison-Wesley Professional, 2012. ISBN: 0-321-62321-5.

  Covers the entire Standard Library, including I/O streams and strings as well as the containers and algorithms. This book is an excellent reference.

- Scott Meyers. *Effective STL: 50 Specific Ways to Improve Your Use of the Standard Template Library*. Addison-Wesley Professional, 2001. ISBN: 0-201-74962-9.

  Written in the same spirit as the author's *Effective* C++ books. This book provides targeted tips for using the Standard Library but is not a reference or tutorial.

- Stephan T. Lavavej. *Standard Template Library (STL)*. `learn.microsoft.com/en-us/shows/c9-lectures-stephan-t-lavavej-standard-template-library-stl-` (accessed August 15, 2023).

  An interesting video lecture series on the C++ Standard Library.

- David R. Musser, Gillmer J. Derge, and Atul Saini. *STL Tutorial and Reference Guide: Programming with the Standard Template Library*, 2nd ed. Addison-Wesley Professional, 2001. ISBN: 0-321-70212-3.

  Similar to the Josuttis text, but covering only parts of the Standard Library, such as containers and algorithms.

C++ Templates

- Herb Sutter. "Sutter's Mill: Befriending Templates." *C/C++ User's Journal*. `www.drdobbs.com/befriending-templates/184403853` (accessed August 15, 2023).

  An excellent explanation of making function templates friends of classes.

- David Vandevoorde, Nicolai M. Josuttis, and Douglas Gregor. *C++ Templates: The Complete Guide*, 2nd ed. Addison-Wesley Professional, 2017. ISBN: 0-321-71412-1.

  Everything you ever wanted to know (or didn't want to know) about C++ templates. This book assumes significant background in general C++.

- David Abrahams and Aleksey Gurtovoy. *C++ Template Metaprogramming: Concepts, Tools, and Techniques from Boost and Beyond*. Addison-Wesley Professional, 2004. ISBN: 0-321-22725-5.

  Delivers practical metaprogramming tools and techniques into the hands of the everyday programmer.

C++11/C++14/C++17/C++20/C++23

- *C++ Standards Committee Papers*. `www.open-std.org/jtc1/sc22/wg21/docs/papers` (accessed August 15, 2023).

  A wealth of papers written by the C++ standards committee.

- Nicolai M. Josuttis. *C++20 - The Complete Guide*. NicoJosuttis, 2022. ISBN: 978-3967300208.

  A book explaining all C++20 features with a focus on how these features impact day-to-day programming, what effect combining features can have, and how you can benefit from them in practice.

- Wikipedia contributors. *C++11*. Wikipedia, The Free Encyclopedia, `en.wikipedia.org/wiki/C%2B%2B11` (accessed August 15, 2023).
- Wikipedia contributors. *C++14*. Wikipedia, The Free Encyclopedia, `en.wikipedia.org/wiki/C%2B%2B14` (accessed August 15, 2023).
- Wikipedia contributors. *C++17*. Wikipedia, The Free Encyclopedia, `en.wikipedia.org/wiki/C%2B%2B17` (accessed August 15, 2023).
- Wikipedia contributors. *C++20*. Wikipedia, The Free Encyclopedia, `en.wikipedia.org/wiki/C%2B%2B20` (accessed August 15, 2023).
- Wikipedia contributors. *C++23*. Wikipedia, The Free Encyclopedia, `en.wikipedia.org/wiki/C%2B%2B23` (accessed August 15, 2023).

  Five Wikipedia articles with a description of new features added to C++11, C++14, C++17, C++20, and C++23.

- Scott Meyers. *Presentation Materials: Overview of the New C++ (C++11/14)*. Artima, 2013. `www.artima.com/shop/overview_of_the_new_cpp` (accessed August 15, 2023).

  A document containing the presentation materials from a Scott Meyers' training course. This is an excellent reference to get a list of all C++11 and select C++14 features.

- *ECMAScript 2017 Language Specification*. `www.ecma-international.org/publications/files/ECMA-ST/ECMA-262.pdf` (accessed August 15, 2023).

  One of the syntaxes of the regular expressions in C++ is the same as the regular expressions in the ECMAScript language, as described in this specification document.

UNIFIED MODELING LANGUAGE

- Russ Miles and Kim Hamilton. *Learning UML 2.0: A Pragmatic Introduction to UML*. O'Reilly Media, 2006. ISBN: 0-596-00982-8.

  A very readable book on UML 2.0. The authors use Java in examples, but they are convertible to C++ without too much trouble.

ALGORITHMS AND DATA STRUCTURES

- Thomas H. Cormen, Charles E. Leiserson, Ronald L. Rivest, and Clifford Stein. *Introduction to Algorithms*, 3rd ed. The MIT Press, 2009. ISBN: 0-262-03384-4.

  One of the most popular introductory algorithms books, covering all the common data structures and algorithms.

- Donald E. Knuth. *The Art of Computer Programming Volume 1: Fundamental Algorithms*, 3rd ed. Addison-Wesley Professional, 1997. ISBN: 0-201-89683-1.
- Donald E. Knuth. *The Art of Computer Programming Volume 2: Seminumerical Algorithms*, 3rd ed. Addison-Wesley Professional, 1997. ISBN: 0-201-89684-2.
- Donald E. Knuth. *The Art of Computer Programming Volume 3: Sorting and Searching*, 2nd ed. Addison-Wesley Professional. 1998. ISBN: 0-201-89685-0.
- Donald E. Knuth. *The Art of Computer Programming Volume 4A: Combinatorial Algorithms, Part 1*. Addison-Wesley Professional, 2011. ISBN: 0-201-03804-8.

  Knuth's four-volume tome on algorithms and data structures. If you enjoy mathematical rigor, there is no better text on this topic. However, it is probably inaccessible without undergraduate knowledge of mathematics or theoretical computer science.

- Kyle Loudon. *Mastering Algorithms with C: Useful Techniques from Sorting to Encryption*. O'Reilly Media, 1999. ISBN: 1-565-92453-3.

  An approachable reference to data structures and algorithms.

RANDOM NUMBERS

- Eric Bach and Jeffrey Shallit. *Algorithmic Number Theory, Efficient Algorithms*. The MIT Press, 1996. ISBN: 0-262-02405-5.
- Oded Goldreich. *Modern Cryptography, Probabilistic Proofs and Pseudorandomness*. Springer, 1999. ISBN: 3-642-08432-X.

  Two books that explain the theory of computational pseudo-randomness.

- Wikipedia contributors. *Mersenne Twister*. Wikipedia, The Free Encyclopedia, `en.wikipedia.org/wiki/Mersenne_twister` (accessed August 15, 2023).

  A mathematical explanation of the Mersenne Twister, used to generate pseudo-random numbers.

OPEN-SOURCE SOFTWARE

- The Open-Source Initiative. `opensource.org` (accessed August 15, 2023).
- The GNU Operating System—Free Software Foundation. `gnu.org` (accessed August 15, 2023).

  Websites where the two main open-source movements explain their philosophies and provide information about obtaining open-source software and contributing to its development.

- The Boost C++ Libraries. `boost.org` (accessed August 15, 2023).

  A huge number of free, peer-reviewed portable C++ source libraries. This website is definitely worth checking out.

- `github.com` and `sourceforge.net` (accessed August 15, 2023).

  Two websites that host many open-source projects. These are great resources for finding useful open-source software.

- `codeguru.com` and `codeproject.com` (accessed August 15, 2023).

  Excellent resources to find free libraries and code for reuse in your own projects.

SOFTWARE ENGINEERING METHODOLOGY

- Robert C. Martin. *Agile Software Development, Principles, Patterns, and Practices*. Pearson, 2003. ISBN: 978-1292025940.

  Written for software engineers "in the trenches," this text focuses on the technology—the principles, patterns, and process—that help software engineers effectively manage increasingly complex operating systems and applications.

- Mike Cohn. *Succeeding with Agile: Software Development Using Scrum*. Addison-Wesley Professional, 2009. ISBN: 0-321-57936-4.

  An excellent guide to start with the Scrum methodology.

- David Thomas and Andrew Hunt, *The Pragmatic Programmer, Your Journey to Mastery*, 2nd ed. Addison-Wesley Professional, 2019. ISBN: 978-0135957059.

  A new edition of a classic book, and a must-read for every software engineer. More than 20 years later, the advice of the first edition is still spot on. It examines the core process—what do you do, as an individual and as a team, if you want to create software that's easy to work with and good for your users.

- Barry W. Boehm, TRW Defense Systems Group. *A Spiral Model of Software Development and Enhancement*. IEEE Computer, 21(5): 61–72, 1988.

  A landmark paper that described the state of software development at the time and proposed the spiral model.

- Kent Beck and Cynthia Andres. *Extreme Programming Explained: Embrace Change*, 2nd ed. Addison-Wesley Professional, 2004. ISBN: 0-321-27865-8.

  One of several books in a series that promote Extreme Programming as a new approach to software development.

- Robert T. Futrell, Donald F. Shafer, and Linda Isabell Shafer. *Quality Software Project Management*. Prentice Hall, 2002. ISBN: 0-130-91297-2.

  A guidebook for anybody who is responsible for the management of software development processes.

- Robert L. Glass. *Facts and Fallacies of Software Engineering*. Addison-Wesley Professional, 2002. ISBN: 0-321-11742-5.

  Discusses various aspects of the software development process and exposes hidden truisms along the way.

- Philippe Kruchten. *The Rational Unified Process: An Introduction*, 3rd ed. Addison-Wesley Professional, 2003. ISBN: 0-321-19770-4.

  Provides an overview of RUP, including its mission and processes.

- Edward Yourdon. *Death March*, 2nd ed. Prentice Hall, 2003. ISBN: 0-131-43635-X.

  A wonderfully enlightening book about the politics and realities of software development.

- Wikipedia contributors. *Scrum*. Wikipedia, The Free Encyclopedia, `en.wikipedia.org/wiki/Scrum_(software_development)` (accessed August 15, 2023).

  A detailed discussion of the Scrum methodology.

- *Manifesto for Agile Software Development*. `agilemanifesto.org` (accessed August 15, 2023).

  The complete agile software development manifesto.

- Wikipedia contributors. *Version control*. Wikipedia, The Free Encyclopedia, `en.wikipedia.org/wiki/Version_control` (accessed August 15, 2023).

  Explains the concepts behind revision control systems and what kinds of solutions are available.

PROGRAMMING STYLE

- Bjarne Stroustrup and Herb Sutter. C++ *Core Guidelines*. `github.com/isocpp/CppCoreGuidelines/blob/master/CppCoreGuidelines.md` (accessed August 15, 2023).

  This document is a set of guidelines for using C++ well. The aim of this document is to help people to use modern C++ effectively.

- Martin Fowler. *Refactoring: Improving the Design of Existing Code*, 2nd ed. Addison-Wesley Professional, 2018. ISBN: 0-134-75759-9.

  A new edition of a classic book that espouses the practice of recognizing and improving bad code.

- Herb Sutter and Andrei Alexandrescu. C++ *Coding Standards: 101 Rules, Guidelines, and Best Practices*. Addison-Wesley Professional, 2004. ISBN: 0-321-11358-0.

  A must-have book on C++ design and coding style. "Coding standards" here doesn't mean "how many spaces I should indent my code." This book contains 101 best practices, idioms, and common pitfalls that can help you to write correct, understandable, and efficient C++ code.

- Diomidis Spinellis. *Code Reading: The Open Source Perspective*. Addison-Wesley Professional, 2003. ISBN: 0-201-79940-5.

  A unique book that turns the issue of programming style upside down by challenging the reader to learn to read code properly in order to become a better programmer.

- Dimitri van Heesch. *Doxygen*. `www.doxygen.nl` (accessed August 15, 2023).

  A highly configurable program that generates documentation from source code and comments.

- John Aycock. *Reading and Modifying Code*. John Aycock, 2008. ISBN 0-980-95550-5.

  A nice little book with advice about how to perform the most common operations on code: reading, modifying, testing, debugging, and writing.

- Wikipedia contributors. *Code refactoring*. Wikipedia, The Free Encyclopedia, `en.wikipedia.org/wiki/Refactoring` (accessed August 15, 2023).

  A discussion of what code refactoring means, including a number of techniques for refactoring.

- Google. *Google C++ Style Guide*. `google.github.io/styleguide/cppguide.html` (accessed August 15, 2023).

  A discussion of the C++ style guidelines used at Google.

COMPUTER ARCHITECTURE

- David A. Patterson and John L. Hennessy. *Computer Organization and Design: The Hardware/Software Interface*, 4th ed. Morgan Kaufmann, 2011. ISBN: 0-123-74493-8.
- John L. Hennessy and David A. Patterson. *Computer Architecture: A Quantitative Approach*, 5th ed. Morgan Kaufmann, 2011. ISBN: 0-123-83872-X.

  Two books that provide all the information most software engineers will ever need to know about computer architecture.

EFFICIENCY

- Dov Bulka and David Mayhew. *Efficient C++: Performance Programming Techniques*. Addison-Wesley Professional, 1999. ISBN: 0-201-37950-3.

  One of the few books to focus exclusively on efficient C++ programming. This book covers both language-level and design-level efficiency.

- GNU gprof. `sourceware.org/binutils/docs/gprof/` (accessed August 15, 2023).

  Information about the gprof profiling tool.

TESTING

- Elfriede Dustin. *Effective Software Testing: 50 Specific Ways to Improve Your Testing*. Addison-Wesley Professional, 2002. ISBN: 0-201-79429-2.

  A book aimed at quality assurance professionals, although any software engineer will benefit from this book's discussion of the software-testing process.

DEBUGGING

- Diomidis Spinellis. *Effective Debugging: 66 Specific Ways to Debug Software and Systems*. Addison-Wesley Professional, 2016. ISBN: 978-0134394794.

  This book helps experienced programmers accelerate their journey to mastery, by systematically categorizing, explaining, and illustrating the most useful debugging methods, strategies, techniques, and tools.

- Microsoft Visual Studio Community Edition. `microsoft.com/vs` (accessed August 15, 2023).

  The Community Edition of Microsoft Visual Studio is a version of Visual Studio free of charge for students, open-source developers, and individual developers to create both free and paid applications. It's also free of charge for up to five users in small organizations. It comes with an excellent graphical symbolic debugger.

- The GNU Debugger (GDB). `www.gnu.org/software/gdb/gdb.html` (accessed August 15, 2023).

  An excellent command-line symbolic debugger.

- Valgrind. `valgrind.org` (accessed August 15, 2023).

  An open-source memory-debugging tool for Linux.

- Microsoft Application Verifier. Part of the Windows SDK, `developer.microsoft.com/windows/downloads/windows-sdk` (accessed August 15, 2023).

  A run-time verification tool for C++ code that assists in finding subtle programming errors and security issues that can be difficult to identify with normal application testing techniques.

DESIGN PATTERNS

- Erich Gamma, Richard Helm, Ralph Johnson, and John Vlissides. *Design Patterns: Elements of Reusable Object-Oriented Software*. Addison-Wesley Professional, 1994. ISBN: 0-201-63361-2.

  Called the "Gang of Four" (GoF) book (because of its four authors), the seminal work on design patterns.

- Andrei Alexandrescu. *Modern C++ Design: Generic Programming and Design Patterns Applied*. Addison-Wesley Professional, 2001. ISBN: 0-201-70431-5.

  Offers an approach to C++ programming that employs highly reusable code and patterns.

- John Vlissides. *Pattern Hatching: Design Patterns Applied*. Addison-Wesley Professional, 1998. ISBN: 0-201-43293-5.

  A companion to the GoF book, explaining how patterns can actually be applied.

- Eric Freeman, Bert Bates, Kathy Sierra, and Elisabeth Robson. *Head First Design Patterns*. O'Reilly Media, 2004. ISBN: 0-596-00712-4.

  A book that goes further than just listing design patterns. The authors show good and bad examples of using patterns and give solid reasoning behind each pattern.

- Wikipedia contributors. *Software design pattern*. Wikipedia, The Free Encyclopedia, `en.wikipedia.org/wiki/Design_pattern_(computer_science)` (accessed August 15, 2023).

  Contains descriptions of a large number of design patterns used in computer programming.

OPERATING SYSTEMS

- Abraham Silberschatz, Peter B. Galvin, and Greg Gagne. *Operating System Concepts*, 10th ed. Wiley, 2018. ISBN: 1-119-45633-9.

  A great discussion on operating systems, including multithreading issues such as deadlocks and race conditions.

MULTITHREADED PROGRAMMING

- Anthony Williams. *C++ Concurrency in Action*, 2nd ed. Manning Publications, 2019. ISBN: 1-617-29469-1.

  An excellent book on practical multithreaded programming, including the C++ threading library.

- Cameron Hughes and Tracey Hughes. *Professional Multicore Programming: Design and Implementation for C++ Developers*. Wrox, 2008. ISBN: 0-470-28962-7.

  A book for developers of various skill levels who are making the move into multicore programming.

- Maurice Herlihy and Nir Shavit. *The Art of Multiprocessor Programming*. Morgan Kaufmann, 2012. ISBN: 0-123-97337-6.

  A great book on writing code for multiprocessor and multicore systems.

Standard Library Header Files

The interface to the C++23 Standard Library consists of 107 header files, 21 of which present the C Standard Library. Starting with C++23, you simply import the named module `std` to get access to the entire Standard Library, as has been done in all examples throughout this book. There is no longer a need to explicitly import or include individual header files, except for certain non-importable header files, such as `<cassert>`. However, if your compiler does not yet support the C++23 `std` named module, then you need to import or include the appropriate header files. In that case, it's often difficult to remember which header files you need to include in your source code, so this appendix provides a brief description of the most useful functionality of each header, organized into eight categories:

- The C Standard Library
- Containers
- Algorithms, iterators, ranges, and allocators
- General utilities
- Mathematical utilities
- Exceptions
- I/O streams
- Threading support library

THE C STANDARD LIBRARY

The C++ Standard Library includes almost the entire C Standard Library. The header files are generally the same, except for these two points:

- The header names are `<cname>` instead of `<name.h>`.
- All the names declared in the `<cname>` header files are in the `std` namespace.

> **NOTE** *You can still include* `<name.h>` *if you want, but that puts the names into the global namespace instead of the* `std` *namespace. Additionally, up until C++23, the use of* `<name.h>` *C Standard Library headers was deprecated. Starting with C++23, their use is no longer deprecated, but discouraged.*

> **NOTE** *The C Standard Library headers are not guaranteed to be importable using an* `import` *statement. Hence, use* `#include <cname>` *instead of* `import <cname>;`*. Of course, using* `import std;` *also makes everything from the C Standard Library available in the* `std` *namespace, except for macros such as* `assert()` *from* `<cassert>`*.*

The following table lists all C Standard Library headers and provides a summary of their most useful functionality. Note that it's recommended to avoid using C functionality, and instead use equivalent C++ features whenever possible:

HEADER	CONTENTS
`<cassert>`	`assert()` macro.
`<cctype>`	Character predicates and manipulation functions, such as `isspace()` and `tolower()`.
`<cerrno>`	Defines `errno` expression, a macro to get the last error number for certain C functions.
`<cfenv>`	Supports the floating-point environment, such as floating-point exceptions, rounding, and so on.
`<cfloat>`	C-style defines related to floating-point arithmetic, such as `FLT_MAX`.
`<cinttypes>`	Defines a number of macros to use with the `printf()`, `scanf()`, and similar functions. This header also includes a few functions to work with `intmax_t`.
`<climits>`	C-style limit defines, such as `INT_MAX`. It is recommended to use the C++ equivalents from `<limits>` instead.
`<clocale>`	A few localization macros and functions like `LC_ALL` and `setlocale()`. See also the C++ equivalents in `<locale>`.
`<cmath>`	Math utilities, including trigonometric functions `sqrt()`, `fabs()`, and others.
`<csetjmp>`	`setjmp()` and `longjmp()`. Never use these in C++!
`<csignal>`	`signal()` and `raise()`. Avoid these in C++.

HEADER	CONTENTS
`<cstdarg>`	Macros and types for processing variable-length argument lists.
`<cstddef>`	Important constants such as `NULL`, and important types such as `size_t` and `byte`.
`<cstdint>`	Defines a number of standard integer types such as `int8_t`, `int64_t` and so on. It also includes macros specifying minimum and maximum values of those types.
`<cstdio>`	File operations, including `fopen()` and `fclose()`. Formatted I/O: `printf()`, `scanf()`, and family. Character I/O: `getc()`, `putc()`, and family. File positioning: `fseek()` and `ftell()`. It is recommended to use C++ streams instead. (See the section "I/O Streams," later in this appendix.)
`<cstdlib>`	Random numbers with `rand()` and `srand()` (deprecated since C++14; use the C++ `<random>` functionality instead). This header includes the `abort()` and `exit()` functions, which you should avoid; C-style memory allocation functions `calloc()`, `malloc()`, `realloc()`, and `free()`; C-style searching and sorting with `qsort()` and `bsearch()`; string to number conversions: `atof()`, `atoi()`; and a set of functions related to multibyte/wide string manipulation.
`<cstring>`	Low-level memory management functions, including `memcpy()` and `memset()`. This header includes C-style string functions, such as `strcpy()` and `strcmp()`.
`<ctime>`	Time-related functions, including `time()` and `localtime()`.
`<cuchar>`	Defines a number of Unicode-related macros, and functions like `mbrtoc16()`.
`<cwchar>`	Versions of string, memory, and I/O functions for wide characters.
`<cwctype>`	Versions of functions in `<cctype>` for wide characters: `iswspace()`, `towlower()`, and so on.

The following C Standard Library headers have been removed since C++20:

HEADER	CONTENTS
`<ccomplex>`	Only included `<complex>`.
`<ciso646>`	In C, the `<iso646.h>` file defines macros `and`, `or`, and so on. In C++, those are keywords, so this header was empty.
`<cstdalign>`	Alignment-related macro `__alignas_is_defined`.
`<cstdbool>`	Boolean type-related macro `__bool_true_false_are_defined`.
`<ctgmath>`	Only included `<complex>` and `<cmath>`.

CONTAINERS

The definitions for the Standard Library containers can be found in 16 header files:

HEADER	CONTENTS
<array>	The array class template
<bitset>	The bitset class template
<deque>	The deque class template
C++23 <flat_map>	The flat_map and flat_multimap class templates
C++23 <flat_set>	The flat_set and flat_multiset class templates
<forward_list>	The forward_list class template
<list>	The list class template
<map>	The map and multimap class templates
C++23 <mdspan>	The mdspan class template (technically not a container, but a multidimensional view over a contiguous sequence of elements stored somewhere else)
<queue>	The queue and priority_queue class templates
<set>	The set and multiset class templates
<span>	The span class template (technically not a container, but a view over a contiguous sequence of elements stored somewhere else)
<stack>	The stack class template
<unordered_map>	The unordered_map and unordered_multimap class templates
<unordered_set>	The unordered_set and unordered_multiset class templates
<vector>	The vector class template and the vector<bool> specialization

Each of these header files contains all the definitions you need to use the specified container, including their iterators. Chapter 18, "Standard Library Containers," describes these containers in detail.

ALGORITHMS, ITERATORS, RANGES, AND ALLOCATORS

The following header files define the available Standard Library algorithms, iterators, and allocators, and the ranges library:

HEADER	CONTENTS
<algorithm>	Prototypes for most of the algorithms in the Standard Library, and min(), max(), minmax(), and clamp(). See Chapter 20, "Mastering Standard Library Algorithms."

HEADER	CONTENTS
<bit>	Defines the endian class enumeration, see Chapter 34, "Developing Cross-Platform and Cross-Language Applications," and provides function prototypes to perform low-level operations on bit sequences, such as bit_ceil(), rotl(), countl_zero(), and more, see Chapter 16, "Overview of the C++ Standard Library."
<execution>	Defines the execution policy types for use with the Standard Library algorithms. See Chapter 20.
<functional>	Defines the built-in function objects, negators, binders, and adaptors. See Chapter 19, "Function Pointers, Function Objects, and Lambda Expressions."
<iterator>	Definitions of iterator_traits, iterator tags, iterator, reverse_iterator, insert iterators (such as back_insert_iterator), and stream iterators. See Chapter 17, "Understanding Iterators and the Ranges Library."
<memory>	Defines the default allocator and function prototypes for dealing with uninitialized memory inside containers. Also provides unique_ptr, shared_ptr, weak_ptr, make_unique(), and make_shared(), introduced in Chapter 7, "Memory Management."
<memory_resource>	Defines polymorphic allocators and memory resources. See Chapter 25, "Customizing and Extending the Standard Library."
<numeric>	Prototypes for some numerical algorithms: accumulate(), inner_product(), partial_sum(), adjacent_difference(), gcd(), lcm(), and a few others. See Chapter 20.
<ranges>	Provides all functionality for the Ranges library. See Chapter 17.
<scoped_allocator>	An allocator that can be used with nested containers such as a vector of strings, or a vector of maps.

GENERAL UTILITIES

The Standard Library contains some general-purpose utilities in several different header files:

HEADER	CONTENTS
<any>	Defines the any class. See Chapter 24, "Additional Vocabulary Types."
<charconv>	Defines the chars_format enumeration, the from_chars() and to_chars() functions, and related structs. See Chapter 2, "Working with Strings and String Views."

continues

(continued)

HEADER	CONTENTS
`<chrono>`	Defines the chrono library. See Chapter 22, "Date and Time Utilities."
`<codecvt>`	Provides code conversion facets for various character encodings. This header is deprecated since C++17.
`<compare>`	Provides classes and functions to support three-way comparisons. See Chapters 1, "A Crash Course in C++ and the Standard Library," and 9, "Mastering Classes and Objects."
`<concepts>`	Provides standard concepts such as `same_as`, `convertible_to`, `integral`, `movable`, and more. See Chapter 12, "Writing Generic Code with Templates."
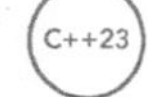 `<expected>`	Defines the `expected` and `unexpected` class templates, the `bad_expected_access` exception, and the `unexpect_t` and `unexpect` tags. See Chapter 24.
`<filesystem>`	Defines all available classes and functions to work with the filesystem. See Chapter 13, "Demystifying C++ I/O."
`<format>`	Provides all functionality for the format library, such as `format()`, `format_to()`, and so on. See Chapter 2.
`<initializer_list>`	Defines the `initializer_list` class template. See Chapter 1.
`<limits>`	Defines the `numeric_limits` class template, and specializations for most built-in types. See Chapter 1.
`<locale>`	Defines the `locale` class, the `use_facet()` and `has_facet()` function templates, and the various facet families. See Chapter 21, "String Localization and Regular Expressions."
`<new>`	Defines the `bad_alloc` exception and `set_new_handler()` function. This header also defines the prototypes for all six forms of `operator new` and `operator delete`. See Chapter 15, "Overloading C++ Operators."
`<optional>`	Defines the `optional` class template. See Chapter 1.
C++23 `<print>`	Defines the `print()`, `println()`, `vprint_unicode()`, and `vprint_nonunicode()` functions. See Chapters 1 and 2.
`<random>`	Defines the random number generation library. See Chapter 23, "Random Number Facilities."
`<ratio>`	Defines the ratio library to work with compile-time rational numbers. See Chapter 22.

HEADER	CONTENTS
`<regex>`	Defines the regular expressions library. See Chapter 21.
`<source_location>`	Provides the `source_location` class. See Chapter 14, "Handling Errors."
 `<stacktrace>`	Provides the `stacktrace` class. See Chapter 14.
`<string>`	Defines the `basic_string` class template and the type aliases `string` and `wstring`. See Chapter 2.
`<string_view>`	Defines the `basic_string_view` class template and the type aliases `string_view` and `wstring_view`. See Chapter 2.
`<system_error>`	Defines error categories and error codes.
`<tuple>`	Defines the `tuple` class template as a generalization of the `pair` class template. See Chapter 24.
`<type_traits>`	Defines type traits for use with template metaprogramming. See Chapter 26, "Advanced Templates."
`<typeindex>`	Defines a simple wrapper for `type_info`, which can be used as an index type in associative containers.
`<typeinfo>`	Defines the `bad_cast` and `bad_typeid` exceptions. Defines the `type_info` class, objects of which are returned by the `typeid` operator. See Chapter 10, "Discovering Inheritance Techniques," for details on `typeid`.
`<utility>`	Defines the `pair` class template and `make_pair()` (see Chapter 1). This header also defines utility functions such as `swap()`, `exchange()`, `move()`, `as_const()`, and more.
`<variant>`	Defines the `variant` class template. See Chapter 24.
`<version>`	Provides implementation-dependent information about the C++ Standard Library that you are using, and exposes all Standard Library feature-test macros. See Chapter 16.

MATHEMATICAL UTILITIES

C++ provides some facilities for numeric processing. These capabilities are not described in detail in this book; for details, consult one of the Standard Library references listed in Appendix B, "Annotated Bibliography":

HEADER	CONTENTS
`<complex>`	Defines the `complex` class template for working with complex numbers.

continues

(continued)

HEADER	CONTENTS
<numbers>	Provides several mathematical constants, such as `pi`, `phi`, `log2e`, and more.
 <stdfloat>	Provides the `float16_t`, `float32_t`, `float64_t`, `float128_t`, and `bfloat16_t` fixed-width floating-point types. See Chapter 1.
<valarray>	Defines `valarray` and related classes and class templates for working with mathematical vectors and matrices.

EXCEPTIONS

Exceptions are covered in Chapter 14. Two header files provide most of the requisite definitions, but some exceptions for specific domains are defined in the header file for that domain:

HEADER	CONTENTS
<exception>	Defines the `exception` and `bad_exception` classes, and the `set_terminate()` and `uncaught_exceptions()` functions.
<stdexcept>	Non-domain-specific exceptions not defined in <exception>.

I/O STREAMS

The following table lists all the header files related to I/O streams in C++. However, normally your applications only need to include <fstream>, <iomanip>, <iostream>, <istream>, <ostream>, and <sstream>. Consult Chapter 13 for details:

HEADER	CONTENTS
<fstream>	Defines the `basic_filebuf`, `basic_ifstream`, `basic_ofstream`, and `basic_fstream` classes. This header declares the `filebuf`, `wfilebuf`, `ifstream`, `wifstream`, `ofstream`, `wofstream`, `fstream`, and `wfstream` type aliases.
<iomanip>	Declares the I/O manipulators not declared elsewhere (mostly in <ios>).
<ios>	Defines the `ios_base` and `basic_ios` classes. This header declares most of the stream manipulators. You rarely have to include this header directly.
<iosfwd>	Forward declarations of the templates and type aliases found in the other I/O stream header files. You rarely need to include this header directly.

HEADER	CONTENTS
<iostream>	Declares cin, cout, cerr, clog, and the wide-character counterparts. Includes <istream>, <ostream>, <streambuf>, and <ios>. Note that it's not just a combination of <istream> and <ostream>.
<istream>	Defines the basic_istream and basic_iostream classes. This header declares the istream, wistream, iostream, and wiostream type aliases.
<ostream>	Defines the basic_ostream class. This header declares the ostream and wostream type aliases.
 <spanstream>	Defines the basic_spanbuf, basic_ispanstream, basic_ospanstream, and basic_spanstream classes. This header declares the spanbuf, wspanbuf, ispanstream, wispanstream, ospanstream, wospanstream, spanstream, and wspanstream type aliases.
<sstream>	Defines the basic_stringbuf, basic_istringstream, basic_ostringstream, and basic_stringstream classes. This header declares the stringbuf, wstringbuf, istringstream, wistringstream, ostringstream, wostringstream, stringstream, and wstringstream type aliases.
<streambuf>	Defines the basic_streambuf class. This header declares the type aliases streambuf and wstreambuf. You rarely have to include this header directly.
<strstream>	Deprecated.
<syncstream>	Defines all classes related to synchronized output streams, such as osyncstream and wosyncstream. See Chapter 27, "Multithreaded Programming with C++."

THREADING SUPPORT LIBRARY

C++ includes a threading support library, which allows you to write platform-independent multithreaded applications. See Chapter 27 for details. The threading support library consists of the following header files:

HEADER	CONTENTS
<atomic>	Defines the atomic types, atomic<T>, and atomic operations.
<barrier>	Defines the barrier class.
<condition_variable>	Defines the condition_variable and condition_variable_any classes.
<coroutine>	Defines all functionality for writing coroutines.

continues

(continued)

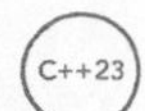

HEADER	CONTENTS
`<future>`	Defines `future`, `promise`, `packaged_task`, and `async()`.
`<generator>`	Defines the `generator` awaitable class.
`<latch>`	Defines the `latch` class.
`<mutex>`	Defines `call_once()` and the different non-shared mutex and lock classes.
`<semaphore>`	Defines the `counting_semaphore` and `binary_semaphore` classes.
`<shared_mutex>`	Defines the `shared_mutex`, `shared_timed_mutex`, and `shared_lock` classes.
`<stop_token>`	Defines the `stop_token`, `stop_source`, and `stop_callback` classes.
`<thread>`	Defines the `thread` and `jthread` classes, and functions `yield()`, `get_id()`, `sleep_for()`, and `sleep_until()`.

Introduction to UML

The Unified Modeling Language (UML) is the industry standard for diagrams visualizing class hierarchies, subsystem interactions, sequence diagrams, and so on. This book uses UML for its class diagrams. Explaining the entire UML standard warrants a book in itself, so this appendix is just a brief introduction to only those aspects of UML that are used throughout this book. There are different versions of the UML standard. This book uses UML 2.

DIAGRAM TYPES

UML defines the following types of diagrams:

- Structural UML diagrams
  - Class diagram
  - Object diagram
  - Package diagram
  - Composite structure diagram
  - Component diagram
  - Deployment diagram
  - Profile diagram
- Behavioral UML diagrams
  - Use case diagram
  - Activity diagram
  - State machine diagram
  - Interaction diagram
    - Sequence diagram

- Communication diagram
- Timing diagram
- Interaction overview diagram

Because this book uses only class and sequence diagrams, those are the only diagrams further discussed in this appendix.

CLASS DIAGRAMS

Class diagrams are used to visualize individual classes and can include data members and member functions. They are also used to show the relationships between different classes.

Class Representation

A class is represented in UML as a box with a maximum of three compartments, containing the following:

- The name of the class
- The data members of the class
- The member functions of the class

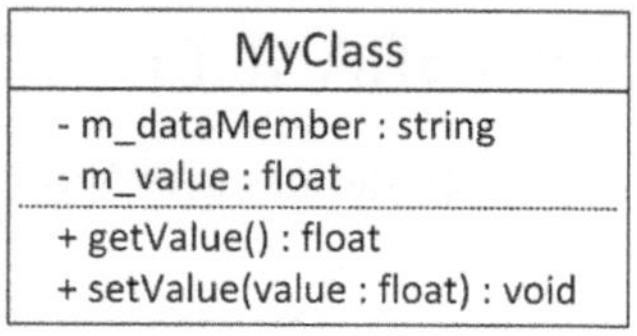

Figure D.1 shows an example. `MyClass` has two data members—one of type `string`, the other of type `float`—and it has two member functions. The plus and minus signs in front of each member specify its visibility. The following table lists the most commonly used visibilities:

MyClass
- m_dataMember : string
- m_value : float
+ getValue() : float
+ setValue(value : float) : void

FIGURE D.1

VISIBILITY	MEANING
+	`public` member
-	`private` member
#	`protected` member

Depending on the goal of your class diagram, sometimes details of members are left out, in which case a class is represented with a box, as shown in Figure D.2. This can, for example, be used if you are only interested in visualizing the relationships between different classes.

MyClass

FIGURE D.2

Relationship Representation

UML 2 supports six kinds of relationships between classes: inheritance, realization/implementation, aggregation, composition, association, and dependency. The following sections introduce these relationships.

Inheritance

Inheritance is visualized using a line starting from the derived class and going to the base class. The line ends in a hollow triangle on the side of the base class, depicting the is-a relationship. Figure D.3 shows an example.

FIGURE D.3

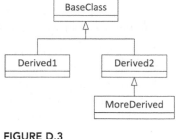

Realization/Implementation

A class implementing an interface is basically inheriting from that interface (is-a relationship). However, to make a distinction between generic inheritance and interface realization, the latter is visualized similar to inheritance but using a dashed instead of a solid line, as shown in Figure D.4. The `ListBox` class is derived from `UIElement` and implements/realizes the `IClickable` and `IScrollable` interfaces.

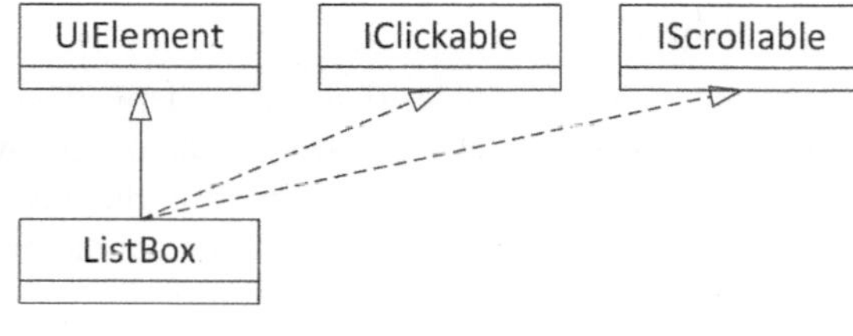

FIGURE D.4

Aggregation

Aggregation represents a has-a relationship. It is visualized using a line with a hollow diamond shape on the side of the class that contains the instance or instances of the other class. In an aggregation relationship, you can also optionally specify the multiplicity of each participant in the relationship. The location of the multiplicity, that is, on which side of the line you need to write it, can be confusing at first. For example, in Figure D.5, a `Class` can contain/aggregate one or more `Students`, and each `Student` can follow zero or more `Classes`. An aggregation relationship means that the aggregated object or objects can continue to live when the aggregator is destroyed. For example, if a `Class` is destroyed, its `Students` are not destroyed.

FIGURE D.5

The following table lists a few examples of possible multiplicities:

MULTIPLICITY	MEANING
`N`	Exactly N instances
`0..1`	Zero or one instance
`0..*`	Zero or more instances
`N..*`	N or more instances

Composition

Composition is similar to aggregation and is visually represented almost the same, except that a full diamond is used instead of a hollow diamond. With composition, in contrast to aggregation, if the class that contains instances of the other class is destroyed, those contained instances are destroyed as well. Figure D.6 shows an example. A `Window` can contain zero or more `Buttons`, and each `Button` has to be contained by exactly one `Window`. If the `Window` is destroyed, all `Buttons` it contains are destroyed as well.

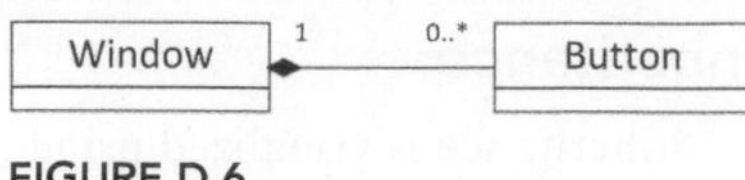

FIGURE D.6

Association

An association is a generalization of an aggregation. It represents a binary link between classes, while an aggregation is a unidirectional link. A binary link can be traversed in both directions. Figure D.7 shows an example. Every `Book` knows who its authors are, and every `Author` knows which books she wrote.

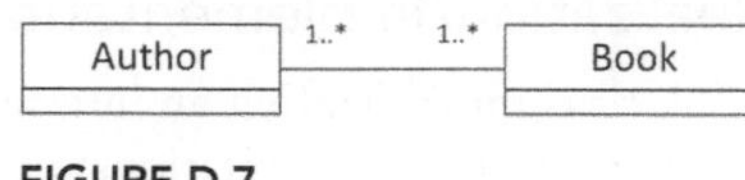

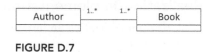

FIGURE D.7

Dependency

A dependency visualizes that a class depends on another class. It is depicted as a dashed line with an arrow pointing toward the dependent class. Usually, some text on the dashed line describes the dependency. To come back to the car factory example of Chapter 33, "Applying Design Patterns," a `CarFactory` is dependent on a `Car` because the factory creates the cars. This is visualized in Figure D.8.

FIGURE D.8

INTERACTION DIAGRAMS

UML 2 supports four types of interaction diagrams: sequence, communication, timing, and interaction overview diagrams. This book uses only sequence diagrams, briefly discussed in the following section.

Sequence Diagrams

A sequence diagram graphically represents which messages are sent between different objects and the order in which these are sent. A sequence diagram consists of the following components:

- **Objects:** Object instances involved in the interactions.
- **Lifelines:** Graphically represent the lifetime of objects.
- **Messages:** Messages are sent from one object to another object.
- **Replies:** When an object receives a message from another object, it sends a reply.
- **Self-messages:** Messages an object sends to itself.
- **Alternatives:** Represent alternative flows, similar to the branching in an `if-then-else` statement.

Figure D.9 shows an example of a sequence diagram. It's a simplified version of the diagram from Chapter 4, "Designing Professional C++ Programs," but this time with labels indicating the meaning of the important parts of the diagram.

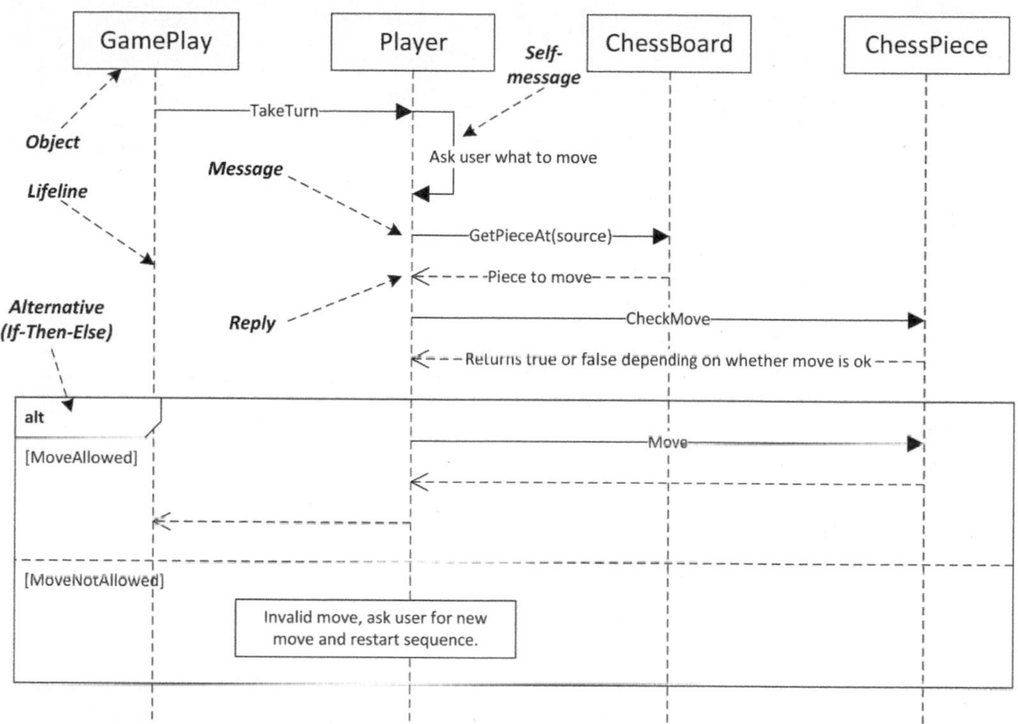

FIGURE D.9

INDEX

Symbols and Nu

A

B

C

D

F

G

H

I

K

L

M

N

P

Q

T

U

V

W

X

Y

Z